MW00423505

# THE
# FATHERS
## OF THE
# CHURCH

# THE FATHERS OF THE CHURCH

## A COMPREHENSIVE INTRODUCTION

### HUBERTUS R. DROBNER

Translated by SIEGFRIED S. SCHATZMANN with

bibliographies updated and expanded for the English edition

by William Harmless, SJ, and Hubertus R. Drobner

**The Fathers of the Church: A Comprehensive Introduction**

English translation © 2007 by Hendrickson Publishers
Hendrickson Publishers, Inc.
P. O. Box 3473
Peabody, Massachusetts 01961-3473

ISBN 978-1-56563-331-5

*The Fathers of the Church: A Comprehensive Introduction,* by Hubertus R. Drobner, with bibliographies updated and expanded for the English edition by William Harmless, SJ, and Hubertus Drobner, is a translation by Siegfried S. Schatzmann of *Lehrbuch der Patrologie.* © Verlag Herder Freiburg im Breisgau, 1994.

*Printed in the United States of America*

*Second Printing — December 2008*

Cover Art: Saints Martin, Clement, Sixtus II, Lawrence, Hippolytus. Byzantine mosaic. Located in the Court of Martyrs, Basilica of Sant'Apollinare Nuovo, Ravenna, Italy.
Photo Credit: Erich Lessing/Art Resource, N.Y. Used with permission.

**Library of Congress Cataloging-in-Publication Data**

Drobner, Hubertus R.
    [Lehrbuch der patrologie. English]
    The fathers of the church : a comprehensive introduction / by Hubertus R. Drobner ; translated by Siegfried S. Schatzmann ; with bibliographies updated and expanded for the English edition by William Harmless, and Hubertus R. Drobner.
        p. cm.
    Includes bibliographical references and indexes.
    ISBN-13: 978-1-56563-331-5 (alk. paper)
    1. Fathers of the church—History and criticism. 2. Church history—Primitive and early church, ca. 30–600—Sources. 3. Theology, Doctrinal—History—Early church, ca. 30–600. I. Schatzmann, Siegfried S. II. Title.
    BR67.D7613 2006
    270.1—dc22
                                        2006010723

# Contents

# Introduction

# Part One
## Apostolic and Postapostolic Literature

# Part Three
## Literature of the Ascending Imperial Church
### (Early Fourth Century to ca. 430)

# Part Four
## Literature of the Transition from Late Antiquity to the Early Middle Ages
### (ca. 430 to the Mid-Eighth Century)

# Part Five
## Literature of the Christian East

# Preface to the German Edition

AN INTRODUCTION IS INTENDED TO PRESENT the essential knowledge of a particular field of study in a way that is easy to remember. Yet it is also meant to facilitate its further, more intensive study by means of an apt selection of the most important references to sources and bibliographies and thus to serve as a textbook for the student as well as an initial reference work for the expert. These goals determine the selection of subject matter, content, structure, and form of the present introduction to the Fathers. The most important authors and works of the early Christian history of literature are presented in their respective political, social, ecclesiastical, and cultural contexts and are organized in terms of bibliographies, editions, English translations, ancillary sources, and relevant literature. In order to make the multiplicity of sources more accessible, they will be further subdivided in terms of the respective works and, in the relevant literature, in terms of lexical articles, introductions, commentaries, collections of essays, general studies, and monographs, as well as special topics. Tables are provided so as to make the overview vivid.

To all those who have accompanied and supported the development of this work, I wish to express my sincere gratitude for their multifaceted support: to Archbishop Dr. Johannes Joachim Degenhardt for granting two semesters as research sabbaticals; to Mrs. Ingrid Wolf for her multifaceted and involved secretarial work; to Joachim Suppelt for his assistance in teaching and for undertaking the initial, basic collection of data; as well as to Jürgen Drüker and Frank Schäffer, who served as research assistants. Special thanks are also due the employees of the Academic Library of Paderborn and of the libraries in Rome, especially the Institutum Patristicum Augustinianum and the Pontificia Università Gregoriana, for their consistently kind helpfulness in collecting and checking bibliographic data.

Paderborn                                                                          Hubertus R. Drobner
Feast of St. Athanasius, 1994

# Preface to the English Edition

THIRTEEN YEARS HAVE PASSED SINCE THE German original of this book was first published in 1994. In our modern world this is a long period of time that brings about manifold changes. Consequently, the present English edition is not just a translation of the original work but the result of years of corrections, additions, updates, and improvements, which gradually shaped the various versions since 1994: Italian (1998, second edition 2002), French (1999), Spanish (1999, second edition 2001), Korean (2001, second edition 2003), and Portuguese (2003).

Apart from numerous smaller additions and changes to the text, the following paragraphs were added to the original:

- Part Two: Introduction
- Tertullian: B. *De anima*, D. *Adversus Marcionem*
- Eusebius of Caesarea: B. Biblical and Exegetical Works, C. Apologetic Works
- Hilary of Poitiers: B. Exegetical Works
- Basil the Great: 3. Letters
- Part Five: Literature of the Christian East

Only the additions and changes made to the second German edition (2004) could not be included, as the editorial process of the English version was too far advanced.

All bibliographies were thoroughly updated and adapted to the English-speaking public with the invaluable help of my colleague and good friend Professor William Harmless, SJ, formerly of Spring Hill College, Mobile, Alabama, now at Creighton University, Omaha, Nebraska. He dedicated himself above all to the selection and evaluation of the English translations and studies, while I continued to care for the publications in other major languages.

In general, the reader has to keep in mind that despite all the changes in details, the basic character of the work has not been altered. It is not a "manual" that intends to cover the entire field in all its details. It is a textbook that presents an overview of the most important authors, works, and themes, imbedded in their historical, political, and ecclesiastical background. For everything beyond this basic aim, the numerous bibliographical data given serve to point the way to further and more specialized studies.

Paderborn                                                                Hubertus R. Drobner

# List of Abbreviations

## I. SECONDARY SOURCES

| | |
|---|---|
| AANL.M | Atti dell'Accademia nazionale dei Lincei: Memorie, classe di scienze morali, storiche, e filologiche, Rome |
| AASF | Annales Academiae Scientiarum Fennicae, Helsinki |
| AASS | *Acta sanctorum quotquot toto orbe coluntur.* Antwerp, 1643– |
| AAST.M | *Atti dell'Accademia delle scienze di Torino: Classe di scienze morali, storiche, e filologiche,* Turin |
| AAWG.PH | Abhandlungen der Akademie der Wissenschaften in Göttingen: Philologisch-historische Klasse, Göttingen |
| ABAW.PH | Abhandlungen der Bayerischen Akademie der Wissenschaften: Philosophisch-historische Abteilung, Munich |
| ABenR | *American Benedictine Review,* Atchison, Kans. |
| ABla | Analekta Blatadon, Thessaloníki |
| ABR | *Australian Biblical Review,* Melbourne |
| ABRL | Anchor Bible Reference Library |
| ACIAC | Actes du Congrès international d'archéologie chrétienne |
| ACO | *Acta conciliorum oecumenicorum.* Edited by E. Schwartz. Berlin, 1914– |
| ACW | Ancient Christian Writers, Westminster, Md., etc. |
| Aev | *Aevum: Rassegna di scienze, storiche, linguistiche, e filologiche,* Milan |
| AGJU | Arbeiten zur Geschichte des antiken Judentums und Urchristentums, Leiden, etc. |
| AGLB | Aus der Geschichte der lateinischen Bibel, Fribourg, Switz. |
| AGWG | Abhandlungen der Gesellschaft der Wissenschaften zu Göttingen, Göttingen |
| AGWG.PH | Abhandlungen der Gesellschaft der Wissenschaften zu Göttingen: Philologisch-historische Klasse, Göttingen, etc. |
| AHAW.PH | Abhandlungen der Heidelberger Akademie der Wissenschaften: Philosophisch-historische Klasse, Heidelberg |
| AHB | *Ancient History Bulletin,* Calgary |
| AHC | *Annuarium historiae conciliorum,* Amsterdam, etc. |
| AHP | *Archivum historiae pontificiae,* Rome |

| | |
|---|---|
| AKG | Arbeiten zur Kirchengeschichte, Berlin, etc. |
| *AKuG* | *Archiv für Kulturgeschichte*, Berlin |
| ALGHJ | Arbeiten zur Literatur und Geschichte des hellenistischen Judentums, Leiden |
| AlOm.A | Alpha-Omega: Lexika, Indizes, Konkordanzen zur klassischen Philologie, Reihe A, Hildesheim, etc. |
| *ALW* | *Archiv für Liturgiewissenschaft*, Regensburg |
| *Ambrosius* | *Ambrosius: Bollettino liturgico ambrosiano*, Milan |
| AnAl | Antichità altoadriatiche, Triest, etc. |
| AnBib | Analecta biblica, Rome |
| *AnBoll* | *Analecta bollandiana*, Brussels |
| *ANCL* | *Ante-Nicene Christian Library*, Edinburgh |
| *ANF* | *Ante-Nicene Fathers* |
| AnGr | Analecta gregoriana, Rome |
| *ANRW* | *Aufstieg und Niedergang der römischen Welt: Geschichte und Kultur Roms im Spiegel der neueren Forschung*. Edited by H. Temporini and W. Haase. Berlin, 1972– |
| Ant. | Antiquitas, Bonn |
| ANTF | Arbeiten zur neutestamentlichen Textforschung, Berlin, etc. |
| APAW.PH | Abhandlungen der Preussischen Akademie der Wissenschaften: Philosophisch-historische Klasse, Berlin |
| *Apocrypha* | *Apocrypha: Le champ des apocryphes*, Turnhout |
| *AR* | *Archiv für Religionswissenschaft*, Leipzig |
| ArAmb | Archivio ambrosiano, Milan |
| ARWAW | Abhandlungen der Rheinisch-Westfälischen Akademie der Wissenschaften, Cologne |
| ASAW.PH | Abhandlungen der Sächsischen Akademie der Wissenschaften: Philologisch-historische Klasse, Leipzig |
| *ASEs* | *Annali di storia dell'esegesi*, Bologna |
| ASNU | Acta Seminarii neotestamentici upsaliensis, Stockholm |
| ASTh | Amsterdam Studies in Theology, Amsterdam |
| *At.* | *Athenaeum: Studi periodici di letteratura e storia dell'antichità*, Pavia |
| ATA | Alttestamentliche Abhandlungen, Munich, etc. |
| ATANT | Abhandlungen zur Theologie des Alten und Neuen Testaments, Zurich |
| ATDan | Acta theologica danica, Århus, etc. |
| *ATh* | *Année théologique*, Paris |
| *AThA* | *Année théologique augustinienne*, Paris |
| ÄThF | Äthiopische Forschungen, Wiesbaden |
| *AThR* | *Anglican Theological Review*, New York |
| ATLA.BS | American Theological Library Association: Bibliography Series, Metuchen, N.J. |
| AUG | Acta Universitatis Gothoburgensis: Göteborgs Universitets Högskolas årsskrift, Göteborg, Swed. |

| | |
|---|---|
| *Aug* | *Augustinianum: Periodicum quadrimestre Instituti Patristici "Augustinianum,"* Rome |
| *AugL* | *Augustinus-Lexikon.* Edited by Cornelius Mayer with Erich Feldmann et al. Revised by Karl Heinz Chelius. Basel, 1986– |
| *Aug(L)* | *Augustiniana: Tijdschrift voor de studie van Sint Augustinus en de Augustijnenorde,* Louvain |
| *AugStud* | *Augustinian Studies,* Villanova, Penn. |
| *Augustinus* | *Augustinus: Revista trimestral publicada por los Padres Agustinos Recoletos,* Madrid |
| AUL.T | Acta Universitatis Lundensis: Afdeling 1, teologi, juridik och humanistiska ämen, Stockholm |
| AUU | Acta Universitatis Upsalensis, Uppsala |
| *AVL* | *Arbeitsberichte der Stiftung: Vetus Latina,* Beuron |
| AWR | Aus der Welt der Religion, Giessen, etc. |
| AzTh | Arbeiten zur Theologie, Stuttgart |
| BAC | Biblioteca de autores cristianos, Madrid |
| *BAIEP* | *Bulletin d'information et de liaison: Association internationale d'études patristiques,* Amsterdam |
| *BALCL* | *Bulletin d'ancienne littérature chrétienne latine,* Maredsous, Belg. |
| BAR | Bonner akademische Reden, Bonn |
| BAug | Bibliothèque augustinienne, Paris |
| BBB | Bonner biblische Beiträge, Bonn, etc. |
| *BBKL* | *Biographisch-bibliographisches Kirchenlexikon,* Hamm |
| BByz.E | Bibliothèque byzantine: Études, Paris |
| *BByz.T* | *Bibliothèque byzantine: Traité d'études byzantines,* Paris |
| BEFAR | Bibliothèque des ècoles françaises d'Athènes et de Rome, Paris |
| BEHE.H | Bibliothèque de l'École des hautes études: Section des sciences historiques et philologiques, Paris |
| BEL.S | Bibliotheca "Ephemerides liturgicae": Subsidia, Rome |
| *Ben.* | *Benedictina: Fascicoli trimestrali di studi benedettini,* Rome |
| *BenM* | *Benediktinische Monatschrift zur Pflege religiösen und geistigen Lebens,* Beuron |
| *BenR* | *Benedictine Review,* Atchison, Kans. |
| BenS | Benedictine Studies, Baltimore |
| BETL | Bibliotheca ephemeridum theologicarum lovaniensium, Louvain |
| BFCT | Beiträge zur Förderung christlicher Theologie, Gütersloh |
| BGAM | Beiträge zur Geschichte des alten Mönchtums und des Benediktinerordens, Münster |
| BGAM.S | Beiträge zur Geschichte des alten Mönchtums und des Benediktinerordens: Supplementband, Münster |
| BGBE | Beiträge zur Geschichte der biblischen Exegese, Tübingen |
| BGBH | Beiträge zur Geschichte der biblischen Hermeneutik, Tübingen |

| | |
|---|---|
| BGL | Benediktinisches Geistesleben, St. Ottilien |
| BGQMA | Beiträge zur Geschichte und Quellenkunde des Mittelalters, Berlin, etc. |
| BGrL | Bibliothek der griechischen Literatur, Stuttgart |
| *BHB* | *Bulletin d'histoire bénédictine*, Maredsous, Belg. |
| *BHG* | *Bibliotheca hagiographica graeca*, Brussels |
| *BHL* | *Bibliotheca hagiographica latina*, Brussels |
| *BHO* | *Bibliotheca hagiographica orientalis*, Brussels |
| BHRom | Bibliotheca helvetica romana, Olten, Switz., etc. |
| BHTh | Beiträge zur historischen Theologie, Tübingen |
| *Bib* | *Biblica: Commentarii periodici ad rem biblicam scientifice investigandam*, Rome |
| BibS(F) | Biblische Studien, Fribourg, Switz. |
| *Bijdr* | *Bijdragen: Tijdschrift voor filosofie en theologie*, Nijmegen, etc. |
| *BIFAO* | *Bulletin de l'Institut français d'archéologie orientale*, Cairo |
| *BJRL* | *Bulletin of the John Rylands University Library of Manchester*, Manchester, Eng. |
| BJS | Brown Judaic Studies, Missoula, Mont., etc. |
| BKAW | Bibliothek der klassischen Altertumswissenschaften, Heidelberg |
| BKP | Beiträge zur klassischen Philologie, Meisenheim, etc. |
| BKV[1] | Bibliothek der Kirchenväter. Edited by O. Bardenhewer, T. Schermann, and C. Weyman. Kempten, 1869–1888 |
| BKV[2] | Bibliothek der Kirchenväter. Edited by O. Bardenhewer, T. Schermann, and C. Weyman. Kempten, 1911–1939 |
| *BLE* | *Bulletin de littérature ecclésiastique*, Toulouse |
| BMus | Bibliothèque du Muséon, Louvain |
| BoBKG | Bonner Beiträge zur Kirchengeschichte, Cologne |
| BPat | Biblioteca patristica |
| *BPatr* | *Bibliographia patristica*, Berlin |
| BPM | Biblia polyglotta matritensia, Madrid |
| *BSAC* | *Bulletin de la Société d'archéologie copte*, Cairo |
| BSal.E | Bibliotheca salmanticensis: Estudios, Salamanca |
| BSHST | Basler und Berner Studien zur historischen und systematischen Theologie, Bern, etc. |
| BSPLi | Beiheft zu den Studia patristica et liturgica, Regensburg |
| BSRel | Biblioteca di scienze religiose, Rome |
| *BSS* | *Bibliotheca sanctorum*, Rome |
| BT | Bibliothèque de théologie, Paris |
| BTeo | Biblioteca de teología, Pamplona |
| BTH | Bibliothèque de théologie historique, Paris |
| *BThAM* | *Bulletin de théologie ancienne et médiévale*, Louvain |
| BThS.F | Bibliotheca theologica salesiana: 1. serie, Fontes, Zurich |
| BTN | Bibliotheca theologica norvegica, Oslo |
| *BVLI* | *Bericht des Instituts: Vetus Latina Institut*, Beuron |

| | |
|---|---|
| BWA(N)T | Beiträge zur Wissenschaft vom Alten (und Neuen) Testament, Stuttgart, etc. |
| *Byzantion* | *Byzantion: Revue internationale des études byzantines*, Brussels |
| *ByzZ* | *Byzantinische Zeitschrift*, Leipzig |
| BZNW | Beihefte zur Zeitschrift für die neutestamentliche Wissenschaft, Berlin, etc. |
| CAnt | Christianisme antique, Paris |
| Cass. | Cassiciacum: Eine Sammlung wissenschaftlicher Forschungen über den heiligen Augustinus und den Augustinerorden sowie wissenschaftlicher Arbeiten von Augustinern aus anderen Wissensgebieten, Würzburg |
| CBLa | Collectanea biblica latina, Rome |
| CBM | Chester Beatty Monographs, London |
| CBQMS | Catholic Biblical Quarterly Monograph Series, Washington, D.C. |
| CChr.ILL | Corpus Christianorum: Instrumenta lexicologica latina, Turnhout, Belg. |
| CChr.SA | Corpus Christianorum: Series apocryphorum, Turnhout, Belg. |
| CCSG | Corpus Christianorum: Series graeca. Turnhout, Belg., 1977– |
| CCSL | Corpus Christianorum: Series latina. Turnhout, Belg., 1953– |
| CCSSM | Convegni del Centro di studi sulla spiritualità medievale, Todi |
| CCWJCW | Cambridge Commentaries on Writings of the Jewish and Christian World, Cambridge |
| *CDios* | *La ciudad de Dios*, El Escorial |
| CdR | Classici delle religioni, Turin |
| CEA | Collection d'études anciennes, Paris |
| *CEAn* | *Cahiers des études anciennes*, Montreal |
| CEFR | Collection de l'École française de Rome, Rome |
| *CEMéd* | *Cahiers d'études médiévales*, Montreal |
| *CF* | *Classical Folia: Studies in the Christian Perpetuation of Classics*, Worcester, Mass. |
| CF | Collectanea friburgensia, Fribourg, Switz. |
| CFi | Cogitatio fidei, Paris |
| *CH* | *Cahiers d'histoire*, Lyon |
| *CHB* | *The Cambridge History of the Bible*, Cambridge |
| *ChH* | *Church History*, Chicago |
| *Chiron* | *Chiron*, Munich |
| *CHR* | *Catholic Historical Review*, Washington, D.C. |
| CistSS | Cistercian Studies Series, Kalamazoo, Mich. |
| CJAn | Christianity and Judaism in Antiquity, Notre Dame, Ind. |
| CJJC | Collection Jésus et Jésus-Christ, Paris |
| *Clar.* | *Claretianum*, Rome |
| CMB | Calwer Missionsblatt, Calw, etc. |
| CollLat | Collection Latomus, Brussels |
| *Comp* | *Compostellanum*, Santiago de Compostela |

| | |
|---|---|
| CoptSt | Coptic Studies, Leiden, etc. |
| *CorpAp* | *Corpus apologetarum christianorum saeculi secundi.* Edited by J. K. T. von Otto. Vols. 1–5. 3d ed. Jena, 1876–1881 |
| CorPat | Corona patrum, Turin |
| *CP* | *Classical Philology,* Chicago |
| CPA | Concordantia in Patres apostolicos |
| CPF | Collection Les pères dans la foi, Paris |
| *CPG* | *Clavis patrum graecorum.* Edited by M. Geerard. 5 vols. Turnhout, Belg., 1974–1987; 2d ed. 2003– |
| *CPL* | *Clavis patrum latinorum.* Edited by E. Dekkers and A. Gaar. 3d ed. CCSL. Steenbrugge, Belg., 1995 |
| CPS | Corona patrum salesiana: Sanctorum patrum graecorum et latinorum opera selecta, Turin |
| *CQ* | *Church Quarterly,* London |
| CRINT | Compendia rerum iudaicarum ad Novum Testamentum, Assen, Neth., etc. |
| *CrSt* | *Cristianesimo nella storia,* Bologna |
| CSCO | Corpus scriptorum christianorum orientalium, Paris, etc. |
| CSEL | Corpus scriptorum ecclesiasticorum latinorum, Vienna |
| CTePa | Collana di testi patristici, Rome |
| CTUN | Colección teológica de la Universidad de Navarra, Pamplona |
| CWS | Classics of Western Spirituality, London, etc. |
| *DA* | *Deutsches Archiv für Erforschung des Mittelalters,* Marburg |
| *DACL* | *Dictionnaire d'archéologie chrétienne et de liturgie.* Edited by F. Cabrol. 15 vols. in 30. Paris, 1907–1953 |
| *DBSup* | *Dictionnaire de la Bible: Supplément,* Paris |
| *DEB* | *Dictionnaire encyclopédique de la Bible,* Turnhout, Belg. |
| DH | Enchiridion symbolorum, definitionum, et declarationum de rebus fidei et morum. Edited by H. Denzinger and P. Hünermann. 37th ed. Fribourg, Switz., 1991 |
| *DHGE* | *Dictionnaire d'histoire et de géographie ecclésiastiques.* Edited by A. Baudrillart et al. Paris, 1912– |
| *Did.* | *Didaskaleion,* Turin |
| *Div.* | *Divinitas,* Rome |
| *DOP* | *Dumbarton Oaks Papers,* Cambridge, Mass., etc. |
| *DPAC* | *Dizionario patristico e di antichità christiane.* Edited by A. di Berardino. 3 vols. Casale Monferrato, 1983–1988 |
| *DR* | *Downside Review,* Bath, Eng. |
| *DSp* | *Dictionnaire de spiritualité ascétique et mystique, doctrine et histoire.* Edited by M. Viller et al. 15 vols. in 21. Paris, 1937–1995 |
| *DT* | *Divus Thomas: Commentarium de philosophia et theologia,* Piacenza |
| *DTC* | *Dictionnaire de théologie catholique,* Paris |
| *DTT* | *Dansk teologisk tidsskrift,* Copenhagen |
| EBib | Études bibliques, Paris |

| ECF | Early Church Fathers |
|---|---|
| *ECl* | *Estudios clásicos,* Madrid |
| *ED* | *Euntes docete,* Rome |
| EdF | Erträge der Forschung, Darmstadt |
| *EEC* | *Encyclopedia of Early Christianity.* Edited by E. Ferguson. 2 vols. 2d ed. New York and London, 1997 |
| *EECh* | *Encyclopedia of the Early Church.* Edited by A. di Berardino. Translated by A. Walford. 2 vols. Cambridge and New York, 1992 |
| *EgT* | *Église et théologie,* Paris |
| EHPhR | Études d'histoire et de philosophie religieuses, Paris |
| EHS.Ph | Europäische Hochschulschriften: Philosophie, Frankfurt |
| EHS.T | Europäische Hochschulschriften: Reihe 23, Theologie, Frankfurt, etc. |
| EichB | Eichstätter Beiträge, Regensburg |
| *EkklPh* | *Ekklesiastikos pharos,* Alexandria |
| *EL* | *Ephemerides liturgicae,* Rome |
| *EO* | *Ecclesia orans,* Rome |
| *EOr* | *Echos d'Orient,* Bucharest |
| EPhM | Études de philosophie médiévale, Paris |
| *EPOM* | *Estudios,* Madrid |
| EPRO | Études préliminaires aux religions orientales dans l'empire romain, Leiden |
| *ErJb* | *Eranos-Jahrbuch,* Zürich |
| ESH | Ecumenical Studies in History, Richmond, Va., etc. |
| ESR | Études de science religieuse, Paris |
| *EstEcl* | *Estudios eclesiásticos,* Madrid |
| EstOn | Estudios onienses, Madrid |
| *EstTrin* | *Estudios Trinitarios,* Salamanca |
| *EtFr* | *Études franciscaines,* Paris |
| ETH | Études de théologie historique, Paris |
| ETHDT | Études et textes pour l'histoire du dogme de la Trinité, Paris |
| *EThL* | *Ephemerides theologicae lovanienses,* Louvain |
| ETHS | Études de théologie et d'histoire de la spiritualité, Paris |
| EThSt | Erfurter theologische Studien, Leipzig |
| EtJ | Études juives, Paris |
| *EuA* | *Erbe und Auftrag: Benediktinische Monatsschrift,* Beuron |
| FBESG | Forschungen und Berichte der Evangelischen Studiengemeinschaft, Stuttgart |
| FC | Fathers of the Church, Washington, D.C., etc. |
| FCCO | Codificazione canonica orientale: Sacra congregazione per la chiesa orientale, Rome |
| FChLDG | Forschungen zur christlichen Literatur- und Dogmengeschichte, Paderborn, etc. |
| FChr | Fontes christiani, Fribourg, Switz. |

| | |
|---|---|
| FGIL | Forschungen zur Geschichte des innerkirchlichen Lebens, Innsbruck |
| FGPP | Forschungen zur Geschichte der Philosophie und der Pädagogik, Leipzig |
| FGTh | Forschungen zur Geschichte der Theologie und des innerkirchlichen Lebens, Innsbruck |
| FKDG | Forschungen zur Kirchen- und Dogmengeschichte, Göttingen |
| FKGG | Forschungen zur Kirchen- und Geistesgeschichte, Stuttgart |
| FlorPatr | Florilegium patristicum, Bonn |
| FP | Fuentes patristicas |
| FRLANT | Forschungen zur Religion und Literatur des Alten und Neuen Testaments, Göttingen |
| FThSt | Fundamentaltheologische Studien, Munich |
| FTS | Frankfurter theologische Studien, Frankfurt, etc. |
| FVK | Forschungen zur Volkskunde, Düsseldorf, etc. |
| *FZPhTh* | *Freiburger Zeitschrift für Philosophie und Theologie*, Fribourg, Switz. |
| GAB | Göppinger akademische Beiträge, Göppingen |
| GCP | Graecitas Christianorum primaeva: Studia ad sermonem graecum pertinentia, Nijmegen |
| GCS | Die griechischen christlichen Schriftsteller der ersten [drei] Jahrhunderte, Berlin, etc. |
| GDK | Gottesdienst der Kirche: Handbuch der Liturgiewissenschaft, Regensburg |
| GFTP | Grenzfragen zwischen Theologie und Philosophie, Bonn |
| *GGA* | *Göttingische Gelehrte Anzeigen*, Göttingen |
| *GK* | *Gestalten der Kirchengeschichte*. Edited by M. Greschat. 12 vols. in 14. Stuttgart: Kohlhammer, 1981–1986 |
| GLCP | Graecitas et latinitas Christianorum primaeva: Supplementa, Nijmegen |
| *Glotta* | *Glotta: Zeitschrift für die griechische und lateinische Sprache*, Göttingen |
| GLS | Alcuin/GROW Liturgical Study |
| *Gn* | *Gnomon*, Munich, etc. |
| GOF | Göttinger Orientforschungen, Wiesbaden |
| GOF.S | Göttinger Orientforschungen: Reihe 1, Syriaca, Wiesbaden |
| *GÖK* | *Geschichte der ökumenischen Konzilien*, Mainz: Matthias Grünewald, 1963– |
| *GOTR* | *Greek Orthodox Theological Review*, Brookline, Mass. |
| *GRBS* | *Greek, Roman, and Byzantine Studies*, Cambridge, Mass. |
| *Greg* | *Gregorianum*, Rome |
| GrTS | Grazer theologische Studien, Graz, Austria |
| GTA | Göttinger theologische Arbeiten, Göttingen |
| GVSH.H | Göteborgs kungi. vetenskaps- och vitterhetssamhälles Handlingar: Ser. A, Humanistiska skrifter, Göteborg |

| | |
|---|---|
| GWZ | Geist und Werk der Zeiten, Zurich, etc. |
| *Gym.* | *Gymnasium: Zeitschrift für Kultur der Antike und humanistische Bildung,* Heidelberg |
| HAW | Handbuch der Altertumswissenschaft, Munich |
| HCO | Histoire des conciles œcuméniques, Paris |
| HDG | *Handbuch der Dogmengeschichte.* Edited by M. Schmaus et al. Fribourg, Switz., 1951– |
| HDIEO | Histoire du droit et des institutions de l'Église en Occident, Paris |
| HDR | Harvard Dissertations in Religion, Missoula, Mont., etc. |
| *Helm.* | *Helmantica: Revista de humanidades clásicas,* Salamanca |
| Hereditas | Hereditas: Studien zur alten Kirchengeschichte, Bonn |
| Hermes.E | Hermes: Zeitschrift für klassische Philologie, Einzelschriften, Wiesbaden |
| *HeyJ* | *Heythrop Journal,* Oxford |
| *HispSac* | *Hispania sacra: Revista de historia ecclesiástica,* Madrid |
| *Hist* | *Historia: Zeitschrift für alte Geschichte,* Wiesbaden |
| Hist.E | Historia: Zeitschrift für alte Geschichte, Ergänzungsband, Wiesbaden, etc. |
| *HJ* | *Historisches Jahrbuch der Görresgesellschaft,* Munich |
| *HLL* | *Handbuch der lateinischen Literatur der Antike.* Edited by Reinhart Herzog and Peter Lebrecht Schmidt. HAW 8. Munich, 1989– |
| HNT | Handbuch zum Neuen Testament, Tübingen |
| HO | Handbuch der Orientalistik, Leiden, etc. |
| *HSCP* | *Harvard Studies in Classical Philology,* Cambridge, Mass. |
| *HTR* | *Harvard Theological Review,* Cambridge, Mass. |
| HTS | Harvard Theological Studies, Cambridge, Mass. |
| HUT | Hermeneutische Untersuchungen zur Theologie, Tübingen |
| *HWP* | *Historisches Wörterbuch der Philosophie,* Basel |
| Hyp. | Hypomnemata: Untersuchungen zur Antike und zu ihrem Nachleben, Göttingen |
| HZ.B | Historische Zeitschrift: Beiheft, Munich |
| ICA | Initiations au christianisme ancien, Paris |
| IP | Instrumenta patristica, Steenbrugge, Belg. |
| *Irén* | *Irénikon,* Chevetogne, Belg. |
| *Istina* | *Istina,* Boulogne-sur-Seine |
| IThS | Innsbrucker theologische Studien, Innsbruck |
| *ITQ* | *Irish Theological Quarterly,* Maynooth |
| *JAC* | *Jahrbuch für Antike und Christentum,* Münster, 1958– |
| JAC.E | Jahrbuch für Antike und Christentum: Ergänzungsbände |
| *JBL* | *Journal of Biblical Literature,* Philadelphia |
| JBTh | Jahrbuch für biblische Theologie, Neukirchen |
| *JEA* | *Journal of Egyptian Archaeology,* London |
| *JECS* | *Journal of Early Christian Studies* |

| JEH | *Journal of Ecclesiastical History,* London |
| JLH | *Jahrbuch für Liturgik und Hymnologie,* Kassel |
| JNG | *Jahrbuch für Numismatik und Geldgeschichte,* Munich |
| JPhST | *Jahrbuch für Philosophie und spekulative Theologie,* Paderborn |
| JRH | *Journal of Religious History,* Sydney |
| JS | *Journal des savants,* Paris |
| JSNTSup | Journal for the Study of the New Testament: Supplement Series, Sheffield |
| JSP | *Journal for the Study of the Pseudepigrapha,* Sheffield |
| JSPSup | Journal for the Study of the Pseudepigrapha: Supplement Series, Sheffield |
| JSSem.S | Journal of Semitic Studies: Supplement |
| JTS | *Journal of Theological Studies,* Oxford |
| JWG | *Jahrbuch für Wirtschaftsgeschichte,* Berlin |
| KAV | Kommentar zu den apostolischen Vätern, Göttingen |
| KGQS | Kirchengeschichtliche Quellen und Studien, St. Ottilien |
| KGS | Kirchengeschichtliche Studien, Münster |
| KHSt | Kerkhistorische studiën behorende bij het Nederlands Archief voor kerkgeschiedenis, The Haag |
| KIG | *Die Kirche in ihrer Geschichte: Ein Handbuch,* Göttingen |
| KKTS | Konfessionskundliche und kontroverstheologische Studien, Paderborn |
| Kl. | *Kleronomia,* Thessaloníki |
| Klio | *Klio: Beiträge zur alten Geschichte,* Leipzig |
| KlT | Kleine Texte, Bonn, etc. |
| Kyrios | *Kyrios: Vierteljahresschrift für Kirchen- und Geistesgeschichte Osteuropas,* Berlin |
| LA | *Late Antiquity: A Guide to the Postclassical World.* Edited by G. W. Bowersock, P. Brown, and O. Grabar. Cambridge and London: Belknap Press of Harvard University Press, 1999 |
| Lat. | Lateranum Monographs, Rome |
| Lat. | *Lateranum,* Rome |
| LCC | Library of Christian Classics. Philadelphia, 1953– |
| LCL | Loeb Classical Library, Cambridge, Mass. |
| LCO | Letture cristiane delle origini: Antologie, Rome |
| LCP | Latinitas Christianorum primaeva, Nijmegen |
| LCPM | Letture cristiane del primo millennio, Turin and Milan |
| Leit. | *Leiturgia: Handbuch des Evangelischen Gottesdienstes,* Kassel |
| LHD | Library of History and Doctrine, Philadelphia, etc. |
| LJ | *Liturgisches Jahrbuch,* Münster |
| LMA | *Lexicon des Mittelalters,* Munich, etc. |
| LO | Lex orandi, Paris |
| LP | Liber pontificalis, Paris |
| LQF | Liturgiegeschichtliche Quellen und Forschungen, Münster |
| LSS | Leipziger semitische Studien, Leipzig |

| | |
|---|---|
| *LTK* | *Lexikon für Theologie und Kirke.* Edited by Walter Kasper and Konrad Baumgartner. 3d ed. Fribourg, Switz., 1993–2001 |
| LWQF | Liturgiewissenschaftliche Quellen und Forschungen, Münster |
| MAB.L | Mémoires de l'Académie royale de Belgique: Classe des lettres et des sciences morales et politiques, Brussels |
| *MAe* | *Medium aevum,* Oxford |
| MAg | Miscellanea agostiniana, Rome |
| *MAH* | *Mélanges d'archéologie et d'histoire,* Paris |
| *MAM* | *Mémoires de l'académie (royale, impériale, nationale) de Metz,* Metz |
| *Man.* | *Manuscripta,* St. Louis, Mo. |
| Mansi | Mansi, G. *Sacrorum conciliorum nova et amplissima collectio.* New ed. 54 vols. in 58. Paris: H. Welter, 1901–1927 |
| *Mar.* | *Marianum: Ephemerides mariologicae,* Rome |
| *MAST.M* | *Memorie della [r.] Accademia delle scienze di Torino: Classe di scienze morali, storiche, e filologiche,* Turin |
| *MB* | *Musée belge: Revue de philologie classique,* Louvain |
| MBM | Münchener Beiträge zur Mediävistik und Renaissance-Forschung, Munich |
| MBPF | Münchener Beiträge zur Papyrusforschung und antiken Rechtsgeschichte, Munich |
| MBTh | Münsterische Beiträge zur Theologie, Münster |
| MCass | Miscellanea cassiense, Monte Cassino, Italy |
| *MCom* | *Miscelánea Comillas,* Santander |
| MCS | Monumenta christiana selecta, Tournai |
| *MD* | *La Maison-Dieu: Revue de pastorale liturgique,* Paris 1, 1945– |
| *MEFRA* | *Mélanges d'archéologie et d'histoire de l'École française de Rome: Série Antiquité,* Paris |
| MFC | Message of the Fathers of the Church. Wilmington, Del., etc. |
| MFCL | Mémoires et travaux publiés par des professeurs des facultés catholiques de Lille, Lille, etc. |
| MGH.AA | Monumenta Germaniae historica inde ab anno Christi quingentesimo usque ad annum millesimum et quingentesimum: Auctores antiquissimi, Berlin |
| MGH.Ep | Monumenta Germaniae historica inde ab anno Christi quingentesimo usque ad annum millesimum et quingentesimum: Epistolae, Hanover |
| MGH.GPR | Monumenta Germaniae historica inde ab anno Christi quingentesimo usque ad annum millesimum et quingentesimum: Gesta pontificum romanorum, Hanover, etc. |
| MGH.SRM | Monumenta Germaniae historica inde ab anno Christi quingentesimo usque ad annum millesimum et quingentesimum: Scriptores rerum merovingicarum, Hanover |
| MGMA | Monographien zur Geschichte des Mittelalters, Stuttgart |

| | |
|---|---|
| *MH* | *Museum helveticum*, Basel |
| ML.H | Museum lessianum: Section historique, Brussels |
| ML.T | Museum lessianum: Section théologique, Brussels, etc. |
| *Mn.* | *Mnemosyne: Bibliotheca classica/Philologica batava*, Leiden |
| Mn.S | Mnemosyne: Bibliotheca classica/Philologica batava, Supplementum, Leiden |
| MPF | Monographien zur philosophischen Forschung, Reutlingen, etc. |
| *MRSt(L)* | *Mediaeval and Renaissance Studies*, London |
| *MScRel* | *Mélanges de science religieuse*, Lille |
| *MSLCA* | *Miscellanea di studi di letteratura cristiana antica*, Catania |
| *MSM* | *Modern Schoolman: A Quarterly Journal of Philosophy*, St. Louis |
| MThS.H | Münchener theologische Studien I: Historische Abteilung, Munich |
| MThS.S | Münchener theologische Studien II: Systematische Abteilung, Munich |
| *MTZ* | *Münchener theologische Zeitschrift*, Munich |
| *MUSJ* | *Mélanges de l'Université Saint-Joseph*, Beirut |
| MüSt | Münsterschwarzacher Studien: Missionsbenediktiner der Abtei Münsterschwarzach, Münsterschwarzach |
| *Mus* | *Muséon: Revue d'études orientales*, Louvain |
| *MySal* | *Mysterium salutis: Grundriss heilsgeschichtlicher Dogmatik*, Einsiedeln, Switz. |
| *NAKG* | *Nederlandsch archief voor kerkgeschiedenis*, 's-Gravenhage |
| NAWG.PH | Nachrichten (von) der Akademie der Wissenschaften in Göttingen: Philologisch-historische Klasse, Göttingen |
| NBA | Nuova biblioteca agostiniana, Rome |
| *NDid* | *Nuovo Didaskaleion*, Catania |
| NGWG.PH | Nachrichten (von) der Gesellschaft der Wissenschaften (zu) in Göttingen: Philologisch-historische Klasse, Berlin, etc. |
| NHC | Nag Hammadi Codices |
| NHS | Nag Hammadi Studies, Leiden, etc. |
| *NMS* | *Nottingham Mediaeval Studies*, Cambridge |
| *NovT* | *Novum Testamentum*, Leiden |
| NovTSup | Novum Testamentum Supplements, Leiden |
| *NPNF[1]* | *Nicene and Post-Nicene Fathers: First Series* |
| *NPNF[2]* | *Nicene and Post-Nicene Fathers: Second Series* |
| *NRS* | *Nuova rivista storica*, Rome |
| NSGTK | Neue Studien zur Geschichte der Theologie und Kirche, Berlin |
| NTAbh | Neutestamentliche Abhandlungen, Münster |
| NTOA | Novum Testamentum et orbis antiquus, Fribourg, Switz. |
| *NTS* | *New Testament Studies*, Cambridge |
| NTTS | New Testament Tools and Studies, Leiden, etc. |

| | |
|---|---|
| OA | Orbis academicus: Problemgeschichten der Wissenschaft in Dokumenten und Darstellungen, Munich |
| OBO | Orbis biblicus et orientalis, Fribourg, Switz. |
| ÖC | Das östliche Christentum, Würzburg |
| *OCP* | *Orientalia christiana periodica,* Rome |
| OCT | Oxford Classical Texts/Scriptorum classicorum bibliotheca oxoniensis, Oxford |
| OECS | Oxford Early Christian Studies, Oxford, etc. |
| OECT | Oxford Early Christian Texts, Oxford |
| *OLP* | *Orientalia lovaniensia periodica,* Louvain |
| *OrChr* | *Oriens christianus,* Rome |
| OrChrAn | Orientalia christiana analecta, Rome |
| OrChr(R) | Orientalia christiana, Rome |
| *Orph.* | *Orpheus: Rivista di umanità classica e cristiana,* Catania |
| *OrSyr* | *L'orient syrien,* Paris |
| *OS* | *Ostkirchliche Studien,* Würzburg |
| OTM | Oxford Theological Monographs, Oxford, etc. |
| *Paideia* | *Paideia: Rivista letteraria di informazione bibliografica,* Genoa |
| *Pallas* | *Pallas: Revue d'études antiques,* Toulouse |
| *PaP* | *Past and Present: A Journal of Scientific History,* London/ Fribourg, Switz. |
| Par. | Paradosis: Études de littérature et de théologie ancienne, Fribourg, Switz. |
| *ParOr* | *Parole de l'orient,* Kaslik, Lebanon |
| PatMS | Patristic Monograph Series, Cambridge, Mass., etc. |
| Patr. | Patristica, Paris |
| Patrologia | Patrologia: Beiträge zum Studium der Kirchenväter, Frankfurt |
| PatSor | Patristica sorbonensia, Paris |
| PatSt | Patristic Studies: Catholic University of America, Washington, D.C. |
| *PBA* | *Proceedings of the British Academy for the Promoting of Historical, Philosophical, and Philological Studies,* London |
| PCRHP.O | Hautes études orientales, Publications du Centre de recherches d'histoire et de philologie, École pratique des hautes études, Geneva |
| PETSE | Papers of the Estonian Theological Society in Exile, Stockholm |
| PFLUS | Publications de la faculté des lettres (et sciences humaines) de l'Université de Strasbourg, Strasbourg, etc. |
| PFLUT | Pubblicazioni della facoltà di lettere e filosofia del l'Università di Torino, Turin |
| PG | Patrologia graeca [= Patrologiae cursus completus: Series graeca]. Edited by J.-P. Migne. 162 vols. Paris, 1857–1886 |
| PGW | Philosophie und Grenzwissenschaften, Innsbruck |
| PhAnt | Philosophia antiqua, Leiden, etc. |

| | |
|---|---|
| *Phil* | *Philologus,* Wiesbaden |
| *PhJ* | *Philosophisches Jahrbuch der Görres-Gesellschaft,* Fulda |
| PIOL | Publications de l'Institut orientaliste de Louvain, Louvain |
| PIRHT | Publications de l'Institut de recherche et d'histoire des textes: Documents, études, et repertoires, Paris |
| PL | Patrologia latina [=Patrologiae cursus completus: Series latina]. Edited by J.-P. Migne. 221 vols. Paris, 1844–1891 |
| PLS | Patrologiae cursus completus: Series latina, supplementum. Edited by A. Hamman. 5 vols. Paris, 1958–1974 |
| PMAAR | Papers and Monographs of the American Academy in Rome, Rome |
| PO | Patrologia orientalis, Paris, etc. |
| *POC* | *Proche-Orient chrétien,* Jerusalem |
| PP | Philosophia patrum, Leiden |
| PRSA | Problemi e ricerche di storia antica, Rome |
| PS | Patrologia syriaca, Paris |
| PTS | Patristische Texte und Studien, Berlin, etc. |
| PUCSC | Pubblicazioni (Edizioni) del l'Università Cattolica del Sacro Cuore, Milan |
| PUM.T | Publications of the University of Manchester: Theological Series, Manchester, Eng. |
| PuP | Päpste und Papsttum, Stuttgart |
| PW | Pauly, A. F. *Paulys Realencyclopädie der classischen Altertumswissenschaft.* New edition. Edited by G. Wissowa. 49 vols. in 58. Stuttgart, 1894–1980 |
| PWSup | Supplement to PW. Stuttgart |
| QD | Quaestiones disputatae, Fribourg, Switz. |
| QVetChr | Quaderni di "Vetera Christianorum," Bari |
| *RAC* | *Reallexikon für Antike und Christentum.* Edited by T. Kluser et al. Stuttgart, 1950– |
| *RAC.S* | *Reallexikon für Antike und Christentum: Supplement,* Stuttgart |
| *RAM* | *Revue d'ascétique et de mystique,* Toulouse |
| *RAMi* | *Rivista di ascetica e mistica,* Florence |
| *RB* | *Revue biblique,* Paris |
| *RBén* | *Revue bénédictine de critique, d'histoire et de littérature religieuses,* Maredsous, Belg. |
| *RBI* | *Revue biblique international,* Paris |
| *RBMA* | *Repertorium biblicum medii aevi,* Madrid |
| *RBS* | *Regulae Benedicti studia: Annuarium internationale,* Hildesheim |
| RBS.S | Regulae Benedicti studia: Annuarium internationale, Supplementa, Hildesheim, etc. |
| *RCSF* | *Rivista critica di storia della filosofia,* Milan |
| *RdE* | *Revue d'égyptologie,* Paris, etc. |
| *REA* | *Revue des études anciennes,* Bordeaux |

| | |
|---|---|
| *REAug* | *Revue des études augustiniennes,* Paris |
| *RechAug* | *Recherches augustiniennes,* Paris |
| *RechTh* | *Recherches théologiques: Par les professeurs de la faculté de théologie protestante de l'Université de Strasbourg,* Paris |
| *Ren.* | *Renovatio: Zeitschrift für das interdisziplinäre Gespräch,* Regensburg |
| *RevScRel* | *Revue des sciences religieuses,* Strasbourg |
| *RFIC* | *Rivista di filologia e di istruzione classica,* Turin |
| *RFNS* | *Rivista di filosofia neo-scolastica,* Milan |
| *RHE* | *Revue d'histoire ecclésiastique,* Louvain |
| *RHEF* | *Revue d'histoire de l'église de France,* Paris |
| *RHPR* | *Revue d'histoire et de philosophie religieuses,* Strasbourg |
| *RHR* | *Revue de l'histoire des religions,* Paris |
| *RHT* | *Revue d'histoire des textes,* Paris |
| *RivB* | *Rivista biblica italiana,* Rome |
| RivLas | Rivista lasalliana, Turin |
| RKAM | Religion und Kultur der alten Mittelmeerwelt in Parallelforschungen, Munich |
| *RMP* | *Rheinisches Museum für Philologie,* Bonn |
| *RPARA* | *Rendiconti della Pontificia Accademia Romana di archeologia,* Rome |
| *RQ* | *Römische Quartalschrift für christliche Altertumskunde und Kirchengeschichte,* Fribourg, Switz. |
| RQ.S | Römische Quartalschrift für christliche Altertumskunde und Kirchengeschichte: Supplementhefte, Fribourg, Switz., etc. |
| *RR* | *Review of Religion,* New York |
| *RSC* | *Rivista di studi classici,* Turin |
| *RSFR* | *Rivista trimestrale di studi filosofici e religiosi,* Assisi |
| *RSLR* | *Rivista di storia e letteratura religiosa,* Florence |
| *RSPT* | *Revue des sciences philosophiques et théologiques,* Paris |
| *RSR* | *Recherches de science religieuse,* Paris |
| *RSSR* | *Ricerche di storia sociale e religiosa,* Rome |
| RSSR.M | Recherches et synthèses de sciences religieuses: Section de morale, Gembloux, Belg. |
| RST | Regensburger Studien zur Theologie, Bern, etc. |
| *RTAM* | *Recherches de théologie ancienne et médiévale,* Louvain |
| *RThom* | *Revue thomiste,* Bruges, Belg. |
| *RTL* | *Revue théologique de Louvain,* Louvain |
| *RTP* | *Revue de théologie et de philosophie,* Lausanne |
| *RUO* | *Revue de l'Université d'Ottawa,* Ottawa |
| RVV | Religionsgeschichtliche Versuche und Vorarbeiten, Giessen, etc. |
| SA | Studia anselmiana, Rome |
| SAC | Studi di antichità cristiana, Rome |
| *SacEr* | *Sacris eruditi: Jaarboek voor Godsdienstwetenschappen,* Steenbrugge, Belg., etc. |

| | |
|---|---|
| *Sal.* | *Salesianum: Pubblicata a cura dei professori del Pontificio Ateneo salesiano di Torino,* Turin |
| *Salm* | *Salmanticensis,* Salamanca |
| SAQ | Sammlung ausgewählter Kirchen- und dogmengeschichtlicher Quellenschriften, Tübingen |
| SBA | Schweizerische Beiträge zur Altertumswissenschaft, Basel |
| SBAW | Sitzungsberichte der Bayerischen Akademie der Wissenschaften, Munich |
| SBAW.PH | Sitzungsberichte der Bayerischen Akademie der Wissenschaften: Philosophisch-historische Klasse, Munich |
| SBAW.PPH | Sitzungsberichte der Bayerischen Akademie der Wissenschaften: Philosophisch-philologische und historische Klasse, Munich |
| SBF.CMi | Studium biblicum franciscanum: Collectio minor, Jerusalem, etc. |
| SC | Sources chrétiennes. Paris: Cerf, 1941– |
| SCA | Studies in Christian Antiquity, Washington, D.C. |
| SCBE | Scriptorum classicorum bibliotheca oxoniensis, Oxford |
| *ScC* | *La scuola cattolica,* Milan |
| *Schol* | *Scholastik,* Fribourg, Switz. |
| *SCO* | *Studi classici e orientali,* Pisa |
| *ScrTh* | *Scripta theologica,* Pamplona |
| SD | Studies and Documents, London |
| SEAug | Studia ephemeridis "Augustinianum," Rome |
| SEC | Studies in Early Christianity |
| *SecCent* | *Second Century,* Abilene, Tex. |
| SEHL | Scriptores ecclesiastici hispano-latini veteris et medii aevi, El Escorial, Spain |
| SeL | Storia e letteratura: Raccolta di studi e testi, Rome |
| *Seminarium* | *Seminarium: Commentarii pro seminariis, vocationibus ecclesiasticis, universitatibus,* Vatican City |
| SGKA | Studien zur Geschichte und Kultur des Altertums, Paderborn |
| SGLG | Studia graeca et latina gothoburgensia, Stockholm, etc. |
| SGTK | Studien zur Geschichte der Theologie und der Kirche, Leipzig |
| SHAW | Sitzungsberichte der Heidelberger Akademie der Wissenschaften, Heidelberg |
| SHAW.PH | Sitzungsberichte der Heidelberger Akademie der Wissenschaften: Philosophisch-historische Klasse, Heidelberg |
| SHCT | Studies in the History of Christian Thought, Leiden, etc. |
| SHG | Subsidia hagiographica, Brussels |
| SHR | Studies in the History of Religions, Leiden |
| *SicGym* | *Siculorum gymnasium: Rassegna semestrale della facoltà di lettere e filosofia dell'Università di Catania,* Catania |
| *Sileno* | *Sileno: Rivista di studi classici e cristiani,* Rome |
| SIM | Studia Instituti Missiologici Societatis Verbi Divini, Nettetal, Ger. |

| | |
|---|---|
| *SJT* | *Scottish Journal of Theology,* Edinburgh |
| SKG.G | Königsberger Gelehrten Gesellschaft: Geisteswissenschaftliche Klasse, Schriften, Halle, etc. |
| SKV | Schriften der Kirchenväter, Munich |
| SLAG | Luther-Agricola-Gesellschaft: Schriften, Helsinki |
| *SMGB* | *Studien und Mitteilungen zur Geschichte des Benediktinerordens und seiner Zweige,* Munich |
| SMH | Studies in Medieval History, Washington, D.C. |
| SMHVL | Scripta minora: Kungliga Humanistiska Vetenskapssamfundet i Lund, Lund |
| SMRH | Studies in Medieval and Renaissance History, Lincoln, Nebr. |
| SMRL | Studies in Medieval and Renaissance Latin Language and Literature, Washington, D.C. |
| *SMSR* | *Studi e materiali di storia delle religioni,* Rome |
| SNVAO.HF | Skrifter utgitt av Det Norske videnskaps-akademi i Oslo: Historisk-Filosofisk Klasse, Oslo |
| *SO* | *Symbolae osloenses,* Oslo |
| SÖAW.PH | Sitzungsberichte der Österreichischen Akademie der Wissenschaften in Wien: Philosophisch-historische Klasse, Vienna |
| SoECT | Sources of Early Christian Thought. Philadelphia, 1980– |
| SPAMP | Studien zur Problemgeschichte der antiken und mittelalterlichen Philosophie, Leiden |
| SPAW.PH | Sitzungsberichte der Preussischen Akademie der Wissenschaften: Philosophisch-historische Klasse, Berlin |
| SPB | Studia patristica et byzantina, Ettal, Ger. |
| *Spec* | *Speculum,* Cambridge, Mass. |
| SPMed | Studia patristica mediolanensia, Milan |
| SpOr | Spiritualité orientale, Bégrolles-en-Mages, France |
| SPS | Salzburger Patristische: Veröffentlichungen des Internationalen Forschungszentrums für Grundfragen der Wissenschaften Salzburg, Salzburg |
| *SROC* | *Studi e ricerche sull'Oriente cristiano,* Rome |
| *SSAM* | *Settimana di studio del Centro italiano di studi sull'alto medioevo,* Spoleto |
| SSL | Spicilegium sacrum lovaniense, Louvain, etc. |
| *SSR* | *Studi di sociologia della religione,* Rome |
| *SSRel* | *Studi storico-religiosi,* L'Aquila |
| SSSR | Society for the Scientific Study of Religion |
| SST | Studies in Sacred Theology, Washington, D.C., etc. |
| *ST* | *Studia theologica,* Lund |
| STA | Studia et testimonia antiqua, Munich |
| StAnsPT | Studia anselmiana philosophica theologica, Rome |
| STG | Studien zur Theologie und Geschichte, St. Ottilien |
| STGL | Studien zur Theologie des geistlichen Lebens, Würzburg |

| | |
|---|---|
| STL | Studia theologica lundensia, Lund, etc. |
| *StLi* | *Studia liturgica,* Rotterdam |
| *StMed* | *Studi medievali,* Turin |
| *StPat* | *Studia patavina,* Padua |
| StPatr | Studia patristica, Berlin, etc. |
| StPB | Studia post-biblica, Leiden, etc. |
| STPIMS | Studies and Texts: Pontifical Institute of Mediaeval Studies, Toronto |
| StPM | Stromata patristica et mediaevalia, Brussels |
| STRT | Studia theologica rheno-traiectina, Utrecht |
| StSil | Studia silensia, Burgos, Spain |
| StSR | Studi di scienze religiose, Parma |
| StT | Studi e testi, Biblioteca Apostolica Vaticana, Vatican City |
| Studia | Studia: Recherches de philosophie et de théologie publiées par les facultés S. J. de Montréal, Paris |
| *StudMon* | *Studia monastica,* Montserrat, Spain |
| *SubBi* | *Subsidia biblica* |
| SubMon | Subsidia monastica, Montserrat, Spain |
| SUC | Schriften des Urchristentums, Darmstadt |
| SuPa | Sussidi patristici, Rome |
| *SUSF* | *Studi urbinati di Storia, filosofia e letteratura,* Urbino |
| SVigChr | Supplements to Vigiliae christianae, Leiden, etc. |
| SVSL | Skrifter utgivna av Vetenskaps-Societeten i Lund, Lund |
| SVTP | Studia in Veteris Testamenti pseudepigrapha, Leiden |
| *SVTQ* | *St. Vladimir's Theological Quarterly,* New York |
| SWR | Studies in Women and Religion |
| TANZ | Texte und Arbeiten zum neutestamentlichen Zeitalter, Tübingen |
| TBAW | Tübinger Beiträge zur Altertumswissenschaft, Stuttgart |
| TBNGP | Texte und Forschungen zur byzantinisch-neugriechischen Philologie, Berlin, etc. |
| TCH | Transformation of the Classical Heritage. Berkeley, Calif. |
| *TDNT* | *Theological Dictionary of the New Testament,* Grand Rapids, Eerdmans |
| TD.T | Textus et documenta: Series theologica, Pontificia Universitas Gregoriana, Rome |
| TEH | Theologische Existenz heute, Munich |
| *Teol* | *Teología,* Buenos Aires |
| Test. | Testimonia: Schriften der altchristlichen Kirche, Düsseldorf |
| TeT | Temi e testi, Rome |
| TET | Textes et études théologiques, Bruges, Belg. |
| Teubner | Bibliotheca scriptorum graecorum et romanorum teubneriana, Leipzig, etc. |
| *TF* | *Theologische Forschung,* Hamburg |
| *TGl* | *Theologie und Glaube,* Paderborn |

| | |
|---|---|
| *Theol(A)* | *Theologia: Epistemonikon periodikon ekdidomenon kata trimenian,* Athens |
| Theol(P) | Théologie, Paris |
| Theoph. | Theophaneia: Beiträge zur Religions- und Kirchengeschichte des Altertums, Bonn, etc. |
| ThH | Théologie historique, Paris |
| *Thought* | *Thought: A Review of Culture and Idea,* New York |
| *THS* | *Transactions of the Royal Historical Society,* London |
| ThSLG | Theologische Studien der Österreichischen Leo-Gesellschaft, Vienna |
| *ThStKr* | *Theologische Studien und Kritiken: Zeitschrift für das gesamte Gebiet der Theologie,* Hamburg |
| TK | Texte und Kommentare: Eine altertumswissenschaftliche Reihe, Berlin |
| TKTG | Texte zur Kirchen- und Theologiegeschichte, Gütersloh |
| *TLG* | *Thesaurus linguae graecae: Canon of Greek Authors and Works.* 3d ed. Oxford, 1990 |
| *TLZ* | *Theologische Literaturzeitung,* Leipzig |
| *TP* | *Theologie und Philosophie,* Fribourg, Switz. |
| TPL | Textus patristici et liturgici, Regensburg |
| *TQ* | *Theologische Quartalschrift,* Tübingen |
| *TRE* | *Theologische Realenzyklopädie.* Edited by G. Krause and G. Müller. Berlin, 1977– |
| TRSR | Testi e ricerche di scienze religiose, Florence, etc. |
| *TRu* | *Theologische Rundschau,* Tübingen |
| TS | Texts and Studies: Contributions to Biblical and Patristic Literature, Cambridge |
| *TS* | *Theological Studies,* Woodstock, Md. |
| TSMÂO | Typologie de sources du Moyen Âge occidental, Turnhout, Belg. |
| TSTP | Tübinger Studien zur Theologie und Philosophie, Mainz |
| TTH | Translated Texts for Historians |
| TThSt | Trierer theologische Studien, Trier |
| TTS | Tübinger theologische Studien, Mainz |
| TU | Texte und Untersuchungen zur Geschichte der altchristlichen Literatur, Leipzig, Berlin |
| *TZ* | *Theologische Zeitschrift: Theologische Fakultät der Universität Basel,* Basel |
| TzF | Texte zur Forschung, Darmstadt |
| UB | Urban-(Taschen-)Bücher, Stuttgart |
| UNHAII | Uitgaven van het Nederlands Historisch-Archeologisch Instituut te Istanbul, Istanbul |
| VAW | Verhandelingen der Koninklijke Akademie van Wetenschappen te Amsterdam, Amsterdam |
| *VC* | *Vigiliae christianae: A Review of Early Christian Life and Language,* Amsterdam |

| | |
|---|---|
| *VetChr* | *Vetera Christianorum*, Bari, Italy |
| *VF* | *Verkündigung und Forschung*, Munich |
| VHAAH.FF | K. vitterhets-, historie- och antikvitets-akademiens, Stockholm handlingar: Filologisk-filosofiska serien, Stockholm |
| VIEG | Veröffentlichungen des Instituts für Europäische Geschichte Mainz, Wiesbaden |
| VieMon | Vie monastique, Bégrolles-en-Mauges, France |
| ViSa | Vite dei santi, Verona, etc. |
| *Vivarium* | *Vivarium: A Journal for Mediaeval Philosophy and the Intellectual Life of the Middle Ages*, Leiden |
| VL | Vetus Latina: Die Reste der altlateinischen Bibel, Fribourg, Switz. |
| VNAW | Verhandelingen der Koninklijke Nederlandsche Akademie van Wetenschappen (te Amsterdam), Amsterdam |
| VRCS | Variorum Reprints: Collected Studies Series, London, etc. |
| VSen | Verba seniorum: Collana di testi patristici e medievali, Albi, etc. |
| *VS.S* | *La vie spirituelle: Supplément*, Paris |
| WBTh | Wiener Beiträge zur Theologie, Vienna |
| WdF | Wege der Forschung, Darmstadt |
| WoodSt | Woodbrooke Studies: Christian Documents in Syriac, Arabic and Garshuni, Cambridge |
| WSA | The Works of Saint Augustine: A Translation for the 21st Century |
| *WSt* | *Wiener Studien: Zeitschrift für klassische Philologie und Patristik*, Vienna |
| WUNT | Wissenschaftliche Untersuchungen zum Neuen Testament, Tübingen |
| WZ(H) | Wissenschaftliche Zeitschrift der Martin-Luther-Universität, Halle-Wittenberg, Halle |
| *ZAC* | *Zeitschrift für antikes Christentum/Journal of Ancient Christianity* |
| *ZDP* | *Zeitschrift für deutsche Philologie*, Berlin |
| *ZDPV* | *Zeitschrift des Deutschen Palästina-Vereins*, Wiesbaden, etc. |
| Zet. | Zetemata. Monographien zur klassischen Altertumswissenschaft, Munich |
| *ZKG* | *Zeitschrift für Kirchengeschichte*, Stuttgart |
| *ZKT* | *Zeitschrift für katholische Theologie*, Vienna |
| *ZNW* | *Zeitschrift für die neutestamentliche Wissenschaft und die Kunde der älteren Kirche*, Berlin |
| *ZPE* | *Zeitschrift für Papyrologie und Epigraphik*, Bonn |
| *ZSRG.K* | *Zeitschrift der Savigny-Stiftung für Rechtsgeschichte: Kanonistische Abteilung*, Weimar |
| *ZTK* | *Zeitschrift für Theologie und Kirche*, Tübingen |
| *ZWT* | *Zeitschrift für wissenschaftliche Theologie*, Jena |

## II. GENERAL

| | |
|---|---|
| b. | born |
| B.C.E. | before the Common Era |
| bk(s). | book(s) |
| c. | century |
| ca. | about |
| C.E. | Common Era |
| cf. | compare |
| ch(s). | chapter(s) |
| com. | commentary |
| d. | died |
| ed(s). | editor(s), edited by, edition |
| esp. | especially |
| ET | English translation |
| f(f). | and the following one(s) |
| frg(s). | fragment(s) |
| LXX | Septuagint |
| n. | note |
| no(s). | number(s) |
| n.a. | no author |
| n.p. | no publisher; no page numbers |
| NS | New Series |
| NT | New Testament |
| OT | Old Testament |
| par. | parallel(s) |
| para. | paragraph |
| pref. | preface |
| pt. | part |
| repr. | reprint |
| rev. | revised (by) |
| trans. | translated by |
| v. | verse |

## III. PRIMARY SOURCES

### A. Old Testament

| | |
|---|---|
| Gen | Genesis |
| Exod | Exodus |
| Num | Numbers |
| Ps(s) | Psalms |

| Prov | Proverbs |
|------|----------|
| Isa | Isaiah |
| Dan | Daniel |

## B. New Testament

| Matt | Matthew |
|------|---------|
| Rom | Rom |
| 1–2 Cor | 1–2 Corinthians |
| Gal | Galatians |
| Phil | Philippians |
| Col | Colossians |
| 1–2 Thess | 1–2 Thessalonians |
| Heb | Hebrews |
| 2 Pet | 2 Peter |
| Rev | Revelation |

## C. Greek and Latin Works

| *1 Apol.* | *Apologia i* of Justin Martyr |
|-----------|-------------------------------|
| *2 Apol.* | *Apologia ii* of Justin Martyr |
| *Apol.* | *Apologeticus* of Tertullian |
| *Autol.* | *Ad Autolycum* of Theophilus |
| *Aux.* | *Sermo contra Auxentium de basilicis tradendis* |
| *Barn.* | *Barnabas* |
| *C. Ar.* | *Orationes contra Arianos* of Athanasius |
| *C. Jul.* | *Contra Julianum* of Augustine |
| *Cael. hier.* | *De caelesti hierarchia* of Pseudo-Dionysius the Areopagite |
| *Comm. Isa.* | *Commentariorum in Isaiam libri XVIII* of Jerome |
| *Conf.* | *Confessiones* of Augustine |
| *Enarrat. Ps.* | *Enarrationes in Psalmos* of Augustine |
| *Ep.* | *Epistulae* |
| *Ep. pasc.* | *Epistulae pascales (Paschal Letters)* of Theophilus of Alexandria |
| *Epist.* | *Epistulae* of Jerome |
| *Haer.* | *Adversus haereses* of Irenaeus |
| *Haer.* | *Refutatio omnium haeresium* of Hippolytus |
| *Hist. eccl.* | *Ecclesiastical History (Historia ecclesiastica)* of Eusebius, Evagrius Scholasticus, Rufinus, or Sozomen |
| *Hom. Luc.* | *Homiliae in Lucam* of Origen |
| Ign. *Rom.* | Ignatius, *To the Romans* |
| Ign. *Smyrn.* | Ignatius, *To the Smyrnaeans* |

| | |
|---|---|
| *Off.* | *De officiis ministrorum* of Ambrose |
| *Or.* | *Orationes* |
| *Or. Bas.* | *Oratio in laudem Basilii* of Gregory of Nazianzus |
| *Pan.* | *Panarion (Adversus haereses)* of Epiphanius |
| *Prax.* | *Adversus Praxean* of Tertullian |
| *Retract.* | *Retractationes* of Augustine |
| *Serm.* | *Sermones* of Augustine |
| *Strom.* | *Stromata* of Clement of Alexandria |
| *Trin.* | *De Trinitate* of Augustine |
| *Vir. ill.* | *De viris illustribus* of Jerome |
| *Vit. Amb.* | *Vita Ambrosii* of Paulinus |
| *Vit. Ant.* | *Vita Antonii* of Athanasius |
| *Vit. Aug.* | *Vita Augustini* of Possidius |
| *Vit. Const.* | *Vita Constantini* of Eusebius |

# General Bibliography

## I. BIBLIOGRAPHIES

*L'année philologique: Bibliographie critique et analytique de l'antiquité gréco-latine* (Paris, 1924–). *[AnPhil]*

> Annual annotated bibliography of classical philology and antiquity, arranged according to authors and fields, also encompassing Christian antiquity and its authors. Its volumes are generally published three years after the date of publication of the works listed.

> Complementary bibliographies: S. Lambrino, *Bibliographie de l'antiquité classique, 1896–1914* (Paris: Belles Lettres, 1951). – J. Marouzeau, *Dix années de bibliographie classique, 1914–1924* (2 vols.; Paris: Belles Lettres, 1927–1928).

*Bibliographia patristica: Internationale patristische Bibliographie* (Berlin, 1956–1990). *[BPatr]*

> Arranged according to authors and fields, without commentary, but including lists of reviews.

*Revue d'histoire ecclésiastique [RHE]. See* VIII. Journals and Yearbooks

Further periodical bibliographies in: *Bulletin d'information et de liaison: Association internationale d'études patristiques* (Amsterdam, 1968–) *[BAIEP]*. – *Bulletin de la Bible latin: Bulletin d'ancienne littérature chrétienne latine* (Maredsous, Belg., 1921–1993). – *Bulletin de théologie ancienne et médiévale* (Louvain, 1929–1996) *[BthAM]*. – *Byzantinische Zeitschrift* (Munich, 1892–) *[ByzZ]*. – *Ostkirchliche Studien* (Würzburg, 1952–) *[OS]*. – *Revue des sciences philosophiques et théologiques* (Paris, 1907–) *[RSPT]*. – *Recherches de science religieuse* (Paris, 1910–) *[RSR]*. – *Salmanticensis: Commentarius de sacris disciplinis cura facultatum Pontificiae Universitatis Ecclesiasticae (Salmanticensis) editus* (Salamanca, 1954–) *[Salm.]*.

T. A. Robinson et al., *The Early Church: An Annotated Bibliography of Literature in English* (Metuchen, N.J.: Scarecrow, 1993).

M. Albert et al., *Christianismes orientaux: Introduction à l'étude des langues et des littératures* (ICA 4; Paris: Cerf, 1993).

> Comprehensive, well-ordered bibliography of Arabic, Armenian, Coptic, Georgian, and Syriac languages and literatures.

*See also* XI. Electronic Databanks, Bibliographies

# II. DICTIONARIES / ENCYCLOPEDIAS

## A. Early Christianity and Literature

*Encyclopedia of the Early Church* (produced by the Institutum Patristicum Augustinianum and edited by A. di Berardino; translated from the Italian by A. Walford; with a foreword and bibliographic amendments by W. H. C. Frend; 2 vols.; Cambridge: James Clarke; New York: Oxford University Press, 1992). *[EECh]*

> = *Dizionario patristico e di antichità cristiane* (ed. A. di Berardino; 3 vols.; Casale Monferrato: Marietti, 1983–1988).

> = *Dictionnaire encyclopédique du christianisme ancien* (ed. F. Vial; 2 vols.; Paris: Cerf, 1990).

> = *Diccionario patrístico y de la antigüedad cristiana* (2 vols.; Salamanca: Sígueme, 1991–1992).

> General dictionary of early Christian literature and related subjects, produced with the collaboration of numerous international specialists, with good select bibliographies to each article. Complemented by synoptic tables, maps, illustrations, and indexes. The French and Spanish editions have been translated unchanged; the English, with supplementary bibliographies; unfortunately, they contain numerous printing errors.

E. Ferguson et al., eds., *Encyclopedia of Early Christianity* (2 vols.; 2d ed.; New York and London: Garland 1997). *[EEC]*

> Dictionary of the patristic age, comparable to the preceding in organization and design.

S. Döpp and W. Geerlings, eds., *Dictionary of Early Christian Literature* (trans. M. O'Connell; New York: Crossroad, 2000).

> A concise, one-volume dictionary of early Christian literature, with basic bibliographical references.

*Reallexikon für Antike und Christentum: Sachwörterbuch zur Auseinandersetzung des Christentums mit der antiken Welt* (ed. T. Klauser et al.; Stuttgart: Hiersemann, 1950–). *[RAC]*

> Fundamental enterprise researching comprehensively the relations between Christendom and the antique world. Initiated by Franz Joseph Dölger, sole editor and author of the periodical *Antike und Christentum* (6 vols.; Münster, 1929–1950). Supplements are published in *Jahrbuch für Antike und Christentum,* later to be collected in supplement volumes.

*Dictionnaire d'archéologie chrétienne et de liturgie* (ed. F. Cabrol; 15 vols.; Paris: Letouzey & Ané, 1907–1953). *[DACL]*

> Comprehensive dictionary of Christian archaeology. Extremely useful for every aspect of the environment of early Christian texts.

# B. General Dictionaries for Theology and Church

*New Catholic Encyclopedia* (2d ed.; 15 vols.; Detroit: Thomson/Gale; Washington, D.C.: Catholic University of America Press, 2003).

F. L. Cross and E. Livingstone, eds., *The Oxford Dictionary of the Christian Church* (3d ed.; New York: Oxford University Press: 1997).

H. Wace and W. Piercy, eds., *A Dictionary of Christian Biography* (4 vols.; London: J. Murray, 1877–1887). Articles pertaining to the early church reprinted as *A Dictionary of Early Christian Biography* (Peabody, Mass.: Hendrickson, 1999).

*Theologische Realenzyklopädie* (ed. G. Krause and G. Müller; Berlin: de Gruyter, 1977–). *[TRE]*

> Comprehensive articles for all of theology, ecclesiastical history, and literature by international specialists, with extensive bibliographies.

*Dictionnaire d'histoire et de géographie ecclésiastiques* (Paris: Letouzey & Ané, 1912–). *[DHGE]*

> Comprehensive dictionary for all of ecclesiastical history, with well-selected bibliographies.

*Dictionnaire de spiritualité ascétique et mystique, doctrine et histoire* (ed. M. Viller; 15 vols. in 21; Paris: Beauchesne, 1937–1995). *[DSp]*

> Dictionary of the most fundamental aspects of Christian spirituality. Nearly all ancient Christian authors and works are included.

# C. General Encyclopedias for Classical Antiquity and Byzantium

A. F. Pauly, *Paulys Realencyclopädie der classischen Altertumswissenschaft* (new ed.; ed. G. Wissowa; 49 vols. in 58; Stuttgart: J. B. Metzler, 1894–1980). [PW]

J. P. Murphy, *Index to the Supplements and Suppl. Volumes of Pauly-Wissowa's R.E.* (2d ed.; Chicago: Ares, 1980).

*Register der Nachträge und Supplemente* (ed. H. Gärtner and A. Wünsch; Munich: A. Druckenmüller, 1980).

> Monumental enterprise to present all of classical antiquity in comprehensive articles, accompanied by fundamental bibliographies.

A. P. Kazhdan, ed., *The Oxford Dictionary of Byzantium* (3 vols.; New York: Oxford University Press, 1991).

# III. PATROLOGIES AND HISTORIES OF LITERATURE

J. Quasten, *Patrology* (3 vols.; Utrecht: Spectrum, 1950–1960).

= *Initiation aux Pères de l'Église* (trans. J. Laporte; 3 vols.; Paris: Cerf, 1955–1963).

= *Patrologia* (2 vols.; Turin: Marietti, 1967–).

= *Patrología* (trans. I. Oñatibia, P. U. Farré, and E. M. Llopart; 4 vols. BAC 206, 217, 422, 605; Madrid: Biblioteca de autores cristianos, 2001–2002).

Continued by:

*Patrology 4: The Golden Age of Latin Patristic Literature, from the Council of Nicea to the Council of Chalcedon* (trans. P. Solari; Institutum Patristicum Augustinianum, Rome; Westminster, Md.: Christian Classics, 1986).

= *Patrologia, vol. 3: Dal concilio di Nicea (325) al concilio di Calcedonia (451): I Padri latini* (ed. A. di Berardino; Turin: Marietti, 1978).

= *Patrología 3: La edad de oro de la literatura patrística latina* (trans. J. M. Guirau; BAC 422; Madrid: Biblioteca de autores cristianos, 1981).

= *Initiation aux Pères de l'Église, vol. 4: Du concile de Nicée (325) au concile de Chalcédoine (451), les Pères latins* (trans. J. Bagot; rev. A. Hamman; Paris: Cerf, 1986).

*Patrologia, vol. 4: Dal concilio di Calcedonia (451) a Beda, i Padri latini* (ed. A. di Berardino; Genoa: Marietti, 1996).

*The Eastern Fathers from the Council of Chalcedon (451) to John of Damascus (750)* (ed. A. di Berardino; trans. Adrian Walford; Cambridge: J. Clarke, 2006).

= *Patrologia, vol. 5: Dal concilio di Calcedonia (451) a Giovanni Damasceno (750), i Padri orientali* (ed. A. di Berardino; Genoa: Marietti, 2000).

Comprehensive and fundamental manual. Introduces all the authors and works of the patristic age with ample bibliographies. Puts emphasis on historical and biographical data and the doctrinal/theological contents of the works.

B. Altaner, *Patrology* (trans. H. C. Graef; New York: Herder, 1961).

= B. Altaner and A. Stuiber, *Patrologie: Leben, Schriften, und Lehre der Kirchenväter* (8th ed.; Fribourg, Switz.: Herder, 1978).

= *Précis de patrologie* (adapted by H. Chirat; Paris: Salvator, 1961).

= *Patrología* (trans. E. Cuevas and U. Domínguez-Del Val; 5th ed.; Madrid: Espasa-Calpe, 1962).

= *Patrologia* (trans. A. Babolin; 7th ed.; Turin: Marietti, 1997).

Manual of the same type as Quasten. Treats the material more succinctly but clearly and reliably, with rich and basic bibliographies.

W. Schmid and O. Stählin, *Geschichte der griechischen Literatur* (HAW 7; Munich: Beck, 1929–); based on W. von Christ, *Geschichte der griechischen Literatur* (6th ed.; 3 vols.; Munich: Beck, 1912–1924).

> Comprehensive history of ancient Greek literature until 530, thus embracing nearly all of the Greek Christian literature as well (vol. II/2, pp. 1105–1492). While the classical literature is ordered by genres, the Christian is arranged according to authors and works.

H.-G. Beck, *Kirche und theologische Literatur im byzantinischen Reich* (2d unaltered ed.; HAW 12.2.1; Munich: Beck, 1977).

> Basic manual for the Christian Byzantine literature from the sixth century to the end of the Byzantine Empire, 1453. Indispensable for understanding the intertwining relationships of ecclesiastical and imperial structures, the imperial church and its organization, liturgy, hagiography, and theology.

L. J. Engels and H. Hofmann, eds., *Spätantike, mit einem Panorama der byzantinischen Literatur* (vol. 4 of *Neues Handbuch der Literaturwissenschaft;* Wiesbaden: AULA, 1997).

> Introduction to the late-ancient literature, arranged by literary genres and topics.

M. Schanz, C. Hosius, and G. Krüger, *Geschichte der römischen Literatur bis zum Gesetzgebungswerk des Kaisers Justinian* (4th ed.; 4 vols. in 5; HAW 8; Munich: Beck, 1927–1959).

> In this Latin counterpart to von Christ's *Geschichte der griechischen Literatur,* Latin Christian literature is treated in vols. 3, pp. 245–61; 4.1, pp. 205–550; 4.2, pp. 360–645.

R. Herzog and P. L. Schmidt, eds., *Handbuch der lateinischen Literatur der Antike* (HAW 8; Munich: Beck, 1989–). *[HLL]*

> Completely revised edition of Schanz-Hosius-Krüger, while adhering to its basic principles. The Christian literature, too, is, wherever possible, inserted in the general division according to literary genres. Collections of sources and bibliographies abound. The treatment of the works, however, is from an exclusively philological point of view.

C. Moreschini and E. Norelli, *Storia della letteratura cristiana antica greca e latina* (2 vols. in 3; Brescia: Morcelliana, 1995–1996).

> = C. Moreschini and E. Norelli, *Early Christian Greek and Latin Literature: A Literary History* (2 vols.; Peabody, Mass.: Hendrickson, 2005).

# IV. SERIES OF EDITIONS

Patrologiae cursus completus: Series graeca (ed. J.-P. Migne; 162 vols.; Paris: Migne, 1857–1886). [PG]

Complemented by:

T. Hoepfner, *Index locupletissimus* (2 vols.; Paris: Librairie Orientaliste Paul Geuthner, 1928–1945).

F. Cavallera, *Indices* (Paris: Garnier, 1912).

Largest collection of Greek patristic texts accompanied by Latin translations, with the intention of being complete until the end of the Byzantine Empire (including the works by Cardinal Bessarion [d. 1472] and Patriarch Gennadius II of Constantinople, † after 1472). Compiled by the French priest and publisher Jacques-Paul Migne. He collected and printed the best available editions of his time, especially those prepared by the Benedictine convent of St. Maur in Paris, the famous Maurists. Despite great efforts to produce new editions according to modern critical standards, many of these texts remain the only or best editions hitherto available. Cf. A.-G. Hamman, *Jacques-Paul Migne: Le retour aux Pères de l'Église* (Paris: Beauchesne, 1975).

*See also* X. Microfiches

*See also* XI. Electronic Databanks

Patrologiae cursus completus: Series latina (ed. J.-P. Migne; 221 vols.; Paris: Migne, 1844–1891 [218–221: Indices]). [PL]

Complemented by:

J.-P. Migne, *Elucidatio in 235 tabulas Patrologiae latinae auctore cartusiensi* (Rotterdam: De Forel, 1952).

P. Glorieux, *Pour revaloriser Migne: Tables rectificatives* (Mélanges de science religieuse: Année 9, 1952: Cahier supplémentaire; Lille: Facultés catholiques, 1952).

Latin counterpart to the Patrologia graeca, up to Pope Innocent III († 1216).

*See also* X. Microfiches

*See also* XI. Electronic Databanks

Patrologiae cursus completus: Series latina, supplementum (ed. A. Hamman; 5 vols.; Paris: Garnier, 1958–1974); vol. 5: *Indices,* ed. A. L. Bailly and J.-P. Bouhot. [PLS]

Comprehensive collection of all texts discovered after Migne's monumental series, arranged in the order of Migne's patrologies.

*See also* X. Microfiches

*See also* XI. Electronic Databanks

Corpus Christianorum: Series latina (Turnhout, Belg.: Brepols, 1954–). [CCSL]

This series intends to become a new Patrologiae cursus completus and therefore, like Migne, in part reedits already existing critical editions; but it also produces new critical editions of the works of Latin patristic authors up to the Venerable Bede

(† 732). Structure and content are reported in the *Clavis patrum latinorum*. (See VI. Reference Works.)

*See also* X. Microfiches

*See also* XI. Electronic Databanks

Corpus Christianorum: Series graeca (Turnhout, Belg.: Brepols, 1977–). [CCSG]

> Parallel series for early Greek Christian literature up to John Damascene († ca. 750). See *Clavis Patrum Graecorum* (VI. Reference Works).

*See also* X. Microfiches

Corpus Christianorum: Series apocryphorum (Turnhout, Belg.: Brepols, 1983–). [CChr.SA]

> The third parallel series for the New Testament Apocrypha. See *Clavis apocryphorum Novi Testamenti* (VI. Reference Works).

*See also* X. Microfiches

Corpus scriptorum ecclesiasticorum latinorum (Vienna: Österreichische Akademie der Wissenschaften, 1866–). [CSEL]

> Collection of critical editions of Latin texts of the patristic age. Like the Corpus Christianorum: Series latina, it intends to replace the texts in Migne's patrologies. A number of works are therefore edited in both series independently.

*See also* X. Microfiches

Die griechischen christlichen Schriftsteller der ersten [drei] Jahrhunderte (Leipzig: Hinrichs; Berlin, etc.: Akademie, etc., 1897–). [GCS]

> Collection of critical editions of Greek texts of the patristic age, parallel to the Corpus scriptorum ecclesiasticorum latinorum. Despite its original limitation to the first three centuries, some later works are included as well.

*See also* X. Microfiches

Sources chrétiennes (founded by H. de Lubac and J. Daniélou; Paris: Cerf, 1941–). [SC]

> Very popular bilingual collection of early Christian and some medieval literature, with French translations and commentaries; in general, not producing new critical editions but reprinting the best existing ones.

Oxford Early Christian Texts (Oxford: Oxford University Press, 1971–). [OECT]

> Open bilingual series of critical editions of early Greek and Latin Christian texts with English translations, without numbering of the volumes or definite overall plan.

Patrologia syriaca (ed. R. Graffin; 3 vols.; Paris, etc.: Firmin-Didot, etc., 1894–1926). [PS]

> First collection of Syriac patristic works.

*See also* X. Microfiches

Patrologia orientalis (ed. R. Graffin, F. Nau, and F. Graffin; Paris, etc.: Firmin-Didot, etc., 1903–). [PO]

> Large and still growing collection of all oriental early Christian literature, formerly with translations into Latin, more recently into a modern language (mostly English, French, or German).

Corpus scriptorum christianorum orientalium (Paris, etc., 1903–). [CSCO]

> Monumental collection of Christian oriental texts, now comprising hundreds of volumes subdivided in series for Ethiopic, Arabic, Armenian, Coptic, Georgian, and Syriac authors; complemented by a studies series (Subsidia). Formerly with translations into Latin, more recently into a modern language (mostly English, French, or German).

Monumenta Germaniae historica inde ab anno Christi quingentesimo usque ad annum millesimum et quingentesimum: Auctores antiquissimi (15 vols.; Berlin: Weidman, 1877–1919). [MGH.AA]

> The first volumes contain, in the given chronological delimitations, critical editions of early Christian Latin authors living in, or important for, German areas, such as Salvianus of Marseille and Gregory of Tours.

# V. SERIES OF TRANSLATIONS

## A. English

The Ante-Nicene Christian Library (24 vols.; Edinburgh: T&T Clark, 1866–1872). [ANCL]

The Ante-Nicene Fathers (10 vols.; Buffalo: Christian Literature, 1885–1896; repr., Grand Rapids: Eerdmans, 1973; Peabody, Mass.: Hendrickson, 1995). [ANF]

The Nicene and Post-Nicene Fathers: First Series (14 vols.; Buffalo: Christian Literature, 1886–1900; repr., Grand Rapids: Eerdmans, 1956; Peabody, Mass.: Hendrickson, 1995). [NPNF¹]

The Nicene and Post-Nicene Fathers: Second Series (14 vols.; New York: Christian Literature, 1886–1900; repr., Grand Rapids: Eerdmans, 1956; Peabody, Mass.: Hendrickson, 1995). [NPNF²]

Ancient Christian Writers (Westminster, Md., etc.: Newman, 1946–). [ACW]

Fathers of the Church (Washington, D.C., etc., 1946–). [FC]

## B. French

Collection Les Pères dans la foi (ed. A.-G. Hamman and M.-H. Congourdeau; Paris: Migne, 1977–). [CPF]

See also IV. Series of Editions: Sources chrétiennes

## C. German

Bibliothek der Kirchenväter (ed. F. X. Reithmayr and V. Thalhofer; 80 vols.; Leipzig: Engelmann, 1869–1888). [BKV$^1$]

Bibliothek der Kirchenväter (ed. O. Bardenhewer, T. Schermann, K. Weyman, J. Zellinger, and J. Martin; 61 vols. and 2 vols. indices; Kempten: Kösel, 1911–1931. 2d series: ed. O. Bardenhewer, J. Zellinger, and J. Martin; 20 vols.; Munich: Kösel & Pustet, 1932–1939). [BKV$^2$]

Bibliothek der griechischen Literatur (ed. P. Wirth and W. Gessel; Stuttgart: A. Hiersemann, 1971–). [BGrL]

Fontes christiani: Zweisprachige Neuausgabe christlicher Quellentexte aus Altertum und Mittelalter (ed. N. Brox et al.; Fribourg, Switz.: Herder, 1991–). [FChr]

## D. Italian

Classici delle religioni (Turin: Unione Tipografico-Editrice Torinese, 1968–). [CdR]

Collana di testi patristici (Rome: Città Nuova, 1976–). [CTePa]

Letture cristiane delle origini (Rome: Edizioni Paoline, 1979–). [LCO]

Letture cristiane del primo millennio (Turin and Milan: Edizioni Paoline, 1987–). [LCPM]

Collana patristica (Rome: Edizioni Paoline, 1992–).

## E. Spanish

Biblioteca de autores cristianos (Madrid: Editorial Católica, 1944–). [BAC]

Biblioteca de patrística (Madrid: Ciudad Nueva, 1986–).

Fuentes patrísticas (Madrid: Ciudad Nueva, 1991–).

## VI. REFERENCE WORKS

J.-C. Haelewyck, *Clavis apocryphorum Veteris Testamenti* (Turnhout, Belg.: Brepols, 1998).

> Inventory of all apocryphal books of the Old Testament in historical sequence, giving the codices, editions, translations, and basic bibliography.

M. Geerard, *Clavis apocryphorum Novi Testamenti* (Turnhout, Belg.: Brepols, 1992).

> Inventory of all apocryphal books of the New Testament in biblical sequence (Gospels, Acts, Epistles, Apocalypses), giving the codices, editions, and basic bibliography and discussing the historical and literary problems. Concludes with analytical indices.

M. Geerard, *Clavis patrum graecorum* (5 vols.; Corpus Christianorum; Turnhout, Belg.: Brepols, 1974–1987; 2d ed., 2003–). *[CPG]*

Complemented by:

> *Clavis patrum graecorum: Supplementum* (ed. M. Geerard, J. Noret, F. Glorie, and J. Desmet; Corpus Christianorum; Turnhout, Belg.: Brepols, 1998).

> Inventory of all Greek patristic authors and writings in chronological sequence, with indications of codices, editions, basic literature, and literary-historical problems. Concludes with indices.

> E. Dekkers and A. Gaar, *Clavis patrum latinorum* (3d ed.; CCSL; Steenbrugge, Belg.: Abbatia Sancti Petri, 1995). *[CPL]*

> Counterpart of the *Clavis patrum graecorum* for the Latin patristic authors and writings.

> J. Machielsen, *Clavis patristica pseudepigraphorum medii aevi* (Turnhout, Belg.: Brepols, 1990–).

> Supplement to the *Clavis patrum latinorum* for all medieval writings attributed to a patristic author up to the Venerable Bede († 732), including authentic patristic writings adapted and thus profoundly changed by medieval writers.

H. J. Frede, *Kirchenschriftsteller—Verzeichnis und Sigel: Repertorium scriptorum ecclesiasticorum latinorum saeculo nono antiquiorum siglis adpositis quae in editione Bibliorum Sacrorum iuxta veterem latinam versionem adhibentur* (4th rev. ed.; VL 1.1; Fribourg, Switz.: Herder, 1995). – H. J. Frede and R. Gryson, *Kirchenschriftsteller—Verzeichnis und Sigel: Aktualisierungsheft 1999 = Compléments 1999* (VL 1.1C; Fribourg, Switz.: Herder, 1999).

> List of the abbreviations of the Latin patristic authors and works used in the critical edition of the Vetus Latina, the fragments of pre-Vulgate Latin translations of the Bible preserved in patristic texts. Indispensable reference work because of the precise and up-to-date indications of editions, chronology, authorship, and authenticity of the writings.

A. Keller, *Translationes patristicae graecae et latinae: Bibliographie der Übersetzungen altchristlicher Quellen* (Stuttgart: A. Hiersemann, 1997–).

> Bibliography of the German, English, French, Italian, and Spanish translations of patristic writings in alphabetical order by author, indicating the most recent editions.

Instrumenta patristica (Steenbrugge, Belg.: Abbatia Sancti Petri, 1959–). [IP]

> Series of reference works for the study of early Christian literature: bibliographies, manuscript catalogues, dictionaries, miscellaneous volumes in honor of various scholars, and monographs.

*See also* X. Microfiches

*See also* XI. Electronic Databanks

## VII. MANUALS (HISTORY, PHILOLOGY, THEOLOGY)

Handbuch der [until 1921: klassischen] Altertumswissenschaft (ed. I. von Müller, W. Otto, and H. Bengtson; Munich: Beck, 1885–). [HAW]

> Comprehensive and basic manual for all aspects of classical antiquity up to the Byzantine period: grammar, rhetoric, history, literature, religion, archaeology, numismatics, etc.

*Aufstieg und Niedergang der römischen Welt: Geschichte und Kultur Roms im Spiegel der neueren Forschung* (ed. H. Temporini and W. Haase; Berlin: de Gruyter, 1972–). *[ANRW]*

> Originally planned as a four-volume homage for Prof. Joseph Vogt of Tübingen, then enlarged to a many-volumed series treating fundamentally all aspects of the Greco-Roman world. Articles are written in various languages (English, French, German, Italian).

*Handbook of Church History* (ed. H. Jedin and J. Dolan; 10 vols.; London: Burns & Oates; New York: Herder, Crossroad, 1965–1982). [HCH] Vols. 2, 5–10 published as *History of the Church*. Includes:

> Vol. 1: K. Baus, *From the Apostolic Community to Constantine* (New York: Herder, 1965; 3d ed.; New York: Seabury, 1980).

> Vol. 2: K. Baus et al., *The Imperial Church from Constantine to the Early Middle Ages* (New York: Seabury, 1980).

> Vol. 3: F. Kempf et al., *The Church in the Age of Feudalism* (New York: Herder, 1969).

> Basic manual for the historical environment of the patristic writings.

Handbuch der Dogmengeschichte (ed. M. Schmaus et al.; Fribourg, Switz.: Herder 1951–). *[HDG]*

> Comprehensive but hitherto unfinished manual of the history of Christian doctrine from the beginnings to modern times in four sections: (a) living according to the faith; (b) Trinity, creation, sin; (c) Christology, soteriology, Mariology, God's kingdom and the church; and (d) sacraments, eschatology. The first volume(s) of each section treat the ancient church.

*See* further bibliographical entries on doctrine and theology in particular in part 3, introduction.

# VIII. JOURNALS AND YEARBOOKS

*Augustinianum: Periodicum quadrimestre Instituti Patristici "Augustinianum"* (Rome, 1961–). *[Aug]*

> General journal for the whole field of patristics in all major languages, with a large review section.

*Jahrbuch für Antike und Christentum* (Münster: Aschendorff, 1958–). *[JAC]*

> Yearbook for articles, reviews, notes, and supplements to the *Reallexikon für Antike und Christentum.*

*Journal of Early Christian Studies* (Baltimore, 1993–). *[JECS]*

> Specialized journal of the North American Patristic Society. Basic, as it reflects ongoing North American patristic research.

*Journal of Ecclesiastical History* (London, 1950–). *[JEH]*

> General journal of ecclesiastical history, including the early church.

*Journal of Theological Studies* (Oxford, 1899–). *[JTS]*

> General journal of theology, including patristics.

*Revue bénédictine de critique, d'histoire et de littérature religieuses* (Maredsous, Belg., 1890–). *[RBén]*

> Historical journal containing numerous fundamental contributions to patrology.

*Revue d'histoire ecclésiastique* (Louvain, 1900–). *[RHE]*

> Journal for the whole field of ecclesiastical history, including early Christian literature. Especially useful because of the annual bibliography, divided according to periods and subjects.

*Vigiliae christianae: A Review of Early Christian Life and Language* (Amsterdam 1947–). *[VC]*

> International journal on Christian antiquity and literature, in all major languages, with reviews.

# IX. MONOGRAPH SERIES

Patristic Studies (Washington, D.C.: Catholic University of America, 1922–). [PatSt]

> Editions and studies, many of them dealing with questions on philology, style etc. of the texts.

Greek, Roman and Byzantine Monographs (Durham, N.C., etc., 1959–).

Initiations au christianisme ancien (Paris: Cerf, 1985–). [ICA]

> Introductory and subsidiary patristic studies.

Jahrbuch für Antike und Christentum: Ergänzungsbände (ed. Franz Joseph Dölger-Institut Bonn; Münster: Aschendorff, 1964–). [JAC.E]

> Monograph series supporting the articles of the *Reallexikon für Antike und Christentum.*

Paradosis: Études de littérature et de théologie ancienne (Fribourg, Switz.: St-Paul, 1947–). [Par.]

Patristic Monograph Series (Cambridge, Mass.: Philadelphia Patristic Foundation, 1975–). [PatMS]

> Series of monographs, conference acts, and patristic texts.

Patristische Texte und Studien (ed. K. Aland, W. Schneemelcher, and E. Mühlenberg; Berlin: de Gruyter, 1964–). [PTS]

Studia ephemeridis "Augustinianum" (Rome: Studium Theologicum "Augustinianum," 1967–). [SEAug]

> Monograph series of the Institutum Patristicum Augustinianum in Rome for the entire field of patristics, including many doctoral dissertations done at the institute. Does not publish texts or reference works.

Studia patristica: Papers Presented to the International Conference on Patristic Studies (Berlin, etc.: Akademie, 1957–). [StPatr]

> Collection of most of the papers presented to the International Conference on Patristic Studies, assembling in Oxford every fourth year since 1951. In various languages, mirrors largely the state of patristic research of the time. Originally the volumes were incorporated in the series Texte und Untersuchungen.

Studia patristica mediolanensia (ed. G. Lazzati and R. Cantalamessa; Milan: Vita e Pensiero, 1974–). [SPMed]

Supplements to Vigiliae christianae (ed. A. F. J. Klijn, C. Mohrmann, G. Quispel, J. H. Waszink, and J. C. M. van Winden; Leiden: Brill, 1987–). [SVigChr] Formerly Philosophia patrum.

Philosophia patrum (ed. by J. H. Waszink and J. C. M. van Winden; 8 vols.; Leiden: Brill, 1971–1986). [PP]

> Series of editions, monographs, bibliographies, and collections of studies in the major international languages, supplementing the journal *Vigiliae christianae.*

Sussidi patristici (Rome: Institutum Patristicum Augustinianum, 1981–). [SuPa]

> Series of short introductions, bibliographies, and collections of texts in English, German, and Italian, intended as study tools

Texte und Untersuchungen zur Geschichte der altchristlichen Literatur (ed. O. von Gebhardt and A. von Harnack; Leipzig: Hinrichs; Berlin: Akademie, 1883–). [TU]

> Famous series containing many extremely important contributions to the field.

Texts and Studies: Contributions to Biblical and Patristic Literature (Cambridge: Cambridge University Press, 1891–). [TS]

*See also* X. Microfiches

# X. MICROFICHES

The major editors of microfiches for patrology are Brepols, Turnhout, Belg.; IDC Microform Publishers, Leiden; and Slangenburg Abbey, Doetinchem, Neth.

## A. Editions

Patrologiae cursus completus: Series graeca (ed. J.-P. Migne; 162 vols.; Paris: Migne, 1857–1866). [PG] [IDC]

Patrologiae cursus completus: Series latina (ed. J.-P. Migne; 221 vols.; Paris: Migne, 1841–1864 [218–221: Indices]). [PL] [IDC]

Corpus scriptorum ecclesiasticorum latinorum (Vienna: Österreichische Akademie der Wissenschaften, 1866–). [CSEL]

Die griechischen christlichen Schriftsteller der ersten [drei] Jahrhunderte (Leipzig: Hinrichs; Berlin: Akademie, 1897–). [GCS]

Patrologia syriaca (ed. R. Graffin; 3 vols.; Paris: Firmin-Didot, 1897–1927). [PS]

## B. Reference Works

*Cartotheca patrologiae graeco-latinae* (ed. Facultate theologica tilburgense; 9244 fiches; Turnhout, Belg.: Brepols, 1984).

> Comprises ca. 3,500 cards with entries in alphabetical order and a thematic index of ca. 6,000 cards.

*Corpus Christianorum, Instrumenta lexicologica latina: Series A–Formae; Series B – Lemmata* (Turnhout, Belg.: Brepols, 1982–).

*Corpus Christianorum, Thesaurus patrum graecorum* (Turnhout, Belg.: Brepols, 1990–).

> The series consists of (a) *Enumeratio formarum* (alphabetical index of all the word forms with reference to their frequency), (b) *Concordantia formarum* (an alphabetical concordance of all the word forms of every word), (c) *Index formarum* a tergo ordinatarum (list of the word forms in alphabetical order of their endings). Series B does the same for the words themselves.

## C. Monograph Series

Texte und Untersuchungen zur Geschichte der altchristlichen Literatur (ed. O. von Gebhardt and A. von Harnack; Leipzig: Hinrichs; Berlin: Akademie, 1883–). [TU]

# XI. ELECTRONIC DATABANKS

## A. Bibliographies

Karlsruhe Virtual Catalog

http://www.ubka.uni-karlsruhe.de/hylib/virtueller_katalog.html

> A very powerful and highly effective general research tool, linking the online catalogs of all major libraries worldwide, among them the Library of Congress, the British Library, and the COPAC, a unified access to the libraries of the major British libraries, including Oxford and Cambridge.

Catalog of the library of the Institutum Patristicum Augustinianum in Rome, Via Paolo VI, 25.

http://portico.bl.uk/gabriel/en/countries/vatican-union-en.html

telnet://librs6k.vatlib.it

> The best und most up-to-date bibliography of early Christian literature, available through personal inspection or in conjunction with the Bibliotheca Vaticana and other Roman libraries via the Roman library network (Urbs) and the Internet.

Bibliographic Information Base in Patristics. Université Laval, Quebec, Canada. [BIBP]

http://www.bibl.ulaval.ca/bd/bibp/english.html

> At present it contains about 29,300 records from 325 journals on all disciplines studying patristic Christianity. Search language is French. Persons wishing to search it in English or some other language are advised to contact Prof. René-Michel Roberge under the E-mail address bibp@ftsr.ulaval.ca or write to Laboratoire BIBP, Faculté de théologie et de sciences religieuses, Université Laval. Quebec, QC, Canada. G1K 7P4.

## B. Editions

L. Berkowitz and K. A. Squitier, with technical assistance from W. A. Johnson, *Thesaurus linguae graecae: Canon of Greek Authors and Works* (Version E; Irvine: University of California, Irvine, 2000). *[TLG]*

Databank of all ancient Greek texts, both classical and Christian, from Homer to about the year A.D. 600, with the appropriate research tools and a list of entries and editions in printed form.

Packard Humanities Institute CD-ROM #5.

Counterpart to the *Thesaurus linguae graecae* (*TLG*) for the ancient Latin literature until A.D. 200, including a selection of later authors and texts with the intention of comprising all of ancient Latin literature. Address: Packard Humanities Institute, 300 Second Street, Suite 201, Los Altos, CA 94022, USA. E-mail: phi@packhum.org.

*Patrologia latina Database CD-ROM* (version 5; Alexandria, Va.: Chadwyck-Healey, 1995).

Complete text of the 221 volumes of the Patrologia latina, including the introductions, notes, and indices on four CDs, with research software.

*Cetedoc Library of Christian Latin Texts CD-ROM* (version 3; Turnhout, Belg.: Brepols, 1996). *[CLCLT]*

Complete collection of the texts published in Corpus Christianorum: Series latina and Continuatio mediaevalis. Also contains complete collections of the works of the most important authors, e.g., Augustine.

## C. Reference Works

*Cetedoc-Index of Latin Forms* CD-ROM (Turnhout, Belg.: Brepols, 1998).

*In principio: Incipit Index of Latin Texts* CD-ROM (Turnhout, Belg.: Brepols, 1993–).

# XII. INTERNET ADDRESSES

Given the rapid development of, and changes in, the Internet, no definite list of patristic Web site addresses can be given; only some collections are listed:

M. Wallraff, "Patristische Arbeitshilfen im Internet," *ZAC* 1 (1997): 127–28.

T. Kuhlmei and T. Krannich, "Arbeitshilfen zur spätantiken und byzantinischen Kunst im Internet," *ZAC* 1 (1997): 302–4.

T. Krannich, "Arbeitshilfen zur Archäologie im Internet," *ZAC* 2 (1998): 299–303.

See especially the collection of links published on the Web site of the North American Patristics Society: http://moses.creighton.edu/napslinks/index.htm.

# Introduction

# Patrology as a Subject

THE TERM "PATROLOGY" IS COMPOSED OF two Greek terms, πατήρ ("father") and λόγος ("teaching"), and hence, literally translated, means the teaching of the Fathers (of the church).

## I. THE CONCEPT "FATHER"

The Christian honorary title "Father" represents the confluence of a host of common, human, OT, and Greco-Roman conceptions, such as (a) the father as progenitor of life and as head of the family, for whose welfare and authoritative leadership he was responsible; and as (b) the guardian and mediator of experience and tradition and thus as the authentic teacher, particularly of the faith. The Roman *pater familias* is the priest of the household cult. The OT understanding of parents is that they function as God's representatives in the family while the patriarchs are guardians of the promise and guarantors of the grace of the covenant with God (cf. Sir 44–50; Luke 1:55), who therefore deserve obedience and admiration.

This natural concept of the father extended to "the fathers" (the forebears), as well as to the "intellectual" and "spiritual father" (teacher, leader of a school of philosophers, rabbi). In this figurative sense the apostles of Christ (cf., e.g., 1 Cor 4:14f.) and the bishops of the church are the fathers of the believers, since in the act of baptism they are the progenitors of the new life, in the proclamation and interpretation of the faith they are their educators and teachers, and as leaders of the community they are the authorities and providers of the "family." Until the fourth century, therefore, the ancient church accorded the title "father" exclusively to bishops; only beginning with the fifth century was it also applied to priests (e.g., Jerome) and deacons (e.g., Ephraim the Syrian). Addressing the priest as "father" continues today in many languages (*pater*, "father," *père, padre*).

## II. CHURCH FATHER – DOCTOR OF THE CHURCH – CHURCH WRITER

The concept of church father highlights one aspect of the complex conception of the father, namely, the bishop as the authentic tradent and guarantor of the true faith who guards the continuity and unity of the faith in the unbroken tradition of the apostles and in communion with the church. He is the reliable teacher of the faith to whom one may appeal when in doubt. Although this authority does not render the respective church father inerrant in every detail—he has to be judged by Scripture as well as the *regula fidei* of the church as a whole— in agreement with the latter, however, he is an authentic witness of the faith and of the teaching of the church. From the fourth century, therefore, the bishops— beginning with the bishops of the Council of Nicea (325)—who distinguished themselves in the transmission, exposition, and defense of the faith were accorded the title "church fathers" or "holy fathers." In his work *De spiritu sancto* (374/375) Basil the Great was the first to attach a list of church fathers (ch. 29) who supported his interpretation in terms of a "legitimation by the fathers" (*argumentatio patristica*). Augustine adopted the same method from 412 on, particularly in the controversy against Pelagianism, and during the Council of Ephesus (431) Cyril of Alexandria, in support of his own orthodoxy, ordered the reading of excerpts from their works, which the council officially accepted and incorporated in its records.[1] Finally, Vincent of Lérins in his *Commonitorium* (434) coined the classical concept of the *magistri probabiles* and developed the theory of legitimation by the fathers (ch. 41).

Because of their special significance as privileged witnesses of the living tradition of the church, the church fathers traditionally were determined by means of four criteria:

a. *Doctrina orthodoxa:* Their theology as a whole had to be in agreement with the church's common teaching, which does not denote absolute inerrancy in every detail.

b. *Sanctitas vitae:* Holiness in the sense of the ancient church, in which the veneration of the saints was not based on explicit canonization but instead on the recognition and admiration of an exemplary life by the community of believers.

c. *Approbatio ecclesiae:* The church's recognition, though not necessarily explicit, of the person and his teaching.

d. *Antiquitas:* They have to belong to the period of the ancient church.

In 1295 Pope Boniface VIII first bestowed the honorary title "doctor of the church" upon the Latin church fathers Ambrose, Jerome, Augustine, and Gregory the Great. Pope Pius V, in his breviary of 1568, accorded the same honor to the Greek fathers Athanasius, Basil the Great, Gregory of Nazianzus, and John Chrysostom. Since that time they have been honored as the "four great Western and Eastern doctors of the church" and as such have found their way into many artistic portrayals. The concept of doctor of the church agrees with that of church

---

[1] Cf. B. Studer, "Argumentation, patristic," *EECh* 1:72; B. Studer, *Epocha patristica* (vol. 1 of *Storia della teologia;* Casale Monferrato: Piemme, 1993), 457–61.

father, though it is not restricted to antiquity. Hence the fourth criterion above is replaced with that of outstanding scholarly achievement (*eminens doctrina*). The church fathers' explicit elevation to the status of doctors of the church intends to highlight and honor their extraordinary significance as outstanding tradents of the faith and of the ecclesiastical teaching: Isidore of Seville (1722), Peter Chrysologus (1729), Leo the Great (1754), Hilary of Poitiers (1851), Cyril of Alexandria and Cyril of Jerusalem (1882), John of Damascus (1890), and Ephraim the Syrian (1920).

Ancient Christian writers who do not meet one or more of the first three criteria of a church father but are part of the Catholic Church are called "church writers." All other ancient Christian, albeit not ecclesiastical, writings (apocrypha, heretical works, etc.) are considered part of the wider circle of "early Christian" or "ancient Christian" literature.

The limitation of the concept of the father to antiquity did not come about until the modern period. Jean Mabillon (1632–1707) still regarded Bernard of Clairvaux (d. 1153) as the last of the Fathers. Jacques-Paul Migne (1800–1875) concluded his monumental collection of the *Patrologia graeca* with Gennadius II of Constantinople (d. after 1472)—and hence included the entire corpus of the Byzantine literature—and that of the *Patrologia latina* with Pope Innocent III (d. 1216). While the limitation to antiquity is generally accepted today, the time frame is by no means beyond dispute. Traditional introductions—including the present one—conclude with Isidore of Seville (d. 636) in the West and with John of Damascus (d. ca. 750) in the East. There are good reasons, however, for the increasing calls to conclude the era of the Fathers in the mid- to late fifth century, though this has not taken hold up to now. (On the division of patristics into periods of time, cf. the introductions of parts 2 to 4).

# III. PATROLOGY – PATRISTICS – HISTORY OF LITERATURE

Throughout the formation of this subject, even within the confessional boundaries of Catholic and Protestant churches, the following three different designations or definitions have developed:

a. Since the seventeenth century, *patristics* has denoted the *theologia patristica*, especially the dogmatics of the Fathers in contrast to the *theologia biblica, scholastica*, etc.

b. The concept of *patrology* was first introduced by the Protestant theologian Johannes Gerhard (d. 1637) as the title of his posthumously published work *Patrologia sive de primitivae ecclesiae christianae doctorum vita ac lucubrationibus* (*Patrology, or the Life and Works of the Early Christian Teachers*) (Jena, 1653), in the sense of historical and literary studies of the Fathers.

c. An animated discussion about the scope and objective of the discipline of patristics arose around the turn of the twentieth century, in the wake of the general upturn in historical and philological research. The prevailing thought was that it had to be considered and treated consistently as part of literary studies in general—that is, as *ancient Christian* or *early Christian literary studies*—without denying its theological character on account of its subject. On the other hand, a second definition of Christian literary studies distinguishes the latter from patrology and patristics as a nontheological discipline of the philology of ancient Christian writers.

On the whole, all three designations for the subject are used more or less without differentiation today; conversely, the discussion about its precise definition does not abate. Since we are not in a position to address in detail here the arguments adduced, the present work will use only the designations "patristics/patristic" and "patrology" as follows:

- *patristics/patristic:* the period of the Fathers/belonging to the time, to the writings, to the thought, etc., of ancient Christian literature.

- *patrology:* the study of ancient Christian literature.

Nevertheless, patrology is not thereby identified with literary studies in general but instead intentionally retains the concept of father in the designation so as to clarify that the subject issue here is necessarily a theological one, the undeniable core element of which is the Fathers of the church and, in the ecclesiastical sense, their writings. Still, since all of ancient Christian literature and its environment have to be considered in order to understand and explain the Fathers in their broader context, modern patrology is the study of ancient Christian literature in its entirety, in all its aspects, bringing all the appropriate methods to bear.

*Encyclopedia Articles:* H. Emonds, "Abt," *RAC* 1:45–55. – L. Wenger and A. Oepke, "Adoption," *RAC* 1:99–112. – G. Schrenk and G. Quell, "πατήρ," *TDNT* 5:945–1104. – A. Hamman, "Padre, Padri della Chiesa," *DPAC* 2:2562. – A. Hamman, "Patrologia, patristica," *DPAC* 2:2708–18. – E. Mühlenberg, *TRE* 26: 97–106.

*Studies:* P. Grech and R. Farina, eds., *Lo studio dei Padri Nella Chiesa oggi* (Rome: Istituto Patristico "Augustinianum," 1977). – E. Bellini, *I Padri nella tradizione cristiana* (ed. L. Saibene; Milan: Jaca, 1982). – E. Cavalcanti, "Quindici anni di studie patristici in Italia (orientamenti metodologici)," in *Metodologie della ricerca sulla tarda antichità: Atti del primo convegno dell'Associazione di studi tardoantichi* (ed. A. Garzya; Naples: D'Auria, 1989), 189–222. – A. Quacquarelli, ed., *Complementi interdisciplinari di patrologia* (Rome: Città Nuova, 1989).

*Teaching the Fathers:* Santa Sede, Congregazione per l'Educazione cattolica, *Istruzione sullo studio dei Padri della Chiesa nella formazione sacerdotale* (Rome: Tipografia Poliglotta Vaticana, 1989). – A. di Berardino, "Alcuni orientamenti negli studi patristici oggi," *Seminarium* 42 (1990): 389–412. – H. R. Drobner, "La patrología en la formación sacerdotal según la 'Instrucción sobre el estudio de los Padres de la Iglesia,'" in *La formación de los sacerdotes en las circunstancias actuales: XI Simposio Internacional de Teología de la Universidad de Navarra* (ed. L. F. Mateo-Seco; CTUN 70; Pamplona: Servicio de Publicaciones de la Universidad de Navarra, 1990), 861–73. – H. R. Drobner, "Die 'Instruktion über das Studium der Kirchenväter in der Priesterausbildung,'" *TGl* 81 (1991): 190–201. – N.a., "Lo studio dei Padri della Chiesa oggi," *Sal.* 53 (1991): 1–148, 219–72. – E. Dal Covolo and A. M. Triacca, eds., *Lo studio dei Padri della Chiesa oggi* (BSRel 96; Rome: LAS, 1991). E. dal Covolo, "I Padri della Chiesa maestri di formazione sacerdotale," *Sal.* 55 (1993): 133–46.

# Part One

# Apostolic and Postapostolic Literature

# The Rise of Christian Literature

## I. ORAL TRADITION AND PRELITERARY FORMS

Twenty years passed between the death and resurrection of Jesus ca. 30 C.E. and the emergence of the earliest Christian literature. Jesus' proclamation of his teaching had been exclusively oral, and even the earliest communities initially did not see any need for a literary record, all the more so since the eyewitnesses who personally knew and heard Jesus lived among them and authentically attested to his gospel. Furthermore, they expected the promised return of the Messiah and the ultimate establishment of his kingdom to be realized in the lifetime of the first generation of disciples (imminent expectation). During this period of time, however, as is probably true of all peoples whose oral transmission of stories, myths, and wisdom gives rise to peculiar structures, there developed so-called pre-literary forms, which we know to the extent that they found their way into later literature. They grew in the soil of the five most important contexts of life of the early communities composed of Jewish and Gentile Christians with their mixtures of culture and environment:

a. In everyday life, as exhortations and instructions for the Christian life (paraenesis), among them the famous catalogs of vices and virtues (Gal 5:19–23), the household codes (Col 3:18–4:2), as well as the doctrine of the two ways, which originated in Judaism, as reflected in the *Letter of Barnabas* and the *Didache,* challenging Christians to walk in the way of good or evil, of light or darkness. The literary paraenesis has its roots and parallels in the popular wisdom tradition of Judaism and in Hellenistic popular philosophy and basically serves to recall and repeat the oral paraenesis.

b. In liturgy, as prayers, hymns, and acclamations, such as "amen," "hallelujah," "hosanna," the Lord's Prayer (Matt 6:9–13), the Magnificat (Luke 1:46–55), and the Benedictus (Luke 1:68–79).

c. In catechesis, for the purpose of passing on the faith within the community and instructing new converts, especially in preparation for baptism, such as the earliest short forms of the confession of faith (Acts 8:37) and the baptismal formula (Matt 28:19).

d. In missionary proclamation, as kerygmatic formulas summarizing missionary sermons (1 Thess 1:9f.) or delimiting Christian monotheism, by polemics and proclamation, over against polytheism (εἷς acclamations, 1 Cor 8:6).

*Study:* P. Vielhauer, *Geschichte der urchristlichen Literatur: Einleitung in das Neue Testament, die Apokryphen, und die Apostolischen Väter* (Berlin and New York: de Gruyter, 1975), 9–57.

e. The oral tradition of the words and deeds of Jesus, representing a separate literary category that has largely, though not entirely, found its way into the four canonical gospels. There are the so-called agrapha (ἄγραφος = unwritten), dominical sayings that are not preserved in the canonical gospels but in other, often much later sources, such as the remaining writings of the NT (e.g., Acts 20:35: "remembering the words of the Lord Jesus, how he said, 'It is more blessed to give than to receive'"), the NT apocrypha, the writings of the church fathers, and even Islamic works. The papyri excavated in 1897–1927 in Oxyrhynchus (130 miles south of Cairo) and the gnostic *Gospel of Thomas,* representing a collection of 114 dominical sayings (cf. ch. 1.I.C) and discovered at Nag Hammadi in 1945, are particularly profitable.

Many agrapha came about as free, tendentious fabrications of certain groups and sects in order to support their own heretical teachings, while others developed as embellishments and derivations of the canonical gospels. Nevertheless, a small number remain that are considered authentic and may be placed alongside the canonical gospels. Although they do not yield any new insights beyond those of the canonical gospels, they do confirm the authentic witnesses to the proclamation of Jesus.

In the agrapha, what is true of the entire oral tradition of Christianity becomes especially clear, namely, that it does not end with the rise of Christian literature but instead parallels it, especially in liturgy and catechesis throughout the centuries. Thus we must continually reckon with oral tradition's influence upon the writings and the theology of the Fathers.

*Bibliography:* J. H. Charlesworth, *The New Testament Apocrypha and Pseudepigrapha: A Guide to Publications, with Excursuses on Apocalypses* (ATLA.BS 17; Metuchen, N.J.: Scarecrow, 1987), 138–55.

*Editions:* A. Resch, *Agrapha: Aussercanonische Evangelienfragmente* (TU 5.4; Leipzig: Hinrichs, 1889). – Idem, *Agrapha aussercanonische Schriftfragmente* (TU 30.4; Leipzig: Hinrichs, 1906). – M. Asin y Palacios, *Logia et agrapha Domini Jesu apud moslemicos scriptores asceticos praesertim usitata,* (2 vols. PO 13.3; Paris: Firmin-Didot, 1916–1926), 1:327–431; 2:529–624. – *Apocrypha 2: Evangelien* (ed. E. Klostermann; KlT 8; Berlin: de Gruyter, 1929); *Apocrypha* (ed. E. Klostermann; KlT 11; Berlin: de Gruyter, 1911). – *Los evangelios apócrifos: Colección de textos griegos y latinos: Versión crítica, estudios introductorios, comentarios, e ilustraciones* (ed. A. de Santos Otero; 7th ed.; BAC 148; Madrid: Biblioteca de Autores Cristianos, 1991), 108–22.

*Encyclopedia Articles:* O. Hofius, *TRE* 2:103–10. – M. G. Mara, "Agraphon," *EECh* 1:18. – G. A. Koch, "Agrapha," *EEC* 1:27–28.

*Studies:* J. H. Ropes, *Die Sprüche Jesu, die in den kanonischen Evangelien nicht überliefert sind: Eine kritische Bearbeitung des von D. Alfred Resch gesammelten Materials* (TU 14.2; Leipzig: Hinrichs, 1896). – J. Jeremias, *Unknown Sayings of Jesus* (2d English ed.; London: SPCK, 1964); trans. of *Unbekannte Jesusworte* (BFCT 45.2; Gütersloh: G. Mohn, 1980). – F. Bovon and H. Koester, *Genèse de l'écriture chrétienne* (Brussels:

Brepols, 1991). – J. K. Elliott, "Non-canonical Sayings of Jesus in Patristic Works and in the New Testament Manuscript Tradition," in *Philologia sacra: Biblische und patristische Studien für Hermann J. Frede und Walter Thiele zu ihrem siebzigsten Geburtstag* (ed. R. Gryson; VL 24.2; Fribourg, Switz.: Herder, 1993), 343–54.

# II. LITERARY GENRES OF APOSTOLIC LITERATURE

The earliest work of Christian literature we possess is the Apostle Paul's first letter to the Thessalonians, written in 51/52 in Corinth, followed by the remaining authentic Pauline letters to the Galatians, Corinthians, Philippians, Philemon, and Romans. Here it is easy to see how Christian literature came about: not with the intention of writing a work of literature but for reasons of practical necessity. The growing expansion of Christianity made personal contact increasingly more difficult; it had to be replaced by the literary form of the letter. The primary letter, however, is not itself considered literature. It becomes so only as it is preserved. This does not mean that letters need to be nonliterary in their form. Long before Christianity existed, Greek and Roman society had developed a culture of writing letters with established literary criteria to which a trained writer adhered, quite apart from such forms as prescript, salutations, forms of greetings, etc. (cf. ch. 4.IV.excursus 2). At the same time, the primary letter demonstrates a certain range, from the private letter, addressed to an individual, to the public letter, addressed to the entire population. Occasionally the author already knows or assumes that his letter will be preserved and given literary status and thus stylizes it accordingly. These distinctions can also be observed in the early Christian letters, some of which are addressed to entire communities, intended to be read publicly in the church service and to be passed on to other communities. Hence they bear the marks of a general Christian letter of proclamation and exhortation.

Roughly twenty years later, beginning ca. 70 C.E., a second genre of Christian literature—the gospels—emerged as a result of a different need for communication, namely, the preservation of the authentic teaching of Christ for posterity. Forty years after Christ's death and resurrection, the Christians were disappointed in their "imminent expectation" of the soon return of the Messiah. More and more of the eyewitnesses died, and with increasing frequency individual groups appealed to divergent oral traditions. This led to the need for the true gospel to be recorded, a task that different authors undertook at different locations and with different presuppositions. Thus the Gospel of Mark was the first one to emerge, in a Hellenistic community ca. 70 C.E., followed by the Gospel of Luke ca. 80 C.E., the Gospel of Matthew in a Jewish-Christian community between 90 and 95, and the Gospel of John ca. 100. They provide an account of the life and teaching of Jesus from his birth, or from his first appearance, to his resurrection, not from a chronological and historicizing interest but inspired by belief, based on the communities' theological reflection and experience, and for the purpose of a theological and catechetical statement of faith. Mark, for instance, intends to explain the messianic secret and for this reason begins with John the Baptist's preparation for the first appearance of the Messiah and with the baptism of Jesus. By contrast, Matthew intends to explain how the OT is fulfilled in the NT, emphasizes the divine Sonship and sovereignty of Jesus, and therefore begins with the genealogy of Jesus, starting with the patriarchs. All of the gospels offer their own selection of content, structure, and manner of presentation, at the same time using the pieces of tradition available to them.

Luke's intention can be seen in that he wrote his gospel as the first book of a two-volume work, of which the Acts of the Apostles was an integral part. The book of Acts itself created a new, third literary genre of the NT. As Luke himself specifies in the proem of his gospel (1:1–4), he intends to provide an accurately researched, historical account of salvation, beginning with the proclamation of the Messiah and culminating with his ascension and the resultant spread of salvation in the whole world through the apostles' actions.

Finally, the fourth genre of apostolic literature to arise was the apocalypse, the first one being Revelation, or the Apocalypse of John, at the end of the first century. Such prophetic revelations of the end times are meant to warn of the impending end of the world but also to provide encouragement during the persecutions and sufferings of this end time. In content and style, they follow the literary examples of apocalyptic writings developed largely in late Judaism.

# CHAPTER ONE

# Biblical Apocrypha

*Studies:* L. Leloir, "Utilité ou inutilité de l'étude des apocryphes," *RTL* 19 (1988): 38–70. – E. Junod, "La littérature apocryphe chrétienne constitue-t-elle un objet d'études?" *REA* 93 (1991): 397–414. – J.-D. Kaestli and D. Marguerat, eds., *Il mistero degli apocrifi: Introduzione a una letteratura da scoprire* (Milan: Massimo, 1996); trans. of *Mystère apocryphe: Introduction à une littérature méconnue* (Geneva: Labor & Fides, 1995).

## INTRODUCTION: FORMATION OF THE BIBLICAL CANON

### A. New Testament

Although the twenty-seven writings making up today's canon (κανών = "standard") of the NT belong to the earliest Christian works of literature, the development of the canon took several centuries. The first five centuries yielded multiple works of the four literary genres of the NT, all of them with the initial intention of providing a literary record of the authentic teaching of Christ. The apostolicity of a writing became the decisive criterion of reliability, since it was able to appeal directly to Christ. Hence, if a writing did not originate from an apostle or an apostolic associate, it was attributed to them, not in the sense of a forgery or a deception but rather to subordinate it to apostolic authority and to indicate that it vouched to contain faith-related truths. Granted, not all writings demonstrated the same quality and reliability, with the result that individual communities, with local variations, admitted only a portion of these writings for public proclamation in the liturgy and acknowledged them as Holy Scripture. By the middle of the second century, therefore, an initial consensus emerged from the tradition, forming a decisive criterion in the formation of the NT canon.

During the second century, heterodox strands in the church—especially the gnostics—began to write and revere "holy books" that they likewise placed under apostolic authority in order to legitimate their heretical doctrines. For this reason, the church was forced to determine authoritatively what books contained the authentic truth of the faith, deserved reverence as Holy Scripture, and could be used in public proclamation. By the end of the second century, this process was largely complete, even if the final boundary of the twenty-seven canonical books was not established until the fourth century. Until then, individual communities or regions had to reckon with minor divergences in what was considered to be canonical. The earliest witness of the NT canon, which demonstrates a remarkably final form, is the *Canon Muratori* (Muratorian Canon), named after Ludovico Antonio Muratori (1672–1750), who discovered it before 1740 in an eighth-century codex in the Bibliotheca Ambrosiana in Milan. This is a list, probably written in Rome ca. 200,[1] that already contains twenty-two of the twenty-seven canonical writings; the only ones missing are Hebrews, James, 1 and 2 Peter, and one of the Johannine letters. The final shape of the NT canon of the Greek church is found first in the thirty-ninth *Festal Letter* of Athanasius at Easter, 367. Its counterpart in the West is contained in part two of the *Decretum gelasianum,* the first three parts of which probably originated in a Roman synod under Pope Damasus in 382, as well as in the documents of a synod held in Hippo Regius in North Africa in 393.

All other works that, in their titles, content, or form, are related to the NT and likewise claim apostolic authority but are not part of the canon are called "apocrypha" by the church. The church thereby adopted a concept that Gnosticism, in continuity with the esoteric mystery religions of antiquity, used for its own sacred writings. Gnosticism held them in such high esteem that only the fully initiated members of the gnostic communities were allowed to attain knowledge from them; they were withheld from everyone else as secret (ἀπόκρυφος). Whereas the term "apocryphal" therefore signified the highest regard within Gnosticism, this term took on, for the orthodox church in its defense, the meaning of "false, heretical, reprehensible." The term was then further applied to all the writings whose origin was unknown, whose attribution was false, or whose content was heretical and finally to all the extracanonical writings in general. The term "apocryphal" itself therefore does not necessarily mean "heretical"; many apocryphal writings contain reliable bases of ecclesiastical theology and piety, such as Mariology, but they were not canonized, partly because they are overgrown with legends and abstruse miracle accounts and, on the whole, therefore do not demonstrate the same reliability as the canonical books.

According to their genre, the biblical books, both canonical and apocryphal, belong to the Christian history of literature, even though this classification is certainly subject to debate. Because of their own significance as foundation for the Christian faith, the biblical writings are treated as a separate theological subject; for this reason, the canonical books of the NT, unlike the apocryphal writings, are not considered part of patrology.

With the fixing of the canon of Scripture, naturally the purpose of the subsequently emerging writings changed, but they continued to relate to the NT in

---

[1] For the most recent argument in favor of a Syrian or Palestinian origin at the end of the fourth century, see G. M. Hahneman, *The Muratorian Fragment and the Development of the Canon* (Oxford: Clarendon, 1992).

terms of their attribution, content, and form. Beginning with the second century, there are three types to be distinguished:

a. books, especially gospels and acts of apostles, that in many ways intend to supplement the incomplete accounts of the canonical books, motivated by theological interests or popular piety (e.g., the childhood of Mary and Jesus, or the fate of an apostle);

b. writings in competition with the canonical books, seeking to legitimate the heretical doctrines of specific groups or sects, or even local customs and traditions;

c. a later group of writings seeking to solve current apologetic or dogmatic problems on the basis of an assumed apostolic authority.

In the most recent edition of his translation of the NT apocrypha, Wilhelm Schneemelcher provides the following summary definition of this literary type:

> The New Testament apocrypha represent those writings which originated in the earliest centuries of the history of the Church and have a certain relationship with the New Testament writings in terms of title, type or content. In the individual apocrypha the relationship with the canonical works is quite varied and has to be determined in each case. Likewise the motives that led to the development of the apocrypha are by no means uniform. The determination of what constitutes New Testament apocrypha has to be particularly attentive to the essential historical framework. This applies not only to the boundary with regards to the hagiographic literature but is especially significant with reference to the relationship to the developing or closed canon of the New Testament. The literature in question involves the following:

> Gospels, which are not only conspicuous because they did not become part of the New Testament but, more importantly, which in part wanted to claim the same position as the canonical gospels (this applies to the earliest texts) or in some way intended to augment the canonical texts.

> Pseudepigraphic letters that were largely intended to disseminate doctrinal supplements and corrections.

> Acts of the apostles, in which the information and legends of the apostles was shaped like a novel (often in great detail) and thereby intended to supplement the inadequate understanding of the apostles' destiny to be gained from the New Testament. This was often influenced by propaganda-related motives of certain theological teachings.

> Apocalypses which partly reworked Jewish texts but partly also further developed the form of "revelations" assumed from Judaism.[2]

---

[2] W. Schneemelcher, ed., *New Testament Apocrypha* (trans. R. McL. Wilson; 2 vols.; 2d ed.; Cambridge: J. Clarke; Louisville: Westminster John Knox, 1991–1992), 1:61.

## Greek New Testament

*Bibliography: Elenchus bibliographicus biblicus* (Rome: Pontifical Biblical Institute, 1920–). *[EBB]*

*Editions:* Nestle-Aland, *Novum Testamentum Graece* (27th rev. ed.; Stuttgart: Deutsche Bibelstiftung, 1993). – Institut für Neutestamentliche Textforschung, ed., *Novum Testamentum graecum: Editio critica maior* (Stuttgart: Deutsche Bibelgesellschaft, 1997–).

*Reference Works and Concordances:* W. F. Moulton and A. S. Geden, *A Concordance to the Greek Testament, according to Westcott and Hort, Tischendorf and the English Revisers* (5th ed., rev. H. K. Moulton; Edinburgh: T&T Clark, 1978). – A. Schmoller, *Handkonkordanz zum griechischen Neuen Testament* (15th ed.; Stuttgart: Württembergische Bibelanstalt, 1973). – H. Bachmann and W. Slaby, *Konkordanz zum griechischen Neuen Testament von Nestle-Aland, 26 Auflage, und zum Greek New Testament, 3d Edition* (3d ed.; Berlin: de Gruyter: 1987). – J. R. Kohlenberger III, *The Exhaustive Concordance to the Greek New Testament* (Grand Rapids: Zondervan, 1995). – R. E. Whitaker and J. R. Kohlenberger III, eds., *The Analytical Concordance to the New Revised Standard Version of the New Testament* (Grand Rapids: Eerdmans, 2000).

*Dictionaries:* R. C. Trench, *Synonyms of the New Testament* (9th ed.; London: Macmillan, 1880; repr., Grand Rapids: Eerdmans, 1953). – J. H. Moulton and G. Milligan, *The Vocabulary of the Greek Testament, Illustrated from the Papyri and Other Non-literary Sources* (London: Hodder & Stoughton, 1930; repr., Grand Rapids: Eerdmans, 1985; repr., Peabody, Mass.: Hendrickson, 1997). – G. Kittel et al., eds. *Theological Dictionary of the New Testament* (trans. G. W. Bromiley; Grand Rapids: Eerdmans, 1964–1976). – F. W. Danker, *A Greek-English Lexicon of the New Testament and Other Early Christian Literature* (3d ed.; Chicago: University of Chicago Press, 2000). – C. Spicq, *Theological Lexicon of the New Testament* (ed. and trans. J. Ernest; 2 vols.; Peabody, Mass.: Hendrickson, 1994). – D. N. Freedman, *The Anchor Bible Dictionary* (6 vols.; New York: Doubleday, 1992).

*Grammars:* J. H. Moulton and N. Turner, *A Grammar of New Testament Greek* (4 vols.; Edinburgh: T&T Clark, 1906–76). – F. Blass, A. Debrunner, and R. W. Funk, *A Greek Grammar of the New Testament and Other Early Christian Literature* (Chicago: University of Chicago Press, 1961) – W. D. Mounce, *Basics of Greek Grammar* (Grand Rapids: Zondervan, 1993). – D. B. Wallace, *Greek Grammar beyond the Basics* (Grand Rapids: Zondervan, 1996).

*Studies:* B. M. Metzger, *The Text of the New Testament: Its Transmission, Corruption, and Restoration* (4th ed.; New York: Oxford University Press, 2005). – K. Aland, ed., *Die alten Übersetzungen des Neuen Testaments—die Kirchenväterzitate und Lektionar: Der gegenwärtige Stand ihrer Erforschung und ihre Bedeutung für die griechische Textgeschichte* (ANTF 5; New York: de Gruyter, 1972). – B. M. Metzger, *The Early Versions of the New Testament: Their Origin, Transmission, and Limitations* (Oxford: Clarendon, 1977).

## Apocrypha

*Bibliographies: Initia biblica, apocrypha, prologi* (vol. 1 of *Repertorium biblicum medii aevi;* ed. F. Stegmüller; Madrid: Consejo Superior de Investigaciones Científicas, Instituto Francisco Súarez, 1950–). – *Supplementum* (vol. 8 of *Repertorium biblicum medii aevi;* ed. F. Stegmüller; Madrid: Consejo Superior de Investigaciones Científicas, Instituto Francisco Súarez, 1950–). – G. Delling et al., *Bibliographie zur jüdisch-hellenistischen und intertestamentarischen Literatur, 1900–1965* (TU 106; Berlin: Akademie, 1969). – J. H. Charlesworth et al., *The New Testament Apocrypha and Pseudepigrapha: A Guide to Publications, with Excursuses on Apocalypses* (ATLA.BS 17; Metuchen, N.J.: Scarecrow, 1987). – J. H. Charlesworth, "Research on the New Testament Apocrypha and Pseudepigrapha," *ANRW* 2.25.5:3919–68.

*Editions:* Corpus Christianorum: Series apocryphorum (Turnhout, Belg.: Brepols, 1983–). – J. A. Fabricius, *Codex apocryphus Novi Testament* (2d ed.; 2 vols.; Hamburg: B. Schiller and J. C. Kisner, 1719–1743). – A. Birch, *Auctarium codicis apocryphi N.T. Fabriciani* (Copenhagen: Arntzen & Hartier, 1804). – M. R. James, ed., *Apocrypha anecdota: A Collection of Thirteen Apocryphal Books and Fragments* (TS 2.3; Cambridge: Cambridge University Press; New York: Macmillan, 1893; repr., Nendeln, Liechtenstein: Kraus Reprint, 1967). – M. R. James, ed., *Apocrypha anecdota: Second Series* (TS 5.1; Cambridge: Cambridge University Press, 1897). – E. Preuschen, ed. and trans., *Antilegomena: Die Reste der ausserkanonischen und urchristlichen Überlieferungen* (2d ed.; Giessen: Töpelmann, 1905). – E. Klostermann, *Apocrypha* (KlT 3, 8, 11; Berlin: de Gruyter, 1911–1933). – *Die apokryphen Briefe des Paulus an die Laodicener und Korinther* (ed. A. von Harnack; 2d ed.; KlT 12; Berlin: de Gruyter, 1931).

*Translations:* W. Schneemelcher, ed., *New Testament Apocrypha* (trans. R. McL. Wilson; 2 vols.; 2d ed.; Cambridge: J. Clarke; Louisville: Westminster John Knox, 1991–1992). – J. K. Elliott, *The Apocryphal New Testament: A Collection of Apocryphal Christian Literature in an English Translation* (Oxford: Clarendon; New York: Oxford University Press, 1993). – J. K. Elliott, *The Apocryphal Jesus: Legends of the Early Church* (Oxford: Oxford University Press, 1996).

## Studies of New Testament Literature and the Canon

*Encyclopedia Articles:* G. Bardy, "Apokryphen," *RAC* 1:516–20. – G. Schrenk, "βιβλίον," *TDNT* 1:615–20. – H. W. Beyer, "κανόν," *TDNT* 3:596–602. – A. Oepke and R. Meyer, "κρύπτω κτλ," *TNDT* 3:957–1000. – R. M. Wilson, "Apokryphen II," *TRE* 3:316–62. – W. Schneemelcher, "Bibel III," *TRE* 6:22–48. – W. Künneth, "Kanon," *TRE* 17:562–70. – J. Gribomont, "Scripture, Holy," *EECh* 2:762–4. – M. G. Mara, "Apocrypha," *EECh* 1:56–58. – D. M. Scholer, "Apocrypha, New Testament," *EEC* 1:74–76. – L. M. McDonald, "Canon," *EEC* 1:205–11.

*Manuals:* A. Sand, *Kanon: Von den Anfängen bis zum Fragmentum Muratori* (*HDG* 1.3a1; Fribourg, Switz.: Herder, 1974). – P. Vielhauer, *Geschichte der urchristlichen Literatur: Einleitung in das Neue Testament, die Apokryphen, und die Apostolischen Väter* (Berlin and New York: de Gruyter, 1978). – F. Gori, "Gli apocrifi e i Padri," in *Complementi interdisciplinari di patrologia* (ed. A. Quacquarelli; Rome: Città Nuova, 1989), 223–72. – A. Ziegenaus, *Kanon: Von der Väterzeit bis zur Gegenwart* (*HDG* 1.3a2; Fribourg, Switz.: Herder, 1990). – P. L. Schmidt and K. Zelzer, *HLL* 4:378–410.

*Collections of Essays:* L. M. McDonald and J. A. Sanders, eds., *The Canon Debate* (Peabody, Mass.: Hendrickson, 2002). – *Aug* 23 (1983): 19–378. – *ANRW* 2.25.1–6.

*Studies:* H. von Campenhausen, *The Formation of the Christian Bible* (Philadelphia: Fortress, 1972). – W. Farmer and D. Farkasfalvy, *The Formation of the New Testament Canon: An Ecumenical Approach* (New York: Paulist, 1983). – H. Y. Gamble, *The New Testament Canon: Its Making and Meaning* (Philadelphia: Fortress, 1985). – D. G. Meade, *Pseudonymity and Canon: An Investigation into the Relationship of Authorship and Authority in Jewish and Earliest Christian Tradition* (WUNT 39; Tübingen: Mohr, 1986). – B. M. Metzger, *The Canon of the New Testament: Its Origin, Development, and Significance* (Oxford: Clarendon, 1987). – F. F. Bruce, *The Canon of Scripture* (Glasgow: Chapter House; Downers Grove, Ill.: InterVarsity, 1988). – L. M. McDonald, *The Formation of the Christian Biblical Canon* (rev. ed.; Peabody, Mass.: Hendrickson, 1995). – M. Pesce, "La trasformazione dei documenti religiosi: Dagli scritti protocristiani al canone neotestamentario," *VetChr* 26 (1989): 307–36. – E. Junod, "'Apocryphes du Nouveau Testament'—Une appellation erronée et une collection artificielle: Discussion de la nouvelle définition proposée par W. Schneemelcher," *Apocrypha* 3 (1992): 17–46. – G. M. Hahneman, *The Muratorian Fragment and the Development of the Canon* (Oxford: Clarendon, 1992). – J. Trebolle Barrera, *La Biblia judía y la Biblia cristiana: Introducción a la historia de la Biblia* (Madrid: Trotta, 1993); [ET] *The Jewish Bible and the Christian Bible: An Introduction to the History of the Bible* (trans. W. G. E. Watson; Leiden: Brill, 1998). – Y.-M. Blanchard, *Aux sources du canon: Le témoignage d'Irénée* (Paris: Cerf, 1993). – J. W. Miller, *The Origins of the Bible: Rethinking Canon History* (New York: Paulist, 1994). – J. T. Lienhard, *The Bible, the Church, and Authority: The Canon of the Christian Bible in History and Theology* (Collegeville, Minn.: Liturgical, 1995). – J. C. VanderKam and W. Adler, eds., *The Jewish Apocalyptic Heritage in Early Christianity* (CRINT 3.4; Minneapolis: Fortress, 1996). – J. Barton, *The Spirit and the Letter: Studies in the Biblical Canon* (London: SPCK, 1997). – G. N. Stanton, "The Fourfold Gospel," *NTS* 43 (1997): 317–46; repr. in *Norms of Faith and Life* (ed. E. Ferguson; Recent Studies in Early Christianity 3; New York: Garland, 1999), 1–30. – John Barton, *People of the Book? The Authority of the Bible in Christianity* (London: SPCK, 1998) = *Holy Writings, Sacred Text: The Canon in Early Christianity* (Louisville: Westminster John Knox, 1998).

# B. Old Testament

The formation of a "New" Testament canon inevitably paralleled the establishment of a canon of the "Old" Testament, the Jewish biblical writings that, until then and on account of the Jewish origin of Christianity, had been its only Scripture. Indeed, the Hebrew canon was not established until close to the end of the first century, that is, at a time when the differentiation between Judaism and Christianity was already progressing. Second-century Christianity, already largely shaped by the Greek language, did not use the Hebrew text as its authentic OT text but instead used its Greek translation, the Septuagint (LXX), which originated in the Judaism of the Hellenistic diaspora between the third and the first centuries B.C.E. The Septuagint was given this name on the basis of the tradition (preserved for us in the *Letter of Aristeas*) that seventy-two inspired scribes from Palestine translated the Pentateuch on behalf of the Egyptian king Ptolemy II (286–285 B.C.E.). Since the Hebrew canon at that time had not yet been finalized, however, it also included a number of OT writings that subsequently were not adopted in the Hebrew canon and that Christianity considered as so-called deuterocanonical works. These comprise the Greek additions to Daniel and Esther, Baruch, the Epistle of Jeremiah, 1 and 2 Maccabees, Judith, Tobit, Sirach, and the Wisdom of Solomon. Protestantism removed them again, deeming them apocryphal, but the Council of Trent, in the *Decretum de libris sacris et de traditionibus recipiendis* (DH 1501), on April 6, 1546, once more affirmed them as component parts of the Holy Scripture of the Catholic Church. Protestantism designates the deuterocanonical books of the OT as apocrypha, and all the remaining extracanonical writings of the OT as pseudepigrapha (ψευδῶς = "falsely," ἐπιγράφειν = "to attribute"). The Catholic Church, conversely, considers all the extracanonical OT writings as apocrypha.

Since the canon was not yet closed, the number of OT books Christianity considered to be canonical varied locally in the early centuries. To the extent that the church fathers used them and many of them were reworked and expanded from the Christian perspective, they too are part of the subject of patrology.

## Septuagint

*Bibliographies:* J. W. Wevers, "Septuaginta Forschungen seit 1954," *TRu* 33 (1968): 18–76. – S. P. Brock, C. T. Fritsch, and S. Jellicoe, *A Classified Bibliography of the Septuagint* (Leiden: Brill, 1973).

*Editions: Septuaginta: Vetus Testamentum graecum, auctoritate Societatis Litterarum Gottingensis editum* (11 vols. in 17; Göttingen: Vandenhoeck & Ruprecht, 1939–1993). – A. Rahlfs, *Septuaginta, id est, Vetus Testamentum graece iuxta LXX interpretes* (2 vols.; 8th ed.; Stuttgart: Württembergische Bibelanstalt, 1965). – N. Fernández Marcos and J. R. Busto Saiz, with M. V. Spottorno, Díaz Caro, and S. P. Cowe, *El texto antioqueno de la Biblia griega* (3 vols.; Madrid: Instituto de Filología, 1989–1996).

*Translations:* L. L. Brenton, *The Septuagint with Apocrypha: Greek and English* (Peabody, Mass.: Hendrickson, 1976). – M. Harl et al., *La Bible d'Alexandrie* (Paris: Cerf, 1986–).

*Reference Works—Concordances:* E. Hatch and H. A. Redpath, *A Concordance to the Septuagint and the Other Greek Versions of the Old Testament (including the Apocryphal Books)* (2d ed.; Grand Rapids: Baker, 2005).

*Dictionaries:* F. Rehkopf, *Septuaginta-Vokabular* (Göttingen: Vandenhoeck & Ruprecht, 1989). – J. Lust, E. Eynikel, and K. Hauspie, with the collaboration of G. Chamberlain, *A Greek-English Lexicon to the Septuagint* (2 vols.; Stuttgart: Deutsche Bibelgesellschaft, 1992–1996). – T. Muraoka, *A Greek-English Lexicon of the Septuagint: Twelve Prophets* (Louvain: Peeters, 1993).

*Grammars:* H. Thackeray, *A Grammar of the Old Testament in Greek according to the Septuagint* (Hildesheim and New York: Olms, 1987). F. C. Conybeare and S. G. Stock, *Grammar of Septuagint Greek* (Peabody, Mass.: Hendrickson, 1988).

*Encyclopedia Articles:* J. L. Coole, "Altes Testament," *RAC* 1 (1950): 354–63. – G. Dorival et al., "Versions anciennes de la Bible," *DEB* 2:1302–25. – C. Cox, *EEC* 2:1048–50.

*Introductions:* H. B. Swete, R. R. Ottley, and H. S. J. Thackeray, *An Introduction to the Old Testament in Greek* (3d ed.; Cambridge: Cambridge University Press, 1913; New York: KTAV, 1968). – S. Jellicoe, *The Septuagint and Modern Study* (Oxford: Clarendon, 1968). – N. Fernández Marcos, *Introducción a las versiones griegas de la Biblia* (2d rev. ed.; Madrid: Consejo Superior de Investigaciones Científicas, 1998). – G. Dorival, M. Harl, and O. Munnich, *La Bible grecque des Septante: Du judaïsme hellénistique au christianisme ancien* (ICA; Paris: Cerf, 1988). – M. Cimosa, *Guida allo studio della Bibbia greca (LXX): Storia–lingua–testi* (Rome: Società Biblica Britannica & Forestiera, 1995). – P. Lamarche, "The Septuagint: Bible of the Earliest Christians," in *The Bible in Greek Christian Antiquity* (ed. P. Blowers; Notre Dame, Ind.: University of Notre Dame Press, 1997), 15–33.

## Apocrypha

*Editions:* J. A. Fabricius, *Codex pseudepigraphus Veteris Testamenti* (2 vols.; Hamburg: Felginer, 1713; 2d rev. ed., 1723). – C. C. L. Schmid, *Corpus omnium veterum apocryphorum extra Biblia* (Hadamar, Ger.: n.p., 1804). – M. R. James, ed., *The Testament of*

*Abraham: The Greek Text* (TS 2.2; Cambridge: Cambridge University Press; New York: Macmillan, 1892). – R. L. Bensley, ed., *The Fourth Book of Ezra* (TS 3.2; Cambridge: Cambridge University Press, 1895; Nendeln, Liechtenstein: Kraus Reprint, 1967).

*Translations:* J. H. Charlesworth, *The Old Testament Pseudepigrapha* (2 vols.; Garden City, N.Y.: Doubleday; London: Darton, Longman & Todd, 1983–1985).

*Reference Works:* A.-M. Denis, *Concordance grecque des pseudépigraphes d'Ancien Testament* (Louvain: Université Catholique de Louvain, Institut Orientaliste, 1987). – W. Strothmann, *Wörterverzeichnis der apokryphen-deuterokanonischen Schriften des Alten Testaments in der Peschitta* (GOF 1.27; Wiesbaden: Harrassowitz, 1988). – W. Lechner-Schmidt, *Wortindex der lateinisch erhaltenen Pseudepigraphen zum Alten Testament* (TANZ 3; Tübingen: Francke, 1990). – A.-M. Denis, *Concordance latine des pseudépigraphiques d'Ancien Testament* (Corpus Christianorum: Thesaurus patrum latinorum; Turnhout, Belg.: Brepols, 1993).

*Encyclopedia Articles:* H.-P. Rüger, "Apokryphen I," *TRE* 3:289–316. – G. Wanke and E. Plümacher, "Bibel I–II," *TRE* 6:1–22. – J. H. Charlesworth, "Pseudepigraphen des Alten Testaments," *TRE* 27:639–45. – K. Zelzer and P. L. Schmidt, *HLL* 4:367–78. – J. J. Collins, "Apocrypha, Old Testament," *EEC* 1:77–78.

*Journals: Journal for the Study of the Pseudepigrapha (and Related Literature)* (Sheffield, 1987–). *[JSP]*

*Collections of Essays: Zum Problem des biblischen Kanons* (ed. P. D. Hanson et al.; Jahrbuch für biblische Theologie 3; Neukirchen-Vluyn: Neukirchener, 1989). – Journal for the Study of the Pseudepigrapha: Supplement Series (Sheffield: JSOT Press, 1988–). [JSPSup] – Studia in Veteris Testamenti pseudepigrapha (Leiden: Brill, 1970–) [SVTP]

*Studies:* H. von Campenhausen, "Das Alte Testament als Bibel der Kirche vom Ausgang des Urchristentums bis zur Entstehung des Neuen Testaments," in idem, *Aus der Frühzeit des Christentums: Studien zur Kirchengeschichte des ersten und zweiten Jahrhunderts* (Tübingen: Mohr, 1963), 152–96. – O. Eissfeldt, *Einleitung in das Alte Testament unter Einschluss der Apokryphen und Pseudepigraphen sowie der apokryphen- und pseudepigraphenartigen Qumran-Schriften* (Tübingen: Mohr, 1934; 3d ed., 1964), 773–864. – L. Rost, *Einleitung in die alttestamentlichen Apokryphen und Pseudepigraphen* (Heidelberg: Quelle & Meyer, 1971). – D. Kaestli and O. Wermelinger, eds., *Le canon de l'Ancien Testament: Sa formation et son histoire* (Geneva: Labor et Fides, 1984). – R. Beckwith, *The Old Testament Canon of the New Testament Church and Its Background in Early Judaism* (London: SPCK; Grand Rapids: Eerdmans, 1985). – J. H. Charlesworth, *The Old Testament Pseudepigrapha and the New Testament: Prolegomena for the Study of Christian Origins* (Cambridge: Cambridge University Press, 1985).

# I. GOSPELS

## A. Literary Genre

Following the pattern of the canonical gospels, the literary genre of the gospel is shaped by the initially orally transmitted sayings and narrative materials of the life, deeds, and teaching of the earthly Jesus. An editor then arranged them together with theological and community-related reflections so as to preserve them authentically as well as to strengthen and spread the faith in Christ. Thus, whereas the shaping of the genre encompasses criteria of content and form, the term εὐαγγέλιον originally described only the message itself—a meaning that was not extinguished when it became common, around the mid-second century, to use this designation for the book containing the message as well. Hence there are many NT apocrypha that have been handed down under the label of "gospel" although they do not fit the definition of the genre. At the same time, writings that do fit the gospel genre are given different titles. Schneemelcher summarizes this in the broadest sense under "Gospels: Non-biblical Material about Jesus" and comes to the following conclusion: "Overall it may be said that there is no independent and standard genre called 'apocryphal gospels.'"[3] Nevertheless, the texts compiled here under this designation belong together, not only because their content is the person and work of Christ, but also because what characterizes them is the diverse way in which they are determined or influenced by the genre of gospel. An overall perspective therefore has to take the following criteria into consideration: content, literary forms, authors, origin, intention, indebtedness, history of transmission, etc., content being the most important aspect on account of the theological nature of the literature.

a. Closest to the canonical gospels are those likewise following the *synoptic tradition*, partly by drawing upon the same sources and partly by assimilating the three canonical gospels, such as the *Gospel of Peter*, the *Gospel of the Nazarenes*, and the *Gospel of the Ebionites*.

b. Concerning their origin, the latter two gospels belong to the *Jewish Christian gospels*, which are close to the Gospel of Matthew and which preserve primarily Jewish traditions or originate from Jewish Christian sects.

c. *Heterodox gospels* aim to legitimate their doctrines that diverge from those of the church at large. This is particularly true of the gnostic movement, from which we possess a wealth of gospel writings since the discovery of the Nag Hammadi library, such as the *Pistis Sophia*, the two *Books of Jeu*, the *Gospel of Thomas*, the *Gospel of Bartholomew*, and many others.

d. Since, in many ways, the canonical gospels did not satisfy popular piety's thirst for knowledge nor later desires for more detailed theological clarity, there arose a large group of writings that *supplemented the canonical gospels*.

They concern mostly the prehistory of the birth and childhood of Jesus because the canonical gospels leave considerable room in these areas. The *infancy gospels* not only answer the questions about Jesus' ancestors and the more detailed, marvelous circumstances of his birth and the years of his childhood; in their theological intent they also stress the deity of the child, which was evident from the beginning, and the true virginity of Mary before, during, and after the birth of Jesus. Most significant among them is the *Protoevangelium of James*, followed by the *Arabic Gospel of the Infancy*, the *Gospel of Pseudo-Matthew*, and the

---

[3] W. Schneemelcher, 5th ed., 5:72.

*Infancy Gospel of Thomas.* The circle of people treated is then expanded to the parents and relatives of Jesus, such as in the *History of Joseph the Carpenter.* No infancy gospel, however, goes beyond Jesus at the age of twelve; the conception of Jesus' development, as indicated in Luke 2:52, "Jesus increased in wisdom and stature," has no place in the apocryphal infancy gospels for a God-man (θεῖος ἀνήρ).

In liturgy, popular piety, and art these works have had extraordinary consequences. This is the origin, for instance, of the names of Mary's parents, namely, Joachim and Anna; of the ox and donkey at Jesus' manger; of the number and names of the magi. They have been retold again and again even in modern times—for instance, in Selma Lagerlöf's *Legends of Christ* (1904) and Felix Timmerman's *Das Jesuskind in Flandern* (1917).

By comparison, the number of gospels that *supplement the passion narrative of Jesus* remains small because the canonical gospels address this much more extensively. Theological reflection and popular pious phantasy, however, concern themselves with the fate of the individuals involved and with Jesus' descent into Hades in the *Acts of Pilate* and the gospels of Nicodemus, Bartholomew, and Gamaliel.

These are followed by the *dialogues of the redeemer,* which aim to augment and state more precisely Jesus' instructions to his disciples after the resurrection. They generally use the form of dialogue, although epistolary and apocalyptic elements may also occur. Examples are the Freer Logion, the *Epistle of the Apostles,* and the letter and the two apocalypses of James.

e. Finally, there are a number of *gospel fragments,* from various papyri, that cannot be classified more accurately; the agrapha discussed above; as well as individually handed down expressions of the oral sayings-tradition of Jesus.

This concludes a brief description of the extant material in broad outline. There are indications in the works of early Christian literature, however, that it must have existed in much larger quantities. A more detailed description of some major examples may clarify the contents, forms, and intentions of the apocryphal gospel literature.

*Editions:* C. von Tischendorf, *Evangelia apocrypha: Adhibitis plurimis codicibus graecis et latinis maximam partem nunc primum consultis atque ineditorum copia insignibus* (rev. ed.; Leipzig: Mendelssohn, 1876). – *Évangile de Pierre* (ed. M. G. Mara; SC 201; Paris: Cerf, 1973) [*Evangelium Petri* Com]. – *Los evangelios apócrifos: Colección de textos griegos y latinos, versión crítica, estudios introductorios, comentarios, e ilustraciones* (ed. A. de Santos Otero; 7th ed.; BAC 148; Madrid: Biblioteca de Autores Cristianos, 1991). – G. Schneider, *Evangelia infantiae apocrypha: = Apocryphe Kindheitsevangelien* (FChr 18; Fribourg, Switz.: Herder, 1995).

*Translations:* A. Walker, trans., "The Protevangelium of James," "The Gospel of Pseudo-Matthew," "The Gospel of the Nativity of Mary," "The History of Joseph the Carpenter," "The Gospel of Thomas," "The Arabic Gospel of the Infancy of the Saviour," "The Gospel of Nicodemus," "The Letter of Pontius Pilate Concerning Our Lord Jesus Christ," "The Report of Pilate the Procurator concerning Our Lord Jesus Christ," "The Report of Pontius Pilate," "The Giving Up of Pontius Pilate," "The Death of Pilate," "The Narrative of Joseph," and "The Avenging of the Saviour," in *ANF* (Peabody, Mass.: Hendrickson, 1995; repr. of 1886 ed.), 8:361–476. – J. A. Robinson and A. Rutherfurd, trans., "The Gospel of Peter," in *ANF* (Peabody, Mass.: Hendrickson, 1995; repr. of 1887 ed.), 9:1–31. – J. K. Elliott, "Fragments of Gospels on Papyrus, Infancy Gospel of Thomas, Gospel of Pseudo-Matthew, Arabic Infancy Gospel, History of Joseph the Carpenter, Secret Gospel of Mark, Gospel of Peter," in idem, *Apocryphal New Testament: A Collection of Apocryphal Christian Literature in an English Translation* (Oxford: Clarendon; New York: Oxford University Press, 1993), 3–163. – B. D. Ehrman, "Gospel of Thomas, Gospel of Peter, Infancy Gospel of Thomas, Secret Gospel of Mark, Papyrus Egerton 2, Gospel of the Ebionites, Gospel of the Nazareans, Gospel according to the Hebrews," in *The New Testament and Other Early Christian Writings: A Reader* (2d ed.; New York; Oxford: Oxford University Press, 2004), 116–142.

*Encyclopedia Articles:* G. Friedrich, εὐαγγελίζομαι, κτλ, *TDNT* 2:707–37. – O. Michel, *RAC* 6:1107–60. – Vielhauer, 613–92.

*Studies:* H. Daniel-Rops, *Die apokryphen Evangelien des Neuen Testaments* (2d ed.; Zurich: Arche, 1956). – Ortensio da Spinetoli, *Introduzione ai vangeli della infanzia* (Brescia: Paideia, 1967). – K. Beyschlag, *Die verborgene Überlieferung von Christus* (Munich: Siebenstern Taschenbuch, 1969). – E. Haenchen, "Neutestamentliche und gnostische Evangelien," in *Christentum und Gnosis* (ed. Walther Eltester; BZNW 37; Berlin: Töpelmann, 1969), 19–45. – H. Köster, "Überlieferung und Geschichte der früh-christlichen Evangelienliteratur," *ANRW* 2.25.2:1463–1542. – R. Laurentin, *I vangeli dell'infanzia di Cristo: Esegesi e semiotica, storicità e teologia* (3d ed.; Milan: Edizioni Paoline, 1989); French trans., *Les évangiles de l'enfance du Christ: Vérité de Noël au-delà des mythes* (Paris: Desclée de Brouwer, 1982). – W. S. Vorster, "Der Ort der Gattung Evangelium in der Literaturgeschichte," *VF* 29.1 (1984): 2–25. – H. Franke-mölle, *Evangelium—Begriff und Gattung: Ein Forschungsbericht* (Stuttgart: Kathol-isches Bibelwerk, 1988). – S. Gero, "Apocryphal Gospels: A Survey of Textual and Literary Problems," *ANRW* 2.25.5:3969–96. – D. Dormeyer, *Evangelium als liter-arische und theologische Gattung* (EdF 263; Darmstadt: Wissenschaftliche Buchgesell-schaft, 1989). – J. P. Meier, *The Marginal Jew: Rethinking the Historical Jesus* (3 vols.; ABRL; New York and London: Doubleday, 1991), 1:112–66.

# *B.* Protoevangelium of James

The so-called *Protoevangelium of James* is one of the gospels seeking to supplement the canonical gospels. It originated in Egypt in the second half of the second century and was later expanded. The Western church rejected it as apoc-ryphal in the *Decretum gelasianum* (ca. 500), with the result that it fell into obliv-ion altogether in the West. The Eastern church, however, continued to cherish it widely, as indicated by its profuse transmission in such versions as the Ethiopic, Arabic, Armenian, Georgian, Coptic, Slavic, and Syriac. It even had its place in lit-urgy, prompting the French Jesuit humanist Guillaume Postel, who brought it back from a trip to the Orient in 1549/1550 and made a Latin translation, to con-sider it canonical. He also gave it its name, on the basis that the writer calls him-self James at the conclusion of the work (para. 25) and thus probably wanted to be regarded as the Lord's brother. Since it deals with the prehistory of the birth of Jesus, chronologically it would have to be ordered as the first (πρῶτον) gospel.

The work divides into three parts. Part one (para. 1–16) narrates the origin, birth, and childhood of Mary up to the conception of Jesus. Joachim and Anna, a wealthy and devout couple suffering childlessness, are miraculously granted a daughter, Mary, by God. They fully dedicate her to God, and from age three on they have her raised as a virgin in the temple of Jerusalem, where she is fed by an angel. At the age of twelve, when Mary begins to mature from childhood to womanhood, she is entrusted to Joseph, a widower who already has adult sons and whom God chooses through a miraculous sign. When all the widowers in Israel are gathered at the temple, a dove comes out of Joseph's rod and flies onto his head. The gospel summarizes the subsequent years, reporting only that together with other temple virgins Mary weaves a veil for the temple; this is followed by the angel's annunciation, her visit with Elizabeth, and Joseph's consternation, upon his return from his lengthy building project, when he finds Mary six months pregnant. "And Mary was sixteen years old when all these mysterious things happened" (para. 12). In keeping with Matt 1:20–23, an angel instructs Joseph about the divine origin of the child, and Joseph and Mary both pass a trial by ordeal in the presence of the high priest. Part two (para. 17–21) starts with the account of the birth of Jesus, in accordance with the canonical models. On the way to Bethlehem to be enrolled in the census, Joseph has to leave Mary behind in a cave near the town because her time has come, and he proceeds to look for a midwife. The midwife shares the experience of the marvelous birth of the child and, to her amazement, discovers Mary's unchanged virginity after the birth. She shares this with a second midwife, named Salome, who reexamines Mary in unbelief and whose hand withers as a result; the infant Jesus, however, heals her. Part three (para. 22–25) adds an account of the martyrdom of Zechariah. Because Herod was deceived by the magi and is not able to seize either Jesus or John, he has Zechariah murdered.

Although the *Protoevangelium of James* belongs with the infancy gospels, the focal point of its theological and narrative interest is Jesus' mother, Mary. As the most significant witness of early Christian Marian piety, this writing is meant to serve as evidence of her divine election from birth and of her perpetual virginity. Its foremost purpose is to counter the legend, found in the pagan polemicist Celsus (ca. 178) and in Jewish literature, that Jesus was the son of Mary from an illegitimate relationship with a Roman soldier called Pantera. At the same time, it was meant to forestall an erroneous interpretation concerning the "brothers of Jesus" mentioned in the canonical gospels (Matt 12:46), by identifying them as sons from Joseph's first marriage. Curiously, however, precisely this interpretation led to the rejection of this gospel because, in order to attribute perpetual virginity to Joseph as well, Jerome regarded them as cousins of Jesus and for this reason polemicized against the gospel of James.

Regarding its literary form, we have here a collection of personal legends, but their presentation is quite guarded and cannot be compared with the virtual obsession with miracles seen in other apocryphal writings. They rely upon OT examples (the births of Samuel and Samson) and make use of the canonical infancy narratives of Matthew and Luke. Their influence upon the foundation of ecclesi-astical Mariology can hardly be overestimated.

*Editions:* E. de Strycker, *La forme la plus ancienne du Protévangile de Jacques: Recherches sur le Papyrus Bodmer 5 avec une édition critique du texte grec et une traduction annotée; en appendice les versions arméniennes traduites en latin par H. Quecke* (SHG 33; Brussels: Société des Bollandistes, 1961). – *Los evangelios apócrifos: Colección de textos griegos y latinos, versión crítica, estudios introductorios, comentarios, e ilustraciones* (ed. A. de Santos Otero; 7th ed.; BAC 148; Madrid: Biblioteca de Autores Cristianos, 1991), 126–76. – G. Schneider, *Evangelia infantiae apocrypha* = *Apokryphe Kindheits evangelien* (FChr 18; Fribourg, Switz.: Herder, 1995), 95–145.

*Translations:* A. Walker, trans., "The Protevangelium of James," in *ANF* (Peabody, Mass.: Hendrickson, 1995; repr. of 1886 ed.), 8:361–67. – J. K. Elliott, *Apocryphal New Testament: A Collection of Apocryphal Christian Literature in an English Translation* (Oxford: Clarendon; New York: Oxford University Press, 1993), 68–83. – B. D. Ehrman, *After the New Testament: A Reader in Early Christianity* (New York and Oxford: Oxford University Press, 1999), 247–54.

*Reference Works:* A. Fuchs with C. Eckmair, *Konkordanz zum Protoevangelium des Jakobus* (Linz, Austria: A. Fuchs, 1978).

*Encyclopedia Articles:* M. P. McHugh, "Protoevangelium of James," *EEC* 2:955–56.

*Studies:* H. R. Smid, *Protevangelium Jacobi: A Commentary* (Assen, Neth.: Van Gorcum, 1965). – E. Cothenet, "Le Protévangile de Jacques: Origine, genre, et signification d'un premier midrash chrétien sur la nativité de Marie," *ANRW* 2.25.6:4252 – 69. – G. Kretschmar, "'*Natus ex Maria virgine*': Zur Konzeption und Theologie des Protoevangeliums Jacobi," in *Anfänge der Christologie: Festschrift für Ferdinand Hahn zum 65. Geburtstag* (ed. C. Breytenbach, H. Paulsen, and C. Gerber; Göttingen: Vandenhoeck & Ruprecht, 1991), 417–28. – P. L. Schmidt, *HLL* 4:381–82.

# C. *Coptic* Gospel of Thomas

The *Gospel of Thomas* is not to be confused with the *Infancy Gospel of Thomas* or with the *Book of Thomas the Contender* (NHC II,7). Until the discovery and publication of the Nag Hammadi Library (1945/1948), it was known only through fragments in Jerome and, without being identified as such, in Oxyrhynchus Papyri 1, 653 and 654. In addition, Origen and Eusebius, among others, reported that it had been used by the gnostics and Manichaeans.

Nag Hammadi codex II,2 contains the complete text of this gospel in a Coptic translation from the original Greek, written in eastern Syria ca. the mid-second century. It contains 114 dominical sayings of divergent literary types: apophthegms (dialogue sayings); *logia* (wisdom sayings); prophetic and apocalyptic sayings; legal sayings and "community sayings"; "I-sayings" and parables, about half of which are paralleled by sayings in the Synoptics, and some of them can be found in the reconstructed sayings-source Q; and the agrapha, some of which have been known for some time while others have been unknown until recently.

The particular significance of the *Gospel of Thomas* is that it represents a collection of Jesus-sayings, demonstrating for the first time the existence of this genre, which previously had been postulated as Q (= *Quelle*, "source") on the basis of the analysis of the Synoptic Gospels of Matthew and Luke. To what extent the *Gospel of Thomas* is part of the gnostic writings is not yet fully established. Although it shows gnostic tendencies, in the Nag Hammadi Library it appears more like a foreign element.

*Bibliographies:* E. Haenchen, "Literatur zum Thomasevangelium," *TRu* 27 (1961): 147–78, 306–38.

*Editions: The Gospel according to Thomas* (ed. A. Guillaumont, H.-C. Puech, G. Quispel, W. Till, and Y. 'Abd al Masih; Leiden: Brill; New York: Harper, 1959). – *Das Evangelium nach Thomas* (ed. J. Leipoldt; TU 101; Berlin: Akademie, 1967). – *Das Thomasevangelium* (ed. M. Fieger; NTAbh NS 22; Münster: Aschendorff, 1991) [Com].

*Translations:* B. Layton, *The Gnostic Scriptures* (ABRL; Garden City, N.Y.: Doubleday, 1987), 376–99. – J. M. Robinson, ed., *The Nag Hammadi Library in English* (4th ed.; Leiden: Brill, 1996), 124–38. – M. Meyer, *The Gospel of Thomas: The Hidden Sayings of Jesus* (San Francisco: HarperSanFrancisco, 1992). – J. K. Elliott, *Apocryphal New Testament: A Collection of Apocryphal Christian Literature in an English Translation* (Oxford: Clarendon; New York: Oxford University Press, 1993), 123–47 [with P. Oxyrhynchus 1 and 654 in parallel]. – B. D. Ehrman, *After the New Testament: A Reader in Early Christianity* (New York and Oxford: Oxford University Press, 1999), 237–44.

*Reference Works:* E. H. Degge, *A Computer-Generated Concordance of the Coptic Text of the Gospel according to Thomas* (Wooster, Ohio: n.p., 1995).

*Commentary:* R. Valantasis, *The Gospel of Thomas* (New Testament Readings; London: Routledge, 1997).

*Encyclopedia Articles:* K. V. Neller, "Gospel of Thomas (Sayings)," *EEC* 1:478–79.

*Studies:* J. A. Fitzmyer, "The Oxyrhynchus Logoi of Jesus and the Coptic Gospel according to Thomas," in idem, *Essays on the Semitic Background of the New Testament* (Missoula, Mont.: Scholars Press, 1974), 355–433. – P. de Suarez, *L'Évangile selon Thomas: Traduction, présentation, et commentaires* (Marsanne, France: Métanoïa, 1974). – J.-E. Ménard, *L'Évangile selon Thomas* (NHS 5; Leiden: Brill, 1975). – M. Lelyveld, *Les logia de la vie dans l'Évangile de Thomas: À la recherche d'une tradition et d'une rédaction* (NHS 34; Leiden: Brill, 1987). – F. T. Fallon and R. Cameron, "The Gospel of Thomas: A Forschungsbericht and Analysis," *ANRW* 2.25.6:4195–4261. – M. Alcalá, *El evangelio copto de Tomás* (Salamanca: Sígueme, 1989). – M. Fieger, *Das Thomasevangelium: Einleitung, Kommentar, und Systematik* (NTAbh NF 22; Münster: Aschendorff, 1991). – J. Meier, *A Marginal Jew: Rethinking the Historical Jesus* (3 vols.; ABRL; New York and London: Doubleday, 1991), 1:123–66. – A. D. De Conick and J. Fossum, "Stripped before God: A New Interpretation of Logion 37 in the Gospel of Thomas," *VC* 45 (1991): 123–50. – R. Trevijano Etcheverría, "La conversión de la escatología en protología (EvTom log. 18, 19, 24, 49 y 50)," *Salm* 40 (1993): 133–63. – A. D. De Coninck, *Seek to See Him: Ascent and Vision Mysticism in the Gospel of Thomas* (SVigChr 33; Leiden: Brill, 1996). – T. Zöckler, *Jesu Lehren im Thomasevangelium* (Nag Hammadi and Manichaean Studies 47; Leiden: Brill, 1999). – R. Valantasis, "Is the Gospel of Thomas Ascetical? Revisiting an Old Problem with a New Theory," *JECS* 7 (1999): 55–82. – A. Siverstev, "The *Gospel of Thomas* and Early Stages in the Development of the Christian Wisdom Literature," *JECS* 8 (2000): 319–40.

# *D.* Epistle of the Apostles

The *Epistle of the Apostles* belongs to the genre of dialogues between the risen one and his disciples; the origin of such dialogues is generally associated with gnostic circles. For this particular *Epistle*, however, precisely the converse is true: it opposes Gnosticism by using Gnosticism's own methods. Secret revelations given to individuals are countered with a dialogue between Christ and all the apostles cited by name, which the latter then publish in the form of a letter. It defends Christ's true deity; the reality of his incarnation and resurrection; the resurrection of the body, together with the soul and the spirit, for judgment; and Jesus' descent into Hades to the saints of the old covenant so as to allow them to share in the forgiveness of sins by baptism. The letter concludes with an apocalyptic view of the end time and with the story of the ascension of Christ.

In literary terms, it is a revelatory address within a framework of evangelistic report and letter. Theologically the *Epistle* offers an orthodox alternative to docetic Christology and to the dualistic anthropology of Gnosticism. In this regard it is, on the whole, successful even if it cannot entirely evade gnostic and syncretistic influences, which, however, can be explained in terms of their place and time of origin, namely, Hellenistic Jewish Christianity in Egypt in the middle of the second century. Beyond this, it contains the earliest attestation of the Christian Passover festival and of the expectation of the Lord's return (Parousia) in the night of the Passover (para. 15[26]).

We do not know whether this writing had any influence in the ancient church, for until the end of the nineteenth century it was entirely unknown; nor was it mentioned anywhere in the remaining literature. It was not until 1895 that Carl Schmidt discovered Coptic fragments of it and J. Bick discovered a page in a Latin palimpsest. Together with Sylvain Grébaut, Louis Fuerrier was able to publish the complete Ethiopic text in 1912. All of the versions, however, are translations of a Greek original.

*Editions: Le Testament en Galilée de Nôtre-Seigneur Jésus-Christ* (ed. L. Guerrier and S. Grébaut; PO 9.3; Paris: Firmin-Didot, 1912; repr., Turnhout, Belg.: Brepols, 2003). – *Gespräche Jesu mit seinen Jüngern nach der Auferstehung* (ed. C. Schmidt and I. Wajnberg; TU 43; Leipzig: Hinrichs, 1919).

*Translations:* J. K. Elliott, *Apocryphal New Testament: A Collection of Apocryphal Christian Literature in an English Translation* (Oxford: Clarendon; New York: Oxford University Press, 1993), 555–588. – B. D. Ehrman, *After the New Testament: A Reader in Early Christianity* (New York and Oxford: Oxford University Press, 1999), 259–63 [selections].

*Studies:* M. Hornschuh, *Studien zur Epistula apostolorum* (PTS 5; Berlin: de Gruyter, 1965). – J. V. Hills, *Tradition and Composition in the Epistula apostolorum* (HDR 24; Minneapolis: Fortress, 1990). – K. Zelzer, *HLL* 4:412–13. – C. E. Hill, "The Epistula apostolorum: An Asian Tract from the Time of Polycarp," *JECS* 7 (1999): 1–53.

# E. Gospel of Nicodemus

The *Gospel of Nicodemus* is composed of two parts, the *Acts of Pilate* (chs. 1–16) and the *Descensus Christi ad inferos* ("Christ's descent into hell"), dealing with the descent of Jesus into the underworld after his death (chs. 17–27), and hence is part of the gospels supplementing Christ's passion. One of the main focal points is Pilate as a person who is to be exonerated and who thereby gains his own significance in hagiography and in the veneration of saints.

In the prologue, the compiler himself notes the date of the final redaction of this work as the "eighteenth year of the reign of our emperor Flavius Theodosius and in the fifth year of the 'Nobility' of Flavius Valentinianus, in the ninth indiction," namely, 425 C.E. The first part, the *Acts of Pilate*, definitely originated before 375/376, since Epiphanius of Constantia (Salamis) cites it. Two references to it in Justin and Tertullian seem to point to an even earlier date of origin, prior to 150. It is possible that its authorship is also associated with the pagan *Acts of Pilate* mentioned by Eusebius, which was to fan the hatred against Christians during the persecution under Maximinus Daia (311/312). In any case, the compilation of 425 is made up of earlier material. Friedrich Scheidweiler questions this merely as far as the *Descensus* is concerned, which he argues was appended later because it is missing in one of the extant Greek versions, whereas the *Acts* is developed in more detail: "The addition is thoroughly out of keeping, since the work is complete and does not admit of any expansion." He views version B as a revision of the original, expanding chs. 10 and 11 considerably while abbreviating ch. 16 significantly in order to be able to add the *Descensus*.[4] Scheidweiler does not thereby achieve a more precise determination of this part's date of origin, however, since he merely deems it a "substantially older fragment" that was "simply added." There might be an indication that the *Descensus* was composed in the late fourth century: the interpretation of Ps 24:7 in terms of the descent to Hades, "Be lifted up, you ancient doors, that the King of glory may come in," which until Gregory of Nyssa seems to have been applied exclusively to the ascension.[5]

The *Acts of Pilate* is composed of two parts. Chapters 1–11, the actual *Acta Pilati*, are an account of Jesus' trial before Pilate, his crucifixion, and his burial. Theologically they are intended as a defense of Jesus' virgin birth over against the Jewish slander (cf. the Pantera legend under B above), his divine authority and innocence confirming his miracles, as well as the depiction of Pilate as an opponent of Jesus' crucifixion; in this context it assimilates a wealth of material from the canonical gospels. Pilate's positive role continues in later writings and excuses

---

    [4] F. Scheidweiler, in *New Testament Apocrypha* (ed. W. Schneemelcher; trans. R. McL. Wilson; 2 vols.; 2d ed.; Cambridge: J. Clarke; Louisville: Westminster John Knox, 1991–1992), 1:447ff., contra Bardenhewer (*Litg.* 1:545, n. 3).
    [5] Cf. H. R. Drobner, "Die Himmelfahrtspredigt Gregors von Nyssa," in *EPMH-NEYMATA: Festschrift für Hadwig Hörner zum sechzigsten Geburtstag* (ed. H. Eisenberger; Heidelberg: Winter, 1990), 106–9.

him for Jesus' death to the extent that the Syrian church venerated him as a saint, and to this day he has a place in the calendar of saints of the Coptic church. The topic of Pilate also evolved in other ways, with him encountering a lamentable end: after his violent death, he was not able to find peace either in the Tiber or in the Rhone because his grave was surrounded by raving spirits from hell, until he was finally cast into a mountain lake. The mountain at that location is therefore named Mount Pilatus in Switzerland to this day.

Originally chs. 12–16 were not part of the *Acta Pilati*. They contain the account of a meeting by the Sanhedrin in Jerusalem after the death of Jesus. During their meeting, the resurrection of Jesus is proclaimed to them, as are his great commission and ascension. As a result, an intense discussion develops, in the course of which Nicodemus and Joseph of Arimathea testify for Jesus, albeit without being able to persuade the Jews.

The final part (chs. 17–27) is claimed to be the testimony of two sons of Simeon who in their deceased state encounter Jesus in Hades, then are raised with him and now write this down in the presence of the high priests in Jerusalem. The account begins with the first ray of light penetrating the darkness of Hades, thus raising hope in the patriarchs, the prophets, and John the Baptist that their predictions concerning the Messiah are now being fulfilled. Hades and Satan end up in a feud because the insatiable Hades swallowed up Jesus although Jesus had demonstrated his divine power in his miracles. Then in the words of Ps 24:7 the call goes out to open the gates of the underworld for the ruler; Hades and Satan are conquered, and the OT saints are raised, baptized in the Jordan, and led into paradise with Christ.

In multiple adaptations and transmissions, this depiction of Christ's descent into Hades permeated all of the Middle Ages up to modern times, as illustrated by the numerous translations into Arabic, Armenian, Coptic, Latin, and Syriac. An Easter Saturday sermon attributed to Epiphanius (PG 43:439–64) has contributed to this by drawing upon the *Gospel of Nicodemus* and describing the struggle of the descent in even greater detail and more magnificently. Even today some excerpts serve as readings in the Roman Catholic breviary at Easter.

*Editions:* C. von Tischendorf, *Evangelia apocrypha: Adhibitis plurimis codicibus graecis et latinis maximam partem nunc primum consultis atque ineditorum copia insignibus* (rev. ed.; Leipzig: Mendelssohn, 1876), 210–486. – M. Vandoni and T. Orlandi, *Vangelo di Nicodemo* (2 vols.; Milan: Instituto Editoriale Cisalpino, 1966). – A. Vaillant, *L'Évangile de Nicodème: Texte slave et texte latin* (PCRHP.O 1; Geneva: Droz, 1968). – H. C. Kim, *The Gospel of Nicodemus—Gesta Salvatoris: Edited from the Codex Einsidlensis Ms. 326* (Toronto: Published for the Centre for Medieval Studies by the Pontifical Institute of Medieval Studies, 1973). – *Los evangelios apócrifos: Colección de textos griegos y latinos, versión crítica, estudios introductorios, comentarios, e ilustraciones* (ed. A. de Santos Otero; 7th ed.; BAC 148; Madrid: Biblioteca de Autores Cristianos, 1991), 396–471.

*Translations:* A. Walker, trans., "The Gospel of Nicodemus," in *ANF* (Peabody, Mass., Hendrickson, 1995; repr. of 1886 ed.), 8:416–67. – J. K. Elliott, *Apocryphal New Testament: A Collection of Apocryphal Christian Literature in an English Translation* (Oxford: Clarendon; New York: Oxford University Press, 1993), 164–205.

*Studies:* R. P. Wülcker, *Das Evangelium Nicodemi in der abendländischen Literatur: Nebst drei Excursen* (Paderborn: F. Schöningh, 1872). – R. A. Lipsius, *Die Pilatus-Acten kritisch untersucht* (2d ed.; Kiel: Haeseler, 1886). – E. von Dobschütz, "Der Process Jesu nach den Acta Pilati," *ZNW* 3 (1902): 89–114. – T. Mommsen, "Die Pilatus-Acten," *ZNW* 3 (1902): 198–205. – J. Kroll, *Gott und Hölle: Der Mythos vom Descensus-Kampfe* (Darmstadt: Wissenschaftliche Buchgesellschaft, 1963). – Z. Izydorczyk, "The Unfamiliar *Evangelium Nicodemi*," *Manuscripta* 33 (1989): 169–91. – J.-D. Dubois, "Les 'Actes de Pilate' au quatrième siècle," *Apocrypha* 2 (1991): 85–98. – K. Zelzer, *HLL* 4:387–90.

# II. ACTS OF THE APOSTLES

## A. *Literary Genre*

In contrast to the apocryphal gospels, the apocryphal acts, extant for the most part only in fragments, do not parallel the canonical Acts of the Apostles written by Luke, nor do they depend on or compete with the latter. Instead they emerged independently in two later phases and, broadly speaking, intended to supplement the canonical Acts. The five important acts originated in the second and third centuries, namely the acts of Andrew, John, Paul, Peter, and Thomas, which the Manichaeans compiled into a corpus and subsequently were construed as a composite work by an author known as Leucius Charinus. The acts arising from the fourth century on have been handed down in large numbers and either rework the five major acts or deal with other apostles, albeit no longer with the original wealth of material and ideas of the earlier ones. All of them are characterized by the common theme of the person, life (travels, deeds), and teaching of one or more of the apostles as θεῖοι ἄνδρες and trustworthy witnesses of the faith. These acts thereby furnish the starting point of later hagiography by handing down martyrdoms and other individual segments separately and detached.

The literary genre of these acts has yet to be determined uniformly because their stylistic forms diverge widely. In all probability they are associated with the ancient novels, namely, the literature known as περίοδοι and πράξεις, although they differ from the latter in that they use not only fiction but also traditional elements, legends, and stories. R. Söder offers an analysis of five major elements:

- the travel theme;

- the aretalogical element, stressing the marvelous virtues (ἀρεταί) and powers (δυνάμεις) of the heroes;

- the teratological element, exhibiting the world of wonders that the apostles encounter (cannibals, talking animals, etc.);

- the persuasive element, displayed especially in the speeches;

- the erotic element, finding expression in proper love motifs but also in ascetic and encratite features.

The apocryphal acts may have to be classified as popular literature whose intent was to provide its readers with Christian entertainment, edification, and instruction, not with a discussion of theological or ecclesiastical problems. The theory that these acts originated in Gnosticism can no longer be sustained, on the basis of the more recent discoveries of gnostic writings and the necessary technical differentiation of "the" gnosis—which does not mean, of course, that some of them do not contain such elements.

*Editions:* Acta Johannis (ed. E. Junod and J.-D. Kaestli; CChr.SA 1–2; Turnhout, Belg.: Brepols, 1983). – *Acta Andreae* (ed. J.-M. Prieur; CChr.SA 5–6; Turnhout, Belg.: Brepols, 1989). – *Acta Philippi* (ed. F. Bovon, B. Bouvier, and F. Amsler; CChr.SA 11–12; Turnhout, Belg.: Brepols, 1999). – R. A. Lipsius and M. Bonnet, *Acta apostolorum apocrypha* (2 vols. in 3; Leipzig: Mendelssohn, 1891–1903).

*Translations:* A. Walker, trans., "Acts of the Holy Apostles Peters and Paul," "Acts of Paul and Thecla," "The Acts of Barnabas," "The Acts of Philip," "Acts and Martyrdom of the Holy Apostle Andrew," "Acts of Andrew and Matthias," "Acts of Peter and Andrew," "Acts and Martyrdom of St. Matthew the Apostle," "Acts of the Holy Apostle Thomas," "Consummation of Thomas the Apostle," "Martyrdom of the Holy and Glorious Apostle Bartholomew," "Acts of the Holy Apostle Thaddaeus," "Acts of the Holy Apostle and Evangelist John the Theologian," in *ANF* (Peabody, Mass.: Hendrickson, 1995; repr. of 1886 ed.), 8:477–564. – J. K. Elliott, *Apocryphal New Testament: A Collection of Apocryphal Christian Literature in an English Translation* (Oxford: Clarendon; New York: Oxford University Press, 1993), 229–349, 431–537 [*Acts of Andrew, Acts of John, Pseudo-Clementine Literature, Acts of Thomas*].

*Reference Works:* M. Lipinski, *Konkordanz zu den Thomasakten* (BBB 67; Frankfurt: Athenäum, 1988).

*Encyclopedia Articles:* E. Plümacher, PWSup 15:11–70. – K. Zelzer and P. L. Schmidt, *HLL* 4:391–405.

*Studies:* R. A. Lipsius, *Die apokryphen Apostelgeschichten und Apostellegenden: Ein Beitrag zur altchristlichen Literaturgeschichte* (2 vols. in 3; Braunschweig: C. A. Schwetschke und Sohn, 1883–1890). – R. Söder, *Die apokryphen Apostelgeschichten und die romanhafte Literatur der Antike* (Stuttgart: Kohlhammer, 1932; repr., 1969). – M. Blumenthal, *Formen und Motive in den apokryphen Apostelgeschichten* (TU 48.1; Leipzig: Hinrichs, 1933). – F. Bovon et al., *Les Actes apocryphes des apôtres: Christianisme et monde païen* (Geneva: Labor et Fides, 1981). – C. W. Müller, "Der griechische Roman," in *Griechische Literatur* (vol. 2 of *Neues Handbuch der Literaturwissenschaft*; Wiesbaden: Akademie Verlagsgesellschaft Athenaion, 1981), 3:377–412. – N. Holzberg, *Der antike Roman: Eine Einführung* (Munich: Artemis, 1986). – T. Hägg, *Eros und Tyche: Der Roman in der antiken Welt* (Mainz: Philipp von Zabern, 1987). – V. Burrus, *Chastity as Autonomy: Women in the Stories of the Apocryphal Acts* (SWR 23; Lewiston, N.Y.: Mellen, 1987). – ANRW 2.25.6:4293–27. – F. Bovon, A. Graham Brock, and C. R. Matthews, eds., *The Apocryphal Acts of the Apostles* (Cambridge, Mass.: Harvard University Center for the Study of World Religions, 1999).

# B. Acts of Peter

The *Acts of Peter,* the earliest of the extant apocryphal acts, originated in Asia Minor or Rome roughly between 180 and 190. About a third of it has been lost; the extensive middle section and the concluding part, as well as two separate stories of the first section, are handed down in the Latin *Actus Vercellenses*, in two Greek manuscripts, and in various fragments. A *Martyrdom of Peter* circulated as well, as attested in a number of Eastern versions.

Part 1 probably took place in Jerusalem, where, according to tradition, Peter lived for twelve years and encountered Simon Magus for the first time (cf. Acts 8:18–24). Part 2 narrates Peter's journey to Rome, in obedience to a divine directive, as well as his activity there. After Paul left Rome on a mission to Spain, Simon is said to have surfaced in Rome and, apart from a few of the faithful, won the local community of believers over to himself by amazing the Romans with his miracles. Peter then takes up the attack against Simon, performing many, even more convincing miracles and finally overcoming him in a head-on, public exhibition of miraculous power. The final scene of this clash, in which Simon wants to demonstrate his flying skills from the top of a tall scaffold but fails on account of Peter's prayer and breaks a leg, has gained notoriety (including in Hollywood films).

The concluding part describes Peter's martyrdom, which, as is frequent in the apocryphal acts, was brought about by means of an erotic and ascetic element. His preaching of chastity attracts the indignation of Agrippa, the Roman prefect, and arouses unrest in the city. Four of Agrippa's concubines leave him, and many wives separate from their husbands or, for the sake of the new chastity, refuse to share in the sexual intimacy of marriage. With arrest impending, Peter flees from Rome on the Via Appia, where Christ appears to him and, upon Peter's question, *Quo vadis, Domine?* responds, "I am going to Rome to be crucified a second time." As a result, Peter returns to Rome and there suffers death by crucifixion; in contrast to Jesus, however, he is crucified upside down. It is precisely in the *Quo vadis* story that one recognizes the popular effect of these acts. To this day the traditional site of the appearance is commemorated in a church built at that location and where Jesus' footprints, which he left behind at his ascension, are venerated in a block of marble. Likewise, the novel *Quo Vadis* brought the Polish author Henryk Sienkiewicz (1846–1916) world fame and in 1905 the Nobel Prize in literature.

From the literary perspective, the *Acts of Peter* belongs to the πράξεις literature. Its aim is not to combat heretics but to depict the miraculous mighty works of Peter, as θεῖος ἀνήρ, which demonstrate God's superior power over evil. The work's structure is determined by the aretalogical element (miracles, visions, etc.), interspersed with speeches, dialogues, and prayers. The account of the journey from Jerusalem to Rome merely links these two scenes and does not supply the work's overall framework; hence it does not belong to the περίοδοι.

*Editions:* R. A. Lipsius and M. Bonnet, *Acta apostolorum apocrypha* (2 vols. in 3; Leipzig: Mendelssohn, 1891–1903), 1:45 – 103. – L. Vouaux, ed., *Les Actes de Pierre* (Paris: Letouzey & Ané, 1922) [Com].

*Translations:* A. Walker, trans., "Acts of the Holy Apostles Peter and Paul," in *ANF* (Peabody, Mass.: Hendrickson, 1995; repr. of 1886 ed.), 8:477–86. – J. K. Elliott, *Apocryphal New Testament: A Collection of Apocryphal Christian Literature in an English Translation* (Oxford: Clarendon; New York: Oxford University Press, 1993), 390–430.

– B. D. Ehrman, *After the New Testament* (New York and Oxford: Oxford University Press, 1999), 263–75.

*Studies:* C. Schmidt, *Die alten Petrusakten im Zusammenhang der apokryphen Apostellitera- tur nebst einem neuentdeckten Fragment* (TU 24.1; Leipzig: Hinrichs, 1903). – C. Schmidt, "Studien zu den alten Petrusakten," *ZKG* 43 (1924): 321–48; 45 (1927): 481–513. – G. Poupon, "Les 'Actes de Pierre' et leur remaniement," *ANRW* 25.6:4363–83. – K. Zelzer and P. L. Schmidt, *HLL* 4:392–94. – J. N. Bremmer, ed., *The Apocryphal Acts of Peter: Magic, Miracles, and Gnosticism* (Louvain: Peeters, 1998).

# C. Acts of Paul

The *Acts of Paul (Acta Pauli)*, which does belong to the περίοδοι and pre- sumably depends on the *Acts of Peter*, was written by a presbyter in Asia Minor ca. 185–195 and narrates the deeds of Paul in the framework of a major travel story. It, too, is not preserved completely, lacking the beginning and a large part in the middle. The remainder has been handed down in different ways and in various fragments, namely, in Greek and Coptic papyri, as the *Acts of Paul and Thecla*, as the correspondence between Paul and the Corinthians (*3 Corinthians*), and as the *Martyrdom of Paul*. On the basis of these, Schneemelcher has reconstructed the original form of the *Acts* as far as possible. The structure of the work is deter- mined by the destinations in Paul's journey: Damascus, Jerusalem, Antioch (Syria?), Iconium, Antioch (Pisidia?), Myra, Sidon, Tyre, and, following a lacuna, Smyrna, Ephesus, Philippi, Corinth, Italy, and Rome. The episodes follow an al- most stereotypical schema: description of the itinerary; Paul's preaching on the resurrection and chastity, which evokes unrest because wives turn away from their husbands; his resultant persecution and miraculous rescue; and continua- tion of the journey.

It may be assumed, on the basis of fragments, that the lost beginning likely described Paul's conversion in Damascus and his initial ministry there and in Je- rusalem. This was followed by an episode in Antioch, extant in fragmentary form, which leads directly into the main section, which has been handed down as the *Acts of Paul and Thecla (Acta Pauli et Theclae)*, in which Paul plays only a minor part. In Iconium the virgin Thecla is persuaded by Paul's preaching and leaves her betrothed, who, together with other men whose wives also left them, brings charges against Paul before the proconsul. As a result, Paul is imprisoned, but at night Thecla gains access to him by bribing the guards so as to continue to be in- structed by Paul. When this becomes public, both are taken to court. Paul is banned from the city and Thecla is condemned to be burned, but the fire does not touch her. In the next city, Antioch, she escapes death in the arena because none of the beasts attacks her; indeed a lioness defends her until the lioness itself per- ishes. Thecla then steps into a pit full of water and baptizes herself; finally, she is officially set free.

The remaining segments are preserved in fragmentary form only and fol- low the same structure. The correspondence between Paul and the Corinthians

(*3 Corinthians*) deals with questions concerning gnostic heresies preached by two men in Corinth, namely, the rejection of the OT and the denial of God's omnipotence, of the resurrection of the flesh, of God as the creator of the world, and of Christ as the Son of God incarnated through Mary. The *Acta* concludes with Paul's martyrdom in Rome, where he arrives as a free man, in contrast to the Lukan Acts. Here the martyrdom is the consequence not of a sermon on chastity but, rather, of the proclamation of Christ as ruler of the aeons, so that Emperor Nero sees his power jeopardized.

The author has merged assumed traditions with his own ideas, creating a new entity, the purpose of which is not theological but the community's edification and enjoyment. The main topics addressed are those of the resurrection and chastity. Whether he was conversant with the canonical Acts remains doubtful. Although many place-names of Paul's itinerary agree and a few reminiscences may be noted, these may be attributed to common roots, for on the whole the shaping of the subject matter of the *Acts of Paul* indicates no dependence at all.

Paul's description as "a man small of stature, with a bald head and crooked legs, in a good state of body, with eyebrows meeting and nose somewhat hooked" (3:2) became determinative for early Christian iconography, in which he is typically depicted as narrow-faced, goateed, and bald. By contrast, Peter is portrayed with a round face, full hair, and a curly, full beard.

*Editions:* R. A. Lipsius and M. Bonnet, *Acta apostolorum apocrypha* (2 vols. in 3; Leipzig: Mendelssohn, 1891–1903), 1:23–44, 104–17, 235–72. – L. Vouaux, *Les Actes de Paul et ses lettres apocryphes* (Paris: Letouzey & Ané, 1913). – C. Schmidt, *Acta Pauli: Aus der Heidelberger koptischen Papyrushandschrift Nr. 1* (2d ed.; Leipzig: Hinrichs, 1905). – C. Schmidt with W. Schubart, eds., *Acta Pauli: Nach dem Papyrus der Hamburger Staats- und Universitäts-Bibliothek* (Glückstadt and Hamburg: J. J. Augustin, 1936). – M. Testuz, *Papyrus Bodmer X–XII* (Cologne: Bibliotheca Bodmeriana, 1959), 7–45. – *Die apokryphen Briefe des Paulus an die Laodicener und Korinther* (ed. A. von Harnack; 2d ed.; KlT 12; Berlin: de Gruyter, 1931), 6–22.

*Translations:* A. Walker, trans., "Acts of Paul and Thecla," in *ANF* (Peabody, Mass.: Hendrickson, 1995; repr. of 1886 ed.), 8:487–92. – J. K. Elliott, *Apocryphal New Testament: A Collection of Apocryphal Christian Literature in an English Translation* (Oxford: Clarendon; New York: Oxford University Press, 1993), 350–389. – B. D. Ehrman, *After the New Testament* (Oxford: Oxford University Press, 1999), 275–84.

*Studies:* W. Schneemelcher, *Gesammelte Aufsätze zum Neuen Testament und zur Patristik* (ed. W. Bienert and K. Schäferdiek; ABla 22; Thessaloníki: Patriarchal Institute for Patristic Studies, 1974), 182–239. – W. Rordorf, "In welchem Verhältnis stehen die apokryphen Paulusakten zur kanonischen Apostelgeschichte und zu den Pastoralbriefen?" in *Text and Testimony: Essays on New Testament and Apocryphal Literature in Honour of A. F. J. Klijn* (ed. T. Baarda; Kampen, Neth.: Kok, 1988), 225–41. – W. Rordorf, "Was wissen wir über Plan und Absicht der Paulusakten?" in *Oecumenica et patristica: Festschrift für Wilhelm Schneemelcher zum 75. Geburtstag* (ed. D. Papandreou et al.; Chambésy-Geneva: Metropolie der Schweiz, 1989), 71–82. – J. N. Bremmer, ed., *The Apocryphal Acts of Paul and Thecla* (Kampen, Neth.: Kok Pharos, 1996). – K. Zelzer and P. L. Schmidt, *HLL* 4:394–96.

# III. LETTERS

## A. *Literary Genre*

For a basic understanding of patrology, the third literary type of the biblical apocrypha, namely, the letters, does not call for an extensive treatment. There are not many of them, and they do not have great importance for early literature and theology. All of them are associated with fictitious and pseudepigraphic epistolary literature and are often handed down within larger works, as, for instance, *3 Corinthians* in the *Acts of Paul* or Jesus' correspondence with King Abgar of Edessa (*Epistle of Christ and Abgar*) in the Abgar legend. In addition, the *Epistle to the Laodiceans* is worth noting because its origin is linked with Paul's comment in Col 4:16: "And when this letter has been read among you, have it read also in the church of the Laodiceans; and see to it that you read also the letter from Laodicea." Mention should also be made of the correspondence between Paul and Seneca the philosopher (*Epistles of Paul and Seneca*), which was intended to commend the Pauline letters, despite their nonclassical style, to the Roman audience through the mouthpiece of the famous philosopher. This writing indeed made a considerable impression upon antiquity.

*Editions:* PLS 1:673–78 [Paul and Seneca]. – PLS 2:1486–87, 1522–42 [Titus]. – *Die apokryphen Briefe des Paulus an die Laodicener und Korinther* (ed. A. von Harnack; 2d ed.; KlT 12; Berlin: de Gruyter, 1931). – *Los evangelios apócrifos: Colección de textos griegos y latinos, versión crítica, estudios introductorios, comentarios, e ilustraciones* (ed. A. de Santos Otero; 7th ed.; BAC 148; Madrid: Biblioteca de Autores Cristianos, 1991), 662–69.

*Translations:* J. K. Elliott, *Apocryphal New Testament: A Collection of Apocryphal Christian Literature in an English Translation* (Oxford: Clarendon; New York: Oxford University Press, 1993), 537–54 [*Letters of Christ and Abgar, Letter of Lentulus, Epistle to the Laodiceans, Correspondence of Paul and Seneca, Epistle to the Alexandrians*]. – B. D. Ehrman, *After the New Testament: A Reader in Early Christianity* (Oxford: Oxford University Press, 1999), 290–96 [*Third Letter to the Corinthians, Correspondence Between Paul and Seneca, Letter to the Laodiceans*].

*Encyclopedia Articles:* H. Leclercq, "Sénèque et s. Paul," DACL 15.1:1193–98. – E. Kirsten, "Edessa," RAC 4:588–93. – A. Hamman, "Seneca and Paul, Correspondence of," EECh 1:767.

*Studies:* E. von Dobschütz, "Der Briefwechsel zwischen Abgar und Jesus," ZWT 43 (1900): 422–86. – J. N. Sevenster, *Paul und Seneca* (Leiden: Brill, 1961). – A. F. J. Klijn, "The Apocryphal Correspondence between Paul and the Corinthians," VC 17 (1963): 2–23. – F. Schnider and W. Stenger, *Studien zum neutestamentlichen Briefformular* (NTTS 11; Leiden: Brill, 1987). – D. Trobisch, *Die Entstehung der Paulusbriefsammlung: Studien zu den Anfängen christlicher Publizistik* (NTOA 10; Fribourg, Switz.: Universitätsverlag, 1989). – I. Ramelli, "L'epistolario apocrifo Seneca–San Paolo: Alcune osservazioni," VetChr 34 (1997): 299–310. – A. Fürst, "Pseudepigraphie und Apostolizität im apokryphen Briefwechsel zwischen Seneca und Paulus," JAC 41 (1998): 77–117. – G. G. Gamba, "Il carteggio tra Seneca e San Paolo: Il 'problema' della sua autenticità," Sal. 60 (1998): 209–50.

# *B.* Letter of Barnabas

Traditionally the *Letter of Barnabas* is classified among the Apostolic Fathers, but it should more appropriately be considered as belonging to the apocrypha, as Eusebius and Jerome thought, since it represents a pseudepigraphic writing in the name of an apostle. In many places in antiquity, the *Letter of Barnabas* was regarded as canonical and hence as one of the biblical books. In the famous Codex Sinaiticus it is directly attached to the NT. Concerning its literary genre, it is a tract in epistolary form, albeit limited to a brief and (for a genuine letter) incomplete salutation at the beginning, to echoes of an epistolary proem, and to fragments of an epistolary conclusion. The identifications of the writer, recipients, and reason for writing, standard in a genuine letter, are missing here.

Although the author of this letter does not mention his name anywhere, tradition, since its earliest attestation in Clement of Alexandria, has attributed it to Barnabas, Paul's companion, whose background was Judaism. The letter, however, demonstrates that its author was a Gentile Christian, and at the time of writing, Barnabas, in all probability, was no longer alive, for 16:3–4 speaks of a temple being rebuilt by those who destroyed it. Klaus Wengst has recently been able to show the probability that this refers to the Jerusalem temple, destroyed in 70 C.E. by Titus, in place of which Emperor Hadrian in 130 sought to erect a temple to Jupiter Capitolinus, thereby precipitating the Bar Kokhba revolt. Since the *Letter of Barnabas* makes no reference to this revolt, Wengst infers a writing date between 130 and 132. The place of writing was traditionally held to be Egypt or, more specifically, Alexandria; currently, however, scholarship tends to favor Asia Minor, Syria, or Palestine.

The letter divides into twenty-one chapters, with the words concluding ch. 17, "So much then for this. But let us pass on to another lesson and teaching," clearly indicating a break between the two main sections. Following a brief salutation and proem (1), the first section (2–17) deals with the knowledge to be gained from Scripture (the OT) concerning God, Christ, the new people of God, and their ethical obligations. The second section (18–20) calls upon the Christian to decide between the ways of light and darkness. This doctrine of the two ways had its origin in Judaism and, in a more systematic form, is found again in the *Didache*. Chapter 21 concludes with admonitions to obey the Lord's commandments, followed by a salutation and benediction. The author uses a broad array of traditional elements that are determined by formal observations. For instance, he does not draw his citations of Scripture directly from the LXX. He has access to a collection of *testimonia*, though it is likely not his only source, as shown by the evident seams, breaks, and discrepancies. The hypotheses of later interpolation should be laid to rest.

The theological significance of the *Letter of Barnabas* is that it constitutes the first comprehensible typological and spiritual interpretation of the entire OT as prophecy pointing to Christ and the Christian lifestyle, albeit in unprecedented radicality. Accordingly, there never existed a covenant between God and the Jewish people, their understanding of the Holy Scripture being a fundamental misunderstanding. Christians alone are the recipients of the covenant and Scripture; they therefore discerned Scripture's christological and spiritual meaning behind the literal.

*Editions: Épître de Barnabé* (ed. P. Prigent and R. A. Kraft; SC 172; Paris: Cerf, 1971) [Com]. – *Epistola di Barnaba* (ed. F. Scorza Barcellona; CorPat 1; Turin: Società Editrice Internazionale, 1975) [Com]. – *Didache (Apostellehre), Barnabasbrief, Zweiter Klemensbrief, Schrift an Diognet* (ed. K. Wengst; Darmstadt: Wissenschaftliche Buchgesellschaft, 1984), 101–202 [Com]. – *Die apostolischen Väter* (ed. Lindemann and Paulsen; Tübingen: Mohr, 1992), 23–75. – *Didaché, Doctrina apostolorum, Epístola del Pseudo-Bernabé* (ed. J. J. Ayán Calvo; FP 3; Madrid: Ciudad Nueva, 1992), 125–231 [Com]. – M. W. Holmes, *The Apostolic Fathers: Greek Texts and English Translations* (rev. ed.; Grand Rapids: Baker, 1999), 274–327.

*Translations:* A. C. Coxe, trans., "The Epistle of Barnabas," in *ANF* (Peabody, Mass.: Hendrickson, 1995; repr. of 1885 ed.), 1:133–49. – *The Apostolic Fathers* (trans. F. X. Glimm, J. M.-F. Marique, and G. G. Walsh; FC 1; Washington, D.C.: Catholic University of America Press, 1947; repr., 1969), 185–222. – *The Didache, The Epistle of Barnabas, The Epistles and The Martyrdom of St. Polycarp, The Fragments of Papias, The Epistle to Diognetus* (trans. J. A. Kleist; ACW 6; Westminster, Md.: Newman, 1948), 27–65, 166–83. – *Early Christian Writings: The Apostolic Fathers* (trans. M. Staniforth; Harmondsworth, Eng.: Penguin, 1968), 187–222. – B. D. Ehrman, *The New Testament and Other Christian Writings: A Reader* (2d ed.; New York: Oxford University Press, 2004), 344–58.

*Reference Works:* A. Urbán, *Barnabae Epistolae concordantia* (AlOm.A 165; Hildesheim and New York: Olms-Weidmann, 1996).

*Encyclopedia Articles:* J. Schmid, *RAC* 1:1212–17. – Vielhauer, 599–612. – K. Wengst, *TRE* 5:238–41. – F. Scorza Barcellona, *EECh* 1:111–12. – K. Zelzer, *HLL* 4:415. – E. Ferguson, *EEC* 1:167–68.

*Commentary:* F. R. Prostmeier, *Der Barnabasbrief* (KAV 8; Göttingen: Vandenhoeck & Ruprecht, 1999) [Com].

*Studies:* P. Prigent, *Les testimonia dans le christianisme primitive: L'Épître de Barnabé I–XVI et ses sources* (Paris: Gabalda, 1961). – E. Robillard, "L'Épître de Barnabé: Trois époques, trois théologies, trois rédacteurs," *RB* 78 (1971): 184–209. – K. Wengst, *Tradition und Theologie des Barnabasbriefes* (AKG 42; Berlin and New York: de Gruyter, 1971). – L. W. Barnard, "The 'Epistle of Barnabas' and Its Contemporary Setting," *ANRW* 2.27.1:159–207. – J. C. Paget, *The Epistle of Barnabas: Outlook and Background* (Tübingen: Mohr, 1994). – R. Hvalvik, *The Struggle for Scripture and Covenant: The Purpose of the Epistle of Barnabas and Jewish-Christian Competition in the Second Century* (Tübingen: Mohr, 1996).

# IV. APOCALYPSES

## A. Literary Genre

The term "apocalypse" can be traced back to the initial words of the first Christian writing of this kind, that is, John's Ἀποκάλυψις Ἰησοῦ Χριστοῦ, which was accepted into the NT canon. The literary genre itself, however, originated in Judaism and produced the book of Daniel as its most significant OT apocalypse. To a large extent, Christian apocalypses follow their Jewish counterparts, which they supply with their own eschatology. Although there are "no formal laws which are applicable to all apocalypses"[6] and the apocalypse of John is accorded a special place among all the apocalypses, it is possible to discern a number of enduring stylistic and content-related features:

a. All apocalypses are written pseudonymously under the name of a significant male of the past who lends the work an authority that the author himself does not possess. This means that an apocalypse is always written from a perspective of fictitious anteriority, as a book that alleges to be ancient already and, because of being sealed up, has to be kept secret until the predetermined time of the end (cf. Dan 12:9; Rev 6). One of the typical features therefore is that they contain precise, verifiable surveys of history in future form (*vaticinia ex eventu*) so as to arouse the reader to confidence in the reliability of the visions of the end as well. Human history is divided into ages, the last one of which has now dawned.

b. The apocalyptic writer receives his message in the form of an ecstatic vision or a dream; for this purpose he is frequently translated into the heavenly world in order to become acquainted with the beyond and then to describe it (cf. Rev 1:10f.). A translation such as this reaches its apex in a throne room vision, in an encounter with God himself that legitimates the seer. The presentation of the message customarily uses the personal I-form.

c. The visions occur in the form of pictures and represent allegories, explained to the seer by a mediator (*angelus interpres*), by God, or by Christ.

d. The apocalypses systematize the confusing wealth of phenomena that have been seen, especially by means of numbers, so as to show their understanding of the divine order.

e. Since the aim of an apocalypse is not esoteric but present and practical, namely, strengthening and guiding the believer to persevere in the tribulation of the end time, it includes such regular components as paraenesis and prayers. These may take the forms of petition and lament as well as praise, thanksgiving, and hymns.

Four major antitheses shape the conceptual world of apocalypses: the dualism of two aeons, universalism and individualism, pessimism and hope in the hereafter, determinism and imminent expectation. According to God's great and unchanging plan of redemption, the history of the world and its ages are predetermined from its creation to its end. The aeon of the world is evil, dominated by Satan, and degenerates from one generation to another, right up to the political and cosmic catastrophies of the end time. Independently of a national expectation of salvation, the individual is to persevere by means of obedience to God. Although the old world of sin, idolatry, and human power has to vanish first before

---

6 W. G. Kümmel, *Introduction to the New Testament* (trans. H. C. Kee; rev. ed.; Nashville: Abingdon, 1975), 454.

the kingdom of God dawns, already in the present life God promises the devout a share in the new world by observing God's commandments. By anticipating salvation in the age to come, the believer draws hope and confidence that his perseverance and faithfulness will be rewarded and the ungodly will be punished. The signs of the time demonstrate the nearness of the world's end determined by God, although its specific date cannot be predicted with precision. Now is thus the time of conversion and of preparation for the age to come.

From the second century on, Christian apocalypses and Christian revisions of Jewish apocalypses arose in this framework, among them the *Testament of Abraham*, the *Greek Apocalypse of Ezra*, and *2 Enoch (Slavonic Apocalypse)*.  Contentwise, of course, early Christian eschatology replaced or reshaped the Jewish conceptions of the hereafter. Among the primary themes of second-century apocalypses are the explanation of the delay of the Parousia, which could not have occurred yet according to God's eschatological plan for the world; the end of the world; and the hereafter. From the fourth century on (third-century apocalypses conspicuously have not been handed down), however, the interest either shifts to the description of heaven and hell, in order to strengthen Christian morality and orthodoxy, or ends up in a curious craving for knowledge of details on the final judgment and the end of the world. The likely reason for this is that ecclesiastical eschatology was already established in its decisive features. In any case, Christian apocalyptists did not enjoy the liberty of their Jewish counterparts to shape largely unformed material independently.

The following are considered to be among the most significant Christian apocalypses: the *Apocalypse of Peter*, the *Martyrdom and Ascension of Isaiah*, the *Apocalypse of Paul*, and the *Apocalypse of Thomas*. Nag Hammadi brought a number of gnostic apocalypses to light as well, but their detailed analysis is still pending.

*Editions:* C. Tischendorf, ed., *Apocalypses apocryphae* (Leipzig: Mendelssohn, 1866; repr., Hildesheim: Olms, 1966). – M. R. James, ed., *Apocrypha anecdota: A Collection of Thirteen Apocryphal Books and Fragments* (TS 2.3; Cambridge: Cambridge University Press; New York: Macmillan, 1893; repr., Nendeln, Liechtenstein: Kraus Reprint, 1967). – A. Böhlig and P. Labib, *Koptisch-gnostische Apokalypsen aus Codex V von Nag Hammadi im Koptischen Museum zu Alt-Kairo* (WZ[H] Sonderband; Halle: Martin-Luther-Universität, 1963).

*Translations:* A. Walker, trans., "Revelation of Moses," "Revelation of Esdras," "Revelation of Paul," "Revelation of John," "The Book of John concerning the Falling Asleep of Mary," and "The Passing of Mary," in *ANF* (Peabody, Mass.: Hendrickson, 1995; repr. of 1886 ed.), 8:565–98. – A. Rutherfurd, trans., "The Revelation of Peter," "The Vision of Paul," "The Apocalypse of the Virgin," "The Apocalypse of Sedrach," "The Testament of Abraham," "The Acts of Xanthippe and Polyxena," and "The Narrative of Zosimus," in *ANF* (Peabody, Mass.: Hendrickson, 1995; repr. of 1887 ed.), 9:139–224. – J. K. Elliott, ed., *The Apocryphal New Testament: A Collection of Apocryphal Christian Literature in an English Translation* (Oxford: Clarendon; New York: Oxford University Press, 1993), 591–688 [*Apocalypse of Peter, Apocalypse of Paul, Apocalypse of Thomas, Questions of Bartholomew, Letter of James*]. – B. D. Ehrman, *After the New Testament: A Reader in Early Christianity* (Oxford: Oxford University Press, 1999), 296–308 [*Apocalypse of Peter, Apocalypse of Paul*].

*Encyclopedia Articles:* A. Oepke: ἀποκαλύπτω, κτλ, *TDNT* 3:563–92. – J. Lebram, K. Müller, A. Strobel, and K.-H. Schwarte, *TRE* 3:192–275. – E. Romero Pose, *EECh* 1:55. – J. J. Collins, "Apocalyptic Literature," *EEC* 1:73–75.

*Collections of Essays:* J. J. Collins, ed., *Apocalypse: The Morphology of a Genre* (Semeia 14; Missoula, Mont.: Society of Biblical Literature, 1979). – K. Koch and J. M. Schmidt, eds., *Apokalyptik* (WdF 365; Darmstadt: Wissenschaftliche Buchgesellschaft, 1982). – J. G. Griffiths, *Apocalypticism in the Mediterranean World and the Near East* (ed. D. Hellholm; Tübingen: Mohr, 1983). – C. Kappler et al., eds., *Apocalypses et voyages dans l'au-delà* (Paris: Cerf, 1987). – J. J. Collins, ed., *The Origins of Apocalypticism in Judaism and Christianity* (vol. 1 of *The Encyclopedia of Apocalypticism*; ed. B. McGinn; New York: Continuum, 1998).

*Studies:* W. Schmithals, *The Apocalyptic Movement* (trans. J. E. Steely; Nashville: Abingdon, 1975); trans. of *Die Apokalyptik: Einführung und Deutung* (Göttingen: Vandenhoeck & Ruprecht, 1973). – D. E. Aune, *Prophecy in Early Christianity and the Ancient Mediterranean* (Grand Rapids: Eerdmans, 1983). – A. J. Beagley, *The "Sitz im Leben" of the Apocalypse with Particular Reference to the Role of the Church's Enemies* (BZNW 50; Berlin: de Gruyter, 1987). – C. Rowland, "Apocalyptic Literature," in *It Is Written—Scripture Citing Scripture: Essays in Honor of Barnabas Lindars, SSF* (ed. D. A. Carson; Cambridge: Cambridge University Press, 1988), 170–89. – A. Yarbro Collins, "Early Christian Apocalyptic Literature," *ANRW* 2.25.6:4665–4711. – R. E. Sturm, "Defining the Word 'Apocalyptic': A Problem in Biblical Criticism," in *Apocalyptic and the New Testament: Essays in Honour of J. Lewis Martyn* (ed. J. Marcus and M. L. Soards; JSNTSup 24; Sheffield: JSOT Press, 1989), 17–48. – W. Zager, *Begriff und Wertung der Apokalyptik in der neutestamentlichen Forschung* (Frankfurt and New York: Lang, 1989). – H. O. Maier, "Staging the Gaze: Early Christian Apocalypses and Narrative Self-Representation," *HTR* 90 (1997): 131–55.

# B. Shepherd of Hermas

The most popular noncanonical writing of the earliest centuries of Christendom was the Shepherd of Hermas, which in many places even enjoyed canonical recognition. It emerged in Rome, in several parts and over a lengthy period of time, roughly between 130 and 140.[7] The author was a freed slave and small-businessman called Hermas. The writing has the name "Shepherd" from the second revealer figure that appears in it. The work is structured into five visions (*visiones*), twelve mandates (*mandata*), and ten parables (*similitudines*) and is also cited in this manner. Visions 1–4, as well as vision 5 to similitude 7, probably originated separately and independently of one another, though by the same author,[8] who in the compilation added similitudes 9 and 10. Vision 5 becomes the introduction to the following books.

The visions begin the narrative that Hermas has been sold as a slave to a certain Rhoda in Rome and later has been released. One day he sees his previous mistress bathing in the Tiber and accompanies her as she ascends from the river.

---

[7] Suggested dates range from the late first century to the end of the second century.
[8] Giet and Nautin assume three different authors.

Seeing her beauty, he wishes deep down that he also had a woman such as this to be his wife. A few days later, while on the way to Cumae, the dwelling place of the sibyl north of Naples, he is translated by the Spirit into a desolate area. There his former mistress appears to him as a heavenly image and informs him that his desire already was sinful adultery in thought. After this there appears an old lady in a brilliant garment, whom Hermas assumes to be the sibyl but about whom he later learns that she represents a personification of the church. She calls Hermas and his entire family to repentance. The second vision occurs a year later at the same place. The old lady hands Hermas a small book, a "heavenly letter" allowing Christianity a final period of repentance, with the mission to copy it and to proclaim this letter, as well as further visions yet to come, to the church in Rome and other cities. In the third vision, the old lady, who becomes increasingly younger, shows Hermas the construction of a tower, which symbolizes the church and whose perfection had to be delayed until all Christians are perfected through repentance. Finally, in vision 5, a second revealer appears, an angel of repentance in the form of a shepherd who in the following mandates and parables shows what ideal Christianity is.

Regarding its literary form, the Shepherd is an apocalypse, indicated, for instance, by the stylistic elements of the first-person narrative, visions, translations, and the heavenly letter. In this, Hermas follows the Jewish apocalyptic traditions. In the case of the figure of the old lady and the shepherd, however, he uses Roman models drawn from the Hermetic literature.[9] In content, it lacks the characteristics of an apocalypse, the unveilings of the eschatological future or of the hereafter, so much so that Vielhauer labels it a "pseudo-apocalypse," whereas Staats prefers to view it as an "original form of an early Catholic Church-related apocalypse."

The primary topic and significance of the Shepherd is seen in its teaching on repentance, which proclaims the possibility of a once-only postbaptismal forgiveness of sins, representing the basic forgiveness of sins in the general Christian view of things. The interpretation and classification of this doctrine of repentance, however, are not assessed uniformly. According to Windisch, Dibelius, and others, it means that in the earliest form of Christianity, prior to Hermas, there was no possibility of a second repentance after baptism. Because of the daily experience of sinfulness, even on the part of baptized Christians, and moving away from the rigorous demands of holiness under the impression of an imminent eschatological expectation, the Shepherd of Hermas opens up a new opportunity to repent. For the sake of consistency, he had to opt for the form of an apocalypse, of an immediate divine revelation and commission, since he was not able to appeal to any tradition of the church or to sufficient authority of his own. On the other hand, for Poschmann and others, the Shepherd of Hermas represents nothing more than the codification of an already existing practice of the church, if not

---

[9] A collection of pagan gnostic wisdom literature attributed to the god Hermes Trismegistos. Cf. G. Filoramo, "Hermetism," *EECh* 1:377; H. J. Sheppard, A. Kehl, and R. McL. Wilson, "Hermetik," *RAC* 14:780–808.

indeed an intensification of the practice of repentance by constricting it to a single occurrence. Norbert Brox summarizes the interpretation to the effect that the church at the time of Hermas indeed allowed repentance only once but that it could be and was deferred. Beyond this, however, Hermas wanted to maintain the enthusiasm of the earliest period of time and proclaimed the one-time opportunity for repentance at the present time.

The subsequent history of repentance in the early church demonstrates that in the case of grave sins it was indeed practice, until the fifth century, to allow only one postbaptismal opportunity to repent in public. The imposed works of repentance became so severe, such as the lifelong renunciation of sexual intimacy in marriage, that repentance was increasingly deferred until the end of life; indeed the Gallic synods barred younger individuals from repentance. Only beginning with the fifth century did the Irish-Scottish mission introduce the development of unlimited private and repeated repentance in the Latin church on the continent.

*Editions: Die apostolischen Väter* (ed. M. Whittaker; 2d ed.; GCS 48; Berlin: Akademie, 1967). – *Le Pasteur* (ed. R. Joly; 2d ed.; SC 53; Paris: Cerf, 1968, repr., 1997) [Com]. – A. Carlini, *Papyrus Bodmer XXXVIII: Erma, Il Pastore (Ia–IIIa visione)* (Cologny-Geneva: Fondation Martin Bodmer, 1991) [Com]. – M. W. Holmes, *The Apostolic Fathers: Greek Texts and English Translations* (rev. ed.; Grand Rapids: Baker, 1999), 329–527. – *Die apostolischen Väter* (ed. A. Lindemann and H. Paulsen; Tübingen: Mohr, 1992), 325–555. – O. Rainieri, *OCP* 59 (1993): 427–64 [Ethiop]. – *Il Pastore di Erma* (ed. A. Vezzoni; Florence: Le Lettere, 1994) [Com]. – *El Pastore* (ed. J. J. Ayán Calvo; FP 6; Madrid: Ciudad Nueva, 1996) [Com].

*Translations:* A. C. Coxe, trans., "The Pastor of Hermas," in *ANF* (Peabody, Mass.: Hendrickson, 1995; repr. of 1885 ed.), 2:1–58. – *The Apostolic Fathers* (trans. F. X. Glimm, J. M.-F. Marique, and G. G. Walsh; FC 1; Washington, D.C.: Catholic University of America Press, 1947, repr., 1969), 223–350. – G. F. Snyder, *The Shepherd of Hermas* (vol. 6 of *The Apostolic Fathers: A New Translation and Commentary;* ed. R. Grant; New York: Nelson, 1968). – B. D. Ehrman, *The New Testament and Other Christian Writings: A Reader* (2d ed.; New York: Oxford University Press, 2004), 386–406 [selections].

*Encyclopedia Articles:* Vielhauer, 513–23. – R. Staats, *TRE* 15:100–108. – A. Hilhorst, *RAC* 14:682–701. – P. Nautin, *EECh* 1:377. – K. Zelzer and P. L. Schmidt, *HLL* 4:415–17. – D. E. Aune, *EEC* 1:521–22.

*Commentaries:* N. Brox, *Der Hirt des Hermas* (KAV 7; Göttingen: Vandenhoeck & Ruprecht, 1991) [Com]. – C. Osiek, *Shepherd of Hermas: A Commentary* (Hermeneia; Minneapolis: Fortress, 1999).

*Studies:* H. O. Maier, *The Social Setting of the Ministry as Reflected in the Writings of Hermas, Clement, and Ignatius* (Waterloo, Ont.: Wilfrid Laurier University Press, 1991). – P. Henne, *La christologie chez Clément de Rome et dans le Pasteur d'Hermas* (Par. 33; Fribourg, Switz.: Éditions Universitaires, 1992). – R. Joly, "Le milieu complexe du 'Pasteur d'Hermas,'" *ANRW* 2.27.1:524–51. – C. Haas, "Die Pneumatologie des 'Hirten des Hermas,'" *ANRW* 2.27.1:552–86. – P. Cox Miller, *Dreams in Late Antiquity: Studies in the Imagination of a Culture* (Princeton, N.J.: Princeton University Press, 1995). – A. Schneider, *"Propter sanctam ecclesiam suam": Die Kirche als Geschöpf, Frau, und Bau im Bußunterricht des Pastor Hermae* (SEAug 67; Rome: Institutum Patristicum Augustinianum, 1999).

*Penance:* B. Poschmann, *Paenitentia secunda—Die kirchliche Buße im ältesten Christentum bis Cyprian und Origenes: Eine dogmengeschichtliche Untersuchung* (Theoph. 1; Bonn: P. Hanstein, 1940), 134–205. – H. Emonds and B. Poschmann, "Buße," *RAC* 2:802–12. – G. A. Benrath, "Buße V," *TRE* 7:452–73. – H. Vorgrimler, *Buße und Krankensalbung* (*HDG* 4.3; Fribourg, Switz.; Herder, 1978), 33–36. – I. Goldhahn-Mueller, *Die Grenze der Gemeinde: Studien zum Problem der zweiten Buße im Neuen Testament unter Berücksichtigung der Entwicklung im 2. Jh. bis Tertullian* (GTA 39; Göttingen: Vandenhoeck & Ruprecht, 1989). – P. Henne, "La pénitence et la rédaction du Pasteur d'Hermas," *RBI* 98 (1991): 358–97.

## C. Christian Sibyllines

The *Sibylline Oracles (Oracula Sibyllina)* represent a distinct form of apocalyptic literature, the origins of which are traced back to the seventh century B.C.E. Initially the sibyl was a mythical prophetess of superhuman age, of oriental, perhaps Persian, origin. Beginning with the fifth century B.C.E., her oracles began circulating in Greece. Later on, reference is made to several sibyls in different locations, such as Erythrae, Delphi, and Cumae. Their prophecies, written in epic hexameters, often contained promises of threat and misfortune and announced a new kingdom through liberation from the present oppression. In this way the oracles developed into political and anti-Roman propaganda.

In the third century B.C.E., Greek Diaspora Judaism adopted the sibylline prophecies and shaped them into religious propaganda with new content. The oracles of the sibyls now became witnesses of monotheism, announced the Last Judgment with its dread and punishment, and called people to repentance. Their links with apocalyptic writings are evident in their use of pseudonymous sayings, fictitious anteriority, and the *vaticinia ex eventu*, that is, historical overviews in the future tense that are intended to prove the truth of everything prophetic. In contrast to the apocalypses, intended for the strengthening of the believers, the Sibyllines turn to propaganda and defense against the world outside. In the second century C.E., Christians adopted this literary type from Judaism, "whose form, topic, and mood seemed very appropriate for the struggle for self-assertion against the outside."[10]

The collection of the *Sibylline Oracles* in twelve books,[11] with which we are familiar today, is a mixture of all three forms and originated roughly between 180 B.C.E.[12] and the third century C.E. Book 6 contains exclusively Christian prophecy and bks. 7 and 8 do so predominantly, but there is evidence of Christian influence in other books as well. Book 6, comprising only twenty-eight verses, is a hymn about the cross of Christ; bk. 7 (162 verses), in gnostic-colored representations,

---

[10] Vielhauer, 494.

[11] Occasionally reference is made to fourteen books because the eighth book was handed down in three parts; hence the books Cardinal Angelo Mai discovered in 1817 were given the numbers 11 to 14.

[12] According to Hamman, 140 B.C.E.

depicts the demise of pagan realms and a golden era at the end of time. Book 8, comprising 500 verses, is the most important and, in Christian antiquity, the most frequently used and attested. It commences with 216 verses of woes against Rome and then develops a Christian eschatology, beginning in v. 217 with the famous ΙΧΘΥΣ acrostic, Ἰησοῦς Χριστὸς Θεοῦ υἱὸς σωτήρ, which Constantine and Augustine cited.

The Sibyllines were cited by many church fathers, and their influence continued into the Middle Ages, as seen in the hymn *Dies irae*, Dante's *Divina commedia*, and Michelangelo's portrayals in the Sistine Chapel.

*Editions:* Die Oracula sibyllina (ed. J. Geffcken; GCS 8; Leipzig: Hinrichs, 1902; repr., New York: Arno, 1979). – *Sibyllinische Weissagungen* (ed. A. Kurfess; Munich: Heimeren, 1951).

*Translations:* J. J. Collins, "Sibylline Oracles," in *Old Testament Pseudepigrapha* (ed. J. H. Charlesworth; 2 vols.; Garden City, N.Y.: Doubleday, 1983), 1:318–472.

*Encyclopedia Articles:* A. Rzach, PW 2A:2073–2183. – A. Hamman, *EECh* 2:614–15. – E. Ferguson, *EEC* 2:1056. – L. Rosso Ubigli, *TRE* 31:240–45.

*Commentaries:* V. Nikiprowetzky, *La troisième Sibylle* (Études juives 9; Paris: Mouton, 1970). – D. S. Potter, *Prophecy and History in the Crisis of the Roman Empire: A Historical Commentary on the Thirteenth Sibylline Oracle* (Oxford: Clarendon, 1990).

*Studies:* J. Geffcken, *Komposition und Entstehungszeit der Oracula sibyllina* (TU 23.1; Leipzig: Hinrichs, 1902). – K. Prümm, "Das Prophetenamt der Sibyllen in kirchlicher Literatur mit besonderer Rücksicht auf die Deutung der 4. Ekloge Virgils," *Schol* 4 (1929): 54–77, 221–46, 498–533. – B. Bischoff, "Die lateinischen Übersetzungen und Bearbeitungen aus den *Oracula sibyllina*," in *Mélanges Joseph de Ghellinck* (2 vols.; ML.H 13; Gembloux, Belg.: J. Duculot, 1951), 1:121–47. – B. Thompson, "Patristic Use of the Sibylline Oracles," *RR* 16 (1951): 115–36. – J. J. Collins, "The Development of the Sibylline Tradition," *ANRW* 2.20.1:421–59. – S. A. Redmond, "The Date of the Fourth Sibylline Oracle," *SecCent* 7 (1990): 129–49. – B. Teyssèdre, "Les représentations de la fin des temps dans le chant V des *Oracles sibyllins*: Les strates de l'imaginaire," *Apocrypha* 1 (1990): 147–65.

# Postapostolic Literature

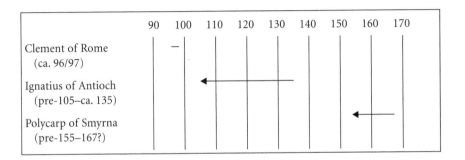

| | 90 | 100 | 110 | 120 | 130 | 140 | 150 | 160 | 170 |
|---|---|---|---|---|---|---|---|---|---|
| Clement of Rome (ca. 96/97) | | | | | | | | | |
| Ignatius of Antioch (pre-105–ca. 135) | | | | | | | | | |
| Polycarp of Smyrna (pre-155–167?) | | | | | | | | | |

MOST MODERN PATROLOGIES DO NOT BEGIN their presentations with the biblical apocrypha but with the so-called Apostolic Fathers because they do not consider the canonical books of the NT as belonging to early Christian literature and they do not belong to the subject of patrology. The biblical apocrypha, rightfully, follow chronologically in a later chapter. But if the exclusion of the canonical books from patrology is a "technical" one, because of the special significance of these works as Scripture—though this does not remove them from early Christian literature in terms of their character—it was necessary to begin with their origin and the rise of the biblical apocrypha that depended on them. An arrangement such as this certainly does violate the chronology, for the development of the apocrypha extended over five centuries, during which patristic literature increasingly blossomed in a multitude of forms. For this reason, it is now incumbent to return to the chronological treatment of the earliest patristic writings.

It is not easy to delimit the categories, nor is it always possible to do so clearly, because the postapostolic literature emerged in the same environment and from the same theological milieu that produced the NT writings. Some of these postapostolic writings even enjoyed canonical value in antiquity. To begin with, the most helpful distinction attributes the genres of gospel, acts, and apocalypse exclusively to the literature of the NT. The fourth type of biblical writing, the letter, occurs commonly in early Christian literature, though all of the apocryphal letters belong to the pseudepigrapha. In the final analysis, however, only the tradition of the church can serve as a decisive criterion.

Postapostolic literature encompassed a time frame from 90 to 160 and shaped four literary genres, partly continuing the NT forms and partly developing new ones. The first to emerge were genuine letters, addressed to entire communities and intended for publication. Additionally, liturgy and community life gave rise to new forms of instruction and proclamation as well as to the beginnings of Christian poetry. These still breathe the spirit of earliest Christianity because they were written by disciples of the apostles or by authors who lived in the proximity of the apostolic age and therefore were able to appeal to immediate apostolic tradition. The structure of the community, expressions of life, theology, and language still are closely linked with the NT writings. "The writers endeavor to show believers, in simple terms, the significance of the salvation that appeared in Christ and to affirm them in their hope in the return of the Lord. They call for obedience to the shepherds of the communities and warn against heresies and schisms. A scholarly explanation of Christianity or of particular doctrines, such as those attempted by the second-century apologists, is foreign to them."[1]

Seven of these authors or writings traditionally constitute the group known as the Apostolic Fathers. In 1672 Jean-Baptiste Cotelier published a collection of the Fathers "who blossomed in postapostolic times," containing the letters of Barnabas, Clement of Rome, Ignatius of Antioch, Polycarp of Smyrna, and the Shepherd of Hermas. At a later point, the fragments of Papias of Hierapolis and *Diognetus* were added, and occasionally the *Didache* and the fragment of Quadratus as well. Since the early twentieth century the designation of this collection has been questioned and may well have to be relinquished despite the attempts to salvage it in a more restrictive and precise form. The Apostolic Fathers do not constitute a uniform body of writings in terms of the categories of literary history. On the one hand, some of them are to be considered biblical apocrypha; on the other, the postapostolic literature encompasses much more than these.

*Editions:* J. B. Lightfoot, *The Apostolic Fathers* (ed. and rev. Michael W. Holmes; 2d ed.; Grand Rapids: Baker, 1998) [Com]. – K. Lake, *Apostolic Fathers* (London: Heinemann, 1925; repr., LCL 24; Cambridge, Mass.: Harvard University Press; London: Heinemann, 1985). – J. A. Fischer, *Die Apostolischen Väter* (8th ed.; SUC 1; Darmstadt: Wissenschaftliche Buchgesellschaft, 1981) [Com]. – K. Wengst, *Didache (Apostellehre), Barnabasbrief, Zweiter Klemensbrief, Schrift an Diognet* (SUC 2; Darmstadt: Wissenschaftliche Buchgesellshaft, 1984) [Com]. – A. Lindemann and H. Paulsen, *Die Apostolischen Väter* (Tübingen: Mohr, 1992). – M. W. Holmes, *The Apostolic Fathers: Greek Texts and English Translations* (rev. ed.; Grand Rapids: Baker, 1999).

*Translations:* A. C. Coxe, trans., "The Epistle of Ignatius to the Ephesians," "The Epistle of Ignatius to the Magnesians," "The Epistle of Ignatius to the Trallians," "The Epistle of Ignatius to the Romans," "The Epistle of Ignatius to the Philadelphians," "The Epistle of Ignatius to the Smyrnaeans," "The Epistle of Ignatius to Polycarp," "Syriac Versions of the Ignatian Epistles," and "Spurious Epistles of Ignatius," in *ANF* (Peabody, Mass.: Hendrickson, 1995; repr. of the 1885 ed.), 1:45–119. – *The Apostolic Fathers* (trans. F. X. Glimm, J. M.-F. Marique, and G. G. Walsh; FC 1; Washington,

---

[1] B. Altaner and A. Stuiber, *Patrologie: Leben, Schriften, und Lehre der Kirchenväter* (8th ed., Fribourg, Switz.: Herder, 1978), 43.

D.C.: Catholic University of America Press, 1947; repr., 1969), 81–127. – R. Grant, *The Apostolic Fathers: A New Translation and Commentary* (6 vols.; New York: Nelson, 1964–1968). – C. C. Richardson, *Early Christian Fathers* (New York: Macmillan, 1970). – M. Staniforth, *Early Christian Writings: The Apostolic Fathers* (rev. A. Louth; London and New York: Penguin, 1987). – B. D. Ehrman, *After the New Testament: A Reader in Early Christianity* (New York: Oxford University Press, 1998) [selections].

*Reference Works:* E. J. Goodspeed, *Index patristicus; sive, Clavis patrum apostolicorum operum* (Leipzig: Hinrichs, 1907; repr., with corrections, Naperville, Ill.: A. R. Allenson, 1960). – H. Kraft, *Clavis patrum apostolicorum* (Munich: Kösel, 1963). – M. Günther, *Einleitung in die Apostolischen Väter* (Frankfurt and New York: Lang, 1997).

*Introduction:* P. Vielhauer, *Geschichte der urchristlichen Literatur: Einleitung in das Neue Testament, die Apokryphen, und die Apostolischen Väter* (Berlin and New York: de Gruyter, 1975).

*Collection of Essays:* ANRW 2.27.1:588–762

*Studies:* H. Köster, *Synoptische Überlieferung bei den Apostolischen Vätern* (TU 65; Berlin: Akademie, 1957). – L. W. Barnard, *Studies in the Apostolic Fathers and Their Background* (Oxford: Blackwell, 1966; New York: Schocken Books, 1967). – J. A. Fischer, "Die ältesten Ausgaben der *Patres apostolici*: Ein Beitrag zu Begriff und Begrenzung der Apostolischen Väter," *HJ* 94 (1974): 157–90; 95 (1975): 88–119. – H. Lohmann, *Drohung und Verheissung: Exegetische Untersuchungen zur Eschatologie bei den Apostolischen Vätern* (BZNW 55; Berlin and New York: de Gruyter, 1989). – R. Grant, *Jesus after the Gospels: The Christ of the Second Century* (Louisville: Westminster John Knox, 1989). – S. Tugwell, *The Apostolic Fathers* (Outstanding Christian Thinkers Series; Harrisburg, Pa.: Morehouse, 1990). – H. E. Lona, *Über die Auferstehung des Fleisches: Studien zur frühchristlichen Eschatologie* (BZNW 66; Berlin and New York: de Gruyter, 1993). – W. H. Wagner, *After the Apostles: Christianity in the Second Century* (Minneapolis: Fortress, 1994). – C. N. Jefford, K. J. Harder, and L. D. Amezaga Jr., *Reading the Apostolic Fathers: An Introduction* (Peabody, Mass.: Hendrickson, 1997).

# I. LETTERS

## A. First Clement

The oldest extant work of Christian literature, apart from the biblical writings, is a letter that both the manuscripts and the earliest tradition of the church have unanimously attributed to Clement, Peter's third successor to the episcopal see of Rome (90/92–101) according to the bishops' list of Irenaeus. This attribution is made despite the fact that the text itself does not mention a name at all. If the letter's reference to "the sudden and repeated calamities and reverses" (1:1) that have prevented the Roman church from attending to the turmoil in Corinth—which Eusebius dates during the reign of Emperor Domitian (81–96)—is taken together with the persecution of the Roman Christians toward the end of Domitian's reign, the letter could have originated in 96/97. We have no further information about the author; whether he can be identified with the Clement who was Paul's fellow worker (Phil 4:3), as Origen and Eusebius insist, is debatable. In any case, *1 Clement* is the work of a single author even though he uses the plural form constantly to refer to himself and even though the Roman community as a whole is to be seen as the sender. Like 1 Corinthians, the letter is occasioned by disputes in the Corinthian community. Some of the older presbyters had been replaced with younger ones; a minority took offense at this, and others did not know what position they should take in this conflict. The Roman community heard about it and decided to take the initiative to intervene.

In all of the sixty-five chapters that comprise this letter, this issue is addressed in a relatively short section (40–58) only; on the basis of the divinely ordained liturgical and hierarchical structure of the church, the deposing of the presbyters is condemned and the rabble-rousers are called to repentance. Following the proem (1–3), which briefly addresses the letter's occasion, the first major section (4–39) is made up of extensive exhortations against jealousy and envy as reasons for the turmoil. Equally prevalent are admonitions to humility, peaceableness, unity, and harmony according to the biblical models, Christ's example, the order of the cosmos, society, and the human body, focusing on the eschatological goal of Christians. The letter ends (59–65) with prayer, a summary of contents, a commendation, and a final salutation.

Opinions differ on the fundamental character of the letter, especially on the issue of whether this is an occasional writing to solve a particular case or whether essential ecclesiological and dogmatic questions are being discussed. Walter Bauer classifies the Corinthian conflict within the frame of the general debate between orthodoxy and heresy.[2] This view finds support from two observations: first, in the second century, *1 Clement* was understood and used as an antiheretical document, and second, this view may explain the unsolicited intervention by the Roman community. It may also be true that the latter, being aware of its authority on the basis of the Petrine succession, sought to extend its influence. The claim of a first witness to the Roman claim to primacy is out of the question, however, since both the monarchical episcopate and the necessary jurisdiction were lacking.

*Editions: Épître aux Corinthiens* (ed. A. Jaubert; rev. ed.; SC 167; Paris: Cerf, 2000). – M. W. Holmes, *The Apostolic Fathers: Greek Texts and English Translations* (rev. ed.; Grand Rapids: Baker, 1999), 23–101 [ET]. – *Epistola ad Corinthios* (ed. G. Schneider; FChr 15; Fribourg, Switz., and New York: Herder, 1994) [Com]. – *Carta a los Corintios* (ed. J. J. Ayán Calvo; FP 4; Madrid: Ciudad Nueva, 1994), 17–155.

*Translations:* A. C. Coxe, trans., "The First Epistle of Clement to the Corinthians," in *ANF* (Peabody, Mass.: Hendrickson, 1995; repr. of the 1885 ed.), 1:1–21. – J. Keith, trans., "The First Epistle of Clement to the Corinthians," in *ANF* 10 (Peabody, Mass.: Hendrickson, 1995; repr. of the 1887 ed.), 9:225–48 [completed and revised reprint from *ANF* 1]. – *The Apostolic Fathers* (trans. F. X. Glimm, J. M.-F. Marique, and G. G. Walsh; FC 1; Washington, D.C.: Catholic University of America Press, 1947; repr.,

---

[2] W. Bauer, *Rechtgläubigkeit und Ketzerei im ältesten Christentum* (BHTh 10; Tübingen: Mohr, 1964), 99–109.

1969), 1–63. – *The Epistles of St. Clement of Rome and St. Ignatius of Antioch* (trans. J. A. Kleist; ACW 1; Westminster, Md.: Newman, 1961), 1–49, 103–17. C. C. Richardson, *Early Christian Fathers* (New York: Macmillan, 1970), 33–73. – M. Staniforth, *Early Christian Writings: The Apostolic Fathers* (rev. A. Louth; London and New York: Penguin, 1987), 19–51.

*Encyclopedia Articles:* A. Stuiber, *RAC* 3:188–97. – Vielhauer, 529–40. – D. Powell, *TRE* 8:113–20. – P. F. Beatrice, *EECh* 1:181. – D. Liebs, *HLL* 4:417–18. – G. Snyder, *EEC* 1:264–65.

*Concordance:* A. Urbán, *Primae epistulae Clementis Romani ad Corinthios concordantia* (AlOm.A 164; CPA 3; Hildesheim and New York: Olms-Weidmann, 1996).

*Commentary:* A. Lindemann, *Die Clemensbriefe* (HNT 17; Tübingen: Mohr, 1992), 3–181.

*Studies:* B. Bowe, *A Church in Crisis: Ecclesiology and Paraenesis in Clement of Rome* (Minneapolis: Fortress, 1988). – H. O. Maier, *The Social Setting of the Ministry as Reflected in the Writings of Hermas, Clement, and Ignatius* (Waterloo, Ont.: Wilfrid Laurier University Press, 1991). – P. Henne, *La christologie chez Clément de Rome et dans le Pasteur d'Hermas* (Par. 33; Fribourg, Switz.: Éditions Universitaires, 1992). – O. B. Knoch, "Im Namen des Petrus und Paulus: Der Brief des Clemens Romanus und die Eigenart des römischen Christentums," *ANRW* 2.27.1:3–54. – A. W. Ziegler and G. Brunner, "Die Frage nach einer politischen Absicht des Ersten Klemensbriefes," *ANRW* 2.27.1:55–76.

# B. Letters of Ignatius of Antioch

Ignatius was a Gentile Christian and, according to Eusebius, Peter's second successor to the episcopal see of Syrian Antioch. On a journey to Rome as a prisoner, he wrote seven letters that are extant in three recensions of different lengths and to which some pseudo-Ignatian writings were added. Until most recently, this transmissional situation has given rise to basic discussions on the authentic number of letters, but none of the delimitation attempts have been successful. Generally, all seven letters in the recension of medium length are considered to be authentic.

In keeping with ancient coastal navigation along Asia Minor, the voyage proceeded in a northerly direction to Cilicia or Pamphylia; from there the journey continued cross-country, stopping in Philadelphia for some time. The detours and stops probably have to be attributed to the guards' further obligations. In Smyrna they again boarded a ship, with the next ports of call being Troas and Grecian Neapolis, near Philippi. During the extended stay at Smyrna, the bishops of Ephesus, Magnesia, and Tralles, together with their communities' delegations, called on Ignatius, who handed each of them a letter addressed to their church. In addition, he sent a letter ahead to the church of Rome, taken there directly by a delegation from Antioch (cf. Ign. *Rom.* 10:2) with the request not to undertake anything that might prevent his martyrdom. In Troas, before crossing over to Greece, Ignatius penned three further letters: to Philadelphia, to Smyrna, and to Smyrna's bishop, Polycarp. In them he expressed his gratitude for the hospitality shown to him and requested that they visit—that is, write to—the church in

*Death by Martyrdom*

Antioch, where persecution had, in the meantime, ceased. In Rome he suffered death by martyrdom, as attested reliably by Polycarp, Origen, and Eusebius.

Beyond this we know nothing about the person and life of Ignatius. Byzantine hagiography identified him as the child whom Jesus displayed to the disciples as an example (Matt 18:2 par.), whereas Jerome took him to be a disciple of the Apostle John. Both reports remain hypothetical, but there is no doubt that as far as his time and theology are concerned, Ignatius was close to the apostles. For a long time it was considered established that the martyrdom of Ignatius, as reported by Eusebius, took place ca. 107–110, during the reign of Emperor Trajan (98–117), as a result of a local persecution of Christians in Antioch. For the sake of the name of Christ, he is said to have been condemned to die in the circus and for this purpose was brought to Rome under guard. This interpretation is being questioned by modern scholarship, suggesting that the time of Ignatius's journey and death can only vaguely be established between 105 and 135. Further, the reason for his trial may not have been a persecution of Christians but rather intracommunity disputes or a charge on the grounds of a *crimen laesae maiestatis,* for which the emperor reserved the final verdict. In any case, Ignatius's intense objection to any assistance in Rome may point to the possibility that the trial indeed was not yet closed by any means nor the death sentence already irreversibly declared.

The historical context shows that the letters are terse occasional writings, authored in keeping with the epistolary and rhetorical rules of antiquity, albeit without comprehensive outline or structure. Three primary themes or concerns are prominent:

a. Warnings against heresies, especially docetism.[3] The incarnation, death, and resurrection of Christ, as well as his presence in the Eucharist, did not take place through a merely simulated external shape but rather in the reality of the humanity of the Son of God.

b. The unity of the theology of Trinitarian monotheism; of ecclesiology; and of the monarchical episcopate, attested here for the first time. The order of the earthly church (called ἡ καθολικὴ ἐκκλησία for the first time in Ign. *Smyrn.* 8:2) mirrors the reflection of the heavenly kingdom. It is structured hierarchically, according to the pattern of the trinity, under the leadership of the bishop, assisted by presbyters and deacons in gradated subordination. The question remains open whether joint leadership of the community, a two-tiered office (bishops/presbyters and deacons), and charismatic offices, as we know them from the Pauline letters, were indeed already outdated in Syria or whether Ignatius merely paints an ideal portrait of what was in process. For Ignatius, the community submits to the bishop as its head, as the entire church as a body submits to Christ, who in turn submits to the Father. The harmony of all is the supreme model. Because of his office, the bishop presides over baptism, the Eucharist, and the mar-

---

[3] From the verb δοκεῖν ("to appear," "to seem"); a heretical doctrine already emerging in the NT and becoming prominent in the second century. It attempted to reconcile the sufferings of the Son of God with his immutable and nonsuffering divinity by explaining that his body only appeared to have been corporeal.

riage ceremony and vouches for orthodoxy; this obligates him to a particularly exemplary life, though the valid exercise of his office is not contingent on it.

c. Theology of, and yearning for, martyrdom. The letter to the Romans, in which Ignatius entreats the community there not to undertake anything that might prevent his martyrdom, indicates the typical yearning for martyrdom that characterized Christianity during the first two centuries. This longing was not merely based on an ascetical and ethical aspiration for perfection but was rooted in the theology of the imitation of Christ. For Ignatius, it even takes on eucharistic features: "I am God's wheat, and I am ground by the teeth of wild beasts that I may be found pure bread [of Christ]" (Ign. *Rom.* 4:1).

The letters of Ignatius were quickly disseminated. Shortly after his death, the Philippian church requested Polycarp of Smyrna to send them copies of the letters available to him, which he did, as the surviving letter that accompanied them shows (cf. C below).

*Bibliographies:* P. Serra Zanetti, "Bibliografia eucaristica Ignaziana recente," in *Miscellanea liturgica in onore di sua eminenza il Cardinale Giacomo Lercaro* (Rome and New York: Desclée, 1966–1967), 341–89. – G. Trentin, "Rassegna di studi su Ignazio di Antiochia," *StPat* 19 (1972): 75–87. – N. Collmar, *BBKL* 2:1251–55.

*Editions: Lettres* (ed. P. T. Camelot; 4th ed.; SC 10; Paris: Cerf, 1969), 9–155. – *Cartas* (ed. J. J. Ayán Calvo; 2d ed.; FP 1; Madrid: Ciudad Nueva, 1999), 31–189. – M. W. Holmes, *The Apostolic Fathers: Greek Texts and English Translations* (rev. ed.; Grand Rapids: Baker, 1999), 129–201 [ET].

*Translation:* A. C. Coxe, trans., "The Epistle of Ignatius to the Ephesians," "The Epistle of Ignatius to the Magnesians," "The Epistle of Ignatius to the Trallians," "The Epistle of Ignatius to the Romans," "The Epistle of Ignatius to the Philadelphians," "The Epistle of Ignatius to the Smyrnaeans," "The Epistle of Ignatius to Polycarp," "Syriac Versions of the Ignatian Epistles," and "Spurious Epistles of Ignatius," in *ANF* (Peabody, Mass.: Hendrickson, 1995; repr. of the 1885 ed.), 1:45–119. – *The Apostolic Fathers* (trans. F. X. Glimm, J. M.-F. Marique, and G. G. Walsh; FC 1; Washington, D.C.: Catholic University of America Press, 1947; repr., 1969), 81–127. – *The Epistles of St. Clement of Rome and St. Ignatius of Antioch* (trans. J. A. Kleist; ACW 1; Westminster, Md., Newman, 1961), 51–99, 118–46. – C. C. Richardson, *Early Christian Fathers* (New York: Macmillan, 1970), 74–120. – M. Staniforth, *Early Christian Writings: The Apostolic Fathers* (rev. A. Louth; London and New York: Penguin, 1987), 53–112.

*Commentary:* W. R. Schoedel, *Ignatius of Antioch: A Commentary on the Letters* (Hermeneia; Philadelphia: Fortress, 1985).

*Encyclopedia Articles:* Vielhauer, 540–52. – H. Paulsen, 1:38–50. – W. R. Schoedel, *TRE* 16:40–45. – P. Nautin, *EECh* 1:404–5. – R. Aubert, *DHGE* 25:684–86. – H. Paulsen, *RAC* 17:933–53. – P. L. Schmidt, *HLL* 4:418. – G. Snyder, *EEC* 1:559–60.

*General Studies:* R. Weijenborg, *Les lettres d'Ignace d'Antioche: Étude critique littéraire et de théologie* (Leiden: Brill, 1969). – H. Paulsen, *Studien zur Theologie des Ignatius von Antiochien* (FKDG 29; Göttingen: Vandenhoeck & Ruprecht, 1978). – R. Joly, *Le dossier d'Ignace d'Antioche* (Brussels: Éditions de l'Université de Bruxelles, 1979). – P. Meinhold, *Studien zu Ignatius von Antiochien* (VIEG 97; Weisbaden: Steiner, 1979). – J. Rius-Camps, *The Four Authentic Letters of Ignatius the Martyr* (OrChrAn 213; Rome: Pontificium Institutum Orientalium Studiorum 1980). – C. Trevett, *A Study of Ignatius of Antioch in Syria and Asia* (Studies in the Bible and Early Christianity 29;

Lewiston, N.Y.: Mellen, 1992). – W. R. Schoedel, "Polycarp of Smyrna and Ignatius of Antioch," *ANRW* 2.27.1:272–358. – C. Munier, "Où en est la question d'Ignace d'Antioche? Bilan d'un siècle de recherches, 1870–1988," *ANRW* 2.27.1:359–484.

*Particular Studies:* K. Bommes, *Weizen Gottes: Untersuchungen zur Theologie des Martyriums bei Ignatius von Antiochien* (Theoph. 27; Köln: P. Hanstein 1976). – L. Wehr, *Arznei der Unsterblichkeit: Die Eucharistie bei Ignatius von Antiochien und im Johannesevangelium* (NTAbh NS 18; Münster: Aschendorff 1987). – J. Rius-Camps, "Ignacio de Antioquia, ¿testigo ocular de la muerte y resurrección de Jesús?" *Bib* 70 (1989): 449–73. – H. O. Maier, *The Social Setting of the Ministry as Reflected in the Writings of Hermas, Clement, and Ignatius* (Waterloo, Ont.; Wilfrid Laurier University Press, 1991). – R. M. Hübner, "Thesen zur Echtheit und Datierung der sieben Briefe des Ignatius von Antiochien," *ZAC* 1 (1997): 44–72. – A. Lindemann, "Antwort auf die 'Thesen zur Echtheit und Datierung der sieben Briefe des Ignatius von Antiochien.'" *ZAC* 1 (1997): 185–94. – T. Lechner, *Ignatius adversus Valentinianos? Chronologische und theologiegeschichtliche Studien zu den Briefen des Ignatius von Antiochien* (SVigChr 47; Leiden and Boston: Brill, 1999). – C. T. Brown, *The Gospel and Ignatius of Antioch* (Studies in Biblical Literature 12; New York: Lang, 2000).

# C. Letters of Polycarp of Smyrna

According to the transmission history, only one letter by Polycarp, bishop of Smyrna, comprising fourteen chapters and addressed to the Philippians, has been preserved, although Irenaeus of Lyon is aware of several letters. But since ch. 9 of this writing already presupposes Ignatius's death whereas ch. 13 solicits new information about his fate, it must be assumed that we are dealing with the compilation of two letters. In this case, ch. 13 represents the brief cover letter for the collection of the Ignatian letters that Polycarp sent to the church in Philippi upon its request.[4] According to Fischer, the following may account for the historical context: While passing through the city, Ignatius had asked the Philippians to write to Antioch; they obliged straightaway by sending the letter to Polycarp in Smyrna for forwarding, with the request to send them copies of the letters of Ignatius that were available to him. Polycarp granted their request and in the cover letter promised to take care of the delivery of the entrusted letter in Antioch; he also inquired about the further plight of Ignatius. This sequence would move ch. 13 into the immediate time frame of Ignatius's journey to his death. In this case, the other chapters would have originated shortly afterward, as an elaborate response to a further letter from Philippi answering the questions of the first letter. Since more recent scholarship no longer dates the death of Ignatius to ca. 107–110, Harrison's dating of ca. 135 also agrees with this sequence of events. Contentwise, the letter represents a general hortatory writing that, after the greeting and a commendation of the church of Philippi, admonishes the

---

[4] P. Nautin, *EECh* 2:701, rejects this hypothesis as "inadequately substantiated," and Dehandschutter and others assume the unity of the letter.

Philippians to faith and upright conduct, reminds them of the duties of the various groups in the church, and warns them against heresy.

We are quite well informed about Polycarp's life from Ignatius's letter addressed to him, remarks by Irenaeus and Eusebius, and an account of his martyrdom (cf. ch. 3.III.B.1). A precise chronology cannot, however, be established with certainty. It depends on the following factors:

a. how strictly one understands the term "disciple of the apostle," i.e., whether the apostle is identified as his mentor John or a presbyter named John who is otherwise unkown to us;

b. whether the martyrdom of Ignatius is more closely associated with 105 or with 135;

c. the year during Anicetus's episcopate in Rome (155–166) to which his encounter with Polycarp is to be dated;

d. whether Polycarp's statement in the *Martyrdom of Polycarp* (21) that he had served Christ eighty-six years includes his entire life or only the period from his conversion to Christianity; and finally,

e. the value attributable to the dating of his martyrdom in the *Martyrdom of Polycarp*, "on the second day of the first part of the month Xanthicus, on the seventh before the kalends of March, on a great sabbath" (21:1), as well as to that of Eusebius (167 C.E.). (Brind' Amour's solution to interpret the "great Sabbath" as Sunday and thereby conclude that the date was February 23, 167, is not convincing).[5]

Polycarp's journey to Rome to consult with Bishop Anicetus about various questions, such as the date of the Easter celebration, was to have a most enduring impact on church history. In the so-called Easter controversy, Bishop Victor of Rome (ca. 189–199), because of local dissent, wanted to obligate all Christian communities worldwide to observe Easter on the Sunday following the first full moon of spring. The Christians in Asia Minor, however, objected, appealing to their original, Johannine tradition of celebrating Easter on 14 Nisan, that is, on the same day as the Jews, without regard for the particular day of the week. For this reason, they were called Quartodecimans. The Eastern churches pointed out that Polycarp and Anicetus had already discussed this and, though they did not reach a consensus, nevertheless had not terminated ecclesial fellowship and

---

[5] W. Rohrdorf, "Zum Problem des 'Grossen Sabbats' im Polykarp- und Pionius-martyrium," in *Pietas: Festschrift für Bernard Kötting* (ed. E. Dassmann and K. Suso Frank; JAC.E 8; Münster: Aschendorff, 1980): 245–49, interprets the "great Sabbath" as a Saturday associated with a public festival, namely, the festival of Terminus on February 23. P. Devos, *"META ΣABBATON"* chez saint Épiphane (AnBoll 108; Brussels: Société des Bollandistes, 1990), 293–306, argues that it does not refer to any day of the week but rather to spiritual rest in Christ from sin. In a personal letter to Devos, Brind' Amour agrees with this interpretation; cf. P. Devos, *Notatio in vitam S. Polycarpi* (AnBoll 110; Brussels: Société des Bollandistes, 1992), 260–62.

peace. For the same reason, Irenaeus of Lyon exhorted Victor to pursue peace, and as a result, the dispute was settled without a definitive conclusion. The Quartodecian practice diminished more and more until the Council of Nicea (325) finally prohibited it.

*Editions: Lettres* (ed. P. T. Camelot; 4th ed.; SC 10; Paris: Cerf, 1969; repr., 1998), 157–93. – *Cartas* (ed. J. J. Ayán Calvo; 2d ed.; FP 1; Madrid: Ciudad Nueva, 1991), 191–229. – M. W. Holmes, *The Apostolic Fathers: Greek Texts and English Translations* (rev. ed.; Grand Rapids: Baker, 1999), 202–21 [ET].

*Translations:* A.C. Coxe, trans., "The Epistle of Polycarp to the Philippians," in *ANF* (Peabody, Mass.: Hendrickson, 1995; repr., of the 1885 ed.), 1:31–36. – *The Apostolic Fathers* (trans. F. X. Glimm, J. M.-F. Marique, and G. G. Walsh; FC 1; Washington, D.C.: Catholic University of America Press, 1947; repr., 1969), 129–43. – *The Didache, The Epistle of Barnabas, The Epistles and the Martyrdom of St. Polycarp, The Fragments of Papias, The Epistle to Diognetus* (trans. J. A. Kleist; ACW 6; Westminster, Md.: Newman, 1948), 67–82, 184–96. – C. C. Richardson, *Early Christian Fathers* (New York: Macmillan, 1970), 121–37. – M. Staniforth, *Early Christian Writings: The Apostolic Fathers* (rev. A. Louth; London and New York: Penguin, 1987), 113–24.

*Encyclopedia Articles:* P. Meinhold, PW 21:1662–93. – Vielhauer, 552–66. – P. Nautin, *EECh* 2:701. – D. Van Damme, *TRE* 27:25–28. – P. L. Schmidt, *HLL* 4:418. – G. Snyder, *EEC* 2:933–34.

*Concordance:* A. Urbán, *Polyarpi et secundae epistulae Clementis Romani concordantiae* (AlOm.A 205; CPA 7; Hildesheim and New York: Olms=Weidmann, 2001).

*Commentary:* J. B. Bauer, *Die Polykarpbriefe* (KAV 5; Göttingen: Vandenhoeck & Ruprecht, 1995).

*Studies:* P. N. Harrison, *Polycarp's Two Epistles to the Philippians* (Cambridge: Cambridge University Press, 1936). – J. A. Fischer, "Die Synoden im Osterfeststreit des 2. Jahrhunderts," *AHC* 8 (1976): 15–39; repr. in J. A. Fischer and A. Lumpe, *Die Synoden von den Anfängen bis zum Vorabend des Nicaenums* (Paderborn: F. Schöningh, 1997), 60–87. – B. Dehandschutter, "Polycarp's Epistle to the Philippians: An Early Example of 'Reception,'" in *The New Testament in Early Christianity = La réception des écrits néotestamentaires dans le christianisme primitif* (ed. J.-M. Sevrin et al.; BETL 86; Louvain: Louvain University Press, 1989), 275–91. – W. R. Schoedel, "Polycarp of Smyrna and Ignatius of Antioch," *ANRW* 2.27.1:272–358.

# II. COMMUNITY TEXTS

## *A. Papias Fragments*

Only fragments are preserved of the *Exposition of the Oracles of the Lord* by Papias, bishop of Hierapolis in Phrygia; they survive in five books, mainly in the *Ecclesiastical History* of Eusebius and in Irenaeus's *Adversus haereses*. Beyond this we have virtually no knowledge at all about Papias as a person, except that he was a friend of Polycarp of Smyrna. On the issue of whether Papias had been a disciple of the Apostle John, views already differed between Irenaeus and Eusebius.

The same is true of the attempts at dating the work, which range from 90 to 140; more recent commentators tend to favor a later date of ca. 130/140. "Apparently the book was a collection and commentary on reports, based on all kinds of sources, on Jesus' words and deeds and was intended to examine the authenticity of the Jesus tradition and to ensure its correct understanding by means of exegesis."[6] This is done with an anti-gnostic tendency; for this reason, Papias does not rely on such biblical books as the gospels of John and Luke or the letters of Paul, all of which the gnostics treasured, but instead primarily on oral traditions as well as those handed down by Mark and Matthew. Given its fragmentary nature, it is not possible to determine the literary genre to which the *Exposition* belonged. Its form, in any case, is very ancient and closely associated with the apostolic era.

*Bibliography:* J. Kürzinger et al., *Papias von Hierapolis und die Evangelien des Neuen Testaments: Gesammelte Aufsätze, Neuausgabe und Übersetzung der Fragmente, kommentierte Bibliographie* (Regensburg: F. Pustet, 1983). – M. W. Holmes, *The Apostolic Fathers: Greek Texts and English Translations* (rev. ed.; Grand Rapids: Baker, 1999), 556–90 [ET].

*Translations:* A. C. Coxe, trans., "Fragments of Papias," in *ANF* (Peabody, Mass.: Hendrickson, 1995; repr., of the 1885 ed.), 1:151–55. – *The Apostolic Fathers* (trans. F. X. Glimm, J. M.-F. Marique, and G. G. Walsh; FC 1; Washington, D.C.: Catholic University of America Press, 1947; repr., 1969), 369–88. – *The Didache, The Epistle of Barnabas, The Epistles and the Martyrdom of St. Polycarp, The Fragments of Papias, The Epistle to Diognetus* (trans. J. A. Kleist; ACW 6; Westminster, Md.: Newman, 1948), 103–24, 204–10.

*Editions:* E. Preuschen, ed. and trans., *Antilegomena: Die Reste der ausserkanonischen Evangelien und urchristlichen Überlieferungen* (2d ed.; Giessen: Töpelmann, 1905), 91–99.

*Encyclopedia Articles:* F. Wotke, PW 18.2:966–76. – Vielhauer, 757–65. – L. Vanyó, *EECh* 2:647. – U. H. J. Körtner, *TRE* 25:641–44. – P. L. Schmidt, *HLL* 4:418–19. – E. Ferguson, *EEC* 2:866.

*Studies:* V. Bartlet, "Papias's 'Exposition': Its Date and Contents," in *Amicitiae corolla: A Volume of Essays Presented to James Rendel Harris, D. Litt., on the Occasion of His Eightieth Birthday* (ed. H. G. Wood; London: University of London Press, 1933), 15–44. – E. Gutwenger, "Papias: Eine chronologische Studie," *ZKT* 69 (1947): 385–416. – K. Beyschlag, "Herkunft und Eigenart der Papiasfragmente," in *Biblica, Patres apostolici, historica* (vol. 2 of *Papers Presented to the Third International Conference on Patristic Studies Held at Christ Church, Oxford, 1959;* ed. F. Cross; StPatr 4; TU 79; Berlin: Akademie, 1961), 268–80. – A. F. Walls, "Papias and Oral Tradition," *VC* 21 (1967): 137–40; repr., *Orthodoxy, Heresy, and Schism in Early Christianity* (ed. E. Ferguson; SEC 4; New York: Garland, 1993), 107–10. – U. H. J. Körtner, *Papias von Hierapolis: Ein Beitrag zur Geschichte des frühen Christentums* (Göttingen: Vandenhoeck & Ruprecht, 1983). – G. Zuntz, "*Papiana,*" *ZNW* 82 (1991): 242–63. – W. R. Schoedel, "Papias," *ANRW* 2.27.1:235–70. – C. E. Hill, "What Papias Said about John (and Luke): A 'New' Papian Fragment," *JTS* NS 49 (1998): 582–629.

---

6 Vielhauer, 761.

# B. Didache

The *Didache* (*Teaching of the Twelve Apostles*) was held in high regard in antiquity. In the modern era, however, its existence was known only through some canonical lists and references in the church fathers until Philotheos Bryennios discovered the full text in Constantinople in 1873. Later on, further strands of tradition were found in other texts, such as the *Apostolic Constitutions and Canons*, the *Doctrina apostolorum*, *Barnabas*, and a few patristic citations.

In the case of the *Didache*, we are dealing with a church manual that likely originated in Syria/Palestine (Egypt?) in the early second century. It is structured in five parts (sixteen chapters) and provides teaching on the community's ethical conduct (1–6), liturgy (7–10), the treatment of itinerant prophets and of Christians who are moving around (11–13), community life (14–15), and eschatology (16). For this reason, it is viewed as an important, albeit not comprehensive, witness in support of an early community structure (Schöllgen). Chapters 1–6, like *Barn.* 18–20, contain a teaching known as "the two ways," and it may be assumed that both draw upon a common source, one influenced by Judaism. In contrast to *Barnabas*, the *Didache* describes the two ways as the ways of life and death respectively (the former used light and darkness) and offers a more extensive and more structured version. Extraordinarily for our knowledge of second-century liturgical and communal structures, the charismatic offices (apostles, prophets, teachers) still enjoy prominence alongside the beginnings of the offices the community recognized by ordination, namely, those of bishops and deacons. The true apostle is an itinerant prophet who is permitted to stay in the community for only one day or, exceptionally, two and for that length of time is entitled to receive support. Apparently the Eucharist is celebrated as a meal with prayers of benediction and blessing but without citing the words of institution.

*Editions: La Didachè: Instructions des apôtres* (ed. J.-P. Audet; EBib; Paris: Librairie Lecoffre, 1958) [Com]. – *La Doctrine des douze apôtres = Didachè* (ed. W. Rordorf and A. Tuilier; SC 248; Paris: Cerf, 1978). – *Didache = Zwölf-Apostel-Lehre* (ed. G. Schöllgen; FChr 1; Fribourg, Switz., and New York: Herder, 1991), 23–139 [Com]. – *Didaché, Doctrina apostolorum, Epístola del Pseudo-Bernabé* (ed. J. J. Ayán Calvo; FP 3; Madrid: Ciudad Nueva, 1992), 17–123. – *Les Constitutions apostoliques* (ed. M. Metzger; 3 vols.; SC 320, 329, 336; Paris: Cerf, 1985–1987). – M. W. Holmes, *The Apostolic Fathers: Greek Texts and English Translations* (rev. ed.; Grand Rapids: Baker, 1999), 246–69 [ET].

*Translations:* A. C. Coxe, trans., "The Teaching of the Twelve Apostles," in *ANF* (Peabody, Mass.: Hendrickson, 1995; repr. of the 1886 ed.), 7:377–83. – *The Apostolic Fathers* (trans. F. X. Glimm, J. M.-F. Marique, and G. G. Walsh; FC 1; Washington, D.C.: Catholic University of America Press, 1947; repr., 1969), 165–84. – *The Didache, The Epistle of Barnabas, The Epistles and the Martyrdom of St. Polycarp, The Fragments of Papias, The Epistle to Diognetus* (trans. J. A. Kleist; ACW 6; Westminster, Md.: Newman, 1948), 1–25, 151–66. – C. C. Richardson, *Early Christian Fathers* (New York: Macmillan, 1970), 161–79. – M. Staniforth, *Early Christian Writings: The Apostolic Fathers* (rev. A. Louth; London and New York: Penguin, 1987), 185–99.

*Concordance:* A. Urbán, *Concordantia in Didachen* (AlOm.A 146; Hildesheim: Olms-Weidmann, 1993).

*Encyclopedia Articles:* J. Schmid, *RAC* 3:1009–13. – Vielhauer, 719–37. – A. Tuilier, *TRE* 8:731–36. – W. Rordorf, *EECh* 1:234–35. – D. Liebs, *HLL* 4:413–14. – E. Ferguson, *EEC* 1:328–29.

*Commentary:* K. Niederwimmer, *The Didache: A Commentary* (trans. L. A. Maloney; Hermeneia; Minneapolis: Fortress 1998); trans. of *Die Didache* (KAV 1; Göttingen: Vandenhoeck & Ruprecht, 1989).

*Collections of Essays:* C. N. Jefford, *The Didache in Context: Essays on Its Text, History, and Transmission* (NovTSup 77; Leiden and New York: Brill, 1995). – J. A. Draper, ed., *The Didache in Modern Research* (AGJU 37; Leiden and New York: Brill, 1996).

*Studies:* F. E. Vokes, *The Riddle of the Didache: Fact or Fiction, Heresy or Catholicism?* (London: SPCK; New York: Macmillan, 1938). – A. Adam, "Erwägungen zur Herkunft der Didache," *ZKG* 68 (1957): 1–47; repr. in *Sprache und Dogma: Untersuchungen zu Grundproblemen der Kirchengeschichte* (ed. G. Ruhbach; Gütersloh: G. Mohn, 1969), 24–70. – B. Layton, "The Sources, Date, and Transmission of *Didache* 1.3b–2.1," *HTR* 61 (1968): 343–83. – A. Vööbus, *Liturgical Traditions in the Didache* (PETSE 16; Stokholm: ETSE, 1968). – S. Giet, *L'énigme de la Didachè* (PFLUS 149; Paris: Ophrys, 1970). – F. E. Vokes, "The Didache—Still Debated," *CQ* 3 (1970): 57–62. – W. Rordorf, "Un chapitre d'éthique judéo-chrétienne: Les deux voies," *RSR* 60 (1972): 109–28; trans. as "An Aspect of the Judeo-Christian Ethic: The Two Ways," in *The Didache in Modern Research* (ed. J. A. Draper; AGJU 37; Leiden and New York: Brill, 1996), 148–64. – A. de Halleux, "Les ministères dans la *Didachè*," *Irén* 53 (1980): 5–29. – G. Schöllgen, "Die Didache als Kirchenordnung: Zur Frage des Abfassungszweckes und seinen Konsequenzen für die Interpretation," *JAC* 29 (1986): 5–26; trans. as "The *Didache* as a Church Order: An Examination of the Purpose for the Composition of the *Didache* and Its Consequences for Its Interpretation," in *The Didache in Modern Research* (ed. J. A. Draper; AGJU 37; Leiden and New York: Brill, 1996), 43–71. – C. N. Jefford, *The Sayings of Jesus in the Teaching of the Twelve Apostles* (SVigChr 11; Leiden and New York: Brill, 1989). – M. Del Verme, "*Didachè* e giudaismo: La ἀπαρχή di Didachè 13,3–7," *VetChr* 28 (1991): 253–65. – F. E. Vokes, "Life and Order in the Early Church: The *Didache*," *ANRW* 2.27.1:209–33. – W. Rordorf, "Die Mahlgebete in Didache Kap. 9–10: Ein neuer *status quaestionis*," *VC* 51 (1997): 229–46.

# III. THE OLDEST SERMON: *SECOND CLEMENT*

Besides the authentic letter by Clement, the Roman bishop discussed earlier, tradition knows of another "letter," *2 Clement*—though it is neither a letter nor written by Clement. The letter owes its name to tradition attaching it to *1 Clement*, despite the fact that Eusebius already questioned its authenticity. Whereas older introductions unanimously classified this writing as the oldest extant Christian sermon, more recently its literary character has been discussed again. Donfried and Stegemann see its origin closely linked with *1 Clement*. According to Donfried, soon after their induction, the old presbyters wrote an exhortation, which one of them then presented to the assembled community. According to Stegemann, an unknown Syrian Christian wanted to spread *1 Clement* between 120 and 160 because of its disciplinary effect and at the same time intended to supplement its Christology and its views on repentance and asceticism. Wengst and Warns contradict both hypotheses.

In any case, this writing consists of an exhortation presented at the conclusion of a reading in the worship service. In twenty-one paragraphs and without rigid structure, it strings together various arguments and examples calling for obedience to Christ's commandments: in return for Christ's redemptive deed, in view of the age to come, by comparing life with a competition, because of the limited possibility of repentance, on account of the good fruits of obedience, etc. The preacher thereby uses a wealth of biblical and extrabiblical citations, for which, besides the LXX and the Synoptic Gospels, he apparently also had access to another, apocryphal gospel unknown to us.

Nothing can be said with certainty about the place of origin; assumptions range from Rome, via Corinth and Syria, all the way to Egypt. The date of origin may have been ca. 120–150.[7]

*Editions:* M. W. Holmes, *The Apostolic Fathers: Greek Texts and English Translations* (rev. ed.; Grand Rapids: Baker, 1999), 103–27 [ET]. – *Carta a los Corintios* (ed. J. J. Ayán Calvo; FP 4; Madrid: Ciudad Nueva, 1994), 157–209.

*Translations:* A. C. Coxe, trans., "An Ancient Homily, Commonly Styled the Second Epistle of Clement," in *ANF* (Peabody, Mass.: Hendrickson, 1995; repr. of the 1886 ed.), 7:509–23. – J. Keith, trans., "The Second Epistle of Clement," in *ANF* (Peabody, Mass.: Hendrickson, 1995; repr. of the 1887 ed.), 9:249–56 [completed and revised reprint of *ANF* 7]. – *The Apostolic Fathers* (trans. F. X. Glimm, J. M.-F. Marique, and G. G. Walsh; FC 1; Washington, D.C.: Catholic University of America Press, 1947; repr., 1969), 65–79. – C. C. Richardson, *Early Christian Fathers* (New York: Macmillan, 1970), 183–202.

*Encyclopedia Articles:* Vielhauer, 737–44. – D. Powell, *TRE* 8:121–23. – P. F. Beatrice, *EECh* 1:181. – G. Snyder, *EEC* 1:264–65.

*Concordance:* A. Urbán, *Polyarpi et secundae epistulae Clementis Romani concordantiae* (AlOm.A 205; CPA 7; Hildesheim and New York: Olms=Weidmann, 2001).

*Commentary:* A. Lindemann, *Die Clemensbriefe* (HNT 17; Tübingen: Mohr, 1992), 183–277.

*Status quaestionis:* E. Baasland, "Der 2. Klemensbrief und frühchristliche Rhetorik: 'Die erste christliche Predigt' im Lichte der neueren Forschung," *ANRW* 2.27.1:78–157.

*Studies:* K. P. Donfried, "The Theology of Second Clement," *HTR* 66 (1973): 487–501; repr. in E. Ferguson, ed., *Literature of the Early Church* (SEC 2; New York: Garland, 1993), 23–37.

# IV. BEGINNINGS OF CHRISTIAN POETRY: *ODES OF SOLOMON*

"Little more than a few fragments of all the wealth of early Christian hymns have been passed down to us, and what we do have is incorporated into other

---

[7] On the basis of the sermon's argument with Valentinian Gnosticism, Warns dismisses a date as early as 130/140 and instead opts for ca. 160 (Warns, 90f).

texts as more or less explicit citations. Early Christianity did not have the Psalms of the Jewish community, nor the Hodayot of Qumran."[8] For this reason, the publication of the forty-two odes of Solomon (except ode 2) by J. Rendel Harris (1909) and F. C. Burkitt (1912), based on two Syriac manuscripts, accordingly aroused attention. Until then only five of them (1, 5, 6, 22, and 26) had been extant in the *Pistis Sophia* in Coptic. In 1959 a further minor fragment of the eleventh ode was found in the third-century Bodmer papyrus XI. The original language of the odes (Greek, Syriac, Aramaic, or Hebrew) has been discussed extensively. Presently the inclination is toward the Syriac again (L. Abramowski). The place of writing is thought to be a Jewish-Christian community in Syria in the second half of the second century.

The odes represent liturgical songs in elevated prose, and the genre agrees with the OT psalms. R. Abramowski arranged them according to their literary forms: didactic poems (23, 24, 31–34), community hymns (4, 6, 8, 9, 13, 30, 39, 41), individual hymns (1, 3, 7, 10, 11, 15, 17, 19, 21, 27–29, 35, 36, 38, 42), prayer poems (22, 25, 26, 37, 40), and mixtures of these (12, 14, 16, 18, 20).

*Bibliography:* G. Kittel, *Die Oden Salomos—überarbeitet oder einheitlich? Mit 2 Beilagen: I. Bibliographie der Oden Salomos, II. Syrische Konkordanz der Oden Salomos* (BWA[N]T 16; Leipzig: Hinrichs, 1914). – M. Lattke, *Die Oden Salomos in ihrer Bedeutung für Neues Testament und Gnosis* (3 vols.; OBO 25.1–3; Fribourg, Switz.: Éditions Universitaires, 1979–1986).

*Editions:* H. Grimme, *Die Oden Salomos, syrisch-hebräisch-deutsch: Ein kritischer Versuch* (Heidelberg: Winter, 1911). – G. Diettrich, *Die Oden Salomos unter Berücksichtigung der überlieferten Stichengliederung aus dem Syrischen ins Deutsche übersetzt und mit einem Kommentar versehen* (NSGTK 9; Berlin: Trowitzsch, 1911). – W. Bauer, *Die Oden Salomos* (KlT 64; Berlin: de Gruyter, 1933). – M. Testuz, *Papyrus Bodmer X–XII* (Cologne: Geneva, 1959), 47–69. – J. H. Charlesworth, *The Odes of Solomon* (Oxford: Clarendon, 1973) [Com].

*Translations:* J. H. Charlesworth, *The Old Testament Pseudepigrapha* (2 vols.; Garden City, N.Y.: Doubleday, 1985), 2:725–71.

*Encyclopedia Articles:* Daniélou, *DBSup* 6:677–84. – Vielhauer, 750–56. – M. Petit, *DSp* 11:602–8. – C. Kannengiesser, *EECh* 2:609–10. – E. Ferguson, *EEC* 2:824–25.

*Concordance:* M. Lattke, *Die Oden Salomos in ihrer Bedeutung für Neues Testament und Gnosis* (3 vols.; OBO 25.1–3; Fribourg, Switz.: Éditions Universitaires, 1979–1986).

*Studies:* R. Abramowski, "Der Christus der Salomooden," *ZNW* 35 (1936): 44–69. – L. Abramowski, "Sprache und Abfassungszeit der Oden Salomos," *OrChr* 68 (1984): 80–90. – M. Franzmann, *The Odes of Solomon: An Analysis of the Poetical Structure and Form* (NTOA 20; Fribourg, Switz.: Vandenhoeck & Ruprecht, 1991). – J. H. Charlesworth, *Critical Reflections on the Odes of Solomon* (JSPSup 22; Sheffield: Sheffield Academic, 1998).

---

[8] Vielhauer, 750.

Part Two

# Literature of the Period of Persecution (Mid-Second to Early Fourth Centuries)

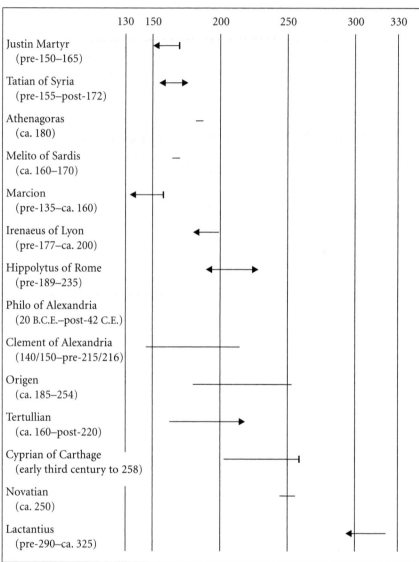

# The Impact of Persecution

IN THE MIDDLE OF THE SECOND century, a fundamental shift in Christian literature occurred as a result of the church's changed circumstances. The writings of the apostolic and postapostolic times had restricted themselves mainly to the preservation and faithful transmission of the gospel of Jesus and to the institutions and rules necessary for the Christian life of the congregations and of each individual. The establishment of basic as well as literary relations with the non-Christian environment seemed unnecessary, since, because of the *Naherwartung* (the expectation of the imminent return of the Messiah), a continuing engagement with this world no longer seemed indicated. The writings restricted themselves to the conduct of everyday life, to missionary activity, and to coping spiritually with the local persecutions that continually flared up and were interpreted as tests. On the other side, the surrounding pagan world had no motivation to concern itself more closely with Christianity in its thought and literature. For that world, it was one of the many small religious communities of the Roman Empire, one that played no role in public life and often enough was not even distinguished, in the public mind, from Judaism, from which it arose.

A hundred years after the death and resurrection of Jesus, however, Christians finally had to acknowledge that the Parousia of the Lord was indeed delayed to an unforeseeable time and so the permanent establishment of Christianity on earth was necessary. At the same time, successful missionary work had so increased the number of Christians in the cities that their presence was noticeable and they came to comprise all levels of the population, not only the uneducated, the easily seduced, as the incipient pagan scholarly criticism was fond of depicting Christians. Rather, educated Christians brought their philosophical and rhetorical learning into the church and began to infuse the faith with it and to establish and protect their faith's reasonableness in confrontation with the traditional religions. Their observations were taken quite seriously by their opponents, the pagan intellectuals, despite the latter's many assertions to the contrary, and were found worthy of even a literary response. Fronto of Cirta, the teacher of Emperor Marcus Aurelius (161–180), delivered a public speech against the Christians, and about 170 the sophist Lucian of Samasota made fun of the Christians in his satire *De morte Peregrini* because of their love of neighbor and unselfishness. About 178 the Alexandrian Platonist Celsus wrote a polemic entitled

*The True Word* ('Αληθὴς λόγος) against the Christians, which Origen answered with his great tract *Contra Celsum.*

The Christian apologetic literature moreover had to combat the attacks that the pagan state carried out on the church, the persecutions of Christians; these writings not only proved the reasonableness and innocuousness of Christianity but substantiated its exclusive claim to truth and endorsed its unique worth for the state because of the model behavior of its members. The persecutions of Christians and, in general, the conflicts of Christianity with the surrounding pagan world from the middle of the second to the beginning of the fourth century fundamentally shaped all Christian literature in such manifold ways that one may include this period under the concept—belonging chiefly to the field of church history rather than the study of literature—of the "literature of the time of persecution." The trials against Christians became its subject, partly as court minutes and partly as reports and accounts of the trials. The great empire-wide persecutions beginning in the middle of the third century raised severe, even theological, problems within the church, and appropriate tracts had to work out and respond to these.

The penetration of ancient philosophical-rhetorical learning into the church shaped not only its discussions with those outside the church but also its inner development, its exegesis, preaching, and dogma, which enjoyed its first great blossoming. If one could accuse the biblical books of an unliterary lack of form and style, Christian literature now experienced a flourishing of masterpieces according to ancient literary art. Included in this literature is the discussion carried out in writing within the church regarding what was the ecclesiastically and theologically correct path for an expanding Christianity—that is, the clarification of what could be accepted in the church as valid (orthodox) theology and what was to be excluded as heretical (heterodox). Around the end of the nineteenth and beginning of the twentieth century, the concept of the "hellenization" of Christianity was introduced to describe this complex process of the enculturation of Christianity in the ancient Hellenistic world—in the sense, indeed, of an inadmissible transformation and falsification of the original, "pure" teaching of Jesus as reflected in the biblical writings. Although the complicated problem of hermeneutics cannot be fully treated here, it can nevertheless be said that recent research has made clear that such a process was and is unavoidable for the worldwide spread of Christianity, that it never remains one-sided, and that it not only happened once in the Hellenistic era but occurs whenever the Christian gospel is "translated" into another language and culture. There is hardly current agreement on what is thereby lost and how much is thereby won for the faith.

The second-and third-century Christian literature that arose on this background was composed chiefly of two large groups: the Greek literature, which alone prevailed until the end of the second century, and the Latin literature, which established itself in North Africa and Rome at the end of the second century. These writings are to be distinguished according to content and literary genre: the apologetic writings; the reports of martyrdom; theological literature in tracts, commentaries, sermons, and so on, in which the discussion about orthodox faith occupied a special position; and works that had a direct application to the practical needs of the life of the community, such as letters, liturgical writings, and moral tracts.

### Fronto of Cirta

*Encyclopedia Articles:* J. H. Waszink, *RAC* 8:520–24. – A. Hamman, *EECh* 1:330.

### Celsus (cf. ch. 3.V.C.4)

*Editions:* G. B. Bozzo and S. Rizzo, *Il discorso della verità: Contro i Christiani/Celso* (Milan: Biblioteca Universale Rizzoli, 1989) [Com].

*Translations: On the True Doctrine: A Discourse against the Christians* (trans. R. J. Hoffmann; New York: Oxford University Press, 1987) [Com].

*Encyclopedia Articles:* P. Merlan, *RAC* 2:954–65. – C. Borret, *Contre Celse* (SC 227; Paris: Cerf, 1976), 9–198. – A. Hamman, *EECh* 1:155.

*Studies:* L. Rougier, *Celse; ou Le conflit de la civilisation antique et du christianisme primitif* (Paris: Éditions du Siècle, 1925). – W. Völker, *Das Bild vom nichtgnostischen Christentum bei Celsus* (Halle: Buchhandlung des Waisenhauses, 1928). – C. Andresen, *Logos und Nomos: Die Polemik des Kelsos wider das Christentum* (AKG 30; Berlin: de Gruyter, 1955). – H.-U. Rosenbaum, "Zur Datierung von Celsus' ΑΛΗΘΗΣ ΛΟΓΟΣ," *VC* 26 (1972): 102–11. – L. Rougier, *Celse: Contre les chrétiens* (Paris: Copernic, 1977). – K. Pichler, *Streit um das Christentum: Der Angriff des Kelsos und die Antwort des Origenes* (RST 23; Frankfurt: Lang, 1980).

### Lucian of Samosata

*Edition: Luciani Opera* (ed. M. D. Macleod; OCT; Oxford: Clarendon, 1972–1980), 3:188–205.

*Studies:* M. Caster, *Lucien et la pensée religieuse de son temps* (Paris: Belles Lettres, 1937). – P. Siniscalco, *EECh* 1:508.

### The Expansion of Christianity

*Encyclopedia Articles:* B. Kötting, *RAC* 2:1138–59. – P. Siniscalco, "Evangelization," *EECh* 1:307–8.

*Studies:* A. von Harnack, *Die Mission und Ausbreitung des Christentums in den ersten drei Jahrhunderten* (2 vols.; 4th ed.; Leipzig: Hinrichs, 1924; repr., Leipzig: Zentral-Antiquariat der Deutschen Demokratischen Republik, 1965). – A. Ehrhard, *Die Kirche der Märtyrer: Ihre Aufgaben und ihre Leistungen* (Munich: Kösel & Pustet, 1932). – A. D. Nock, *Conversion: The Old and the New in Religion from Alexander the Great to Augustine of Hippo* (Oxford: Oxford University Press, 1933; repr., Lanham, Md.: University Press of America, 1988). – K. S. Latourette, *The First Five Centuries* (vol. 1 of *A History of the Expansion of Christianity;* New York and London: Harper & Brothers, 1937). – A. G. Hamman, *La vie quotidienne des premiers chrétiens (95–197)* (3d rev. ed.; Paris: Hachette, 1979); Spanish: *La vida cotidiana de los primeros*

*Cristianos* (Madrid: Palabra, 1989; German: *Die ersten Christen* (Stuttgart: P. Reclam, 1985). – A. Orbe, *Introducción a la teología de los siglos II y III* (2 vols.; AnGr 248; Rome: Editrice Pontificia Università Gregoriana, 1987). – G. Bardy, *La conversion au christianisme durant les premiers siècles* (Theol[P] 15; Paris: Aubier, 1949); German: *Menschen werden Christen* (ed. J. Blank; Frankfurt, 1988).

## Christianity and the Pagan World / Philosophy / Culture

*Editions:* W. den Boer, *Scriptorum paganorum I–IV saec. de Christianis testimonia* (rev. ed.; Textus minores 2; Leiden: Brill, 1965).

*Encyclopedia Articles:* C. Andresen, "Antike und Christentum," *TRE* 3:50–99. – M. Pellegrino, "Classical Culture and Christianity," *EECh* 1:176–8. – S. Lilla, "Hellenism and Christianity," *EECh* 1:372–73. – R. J. De Simone, "Philosophy and the Fathers," *EECh* 2:683. – A. Quacquarelli, "Rhetoric," *EECh* 2:735–36.

*Collections of Essays:* ANRW 2.23.1–2. – G. Gottlieb and P. Barcelo, eds., *Christen und Heiden in Staat und Gesellschaft des zweiten bis vierten Jahrhunderts* (Munich: E. Vögel, 1992).

*Studies:* J. Geffcken, *Das Christentum im Kampf und Ausgleich mit der griechisch-romischen Welt: Studien und Charakteristiken aus seiner Werdezeit* (Leipzig: n.p., 1920). – W. Nestle, "Die Haupteinwände des antiken Denkens gegen das Christentum," *AR* 37 (1941): 51–100. – P. de Labriolle, *La réaction païenne: Étude sur la polémique anti-chrétienne du Ier au VIe siècle* (10th ed.; Paris: L'Artisan du Livre, 1948). – J. Daniélou, *Message évangélique et culture hellénistique aux IIe et IIIe siècles* (BT 2; Paris: Desclée, 1961); [ET] *Gospel Message and Hellenistic Culture* (London: Darton, Longman & Todd; Philadelphia: Westminster, 1973). – W. Jaeger, *Das frühe Christentum und die griechische Bildung* (Berlin: de Gruyter, 1963). – H. A. Wolfson, *Faith, Trinity, Incarnation* (vol. 1 of *The Philosophy of the Church Fathers;* 3d rev. ed.; London and Cambridge, Mass.: Harvard University Press, 1976). – E. von Ivánka, *Plato christianus: Übernahme und Umgestaltung des Platonismus durch die Väter* (Einsiedeln, Switz.: Johannes, 1964). – E. R. Dodds, *Pagan and Christian in an Age of Anxiety: Some Aspects of Religious Experience from Marcus Aurelius to Constantine* (Cambridge: Cambridge University Press, 1965; New York: Norton, 1970). – P. Kerestzes, *From the Severi to Constantine the Great* (vol. 2 of *Imperial Rome and the Christians;* Lanham, Md. and London: University Press of America, 1989). – G. Jossa, *I Cristiani e l'impero romano: Da Tiberio a Marco Auelio* (Naples: Carroci, 1991).

## Jews and Christians

*Studies:* C. Munier, "Jews and Christians," *EECh* 1:436–37. – J. M. Lieu, *Image and Reality: The Jews in the World of the Christians in the Second Century* (Edinburgh: T&T Clark, 1996).

## "Hellenization" of the Christian Faith

*Studies:* J. Hessen, *Griechische oder biblische Theologie? Das Problem der Hellenisierung des Christentums in neuer Beleuchtung* (2d ed.; Munich: E. Reinhardt, 1962). – M. C. Bartolomei, *Ellenizzazione del cristianesimo: Linee di critica filosofica e teologica per una interpretazione del problema storico* (L'Aquila and Rome: L.U. Japadre, 1984). – E. P. Meijering, *Die Hellenisierung des Christentums im Urteil Adolf von Harnacks*

(VNAW) 128; Amsterdam: North-Holland, 1985). – C.-F. Geyer, *Religion und Diskurs: Die Hellenisierung des Christentums aus der Perspektive der Religionsphilosophie* (Stuttgart: Steiner, 1990).

## Christianity and the Roman Empire / Persecutions

*Encyclopedia Articles:* J. Vogt and H. Last, *RAC* 2:1159–1228. – R. Freudenberger, *TRE* 8:23–29. – W. H. C. Frend, *EECh* 2:671–74.

*Studies:* J. Moreau, Die *Christenverfolgung im römischen Reich* (AWR NS 2; Berlin: A. Töpelmann, 1961). – W. H. C. Frend, *Martyrdom and Persecution in the Early Church: A Study of a Conflict from the Maccabees to Donatus* (Oxford: Blackwell, 1965; repr., Grand Rapids: Baker, 1981). – R. Freudenberger, *Das Verhalten der römischen Behorden gegen die Christen im 2. Jahrhundert, dargestellt am Brief des Plinius an Trajan und den Reskripten Trajans und Hadrians* (MBPF 52; Munich: Beck, 1969). – A. Wlosok, *Rom und die Christen: Zur Auseinandersetzung zwischen Christentum und römischem Staat* (Stuttgart: E. Klett, 1970). – R. Klein, ed., *Das frühe Christentum im römischen Staat* (WdF 267; Darmstadt: Wissenschaftliche Buchgesellschaft, 1971). – J. Molthagen, *Der römische Staat und die Christen im zweiten und dritten Jahrhundert* (2d ed.; Hyp. 28; Göttingen: Vandenhoeck & Ruprecht, 1975). – C. Munier, *L'Église dans l'empire romain (IIe–IIIe siècles): Église et cité* (HDIEO 2.3; Paris: Cujas, 1979).

## Theology

*Studies:* A. Orbe, *Introducción a la teología de los siglos II y III* (2 vols.; AnGr 248; Rome: Editrice Pontificia Università Gregoriana, 1987). – M. Simonetti, *Studi sulla cristologia del II e III secolo* (SEAug 44; Rome: Institutum Patristicum Augustinianum, 1993).

# CHAPTER THREE

# Greek Literature

## INTRODUCTION: CHRISTIAN GREEK

Until 180 all of Christian literature used only the common colloquial language of the Roman empire, namely, Koine Greek (κοινὴ διάλεκτος = "common language"). Its use in the proclamation of the Christian message, however, was the result of the development of a Christian "special language"—a phenomenon that can be observed in all special groups of any society. Earliest Christianity thereby continued an already existing Greek special language, the language of Hellenistic Diaspora Judaism. There the Hebrew Bible had been translated into Greek (Septuagint), and in the worship services homilies were given in Greek, thus permeating the Jewish-Greek special language with biblical and Semitic concepts and terms. The Septuagint served early Christianity as its original OT, so that Christianity directly adopted its Semitisms in vocabulary and syntax. In addition, it had to introduce new terms for the specifically Christian gospel message or modify already existing ones. Vulgar Greek expressions found their way into Christian Greek because many of the early Christians came from the lower social strata. Finally, terms with a particular pagan-cultic meaning were removed from the Christian vocabulary. The following changes are particularly noteworthy:

- adoption of biblical and liturgical terms, such as "hosanna," "hallelujah," "amen";

- reinterpretation of already existing concepts by aligning the meaning with Hebrew biblical thought (e.g., δόξα = *kabod* = glory of God; διαθήκη = *berith* = covenant of God with humans, "testament");

- syntactical changes, such as the pleonastic use of οὐρανοί or εἰς τοὺς αἰῶνας τῶν αἰώνων; qualifying genitives instead of adjectives (e.g., ἄν-θρωπος τῆς ἀνομίας); periphrastic constructions of ἐστίν plus a participle instead of a finite verb form; and copying the Hebrew b^e construction with ἐν (e.g., ἐν σαρκὶ ἔρχεσθαι).

Otherwise the vocabulary changes take place primarily by:

- narrowing the meaning (e.g., ἐκκλησία = gathering of the church; ἀπόστολος = apostle belonging to the circle of the Twelve) and

- introducing new technical terms (e.g., βαπτισμός = "baptism"; εὐχαριστία = "Eucharist"; γραφή = Holy Scripture).

The usage of Greek by the Fathers furthermore reflected the general linguistic evolution of the time:

- *itacism:* the uniform pronunciation of all the *i*-vowels and diphthongs (ι, η, υ) as *i;*

- *isochronism:* standardization of the length and shortness (quantities) of the respective vowels and diphthongs;

- *transition* from musical accents, indicating pitch, to expiratory accents, denoting emphasis;

- *softening* of the consonant β to *w.*

Hence most of the patristic texts originally might well have been pronounced like modern Greek rather than like the classical Attic Greek, unless there is evidence of intentional Atticisms. A good example of a development that did not at all happen uniformly or in a straight line can be seen in the name David, which is written in three distinct ways: Δαυίδ (υ = *u*), Δαβίδ (β = *w*), Δαυείδ (ει = *i*).

The decisive impetus for researching the Christian special languages of antiquity was given by Josef Schrijnen, a Dutch classical philologist of the 1930s. His work is continued into the present by his students; among them Christine Mohrmann has been particularly outstanding.

*Thesaurus:* H. Stephan, *Thesaurus graecae linguae* (10 vols.; rev. ed.; London: In Aedibus Valpianis, 1816–1828; repr. of 1852 ed., Athens: Epikairoteta, 1998).

*Dictionaries:* C. du Cange, *Glossarium ad scriptores mediae et infimae graecitatis* (2 vols.; Lyon, 1688; repr., Graz: Akademische Druck, 1958). – E. A. Sophocles, *Greek Lexicon of the Roman and Byzantine Periods (from B.C. 146 to A.D. 1100)* (Cambridge, Mass.: Harvard University Press, 1900). – H. Liddell, R. Scott, H. S. Jones, and R. McKenzie, *A Greek-English Lexicon* (9th ed. with revised supplement, by P. G. W. Glare and A. A. Thompson; Oxford: Clarendon, 1996). – G. W. H. Lampe, *A Patristic Greek Lexicon* (Oxford: Clarendon, 1961; repr., 1976). – F. W. Danker, W. Bauer, W. F. Arndt, and F. W. Gingrich, *A Greek-English Lexicon of the New Testament and Other Early Christian Literature* (3d ed.; Chicago: University of Chicago Press, 2000); based on W. Bauer, *Griechisch-deutsches Wörterbuch* (6th ed.; Berlin: de Gruyter, 1988).

*Grammars:* F. Blass, A. Debrunner, and R. W. Funk, *A Greek Grammar of the New Testament and Other Early Christian Literature* (Chicago: University of Chicago Press, 1961). – R. Kühner, F. Blass, and B. Gerth, *Ausführliche Grammatik der griechischen Sprache* (4 vols.; 3d ed.; Hannover: Hahnsche Buchhandlung, 1890–1904). – E. Schwyzer, *Griechische Grammatik* (4 vols.; 2d ed.; HAW 2.1.1–4; Munich: Beck, 1950–1971). – F. Blass, A. Debrunner, and F. Rehkopf, *Grammatik des neutestamentlichen Griechisch* (17th ed.; Göttingen: Vandenhoeck & Ruprecht, 1979). – W. D. Mounce, *Basics of Greek Grammar* (Grand Rapids: Zondervan, 1993). – D. B. Wallace, *Greek Grammar beyond the Basics* (Grand Rapids: Zondervan, 1996).

*Encyclopedia Articles:* V. Loi, "Greek, Christian," *EECh* 1:360–61. – P. Siniscalco, "Languages of the Fathers," *EECh* 1:472.

*Studies:* Graecitas Christianorum primaeva: Studia ad sermonem graecum pertinentia (Nijmegen: Dekker & van de Vegt, 1962–1977) [GCP]. – Graecitas et latinitas Christianorum primaeva: Supplementa (Nijmegen: Dekker & van de Vegt, 1964–) [GLCP]. – G. Bardy, *La question des langues dans l'Église ancienne* (Paris: Beauchesne, 1948). – H. Poeschel, *Die griechische Sprache: Geschichte und Einführung* (Munich: Heimeran, 1950; 4th ed., 1961). – O. Hoffmann and A. Debrunner, *Geschichte der griechischen Sprache* (ed. A. Scherer; 4th ed.; Berlin: de Gruyter, 1969). – P. Chantraine, *Morphologie historique du grec* (3d ed.; Paris: Librairie C. Klincksieck, 1991). – W. D. Mounce, *The Morphology of Biblical Greek* (Grand Rapids: Zondervan, 1994).

# I. GREEK APOLOGISTS

Since Christianity had to deal with its environment from the start, first with the Jewish and then with the Hellenistic, we already find apologetic elements in the NT writings themselves—for instance, the accusation against the Jews that they had not recognized the Messiah and therefore forfeited the right to inherit the promise, a promise that had now been redirected to Christians; or Paul's speech on the Areopagus in Athens (Acts 17:19–34), which skillfully linked up with the current conception of the "unknown God" and proclaimed the one true God in contrast with all the others. It was not until the second century, however, that apologetics evolved into a literary genre of its own because the church's situation had changed. For this reason, the initial authors of the second half of the second century, whose extant literary work consists primarily or entirely of apologias, are called the Greek apologists (ἀπολογεῖν = "to defend"). Subsequently apologias emerged in the Greek and Latin churches throughout the patristic era, but they did not play as sweeping and fundamental a role as did those of the second century.

Because of the origin and environment of early Christianity, apologetics was directed at two opponents, the Jews and the pagans. The anti-Jewish polemic (which has nothing to do with anti-Semitism, since the issue is not race but faith!) has a twofold goal:

a. Separating Christianity from its origin in Judaism. An important part of this is acknowledgment of Jesus as the Messiah and interpretation of the OT as announcing him. Hence the old covenant's only significance was to serve as a forerunner and signpost pointing to him, and in the light of the new covenant, it has to be interpreted christologically. In this way apologetics provides Christians with arguments for debate with the Jews, strengthens them in the awareness that they are the fulfillment of God's will prepared in Judaism, and prevents Judaizing tendencies in Christianity.

b. It also aspires to convert Jews by convincing them of the validity of faith in the Messiah on the basis of the OT itself. Given the relatively scant opposition, anti-Jewish apologetics takes up negligible space in early Christian literature. Its importance becomes apparent, however, when we consider that at the end of the fourth century, John Chrysostom, for instance, still had to warn his church in several sermons against converting to Judaism, whose success in gaining converts was apparently quite substantial at that time.

From the Hellenistic environment, as well as the state, the most threatening oppression of Christianity came by means of frequently erupting persecution of believers. Granted, until the persecution by Decius (250/251), these persecutions were merely local and of limited duration; but they did not affect Christians any less, all the more so since they occurred unpredictably because of envy, slander, misunderstanding, and unjustified accusations, and Christians were not aware of any guilt. Furthermore, until the empirewide edict by Decius to offer sacrifices to the emperor and the corresponding sanctions for refusing such sacrifice, there was no clear-cut Roman legal basis for persecutions. On most occasions, it seems that Christian existence itself, the *nomen christianum*, was the reason for punishment. Only the emperor was able to bring about an empirewide, uniform legal basis and protect Christians from unjustified persecution. For this reason, the apologias of the second century were directed to the emperor or emperors and above all else pointed out two legal inconsistencies: If being a Christian per se were an offense, the state would have to persecute Christians continuously and not only when they are reported, as in the case of Trajan, for instance, who ruled on this basis in his correspondence with Pliny the Younger in 112. In addition, it would have to be demonstrated what crime they were guilty of for being Christian. Although the charges made against Christians were many, primarily godlessness, incest, cannibalism, and murder of children, they could never be proven in any case.

In terms of content, therefore, the argumentation was intended to clarify the misconceptions and wrong ideas regarding Christians among the people who fanned the flames of the persecutions. Christianity had to be presented not only as an acceptable conviction of faith that was compatible with the welfare and laws of the state but as a faith that promoted the latter when Christians prayed for the emperor, participated in public life, carefully heeded justice because of their Christian moral obligations, etc. The real and absolute impetus, however, always was the conviction Christians held that they revered the only true God—a conviction that prevented them from participating in the public worship of idols. Hence Christian apologetics after all had to substantiate clearly the reasonableness and superiority of the faith, which, in turn, led to laying the foundation for theology in the church's development.

Giving an account for the faith with reference to the outside world was not difficult, since the apologists' enlightened, philosophically informed contemporaries had long ceased to believe in the myths about the gods and instead developed their own transcendental understanding of God that determined their worldview and ethical behavior. This provided a suitable starting point for Christian teaching, which proclaimed the one eternal God and could point to the superior ethical quality of the Christian life. In the Roman Empire, however, the intellectual turning away from the mythical belief in gods evoked a strange conflict between inner conviction and outward conduct: participation in the imperial cult for the benefit of the state did not affect the inner conviction, the philosophy one followed.

For this reason, the claim of absoluteness on the part of Christian "philosophy," which kept Christians away from state-related sacrifices and from participating in public festivals dedicated to the gods, remained incomprehensible. On this level, Christianity had to demonstrate that it was the only reasonable philosophy, the greatest and oldest of all. The argument of antiquity was particularly important in the ancient world, given that truth had enduring validity. On this issue, Christian apologetics coincided with its Jewish counterparts in Flavius Josephus and Philo of Alexandria. Judaism had indeed developed an extensive apologetic because it sought to preserve its consciously separate status; where it was embedded in a Hellenistic environment, however, it was forced to discuss the question of who was more ancient, Homer or Moses.

Early Christian apologetics essentially fulfilled three tasks:

a. defending against violent and argumentative attacks directed against Christianity by proving their lack of justification or power of persuasion;

b. clearing up false conceptions about Christianity by explaining the actual circumstances;

c. providing a logical reason and justification for the Christian faith by proving the inferiority of the opposition's faith stance; this was often aided by a missionary zeal to convert an opponent to Christianity.

Approximately half of the apologias of which we are aware have perished; that is, they are only preserved in a few fragments, mostly in the *Ecclesiastical History* of Eusebius. The earliest apologia known to us is that of Quadratus, who presented it to Hadrian during one of Hadrian's visits to Asia Minor (123/124 or 129) or Athens (125/126 or 129). Miltiades, the rhetorician of Asia Minor, Apollinaris of Hierapolis, and Melito of Sardis addressed apologias to Marcus Aurelius (161–180) and his coregent Lucius Verus (161–169). Finally, we know that ca. 140 Ariston of Pella addressed a Christian apologia to the Jews entitled *Dialogue of Papiscus and Jason concerning Christ*. All of these writings have perished, however.

Apart from those examined here in greater detail, the following are also extant:

a. an apologia of Aristides, the philosopher of Athens, addressed to Hadrian (117–138) or Antonius Pius (138–169) in the early years of the respective emperor's reign;

b. three books by Theophilus of Antioch, addressed to Autolycus (shortly after 180), in which he seeks to demonstrate the credibility of Christianity to his friend;

c. a "satire on non-Christian philosophers" by Hermias, probably from the third century, who denounces the inconsistencies of belief in pagan idols and of philosophy;

d. three apologias by unknown third-century authors, namely, *Cohortatio ad Graecos, De monarchia,* and *Oratio ad Graecos,* which were incorporated into the *Corpus Justini* soon thereafter, for Eusebius was already conversant with them before 311/312 as the works of Justin.

*Editions:* J. K. T. von Otto, *Corpus apologetarum christianorum saeculi secundi* (9 vols.; Jena: Maukii, 1847–1881) *[CorpAp]. –* J. Geffcken, *Zwei griechische Apologeten* (Leipzig: Teubner, 1907) [Aristides, Athenagoras]. – E. J. Goodspeed, *Die ältesten Apologeten: Texte mit kurzen Einleitungen* (Göttingen: Vandenhoeck & Ruprecht, 1914) [Aristides, Athenagoras, Justin, Tatian]. – G. Ruhbach, *Altkirchliche Apologeten* (TKTG 1; Gütersloh: G. Mohn, 1966) [Aristides, Athenagoras, Melito, Quadratus]. – R. M. Grant, *Theophilus of Antioch ad Autolycum* (OECT; Oxford: Clarendon, 1970). – C. Alpigiano, *Aristide di Atene, Apologia* (BPat 11; Florence: Edizioni Dehoniane, 1988). – M. Marcovich, *Pseudo-Iustinus, Cohortatio ad Graecos, De monarchia, Oratio ad Graecos* (PTS 32; Berlin and New York: de Gruyter, 1990). – M. Marcovich, *Theophili Antiocheni Ad Autolycum* (PTS 44; Berlin and New York: de Gruyter, 1995).

*Translations:* A. C. Coxe, trans., "Theophilus to Autolycus," in *ANF* (Peabody, Mass.: Hendrickson, 1995; repr. of the 1885 ed.), 2:85–121 [Theophilus, *To Autolycus*]. – D. M. Kay, trans., "The Apology of Aristides the Philosopher," in *ANF* (Peabody, Mass.: Hendrickson, 1995; repr. of the 1887 ed.), 9:257–79.

*Index:* E. J. Goodspeed, *Index apologeticus* (Leipzig: Hinrichs, 1912).

*Encyclopedia Articles:* G. Bardy, "Apologetik," *RAC* 1:533–43. – L. W. Barnard, "Apologetik I," *TRE* 3:371–411. – M. Pellegrino, "Apologists–Apologetic (general characteristics)," *EEC* 1:60. – P. Siniscalco, "Aristides," *EEC* 1:72–73. – P. Siniscalco, "Hermias," *EEC* 1:378. – P. Nautin, "Theophilus of Antioch," *EEC* 2:831–32. – H. Gamble, "Apologetics," *EEC* 1:81–87.

*General Studies:* A. Puech, *Les apologistes grecs du IIe siècle de notre ère* (Paris: Hatchette, 1912). – J.-R. Larin, *Orientations maîtresses des apologistes chrétiens de 270 à 361* (AnGr 61; Rome: Apud Aedes Universitatis Gregorianae, 1954). – R. M. Grant, *Greek Apologists of the Second Century* (Philadelphia: Westminster, 1988). – E. Ferguson, ed., *The Early Church and Greco-Roman Thought* (SEC 8; New York: Garland, 1993). – B. Pouderon and J. Doré, eds., *Les apologistes chrétiens et la culture grecque* (ThH 105; Paris: Beauchesne, 1998). – M. Edwards, M. Goodman, and S. Price, with C. Rowland, eds., *Apologetics in the Roman Empire: Pagans, Jews, and Christians* (Oxford and New York: Oxford University Press, 1999).

*Studies on Particular Aspects:* R. M. Grant, "The Chronology of the Greek Apologists," *VC* 9 (1955): 25–33. – R. Joly, *Christianisme et philosophie: Études sur Justin et les apologistes grecs du deuxième siècle* (Brussels: Éditions de l'Université de Bruxelles, 1973). – D. W. Palmer, "Atheism, Apologetic, and Negative Theology in the Greek Apologists of the Second Century," *VC* 37 (1983): 234–59. – R. M. Grant, "Five Apologists and Marcus Aurelius," *VC* 42 (1988): 1–17. – A. J. Droge, *Homer or Moses? Early Christian Interpretation of the History of Culture* (HUT 26; Tübingen: Mohr, 1989). – W. Kinzig, "Der 'Sitz im Leben' der Apologie in der alten Kirche," *ZKG* 100 (1989): 291–317. – P. Pilhofer, *PRESBYTERON KREITTON: Der Altersbeweis der jüdischen und christlichen Apologeten und seine Vorgeschichte* (WUNT 2.39; Tübingen: Mohr, 1990). – J. J. Walsh, "On Christian Atheism," *VC* 45 (1991): 255–77. – M. Rizzi, *Ideologia e retorica negli "exordia" apologetici: Il problema dell' "altro" (II–III secolo)* (SPMed 18; Milan: Vita e Pensiero, 1993). – J. W. Hargis, *Against the Christians: The Rise of Early Anti-Christian Polemic* (Patristic Studies 1; New York: Lang, 1999) [on Celsus, Porphyry, and Julian the Apostate].

*Judaism and Early Christian Apologetic:* A. L. Williams, *Adversus Judaeos: A Bird's-Eye View of Christian Apologiae until the Renaissance* (Cambridge: Cambridge University Press, 1935). – M. Simon, *Verus Israël: A Study of the Relations between Christians and Jews in the Roman Empire (135–425)* (trans. H. McKeating; London and Portland, Oreg.: Vallentine Mitchell, 1996); trans. of *Verus Israël: Étude sur les relations entre chrétiens et juifs dans l'empire romain, 135–425* (Paris: de Boccard, 1948). R. Wilde, *The Treatment of the Jews in the Greek Christian Writers of the First Three Centuries* (PatSt 81; Washington, D.C.: Catholic University of America Press, 1949). – H. Schreckenberg, *Die christlichen Adversus-Judaeos-Texte und ihr literarisches und historisches Umfeld (1.-11. Jh.)* (2d rev. ed.; Frankfurt and New York: Lang, 1991). – E. Ferguson, ed., *Early Christianity and Judaism* (SEC 6; New York: Garland, 1993). – C. Setzer, *Jewish Responses to Early Christians: History and Polemics, 30–150 C.E.* (Minneapolis: Fortress, 1994).

# A. Diognetus

The writing addressed to a certain Diognetus, about whom we have no detailed information, is traditionally included among the Apostolic Fathers. Ever since its 1592 *editio princeps* by Henricus Stephanus (Henri Estienne), it has been known as the epistle or letter to Diognetus. This is an apologetic writing, however, and lacks the formal features of an ancient letter despite the fact that it addresses Diognetus. It is not attested anywhere in antiquity or in the Middle Ages; its only occurrence is in a single codex from the thirteenth or fourteenth century, the exemplar of which may have originated in the sixth or seventh century. Discovered accidentally in the shop of a fish dealer in Constantinople in the first half of the fifteenth century, it ended up in the public library of Strasbourg in the late eighteenth century. During the Franco-Prussian War, however, it was destroyed by fire when the Prussians bombarded the city on August 24, 1870. Fortunately, the codex can be reconstructed reliably on the basis of earlier copies, collations, and critical editions despite the fact that this has also led to numerous instances where the text is in question.

The introduction to the apologia (1.1) cites three questions about which Diognetus wants to be better informed: (a) the identity of the Christians' God, how Christians revere him, why they have scant regard for death, and why they do not adhere to the Greek or Jewish cults; (b) what their love of the neighbor is all about; and (c) why their faith became public only now and not earlier. Chapters 2–4 are skillfully linked with a philosophical concept of God with which Diognetus would readily agree, in order to demonstrate, in answer to the first question, that the pagan gods are nothing more than the material product of humans and worshiping them is senseless. The Jews do indeed worship the one true God as well, albeit in an erroneous manner because they present their sacrifices superstitiously and meticulously adhere to ludicrous requirements of the law. Chapters 5–6 describe the lifestyle Christians practice: they are people on earth like everyone else, but by belonging to Christ, they already are citizens of heaven. Hence they surpass the world in existence and conduct, just as the soul surpasses the body. Chapters 7–8 explain the Christians' understanding of their God, who is omnipotent, Creator of all, invisible, and good, by critiquing the various philosophical conceptions of God and thereby substantiating the faith and life of Christians and establishing the premise for the response to the third question, which follows (chs. 9–10).

The redemptive plan of God and his Son had preordained from eternity that the Son should be sent to redeem humans from sin and death only when humankind had become convinced of its unrighteousness and realized how impossible self-redemption was. Chapter 10 concludes this work with an appeal to Diognetus to become a Christian himself by coming to know and emulating God. In this way, *Diognetus* tends to become a "writing to recruit for Christianity," rather than remaining an apologia proper.

In many respects, the formulation of the questions by Diognetus and the argumentation of the apologia may well be considered typical of early Christian apologetics. On the one hand, the questions call for information about the basis of this new religion (the concept of God) and its most conspicuous phenomena (love of neighbor), but on the other, they are critical inquiries that call for a justification of the faith. Why do Christians not participate in the cult of the state like all other authorized religions in the Roman Empire, or if this is not what they want to do, why did they not remain true to their Jewish roots? The Jews were exempted from such participation, after all; so why opt for a new, third way instead? The same applies to the question concerning the truth claim of a new religion. Since truth is considered to be eternal, does truth not have to be traditional? Can anything new be superior to the enduring tradition of the fathers, the *mos maiorum*?

The structural features of the responses addressed to Diognetus are no less typical. To begin with, the responses take up common convictions (a philosophical, not a mythical, concept of God; the rejection of Jewish traditions) and then present Christianity as positive and superior by means of philosophical concepts (e.g., the comparison between body and soul), distancing themselves, however, from unacceptable philosophical positions. They also substantiate Christianity's late, yet uniquely true, mission and finally encourage the recipient to convert.

Chapters 11 and 12 are generally considered to be additions by another hand, but Andriessen, Marrou, and recently Rizzi deem them to be authentic, whereas Barnard views them as a further segment by the same author and attached in the course of transmission. The author himself remains unknown; Andriessen's hypothesis that *Diognetus* is identical to the lost apologia of Quadratus has little to commend itself. The place and date of writing remain equally uncertain. The majority date it ca. 200; Marrou suggests Alexandria as the likely place. Yet Barnard and others date it ca. 140, before the Marcionite controversy. In any case, dating it to the post-Constantinian era should prove to be an implausible prospect.

*Editions: Der Brief an Diognetos* (ed. J. Geffcken; Heidelberg: Winter, 1928) [Com]. – *Die apostolischen Väter* (ed. K. Bihlmeyer; Tübingen: Mohr, 1970), 141–49. – *The Epistle to Diognetus* (ed. H. G. Meecham; PUM.T 7; Manchester, Eng.: Manchester University Press, 1949) [ET/Com]. – *À Diognète* (ed. H.-I. Marrou; 2d ed.; SC 33; Paris: Cerf, 1965). – *Didache (Apostellehre), Barnabasbrief, Zweiter Klemensbrief, Schrift an Diognet* (ed. K. Wengst; Darmstadt: Wissenschaftliche Buchgesellschaft, 1984), 281–348 [Com]. – *Die apostolischen Väter* (ed. Lindemann and Paulsen; Tübingen: Mohr, 1992), 304–323.

*Translations:* A. C. Coxe, trans., "The Epistle of Mathetes to Diognetus," in *ANF* (Peabody, Mass.: Hendrickson, 1995; repr. of the 1885 ed.), 1:23–30. – *The Apostolic Fathers* (trans. F. X. Glimm, J. M.-F. Marique, and G. G. Walsh; FC 1; New York: Cima, 1947; repr., 1969), 351–67. – *The Didache, The Epistle of Barnabas, The Epistles and the Martyrdom of St. Polycarp, The Fragments of Papias, The Epistle to Diognetus* (trans. J. A. Kleist; ACW 6; Westminster, Md.: Newman, 1948), 125–47, 210–21. – M. Staniforth, *Early Christian Writings: The Apostolic Fathers* (rev. A. Louth; London and New York: Penguin, 1987), 139–51. – B. D. Ehrman, ed. *After the New Testament: A Reader in Early Christianity* (New York: Oxford University Press, 1999), 71–75.

*Concordance:* A. Urbán, *Concordantia in Epistulam ad Diognetum* (AlOm.A 135; Hildesheim and New York: Olms-Weidmann, 1993).

*Encyclopedia Articles:* S. Zincone, *EECh* 1:237.

*Studies:* E. Molland, "Die literatur- und dogmengeschichtliche Stellung des Diognetbriefes," *ZNW* 33 (1934): 289–312, repr. in idem, *Opuscula patristica* (BTN 2; Oslo: Universitets-förlaget, 1970), 79–101. – W. Eltester, "Das Mysterium des Christentums: Anmerkungen zum Diognetbrief," *ZNW* 61 (1970): 278–93. – C. M. Nielsen, "The Epistle to Diognetus: Its Date and Relationship to Marcion," *AThR* 52 (1970): 77–91. – J. T. Lienhard, "The Christology of the Epistle to Diognetus," *VC* 24 (1970): 280–89. – R. Brändle, *Die Ethik der "Schrift an Diognet": Eine Wiederaufnahme paulinischer und johanneischer Theologie am Ausgang des zweiten Jahrhunderts* (ATANT 64; Zurich: Theologischer Verlag, 1975). – A. L. Townsley, "Notes for an Interpretation of the *Epistle to Diognetus*," *RSC* 24 (1976): 5–20. – A. Lindemann, "Paulinische Theologie im Brief an Diognet," in *Kerygma und Logos—Beiträge zu den geistesgeschichtlichen Beziehungen zwischen Antike und Christentum: Festschrift für Carl Andresen zum 70. Geburtstag* (ed. A. M. Ritter; Göttingen: Vandenhoeck & Ruprecht, 1979), 337–50. – R. G. Tanner, "The Epistle to Diognetus and Contemporary Greek Thought," in *Papers Presented to the Seventh International Conference on Patristic Studies Held in Oxford, 1975* (ed. E. Livingstone; StPatr 15; TU 128; Berlin: Akademie, 1984), 495–508. – T. Baumeister, "Zur Datierung der Schrift an Diognet," *VC* 42 (1988): 105–11. – M. Rizzi, *La questione dell'unità dell' "Ad Diognetum"* (SPMed 16; Milan: Vita e Pensiero, 1989). K. Schneider, "Die Stellung der Juden und der Christen in der Welt nach dem Diognetbrief," *JAC* 42 (1999): 20–41.

# B. Justin Martyr

From the autobiographical references in his own works, from an account of his martyrdom, and from reports in the *Ecclesiastical History* of Eusebius and in Epiphanius, we are fairly familiar with Justin's life. He was born in Flavia Neapolis (ancient Shechem, modern Nablus) in Samaria. His father's name was Priscus, his grandfather's Bacchius, which may indicate that he descended from a family of Roman or Greek settlers. In any case, he was uncircumcised, and his work does not disclose any conversance with Samaritan Judaism at all. He searched for answers on vital issues among various groups in succession, with the Stoics, Peripatetics, and Pythagoreans, and finally found his "contentment" in (middle) Platonic philosophy. But even within this security, he became unsettled by a conversation with an old man who pointed him in the direction of the books of the prophets. This ultimately was where he recognized the truth, and from then on he wore a philosopher's cloak to indicate that he was a Christian itinerant preacher. To what extent the historicity of the details of this autobiography can be accepted is a matter of debate, since it contains numerous very stylized elements. Conversely there is no compelling argument against accepting that this "typical" life essentially traces Justin's path. He spent the final years of his life in Rome, where he likely also wrote most of his works—the three extant ones, in any case. There he had a serious clash with Crescens the Cynic, and as a result he had a presentiment of his death by martyrdom. Whether Crescens indeed was the reason for his execution under the prefect Rusticus (163–167), however, remains uncertain. At any rate, the year of his death, 165, handed down in the *Chronicon paschale*, may be accepted as accurate.

In his *Ecclesiastical History* Eusebius offers a list of Justin's works (4.18.2–6). Of all the texts attributed to him in the manuscript tradition, only three, written between 150 and 160, are accepted as authentic, namely, two apologias and the *Dialogue with Trypho*, together with a few fragments. Since his works are best classified as occasional writings in terms of literary type, it is impossible to expect them to yield a systematically constructed theology. Nevertheless it is possible to extrapolate several important statements, for instance, on the Trinity, Christology, the doctrine of creation, and exegesis.

*Bibliographies:* L. W. Barnard, "Justin Martyr in Recent Study," *SJT* 22 (1969): 152–64. – O. Skarsaune, "Trekk fra nyere Justin-forskning," *DTT* 39 (1976): 231–57. – J. Morales, "La investigación sobre san Justino y sus escritos," *ScrTh* 16 (1984): 869–96. – B. Wildermuth, *BBKL* 3:888–95.

*Translations: The First Apology; The Second Apology; Dialogue with Trypho; Exhortation to the Greeks; Discourse to the Greeks; The Monarchy, or the Rule of God* (trans. T. B. Falls; FC 6; Washington, D.C.: Catholic University of America Press in association with Consortium Books, 1948; repr., 1977) [*Opera omnia*].

*Encyclopedia Articles:* C. P. Bammel, 1:51–68. – O. Skarsaune, *TRE* 17:471–78. – R. J. DeSimone, *EECh* 1:462–64. – T. Stylianopoulous, *EEC* 1:647–50.

*General Studies:* H. Chadwick, *Early Christian Thought and the Classical Tradition: Studies in Justin, Clement, and Origen* (2d ed.; Oxford: Clarendon; New York: Oxford University Press, 1984), 1–30. – L. Barnard, *Justin Martyr: His Life and Thought* (London: Cambridge University Press, 1967). – E. F. Osborn, *Justin Martyr* (BHTh 47; Tübingen: Mohr, 1973).

*Studies on Justin and the Bible:* P. Prigent, *Justin et l'Ancien Testament: L'argumentation scripturaire du traité de Justin contre toutes les hérésies comme source principale du Dialogue avec Tryphon et de la première Apologie* (EBib; Paris: Librairie Lecoffre, 1964). – A. J. Bellinzoni, *The Sayings of Jesus in the Writings of Justin Martyr* (NovTSup 17; Leiden: Brill, 1967). – D. Bourgeois, *La sagesse des anciens dans le mystère du Verbe: Évangile et philosophie chez saint Justin philosophe et martyr* (Paris: Téqui, 1981). –

O. Skarsaune, *The Proof from Prophecy: A Study in Justin Martyr's Proof-Text Tradition: Text-Type, Provenance, Theological Profile* (NovTSup 56; Leiden: Brill, 1987).

*Chronology:* A. G. Hamman, "Essai de chronologie de la vie et des œuvres de Justin," *Aug* 35 (1995): 231–39.

*Philosophy:* C. Andresen, "Justin und der mittlere Platonismus," *ZNW* 44 (1952–1953): 157–95. – R. Holte, *Logos spermatikos: Christianity and Ancient Philosophy according to St. Justin's Apologies* (trans. T. Pierce; STL 12; Lund, Swed.: Gleerup, 1958): 109–68. – A. J. Droge, "Justin Martyr and the Restoration of Philosophy," *ChH* 56 (1987): 303–19; repr. in *The Early Church in Greco-Roman Thought* (ed. E. Ferguson; SEC 8; New York: Garland, 1993), 65–81. – E. Robillard, *Justin: L'itinéraire philosophique* (Montreal: Bellarmin; Paris: Cerf, 1989). – M. J. Edward, "On the Platonic Schooling of Justin Martyr," *JTS* NS 42 (1991): 17–34. – G. Girgenti, *Giustino Martire: Il primo cristiano platonico* (Milan: Vita e Pensiero, 1995).

*Theology:* E. R. Goodenough, *The Theology of Justin Martyr: An Investigation into the Conceptions of Early Christian Literature and Its Hellenistic and Judaistic Influences* (Jena: Frommann, 1923; repr., Amsterdam: Philo, 1968). – J. J. Ayán Calvo, *Antropología de san Justino: Exégesis del mártir a Gen I–III* (Santiago de Compostela: Instituto Teologico Compostelano, 1988). – G. A. Nocilli, *La catechesi battesimale ed eucaristica di San Giustino Martire* (Bologne: Edizioni Francescane Bologna, 1990). – P. Merlo, *Liberi per vivere secondo il Logos: Principi e criteri dell'agire morale in San Giustino filosofo e martire* (BSRel 111; Rome: LAS, 1995). – M. J. Edwards, "Justin's Logos and the Word of God," *JECS* 3 (1995): 261–80.

# 1. First Apology

The *First Apology* (written ca. 153–155) consists of two main parts. Chapters 1–29 contain a defense against the charge that Christians are atheists. Justin concedes that Christians do not pay homage to the gods, since they acknowledge that gods in reality are evil demons that by terror and torment entice humans to revere them as gods. Jesus Christ, the Logos and Son of God, unmasked this demonic deceit; now people throughout the world will become truly God-fearing through him. Chapters 30–60 provide scriptural support from the OT that Jesus indeed is the Son of God and not a magician. Chapters 61–67 offer a description of a baptismal service and of the Sunday eucharistic celebration. Chapter 68 concludes the work with the rendering of a rescript by Emperor Hadrian.

This work is constructed quite loosely. The digressions typical in Justin's writings may be the result of his strict adherence to his sources, so much so that their structure breaks his own. His train of thought, however, is tight and clear. He begins with a twofold assumption: first, the ideal of the god-fearing life, which he shares with the philosophers; second, the apparent rejection of this ideal by Christians because they refuse to participate in the cult of the state, which was considered to be necessary, both socially and politically. Linking up with the philosophical critique of religion, Justin defends by attacking the deities. Accordingly, the actions of the Homeric gods are abominable and immoral, and those who imitate them become enslaved to the most hideous of sins. Worshiping lifeless images of the gods is irrational nonsense. Hence behind the Homeric gods

Justin sees demonic actions. In contrast to the gods of the poets, the true God is not conceived, nor is he subject to passions. By means of his life and resurrection, Christ overcame the demons, whose ringleader is Satan. Now Christ liberates from the dominion of demons all humans who desire to believe in him. Yet Christ was not only effective against the demonic as the incarnate Logos and wisdom of God; as the agent of creation, the Logos also implanted the seed of truth, the λό γος σπερματικός, in all humans, on account of which pre-Christian philosophers were already Christian in their thought and behavior. The example par excellence is Socrates, who uncovered the demons' deception and challenged people to seek the true God, on account of which he had to suffer a martyr's death.

## 2. Second Apology

The *Second Apology* follows the first one in quick succession because of a current event. The Roman prefect Urbicus ordered the execution of three Christians for the sole reason of confessing the *nomen christianum*. Consequently, Justin appeals to the Roman public against this unjustified cruelty and, in doing so, refutes several points of criticism. For instance, he responds to the derisive question why Christians prohibit suicide if this is the quickest way to bring them to their God. Persecutions are the work of demons that hate truth and virtue. The same enemies had already tormented the righteous of the OT era and of the ancient pagan world. They would have no power over Christians, however, if God were not intending to lead his disciples to virtue and reward through trials and difficulties. At the same time, persecutions offer Christians an opportunity to demonstrate convincingly the superiority of their faith. Finally, Justin appeals to the emperor not to allow anything to prompt him in evaluating Christians other than their righteousness, piety, and love for the truth.

Justin makes use of several typical arguments of early Christian apologetics: appealing to the emperor not to be motivated by popular prejudice of the masses against Christians but rather only by justice and his own wisdom; analyzing the reason for persecuting Christians in terms of the evil adversary's envy regarding the truth and virtue of Christians, just as it has always been the case over against the righteous; assessing that God allows persecution in order to test Christians on the path to perfection; and, finally, attesting that the perseverance of Christians undergoing persecution is evidence of the superiority of their faith, which cannot be suppressed by anything, not even by death.

*Editions: Apologies* (ed. A. Wartelle; Paris: Études Augustiniennes, 1987) [Com]. – *Iustini Martyris Apologiae pro Christianis* (ed. M. Marcovich; PTS 38; Berlin and New York: de Gruyter, 1994). – *Saint Justin Apologie pour les chrétiens* (ed. C. Munier; Par. 39; Fribourg, Switz.: Éditions Universitaires, 1995). – *Giustino Martire: Il primo cristiano platonico* (ed. G. Girgenti; Milan: Vita e Pensiero, 1995).

*Translations:* A. C. Coxe, trans., "The First Apology of Justin" and "The Second Apology of Justin," in *ANF* (Peabody, Mass.: Hendrisckson, 1995; repr. of 1885 ed.), 1:163–93. – *The First and Second Apologies* (trans. L. W. Barnard; ACW 56; New York: Paulist, 1997).

*Studies:* H. Chadwick, "Justin Martyr's Defense of Christianity," *BJRL* 47 (1965): 275–97; repr. in *The Early Church in Greco-Roman Thought* (ed. E. Ferguson; SEC 8; New York: Garland, 1993), 23–45. – L. Alfonsi, "La struttura della l' *'Apologia'* di Giustino," in *Paradoxos politeia: Studi patristici in onore Giuseppe Lazzati* (ed. R. Cantalamessa and L. F. Pizzolato; SPMed 10; Milan: Vita e Pensiero,1979), 57–76. – C. Saldanha, *Divine Pedagogy: A Patristic View of Non-Christian Religions* (BSRel 57; Paris: LAS, 1984), 39–73. – C. Munier, "À propos des Apologies de Justin," *RevScRel* 61 (1987): 177–86. – C. Munier, "La méthode apologétique de Justin le Martyr," *RevScRel* 62 (1988): 90–100, 227–39. – G. W. Latrop, "Justin, Eucharist, and 'Sacrifice': A Case of Metaphor," *Worship* 64 (1990): 30–48. – S. A. Panimolle, "Storicità e umanità del Cristo nelle *Apologie* di S. Giustino Martire," *RivB* 38 (1990): 191–223. – A. J. Guerra, "The Conversion of Marcus Aurelius and Justin Martyr: The Purpose, Genre, and Content of the First Apology," *SecCent* 9 (1992): 129–87. – C. Munier, *L'Apologie de saint Justin philosophe et martyr* (Par. 38; Fribourg, Switz.: Éditions Universitaires, 1994).

## 3. Dialogue with Trypho

The *Dialogue with Trypho* is the oldest extant anti-Jewish apology; the introduction and a considerable part of ch. 74, however, are lost. This work must have been written after the apologias, since ch. 120 cites the *First Apology*. The dialogue reports a two-day conversation between Justin and an educated Jew by the name of Trypho. Its literary model was provided by the Platonic dialogues; therefore the work should not be understood as a literal record but rather as a literarily shaped record of the conversation.

The dialogue comprises 142 chapters. In the introduction (2–8), Justin reports autobiographically about his education and conversion. The first major part (9–47) explains the OT from the Christian perspective. The validity of the Mosaic law was temporally limited whereas Christianity presents the new and eternal law of humanity as a whole. The second major part (48–108) justifies revering Christ as God; the third part (109–142) shows that the nations believing in Christ and observing his law represent the new Israel and the true, chosen people of God.

Contentwise the development of the dialogue differs from that of the apologias because the addressees are different, though in terms of method it essentially conforms. Whereas Justin justifies the novelty of Christianity over against Gentiles by pointing to a progressive revelation of God—in general among the philosophers but specially in Christ—in the case of the Jews, he is able to build upon a much more concrete continuity, the same God's preparation of the Jewish people for the coming of the Messiah. He therefore establishes his reasoning upon the OT and cites particularly the prophets in order to demonstrate how Christian truth was prepared under the old covenant.

*Editions: Diologus cum Tryphone* (ed. M. Marcovich; PTS 47; Berlin and New York: de Gruyter, 1997).

*Translations:* A. C. Coxe, trans., "Dialogue of Justin, Philosopher and Martyr, with Trypho, a Jew," in *ANF* (Peabody, Mass.: Hendrickson, 1995; repr. of 1885 ed.), 1:194–270.

*Studies:* N. Hyldahl, *Philosophie und Christentum: Eine Interpretation der Einleitung zum Dialog Justins* (ATDan 9; Copenhagen: Munksgaard, 1966). – J. C. M. van Winden,

*An Early Christian Philosopher: Justin Martyr's Dialogue with Trypho, Chapters One to Nine* (PP 1; Leiden: Brill, 1971). – J. Nilson, "To Whom Is Justin's *Dialogue with Trypho* Addressed?" *TS* 38 (1977): 538–46. – G. Otranto, "Note sull'itinerario spirituale di Giustino: Fede e cultura in 'Dialogo' 1–9," in *Crescita dell'uomo nella catechesi dei Padri (età prenicena)* (ed. S. Felici; BSRel 78; Rome: LAS, 1987), 29–39. – E. dal Covolo, "'Regno di Dio' nel Dialogo di Giustino con Trifone Giudeo," *Aug* 28 (1988): 111–23. – S. A. Panimolle, "L''ora' del Cristo nel 'Dialogo con Trifone,'" *VetChr* 27 (1990): 303–32. – S. A. Panimolle, "Storicità dell'incarnazione del Verbo e vangelo dell'infanzia nel *Dialogo con Trifone* di San Giustino," *Mar.* 52 (1990): 63–85. – S. A. Panimolle, "Il ministero pubblico di Gesù nel *Dialogo con Trifone* di Giustino," *Aug* 31 (1991): 277–307. – A. Rudolph, "*Denn wir sind jenes Volk . . .*": Die neue Gottesverehrung in Justins Dialog mit dem Juden Tryphon in historisch-theologischer Sicht (Hereditas 15; Bonn: Borengässer, 1999).

# Excursus: Dialogue as a Genre in Antiquity and Christianity

The genre of the dialogue, flourishing in both Greek and Latin literature since the classical period, was first adopted into Christian literature by the Greek apologists. The lost *Dialogue of Papiscus and Jason concerning Christ* by Ariston of Pella (ca. 140), as mentioned above, represents the first example known to us. The earliest extant example is the *Dialogue with Trypho* (150–160), just discussed; the dialogue then persists throughout the patristic era in a wide variety of forms and themes. In both the classical and the Christian eras, dialogues are hardly ever recordlike transcripts of actual conversations; if they are at all, then they are in the form of a literary adaptation. Generally the form of the fictitious dialogue served the purpose of presenting an ethical, philosophical, or historical topic more vividly and more memorably than would have been possible with the form of the treatise. The greatest examples and models of this genre, even for the Christian authors, come from the pen of Plato and Cicero.

Formwise, literary dialogues may be arranged dramatically as direct, vivid conversations. Yet the dialogue partners might also be pushed into the background when the dialogue takes on the form of a monologue in which only one person continues to speak after a vivid introductory speech and the others do not voice support until near the conclusion. The dialogue can also be based on a third-party report in which the narrative frame supports the source. Finally, the dialogue may move in the direction of a pure treatise where the audience only appears in occasionally inserted expressions of approval for an individual's presentation. In this way the dialogue approaches the diatribe, introducing an imaginary interlocutor in order to press the question in the argument ("Someone might object . . .").

Because they had to confront the mindset of their times, Christian dialogues almost exclusively follow the classical examples of Plato and Cicero, both in their form and in their philosophical and ethical thought patterns. Methodius of Olympus shaped his *Symposium* after Plato's, and Gregory of Nyssa his *Dialogue on the Soul and the Resurrection* after Plato's *Phaedo*. Minucius Felix's *Octavius* is based on Cicero's *De natura deorum,* and the influence of Cicero's

*Hortensius* on Augustine is well-known. Christianity did not continue with the biblical dialogue forms of the book of Job, the rabbinic discussions of late Judaism, or the early diatribe and dialogue forms of Acts and the NT letters.[1]

The content of the Christian dialogues developed in four forms[2]:

a. The *apologetic dialogue* addresses primarily the Jews, but also the Gentiles, to convince them of the meaning of the OT as messianic prophecy, that is, the meaningfulness of faith in Christ. This extends from Ariston and Justin on the Greek side and Minucius Felix on the Latin side to the Byzantine and medieval periods.

b. The *theological dialogue* deals mainly with intraecclesiastical problems and heterodox currents. Excellent examples of this form are the following: Origen's *Dialogue with Heraclides* (and his bishop concerning the Father, the Son, and the soul), based on an actual discussion; the *Symposium* (also called the *Banquet of the Ten Virgins* or *Concerning Virginity*) by Methodius of Olympus, aimed at the Encratites; Nestorius's *Liber Heraclidis* in defense of his Christology; and the *Eranistes* by Theodoret of Cyrus, directed against the Monophysites.

c. The *philosophical dialogue* best reflects the association with the classical dialogue. Among the most important examples are the *Dialogue on the Soul and the Resurrection* (with his sister Macrina) by Gregory of Nyssa, mentioned above; the early Cassiciacum dialogues of Augustine, namely, *Contra Academicos, De vita beata,* the *Soliloquia, De libero arbitrio;* and the *Consolatio philosophiae* by Boethius.

d. The final form to arise, for which there is no model in classical antiquity, was the *biographical dialogue*. Its aim is to shape the reading material for the lives of the saints more attractively and vividly; examples are Sulpicius Severus's *Vita* of St. Martin and the *Dialogues* of Gregory the Great on the life and miracles of the Latin saints, the second volume of which is dedicated to St. Benedict.

*Encyclopedia Articles:* A. Hermann and G. Bardy, *RAC* 3:928–55. – P. F. Beatrice, *EECh* 1:233–24.

*Studies:* M. Hoffmann, *Der Dialog bei den christlichen Schriftstellern der ersten vier Jahrhunderte* (TU 96; Berlin: Akademie, 1966). – B. R. Voss, *Der Dialog in der frühchristlichen Literatur* (STA 9; Munich: Fink, 1970). – P. Perkins, *The Gnostic Dialogue: The Early Church and the Crisis of Gnosticism* (New York: Paulist,1980).

# C. Tatian of Syria

The life of Tatian, about which we know very few details, resembled that of Justin in many ways, and the paths of the two converged. According to the autobiographical references in his apology, he was born "in the land of the Assyrians," that is, in Mesopotamia or Syria, though his upbringing was Hellenistic. After several journeys and searching for the truth among the philosophers and the mysteries, he, like Justin, came across the Bible and converted to Christianity. He spent at least the

---

[1] Otherwise, Beatrice, *EECh* 1:233.
[2] The fifth form of the biblical dialogue is not sufficiently supported. Cf. Bardy, *RAC* 3:954.

period immediately after his conversion with Justin in Rome and was regarded as his student. Together they became engaged in the debate with Crescens. After Justin's death (165) Tatian distanced himself from the Catholic Church and became a leader of Encratism (ἐγκράτεια = "abstinence"), a heretical movement with pre-Christian roots that, because of a misconstrued opposition to the world and the body, argued for rigorous asceticism. It considered especially the abstention from meat, wine, and marriage as an indispensable precondition for Christianity. Epiphanius (*Panarion* 46.1) reports that even in the celebration of the Eucharist he replaced the wine with water. When he was excommunicated in Rome (ca. 170) on account of this, he returned to his native country, where his principles were not considered heretical, and ministered in Syria, Cilicia, and Pisidia.

*Bibliography:* K.-G. Wesseling, *BBKL* 11:552–71.

## 1. *Oratio ad Graecos*

Tatian's forty-two-chapter apology, written between 155 and 170, is directed against all "Greeks," that is, the world shaped by Hellenism, their gods, their philosophy, and their culture, in order to demonstrate the superiority of Christianity. Since the Hellenistic world was convinced of the superiority of its culture over everything "barbaric," including Christianity as far as its origin was concerned, Tatian seeks to demolish this illusion in the introduction (1–3). He seeks to demonstrate that all the great achievements of which the Greeks were so proud had been borrowed from the barbarians after all: the alphabet from the Phoenicians, historiography from the Egyptians, flute playing from Marsyas, etc. Furthermore their rhetoric, poetry, and philosophy were worthless, since they had not yielded anything sublime. Chapters 4–8 present a positive depiction of God and God's creation; chs. 9–16 discuss demonology, pneumatology, psychology, and soteriology; and chs. 17–28 demonstrate the foolishness and reprehensibleness of Greek deities, medicine, theatrical plays, politics, and morality. After two autobiographical chapters (29–30), Tatian adduces the proof of age (31–41) to demonstrate that Moses was older than Homer and all of the Greek writers; for this reason, Christianity, originating from Judaism, was able to claim the originality of truth for itself. The work concludes with Tatian's call for discussion, for which he would always be ready (42).

The structure of the work is difficult to grasp in its details because it repeatedly digresses into lengthy excursuses; yet the purpose of the latter is to provide more detailed explanations on particular points in the form of "remarks." Tatian's theology is made up of a blend of ecclesiastical and heretical bodies of thought that is equally difficult to disentangle. He rejected the entire OT as the work of an evil demiurge, rather than of God the Father of Jesus Christ, and equally rejected a number of the Pauline letters.

*Editions: Oratio ad Graecos and Fragments* (ed. M. Whittaker; OECT; Oxford and New York: Clarendon, 1982) [ET]. – *Tatiani Oratio ad Graecos* (ed. M. Marcovich; PTS 43; Berlin and New York: de Gruyter, 1995).

*Translations:* J. E. Ryland, trans., "Address of Tatian to the Greeks," in *ANF* (Peabody, Mass.: Hendrickson, 1995; repr. of 1885 ed.), 2:59–83.

*Encyclopedia Articles:* F. Bolgiani, *EECh* 2:815.

*Studies:* M. Elze, *Tatian und seine Theologie* (FKDG 9; Göttingen: Vandenhoeck & Ruprecht, 1960). – H. Chadwick, "Enkrateia," *RAC* 5:352–53. – L. W. Barnard, "The Heresy of Tatian," in *Studies in Church History and Patristics* (ABla 26; Thessaloníki: Patriarchikon Hidryma Paterikōn Meletōn, 1978), 181–93. – W. L. Petersen, "Textual Evidence of Tatian's Dependence upon Justin's ΑΠΟΜΝΗΜΟΝΕΥΜΑΤΑ," *NTS* 36 (1990): 512–34. – M. McGehee, "Why Tatian Never Apologized to the Greeks," *JECS* 1 (1993): 143–58.

## 2. Diatessaron

The second work of Tatian known to us is a unifying compilation (harmony) of the four canonical gospels known as the *Diatessaron* (τὸ διὰ τεσσάρων εὐαγγέλιον). Although it may not qualify as the first such effort, it is nevertheless the most successful one and the apex of this genre, and it continued to be used liturgically in the oriental churches until the fifth century. The original form of the work is not extant, but on the basis of its extensive transmission, it is possible to reconstruct it to a large extent. The main witness in this case is an Armenian translation of a commentary on the *Diatessaron* by Ephraim of Syria, followed by Arabic, Persian, and Latin translations, Armenian and Georgian gospel texts, and various patristic citations.

Many questions concerning the *Diatessaron* have not received conclusive answers. Although the title suggests a Greek original, of which, however, only a small fragment is extant, the history of transmission more likely points to a Syriac origin. Determinination of the date of origin (before or after Tatian turned his back on the church at large) also affects the place of origin (Rome or Syria). In any case, the *Diatessaron* must have been written at a time in the history of the canon when the canon of the four gospels, while already well developed, was not yet sacrosanct. To what extent Tatian wrote the *Diatessaron* "in a certain contrast to Marcion's gospel, whose teachings he did not share by any means,"[3] calls for further examination.

This harmony of the gospels intends to offer a continuous and uniform presentation of the life of Jesus in the chronological framework of John's gospel. For this, it selects from the four gospels relatively freely; it transposes and supplements even from apocryphal sources with encratite, anti-Jewish, and docetic tendencies. Perhaps Tatian's motive was to prepare a suitably functional form of the Bible that would justify its widespread acceptance. According to Elze, his basic theological conception was the principle of the oneness of God and of the indivisible truth of Christianity. The work's significance is found in the insights it is able to provide into the earliest history of the gospel texts, despite the fact that the

---

[3] H. von Campenhausen, *Die Entstehung der christlichen Bibel* (BHTh 39; Tübingen: Mohr, 1968), 206.

problems of the various forms of transmission of the text continue to be extremely complex. Even in the Middle Ages the *Diatessaron* had an extraordinary impact, for instance, on the Dutch, Italian, Old English, and Old German harmonies of the gospels and on the *Heliand* and the *Life of Christ* by the German mystic Ludolf of Saxony (ca. 1300–1377).

*Editions:* D. Ploij, C. A. Phillips, A. H. A. Bakker, and A. J. Barnouw, *The Liège Diatessaron* (8 vols.; VAW NS 31; Amsterdam: NP, 1929–1970) [ET]. – C. H. Kraeling, *A Greek Fragment of Tatian's Diatessaron from Dura* (SD 3; London: Christophers, 1935). – L. Leloir, ed. and trans., *Saint Éphrem: Commentaire de l'évangile concordant: Version arménienne* (2vols.; CSCO 137, 145; Louvain: Durbecq, 1953–1954). – E. Sievers, *Tatian: Lateinisch und altdeutsch mit ausführlichem Glossar* (2d rev. ed.; Paderborn: Wissenschaftliche Buchgesellschaft, 1961). – L. Leloir, *Saint Éphrem, Commentaire de l'évangile concordant: Texte syriaque (manuscrit Chester Beatty 709)* (2 vols.; CMB 8; Dublin: Hodges Figgis, 1963–1990). – I. Ortiz de Urbina, *Vetus Evangelium Syrorum et exinde excerptum Diatessaron Tatiani* (BPM 6; Madrid: Consejo Superior de Investigaciones Científicas, 1967) 207–99. – J. Molitor, "Tatians Diatessaron und sein Verhältnis zur altsyrischen und altgeorgischen Überlieferung," *OrChr* 53 (1969): 1–88; 54 (1970): 1–75; 55 (1971): 1–61.

*Translations:* H. W. Hogg, trans., "The Diatessaron of Tatian," in *ANF* (Peabody, Mass.: Hendrickson, 1995; repr. of 1885 ed.), 9:33–129.

*Encyclopedia Articles:* D. Wünsch, "Evangelienharmonie," *TRE* 10:626–36. – F. Bolgiani, *EECh* 1:234. – K. Zelzer, *HLL* 4:351–52.

*Studies:* E. Preuschen, *Untersuchungen zum Diatessaron Tatians* (SHAW.PH 15; Heidelberg: Winter, 1918). – C. Peters, *Das Diatessaron Tatians: Seine Überlieferung und sein Nachwirken in Morgen- und Abendland sowie der heutige Stand seiner Erforschung* (OrChrAn 123; Rome: Pontificium Institutum Orientalium Studiorum, 1939). – L. Leloir, "Le Diatessaron de Tatien," *OrSyr* 1 (1956): 208–31, 313–35. – L. Leloir, *Doctrines et méthodes de S. Éphrem d'après son Commentaire de l'évangile concordant* (CSCO 220; Louvain: SCO, 1961). – L. Leloir, *Le témoignage d'Éphrem sur le Diatessaron* (CSCO 227; Louvain: SCO, 1962). – G. Quispel, *Tatian and the Gospel of Thomas: Studies in the History of the Western Diatessaron* (Leiden: Brill, 1975). – T. Baarda, *Early Transmission of Words of Jesus: Thomas, Tatian and the Text of the New Testament* (ed. J. Helderman and S. J. Noorda; Amsterdam: VU, 1983). – W. L. Petersen, "New Evidence for the Question of the Original Language of the Diatessaron," in *Studien zum Text und zur Ethik des Neuen Testaments: Festschrift zum 80. Geburtstag von Heinrich Greeven* (ed. W. Schrage; BNZW 47; Berlin and New York: de Gruyter, 1986), 325–43. – M.-É. Boismard and A. Lamouille, *Le Diatessaron: De Tatien à Justin* (EBib NS 15; Paris: Gabalda, 1992). – T. Baarda, *Essays on the Diatessaron* (Kampen, Neth.: Kok Pharos, 1994). – W. L. Petersen, *Tatian's Diatessaron: Its Creation, Dissemination, Significance, and History in Scholarship* (SVigChr 25; Leiden and New York: Brill, 1994).

# D. Athenagoras

Very little is known for sure about the person and life of Athenagoras, since he apparently did not make a lasting impression in antiquity. In the manuscript of his two extant works, the Arethas Codex Parisinus 451 of 914 C.E., the heading of *Legatio pro Christianis*, calls him a "philosopher from Athens," but it is not possible to establish with certainty whether this title originated in antiquity or only at the time when the codex was prepared. Another manuscript, from the fourteenth century, containing an excerpt of a work by Philip of Side (fifth century), however, reports that Athenagoras had been the first head of the Alexandrian school. Yet Philip of Side is not always considered a reliable witness. W. H. C. Frend surmises that Athenagoras may have hailed from Asia Minor.[4]

Accordingly the dating of his two extant works, *Legatio pro Christianis* ("Petition on behalf of the Christians") and *De resurrectione* ("On the Resurrection of the Dead") is debatable, as is the authenticity of the latter. Whereas there are ancient witnesses to his authorship of *Legatio pro Christianis*, the attribution of *De resurrectione* to him is made merely because at the conclusion of *Legatio* Athenagoras remarks that he wanted to postpone addressing the issue of the resurrection of the dead until a later time and because in the Arethas Codex *De resurrectione* follows with the designation "by the same." Hence in recent years there has been a renewed interest in discussing more thoroughly the question of its authenticity—a pursuit still in progress (cf. bibliography on 2 below).

*Editions: Legatio and De resurrectione* (ed. W. R. Schoedel; OECT; Oxford: Clarendon, 1972) [ET]. – *Supplique au sujet des chrétiens et Sur la résurrection des morts* (ed. B. Pouderon; SC 379; Paris: Cerf, 1992) [Com].

*Translations:* B. Pratten, trans., "A Plea for the Christians" and "The Resurrection of the Dead," in ANF (Peabody, Mass.: Hendrickson, 1995; repr. of 1885 ed.), 2:123–62. – *Embassy for the Christians; The Resurrection of the Dead* (trans. J. H. Crehan; ACW 23; Westminster, Md.: Newman, 1956).

*Encyclopedia Articles:* P. Keseling, *RAC* 1:881–88. – P. Nautin, *EECh* 1:95. – H. Stander, *EEC* 1:140–41.

*Studies:* J. L. Rauch, *Greek Logic and Philosophy and the Problem of Authorship in Athenagoras* (Chicago; University of Chicago Press, 1968). – W. R. Schoedel, "Apologetic Literature and Ambassadorial Activities," *HTR* 82 (1989): 55–78. – B. Pouderon, *Athénagore d'Athènes, philosophe chrétien* (ThH 82; Paris: Beauchesne, 1989). – B. Pouderon, *D'Athènes à Alexandrie: Études sur Athénagore et les origines de la philosophie chrétienne* (Québec: Presses de l'Université Laval; Louvain: Peeters, 1998).

# 1. *Legatio pro Christianis*

*Legatio pro Christianis*, an apology, addresses Emperor Marcus Aurelius as well as his son and coregent, Commodus, and therefore must have been written between November 27, 176 (beginning of the coregency of Commodus), and March 17, 180 (Marcus Aurelius's death). Depending on one's interpretation of the note in ch. 1 that there is peace throughout the earth, on whether one classifies *Legatio* as a writing presented in person or construes the dedication to the

---

4 W. H. C. Frend, *Martyrdom and Persecution in the Early Church: A Study of a Conflict from the Maccabees to Donatus* (Oxford: Blackwell, 1965; repr., Grand Rapids: Baker, 1981), 285f.

emperors as a merely literary convention, and on what location one accepts as Athenagoras's place of residence, the following dates deserve consideration: before the Teutonic campaign on August 3, 178; September 176 in Athens; or the winter of 175/176 in Alexandria on the occasion of the visits of Marcus Aurelius. Porta postulates that the *Legatio* of Athenagoras might have been written as a reaction to the letter of the persecuted communities of Vienne and Lyon of August 177.[5]

*Legatio pro Christianis* combats the three popular charges against Christians: atheism, incest, and cannibalism. The weight Athenagoras lends to the respective accusations can be discerned from the structure of the apology: twenty-eight chapters focus on atheism, three on incest, and two on cannibalism. The relative weight given to each charge is comprehensible if it is understood that an atheist was regarded as an enemy of the state, without regard for the quality of his behavior otherwise. Athenagoras begins with a *captatio benevolentiae* addressed to the rulers, with a description of the highly diverse religious customs in the Roman Empire, and with praise for their magnanimous tolerance and love of peace. Thereafter he explains in part 1 (4–12) that the Christian faith is not atheistic but monotheistic, a stance that had already been taken by the Greek poets and philosophers. Christianity is the now-revealed religion of this one true deity. After this argument from tradition, Athenagoras in ch. 8 adduces the so-called topological proof for God for the first time: By definition God is uncreated and indivisible. If there were a plurality of gods, all of them would have to be distinct from, and independent of, one another. Further, if the Creator of the world fills the space above and beyond his creation, there is no room left for a further, equally independent god. Consequently, Christians refuse to join in idolatry, since gods are nothing more than the work of humans— humans or natural phenomena elevated by humans to the level of deity—and since at best it is demons that are at work in them (13–30). Finally, Athenagoras brushes aside the accusations of incest and cannibalism as bursts of hatred by the depraved against the virtue of Christians (31–36).

If Athenagoras's manner of argumentation is compared with the preceding apologists, it becomes apparent that the basic methodological structure is consistent despite all of the differences in matters of detail. First of all there is the endeavor to win the emperor's favor; then it is particularly important to refute the charge of atheism by demonstrating that the Christian faith is not only reasonable but, *in nuce,* is already found in Greco-Roman philosophy (this makes skillful use of the contrast between philosophical belief in God and practical veneration of mythical deities). Once the essential acceptability of Christianity is demonstrated in this manner, all other charges are easily dismissed as the usual resentment of the depraved toward those living virtuously. In his apology Athenagoras cites a large number of ancient authors even though he probably knows most of them only secondhand. He thereby gains the attention of the educated pagan reader, who, on the level of a rational, philosophical argument, expected his counterpart to have such a philosophical and literary education.

---

[5] G. Porta, "La dedica e la data della Πρεσβεία di Atenagora," *Did* 5 (1916): 53–70.

*Editions: Legatio pro Christianis* (ed. M. Marcovich; PTS 31; Berlin and New York: de Gruyter, 1990).

*Translations: See* above.

*Studies:* A. J. Malherbe, "The Structure of Athenagoras, '*Supplicatio pro Christianis*,'" VC 23 (1969): 1–20; repr. in *Literature of the Early Church* (ed. E. Ferguson; SEC 2; New York: Garland, 1993), 107–26. – L. W. Barnard, *Athenagoras: A Study in Second Century Christian Apologetic* (ThH 18; Paris: Beauchesne, 1972). – T. D. Barnes, "The Embassy of Athenagoras," *JTS* NS 26 (1975): 111–14.

## 2. De resurrectione

Quite apart from the fact that in more recent discussions it is accepted as authentic, the second work of Athenagoras is perhaps even more significant than his apology for the modern perspective on the history of theology. He needs to defend the possibility and reasonableness of the resurrection of the dead with heart and soul against two apparently common objections of the time: that the resurrection of the dead is irrational and that the resurrection occurs only for the purpose of judgment. Against this, Athenagoras begins with the fundamental premise, presented in detail in part 2, that the purpose and goal of the creation of the human are eternal life as a complete person—that is, with soul and body. Therefore, in keeping with the destiny of all humans, if in death the mortal body is separated from the immortal soul so as to be decomposed in the ground, the resurrection necessarily has to bring together both body and soul once more (11.3–25). This is not merely reasonable but by all means possible, God-honoring, and consistent with God's will, since as the Creator he is certainly able to reunite all the elements of every decomposed body consistently with his original creation. The problem, presented very concretely, physically and materially, of what will happen with elements belonging equally to several persons—for instance, in the case of a person devoured by an animal, which in turn was consumed by humans, or in the case of cannibalism—he solves by means of a postulate, taken from the natural sciences and medicine, according to which elements of a human body can be assimilated neither by an animal nor by another human; instead they are removed unchanged (2–11.2).

We have no knowledge about the immediate consequences of this first patristic tractate on the resurrection of the dead. Nevertheless it represents the first attempt at addressing many of the questions that in subsequent centuries played a significant part in the discussion of this topic.

*Translations: See* above.

*Studies:* E. Gallicet, "Atenagora o pseudo-Atenagora?" *RFIC* 104 (1976): 420–35. – L. W. Barnard, "The Authenticity of Athenagoras' *De resurrectione*," in *Papers Presented to the Seventh International Conference on Patristic Studies Held in Oxford, 1975* (ed. E. Livingstone; StPatr 15.1; TU 128; Berlin: Akademie, 1984), 39–49. – B. Pouderon, "L'authenticité du traité sur la résurrection attribué à l'apologiste Athénagore," *VC* 40 (1986): 226–44. – B. Pouderon, "La chaine alimentaire chez Athénagore: Confrontation de sa théorie digestive avec la science médicale de son temps," *Orph.* 9 (1988):

219–37. – B. Pouderon, "Athénagore et Tertullien sur la resurrection," *REAug* 35 (1989): 209–30. – B. Pouderon, "'La chair et le sang': Encore sur l'authenticité du traité d'Athénagore," *VC* 44 (1990): 1–5. – H. E. Lona, "Die dem Apologeten Athenagoras zugeschriebene Schrift '*De resurrectione mortuorum*' und die altchristliche Auferstehungsapologetik," *Sal.* 52 (1990): 525–78. – D. T. Ruina, "*Verba philonica*, ΑΓΑΛΜΑΤΟΦΟΡΕΙΝ, and the Authenticity of the *De resurrectione* Attributed to Athenagoras," *VC* 46 (1992): 313–27. – N. Zeegers, "La paternité athénagorienne du *De resurrectione*," *RHE* 87 (1992): 333–74. – B. Pouderon, "*Apologetica*: Encore sur l'authenticité du '*De resurrectione*' d'Athénagore," *RevScRel* 67 (1993): 23–40; 68 (1994): 19–38.

# II. PASCHAL SERMON OF MELITO OF SARDIS

Because of his apologia addressed to Emperor Marcus Aurelius (161–180), Melito, the bishop of Sardis in Lydia in the second half of the second century, is held to be one of the apologists. As in the case of all his other works cited in Eusebius's *Ecclesiastical History* (4.26.1–14), however, the apologia is no longer extant, apart from a few fragments found in catenas. The list of his writings demonstrates how prolific an author he was on widely diverse theological topics. Melito became famous in 1940 when C. Bonner published the all-but-complete text of his newly discovered paschal sermon, which until then had likewise been known only through a few fragments. An ancient sermon alone would likely not have aroused such attention—the second letter of Clement contains a considerably older sermon—had it not upset a theory, commonly held for centuries, about the development of the church and its literature. On the basis of the textual evidence up to that point, it was assumed, especially in Protestantism, beginning with Luther, that the development of the state church and the intrusion of rhetoric in its proclamation signaled the beginning of the church's decline at the beginning of the fourth century. Melito's paschal sermon, however, offers an example of brilliantly stylized Asian rhetoric as early as the second century. This immediately gave rise to intense scholarly research, culminating in the 1960s and 1970s but still continuing today. The objective was not only the production of a critically secured text by filling the remaining lacunae on the basis of newly discovered texts, and its translation into modern languages with commentaries, but beyond this a detailed analysis of the language, style, and general theology of the sermon and of its relationship to other Easter sermons that are dependent on it.

Both from the sermon itself and from the sources on the somewhat later Easter controversy (Eusebius, *Hist. eccl.* 5.24.2–6),[6] it becomes apparent that Melito's community in Asia Minor celebrated Easter in keeping with the original tradition, passed on to them by the Apostle John, without regard for the day of the week on which the first new moon of spring occurred—in other words, in common with the Jews, on 14th Nisan. From the Easter controversy onward, therefore, they were called Quartodecimans. For this reason, it may be more ap-

---

[6] Cf. also ch. 2.I.C on Polycarp of Smyrna and ch. 3.IV.B.1 on Irenaeus of Lyon.

propriate to speak of the celebration of a Christian Passover festival, the primary content of which focused on the remembrance of the fulfillment of the OT Passover (Exod 12) in the suffering, death, and resurrection of Christ.

This typology is the topic of Melito's paschal sermon, delivered ca. 160–170 and composed of four parts (105 paragraphs), each of them concluding with a doxology. The terse prologue (1–10) relates first to the discourse on the reading of Exod 12 in order to laud the mystery of the old and new Passover. By paraphrasing the text, part 2 (11–45) interprets the OT Passover, highlighting the dramatic shaping of the event and the explanation of its typological meaning. Part 3 (46–65) then elucidates the foundation and preparation for Christ, the paschal sacrifice—namely, Adam's fall and the resultant proliferation of the tyrannizing rule of sin over all people, the types of Christ in history, and Israel's prophets with rules for their interpretation. Finally, the fourth and largest part (66–105) interprets the new Passover of Christ: Christ as the fulfillment of the *topoi* and his triumph in the resurrection. Christ's killing does indeed provide Melito with the occasion for an extended anti-Jewish invective (72–99), in which he vividly portrays the paradox of the murder of God on account of his good deeds, and the public sentencing of Israel.

Stylistically conspicuous and characteristic of the sermon throughout is the accumulation of stylistic means drawn from Asian rhetoric, including isocolons, chiasmi, antitheses, homoeoteleutons, paradoxes, oxymora, alliterations, anaphoras, and many others. Several attempts have been made to fit this type of style in with Jewish and classical antecedents, albeit without clear results. At present the sermon can only be described as representing a thoroughgoing, rhetorically stylized, exegetical homily with hymnic elements.

It is not appropriate to expect a festal sermon such as this to furnish a systematically constructed theology. On the basis of the feast's central mystery, however, a wealth of individual statements have already been researched in detail, such as the concept of God, the doctrine of creation, salvation history, Mariology, and exegesis.

*Bibliographies:* R. M. Mainka, "Melito von Sardes: Eine bibliographische Übersicht," *Clar.* 5 (1965): 225–55. – H. R. Drobner, "15 Jahre Forschung zu Melito von Sardes (1965–1980): Eine kritische Bibliographie," *VC* 36 (1982): 313–33. – M. Frenschkowski, *BBKL* 5:1219–23.

*Editions: Sur la Pâque* (ed. O. Perler; SC 123; Paris: Cerf, 1966). – *Homilia sobre la Pascua* (ed. J. Ibáñez Ibáñez and F. Mendoza Ruiz; BTeo 11; Pamplona: Ediciones Universidad de Navarra, 1975) [Com]. – *On Pascha and Fragments* (ed. S. G. Hall; OECT; Oxford: Clarendon, 1979) [ET].

*Translations:* B. D. Ehrman, trans., "Melito of Sardis: On the Passover," in *After the New Testament: A Reader in Early Christianity* (New York: Oxford University Press, 1999), 115–28.

*Encyclopedia Articles:* O. Perler, *DSp* 10:979–90. – A. Hamman, *EECh* 1:551. – S. G. Hall, *TRE* 22: 424–28.

*Studies:* B. Lohse, *Das Passafest der Quartadezimaner* (BFCT 2.54; Gütersloh: Bertelsmann, 1953). – P. Nautin, *Le dossier d'Hippolyte et de Méliton dans les florilèges dogmatiques et chez les historiens modernes* (Patr. 1; Paris: Cerf, 1953). – O. Perler, *Ein Hymnus zur Ostervigil von Meliton? (Papyrus Bodmer XIII)* (Par. 15; Fribourg, Switz.: Universitätsverlag, 1960). – W. Huber, *Passa und Ostern: Untersuchungen zur Osterfeier der alten Kirche* (BZNW 35; Berlin: Töpelmann, 1969). – R. L. Wilken, "Melito, the Jewish Community at Sardis, and the Sacrifice of Isaac," *TS* 37 (1976): 53–69. – I. Angerstorfer, "Melito und das Judentum" (PhD diss., Universität Regensburg, 1985). – F. Trisoglio, "Dalla Pasqua ebraica a quella cristiana in Melitone di Sardi," *Aug* 28 (1988): 151–85. – H. R. Drobner, "Der Aufbau der Paschapredigt Melitos von Sardes," *TGl* 80 (1990): 205–7. – A. Stewart-Sykes, *The Lamb's High Feast: Melito, Peri Pascha, and the Quartodeciman Paschal Liturgy at Sardis* (SVigChr 42; Leiden: Brill, 1998).

# III. ACCOUNTS OF MARTYRDOM

The writings of the martyrs emerged, from the mid-second century on, as the second literary genre of the period of persecution and as a direct result of the persecution of Christians. This genre comprises three subgroups: *acta, passiones/ martyria,* and legends. The *acta* represent documents of the legal proceedings, typically conducted before the proconsul and recorded by clerks of the court and reproducing the examination verbatim. This does not rule out that they were augmented and revised at a later time by a Christian editor. In the *passiones* and *martyria,* on the other hand, Christian writers give an account of the final days and the death of martyrs, often with a decidedly theological interpretation. The legends, although they do not lack a historical core, also contain many elements of pious fantasy. They constitute the beginning of hagiographic literature; but since they did not emerge until the fourth century, they cannot be considered here.

Generally the documents of the martyrs begin with a reference to the date, the names of the judge and the accused, and the accusation. The Christian adaptation of the setting can be seen in the characterization of individuals as "holy martyrs" and "dastardly emperor" or the qualification of the law as "unjust." The proconsul opens the hearing by establishing the identity of the accused; occasionally the latter do not divulge their civil names but instead offer only the confession *Christianus/a sum* as the only true name of a Christian. The proceedings do not discuss Christianity's content but instead seek either to prove the alleged crimes committed by Christians or to appeal to them to swear by the genius of the emperor, to offer up a supplication (*supplicatio*) for him—in short, to return to the traditional and reasonable religion of the Romans. The proconsul attempts to persuade the accused by appealing to them on account of their youth or their old age and their familial and other obligations, by promising them riches, honors, and offices, or by threatening them with torture and death. Not only is this normally unsuccessful, but the martyrs themselves take the initiative to persuade others of their Christian faith, or they threaten the judge and the audience with divine retribution. Thus the only thing remaining in the end is the confession *Christianus/a sum* and the refusal of the pagan cult, whereupon the death sentence is handed down. This takes place *ex tabella,* read from a small slate; that is, the verdict is prepared and in principle is fixed.

The *martyria* and *passiones* make use of the *acta,* but now it is a Christian author who speaks and presents the entire event—the circumstances of the arrest, the conditions in prison, the characterization of the people involved, the description of the torture and of the miracles taking place during it. He adds theological and spiritual reflection, cites the Bible, and takes pains to make clear the goal of the tradition, namely, to edify the believers and to strengthen those who later have to face martyrdom as well.

The following presentation points up a peculiar characteristic of the literary genre of the martyrdom accounts. All of the other writings of the second and third centuries can be categorized according to the various language groups and authors in keeping with their literary-historical contexts. The martyrdom accounts, however, as far as language and authorship are concerned, constitute such a uniform entity that they must be considered together.

The "pagan martyrdom accounts," so labeled by Ulrich von Wilamowitz-Moellendorff (1898), cannot be treated as equivalent to the Christian martyrdom accounts, nor are they to be considered their forerunners or their parallels in paganism. Instead they represent the extant propaganda writings on the resistance of Greek citizens in Alexandria against Roman rule, contained in twenty-two papyrus fragments dating from the first to the third century. These writings resemble Christian martyrdom accounts only to the extent that they also choose the record of court proceedings as their form and describe the resistance against the authority of the state, even to the point of death, for the sake of an ideal. For Christianity, they had further importance only insofar as Christians might have been inspired by these examples—for instance, Tertullian (e.g., *Apol.* 50.5–9), who presents non-Christian heroes as exemplary. Conversely, Justin (*2 Apol.* 10.8), Clement of Alexandria (*Strom.* 4.17.1–3), and John Chrysostom (*De sancto hieromartyre Babyla* [PG 50:543]) clearly pointed out the differences, arguing that they were indeed not martyrs on account of their faith and that their motives were radically different from those of the Christians. This type of literature therefore is more appropriately given the neutral designation *Acta Alexandrinorum.*

*Editions: Acta sanctorum quotquot toto orbe coluntur Database on CD Rom* (version 4; Cambridge and Alexandria, Va.: Chadwyck-Healey, 2002; print ed., Antwerp: Apud Joannem Mevrsium, 1643–). – H. A. Musurillo, *The Acts of the Pagan Martyrs: Acta Alexandrinorum* (Oxford: Clarendon, 1954; special ed., 2000) [ET/Com]. – H. Musurillo, *Acta Alexandrinorum: De mortibus Alexandriae nobilium fragmenta papyracea graeca* (Bibliothèque de théologie; Leipzig: Teubner, 1961). – H. Musurillo, *The Acts of the Christian Martyrs* (Oxford: Clarendon, 1972; special ed., 2000) [ET]. – G. Degli Agosti, *Martiri sotto processo: Scelta di testi tradotti e commentati* (Milan: Istituto Propaganda Libraria, 1986). – A. A. R. Bastiaensen et al., *Atti e passioni dei martiri* (2d ed.; Milan: Fondazione Lorenzo Valla, 1990) [Com].

*Translations: See* above.

*Encyclopedia Articles:* H. Leclercq, "Actes des martyrs," *DACL* 1.1:373–446. – H. Leclercq, "Martyr," *DACL* 10.2:2359–2512. – V. Saxer, "Martyr–Martyrdom III: Acts, Passions, Legends," *EECh* 1:533–35. – A. Wlosok, *HLL* 4:419–21. – E. Ferguson, "Martyrs, Martyrdom," *EEC* 2:724–28. – R. L. Williams, "Persecution," *EEC* 2:895–900.

*Studies:* H. Delehaye, *Les passions des martyrs et les genres littéraires* (2d rev. ed.; Brussels: Société des Bollandistes, 1966). – G. E. M. de Ste Croix, "Why Were the Early Christians Persecuted?" *PaP* 26 (1963): 6–38; repr. in *Church and State in the Early Church* (ed. E. Ferguson; SEC 7; New York: Garland, 1993), 16–48. – W. H. C. Frend, *Martyrdom and Persecution in the Early Church: A Study of a Conflict from the Maccabees to Donatus* (Oxford: Blackwell, 1965; repr., Grand Rapids: Baker, 1981). – G. Lanata, *Gli atti dei martiri come documenti processuali* (Milan: Giuffrè, 1973). – V. Saxer, *Bible et hagiographie: Textes et thèmes bibliques dans les actes des martyrs authentiques des premiers siècles* (Bern: Lang, 1987). – G. A. Bisbee, *Pre-Decian Acts of Martyrs and Commentarii* (HDR 22; Philadelphia: Fortress, 1988). – D. Frankfurter, "The Cult of the Martyrs in Egypt before Constantine," *VC* 48 (1994): 25–47. – A. McGowan, "Eating People: Accusations of Cannibalism against Christians in the Second Century," *JECS* 2 (1994): 413–42. – R. Cacitti, *Grande Sabato: Il contesto pasquale quartodecimano nella formazione della teologia del martirio* (SPMed 19; Milan: Vita e Pensiero, 1994). – C. Butterweck, *"Martyriumssehnsucht" in der alten Kirche? Studien zur Darstellung und Deutung frühchristlicher Martyrien* (BHTh 87; Tübingen: Mohr, 1995). – G. W. Bowersock, *Martyrdom and Rome* (Cambridge and New York: Cambridge University Press, 1995). – B. D. Shaw, "Body/Power/Identity: The Passion of the Martyrs," *JECS* 4 (1996): 269–312.

# A. Acta

## 1. Acta Justini

According to the *Chronicon paschale,* Justin suffered martyrdom in Rome in 165 (cf. I.B). According to the *Acta Justini,* he and five other men, as well as a woman, who likely were among his disciples, appeared in court before the Roman city prefect Quintus Iunius Rusticus. The shortest of the three extant recensions of the records (A) is probably to be regarded as the original one, for it presents the typical portrayal of court proceedings, introduced with references to date and names by a Christian editor and concluded with a note about the execution. At the same time he does not forget to characterize the Roman anti-Christian laws as illegal (ἄνομος) and the accused as saints. The reference to such laws, appearing later also in the prefect's reasons for his judgment, is surprising, however, since we are not aware of particular laws before Decius prescribing Christians to sacrifice to gods.

A cursory reading indicates that the examination's structure is quite simple. The prefect asks the accused, "What is your lifestyle?" "What do you teach?" "Where is your gathering place?" "Are you a Christian?" Then he threatens with a whipping and decapitation in case they do not comply with the order to render sacrifice required by imperial law. At the same time, he inquires whether the accused in fact do believe in a resurrection justifying a risk such as this. Since they respond affirmatively to every question, he pronounces the death sentence.

Behind this straightforward structure, however, both the answers of the accused and the sequence of the questions reveal implied thought patterns by both parties. Thus Justin's answer to the question concerning their lifestyle is that they lead an innocent life; hence behind the general question he suspects the popular accusation of crimes committed by Christians. On the issue of teaching, he first points out that he is conversant with all of the philosophies (which is consistent with what we know about his life) but ultimately became persuaded by the veracity of Christianity. In doing so, he presents himself as erudite as the prefect, if not superior, and at the same time declares Christianity to be the only true philosophy to which one attains when all the others have been tested and rejected. As for Justin's presentation of the essential features of Christian faith—God as the Creator of the world; Christ as the Son of God, savior of the world, and teacher of what is good; the prophets as his proclaimers—the prefect simply passes over it all without a response. Instead he immediately asks about the location where the Christians meet. Hence the issue is not a discussion of the substance of Christianity; Christians are merely to be shown as guilty of a crime. Since the prefect was unsuccessful in substantiating this on the basis of their lifestyle, the question regarding location takes aim at a punishable secret gathering of a conspiratorial kind. This is precisely how Justin responds: "It has always been public, known by and accessible to all." Thus remains the final question: "Are you a Christian?"

The prefect concludes his dialogue with Justin in this way and turns to each of the accused with the same question, albeit with the additional one of whether they had been converted (or misled) to Christianity by Justin. He thereby opens up the possibility of a retraction by the others while at the same time running the chance of a partial success in having dissuaded at least some from their superstition (*superstitio*). Since this is also unsuccessful, the investigation of each individual concludes with the essential question, "Are you a Christian?" and with the death sentence for all. The verdict, however, is not rendered on account of the *nomen christianum* but on account of the refusal to sacrifice as prescribed by the law. It thus appeals to a concrete legal basis, with the tacit assumption that a confessing Christian does not offer sacrifices. From the extant sources, however, it remains doubtful whether a law such as this in fact existed or whether it was indeed not exclusively the *nomen christianum* that was regarded to be worthy of death when it was impossible to adduce evidence of other specific crimes.

Recension B of the *Acta* expands the presentation with interpretive comments on the text. The legal codes are turned into explicit imperial orders; the prefect specifically commands the Christians to comply, and after the question about their meeting place, Justin supplements his response with a reference to the omnipresence of God. Finally, recension C shapes the *Acta* into a composite literary work. The emperor and the prefect are characterized as wicked and godless. The cruel whipping of the martyrs, with the aim of breaking their will, is described in detail. The precise date of death (June 1) is given, and their honorable burial is reported, with a concluding prayer on behalf of the martyrs. Although it has been assumed until now that recensions B and C depended on A, Bisbee recently postulated that A and B possibly originated from a common prototype; this hypothesis awaits further analysis.

*Editions: Saint Justin: Apologies* (ed. A. Wartelle; Paris: Études Augustiniennes, 1987), 226–33, 316–17 [Com]. – G. Girgenti, *Giustino Martire: Il primo cristiano platonico* (Milan: Vita e Pensiero, 1995), 147–53.

*Translations:* A. C. Coxe, trans., "The Martyrdom of the Holy Martyrs, Justin, Chariton, Charites, Paeon, and Liberianus, Who Suffered at Rome," in *ANF* (Peabody, Mass.: Hendrickson, 1995; repr. of 1885 ed.), 1:303–6. – J. Stevenson, trans., "Martyrdom of Justin and His Companions," in *A New Eusebius: Documents Illustrative of the History of the Church* (rev. ed.; London: SPCK, 1987), 32–34.

*Studies:* G. Lazzati, "Gli Atti di S. Giustino Martire," *Aev* 27 (1953): 473–97. – R. Freudenberger, "Die Acta Justini als historisches Dokument," in *Humanitas–Christianitas: Walther von Loewenich zum 65. Geburtstag* (ed. K. Beyschlag, G. Maron, and E. Wölf; Witten: Luther), 24–31. – G. A. Bisbee, "The Acts of Justin Martyr: A Form-Critical Study," *SecCent* 3 (1983): 129–57.

# 2. *Acts* of the Martyrs of Scilli

The *Acts* of the martyrs of Scilli represents the earliest extant Latin document of the ancient church. But since this is also the first document mentioning a Latin translation of the Bible, the latter precedes the former and, as far as we know, should be regarded as the earliest Latin Christian literature (cf. ch. 4.I). Scilli's exact location remains unknown, although it may be assumed that it was situated in North Africa. The date of the martyrdom, however, can be determined accurately on the basis of the introductory sentence of the *Acts:* "When Praesens, for the second time, and Claudianus were consuls, on the 16th day before the calends of August . . . ," that is, July 17, 180.

The *Acts* represents a brief, authentic court record in seventeen paragraphs and, in its form, comes close to the original proconsular records despite certain revisions. According to para. 16, seven men and five women stand trial; only two of them, Speratus and Saturninus, function as spokesmen, and six of them do not even respond during the proceedings. Since these six are not mentioned by name at the outset either (1), the question of whether their names were added later remains ultimately unresolved despite various argumentations.

In keeping with such records, the *Acts* begins with references to the date, the names of the judge and of the accused, and the issue of the trial. This is followed by a dialogue between the proconsul and the two spokesmen, exposing their diverse ways of thinking and styles of delivery in exemplary fashion, as well as the fundamental reasons for the trial. For the proconsul, Christianity is madness (*dementia*) and bad persuasion (*mala persuasio*), though apparently he does not consider it atheism. When the accused aver that they never committed injustice and were praying for the emperor's welfare, he accepts this as *religiosus* even though the true religion of the Romans simply calls for swearing by the emperor's genius and offering up a sacrifice of supplication (*supplicatio*) on his behalf. The contrasting views of the parties are continued in the concepts of the *mysterium simplicitatis* = sacrifice to the emperor vs. Christianity; *imperium* = empire vs. kingdom of heaven; *mala persuasio* = Christianity vs. murder and perjury; *honor* and *timor* to the emperor vs. *honor* to the emperor but *timor* only to God. Typical of the structure of the trial is the proconsul's singular goal to dissuade the Christians in order to "bring them to their senses" (*ad bonam mentem redire*) while not engaging them in a content-related discussion. In the final analysis, the trial boils down to the Christians' confession, their perseverance in their faith (*Christianus/ a sum*). A time to reconsider is rejected, the death sentence by beheading is read from a slate (*ex tabella*), and the condemned give thanks to God for it. The Christian editor of the *Acts* then adds (17) the execution: "And they were beheaded at once for the sake of the name of Christ. Amen."

*Editions:* F. Corsaro, "Note sugli '*Acta martyrum scillitanorum*,'" *NDid* 6 (1956): 5–51 [Com]. – F. Ruggiero, ed., *Atti dei martiri scilitani* (AANL.M 9.1.2; Rome: Accademia Nazionale di Lincei, 1991) [Com].

*Translations:* A. Rutherfurd, trans., "The Passion of the Scillitan Martyrs," in *ANF* (Peabody, Mass.: Hendrickson, 1995; repr. of 1887 ed.), 9:281–85. – J. Stevenson, trans., "The Martyrs of Scilli in Africa Proconularis, 17 July 180," in *A New Eusebius: Documents Illustrative of the History of the Church to 337* (rev. ed.; London: SPCK, 1987), 44–45. – B. D. Ehrman, trans., "The Acts of the Scillian Martyrs," in *After the New Testament: A Reader in Early Christianity* (New York: Oxford University Press, 1999), 41–42.

*Encyclopedia Articles:* H. Leclercq, *DACL* 15.1:1014–21. – V. Saxer, *EECh* 2:762. – A. Wlosok, *HLL* 4:422–23.

*Studies:* H. Karpp, "Die Zahl der scilitanischen Märtyrer," *VC* 15 (1961): 165–72. – H. A. Gärtner, "Die *Acta Scillitanorum* in literarischer Interpretation," *WSt* 102 (1989): 149–67.

## 3. Acta Cypriani

The records of the trial of Bishop Cyprian of Carthage are composed of two parts, reporting two different hearings and judgments. In an edict of August 257 Emperor Valerian had prohibited any Christian gathering, even in cemeteries, and ordered the exile of the bishops in order to break the solidarity of the Christians and rob them of leadership. The initial paragraph (1) establishes the trial of Cyprian by the proconsul Aspasius Paternus of Carthage on August 30, 257. This first part of the records does not appear to have undergone any tampering by an editor. In typical fashion, it begins by noting the date, the people involved, and the reason for the proceedings. This is followed by the proconsul's question of whether Cyprian persists in Christianity, the latter's response, *Christianus sum*, and the sentence of exile to Curubis, a town on the North African coast near Cyrenaica. This is preceded exceptionally by an appeal to Cyprian to hand over the names of his presbyters, which he, of course, refuses.

A second edict by Valerian, issued in July 258, intensified the order to execute bishops, priests, and deacons immediately, whereupon the new proconsul of Carthage, Galerius Maximus, ordered the recall of Cyprian from exile. The trial took place on September 14, 258, on an estate where the proconsul was vacationing. This second part of the records is replete with linking and explanatory terms by the Christian editor, who describes the recall first (2.1–3.2). The trial commences with the usual notation of the identity of the accused, followed by the proconsul's order for Cyprian to render sacrifice in accordance with the imperial decree, which Cyprian rejects. After a further appeal and rejection, the verdict is handed down, the rationale for which is instructive—sacrilege, conspiracy with criminals, enmity to the Roman deities, and consequently a "dastardly crime" (*nequissimum crimen*), to be punished with beheading (3.3–4). The editor concludes with the account of Cyprian's martyrdom.

*Editions:* S. *Thasci Caecili Cypriani Opera omnia* (ed. G. Hartel; 3 vols.; CSEL 3; 3 vols.; Vienna: Apud C. Geroldi Filium, 1871), 3:110–14.

*Translations:* E. Wallis, trans., "The Life and Passion of Cyprian, Bishop and Martyr," in *ANF* (Peabody, Mass.: Hendrickson, 1995; repr. of 1885 ed.), 5:267–74.

*Encyclopedia Articles:* V. Saxer, *EECh* 1:212. – A. Wlosok, *HLL* 4:426–27.

*Studies:* R. Reitzenstein, *Die Nachrichten über den Tod Cyprians: Ein philologischer Beitrag zur Geschichte der Märtyrerliteratur* (SHAW.PH; Heidelberg: Winter, 1913). – P. Corssen, "Das Martyrium des Bischofs Cyprian," *ZNW* 15 (1914): 221–33, 285– 316; 16 (1915): 54–92, 198–230; 17 (1916): 189–206; 18 (1917–1918): 118–39, 202–23, 249–72. – J. Martin, "Die *Vita et passio Cypriani*," *HJ* 39 (1918–1919): 674–712. – R. Reitzenstein, *Nachträge zu den Akten Cyprians* (vol. 2 of *Bemerkungen zur Märtyrienliteratur;* NGWG.PH; Göttingen; 1916–1919), 177–219. – H. Montgomery, "Saint Cyprian's Postponed Martyrdom: A Study of Motives," *SO* 63 (1988): 123–32. – W. Wischmeyer, "Der Bischof im Prozess: Cyprian als *episcopus, patronus, advocatus,* und *martyr* vor dem Prokonsul," in *Fructus centesimus: Mélanges offerts à Gerard J. M. Barelink à l'occasion de son soixante-cinquième anniversaire* (ed. A. A. R. Bastiaensen, A. Hilhorst, and C. H. Knepkens; IP 23; Steenbrugge, Belg.: Abbatia Sancti Petri, 1989), 363–71. – W. Wischmeyer, "*Cyprianus episcopus 2:* Der 2. Teil der *Acta Cypriani*," in *Eulogia: Mélanges offerts à Antoon A. R. Bastiaensen à l'occasion de son soixante-cinquième anniversaire* (ed. G. J. M. Bartelink; IP 24; Steenbrugge, Belg.: Abbatia Sancti Petri, 1991), 407–19. – C. Bobertz, "An Analysis of *Vita Cypriani* 3.6–10 and the Attribution of *Ad Quirinum* to Cyprian of Carthage," *VC* 46 (1992): 112–28.

# B. Martyria *and* Passiones

## 1. *Martyrdom of Polycarp*

The date of the death of Bishop Polycarp of Smyrna cannot be established precisely from the references in the account of his martyrdom (cf. ch. 2.I.C). The account is addressed, in the form of a letter, from the church of Smyrna to the church in Philomelium and beyond that generally to all the Christian churches. The reference to the subject matter of the account (1) ushers directly into the theological purpose and method of the presentation: Polycarp's martyrdom mirrors his discipleship of Christ according to the gospel, in order to encourage others to imitate it. This is followed by a eulogy in praise of the martyrs who brave torture, threats, admonitions, and promises intended to move them to recant (2–3), but also frightening examples of Christians who left the faith during persecution (4).

Polycarp's martyrdom is highlighted against this backdrop. Upon the request of his community, he withdraws to an estate outside the city and even changes his location again in order to remain close to the church. Under torture a slave betrays him, and a troop of soldiers is sent to arrest him. In this situation Polycarp shows himself to be a courteous host to his enemies, serves them a meal, and withdraws to pray for two hours. While still on the way to the amphitheater, the captain of police seeks to persuade him to recant, unsuccessfully, of course (5–8).

When he enters the stadium, a voice from heaven encourages him, and the trial unfolds following the customary pattern. The proconsul asks for his name, attempts to persuade him to denial "using the customary means," and finally commands him to swear by the genius of the emperor (9). The response given is equally customary, namely, *Christianus sum,* linked with an offer to instruct the proconsul in the faith (10). Not only do the further threats of torture and death remain ineffective, Polycarp turns them upon the prosecutor, threatening him with the eternal fire of hell (11). Then Gentiles and Jews prepare the pyre, but because the flames do not consume Polycarp, a *confector* (executioner) stabs him (12–16). On the instigation of the Jews, his body is burnt to ashes, but the Christians reverently inter his remains (17–18). The conclusion of the letter echoes the beginning with praise for the martyr and with an appeal for imitation (*imitatio*) of him (19–20).

Conzelmann, as von Campenhausen before him, has attributed the dating and the prayer (21–22) that follow to the so-called "gospel editor." According to this view, the initial account dealt with twelve martyrs, in which the *Martyrium Polycarpi* merely represented the climax. The editor has focused on Polycarp and shaped the work in keeping with his own theological conception, conforming it to the *imitatio Christi* of the gospels. Conversely, Dehandschutter, with whom Buschmann concurs, argues for the redactional unity of the entire text, with para. 21 representing a relatively early supplement.

The typical elements of martyrdom accounts can be recognized in Polycarp's conduct, in the miraculous events associated with his martyrdom, and in the theological and spiritual interpretation of the events. The strongly anti-Jewish note, however, has to be considered as extraordinary; elsewhere this occurs only in the martyrdom of Pionius.

*Editions:* A. Lindemann and H. Paulsen, eds., *Die apostolischen Väter: Griechisch-deutsche Parallelausgabe* (Tübingen: Mohr, 1992), 258–85. – *Cartas* (ed. J. J. Ayán Calvo; 2d ed.; FP 1; Madrid: Ciudad Nueva, 1999), 231–75 [Com].

*Translations:* A. C. Coxe, trans., "The Encyclical Epistle of the Church at Smyrna concerning the Martyrdom of the Holy Polycarp," in *ANF* (Peabody, Mass.: Hendrickson, 1995; repr. of 1885 ed.), 1:37–44. – *The Apostolic Fathers* (trans. F. X. Glimm, J. M.-F. Marique, and G. G. Walsh; FC 1; Washington, D.C.: Catholic University of America Press, 1947; repr., 1969), 145–63. – *The Didache, The Epistle of Barnabas, The Epistles and the Martyrdom of St. Polycarp, The Fragments of Papias, The Epistle to Diognetus* (trans. J. A. Kleist; ACW 6; Westminster, Md.: Newman, 1948), 83–102, 197–204. – M. Staniforth, *Early Christian Writings: The Apostolic Fathers* (rev. A. Louth; London and New York: Penguin, 1987), 125–35. – B. D. Ehrman, *After the New Testament: A Reader in Early Christianity* (New York: Oxford University Press, 1999), 30–35.

*Studies:* H. von Campenhausen, *Bearbeitungen und Interpolationen des Polykarpmartyriums* (SHAW 1957.3; Heidelberg: Winter, 1957). – H. Conzelmann, *Bemerkungen zum Martyrium Polykarps* (NAWG.PH 1978.2: Göttingen: Vandenhoeck & Ruprecht, 1978), 42–58. – B. Dehandschutter, *Martyrium Polycarpi: Een literar-kritische studie* (BETL 52; Louvain: Universitaire Pers Leuven, 1979). – P. Brind' Amour, "La date du martyre de saint Polycarpe (le 23 février 167)," *AnBoll* 98 (1980): 456–62. – S. Ronchey, *Indagine sul martirio di San Policarpo: Critica storica e fortuna agiografica di un caso giudiziario in Asia Minore* (Rome: Nella Sede dell'Istituto Palazzo Borromini, 1991). – B. Dehandschutter, "The Martyrium Polycarpi: A Century of Research," *ANRW* 2.27.1:485–522. – G. Buschmann, *Martyrium Polycarpi—eine formkritische Studie: Ein Beitrag zur Frage nach der Entstehung der Gattung Märtyrerakte* (BZNW 70; Berlin and New York: de Gruyter, 1994).

## 2. Letter of the Churches of Vienne and Lyon

Ten years after Polycarp's death, we hear of a persecution of Christians in the Gallic churches of Vienne and Lugdunum (modern Lyon) from a letter that is preserved in Eusebius's *Ecclesiastical History* (5.1.3–2.8) and that they addressed to the "brothers in Asia and Phrygia." Presumably, the latter represent their mother churches, since evidently many members of these communities migrated from Asia Minor.

The letter begins with the usual prescript (1.3) and then provides an account of the general prohibition, which preceded the persecution, for the Christian community to assemble (1.4–5). The presentation of the martyrdoms per se, which lasted from early April until August 3, 177, according to Audin, interprets them, first of all, as combat against the devil (1.6). Then follows the badgering by the tumultuous mob, the interrogation by the magistrate in the forum, the martyrs' confession, and their being threatened with instruments of torture (1.7–10). The accused are then imprisoned and await the arrival of the governor to commence the trial. The accusation refers to atheism and failure to venerate the gods (ἄθεος, ἀσεβής). Some thereupon fall away, and some pagan slaves of Christian masters even bear false witness to the popular suspicions against Christians, namely, Oedipal marriages and Thyestean feasts.[7] The editor comments on this by citing John 16:2, "a time is coming when anyone who kills you will think he is offering a service to God" (1.11–15).

The sections in 1.16–63 recount the martyrdom of the four central figures, namely, Sanctus of Vienne, the deacon; Maturus, the neophyte; Attalus and Blandina; and a number of not explicitly named fellow sufferers. All of them confess their faith and for this reason are subjected to the most gruesome kinds of torture for days, intended to elicit a renunciation, that is, an admission of their crime. Many of them die in prison after this torture, among them Photinus, the

---

[7] Referring to the Greek myths of Oedipus, who married his mother, and of Thyestes, who ate his own children.

bishop of Lyon, who is more than ninety years old. Others, however, are miraculously healed, and apostates are reconverted because of the steadfast witness of the martyrs and because they are not faring any better, despite their renunciation, for now they are to be punished for the crimes with which Christians are generally charged. The editor interprets all of these events on the basis of the Bible and with theological reflections concerning the purpose and value of martyrdom as the predicted persecutions of the apocalyptic beast. Finally, the sentence of beheading is handed down and carried out without delay. Yet even the martyrs' corpses are not left in peace. They are not buried but left to be devoured by dogs; the remains are burned and their ashes scattered on the Rhone so as to destroy the Christian hope of the resurrection.

The letter concludes with a brief section on the situation after the end of the persecution (2.1–8). Those who survived categorically decline the honorable designation of "martyr," since it was only to be attributed to Christ and those who died as martyrs; the survivors wish to be known only as *confessores* (ὁμόλογοι)—a distinction that became established at this point. At the same time, they demonstrate compassion with those who weakened, and they pray for them. This course of events was to become significant in later persecutions, especially the one under Decius in 250/251, when the suffering of the *confessores* was placed on the scales as vicarious atonement, as it were, for the apostasy of others. The latter implications especially point to a possible revision of the letter (which, on the whole, is to be considered authentic) during the persecution under Emperor Decius, with the purpose of strengthening Christians in their current trials.

*Editions:* M. J. Routh, ed., *Reliquiae sacrae* (5 vols.; rev. ed.; Oxford: E Typographeo Academico, 1846–1848; repr., Hildesheim and New York: Olms, 1974), 1:285–371 [Com]. – Knopf, Krüger, and Ruhbach, 18–28. – *The Acts of the Christian Martyrs* (ed. and trans. H. Musurillo; Oxford and New York: Oxford University Press, 2000), 60–85.

*Translation:* J. Stevenson, trans., "The Martyrs of Lyons and Vienne, 177," in *A New Eusebius: Documents Illustrative of the History of the Church* (rev. ed.; London: SPCK, 1987), 34–44. – B. D. Ehrman, trans., "The Letter of the Churches of Vienne and Lyons," in *After the New Testament: A Reader in Early Christianity* (New York: Oxford University Press, 1999), 35–41.

*Encyclopedia Articles:* P. Nautin, "Letter of the Church of Lyons and Vienne," *EECh* 1:483–84. – V. Saxer, "Lyons," *EECh* 1:512–13. – C. Pietri, "Vienne," *EECh* 2:869.

*Studies:* A. Chagny, *Les martyrs de Lyon de 177* (Lyon: Vitte, 1936). – E. Griffe, *Des origines chrétiennes à la fin du IVe siècle* (vol. 1 of *La Gaule chrétienne à l'époque romaine;* rev. ed.; Paris: Letouzey & Ané, 1964). – J. Colin, *L'empire des Antonins et les martyrs gaulois de 177* (Ant. 1.10; Bonn: R. Habelt, 1964). – A. Audin, "Les martyrs de 177," *CH* 11 (1966): 343–67. – *Les martyrs de Lyon (177): Colloque international du Centre nationale de la recherche scientifique, Lyon, 20–23 septembre 1977* (Paris: C.N.R.S., 1978). – C. Saumagne and M. Meslin, "De la légalité du procès de Lyon de l'année 177," *ANRW* 2.23.1:316–39. – W. A. Löhr, "Der Brief der Gemeinden von Lyon und Vienne (Eusebius, h. e. V,1–2[4])," in *Oecumenica et patristica: Festschrift für Wilhelm Schneemelcher zum 75. Geburtstag* (ed. D. Papandreou et al.; Stuttgart: Kohlhammer, 1989), 135–49.

## 3. *Passio Perpetuae et Felicitatis*

Perhaps the most moving and, for the subsequent centuries, most exemplary document of martyrdom is encountered in the *Passio Perpetuae et Felicitatis* (*Passion of Perpetua and Felicitas*), which, in terms of form, also became the archetype of all later martyrdom accounts. This is also the reason for the widespread veneration of these saints, so that even today their names are associated with the Roman eucharistic prayer. The *Passio* tells about the martyrdom of Vibia Perpetua, a young woman twenty-two years of age from a noble family of the North African city of Thuburbo; of her young, very pregnant slave Felicitas, who is a catechumen; of the slave Revocatus, also a catechumen; and of two men, Saturus and Secundulus. On the basis of the references in the *Passio* (7), they suffered martyrdom *in natali Getae Caesaris,* which does not refer to the day of his accession, according to general opinion, but to the emperor's birthday. Traditionally it is assumed that the year was 203.

The *Passio Perpetuae et Felicitatis* represents an extraordinary piece of literature, for in its twenty-one sections it combines the account of the martyrs with Perpetua's and Saturus's own words, as well as with apocalyptic elements very reminiscent of John and the Shepherd of Hermas. In the introduction the editor first provides a reflection on martyrdom; the vocabulary has affinities with Montanism, with the resultant suspicion that Tertullian might perhaps have been the author (1). The examples of the earlier martyrs certainly had their importance in attesting to the grace of God and to the upbuilding of the faithful; but the new work of the Spirit, the new prophecies and visions have to be considered as more significant ("new prophecy" is what Montanism is called [cf. IV.A.3]). This is followed by a factual introduction providing the names and familial circumstances of the martyrs (2), then by the first major section (3–10), containing Perpetua's autobiographical, first-person account.

The external events of her father's threefold, futile attempt at persuading her to turn back, the trial at the forum, her Christian confession, and the death sentence *ad bestias* remain in their customary framework. The three visions Perpetua had in prison, however, are quite strange and extraordinary: In vision 1, there is a Jacob's ladder, at the foot of which a dragon seeks to deter everyone from ascending. But following Saturus, Perpetua ascends without fear by using even the dragon's head as the lowest rung and enters into a (paradise-like) garden, where she is received by a shepherd (Christ/angel—cf. Shepherd of Hermas [ch. 1.IV.B]), who offers her sweet milk (milk and honey of the baptismal liturgy). From this she concludes that she will be following Saturus in suffering martyrdom and standing the test. In vision 2, she sees her brother Dinocrates, who died of cancer at the age of seven, suffer agony and prays for him daily, with the result that he appears healed and delivered. On the day before her martyrdom, she sees herself entangled with the devil in a victorious fistfight in the amphitheater; she takes this as a sign of her victorious martyrdom (3). Sections 11–13 contain similar heavenly visions of Saturus, who in his own words speaks of encounters with martyrs who died earlier. Section 14 concludes the framework of the visions. In sections 15–21 the editor concludes his account of the martyrdom of the saints by appealing to Perpetua's explicit mandate to do so. In answer to her prayer, Felicitas gives birth prematurely in the eighth month so as not to be excluded from martyrdom. The martyrs are threatened and whipped, are thrown to wild animals, which frequently do not touch them, and finally die by the sword. The death of Saturus, before whom all of the animals recoil until he calls for a panther that tears him apart and who dips a ring in his own blood while dying and hands it to a soldier in memory of him—all this Cardinal Nicholas Wiseman took up over a century ago as the model of Pancratius, the hero of his popular work *Fabiola: or, The Church of the Catacombs*, which was translated into many languages. As a result, this martyrdom account was (incorrectly) transferred to the Roman martyr Pancratius during the persecution under Diocletian; Pancratius therefore has been depicted since then with a panther at his feet.

*Editions:* J. A. Robinson, *The Passion of S. Perpetua, Together with an Appendix Containing the Original Latin Text of the Scillitan Martyrdom* (TS 1.2; Cambridge: Cambridge University Press, 1891; repr., Nendeln, Liechtenstein: Kraus Reprint, 1967) [Com]. – *La Passio SS. Perpetuae et Felicitatis* (ed. P. Franchi de' Cavalieri; RQ.S 5; Rome: In commission der Herder'schen Verlagshandlung zu Freiburg im Breisgau und der Buchhandlung Spithöver zu Rome, 1896); repr. in P. Franchi de' Cavalieri, *Scritti agiografici* (StT 221; Vatican City: Biblioteca Apostolica Vaticana, 1962–), 1:41–155 [*Index verborum*]. – C. I. M. I. van Beek, *Passio Sanctarum Perpetuae et Felicitatis* (Nijmegen: Dekker & van de Vegt, 1936–), vol. 1 [*Index verborum*]. – *Passion de Perpétue et de Félicité* (ed. J. Amat; SC 417; Paris: Cerf, 1996).

*Translations:* B. D. Ehrman, trans., "The Martyrdom of Perpetua and Felicitas," in *After the New Testament: A Reader in Early Christianity* (New York: Oxford Universtiy Press, 1999), 42–50.

*Encyclopedia Articles:* E. Romero Pose, *EECh* 2:670–71. – A. Wlosok, *HLL* 4:423–26.

*Studies:* A. H. Salonius, *Passio S. Perpetuae: Kritische Bemerkungen mit besonderer Berücksichtigung der griechisch-lateinischen Überlieferung des Textes* (Helsinki: Centraltryckeri och Bokbinderi Aktiebolag, 1921). – E. Corsini, "Proposte per una lettura della '*Passio Perpetuae*,'" in *Forma futuri: Studi in onore Cardinale Michele Pellegrino* (Turin: Bottega d'Erasmo, 1975), 481–541. – R. Braun, "Nouvelles observations linguistiques sur le rédacteur de la *Passio Perpetuae*," *VC* 33 (1979): 105–77. – L. F. Pizzolato, "Note alla *Passio Perpetuae et Felicitatis*," *VC* 34 (1980): 105–19. – M. A. Rossi, "The Passion of St. Perpetua: Everywoman of Late Antiquity," in *Pagan and Christian Anxiety: A Response to E. R. Dodds* (ed. R. C. Smith and J. Lounibos; Lanham, Md.: University Press of America, 1984), 53–86. – A. Pettersen, "Perpetua, Prisoner of Conscience," *VC* 41 (1987): 139–53. – J. Amat, "L'authenticité des songes de la Passion de Perpétue et de Félicité," *Aug* 29 (1989): 177–91. – J. W. Halporn, "Literary History and Generic Expectations in the *Passio* and *Acta Perpetuae*," *VC* 45 (1991): 223–41. – P. Habermehl, *Perpetua und der Ägypter, oder Bilder des Bösen im frühen afrikanischen Christentum: Ein Versuch zur Passio Sanctarum Perpetuae et Felicitatis* (TU 140; Berlin: Akademie, 1992). – C. M. Robeck, *Prophecy in Carthage: Perpetua, Tertullian, Cyprian* (Cleveland, Ohio: Pilgrim, 1992). – B. D. Shaw, "The Passion of Perpetua," *PaP* 139 (1993): 3–45. – J. E. Salisbury, *Perpetua's Passion: The Death and Memory of a Young Roman Woman* (New York: Routledge, 1997).

# IV. HERETICAL AND ANTIHERETICAL LITERATURE

## Introduction: Orthodoxy and Heresy in the Early Church

From a later, orthodox perspective, a heresy (αἵρεσις = "selection," "choice") is based on a selectively accepted article of faith, either by giving it a one-sided bias or by radically overstating it. This may occur in the form of a progression, that is, by developing new theologoumena, or in the form of a retrogression, by stubbornly holding on to antiquated expressions that have meantime undergone further development. In its historical development, of course, heresy arises in the same way orthodox theology does, namely, by endeavoring to discover and interpret as precisely and accurately as possible the content of faith that has been handed down, with the goal of grasping faith better and more adequately and thus rising ever more to the challenge of following Christ in one's life. In the final analysis, the factual distinction between heresy and orthodoxy is that in the case of heresy, either indispensable doctrinal principles are jeopardized, if not jettisoned, or such jeopardy is the consequence of heresy. The early church's difficulty in determining this was that both the criteria for separating heresy from orthodoxy and the clear awareness of the appropriate authority to make such decisions developed only during the respective debates themselves. The criterion—to express this from a finally clarified Catholic perspective—is the *regula fidei*, that is, the content of faith established in Scripture, handed down by the tradition of the church, and approved by it. The further question of who ultimately determines the authentic interpretation and approval leads to the authority of the office of Peter, not in the sense of a ruling's arbitrariness, but in the unity and consensus of the sister churches with the church of Rome. This is particularly applicable to the ancient church, in which a theology of primacy was still developing. Of course, during the early centuries, the recognition and theological appraisal of this systematic definition emerged only gradually. Indeed the latter is itself part of the controversies about orthodoxy and heresy.

*Encyclopedia Articles:* H. D. Betz, A. Schindler, and W. Huber, *TRE* 14:313–48. – N. Brox, *RAC* 13:248–97. – V. Grossi, *EECh* 1:376–77.

*Collections of Essays:* n.a., "Eresia ed eresiologia nella Chiesa antica," *Aug* 25 (1985): 579–903.

*Studies:* A. Hilgenfeld, *Die Ketzergeschichte des Urchristentums urkundlich dargestellt* (Leipzig: Fues, 1887). – J. Brosch, *Das Wesen der Häresie* (GFTP 2; Bonn: P. Hanstein, 1936). – H. E. W. Turner, *The Pattern of Christian Truth: A Study in the Relations between Orthodoxy and Heresy in the Early Church* (London: Mowbray, 1954; repr., New York: AMS, 1978). – W. Bauer, *Orthodoxy and Heresy in Earliest Christianity* (ed. R. A. Kraft and G. Krodel; Philadelphia: Fortress, 1971; repr., Mifflintown, Pa.: Sigler, 1996). – M. Elze, "Häresie und Einheit der Kirche im 2. Jahrhundert," *ZTK* 71 (1974): 389–409. – A. Le Boulluec, *La notion d'hérésie dans la littérature grecque, IIe–IIIe siècles* (2 vols.; Paris: Études Augustiniennes, 1985). – T. A. Robinson, *The Bauer Thesis Examined: The Geography of Heresy in the Early Christian Church* (Lewiston, N.Y.: Mellen, 1988). – R. M. Grant, *Heresy and Criticism: The Search for Authenticity in*

Early Christian Literature (Louisville: Westminster John Knox, 1993). – M. Simonetti, Ortodossia ed eresia tra I e II secolo (Messina: Rubbettino, 1994). – G. Lüdemann, Heretics: The Other Side of Early Christianity (trans. J. Bowden; Louisville: Westminster John Knox, 1996).

# A. Heretical Currents

## 1. Gnosticism

The most powerful, most ominous, and, as far as its proclamation is concerned, most attractive movement with which the church of the second and third centuries had to deal was called "gnosis" (γνῶσις = "knowledge"), and it appeared in multiple and very diverse systems. Fundamentally this was a soteriology incorporating more ancient elements and competing with Christianity; its primary focus was the explanation of evil in the world, the situation of the human in the world, and the possibility of a human's redemption. It assumed an unknown, altogether transcendent God who had no immediate involvement with the creation. The world was created by a demiurge who separated himself from the true God in a prehistoric fall and who is to be identified as the God of the OT. The world he created, therefore, was intrinsically evil. As far as a human's true nature was concerned, however, he shared the nature of the true God, but the divine spark in him had become subjected to the demiurge because he was closely attached to the world by means of his physical body. For this reason, the yearning and goal of the human are to be freed from matter and to return to the true God, which could only be attained by knowledge and was reserved for the elect. Since Christ is not responsible for evil in the world, he does not redeem the human from sin through his death on the cross but in his gospel merely revealed the knowledge necessary for a person's redemption.

As straightforwardly as this traces the essential features of the many and diverse gnostic systems, further investigation proves comparatively difficult because of the scarcity of sources. Given the fact that the gnostic apocryphal writings were the primary reason for delimiting the sacred writings of Christianity and that an existential threat for the Catholic Church began with Gnosticism, it is understandable that the church in the following period almost completely stopped the transmission of gnostic writings. Consequently, until the middle of the twentieth century, the only understanding of Gnosticism we had came from the accounts and citations of the apologetic writings of the church fathers, namely, Irenaeus, Hippolytus, Clement of Alexandria, Tertullian, and Epiphanius, and always with the proviso of their conscious or unconscious falsification because of their opposing view.

### a. Gnostic Library of Nag Hammadi
When in 1948 Henri-Charles Puech and Jean Doresse informed the public of the discovery of a substantial gnostic library in Egypt, this turned out to be a

scholarly sensation of the time. In December 1945 fellah Mohammed Ali es-Samman, together with two of his younger brothers, found a clay jar with thirteen Coptic papyrus codices in the vicinity of Nag Hammadi (ca. 60 miles north of Luxor). They sold it in Cairo, where today codices 2–13 are held in the Coptic museum. In 1952 codex 1 was sold to the C. G. Jung Institute in Zurich, hence its name, Codex Jung.

The codices, which are very well, if not completely, preserved, are dated from the fourth century, even though the works collected in them are older throughout. These comprise fifty-two mostly Greek gnostic writings in Coptic translation—gospels, acts, dialogues, apocalypses, wisdom books, letters, and sermons, the titles of which do not always agree with the actual literary genres of the texts, however. The two most significant works are the *Gospel of Truth* and the Coptic *Gospel of Thomas* (cf. ch. 1.I.C). Their unique significance for a first-time, firsthand, more in-depth understanding immediately led to lively scholarly investigation. Since then critical editions, translations, and scholarly assessments of the texts have progressed significantly, but they are yet to be completed. The Nag Hammadi writings have broadened our knowledge of Gnosticism considerably and, among other things, have confirmed the reliability of Irenaeus, even if the missing original documents remain irreplaceable.

*Bibliographies:* D. M. Scholer, *Nag Hammadi Bibliography, 1948–1969* (NHS 1; Leiden: Brill, 1971). – D. M. Scholer, *Nag Hammadi Bibliography, 1970–1994* (NHS 32; Leiden and New York: Brill, 1997).

*Editions:* Nag Hammadi Studies (Leiden, etc.: Brill, 1971–) [NHS]. – *The Facsimile Edition of the Nag Hammadi Codices* (11 vols.; Leiden: Brill, 1972–1984). – Bibliothèque copte de Nag Hammadi: Section "Textes" (Québec: Presses de l'Université Laval, 1977–). – *The Teachings of Sylvanus (Nag Hammadi Codex VII, 4)* (ed. J. Zandee; Leiden: Nederlands Instituut voor het Nabije Oosten, 1991) [NHC VII,4 ET/Com]. – *Der Brief des Petrus an Philippus: Ein neutestamentliches Apokryphon aus dem Fund von Nag Hammadi* (NHC VIII,2) (ed. H.-G. Bethge; TU 141; Berlin: Akademie, 1997) [NHC VIII,2 Com]. – *Die Auslegung der Erkenntnis: (Nag Hammadi Codex XI,1)* (ed. U.-K. Plisch; TU 142; Berlin: Akademie, 1996) [NHC XI,1 Com]. – *Das Philippus-Evangelium (Nag Hammadi Codex II,3)* (ed. H.-M. Schenke; TU 143; Berlin: Akademie, 1997) [NHC II,3 Com].

*Translations:* J. M. Robinson, *The Nag Hammadi Library in English* (4th rev. ed.; Leiden and New York: Brill, 1996) [NHL].

*Reference Works:* F. Siegbert, *Nag-Hammadi-Register: Wörterbuch zur Erfassung der Begriffe in den koptisch-gnostischen Schriften von Nag-Hammadi mit einem deutschen Index* (WUNT 26; Tübingen: Mohr, 1982). – Bibliothèque copte de Nag Hammadi: Section "Concordances" (Québec: Presses de l'Université Laval, 1992–). – C. A. Evans, R. L. Webb, and R. A. Wiebe, *Nag Hammadi Texts and the Bible: A Synopsis and Index* (NTTS 18; Leiden and New York: Brill, 1993).

*Encyclopedia Articles:* G. Filoramo, *EECh* 2:581. – H.-M. Schenke, *TRE* 23:731–36. – P. Perkins, *EEC* 2:796–97.

*Collections of Essays:* C. W. Hedrick and R. Hodgson, *Nag Hammadi, Gnosticism, and Early Christianity* (Peabody, Mass.: Hendrickson, 1986). – J. D. Turner and A. McGuire, eds., *The Nag Hammadi Library after Fifty Years* (Nag Hammadi and Manichaean Studies 44; Leiden and New York: Brill, 1997).

*Studies:* W. C. van Unnik, *Evangelien aus dem Nilsand: Mit einem Beitrag "Echte Jesusworte?" von J. B. Bauer und mit einem Nachwort "Die Edition der koptisch-gnostischen Schriften von Nag-Hammadi" von W. C. Till* (Frankfurt: Heinrich Scheffler, 1960). – C. Colpe, "Heidnische, jüdische, und christliche Überlieferung in den Schriften aus Nag Hammadi I–X," *JAC* 15 (1972): 5–18; 16 (1973): 106–26; 17 (1974): 109–25; 18 (1975): 144–65; 19 (1976): 120–38; 20 (1977): 149–70; 21 (1978): 125–46; 22 (1979): 98–122; 23 (1980): 108–27; 25 (1982): 65–101. – M. Krause, "Die Texte von Nag Hammadi," in *Nag Hammadi, Gnosticism, and Early Christianity* (ed. C. W. Hedrick and R. Hodgson; Peabody, Mass.: Hendrickson, 1986). – C. M. Tuckett, *Nag Hammadi and the Gospel Tradition: Synoptic Tradition in the Nag Hammadi Library* (Edinburgh: T&T Clark, 1986). – C. Scholten, *Martyrium und Sophiamythos im Gnostizismus nach den Texten von Nag Hammadi* (JAC.E 14; Münster: Aschendorff, 1987). – A. Khosroyev, *Die Bibliothek von Nag Hammadi: Einige Probleme des Christentums in Ägypten während der ersten Jahrhunderte* (Altenberge: Oros, 1995). – M. Franzmann, *Jesus in the Nag Hammadi Writings* (Edinburgh: T&T Clark, 1996). – A. Böhlig, "Die Bedeutung der Funde von Medinet Madi und Nag Hammadi für die Erforschung des Gnostizismus," *Gnosis und Manichäismus: Forschungen und Studien zu Texten von Valentin und Mani sowie zu den Bibliotheken von Nag Hammadi und Medinet Madi* (ed. A. Böhlig and C. Markschies; BZNW 72; Berlin and New York: de Gruyter, 1994), 113–242.

The discoveries at Nag Hammadi have brought to light both Christian and non-Christian gnostic works; in both instances one has to assume interaction—namely, that pagan gnostic writings were christianized and Christian writings were paganized or repaganized. In any case, they do not facilitate any conclusions about the phases of development of gnosis prior to the second century. The origins therefore still remain obscure; the only thing that can be said with certainty is that in Gnosticism the fundamental pursuit of knowledge by the pre-Christian Hellenistic world continued. Beyond this, all attempts at explaining it on the basis of Greek philosophy and religion, Judaism, Persian sources, the NT, etc., especially those representative of the history-of-religions school of R. Reitzenstein and W. Bousset, as well as of the school of R. Bultmann, cannot be considered secure. The existence of a pre-Christian gnosis is fundamentally in doubt, so that it has to be assumed, in agreement with the English school and the more recent work of C. Colpe, that the gnostic movement did not emerge before the first century and hence existed alongside, and in competition with, Christianity. In retrospect it is certainly the case that a number of earlier elements can be discovered in the developed gnostic systems of the second century—for instance, in Platonic philosophy, mythology, Judaism, and oriental religions. Until now, however, no compelling evidence has been found that these elements had gnostic meaning before they were adopted by later unified Gnosticism.

For this reason, contemporary scholarship distinguishes terminologically between gnosis as a system of knowledge and Gnosticism as soteriology, which presupposes a gnostic system and not only individual elements or myths about it. As far as it can be ascertained today, this Gnosticism, in a multitude of Christian and non-Christian systems, did not exist in its fully developed form until the second century and knows no common originating source. The conviction handed down by the church fathers that Simon Magus was the first gnostic is entirely inaccurate. Gnosticism reached its peak in two highly different systems in the second century, namely, those of Basilides and Valentinus.

*Bibliography:* A. Adam, "Neuere Literatur zum Problem der Gnosis," *GGA* 215 (1963): 22–46. – G. Giurovich, "Bibliografia sullo gnosticismo," *ScC* (1970), supplement, 1:39–54. – K. Rudolf, "Gnosis und Gnostizismus: Ein Forschungsbericht," *TRu* 34 (1969): 121–75, 181–231, 358–61; 36 (1971): 1–61, 89–124; 37 (1972): 289–360; 38 (1974): 1–25. – D. M. Scholer, "Bibliographia gnostica, supplementum," *NovT* 13 (1971): 322–36 – R. van den Broeck, "The Present State of Gnostic Studies," *VC* 37 (1983): 41–71. – G. Filoramo, *Il risveglio della gnosi ovvero diventar dio* (Bari: Laterza, 1990). – K. Rudolph, "Die Gnosis: Texte und Übersetzungen," *TRu* 55 (1990): 113–52.

*Editions:* W. Völker, *Quellen zur Geschichte der christlichen Gnosis* (SAQ NS 5; Tübingen: Mohr, 1932). – C. Schmidt, ed., *Die Pistis Sophia, die beiden Bücher des Jeû, unbekanntes altgnostisches Werk* (vol. 1 of *Koptisch-gnostische Schriften;* 4th ed.; GCS 45; Berlin: Akademie, 1981). – Ptolemy, *Lettre à Flora* (ed. G. Quispel; 2d ed.; SC 24; Paris: Cerf, 1966). – Clement of Alexandria, *Théodote* (ed. F. Sagnard; SC 23; Paris: Cerf, 1970). – M. Simonetti, *Testi gnostici in lingua greca e latina* (Vincenza: Fondazione Lorenzo, 1993) [Com].

*Translations:* B. Layton, *The Gnostic Scriptures: A New Translation with Annotations and Introductions* (ABRL; Garden City, N.Y.: Doubleday, 1987). – H.-J. Klimkeit, *Gnosis on the Silk Road: Gnostic Parables, Hymns, and Prayers from Central Asia* (San Francisco: HarperSanFrancisco, 1994).

*Reference Works:* M. Tardieu and J.-D. Dubois, *Histoire du mot "gnostique"; Instruments de travail; Collections retrouvées avant 1945* (vol. 1 of *Introduction à la littérature gnostique;* Paris: Cerf, 1986).

*Encyclopedia Articles:* É. Cornelis, *DSp* 6:508–41. – R. Mortley and C. Colpe, *RAC* 11:446–659. – K. Berger and R. M. Wilson, *TRE* 13 (1984): 519–50. – G. Filoramo, *EECh* 1:352–54. – P. Perkins, *EEC* 1:465–70.

*Collections of Essays:* B. A. Pearson, *Gnosticism, Judaism, and Egyptian Christianity* (Minneapolis: Fortress, 1990). – J. Goehring, *Gnosticism and the Early Christian World: In Honor of James M. Robinson* (Sonoma, Calif.: Polebridge, 1990). – D. M. Scholer, ed., *Gnosticism in the Early Church* (SEC 5; New York: Garland, 1993).

*Introductions and Surveys:* H. Jonas, *Gnosis und spätantiker Geist; Die mythologische Gnosis* (vol. 1 of FRLANT 51, 63; Göttingen: Vandenhoeck & Ruprecht, 1964). – K. Rudolph, ed., *Gnosis und Gnostizismus* (WdF 262; Darmstadt: Wissenschaftliche Buchgesellschaft, 1975). – B. Layton, ed., *The Rediscovery of Gnosticism* (2 vols.; SHR 41; Leiden: Brill, 1980–1981). – H. Leisegang, *Die Gnosis* (5th ed.; Stuttgart: Kröner, 1985). – G. Filoramo, *A History of Gnosticism* (trans. A. Alcock; Cambridge, Mass. and Oxford: Blackwell, 1990). – K. Rudolph, *Gnosis: The Nature and History of an Ancient Religion* (trans. R. M. Wilson; Edinburgh: T&T Clark, 1983). – A. H. B. Logan, *Gnostic Truth and Christian Heresy: A Study in the History of Gnosticism* (Edinburgh: T&T Clark, 1996).

*Research Reports:* K. W. Tröger, "Zum gegenwärtigen Stand der Gnosis- und Nag-Hammadi-Forschung," in *Altes Testament–Frühjudentum–Gnosis: Neue Studien zu "Gnosis und Bibel"* (ed. K. W. Tröger; Gütersloh: Mohn, 1980), 11–13. – H.-M. Schenke, "Gnosis: Zum Forschungsstand unter besonderer Berücksichtigung der religionsgeschichtlichen Problematik," *VF* 32 (1987): 2–21. – M. J. Edwards, "Neglected Texts in the

Study of Gnosticism," *JTS* NS 41 (1990): 26–50. – M. A. Williams, *Rethinking "Gnosticism": An Argument for Dismantling a Dubious Category* (Princeton, N.J.: Princeton University Press, 1996).

*Monographs:* C. Colpe, *Die religionsgeschichtliche Schule: Darstellung und Kritik ihres Bildes vom gnostischen Erlösermythus* (FRLANT 78; Göttingen: Vandenhoeck & Ruprecht, 1961). – G. van Groningen, *First Century Gnosticism: Its Origin and Motifs* (Leiden: Brill, 1967). – R. M. Wilson, *Gnosis and the New Testament* (Oxford: Blackwell, 1968). – A. Orbe, *Cristología gnóstica: Introducción a la soteriología de los siglos II y III* (2 vols.; BAC 384–385; Madrid: Editorial Católica, 1976). – P. Perkins, *The Gnostic Dialogue: The Early Church and the Crisis of Gnosticism* (New York: Paulist, 1980). – G. A. G. Stroumsa, *Another Seed: Studies in Gnostic Mythology* (NHS 24; Leiden: Brill, 1984). – H. A. Green, *The Economic and Social Origins of Gnosticism* (Society of Biblical Literature Dissertation Series 77; Atlanta: Scholars Press, 1985). – J. Ménard, *De la gnose au manichéisme* (Paris: Cariscript, 1986). – D. J. Good, *Reconstructing the Traditions of Sophia in Gnostic Literature* (Society of Biblical Literature Monograph Series 32; Atlanta: Scholars Press,1987). – W. G. Röhl, *Die Rezeption des Johannesevangeliums in christlich-gnostischen Schriften aus Nag Hammadi* (EHS.T 428; Frankfurt and New York: Lang, 1991). – D. Voorgang, *Die Passion Jesu und Christi in der Gnosis* (EHS.T 432; Frankfurt and New York: Lang, 1991). – G. Iacopino, *Il Vangelo di Giovanni nei testi gnostici copti* (SEAug 49; Rome: Institutum Patristicum Augustinianum, 1995). – A. Magris, *La logica del pensiero gnostico* (Brescia: Morcelliana, 1997).

*Gnosis and Christianity:* E. Haenchen, "Gab es eine vorchristliche Gnosis?" *ZTK* 49 (1952): 316–349. – R. M. Grant, *Gnosticism and Early Christianity* (2d rev. ed.; New York: Harper & Row, 1966). – E. M. Yamauchi, *Pre-Christian Gnosticism: A Survey of the Proposed Evidences* (2d ed.; Grand Rapids: Baker, 1983). – K. Koschorke, *Die Polemik der Gnostiker gegen das kirchliche Christentum: Unter besonderer Berücksichtigung der Nag-Hammadi-Traktate "Apokalypse des Petrus" (NHC VII,3) und "Testimonium Veritatis" (NHC IX,3)* (NHS 12; Leiden: Brill, 1978). – S. Pétrement, *A Separate God: The Christian Origins of Gnosticism* (trans. C. Harrison; San Francisco: HarperSanFrancisco, 1990). – M. Simonetti, "Alcune riflessioni sul rapporto tra gnosticismo e cristianesimo," *VetChr* 28 (1991): 337–74. – D. L. Hoffman, *The Status of Women and Gnosticism in Irenaeus and Tertullian* (SWR 36; Lewiston, N.Y.: Mellen, 1995), 23–77.

*Simon Magus:* K. Beyschlag, *Simon Magus und die christliche Gnosis* (WUNT 16; Tübingen: Mohr, 1974). – G. Lüdemann, *Untersuchungen zur simonianischen Gnosis* (GTA 1; Göttingen: Vandenhoeck & Ruprecht, 1975). – K. Rudolph, "Simon-Magus oder Gnosticus? Zum Stand der Debatte," *TRu* 42 (1977): 279–359. – A. H. B. Logan, "Simon Magus," *TRE* 31:272–76.

### b. Basilides

We have hardly any knowledge about the person and life of Basilides. Clement of Alexandria (*Strom.* 7.106.6) maintains—and other sources confirm—that he worked in Alexandria during the reigns of Hadrian and Antoninus Pius (117–161). Any further data remain tentative. His work included a gospel commentary in twenty-four volumes, and also psalms or odes; it is not clear, however, which gospel he addressed in the commentary. Origen (*Hom. Luc.* 1) insists that he wrote his own gospel.

Further, it is not possible to obtain a uniform picture of the doctrinal system of Basilides, since various Christian authors write about it in radically different ways and it is not possible to determine whether they represent differing elements of one and the same system or competing presentations. Clement, whose account is generally considered to be reliable (*Strom.* 4.81–83), critiques Basilides for his teaching that a person's suffering is always the individual's fault. Even if a person was not actively culpable, one's inherent tendency to culpability remains; children suffering "innocently," martyrs, and even Christ himself suffered for this tendency to culpability. Martyrdom does indeed purge sin, even the inherent tendency to sin; hence it has to be viewed as a divine favor accorded to only a few of the elect.

The reliability of the description by Hippolytus (*Haer.* 7.20–27), however, has given rise to a number of controversies. According to him, Basilides held an elaborate doctrine of emanations. In the beginning was nothingness; even God himself was a nonbeing who, in order to create the world, first made a world seed containing everything in itself. Out of this evolved three levels of subordinate sonships that were decreasingly Godlike in essence and that endeavored to return to the pure God. Whereas the first and second sonship succeeded in returning to the Father, the third had to undergo purification first. From the mass of seed there emerged the "great archon" who created the world, followed by a second archon of whom the OT prophets spoke and who was the God of the OT from Adam to Moses. Finally, in order to set the third sonship free, the gospel entered the world and first enlightened Jesus, the son of the first archon, concerning the existence of God the Father. Through him the third sonship was redeemed, and the entire creation was brought back to the Father (ἀποκατάστασις).

Other sources, however, speak of angels as the creators of 365 heavens and assert that it was not Christ who died on the cross but Simon of Cyrene who took his place. Although the preserved accounts make it difficult for us today to ascertain Basilides' system, in his time it nevertheless ushered in an era when Gnosticism blossomed—so much so in fact that it threatened to oust orthodox teaching.

*Editions:* W. Völker, *Quellen zur Geschichte der christlichen Gnosis* (SAQ NS 5; Tübingen: Mohr, 1932), 38–57.

*Translations:* B. Layton, *The Gnostic Scriptures* (ABRL; Garden City, N.Y.: Doubleday, 1987), 417–44.

*Encyclopedia Articles:* J. H. Waszink, *RAC* 1:1217–24. – E. Mühlenberg, *TRE* 5:296–301. – A. Monaci Castagno, *EECh* 1:113. – F. Norris, *EEC* 1:176–77.

*Studies:* P. Hendrix, *De Alexandrijnsche Haeresiarch Basilides: Een Bijdrage tot de Geschiedenis der Gnosis* (Amsterdam: H. J. Paris, 1926). – G. Quispel, "L'homme gnostique (la doctrine de Basilide)," *ErJb* 16 (1948): 89–139; repr. as "Gnostic Man: The Doctrine of Basilides," in *Gnostic Studies* (UNHAII 34.1; Istanbul: Nederlands Historisch-Archaeologisch Instituut in het Nabije Oosten, 1974–), 1.103–33. – W. Foerster, "Das System des Basilides," *NTS* 9 (1962–1963): 233–55. – W.-D. Hauschild, "Christologie und Humanismus bei dem 'Gnostiker' Basilides," *ZNW* 68 (1977): 67–92. – R. M. Grant, "Place de Basilide dans la théologie chrétienne ancienne," *REAug* 25 (1979): 201–16. – B. Layton, "The Significance of Basilides in Ancient Christian Thought," *Representations* 28 (1989): 135–51. – D. Vigne, "Enquête sur Basilide," in *Recherches et tradition: Mélanges patristiques offerts a Henri Crouzel* (ed. A. Dupleix; ThH 88; Paris: Beauchesne, 1992), 285–313. – W. A. Löhr, *Basilides und seine Schule: Eine Studie zur Theologie- und Kirchengeschichte des zweiten Jahrhunderts* (WUNT 83; Tübingen: Mohr, 1996).

## c. Valentinus

Valentinus, also about whom we do not have any detailed information—though more than on Basilides—was the second great gnostic of this period. We are more conversant with Valentinus's system than with Basilides'. He originally was from Egypt and, according to Irenaeus (*Haer.* 3.4.3) and Eusebius (*Hist. eccl.* 4.11.1), came to Rome in 140. There he turned away from orthodoxy and founded a school of his own. After 155 he left for the East, perhaps for Cyprus. Having returned to Rome, he died shortly after 160. Only a few fragments of his works are extant, mainly in Clement of Alexandria. He wrote homilies, psalms, and letters. Hippolytus (*Haer.* 6.37.7) has preserved one of his hymns. Among the writings discovered at Nag Hammadi, none can be traced back to him.

On the basis of the accounts of Gnosticism's opponents, however, we are fairly well informed about the Valentinian doctrinal system as received and applied by his disciples. Nevertheless some doubts have been voiced recently on whether this indeed is the original system of Valentinus. The following essential features can be ascertained: The divine pleroma[8] consists of thirty aeons formed in pairs. The initial four pairs are the most important and constitute the original ogdoad from whom all other aeons originate. Sin severed the unity of these syzygies, as a result of which the spiritual person has to be reunited with his heavenly partner. The sin in question is committed by Sophia, the final aeon, because of its excessive desire to know the eternal, unknown Father, with the result that the divine elements in the world are degraded. At the same time, the heavenly redeemer initiates the salvation of the divine part, thus ultimately leading to the reunification of the pleroma. Humanity is made up of three groups: pneumatics, psychics, and hylics. The first of these is saved completely and reunited with the pleroma, the second is only partially saved, and the third perishes.

*Editions:* W. Völker, *Quellen zur Geschichte der christlichen Gnosis* (SAQ NS 5; Tübingen: Mohr, 1932), 57–141.

*Translations:* B. Layton, *The Gnostic Scriptures* (ABRL; Garden City, N.Y.: Doubleday, 1987), 215–64.

*Encyclopedia Articles:* C. Gianotto, *EECh* 2:859–60. – K. King, *EEC* 2:1155–56.

*Studies:* W. Foerster, *Von Valentin zu Herakleon: Untersuchungen über die Quellen und die Entwicklung der valentinianischen Gnosis* (BZNW 7; Giessen: A. Töpelmann, 1928). – F.-M. Sagnard, *La gnose valentinienne et le témoignage de saint Irénée* (EPhM 36; Paris: J. Vrin, 1947). – A. Orbe, *Estudios Valentinianos* (5 vols.; AnGr 65, 83, 99, 100, 113, 158; Rome: Libreria Editrice dell'Università Gregoriana, 1955–1966). – M. Simonetti, "ΨΥΧΗ e ΨΥΧΙΚΟΣ nella gnosi valentiniana," *RSLR* 2 (1966): 1–47. – G. C. Stead, "The Valentinian Myth of Sophia," *JTS* NS 20 (1969): 75–104. – M. J. Edwards, "Gnostics and Valentinians in the Church Fathers," *JTS* NS 40 (1989): 26–47. – M. R. Desjardins, *Sin in Valentinianism* (Atlanta: Scholars Press, 1990). – C. Markschies, *Valentinus Gnosticus? Untersuchungen zur valentinischen Gnosis mit einem Kommentar zu den Fragmenten Valentins* (WUNT 65; Tübingen: Mohr, 1992). – H. Strutwolf, *Gnosis als*

---

[8] Πλήρωμα = "fullness"; αἰών = "time"; ὀγδοάς = "eightfold"; συζυγία = "pair"; σοφία = "wisdom"; πνεῦμα = "spirit"; ψυχή = "soul"; ὕλη = "matter."

*System: Zur Rezeption der valentinianischen Gnosis bei Origenes* (FKDG 56; Göttingen: Vandenhoeck & Ruprecht, 1993). – J. Holzhausen, *Der "Mythos vom Menschen" im hellenistischen Ägypten: Eine Studie zum "Poimandres" (= CH I), zu Valentin und dem gnostischen Mythos* (Theoph. 33; Bodenheim: Athenaum Hain Hanstein, 1994). – G. Quispel, "The Original Doctrine of Valentinus the Gnostic," *VC* 50 (1996): 327–52.

The orthodox church reacted in two ways against this gnostic teaching of self-redemption by knowledge that is reserved for only a few of the elect. As an organization, the church had to expel adherents of Gnosticism because their theology endangered the essentials of the Christian faith, namely, the God of the OT as the Creator of the world and the Father of Jesus Christ, the redemption of the human person through the sacrificial death of Christ, and the election of all to salvation. On the one hand, the literary battle against Gnosticism unmasked the falsehood of this teaching; on the other, it positively developed a "true gnosis" of Christianity, namely, the integration of the rational and philosophical progression of knowledge in matters of faith into the biblical and traditional theology of the church. The primary representatives of the former orientation in the Greek church of the second and third centuries were Irenaeus of Lyon and Hippolytus of Rome; the latter orientation is represented by the first great theologians of the Alexandrian school, Clement of Alexandria and Origen. Their battle, however, also focused on several other influential heresies of the second and third centuries, namely Marcion, Montanism, and Monarchianism.

## 2. Marcion

Nothing has been preserved of Marcion's work, the *Antitheses* (between OT and NT), nor of the writings of his immediate followers. Consequently, for everything we know about his person and teaching, we are indebted to the works of his opponents, primarily Irenaeus, Tertullian, Hippolytus, and Clement of Alexandria. Marcion hailed from Sinope, a town on the southern coast of the Black Sea. According to Epiphanius (*Pan.* 42.1), the local bishop, his father, excommunicated him, allegedly because he violated a virgin; this may have to be regarded, however, as a later legend to disparage the heretic. Other sources and interpretations instead point to dogmatic disputes as the reason for the excommunication. Subsequently, in 138, Marcion went to Rome, where the Christian community received him, only to be excommunicated again in July 144 because of his unorthodox teachings. He then established a church of his own, which, according to Justin (*1 Apol.* 25.6), had already spread widely within ten years and continued until the fifth century. Marcion likely died ca. 160.

His theological error arises from a theological dilemma that is difficult to resolve and from an at first thoroughly orthodox conviction, namely, how the good God whom Jesus Christ proclaimed can be identified as the God who is just and who punishes, as we encounter him in the OT. By rendering the good God absolute, Marcion is unable to reconcile him with the God who punishes, and he consequently rejects the identity of both and thereby the OT as a whole, as well as all of the NT passages referring to the OT. Thus his Bible is reduced to the Gospel of Luke and the letters of Paul (without Hebrews and the Pastoral Letters), and even these with appropriate abridgements. The theological consequence is that both the world and the human were not created by the good God but—as in Gnosticism—by a demiurge, so that the latter, together with the world, is to be rejected. Salvation is contingent upon stringent separation from the world through rigorous asceticism and flight from the world. For Marcion this even extends to prohibiting the use of wine in the Eucharist (while otherwise adopting the liturgical rites of the church), as well as marriage and procreation.

Consequently, the separation of the two Testaments does not allow Christ to redeem from Adam's sin but instead offers humanity the message of the good God who has been unknown hitherto and who has nothing to do with the world. In this context it was sufficient for Christ to have a phantom body; Christ's actual birth by Mary is denied, since this would defile the Son of God with the world.

The Fathers considered Marcion a gnostic, and many features of his teaching do indeed point in this direction, especially the separation of the two gods, the rejection of the world, and the role of Christ as the one who proclaims the knowledge of salvation. Other features of his teaching, however, are altogether foreign to Gnosticism, such as the founding of his own church, so that it may be necessary to assess Marcion as a unique phenomenon apart from Gnosticism. By rejecting the OT and establishing his own canon of Scripture, he certainly contributed to the eventual clarification of the NT canon, though likely without being the reason for it.

*Encyclopedia Articles:* G. Pelland, *DSp* 10:311–21. – K. Beyschlag, 1:69–81. – B. Aland, *EECh* 1:523–24. – B. Aland, *TRE* 22:89–101. – K. Zelzer, *HLL* 4:350–51. – H. Stander, *EEC* 2:715–17.

*General Studies:* A. von Harnack, *Marcion—das Evangelium vom fremden Gott: Eine Monographie zur Geschichte der Grundlegung der katholischen Kirche* (2d ed.; TU 45; Leipzig: Hinrichs, 1924; repr., Darmstadt: Wissenschaftliche Buchgesellschaft, 1960). – A. von Harnack, *Neue Studien zu Marcion* (TU 44.4; Leipzig: Hinrichs, 1923). – R. S. Wilson, *Marcion: A Study of a Second-Century Heretic* (London: James Clarke, 1933). – E. C. Blackman, *Marcion and His Influence* (London: SPCK, 1948; repr., New York: AMS, 1978). – D. Balás, "Marcion Revisited: A 'Post-Harnack' Perspective," in *Texts and Testaments: Critical Essays on the Bible and Early Church Fathers* (ed. W. E. March; San Antonio, Tex.: Trinity University Press, 1980), 95–108. – R. J. Hoffmann, *Marcion, on the Restitution of Christianity: An Essay on the Development of Radical Paulinist Theology in the Second Century* (Chico, Calif.: Scholars Press, 1984).

*Particular Studies:* J. Knox, *Marcion and the New Testament: An Essay in the Early History of the Canon* (Chicago: University of Chicago Press, 1942). – P. G. Verweijs, *Evangelium und neues Gesetz in der ältesten Christenheit bis auf Marcion* (STRT 5; Utrecht: Kemink en Zoon, 1960). – J. Woltmann, "Der geschichtliche Hintergrund der Lehre Markions vom 'Fremden Gott,'" in *Wegzeichen: Festgabe zum 60. Geburtstag von Prof. Dr. Hermenegild M. Biedermann* (ed. E. C. Suttner and C. Patock; ÖC NS 25; Würzburg: Augustinus, 1971), 15–42. – B. Aland, "Marcion: Versuch einer neuen Interpretation," *ZTK* 70 (1973): 420–47. – G. May, "Marcion in Contemporary Views: Results and Open Questions," *SecCent* 6 (1987–1988): 129–51; repr. in *Orthodoxy, Heresy, and Schism in Early Christianity* (ed. E. Ferguson; SEC 4; New York: Garland,

1993), 259–81. – J. J. Clabeaux, *A Lost Edition of the Letters of Paul: A Reassessment of the Text of the Pauline Corpus Attested by Marcion* (CBQMS 21; Washington, D.C.: Catholic Biblical Association of America, 1989). – D. S. Williams, "Reconsidering Marcion's Gospel," *JBL* 108 (1989): 477–96. – H. J. W. Drijvers, "Christ as Warrior and Merchant: Aspects of Marcion's Christology," in *Papers Presented to the Tenth International Conference on Patristic Studies Held in Oxford, 1987* (ed. E. Livingstone; StPatr 21; Louvain: Peeters, 1989), 73–85. – A. Orbe, "En torno al modalismo de Marción," *Greg* 71 (1990): 43–65. – A. Orbe, "Marcionitica," *Aug* 31 (1991): 195–244. – G. May, "Marcione nel suo tempo," *CrSt* 14 (1993): 205–20. – U. Schmid, *Marcion und sein Apostolos: Rekonstruktion und historische Einordnung der marcionitischen Paulusbriefausgabe* (ANTF 25; Berlin and New York: de Gruyter, 1995). – E. Norelli, "Note sulla soteriologia di Marcione," *Aug* 35 (1995): 281–305. – W. A. Löhr, "Die Auslegung des Gesetzes bei Markion, den Gnostikern, und den Manichäern," in *Stimuli—Exegese und ihre Hermeneutik in Antike und Christentum: Festschrift für Ernst Dassmann* (ed. Georg Schöllgen and Clemens Scholten; JAC.E 23; Münster: Aschendorff, 1996), 77–95.

## 3. Montanism

The movement today labeled Montanism called itself "prophecy"—an apt self-designation based on its primary mission. This name was not altered until its opponents augmented it as "the new prophecy," thereby indicating that it had separated itself from the ecclesiastical tradition; else they designated it Montanism because of its founder, or "the heresy of the Phrygians," based on its place of origin. In his native village of Ardabau in Phrygia, Montanus ca. 170 declared himself the mouthpiece of the Paraclete (John 14:26; 16:7), promised in the gospel, who was about to usher all of Christianity into the full truth. He was joined by two prophetesses, Prisc(ill)a and Maximilla, of whom some oracles have been indirectly handed down, but no original works. Our understanding of Montanism is therefore largely based on the writings directed against them (especially those of Eusebius and Epiphanius), the records of the synods, and the Montanist writings of Tertullian.

Apart from his self-aggrandizement, which even Tertullian rejected, Montanus intended to address one of the pressing problems of the second-century church. The expectation of the imminent return of the Messiah and the exuberance of the earliest communities, expressed through prophets and those empowered by the Spirit, had receded and began to give way to an institutional church. Montanus and his followers wanted to fan this enthusiasm into flame again by proclaiming the imminent end of the world and calling upon Christians to prepare for it by turning away from the world. In line with this, they recommended rigorous fasting, celibacy and sexual continence, generous almsgiving, and a longing for martyrdom, though these demands were gradually toned down by limiting the days set aside for fasting and by rejecting only remarriage. The new Jerusalem was to descend in Phrygian Pepuza or Tymion, and according to the proclamation of Maximilla, this was to take place immediately after her death.

To the extent that Montanism thereby did indeed pursue ecclesiastical goals, it was not initially identified or condemned as heresy. In 177 the martyrs of

✠  － *Martyr defense ?*

Lyon even sent Irenaeus to Rome with a letter in defense of the Montanists. The long-term consequences of Montanist rigorism, however, had to be recognized as dangerous, namely, the sole authority of the prophet, excluding that of the ecclesiastical officeholders and hierarchy; the rigorist demands on all Christians, excluding many from the universal redemptive will of God; and the rejection of the authority of Scripture over the prophets. The earliest known synods of the ancient church therefore condemned Montanism as heretical in the late second century and early third century.

When the end of the world was not realized after the death of Maximilla in 179 and the imminent expectation of the new Jerusalem suffered a severe setback, Montanism began to focus single-mindedly on its rigorist moral demands. From ca. 200 on, it established itself in the West, primarily because of Tertullian's conversion to this sect. Subsequently Montanism gradually disappeared, even though there is evidence of its traces in the East until the ninth century.

*Editions:* P. de Labriolle, *Les sources de l'histoire du montanisme: Textes grecs, latins, syriaques* (Collectanea friburgensia 24; Fribourg, Switz.: Librairie de l'Université, 1913) [Com]. – N. Bonwetsch, *Texte zur Geschichte des Montanismus* (KlT 129; Bonn: A. Marcus & E. Weber, 1914). – R. E. Heine, *The Montanist Oracles and Testimonia* (PatMS 14; [Louvain]: Peeters; Macon, Ga.: Mercer University Press, 1989) [ET]. – W. Tabbernee, *Montanist Inscriptions and Testimonia: Epigraphic Sources Illustrating the History of Montanism* (PatMS 16; Macon, Ga.: Mercer University Press, 1997) [ET/Com].

*Encyclopedia Articles:* H. Bacht, *DSp* 10:1670–76. – B. Aland, *EECh* 1:570–71. – W. H. C. Frend, *TRE* 23:271–79. – D. Groh: *EEC* 2:778–80.

*Studies:* N. Bonwetsch, *Die Geschichte des Montanismus* (Erlangen: A. Deichert, 1881). – P. de Labriolle, *La crise montaniste* (Paris: E. Leroux, 1913). – W. Schepelern, *Der Montanismus und die phrygischen Kulte: Eine religionsgeschichtliche Untersuchung* (trans. W. Bauer; Tübingen: Mohr, 1929). – H. Kraft, "Die altkirchliche Prophetie und die Entstehung des Montanismus," *TZ* 11 (1955): 249–71. – K. Aland, "Bemerkungen zum Montanismus und zur frühchristlichen Eschatologie," *Kirchengeschichtliche Entwürfe: Alte Kirche, Reformation und Luthertum, Pietismus und Erweckungsbewegung* (Gütersloh: Gütersloher Verlagshaus, 1960), 105–48. – T. D. Barnes, "The Chronology of Montanism," *JTS* NS 21 (1970): 403–8. – J. A. Fischer, "Die antimontanistischen Synoden des 2./3. Jahrhunderts," *AHC* 6 (1974): 241–73; repr. in J. A. Fischer and A. Lumpe, *Die Synoden von den Anfängen bis zum Vorabend des Nicaenums* (Paderborn: F. Schöningh, 1997), 23–59. – F. Blanchetière, "Le montanisme original," *RevScRel* 52 (1978): 118–34; 53 (1979): 1–22. – A. Strobel, *Das heilige Land der Montanisten: Eine religionsgeschichtliche Untersuchung* (RVV 37; Berlin and New York: de Gruyter, 1980). – W. H. C. Frend, "Montanism, Research and Problems," *RSLR* 30 (1984): 521–37. – W. H. C. Frend, "Montanism: A Movement of Prophecy and Regional Identity in the Early Church," *BJRL* 70 (1988): 25–34. – W. Tabbernee, "Remnants of the New Prophecy: Literary and Epigraphical Sources of the Montanist Movement," in *Papers Presented to the Tenth International Conference on Patristic Studies Held in Oxford, 1987* (ed. E. Livingstone; StPatr 21; Louvain: Peeters, 1989), 193–201. – W. Tabbernee, "Montanist Regional Bishops: New Evidence from Ancient Inscriptions," *JECS* 1 (1993): 249–80. – C. Trevett, *Montanism: Gender, Authority, and the New Prophecy* (Cambridge and New York: Cambridge University Press, 1996).

## 4. Monarchianism

The first occurrence of the term "Monarchianism" is found in Tertullian (*Prax.* 10.1). It does not denote a uniform theological system or a school of thought; instead it circumscribes all of the endeavors that—on the basis of the monotheism inherited from Judaism and in defense against pagan polytheism and gnostic conceptions, which threatened to divide God the Father and the Son into two separate deities—proclaimed God a strict *monarchia* (μόνος = "only," ἀρχή = "source," "principle"), that is, as the only and indivisible origin of the universe. In its moderate, orthodox form, Monarchianism did not contribute insignificantly to the definition of the Son as being of the same essence as the Father (ὁμοούσιος) at the Council of Nicea (325). Nevertheless, because of its rigorous interpretation of the oneness of God and because it thereby relinquished the Son's unique being in relation to the Father, Monarchianism strayed into heresy.

Heretical Monarchianism evolved into several different movements, which were labeled in keeping with their theology, on the one hand, and with their main representatives, on the other. Theologically, two basic expressions should be distinguished:

a. *Adoptionism.* This endeavored to preserve the oneness of God by arguing that Christ was born and raised as a mere human. Only at his baptism in the Jordan River or after his resurrection did God the Father accept him as Son on the merits of his work. Adoptionism can be traced back to Theodotus, a second-century tanner of Byzantium, and was later taken up by Paul of Samosata (ca. 260–270) and possibly by Photinus of Sirmium (mid-fourth century), but it had little success.

b. *Patripassianism* (*pater* = "Father," *passio* = "suffering") or *Modalism* (*modus* = "manner," "way"). This perceived God the Father and the Son merely as different manifestations of the one God, so that the Father himself suffered on the cross in the form of the Son. This expression of Monarchianism was brought to Rome by Noetus of Smyrna toward the end of the second century; Hippolytus took action against it in literary form (a fragment of *Contra Noetum*). There Sabellius took it up and in the mid-third century introduced it in Egypt (Sabellianism). In the early third century, Praxeas spread it in North Africa and precipitated Tertullian's first fundamental work of Trinitarian theology of the patristic era, *Adversus Praxean*. In the fourth century it also showed up in Asia Minor, in the theology of Marcellus of Ancyra.

*Encyclopedia Articles:* M. Simonetti, "Adoptianists," *EECh* 1:11. – M. Simonetti, "Monarchians," *EECh* 1:566. – M. Simonetti, "Patripassians," *EECh* 2:653–54. – M. Simonetti, "Sabellius–Sabellianism," *EECh* 2:748–49. – M. Simonetti, "Theodotus of Byzantium," *EECh* 2:830. – R. Lyman, *EEC* 2:764–66.

*Studies:* J. N. D. Kelly, *Early Christian Doctrines* (rev. ed.; San Francisco: Harper & Row, 1976), 113–23. – M. Simonetti, "Sabellio e il sabellianismo," *SSR* 4 (1980): 7–28. – M. Decker, *Die Monarchianer: Frühchristliche Theologie im Spannungsfeld zwischen Rom und Kleinasien* (Hamburg: n.p., 1987). – W. A. Bienert, "Sabellius und Sabellianismus als historisches Problem," in *Logos: Festschrift für Luise Abramowski zum 8. Juli 1993* (ed. H. C. Brennecke, E. L. Grasmück, and C. Markschies; BZNW 67; Berlin: de Gruyter, 1993), 124–39. – G. Uríbarri Bilbao, *Monarquía y Trinidad: El concepto teológico "monarchia" en la controversia "monarquiana"* (Madrid: UPCO, 1996).

# B. Orthodox Responses

## 1. Irenaeus of Lyon

Only at a few points do his works and the references Eusebius extracted from his works (*Hist. eccl.* 5.3–25) shed light on Irenaeus's life. He came from Asia Minor, where, as a young man, he had heard Polycarp of Smyrna and from where, like many other members of the community of Lyon, he had migrated to Gaul on the established trade routes. Around 177 the church sent him to Rome as a presbyter, carrying a letter from the believers in Lyon to counsel Bishop Eleutherus (ca. 174–189) to maintain fellowship with the Montanists (cf. IV.A.3). Soon after his return, Lyon chose him as the successor to Photinus, their bishop, who suffered martyrdom (cf. III.B.2). Subsequently we hear of Irenaeus through a second letter of peace during the Easter controversy under Victor, bishop of Rome (ca. 189–ca. 199). By appealing to Polycarp, who, despite their differing views of the date of Easter, had parted peaceably from Anicetus, then bishop of Rome, he fought for maintaining fellowship with the Quartodecimans instead of carrying out the threat of their excommunication (cf. ch. 2.I.C). Irenaeus probably died ca. 200; the notion of his martyrdom, however, does not surface until Jerome (*Comm. Isa.* 17.64).  → written in as a martyr.

Eusebius is aware of a whole range of works by Irenaeus and also passes on some fragments. Only two are extant, however: his main work, *Adversus haereses (Against Heresies)*; and *Epideixis tou apostolikou kērygmatos (Demonstration of the Apostolic Preaching)*.

*Bibliographies:* M. A. Donovan, "Irenaeus in Recent Scholarship," *SecCent* 4 (1984): 219–41. – N. Collmar, *BBKL* 2:1315–26.

*Editions:* H. Jordan, *Armenische Irenaeusfragmente mit deutscher Übersetzung nach W. Lüdtke* (TU 36.2; Leipzig: Hinrichs, 1913). – *Nouveaux fragments arméniens de l'Adversus haereses et de l'Epideixis* (ed. C. Renoux; PO 39; Turnhout, Belg.: Brepols, 1978), 1–164 [Com].

*Translations:* D. N. Power, *Irenaeus of Lyons on Baptism and Eucharist: Selected Texts* (GLS 65; Bramcote, Nottingham: Grove, 1991) [selections]. – R. M. Grant, *Irenaeus of Lyons* (Early Church Fathers; London and New York: Routledge, 1997) [selections].

*Encyclopedia Articles:* L. Doutreleau and L. Regnault, *DSp* 7.2:1923–69. – N. Brox, 1:82–96. – H.-J. Jaschke, *TRE* 16:258–68. – A. Orbe, *EECh* 1:413–16. – R. Aubert, *DHGE* 25:1477–79. – M. Clark, *EEC* 1:587–89.

*Collections of Essays:* "Eirenaios" = Études irénéennes: Irenäische Studien (Rome: Editiones Academiae Alfonsianae, 1979–).

*Introductions/Surveys:* D. Minns, *Irenaeus* (Outstanding Christian Thinkers; London and Washington, D.C.: Georgetown University Press, 1994). – R. M. Grant, *Irenaeus of Lyons* (Early Church Fathers; London and New York: Routledge, 1997).

*Studies:* A. Orbe, *Parábolas evangélicas en san Ireneo* (2 vols.; Madrid: Editorial Católica, 1972). – H.-J. Jaschke, *Der Heilige Geist im Bekenntnis der Kirche: Eine Studie zur Pneumatologie des Irenäus von Lyon im Ausgang vom altkirchlichen Glaubensbekenntnis* (MBTh 40: Münster: Aschendorff, 1976). – P. Bacq, *De l'ancienne à la nouvelle alliance selon saint Irénée* (Paris: Lethielleux, 1978). – C. Saldanha, *Divine Pedagogy: A Patristic View of Non-Christian Religions* (BSRel 57; Rome: LAS, 1984), 75–102. – A. Orbe, *Espiritualidad de san Ireneo* (AnGr 256; Rome: Editrice Pontificia Università Gregoriana, 1989). – R. A. Norris Jr., "Irenaeus' Use of Paul in His Polemic against the Gnostics," in *Paul and the Legacies of Paul* (ed. W. S. Babcock; Dallas: Southern Methodist University Press, 1990), 79–98. – A. Faivre, "Irénée: Premier théologien 'systématique'?" *RevScRel* 65 (1991): 11–32. – M. Blanchard, *Aux sources du canon: Le témoignage d'Irénée* (CFi 175; Paris: Cerf, 1993). – J. de Roulet, "Saint Irénée évêque," *RHPR* 73 (1993): 261–80. – R. Noormann, *Irenäus als Paulusinterpret: Zur Rezeption und Wirkung der paulinischen und deuteropaulinischen Briefe im Werk der Irenäus von Lyon* (WUNT 2.66; Tübingen: Mohr, 1994).

*Anthropology:* A. Orbe, *Antropología de san Ireneo* (BAC; Madrid: Editorial Católica, 1969). – Y. de Andia, *Homo vivens: Incorruptibilité et divinisation de l'homme selon Irénée de Lyon* (Paris: Études Augustiniennes, 1986). – J. Fantino, *L'homme image de Dieu chez saint Irénée de Lyon* (Paris: Cerf, 1986). – J. Birrer, *Der Mensch als Medium und Adressat der Schöpfungsoffenbarung: Eine dogmengeschichtliche Untersuchung zur Frage der Gotteserkenntnis bei Irenaeus von Lyon* (BSHST 59; Bern and New York: Lang, 1989). – D. L. Hoffman, *The Status of Women and Gnosticism in Irenaeus and Tertullian* (SWR 36; Lewiston, N.Y.: Mellen, 1995), 79–143.

*Christology:* A. Houssiau, *La christologie de saint Irénée* (Louvain: Publications Universitaires de Louvain, 1955). – G. Joppich, *Salus carnis: Eine Untersuchung der Theologie des hl. Irenäus von Lyon* (Münsterschwarzach: Vier-Türme-Verlag, 1965). – J. T. Nielsen, *Adam and Christ in the Theology of Irenaeus of Lyons* (Assen: Van Gorkum, 1968). – J. I. González Faus, *Carne de Dios: Significado salvador de la encarnación en la teología de san Ireneo* (Barcelona: Herder, 1969). – H. Lassat, *Promotion de l'homme en Jésus-Christ: D'après Irénée de Lyon, témoin de la tradition des apôtres* (Paris: Mame, 1974).

*Theology:* A. Benoit, *Saint Irénée: Introduction à l'étude de sa théologie* (EHPhR 52; Paris: Presses Universitaires de France, 1960). – W. R. Schoedel, "Theological Method in Irenaeus," *JTS* NS 35 (1984): 31–49; repr. in *Personalities of the Early Church* (ed. E. Ferguson; SEC 1; New York: Garland, 1993), 127–45. – Y. Torisu, *Gott und Welt: Eine Untersuchung zur Gotteslehre des Irenäus von Lyon* (SIM 52; Nettetal: Steyler, 1991). – J. Fantino, *La théologie d'Irénée: Lecture des Écritures en réponse à l'exégèse gnostique—une approche trinitaire* (Pairs: Cerf, 1994).

### *a.* Adversus haereses

The title of the extensive, five-volume tractate "Detection (ἔλεγχος) and Overthrow (ἀνατροπή) of the False Knowledge," written in Greek ca. 180 but extant only in a third- or fourth-century Latin translation (*Adversus haereses*) and in Greek, Armenian, and Syriac fragments, accurately captures the work's intent and structure. It is directed mainly against Valentinian Gnosticism and all of the preceding heresies, which Irenaeus views as preliminary stages. He fundamentally denies its right to be called gnosis, for Christ had proclaimed the only true and complete knowledge of faith to the apostles, who in turn wrote it down in the writings of the NT. Beyond this the secret writings to which gnostics appeal, or even individually inspired knowledge, have to be seen as fundamentally in error and therefore heretical. By means of a detailed critique of their system, it is important to convict this "gnosis" (bks. 1–2) of its falsehood with such force that its representatives ultimately have to give up in defeat because they are incapable of finding further reasonable responses to Irenaeus's questions and objections. The consistent rejection of Gnosticism (bks. 3–4), which has been demonstrated to be false, is replaced with a positive presentation and substantiation of the true gnosis, that is, the traditional, orthodox Christian faith.

Book 1, therefore, begins with the presentation of the system of Ptolemy, the gnostic (1–9), in order to counter it with the uniform faith of the church and the *regula veritatis* (10–22) and to expose the precursors and origin of Valentinianism (23–31). In its first part, bk. 2 (1–11) rejects the basic Valentinian hypothesis of a superordinate pleroma beyond the Creator God, for this would mean relinquishing both Christian monotheism and the concept of God itself. Events outside the one God would logically set limits to God. Part 2 (12–19) deals with the aeons, the seed concept, and the suffering of wisdom. Part 3 (20–28) refutes the Valentinian speculation with numbers, and part 4 (29–30) refutes its eschatology. Finally, part 5 (31–35) concerns itself with a series of non-Valentinian gnostic theories.

Following a lengthy introduction on the exclusive and comprehensive truth content of the Scripture (1–5), preserved in the ecclesiastical tradition alone, the first part (6–15) of bk. 3 substantiates the Creator God as the only existing one. Part 2 (16–23) substantiates Christ as his Son and the redeemer of creation in the reality of the incarnation. Chapters 24–25 conclude with a recapitulation of the introduction and with the warning against rejecting the proclamation of the church. Book 4 continues with the basic delineation of Catholic theology by demonstrating the unity of the OT and the NT through Jesus' own words (1–19), the meaning of the OT as prophecy of the NT (20–35), and the evidence of this unity on the basis of Jesus' parables (36–41). Book 5 concludes this extensive work with three further essential individual topics of Christian doctrine, namely, the resurrection of the body, according to the letters of Paul (1–14); the identity of the Creator God with the Father of Jesus Christ, which can be demonstrated from the healing of the blind and the crucifixion and temptation of Christ (15–24); and the reiterated proof of the identity of the Creator and Father based on the eschatological statements of the Bible (25–36).

Hans-Jochen Jaschke calls Irenaeus the "founder of dogmatics,"[9] which does not overstate the case. *Adversus haereses* represents the first comprehensive theological system, which in many respects remained exemplary and influential for the future. Even if there was no officially recognized, generally reliable canon

---

[9] H.-J. Jaschke, *TRE* 16:266.

of the NT at the time of Irenaeus and if we do not know specifically what books he considered canonical, on the basis of his argumentation it may be assumed, in any case, that in his view the canon was already firmly established and the gnostic writings were excluded as apocryphal. The NT constitutes the exclusive foundation of the true faith, for in it the apostles inscribed the unabridged, complete truth they had heard directly from Christ. The only thing ensuring that this original truth is preserved without error is the faithful tradition of the church of Rome, linked as it is to the unbroken sequence of its bishops as successors of the apostles. To support this, Irenaeus offers the first list of Roman bishops beginning with Peter (3.3.3). The criteria for orthodox churches are two concepts Irenaeus introduces: *canon veritatis* ("canon of truth") and *regula fidei* ("rule of faith"). Gnostics lacked both. The latter is determined by the message of Scripture, the baptismal faith, and the confession of faith in fellowship with the church of Rome. "Because of its worthy origin, every church, that is, all believers, wherever they come from, must agree with this church; in it the tradition going back to the apostles has been preserved by the believers all over the world" (3.3.2). Irenaeus thus established foundations of theological and ecclesiastical criteria for truth, ecclesiology, and the theology of primacy that endure to the present day.

One of his christological definitions also found an echo for centuries, namely, the description of the union of the two natures of Christ as "one and the same" (εἷς καὶ αὐτός). It was replaced only when Augustine's formulation, "the one person of Christ" (*Christus una persona*), gained acceptance. Further, his striking theology of the incarnation as the descent of God for the sake of the human being's ascent has also endured for centuries in many reformulations: "The Son of God became the Son of Man that through him we may receive adoption" (3.16.3).

*Editions: Contre les hérésies* (ed. A. Rousseau, L. Doutreleau, C. Mercier, and B. Hemmerdinger; 10 vols.; SC 100, 152, 153, 210, 211, 263, 264, 293, 294; Paris: Cerf, 1965–1982). – *Epideixis: Adversus haereses* (ed. N. Brox; FChr 8.1–4; Fribourg, Switz.: Herder, 1993–2001).

*Translations:* A. C. Coxe, trans., "Irenaeus Against Heresies," in *ANF* (Peabody, Mass.: Hendrickson, 1995; repr. of 1885 ed.), 1:307–567. – *St. Irenaeus of Lyons Against the Heresies* (trans. D. J. Unger and J. J. Dillon; ACW 55; New York: Paulist,1992).

*Dictionary:* B. Reynders, *Lexique comparé du text grec et des versions latines, arménienne et syriaque de l' "Adversus haereses" de saint Irénée* (2 vols.; CSCO 141–42; Louvain: Durbecq, 1954).

*Commentaries:* E. Lanne, "L'église de Rome '*a gloriosissimis duobus apostolis Petro et Paulo Romae fundatae et constitutae ecclesiae*' (Adv Haer. III,3,2)," *Irén* 49 (1976): 275–322. – A. Orbe, *Teología de san Ireneo: Comentario al libro V del "Adversus haereses"* (3 vols.; BAC 25, 29, 33; Madrid: Biblioteca de Autores Cristianos, 1985–1988). – M. Sciatella, "Antropologia e cristologia in S. Ireneo di Lione: *Adversus haereses* V,1–2, analisi strutturale teologica e scritturistica del testo," *Div.* 32 (1989): 269–85. – D. H. Tripp, "The Original Sequence of Irenaeus *Adversus haereses*, I: A Suggestion," *SecCent* 8 (1991): 157–62. – A. Orbe, "El Dios revelado por el Hijo: Análisis de Ireneo, *Adv. haer.* IV,6," *Aug* 32 (1992) 5–50. – A. Orbe, "*Gloria Dei vivens homo* (Análisis de Ireneo, *adv.*

*haer.* IV,20,1–7)," *Greg* 73 (1992): 205–68. – A. Orbe, "Los hechos de Lot: Mujer e hijas vistos por san Ireneo (*adv. haer.* IV, 31, 1, 15/3, 71)," *Greg* 75 (1994): 37–64.

*Studies:* N. Brox, *Offenbarung, Gnosis, und gnostischer Mythos bei Irenäus von Lyon: Zur Charakteristik der Systeme* (SPS 1; Salzburg: A. Pustet, 1966). – G. Jossa, *Regno di Dio e Chiesa: Ricerche sulla concezione escatologica ed ecclesiologica dell'Adversus haereses di Ireneo* (Naples: D'Auria, 1970). – V. Grossi, "Regula veritatis e narratio battesimale in Sant'Ireneo," *Aug* 12 (1972): 437–63. – P. M. Bräuning, "Die '*principalitas*' der römischen Gemeinde nach Irenäus" (PhD diss.; Halle, 1975). – A. Orbe, *Cristología gnóstica: Introducción a la soteriología de los siglos II y III* (BAC 384–85; Madrid: Editorial Católica, 1976). – E. Lanne, "'La règle de la vérité': Aux sources d'une expression de saint Irénée," in *Lex orandi, lex credendi: Miscellanea in onore di p. Cipriano Vagaggini* (ed. G. J. Békés and G. Farnedi; SA 79; Rome: Editrice Anselmiana, 1980), 57–70. – W. Overbeck, *Menschwerdung: Eine Untersuchung zur literarischen und theologischen Einheit des fünften Buches 'Adversus haereses' des Irenäus von Lyon* (Bern and New York: Lang, 1995). – M. A. Donovan, *One Right Reading? A Guide to Irenaeus* (Collegeville, Minn.: Liturgical, 1997).

## *b.* Epideixis tou apostolikou kērygmatos

The substantially smaller *Epideixis tou apostolikou kērygmatos (Demonstration of the Apostolic Preaching)* has been preserved only in an Armenian translation, from ca. 575–580, which was not discovered until 1904, although we have been aware of the existence of this writing from Eusebius's *Ecclesiastical History* (5.26). It contains an abridged version of the theology of Irenaeus against all of the heresies of the time, addressed to a certain Marcion. After a brief prescript introduction (1–3), the first part presents a theology of the history of salvation: God and creation (4–16), human sin and God's mercy (17–30), and the fulfillment of the redemption through Jesus Christ (31–42). Part 2 aims to demonstrate the truth of salvation history from the revelation of Scripture: the preexistence and incarnation of the Son of God (43–51), the fulfillment of prophecies concerning Jesus (52–84), and Christianity as the fulfillment of messianic predictions (85–97). Chapters 98–100 conclude with the admonitions to live by faith and to resist heresy.

Thus, in contrast to Irenaeus's major work, the *Epideixis* represents an abridged outline of Christian doctrine against the backdrop of Gnosticism, albeit without its detailed refutation. "The tractate of Irenaeus is dedicated to solving a task that today is assigned to foundational theology. Its character is apologetic, not only in the sense of a refutation of the opponents but also in the sense of establishing the rationality of the faith in general."[10]

*Editions: Des heiligen Irenäus Schrift zum Erweise der apostolischen Verkündigung: Eis epideixin tou apostolikou kērygmatos* (ed. K. Ter-Měkěrttschian and E. Ter-Minassiantz; notes and epilogue, A. von Harnack; TU 31.1; Leipzig: Hinrichs, 1907). – *The Proof of the Apostolic Preaching—with Seven Fragments: Armenian Version* (ed. K. Ter-Měkěrttschian, S. G. Wilson, J. Barthoulot, and J. Tixeront; PO 12; Paris: Firmin-Didot, 1913), 655–802. – *Demostración de la predicación apostólica* (ed. E. R. Pose; FP 2; Madrid: Ciudad Nueva, 1992). – *Epideixis: Adversus haereses* (ed. N. Brox; 5 vols.;

---

10 Weber, BKV² 4:xiv.

FChr 8.1; Fribourg, Switz., and New York: Herder, 1993–2001), 21–97. – *Démonstration de la prédication apostolique* (ed. A. Rousseau; SC 406; Paris: Cerf, 1995).

*Translations: Proof of the Apostolic Preaching* (trans. J. P. Smith; ACW 16; Westminster, Md.: Newman, 1952). – *On the Apostolic Preaching* (trans. J. Behr; Crestwood, N.Y.: St. Vladimir's Seminary Press, 1997).

*Word Index:* B. Reynders, *Vocabulaire de la "Démonstration" et des fragments de saint Irénée* (Chevetogne, Belg.: Chevetogne, 1958).

## 2. Hippolytus of Rome

Hippolytus was the last of the Western fathers to write his works in Greek; after him Latin became the exclusive literary language of the West, even though knowledge of Greek, indeed bilingualism, was maintained until the end of the fourth century. As far as we are able to gather from his own writings, Hippolytus lived in Rome during the pontificates extending from Victor to Pontianus (ca. 189–235), first as a presbyter, then, after the death of Calixtus (222), according to his own claim (*Haer.* pref. 6; 9.12.21), as bishop (from 217 on?). If this information is accepted as accurate, he must have been an antibishop, possibly as a result of his debates with Calixtus. While he himself was a fierce opponent of Noetus and Sabellius, he charged Calixtus with being Monarchian, whereas the latter called him a ditheist. In addition, Hippolytus wanted to make more stringent the lenient penitential practice that Calixtus imposed when readmitting someone to the sacraments. Penance & Power

The schism lasted until 235, when, upon taking office, Emperor Maximinus Thrax immediately banished both bishops of Rome, Pontianus and Hippolytus, to Sardinia. Both died in exile but apparently were reconciled, as were the Roman parties under Bishop Antherus (235–236), for Bishop Fabian (236–250) had both of them moved to Rome and interred them on the same day (August 13). The church venerated them jointly as saints. In 1973 P. Testini may have found the sarcophagus of Hippolytus under the basilica of the Isola Sacra near Fiumicino, where he must have been taken after his initial interment on the Via Tiburtina.

In 1551 a headless marble statue sitting on a cathedra was discovered, on the pedestal of which an incomplete list of Hippolytus's works, as well as his *Canon paschalis*, are engraved. Since this was subsequently considered to be an image of Hippolytus, the statue was supplied with a male head. According to M. Guarducci, however, the figure is that of a Greek female philosopher, and the statue is a copy of one dating from the first decade of the second century, patterned after sitting female philosophers, such as the Lampsakos. The statue was in the Lateran Museum until 1959; since then it has been in the entrance hall of the Vatican Library.

Hippolytus had been a prolific writer whose works, among others, included a complete commentary on the Song of Songs (currently extant only in an Old Georgian translation), a commentary on the book of Daniel, and a chronicle of the history of the world until 234/235. But his extraordinary significance for church history and patrology is based on his two main works, the *Refutatio omnium haeresium (Refutation of All Heresies)* and the *Traditio apostolica (Apostolic*

What does he say about Resurrection here?

*Tradition*). P. Nautin suspected that the familiar works of Hippolytus should not be attributed to Hippolytus alone but partly to a second, otherwise unknown author by the name of Josephus or Josippus. This theory, however, has hardly been accepted up to now.

*Bibliographies:* G. Kretschmar, "Bibliographie zu Hippolyt von Rom," *JLH* 1 (1955): 90–95. – F. W. Bautz, *BBKL* 2:888–93.

*Editions:*
*Antichrist* (ed. E. Norelli; BPat 10; Florence: Edizioni Dehoniane, 1987).
*Benedictiones* (ed. M. Brière, L. Mariès, and B.-C. Mercier; PO 27.1–2; Paris: Firmin-Didot, 1954) [Com].
*Benedictiones Isaac et Jacob, In Danielem* (ed. C. Diobouniotis and N. Beïs; TU 38.1; Leipzig: Hinrichs, 1911).
*Chronicon: Die Chronik des Hippolytos im Matritensis graecus 121, nebst einer Abhandlung über den Stadiasmus maris magni von O. Cuntz* (ed. A. Bauer; TU 29.1; Leipzig: Hinrichs, 1905) [Com]. – *Die Chronik* (ed. A. Bauer and R. Helm; vol. 4 of *Hippolytus Werke;* 2d ed.; GCS 46; Berlin: Akademie, 1955; 1st ed. published as GCS 36).
*Contra Noetum* (ed. and trans. R. Butterworth; London: Heythrop College [University of London] Press, 1977) [ET].
*Fragments of Contra Noetum, Adversus Judaeos:* E. Schwartz, *Zwei Predigten Hippolyts* (SBAW.PPH 3; Munich: Verlag der Bayerischen Akademie der Wissenschaften, 1936).
*In Canticum canticorum, In Danielem, Exegetical and Homiletical Works: Exegetische und homiletische Schriften* (ed. G. N. Bonwetsch and H. Achelis; vol. 1 of *Hippolytus Werke;* GCS; Leipzig: Hinrichs, 1897).
*In Danielem: Commentaire sur Daniel* (ed. G. Bardy and M. Lefèvre; SC 14; Paris: Cerf, 1947).
*De David et Goliath, In Canticum canticorum, De antichristo: Traités d'Hippolyte sur David et Goliath, sur le Cantique des cantique et sur l'antéchrist* (ed G. Garitte; CSCO 263–264; Louvain: SCO, 1965).

*Translations:* A. C. Coxe, trans., "The Refutation of All Heresies," "The Extant Works and Fragments of Hippolytus: Exegetical," and "The Extant Works and Fragments of Hippolytus: Dogmatical and Historical," in *ANF* (Peabody, Mass.: Hendrickson, 1995; repr. of 1885 ed.), 5:1–259 [*Opera omnia*].

*Encyclopedia Articles:* M. Richard, *DSp* 7.1:531–71. – M. Marcovich, *TRE* 15:381–87. – C. Scholten, *RAC* 15:492–551. – P. Nautin, *EECh* 1:383–85. – E. Ferguson, *EEC* 1:531–32.

*Collections of Essays:* M. Richard, *Opera minora* (3 vols.; Turnhout, Belg.: Brepols, 1976–1977), nos. 10–20. – *Ricerche su Ippolito* (SEAug 13; Rome: Institutum Patristicum Augustinianum, 1977). – *Nuove ricerche su Ippolito* (SEAug 30; Rome: Institutum Patristicum Augustinianum, 1989).

*Studies:* G. N. Bonwetsch, *Studien zu den Kommentaren Hippolyts zum Buche Daniel und Hohen Liede* (TU 16.2; Leipzig: Hinrichs, 1897). – E. Schwartz, *Christliche und jüdische Ostertafeln* (AGWG.PH NS 8.6; Berlin: Weidmann, 1905). – A. d'Alès, *La théologie de saint Hippolyte* (BTH; Paris: Beauchesne, 1906). – P. Nautin, *Le dossier d'Hippolyte et de Méliton dans les florilèges dogmatiques et chez les historiens modernes* (Patr. 1; Paris: Cerf, 1953). – A. Zani, *La cristologia di Ippolito* (Brescia: Morcelliana, 1983). – C. Osborne, *Rethinking Early Greek Philosophy: Hippolytus of Rome and the Presocratics* (London: Duckworth; Ithaca, N.Y.: Cornell University Press, 1987). – A. Whealey, "Hippolytus' Lost *De universo* and *De resurrectione*: Some New Hypotheses," *VC* 50 (1996): 244–56.

*Archaeology:* P. Testini, "Sondaggi a S. Ippolito all'Isola Sacra: I depositi reliquiari scoperti sotto l'altare," *RPARA* 46 (1973–1974): 165–77. – M. Guarducci, "La statua di 'Sant'Ippolito' in Vaticano," *RPARA* 47 (1974–1975): 163–90. – P. Testini, *La basilica di S. Ippolito: Ricerche archeologiche nell'Isola Sacra* (Rome: Istituto Nazionale d'Archeologia e Storia dell'Arte, 1975), 41–132. – E. Prinzivalli, "Hippolytus, statue of," *EECh* 1:385. – E. dal Covolo, "Ancora sulla 'statua di Sant'Ippolito': Per una 'messa a punto' dei rapporti tra i Severi e il cristianesimo," *Aug* 32 (1992): 51–59. – M. Guarducci, *San Pietro e Sant'Ippolito: Storia di statue famose in Vaticano* (Rome: Instituto Poligrafico e Zecca dello Stato, Libreria dello Stato, 1991). – A. Brent, *Hippolytus and the Roman Church in the Third Century: Communities in Tension before the Emergence of a Monarch-Bishop* (SVigChr 31; Leiden and New York: Brill, 1995).

*Authorship:* P. Nautin, *Hippolyte et Josipe: Contribution à l'histoire de la littérature chrétienne du troisième siècle* (ETHDT 1; Paris: Cerf, 1947). – M. Richard, "Dernières remarques sur s. Hippolyte et le soi-disant Josipe," *RSR* 43 (1955): 379–94. – P. Nautin, "L'homélie d'Hippolyte sur le psautier et les oeuvres de Josipe," *RHR* 179 (1969): 137–79. M. Simonetti, "Una nuova proposta su Ippolito," *Aug* 36 (1996): 13–46.

*Contra Noetum:* J. Frickel, "Der Antinoetbericht des Epiphanius als Korrektiv für den Text von Hippolyts *Contra Noetum,*" *Comp* 35 (1990): 39–53. – J. Frickel, "Hippolyts Schrift *Contra Noetum:* Ein Pseudo-Hippolyt," in *Logos: Festschrift für Louise Abramowski zum 8. Juli 1993* (ed. H. C. Brennecke, E. L. Grasmück, and C. Markschies; BZNW 67; Berlin and New York: de Gruyter, 1993), 87–123.

## *a.* Refutatio omnium haeresium

Following and using Irenaeus's great work against the gnostics, *Adversus haereses,* as well as a number of other sources, Hippolytus wrote the *Refutatio* in ten volumes. This work primarily seeks to demonstrate that the gnostics did nothing more than plagiarize Greek philosophy and mythology and thus had nothing to do with the Christian heritage of faith. Books 1–4 offer a structured survey of the whole breadth of Greek and Hellenistic philosophy, from the pre-Socratics to the time of Hippolytus, in order to afford the reader a sound comparison with the gnostic heresies, their precursors and parallels, which follow in bks. 5–9. Finally, bk. 10 offers a terse summary of the work ("epitome").

Its form as a compendium has given the work a unique history of transmission. Early on, bk. 1 was handed down separately as an introduction to philosophy entitled *Philosophoumena;* in 1701 it was rediscovered and attributed to Origen. Books 2, 3, and the beginning of 4 are lost, but their content, namely, the Greek and Near Eastern mystery cults and mythologies, can be roughly reconstructed on the basis of what precedes and follows. Books 4–10 were found in 1842 and also were initially attributed to Origen; since 1851, however, the entire work has been restored to Hippolytus.

*Editions: Refutation of All Heresies* (ed. M. Marcovich; PTS 25; New York; Berlin: de Gruyter, 1986).

*Studies:* K. Koschorke, *Hippolyts Ketzerbekämpfung und Polemik gegen die Gnostiker: Eine tendenzkritische Untersuchung seiner "Refutatio omnium haeresium"* (GOF 6.4; Wiesbaden: Harrassowitz, 1975). – J. Frickel, *Das Dunkel um Hippolyt von Rom—ein Lösungsversuch: Die Schriften Elenchos und Contra Noëtum* (GrTS 13; Graz, Austria:

Eigenverlag des Instituts für Ökumenische Theologie und Patrologie an der Universität Graz, 1988). – J. Mansfeld, *Heresiography in Context: Hippolytus' Elenchos as a Source for Greek Philosophy* (PhAnt 56; Leiden and New York: Brill, 1992).

## b. Traditio apostolica

The *Traditio apostolica (Apostolic Tradition)* by Hippolytus, originating ca. 215, frequently is not treated under his name but in the framework of other early church rules (*Didache, Didascalia apostolorum*) because it is lost in its original form and is extant only in Coptic, Arabic, Ethiopic, and Latin versions discovered in the nineteenth century. For this reason, the authorship of Hippolytus is still not uniformly accepted. Yet it may be assumed that, in spite of all the differences, the versions are based on one and the same textual source, which G. Dix (1937) and B. Botte (1963) reconstructed as far as possible. After the *Didache*, it represents the most significant witness of early Christian community life and liturgy, beginning with the rite of selecting and consecrating bishops, priests, and deacons; eucharistic prayers; and the appointing of the offices and ministries of widows, readers, virgins, subdeacons, and those gifted in healings. Here one recognizes the ministries and ranks in the early church, which were then much more multifaceted than today and officially commissioned by the church. This is followed by the initiation procedures in the community, the candidature, the catechumenate, the baptismal rite, confirmation, and the Eucharist, and by a detailed list of morally offensive occupations and practices associated with the pagan cult of the gods, which a Christian was no longer able to practice (e.g., owning a brothel, prostitution, acting, being a gladiator or an astrologer). The conclusion orders further liturgical tasks to be performed: the agape, fasting, burials, times of daily prayer, catechesis, and the use of the sign of the cross.

*Editions: The Treatise on the Apostolic Tradition of St. Hippolytus of Rome, Bishop and Martyr* (ed. G. Dix; rev. ed. with corrections, preface, and bibliography by H. Chadwick; London: Alban; Ridgefield, Conn.: Morehouse, 1992) [ET]. – *La Tradition apostolique de Saint Hippolyte* (ed. and trans. B. Botte; rev. ed. A. Gerhards and S. Felbecker; LQF 39; Münster: Aschendorffsche Verlagsbuchhandlung, 1989). – *Didascaliae apostolorum, Canonum ecclesiasticorum, Traditionis apostolicae versiones latinae* (ed. E. Tidner; TU 75; Berlin: Akademie, 1963), 115–50. – Ethiopic: *Der aethiopische Text der Kirchenordnung des Hippolyt* (ed. and trans. H. Duensing; AGWG.PH 3.32; Göttingen: Vandenhoeck & Ruprecht, 1946). – Arabic: *Les "127 canons des apôtres": Texte arabe* (ed. J. and A. Périer; PO 8.4; Paris: Firmin-Didot, 1912). – Coptic: *Der koptische Text der Kirchenordnung Hippolyts* (ed. W. Till and J. Leipoldt; TU 58.5; Berlin: Akademie, 1954). – *Didache = Zwölf-Apostel-Lehre; Traditio apostolica = Apostolische Überlieferung* (ed. G. Schöllgen and W. Geerlings; FChr 1; Fribourg, Switz., and New York: Herder, 1991), 141–313 [Com].

*Translations:* G. J. Cuming, *Hippolytus: A Text For Students* (2d ed.; GLS; Bramcote, Nottingham: Grove, 1987) [Com].

*Dictionary:* J. Blanc, "Lexique comparé des versions de la *Tradition apostolique* de Hippolyte," *RTAM* 22 (1955): 173–92.

*Encyclopedia Articles:* P. F. Bradshaw, "Kirchenordnungen I," *TRE* 18:662–70. – P. Nautin, *EECh* 1:63.

*General Studies:* H. Elfers, *Die Kirchenordnung Hippolyts von Rom: Neue Untersuchungen unter besonderer Berücksichtigung des Buches von R. Lorentz—"De Egyptische Kerkordening en Hippolytus van Rome"* (Paderborn: Bonifacius, 1938). – A. G. Martimort, "Nouvel examen de la 'Tradition apostolique' d'Hippolyte," *BLE* 88 (1987): 5–25.

*Particular Studies:* J. M. Hanssens, *La liturgie d'Hippolyte: Ses documents, son titulaire, ses origines, et son caractère* (OrChrAn 155; Rome: Pontificium Institutum Orientalium Studiorum, 1959). – J. M. Hanssens, *La liturgie d'Hippolyte: Documents et études* (Rome: Libreria Editrice dell'Università Gregoriana, 1970). – A. F. Walls, "The Latin Version of Hippolytus' Apostolic Tradition," in *Papers Presented to the Third International Conference on Patristic Studies Held at Christ Church, Oxford, 1959* (ed. F. Cross; StPatr 3; TU 78; Berlin: Akademie, 1961), 155–62. – J. Magne, *Tradition apostolique sur les charismes et Diataxeis des saints apôtres: Identification des documents et analyse du rituel des ordinations* (Paris: Magne, 1975). – P. F. Bradshaw, E. C. Whitaker, and G. J. Cuming, *Essays on Hippolytus* (GLS 15; Bramcote, Nottinghamshire, 1978). – A. Jilek, *Initiationsfeier und Amt: Ein Beitrag zur Struktur und Theologie der Ämter und des Taufgottesdienstes in der frühen Kirche (Traditio apostolica, Tertulliano, Cipriano)* (EHS.T 130; Frankfurt and Cirencester, Eng.: Lang, 1979). – M. Metzger, "Nouvelles perspectives pour la prétendue *Tradition apostolique*," *EO* 5 (1988): 241–59. – A. G. Martimort, "Encore Hippolyte et la '*Tradition apostolique*,'" *BLE* 92 (1991): 133–37.

# V. BEGINNINGS OF CHRISTIAN SCHOOLS

Regarding schools in antiquity, it is fundamentally important first to distinguish, regardless of further differentiation, between a school as an educational establishment and a school figuratively, in the sense of a particular common viewpoint, whether in the Christian or non-Christian realm. The three-stage Hellenistic-Roman education began at age six or seven with elementary instruction in reading, writing, and arithmetic under the tutelage of a private tutor or in an elementary school of a *litterator/ludi magister* (γραμματεύς). This was followed by the instruction of a *grammaticus,* who taught the first of the seven "liberal arts," grammar, that is, the foundations of language, through the most important literary works of antiquity, especially Homer and Virgil. The *rhetor* continued the instruction in the six remaining subjects: dialectics, rhetoric, arithmetic, music, geometry, and astronomy. To this point, all of the educated in antiquity shared the same educational foundation. Although a number of church fathers (e.g., Tertullian) complained that children of Christians were made to learn the useless, indeed damaging, pagan myths in these schools, at no point in antiquity is there evidence of Christian schools offering general education. The uniform literary education became the foundation for all educated professions, such as the *rhetor* (teacher), lawyer, and politician, all of which presupposed an excellent command of language. Finally, beyond this there was philosophy, the "grad school" of thought and of understanding the world. At this point the concept of "school" became differentiated. It was possible to attend the instruction of a philosopher (the most famous and most significant school of philosophy, dating from 387 B.C.E. to 529 C.E.—and thus likely the longest-lasting school in the history of the world—was the Platonic Academy in Athens, where some of the outstanding church fathers studied, such as Basil the Great and Gregory of Nazianzus), but it was also possible to join one of the philosophical viewpoints ("schools") without this.

In the Christian realm, the third century saw the development of episcopal schools for the purpose of instructing catechumens in the essentials of the Christian faith. The earliest institution of this kind known to us was led by Origen, in Alexandria, beginning in 217. Before and alongside these institutional schools were independent Christian teachers and "philosophers" (such as Justin) who gathered Christian as well as non-Christian students around them, in keeping with the profane schools of philosophy. They intended partly to lead to conversion and partly to deepen understanding of the faith, but always to ponder the meaning and praxis of the world and life. It should not be ignored that, for an individual in antiquity, a reasonable religion such as Christianity was categorized as  a "philosophy," that is, a system of interpreting the world and of leading one's life.

Special importance was attained by the Christian "philosophical schools" that arose, generally without episcopal commission, in cultural centers and where a sufficient number of educated Christians gathered and had a large library available to support their study. About 180, Pantaenus, from Sicily, gathered students around him in Alexandria; the same was true, perhaps even at the same time, of Clement of Alexandria and later of Origen. When the latter fell out with the bishop of Alexandria in 230, he founded a new school in Caesarea in Palestine, sanctioned by the local bishop; this school would attain greatness in the fourth century. In its initial phase, beginning ca. 260, the Antiochene school probably was not as much an institution as it was a theology, traced back to Lucian of Antioch, that strongly influenced the school already established in Edessa in the early third century. The institution was not established until Diodore of Tarsus; the school attained its peak in the fourth century during his tenure and that of his master students.

The Alexandrian and Antiochene schools became prominent in the figurative sense as well—namely, in their exegetical methods and, beginning with the fourth century, in the dogmatic disputes regarding the doctrine of the Trinity and Christology. The Antiochenes attached particular importance to the historical or literal meaning (without restricting themselves to this). Conversely, the Alexandrians intensively attended to the allegorical, moral, and anagogical meaning of Scripture and thereby endeavored to discover a deeper, secret meaning of the biblical writings. This pursuit was linked with their view of Christianity as the "true gnosis," which has no need of esoteric, secret writings but instead unveils the mysteries contained in the writings that have been handed down and accepted by the church. In dogmatic theology the Antiochenes were more inclined to highlight the distinctions between God and Christ ("Christology of separation"), whereas the Alexandrians were more emphatic on the unity of the three persons of the Godhead and of the two natures of Christ ("Christology of oneness"). Of course, this rough characterization of the schools offers only a point of reference on the essential orientation and should not be superimposed mechanically; in particulars, every statement of the schools is to be tested and evaluated carefully.

*Encyclopedia Articles:* K. Müller, "Allegorische Dichtererklärung," PWSup 16–22. – H. Fuchs, "Bildung," *RAC* 2:346–62. – H. Fuchs, "Enkyklios Paideia," *RAC* 5:365–98. – K. Thraede, "Epos," *RAC* 5:984–1007. – P. Blomenkamp, "Erziehung," *RAC* 6:502–59. – C. D. G. Müller, "Alexandrien I," *TRE* 2:248–61. – B. Drewery, "Antiochien II," *TRE* 3:103–13. – H. J. W. Drijvers, "Edessa," *TRE* 9:277–88. – W. Liebeschütz, "Hochschule," *RAC* 15:858–911. – M. Simonetti, "Alexandria II. School," *EECh* 1:22–23. – M. Simonetti, "Antioch V. School," *EECh* 1:50–51. – S. Pricoco, "School," *EECh* 2:759–62. – H. Heinen, "Alexandria in Late Antiquity," in *The Coptic Encyclopedia* (ed. A. S. Atiya; 8 vols.; New York: Macmillan, 1991), 1:95–103.

*General Studies:* R. Nelz, *Die theologischen Schulen der morgenländischen Kirchen während der sieben ersten christlichen Jahrhunderte in ihrer Bedeutung für die Ausbildung des Klerus* (Bonn: Rhenania, 1916). – G. Bardy, "L'Église et l'enseignement dans les trois premiers siècles," *RevScRel* 12 (1932): 1–28. – W. Jaeger, *Early Christianity and Greek Paideia* (Cambridge, Mass.: Belknap Press of Harvard University Press, 1961; German trans., *Das frühe Christentum und die griechische Bildung* [trans. Walther Eltester; Berlin: de Gruyter, 1963]). – A. Quacquarelli, *Scuola e cultura dei primi secoli cristiani* (Brescia: La Scuola, 1974). – H.-T. Johann, ed., *Erziehung und Bildung in der heidnischen und christlichen Antike* (WdF 377; Darmstadt: Wissenschaftliche Buchgesellschaft, 1976). – H.-I. Marrou, *History of Education in Antiquity* (trans. G. Lamb; New York: Sheed & Ward, 1956; repr., Madison: University of Wisconsin Press, 1982). – H.-I. Marrou, *Saint Augustin et la fin de la culture antique* (4th ed.; BEFAR 145; Paris: de Boccard, 1958). – U. Neymeyr, *Die christlichen Lehrer im zweiten Jahrhundert: Ihre Lehrtätigkeit, ihr Selbstverständnis, und ihre Geschichte* (SVigChr 4; Leiden and New York: Brill, 1989).

*Alexandria:* W. Bousset, *Jüdisch-christlicher Schulbetrieb in Alexandrien und Rom: Literarische Untersuchungen zu Philo und Clemens von Alexandria, Justin, und Irenäus* (FRLANT NS 6; Göttingen: Vandenhoeck & Ruprecht, 1915; repr., Hildesheim and New York: Olms, 1975). – G. Bardy, "Aux origines de l'école d'Alexandrie," *RSR* 27 (1937): 65–90. – E. Molland, *The Conception of the Gospel in the Alexandrinian Theology* (SNVAO.HF; Oslo: I kommisjon hos J. Dybwad, 1938). – P. Brezzi, *La gnosi cristiana di Alessandria e le antiche scuole cristiane* (Rome: Edizioni italiane, 1950). – M. Hornschuh, "Das Leben des Origenes und die Entstehung der alexandrinischen Schule," *ZKG* 71 (1960): 1–25, 193–214.

*Antioch:* G. Bardy, *Recherches sur saint Lucien d'Antioche et son école* (ETH; Paris: Beauchesne, 1936).

*Caesarea:* A. Knauber, "Das Anliegen der Schule des Origenes zu Cäsarea," *MTZ* 19 (1968): 182–203.

*Edessa:* E. R. Hayes, *L'école d'Édesse* (Paris: Presses Modernes, 1930).

*Nisibis:* A. Vööbus, *History of the School of Nisibis* (CSCO 266; Louvain: SCO, 1965). – H. J. W. Drijvers, *TRE* 24: 573–76.

### Exegesis

*Bibliographies: Elenchus biblicus* (Rome: Pontifical Biblical Institute, 1920–). *[EBB]* – H. J. Sieben, *Exegesis patrum: Saggio bibliografico sull'esegesi biblica dei Padri della Chiesa* (SuPa 2; Rome: Istituto Patristico "Augustinianum," 1983).

*Translations:* J. W. Trigg, *Biblical Interpretation* (MFC 9; Wilmington, Del.: Glazier; 1989). – K. Froelich, *Biblical Interpretation in the Early Church* (SoECT; Philadelphia: Fortress, 1984).

*Reference Works: Biblia patristica: Index des citations et allusions bibliques dans la littérature patristique* (Paris: Centre National de la Recherche Scientifique, 1975–) [BiPa]. – G. Rinaldi, *Biblia gentium: Primo contributo per un indice delle citazioni, dei riferimenti, e delle allusioni alla Bibbia negli autori pagani, greci e latini, di età imperiale* (Rome: Libreria Sacre Scritture, 1989). – H. J. Sieben, *Kirchenväterhomilien zum Neuen Testament: Ein Repertorium der Textausgaben und Übersetzungen* (IP 22; The Hague: Abbatia Sancti Petri, 1991).

*Journals: Annali di storia dell'esegesi* (Bologna, 1984–). *[ASes]*

*Encyclopedia Articles:* J. C. Joosen and J. H. Waszink, "Allegorese," *RAC* 1:283–87. – H. Schreckenberg, "Exegese I," *RAC* 6:1174–94. – W. E. Gerber, "Exegese III (NT u. Alte Kirche)," *RAC* 6:1211–29. – H. Karpp, "Bibel IV: Die Funktionen der Bibel in der alten Kirche 1: Alte Kirche," *TRE* 6:48–58. – J. Pépin and K. Hoheisel, "Hermeneutik," *RAC* 14:722–71. – M. Simonetti, "Exegesis, patristic," *EECh* 1:309–11. – J. Gribomont, "Scripture, holy," *EECh* 2:762–64.

*Collections of Essays: La Bible et les Pères* (Paris: Presses Universitaires de France, 1971). – *La monde grec ancient et la Bible, La monde latin antique et la Bible,* and *Saint Augustin et la Bible* (vols. 1–3 of *Bible de tous les temps;* Paris: Beauchesne, 1984–1986). – M. Tardieu, ed., *Les règles de l'interprétation* (Paris: Cerf, 1987). – *Cahiers de Biblia patristica* (ed. Michel Tardieu; Paris: Cerf, 1987). – J. van Oort and U. Wickert, eds., *Christliche Exegese zwischen Nicaea und Chalcedon* (Kampen, Neth.: Kok Pharos, 1992). – S. Felici, ed., *Esegesi e catechesi nei Padri (secc. II–IV)* (BSRel 106; Rome: LAS, 1993). – E. Norelli, ed., *Da Gesù a Origene* (vol. 1 of *La Bibbia nell'antichità cristiana;* Bologna: EDB, 1993). – S. Felici, ed., *Esegesi e catechesi nei Padri (secc. IV–VII)* (BSRel 112; Rome: LAS, 1994). – T. Finan and V. Twomey, ed., *Scriptural Interpretation in the Fathers: Letter and Spirit* (Dublin and Portland, Oreg.: Four Courts, 1995). – G. Schöllgen and C. Scholten, eds., *Stimuli: Exegese und ihre Hermeneutik in Antike und Christentum Festschrift für Ernst Dassmann* (JAC.E 23; Münster: Aschendorff, 1996). – P. M. Blowers, *The Bible in Greek Christian Antiquity* (Notre Dame, Ind.: University of Notre Dame Press, 1997).

*Studies:* A. B. Hersmann, *Studies in Greek Allegoric Interpretation* (Chicago: Blue Sky, 1906). – H. Dachs, "'Die λύσις ἐκ τοῦ προσώπου: Ein exegetischer und kritischer Grundsatz Aristarchs und seine Neuanwendung auf Ilias und Odyssee" (PhD diss., Erlangen, 1913). – F. Wehrli, *Zur Geschichte der allegorischen Deutung Homers im Altertum* (Borna and Leipzig: R. Noske, 1928). – J. Pépin, *Mythe et allégorie: Les origines grecques et les contestations judéo-chrétiennes* (2d rev. ed.; Paris: Études Augustiniennes, 1977). – *The Cambridge History of the Bible* (3 vols.; Cambridge: Cambridge University Press, 1963–1970). – H. de Lubac, *L'Écriture dans la tradition* (Paris: Aubier, 1966). – H. Dörrie, "Zur Methodik antiker Exegese," *ZNW* 65 (1974): 121–38. – M. Simonetti, *Lettera e/o allegoria: Un contributo alla storia dell'esegesi patristica* (SEAug 23; Rome: Institutum Patristicum Augustinianum, 1985). – J. Pépin, *La tradition de l'allégorie de Philon d'Alexandrie à Dante: Études historiques* (Paris: Études Augustiniennes, 1987). – A. Pollastri and F. Cocchini, *Bibbia e storia nel cristianesimo latino* (Rome: Borla, 1988). – B. Studer, *"Delectare et prodesse:* Zu einem Schlüsselwort der patristischen Exegese," *SEAug* 27 (1988): 555–81; repr. in idem, *Dominus Salvator: Studien zur Christologie und Exegese der Kirchenväter* (SA 107; Rome: Pontificio Ateneo S. Anselmo, 1992), 431–61. – H. Graf Reventlow, *Epochen der Bibelauslegung* (3 vols.; Munich: C. H. Beck, 1990–1996). – C. Blönnigen, *Der griechische Ursprung der jüdisch-hellenistischen Allegorese und ihre Rezeption in der alexandrinischen Patristik* (Frankfurt and New York: Lang, 1992). – D. Dawson,

*Allegorical Readers and Cultural Revision in Ancient Alexandria* (Berkeley: University of California Press, 1992). – F. Siegert, "Homerinterpretation–Tora-Unterweisung–Bibelauslegung: Vom Ursprung der patristischen Hermeneutik," in *Papers Presented at the Eleventh International Conference on Patristic Studies Held in Oxford, 1991* (ed. E. Livingstone; StPatr 25; Louvain: Peeters, 1993), 159–71. – B. de Margerie, *An Introduction to the History of Exegesis* (trans. P. de Fontnouvelle; 3 vols.; Petersham, Mass.: St. Bede's, 1991–1993); trans. of *Introduction à l'histoire de l'exégèse* (4 vols.; Paris: Cerf, 1980–1990). – M. Simonetti, *Biblical Interpretation in the Early Church: An Historical Introduction to Patristic Exegesis* (trans. J. A. Hughes; Edinburgh: T&T Clark, 1994); trans. of *Profilo storico dell'esegesi patristica* (SuPa 1; Rome: Istituto Patristico "Augustinianum," 1981).

# A. Philo of Alexandria

The initial basis of Alexandrian exegesis was already established before Christianity by the Alexandrian Jew Philo (20 B.C.E. until after 42 C.E.). In keeping with the Platonic and Stoic worldview that the visible world is the copy of the real world of ideas, he discovered the deeper, spiritual meaning behind the literal meaning of Scripture (OT). In doing so, he followed the profane exegesis of Homer and other poets and myths taught by the schools. Because of enlightened philosophy, they could no longer be understood literally, so the allegorical explications elevated the deeper, philosophical and moral, meaning. Philo thus combined Hellenistic philosophy and education with Jewish exegesis and theology. The metropolis of Alexandria offered this enterprise particularly favorable conditions, as a melting pot of Hellenism and the home of the largest Jewish Diaspora of the Roman Empire, which was already exemplified in the second century B.C.E. with the translation of the Hebrew OT into Greek (Septuagint).

About sixty works have been attributed to Philo, mainly commentaries on the Pentateuch and philosophical writings, which Clement of Alexandria, Origen, Gregory of Nyssa, Ambrose, and Jerome knew and analyzed in the original and which influenced many other church fathers. Eusebius and Jerome valued Philo's importance for Christianity so highly that they dealt with him as if he were a Christian. He represents the most prominent example of the adoption of Jewish theology in Christianity, on the basis not of their common Semitic origin but of their common Hellenistic culture—a question pertinent to the investigation of "Jewish Christianity" that has attracted more focused attention in recent years.

*Bibliographies:* H. L. Goodhart and E. R. Goodenough, "A General Bibliography of Philo Judaeus," in E. R. Goodenough, *The Politics of Philo Judaeus: Practice and Theory* (New Haven: Yale University Press; London: H. Milford, Oxford University Press, 1938), 125–321. – E. Hilgert, "*Bibliographia philoniana* 1935–1981," ANRW 2.21.1:47–97. – R. Radice et al., *Philo of Alexandria: An Annotated Bibliography, 1937–1986* (2d ed.; SVigChr 8; Leiden and New York: Brill, 1992). – D. T. Runia, R. Radice, and D. Satran, "Philo of Alexandria: An Annotated Bibliography 1986–1987," in *Studia Philonica Annual: Studies in Hellenistic Judaism* 2 (1990): 141–75. – D. T. Runia, R. Radice, and P. A. Cathey, "Philo of Alexandria: An Annotated Bibliography," in *Heirs of the Septuagint—Philo, Hellenistic Judaism, and Early Christianity: Festschrift for Earle Hilgert* (ed. D. T. Runia, D. M. Hay, and D. Winston; BJS 230; Atlanta: Scholars Press, 1991), 347–74.

*Editions:* L. Cohn and P. Wendland, *Philonis Alexandrini Opera quae supersunt* (8 vols.; Berlin: G. Reimer, 1896–1930; repr., Berlin: de Gruyter, 1962–1963). – *Philo* (ed. F. H. Colson and G. H. Whitaker; 12 vols.; LCL; Cambridge, Mass.: Harvard University Press, 1929–1962) [ET]. – R. Arnaldez, C. Mondésert, J. Pouilloux, et al., eds., *Les Oeuvres de Philon d'Alexandrie* (36 vols.; Paris: Cerf, 1961–1992). – E. M. Smallwood, ed., *Legatio ad Gaium Philonis Alexandrini* (2d ed.; Leiden: Brill, 1970) [ET/Com]. – P. Graffigna, *La vita contemplativa* (Genoa: Melangolo, 1992) [Com].

*Translations:* The *Contemplative Life, The Giants, and Selections* (ed. J. Dillon; trans. and introd. D. Winston; CWS; New York: Paulist, 1981).

*Indexes:* G. Mayer, *Index philoneus* (Berlin and New York: de Gruyter, 1974). – *Biblia patristica, supplément: Philon d'Alexandrie* (Paris: Centre National de la Recherche Scientifique, 1982). – D. T. Runia, "An *Index locorum philonicorum* to Völker," in *Studia philonica Annual: Studies in Hellenistic Judaism* 1 (1990): 82–93. – D. T. Runia, "How to Search Philo," *Studia philonica Annual: Studies in Hellenistic Judaism* 2 (1990): 106–39. – P. Borgen, K. Fuglseth, and R. Skarsten, *The Philo Index: A Complete Greek Word Index to the Writings of Philo of Alexandria* (Grand Rapids and Cambridge: Eerdmans, 2000).

*Encyclopedia Articles:* V. Nikiprowetzky and A. Solignac, *DSp* 12.1:1352–74. – H. Crouzel, *EECh* 2:682–83. – M. Mach, *TRE* 26:523–31. – R. Berchman, *EEC* 2:913–14.

*Introductions:* E. R. Goodenough, *An Introduction to Philo Judaeus* (2d ed.; Oxford: B. Blackwell, 1962; repr., Lanham, Md.: University Press of America, 1986). – S. Sandmel, *Philo of Alexandria: An Introduction* (Oxford and New York: Oxford University Press, 1979).

*Collections of Essays:* Studia philonica (1980). – *ANRW* 2.21.1. – *Studia philonica Annual: Studies in Hellenistic Judaism* (1990). – D. T. Runia, *Exegesis and Philosophy: Studies in Philo of Alexandria* (Collected Studies 332; Aldershot, Hampshire, Eng.: Variorum; Brookfield, Vt.: Gower, 1990–1991). – D. T. Runia, *Philo and the Church Fathers: A Collection of Papers* (SVigChr 32; New York: Brill, 1995).

*General Studies:* M. Pohlenz, *Philon von Alexandreia* (NAWG.PH 5; Göttingen: Vandenhoeck & Ruprecht, 1942), 409–87; repr. in *Kleine Schriften* (ed. H. Dörrie; 2 vols.; Hildesheim, Olms, 1965), 2:305–83. – J. Daniélou, *Philon d'Alexandrie* (Paris: A. Fayard, 1958). – A. Maddallena, *Filone Alessandrino* (Milan: U. Mursia, 1970). – R. Williamson, *Jews in the Hellenistic World: Philo* (CCWJCW 1.2; Cambridge and New York: Cambridge University Press, 1989). – D. T. Runia, *Philo in Early Christian Literature: A Survey* (CRINT 3.3; Assen: Van Gorkum; Minneapolis: Fortress, 1993).

*Particular Studies:* P. Heinisch, *Der Einfluss Philos auf die älteste christliche Exegese (Barnabas, Justin, und Clemens von Alexandria): Ein Beitrag zur Geschichte der allegorisch-mystischen Schriftauslegung im christlichen Altertum* (ATA 1.2; Münster: Aschendorff, 1908). – W. Völker, *Fortschritt und Vollendung bei Philo von Alexandrien: Eine Studie zur Geschichte der Frömmigkeit* (TU 49.1; Leipzig: J. C. Hinrich, 1938). – I. Christiansen, *Die Technik der allegorischen Auslegungswissenschaft bei Philo von Alexandrien* (BGBH 7; Tübigen: Mohr, 1969). – J. P. Martín, *Filón de Alejandría y la génesis de la cultura occidental* (Buenos Aires: Depalma, 1986). – D. T. Runia, *Philo of Alexandria and the Timaeus of Plato* (PhAnt 44; Leiden: Brill, 1986). – P. Borgen, *Philo, John, and Paul: New Perpectives on Judaism and Early Christianity* (Atlanta: Scholars Press, 1987). – J. Ménard, *La gnose de Philon d'Alexandrie* (Paris: Cariscript, 1987). – H. Burkhardt, *Die Inspiration heiliger Schriften bei Philo von Alexandrien* (Giessen: Brunnen, 1988). – R. Radice, *Platonismo e creazionismo in Filone di Alessandria* (Milan: Vita e Pensiero, 1989). – J. Laporte, *Théologie liturgique de Philon d'Alexandrie et d'Origène* (Paris:

Cerf, 1995). – G. Kweta, *Sprache, Erkennen, und Schweigen in der Gedankenwelt des Philo von Alexandrien* (EHS.Ph 403; Frankfurt and New York: Lang, 1996). – P. Borgen, *Philo of Alexandria: An Exegete for His Time* (NovTSup 86; Leiden: Brill, 1997). – P. Frick, *Divine Providence in Philo of Alexandria* (Tübingen: Mohr, 1999).

# B. Clement of Alexandria

Titus Flavius Clemens was born ca. 140–150 in Athens or Alexandria and undertook a philosophical education, in keeping with the peripatetic philosophers of that time, with various teachers in Greece, southern Italy, Syria, Palestine, and Alexandria. Roughly between 180 and 190 he settled in Alexandria, where he heard Pantaenus and established his own school of philosophy. For a long time it had been assumed that this school was to be identified with a catechetical school founded by Pantaenus and commissioned by the bishop, the leadership of which Clement took over and later passed on to Origen. Today, however, the tendency is to view the school of Clement as an independent Christian school of philosophy, like that of Justin in Rome, which reflected on the faith by means of philosophical methods but, as a rule, did not train catechumens or act expressly on behalf of the church. Clement did not become a Christian until he was a young adult; whether he ever was ordained to the priesthood remains uncertain. At the onset of the persecution of Christians under Septimius Severus (202/203), Clement was forced to leave Alexandria and traveled to Palestine (Cappadocia?) to his friend Alexander, the future bishop of Jerusalem. There he died before 215/216, as may be gathered from a letter of Alexander addressed to Origen.[11]

Clement devoted his life's work to proclaiming Christianity to the rich and highly cultured upper strata of Alexandria as the progressive and superior religion, its investigation and formulation being assisted by Platonic and Stoic philosophy. He addressed educated pagans who were looking for an understanding of the meaning of life, as well as Christians who wanted to reflect their faith spiritually beyond pious practices. His three great writings, the *Protrepticus (Exhortation to the Greeks)*, the *Paedagogus (Christ the Educator)*, and the *Stromata (Miscellanies)*, presuppose a readership of this kind. The precise dates of composition for these works remain uncertain. According to Eusebius's chronicles, Clement wrote them in 203, though his heyday had begun in 193. This agrees with the first book of the *Stromata*, which contains a historical survey up to the death of Emperor Commodus in 192.

*Bibliographies:* F. W. Bautz, *BBKL* 1:1063–66. – E. Osborn, "Clement of Alexandria: A Review of Research, 1958–1982," *SecCent* 3 (1983): 219–44.

---

[11] P. Nautin, *Lettres et écrivains chrétiens des IIe et IIIe siècles* (Patr. 2; Paris: Cerf, 1962), 138–41, argues for a number of peculiar viewpoints: Clement was a priest and did not leave Alexandria in 202 because of the persecution but at an unknown point in time prior to 215; like Origen, he was forced to leave because of difficulties with Demetrius, the bishop; he did not stay in Cappadocia, and the letter is to be dated to 230/231.

*Editions: Clemens Alexandrinus* (ed. O. Stählin, L. Früchtel, and U. Treu; 4 vols.; GCS; Berlin: Akademie, 1905–1936). – *Estratti profetici = Eclogae propheticae* (ed. C. Nardi; BPat; Florence: Nardini, Centro Internazionale del Libro, 1985). – *Extraits de Théodote* (ed. F. Sagnard; SC 23; Paris: Cerf, 1970) *[Excerpta ex Theodoto]*.

*Translations:* A. C. Coxe, trans., "Exhortation to the Heathen," "The Instructor," "The Stromata, or Miscellanies," and "Fragments," in *ANF* (Peabody, Mass.: Hendrickson, 1995; repr. of 1885 ed.), 2:163–605. – W. Wilson, trans., "Excerpts of Theodotus," in *ANF* (Peabody, Mass.: Hendrickson, 1995; repr. of 1886 ed.), 8:39–50. – G. W. Butterworth, ed., *The Exhortation to the Greeks, The Rich Man's Salvation, To the Newly Baptized* (LCL; Cambridge, Mass.: Harvard University Press, 1919; repr., 1968).

*Encyclopedia Articles:* L. Früchtel, *RAC* 3:182–88. – L. W. Barnard, "Apologetik I," *TRE* 3:390–91. – A. Méhat, *TRE* 8:101–13. – A. M. Ritter, 1:121–33. – M. Mees, *EECh* 1:179–81. – W. Wagner, *EEC* 1:262–4.

*Studies:* R. B. Tollinton, *Clement of Alexandria: A Study in Christian Liberalism* (2 vols.; London: Williams & Norgate, 1914). – M. von Pohlenz, *Klemens von Alexandreia und sein hellenisches Christentum* (NGWG.PH 1943.3; Göttingen: Vandenhoeck & Ruprecht, 1943), 103–80; repr. in *Kleine Schriften* (ed. H. Dörrie; 2 vols.; Hildesheim: Olms, 1965), 1:481–558. – C. Mondésert, *Clément d'Alexandrie: Introduction à l'étude de sa pensée religieuse à partir de l'Écriture* (Theol[P] 4; Paris: Aubier, 1944). – P. T. Camelot, *Foi et gnose: Introduction à l'étude de la connaissance mystique chez Clément d'Alexandrie* (ETHS 3; Paris: Vrin, 1945). – J. Moingt, "La gnose de Clément d'Alexandrie dans ses rapports avec la foi et la philosophie," *RSR* 37 (1950): 195–251, 398–421, 537–64; 38 (1951): 82–118. – W. Völker, *Der wahre Gnostiker nach Clemens Alexandrinus* (TU 57; Berlin: Akademie, 1952). – E. F. Osborn, *The Philosophy of Clement of Alexandria* (TS NS 3; Cambridge: Cambridge University Press, 1957). – H. Chadwick, *Early Christian Thought and the Classical Tradition: Studies in Justin, Clement, and Origen* (Oxford: Clarendon; New York: Oxford University Press, 1966; repr., 1984), 29–65. – J. Bernard, *Die apologetische Methode bei Klemens von Alexandrien: Apologetik als Entfaltung der Theologie* (EThSt 21; Leipzig: St. Benno, 1968). – S. R. C. Lilla, *Clement of Alexandria: A Study in Christian Platonism and Gnosticism* (OTM; London: Oxford University Press, 1971). – R. Mortley, *Connaissance religieuse et herméneutique chez Clément d'Alexandrie* (Leiden: Brill, 1973). – J. Ferguson, *Clement of Alexandria* (New York: Twayne, 1974). – C. Saldanha, *Divine Pedagogy: A Patristic View of Non-Christian Religions* (BSRel 57; Rome: LAS, 1984), 103–50. – D. Ridings, *The Attic Moses: The Dependency Theme in Some Early Christian Writers* (SGLG 59; Göteborg, Sweden: AUG, 1995), 29–139. – L. Rizzero, *Clemente di Alessandria e la "fusiologiva veramente gnostica": Saggio sulle origini e le implicazioni di un' epistemologia e di un' ontologia "cristiane"* (Recherches de théologie ancienne et médiévale: Supplementa 6; Louvain: Peeters, 1996). – P. Karavites, *Evil, Freedom, and the Road to Perfection in Clement of Alexandria* (SVigChr 43; Leiden: Brill, 1999). – D. Kimber Buell, *Making Christians: Clement of Alexandria and the Rhetoric of Legitimacy* (Princeton, N.J.: Princeton University Press, 1999). – U. Schneider, *Theologie als christliche Philosophie: Zur Bedeutung der biblischen Botschaft im Denken des Clemens von Alexandria* (AKG 73; Berlin and New York: de Gruyter, 1999).

# 1. *Protrepticus*

The *Protrepticus* belongs to the literary genre of philosophical admonitions, as we know them, for instance, from Aristotle. This work aims at convincing pagans to turn to the true Logos; in doing so, Clement agrees with the apologists in intent and structure. On the one hand, persuasive argumentation has to present the Christian faith positively; thus the first chapter develops a comprehensive picture of Christ, of the economy of salvation, and of redemption. This is the initial appeal of the meaning of Logos for an individual. As evidence for its truth and age, this is linked with the Greek philosophers and poets who had already pointed to the one true God. On the other hand, it is necessary to critique the convictions and cults of pagans, which Clement does in chs. 2–7. Finally, in an entirely Platonic manner, chs. 8–12 call for perfect conversion to the Logos, for being divinized with the one who manifested himself as human among humans and is the leader of every soul.

Clement's education and argumentative skill are also evident in the elegant, rhetorically polished, and at times even poetic, style whereby he encounters his cultured readers. If one considers the high status that rhetoric and literary finesse held in the ancient world, and how much even Augustine was initially repulsed by the style of the Bible, perceiving it as barbaric, one comes to appreciate the appropriateness of a style such as this in Clement's proclamation.

*Editions:* C. Mondésert, ed., *Protrepticus* (2d ed., rev. and augmented by C. Mondésert and A. Plassart; SC 2; Paris: Cerf, 1949). – M. Marcovich, ed., *Clementis Alexandrini Protrepticus* (SVigChr 34; Leiden and New York: Brill, 1995).

*Studies:* H. Steneker, *ΠΕΙΘΟΥΣ ΔΗΜΙΟΥΡΓΙΑ: Observations sur la fonction du style dans le Protreptique de Clément d'Alexandrie* (GCP 3; Nijmegen: Dekker & van de Vegt, 1967). – M. Galloni, *Cultura, evangelizzazione, e fede nel "Protrettico" di Clemente Alessandrino* (VSen NS 10; Rome: Studium, 1986).

## 2. Paedagogus

At the very beginning of the *Paedagogus,* Clement defines the structure and roles of the Logos: "As there are these three things in the case of man, habits, actions, and passions; habits are the department appropriated by *hortatory* discourse, the guide to piety. . . . All actions, again, are the province of *preceptive* discourse; while *persuasive* discourse applies itself to heal the passions" (1.1–3). Thus the theme of the three books of the *Paedagogus* is an individual's actions, that is, ethics and morality, just as in everyday life a slave of the household as the pedagogue led the children to school and as *repetitor* also taught them right behavior at home. The *Paedagogus,* then, addresses those already converted to Christianity who are now to be instructed, as the second step in the school of perfection, in what is the appropriate Christian lifestyle.

Book 1 introduces both the educator and the principles of education: the goal of education, the educator's love for the people, the universality of education, reward, and punishment. Books 2 and 3 then deal with particular regulations in the form of a diatribe: eating and drinking, living, sleeping, fellowship, sexuality, personal hygiene, ownership, and many other aspects.

*Editions:* H.-I. Marrou and M. Harl, eds., *Paedagogus* (3 vols.; SC 70, 108, 158; Paris: Cerf, 1960–1970). – *El Pedagogo* (ed. M. Merino and E. Redondo; FP 5; Madrid: Ciudad Nueva, 1994) [Com].

*Translations: Christ the Educator* (trans. S. P. Wood; FC 23; Washington, D.C.: Catholic University of America Press, 1954).

*Studies:* J. M. Blázquez, "El uso del pensamiento de la filosofía griega en El Pedagogo (I–II) de Clemente de Alejandría," *Anuario de historia de la Iglesia* 3 (1994): 49–80.

## 3. Stromata

Ever since the *editio princeps* of Clement's works by Pier Vittori (1550), the viewpoint has been maintained that the *Protrepticus, Paedagogus,* and *Stromata* were a trilogy leading one to faith. Thus the *Protrepticus* converts the nonbeliever to faith; the *Paedagogus,* so to speak, is the elementary teacher of the correct Christian life; and in the *Stromata* the one who speaks is the διδάσκαλος, the teacher of perfection. The content and structure of the *Stromata,* however, do not justify such an assumption. Rather, the title of the book, στρωμάτεις (= "patchwork"), points to the literary genre of the *hypomnemata* or *miscellanea,* hence of miscellaneous writings in which the most diverse components are collected. The *Stromata* therefore contains a varied mixture of apologetic, ethical, and practical themes rather than a systematic doctrine of the true gnosis. In the same way, the description of the life of a true gnostic remains largely restricted to this level.

Book 1, parts of bks. 2 and 6, and the conclusion of bk. 7 address apologetic topics, both internal and external. The pagan language, philosophy, and culture had prepared for Christianity by borrowing from the considerably older OT. Knowledge of philosophy is useful, on the one hand, for the purpose of extracting the seed of truth from it and, on the other, for knowing what is to be rejected. Against the gnostics Valentinus and Basilides Clement posits the virtues of the true gnostic and the right relationship between faith and knowledge. The conclusion of bk. 7 provides reasons for the rise of heresies in the church and describes their errors.

Book 3 deals exclusively with ethics, especially the correct estimation of marriage between the extremes of its rejection and license. The remaining parts deal with the gnostic, though largely in connection with ethical issues. His basic virtues are righteousness and love, which direct him in all the trials of life, including pain, illness, and martyrdom. For participation in asceticism, in the life of virtue, and in the ideal of passionlessness (ἀπάθεια), there is also no difference between the sexes; both are in like manner called to it and qualified for it (bk. 4). The true gnostic attains to the knowledge of faith by penetrating the knowledge of truth through the images and allegories of proclamation (bk. 5). The true gnostic (bks. 6 and 7) battles against sin and passions (πάθη) and, through faith and a virtuous life, gradually ascends to perfection. This he attains in gnosis, and it is then evidenced in practical life, in agape, ἀπάθεια, prayer, martyrdom, in short, in his deification (θεοποίησις). In this theory of the true gnostic and in his exegesis, Clement owes much to Philo of Alexandria, who presented this ideal similarly, albeit not with as much elaboration.

The ordering of the *Stromata* appears to be accidental or arbitrary. Méhat,[12] however, finds in it (*Strom.* 1.15.2; 6.103.1) an "ἀκολουθία physique," a natural, proper ordering of the search for the truth, unlike what the heretics whom Clement critiques undertake.

*Editions: Stromate* (ed. C. Mondésert, M. Caster, P. T. Camelot, A. Le Boulluec, P. Voulet, and P. Descourtieux; 6 vols. in 7; SC 30, 38, 278–279, 428, 446, 463; Paris: Cerf, 1951–2001 [*Stromata 1–2, 4–7*]). – *Stromata* (ed. M. Merino Rodríguez; FP 7; Madrid: Ciudad Nueva, 1996) [Com].

*Translations: Stromateis 1–3* (trans. J. Ferguson; FC 85; Washington, D.C.: Catholic University of America Press, 1991).

*Studies:* A. Méhat, *Étude sur les "Stromates" de Clément d'Alexandrie* (PatSor 7; Paris: Seuil, 1966). – L. Roberts, "The Literary Form of the *Stromateis*," *SecCent* 1 (1981): 211–22. – D. Wyrwa, *Die christliche Platonaneignung in den Stromateis des Clemens von Alexandrien* (AKG 53; Berlin and New York: de Gruyter, 1983). – A. van den Hoek, *Clement of Alexandria and His Use of Philo in the Stromateis: An Early Christian Reshaping of a Jewish Model* (SVigChr 3; Leiden and New York: Brill, 1988).

# C. Origen

We are more conversant with the life of Origen than with any other Christian writer before him, on the basis of the extensive information in Eusebius (*Hist. eccl.* 6), Jerome (*Vir. ill.* 54; 62; *Epist.* 33; 44.1), and Photius (*Bibliotheca* 118), who draw upon some of Eusebius's lost works. Further information is gained from an oration of gratitude by Gregory Thaumaturgus, one of Origen's students in Caesarea. He was born ca. 185 to a Christian family in Alexandria and, together with a thorough education in keeping with the *curriculum* of his time, he also enjoyed a solid Christian upbringing. When Leonides, his father, suffered martyrdom during the persecution under Septimius Severus in 201, his mother was able to restrain Origen from his youthful zeal for martyrdom only by hiding his clothes, so that he was unable to leave the house. This character trait of burning Christian zeal accompanied Origen throughout his life and plunged him into many difficulties.

Since the magistrate confiscated the family's possessions after the father's martyrdom, Origen began a school in Alexandria in order to provide for his mother and six younger brothers. In addition to this grammar school, the bishop, Demetrius, entrusted him with the instruction of the catechumens, to which he dedicated himself fully shortly afterward. In his radical zeal, he sold all his secular books so as to devote himself fully to Christianity. To penetrate the message of faith, however, he had to return to philosophy soon thereafter and took instruction from Ammonius Saccas, the founder of Neoplatonism. In his youthful and radical exuberance, he also took literally the saying about the eunuch for the sake

---

[12] *Études*, 35–41.

of the kingdom (Matt 19:12) and emasculated himself. His school registered such remarkable success that he entrusted the instruction of the catechumens to his student Heracles and devoted himself fully to teaching philosophy and theology. Like Clement before him, he also turned to educated pagans with missionary intent. His most famous conversion success was a rich man by the name of Ambrose, whom he won from Gnosticism and who supported him with substantial amounts of money.

In his thirties, Origen began to write and went on numerous research trips to Rome, where he met with Hippolytus. He traveled to Caesarea in Palestine and to Jerusalem, where he made friends with the local bishops, who charged him with the preaching of the gospel although he was a layman, thus inviting the protest of Demetrius, the bishop of his hometown. On the invitation of the governor, he visited Jordan and then went to Antioch to see Julia Mammaea, the emperor's mother. These numerous contacts with high ecclesiastical and governmental dignitaries indicate already the level of fame and esteem he enjoyed. Yet they also laid the groundwork for serious disputes and for the later break with the bishop of Alexandria.

About 231 the bishops of Achaia (Greece) invited him to a disputation with the local heretics. On his journey by land, via Palestine, his episcopal friends in Caesarea ordained him to the priesthood without asking Demetrius for permission and despite his emasculation, which in fact barred him from the priesthood. Upon his return to Alexandria, therefore, Bishop Demetrius had a synod remove him from the priesthood and expel him from the country. Origen then withdrew to Caesarea in Palestine, where the Alexandrian verdict was disregarded; there he founded a new school spreading Alexandrian thought, exegesis, and theology in the Near East. He also exercised his preaching ministry almost daily; only a fraction of the many hundreds of sermons he preached are preserved, despite the seven or more stenographers in the service of Ambrose who took down the sermons in shorthand.

Although he escaped a martyr's death when he was young, he suffered severely under the Decian persecution (250/251). He was imprisoned and tortured but not killed because the authorities wanted to induce him to a public recantation, which would have had an immense, widespread impact because he was so popular. He withstood all of the agony, however, without bending and was set free again after a relatively brief but severe persecution. But his health was broken, and he died (probably in 254) shortly afterward and was given his final resting place in Tyre, where his tomb was still evident in the thirteenth century.

Apart from Augustine, with whom he shares numerous character traits and circumstances of life, Origen was the most prolific writer of the ancient church. Because of later disputes about his person and work, many of his writings are, unfortunately, lost entirely, and the Greek originals of the extant writings largely so. Further, the Latin translations by Rufinus should only be used with caution because he changed theologically problematic statements with current fourth-century meanings favoring Origen. Despite all this, an impressive number of Origen's works are extant, besides lists of his writings and countless fragments.

The fragments are found mainly in the catenas, in the *Philocalia* (a collection of dogmatic pericopes from the works of Origen promoted by Basil the Great and Basil's friend Gregory of Nazianzus ca. 360), in the *Apology for Origen* by Pamphilus of Caesarea (in Rufinus's Latin translation), in the works of friends and opponents, and in the exegetical writings of Jerome, which are significantly inspired by Origen.

*Bibliography:* H. Crouzel, *Bibliographie critique d'Origène* (IP 8; Steenbrugge, Belg.: Abbey of St. Peter, 1971). H. Crouzel, *Bibliographie critique d'Origène: Supplément I* (IP 8A; Steenbrugge, Belg.: Abbey of St. Peter, 1982). – H. Crouzel, *Bibliographie critique d'Origène: Supplément II* (IP 8B; Steenbrugge, Belg.: Abbey of St. Peter, 1996) [until 1992]. – H. G. Hödl, *BBKL* 6:1255–71. – L. Lies, "Zum derzeitigen Stand der Origenesforschung," *ZKT* 115 (1993): 37–62, 145–71.

*Editions:*
*Opera omnia* (PG 11–17). – E. Lommatzsch, ed., *Origenous ta heuriskomena panta: Origenis Opera omnia quae graece vel latine tantum exstant et ejus nomine circumferuntur* (25 vols.; Berlin: Haude & Spener, 1831–1848).
*De pascha:* O. Guéraud and P. Nautin, eds., *Sur la Pâque: Traité inédit publié d'après un papyrus de Toura* (CAnt 2; Paris: Beauchesne, 1979) [Com]. – B. Witte, ed., *Die Schrift des Origenes "Über das Passa": Textausgabe und Kommentar* (Altenberge: Oros, 1993). [Com].
*Disputatio cum Heracleida:* J. Scherer, ed., *Dialog with Heraclides* (SC 67; Paris: Cerf, 1960).
*Epistula ad Gregorium Thaumaturgum:* H. Crouzel, ed., *Remerciement à Origène, suivi de la lettre d'Origène à Grégoire* (SC 148; Paris: Cerf, 1969).
*Exhortatio ad martyrium, Contra Celsum, De oratione:* P. Koetschau, ed., vols. 1–2 of *Origenes Werke* (12 vols. in 13; GCS Or 2–3; Leipzig: Hinrichs, 1899–1955).
*Fragments of Ps 118:* M. Harl, ed., *La chaîne palestinienne sur le psaume 118 (Origène, Eusèbe, Didyme, Apollinaire, Athanase, Théodoret)* (2 vols.; SC 189–190; Paris: Cerf, 1972).
*Homiliae in Psalmos 36–38:* E. Prinzivalli, ed., *Omelie sui Salmi: Homiliae in psalmos XXXVI, XXXVII, XXXVIII* (BPat 18; Florence: Nardini, 1991).
*Philocalia, Epistula ad Africanum:* É. Junod, ed., *Sur le libre arbitre: Philocalie 21–27* (SC 226; Paris: Cerf, 1976). – M. Harl and N. de Lange, eds., *Sur les Écritures: Philocalie, 1–20 et la lettre à Africanus sur l'histoire de Suzanne* (SC 302; Paris: Cerf, 1983).

*Translations:* F. Crombie, A. Menzies, and J. Patrick, trans., "Origen De principiis," "Africanus to Origen," "Origen to Africanus," "Origen to Gregory," "Origen against Celsus," "Origen's Commentary on the Gospel of John," and "Origen's Commentary on the Gospel of Matthew," in *ANF* (Peabody, Mass.: Hendrickson, 1995; repr. of 1885 ed.), 4:221–669; 9:297–512. – J. E. L. Oulton and H. Chadwick, *Alexandrian Christianity* (LCC 2; London: SCM, 1954), 180–455 [*On Prayer, Exhortation to Martyrdom, Dialogue with Heraclides*]. – J. J. O'Meara, ed., *Prayer, Exhortation to Martyrdom* (ACW 19; Westminster, Md.: Newman, 1954). – R. A. Greer, ed., *Origen* (CWS; New York: Paulist, 1979) [*Exhortation to Martyrdom, On Prayer, On First Principles IV, The Prologue to the Commentary on the Song of Songs, Homily XXVII on Numbers*]. – R. J. Daly, ed., *Treatise on the Passover and Dialogue of Origen with Heraclides and his Fellow Bishops on the Father, the Son, and the Soul* (ACW 54; New York: Paulist, 1992). – J. W. Trigg, *Origen* (Early Church Fathers; London and New York: Routledge, 1998) [selections].

*Encyclopedia Articles:* H. Crouzel, *DSp* 11:933–61. – H. Chadwick, 1:134–57. – H. Crouzel, *EECh* 2:619–23. – R. Williams, *TRE* 25:397–420. – R. J. Daly, *EEC* 2:835–37.

*General Studies:* J. Daniélou, *Origen* (trans. W. Mitchell; New York: Sheed & Ward, 1955). – P. Nautin, *Lettres et écrivains chrétiens des IIe et IIIe siècles* (Patr. 2; Paris: Cerf, 1961). – P. Nautin, *Origène: Sa vie et son œuvre* (Paris: Beauchesne, 1977). – U. Berner, *Origenes* (EdF 147; Darmstadt: Wissenschaftliche Buchgesellschaft, 1981). – H. Crouzel, *Origen* (trans. A. S. Worall; Edinburgh: T&T Clark, 1989; repr., 1998). – J. W. Trigg, *Origen* (Early Church Fathers; London and New York: Routledge, 1998).

*Collections of Essays:* International Origen Congresses have been held every four years since 1973 and have published the leading papers in the following volumes: H. Crouzel, G. Lomiento, and J. Rius-Camps, *Origeniana* (Bari: Istituto di Letteratura Cristiana Antica, Università di Bari, 1975). – H. Crouzel and Antonio Quacquarelli., *Origeniana secunda* (Rome: Ateneo, 1980). – R. Hanson and H. Crouzel, *Origeniana tertia* (Rome: Ateneo, 1985). – L. Lies, *Origeniana quarta* (Innsbruck: Tyrolia, 1987). – R. J. Daly, *Origeniana quinta* (Louvain: Louvain University Press, 1992). – G. Dorival and A. Le Boulluec, *Origeniana sexta* (Louvain: Louvain University Press, 1950). – W. A. Bienert and U. Kühneweg, *Origeniana septima* (Louvain: Louvain University Press, 1999). Other collections: A. Dupleix, ed., *Recherches et tradition: Mélanges patristiques offerts a Henri Crouzel* (ThH 88; Paris: Beauchesne, 1992). – C. Kannengiesser and W. L. Petersen, eds., *Origen of Alexandria: His World and His Legacy* (Notre Dame, Ind.: University of Notre Dame Press, 1988). – H. Crouzel, *Les fins dernières selon Origène* (VRCS 320; Aldershot, Hampshire, Eng.: Variorum; Brookfield, Vt.: Gower, 1990).

*Biographies:* M. Hornschuh, "Das Leben des Origenes und die Entstehung der alexandrinischen Schule," *ZKG* 71 (1960): 1–25, 193–214. – A. Knauber, "Das Anliegen der Schule des Origenes zu Cäsarea," *MTZ* 19 (1968): 182–203. – J. Fischer, "Die alexandrinischen Synoden gegen Origenes," *OS* 28 (1979): 3–16; repr. in J. Fischer and A. Lumpe, *Die Synoden von den Anfängen bis zum Vorabend des Nicaenums* (Paderborn: F. Schöningh, 1997), 111–26. – J. W. Trigg, *Origen: The Bible and Philosophy in the Third-Century Church* (Atlanta: John Knox, 1983). – A. Monaci Castagno, *Origene predicatore e il suo pubblico* (Milan: F. Angeli, 1987). – A. Orbe, "Orígenes y los monarquianos," *Greg* 72 (1991): 39–72.

*Philosophy:* H. Crouzel, *Origène et la philosophie* (Theol[P] 52; Paris: Aubier,1962). – H. Crouzel, *Origène et Plotin: Comparisons doctrinales* (Paris: Téqui, 1992). – M. Edwards, "Christ or Plato? Origen on Revelation and Anthropology," in *Christian Origins: Theology, Rhetoric, and Community* (ed. L. Ayres and G. Jones; London and New York: Routledge, 1998), 11–25. – D. Dawson, "Allegorical Reading and the Embodiment of the Soul in Origen," in *Christian Origins: Theology, Rhetoric, and Community* (ed. L. Ayres and G. Jones; London and New York: Routledge, 1998), 26–44.

*Theology:* L. G. Patterson, "Origen: His Place in Early Greek Christian Thought," in *Proceedings of the Eighth International Conference on Patristic Studies, Oxford, 3–8 September 1979* (ed. E. Livingstone; 3 vols.; StPatr 17; Oxford and New York: Pergamon, 1982), 2:924–43. – W. Schütz, *Der christliche Gottesdienst bei Origenes* (Stuttgart: Calwer, 1984). – H. Chadwick, *Early Christian Thought and the Classical Tradition: Studies in Justin, Clement, and Origen* (Oxford and New York: Oxford University Press, 1966; repr., 1984), 66–94. – J. N. Rowe, *Origen's Doctrine of Subordination: A Study of Origen's Christology* (EHS.T 272; Bern and New York: Lang, 1987). – H. Pietras, *L'amore in Origene* (SEAug 28; Rome: Institutum Patristicum Augustinianum, 1988). – E. Schockenhoff, *Zum Fest der Freiheit: Theologie des christlichen Handelns bei Origenes* (TTS 33; Mainz: Matthias-Grünewald-Verlag, 1990). – J. Hammerstaedt, "Der trinitarische Gebrauch des Hypostasisbegriffes bei Origenes," *JAC* 34 (1991): 12–20. – B. E. Daley, *The Hope of the Early Church: A Handbook of Patristic Eschatology* (Cambridge and New York: Cambridge University Press, 1991; repr.,

Peabody, Mass.: Hendrickson, 2003), 47–64. – R. Lyman, *Christology and Cosmology: Models of Divine Activity in Origen, Eusebius, and Athanasius* (Oxford: Clarendon; New York: Oxford University Press, 1993). – K. McDonnell, "Does Origen Have a Trinitarian Doctrine of the Holy Spirit?" *Greg* 75 (1994): 5–35. – H. S. Benjamins, *Eingeordnete Freiheit: Freiheit und Vorsehung bei Origenes* (SVigChr 28; Leiden and New York: Brill, 1994). – M. Fédou, *La sagesse et le monde: Essai sur la christologie d'Origène* (Paris: Desclée, 1994). – P. Widdicombe, *The Fatherhood of God from Origen to Athanasius* (Oxford: Clarendon; New York: Oxford University Press, 1994), 7–120. – H. Ziebritzki, *Heiliger Geist und Weltseele: Das problem der dritten Hypostase bei Origenes, Plotin, und ihren Vorläufern* (BHTh 84; Tübingen: Mohr, 1994). – J. Laporte, *Théologie liturgique de Philon d'Alexandrie et d'Origène* (Paris: Cerf, 1995). – D. Gemmiti, *La donna in Origene: Con testimonianze dei primi tre secoli* (Naples: L. E. R., 1996). – T. Hermans, *Origène: Théologie sacrificielle du sacerdoce des chrétiens* (ThH 102; Paris: Beauchesne, 1996). – G. Masi, *Origène, o, Della riconciliazione universale* (Bologna: CLUEB, 1997). – S. Fernández, *Cristo médico, según Orígenes: La actividad médica como metáfora de la acción divina* (SEAug 64; Rome: Institutum patristicum Augustinianum, 1999).

# 1. Exegetical Writings

The great majority of Origen's works are commentaries on the Bible. Although by reputation he is acknowledged as a master of allegory, Origen too began with the literal meaning of the biblical text, which he established on a philological-critical basis. For this purpose, he compiled a synopsis of six versions of the OT ca. 230, namely, the original Hebrew text, the same in Greek transcription, and the Greek translations of Aquila, Symmachus, the Septuagint, and Theodotion. Hence it was given the name *Hexapla* (= "sixfold") even though, in the case of the Psalms, for instance, he consulted up to three further Greek translations. The goal was to establish the text of the Septuagint as accurately as possible—a text that the Fathers accepted as verbally inspired.

Origen's exegetical premises are explained in his *De principiis* 4.1.11–12:

> The individual ought, then, to portray the ideas of holy Scripture in a threefold manner upon his own soul in order that the simple man may be edified by the "flesh," as it were, of the Scripture, for so we name the obvious sense; while he who has ascended a certain way (may be edified) by the "soul," as it were. The perfect man . . . (may receive edification) from the spiritual law, which has *a shadow of good things to come* [Col 2:17; Heb 10:1]. For as man consists of body, and soul, and spirit, so in the same way does Scripture. . . . But as there are certain passages . . . that do not at all contain the "corporeal" sense . . . there are also places where we must seek only for the "soul," as it were, and "spirit" of Scripture (italics mine).

Thus Origen assumes three senses of the text: the corporeal or literal sense, the psychic or moral sense, and the spiritual or mystical sense. The literal sense refers exclusively to the immediate, concrete meaning of words, not to their symbolic or figurative use, which occurs frequently in the Bible. Hence for Origen the latter biblical passages have no literal sense. But since every individual word of the biblical text *has to* have a sense worthy of, and corresponding to, God because of the verbal inspiration by the Holy Spirit, this sense is to be sought at higher levels.

The moral sense draws from the Bible the concrete instructions on behavior in the Christian life that go beyond the commandments and literal regulations, as the community expects particularly in the proclamation. Finally, the mystical sense fulfills three functions: it unfolds the OT typologically as prophecy in anticipation of Christ; it interprets the faith statements of salvation history; and it explains the Christians' eschatological hope. The center and key of the mystical meaning is Christ himself, who fulfilled the OT promises in his life and at the same time pointed to his return. The gospel thus reflects the reality (cf. 1 Cor 13:12 and Plato's parable of the cave). But since the earthly gospel is identical to the eternal, Christians already share in the truth of Christ through the gospel and the sacraments of the church.

On this basis, John Cassian formulated a fourfold sense of Scripture, which Augustine of Denmark (d. 1282) rendered in this famous hexameter:

*Littera gesta docet, quid credas allegoria,*
*Moralis quid agas, quo tendas anagogia.*

The letter teaches facts, allegory what you are to believe,
The moral meaning what you ought to do, anagogy what you should strive for.

The practical implementation of this exegesis has often led to curious and eccentric interpretations for modern understanding. The validity of its principles does not yield to doubt, however, for it was already applied in the NT (e.g., in the meaning of Jonah with reference to Christ [Matt 12:39f.] or in the spiritual meaning of circumcision [Rom 2:29]), and no reader and interpreter can manage without it in the present.

On the basis of a philological-critical construction of the correct biblical text and by applying his exegetical rules, Origen wrote a wealth of exegetical works on almost all books of the Bible in three literary genres:

- τόμοι = scholarly theological commentaries;

- σχόλια = individual explanations, marginal comments on the biblical text; and

- ὁμιλίαι = public sermons, written by stenographers and later published after being edited in part.

None of the commentaries is preserved in full, however; only eight books of the commentary on Matthew and nine on John are extant in the Greek original, whereas in the Latin translation there are four books on the Song of Songs, the second half of the commentary on Matthew, and ten books on the Letter to the Romans. The scholias are found only among the fragments, and of the homilies, a total of 279 have been handed down, though only 21 of them in the Greek original.

*Editions:*
F. Field, ed., *Origenis Hexaplorum quae supersunt* (2 vols.; Oxford: Clarendon, 1867–1871).
*Commentarius in Canticum canticorum: Commentaire sur le Cantique des cantiques* (ed. L. Brésard, H. Crouzel, and M. Borret; SC 375–76; Paris: Cerf, 1991–1992).

*Commentarii in evangelium Johannis:* E. Preuschen, ed., *Der Johanneskommentar* (vol. 4 of *Origenes Werke;* GCS 10; Leipzig: Hinrichs, 1903). – C. Blanc, ed., *Commentaire sur saint Jean* (5 vols.; SC 120, 157, 222, 290, 385; Paris: Cerf, 1964–1992).

*Commentarii in Romanos:* C. P. Hammond Bammel, ed., *Der Römerbriefkommentar des Origenes* (3 vols.; VL 16, 33, 34; Fribourg, Switz., Herder, 1990–1998).

*Commentarium in evangelium Matthaei:* E. Klostermann, E. Benz, and L. Früchtel, eds., *Origenes Matthäuserklärung* (vols. 10, 11, and 12.1–2 of *Origenes Werke;* 3 vols. in 4; GCS 38, 40, 41; Leipzig: Hinrichs, 1935–1955; vol. 3 rev. U. Treu, 1968). – R. Girod, ed., *Commentaire sur l'Évangile selon Matthieu* (SC; Paris, Cerf, 1970), vol. 1 [*X–XI*].

*De engastrimytho:* E. Klostermann, ed., *Origenes, Eustathius von Antiochien, und Gregor von Nyssa über die Hexe von Endor* (KlT 83; Bonn: Marcus & Weber, 1912), 3–15.

*Homiliae et Commentarii in Lucam:* M. Rauer, ed., *Die Homilien zu Lukas in der Übersetzung des Hieronymus und die griechischen Reste der Homilien und des Lukas-Kommentars* (vol. 9 of *Origenes Werke;* GCS 49; Leipzig: Hinrichs, 1930). – H. Crouzel, F. Fournier, and P. Périchon, eds., *Homélies Luc: Texte latin et fragments grecs* (SC 87; Paris: Cerf, 1962).

*Homiliae in Canticum canticorum:* O. Rousseau, ed., *Homélies sur le Cantique des cantiques* (SC 37; Paris: Cerf, 1954).

*Homiliae in Exodum:* M. Borret, ed., *Homélies sur l'Exode* (SC 321; Paris, Cerf, 1985).

*Homiliae in Ezechielem:* M. Borret, ed., *Homélies sur Ézéchiel* (SC 352; Paris, Cerf, 1989).

*Homiliae in Genesim:* H. de Lubac and L. Doutreleau, eds., *Homélies sur la Genèse* (2d ed.; SC 7; Paris, Cerf, 1976).

*Homiliae in Hexateuchum:* W. A. Baehrens, ed., *Homilien zum Hexateuch in Rufins Übersetzung* (vols 6–7 of *Origenes Werke;* GCS 29–30; Leipzig: Hinrichs, 1920–1921).

*Homiliae in Jeremiam:* P. Husson and P. Nautin, eds., *Homélies sur Jérémie* (2 vols.; SC 232, 238; Paris, Cerf, 1976–1977).

*Homiliae in Jeremiam, Commentarii in Lamentationes, Samuelem, Regna:* E. Klostermann, ed., *Jeremiahomilien; Klageliederkommentar; Erklärung der Samuel- und Königsbücher* (vol. 3 of *Origenes Werke;* GCS; Leipzig: Hinrichs, 1901).

*Homiliae in Jesu Nave:* A. Jaubert, ed., *Homélies sur Josué* (SC 71; Paris, Cerf, 1960).

*Homiliae in Judices:* P. Messié, L. Neyrand, and M. Borret, eds., *Homélies sur les Juges* (SC 389; Paris, Cerf, 1993).

*Homiliae in Leviticum:* M. Borret, ed., *Homélies sur le Lévitique* (2 vols.; SC 286–287; Paris, Cerf, 1981).

*Homiliae in Numeros:* L. Doutreleau, ed., *Homélies sur les Nombres* (SC 415, 442, 461; Paris, Cerf, 1996–2001) [*I–XXVIII*].

*Homiliae in Psalmos:* E. Prinzivalli, H. Crouzel, and L. Brésard, eds., *Homélies sur les psaumes 36 à 38* (SC 411; Paris, Cerf, 1995).

*Homiliae in Samuelem:* P. Nautin and M.-T. Nautin, eds., *Homélies sur Samuel* (SC 328; Paris, Cerf, 1986).

*Homiliae in Samuelem I, Canticum canticorum, Prophetas, Commentarius in Canticum canticorum:* W. A. Baehrens, ed., *Homilien zu Samuel I, zum Hohelied, und zu den Propheten; Kommentar zum Hohelied, in Rufins und Hieronymus' Übersetzung* (vol. 8 of *Origenes Werke;* GCS 33; Leipzig: Hinrichs, 1925).

*Translations:* A. Menzies, trans., "Origen's Commentary on the Gospel of John" and "Origen's Commentary on the Gospel of Matthew," in *ANF* (Peabody, Mass.: Hendrickson, 1995; repr. of 1887 ed.), 9:287–512. – R. P. Lawson, trans., *The Song of Songs: Commentary and Homilies* (ACW 26; Westminster, Md.; Newman, 1957). – R. E. Heine, trans., *Homilies on Genesis and Exodus* (FC 71; Washington, D.C.: Catholic University of America Press, 1982). – R. E. Heine, trans., *Commentary on the Gospel according to John* (2 vols.; FC 80, 89; Washington, D.C.: Catholic University of America Press, 1989–1993). – G. W. Barkley, trans., *Homilies on Leviticus: 1–16* (FC 83; Washington, D.C.: Catholic University of America Press, 1990). – J. T. Lienhard, trans., *Homilies on Luke; Fragments on Luke* (FC 94; Washington, D.C.: Catholic University of America Press, 1996). – J. C. Smith, trans., *Homilies on Jeremiah; Homily on 1 Kings 28* (FC 97; Washington, D.C.: Catholic University of America Press, 1998).

*Reference Works:* B. D. Ehrman, G. D. Fee, and M. W. Holmes, *The Text of the Fourth Gospel in the Writings of Origen* (Atlanta: Scholars Press, 1992–). – D. D. Hannah, *The Text of I Corinthians in the Writings of Origen* (Atlanta: Scholars Press, 1997).

*Encyclopedia Articles:* S. P. Brock, "Bibelübersetzungen I," *TRE* 6:165–66.

*Collections of Essays:* G. Dorival, A. Le Boulluec, et al., eds., *Origeniana sexta: Origène et la Bible = Origen and the Bible* (BETL 118; Louvain: Peeters, 1995). – A. Salvesen, ed., *Origen's Hexapla and Fragments* (Tübingen: Mohr, 1998). – E. dal Covolo and L. Perrone, eds., *Mosè ci viene letto nella Chiesa: Lettura delle Omelie di Origene sulla Genesi* (BSRel 153; Rome: LAS, 1999).

*General Studies:* H. de Lubac, *Histoire et esprit: L'intelligence de l'Écriture d'après Origène* (Theol[P] 16; Paris: Aubier, 1950). – R. P. C. Hanson, *Allegory and Event: A Study of the Sources and Significance of Origen's Interpretation of Scripture* (Richmond: John Knox, 1959; repr., Louisville, Ky.: Westminster John Knox, 2002). – H. de Lubac, *Medieval Exegesis: The Four Senses of Scripture* (trans. M. Sebanc; Grand Rapids: Eerdmans; Edinburgh: T&T Clark, 1998–); trans. of *Exégèse médiévale: Les quatres sens de l'Écriture* (2 vols. in 4; Theol[P] 41; Paris: Aubier, 1959–1964). – R. Gögler, *Zur Theologie des biblischen Wortes bei Origenes* (Düsseldorf: Patmos, 1963). – M. Harl, "Origène et les interprétations patristiques grecques de l'obscurité' biblique," *VC* 36 (1982): 334–71. – E. Nardoni, "Origen's Concept of Biblical Inspiration," *SecCent* 4 (1984): 9–23. – K. Torjesen, *Hermeneutical Procedure and Theological Method in Origen's Exegesis* (PTS 28; Berlin and New York: de Gruyter, 1985). – B. Neuschäfer, *Origenes als Philologe* (2 vols.; SBA 18.1–2; Basel: Friedrich Reinhardt, 1987). – J. T. Lienhard, "Origen as Homilist," in *Preaching in the Patristic Age: Studies in Honor of Walter J. Burghardt, S.J.* (ed. D. Hunter; New York: Paulist, 1989), 36–52. – F. Cocchini, *Il Paolo di Origene: Contributo alla storia della recezione delle epistole paoline nel III secolo* (VSen NS 11; Rome: Studium, 1992). – B. Studer, "L'esegesi doppia in Origene," *ASEs* 10.2 (1993): 427–37.

*Studies of Single Works:* C. P. Bammel, "Die Hexapla des Origenes: *Die hebraica ueritas* im Streit der Meinungen," *Aug* 28 (1988): 125–49. – V. Peri, *Omelie Origeniane sui Salmi: Contributo all'identificazione del testo latino* (StT 289; Vatican City: Biblioteca Apostolica Vaticana, 1980). – G. Lomiento, *L'esegesi origeniana del Vangelo di Luca* (Bari: Istituto di Letteratura Cristiana Antica, Università di Bari, 1966). – J. M. Poffet, *La méthode exégétique d'Héracléon et d'Origène commentateurs de Jn 4: Jésus, la Samaritaine, et les Samaritains* (Par. 28; Fribourg, Switz.: Éditions Universitaires, 1985). – H. J. Vogt, "Beobachtungen zum Johannes-Kommentar des Origenes," *TQ* 170 (1990): 191–208. – R. Roukema, *The Diversity of Laws in Origen's Commentary on Romans* (Amsterdam: Free University Press, 1988). – T. Heither, *Translatio religionis: Die Paulusdeutung des Origenes in seinem Kommentar zum Römerbrief* (BoBKG 16; Cologne: Böhlau, 1990). – J. R. Díaz Sánchez-Cid, *Justicia, pecado, y filiación: Sobre el Comentario de Orígenes a los Romanos* (Toledo: Estudio Teologico de San Ildefonso, 1991). – G. Bendinelli, *Il Commentario a Matteo di Origene: L'ambito della metodologia scolastica dell'antichità* (SEAug 60; Rome: Institutum patristicum Augustinianum, 1997).

## 2. Spiritual Theology

Origen's spiritual theology unfolds in all of his exegetical writings but especially in the homilies. In the commentary on the Song of Songs, he interprets the bride as the church, on the one hand, and as the soul of the person uniting with God, on the other—the two fundamental interpretations of the entire patristic era. The true gnostic (here one observes the close association with Philo and Clement) spiritually ascends to God, just as the apostles did with Christ on the mount of transfiguration, in order to behold him there. To this end he is to lay aside vices (πάθη) through prayer and exercise of the virtues and to develop his senses spiritually on the journey. Just as he possesses five physical senses, he is to gain inner senses in order to see God, hear God, and so forth. In this way, the person also regains his full *imago dei* (according to Gen 1:26f.), which was obscured in the fall.

*Translations:* H. U. von Balthasar, *Origen—Spirit and Fire: A Thematic Anthology of His Writings* (trans. R. J. Daly; Washington, D.C.: Catholic University of America Press, 1984; Edinburgh: T&T Clark, 2001) [selections].

*Studies:* W. Völker, *Das Vollkommenheitsideal des Origenes: Eine Untersuchung zur Geschichte der Frömmigkeit und zu den Anfängen der christlichen Mystik* (BHTh 7; Tübingen: Mohr, 1931). – K. Rahner, "Le début d'une doctrine des cinq sens spirituels chez Origène," *RAM* 13 (1932): 113–45. – A. Lieske, *Die Theologie der Logosmystik bei Origenes* (MBTh 22; Münster: Aschendorff, 1938). – H. Crouzel, *Théologie de l'image de Dieu chez Origène* (Theol[P] 34; Paris: Aubier, 1956). – H. U. von Balthasar, *Parole et mystère chez Origène* (Paris: Cerf, 1957). – H. Crouzel, *Origène et la "connaissance mystique"* (ML.T 56; Paris: Desclée de Brouwer, 1961). – G. Gruber, Ζωή: *Wesen, Stufen, und Mitteilung des wahren Lebens bei Origenes* (MThS.S 23; Munich: Huber, 1962). – H. Crouzel, *Virginité et mariage selon Origène* (ML.T 58; Paris: Desclée de Brouwer, 1963). – J. Dupuis, *"L'ésprit de l'homme": Étude sur l'anthropologie religieuse d'Origène* (ML.T 62; Paris: Desclée de Brouwer, 1967). – J. Chênevert, *L'Église dans le Commentaire d'Origène sur le Cantique des cantiques* (Studia 24; Brussels: Desclée de Brouwer; Montreal: Bellarmin, 1969). – M. Eichinger, *Die Verklärung Christi bei Origenes: Die Bedeutung des Menschen Jesus in seiner Christologie* (WBTh 23; Vienna: Herder, 1969). – W. Gessel, *Die Theologie des Gebetes nach "De oratione" von Origenes* (Munich: Schöningh, 1975). – J. J. Alviar, *Klesis: The Theology of the Christian Vocation according to Origen* (Dublin and Portland, Oreg.: Four Courts, 1993). – F. Cocchini, ed., *Il dono e la sua ombra—ricerche sul ΠΕΡΙ ΕΥΧΗΣ di Origene: Atti del I Convegno del Gruppo italiano di ricerca su "Origene e la tradizione Alessandrina"* (SEAug 57; Rome: Institutum Patristicum Augustinianum, 1997).

## 3. De principiis (On First Principles)

Περὶ ἀρχῶν (ἀρχή = "foundation," "principle") is the heading Origen appropriately gave to his primary theological work of four volumes, in which he presented the essential assertions of his theology between 220 and 230. Book 1 covers the world prior to creation, that is, the Trinity and spiritual creation (angels); bk. 2, the identity of the Creator God with God as Father, and the creation and redemption of the world and of the human person; bk. 3, the free will of the human person, temptation, sin, and the eschatological restoration of all things in God; bk. 4, inspiration and the interpretation of Scripture as the source of faith.

As Origen states in the preface, the basis of all theology is found in Scripture and the *regula fidei*. Thus he makes clear that his theology is to be seen as orthodox and rooted in the ecclesiastical tradition. This is also seen in his statements against the heresies of his time. Against the Marcionites he reaffirms the goodness of the Creator, the Creator's identity with the Father of Jesus, and the unity of the two Testaments. Against the Valentinians he affirms free will and the personal accountability for sin; against docetism, the true incarnation of Christ as the prerequisite for redemption; against the modalists, the individuality of each of the divine persons; and against the adoptionists, the eternal generation of the Son.

Conversely, this work contains theologoumena that subsequently were no longer considered orthodox and became the cause of the quarrels concerning Origen:

a. His doctrine of the Trinity is subordinationist in that, although it clearly distinguishes between Father and Son, it views the Son's authority as subordinate.

b. The doctrine of the soul's preexistence: The souls of humans were created before the creation of the world. But since they deviated from God (ψυχή is derived from ψύχεσθαι = "to grow cold"), they were exiled in bodies.

c. The doctrine of the ἀποκατάστασις: The Son's act of redemption ultimately leads every being, including Satan, back to its eternal state, according to 1 Cor 15:23–26.

Besides a few Greek fragments, *De principiis* has been preserved in full only in the Latin translation of Rufinus, which should be interpreted with caution regarding Origen's own theology. It originated in 397 as a result of the first major conflict concerning the theology of Origen and tends to smooth out offensive statements. Unfortunately, the literal translation, undertaken by Jerome in 399 to offset it, is lost.

*Editions:* P. Koetschau, ed., *De principiis* (vol. 5 of *Origenes Werke;* GCS 22; Leipzig: Hinrichs, 1913). – H. Görgemanns and H. Karpp, eds., *Vier Bücher von den Prinzipien* (TzF 24; Darmstadt: Wissenschaftliche Buchgesellschaft, 1976) [Com]. – H. Crouzel and M. Simonetti, eds., *Traité des principes* (5 vols.; SC 252, 253, 268, 269, 312; Paris: Cerf, 1978–1984).

*Translations:* F. Crombie, trans., "Origen De principiis," in *ANF* (Peabody, Mass.: Hendrickson, 1995; repr. of 1885 ed.), 4:237–384. – G. W. Butterworth, *Origen on First Principles: Being Koetschau's Text of the De principiis Translated into English, Together with an Introduction and Notes* (London: SPCK, 1936; repr., Gloucester, Mass.: P. Smith, 1973).

*Studies:* G. Bardy, *Recherches sur l'histoire du texte et des versions latines du De principiis d'Origène* (MFCL 25; Paris: Champion, 1923). – M. Harl, *Origène et la fonction révélatrice du Verbe incarné* (PatSor 2; Paris: Seuil, 1958). – F. H. Kettler, *Der ursprüngliche Sinn der Dogmatik des Origenes* (BZNW 31; Berlin: A. Töpelmann, 1966). – H. J. Vogt, *Das Kirchenverständnis des Origenes* (BoBKG 4; Vienna: Böhlau, 1974). – H. Crouzel, "Qu'a voulu faire Origène en composant le *Traité des principes?*"

*BLE* 76 (1975): 161–86, 241–60. – G. Dorival, "Nouvelles remarques sur la forme du *Traité des principes* d'Origène," *RechAug* 22 (1987): 67–108. – J. Rius-Camps, "Los diversos estratos redaccionales del *Peri archon* de Orígenes," *RechAug* 22 (1987): 5–65. – P. Heimann, *Erwähltes Schicksal: Präexistenz der Seele und christlicher Glaube im Denkmodell des Origenes* (Tübingen: Katzmann, 1988). – A. Scott, *Origen and the Life of the Stars: A History of an Idea* (Oxford: Clarendon; New York: Oxford University Press, 1991). – N. Pace, *Ricerche sulla traduzione di Rufino del "De principiis" di Origene* (Florence: Nuova Italia, 1990). – L. Lies, *Origenes' "Peri archon": Eine undogmatische Dogmatik* (Darmstadt: Wissenschaftliche Buchgesellschaft, 1992). – B. E. Daley, "Origen's *'De principiis'*: A Guide to the 'Principles' of Christian Scriptural Interpretation," in *Nova et vetera: Patristic Studies in Honor of Thomas Patrick Halton* (ed. J. F. Petruccione; Washington, D.C.: Catholic University of America Press, 1998), 3–21.

## 4. *Contra Celsum*

As outlined in the introduction, one form of dispute between Christianity and paganism in the pre-Constantinian era was the literary controversy among intellectuals. Origen was not able to escape it, although he did not relish taking part. About 178, Celsus, a pagan philosopher, wrote a book against Christians, titled Ἀληθὴς λόγος (*The True Logos*), that had no intention of repeating the usual popular prejudices. Instead he gathered detailed information about Christianity and then attacked from what he considered to be a philosophically superior position. He certainly acknowledged the Christians' doctrine of the Logos, which could easily be reconciled with the Platonic or syncretistic philosophy of the time, and their high ethics and exemplary lifestyle, which were also the goals of correct philosophy. Nevertheless he considered the Jewish-Christian figure of a Messiah and his personification in Jesus to be too absurd. Christ had merely been a deceiver and magician, and his disciples merely fabricated the myth of his resurrection. By comparison, he considered the rationality of the Hellenists' philosophical belief in God as far superior to Christianity.

Although *The True Logos* hardly seems to have reached its intended audience among the Christians, Ambrose urged Origen to provide a response in order to preempt possible damage. Origen initially resisted because he was of the persuasion that false accusations are best punished with noble disdain and the firmly established Christian would not be challenged by them. Ultimately, however, he acquiesced "for such as are either wholly unacquainted with the Christian faith, or for those who, as the apostle terms them, are 'weak in the faith' [Rom 14:1]" (preface 6).

And so ca. 245–248 the eight books of *Contra Celsum* were written. They painstakingly followed the argumentation of Celsus and cited extensive sections of Celsus's work. As a result, about three-fourths of the otherwise lost original of *The True Logos* can be reconstructed from this response against it. It was likely composed of three major parts:

a. Christianity as a sect broken away from Judaism and traced back to suspect human, rather than divine, origins;

b. the impossibility of the Messiah's existence predicated upon the condescension of the Son of God; and

c. the worthlessness of the Christian teaching, which in every respect is inferior to the traditional philosophies and which disqualifies itself on account of its sectarian monotheism.

Origen's eight books likewise begin with the origin of Christianity out of Judaism and also with the doctrine of God and the incarnation (1–2); then he compares Christ with the cults of Greek heroes and gods (3). Books 4–6 explain the essential features of the Christian faith: the Trinity, creation, good and evil, God and the world, worship and church, Christian life, and eschatology. Finally, bks. 7 and 8 return to the fundamental question of the veneration of God by pagans, Jews, and Christians and to the evidence of the one true God and his worship. Origen demonstrates the divinity of Christ primarily from Christ's miracles, and the truth of Christianity from the fact that Christians still work miracles.

*Editions:* M. Borret, ed., *Contre Celse* (5 vols.; SC 132, 136, 147, 150, 227; Paris, Cerf, 1967–1976).

*Translations:* F. Crombie, trans., "Origen against Celsus," in *ANF* (Peabody, Mass.: Hendrickson, 1995; repr. of 1885 ed.), 4:395–667. – H. Chadwick, *Contra Celsum* (Cambridge: Cambridge University Press, 1953; repr., Cambridge and New York: Cambridge University Press, 1980).

*Encyclopedia Articles:* L. W. Barnard, "Apologetik I," *TRE* 3:391–94.

*Collections of Essays:* L. Perrone, ed., *Discorsi di verità: Paganesimo, giudaismo e cristianesimo a confronto nel Contro Celso di Origine* (SEAug 61; Rome: Institutum Patristicum Augustinianum, 1998).

*Studies:* A. Miura-Stange, *Celsus und Origenes: Das Gemeinsame ihrer Weltanschauung nach den acht Büchern des Origenes gegen Celsus: Eine Studie zur Religions- und Geistesgeschichte des 2. und 3. Jahrhundertes* (BZNW 4; Giessen: A. Töpelmann, 1926). – F. Mosetto, *I miracoli evangelici nel dibattito tra Celso e Origene* (BSRel 76; Rome: LAS, 1986). – M. Fédou, *Christianisme et religions païennes dans le Contre Celse d'Origène* (ThH 81; Paris: Beauchesne, 1988). – L. H. Feldmann, "Origen's *Contra Celsum* and Josephus' *Contra Apionem:* The Issue of Jewish Origins," *VC* 44 (1990): 105–35. – L. Lies, "Vom Christentum zu Christus nach Origenes' *Contra Celsum,*" *ZKT* 112 (1990): 150–77. – H. M. Jackson, "The Setting and Sectarian Provenance of the Fragment of the *Celestial Dialogue* Preserved by Origen from Celsus's Ἀληθὴς λόγος," *HTR* 85 (1992): 273–305. – C. Reemts, *Vernunftgemässer Glaube: Die Begründung des Christentums in der Schrift des Origenes gegen Celsus* (Hereditas 13; Bonn: Borengässer, 1998).

# 5. Disputes regarding Origen

The dissemination and influence of Origen's theology can scarcely be overestimated for the subsequent centuries, up into the Middle Ages. Toward the end of the fourth century, however, debates about him began to emerge, and they continued for centuries, precipitated by Epiphanius, bishop of Constantia (Salamis). After he had already included Origen in his *Panarion* (written 374–377), a work encompassing all of the heresies that appeared until then, he accused John, bishop of Jerusalem, of Origenism in the sermons preached at the dedication of a church in Jerusalem in 393, and he challenged him to condemn Origen. Shortly thereafter a certain Atarbios visited the monasteries in Palestine to solicit support. Rufinus rejected him, but Jerome benevolently received him. This gave rise to the first major dispute concerning Origen between Epiphanius, Jerome, and Theophilus of Alexandria, on one side, and Rufinus and John of Jerusalem, on the other, primarily concerning the theology of *De principiis*.

The disputes regarding Origen reached their climax and conclusion in the sixth century, when the monks of the two Laura monasteries at Sinai fell out with one another over his theology. In 543 Emperor Justinian issued an edict against Origen, to which neither the pope nor the patriarchs objected. The imperial police then confiscated and destroyed all of Origen's writings they were able to secure; this is the reason for the incompleteness of the sources today. The second Council of Constantinople (553) did indeed include Origen among the heretics in canon 11, but his name is not included in the emperor's draft or in the letter of Pope Vigilius, whereby he sanctioned the council. It has to be assumed, therefore, that this council did not condemn Origen and thus did not consider his theology as heretical.

*Encyclopedia Articles:* G. Fritz, *DTC* 11.2:1565–88. – H. Crouzel, *EECh* 2:623–24. – R. Williams, *TRE* 25:414–20. – E. Clark, *EEC* 2:837–39.

*Studies:* F. Diekamp, *Die origenistischen Streitigkeiten im sechsten Jahrhundert und das fünfte allgemeine Concil* (Münster: Aschendorff, 1899). – F. Cavallera, *Saint Jérôme: Sa vie et son œuvre* (2 vols.; SSL 1–2; Paris: Champion, 1932). – H. Crouzel, "Qu'a voulu faire Origène en composant le *Traité des principes?*" *BLE* 76 (1975): 161–86, 241–60. – W. A. Bienert, *Dionysius von Alexandrien: Zur Frage des Origenismus im dritten Jahrhundert* (PTS 21; Berlin and New York: de Gruyter, 1978). – J. F. Dechow, *Dogma and Mysticism in Early Christianity: Epiphanius of Cyprus and the Legacy of Origen* (PatMS 13; [Belgium]: Peeters; Macon, Ga.: Mercer University Press, 1988). – W. A. Bienert, "Der Streit um Origenes: Zur Frage nach den Hintergründen seiner Vertreibung aus Alexandria und den Folgen für die Einheit der Kirche," in *Einheit der Kirche in vorkonstantinischer Zeit* (ed. F. von Lilienfeld and A. M. Ritter; Erlangen: [n.p.], 1989), 93–106. – F. X. Murphy and P. Sherwood, *Constantinople II et Constantinople III* (HCO 3; Paris: Orante, 1973). – E. A. Clark, *The Origenist Controversy: The Cultural Construction of an Early Christian Debate* (Princeton, N.J.: Princeton University Press, 1992). – G. E. Gould, "The Image of God and the Anthropomorphite Controversy in Fourth Century Monasticism," in *Origeniana quinta* (ed. R. J. Daly; Louvain: Louvain University Press, 1992), 549–57. – R. Williams, "*Damnosa haereditas:* Pamphilus' Apology and the Reputation of Origen," in *Logos: Festschrift für Luise Abramowski zum 8. Juli 1993* (ed. H. C. Brennecke, E. L. Grasmück, and C. Markschies; BZNW 67; Berlin and New York: de Gruyter, 1993), 151–69. – B. E. Daley, "What Did 'Origenism' Mean in the Sixth Century?" in *Origeniana sexta* (ed. G. Dorival and A. Le Boulluec; Louvain: Louvain University Press; Peeters, 1995), 627–38.

# CHAPTER FOUR

# Beginnings of Latin Literature

*Bibliography:* G. May, "Lateinische Patristik, Hilfsmittel, Handbücher, Literatur- und Auslegungsgeschichte," *TRu* 53 (1988): 250–76.

*Studies:* J. Daniélou, *Les origines du christianisme latin* (vol. 3 of *Histoire des doctrines chrétiennes avant Nicée;* 2d ed.; Paris: Cerf, 1991); [ET] *The Origins of Latin Christianity* (trans. D. Smith and J. A. Baker; London: Barton, Longman & Todd; Philadelphia: Westminster, 1977). – K. Sallmann, ed., *Die Literatur des Umbruchs: Von der römischen zur christlichen Literatur* (HAW 8.4; Munich: C. H. Beck, 1997), 341–584.

## INTRODUCTION: CHRISTIAN LATIN

Since the conquest of Greece by the Romans (concluded with the conquest of Corinth in 147 B.C.E.), Greek had become the common colloquial language (κοινὴ διάλεκτος) of the whole empire, so that also in the West the Christian liturgy and literature at first used Greek. This does not mean that the respective national languages outside Greece were not maintained. In the West, Latin continued to serve as the official language, the literary language, and the everyday language. Especially in North Africa, Greek never took hold, and the simple (rural) population, in any case, only rarely learned a language other than the local mother tongue. Since the success of Christian missions in the second century included the ordinary classes of people, perhaps at first predominantly so, this led to the rise of Latin Christian literature at the end of the second century, beginning with the translation of the essential texts of Christian proclamation and praxis: liturgy and Bible. Significantly, the first witnesses of Latin Christian literature known to us came from Africa: the *Acta Scillitanorum,* 180 (cf. ch. 3.III.A.2), and Tertullian, from 197 on (cf. II).

Like their Greek-speaking counterparts, Latin-speaking Christians sensed that "classical" (pagan) Latin could not do justice to the Christian subject. What developed from the start, therefore, was a special Christian Latin language, into which poured many vernacular peculiarities based on the origin of the translators and recipients; these peculiarities remained noticeable even with later, highly educated writers. Principally, there are three phenomena to be observed here:

a. lexicographic—formation of new words by means of

1) Hebrew or Greek loanwords (*halleluiah, amen, episcopus, eucharistia*);

2) the attachment of new suffixes to Latin words (e.g., *devoratio, glorificare, corruptela*);

3) the use of vernacular terms (e.g., *ambulare* instead of *ire, manducare* instead of *edere*);

4) the translation of Greek words (e.g., πρωτότοκος = *primogenitus;* εὐλογία = *benedictio*);

5) the formation of new semantic fields (e.g., σάρξ = *caro* = *carnalis, carneus, incarnari*);

b. semasiological—expansion or constriction of a word's meaning so that it becomes a technical term (e.g., *caritas* = Christian love and care; *figura* = an OT model of the NT);

c. syntactical—new sentence structure or combination of words:

1) the borrowing of Hebrew syntax (e.g., *saecula saeculorum, vanitas vanitatum*);

2) more specific genitival modifiers (e.g., *plebs fidelium, terra promissionis*);

3) word combinations with new meanings (e.g., *operari virtutes* = "to work miracles"); and

4) the alteration of formerly fixed constructions (e.g., subordinate clauses with *quia, quod, quoniam* instead of accusative with infinitive).

*Bibliography:* G. Sanders and M. Van Uytfanghe, *Bibliographie signalétique du latin des chrétiens* (Corpus Christianorum: Lingua patrum 1; Turnhout, Belg.: Brepols, 1989).

*Thesaurus: Thesaurus linguae latinae* (Leipzig: Teubner, 1900–). – A. Ferrua, *Note al Thesaurus linguae latinae: Addenda et corrigenda (A–D)* (Bari; Edipuglia, 1986). – A. Blaise, *Le vocabulaire latin des principaux thèmes liturgiques* (Brepols: Turnhout, 1966).

*Dictionaries:* C. du Cange, *Glossarium mediae et infimae latinitatis* (ed. L. Favre; 10 vols. in 5; Graz: Akademische Druck- u. Verlagsanstalt, 1954; repr. of 1883–1887 ed.). – K. E. Georges, *Ausführliches lateinisch-deutsches Handwörterbuch* (2 vols.; 13th ed.; Hannover: Hahnsche Buchhandlung, 1972). – A. Souter, *A Glossary of Later Latin to 600 A.D.* (Oxford: Clarendon, 1949, repr., 1997). – A. Blaise, *Manuel du latin chrétien* (Strassbourg: Latin Chrétien, 1955; Turnhout, Belg.: Brepols, 1986). – A. Blaise and H. Chirat, *Dictionnaire latin-français des auteurs chrétiens* (Turnhout, Belg.: Brepols, 1964). – A. Blaise, *Dictionnaire latin-français des auteurs du moyen-âge* (Corpus Christianorum: Continuatio mediaevalis; Turnhout, Belg.: Brepols, 1975). – J. F. Niermeyer, C. van den Kieft, and G. S. M. M. Lake-Schoonebeek, *Mediae latinitatis lexicon minus* (Leiden: Brill, 1976). – P. G. W. Glare, *Oxford Latin Dictionary* (rev. ed.; Oxford: Clarendon; New York: Oxford University Press, 1996).

*Grammars:* R. Kühner, F. Holzweissig, and C. Stegmann, *Ausführliche Grammatik der lateinischen Sprache* (3 vols.; 2d ed. of part 1; 5th ed. of part 2; Hannover: Hahnsche Buchhandlung, 1982). – A. Ernout, *Morphologie historique du latin* (3d rev. ed.; Paris: C. Klincksieck, 1974). – M. Leumann, J. B. Hofmann, and A. Szantyr, *Lateinische Grammatik* (3 vols.; HAW 2.2.1–3; Munich: Beck, 1977–1979).

*Encyclopedia Articles:* P. Siniscalco, "Languages of the Fathers," *EECh* 1:472. – V. Loi, "Latin, Christian," *EECh* 1:474. – M. P. McHugh, *EEC* 2:664–65.

*Studies:* Graecitas et latinitas Christianorum primaeva. Supplementum (Nijmegen: Dekker & van de Vegt, 1964–). [GLCP] – Latinitas Christianorum primaeva (ed. J. Schrijnen; Louvain and Nijmegen: Dekker en van de Vegt, 1932–1972). [LCP] – G. Koffmane, *Geschichte des Kirchenlateins* (2 vols.; Breslau: W. Koebner, 1879–1881). – M. A. Sainio, *Semasiologische Untersuchungen über die Entstehung der christlichen Latinität* (Annales Academiae Scientiarum Fennicae 47.1; Helsinki: Finnische Literaturgesellschaft, 1940). – G. Devoto, *Storia della lingua di Roma* (2d ed.; Bologna: L. Cappelli, 1944; repr., 1991). – G. Bardy, *La question des langues dans l'église ancienne* (Paris: Beauchesne, 1948). – C. Mohrmann, *Études sur le latin des chrétiens* (4 vols.; SeL 65, 87, 103, 143; Rome: Storia e letteratura, 1958–1977). – E. Löfstedt, *Late Latin* (Oslo: Aschehoug; Cambridge, Mass.: Harvard University Press, 1959). – G. B. Pighi, *Storia della lingua latina* (Turin: Società Editrice Internazionale, 1968). – L. Leone, *Latinità cristiana: Introduzione allo studio del latino cristiano* (Lecce: Milella, 1971). – F. Stolz, A. Debrunner, and W. P. Schmid, *Storia della lingua latina* (rev. ed.; Bologna: Pàtron, 1982). – J. Schrijnen, *I caratteri del latino cristiano antico* (with an appendix by C. Mohrmann; Bologna: Pàtron, 1977; 4th ed.; Bologna: Pàtron, 2002) [appendix pp. 367–404]; translation of *Charakteristik des altchristlichen Latein* (LCP 1; Nijmegen: Dekker & van de Vegt, 1932). – V. Loi, *Origini e caratteristiche della latinità cristiana* (Rome: Accademia Nazionale dei Lincei, 1978). – O. García de la Fuente, *Antología del latín bíblico y cristiano* (Málaga: Edinford, 1990). – A. De Prisco, *Il latino tardoantico e altomedievale* (Rome: Jouvence, 1991). – O. García de la Fuente, *Latín bíblico y latín cristiano* (Madrid: CEES, 1994).

# I. EARLIEST LATIN TRANSLATIONS OF THE BIBLE

The earliest Latin translations of the Bible preceded all Latin Christian literature, as far as we are conversant with it. This is shown from the fact that the earliest writings already refer to or use them. In the *Acta Scillitanorum* Saturninus, the proconsul, asks the accused, "What kinds of things do you have in your container of scrolls [*capsa*]?"[1] Seratus responds, "Books and letters of Paul, a righteous man" (12). Since the accused are speaking Latin and come from a population stratum in which a knowledge of Greek cannot be taken for granted, it is generally assumed that the reference is to a Latin version of the Pauline letters. Although Tertullian basically provides his own translations from the Greek, his NT citations show such close parallelism with other traditions that he likely also had Latin translations available to him. Hence in the second half of the second century, at least in North Africa, there existed Latin translations of the NT. The earliest witness to Latin versions of the OT is found in the works of Cyprian about half a century later, although this may merely offer a *terminus ante quem*. In any case, it may be assumed that the OT was not translated from the Hebrew but from the Septuagint.

---

[1] Generally a round, wooden container used to preserve and transport scrolls. In depictions it is used as an attribute of philosophers, teachers, and writers, e.g., in the mosaic of the evangelists in the Basilica of San Vitale in Ravenna. Cf. J. Kollwitz, "Capsa," *RAC* 2:891–93.

The translators did not come from a class of society that was highly educated in literature, for many vernacular expressions and forms found their way
into the Latin Bible and its style thereby remained unpolished, so that Augustine
initially was repulsed by it. Nevertheless this type of Latin had a formative influence on the early Latin Christian language.

Both Jerome, in his *praefatio* to the Gospels (reproduced in the Vulgate editions), and Augustine (*De doctrina christiana* 2.11) refer to a multitude of Latin
translations. Only fragments have been preserved of these, however, mainly in citations by the Fathers, because from the late fourth century on, the Vulgate, a
"universally disseminated edition" of the Bible based on Jerome's predominantly
new translation, superseded all others. An attempt has been made to establish different translation types among the fragments, namely African (*Afra*), Italic
(*Itala*), and Spanish (*Hispana*), but all of them are closely linked, and all of
the pre-Jerome versions are frequently brought together under the label *Itala*.
Whether various parent texts and translations existed is very difficult to determine from the fragments preserved today. In any case, the Vetus Latina Institute
in Beuron, Germany, which since 1951 has been directed by Bonifatius Fischer
and publishes the fragments of the Old Latin Bible following the standard edition
of Petrus Sabatier (1743), proceeds from a prototype for the NT.

*Bibliography: Bulletin de la Bible latin: Bulletin d'ancienne littérature chrétienne latine*
(Maredsous, Belg., 1921–1993).

*Editions: Vetus Latina: Die Reste der altlateinischen Bibel* (Fribourg, Switz.: Herder, 1949–)
[*VL*]. – P. Sabatier, *Bibliorum Sacrorum latinae versiones antiquae seu Vetus Italica* (3
vols.; Paris: apud Franciscum Didot, 1751; repr. of 1743–1749 ed.). – A. Jülicher,
W. Matzkow, and K. Aland, *Itala: Das Neue Testament in altlateinischer Überlieferung*
(4 vols.; 2d ed.; Berlin and New York: de Gruyter, 1970–1976).

*Reference Works: Arbeitsberichte (Stiftung Vetus Latina)* (Beuron: Stiftung Vetus Latina,
1952–) [*AVL*]. – *Bericht des Instituts: Vetus Latina Institut der Erzabtei Beuron* (Beuron:
Stiftung Vetus Latina; note: Since 1971, the *Arbeitsberichte* of the Stiftung Vetus Latina
and the *Bericht* of the Vetus Latina Institut are published in one issue) [*BVLI*]. –
Annuali, in vendita presso: Vetus-Latina-Institut, Beuron. – H. J. Frede, *Kirchenschriftsteller: Verzeichnis und Sigel* (4th ed.; VL 1.1; Fribourg, Switz.: Herder, 1995).

*Encyclopedia Articles:* V. Rechmann and S. P. Brock, *TRE* 6:172–78. – K. Zelzer, *HLL*
4:352–67.

*Collections of Essays:* J. Fontaine and C. Pietri, eds., *Le monde latin antique et la Bible* (Paris:
Beauchesne, 1985). – R. Gryson and P.-M. Bogaert, eds., *Recherches sur l'histoire de la
Bible latine* (Cahiers de la Revue théologique de Louvain 19; Louvain: Peeters, 1987).

*Studies: Aus der Geschichte der lateinischen Bibel* (Fribourg, Switz.: Herder, 1957–). [*AGLE*]
– F. Stummer, *Einführung in die lateinische Bibel: Ein Handbuch für Vorlesungen und
Selbstunterricht* (Paderborn: F. Schöningh, 1928). – B. Fischer, "Das Neue Testament
in lateinischer Sprache: Der gegenwärtige Stand seiner Erforschung und seine Bedeutung für die griechische Textgeschichte," in *Die alten Übersetzungen des Neuen Testaments: Die Kirchenväterzitate und Lektionare* (ed. K. Aland; ANTF 5; New York: de
Gruyter, 1972), 1–92; repr. in B. Fischer, *Beiträge zur Geschichte der lateinischen
Bibeltexte* (AGLB 12; Fribourg, Switz.: Herder, 1986), 156–274. – E. Valgiglio, *La
antiche versioni latine del Nuovo Testamento: Fedeltà e aspetti grammaticali* (Koinonia
11; Naples: D'Auria, 1985).

# II. TERTULLIAN

Although Quintus Septimus Florens Tertullianus, the earliest Latin Christian writer known to us, has left an extensive oeuvre, of which only a small part was lost over the centuries, we know relatively little about his life. His writings contain but few references, and Jerome scarcely offers more in his work dealing with literary history, *De viris illustribus* (53). Tertullian was born into a pagan family in Carthage in 160. His father was an officer in the Roman army with a corresponding societal standing and a good livelihood. He provided his son with a diligent education that, in his works, is reflected in an excellent mastery of rhetoric, law, and Greek. Tertullian's two earliest writings, *Ad nationes* and *Apologeticus*, are dated to 197; we do not know exactly when he was converted to Christianity before this. In the following decade, he penned about twenty apologetic writings against pagans and Jews, of a dogmatic-polemical kind against the gnostics and other heretics, and practical and ascetical works concerning such issues as theatrical plays, prayer, repentance, and baptism. Beginning in 207, Tertullian increasingly sympathized with the rigors of Montanism until he severed his ties with the Catholic Church ca. 213 because he accused it of laxity, especially in matters of repentance. This "changing of sides" did not interrupt his prolific literary output, however; it merely changed the content. From 207 on, he wrote works against Marcion and against the Valentinians, and other writings addressing ascetical and dogmatic issues were now directed, in their rigor, against the Catholic Church. After 220 we lose track of Tertullian. We do not know when and where he died. It may be assumed that he died in Carthage, since, apart from a brief trip to Rome in his younger years, he did not leave the city. According to Jerome, he lived *ad decrepitam aetatem* and hence was at least sixty-three years old.

Tertullian's work as a whole is significant for our knowledge of the time, society, culture, church, and theology of North Africa. Besides his theology, P. Siniscalco pinpoints three major sets of questions regarding Tertullian's person and work that have been the focal point of interest in recent years:

a. Tertullian's relation to the Roman society and culture around him. As much as he was shaped by it, his works contain many indications that he rejected everything associated with this culture. Thus he rejected a pagan education and military service, among other things, so that for him Christianity and *romanitas* seemed to be irreconcilable. Yet other voices see him as pioneering the harmonization of Christianity and the *civitas romana*. In this context, one has to take into account Africa's particular position in the Roman Empire, which shaped Tertullian's attitude and thought. North Africa paid closer attention to its own origins and traditions than it did to Rome. North African Christianity was unable to escape this disposition in spite of the tradition that its origins came from Rome (other indicators, however, point to missionizing from the eastern Mediterranean region).

b. Tertullian's relation to philosophy. Here, too, his verbal rejection of philosophy is juxtaposed to his employment of it in developing his theological conceptions.

c. The significant contribution Tertullian made in developing Christian Latin. Although he may not be seen as the founder of Christian Latin as such, he nevertheless may be viewed as the founder of Christian theological Latin. Furthermore, given his education, he introduces the ancient literary forms and its rhetoric from the outset.

In many respects, Tertullian's theology has become foundational and revolutionary, although he effectively succumbed to a *damnatio memoriae* after his departure to Montanism. In spite of this the history of his reception shows that he continued to be read into the Middle Ages. Esteem for him was such that Cyprian, according to Jerome's account (*Vir. ill.* 53), read Tertullian's works daily and, when he wanted to take them in hand, he had only to say to his *notarius*, "Bring me the master!" Four altogether different tractates particularly stand out and are the most important for an initial understanding of Tertullian's theology: *Ad nationes, Apologeticus, De praescriptione haereticorum,* and *Adversus Praxean.*

*Bibliographies:* "Bibliographia chronica tertullianea," *REAug* 22 (1976): n.p. – R. D. Sider, "Approaches to Tertullian: A Study of Recent Scholarship," *SecCent* 2 (1982): 228–60. – M. Frenschkowski, *BBKL* 11:695–720. – R. Braun et al., eds., *Chronica tertullianea et cyprianea, 1975–1994: Bibliographie critique de la première littérature latine chrétienne* (Paris: Études Augustiniennes, 1999).

*Editions:*
*Opera omnia:* A. Reifferscheid, G. Wissowa, A. Kroymann, H. Hoppe, V. Bulhart, and P. Borleffs, eds., *Quinti Septimi Florentis Tertulliani Opera ex recensione Augusti Reifferscheid et Georgii Wissowa* (5 vols.; CSEL 20, 47, 69, 70, 76; Vienna: F. Tempsky, 1890–1957). – *Opera* (CCSL 1–2; Turnhout, Belg.: Brepols, 1954).
*Ad uxorem:* C. Munier, ed., *A son épouse* (SC 273; Paris: Cerf, 1980).
*Adversus Hermogenem:* F. Chapot, ed., *Contre Hermogène* (SC 439; Paris: Cerf, 1999).
*Adversus Valentinianos:* J.-C. Fredouille, ed., *Contre les Valentiniens* (SC 280–281; Paris: Cerf, 1980–1981).
*De baptismo:* R. F. Refoulé and M. Drouzy, eds., *Traité du baptême* (rev. ed.; SC 35; Paris: Cerf, 2002). – E. Evans, ed., *Tertullian's Homily on Baptism* (London: SPCK, 1964) [ET/Com].
*De carne Christi:* E. Evans, ed., *Tertullian's Treatise on the Incarnation* (London: SPCK, 1956) [ET/Com]. – J.-P. Mahé, ed., *La chair du Christ* (2 vols.; SC 216–217; Paris: Cerf, 1975).
*De carnis resurrectione:* E. Evans, ed., *Tertullian's Treatise on the Resurrection* (London: SPCK, 1960) [ET].
*De cultu feminarum:* M. Turcan, ed., *La toilette des femmes* (SC 173; Paris: Cerf, 1971). – S. Isetta, ed., *L'eleganza delle donne* (BPat 6; Florence: Centro Internazionale del Libro, 1986).
*De exhortatione castitatis:* C. Moreschini and J.-C. Fredouille, eds., *Exhortation à la chasteté* (SC 319; Paris: Cerf, 1985).
*De idololatria:* J. H. Waszink and J. C. M. van Winden, eds., *De idololatria: Critical Text, Translation, and Commentary* (SVigChr 1; Leiden and New York: Brill, 1987) [ET/Com].
*De monogamia:* P. Mattei, ed., *Le mariage unique* (SC 343; Paris: Cerf, 1988). – R. Uglione, ed., *Le uniche nozze* (CorPat 15; Turin: Società Editrice Internazionale, 1993).

*De oratione:* E. Evans, ed., *De oratione liber: Tract on the Prayer* (London: SPCK, 1953) [ET].
*De paenitentia:* C. Munier, ed., *La pénitence* (SC 316; Paris: Cerf, 1984).
*De patientia:* J.-C. Fredouille, ed., *De la patience* (rev. ed.; SC 310; Paris: Cerf, 1999).
*De pudicitia:* C. Micaelli and C. Munier, eds., *La pudicité* (2 vols.; SC 394–395; Paris: Cerf, 1993).
*De spectaculis:* M. Turcan, *Les spectacles* (SC 332; Paris: Cerf, 1986). – K.-W. Weber, ed., *De spectaculis* (Stuttgart: Reclam, 1988) [Com].
*De testimonio animae:* C. Tibiletti, ed., *La testimonianza dell'anima* (BPat 1; Florence: Centro Internazionale del Libro,1984).
*De virginibus velandis:* C. Stücklin, ed., *De virginibus velandis* (EHS.T 26; Frankfurt: Lang, 1974) [Com]. – E. Schulz-Flügel and P. Mattei, eds., *Le voile des vierges* (SC 424; Paris: Cerf, 1997).
*Scorpiace:* G. Azzali Bernardelli, ed., *Scorpiace* (BPat 14; Florence: Nardini, 1990).

*Translations:* A. C. Coxe, trans., "The Writings of Tertullian," in *ANF* (Hendrickson: Peabody, Mass., 1995; repr. of 1885 ed.), 3; 4:3–126 [*Opera omnia*]. – *Tertullian concerning the Resurrection of the Flesh* (ed. and trans. A. Souter; London: SPCK; New York: Macmillan, 1922) [*De carnis resurrectione*]. – *Apology, De spectaculis* (ed. and trans. T. R. Glover; LCL 250; London: Heinemann; Cambridge, Mass.: Harvard University Press, 1960; repr. of 1931 ed.), 1–301. – *Treatises on Marriage and Remarriage: To His Wife, An Exhortation to Chastity, Monogamy* (trans. W. P. Le Saint; ACW 13; Westminster, Md.: Newman, 1951). – *The Treatise against Hermogenes* (trans. J. H. Waszink; ACW 24; Westminster, Md.: Newman, 1956). – *Treatises on Penance: On Penitence and On Purity* (W. P. Le Saint; ACW 28; Westminster, Md.: Newman, 1959). – *Disciplinary, Moral, and Ascetical Works* (ed. R. Arbesmann, E.J. Daly, and E. A. Quain; FC 40; New York: Fathers of the Church, 1959) [*To the Martyrs, Spectacles, The Apparel of Women, Prayer, Patience, The Chaplet, Flight in the Time of Persecution*].

*Reference Works:* G. Claesson, *Index tertullianeus* (3 vols.; Paris: Études Augustiniennes, 1974–1975). – H. Quellet, *Concordance verbale du De corona de Tertullien: Concordance, index, listes de fréquence* (AlOm.A 23; Hildesheim and New York: Olms, 1975); *Concordance verbale du De cultu feminarum de Tertullien* (AlOm.A 60; Hildesheim and New York: Olms-Weidmann, 1986); *Concordance verbale du De patientia de Tertullien* (AlOm.A 97; Hildesheim and New York: Olms-Weidmann, 1988); *Concordance verbale du De exhortatione castitatis de Tertullien* (AlOm.A 131; Hildesheim and New York: Olms-Weidmann, 1992); *Concordance verbale de l'Ad uxorem de Tertullien* (AlOm.A 152; Hildesheim and New York: Olms-Weidmann, 1994).

*Encyclopedia Articles:* H. von Campenhausen, 1:97–120. – C. Munier, *DSp* 15:271–95. – P. Siniscalco, *EECh* 2:818–20. – H. Tränkle, *HLL* 4:438–511. – R. Sider, *EEC* 2:1107–9.

*Introductions/Surveys:* P. Monceaux, *Tertullien et les origines* (vol. 1 of *Histoire littéraire de l'Afrique chrétienne depuis les origines jusqu'à l'invasion arabe;* Paris: E. Leroux, 1901). – B. Nisters, *Tertullian: Seine Persönlichkeit und sein Schicksal—ein charakterologischer Versuch* (MBTh 25; Münster: Aschendorff, 1950). – J. Steinmann, *Tertullien* (Paris: Chalet, 1967). – T. D. Barnes, *Tertullian: A Historical and Literary Study* (rev. ed.; Oxford: Clarendon; New York: Oxford University Press, 1985).

*Collections of Essays:* J. Granarolo and M. Biraud, eds., *Autour Tertullien* (vol. 2 of *Hommage à René Braun;* Paris: Belles Lettres, 1990). – R. Braun, *Approches de Tertullien: Vingt-six études sur l'auteur et sur l'œuvre (1955–1990)* (Paris: Études Augustiniennes, 1992).

*Theology:* A. d'Alès, *La théologie de Tertullien* (BTH; Paris: Beauchesne, 1905). – R. E. Roberts, *The Theology of Tertullian* (London: Epworth [J. A. Sharp], 1924). – W. Bender,

*Die Lehre über den Heiligen Geist bei Tertullian* (MThS.S 18; Munich: M. Hueber, 1961). – R. Cantalamessa, *La cristologia di Tertulliano* (Par. 18; Fribourg, Switz.: Edizioni Universitarie Friburgo, 1962). – J. Moingt, *Théologie trinitaire de Tertullien* (4 vols.; Theol[P] 68–70, 75; Paris: Aubier, 1966–1969). – R. Braun, *Deus Christianorum: Recherches sur le vocabulaire doctrinal de Tertullien* (2d ed.; Paris: Études Augustiniennes, 1977). – G. L. Bray, *Holiness and the Will of God: Perspectives of the Theology of Tertullian* (Atlanta: John Knox, 1979). – C. Rambeaux, *Tertullien face aux morales des trois premiers siècles* (Paris: Belles Lettres, 1979). – G. Hallonsten, *Satisfactio bei Tertullian: Überprüfung einer Forschungstradition* (STL 39; Malmö: CWK Gleerup, 1984). – A. Viciano, *Cristo salvador y liberador del hombre: Estudio sobre la soteriología de Tertuliano* (CTUN 51; Pamplona: Ediciones Universidad de Navarra, 1986). – G. Azzali Bernardelli, *Quaestiones tertullianae criticae* (Mantova: n.p., 1990). – C. B. Daly, *Tertullian—the Puritan and His Influence: An Essay in Historical Theology* (Dublin: Four Courts, 1993). – C. M. Robeck, *Prophecy in Carthage: Perpetua, Tertullian, Cyprian* (Cleveland: Pilgrim, 1992). – D. Rankin, *Tertullian and the Church* (Cambridge and New York: Cambridge University Press, 1995). – E. Osborn, *Tertullian: First Theologian of the West* (Cambridge and New York: Cambridge University Press, 1997). – M. Wellstein, *Nova verba in Tertullians Schriften gegen die Häretiker aus montanistischer Zeit* (Stuttgart: Teubner, 1999).

*Cultural Context:* R. Klein, *Tertullian und das römische Reich* (Heidelberg: Winter, 1968). – R. D. Sider, *Ancient Rhetoric and the Art of Tertullian* (OTM; London: Oxford University Press, 1971). – J.-C. Fredouille, *Tertullien et la conversion de la culture antique* (Paris: Études Augustiniennes, 1972). – E. I. Kouri, *Tertullian und die römische Antike* (Luther-Agricola-Gesellschaft: Schriften A.21; Helsinki: Luther-Agricola-Gesellschaft, 1982). – G. Schöllgen, *Ecclesia sordida? Zur Frage der sozialen Schichtung christlicher Gemeinden am Beispiel Karthagos zur Zeit Tertullians* (JAC.E 12; Münster: Aschendorff, 1984). – D. L. Hoffman, *The Status of Women and Gnosticism in Irenaeus and Tertullian* (SWR 36; Lewiston, N.Y.: Mellen, 1995), 145–207. – G. D. Dunn, "The Universal Spread of Christianity as a Rhetorical Argument in Tertullian's *Adversus Judaeos*," *JECS* 8 (2000): 1–19.

# A. Ad nationes *and* Apologeticus

Tertullian's two initial works, written in the spring of 197 and in the latter part of 197 respectively, by no means leave the impression of being written by a novice. This is not surprising, considering that by this time Tertullian was already almost forty years of age and, given his education and professional work, had considerable literary and rhetorical skills. Both are apologies against the unjust persecution of Christians, with *Ad nationes* being virtually a smaller preparatory work for the larger *Apologeticus*. The argumentation develops in a manner typical of the legally trained Tertullian. In bk. 1 of *Ad nationes*, he unmasks the proceedings of the Roman authorities against Christians as illegal, since the *nomen christianum* apparently is sufficient cause for punishment without a detailed investigation of the other suspicions and popular accusations (1.1–6). Chapters 7–20 then focus on the concrete accusations and demonstrate not only that the latter are absurd but that the accusers are guilty of even more serious offenses and therefore had no right to sit in judgment of Christians. In bk. 2 he launches a counterattack by demonstrating the religious and moral reprehensibility of the gods from their own myths. Furthermore, the gods are either deified humans or actions and for this reason could not have been responsible for the greatness of Rome. Consequently, failure to observe their cult cannot hurt the state. What one finds here, then, is the usual repertoire of Christian apologetics. On the whole, *Ad nationes* gives the impression of being unfinished, and the *Apologeticus*, written shortly after, resumes its topic, sometimes abridged and summarized and at other times in greater detail.

The *Apologeticus* is addressed directly to the proconsul of Carthage and to the provincial governors of North Africa. Tertullian's reason for writing a new, more extensive defense so quickly may have been associated with a new persecution threatening Africa, so that an amnesty request addressed to the authorities seemed more appropriate than a general apology addressed to the pagans. The work contains fifty chapters; to start, chs. 1–9 focus on the reasons and legality of the persecution of Christians. These are predicated on ignorance and unsubstantiated hatred without any ability to prove a concrete crime. The laws directed at Christians have been issued by bad emperors only, and thus the merit of these laws is suspect. Furthermore, the pagans themselves perpetrate what they accuse the Christians of doing, namely, the murder of children, Thyestean feasts, and incest. Chapters 10–27 turn to the accusation of atheism. Since pagan gods are merely humans or demons, the refusal to sacrifice does not represent atheism at all; on the contrary, it is in fact the only correct and useful conduct. For this reason, the Romans owe the gods nothing at all, and the only one worthy of worship is the God revealed in the Bible, an authority more ancient than all of the philosophers; the pagans are wrong in their ideas about God. Chapters 28–45 continue the defense against the accusation, predicated upon atheism, of the *crimen laesae maiestatis* and of behavior that is detrimental to the state. Since the pagan gods are of no value to the emperor and the state, Christians are most useful to them by means of their prayers to the true God and their loyal civic conduct. Even under persecution, they remain within the state. They do not commit crimes; indeed their faith obligates them to virtuous behavior. Chapters 46–50 conclude with the elevation of Christianity above all the philosophies because of its divine origin. Yet even if Christianity were placed on the same level as the philosophies, it should be equally tolerated.

Thus, in the customary apologetic methodology, the *Apologeticus* offers a systematic response to all the attacks against Christians at that time—hatred of the *nomen christianum*, accusation of crimes, anti-Christian laws, atheism, offending the imperial majesty, detriment to the state through the refusal to offer sacrifices—followed by evidence of the positive role of Christians as citizens and the superiority of the one true God and his religion above all other "philosophies," that is, instructions on right living. The *Apologeticus* may well be identified as Tertullian's most outstanding work and, in the following era, justifiably the most copied and disseminated one.

The work has a unique history of transmission, however, for it has been preserved in two different versions that at many points diverge, to the extent that the differences cannot be explained on the basis of the history of transmission (copying errors, etc.). Instead it has to be assumed that Tertullian himself wrote both of them. In principle, the revising of works in antiquity is not a rarety; but normally earlier versions were lost or withdrawn from the market in antiquity.

*Editions: Apologeticum, Verteidigung des Christentums: Lateinisch und deutsch* (ed. and trans. C. Becker; Munich: Kösel, 1952) [Com]. – A. Schneider, *Ad nationes I* (BHRom 9; Rome: Institut Suisse, 1968) [Com].

*Translations:* P. Holmes, trans., "Ad nationes," in *ANF* (Peabody, Mass.: Hendrickson, 1995; repr. of 1885 ed.), 3:109–47. – S. Thelwall, trans., "Apology," in *ANF* (Peabody, Mass.: Hendrickson, 1995; repr. of 1885 ed.), 3:17–55. – *Apology, De spectaculis* (trans. T. Glover; LCL; Cambridge, Mass.: Harvard University Press; London: Heinemann, 1977; repr. of 1931 ed.). – *Apologetical Works* (trans. E. J. Daly; FC 10; New York: Fathers of the Church, 1950), 7–126.

*Studies:* J. Lortz, *Tertullian als Apologet* (2 vols.; MBTh 9–10; Münster: Aschendorff, 1927–1928). – J. P. Waltzing, *Apologétique: Commentaire analytique, grammatical, et historique* (Paris: Belles Lettres, 1931). – C. Becker, *Tertullians Apologeticum: Werden und Leistung* (Munich: Kösel, 1954). – G. Eckert, *Orator christianus: Untersuchungen zur Argumentationskunst in Tertullians Apologeticum* (Stuttgart: Steiner, 1993).

# *B.* De anima

It is well known that the Platonic teaching on the soul—mixed, in the popular philosophy of late antiquity, with elements of other systems, such as Stoicism—stamped anthropology for centuries. Although the ancient church employed philosophy stamped with Platonism to investigate and explain its theology, it was not able to adopt it uncritically in all areas. The teachings on the preexistence of the soul, the ensoulment of the body only after birth, and the transmigration of the soul cannot be reconciled with the Christian belief in creation and redemption. Tertullian's tractate *De anima*, written after 203, reflects part of the controversial history of reception. He opposes the philosophers' unacceptable statements, for thereby they become *patriarchae haereticorum*—referring mainly to the (Valentinian) gnostics (3.1).

The fifty-eight chapters of this work are contained in three main sections. By means of a detailed critique of Phaidon and Platonic philosophy, the introduction (1–3) provides the overall theme and goal of the treatise and, as the irrefutable premise for everything, establishes that the breath of God creates the soul, according to Gen 2:7. Tertullian indicates that he had already delineated this in his now lost writing *De censu animae*, directed against Hermogenes.

The first main section (4–21) discusses the characteristics of the soul. From the Stoic Zeno, Tertullian accepts the definition of the soul as συμφυὲς πνεῦμα. Following Luke 16:22–24 (the rich man in hell who begs poor Lazarus, who is in Abraham's bosom, for a cooling drop of water), he accepts the conception of its—albeit special—corporeality. Although the Platonic structuring of the soul into a rational and an irrational part is deemed acceptable, it does not correspond to God's original intent. God created the soul as a rational whole; only the fall caused part of it to become irrational. Consequently, the basic wholeness of the soul does not allow for differing parts of the soul, all depending on its function; rather, it functions only in differing powers distributed throughout the body. The distinctions between peoples and among individuals therefore do not originate from differing parts of the soul but from their environment, their respective bodily constitutions, and especially their individual upbringing.

The second main section (22–41) opposes the soul's preexistence, whatever its nature might be, and the corresponding Platonic teaching of the ἀνάμνησις, the shadowy memory of its prenatal contemplation of truth. The soul, together with the body, comes into being at conception. The Stoic viewpoint, that the soul is only given after birth together with the first breath of cold air, contradicts both the witness of Scripture and the experience of women. This also excludes all forms of migration on the part of the soul. From the beginning, soul and body grow up and jointly enter puberty at age fourteen, when good and evil are awakened equally, namely, the sense of shame but also the proclivity to evil arising from the original sin. The soul is thereby divided, though what is good can never be destroyed completely.

Finally, the third main section (42–58) explains the soul's destiny in death and, in doing so, links up with the common human experience of sleep and dreams. He explains sleep in traditional terms as the brother of death but also as a symbol of the resurrection, whereas dreams are signs of the soul's unceasing activity. With the exception of the souls of martyrs, which enter paradise at once, the souls of all anticipate the resurrection beneath the soil (cf. Matt 12:40, "in the heart of the earth"). This is also the place where the recompense for deeds done on earth already begins before the resurrection of the bodies because, for the most part, the responsibility for this is the soul's. Tertullian, however, categorically rejects the notion that the souls of those not buried, those who commit suicide, and those who are murdered have to roam the earth restlessly.

Tertullian draws much from the writing Περὶ ψυχῆς by the physician Soranus (early second century C.E.), whom he mentions by name several times (e.g., 6.6; 8.3; 14.2). The continuing influence of his own work, however, which in and of itself and during his time certainly was important, remained rather limited because the viewpoints and formulation of the question on the topic changed rapidly.

*Editions:* Quinti Septimi Florentis Tertulliani De anima (ed. J. H. Waszink; rev. ed.; Amsterdam: J. M. Meulenhoff, 1947) [Com].

*Translations:* P. Holmes, trans., "A Treatise on the Soul," in *ANF* (Peabody, Mass.: Hendrickson, 1995; repr. of 1885 ed.), 3:181–235. – *Apologetical Works* (trans. E. A. Quain; FC 10; New York: Fathers of the Church, 1950), 179–309.

*Index:* J. H. Waszink, *Index verborum et locutionum* (rev. ed.; Hildesheim and New York: Olms, 1971).

*Studies:* G. Esser, *Die Seelenlehre Tertullians* (Paderborn: F. Schöningh, 1893). – H. Karpp, "Sorans vier Bücher 'Περὶ ψυχή' und Tertullians Schrift *De anima*," *ZNW* 33 (1934): 31–47. – H. Karpp, *Probleme altchristlicher Anthropologie: Biblische Anthropologie und philosophische Psychologie bei den Kirchenvätern des 3. Jahrhunderts* (BFCT 44.3; Gütersloh: C. Bertelsmann, 1950); 41–91. – A. J. Festugière, "La composition et l'esprit du *De anima* de Tertullien," *RSPT* 33 (1949): 129–61. – A. D. Nock, "Tertullian and the Ahori," *VC* 4 (1950): 129–41; repr. in *Arthur Darby Nock: Essays on Religion and the Ancient World* (2 vols.; Oxford: Clarendon, 1972), 2:712–19. – J. H. Waszink, "The Technique of the *clausula* in Tertullian's *De anima*," *VC* 4 (1950): 212–45. – J. Amat, *Songes et visions: L'au-delà dans la littérature latine tardive* (Paris: Études Augustiniennes, 1985), 39–50, 93–104, 148–53. – R. Polito, "I quattro libri sull'anima di Sorano e lo scritto *De anima* di Tertulliano," *RCSF* 49 (1994): 423–68.

# C. De praescriptione haereticorum

In his *De praescriptione haereticorum*, the *Prescription against Heretics*, we encounter probably Tertullian's most unusual work and, in any case, a unique apologia in terms of its type. Whereas until now, in the confrontation with those who believed differently and with Christian heretics, arguments were made in substance and the effort was to present the truth of Christianity convincingly, Tertullian here applies to the feud between orthodoxy and heresy a formality of Roman law governing civil action, namely, the *praescriptio*. If the parties of a case were able to posit valid objections against it before the opening of the legal proceedings, the latter were not opened. Here one distinguishes between the *praescriptio pro actore* (in favor of the accuser) and the *praescriptio pro reo* (in favor of the accused). The former demanded the broadening of the accusation because an important circumstance had not been considered; the latter sought the truncation, weakening, or dismissal of the case. Admissible, for instance, were the *praescriptio temporis* (limitation), the *praescriptio fori* (incompetence of the court), the *praescriptio mendaciorum* (evident falsity or incompleteness of data on the part of the accuser), and the *praescriptio militiae* (diplomatic immunity). Tertullian now applies this procedure to the treatment of heretics, though not in a strictly juridical sense. It is not permitted to enter into a discussion with them with regard to substance because any dispute with them was to be established upon the Scripture and the tradition of the church. The heretics have no claim to either of these, however, because they falsify the Scripture and are not in good standing with the tradition of the church. Thus the premise for any discussion is taken away.

Before this central statement in chs. 15–40, Tertullian clarifies two preliminary questions (1–14): 1. Why do heresies exist and why are they successful (1–5)? 2. What constitutes heresy and from what does it arise (6–14)? Christ had already predicted heresies (Matt 7:15: "Beware of false prophets"); they arise from philosophies (Col 2:8: "See to it that no one takes you captive through . . . philosophy") and from an exaggerated search for truth. The devil, in any case, twists the truth. Heresy (from αἵρεσις = *electio*) selects from the corpus of truth only the parts that suit it; yet for the one who is established in the faith this poses only a test.

The final four chapters (41–44) support the outcome by referring to the heretics' lack of church discipline, which of itself already indicates that they are not capable of representing the true church. The work, as a whole, bears the imprint of sharp logic and polemic throughout, as commonly used by a lawyer: "How frivolous it is, how worldly, how merely human (heresy), without seriousness, without authority, without discipline" (41.1). It is not possible to engage in a dispute with heretics "because a controversy over the Scriptures can, clearly, produce no other effect than help to upset either the stomach or the brain" (16.2).

*Editions:* R. F. Refoulé and P. de Labriolle, eds., *Traité de la prescription contre les hérétiques* (SC 46; Paris: Cerf, 1957).

*Translations:* P. Holmes, trans., "The Prescription against Heretics," in *ANF* (Peabody, Mass.: Hendrickson, 1995; repr. of 1885 ed.), 3:243–65. – *Early Latin Theology: Selections from Tertullian, Cyprian, Ambrose, and Jerome* (trans. S. L. Greenslade: LCC; Philadelphia: Westminster, 1956; repr., 1978), 31–64.

*Studies:* A. Beck, *Römisches Recht bei Tertullian und Cyprian: Eine Studie zur frühen Kirchenrechtsgeschichte* (2d ed.; SKG.G 7.2; Aalen: Scientia, 1967). – J. K. Stirnimann, *Die Praescriptio Tertullians im Lichte des römischen Rechts und der Theologie* (Par. 3; Fribourg, Switz.: Paulusverlag, 1949). – D. Michaelides, *Foi, écritures, et tradition: Les "Praescriptiones" chez Tertullien* (Theol[P] 76; Paris: Aubier, 1969). – J. A. Alcaín, "Las normas de lo cristiano en el '*De praescriptione*' de Tertuliano," *Comp* 35 (1990): 71–92.

# *D.* Adversus Marcionem

In historical retrospect, Marcion (cf. ch. 3.IV.A.2) certainly appears to be an important figure, who is worth mentioning in the history of the ancient church. However, if his writings are compared to contemporary currents of Gnosticism, for instance, he is worth mentioning as one of many heretics. For Tertullian and his era, however, the situation was quite the converse; indeed, for them, Marcion's teaching represented the most dangerous of all heresies. This is demonstrated by the fact that although Tertullian indeed also wrote a book titled *Adversus Valentinianos,* his most comprehensive work was that in five volumes against Marcion. Beginning in 207–208, Tertullian took the additional trouble of producing three further editions, each of which was improved and expanded. In addition, according to G. Quispel's analysis, he was able to draw from the writings of Justin, Theophilus of Antioch, and Irenaeus, all of whom had already opposed Marcion.

Corresponding to the two essential problems of Marcion's heresy, Tertullian's *Adversus Marcionem* is composed of two major parts. The theological section is directed against Marcion's teaching concerning a good God who had been unknown before the sending of his Son Jesus, who is not identical to the just and punitive Creator God of the OT, that this God had nothing to do with the evil creation and his Son therefore could not have become a human being *materialiter* in order to deliver from Adam's sin, that he instead merely took on what appeared to be a body so as to proclaim his Father's message of salvation without being tainted with evil matter (1–3). The exegetical section is directed against Marcion's truncated Bible, reduced to the passages that do not refer to the OT Creator God (4–5).

After a brief introduction dealing with the three recensions of the work and with the person and teaching of Marcion (1.1–2), bk. 1 contradicts, for three reasons, the possibility of the unknown God postulated by Marcion. First, based on the premise that God is the *summum magnum*, logically there can only be one single God and not the Father of Jesus and alongside him the demiurge of the OT (1.3–7). Second, apart from the logical impossibility, it would also be unbecoming for this alleged unknown God to have left creation to an evil demiurge for so long and to have revealed himself only much later (1.8–21). Third, upon careful examination, Marcion's unknown God does not prove to be good at all, since he never punishes and especially because for their salvation he imposes on humans such inhumane conditions as forbidding them to marry (1.22–29).

After Tertullian's demonstration that the God whom Marcion postulated cannot exist and is not able to fulfill the imposed criteria, bk. 2, after a transitional prologue (2.1–2), proves from the OT itself that the Creator is perfectly identical to the God of Jesus. He is by no means only a God who punishes, but righteousness and goodness form an intrinsic unity in him. This can already be seen in the creation itself, in the commandment that God gave the first human (2.3–4), and in the facts that Adam's sin goes back to his free will alone (2.5–10) and that even the supposedly offensive commands of God in the OT arise from his goodness and righteousness (2.10–21). Therefore, it is necessary to stand up for him against Marcion's reproach that in many ways his conduct is far too human: God in this way simply approaches humankind for its salvation (2.22–27). In conclusion, Tertullian's theology is summarized in his "counter-antitheses" against Marcion's antitheses (2.28–29).

Finally, bk. 3 shows that Jesus clearly is the Son of this one God of the OT and that he became human in order to redeem Adam's sin and did not merely assume a phantom body. Part 1 (3.1–11) critiques the weak points of Marcion's soteriology: God chose the conceivably worst point in time for a redemption for which no preparation was made, and a redeemer in a phantom body is a farce. Part 2 (3.12–24) then demonstrates with detailed comparisons that the biography of Jesus completely agrees with the OT prophecies concerning the Messiah, including his second coming at the end of time, which Tertullian construes in millenarian terms. Because this had been a fundamental apologetic argument since NT times for establishing a distinction from Judaism and for proving the election of Christians as the messianic people, Tertullian here provides a largely verbatim repetition of the arguments found in his earlier writing, *Adversus Judaeos* 9–14 (ca. 197).

Books 4 and 5 follow Marcion's rudimentary biblical text piece by piece, emphasizing again and again the arbitrariness and groundlessness of the selection. Their primary goal, however, is to demonstrate that even the texts Marcion accepted as revelatory attest to the Creator God he rejected. Hence there is no biblical premise at all for him to claim for his theology; this is the sole prerogative of the church as a whole—a claim very similar to the argumentation in *De praescriptione haereticorum*, which does not allow a heretic to appeal to the Bible, since the latter is the sole property of the one true church.

*Editions: Adversus Marcionem* (ed. C. Moreschini; Milan: Istituto Editoriale Cisalpino, 1971). – *Adversus Marcionem* (ed. and trans. E. Evans; 2 vols.; Oxford: Clarendon, 1972) [ET]. – *Contre Marcion* (5 vols.; ed. R. Braun; SC 365, 368, 399, 456, 483; Paris: Cerf, 1990–2004).

*Translations:* P. Holmes, trans., "The Five Books against Marcion," in *ANF* (Peabody, Mass.; Hendrickson, 1995; repr. of 1885 ed.), 3:271–474.

*Studies:* V. Naumann, "Das Problem des Bösen in Tertullians 2. Buch gegen Marcion," *ZKT* 58 (1934): 311–63, 533–51. – G. Quispel, *De bronnen van Tertullianus' Adversus Marcionem* (Templum Salomonis, Neth.: Burgersdijk & Niermans, 1943). – C. Moreschini, "Temi e motivi della polemica antimarcionita di Tertulliano," *SCO* 17 (1968): 149–86. – E. P. Meijering, *Tertullian Contra Marcion—Gotteslehre in der Polemik: Adversus Marcionem I–II* (PP 3; Leiden: Brill, 1977).

# *E.* Adversus Praxean

Tertullian writes that Praxeas was the first to take the doctrine of Monarchianism from Asia to Rome. He describes him as "a man of generally restless disposition, and above all inflated with the pride of confessorship simply and solely because he had to bear for a short time the annoyance of a prison" (1). His teaching reached Africa through one of his students, was soon recognized as heretical, and was restrained under Tertullian's leadership. When it flared up again (ca. 213), Tertullian felt compelled to write against its premises and so against Praxeas.

Praxeas represented modalism of the Noetus type, and thus Patripassianism. Tertullian commences his refutation, thirty-one chapters in all, with a description of the circumstances under which the teaching of Praxeas came to Africa (1–2). He then explains traditional monotheism, which is to be defended in two lines of argument, one for the simpler minds and the other for those with greater understanding. The simple explanation starts from the concept of *monarchia*. The trinity and unity of God are to be compared to the Roman emperor, who governs the empire together with his sons as coregents; this does not divide the unity of the empire, however. For those with greater understanding, Tertullian draws upon Scripture. According to Exod 33:20, no human can see God and live; in other words, a God who can be seen cannot be the Father. Against the Scripture references to which Monarchians appeal, such as Isa 45:5, "I am the LORD, and there is no other; apart from me there is no God"; John 10:30, "I and the Father are one"; and John 14:9–11: "Anyone who has seen me has seen the Father," Tertullian sets gospel citations addressing the differentiation between Father and Son, such as Matt 27:46, "My God, my God, why have you forsaken me?" and Luke 23:46, "into your hands I commit my spirit." The exaltation by the Father, the sitting at the right hand of God, the sending of the Spirit from the Father through the Son—all this points to the differentiation between Father and Son.

In the light of later theology, a statement from 27.11 is significant: *Videmus duplicem statum, non confusum sed coniunctum in una persona, deum et hominem*

*Iesum* ("We see plainly the twofold state, which is not confounded but conjoined in one person—Jesus, God and man"). Later on, this statement was regarded as the original kernel of the christological definition of the Council of Chalcedon (451). This is subject to question, however, for it is not cited until Augustine and had no influence upon theology at all. Nevertheless this early formulation of the one person of Christ with two natures is surprising.

*Editions:* Q. *Septimii Florentis Tertulliani Adversus Praxean liber* (ed. and trans. E. Evans; London: SPCK, 1948) [ET/Com]. – *Contro Prassea* (ed. and trans. G. Scarpat; CorPat 12; Turin: Società Editrice Internazionale, 1985).

*Translations:* P. Holmes, trans., "Against Praxeas," in *ANF* (Peabody, Mass.: Hendrickson, 1995; repr. of 1885 ed.), 3:597–627. – *Tertullian against Praxeas* (trans. A. Souter; London: SPCK; New York: Macmillan, 1920).

*Studies:* R. Cantalamessa, "Prassea e l'eresia monarchiana," *ScC* 90 (1962): 28–50. – M. Simonetti, *EECh* 2:706.

# III. MINUCIUS FELIX

The dialogue *Octavius* by Marcus Minucius Felix begins with the description of its occasion, the individuals involved, and the surroundings in which it was held (1–4). After the death of his friend Octavius, Minucius Felix recalls their friendship and especially a conversation during the Roman vintage holidays. Octavius had come for a visit from Africa to Rome, and they used this opportunity to travel to Ostia together with another companion by the name of Caecilius. Minucius Felix likely also originally came from Africa, and all three of them were jurists professionally, which shapes the dialogue structurally and stylistically. En route to the seashore at dawn, Caecilius blows a hand kiss to a roadside statue of Serapis, for which Octavius reprimands him; Octavius, like Minucius Felix, is already a Christian. It is not fitting for an educated man to adhere to the religious ignorance of the common people. At first Caecilius does not respond, but he cannot stop thinking about it while walking along the shore, so he proposes a disputation on the way back, with Minucius Felix serving as arbiter. They sit on a wall, with Minucius Felix in the middle, Octavius to his right, and Caecilius to his left. Thus unfolds the discussion.

In an entertaining and rhetorically brilliant form, Caecilius (5–13) presents his objections against Christianity, which fail to go beyond the routine accusations known from the other apologias and martyrdom records. The Christian faith in one God as the Creator and guide of the world is refuted by the obvious situation of the world, which is clearly ruled by pure chance. Furthermore, it is part of the most sublime philosophical knowledge that the divine is unsearchable. The traditional belief in the gods at least has demonstrated its practicability, for through it Rome rose to become a world power. (Caecilius fails to notice or overplays the logical inconsistency that the gods would be those guiding the world all the same.) This is followed by the old and new accusations that the

Christian religion only stultifies the ignorant and feeds them with hopes of a better hereafter without being able to improve the miserable life of the present. In addition, Christians are shady and hence have something to hide, namely incest, the murder of children, and Thyestean feasts, the worship of a donkey's head on the cross,[2] feasts, revelries, and fornication. Their faith in an omnipresent God, the end of the world, and the judgment is ridiculous. In conclusion, Caecilius, confident of victory, derisively challenges Octavius to reply, for which Minucius Felix reprimands him with his brilliant rhetoric (14–15). The disputation can only be concerned with the objective discovery of the truth.

Octavius responds to the arguments of Caecilius in sequence (16–38): The gift of reason and knowledge has been given to every human being so that he can infer the necessarily one Creator from the order of the world, which the philosophers had also recognized. Conversely, as the historians attested, the Greek gods are deified humans or demons, interwoven with shameless fables and customs. Not the gods but brutal force had brought Rome to greatness. Finally, Octavius rejects the suspicions against Christians and substantiates the Christian faith in God and its eschatology, which are evidenced primarily in the Christians' exemplary conduct. Caecilius is depicted as so convinced of this that he declares defeat, even without the verdict of Minucius Felix, and converts to Christianity (39–40).

*Octavius,* perfectly worked out rhetorically and stylistically to the last detail, presents perhaps the finest witness of early Christian apologetics by establishing Christianity exclusively on the basis of reason (neither citing the Bible nor mentioning the name of Christ) and by defending it against the untenable rumors about the crimes committed by Christians. Only the dialogue's date of composition is frequently contested today. What is uncontested is its close association with Tertullian's *Apologeticus* and his *Ad nationes,* both written in 197. Most of the arguments seem to point to the priority of Tertullian, although convincing evidence for this has not been produced up to the present. The earliest date for its composition is established to be that of Fronto of Cirta's writing against the Christians (mid-second century), to which the dialogue makes reference; the latest is Cyprian's *Quod idola dii non sint,* which in its turn cites the dialogue (shortly after 246).

*Bibliographies:* J. P. Waltzing, "Bibliographie des Minucius Felix," *MB* 6 (1902): 5–49. – M. Frenschkowski, *BBKL* 5:1564–67.

*Editions: Minucii Felicis Octavius; Iulii Firmici Materni liber De errore profanarum religionum* (ed. C. Halm; CSEL 2; Vienna: Geroldi, 1867), 1–71. – *Octavius* (ed. J. Beaujeu; Paris: Belles Lettres, 1964) [Com]. – *Octavius* (ed. B. Kytzler; Munich: Kösel, 1965; repr., Stuttgart: Teubner, 1992) [Com]. – *M. Minuci Felicis Octavius* (ed. B. Kytzler; corrected ed.; Stuttgart: Teubner, 1992). – *Octavius: Lateinisch und Deutsch* (ed. B. Kytzler; Stuttgart: P. Reclam Jun., 1983) [Com].

---

[2] A telling witness for this is a third-century graffito discovered on the Palatine in Rome, depicting a man who, in a posture of prayer, beholds someone crucified with the head of a donkey, with the subscription "Alexamenos worships his god." For a recent discussion, cf. W. Schäfke, "Frühchristlicher Widerstand," *ANRW* 2.23.1 (1979): 596–99.

*Translations:* R. E. Wallis, trans., "The Octavius of Minucius Felix," in *ANF* (Peabody, Mass.: Hendrickson, 1995; repr. of 1885 ed.), 4:167–98. – *Tertullian, Minucius Felix* (trans. G. H. Rendall; LCL 520; Cambridge, Mass.: Harvard University Press; London: Heinemann, 1931; repr., 1977), 303–437. – *The Octavius of Marcus Minucius Felix* (trans. G. W. Clarke; ACW 39; New York: Newman, 1974).

*Reference Works:* J. P. Waltzing, *Lexicon minucianum* (Liège: Vaillant-Carmanne, 1909). – B. Kytzler, D. Najock, and A. Nowosand, *Concordantia in Minuci Felicis Octavium* (AlOm.A 72; Hildesheim and New York: Olms-Weidmann, 1991).

*Encyclopedia Articles:* L. W. Barnard, "Apologetik I," *TRE* 3:402. – A. Solignac, *DSp* 10:1268–72. – P. Siniscalco, *EECh* 1:562–63. – B. Kytzler, *TRE* 23:1–3. – E. Heck, *HLL* 4:512–19.

*Studies:* R. Beutler, *Philosophie und Apologie bei Minucius Felix* (Weida: Thomas & Hubert, 1936). – B. Axelson, *Das Prioritätsproblem Tertullian–Minucius Felix* (Skrifter utgivna av Vetenskapssocieteteni Lund 27; Lund, Swed.: H. Ohlssons Boktryckeri, 1941). – G. W. Clarke, "The Literary Setting of the *Octavius* of Minucius Felix," *JRH* 3 (1965): 195–211 – G. W. Clarke, "The Historical Setting of the *Octavius* of Minucius Felix," *JEH* 4 (1967): 267–86; repr. in E. Ferguson, ed., *Literature of the Early Church* (SEC 2; New York: Garland, 1993), 127–64. – W. Fausch, *Die Einleitungskapitel zum "Octavius" des Minucius Felix: Ein Kommentar* (Zurich: City, 1966). – C. Becker, *Der "Octavius" des Minucius Felix: Heidnische Philosophie und frühchristliche Apologetik* (SBAW.PPH 1967.2; Munich: Bayerische Akademie der Wissenschaften, Beck im Kommission, 1967). – M. Rizzi, "Amicitia e veritas: Il prologo dell'*Octavius* di Minucio Felice," *Aevum antiquum* 3 (1990): 245–68. – A. Fürst, "Der philosophiegeschichtliche Ort von Minucius Felix' Dialog 'Octavius,'" *JAC* 42 (1999): 42–49.

# IV. CYPRIAN OF CARTHAGE

In the Latin church, the middle part of the third century brought two personalities to prominence whose life, work, and significance were entirely shaped by the first major, empirewide persecutions of Christians during the reigns of Decius and Valerian, namely, Caecilius Cyprianus Thascius, bishop of Carthage, and Novatian, presbyter and schismatic bishop of Rome. They never met but were in correspondence with one another and had to attend to the same theological and pastoral problems in their respective cities. We are conversant with Cyprian's life primarily from his own writings, namely the brief *Ad Donatum*, serving as an apologia, as it were, of his conversion to Christianity, addressed to a noble and erudite friend in Carthage; the corpus of eighty-one letters; the *Acta* of his martyrdom, discussed above (ch. 3.III.A.3); and the *Vita* written shortly after his death by Pontius, his deacon—a work that is more panegyric than historical.

Cyprian was born into a noble and prosperous family in Carthage in the early part of the third century. He was given an excellent education in keeping with the norms of the time, which enabled him to become a successful orator. Whether he utilized this formation for the *cursus honorum*, the career of a Roman civil servant, as a court orator or as a teacher of rhetoric, as Jerome claims, remains uncertain. In any case, he may have been part of the senatorial nobility, which would explain the support of his noble friends during the times of persecution as well as the extremely considerate disposition of the authorities toward him. About 246 Cyprian turned to Christianity under the influence of the Carthaginian priest Caecilianus, freely distributed his wealth among the poor of the community, and gave up the profession he held in order to devote his life to Christianity alone. He thereby quickly gained the affection of many, so that it was not long before he was ordained to the priesthood and, in 248/249, appointed bishop of Carthage. By 253 he had also been able to overcome the initial opposition of five Carthaginian priests who were jealous of his quick ascent.

In the fall of 249, Decius, the emperor, ordered an empirewide sacrifice of petition (*supplicatio*) in view of the empire's critical situation, which he interpreted as a sign of the wrath of the gods. Specifically appointed committees supervising the offerings confirmed participation by means of a *libellus*, of which numerous examples have been preserved on papyrus in the desert sands.[3] These typically began with the address of the committees, to which the request for confirmation was made, with the precise indication of the location. This was followed by the name of the applicant in the form of official records providing the name of father and mother, place of birth and of residence, and the age and description of the person. By affirming that the gods had consistently been venerated, the committee was petitioned to certify the sacrifice that had been properly offered in their presence. This was followed by the signatures of the petitioner and the committee and the date.

Refusing the sacrifice meant imprisonment, confiscation of property, torture, exile, or even death. Whether the Decian edict was directed specifically against Christians cannot be determined, since it obligated all inhabitants of the empire to sacrifice. It was precisely for the Christians that it had the most devastating consequences, however, since the practice of a cultus other than their own was not permitted. Under this kind of pressure, many Christians did indeed actually or apparently carry out the sacrifice. Some brought a burnt offering (*sacrificati*) or a smoke offering (*thurificati*), whereas others attained the necessary *libellus* by bribery or connections without really having brought an offering (*libellatici*). A third group, Cyprian among them, escaped the persecution by fleeing. In doing so, Cyprian was not motivated by concern for his own life as much as by the well-being of his community, which he did not want to deprive of their shepherd, for already, by the beginning of 250, the bishops of Rome, Jerusalem, and Antioch had died in prison. Cyprian led his church by means of numerous letters, but this did not save him from criticism of his escape. The Roman church admonished him that he should rather have suffered martyrdom, as did their own bishop—a disposition that Tertullian still maintained in his *De fuga in persecutione* and that agreed with early Christianity's longing for martyrdom.

Fortunately, the persecution had already abated by the end of 250, and by Easter 251 it had practically come to an end. But this only ushered in the pastoral and theological problems of coping with the consequences. Most Christians who actually or apparently brought sacrifices had quickly repented of their apostasy

---

[3] Cf. H. Leclercq, "Dèce," *DACL* 4:317–30; idem, "*Libelli*," *DACL* 9:80–85; A. di Bernardino, "*Libellus*," *EECh* 1:484.

and requested readmission into the church. In some cases, this happened immediately on the basis of letters of peace from the *confessores,* hence by vicarious consideration of the merits of those who suffered persecution but stood firm; in other cases, the *lapsi* were readmitted even without observing a period of repentance, provided they were repentant. From his exile Cyprian prohibited this procedure and strove for a uniform resolution after the persecution had ended, since this affected the church empirewide. This took place during a synod in Carthage in early April 251, readmitting the *libellicati* forthwith, given appropriate repentance, whereas the *sacrificati* and *thurificati* were subjected to a more extended period of repentance and offered immediate reconciliation only in cases of serious illness. But when new persecutions threatened a year later, all were readmitted. An opposing party promoting laxity, directed by Felicissimus, a deacon, and Fortunatus, an antibishop, and a rigorist opposition party, led by Maximus, an antibishop, remained insignificant.

In Rome the theological development was quite similar, but not the church politics. After the election of Cornelius as the bishop of Rome in March 251, a Roman synod established the same procedure as Carthage. Novatian, however, who had approved Cyprian's prohibition of untested reconciliation, could not agree with a practice of repentance that he viewed as far too lax. He had himself elevated to become the bishop of the rigorist opposition party; this developed into the Novatian schism, which encompassed large parts of the empire and lasted until the sixth century.

During the pontificate of Stephen, the bishop of Rome (March 254–256), there were serious differences of opinion between him and Cyprian concerning the validity of baptism by heretics and schismatics. Whereas Stephen was of the opinion that the validity of baptism was contingent solely on the correct administration and the baptizand's correct intention (which later was to win out as the church's normative teaching), Cyprian, like Tertullian before him and in keeping with North African tradition, took the view that since the Spirit of God is not at work outside the church, baptism could not be administered validly and so heretics were to be rebaptized. This feud was never settled, and the fellowship between the churches of Rome and Carthage remained unresolved because Stephen died in 257 and Cyprian on September 14, 258, during the Valerian persecution.

On the basis of Cyprian's career and the nature of his death, three of his numerous writings have been accorded particular importance: two works written in 251—*De lapsis* and *De catholicae ecclesiae unitate*—and his correspondence.

*Bibliographies:* F. W. Bautz, *BBKL* 1:1178–83. – *"Chronica cyprianea,"* *REAug* 32 (1986): n.p. – R. Braun et al., eds., *Chronica tertullianea et cyprianea, 1975–1994: Bibliographie critique de la première littérature latine chrétienne* (Paris: Études Augustiniennes, 1999).

*Editions: Opera omnia: S. Thasci Caecili Cypriani Opera omnia* (ed. W. Hartel; 3 vols.; CSEL 3.1–3; Vienna: Geroldi, 1868–1871). – *Sancti Cypriani episcopi Opera* (ed. R. Weber, M. Bévenot, M. Simonetti, C. Moreschini, G. F. Diercks, and G. W. Clarke; CCSL; Turnhout, Belg.: Brepols, 1972–). – *A Demetriano (Ad Demetrianum)* (ed. E. Gallicet; CorPat 4; Turin: Società Editrice Internazionale, 1976). – *Ad Donatum, De bono patientiae: A Donat et La vertu de patience* (ed. J. Molager; SC 291; Paris: Cerf, 1982). –

Vita: Vita di Cipriano; Vita di Ambrogio; Vita di Agostino (ed. A. A. R. Bastieaensen; trans. L. Canali and C. Carena; intro. C. Mohrmann; 4th ed.; ViSa 3; Milan: Fonazione Lorenzo Valla–A. Mondadori, 1997), 1–49. – *De opere et eleemosynis: La bienfaisance et les aumônes* (ed. M. Poirier; SC 440; Paris: Cerf, 1999).

*Translations:* E. Wallis, trans., "The Epistles of Cypran," "The Treatises of Cyprian," "The Seventh Council of Carthage under Cyprian," and "Treatises Attributed to Cyprian on Questionable Authority," in *ANF* (Peabody, Mass.: Hendrickson, 1995; repr. of 1885 ed.), 5:275–596 [*Opera omnia*]. – *Treatises* (trans. R. J. Deferarri, A. E. Keenan, M. H. Mahoney, and G. E. Conway; FC 36; Washington, D.C.: Catholic University of America Press, 1958; repr., 1977) [*Treatises*].

*Reference Works:* P. Bouet, P. Fleury, A. Goulon, M. Zuinghedau, and P. Dufraigne, *Cyprien, Traités: Concordance—documentation lexicale et grammaticale* (2 vols.; Hildesheim and New York: Olms-Weidmann, 1986). – *Thesaurus Sancti Cypriani* (Turnhout: Brepols, 1997–).

*Encyclopedia Articles:* A. Stuiber, *RAC* 3:463–66. – M. Bévenot, *TRE* 8:246–54. – U. Wickert, 1:158–75. – V. Saxer, *EECh* 1:211–12. – P. L. Schmidt, "*Vita Cypriani*," *HLL* 4:433–35. – H. Gülzow, A. Wlosok, and P. L. Schmidt, *HLL* 4:532–75. – R. Sider, *EEC* 1:306–9.

*Introductions and Surveys:* E. W. Benson, *Cyprian: His Life, His Times, His Work* (New York: Appleton; London: Macmillan, 1897). – P. Monceaux, *Saint Cyprien et son temps* (vol. 2 of *Histoire littéraire de l'Afrique chrétienne depuis les origines jusqu'à l'invasion arabe;* Brussels: Culture et civilisation, 1963; repr. of 1901–1923 ed.). – M. Sage, *Cyprian* (PatMS 1; Cambridge, Mass.: Philadelphia Patristic Foundation [sole distributors, Greeno, Hadden], 1975). – C. Saumagne, *Saint Cyprien, évêque de Carthage, "pape" d'Afrique (248–258): Contribution à l'étude des "persécutions" de Dèce et de Valérien* (Paris: Centre National de la Recherche Scientifique, 1975).

*Particular Studies:* J. Ernst, *Papst Stephan I. und der Ketzertaufstreit* (FChLDG 5.4; Mainz: Kirchheim, 1905). – A. von Harnack, *Das Leben Cyprians von Pontius, die erste christliche Biographie* (TU 39.3; Leipzig: Hinrichs, 1913). – A. d'Alès, *La théologie de saint Cyprien* (2d ed.; BTH; Paris: Beauchesne, 1922). – H. Koch, *Cyprianische Untersuchungen* (AKG 4; Bonn: A. Marcus & E. Weber, 1926). – M. Wiles, "The Theological Legacy of St. Cyprian," *JEH* 14 (1963): 139–49; repr. in E. Ferguson, ed., *Personalities of the Early Church* (SEC 1; New York: Garland, 1993), 185–95. – G. S. M. Walker, *The Churchmanship of St. Cyprian* (ESH 9; London: Lutterworth, 1968). – V. Saxer, *Vie liturgique et quotidienne à Chartage vers le milieu du IIIe siècle: Le témoignage de saint Cyprien et de ses contemporains d'Afrique* (SAC 29; Vatican City: Pontificio Istituto di Archeologia Cristiana, 1969). – M. A. Fahey, *Cyprian and the Bible: A Study in Third-Century Exegesis* (BGBH 9; Tübingen: Mohr, 1971). – B. Kötting, "Die Stellung des Konfessors in der Alten Kirche," *JAC* 19 (1976): 7–23. – M. Bévenot, "Cyprian's Platform in the Rebaptism Controversy," *HeyJ* 19 (1978): 123–42. – J. A. Fischer, "Die Konzilien zu Karthago und Rom im Jahr 251," *AHC* 11 (1979): 263–86; repr. in *Die Synoden von den Anfängen bis zum Vorabend des Nicaenums* (Paderborn: F. Schöningh, 1997), 165–89 – P. R. Amidon, "The Procedure of St. Cyprian's Synods," *VC* 37 (1983): 328–339; repr. in E. Ferguson, ed., *Church, Ministry, and Organization in the Early Church Era* (SEC 13; New York: Garland, 1993), 224–35. – S. Cavallotto, "Il magistero episcopale di Cipriano di Cartagine: Aspetti metodologici," *DT* 91 (1988): 375–407. – C. Bobertz, "An Analysis of *Vita Cypriani* 3.6–10 and the Attribution of *Ad Quirinum* to Cyprian of Carthage," *VC* 46 (1992): 112–28. – C. M. Robeck, *Prophecy in Carthage: Perpetua, Tertullian, Cyprian* (Cleveland: Pilgrim, 1992). – J. P. Burns, "On Rebaptism: Social Organization in the Third Century Church," *JECS* 1 (1993): 367–493. – J. H. D. Scourfield, "The *De mortalitate* of Cyprian: Consolation and Context," *VC* 50 (1996): 12–41.

# A. De lapsis

Cyprian wrote the tractate *De lapsis (The Lapsed)* in the spring of 251, after his return to Carthage, in order to substantiate a uniform resolution for the treatment of the *lapsi*. It was read either before the Carthaginian community or (as is widely assumed) before the assembled synod and accepted as the basis of the joint procedure of the North African churches. The confessors of Rome received a copy in order to confirm them in supporting Cornelius, their bishop.

The writing is organized into thirty-six chapters; in the introduction (1–3) Cyprian initially expresses his joy at the end of the persecution with gratitude to God, praises the confessors for their perseverance in the persecution, but also defends fleeing as a legitimate means to preserve the faith. The main part (4–28) contrasts this right conduct with the *lapsi*. First (4–7) he confirms the persecution as a test of faith, as punishment for the deplorable state of affairs in the church, and as in keeping with the prophecies of Holy Scripture. Nevertheless (8–12) many did not escape the persecution by fleeing because they feared for their possessions. The treatment of the *lapsi* is divided into various categories: 1) Against those who submitted themselves immediately to the command to render sacrifice, it is necessary to proceed decisively; leniency is appropriate only in the case of those who relented under torture (13–17). 2) For this reason, confessors cannot lightly readmit sinners (18–20). 3) Unjustified readmissions and those against the will of the bishop incur the punishment of God often already here on earth, as Cyprian explains with several examples (21–26). 4) The *libellatici*, too, had sinned because in appearance they had fallen away and therefore had to take up repentance (27–28). The conclusion (29–36) regulates in detail the periods of repentance, calls for a change in one's ways, and promises God's grace to the repentant.

*Editions: De lapsis and De ecclesiae catholicae unitate* (ed. and trans. M. Bévenot; OECT; Oxford: Clarendon, 1971), 1–55 [ET/Com].

*Translations: The Lapsed; The Unity of the Catholic Church* (trans. M. Bévenot; ACW 25; Westminster, Md.: Newman, 1957). – *Treatises* (trans. R. J. Deferrari; FC 36; New York: Fathers of the Church, 1958), 55–88.

*Studies:* M. Bévenot, "The Sacrament of Penance and St. Cyprian's *De lapsis*," *TS* 16 (1955): 175–213. – B. Poschmann, *Paenitentia secunda: Die kirchliche Busse im ältesten Christentum bis Cyprian und Origenes* (Theoph. 1; Bonn: P. Hanstein, 1940), 368–424. – V. Fattorini and G. Picenardi, "La riconciliazione in Cipriano di Cartagine (*ep. 55*) e Ambrogio di Milano (*De paenitentia*)" *Aug* 27 (1987): 377–406.

# B. De catholicae ecclesiae unitate

The tractate *De catholicae ecclesiae unitate (The Unity of the Catholic Church)*, composed of twenty-seven chapters, has gained fame mainly because of the fourth chapter, which has been handed down in two versions. In one version

(PT = primacy text), Cyprian explicitly speaks of the primacy of the bishop of Rome: "Although the others were what Peter was, the primacy was given to Peter." The somewhat longer parallel text (TR = *Textus receptus*) softens this theology and speaks of Peter only as the origin of unity: "Although the other apostles were what Peter was, equipped with the same fellowship and honor and power, the beginning assumes unity, in order that the one church of Christ might become manifest." The classification and evaluation of the two versions is not undisputed today. Whereas PT previously was considered a later interpolation, M. Bévenot in various publications has argued for the viewpoint that both are genuine redactions from the hand of Cyprian. Written in an entirely different context in 251, PT was used by the Romans in the dispute concerning baptism by heretics by interpreting it with such stringency against Cyprian that he decided to make a correction in order to express more clearly the originally intended meaning. There is much that favors the argumentation of Bévenot, even if it has been questioned again more recently (Campeau, Wickert).

Drawing upon the contemporary situation of the factions in Rome and Carthage after the Decian persecution, the tractate as a whole offers an ecclesiology of unity in a logical-associative progression rather than in a systematically structured sequence. Chapters 1–3 warn against Satan's tricks of temptation: among watchful believers who are victorious over him because of their obedience to the commandments of Christ, he is unable to gain power in any form other than by appearing in the form of Jesus himself and thus causing division in the church. The criterion of the true church is the fellowship with the see of Rome (4–5), in which the bishops have to lead the way, even if the authority of each of them stems from Christ himself. Each one is responsible for his part of the church and is accountable to God alone. The unity of the church is symbolized in the portraits of the pure bride, who dwells in only one house, the seamless garment of Christ, the OT Passover in one house, and the Holy Spirit in the form of the peaceable dove (6–9). Heresies and schisms arise from discord and are tolerated only as tests that the Lord permits. Among them there is neither a valid baptism nor Eucharist, neither martyrdom nor eschatological perfection (10–14). The spread of schisms brings to the fore self-proclaimed priests, such as Korah, Dathan, and Abiram formerly (Num 16:1–33), and even the fall of *confessores*. On the other hand, it is necessary to understand that suffering for the faith is only the beginning of a path leading to perfection, on which even the Apostle Judas stumbled, which should not diminish the steadfastness of the others (15–22). Cyprian concludes with admonitions to unity, based on the example of the earliest church, to obedience to God's commandments, and to watchfulness in expectation of the bridegroom (23–27).

The ecclesiology of the tractate is entirely orthodox and consequently lays the groundwork for the later dispute concerning baptism by heretics. Since Cyprian sees the bishops as the guarantors of the unity of the church, and in order to protect the integrity of the church, he is bound to reject categorically any validity in the exercise of office by bishops who were not ordained legitimately and who are not in fellowship with the remaining bishops of the Catholic Church.

*Editions: De lapsis* and *De ecclesiae catholicae unitate* (ed. and trans. M. Bévenot; OECT; Oxford: Clarendon, 1971), 56–99 [ET/Com].

*Translations: The Lapsed; The Unity of the Catholic Church* (trans. M. Bévenot; ACW 25; Westminster, Md.: Newman, 1957). – S. L. Greenslade, *Early Latin Theology: Selections from Tertullian, Cyprian, Ambrose, and Jerome* (LCC 5; Philadelphia: Westminster, 1956; repr., 1978), 119–42. – *Treatises* (trans. R. J. Deferarri; FC 36; New York: Fathers of the Church, 1958), 91–121.

*Studies:* A. Beck, *Römisches Recht bei Tertullian und Cyprian: Eine Studie zur frühen Kirchenrechtsgeschichte* (2d ed.; SKG.G 7.2; Aalen: Scientia, 1967). – U. Wickert, *Sacramentum unitatis: Ein Beitrag zum Verständnis der Kirche bei Cyprian* (BZNW 41; Berlin and New York: de Gruyter, 1971). – P. Hinchcliff, *Cyprian of Carthage and the Unity of the Catholic Church* (London: G. Chapman, 1974).

*Studies on Primacy:* H. Koch, *Cyprian und der römische Primat: Eine kirchen- und dogmengeschichtliche Studie* (TU 35.1; Leipzig: Hinrichs, 1910). – J. Ernst, *Cyprian und das Papsttum* (Mainz: Kirchheim, 1912). – H. Koch, *Cathedra Petri: Neue Untersuchungen über die Anfänge der Primatslehre* (BZNW 11; Giessen: A. Töpelmann, 1930). – B. Poschmann, *Ecclesia principalis: Ein kritischer Beitrag zur Frage des Primats bei Cyprian* (Breslau: Franke, 1933). – O. Perler, "Zur Datierung der beiden Fassungen des vierten Kapitels *De unitate ecclesiae,*" *RQ* 44 (1936): 1–44. – O. Perler, "*De catholicae ecclesiae unitate* cap. 4–5: Die ursprünglichen Texte, ihre Überlieferung, ihre Datierung," *RQ* 44 (1936): 151–68. – M. Bévenot, *St. Cyprian's De unitate chap. 4 in the Light of the Manuscripts* (AnGr 11; Rome: Apud aedes Universitatis Gregorianae, 1937; London: Burns, Oates & Washbourne, 1938). – L. Campeau, "Le texte de la primauté dans le '*De catholicae ecclesiae unitate*' de S. Cyprien," *Sciences ecclésiastiques* 19 (1967): 81–110, 255–75. – H. Montgomery, "Subordination or Collegiality? St. Cyprian and the Roman See," in S.-T. Teodorsson, ed., *Greek and Latin Studies in Memory of Caius Fabricius* (SGLG 54; Göteborg, Swed.: AUG, 1990), 41–54. – A. Adolph, *Die Theologie der Einheit der Kirche bei Cyprian* (EHS.T 460; Frankfurt and New York: Lang, 1993).

# C. Corpus of Letters

For the first time since the collection of the Pauline letters and those of Ignatius, the origin, occasion, and topic of which belong to the apostolic era and reflect the particular situations of, for example, the first mission or a journey to death, Cyprian's corpus comprises extensive correspondence from the tenure of an educated bishop. This corpus, for instance, contains occasional letters, letters of pastoral or theological content arising from concrete situations, personal and synodal letters, and several pieces of correspondence addressed to Cyprian. Such collections, preserved more frequently beginning in the fourth century, offer direct insight into the writers as individuals, the history of the time, and their theology and therefore represent one of the most valuable sources of patrology.

Of the eighty-one letters of Cyprian's corpus, fifty-nine come from his own hand (1–3, 5–7, 9–20, 25–29, 32–35, 37–41, 43–48, 51, 52, 54–56, 58–63, 65, 66, 68, 69, 71, 73, 74, 76, 80, 81); six are letters to synods, edited by him (4, 57, 64, 67, 70, 72); and sixteen are addressed to him (8, 21–24, 30, 31, 36, 42, 49, 50, 53, 75,

77–79). All of them are dated from his tenure as bishop and can be structured chronologically and contentwise as follows (cf. Duquenne):

a. Letters written by Cyprian during and after the Decian persecution from his hiding place outside Carthage:

1) to his church in Carthage (5–7, 10–19);
2) to Rome during the vacancy of the Roman see (8, 9, 20–22, 27, 28, 30, 31, 35–37);
3) to his church after the persecution concerning the problems of the letters of peace of the *confessores* and of the schism by Felicissimus (41–43).

b. Letters dealing with the restoration of ecclesiastical discipline in Carthage and with the Novatian schism:

1) concerning the election of Cornelius as bishop of Rome and the Novatian schism (44–55);
2) concerning the reinstatement of the repentant, and sundry topics during the reign of Emperor Trebonius Gallus (56–61, 64–66);
3) to Gaul and Spain during the time of Stephen, bishop of Rome (67, 68).

c. Letters dealing with the dispute on baptism by heretics (69–75).

d. Letters from the time of the Valerian persecution (76–81).

e. Letters of an uncertain date, concerning matters of discipline (1–4); in the form of a cover letter, concerning one hundred thousand sesterces of ransom money for Christian prisoners of Numidian Berbers (62); and concerning the necessary celebration of the Eucharist with wine, against the Aquarians (63).

It is clear from Cyprian's oeuvre that numerous letters have been lost. The form and style of the letters are consistent with the history of ancient—Christian and non-Christian—epistolary literature.

For the eucharistic theology and praxis of the church, *Ep.* 63, which has been studied frequently, deserves particular attention as a pioneering writing. It does not simply dismiss the Aquarians' practice of using only water in the celebration of the Eucharist instead of water mixed with wine, but posits this question in the overall context of the significance of the Eucharist for the church. It represents the mystical presence of Christ's sacrifice in the church, offered by the priest as his representative, and is the sacrament of unity. The strong emphasis on the strict observance and authentic passing on of the tradition established by Christ himself, presaged already in the OT by the patriarchs and prophets and clearly attested in the NT by the evangelists and apostles, moves the letter closer (possibly in terms of its date as well) to Cyprian's *De catholicae ecclesiae unitate.*

*Translations:* E. Wallis, trans., "The Epistles of Cyprian," in *ANF* (Peabody, Mass.: Hendrickson, 1995; repr. of 1885 ed.), 5:275–409. – *Letters (1–81)* (trans. R. B. Donna; FC 51; Washington, D.C.: Catholic University of America Press, 1964). – *The Letters of St. Cyprian of Carthage* (trans. G. W. Clark; 4 vols.; ACW 43, 44, 46, 47; New York: Newman, 1984–1989).

*Studies:* A. von Harnack, *Über verlorene Briefe und Aktenstücke, die sich aus der cyprianischen Briefsammlung ermitteln lassen* (TU 23.2; Leipzig: Hinrichs, 1902). – J. Schrijnen and C. Mohrmann, *Studien zur Syntax der Briefe des hl. Cyprian* (2 vols.; LCP 5–6; Nijmegen: Dekker & van de Vegt, 1936–1937). – L. Duquenne, *Chronologie des lettres de S. Cyprien: Le dossier de la persécution de Dèce* (SHG 54; Brussels: Société des Bollandistes, 1972). – H. Gülzow, *Cyprian und Novatian: Der Briefwechsel zwischen den Gemeinden in Rom und Karthago zur Zeit der Verfolgung des Kaisers Decius* (BHTh 48; Tübingen: Mohr, 1975). – R. Seagraves, *Pascentes cum disciplina: A Lexical Study of the Clergy in the Cyprianic Correspondence* (Par. 37; Fribourg, Switz.: Éditions Universitaires, 1993). – P. Siniscalco, "La lettera 63 di Cipriano sull'eucarestia: Osservazioni sulla cronologia, sulla simbolologia, e sui contenuti," in F. Israel et al., eds., *Storia e interpretazione degli antichi testi eucaristici* (Geneva: DARFICLET, 1995), 69–82.

# Excursus: Letters in Antiquity and Christianity

## 1. Private Letters

The original form of the letter as "half of a conversation" (Demetrius, *De elocutione* 223) or as "speech of those not present" (Ambrose, *Ep.* 66.1)—in other words, as a transitory, occasional writing for the sole purpose of substituting for an oral statement rendered impossible by geographical distance—does not belong to literature. Only by chance have such letters of antiquity been preserved in Egyptian papyri and, as such, are extremely valuable in terms of cultural history. They are, however, objects of the history of literature only insofar as they gave rise to the literary letter, and a comparison of the two reveals distinctive features as well as commonalities between them. The transitoriness of the ancient private letter in principle is shown by the use of the writing material. Initially it was written on conjoined wooden tablets, deepened on the inside and covered with a layer of wax; they generally were returned to the sender with the response. Later the preferred material was the pith of the papyrus plant, particularly if the letter was to remain with the recipient. Expensive and durable writing materials, such as parchment, were not used unless there was no papyrus available, as Jerome (*Epist.* 7.2) and Augustine (*Ep.* 15.1) report. The letter was given a name in keeping with the material used or with its purpose, as follows:

- γραμμάτων/σύγγραμμα—*litterae* (writing);

- δέλτος/δελτίον/δίπτυν—*tabula/tabellae* ("tablet");

- ἐπιστολή/ἐπιστόλιον—*epistula* ("letter");

- βιβλίον—*charta/codicillus/libellus* (leaf, sheet of paper).

The tablets were tied together, sometimes through a hole in the center, and the ends of the string were sealed; in the case of less important correspondence, they were also left open. The *charta* sheet was folded or rolled up and then also tied up, with the string pulled through the sheet for security's sake. The outside of the letter, if not left entirely blank, had the name of the sender affixed, introduced by ἀπό or *ab* ("from"), for instance.

An ancient letter began by providing the name of the sender in the nominative case and that of the addressee in the dative case, as well as a salutation: "Paul, an apostle of Christ Jesus by the will of God, and Timothy our brother, to the church of God in Corinth, together with all the saints throughout Achaia: Grace and peace to you from God our Father and the Lord Jesus Christ" (2 Cor 1:1f.). The more formal the letter, the more this introductory formula was expanded, as seen at the beginning of the Letter to the Romans, for instance (1:1–7). The letter also concluded with a greeting and, in the case of more important and formal letters, with an additional reference to the date and place of writing. When distinguished and busy persons and magistrates dictated their letters and had secretaries write them, it was deemed polite to add at least the final greeting by hand: "I, Paul, write this greeting in my own hand. . . . The grace of the Lord Jesus be with you" (1 Cor 16:21, 23).

Private letters were carried privately by the sender's slaves, who were then able to provide additional information orally, or by traveling acquaintances and merchants, who often collected the letters in bundles (*fasciculi*). Official correspondence likewise was carried by its own courier; the *cursus publicus* was not introduced until the time of Emperor Augustus, who had runners, riders, and carts ready at stations along the major military routes for the imperial mail or for mail expressly approved by him through *evectio* (post-warrant). In this way, urgent news traveled almost a hundred miles a day. For the patristic era, the imperial mail, after the Constantinian transition, was even used to transport official ecclesiastical letters and persons, such as bishops, who attended councils.

Official letters take an intermediate position between private and literary letters, since they normally are not considered part of the epistolary literature yet they were often meant for publication and preserved in archives. This type of literature developed an official style of its own, and from Hadrian on, the imperial chancellery was occupied by literati; as a result, these writings point to a high literary quality.

## 2. Literary Letters

Literary letters are composed of two groups:

a. Genuine private letters that were not originally intended for publication because they were representative of everyday life but that "later, either during the writer's or recipient's lifetime or after his death, were published because of their content and thus were considered part of this genre and read and imitated as such."[4] Whereas private correspondence initially was published only after the

---

[4] J. Sykutris, "Epistolographie," PWSup 5:187.

writer's death, Cicero was not reluctant to see his letters to Atticus already disseminated during his lifetime. Pliny the Younger and Gregory of Nazianzus began
to publish their collected letters themselves.

b. The actual literary letters (in the scholarly literature also distinguished as
"epistles") were intended for publication by the author from the start. These
could take the form of genuine letters, appropriately shaped and stylized, or of literary fiction that merely opted for the epistolary format. The latter allowed for
less concern with adherence to literary conventions applicable to other genres of
presentation and made it possible to address the reader personally, as it were. The
literary letter, inter alia, developed the following forms, which Christianity continued to modify and adapt for Christian topics and purposes:

1) There were no newspaper articles in antiquity. If one wanted to address a
certain social or political issue publicly, this could be done by means of a speech
or a *journalistic letter,* akin to the former, that we would label an "official letter"
today. It flourished naturally in times of democracy and crisis, such as during the
Roman civil war (Caesar, Sallust, Anthony), and effectively came to a standstill
during Rome's imperial era. Christianity then caused it to flourish again by publicly opposing even rulers on the basis of its faith.

2) The *letter of instruction* of an older to a younger person (father to son,
teacher to pupil) contained philosophical and ethical admonitions and instructions on an appropriate lifestyle. If they were genuine letters based on a concrete
situation, they offered such generally valid wisdom and rules of life that they were
disseminated more widely. Besides this, philosophers were fond of this form in
which to couch their works; Epicurus and Seneca, in his letters to Lucilius, are
their masters. Paul made the paraenetic and devotional didactic letter the first
Christian literary form, and it was maintained in episcopal letters throughout the
patristic era.

3) *Scholarly treatises in letter form,* closely linked with the didactic letter,
initially developed from actual communications of new insights to colleagues
and friends but opted for the letter as a less restrictive form for shorter treatises,
in which the prescript took on the function of a dedication and which today
might be comparable to journal articles. In Christianity, these continued in the
form of epistolary theological works.

4) *Letters from heaven,* which were also attributed power to heal, allegedly
originated from the hand of the gods themselves and, as a "didactic letter of the
gods," contained their revelation of a moral-religious kind. Generally they were
composed of three parts: a description of their discovery or presentation to the
writer; admonitions and warnings, including threats of punishment; and, finally,
information about (magic) prophylaxes. In his *Dialogue of the Gods* Lucian of
Samosata (second century C.E.) turned this form into satire; in Christianity, however, it had already been adopted again as a form of divine revelation in John's
Revelation.

5) Unless they are explicitly identified as such, *poetic letters* in verse form
become blurred with characteristics of a poem, which can use the salutation and
dedication as well. The Romans favored them (Ovid), and only later did they

penetrate Christian literature with Paulinus of Nola (355–431), through his teacher Ausonius, the poet.

6) The *pseudonymous letter*, under the name of a famous person, was already common in the classical period (Alexander the Great, Socrates, Plato, Aristotle, etc.). According to ancient conventions, these were rarely viewed as forgeries but rather as imitations, supplementing and passing on the authority of a famous and valued author. In this sense, it won particular importance for Christianity because, primarily in early Christianity, didactic letters were placed under the authority of the apostles.

*Encyclopedia Articles:* C. Dziatzko, "Brief," PW 3:836–43. – O. Seeck, "*Cursus publicus,*" PW 4:1846–63. – J. Sykutris, "Epistolographie," PWSup 5:185–220. – J. Schneider, "Brief," *RAC* 3:564–85. – E. Kornemann, "Postwesen," PW 22.1:988–1014. – H. Zilliacus, "Anredeformen," *JAC* 7:157–82; repr. in *RAC.S* 1:465–97. – M. P. Ciccarese, "Letter, Epistle," *EECh* 1:483. – E. Peretto, "Letters of Communion," *EECh* 1:484.

*Studies:* G. Luck, "Brief und Epistel in der Antike," *Altertum* 7 (1961): 77–84. – K. Thraede, *Grundzüge griechisch-römischer Brieftopik* (Zet. 48: Munich, Beck, 1970). – E. Suárez de la Torre, "La epistolografía griega," *ECl* 23 (1979): 19–46. – G. Tibiletti, *Le lettere private nei papiri greci del III e IV secolo d. C.: Tra paganesimo e cristianesimo* (Milan: Vita e Pensiero, 1979). – P. Cugusi, *Evoluzione e forme dell'epistolografia latina nella tarda antichità e nei primi due secoli dell'impero: Con cenni sull'epistolografia preciceroniana* (Rome: Herder, 1983). – A. Garzya, "L'epistolografia letteraria tardoantica," in *Il mandarino e il quotidiano: Saggi sulla letteratura tardoantica e bizantina* (Naples: Bibliopolis, 1985), 113–48. – S. K. Stowers, *Letter Writing in Greco-Roman Antiquity* (Philadelphia: Westminster, 1986). – J. L. White, *Light from Ancient Letters: Foundation and Facets* (Philadelphia: Fortress, 1986). – P. Cugusi, "L'epistolografia: Modelli e tipologie di comunicazione," in *Lo spazio letterario di Roma antica II* (ed. G. Cavallo, P. Fedeli, and A. Giardina; Rome: Salerno, 1989), 379–419. – M. Zelzer, "Die Briefliteratur," in *Spätantike* (vol. 4 of *Neues Handbuch der Literaturwissenschaft;* ed. J. Engels, H. Hofmann, et al.; Wiesbaden: AULA, 1997), 321–53.

# 3. Letters in Christianity

Christian literature begins with the letters of Paul, which straddle the fence between the nonliterary private letter and the public, didactic letter. On the one hand, as genuine letters, they were originally intended to overcome distance to the communities in matters of real concern and without the intent of their dissemination. On the other hand, they are addressed to the "public" of entire communities and contain essential expositions of Christian teaching, so that they bear the marks of general didactic writings. The letters of the postapostolic period, namely *1 Clement* and the letters of Ignatius of Antioch and Polycarp of Smyrna, also belong to the latter group. The first letter of Peter continues the genre of the public letter, and Hebrews, as a theological treatise concerning the high priesthood of Christ, continues the scholarly treatise in letter form. The genre of the heavenly letters has been preserved in the letters of Christ in John's Revelation and in the Shepherd of Hermas. At the same time, the pseudonymous letters of the NT and of the NT apocrypha flourished as well; they partly intended to appeal to the authority of the apostles and partly wanted to satisfy the pious thirst for knowledge, as in *3 Corinthians*, the *Epistle to the Laodiceans*, the *Epistle of Christ and Abgar* (correspondence between Jesus and Abgar, king of Edessa), the letter of Pontius Pilate to Emperor Claudius, the *Epistles of Paul and Seneca, Barnabas*, the *Epistle of the Apostles*, and the writings of Pseudo-Ignatius. The classification of *Diognetus* and the martyrdom accounts in the form of a letter (the *Martyrdom of Polycarp*, the letter of the churches of Lyon and Vienne) cannot be determined accurately because there is no antecedent for them in classical literature. They should be placed, however, near the private letter or the public letter.

Even if we know much about it indirectly, there is little that has been preserved of the other Christian epistolary literature of the first three centuries. As an apology, Tertullian's letter to Scapula takes the form of an "open letter"; Origen used the form of a letter to discuss theological issues. Between Dionysius, bishop of Corinth (second half of second century), and Dionysius of Alexandria, a student of Origen (bishop 248–264/265), there developed an extensive episcopal correspondence. We encounter this type first in Cyprian's corpus of letters, which are associated with the most diverse genres: private letters, literary private letters, public letters, didactic writings, theological treatises, and official letters. They derive their peculiar characteristic—often in reply to inquiries—from the treatment of a host of relevant and fundamental theological and ecclesiastical issues, and they thereby shaped ecclesiastical life in dogma, ethics, morality, discipline, and practice. Beginning with the fourth century, this kind of correspondence is represented in the major corpora of letters by the Cappadocians, Jerome, Ambrose, Augustine, John Chrysostom, and Cyril of Alexandria. Their editions are based upon notebooks preserving the drafts of letters, and in order to better understand and supplement their own letters, they normally include letters received as well. In the fourth century also, classical epistolary theory increasingly filters into Christian letters, including the poetic letters of Paulinus of Nola.

Synodal letters developed as particular official writings informing the churches that were not represented at the synods of their decisions and at the same time expressing the fellowship of the churches. A newly elected bishop thus also sent out *letters of ecclesiastical communion* whereby he notified his colleagues of his assumption of office and requested their fellowship; in times of dogmatic dispute, this also included his own confession of faith. The *letters of peace* of the *confessores* from the time of the Decian persecution and later likewise belong to the category of letters of fellowship in the sense that they petitioned for readmission of the *lapsi* into the fellowship of the church on the basis of their own merits during the time of persecution. The *Easter letters* (often known as the "festal letters") originated in Alexandria in the third century because of the necessity of establishing a uniform Christian date for Easter, independent of the Jewish Passover date, on the Sunday following the first full moon of spring. The astronomers of Alexandria, deemed the best in the empire, determined the date, and the patriarch communicated it to the bishops of his patriarchy by letter, and later to Rome as well. He used this opportunity to supplement the purely technical information with theological and spiritual explanations, just as bishops today write pastoral letters at the beginning of Lent. Festal letters such as this are extant from

Athanasius (the thirty-ninth, from the year 367, for the first time includes the definitive canon of the NT), Theophilus (385–412), and Cyril of Alexandria (412–444).

The *papal letters* constitute a final group, that is, official edicts on matters of ecclesiastical life that initially use the brotherly, devotional style of the private letter but then bring to bear the genre of the *responsum* and the papal decree in keeping with the secular administrative style. This is especially true of Pope Siricius (384–399), Innocent (402–417), and Zosimus (417–418). From then on, such official letters are preserved by all the popes; the most important corpora of letters are associated with Leo the Great (440–461), Gelasius (492–496), and Gregory the Great (590–604).

*Bibliography:* C. Burini, G. Asdrubali Pentiti, M. C. Spadoni Cerroni, and F. Sillitti, *Epistolari cristiani (secc. I–V): Repertorio bibliografico* (3 vols.; Rome: Benedictina Editrice, 1990).

*Encyclopedia Articles:* H. Leclercq, "Lettres chrétiennes," *DACL* 8.2:2683–2885. – T. Klauser, "Festankündigung," *RAC* 7:767–85.

*Studies:* H. Jordan, *Geschichte der altchristlichen Literatur* (Leipzig: Quelle & Meyer, 1911), 128–72. – G. Ghedini, *Lettere cristiane dai papiri greci del III e IV secolo* (Milan: Aegyptus, 1923). – D. Gorce, *Les voyages, l'hospitalité ,et le port des lettres dans le monde chrétien des IVe et Ve siècles* (Paris: A. Picard, 1925). – A. von Harnack, *Die Briefsammlung des Apostels Paulus und die anderen vorkonstantinischen christlichen Briefsammlungen* (Leipzig: Hinrichs, 1926). – A. A. R. Bastiaensen, *Le cérémonial épistolaire des chrétiens latins: Origine et premiers développements* (GLCP 2.1; Nijmegen: Dekker & van de Vegt, 1964). – C. Andresen, "Zum Formular frühchristlicher Gemeindebriefe," *ZNW* 56 (1965): 233–59. – M. Naldini, *Il cristianesimo in Egitto: Lettere private nei papiri dei secoli II–IV* (2d ed.; Florence: Nardini, 1998). – H. Y. Gamble, *Books and Readers in the Early Church: A History of Early Christian Texts* (New Haven: Yale University Press, 1995). – K. Haines-Eitzen, "'Girls Trained in Beautiful Writing': Female Scribes in Roman Antiquity and Early Christianity," *JECS* 6 (1998): 629–46.

## 4. Ancient Epistolary Theory

Cicero basically organized letters as *litterae privatae* and *publicae* or as *litterae familiares* and *negotiales*. He assumed an epistolary theory based on custom and the feel for what was proper, as far as it can be reconstructed from scattered references by ancient literati. In the rhetorical manuals of ancient classicism, however, no space was accorded to epistolary theory on its own right. The rules applicable to business and public letters were those governing rhetoric; for treatises in the form of letters, the applicable rules were those of discourses or tractates, though always in a less restrictive form. By adopting the classical rules, Gregory of Nazianzus presented the stylistic criteria for the private letter with remarkable clarity in *Ep.* 51 to Nicoboulos: Three characteristics are to shape it, namely χρεία/συντομία (appropriate brevity), σαφήνεια (clarity), and χάρις (grace). The length of the letter had to agree with the scope and importance of the content. Significant matters were not to be treated too briefly, nor trivialities inordinately extensively. The tone is to be informal, simple, and clear. It attains its ideal when it addresses the erudite and the uneducated at the same time. The letter is not to be written entirely without rhetorical adornment and sophistication; yet the figures of speech should be used only sparingly and, at the same time, with ease. On the whole, the personal character of the writer is to shine through. Gregory of Nazianzus himself adhered to these conventions, as did, at least from the fourth century on, all writers of Christian letters, especially since almost all bishops commanded a corresponding scholastic and rhetorical background.

*Studies:* A. J. Malherbe, *Ancient Epistolary Theorists* (Atlanta: Scholars Press, 1988).

# V. NOVATIAN

Given that Novatian played such a prominent role in the mid-third-century Roman church, we know comparatively little else about his life. Likely a Roman by birth, he was baptized while in danger of death, according to Eusebius (*Hist. eccl.* 6.43.13–17), but not confirmed; hence the clergy and people of Rome resisted his ordination to the priesthood by Bishop Fabian. He was very well educated, as his writings demonstrate, and may well be characterized as a born leader. Until the Decian persecution erupted, he lived a secluded life, perhaps as a hermit. Only in the summer of 250, after Fabian's death, did he become active in the church, and he immediately assumed a leading position. The correspondence with Carthage ensued under his overall responsibility; three of his letters are preserved in Cyprian's corpus of letters (30, 31, 36), in which he supports Cyprian's position on the issue of the *lapsi*. When he, as perhaps the most prominent presbyter of Rome, was not elected bishop of Rome in 251 but instead Cornelius, who demonstrated the same more moderate position toward the *lapsi* as did Cyprian following the persecution, he declared himself the head of the rigorist party and allowed himself to be ordained as an antibishop. He strove for the ideal of a "pure" church, whose members necessarily had to be equally pure. Thus, if someone committed another grave sin after the foundational forgiveness of sins in baptism, he could no longer belong to the church. Underneath this, however, Novatian seems to be more indebted to Stoic conceptions than to just biblical ones. Socrates, the church historian, reports in his church history (4.28) that Novatian died a martyr, likely in the Valerian persecution. In 1932 an inscription was found in a small catacomb near San Lorenzo with the following words: *Novatiano beatissimo martyri Gaudentius diaconus fecit.* The information of Socrates and the connection between the inscription and Novatian the antibishop, however, remain in doubt.

*Editions: Opera* (ed. G. F. Diercks; CCSL 4; Turnhout, Belg.: Brepols, 1972).

*Translations:* R. E. Wallis, trans., "A Treatise of Novatian concerning the Trinity" and "On the Jewish Meats," in *ANF* (Peabody, Mass.: Hendrickson, 1995; repr. of 1885 ed.), 5:605–50. – *The Trinity, The Spectacles, Jewish Foods, In Praise of Purity, Letters* (trans.

R. J. Desimone; FC 67; Washington, D.C.: Catholic University of America Press in association with Consortium Press, 1974), 157–76.

*Reference Works: Thesaurus Novatiani* (Turnhout, Belg.: Brepols, 1999).

*Encyclopedia Articles:* R. J. Desimone, *DSp* 11:479–83. – H. J. Vogt, "Novatian," *EECh* 2:603–4. – R. J. Desimone, "Novatianists," *EECh* 2:604. – J. S. Alexander, *TRE* 24:678–82. – H. Gülzow, *HLL* 4:519–28. – H. J. Vogt, *EEC* 2:819–20.

*Studies:* A. d'Alès, *Novatien: Étude sur la théologie romaine au milieu du IIIe siècle* (ETH; Paris: Beauchesne, 1924). – H. Vogt, *Coetus sanctorum: Der Kirchenbegriff des Novatian und die Geschichte seiner Sonderkirche* (Theoph. 20; Bonn: P. Hanstein, 1968). – H. Gülzow, *Cyprian und Novatian: Der Briefwechsel zwischen den Gemeinden in Rom und Karthago zur Zeit der Verfolgung des Kaisers Decius* (BHTh 48; Tübingen: Mohr, 1975). – P. Mattei, "L'anthropologie de Novatien: Affinités, perspectives, et limites," *REAug* 38 (1992): 235–59.

# De Trinitate

In content and structure, Novatian's principal work on the Trinity, written ca. 240, reflects the numerous theological disputes of his time. Part 1 (1–8) defends the identity of God the Father with the Creator of the world against Gnosticism. Part 2 (9–28), dealing with the Logos, takes up the largest part of the work. Against the Marcionites, he supports Jesus as the true Son of the Creator God (9); against the docetists, his true incarnation (10); against the adoptionists, his true divinity (11–25); and against the modalists, his distinction from the Father (26–28). Chapter 29 briefly treats the Holy Spirit; and chs. 30–31, the oneness of God in the distinction of the two divine persons of the Father and the Son.

Although the concept of *trinitas* had already been shaped by Tertullian, Novatian does not make use of it but borrows from him such terms as *una substantia, tres personae,* and *ex substantia dei* and introduces such terms as *incarnari* (*De Trinitate* 138) and *praedestinatio* (*De Trinitate* 94) into the Latin language. It should not be surprising that he accords such little space to the Holy Spirit and does not explicitly call him God and the Third Person of the Trinity, or that he does not include the Spirit in the discussion on the oneness of God. The development of theological reflection did not reach that point until the second half of the fourth century, especially with Basil the Great. He sees the Holy Spirit mainly as the source of holiness, inspiration, and immortality, who, as the source of all virtue by indwelling the individual on the basis of baptism, protects him from sin. Nevertheless, hardly anything is known about the effects of this first great tractate of the first Roman theologian.

*Editions: De Trinitate* (ed. H. Weyer; Test. 2; Düsseldorf: Patmos, 1962) [Com]. – *La trinità* (ed. V. Loi; CorPat 2; Turin: Società Editrice Internazionale, 1975). – *La Trinidad* (ed. C. Granado; FP 8; Madrid: Ciudad Nueva, 1996).

*Translations: The Trinity, The Spectacles, Jewish Foods, In Praise of Purity, Letters* (trans. R. J. Desimone; FC 67; Washington, D.C.: Catholic University of America Press in association with Consortium Press, 1974).

*Studies:* R. J. DeSimone, *The Treatise of Novatian the Roman Presbyter on the Trinity: A Study of the Text and the Doctrine* (SEAug 4; Rome: Institutum Patristicum Augustinianum, 1970). – R. J. DeSimone, "Again the Kenosis of *Phil.* 2,6–11: Novatian, *Trin.* 22," *Aug* 32 (1992): 91–104. – P. Mattei, "Novatien, *De Trinitate* 31: Texte et traduction, commentaire philologique et doctrinale," *MAST.M* 20 (1996): 159–257.

# VI. LACTANTIUS

Lucius Caecilius Firmianus Lactantius was the last great Latin church father who was personally impacted by the persecution of Christians and whose work was significantly shaped by them; subsequently he was also called "the Christian Cicero" because of his excellent classical style. He came from Africa, where the famous rhetor Arnobius trained him and he himself functioned as a teacher of rhetoric. He so distinguished himself that between 290 and 300 Emperor Diocletian appointed him teacher of Latin rhetoric at his new residence in Nicomedia of Bithynia. There the future emperor, Constantine the Great, who stayed in Nicomedia until 306, may also have been among his students. In any case, he knew Lactantius there, which explains his later appointment as teacher of Crispus, Constantine's eldest son.

The precise date of Lactantius's conversion to Christianity is unknown, but it may have been before 303, for when the Diocletian persecution began in February 303, he relinquished his office as rhetor and lived in humble circumstances in or near Nicomedia during the persecution. This is the time when his fruitful engagement as a Christian writer began. In 303/304 he wrote an apologetic work, *De opificio Dei,* and in 304–311 *Divinarum institutionum libri VII,* his magnum opus. After the persecution ended in 313, Constantine appointed him in 314/315 as teacher of his son Crispus in Trier. There he completed *De mortibus persecutorum* and wrote an apology, *De ira Dei,* as well as a short edition of the *Institutiones (Epitome divinarum institutionum).* The latter was likely to be published in a second edition with dedicatory salutations addressed to Constantine, who was already sole ruler in 324. Since Lactantius did not complete it, he likely died ca. 325.

*Bibliographies:* B. Kettern, *BBKL* 4:952–65.

*Editions: Opera omnia:* (ed. S. Brandt; 3 vols. in 2; CSEL 19, 27; Vienna: F. Tempsky, 1890–1897). – *Vom Zorne Gottes [= De ira Dei]* (ed. H. Kraft and A. Wlosok; 2d ed.; TzF 4; Darmstadt: Wissenschaftliche Buchgesellschaft, 1971) [Com]. – *La colère de Dieu* (ed. C. Ingremeau; SC 289; Paris: Cerf, 1982). – *L'ouvrage du Dieu créateur [= De opificio Dei]* (ed. M. Perrin; SC 213–14; Paris: Cerf, 1974).

*Translations:* W. Fletcher, trans., "The Divine Institutes," "The Epitome of the Divine Institutes," "A Treatise on the Anger of God," "On the Workmanship of God, or the Formation of Man," "Of the Manner in Which the Persecutors Died," "Fragments of Lactantius," "The Phoenix," and "A Poem on the Passion of the Lord," in *ANF* (Peabody, Mass.: Hendrickson, 1995; repr. of 1886 ed.), 7:9–328 [*Opera omnia*]. – *Minor Works* (trans. M. F. McDonald; FC 54; Washington, D.C.: Catholic University of America Press, 1965).

*Reference Works: Thesaurus Lactantii* (Turnhout, Belg.: Brepols, 1998).

*Encyclopedia Articles:* É. Lamirande, *DSp* 9:48–59. – V. Loi, *DPAC* 2:1905–8. – A. Wlosok, *GK* 1:176–88. – A. Wlosok, *HLL* 5:375–404. – A. Wlosok, *TRE* 20:370–74. – M. P. Mchugh, *EEC* 2:660–61.

*Collections of Essays:* J. Fontaine and M. Perrin, eds., *Lactance et son temps: Recherches actuelles* (ThH 48; Paris: Beauchesne, 1978).

*Studies:* A. Wlosok, *Laktanz und die philosophische Gnosis: Untersuchungen zu Geschichte und Terminologie der gnostischen Erlösungsvorstellung* (AHAW.PH 1960.2; Heidelberg: Winter, 1960). – V. Loi, *Lattanzio nella storia del linguaggio e del pensiero teologico pre-niceno* (BThS.F 5; Zurich: Pas, 1970). – M. Perrin, *L'homme antique et chrétien: L'anthropologie de Lactance, 250–325* (ThH 59; Paris: Beauchesne, 1981). – P. Monat, *Lactance et la Bible: Une propédeutique latine à la lecture de la Bible dans l'Occident constantinien* (2 vols.; Paris: Études Augustiniennes, 1982). – P. McGuckin, "The Christology of Lactantius," in *Proceedings of the Eighth International Conference on Patristic Studies, Oxford, 3–8 September, 1979* (ed. E. Livingstone; 3 vols.; StPatr 17; Oxford and New York: Pergamon, 1982), 2:813–20. – C. Ocker, "*Unius arbitrio mundum regi necesse est:* Lactantius' Concern for the Preservation of Roman Society," *VC* 40 (1986): 348–64. – E. DePalma Digeser, *The Making of a Christian Empire: Lactantius and Rome* (Ithaca, N.Y.: Cornell University Press, 2000).

# Divinarum institutionum *and* Epitome divinarum institutionum

On account of its origin and purpose at the end of the period of the persecutions, the "divine instructions" of Lactantius remained the only work of its kind in Latin Christian literature. The persecution of Christians under Diocletian was intended not only to compel them to return to the ancient cult of the gods but also to persuade them by enlightenment. Soon after the persecution began in 303, therefore, pagan philosophers and literati published pamphlets that presented Christians in the traditional way, as uneducated and misled by an irrational heresy. Lactantius responded in the same way Greek apologists had done before him. He wrote an apologia rejecting the accusations against Christians, on the one hand, and aiming, through logical and philosophical argumentation, to demonstrate and convince the educated pagan of the education of Christians, on the other. Structured in the classical style of Cicero, *Divinarum institutionum* thus offers fundamental Christian religious instruction, formulated according to the opponents' imagination and conceptuality, in order to demonstrate that it is not pagan belief in gods and philosophy but Christianity alone that is able to lay claim to the truth. The title, chosen in parallel with juridical textbooks, points to the essential character of the work: Like the *pater familias* according to Roman law, God is Father and Lord, provider and judge, and this fundamentally orders his relationship with people. God's commandments make demands upon the individual, who is expected to obey and, in return, receives the reward he deserves.

The seven books progress from error to truth and to ever-increasing closeness to God. Book 1 (*De falsa religione*) refutes polytheism. Since the concept of God includes the indivisible *summa potestas,* there can be only one God logically, and this is then also supported with witnesses from pagan literature. There follows the usual critique of the gods, namely, that they are merely deified humans and, because of their shameful morality, are ill suited to be ethical models for the individual. Book 2 (*De origine erroris*) explains the origin of the false cults of the gods as demonic, which the true God only tolerates for the purpose of testing the person. Book 3 (*De falsa sapientia*) is meant to convict philosophers of ignorance on the basis of their teachings on ethics. The virtues themselves are not the goal of life (as the Stoics insist), but instead they are merely a means to attaining immortality. Wisdom and religion are inseparable. Book 4 (*De vera sapientia*) describes the Christian revelation through Christ as the true wisdom; he represents the *exemplum* of the perfected sage—a goal that philosophers never reached. As the philosophers (Platonism) realized correctly, God, in principle, is unknowable, and truth is attainable only through the path of revelation. Christ alone mediates perfect knowledge of salvation. Book 5 (*De iustitia*) objects to the prosecutors' claim of *pietas* and *iustitia*, whereby they justified their actions. He uses Aeneas to show that not even this hero, whom the Romans revered so highly as an example, acted in accordance with *pietas*. The only true piety and righteousness are to be found among Christians and are misjudged as mere folly by pagans. Book 6 (*De vero cultu*) introduces the ethics of Christianity, based upon the laws of God (not upon those of the Roman *ius civile*), though entirely in the form of Ciceronic-Stoic teaching on duties, structuring righteousness in terms of obligations toward God and human beings. This also includes the teaching of the two ways, as it was already present in *Barnabas* and the *Didache*, as well as detailed lists of vices and virtues. Book 7 (*De vita beata*) concludes with eschatology in the millenarian tradition of Revelation. Of the six thousand years in the age of the earth, two hundred are yet to come; then follows the millennial kingdom of God on earth, in which the "golden age," as the poets describe it, will be realized. After the subsequent final battle between good and evil, the ultimate kingdom of God will finally be established, which is also the goal of all of human history.

The *Epitome* does not represent a summary of the *Divinarum institutionum* as much as an abridged and improved version with substantial changes and expansions in matters of detail. Many references are deleted, original Greek citations are translated, and the argumentation and presentation overall are smoothed out and presented more clearly.

*Editions: Institutions divines* (ed. P. Monat; rev. ed.; SC; Paris: Cerf, 1973–; repr., 2000–) [I, II, IV, V]. – *Épitomé des institutions divines* (ed. M. Perrin; SC 335; Paris: Cerf, 1987). – *L. Caeli Firmiani Lactanti Epitome divinarum institutionum* (ed. E. Heck and A. Wlosok; Teubner; Stuttgart: Teubner, 1994).

*Translations: The Divine Institutes, Books I–VII* (trans. M. F. McDonald; FC 49; Washington, D.C.: Catholic University of America Press, 1964).

*Studies:* O. P. Nicholson, "The Source of the Dates in Lactantius' *Divine Institutes*," *JTS* NS 36 (1985): 291–310. – O. P. Nicholson, "Flight from Persecution as Imitation of Christ: Lactantius' Divine Institutes IV,18,1–2," *JTS* NS 40 (1989): 48–65. – C. Lo Cicero, "Una 'citazione' di Seneca in Lattanzio e l'epilogo del V libro delle *Divinae institutiones*," *Orph.* 12 (1991): 378–410. – E. DePalma Digeser, "Lactantius and Constantine's Letter to Arles: Dating the Divine Institutes," *JECS* 2 (1994): 33–52.

Part Three

# Literature of the Ascending Imperial Church (Early Fourth Century to ca. 430)

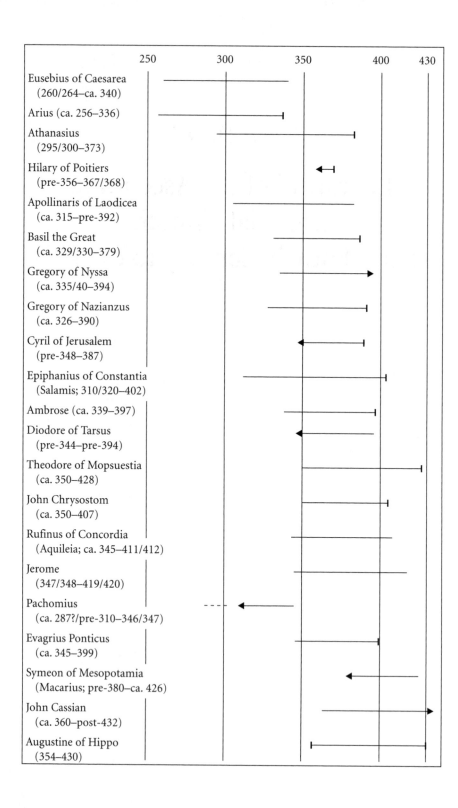

# Essential Features of the History of the Fourth Century

THERE IS NO QUESTION THAT THE so-called Constantinian shift (313) meant the dawning of a new era for the Christian church as well as for its literature. It was now able to develop freely and in safety, and it fully integrated itself into the Roman state and culture in increasingly significant ways. With the influx of increasing numbers of people into the church, it was not only its tasks and influence that grew; increasing numbers of intellectuals joined, and communities and diocesan towns multiplied as well. The multitude of educated bishops accounts for the majority of the writers in this era of patristic literature, in which they responded to the theological, pastoral, and spiritual needs of their time. At no other time of the patristic era were there more numerous and overall more significant works written than in the fourth and fifth centuries; hence this period tends to be called the "heyday" or the "golden era" of patristics. This terminology, however, is predicated upon the traditional scheme of "rise-apex-decline" and therefore brings ideologically charged categories to bear on the literature instead of deriving structural criteria from it. Rather, the specific characteristic of the literature of the fourth and early fifth centuries is that it not only mirrors the multifaceted ecclesiastical life in its development from toleration (313) to state church (396) but was in fact shaped by this development. In all of its rich forms, therefore, it is "the literature of the ascending imperial church."

Traditionally the councils of Nicea (325) and Chalcedon (451) constitute the boundaries of this period because the original orientation of patrology was shaped by the history of dogma. Historians generally also agree that in many areas the first half of the fifth century saw the convergence of decisive factors separating the two periods; here too, however, the periodization of literary history ought to draw its criteria from the development of the literature itself. In this context, it seems that, even from the perspective of the history of dogma, it was not the Council of Chalcedon (451) that constituted the break but roughly the year 430, for several reasons.

a. The Visigoth conquest of Rome by Alaric (410) ushered in the disintegration of the empire's political unity of East and West. Although Roman emperors of the West ruled nominally until 476 and many imperial structures, such as the Roman senate, persisted until the sixth century, the essential reshaping of the

West under "barbarian" rulers began inexorably at this point. Literature likewise began to address these issues practically, historically, and theologically, starting with Augustine's tractate *De civitate Dei*.

b. The linguistic and thus cultural and literary integrity of the Roman Empire also began to disintegrate no later than with Augustine's death. Augustine still had basic, albeit not fluent, Greek language skills; after him, however, because of the lack of the necessary linguistic skills, the West no longer took notice of Greek literature except when it was translated into Latin.

c. The Council of Chalcedon did not conclude any period in terms of the history of theology and literature but, rather, represented the period's apex and resulted in painful after-effects. Issues concerning the acceptance of this council lasted for centuries. In my view, the Nestorian controversy beginning in 428 has to be seen as the starting point of a new period.

Although a precise year cannot be given, the year of Augustine's death (430) may be considered the point of reference for the new period, for, on the one hand, he embodied the apex of the literature of the imperial church and, on the other, his life and work nevertheless already signaled the new era, according to the criteria cited above: *De civitate Dei*, the conquest of North Africa by the Vandals, linguistic skill, the problem of the "pre-Nestorian" Christology of Leporius, and the summons to the Council of Ephesus (431).

The period thus delimited, from the beginning of the fourth century to roughly 430, saw the rise of most of the works of patristic literature relative to all of the church's expressions of life:

- understanding of Holy Scripture as the basis of faith;

- philosophical grounding and investigation of the faith;

- continuation of theology and development of the basic dogmas in the context of disputes with heterodoxies and with the state turned Christian, which also called for a new understanding of the church;

- historiography in the context of a "kingdom of God" that has already begun;

- theology of the sacraments and liturgical praxis: baptismal catechesis, liturgy of the Mass, penance, marriage, including liturgical texts and Christian poetry;

- spiritual life/piety, ecclesiastical offices, and monasticism/asceticism;

- correct behavior (ethics/morality) in everyday life, including Christian legislation;

- the sermon, encompassing all the topics and rubrics mentioned.

The difficulty of giving a clear historical presentation of this literature is evident, not only because of its wealth and variety but also because no single church father can be associated any longer with one particular category. Therefore, if a presentation rigidly follows a chronological approach, it tears apart the factual cor-relations; conversely, if it presents the content in diachronic, content-related longi-tudinal sections, the understanding of the overall historical development is lost. In particular, a purely dogmatic-historical or regional classification of the authors cannot suffice. The structure to be presented here assumes that, beginning with the fourth century, Christian literature makes known three major areas:

a. theology and especially dogmatics, which also determined the major inter-nal church controversies, which at the same time became disputes between the church and the Roman state because of the understanding of the rela-tionship between the two;

b. pastoral care for the Christian communities, encompassing all practical ex-pressions of the church's life, namely, missions, conversion, catechesis, proclamation, liturgy, sacraments, social care, and many others;

c. ascetic and monastic forces, as elements of an independent Christian way of life, integrated into the life of the community, on the one hand, or with-drawn from the same, on the other.

These serve as the fundamental organizing principle to which individuals and writings are related chronologically. It is important to remember that all three areas are at work simultaneously in all of the writers addressed. Their association with one category or another merely accentuates their primary significance so as not to lose the factual context that is necessary for an overview. Augustine, of course, is beyond a classification such as this. He himself summed up his time by addressing all of the ecclesiastical and theological currents and pointing to the way ahead for them. For this reason, he requires a chapter of his own.

The relevant political, ecclesiastical, and theological background necessary for an understanding of fourth-century Christian literature is so varied and com-plex that it is necessary to provide an overview, in summary fashion, of the history of the fourth century before endeavoring to present the literature of this period. The corresponding analysis will select, classify, and evaluate the material by consid-ering three perspectives: state politics, ecclesiastical and ecclesiastical-political events, and theological questions. It thus aims to consider the same material, which is inseparable in history, from three separate ideological vantage points, so as to let the structures and trajectories necessary for understanding emerge, with the goal of providing a portrait that is as close to the historical reality as possible.

# I. POLITICAL HISTORY

*Bibliography:* K. Christ et al., *Römische Geschichte: Eine Bibliographie* (Darmstadt: Wissen-schaftliche Buchgesellschaft, 1976).

*Reference Works:* V. Grumel, *La chronologie* (Bibliothèque byzantine: Traité d'études byzantines 1; Paris: Presses Universitaires de France, 1958). – A. H. M. Jones, J. R. Martindale, and J. Morris, *The Prosopography of the Later Roman Empire* (3 vols.;

Cambridge: Cambridge University Press, 1971–1992). – G. W. Bowersock, P. Brown, and O. Grabar, *Late Antiquity: A Guide to the Postclassical World* (Cambridge, Mass.: Belknap Press of Harvard University Press, 1999).

*Studies:* A. H. M. Jones, *The Later Roman Empire, 284–602: A Social, Economic, and Administrative Survey,* vol. 1 (2 vols.; Norman: University of Oklahoma Press, 1964; repr., Baltimore: Johns Hopkins University Press, 1986). – W. Schneemelcher, *Kirche und Staat im 4. Jahrhundert. Rede z. Antritt d. Rektorates d. Rhein. Freidrich-Wilhelms-Univ. zu Bonn am 28. Okt. 1967* (BAR 37; Bonn: Hanstein, 1970). – K. Christ, *Römische Geschichte: Einführung, Quellenkunde, Bibliographie* (3d ed.; Die Altertumswissenschaft; Darmstadt: Wissenschaftliche Buchgesellschaft, 1980). – G. Bonamente and A. Nestori, eds., *I Cristiani e l'impero nel IV secolo: Colloquio sul cristianesimo nel mondo antico, atti del convegno (Macerata 17–18 dicembre 1987)* (Pubblicazioni della Facoltà di lettere e filosofia 47; Atti di convegni 9; Macerata: Università degli Studi di Macerata, 1988). – A. Demandt, *Die Spätantike: Römische Geschichte von Diocletian bis Justinian, 284–565 n. Chr.* (HAW 3; Munich: Beck, 1989). F. Heim, *La théologie de la victoire: De Constantin à Théodose* (ThH 89; Paris: Beauchesne, 1992). – A. Cameron, *The Later Roman Empire: AD 284–430* (Cambridge, Mass.: Harvard University Press, 1993). – F. Paschoud and J. Szidat, eds., *Usurpationen in der Spätantike: Akten des Kolloquiums "Staatsstreich und Staatlichkeit," 6.–10. März 1996, Solothurn/Bern—elf Beiträge* (Hist.E 111; Stuttgart: Steiner, 1997). – A. Cameron and P. Garnsey, eds., *The Late Empire: A.D. 337–425* (Cambridge Ancient History 13; Cambridge: Cambridge University Press, 1998).

# *Introduction: Sacral Notion of the Empire*

If one speaks of politics in the context of the history of the church and the theology of the fourth century, the reference is almost exclusively to the politics of the Roman emperor. This extends from the first Christian emperor and autocrat, Constantine the Great (306/324–337), to the last absolute dictator of the entire realm, Theodosius the Great (379/388–395). They mark not only the boundaries of the development of the empire in the fourth century but also its basic problems. The notion of the Roman Empire was a notion of unity: one realm, one emperor, one god or uniform deities of the state, in which the dynastic-sacral concept of the realm is made manifest in the person of the emperor. He was not only the supreme ruler, guardian of the unity and promoter of the welfare of the empire, but also the supreme priest, indeed god, who embodied the unity and welfare of the state guaranteed by the deities of the empire. The broad expansion of the empire, however, and the increasing encroachment by Germanic, Slavic, Gothic, and Eastern peoples upon the empire forced Diocletian in 285 to establish a tetrarchy. While it did not eliminate the notion of unity of the Roman Empire—it was embodied by the *senior Augustus*—it did bear the seed of the empire's division and of the power struggles among the emperors themselves. This is already evident in the case of Diocletian's coregent, Maximian, who in 305 resigned, though reluctantly, in accordance with the rules of the tetrarchy but then had himself declared emperor on two further occasions (308 and 310). After Diocletian the tetrarchy no longer functioned in keeping with its original plan.

Constantine (306/324–337), Constantius II (353–361), and Julian (388–395) did indeed rule the empire on their own, but otherwise there always were legitimate or illegitimate coregents (usurpers). If they were supportive commanders, such as Licinius, Constans, or Julian, who were appointed to secure the extensive borders of the realm, this also bore the seed of civil war. If they were minors, such as Gratian and Valentinian II, who had been appointed to coregency early on for the purpose of securing the dynastic line of succession, the foreign-policy threat increased, as did the danger of usurpation. Only in the case of brothers, namely, Valentinian I and Valens, as well as Theodosius, was peaceful cooperation achieved because of family ties that had been respected with trust.

All of this sometimes confusing history of the various emperors would be unimportant for the history of the church and the theology of the fourth century had religion not been bound up inseparably with the Roman notion of emperor and empire. The gods had made Rome great, had guarded and protected it, and in the emperor's political fortune, in his successful battles, and in the welfare of the empire, their activity and the true divine worship were made manifest. When Constantine turned to Christianity in 312, he relinquished the ancient gods of the empire but not the underlying imperial notion. Thus the ancient deities were merely replaced with the Christian God. In Constantine's battle against Maxentius at the Milvian Bridge outside Rome, the Christian God had proved himself to be more powerful and hence was the true God who now guaranteed the empire's continued existence and welfare. As emperor, Constantine was the agent of this God as leader of the political-sacral unity of the empire, as were the emperors before him in the name of the ancient gods. For this reason, Eusebius called Constantine κοινὸς ἐπίσκοπος (Vit. Const. 1.44.2), while he called himself ἐπὶ σκοπος τῶν ἐκτός (Vit. Const. 4.24). This title corresponds to the old title of pontifex maximus, which the Christian emperors owned as well until Theodosius, even if it did not encompass any priestly function in the Christian church. But the sacral notion of the emperor entitled and obligated the ruler to care for the political and religious welfare of his people.

For this reason, Christian emperors also acted as leaders of the church; summoned councils; promoted, confirmed, or rejected their decisions; and approved the choice of bishops or deposed them. Indeed, after consultation with synods and theologians, they established the correct and binding faith until Theodosius elevated it even to the level of state law in 381. The issue was not merely the settling of public uprisings, which occurred repeatedly in the fourth century, from the Donatists through the Arians and Nicenes to the Priscillians, but the realization of the notion of the empire, which could tolerate only one official cult of the state and had to restore and protect its correctness and uniformity for the sake of the state's welfare. Other religions and confessions could be brooked alongside it only to the extent that they did not endanger the welfare of the state.

This general notion of the empire, as well as the essential goal of the empire's unity and welfare, could take on quite different, concrete shapes, and it did so in the fourth century, not only in the transition from paganism to Christianity under Constantine and vice versa under Julian the Apostate but also within different Christian confessions. This did not depend so much on the emperor's personal conviction of faith—a "dogmatic" holding on to doctrine without regard for its practical consequence did not exist among the emperors of the fourth century—but on competition for political opportunity. Political success demonstrated the favor of the gods and thereby the correctness of the conviction of faith. For this reason, the emperors' politics of religion was part of their power politics; hence church and faith could be brought into play without misgivings, as instruments of power struggles. If imperial politics and the politics of religion are interpreted from this perspective, the otherwise rather confusing, indeed often contradictory, behavior of the emperors proves to be politically consistent.

*Translation:* P. R. Colman-Norton, *Roman State and Christian Church: A Collection of Legal Documents to A.D. 535* (3 vols.; London: SPCK, 1966).

*Studies:* M. Vogelstein, *Kaiseridee-Romidee und das Verhältnis von Staat und Kirche seit Constantin* (Historische Untersuchungen 7; Breslau: Marcus, 1930). – W. Ensslin, *Gottkaiser und kaiser von Gottes gnaden* (SBAW.PH 1943.6; Munich: Verlag der Bayerischen Akademie der Wissenschaften in Kommission bei Beck, 1943). – H. Berkhof, *Kirche und Kaiser: Eine untersuchung der Entstehung der byzantinischen und der theokratischen Staatsauffassung im vierten Jahrhundert* (trans. G. W. Locher; Zurich: Evangelischer Verlag, 1947). – F. Dvornik, *Early Christian and Byzantine Political Philosophy: Origins and Background* (Dumbarton Oaks Studies 9; Washington, D.C.: Dumbarton Oaks Center for Byzantine Studies; Trustees of Harvard University, 1966). – J. Ziegler, *Zur religiösen Haltung der Gegenkaiser im 4. Jh. n. Chr.* (FTS 4; Kallmünz: Lassleben, 1970). A. Piganiol, *L'empire chrétien (325–395)* (2d ed.; ed. A. Chastagnol; Collection Hier; Paris: Presses Universitaires de France, 1972). – J. R. Fears, *Princeps a diis electus: The Divine Election of the Emperor as a Political Concept at Rome* (PMAAR 26; Rome: American Academy in Rome, 1977). – J. H. W. G. Liebeschuetz, *Continuity and Change in Roman Religion* (Oxford: Clarendon; New York: Oxford University Press, 1979). – S. Elbern, *Usurpationen im spätrömischen Reich* (Habelts Dissertationsdrucke: Reihe Alte Geschichte 18; Bonn: R. Habelt, 1984). A. Dihle, ed., *L'Église et l'empire au IVe siècle: Sept exposés suivis de discussions* (Entretiens sur l'antiquité classique 34; Geneva: Fondation Hardt, 1989). – A. Cameron, *Christianity and the Rhetoric of Empire: The Development of Christian Discourse* (Sather Classical Lectures 55; Berkeley: University of California Press: 1991). – P. Brown, *Power and Persuasion in Late Antiquity: Toward a Christian Empire* (Curti Lectures; Madison: University of Wisconsin Press, 1992). – G. Fowden, *Empire to Commonwealth: Consequences of Monotheism in Late Antiquity* (Princeton, N.J.: Princeton University Press, 1993).

## A. Constantine the Great (306/324–337)

In the power struggle against Maxentius in 312, Constantine changed his god, and his success vindicated him; the same was true against Licinius in 324. After achieving autocracy, it had to be Constantine's most noble goal to protect the one empire, under the one ruler, with the favor of the one God and his church, against external enemies and to cause it to blossom within. In this pursuit, the uprising of Arius, who threatened this sacral unity of the empire, affected

## Roman Emperors of the Fourth Century (usurpers in italics)

| | Western Part | | Eastern Part | |
|---|---|---|---|---|
| | **Augustus** | **Caesar** | **Augustus** | **Caesar** |
| Dioceses | Italy, Rhaetia, Africa | Gaul, Britain, Spain | Thrace, Asia, Syria, Egypt, Libya, | Illyricum, Greece, Dalmatia, Pannonia, |
| Courts | Milan, Aquileia | Trier, York | Nicomedia | Sirmium, Thessalonica |
| 305 | Abdication of the First Tetrarchy under Diocletian, Second Tetrarchy: | | | |
| | Constantius Chlorus (d. 306) (father of Constantine) | Severus | Galerius (d. 311) | Maximinus Daia (d. 313) |
| 306 | Severus (d. 307) | Constantine | | |
| 306 | *Maxentius* (d. 312) | | | |
| 307 | Constantine | | | |
| 308 | Licinius | Constantine | | |
| 311 | | | Licinius (d. 325) | |
| 312 | Constantine | | | |
| 313 | | | | Licinius (d. 325) |
| 324 | Constantine the Great, sole ruler (d. 337) | | | |
| 337 | Constans (Caesar): Italy, Africa, Pannonia, Dalmatia | Constantine II (d. 340) | Flavius Dalmatius (Caesar): Thrace with Constantinople (d. 337) | Constantius II: East, incl. Egypt |
| 9–9–337 | (Augustus) | (Augustus) | | (Augustus) |
| 338 | | | Divided between Constans (western Illyricum) and Constantinus II (eastern Illyricum and Thrace) | |
| 340 | Constans, sole ruler of the Western empire (d. 350) | | | |
| 350 | *Magnentius* (d. 353) | | | |
| 353 | Constantius II, sole ruler (d. 361) | | | |
| 355 | Julian (Caesar) | | | |
| 360 | (Augustus) | | | |
| 361 | Julian the Apostate, sole ruler (d. 363) | | | |
| 363 | Jovian, sole ruler (d. 364) | | | |
| 364 | Valentinian (d. 375) and his younger | | Valens (d. 378) | |
| 367 | brother Gratian, eldest son of Valentinian 2d Augustus in the West | | | |
| 375 | Valentinian II (2d son) (d. 392) (within the boundaries of Diocletian's tetrarchy) | Gratian (d. 383) | | |
| 379 | | | Theodosius | |
| 383 | | *Maximus* (d. 388) | | |
| 388 | Theodosius the Great, sole ruler (d. 395) | | | |

Constantine all the more painfully. When he had to convince himself that it was not a matter of a politically irrelevant "philosophical" dispute of various theological schools, as initially assumed, but a split in the church and hence a public one, he endeavored to resolve the conflict himself. He summoned the Council of Nicea (325), led it, and perhaps even proposed the solution to the theological issue of the divinity of Christ through the concept of ὁμοούσιος. The council closed with the bishops' almost unanimous agreement on the council's creed; the emperor exiled the three objectors.

This could have ended the dispute and, in Constantine's mind, should have done so. But when it did not subside, Constantine did not pursue the rigorous implementation of the resolutions of Nicea as his highest goal, for precisely these attempts contributed to evoking disquiet, but instead sought the restoration of peace in church and empire, in accordance with the ideal of a uniform cult of the empire and with the political necessity for internal unity in the empire. It is not entirely certain whether there was a follow-up synod in Nicea in 327 to rehabilitate Arius. In any case, the radicals of both parties, in the long run, jeopardized the imperial goals and therefore had to be exiled after a further (failed) attempt at suppressing Arius (333). This included Eustathius of Antioch (330), Athanasius of Alexandria (335), and Marcellus of Ancyra (336). The protagonists of the hour who were acceptable to the emperor and who promoted his endeavors were men such as Eusebius of Caesarea and Eusebius of Nicomedia, who took a line that was politically-theologically mediating and conciliatory. Arius's reconciliation by a synod in Jerusalem in 335, after he had presented a confession of faith that seemed acceptable and conciliatory, thus represents the logical consequence of Constantine's policy of unity. The appeal of the emperor, who was personally present at the council, to the churches of Alexandria and Egypt henceforth to end the divisions makes his fundamental intentions very clear.

Constantine died on May 22, 337, without having resolved the problem of the Arian dispute. In the main, the western half of the empire, where Athanasius had been exiled and Marcellus had moved, accepted the Nicene position, whereas the eastern half predominantly accepted Arianism or a *via media* between the two extremes.

*Edition:* V. Keil, *Quellensammlung zur Religionspolitik Konstantins des Grossen* (TzF 54; Darmstadt: Wissenschaftliche Buchgesellschaft, 1989).

*Encyclopedia Articles:* J. Vogt, *RAC* 3 (1957): 306–79. – T. Schleich, "Konstantin der Grosse," *GK* 1 (1984): 189–214. – St. G. Hall, *TRE* 19 (1990): 489–500. – M. Forlin Patrucco, *EECh* I:193. – R. M. Grant, *EEC* I:280f. – H. D. Drake, "Constantine," *LA* 389–91.

*General Studies:* H. Dörries, *Das Selbstzeugnis Kaiser Konstantins* (AAWG.PH 34; Göttingen: Vandenhoeck & Ruprecht, 1954). – H. Dörries, *Konstantin der Grosse* (UB 29; Stuttgart: Kohlhammer, 1958). – J. Vogt, *Constantin der Grosse und sein Jahrhundert* (2d ed; Munich: Bruckmann, 1960). – A. H. M. Jones, *Constantine and the Conversion of Europe* (new rev. ed.; Men and History; New York: Collier, 1962; repr., Mediaeval Academy Reprints for Teaching 4; Toronto and Buffalo: University of Toronto Press in association with the Mediaeval Academy of America, 1978). – T. D. Barnes, *Constantine and Eusebius* (Cambridge, Mass.: Harvard University Press, 1981). –

M. Clauss, *Konstantin der Grosse und seine Zeit* (C.H. Beck Wissen in der Beck'schen Reihe 2042; Munich: Beck, 1996). – H. A. Pohlsander, *The Emperor Constantine* (Lancaster Pamphlets; London and New York: Routledge, 1996). – T. G. Elliott, *The Christianity of Constantine the Great* (Scranton, Pa.: University of Scranton Press; Bronx, N.Y.: Marketing and Distribution, Fordham University Press, 1996). – H. D. Drake, *Constantine and the Bishops: The Politics of Intolerance* (Ancient Society and History; Baltimore: Johns Hopkins University Press, 2000).

*Collections of Essays:* H. Kraft, ed., *Konstantin der Grosse* (WdF 131; Darmstadt: Wissenschaftliche Buchgesellschaft, 1974). – G. Bonamente and F. Fusco, eds., *Costantino il Grande—dall'antichità all'umanesimo: Colloquio sul cristianesimo nel mondo antico, Macerata, 18–20 dicembre 1990* (2 vols; Università degli studi di Macerata, Facoltà di lettere e filosofia 67; Macerata: Università degli Studi di Macerata; Rome: Distribuzione, E.G.L.E., 1992–1993).

*Studies:* A. Alföldi, *The Conversion of Constantine and Pagan Rome* (trans. H. Mattingly; Oxford: Clarendon, 1948). – V. C. de Clercq, *Ossius of Cordova: A Contribution to the History of the Constantinian Period* (SCA 13; Washington, D.C.: Catholic University of America Press, 1954). – H. Kraft, *Kaiser Konstantins religiöse Entwicklung* (BHTh 20; Tübingen: Mohr, 1955). – K. Aland, "Die religiöse Haltung Kaiser Konstantins," in *Studia patristica: Papers Presented to the Second International Conference on Patristic Studies Held at Christ Church, Oxford, 1955* (ed. K. Aland and F. L. Cross; StPatr 1; TU 63–64; Berlin: Akademie, 1957), 547–600; repr. in idem, *Kirchengeschichtliche Entwürfe: Alte Kirche, Reformation und Luthertum, Pietismus und Erweckungsbewegung* (Gütersloh: Gütersloher Verlagshaus, 1960), 202–39. – J. Straub, "Constantine as ΚΟΙΝΟΣ ΕΠΙΣΚΟΠΟΣ: Tradition and Innovation in the Representation of the First Christian Emperor's Majesty," *DOP* 21 (1967): 37–56; repr. in idem, *Regeneratio imperii: Aufsätze über Roms Kaisertum u. Reich im Spiegel d. heidn. u. christl. Publizistik* (Darmstadt: Wissenschaftliche Buchgesellschaft, 1972), 134–58. – A. Lippold, "Bischof Ossius von Cordova und Konstantin de Grosse," *ZKG* 92 (1981): 1–15. – R. Lane Fox, *Pagans and Christians* (New York: Knopf, 1987), 609–62. – Ø. Norderval, "The Emperor Constantine and Arius: Unity in the Church and Unity in the Empire," *ST* 42 (1988): 113–50. – T. Grünewald, *Constantinus Maximus Augustus: Herrschaftspropaganda in der zeitgenössischen Überlieferung* (Hist.E 64; Stuttgart: Steiner, 1990). – K. M. Girardet, "Kaiser Konstantin d. Gr. als Vorsitzender von Konzilien: Die historischen Tatsachen und ihre Deutung," *Gym.* 98 (1991): 548–60. – J. Bleicken, *Constantin der Grosse und die Christen: Überlegungen zur konstantinischen Wende* (HZ.B NS 15; Munich: Oldenbourg, 1992). – R. Leeb, *Konstantin und Christus: Die Verchristlichung der imperialen Repräsentation unter Konstantin dem Grossen als Spiegel seiner Kirchenpolitik und seines Selbstverständnisses als christlicher Kaiser* (AKG 58; Berlin and New York: de Gruyter, 1992). – B. Bleckmann, *Konstantin de Grosse* (Rowohlts Monographien 55; Reinbeck; Hamburg: Rowohlt, 1996). – D. R. Williams, "Constantine, Nicaea, and the 'Fall' of the Church," in *Christian Origins: Theology, Rhetoric, and Community* (London and New York: Routledge, 1998), 117–36.

# B. *Constantine's Sons (337–361)*

## 1. Era of Coregency (337–353)

Constantine left the empire to his three sons, Constantine II, Constantius II, and Constans, as well as to Flavius Dalmatius, his nephew, as four caesars with equal rights in their respective administrative districts. In this way, he created a constellation that almost inevitably had to lead to a struggle for supremacy, which occurred almost immediately. Already in 337 Flavius Dalmatius was deprived of power and, together with most of the members of his family, lost his life; his district was divided between Constantius and Constans, whereas Constantine II was passed over. On September 9, 337, therefore, all three of them assumed the title "Augustus." Just a few years later (340), in a conflict with Constans, Constantine II likewise lost his life, so that there were only two emperors left: Constans in the West and Constantius II in the East. Their rivalry, however, continued to smolder, bringing to bear also the politics of religion. Constans adhered to the pro-Nicene views of the West, whereas Constantius II sided with the (moderate) Arians.

Indeed, neither Constans nor Constantius succeeded in gaining a decisive dominance over his competitor, so that the church's situation also remained undecided. Through the usurpation of the Western empire by Magnentius and the murder of Constans (350), the scales finally tipped in favor of Constantius. Though a pagan, Magnentius favored the Western Nicene church, but the fortunes of battle did not favor him. Constantius emerged victorious from the two decisive battles in 351 and 353 and thereby united the empire again under one hand. How closely the victory in battle was, for Constantius, linked with his faith in God can be seen in the report that he did not take part in the battle but spent his time in a chapel praying.

## 2. Constantius II as Sole Ruler (353–361)

The anti-Nicene reaction began immediately, or more appropriately, the emperor now endeavored to support the political unity of the empire, in accordance with the notion of the empire, by means of a uniform confession of faith; and everyone who resisted this goal or appeared to jeopardize it had to give way. The councils of Arles (353) and Milan (355) condemned the uncompromising Athanasius—perhaps also because of his connections with Magnentius, which Constantius deemed treasonous—and his followers with him, namely, Lucifer of Calaris, Hilary of Poitiers, Ossius of Córdoba, and Liberius of Rome. Nor did the emperor shy away from a military campaign to carry out his goals in Alexandria (356), expel Athanasius, and appoint George, an Arian from Cappadocia, as bishop.

The first attempt at unity in the synod of Sirmium (357) failed because it prohibited entirely the discussion of the concepts of ὁμοούσιος and ὁμοιούσιος and thus practically denied the issue. The following double council of Ariminum (Rimini) and Seleucia (359) did not achieve, in either of its parts, the result the emperor wished for. But since he now was determined to bring unity even by using force, he compelled the delegations of both parts of the council to sign a Homoean formula at Nike (Thrace), in accordance with the synod of Sirmium; this was subsequently confirmed by the Council of Constantinople in 360. A further synod, meeting in Paris (360/361), interpreted the Nicene ὁμοούσιος in terms of a *similitudo,* hence as ὁμοίωσις.

Except for the remains of a stubborn resistance around Athanasius, the unity of faith could have thus been stabilized for a second time, after Constantine, through imperial intervention, albeit on a Homoean middle ground, had Constantius not died during a military campaign in Persia on November 3, 361.

*Constans:* J. Moreau, *JAC* 2 (1959): 179–84. – M. Forlin Patrucco, "Constans I," *EECh* 1:192. R. M. Grant, "Constans (ca. 323–350)," *EEC* 1:279 f.

*Constantine II:* J. Moreau, *JAC* 2 (1959): 160 f. – M. Forlin Patrucco, "Constantine II," *EECh* 1:193.

*Constantius II:* K. Kraft, "Die Taten der Kaiser Constans und Constantius II," *JNG* 9 (1958): 141–86. – J. Moreau, *JAC* 2 (1959): 162–79. – K. M. Girardet, "Kaiser Konstantius als 'episcopus episcoporum' und das Herrscherbild des kirchlichen Widerstandes (Ossius von Corduba und Lucifer von Calaris)," *Hist* 26 (1977): 95–128. – R. Klein, *Constantius II. und die christliche Kirche* (Impulse der Forschung 26; Darmstadt: Wissenschaftliche Buchgesellschaft [Abt. Verl.], 1977). – M. M. Mudd, *Studies in the Reign of Constantius II* (New York: Carlton, 1989). – M. Forlin Patrucco, "Constantius II," *EECh* 1:198. – R. M. Grant, "Constantius II (317–361)," *EEC* 1:286 f.

# C. Julian the Apostate (361–363) and Jovian (363–364)

Julian, who publicly declared himself in favor of the ancient deities and hence was given the epithet *apostata* (apostate) by the Christians, ushered in a final, brief renaissance of the ancient belief in gods. On these renewed foundations, Julian intended to secure the troubled *imperium romanum* and therefore sought to diminish the Christian churches, regardless of confession, and to strengthen the ancient cult, which the Christian emperors until now had subjected to creeping atrophy, if not openly combating it. In doing so, he merely turned back, of course, to the ancient gods; the underlying notion of the empire with its goals remained the same. He was apathetic toward Christianity and tolerated it as long as it did not impede the welfare of the state. He therefore repealed the verdicts of exile pronounced by Constantius based on Christian motives, not to give preferential treatment but out of disinterest. At the same time, it was far from his mind to restore the returning bishops to their offices or to renew the church's privileges. In accordance with the notion of a uniform religion of the empire, Christianity was to become insignificant as far as the state was concerned—for instance, by means of fragmentation. Only when public unrest arose among ecclesiastical groups because of quarrels did the authority of the state intervene for reasons of state, whatever the factions. Hence the further exile of Athanasius on October 24, 362, may be traced back to the unrest he precipitated in Alexandria rather than to his successes in the religious politics at the council held there.

The pagan reaction of Julian (d. June 26, 363) and the Catholic period of his successor, Jovian (d. February 17, 364), who restored all of the church's privileges and allowed Athanasius to return, indeed remained merely episodes because of their brief reigns.

*Jovian:* G. Wirth, "Jovian: Kaiser und Karikatur," in *Vivarium: Festschrift Theodor Klauser zum 90. Geburtstag* (JAC.E 11; Münster: Aschendorff, 1984), 353–84. – P. Siniscalco, *EECh* 1:454. – F. W. Norris, *EEC* 1:633.

*Julian the Apostate:*
*Bibliography:* M. Caltabiano, "Un quindicennio di studi sull'imperatore Giuliano (1965–1980), III," *Koinonia* 8 (1984): 1:17–31.

*Edition:* W. C. F. Wright, *The Works of the Emperor Julian, with an English Translation by Wilmer Cave Wright* (3 vols.; LCL; London: Heinemann; New York: Macmillan, 1923–1953).

*Literature:* P. Allard, *Julien l'Apostat* (3 vols.; 2d ed.; Paris: Lecoffre, 1900–1903). – J. Bidez, *Julian der Abtrünnige* (Munich: Rinn, 1947). – G. W. Bowersock, *Julian the Apostate* (Cambridge, Mass.: Harvard University Press, 1978). – R. Klein, ed., *Julian Apostata* (WdF 509; Darmstadt: Wissenschaftliche Buchgesellschaft, 1978). – R. L. Wilken, "Julian the Apostate: Jewish Law and Christian Truth," in *The Christians as the Romans Saw Them* (New Haven, Conn.: Yale University Press, 1984; 2d ed., 2003), 164–96. – C. Fouquet, *Julien: La mort du monde antique* (Confluents; Paris: Belles Lettres, 1985). – B. Gentili, ed., *Giuliano imperatore: Atti del Convegno della S.I.S.A.C., Messina, 3 aprile 1984* (Atti di convegni 3; Urbino: QuattroVenti, 1986). – J. Bouffartigue, *L'empereur Julien et la culture de son temps* (Collection des études augustiniennes: Série Antiquité 133; Paris: Institut d'Études Augustiniennes; Turnhout, Belg.: Brepols, 1992). – M. L. Angrisani Sanfilippo, *EECh* 1:459 f. – E. L. Grasmück, "Kaiser Julian und der θεὸς λόγος der Christen," in *Logos: Festschrift für Luise Abramowski zum 8. Juli 1993* (ed. H. C. Brennecke, E. L. Grasmück, and C. Markschies; BNZW 67; Berlin and New York: de Gruyter, 1993), 297–327. – P. Athanassiadi, *Julian: An Intellectual Biography* (Classical Lives; London and New York: Routledge, 1992; repr. of *Julian and Hellenism* [Oxford: Clarendon, 1981]). – R. B. E. Smith, *Julian's Gods: Religion and Philosophy in the Thought and Action of Julian the Apostate* (London and New York: Routledge, 1995). – D. B. Levenson, "Julian (331/2–363)," *EEC* 1:640–42.

# D. Valentinian (364–375) and Valens (364–378)

The confessional division of the empire continued under the brothers Valentinian and Valens. Valens pursued the Homoean line of Constantius and tried everything to lead this confession to victory, especially by filling appropriate episcopal sees, but also by public pressure and threat. As the time of Athanasius (d. 373) in Alexandria drew to a close, beginning with 370, Cappadocia emerged as the new center of Nicene resistance, led by Basil, the metropolitan of Caesarea. He not only resisted the emperor (372) face to face; he also understood how to secure his diocese by appointing brothers and friends who shared his view. His younger brother Gregory became the bishop of Nyssa in 371; the youngest brother, Peter, bishop of Sebaste in 381; his friend at studies, Gregory, bishop of Sasima in 372 and of Nazianzus in 374; and Amphilochius, bishop of Iconium in 373/374.

Under Valentinian the West remained calm and Nicene until the disputes, resembling a civil war, between Damasus, bishop of Rome, and Ursinus, a deacon. This was also true for Gratian, his eldest son, who, as Caesar, ruled with his father beginning in 367 and after Valentinian's death (375) ruled Gaul, Britain, and Spain. The other administrative district of the West (following the Diocletian structure: Italy, Rhaetia, and Africa) installed Valentinian II, the other son of Valentinian, as Caesar, who together with his mother, Justina, professed Arianism. Out of this arose the famous disputes between the Arian imperial court in Milan and the intransigent Nicene bishop of Milan, Ambrose (374–397), who already under Gratian had actively and successfully proceeded against the Arians. Twice in 385/386 Ambrose steadfastly refused to surrender any church to the Arians and was successful. Valentinian in 387 fled from Maximus, the usurper who supported the Nicenes, to Theodosius in the East, under whose influence he was converted to orthodox Christianity; thus ended the final support of Arianism by a Roman ruler.

*Gratian:* M. Fortina, *L'imperatore Graziano* (Turin: Società Editrice Internazionale, 1953). – G. Gottlieb, *Ambrosius von Mailand und Kaiser Gratian* (Hyp. 40; Göttingen: Vandenhoeck & Ruprecht, 1973). – G. Gottlieb, *RAC* 12 (1983): 718–32. – G. Gottlieb, "Der Mailänder Kirchenstreit von 385/386: Datierung, Verlauf, Deutung," *MH* 42 (1985): 37–55. – M. G. Mara, "Gratian," *EECh* 1:360. – M. P. McHugh, "Gratian (359–383)," *EEC* 1:483 f.

*Valens:* R. Snee, "Valens' Recall of the Nicene Exiles and Anti-Arian Propaganda," *GRBS* 26 (1985): 395–419. – D. Woods, "The Baptism of the Emperor Valens," *Classica et mediaevalia* 45 (1994): 211–21. – M. G. Mara, "Valens, emperor," *EECh* 2:858. – M. P. McHugh, "Valens (ca. 383–387)," *EEC* 2:1153.

*Valentinian I:* W. Heering, "Kaiser Valentinian I (364–375 n. chr.)" (diss., Thüringische Lande-Universität Jena; Magdeburg: Faber'sche Buchdruckerei, 1927). – M. G. Mara, "Valentinian I," *EECh* 2:858. – M. P. McHugh, "Valentinian I (321–375)," *EEC* 2:1154.

*Valentinian II:* M. G. Mara, "Valentinian II," *EECh* 2:858 f. – M. P. McHugh, "Valentinian II (371–392)," *EEC* 2:1154 f.

# E. Theodosius the Great (379/388–395)

The real victory for the Nicene creed was won on January 19, 379, when Theodosius came to power in the East after Valens died in the battle of Adrianople against the Visigoths. Theodosius hailed from Spain, had grown up as a pro-Nicene Christian, and so declared Nicea's creed to be the religion of the empire soon after he came to power. It is probably not appropriate to view this as originating from his personal faith stance alone but rather also from the consciousness that this gave the empire a uniform creed in accord with Rome's position. On August 3, 379, he ordered that the Nicene creed alone was permitted, and on February 27, 380, he issued an appeal to the entire empire to profess the Christian faith as taught in Rome and Alexandria. When the emperor entered Constantinople, the basic religiopolitical decisions had already been made. He immediately replaced Demophilus, the Arian patriarch, with Gregory of Nazianzus, and when the latter failed to prove up to the task, he was replaced with Nectarius, a senator, in 381. At the same time, the second ecumenical council, which Theodosius summoned to Constantinople, dealt with the remaining theological issues of neo-Arianism associated with Aëtius and Eunomius, with Apollinarianism, but also with the Pneumatomachians and Macedonians; formulated Nicenism more precisely regarding the divinity of the Holy Spirit; and helped Nicenism to succeed.

By his victory over the usurper Maximus (388), Theodosius was able to unite the entire empire under one rule for one last time, and he drew the religiopolitical conclusion to prohibit the ancient pagan cult in all its forms. Thus the Christianity that subscribed to the Nicene creed became the official religion of the state. This was followed by a thoroughgoing destruction of temples and idols, although this had already proceeded since 384. Even renowned edifices, such as the Serapeum in Alexandria, were not spared, whereby important works of art and cultural treasures were destroyed, much to the regret even of many Christians. Even traditional institutions associated with the cult of the gods ceased, the centuries-old Olympic Games among them. Theodosius's ultimate, empirewide decision for the Christian God was ratified politically with his conquest—which was commonly interpreted as divine approval—of the pagan usurpers Arbogast and Eugenius in the battle at the river Frigidus (Vipacco) on September 6, 394.

Under Valentinian II and Theodosius, the relationship between emperor and church in the West also changed fundamentally, however. Although the sacral idea of the emperor and his competence in ecclesiastical matters were not questioned, purely faith-related decisions began to be considered as outside his power. Although bishops had previously resisted imperial decisions and persisted unflinchingly in their conviction of faith, the emperor had never consented to them. Ambrose was the first to succeed in this against Valentinian II in Milan and later even against Theodosius, who, in 390, was required to submit to public penance after a massacre in Thessalonica. Thus in the West the course was already set for a church emancipating itself from the emperor, indeed a church that itself assumed his tasks. The political evolution beginning with the death of Theodosius (395) until the end of the Western Roman Empire promoted this process even further.

*Literature:* W. Ensslin, *Die Religionspolitik des Kaisers Theodosius d. Gr.* (SBAW.PH 1953.2; Munich: Verlag der Bayerischen Akademie der Wissenschaften, in Kommission bei der C. H. Beck'schen Verlagsbuchhandlung, 1953). – N. Q. King, *The Emperor Theodosius and the Establishment of Christianity* (LHD; London: SCM, 1961). – A. Lippold, *Theodosius der Grosse und seine Zeit* (2d ed.; Beck'sche schwarze Reihe 209; Munich: Beck, 1980). – A. Lippold, "Theodosius der Grosse," *GK* 2: 75–86. – M. G. Mara, "The Great," *EECh* 2:828 f. – S. Williams and G. Friell, *Theodosius: The Empire at Bay* (London: Batsford, 1994; repr., New Haven, Conn.: Yale University Press, 1995). – T. E. Gregory, "Theodosius I (346/7–395)," *EEC* 2:1119 f.

# II. CHURCH HISTORY

The ecclesiastical relationships of the fourth century are best presented through the four ancient ecclesiastical patriarchates and the numerous synods, which were frequently held several times a year. However much the emperors determined ecclesiastical politics, they never did this by exercising absolute power but always presupposed legitimation by an assembly of bishops or brought it about by summoning synods, presiding over them, and directing their decisions. The four patriarchates, ordered by rank, were Rome, Constantinople, Alexandria, and Antioch; they were partly the sources and centers of controversies and partly, as the seats of the ecclesiastical or secular leader, the necessary points of crystallization. In this respect, Rome played a relatively minor part because the disputes of the fourth century originated—and in the main were dealt with—in the East, although they also spread to the Western church.

*Literature:* J. R. Palanque et al., *The Church in the Christian Roman Empire* (trans. E. C. Messenger; 2 vols.; London: Oates & Washbourne, 1949–1952). – H. G. Beck, *Kirche und theologische Literatur im Byzantinischen Reich* (HAW 12.2.1; Munich: Beck, 1959). – R. Lorenz, *Das vierte bis sechste Jahrhundert (Westen)* (*KIG* 1.C.1; Göttingen: Vandenhoeck & Ruprecht, 1970). – K. F. Morrison, ed., *The Church in the Roman Empire* (University of Chicago Readings in Western Civilization 3; Chicago: University of Chicago Press, 1986). – R. Lorenz, *Das vierte Jahrhundert (Der Osten)* (*KIG* 1.C.2; Göttingen: Vandenhoeck & Ruprecht, 1992). – E. Contreras and R. Peña, *El contexto histórico eclesial de los Padres latinos: Siglos IV–V* (Luján, Argentina: ECUAM, 1993). – J. Ulrich, *Die Anfänge der abendländischen Rezeption des Nizänums* (PTS 39; Berlin and New York: de Gruyter, 1994).

# A. Patriarchates

## 1. Alexandria

In Alexandria the beginnings of the fourth-century controversies antedate the Constantinian shift. The local Meletian schism, which preceded Arianism but did not play an insignificant role in the latter, arose from theological and practical pastoral differences between Peter, the patriarch of Alexandria (300–311), and Meletius, the bishop of Lycopolis in Upper Egypt. Although Peter himself eluded persecution by fleeing and approved of this conduct in the case of other bishops as well, Meletius regarded these bishoprics as vacant. He therefore assumed the authority to fill them with candidates that suited him, as a result of which Peter excommunicated him and his followers.

About 318 Arius, perhaps not without help from the Meletian party, triggered the Arian controversy, named after him. With the support of Athanasius, his deacon at the time and later episcopal successor, Alexander asserted his position both in Alexandria and at the Council of Nicea; Arius was condemned and excommunicated, first by a synod in Alexandria and then in Antioch (324/325), as well as in Nicea (325).

Athanasius (328–373) formed the head of the anti-Arian, Nicene resistance for four decades, as a result of which he had to leave his diocese no less than five times and four Arian anti-bishops were appointed in succession in his place. After his final return in 366, the leadership of the Nicene resistance, from 370 on, went over to Basil of Caesarea and the Cappadocians. The successor of Athanasius, Peter II of Alexandria (378–380), was also exiled under Valens; the patriarchs of Alexandria subsequently only came to prominence again, however, in the dispute about John Chrysostom (407) and in the dogmatic disputes concerning Nestorius and Eutyches, which led to the councils of Ephesus (431) and Chalcedon (451).

*Encyclopedia Articles:* C. D. G. Müller, "Ägypten IV," *TRE* 1:512–33. – C. Kannengiesser, "Alexander of Alexandria," *EECh* 1:20. – T. Orlandi, M. Simonetti, and M. Falla Castelfranchi, "Alexandria," *EECh* 1:22–25. – M. Naldini, "Egypt I: Origins of Christianity," *EECh* 1:264. – M. Simonetti, "Melitius of Lycopolis, Melitian Schism," *EECh* 1:551. – M. Simonetti, "Peter I of Alexandria," *EECh* 2:677 f. – M. Simonetti, "Peter II of Alexandria," *EECh* 2:678. – E. Ferguson, "Alexander of Alexandria," *EEC* 1:30. – F. W. Norris, "Alexandria," *EEC* 1:30–34. – J. E. Goehring, "Egypt," *EEC* 1:363–66. – M. P. McHugh, "Melitus of Lycopolis," *EEC* 2:745. – E. Ferguson, "Peter of Alexandria," *EEC* 2:907. – C. Haas, "Alexandria," in *LA*, 285–87.

*Studies:* W. Telfer, "Melitius of Lycopolis and Episcopal Succession in Egypt," *HTR* 48 (1955): 227–37. – E. Schwartz, "Die Quellen über den melitianischen Streit," in *Zur Geschichte des Athanasius* (His Gesammelte Schriften 3; Berlin: de Gruyter, 1959), 87–116. – A. Martin, "Athanase et les mélitiens (325–335)," in *Politique et théologie chez Athanase d'Alexandrie: Actes du colloque de Chantilly, 23–25 septembre 1973* (ed. C. Kannengiesser; ThH 27; Paris: Beauchesne, 1974), 31–61. – R. Williams, "Arius and the Melitian Schism," *JTS* NS 37 (1986): 35–52. – T. Vivian, *St. Peter of Alexandria: Bishop and Martyr* (Studies in Antiquity and Christianity; Philadelphia: Fortress, 1988). – A. Martin, "Les relations entre Arius et Melitios dans la tradition alexandrine: Une histoire polémique," *JTS* NS 40 (1989): 401–13. – C. W. Griggs, *Early Egyptian Christianity from Its Origins to 451 C.E.* (CoptSt 2; Leiden and New York: Brill, 1990). – C. Haas, *Alexandria in Late Antiquity: Topography and Social Conflict* (Ancient Society and History; Baltimore: Johns Hopkins University Press, 1997).

# 2. Antioch

### a. From Eustathius (324–ca. 327) to Eudoxius (359)

From the start, the second focal point of the fourth-century disputes was almost inevitably situated at Antioch, the other ancient patriarchate of the East. By 268 the ὁμοούσιος concept—later taken up again at Nicea—had, in fact, been condemned in Antioch in connection with the case of Paul of Samosata. Arius turned here for support after his condemnation in Alexandria, but instead he was convicted by a synod, led by Ossius of Córdoba (324/325), which appointed Eustathius to fill the vacant see of the city; the latter was to play a prominent role at the Council of Nicea (325). When the anti-Nicene reaction set in, Eustathius was deposed by a synod meeting in Antioch itself and led by Eusebius of Caesarea (328 or 329). Until recently it had been assumed that he was charged with disciplinary misdemeanors (immorality, abuse of power); according to Hanson's investigation, however, the reason seems to have been Sabellianism. In any case, the real reason was that he, like Athanasius and Marcellus, was a rigorous defender of Nicea and therefore stood in the way of Constantine's politics of unity and compromise.

All of his successors were supporters of the Eusebian party, and several times Antioch was the arena of decisive synods that in theology consistently maintained the Eusebian *via media*. In 344 the synod deposed Stephen, bishop of Antioch, for obstructing Roman legates; he was followed by Leontius (344–358), who inclined toward radical Arianism and ordained Aëtius, the founder of neo-Arianism, to the diaconate. Eudoxius, his successor, who had previously been bishop of Germanicia in Syria, also followed wholly the anomoean course of his predecessor and so favored Aëtius and Eunomius, his student, with his radical assertion that the Son is dissimilar to the Father in every way, that in fact he was not even truly generated by the Father. This radical Arian line of thought ran counter to Constantius's Homoean policy of compromise, so Eudoxius was deposed by the synod he summoned to Antioch in 358. Nevertheless he was successful in regaining the emperor's favor by falling in line with the emperor and Acacius of Caesarea at the synods of Seleucia (359) and Constantinople (360). He even succeeded in being transferred to the bishopric of the capital, which had been vacated when Macedonius was deposed; despite numerous hostilities after the death of Constantius, he held on to it, with the favor of Valens, until his death (370).

*Encyclopedia Articles:* B. Drewery, "Antiochia II," *TRE* 3:103–13. – R. Lorenz, "Eustathius von Antiochien," *TRE* 10:543–46. – O. Pasquato and M. Simonetti, "Antioch," *EECh* 1:47–51. – M. Simonetti, "Eudoxius," *EECh* 1:295 f. – M. Simonetti, "Eustathius of Antioch," *EECh* 1:303. – F. W. Norris, "Antioch," *EEC* 1:66–70. – R. A. Greer, "Eustathius of Antioch," *EEC* 1:403. – P. L. Galtier, "Antioch," in *LA*, 303–4.

*Studies:* P. Krause, "Eustathius von Antiochien," (diss., Universität Breslau, 1921). – E. Burn, *S. Eustathius of Antioch* (London: Faith, 1926). – R. V. Sellers, *Eustathius of Antioch and His Place in the Early History of Christian Doctrine* (Cambridge: University Press, 1928). – E. Schwartz, "Zur Kirchengeschichte des vierten Jahrhunderts," *ZNW* 34 (1935): 129–213; repr. in *Zur Geschichte der alten Kirche und ihres Rechts* (His Gesammelte Schriften 4; Berlin: de Gruyter, 1960), 1–110. – R. Devreesse, *Le patriarcat d'Antioche, depuis la paix de l'Église jusqu'a la conquête arabe* (Études palestiniennes et orientales; Paris: Gabalda, 1945). – M. Spanneut, *Recherches sur les écrits d'Eustathe d'Antioche: Avec une édition nouvelle des fragments dogmatiques et exégétiques* (MFCL 65; Lille: Facultés Catholiques, 1948). – G. Downey, *A History of Antioch in Syria from Seleucus to the Arab Conquest* (Princeton, N.J.: Princeton University Press, 1961). – D. S. Wallace-Hadrill, *Christian Antioch: A Study of Early Christian Thought in the East* (Cambridge and New York: Cambridge University Press, 1982). – R. P. C. Hanson, "The Fate of Eustathius in Antioch," *ZKG* 95 (1984): 1171–79.

### b. Meletian Schism

During the final forty years of the fourth century, Antioch remained divided in the so-called Meletian schism, which saw not only a Catholic and an Arian bishop in Antioch but, alongside the Arian community, two Nicene communities competing with one another. It is difficult to disentangle the beginnings of the schism, especially theologically. Acacius, who in 340 succeeded Eusebius as bishop of Caesarea and continued the Homoean policy, which the latter shared with the emperor, presented Meletius, a like-minded individual (360), as successor of Eudoxius to the see of Antioch. Shortly afterward, in a sermon preached in the presence of Constantius, Meletius turned out to be anti-Arian and a Homoi-ousian. For this reason, a synod deposed him at Antioch in 360/361, and in his place it appointed Euzoius, the old companion of Arius, who had joined the emperor's Homoean party. Since Constantius died in 361, Meletius returned to Antioch (362), in order to reorganize his community. During the same year, however, Lucifer of Calaris consecrated Paulinus, the head of the Nicene party in Antioch since 350, as bishop; this meant that there were now three bishops in Antioch: Euzoius, the Homoean; Meletius, the anti-Arian (Homoiousian); and Paulinus, the Nicene rigorist. Meletius, however, moved closer and closer to the Nicene creed. A synod made up of Homoean and Homoiousian bishops, which he summoned to Antioch in 363 and which he led, accepted the Nicene ὁμοούσιος, though interpreted in a Homoiousian way, like the synod of Paris in 360/361, influenced by Hilary. As a result, most of the anti-Arian bishops acknowledged Meletius, Basil the Great among them, and charged Paulinus with Sabellianism. But Egypt, under Athanasius, and the West, under the leadership of Felix II, bishop of Rome, acknowledged Paulinus exclusively as the city's legitimate Catholic bishop. In their famous *Tomus ad Antiochenos,* Athanasius and the Alexandrian synod challenged Antioch in 362 to unite with the church of Paulinus.

Under the Arian policy of Valens, Meletius was exiled twice (365 and 369) but was able to return shortly before the former died (378). A synod of ca. 150 bishops meeting in Antioch (379) recognized him as the leader of the Eastern episcopate after his prestige had grown further from his proving of himself in exile; a simultaneous attempt at a settlement with Paulinus came to naught. Since Basil the Great had died on January 1, 379, Meletius continued to act as the head of the Nicene episcopate of the East and in 381 presided over the Council of Constantinople, in the course of which he passed away.

Although Euzoius, the Arian bishop of Antioch, died in 375 and Dorotheus, his successor, had to resign in 381 because of the anti-Arian laws of Emperor Theodosius, Paulinus failed to be recognized as the only legitimate bishop of Antioch despite massive Western support. Meletius was succeeded by Flavian (381–404), the teacher of John Chrysostom. Evagrius (383–ca. 394) succeeded Paulinus, who ordained him on his deathbed (d. 383). It was not until after Evagrius's death that his community united with Flavian's and thus ended the schism.

Studies: F. Cavallera, *Le schisme d'Antioche (iv–v siècle)* (Paris: Picard, 1905). – M. Simon-etti, "Acacius of Caesarea," *EECh* 1:5. – M. Simonetti, "Euzoius of Antioch," *EECh* 1:305. – M. Simonetti, "Meletius of Antioch," *EECh* 1:530. – M. Simonetti, "Paulinus of Antioch," *EECh* 2:660. – F. W. Norris, "Acacius of Caesarea," *EEC* 1:9. – M. P. McHugh, "Meletius of Antioch," *EEC* 2:745.

## 3. Constantinople

The episcopal see of the capital city, understandably, reflected the imperial politics of the fourth century most faithfully, so that from the death of Constantine (337) until Theodosius came to power in 379, the bishops in charge were almost exclusively Arian. Alexander, the first bishop of Constantinople (established in 330), who radically followed the faith of Nicea and, like Athanasius, adamantly resisted a reconciliation with Arius in 335 without being forced into exile, died shortly after Constantine in 337. He was succeeded by Paul, who was exiled in 339 and replaced by an Arian, Eusebius of Nicomedia.

By this time, Eusebius could already look back over a long history in Arianism. He had been a student of Lucian of Antioch, whom Arius identified as his teacher as well (hence the group of Lucian's Arian students called itself or was given the name *Sylluciani*). Initially the bishop of Berytus (modern Beirut), he was called to the imperial residence of Licinius in Nicomedia just before 318, from where he supported Arius and in his letters disputed with Alexander of Alexandria. Although he had held a synod in Bithynia in favor of Arius in 324 and later acted as spokesman for the Arians as well, in Nicea in 325 he signed both the creed and the condemnation of Arius, which may well be regarded as a purely ecclesiastical-political calculation. Although he was exiled all the same after the council, he led the Arian reaction beginning with the follow-up synod of Nicea in 327 and achieved the removal of Eustathius from Antioch in 329, of Athanasius in 335, and of Marcellus of Ancyra in 336. Thus he drove out the leading bishops of the *fides nicaena;* his attempts at ousting Alexander, the elderly bishop, from Constantinople, however, in order to claim the bishopric of the capital for himself, failed. Only under Paul, the latter's successor (339), did he achieve his goal, after Constantius II unequivocally sided with the Arians and did not merely pursue a political compromise between Nicenes and Arians, as did Constantine. On his deathbed Constantine was baptized by Eusebius of Nicomedia, whose star rose so high from 339 on because Eusebius of Caesarea, the great confidante and counselor of Constantine, died during the same period (339/340). He resisted all endeavors by Julius of Rome to summon an ecumenical synod; only after his death in 341 was Constans able to issue the invitation to gather in Serdica (Sofia) (343). Eusebius of Nicomedia's action having the farthest-reaching impact on the future of the church was the consecration of Ulfilas, a Goth, as bishop (341) shortly before Eusebius died, as a result of which the Goths accepted the Arian-Christian confession.

In the following years and depending on the political situation, Paul and Macedonius, the Homoiousian, took turns occupying the episcopal see of Constantinople. The latter pushed the question of the divinity of the Holy Spirit, which he and his followers (the Macedonians) rejected (Pneumatomachians) and which was to play a significant role among the Cappadocians and at the Council of Constantinople in 381. Eudoxius, who transferred from the bishopric of Antioch and now pursued a moderate Homoiousian line, ruled from 360 to 370. Demophilus ruled from 370 to 380. He was unable to accept the final decision in favor of the Nicene creed under Theodosius (380) and thus lost his diocese. Theodosius appointed Gregory of Nazianzus to be his successor, but Gregory soon resigned during the Council of Constantinople in 381 because he did not feel up to the task as bishop of the capital city. The emperor then chose a senator by the name of Nectarius, who was only a catechumen at the time. The council concurred, and the choice proved to be a very good one. He ruled without further problems until he died in 397. He was followed by John Chrysostom (398–407).

*Encyclopedia Articles:* J. Meyendorff, "Byzanz," *TRE* 7:500–531. – G. Schmalzbauer, "Konstantinopel," *TRE* 19:503–18. – C. Kannengiesser, "Alexander of Constantinople," *EECh* 1:21. – I. Dujcev, M. Simonetti, and C. Kannengiesser, "Constantinople (Istanbul)," *EECh* 1:194–98. – C. Kannengiesser, "Eusebius of Nicomedia," *EECh* 1:301 f. – M. Simonetti, "Macedonians," *EECh* 1:516. – D. Stiernon, "Nectarius," *EECh* 2:584. – M. Simonetti, "Paul of Constantinople," *EECh* 2:662 f. – F. W. Norris, "Constantinople," *EEC* 1:281–85. – G. J. Johnson, "Eusebius of Nicomedia," *EEC* 1:402. f. – F. W. Norris, "Nectarius," *EEC* 2:799 f. – A. Ricci, "Constantinople," *LA* 1999, 391–92.

*Studies:* A Lichtenstein, *Eusebius von Nikomedien: Versuch einer Darstellung seiner Persönlichkeit und seines Lebens unter besonderer Berücksichtigung seiner Führerschaft im arianischen Streit* (Halle: Niemeyer, 1903). – F. Winckelmann, "Die Bischöfe Metrophanes und Alexander von Byzanz," *ByZ* 59 (1966): 47–71. – G. Dagron, *Naissance d'une capitale: Constantinople et ses institutions de 330 à 451* (BByz.E 7; Paris: Presses Universitaires de France, 1974). – C. Luibhéid, "The Arianism of Eusebius of Nicomedia," *ITQ* 43 (1976): 2–23.

# 4. Rome

By rank, the Roman bishopric was the first patriarchate of the Roman Empire. It had only a minor part in the fourth-century controversies because, first, the origin and center of the dogmatic disputes were located in the East and, second, all of the Roman bishops adhered to the Nicene creed, as did most of the West and its emperors in general.

Bishop Silvester (314–335) sent two presbyters to the Council of Nicea (325) and may also have appointed Ossius of Córdoba to represent his interests; beyond this, however, he did not participate in the Arian dispute. Only Julius (337–352), his second successor, actively intervened against the Eusebians by siding with Athanasius. A synod in Rome (341) rehabilitated Athanasius and Marcellus of Ancyra and prompted Constans to summon the Council of Serdica (343). Liberius (352–366) happened to rule during the reign of Constantius II, the Homoean emperor. Because he was unwilling to submit to the emperor's wishes, the latter exiled him to Thrace in 355 and thus broke his resistance. At the instigation of Constantius, Felix, a Roman archdeacon, consented to becoming the Arian antipope. In 358 Liberius was allowed to return first to Sirmium, then to Rome, and although he probably did not sign the "second Sirmian formula" of 357, Athanasius and Hilary accused him of softness, since he at least no longer mustered active resistance. At the double synod of Ariminum and Seleucia (359), in which the emperor forced unity, Rome was completely ignored; legates had not even been invited. After the death of Constantius, Liberius affirmed his Nicene position in a letter to the bishops of Italy (362/363). His name survives mainly as the builder of the Basilica Liberiana, the famous Basilica of Santa Maria Maggiore in Rome, which, according to legend, he constructed because of a miracle of snow in midsummer (feast of the dedication of the Basilica of Saint Mary Major, August 5).

Under the Catholic emperors Valentinian I and Theodosius, Pope Damasus (366–384) completed the Nicene restoration of the West when, together with

Ambrose of Milan, he regained the Homoiousian episcopate of northern Italy and Illyricum. A synod in Rome (370) confirmed the condemnation of Auxentius of Milan; a further synod in 377 rejected the Apollinarians and Pneumato-machians through the efforts of Basil the Great. A synod that Ambrose summoned to Aquileia (378) put in order the ecclesiastical affairs of northern Italy. Despite all the efforts of Basil, Damasus did not enter into ecclesiastical communion with Meletius but recognized Paulinus alone as the legitimate bishop of Antioch. For church history and patrology, Damasus is further significant as the promoter of the cult of the saints in Rome, as the one who opened the catacombs, and because of his commissioning of Jerome, his temporary secretary (?), to prepare a new Latin translation of the Bible (Vulgate).

*Editions:* T. Mommsen, *Libri pontificalis pars prior* (vol. 1 of *Gestorum pontificum romanorum;* MGH.GPR 1; Berlin: Weidmann, 1898). – L. Duchesne, *Le Liber pontificalis: Texte, introduction, et commentaire* (3 vols.; BEFAR 2d ser. 3; Paris: Thorin, 1886–1957). – K. Aland and C. Mirbt, *Quellen zur Geschichte des Papsttums und des römischen Katholizismus* (6th ed.; Tübingen: Mohr, 1967–).

*Translation:* R. Davis, trans., *The Book of Pontiffs (Liber pontificalis): The Ancient Biographies of the First Ninety Bishops to AD 715* (Translated Texts for Historians: Latin Series 5; Liverpool: Liverpool University Press, 1989).

*Encyclopedia Articles:* C. Pietri, "Damascus," *EECh* 1:218 f. – B. Studer, "Julius I," *EECh* 1:460. – B. Studer, "Liberius," *EECh* 1:485. – B. Studer and M. Spinelli, "Papacy," *EECh* 2:640–46. – C. Pietri, U. Dionisi, and P. Rouillard, "Rome," *EECh* 2:740–45. – M. P. McHugh, "Damascus," *EEC* 1:316 f. – E. Ferguson, "Julius I," *EEC* 1:644. – M. P. McHugh, "Liberius," *EEC* 2:680. – R. B. Eno, "Papacy," *EEC* 2:860–66. – R. W. Mathisen, "Rome," *EEC* 2:997–1002. – D. Kinney, "Rome," *LA,* 673 f. – T. Noble, "Papacy," *LA,* 633–35.

*Studies: Archivum historiae pontificiae [AHP].* – E. Caspar, *Geschichte des Papsttums von den Anfängen bis zur Höhe der Weltherrschaft* (Tübingen: Mohr, 1930–1933), 103–295. – M. A. Norton, "Prosopography of Pope Damasus," in *Leaders of Iberian Christianity, 50–650 A.D.* (ed. J. M. F. Marique; Boston: St. Paul, 1962), 13–80 = *Folia* 4 (1950): 13–51; 5 (1951): 30–55; 6 (1952): 16–39. – J. Taylor, "St. Basil the Great and Pope St. Damasus I," *DR* 91 (1973): 186–203, 262–74. – A. C. Piepkorn, "The Roman Primacy in the Patristic Era II: From Nicea to Leo the Great," in *Papal Primacy and the Universal Church* (ed. P. Empie and A. Murphy; Lutherans and Catholics in Dialogue 5; Minneapolis: Augsburg, 1974), 73–97. – W. Gessel, "Das primatiale Bewusstsein Julius' I: Im Lichte der Interaktionen zwischen der Cathedra Petri und den zeitgenössischen Synoden," in *Konzil und Papst: Historische Beiträge zur Frage der höchsten Gewalt in der Kirche (Festgabe für Hermann Tüchle)* (Munich, Paderborn, and Vienna: Schöningh, 1975). – C. Pietri, *Roma christiana: Recherches sur l'église de Rome, son organisation, sa politique, son idéologie de Miltiade à Sixte III (311–440)* (BEFAR 224; Rome: École Française de Rome, 1976–). – M. Wojtowytsch, *Papsttum und Konzile von den Anfängen bis zu Leo I. (440–461): Studien zur Entstehung der Überordnung des Papstes über Konzile* (PuP 17; Stuttgart: Hiersemann, 1981). – J. N. D. Kelly, *The Oxford Dictionary of Popes* (Oxford and New York: Oxford University Press, 1986). – R. B. Eno, *The Rise of the Papacy* (Theology and Life 32; Wilmington, Del.: Glazier, 1990). – E. Duffy, *Saints and Sinners: A History of the Popes* (New Haven, Conn.: Yale University Press in association with S4C, 1997). – R. Curran, *Pagan City and Christian Capital: Rome in the Fourth Century* (Oxford Classical Monographs; Oxford: Clarendon; New York: Oxford University Press, 2000).

## The Bishops of the Four Patriarchates of the Fourth Century

| Rome | |
| --- | --- |
| *Nicenes* | *Arians* |
| Silvester (314–335) Marcus (336) Julius (337–352) Liberius (352–366; 355–358, exiled) Damasus (366–384) | Felix II (355–358, d. 365) |

| Constantinople[1] | |
| --- | --- |
| *Nicenes* | *Arians* |
| Alexander (330–337) Paul (337–339, deposed)<br><br>Paul (341–342, deposed)<br><br>Paul (346–352, deposed)<br><br><br>Evagrius (370) Gregory of Nazianzus (379–381, resigned) Nectarius (381–397) John Chrysostom (398–404, deposed) | Eusebius of Nicomedia (339–341)<br><br>Macedonius (342–346, deposed)<br><br>Macedonius (351–360) Eudoxius of Antioch (360–370) Demophilus (370–380, deposed) |

| Alexandria | |
| --- | --- |
| Peter (300–311) | |
| *Nicenes* | *Arians* |
| Alexander (until 328) Athanasius (328–373) (exiled 335–337, 339–346, 356–362, 362/363, 365/366) | Pistos (336 or 338) Gregory (339–344 or 348) George (357–358, 361, murdered) Lukios (365) |

| Antioch | |
| --- | --- |
| *Nicenes* | *Eusebians (Homoiousians)* |
| Eustathius (324/325–328/329, deposed) | Stephen (until 344) Leontius (344–358) Eudoxius (358–360, transferred to Constantinople) Meletius (360–381) |

---

[1] The question whether the council met in 342 or 343 is still without a unanimously accepted response.

**The Bishops of the Four Patriarchates of the Fourth Century (continued)**

| The Meletian Schism | | |
|---|---|---|
| | | *Homoeans* |
| Paulinus (362–383) | Meletius (360–381, 360/361–362, deposed; from 363, Homoousian) | Euzoius (360/361–375) Dorotheus (375–381, deposed) |
| Evagrius (383–ca. 394) | Flavian (381–404) | |

# B. Synods

The primary ecclesiastical-political and theological developments took place in the numerous fourth-century synods. On the basis of their historical significance, they can be divided into two groups, namely, those making the important theological decisions and those confirming these decisions, executing them, and extrapolating the disciplinary consequences, such as appointing and removing bishops.

The two great cornerstones of this development were the first two "ecumenical" councils of Nicea (325) and Constantinople (381). The former countered Arius with the ὁμοούσιος and thereby set in motion the battle for its acceptance, which lasted more than half a century. The latter, under the leadership of Theodosius, conclusively established the Nicene creed as binding on all but also dealt with resultant problems: the "Young Arians" around Eunomius; the Pneumatomachians, who did not accept the divinity of the Holy Spirit (this issue, until Basil the Great, had not been articulated as a central theme by either side of the Arian dispute because initially it concerned only the relationship of the Father and the Son, but it followed inevitably as a result); and, with Apollinaris of Laodicea, the christological issue of the completeness of the two natures of Christ.

The following are the synods that made substantial dogmatic decisions between these two councils:

- Antioch, 341
- Serdica, 343
- Sirmium, 351 and 357
- Ancyra, 358
- Ariminum and Seleucia, 359
- Alexandria, 362

The twenty-one other synods, which were by no means insignificant in ecclesiastical-political terms, took place several times a year in the most diverse cities of the empire. They were geared more to the practical implementation of the political and theological decisions, and between 323 and 360/361, like a string of pearls, they mark the ecclesiastical path between the great "ecumenical" councils of Nicea (325) and Constantinople (381):

- Alexandria, 323

- Antioch, 324/325

- Nicea, 327 (?)

- Antioch, ca. 327

- Tyre, 335

- Jerusalem, 335

- Rome, 341

- Antioch, 344

- Milan, 345

- Sirmium, 347

- Antioch, 352

- Egypt, 352

- Rome, 353

- Arles, 353

- Milan, 355

- Béziers, 356

- Antioch, 358

- Gaul, 358

- Constantinople, 360

- Paris, 360/361

- Antioch, 360/361

*Bibliographies: Annuarium historiae conciliorum* (Amsterdam, etc., 1969–) *[AHC]*.

*Editions:* Mansi 2:1081–1379; 3:1–520. – C. Munier, *Concilia Galliae: A. 314–A. 506* (CCL 148; Turnhout, Belg.: Brepols, 1963). – *Conciles gaulois du IVe siècle* (ed. J. Gaudmet; trans. C. Munier; SC 241; Paris: Cerf, 1977).

*Translations:* J. Stevenson, *Creeds, Councils, and Controversies: Documents Illustrating the History of the Church, AD 377–461* (rev. ed with additional documents; ed. W. H. C. Frend; London: SPCK, 1989), 5–51 [Selections].

*Literature:* C. J. Hefele and H. Leclercq, *Histoire des conciles: D'après les documents originaux* (Paris: Letouzey & Ané, 1907), vols. 1/1–2/1. – G. Roethe, *Geistige Grundlagen römischer Kirchenpolitik* (vol. 2 of *Zur Geschichte der römischen Synoden im 3. und 4. Jahrhundert;* FKGG 11.2; Stuttgart: Kohlhammer, 1937). – P. Palazzini, ed.,

*Dizionario dei concili* (6 vols.; Rome: Città Nuova, 1963–1968). – L. D. Davis, *The First Seven Ecumenical Councils (325–787)* (Theology and Life 21; Wilmington, Del.: Glazier, 1983; repr., Collegeville, Minn.: Liturgical, 1990). – L. Perrone, in *Storia dei concili ecumenici* (ed. G. Albergio et al.; Brescia: Queriniana, 1990), 45–56. – C. Munier, "Council," *EECh* 1:205.

# 1. To the Synod of Antioch (341)

The synod of Antioch in 268 was a prelude to the theological problems of the fourth century, although it was not directly involved with them. It condemned Paul of Samosata, the bishop of Antioch at the time, because of, among other things, his Monarchian doctrine of the Trinity, which did not sufficiently uphold the Son's distinction from the Father. Hilary (*De synodis* 81) reports that Paul used the term ὁμοούσιος in this context and for this reason the synod rejected it as well.[2] At Nicea, and subsequently, the danger of the term ὁμοούσιος was indeed seen in the possibility of interpreting it in the sense of Monarchianism or Sabellianism. The Nicenes were frequently accused of this, and it rendered the word unacceptable to its opponents.

The Arian controversy began in Alexandria, with the synod that excommunicated Arius (323), and with the synod of Antioch (324/325), which confirmed the verdict and continued to apply it. No new, original theology was developed at either of the two synods; they merely rejected the theology of Arius and confirmed the traditional baptismal faith. The same also applies to the synods following the Council of Nicea (325), though under different circumstances. Whether there ever was a second synod convening in Nicea (327), which in some way rehabilitated Arius, is still not resolved beyond doubt today. In any case, the synod of Antioch (328 or 329), under the leadership of Eusebius of Caesarea, did rehabilitate him and deposed Eustathius from Antioch and Asclepas from Gaza. On the instigation of the two Eusebiuses of Caesarea and Nicomedia, the synod of Tyre (335), under the leadership of Flacillus of Antioch, the new Eusebian bishop, deposed Athanasius. At the synod of Jerusalem (September 17, 335), meeting just a few days later, Arius was reconciled in the presence of Constantine and the two Eusebiuses after he presented them with an acceptable confession of faith, and the synod asked the churches of Alexandria and Egypt to end the division.

Theological progress was not attained until the "dedication synod" in Antioch, on the occasion of the dedication of a large church in Antioch on January 6, 341. Under the leadership of Flacillus of Antioch, ninety-seven Eusebian bishops met, passing three formulas, the second of which (later called the "second Antiochene formula" for short) was to have sustained theological influence. In the endeavor to find an acceptable middle ground between radical Arianism and the equally rigid insistence upon the Nicene creed, it condemned anomoeanism

---

[2] Following Grumel, 434f. and Demandt, 498 (cf. I, "Political History"). Otherwise A. Hohlweg in Beck, 803f. (cf. general bibliography, C).

but ignored the ὁμοούσιος position. In doing so, it stressed the Son's deity, though in slight subordination to the Father, and propagated Origen's doctrine of the three hypostases in God; at a later point, through the synod of Alexandria in 362, this was to become the definitive, orthodox formula for the Cappadocians.

When the West put Constans under pressure to summon a general council, the East proposed a modified version of the second Antiochene formula, the so-called fourth Antiochene formula. Its origin is unknown; nevertheless, in continuity with the second formula, it was to become a further theological premise of the dialogue between East and West. The formulation of its anti-Arian passages follows the Nicene version closely, and offensive Origenisms are eliminated, especially the doctrine of the three hypostases. But the ὁμοούσιος concept continues to be conspicuous by its absence.

The Roman synod, meeting a little later the same year, initially not under the leadership of Julius[3] of Rome, as assumed until recently, rehabilitated Athanasius and Marcellus, who were in attendance. The Eastern bishops declined to participate.

*Editions:* Mansi 2:1081–1368.

*Studies:* C. J. Hefele and H. Leclercq, *Histoire des conciles: d'Après les documents originaux* (Paris: Letouzey & Ané, 1907), 1/2:633–736.

*Paul of Samosata:*
*Bibliography:* L. Perrone, "L'enigma di Paolo di Smosata—dogma, Chiesa, e società nella Siria del III secolo: Prospettive di un ventennio di studi," *CrSt* 13 (1992): 253–327.
*Studies:* F. Loofs, *Paulus von Samosata: Eine Untersuchung zur altkirchlichen Literatur- und Dogmengeschichte* (TU 44.5; Leipzig: Hinrichs, 1924). – G. Bardy, *Paul de Samosate: Étude historique* (SSL 4; Louvain: "Spicilegium Sacrum Lovaniense," Bureaux; Paris: Champion, 1929). – H. de Riedmatten, *Les Actes du process de Paul de Samosate: Étude sur la christologie du IIe au IVe siècle* (Par. 6; Fribourg, Switz.: St-Paul, 1952). – H. C. Brennecke, "Zum Prozess gegen Paul von Samosata: Die Frage nach der Veruteilung des Homoousios," *ZNW* 75 (1984): 270–90. – F. W. Norris, "Paul of Samosata: *Procurator ducenarius,*" *JTS* NS 35 (1984): 50–70. – J. A. Fischer, "Die antiochenischen Synoden gegen Paul von Samosata," *AHC* 18 (1986): 9–30; repr. in *Die Synoden von den Anfängen bis zum Vorabend des Nicaenums* (Konziliengeschichte: Reihe A, Darstellungen; Paderborn: Schöningh, 1997), 351–78. – M. Simonetti, "Paul of Samosata," *EECh* 2:663. – F. W. Norris, "Paul of Samosata (Third Century)," *EEC* 2:885.

*Nicea, 327:* R. Lorenz, "Das Problem der Nachsynode von Nicäa (327)," *ZKG* 90 (1979): 22–40. – C. Luibhéid, "The Alleged Second Session of the Council of Nicaea," *JEH* 34 (1983): 165–74. – C. Kannengiesser, "Nicaea," *EECh* 2:594 f.

*Tyre, 335:* M. Simonetti, "Tyre," *EECh* 2:854 f.

*Antioch 341:* M. Tetz, "Die Kirchweihsynode von Antiochien (341) und Marcellus von Ancyra: Zu den Glaubenserklärung des Theophronius von Tyana und ihren Folgen," in *Oecumenica et patristica: Festschrift für Wilhelm Schneemelcher zum 75. Geburtstag* (ed. D. Papandreou, W. A. Bienert, and K. Schäferdiek; Stuttgart: Kohlhammer, 1989), 199–217.

---

[3] Cf. Brennecke's fundamental critique of this, "Zum Prozess gegen Paul von Samosata: Die Frage nach der Verurteilung des Homoousios," *ZNW* 75 (1984): 270–90.

## 2. Synod of Serdica (343)

When the Eastern party had weakened because of the death of their leader, Eusebius of Nicomedia (341), Constans, urged on by the Western bishops, succeeded in summoning a general synod,[4] which met in Serdica (Sofia), in the Eastern part of the empire. Instead of achieving the unity hoped for, however, this synod actually fostered the breakup between East and West. Apparently the two primary items on the synod's agenda should have been the dogmatic issue of the *fides nicaena* and personnel matters, such as those concerning Athanasius and Marcellus. But since the Western bishops had already restored Athanasius and Marcellus to the church before the arrival of their Eastern counterparts, the joint session never took place. Each of the two rump councils excommunicated the other.

*Editions:* Mansi 3:1–40. – DH 133–35.

*Studies:* C. J. Hefele and H. Leclercq, *Histoire des conciles: D'après les documents originaux* (Paris: Letouzey & Ané, 1907), 1/2:737–823. – H. Hess, *The Canons of the Council of Sardica, A.D. 343: A Landmark in the Early Development of Canon Law* (OTM 1; Oxford: Clarendon, 1958). – L. W. Barnard, "The Council of Serdica: Some Problems Re-assessed," *AHC* 12 (1980): 1–25. – L. W. Barnard, *The Council of Serdica, 343 A.D.* (Sofia: Synodal, 1983). – L. W. Barnard, "The Council of Serdica: Two Questions Reconsidered," in *Ancient Bulgaria: Papers Presented to the International Symposium on the Ancient History and Archaeology of Bulgaria, University of Nottingham, 1981* (ed. A. G. Poulter; University of Nottingham Department of Classical and Archaeological Studies [Archaeology Section] Monograph Series 1; Nottingham: University of Nottingham, Department of Classical and Archaeological Studies, Archaeology Section, 1983), 215–31. – M. Tetz, "*Ante omnia de sancta fide et de integritate veritatis,* Glaubensfragen auf der Synode von Serdika (342)," *ZNW* 76 (1985): 243–69. – T. G. Eliot, "The Date of the Council of Serdica," *AHB* 2 (1988): 65–72. – S. G. Hall, "The Creed of Serdica," *StPatr* 19 (1989): 173–84. – M. Simonetti, "Sardica II: Council," *EECh* 2:756 f.

## 3. From Antioch (344) to Sirmium (351): Photinianism

A synod, meeting in Antioch (344), deposed Stephen of Antioch and probably formulated the *Ekthesis makrostichos*, which was presented to the synod of Milan (345) in the following year. It was composed of the fourth formula of Antioch, the anathema declarations of Serdica, and seven further theological declarations.

The synod that Constans summoned to meet in Milan for the first time concerned itself with a "sideshow" of the controversy, namely, the case of Photinus, bishop of Sirmium. He was a student of Marcellus of Ancyra and was condemned for radical Monarchianism. He may have understood the Logos more

---

[4] Cf. H. C. Brennecke, *Hilarius von Poitiers und die Bischofsopposition gegen Konstantius II* (PTS 26; Berlin and New York: de Gruyter, 1984), 7f., against the widespread assumption of the converse sequence.

in terms of an impersonal force (δύναμις) of the Father, through which the Father works, as in the theophanies of the OT, for instance. According to Hilary (*Fragmenta historica* B 2.9.1), another synod that met in Sirmium (347) confirmed this decision; the same was surely true of the Sirmium synod of 351, at which Constantius was present and Basil of Ancyra was the spokesman and which also deposed and exiled him.

*Editions:* Mansi 3:141–184. – DH 139.

*Studies:* C. J. Hefele and H. Leclercq, *Histoire des conciles: D'après les documents originaux* (Paris: Letouzey & Ané, 1907), 1/2:825–62. – M. Simonetti, "Ekthesis makrostichos," *EECh* 1:268. –A. di Berardino, "Milan," *EECh* 1:559. – M. Simonetti, "Photinus of Sirmium," *EECh* 2:685 f. – M. Simonetti, "Sirmium," *EECh* 2:783. – F. W. Norris, "Photinus," *EEC* 2:919 f.

## 4. From Antioch (352) to Sirmium (357)

All of the following synods concerned themselves with decisions for or against Athanasius without achieving dogmatic progress. Only the synod of Sirmium (357) marks another important break, in terms of both the church policy of Constantius and theological development. The emperor's single-minded attention was aimed at a binding formulation of faith for the entire empire after he, like Constantine, his father, had succeeded in unifying the empire again under one ruler. Under the leadership of the court bishops, Valens, Ursacius, and Germinius, the synod decided on the "second Sirmian formula" (following the first one in 351). It prohibited any speculation about the terms οὐσία/*substantia* and the use of the derived words ὁμοούσιος and ὁμοιούσιος. Only biblically attested statements were to be deemed valid, and the synod interpreted these in terms of the clear distinction between Father and Son and the subordination of the Son to the Father. Nevertheless the Son continues to be God as well. This was the first time that a synod had taken up the ὁμοούσιος concept, which is central to the Faith of Nicea.

*Edition:* Mansi 3:231–66.

*Studies:* C. J. Hefele and H. Leclercq, *Histoire des conciles: D'après les documents originaux* (Paris: Letouzey & Ané, 1907), 1/2:863–902. – É. Griffe, *Des origines chrétiennes à la fin du IVe siècle* (vol. 1 of *La Gaule chrétienne à l'époque romaine;* rev. ed.; Paris: Letouzey & Ané, 1964–). – M. Meslin, *Les ariens d'Occident, 335–430* (PatSor 8; Paris: Seuil, 1967). – M. Simonetti, "Arianesimo latino," *StMed* 3.8 (1967): 663–744. – M. Simonetti, "Germinius of Sirmium," *EECh* 1:350. – M. Simonetti, "Valens of Mursa and Ursacius of Singidunum," *EECh* 2: 858. – D. H. Williams, "Another Exception to the Later Fourth-Century 'Arian' Typologies: The Case of Germinius of Sirmium," *JECS* 4 (1996): 335–58.

## 5. Ancyra (358) and the Double Synod of Ariminum/Seleucia (359)

The synods of Ancyra and Ariminum/Seleucia denote the successful conclusion of the unity efforts of Constantius, who lived until 361. Shortly before

Easter 358, Basil of Ancyra issued an invitation to a synod during the consecration of a church; because of the cold weather at that time of the year, however, only twelve bishops attended. In contrast to the Homoeans and the Nicenes, they were the first to posit a compromise confession. The Son is ὅμοιος κατ᾽ οὐσίαν, that is, "similar in essence" to the Father. Basil succeeded in convincing the emperor of this position, especially because, for the first time since the synod of Antioch in 268, the condemnation of the Nicene ὁμοούσιος was introduced into the argument. As a result, the emperor pushed through the Homoean position politically by deposing and exiling seventy reluctant bishops. He also summoned a double synod to meet in 359 in Ariminum in the West and in Seleucia in the East, that is, two partial councils of the Homoousian bishops of the West and of their Homoiousian counterparts of the East. Neither of the two synods certainly showed any willingness to comply with the emperor's wishes; instead they insisted upon their respective positions. In Nike (Thrace), however, the emperor forced both to subscribe to a neutral, and hence also meaningless, formula of reunion, proposed by his court bishops, according to which the Son is ὅμοιος κατὰ τὰς γραφάς, "similar according to the Scriptures" to the Father. A subsequent synod in Constantinople (360) ratified this decision. Only the synod of Paris of 360/361, which was able to meet under the leadership of Emperor Julian, opposed it and subscribed to the ὁμοούσιος, albeit with a conciliatory meaning that compared it to the concept of *similitudo* (ὁμοιουσία).

*Editions:* Mansi 3:256–336.

*Literature:* C. J. Hefele and H. Leclercq, *Histoire des conciles: D'après les documents originaux* (Paris: Letouzey & Ané, 1907), 1/2:903–62. – Y.-M. Duval, "La 'manœuvre frauduleuse' de Rimini: À la recherché du *Liber adversus Ursacium et Valentem*," in *Hilaire et son temps: Actes du colloque de Poitiers, 29 septembre–3 octobre 1968, à l'occasion du XVIe centenaire de la mort de saint Hilaire* (Paris: Études Augustiniennes, 1969), 51–103. – D. Stiernon, "Ancyra," *EECh* 1:37. – M. Simonetti, "Basil of Ancyra," *EECh* 1:113. – M. Simonetti, "Rimini, Council of," *EECh* 2:737. – M. Simonetti, "Seleucia in Isauria, Council of," *EECh* 2:766 f.

# 6. Alexandria (362)

The death of Constantius (361) and the basic apathy of Julian the Apostate, the new emperor, toward intra-church affairs facilitated the synod that met in Alexandria in 362; it was the final one dealing with the Arian controversy in a decisive way before the Council of Constantinople. In its *Tomus ad Antiochenos*, it published for the first time the theological *via media* that Basil the Great and his companions would develop into the orthodox solution by the time of the Council of Constantinople. It stressed the divinity of the Holy Spirit and, for the first time, along with the assertion of the one hypostasis in God, allowed the formulation of three hypostases and thus, for the first time, provided the grounds for a differentiated understanding of ὑπόστασις as person and not solely as substance.

No further important synods took place within this line of development of the Arian controversy because Valens (364–378) followed entirely the line of the

Homoean formula of reunion adopted at Ariminum and Seleucia. He sought to enforce it with purely political measures against both the Nicenes and the Homoiousians. Beginning in 379, Theodosius ended the political dimension of the dispute. Under the leadership of Eunomius of Cyzicus, the anomoeans, or "Young Arians," did play a major part in the theological dispute with the Nicenes, especially with Basil the Great and Gregory of Nyssa; in terms of ecclesiastical politics, however, they were merely a sect.

*Editions:* Mansi 3:343–58.

*Encyclopedia Articles:* C. J. Hefele and H. Leclercq, *Histoire des conciles: D'après les documents originaux* (Paris: Letouzey & Ané, 1907), 1/2:963–69. – H. Köster, "Ὑπόστασις," *TDNT* 8:572–89. – B. Studer, "Hypostase," *HWP* 3 (1974): 1255–59. – B. Studer, "Hypostasis," *EECh* 1:401. – G. C. Stead, "Ousia," *EECh* 2:636 f. – J. Hammerstaedt, "Hypostasis," *RAC* 16 (1993): 986–1035.

*Studies:* R. E. Witt, "Ὑπόστασις," in *Amicitiæ corolla: A Volume of Essays Presented to James Rendel Harris, D. LITT., on the Occasion of His Eightieth Birthday* (ed. H. G. Wood; London: University of London Press, 1933), 319–43. – M. Richard, "L'introduction du mot 'hypostase' dans la théologie de l'incarnation," *MScRel* 2 (1945): 5–32, 243–70. – H. Kraft, "ΗΟΜΟΟΥΣΙΟΣ" *ZKG* 66 (1954/1955): 1–24. – H. Dörrie, "*Hypostasis: Wort- und Bedeutungsgeschichte* (NAWG.PH 1955.3; Göttingen: Vandenhoeck & Ruprecht, 1955), 35–92. – C. Stead, *Divine Substance* (Oxford: Clarendon, 1977). – A. de Halleux, "'Hypostase' et 'personne' dans la formation du dogme trinitaire (ca. 375–381)," *RHE* 79 (1984): 313–69, 625–70. – M. Tetz, "Ein enzyklisches Schreiben der Synode von Alexandrien (362)" *ZNW* 79 (1988): 262–81.

# III. THEOLOGY

In the history of the church, it was customary from the start to identify a doctrine either by its content or by the person or place of origin. Both of these categories inevitably overlap because the same notions were often espoused by several groups. Therefore, in what follows, for better understanding, first the descriptions of the doctrines will find use as a principle of arrangement in order then to furnish them with their various historical developments and group identifications.

In the case of the Arian controversy, essentially four lines of thought need to be distinguished in the chronological sequence of their appearance: the anomoeans, the Homoousians, the Homoiousians, and the Homoeans. After 360 they are joined by the Apollinarians and Pneumatomachians. It is to be noted that in the case of Apollinarianism no technical theological term gained currency.

## History of Theology

*Collection of Essays:* E. Ferguson, ed., *Doctrines of God and Christ in the Early Church* (SEC 9; New York: Garland, 1993).

*Studies:* B. Lohse, *Epochen der Dogmengeschichte* (Stuttgart: Kreuz, 1963): [ET] *A Short History of Christian Doctrine* (trans. E. Stoeffler; Philadelphia: Fortress, 1966). – L. Scheffczyk, "Lehramtliche Formulierungen und Dogmengeschichte der Trinität," *MySAl* 2 (1967): 146–220. – A. Adam, *Die Zeit der Alten Kirche* (vol. 1 of *Lehrbuch der Dogmengeschichte;* 2d ed.; Gütersloh:. Mohn, 1970–). – J. Pelikan, *The Emergence of the Catholic Tradition (100–600)* (vol. 1 of *The Christian Tradition: a History of the Development of Doctrine;* Chicago: University of Chicago Press, 1971–1989). – J. N. D. Kelly, *Early Christian Doctrines* (5th rev. ed.; London: Black, 1977). – C. Andersen et al., eds., *Die Lehrentwicklung im Rahmen der Katholizität* (Handbuch der Dogmen- und Theologiegeschichte 1; Göttingen: Vandenhoeck & Ruprecht, 1982). – K. Bey-schlag, *Gott und Welt* (vol. 1 of *Grundriss der Dogmengeschichte;* Grundrisse 2–3.1; Darmstadt: Wissenschaftliche Buchgesellschaft, 1982–). – R. P. C. Hanson, *The Search for the Christian Doctrine of God: The Arian Controversy, 318–381* (Edinburgh: T&T Clark, 1988). – L. Padovese, *Introduzione alla teologia patristica* (Introduzione alle discipline teologiche 2; Casale Monferrato: Piemme, 1992). – A. di Berardino and B. Studer, eds. *History of Theology I: The Patristic Period* (trans. M. J. O'Connell; Collegeville, Minn.: Liturgical, 1996).

## Soteriology

*Literature:* C. Andersen, *RAC* 6 (1966): 54–219. – B. Studer and B. Daley, *Soteriologie: In der Schrift und Patristik* (*HDG* 3.2a; Fribourg, Switz.: Herder, 1978). – B. Studer, *EECh* 2:788 f. – B. Studer, *Trinity and Incarnation: The Faith of the Early Church* (ed. A. Louth; trans. M. Westerhoff; Edinburgh: T&T Clark; Collegeville, Minn.: Liturgical, 1993).

## Trinitarian Theology

*Bibliographies: Estudios Trinitarios* (Salamanca: Secretariado Trinitario, 1967–) *[EstTrin].* – V. Venanzi, "Dogma e linguaggio trinitario nei Padri della Chiesa: Un panorama bibliographico, 1960–1972," *Aug* 13 (1973): 425–53. – E. Schadel et al., eds., *Bibliotheca trinitariorum: Internationale Bibliographie trinitarischer Literatur* (2 vols.; Munich and New York: Saur, 1984–1988).

*Translations:* E. R. Hardy, *Christology of the Later Fathers* (LCC 3; Philadelphia: Westminster, 1954) [Anthology]. – W. R. Rusch, ed. and trans., *The Trinitarian Controversy* (SoECT; Philadelphia: Fortress, 1980.

*Encyclopedia Articles:* B. Studer, *EECh* 2:851–53. – D. F. Wright, *EEC* 2:1142–47.

*Studies:* B. de Margerie, *La Trinité chrétienne dans l'histoire* (ThH 31; Paris: Beauchesne, 1975). – J. Barbel, *Der Gott Jesu im Glauben der Kirche: Die Trinitätslehre bis zum 5. Jahrhundert* (ed. A. Fries; Der Christ in der Welt 5.15e; Aschaffenburg: Pattloch, 1976). – M. O'Carroll, *Trinitas: A Theological Encyclopedia of the Holy Trinity* (Wilmington, Del.: Glazier, 1987). – F. Courth, *Trinität in der Schrift und Patristik* (*HDG* 2.1a; Fribourg, Switz.: Herder, 1988). – T. F. Torrance, *The Trinitarian Faith: The Evangelical Theology of the Ancient Catholic Church* (Edinburgh: T&T Clark, 1988). – M. R. Barnes and D. H. Williams, eds., *Arianism after Arius: Essays on the Development of the Fourth Century Trinitarian Conflicts* (Edinburgh: T&T Clark, 1993). – B. Sesböüe, ed., B. Meunier, trans., *Dieu peut-il avoir un Fils? Le débat trinitaire du IVe siècle* (Textes en main; Paris: Cerf, 1993). – M. R. Barnes, "The Fourth Century as Trinitarian Canon," in *Christian Origins: Theology, Rhetoric, and Community* (eds. L. Ayres and G. Jones; London and New York: Routledge, 1998), 47–67. – J. T. Lienhard,

"*Ousia* and *hypostasis:* The Cappadocian Settlement and the Theology of 'One *hypostasis,*'" in *The Trinity: An Interdisciplinary Symposium on the Trinity* (ed. S. T. Davis, D. Kendall, and G. O'Collins; Oxford and New York: Oxford University Press, 1999), 99–121.

## Christology

*Translations:* E. R. Hardy and C. C. Richardson, eds., *Christology of the Later Fathers* (LCC 3; Philadelphia: Westminster, 1954) [Anthology]. – R. A. Norris, ed. and trans., *The Christological Controversy* (SoECT; Philadelphia: Fortress, 1980) [Anthology]. – G. H. Ettlinger, *Jesus, Christ and Savior* (MFC 2; Wilmington, Del.: Glazier, 1987) [Anthology].

*Encyclopedia Articles:* R. Williams, *TRE* 16:726–45. – M. Simonetti, *EECh* 1:163–65. – F. W. Norris, *EEC* 1:242–51.

*Studies:* R. V. Sellers, *Two Ancient Christologies: A Study in the Christological Thought of the Schools of Alexandria and Antioch in the Early History of Christian Doctrine* (Church Historical Society, Publications 39; London: SPCK, 1954). – J. Liébart, *Christologie: Von der apostolischen Zeit bis zum Konzil von Chalcedon (451)* (*HDG* 3.1a; Fribourg, Switz.: Herder, 1965). – P. Smulders, "Dogmengeschichtliche und lehramtliche Entfaltung der Christologie," *MySal* 3 (1970): 389–476. – L. Scipioni, "Il Verbo e la sua umanità: Annotazioni per una cristologia patristica," *Teol* 2(1977): 3–51. – M. Serenthà, "Cristologia patristica: Per una precisazione dell'attuale 'status quaestionis," *ScC* 106 (1978): 3–36. – A. Grillmeier, *Christ in Christian Tradition* (2d rev. ed; trans. J. Bowden; London: Mowbray, 1975–), vol. 1. – A. Grillmeier, *From the Council of Chalcedon (451) to Gregory the Great (590–604): Reception and Contradiction—the Development of the Discussion about Chalcedon from 451 to the Beginning of the Reign of Justinian* (vol. 2, part 1 of *Christ in Christian Tradition;* trans. P. Allen and J. Cawte; London: Mowbray, 1987). – A. Grillmeier, *From the Council of Chalcedon (451) to Gregory the Great (590–604): The Church of Constantinople in the Sixth Century* (vol. 2, part 2 of *Christ in Christian Tradition;* trans. J. Cawte and P. Allen; London: Mowbray, 1995). – A. Grillmeier, *The Church of Alexandria with Nubia and Ethiopia after 451* (vol. 2, part 4 of *Christ in the Christian Tradition;* trans. O. C. Dean Jr.; London: Mowbray; Louisville: John Knox, 1996). – A. Gilg, *Weg und Bedeutung der altkirchlichen Christologie* (Munich: Kaiser, 1989). – K. Beyschlag, *Gott und Mensch* (vol. 2 of *Grundriss der Dogmengeschichte;* Grundrisse 3.1; Darmstadt: Wissenschaftliche Buchgesellschaft, 1991).

### Theological Method

*Study:* B. Studer, *Schola christiana: Die Theologie zwischen Nizäa (325) und Chalcedon (451)* (Paderborn: Ferdinand Schöningh, 1998).

# *A. Anomoeans (Arians, Neo-Arians, Eunomians)*

The anomoean doctrine claims that the Son of God is unlike the Father in every respect (ἀνόμοιος). If we may indiscriminately follow Athanasius, who handed down this statement (*C. Ar.* 1.6), the teaching of Arius was that the Son is ἀλλότριος μὲν καὶ ἀνόμοιος κατὰ πάντα τῆς τοῦ πατρὸς οὐσίας καὶ ἰδιότητος ("alien and unlike in all things to the Father's essence and individuality"). In the original sense of the term, the adherents of this teaching were the Arians. But since Athanasius did not gauge this designation by Arius's teaching but used it to designate all of the non-Nicenes, it took on an expanded meaning. The immediate reaction to the denial of any similarity of the οὐσίαι of the Father and the Son was expressed by the ὁμοούσιος concept, that is, the affirmation of an equality of being. The historical development in the subsequent decades distanced itself from the two concepts and moved toward expressions of similarity (ὁμοιούσιος, ὅμοιος).

The strict anomoean doctrine was not taken up again until ca. 355 by Aëtius, the Antiochene deacon, and by his secretary and student, Eunomius, later the bishop of Cyzicus. Aëtius must have been a brilliant orator and a persuasive dialectician; the story is told that in a public discussion he silenced Basil of Ancyra and Eustathius of Sebaste. The synod of Constantinople (360) condemned Aëtius but at the same time consecrated Eunomius to be bishop.

This neo-Arian, or Young Arian, teaching, as it came to be known before long because differences with the theology of Arius were noticed, differed from the latter in two ways in particular and thereby also became more perilous. For one, the proclamation of its theology proper was altogether rationalistic. Accordingly God's οὐσία is by all means accessible to the human cognitive faculty provided that one ponders and applies the biblical-dogmatic premises in a logically correct manner. The second aspect asserted the agreement of concept and reality, so that one can safely infer the nature of the described reality from the concept. Hence things described by different concepts are also different by nature. Therefore, if the predicate ἀγέννητος is accorded exclusively to the Father's nature, while the Son is γεννητός, their οὐσίαι must necessarily be distinct: ἀνόμοιος τῷ πατρὶ [καὶ] κατ' οὐσίαν. The logical unity of this system left a marked impression, and a number of great theologians (Basil the Great, Gregory of Nyssa, Didymus of Alexandria, Apollinaris of Laodicea, Theodore of Mopsuestia) had difficulties refuting it.

Theodosius's Nicene policy of religion brought the Arian school of thought to an end. Eunomius, who had attempted to establish his own rival church and even severed his ties with Eudoxius of Antioch (Constantinople), who consecrated him, because he did not consider him to be sufficiently radical, was condemned in 383 and exiled to Moesia and then to Caesarea in Cappadocia. He died ca. 394 on one of his estates.

*Editions:* Contre Eunome, II: Livres II–III (ed. and trans., B. Sesboüé, with G.-M. de Durand and L. Doutreleau; SC 305; Paris: Cerf, 1983), 177–299 [Eunomius, *Apologiae*]. – R. P. Vaggione, *Eunomius: The Extant Works* (OECT; Oxford and New York: Clarendon, 1987) [ET].

*Encyclopedia Articles:* L. Abramowski, "Eunomios," *RAC* 6:936–47. – H. C. Brennecke, "Stellenkonkordanz zum Artikel 'Eunomios,'" *JAC* 18 (1975): 202–5. – A. M. Ritter, "Eunomius," *TRE* 10:525–28. – M. Simonetti, "Aetius of Antioch," *EECh* 1:13. – M. Simonetti, "Anomoeans, Anomoeism," *EECh* 1:42. – M. Simonetti, "Eunomius of Cyzicus," *EECh* 1:297. – R. P. Vaggione, "Aetius," *EEC* 1:21 f. – R. P. Vaggione, "Anomeans," *EEC* 1:58 f. – R. P. Vaggione, "Eunomius of Cyzicus," *EEC* 1:399.

*Studies:* M. Albertz, "Zur Geschichte der jung-arianischen Kirchengemeinschaft," *ThStKr* 82 (1909): 205–78. – G. Bardy, "L'héritage littéraire d'Aétius," *RHE* 24 (1928): 809–27. – L. R. Wickham, "The *Syntagmation* of Aetius the Anomoean," *JTS* NS 19 (1968): 532–69. – L. R. Wickham, "Aetius and the Doctrine of Divine Ingeneracy," in *Papers Presented to the Fifth International Conference on Patristic Studies held in Oxford, 1967* (ed. F. L. Cross; StPatr 11; TU 108; Berlin: Academie-Verlag, 1972), 259–63. – E. Cavalcanti, *Studi Eunomiani* (OrChrAn 202; Rome: Pontificum Institutum Orientalium Studiorum, 1976). – T. A. Kopecek, *A History of Neo-Arianism* (PatMS 7; Cambridge, Mass.: Philadelphia Patristic Foundation, 1979). – T. A. Kopecek, "Neo-Arian Religion: The Evidence of the Apostolic Constitutions," in *Arianism—Historical and Theological Reassessments: Papers from the Ninth International Conference on Patristic Studies, September 5–10, 1983, Oxford, England* (PatMS 11; Cambridge, Mass.: Philadelphia Patristic Foundation, 1985), 153–79. – M. Wiles, "Eunomius: Hair-Splitting Dialectician or Defender of the Accessibility of Salvation?" in *The Making of Orthodoxy: Essays in Honor of Henry Chadwick* (ed. R. Williams; Cambridge and New York: Cambridge University Press, 1989), 157–72. – K.-H. Uthemann, "Die Sprache der Theologie nach Eunomius von Cyzicus," *ZKG* 104 (1993): 143–75.

# B. Homoousians (Nicenes)

In Arian terminology, "Homoousians" (*homousiani;* ὁμοουσιασταί) was the designation applied to those who adhered to the Nicene creed without any strictures. Prominent among them were Athanasius, Ossius of Córdoba, Marcellus of Ancyra, Lucifer of Calaris, Eusebius of Vercellae, the three great Cappadocians— Basil, Gregory of Nazianzus, and Gregory of Nyssa—but undoubtedly also Photinus of Sirmium and Apollinaris of Laodicea, who at a later time were condemned as heretics, albeit for different reasons.

Two problems were bound up with the concept of ὁμοούσιος, which ultimately was to be successful under Theodosius and the Council of Constantinople (381). For one, the Council of Nicea had adopted this term without being aware that it had already been condemned in Antioch in 268, together with Paul of Samosata. And when Basil of Ancyra presented this information in 358, the Nicenes found it difficult to substantiate their opposition. The condemnation of 268 had a much greater impact upon the second theological problem, however. The concept of ὁμοούσιος had been perceived as Sabellian, that is, as blurring the distinction between Father and Son as persons. Up to the synod of Alexandria (362) and the theology of the Cappadocians, the fourth-century discussion did indeed suffer from the unresolved delineation of the concepts of οὐσία and ὑπό στασις, which all too often had been treated as synonymous. Conversely, if οὐσία was understood as "being" and ὑπόστασις as "substance," Origen's way of referring to God in τρεῖς ὑποστάσεις was rendered impossible. Yet the lack of a term to distinguish between the divine persons could lead to Sabellian misinterpretations of ὁμοούσιος. The Nicenes thus had to undergo this reproach rather often, and Marcellus of Ancyra and Photinus of Sirmium were condemned.

*Encyclopedia Articles:* M. Simonetti, "Homoousians," *EECh* 1:396. – M. Simonetti, "Homoousios," *EECh* 1:396. – C. Kannengiesser, "Marcellus of Ancyra," *EECh* 1:522. –

K. Seibt, "Marcell von Ankyra," *TRE* 22:83–89. – G. C. Stead, "Homoousios," *RAC* 16:364–433.

*Studies:* M. Tetz, "Zur Theologie des Markell von Ankyra I–III," *ZKG* 75 (1964): 217–70; 79 (1968): 3–42; 83 (1972): 145–94. – M. Simonetti, "Su alcune opre attribuite di recente a Marcello d'Ancira," *RSLR* (1973): 313–29. – M. Tetz, "Markellianer und Athanasios von Alexandrien: Die markellische *Expositio fidei ad Athanasium* des Diakons Eugenios von Ankyra," *ZNW* 64 (1973): 75–121. – F. Dinsen, *Homoousios: Die Geschichte des Begriffs bis zum Konzil von Konstantinopel (381)* (Kiel: n.p., 1976). – W. A. Bienert, "Das vornicaenische ὁμοούσιος als Ausdruck der Rechtgläubigkeit," *ZKG* 90 (1979): 151–75. – L. Barnard, "Marcellus of Ancyra and the Eusebians," *GOTR* 25 (1980): 63–76. – M. Simonetti, "Ancora su *homoousios* a prosposito di due recenti studi," *VetChr* 17 (1980): 85–98. – J. T. Leinhard, "Marcellus of Ancyra in Modern Research," *TS* 43 (1982): 486–503. – J. T. Leinhard, "Acacius of Caesarea, *Contra Marcellum:* Historical and Theological Considerations," *CrSt* 10 (1989): 1–21. – J. T. Leinhard, "Basil of Caesarea, Marcellus of Ancyra, and 'Sabellius,'" *ChH* 58 (1989): 157–67. – G. Feige, *Die Lehre Markells von Ankyra in der Darstellung seiner Gegner* (EThST 58; Leipzig: Benno, 1991). – K. Seibt, *Die Theologie des Markell von Ankyra* (AKG 59; Berlin and New York: de Gruyter, 1994). – J. T. Leinhard, *Contra Marcellum: Marcellus of Ancyra and Fourth Century Theology* (Washington, D.C.: Catholic University of America Press, 1999).

# *C. Homoiousians (Eusebians, Semi-Arians)*

The most enigmatic position in the Arian controversy of the fourth century is seen in the theology of those who are described as "Homoiousians" in the Latin Arian documents but as "Semi-Arians" on the Greek side. Of course, the Nicenes shaped this label with tendentious intent, for the Homoiousians were anti-Arian and not infrequently Homoousians at the same time. In the broadest sense, the designation "Homoiousians" encompasses all of those who were looking for a *via media* between Arianism and the Nicene position, beginning with the three Eusebiuses (of Caesarea, Emesa, and Nicomedia—hence the label "Eusebians"), without being familiar with or using the concept of ὁμοιούσιος. We do not know where it originated. It occurs first in the second formula of Sirmium (357), where its use, as well as that of ὁμοούσιος, was forbidden. The concept of ὁμοιούσιος really belongs to the theology and faction of Basil of Ancyra, who at the synod of Ancyra (358) pushed through the formula of ὅμοιος κατ' οὐσίαν. He construed οὐσία as an individual substance, thus arguing for three ὑποστάσεις and three οὐσίαι in the Deity. The οὐσία of the Son is similar to the Father's insofar as it is divine as well. With the favor of Constantius, this orientation flourished briefly in the East, but because the emperor turned to the Homoeans beginning with the formula of Nike (359) and the synod of Constantinople (360), it quickly became a thing of the past.

The Homoiousian orientation gained more importance by joining forces with the Homoousian doctrine. Hilary of Poitiers brought it with him to the West from his exile and interpreted ὁμοούσιος in this way, as did the synod of Paris in 360/361. Likewise in the East, part of the Homoiousian faction merged with the

Homoousians through the mediation of Basil the Great and Meletius of Antioch. The other part adhered to the Antiochene formula of 341 and, beginning in 360, underwent a further split on the issue of the divinity of the Spirit. The Macedonians were part of this group.

*Studies:* J. Gummerus, *Die homöusianische Partei bis zum Tode des Konstantius: Ein Beitrag zur Geschichte des arianischen Streites in den Jahren 356–361* (Leipzig: A. Deichert'sche [Georg Böhme], 1900). – W. A. Löhr, *Die Entstehung der homöischen und homöusianischen Kirchenparteien: Studien zur Synodalgeschichte des 4. Jahrhunderts* (Beiträge zur Religionsgeschichte/Witterschlick; Bonn: Wehle; Bonn: Verlag für Kultur und Wissenschaft, 1986). – M. Simonetti, *EECh* 1:395. – A. M. Ritter, *DHGE* 24:1507–10.

# D. Homoeans

The term "Homoean" is of modern origin, shaped by the dogmatic formulation that the Son is ὅμοιος κατὰ τὰς γραφάς to the Father. Its author was Acacius of Caesarea, the successor of Eusebius and promoter of Meletius of Antioch. He suggested this formulation as the broadest possible and most noncommittal uniform formula, which Constantius accepted; the latter then pressured the double synod of Ariminum and Seleucia to decide in its favor at Nike and had it ratified by a synod in Constantinople in 360. But since it denoted a purely politically imposed formula that offered no theologically satisfactory solution, it could be sustained only as long and as broadly as the imperial power promoted it. After Constantius (d. 361), Valens continued to adhere to it in the East (364–368). Yet with the synod of Alexandria (362), Apollinaris of Laodicea, and the Cappadocians, the theological development moved toward other solutions. Because of a number of difficulties in domestic and foreign affairs precipitated by Procopius, a usurper, and by the Goths and the Persians, Valens was unable to enforce his religiopolitical line against the massive and open resistance of many bishops.

Based on these historical and theological constellations, a new phase of controversies and theological developments began in 360/362, which were also pursued in Christian literature, namely, neo-Arianism by Eunomius, Apollinarianism, and the battle against them, undertaken by Basil the Great of Caesarea, Gregory of Nazianzus, and Gregory of Nyssa. They further developed satisfactory theological solutions, which the Council of Constantinople accepted together with the Nicene creed.

*Studies:* H. C. Brennecke, *Studien zur Geschichte der Homöer: Der Osten bis zum Ende der homöischen Reichskirche* (BHTh 73; Tübingen: Mohr, 1988). – M. Simonetti, "Homoeans," *EECh* 1:395. – R. A. Greer, "Homoeans," *EEC* 1:540–41.

# CHAPTER FIVE

# First Phase of Arianism

## I. EUSEBIUS OF CAESAREA

Eusebius, also called Pamphilus, a name he adopted in honor of his mentor, died as a martyr (February 16, 309 or 310) during the Diocletian persecution. He was part of the generation of church fathers, as was Lactantius, who experienced and helped to shape the change from persecution to toleration and finally to acceptance of Christianity. Whereas Lactantius never occupied an ecclesiastical office and personally did not experience anything beyond the triumph of Constantine's autocratic rule (324), Eusebius functioned as bishop of Caesarea, the metropolis of Palestine, throughout Constantine's reign. He also served as a close confidante and advisor to the emperor, developed the historical theology of the Christian empire, and took a decisive part in the first great theological and ecclesiastical crisis of this empire, namely, the debate concerning Arius and his teaching.

Eusebius was born between 260 and 264, possibly in Caesarea itself, and probably began to study history in his early years. As a coworker of Pamphilus, he was devoted to taking care of the library of Caesarea, which Origen had established, and to studying the Bible. He took several research trips to Antioch, Caesarea Philippi, and Jerusalem. Together with Pamphilus, who during the Diocletian persecution was imprisoned in Caesarea from November 307 on, he wrote the first five volumes of an apologia for Origen; the sixth and final volume was not completed until after his teacher's death. The only extant volume is the first, in a Latin translation by Rufinus, which was to become significant in the debate between Rufinus and Jerome over Origen. During the persecution, Eusebius resided in Tyre and Thebais in Egypt, among other places; whether he also suffered incarceration cannot be established with certainty. In any case, later accusations of apostasy seem untenable, given that soon after the persecution ended, the church of Caesarea consecrated him to be its bishop in 313. For the next decade, he was more occupied with pastoral work in rebuilding the life of the church than with literary activity.

When an Alexandrian synod, under the leadership of Bishop Alexander, excommunicated Arius,[1] the latter sought support with the Eastern bishops. In a

---

[1] The precise chronology of the beginning of the Arian controversy between 318 and 323 is still subject to debate today; even the date of Arius's excommunication can only be determined more accurately by means of the *terminus ante quem* of 324.

letter addressed to Alexander, Eusebius expressed his support for Arius; a synod in Caesarea likewise declared itself in his favor. Conversely, a synod held in Antioch in late 324 or early 325 excommunicated Arius and his followers, Eusebius among them. This decision was only to be considered provisional, however, until a final decision would be reached at the synod in Ancyra in the spring of 325. This synod finally gathered in Nicea as the first "ecumenical" council and defined the formula of the "same nature" (ὁμοούσιος) of God the Father and the Son. Eusebius defended his own orthodoxy on the basis of the *symbolum* of the church of Caesarea and accepted the ὁμοούσιος, though reluctantly. His concern was that this concept contained Sabellian tendencies that did not adequately distinguish between God as Father and as Son. The council accepted Eusebius's explanation of his orthodoxy; subsequent years were to confirm his fears of an interpretation of ὁμοούσιος with Sabellian tendencies.

Eusebius's stance in the further development of the Arian dispute has given rise to many controversial interpretations. He had officially accepted the Nicene creed and no longer supported Arius, and officially his orthodoxy was no longer questioned. On the other hand, he participated in the measures taken against the leaders of the Nicene party. He instigated the removal of Eustathius, the bishop of Antioch, because of Sabellianism (ca. 330) but declined the offer to transfer to this bishopric by referring to canon 15 of the Council of Nicea, which prohibited the change of bishoprics. In 335 he led a synod in Tyre in which Athanasius was called to account, although he did not participate in hounding him. Shortly after this, on behalf of the emperor, he drafted two writings (*Contra Marcellum, De ecclesiastica theologia*) to refute the theology of Marcellus of Ancyra, who in 336 was deposed as an uncompromising anti-Arian. Despite all this, it may not be appropriate to qualify his stance simply as "ambivalent," "conflicting," or as predicated only on political calculation (even though he undoubtedly had outstanding political skills) without allowing himself to be led by his own theological conviction. He endeavored to point in the direction of a *via media*, shaped by an Alexandrian theological orientation (mainly through Dionysius of Alexandria, a student of Origen), between Arian and Nicene theology. He was not successful in this regard because his own theological conceptuality did not prove to be sufficiently sustainable.

Without underestimating the value of Eusebius's exegetical-apologetic writings, such as the *Praeparatio evangelica*, the *Demonstratio evangelica*, and the *Commentary on Isaiah*, his justified fame as an ecclesiastical writer rests on his historical works, which earned for him the honorary title "father of church history." In this he became the custodian of incalculable source material for the first three centuries, the theoretician of a Christian history of salvation, culminating in Constantine's empire, and the more or less official historian of this empire and its ideas. He died ca. 340, soon after Constantine, whose *Vita* he had written after the death of the latter (337).

*Bibliography:* F. W. Bautz, *BBKL* 1:1561–64.

*Editions: Opera omnia:* PG 19–24.

*Reference Works: Biblia patristica: Index des citations et allusions bibliques dans la littérature patristique.* Vol. 4, *Eusèbe de Césarée, Cyrille de Jérusalem, Epiphane de Salamine* (Paris: Éditions du Centre National de la Recherche Scientifique, 1987).

*Encyclopedia Articles:* J. Moreau, *RAC* 6:1052–88. – D. S. Wallace-Hadrill, *TRE* 10:537–43. – G. Ruhbach, "Euseb von Caesarea," *GK* 1:224–35. – C. Curti, *EECh* 1:299–301. – R. Lyman, *EEC* 1:399–402.

*Introductions and Surveys:* F. J. Foakes-Jackson, *Eusebius Pamphili, Bishop of Caesarea in Palestine and First Christian Historian: A Study of the Man and His Writings* (Cambridge: Heffer, 1933). – D. S. Wallace-Hadrill, *Eusebius of Caesarea* (London: Mowbray, 1960; Westminster, Md.: Canterbury, 1961). – T. D. Barnes, *Constantine and Eusebius* (Cambridge, Mass.: Harvard University Press, 1981).

*Collections of Essays:* G. Ruhbach, ed., *Die Kirche angesichts der konstantinischen Wende* (WdF 306; Darmstadt: Wissenschaftliche Buchgesellschaft, 1976). – H. W. Attridge and G. Hata, eds., *Eusebius, Christianity, and Judaism* (StPB 42; Leiden and New York: Brill, 1992).

*Studies:* H. Berkhof, *Die Theologie des Eusebius von Caesarea* (Amsterdam: Uitgeversmaatschappij Holland, 1939). – J.-R. Laurin, *Orientations mâitresses d'apologistes chrétiens de 270 à 361* (AnGr 61; Rome: Apud Aedes Universitatis Gregorianae, 1954), 94–145, 344–401. – A. Weber, *'APXH: Ein Beitrag zur Christologie des Eusebius von Cäsarea* (Munich: Neue Stadt, 1965). – D. L. Holland, "Die Synode von Antiochien (324/25) und ihre Bedeutung für Eusebius von Caesarea und das Konzil von Nizäa," *ZKG* 81 (1970): 163–81. – G. C. Stead, "Eusebius and the Council of Nicaea," *JTS* NS 24 (1973): 85–100; repr. in E. Ferguson, ed., *Doctrines of God and Christ in the Early Church* (SEC 9; New York: Garland, 1993), 111–26. – L. Abramowski, "Die Synode von Antiochien 324/25 und ihr Symbol," *ZKG* 86 (1975): 356–66. – H. von Campenhausen, "Das Bekenntnis Eusebs von Caesarea (Nicaea 325)," *ZNW* 67 (1976): 123–39. – C. Luibhéid, *Eusebius of Caesarea and the Arian Crisis* (Dublin: Irish Academic Press, 1981). – S. Gero, "The True Image of Christ: Eusebius's Letter to Constantine Reconsidered," *JTS* NS 32 (1981): 460–70. – D. Ridings, *The Attic Moses: The Dependency Theme in Some Early Christian Writers* (SGLG 59; Göteborg, Sweden: AUG, 1995), 141–96. – H. Strutwolf, *Die Trinitätstheologie und Christologie des Euseb von Caesarea: Eine dogmengeschichtliche Untersuchung seiner Platonismusrezeption und Wirkungsgeschichte* (FKDG 72; Göttingen: Vandenhoeck & Ruprecht, 1999). – J. Ulrich, *Euseb von Caesarea und die Juden: Studien zur Rolle der Juden in der Theologie des Eusebius von Caesarea* (PTS 49; Berlin: de Gruyter, 1999).

# A. Historical Works

## Introduction: Christian Chronography and Theological History

Before Eusebius church historiography did not exist as a genre. Ever since Herodotus and Thucydides (second half of fifth century B.C.E.), however, the secular literature of antiquity was conversant with a highly developed historiography. The reason for this may be traced back to the church's tenuous situation during the first three centuries. Most likely, however, there was a historical awareness and the beginnings of theological history and chronography in Christianity from the start, all the more so since the church was founded on the historical person of Jesus, the incarnate Son of God, and not on a myth. Although the character of the NT writings first and foremost is proclamational, not historiographic, the writings are nevertheless predicated upon concrete, historically verifiable, references to dates and places (e.g., Luke 1:5, "in the time of Herod king of Judea"; Luke 2:1, "In those days Caesar Augustus issued a decree"; John 18:13, "Annas, who was the father-in-law of Caiaphas, the high priest that year"), and they arrange the salvific events, interpreted through Christ, into the history of God with humans, especially with the Jewish nàtion (e.g., the genealogy of Jesus [Matt 1:1–17]; "but when the time had fully come, God sent his Son" [Gal 4:4]). The church adopted its expectation of the end time from Judaism, including such historical-theological concepts as the schema of the four kingdoms (Dan 2:1–49) and chiliastic calculations of the time of the world, based on Ps 90:4 ("a thousand years in your sight are like a day that has just gone by"; cf. 2 Pet 3:8) and on the six-days schema of creation, according to which the world, from creation to the establishment of the final kingdom of God, will endure for six thousand years (cf. Rev 20:1–6).

The second and third centuries developed these conceptions and expressed them in concrete terms in the discussion with the pagan world, which perceived itself as older and superior, on the one hand, and with currents within the church that strayed into heresy, on the other (e.g., Montanism, cf. ch. 3.IV.A.3), predicting the world's impending end in the context of a new outbreak of its expectation. The apologists compared pagan and biblical chronologies, and this provided the evidence of Christianity's antiquity because Moses and the OT are to be dated to before the oldest of the cultures and philosophers; indeed the latter merely plagiarized the OT (cf. ch. 3.I). Theophilus of Antioch (*Autol.* 3.16–30), Clement of Alexandria (*Strom.* 1.21), and the writer of the first Christian chronicle of the world, Julius Africanus, calculated the world's time that had already passed, down to the year and day, since Christ was born in the middle of the sixth and final millennium. Julius Africanus (d. ca. 240) created a new Christian literary genre with his work Χρονογραφίαι, of which, granted, only fragments have been preserved; he provided a comparison of dates and events of biblical and secular history from the creation of the world to his own time (221) in chronological and synchronic order. A little later this was followed by the (extant) chronicles of Hippolytus, using the same schema up to the year 235. All other kinds of works, such as bishops' lists or descriptions of the various heresies, although they are indispensable source material for the historian, do not belong to the literary genre of historiography because they were written for dogmatic purposes.

*Studies:* F. Winkelmann, "Historiographie," *RAC* 15:724–65. – H. Hofmann, "Die Geschichtsschreibung," in *Spätantike* (vol. 4 of *Neues Handbuch der Literaturwissenschaft;* Wiesbaden: AULA, 1997), 403–67.

## 1. Chronicle

Eusebius likewise began his historical work by constructing a chronicle, drawing its data from the Bible, the chronicle of Julius Africanus, Flavius

Josephus, Hellenistic chronographers, and Greek historians, as well as from other Christian writers. Besides from his unusually critical selection of sources, his important innovation in Christian chronography was to turn away from addressing not only world history from its creation but also millenarian conceptions. He began his *Chronicle* with events he considered datable (Abraham's birth in 2016/2015 B.C.E.) and established the birth of Christ in the year 5200 after creation, but did not include an eschatological date for the end of the world. His intention was no longer to provide an indication of the approaching fulfillment of time but instead to demonstrate that world history had reached its intended apex in the empire of Constantine, the end of which could not be foreseen. This also includes the traditional apologetic proof of antiquity.

The *Chronicle* is composed of two parts. Part 1 (χρονογραφία) examines the chronology of the most significant peoples of antiquity—the Chaldeans, Assyrians, Hebrews, Egyptians, Greeks, and Romans. Building upon this and in parallel columns, he listed in part 2 (χρονικοὶ κανόνες) the most important events of history, thereby clarifying their arrangement in accordance with the various chronological systems, especially in their relationship to the sacred history of Judaism in preparation for Christianity.

The *Chronicle* of Eusebius appeared in two editions, the second of which went up to Constantine's *vicennalia* celebration of 325/326. According to an older viewpoint, the first edition went up to 303. More recently, however, Barnes,[2] in agreement with two other researchers,[3] assumes that it ended with the year 276/277 and was already published before the end of the third century. Whether the year of publication can be pushed back very close to the final year treated[4] calls for careful examination. Even if Eusebius began his historical studies when he was still very young, the completion of a work such as this requires several years of work. The original form of the *Chronicle* has been lost but can be reconstructed quite reliably with excerpts from later chronographers, a sixth-century Armenian translation, and especially Jerome's Latin translation. Jerome became acquainted with it during a stay in Constantinople in 380/381, translated the first part (up to the fall of Troy) verbatim into Latin, then added his own material, from Roman history and literature, for the period ending with Constantine's *vicennalia* celebration and extended it to 378. It thus became the model for the world chronicles by Sulpicius Severus (to 400), Prosper of Aquitaine (to 455), and Isidore of Seville (to 615) and continued to be influential well into the Latin Middle Ages.

*Editions: Die Chronik* (vol. 5 of *Eusebius Werke;* ed. J. Karst; GCS; Leipzig: Hinrichs, 1911). – *Die Chronik des Hieronymus* (vol. 7 of *Eusebius Werke;* ed. R. Helm; 3d ed.; GCS; Leipzig: Hinrichs, 1984). – G. Brugnoli, *Curiosissimus excerptor: Gli "Additamenta" di Girolamo ai "Chronica" di Eusebio* (Pisa: ETS, 1995) [Com].

---

2 T. D. Barnes, *Constantine and Eusebius* (Cambridge, Mass.: Harvard University Press, 1981), 111.

3 D. S. Wallace-Hadrill, *TRE* 10:539; F. Winkelmann, "Historiographie," *RAC* 15:752.

4 Wallace-Hadrill, *TRE* 10:539: "already finalized by 280," although he establishes the date of Eusebius's birth as only "around 264."

*Studies:* R. Helm, *Hieronymus' Zusätze in Eusebius' Chronik und ihr Wert für die Literatur-geschichte* (Philologus: Supplementband 21.2; Leipzig: Dieterich'sche Verlagsbuch-handlung, 1929). – D. S. Wallace-Hadrill, "The Eusebian Chronicle: The Extent and Date of Composition of Its Early Editions," *JTS* NS 6 (1955): 248–53. – A. A. Moss-hammer, *The Chronicle of Eusebius and Greek Chronographic Tradition* (Lewisburg, Pa.: Bucknell University Press, 1979). – P. Siniscalco, "Chronography–Chronology," *EECh* 1:166–67.

## 2. Ecclesiastical History

Using the *Chronicle* as preparatory material, Eusebius created the first opus of the ecclesiastical history genre; even so it reflects such mastery that it continues to be influential to this day and for the first three centuries provides unique source material. There has been a lot of discussion since the early twentieth century on the history of its origin. Today it may be assumed that bks. 1–7, dealing with the history of Christianity from its beginning to the Diocletian persecution, were already published before 303, possibly even before the end of the third century, and were revised and expanded in later editions. By 325 Eusebius added bks. 8–10, from the Diocletian persecution to Constantine's conquest over Licinius (324), for which we must reckon with several revisions, arising out of changing points of view of the times, and with a final revision. This alters the assessment of Eusebius's original presentational intent considerably. As long as one assumes a first edition after 311, the *Ecclesiastical History* could, from the outset, be considered an apologia for Christianity; its victory, under Constantine, over all of the hostile forces provided the evidence of its divine origin and its providential, divine guidance through all adversities, in what was intended from the start to be a history of salvation. If the books were published before the Diocletian persecution, however, this historical picture, as it appears in the final redaction that we now have, may only gradually have developed.

This new method of the *Ecclesiastical History* of Eusebius is one of organization according to the years of emperors and pontificates, together with analysis and elaborate citation of rich source materials. These sources were accessible to him in the extensive libraries of Caesarea and Jerusalem, and much is preserved for us by Eusebius alone. In his view, the historian's primary task is collecting authentic texts and arranging them contextually by means of brief explanations; it is not a personal, vivid analysis of sources or an organic presentation, originating from them, of the historical processes. His use of sources has frequently been criticized, however, because he does not distinguish between primary and secondary sources, deletes and paraphrases passages, and analyzes the more orthodox Christian writers, as well as the more famous rather than little-known secular writers. The presentations are not always proportionate to the importance of the content, and many opinions seem superficial or biased. Even if Eusebius did not work according to modern historical standards, this does not demonstrate an essential, let alone conscious, falsification of the material. In any case, even his opponents in the field of history recognized him as *the* authority. More crucial is the fact that in the later books (8–10), dealing with his own lifetime, he substantiates less and his writing is sketchy and panegyrical instead of displaying objective sobriety.

Many of the later church historians of the patristic era consider themselves indebted to the Eusebian *Ecclesiastical History,* so much so that they merely translate and expand: Rufinus of Concordia (Aquileia) (to 395), Sozomen (to 425), Theodoret of Cyrhus (to 428), and Socrates Scholasticus (to 439).

*Editions: Die Kirchengeschichte* (vol. 2/1–3 of *Eusebius Werke;* ed. E. Schwartz and T. Mommsen; 2d ed.; GCS; Berlin: Akademie, 1999). – *The Ecclesiastical History* (ed. K. Lake and J. E. L. Oulton; 2 vols.; LCL; Cambridge, Mass.: Harvard University Press, 1926–1932; repr., 1964–1965, 1980) [ET]. – *Histoire ecclésiastique* (ed. G. Bardy and P. Périchon; 4 vols.; 4th ed.; SC 31, 41, 55, 73; Paris: Cerf, 1993–2001) [*Historia ecclesiastica, De martyribus Palaestinae*].

*Translations:* A. C. McGiffert, trans., "The Church History of Eusebius," in *NPNF²* (Peabody, Mass.: Hendrickson, 1995; repr. of 1890 ed.), 1:81–403. – *Ecclesiastical History* (trans. R. J. Deferrari; 2 vols.; FC 19, 29; Washington, D.C.: Catholic University of America Press, 1953–1955; repr., 1965–1969). – *The History of the Church from Christ to Constantine* (trans. G. A. Williamson; rev. and ed. A. Louth; London and New York: Penguin, 1989).

*Studies:* M. Gödecke, *Geschichte als Mythos: Eusebs "Kirchengeschichte"* (Frankfurt and New York: Lang, 1987). – D. Timpe, "Was ist Kirchengeschichte? Zum Gattungscharakter der *Historia ecclesiastica* des Eusebius," in *Festschrift Robert Werner: Zu seinem 65. Geburtstag* (ed. W. Dalheim et al.; Konstanz: Universitätsverlag Konstanz, 1989), 171–204. – A. Louth, "The Date of Eusebius' *Historia ecclesiastica,*" *JTS* NS 41 (1990): 111–23. – W. Tabbernee, "Eusebius' 'Theology of Persecution': As Seen in the Various Editions of His Church History," *JECS* 5 (1997): 319–34. – D. Mendels, *The Media Revolution of Early Christianity: An Essay on Eusebius's Ecclesiastical History* (Grand Rapids: Eerdmans, 1999).

# 3. *Vita Constantini*

Eusebius's *Vita Constantini,* written in four books after the emperor's death (337), contains what is likely the most popular piece of his entire oeuvre, namely, the sign of the cross before the battle against Maxentius at the Milvian Bridge in Rome (1.28–31). Constantine himself reported that around noon he had prayed to the Christian God for victory when the *tropaion*[5] of a cross of light appeared above the sun in the sky with the words "In this sign you will conquer." Since he did not readily grasp the meaning of this sign, however, Christ appeared to him in a dream and commissioned him to have the sign he had seen reproduced as an emblem (similarly Lactantius, *De mortibus persecutorum* 44). This gave rise to the labarum, a cross-like staff covered in gold, with the tip formed by a wreath of gold and precious stones around the Chi-Rho, the monogram of Christ. A square

---

[5] From time immemorial, the *tropaion* (τρέπειν = "to turn"), shaped like a T, was a rack that was erected as a sign of victory at the place in the battle where the enemy turned to flee. On the arms of the T, they pegged captured armor. Hence the form and meaning of the concept were transferred to the cross of Christ.

piece of purple fabric, interwoven with gold and studded with sparkling gems, hung from the crossbar, and underneath it the golden half-length portraits of the emperor and his sons were affixed. In 324 this labarum became the standard for the empire as a whole.

What is not found in Eusebius, however, is the famous legend of Constantine's conversion by Pope Silvester (314–335), which is depicted in the sequence of pictures in a chapel of the Santi Quattro Coronati Basilica in Rome. The legend is that Constantine contracted leprosy and believed, in line with ancient tradition, that he could be cleansed from it by bathing in the blood of innocent children. Then Pope Silvester instructed him about the power of the Christian God and of the healing power of baptism, and Constantine was indeed healed of leprosy when Pope Silvester administered baptism to him. This legend did not arise until the fifth century in Rome, but in the eighth century it became the basis for the so-called Donation of Constantine, which sought to justify the imperial power of the medieval papacy over the power of the emperors. According to this, Constantine, on the basis of his miraculous healing, recognized the power with which Christ had equipped Peter and consequently established the primacy of the pope over the worldwide church, granted Pope Silvester the Lateran Palace, and bestowed upon him the authority over Rome and the western part of the Roman Empire, as well as the imperial insignia.[6]

The intent and content of the *Vita Constantini* poses serious problems regarding the author's historical objectivity, to the extent that many researchers reject the Eusebian authorship, although their arguments have not been deemed persuasive to date. In this work Eusebius seeks to define and interpret theologically the position of the emperor in the Roman Empire, which is now Christian. The emperor reflects the image of God as ruler and emulates the Logos. The relationship is similar to that of the Father and the Son in the Trinity; hence the emperor functions as God's representative ruler on earth and as the teacher of all his subjects, so that he can also be called "bishop of those outside the church" (ἐπί σκοπος τῶν ἐκτός). Christianity continues the original faith of the patriarchs, whereas the period of the Jewish law only served the purpose of training and preparing the people. The Roman Empire, which had attained its highest position of power at the time of Christ, had been chosen to promote the spread of Christianity first through the *pax romana* but then through Constantine to create a new union between state and church, in which the emperor is the head of the empire *and* the church (Caesaropapism).

Thus the *Vita Constantini* becomes a kind of panegyric on the emperor, expressly intended "to speak and write of those circumstances only which have reference to his religious character" and "to celebrate in every way the praises of this truly blessed prince" (1.11). Constantine is portrayed as the leader, like Moses, chosen by God to lead his people, who on behalf of God and by God's power was victorious over all the enemies of Christianity. After this he organized church and state

---

[6] Cf. H. Fuhrmann, "Constitutum Constantini," *TRE* 8:196–202.

into the aspired kingdom of God by his own piety, through laws and active promotion of the church, and provided for the true doctrine and unity of the church, especially at the Council of Nicea. For this reason, God blessed him with all wealth
and dignity and granted him an exemplary, blessed end. "The most justice is done
to this work if it is read as a treatise on political philosophy (Baynes), as a purely
theological work (Winkelmann), or as a study on the ideal ruler (Farina)."[7]

*Edition: Über das Leben des Kaisers Konstantin* (vol. 1/1 of *Eusebius Werke;* ed. F. Winkelmann; GCS; Berlin: Akademie, 1975).

*Translations:* E. C. Richardson, trans., "Life of Constantine," "Constantine's Oration to the
Assembly of the Saints," and "Oration in Praise of Constantine," in *NPNF²* (Peabody,
Mass.: Hendrickson, 1995; repr. of 1890 ed.), 1:481–610. – H. A. Drake, *In Praise of
Constantine: A Historical Study and New Translation of Eusebius' Tricennial Orations*
(Berkeley: University of California Press, 1976). – *Life of Constantine* (trans. A. Cam-
eron and S. G. Hall; Oxford: Clarendon, 1999) [Com].

*Authenticity, Textual Problems:* F. Winkelmann, *Die Textbezeugung der Vita Constantini des
Eusebius von Caesarea* (TU 84; Berlin: Akademie, 1962). – F. Winkelmann, "Zur
Geschichte des Authentizitätsproblems der *Vita Constantini,*" *Klio* 40 (1962): 187–
243. – M. R. Cataudella, "Sul problema della 'Vita Constantini' attribuita a Eusebio di
Cesarea," *MSLCA* 13 (1963): 41–59. – M. R. Cataudella, "La 'persecuzione' di Licinio e
l'autenticità della '*Vita Constantini,*'" *At.* NS 48 (1970): 46–83, 229–50. – H. A. Drake,
"What Eusebius Knew: The Genesis of the *Vita Constantini,*" *CP* 83 (1988): 20–38. –
M. J. Hollerich, "Myth and History in Eusebius' *De vita Constantini: Vit. Const.* 1.12
in Its Contemporary Setting," *HTR* 82 (1989): 421–45. – T. G. Elliott, "Eusebian
Frauds in the *Vita Constantini,*" *Phoenix* 44 (1990): 162–71. – S. G. Hall, "Eusebian
and Other Sources in *Vita Constantini* I," in *Logos: Festschrift für Luise Abramowski
zum 8. Juli 1993* (ed. H. C. Brennecke, E. L. Grasmück, and C. Markschies; BZNW 67;
Berlin: New York: de Gruyter, 1993), 239–63.

*History of Theology:* H. Eger, "Kaiser und Kirche in der Geschichtstheologie Eusebs von
Cäsarea," *ZNW* 38 (1939): 97–115. – R. Farina, *L'impero e l'imperatore cristiano in
Eusebio di Cesarea: La prima teologia politica del cristianesimo* (BThS.F 2; Zurich: Pas,
1966). – J.-M. Sansterre, "Eusèbe de Césarée et la naissance de la théorie 'césaro-
papiste,'" *Byzantion* 42 (1972): 131–95, 532–94. – K. M. Girardet, "Das christliche
Priestertum Konstantins d. Gr.: Ein Aspekt der Herrscheridee des Eusebius von
Caesarea," *Chiron* 10 (1980): 569–92. – T. D. Barnes, "Panegyric, History, and Hagiography in Eusebius' *Life of Constantine,*" in *The Making of Orthodoxy Essays in Honour
of Henry Chadwick* (ed. R. Williams; Cambridge and New York: Cambridge University Press, 1989), 94–123. – M. J. Hollerich, "Religion and Politics in the Writings of
Eusebius: Reassessing the First 'Court Theologian,'" *ChH* 59 (1990): 309–25.

**Historical Works**

*Editions: Über das Leben Constantins, Constantins Rede an die heilige Versammlung, Tricen-
natsrede an Constantin* (vol. 1 of *Eusebius Werke;* ed. I. A. Heikel; GCS; Leipzig:
Hinrichs, 1902) [*Vita Constantini, Oratio ad sanctorum coetum, Laudes Constantini*].

---

[7] Wallace-Hadrill, *TRE* 10:541.

*Translations: The Ecclesiastical History and the Martyrs of Palestine* (trans. H. J. Lawlor and J. E. L. Oulton; 2 vols.; London: SPCK; New York and Toronto: Macmillan, 1928; repr., 1954).

*Studies:* R. Laqueur, *Eusebius als Historiker seiner Zeit* (AKG 11; Berlin and Leipzig: de Gruyter, 1929). – J. Sirinelli, *Les vues historiques d'Eusèbe de Césarée durant la période préniceénne* (Dakar: Université de Dakar, Section de Langues et Littératures, 1961). – R. M. Grant, *Eusebius as Church Historian* (Oxford: Clarendon; New York: Oxford University Press, 1980). – G. F. Chesnut, *The First Christian Histories: Eusebius, Socrates, Sozomen, Theodoret, and Evagrius* (2d. ed.; Macon, Ga.: Mercer University Press, 1986). – F. Winkelmann, *Euseb von Kaisareia: Der Vater der Kirchengeschichte* (Berlin: Verlags-Anstalt Union, 1991). – R. W. Burgess, with the assistance of W. Witakowski, *Studies in Eusebian and Post-Eusebian Chronography* (Hist.E 135; Stuttgart: Steiner, 1999).

*Historiography:* F. Overbeck, *Über die Anfänge der Kirchengeschichtsschreibung* (Basel: L. Reinhardt, 1892). – A. Momigliano, "Pagan and Christian Historiography in the Fourth Century A.D.," in *The Conflict between Paganism and Christianity in the Fourth Century* (ed. A. Momigliano; Oxford: Clarendon, 1963), 79–99; repr. in A. Momigliano, *Essays in Ancient and Modern Historiography* (Oxford: Blackwell; Middletown, Conn.: Wesleyan University Press, 1977), 107–26. – P. Meinhold, *Geschichte der kirchlichen Historiographie* (2 vols.; OA 3.5; Fribourg, Switz.: Alber, 1967), 1:19–185. – A. Kehl and H.-I. Marrou, "Geschichtsphilosophie," *RAC* 10:703–79. – B. Croke and A. M. Emmett, eds., *History and Historians in Late Antiquity* (Sydney and New York: Pergamon, 1983). – E. Stöve, *TRE* 18:535–60. – F. Winkelmann, "Historiographie," *RAC* 15:724–65. – P. Siniscalco, *EECh* 1:388–90.

# B. Biblical and Exegetical Works

Of the exegetical works of Eusebius, those deserving special emphasis are the two commentaries, on the Psalms and Isaiah, and the *Onomasticon*. The significance of the *Commentary on the Psalms (Commentarius in Psalmos)*, presumably one of Eusebius's works written after 327–328, can be gauged already by the fact that both Hilary of Poitiers and Eusebius of Vercelli deemed it worthwhile enough to translate into Latin. Although it is not extant in full, significant parts of it have been preserved (for Ps 51–95 entirely, the rest in fragmentary form) and might perhaps be reconstructed completely from the frequent excerpts found in the catenas. The same applies to the *Commentary on Isaiah (Commentarius in Isaiam)*.

The *Onomasticon*, an alphabetical index of biblical place-names with geographical and historical comments, to date represents the most important historical source for the Holy Land. The *Onomasticon* enjoyed such popularity that Jerome translated it into Latin, with further corrections and additions. Since Eusebius wrote it upon the recommendation of Paulinus, bishop of Tyre, it must have been written before the latter's death in 331. According to the information in the *praefatio*, its present form comprises only the fourth book of the entire work. Book 1 contained the Greek translation of the ethnological concepts of the Hebrew Bible; bk. 2, a topography of ancient Judea and the territory of the twelve tribes; and bk. 3, a map of Jerusalem and the temple district, including comments on the same.

The exegesis of Eusebius proceeds largely from the historical meaning of Scripture. For him, the reason for adding an allegorical or typological interpretation is that the Psalms and the prophecies communicate on two levels, first to the author's contemporaries and then to future readers. For this reason, he emphatically opposes an arbitrary separation of the spiritual interpretation of the text (θεωρία) from its historical meaning.

*Editions: Das Onomastikon* (vol. 3/1 of *Eusebius Werke;* ed. E. Klostermann; 2d ed.; GCS; Leipzig: Hinrichs, 1992). – *Der Jesajakommentar* (vol. 9 of *Eusebius Werke;* ed. J. Ziegler; GCS; Leipzig: Hinrichs, 1975) [*Commentarii in Isaiam*].

*Studies:*
*Commentarii in Isaiam:* M. Simonetti, "Esegesi e ideologia nel *Commento a Isaia* di Eusebio," *RSLR* 19 (1983): 3–44. – M. Hollerich, *Eusebius of Caesarea's Commentary on Isaiah: Christian Exegesis in the Age of Constantine* (OECS; Oxford: Clarendon; New York: Oxford University Press, 1999).
*Commentarii in Psalmos:* C. Curti, *Eusebiana I: Commentarii in Psalmos* (2d ed.; Catania: Centro di Studi sull'Antico Cristianesimo, Università di Catania, 1989). – C. Curti, "La cronologia dei *Commentarii in Psalmos* di Eusebio di Cesarea," *Quaderni catanesi di studi classici e medievali* 2 (1990): 53–65.
*Onomasticon:* E. Klostermann, *Eusebius' Schrift* ΠΕΡΙ ΤΩΝ ΤΟΠΙΚΩΝ ΟΝΟΜΑΤΩΝ ΤΩΝ ΕΝ ΤΗ ΘΕΙΑ ΓΡΑΦΗ (TU 23.2b; Leipzig: Hinrichs, 1902). – P. Thomsen, "Palästina nach dem Onomastikon des Eusebius," *ZDPV* 26 (1903): 97–141, 145–88. – M. Noth, "Die topographischen Angaben im Onomastikon des Eusebius," *ZDPV* 66 (1963): 32–63. – C. U. Wolf, "Eusebius of Caesarea and the Onomasticon," *Biblical Archaeologist* 27 (1964): 66–96.

*Exegesis:* C. Sant, *The Old Testament Interpretation of Eusebius of Caesarea: The Manifold Sense of the Holy Scripture* (Malta: Royal University of Malta Press, 1967). – É. des Places, *Eusèbe de Césarée commentateur: Platonisme et Écriture sainte* (ThH 63; Paris: Beauchesne, 1982). – C. Curti, "L'esegesi di Eusebio di Cesarea: Caratteri e sviluppo," in *Le trasformazioni della cultura nella tarda antichità I* (ed. C. Giuffrida and M. Mazza; Rome: Jouvence, 1985), 459–78.

# C. Apologetic Works

Among the apologetic writings of Eusebius, the major two-volume work of the *Praeparatio evangelica* and the *Demonstratio evangelica* is particularly important. The groundwork for it was the "basic, general introduction to the Gospel," written before Eusebius's consecration as bishop (ca. 313), a compilation of OT messianic prophecies with comments, in ten books. Only the second half of it (bks. 6–9) and some fragments have been preserved under the separate name *Eclogae propheticae.*

The occasion for writing the *Praeparatio* and the *Demonstratio evangelica,* as the many citations indicate, was the attacks of the famous Neoplatonist Porphyry (d. 305) against the Christians. They were written after 270 and comprised fifteen books, all of which are lost today. Porphyry was only one, albeit very prominent, voice of a much more extensive polemic against Christians in the third century; against a polemic such as this, early Christian apologetics of necessity pursued a twofold goal from the start: to refute and, if possible, convince the opponent; and to establish and strengthen Christians' faith in order to counter or confront their insecurity and at the same time enable them to hold their own argumentatively in discussions (cf. ch. 3.I).

Eusebius pursues this twofold strategy as well. He responded to the work of Porphyry with a separate writing addressed to him, but it, too, has been lost. Only a smaller book that preceded it has been preserved; it was written between 311 and 313, against a polemical writing of the Bythinian governor Hierocles that supported the superiority of Apollonius of Tyana over Jesus Christ. The *Praeparatio* and the *Demonstratio evangelica* secondarily address Christians and—as Eusebius emphasizes—among them especially those who have just recently been converted from paganism. This apologetic catechesis in turn is divided into two parts in order to provide the reason why, in spite of all anti-Christian, often apparently extremely reasonable polemic, neither the pagan veneration of deities nor Judaism—regardless of the fact that both Jews and Christians worship the same God and Christianity grew out of Judaism—can be considered true faith.

Thus, with the customary apologetic arguments, the *Praeparatio evangelica* in fifteen books critiques pagan polytheism and ancient philosophy, which, as the older religion, claims to be the true one. Against this Eusebius adduces the already traditional apologetic evidence of antiquity. It was the Jewish nation that God chose for the preparation of the Messiah and his gospel (hence the title *Praeparatio evangelica*), for Moses had lived before Homer, and if there truly was a kernel of truth to be found in Greek philosophy, it would be found only where it draws from the Bible. At the outset of the final book (15), Eusebius himself summarizes the structure and content of this opus composed of two major sections. To begin with, bks. 1–6 reject the pagan belief in gods, by criticizing first, in the traditional fashion of early Christian apologetics, the immorality and absurdity of pagan myths about gods (1–3), then the foolishness of pagan oracles (4–5) and faith in blind fate, at the mercy of which the human finds himself (6). The second section (7–13), likewise using the traditional apologetic arguments, explains positively that the Christians rightly relinquished Greek philosophy and religion and in their place accepted the scripture of the Hebrews, because Moses and the prophets had lived before the Greek philosophers. The latter, especially Plato, had merely drawn from the former (the evidence of antiquity). In conclusion, bks. 14–15 emphasize the contradictions and errors of the various Greek philosophers.

Like the pagans' own myths and philosophy in the dispute with paganism, in the *Demonstratio evangelica* it is the Jews' own Bible, which the Christians had adopted as "the Old Testament," that constitutes the basis of refutation. The Jews reproach Christians for having appropriated the OT merely as a pretence in order to unjustly claim possession of the promises given to the elect people of God, for if Christians were really serious, they would also have to observe the law. Against this Eusebius has to demonstrate (*demonstrare*) on the basis of the OT that Christ is the expected Messiah, the gospel is the final form of the revelation of the one God, and the law only served as preparation for the gospel. Books 1–2 of the original twenty (only bks. 1–10 and a major fragment of bk. 15 are extant) show how the OT itself had already anticipated the end of the law and the calling of the Gen-

tiles. Books 3–10 address the prophetic witnesses of the OT regarding the humanity (3), the divinity (4–5), the incarnation and earthly life (6–9), and the suffering
and death (10) of the Messiah. The ten books that are lost most likely continued
this messianic salvation history, prophesied in the OT, through the resurrection,
the ascension, and the sending of the Spirit, up to the founding of the church. The
fragment from bk. 15 explains the four kingdoms in the book of Daniel.
    Both tractates probably originated before 325, the *Praeparatio evangelica*
perhaps ca. 312–322 and the *Demonstratio* immediately afterward, since nothing
internally points to the Arian controversy and the Council of Nicea (325).
    Cf. also the bibliography of ch. 3.I.

*Editions: Contra Hieroclem: Contre Hiéroclès* (ed. M. Forrat and É. des Places; SC 333; Paris:
    Cerf, 1986). – *Contra Marcellum, De ecclesiastica theologia: Gegen Marcell; Über die
    kirchliche Theologie; Die Fragmente Marcells* (vol. 4 of *Eusebius Werke;* ed. E. Kloster-
    mann; 2d ed.; GCS; Leipzig: Hinrichs, 1972). – *Die Demonstratio evangelica* (vol. 6 of
    *Eusebius Werke;* ed. I. A. Heikel; GCS; Leipzig: Hinrichs, 1913). – *Die Praeparatio
    evangelica* (vol. 8/1–2 of *Eusebius Werke;* ed. K. Mras and É. des Places; 2d ed.; GCS;
    Berlin: Akademie, 1982–1983). – *La préparation évangélique* (ed. J. Sirinelli et al.; 15
    vols. in 9; SC 206, 215, 228, 262, 266, 292, 307, 338, 369; Paris: Cerf, 1974–1991). –
    *Theophania: Die Theophanie* (vol. 3/2 of *Eusebius Werke;* ed. H. Gressmann; GCS;
    Leipzig: Hinrichs, 1904; ed. A. Laminski; 2d ed.; Berlin: Akademie, 1992).*

*Translations: Preparation for the Gospel* (trans. E. H. Gifford; Oxford: Clarendon, 1903;
    repr., Eugene, Oreg.: Wipf & Stock, 2002). – *The Proof of the Gospel: Being the Dem-
    onstratio evangelica of Eusebius of Caesarea* (trans. W. J. Ferrar, 2 vols.; London: SPCK;
    New York: Macmillan, 1920; repr., Eugene, Oreg.: Wipf & Stock, 2001).*

*Studies:* H. Gressmann, *Studien zu Eusebs Theophanie* (TU 23.3; Leipzig: Hinrichs, 1903). –
    H. Doergens, *Eusebius von Cäsarea als Darsteller der griechischen Religion: Eine Studie
    zur altchristlichen Apologetik* (FChLDG 12.5; Paderborn: F. Schöningh, 1922). –
    P. Henry, *Recherches sur la Préparation évangelique d'Eusèbe et l'édition perdue des
    œuvres de Plotin publiées par Eustochius* (Paris: E. Leroux, 1935). – J. J. O'Meara, "Por-
    phyry's 'Philosophy from Oracles' in Eusebius' *Praeparatio evangelica* and Augustine's
    Dialogues of Cassiciacum," *RechAug* 6 (1969): 103–39. – G. F. Chesnut, "Fate, For-
    tune, Free Will, and Nature in Eusebius of Caesarea," *ChH* 42 (1973): 165–82; repr. in
    E. Ferguson, ed., *Doctrines of Human Nature, Sin, and Salvation in the Early Church*
    (SEC 10; New York: Garland, 1993), 13–30. – M. Kertsch, "Traditionelle Rhetorik und
    Philosophie in Eusebius' Antirrhetikos gegen Hierokles," *VC* 34 (1980): 145–71. –
    E. V. Gallagher, "Eusebius the Apologist: The Evidence of the *Preparation* and the
    *Proof,*" in *Papers Presented at the Eleventh International Conference on Patristic Studies
    Held in Oxford, 1991* (ed. E. Livingstone; StPatr 26; Louvain: Peeters, 1993), 251–60.

# II. ARIUS

    Arius, in whose disputes Eusebius had been involved practically from the be-
ginning, probably came from Libya. It is estimated that he was born ca. 256. From
the early years of the Diocletian persecution, he lived in Alexandria, but he called
himself a student of Lucian of Antioch. The shape of his theology, however, points
rather to Origen and Alexandria. He was ordained to the diaconate by Bishop Peter

(ca. 300–311), who later excommunicated him because he supported Meletius of Lycopolis in the Meletian schism. Bishop Achillas (311/312) readmitted him into the community, however, and even consecrated him to the priesthood. Under Bishop Alexander (312–328), he was in charge of one of the city's churches, which (because of its form?) was called ἡ βαύκαλις (= a sturdy earthenware vessel with a narrow bottleneck). In this charge he proved himself a good preacher as well as a particularly assiduous pastor and was held in high regard.

During these years Arius developed his subsequently disputed and ultimately condemned theology of the relationship of the Son of God to the Father. In this pursuit he was led by the intention to offer a clear interpretation of Origen's doctrine of the Trinity. To God the Father, Son, and Spirit, Origen had attributed a hypostasis to each, but he subordinated the Son and the Spirit to the Father (subordinationism) so as to maintain the oneness of God in the sense of Monarchianism but at the same time to emphasize the distinction of the Trinity against every kind of Sabellianism. The resultant question of the precise relationship of the Trinity to one another had not been answered by then, however. This is what Arius now wanted to undertake on the basis of middle-Platonic or Neoplatonic principles. This Platonism taught that there is only one origin of being (τὸ ἕν), which alone is without beginning and alone possesses substance (ὑπόστασις) in the true sense of the word, that is, independent of anyone or anything. Arius transferred this conception to God the Father. He alone is the one God, the origin of all, without beginning (ἄναρχος), that is, alone unbegotten (ἀγέννητος) and uncreated (ἀγένητος)—previously these concepts had described an identical process. Hence he alone is eternal (ἀΐδιος), unchanging (ἄτρεπτος), and immutable (ἀναλλοίωτος). He alone possesses the unique divine hypostasis, that is, the divine nature (previously the concepts ὑπόστασις and οὐσία had not been distinguished clearly). The doubling of this divine attribute, according to this pattern of thinking, would conjure up ditheism, so Arius explained Origen's open-ended Trinitarian theology in a way that clearly placed the Son on the side of the created. The Son is begotten (γεν[ν]ητός), hence created (κτίσμα, ποίημα), with all of the implications. Ἦν ποτε ὅτε οὐκ ἦν—"At one time he did not exist"—became the slogan that best expresses the core of his theology, which he shaped in the Thalia (θάλεια = "banquet"), his main work, which is cited in almost all of the sources dealing with Arius.

In view of the biblical witness concerning Jesus, Arius explained his position to this effect, that the Son of God nonetheless assumes a special status that is uniquely outstanding among all creatures. He had been created before time began, and everything else had been created only through him. He takes precedence over all of creation (Prov 8:22–31). He also bears the names God, Logos, Sophia, and Dynamis, though not on account of his nature but on account of grace. God foresaw that Christ, despite his changeable nature (τρεπτός), would always bring together the freedom of his will (αὐτεξούσιος) with the will of God; therefore God bestowed glory (δόξα) upon him from the start, a glory that the human must attain only through moral excellence (ἀρετή) in life. However much this conception elevates the Son above all creatures, it does little to bridge the essential and absolute chasm between God the Father, on one side, and the Son, together with all the remaining creatures, on the other. According to Arius's model, the Son is God, though not "true God" (ἀληθινὸς θεός) because he does not share in the Father's nature (οὐσία/ὑπόστασις) and therefore is subordinate in terms of rank, authority, and glory. For this reason, the concepts of ὁμοούσιος and "equally eternal" are to be rejected because the latter, with the division of οὐσία, introduces materialistic conceptions and the latter presupposes two beings without beginning. The Son is and remains "alien and dissimilar in every way to the essence and selfhood of the Father" (ἀλλότριος μὲν καὶ ἀνόμοιος κατὰ πάντα τῆς τοῦ πατρὸς οὐσίας καὶ ἰδιότητος).

Hans Opitz pinpointed the beginning of the disputes to 318 and their initial phase to 318–322. The Meletians accused Arius of dogmatic innovations before the bishop, and in return Arius polemicized against the bishop's teaching that the Logos is "equally eternal" with the Father. At the same time, he wrote the *Thalia*, which is extant in fragments only. About 320 he wrote a letter addressed to Alexander with the joint signatures of several presbyters and deacons, and in late 327, together with Euzoius, an Alexandrian deacon and later his companion of many years, he sent a letter to Constantine to demonstrate his orthodoxy. Bishop Alexander at first reacted with great restraint in an encyclical and a letter to Alexander of Thessalonica or Byzantium, and Constantine initially viewed the quarrel only as an intra-church difference of opinion—comparable to the quarreling of philosophers—that unnecessarily jeopardized the unity of the church, which is important to the state.

Since Arius very quickly gained popularity and support beyond Egypt, a synod in Alexandria excommunicated him (323). This certainly did not settle the dispute, so Constantine, after gaining autocratic power, sent Ossius, bishop of Córdoba, to Alexandria on an official mission of peace in September 324. By the time the latter returned to the imperial residence in Nicomedia at the end of 324, his attempt at mediation had failed, but he had come to recognize the fundamental significance of the dispute, which transcended Alexandria. He also understood the confused situation of the vacancy of the see he encountered in Antioch on his return trip. Under his leadership, a synod undertook to fill the vacancy and at the same time addressed itself to the theology of Arius and condemned him, together with three of his followers, Eusebius of Caesarea among them, subject to the decision's confirmation by a larger synod. The following year a synod was initially invited to meet in Ancyra, but it ultimately gathered in Nicea and formulated an ecumenical creed, in which it introduced the ὁμοούσιος ("of the same essence") concept (cf. III.A).

Constantine's politics for resolving the issue described earlier (cf. 3.I.A) changed Arius's fate several times. In 328 the emperor recalled him from exile in Illyricum and strongly supported the quest for a reconciliation with Athanasius, Alexander's successor as bishop of Alexandria, who uncompromisingly turned him away. In 333 the emperor issued a further edict against Arius, decreeing the burning of his writings and his *damnatio memoriae*. Under the leadership of Eusebius of Caesarea and Eusebius of Nicomedia, however, a synod in Jerusalem came out in favor of restoring Arius, but he died just shortly before this was to be done, in 336. The ultimate failure of Arianism led to the far-reaching destruction of his works, as a result of which hardly anything of them has been preserved.

*Bibliographies:* A. M. Ritter, *"Arius redivivus?* Ein Jahrzwölft Arianismusforschung," *TRu* 55 (1990): 153–87. – A. M. Ritter, "Arius in der neueren Forschung," in *Homo imago et amicus Dei: Miscellanea in honorem Ioannis Golub* (ed. R. Perič; Rome: Pontificium Collegium Croaticum Sancti Hieronymi, 1991), 423–39.

*Editions:* E. Schwartz, "Die Dokumente des arianischen Streits bis 325: Die Quellen über den melitianischen Streit," NGWG.PH (1905): 3.257–99; repr. in idem, *Gesammelte Schriften* (5 vols.; Berlin: de Gruyter, 1938–1963), 3:117–68. – E. Schwartz, "Das antiochenische Synodal-Schreiben von 325," NGWG.PH (1908): 3.305–74; repr. in part, *Gesammelte Schriften* (5 vols.; Berlin: de Gruyter, 1938–1963), 3:169–87. – *Urkunden zur Geschichte des arianischen Streites: 318–321* (vol. 3/1 of *Athanasius Werke;* ed. H. G. Opitz; Berlin: de Gruyter, 1934–).

*Translations:* J. Stevenson, *A New Eusebius: Documents Illustrative of the History of the Church to A.D. 337* (rev. ed.; London: SPCK, 1987), 321–32.

*Encyclopedia Articles:* A. M. Ritter, *TRE* 3:692–719. – A. M. Ritter, "Arius," *GK* 1:215–23. M. Simonetti, "Arius–Arians–Arianism," *EECh* 1:76–78. – R. Williams, "Arianism," *EEC* 1:107–11 – C. Kannengiesser, "Arius," *EEC* 1:114–15.

*General Studies:* M. Simonetti, *Studi sull'arianesimo* (VSen NS 5; Rome: Studium, 1965). – E. Boularand, *L'hérésie d'Arius et la "foi" de Nicée* (2 vols.; Paris: Letouzey & Ané, 1972). – M. Simonetti, *La crisi ariana nel IV secolo* (SEAug 11; Rome: Institutum Patristicum Augustinianum, 1975). – R. C. Gregg, ed., *Arianism: Historical and Theological Reassessments* (PatMS 11; Cambridge, Mass.; Philadelphia Patristic Foundation, 1985). – J. T. Lienhard, "The 'Arian' Controversy: Some Categories Reconsidered," *TS* 48 (1987): 415–37. – R. Williams, *Arius: Heresy and Tradition* (rev. ed.; Grand Rapids: Eerdmans, 2002). – A. Martin, "Le fil D'Arius: 325–335," *RHE* 84 (1989): 297–333. – A. Martin, "Les relations entre Arius et Melitios dans la tradition alexandrine: Une histoire polémique," *JTS* NS 40 (1989): 401–13. – C. Kannengiesser, "Alexander and Arius of Alexandria: The Last Ante-Nicene Theologians," *Comp* 35 (1990): 93–105. – G. C. Stead, "Arius in Modern Research," *JTS* NS 45 (1994): 24–36.

*Chronology/Origins of the Controversy:* H.-G. Opitz, "Die Zeitfolge des arianischen Streites von den Anfängen bis zum Jahre 328," *ZNW* 33 (1934): 131–59. – W. Telfer, "When Did the Arian Controversy Begin?" *JTS* 47 (1946): 129–42. – W. Schneemelcher, "Zur Chronologie des arianischen Streites," *TLZ* 79 (1954): 393–400. – T. E. Pollard, "The Origins of Arianism," *JTS* NS 9 (1958): 103–11. – M. Simonetti, "Le origini dell'arianesimo," *RSLR* 7 (1971): 317–30. – U. Loose, "Zur Chronologie des arianischen Streites," *ZKG* 101 (1990): 88–92.

*Philosophy:* L. W. Barnard, "What Was Arius' Philosophy?" *TZ* 28 (1972): 110–17. – F. Ricken, "Zur Rezeption der platonischen Ontologie bei Eusebios von Kaisareia, Areios, und Athanasios," *TP* 53 (1978): 321–52. – R. D. Williams, "The Logic of Arianism," *JTS* NS 34 (1983): 56–81.

*Prehistory:* G. Bardy, *Recherches sur saint Lucien d'Antioche et son école* (ETH; Paris: Beauchesne, 1936). – L. W. Barnard, "The Antecedents of Arius," *VC* 24 (1979): 172–88. – *Logos: Festschrift für Luise Abramowski zum 8. Juli 1993* (ed. H. C. Brennecke, E. L. Grasmück, and C. Markschies; BZNW 67; Berlin: de Gruyter, 1993), 170–92.

*Synod of 324/325 (Antioch):* L. Abramowski, "Die Synode von Antiochien 324/25 und ihr Symbol," *ZKG* 86 (1975): 356–66.

*Thalia:* C. Kannengiesser, "Où et quand Arius composa-t-il la *Thalie?*" in *Kyriakon: Festshrift Johannes Quasten* (ed. P. Granfield and J. A. Jungmann; Münster: Aschendorff, 1970), 346–51. – G. C. Stead, "The *Thalia* of Arius and the Testimony of Athanasius," *JTS* NS 29 (1978): 20–52. – K. Metzler, "Ein Beitrag zur Rekonstruktion der '*Thalia*' des Arius," in K. Metzler and F. J. Simon, *Ariana et Athanasiana: Studien zur Überlieferung und zu philologischen Problemen der Werke des Athanasius von Alexandrien* (Opladen: West-deutscher Verlag, 1991), 11–45. – A. Pardini, "Citazioni letterali dalla 'θάλεια' in Atanasio, Ar. 1,5–5," *Orph.* 12 (1991): 411–28. – T. Böhm, "Die *Thalia* des Arius: Ein Beitrag zur fruehchristlichen Hymnologie," *VC* 46 (1992): 334–55.

*Theology:* A. Tulier, "Le sense du terme ὁμοούσιος dans le vocabulaire théologique d'Arius et de l'école d'Antioche," in *Papers Presented to the Third International Conference on Patristic Studies Held at Christ Church, Oxford, 1959* (ed. F. Cross; StPatr 3; TU 78; Berlin: Akademie, 1961), 421–30. – E. P. Meijering, "ΗΝ ΠΟΤΕ ΟΤΕ ΟΥΚ ΗΝ Ο ΥΙΟΣ: A Discussion on Time and Eternity," *VC* 28 (1974): 161–68. – R. Lorenz, *Arius judai-zans? Untersuchungen zur dogmengeschichtlichen Einordnung des Arius* (FKDG 31; Göttingen: Vandenhoeck & Ruprecht, 1979). – R. C. Gregg and D. E. Groh, *Early Arianism: A View of Salvation* (Philadelphia: Fortress, 1981). – T. Böhm, *Die Christo-logie des Arius: Dogmengeschichtliche Überlegungen unter besonderer Berücksichtigung der Hellenisierungsfrage* (St. Ottilien: EOS, 1991).

# III. COUNCIL OF NICEA (325)

Having attained autocracy in 324, Constantine summoned the first ecu-menical council in the history of the church, primarily for the purpose of settling the dispute with Arius. He initially summoned it to meet in Ancyra and then moved the location to Nicea, which was closer to his residence in Nicomedia. It is considered the first *ecumenical* council not only because it decided in a generally binding manner on an issue concerning the entire church but also because its composition represented the church as a whole. Constantine himself solemnly opened it in the main hall of his palace on May 20, 325, and exerted considerable influence upon its discussions and decisions. The emperor's function as leader can be explained on the basis of his understanding of power as the responsible guarantor of the unity of church and state, as Eusebius of Caesarea presented it, especially in the *Vita Constantini,* and this leadership was also continued by his suc-cessors. Later tradition claims that exactly 318 bishops participated in the Coun-cil of Nicea, bearing the title "holy fathers" for the first time (cf. introduction II). Even if this reference might come close to the actual number of participants of between 200 and 300 bishops, the precise number 318 refers symbolically to the 318 servants of Abraham (Gen 14:14) or to the interpretation of the Greek nu-meral 300, written as a τ (= cross of Christ) and of 18, written as ιη (= Jesus).[8] The prominent protagonists of the council were the following:

---

[8] On this, cf. M. Aubineau, "Les 318 serviteurs d'Abraham (Gen., XIV, 14) et le nombre des pères au concile de Nicée (325)," *RHE* 61 (1966): 5–43; H. Chadwick, "Les 318 pères de Nicée," *RHE* 61 (1966): 808–11.

- Ossius, bishop of Córdoba, who had already attempted mediation in Alexandria on behalf of the emperor and chaired the synod of Antioch in 324/325. Various evidence indicates that at Nicea he may have functioned not only as a confidante of the emperor but, together with two Roman presbyters, as official representative of the bishop of Rome.

- Alexander, patriarch of Alexandria, together with Athanasius, his deacon and later successor, who for half a century was to become the leader of the Nicene party and the soul of the anti-Arian resistance.

- Patriarch Eustathius, newly installed in the bishopric of Antioch, who in 330 was exiled precisely for his uncompromising Nicene position.

- Eusebius, bishop of Caesarea, who after his provisional excommunication by the synod of Antioch initially had to defend himself before the council but subsequently fulfilled an important political role in the search for a tenable compromise between Arianism and adamant Nicenism.

- Nicolas, bishop of Myra, who continues to be popular today (as St. Nicholas), may have participated in the council but without assuming prominence.

- The Arian position was represented mainly by Arius himself, together with Eusebius, bishop of Nicomedia, and other students of Lucian of Antioch.

It is impossible to know precisely how long the council met. It may have concluded on June 19, 325, or with the celebration of the twentieth anniversary of the reign of Constantine (*vicennalia*), which began on July 25, 325. It may be assumed that minutes were kept of the sessions of the council; no records of the council have been preserved, however. Its decisions are handed down only indirectly. It issued four documents: a creed (*symbolum*), which was signed by everyone except Arius and two of his followers, who were excommunicated for it and exiled to Illyricum; a decree concerning the correct and ecumenically binding date of Easter; twenty canons on matters of discipline; and a letter of the synod to communicate the results of the council to the fellow churches.

*Editions:* Mansi 2:635–1082. – C. H. Turner, ed., *Ecclesiae occidentalis monumenta iuris antiquissima: Canonum et conciliorum graecorum interpretationes latinae* (2 vols. in 5; Oxford: Clarendon, 1899–1939), 1/1:97–280, 297–368. – N. P. Tanner and G. Alberigo, *Decrees of the Ecumenical Councils* (London: Sheed & Ward; Washington, D.C.: Georgetown University Press, 1990), 1–19. [ET].

*Encyclopedia Articles:* C. Kannengiesser, *EECh* 2:595 – H. C. Brennecke, *TRE* 24:429–41. – H. Vogt, *EEC* 2:810–12.

*Manuals:* J. Hefele and H. Leclercq, *Histoire des conciles: D'après les documents originaux* (Paris: Letouzey & Ané, 1907–), 1/1:335–632. – I. Ortiz de Urbina, *Nicée et Constantinople* (HCO 1; Paris: Orante, 1963), 13–136. – C. Luibhéid, *The Council of Nicaea*

(Galway, Ireland: Officina Typographica, Galway University Press, 1982). – L. D. Davis, *The First Seven Ecumenical Councils (325–787): Their History and Theology* (Wilmington, Del.: Glazier, 1983; repr., Collegeville, Minn.: Liturgical, 1990). – L. Perrone, in *Storia dei concili ecumenici* (ed. G. Alberigo et al.; Brescia: Queriniana, 1990), 23–45.

*Studies:* F. Ricken, "Nikaia als Krisis des altchristlichen Platonismus," *TP* 44 (1969): 321–41. – F. Ricken, "Das Homousios von Nikaia als Krisis des altchristlichen Platonismus," in *Zur Frühgeschichte der Christologie: Ihre biblischen Anfänge und die Lehrformel von Nikaia* (ed. B. Welte; QD 51; Fribourg, Switz.: Herder, 1970), 74–99. – M. Simonetti, "Teologia alessandrina e teologia asiatica al concilio di Nicea," *Aug* 13 (1973): 369–98. – G. C. Stead, "Eusebius and the Council of Nicaea," *JTS* NS 24 (1973): 85–100; repr. in E. Ferguson, ed., *Doctrines of God and Christ in the Early Church* (SEC 9; New York: Garland, 1993), 111–26. – H. von Campenhausen, "Das Bekenntnis Eusebs von Caesarea (Nicaea 325)," *ZNW* 67 (1976): 123–39; repr. in idem, *Urchristliches und Altchristliches* (Tübingen: Mohr, 1979), 278–99. – B. Lonergan, *The Way to Nicea: The Dialectical Development of Trinitarian Theology* (trans. C. O'Donovan; London: Darton, Longman & Todd, 1982; trans. of *De Deo Trino*; Rome: Apud Aedes Universitatis Gregorianae, 1964). – T. F. Torrance, *The Trinitarian Faith: The Evangelical Theology of the Ancient Catholic Church* (Edinburgh: T&T Clark, 1988). – M. Tetz, "Zur strittigen Frage arianischer Glaubenserklärung auf dem Konzil von Nicaea (325)," in *Logos: Festschrift für Luise Abramowski zum 8. Juli 1993* (ed. H. C. Brennecke, E. L. Grasmück, and C. Markschies; BZNW 67; Berlin: de Gruyter, 1993), 220–38.

# A. Symbolum

The council's main issue was to clarify theologically and pin down in an ecclesiastically binding way belief in the Trinity in confrontation with the theology of Arius. The fathers of the council did this for the first time, not in theological propositions but in the form of a creed *(symbolum)*. Previously there existed only local churches' *symbola*, which had developed from brief statements of faith, such as those already contained in the NT. In the life of the communities, they had their setting in the baptismal liturgy, during which the baptizand was questioned about his faith and which is still practiced on Easter eve. Originally this baptismal confession was interrogative rather than declarative in form, and even the name *symbolum* probably goes back to the function of the baptismal confession as a proof of identity that had to be presented in order to receive baptism. The decree of an ecumenically binding credo turned it into the test for orthodoxy, into a *regula fidei* in a new sense.

As a basis for its *symbolum,* the council took up either the baptismal confession of the church of Caesarea, which Eusebius presented—and which was accepted—as evidence of his orthodoxy, or that of another Syro-Palestinian city, and then supplemented it with statements that were more precise, excluding the Arian interpretation as much as possible. Besides biblical concepts, they also introduced technical philosophical terms, the most important among them being that of ὁμοούσιος:

| | |
|---|---|
| Πιστεύομεν εἰς ἕνα θεὸν | We believe in one God, |
| πατέρα παντοκράτορα | the Father almighty, |
| πάντων ὁρατῶν τε καὶ ἀοράτων | maker of all things visible and invisible; |
| ποιητήν. | |
| Καὶ εἰς ἕνα κύριον Ἰησοῦν Χριστόν | And in one Lord Jesus Christ, |
| τὸν υἱὸν τοῦ θεοῦ | the Son of God, |
| γεννηθέντα ἐκ τοῦ πατρὸς μονογενῆ | begotten from the Father, only-begotten, |
| τουτέστιν ἐκ τῆς οὐσίας τοῦ πατρός, | that is, from the substance of the Father, |
| θεὸν ἐκ θεοῦ | God from God, |
| φῶς ἐκ φωτός | light from light, |
| θεὸν ἀληθινὸν ἐκ θεοῦ ἀληθινοῦ, | true God from true God, |
| γεννηθέντα οὐ ποιηθέντα, | begotten not made, |
| ὁμοούσιον τῷ πατρί, | of one substance with the Father, |
| δι' οὗ τὰ πάντα ἐγένετο, | through whom all things came into being, |
| τά τε ἐν τῷ οὐρανῷ καὶ τὰ ἐν τῇ γῇ | things in heaven and things on earth, |
| τὸν δι' ἡμᾶς τοὺς ἀνθρώπους | who for us humans |
| καὶ διὰ τὴν ἡμετέραν σωτηρίαν | and for our salvation |
| κατελθόντα καὶ σαρκωθέντα, | came down and became incarnate, |
| ἐνανθρωπήσαντα | becoming human, |
| παθόντα | suffered |
| καὶ ἀναστάντα τῇ τρίτῃ ἡμέρᾳ, | and rose again on the third day, |
| ἀνελθόντα εἰς τοὺς οὐρανούς, | ascended to the heavens, |
| ἐρχόμενον κρῖναι ζῶντας καὶ νεκρούς. | will come to judge the living and the dead; |
| Καὶ εἰς τὸ ἅγιον πνεῦμα. | And in the Holy Spirit. |
| Τοὺς δὲ λέγοντας ἦν ποτε ὅτε οὐκ ἦν | But as for those who say, "There was when he was not," |
| καὶ πρὶν γεννηθῆναι οὐκ ἦν | and "Before being born He was not," |
| καὶ ὅτι ἐξ οὐκ ὄντων ἐγένετο | and that He came into existence out of nothing, |
| ἢ ἐξ ἑτέρας ὑποστάσεως | or who assert that the Son of God is of a different hypostasis |
| ἢ οὐσίας φάσκοντας εἶναι | or substance, |
| [ἢ κτιστὸν] | or is subject to alteration |
| ἢ τρεπτὸν | or change— |
| ἢ ἀλλοιωτὸν τὸν υἱὸν τοῦ θεοῦ, | |
| τοὺς ἀναθεματίζει ἡ καθολικὴ | these the catholic |
| καὶ ἀποστολικὴ ἐκκλησία. | and apostolic church anathematizes.[9] |

The creed is composed of three parts, with the third part, dealing with the Holy Spirit, remaining a simple assertion: "and in the Holy Spirit." The latter is part of the baptismal formula, but the doctrine of the Spirit had until then nei-

---

[9] The translation is a slightly modified version of that found in J. N. D. Kelly's *Early Christian Creeds* (3d ed; London: Longman, 1972), 215–16.

ther become problematic nor been developed further. In fact, other *symbola* are only bipartite (Father-Son) or purely christological, which aptly indicates the original concern of theology and creed—redemption through Jesus Christ. Afterwards, the perspective broadens, albeit in a subordinated way, to the Father as Creator of the world and sender of the Son and finally to the Spirit. For this reason also, the christological section takes up the major part of all creeds, and controversies are ignited on this section. The statements about God the Father are hardly in question. In any case, the name of God befits the Father first and foremost; he is the Father, omnipotent and Creator of the universe. All other divine attributes derive logically from this.

In the christological section of the Nicene *symbolum*, the ὁμοούσιος ("of the same substance") concept has become a catchword constituting the core of the anti-Arian confession; it aligns the Son clearly and irrevocably with God, and every further statement of precision inserted by the council follows from it. This also made it possible to differentiate clearly two terms that had been considered synonymous, γεννηθείς ("begotten") and γενηθείς ("created"); the former now refers to the eternal generation of the Son from the οὐσία (not from the will) of the Father, whereas the latter only describes creatureliness (ποιηθείς). Thus Christ is not only God in the derived sense (from the Father) but "true God of true God." For this reason, the final anathema concluding the creed lists all of the Arian theologoumena to be rejected for assuming that the Son, however exceptional, is nevertheless a creature. (The tradition of concluding the doctrinal decisions of a council with an anathema invoked on opponents was not relinquished until the Second Vatican Council).

Since both parties were first of all concerned with protecting and correctly interpreting the biblical kerygma, nonbiblical concepts were fundamentally suspect and only reluctantly adopted. By resolving the question of the Son's divinity philosophically by way of the Father's οὐσία, the council implied two problems with which the dispute on accepting this *symbolum* would be concerned:

1) Because of the unclear delimitation of the two terms, the possible identification of οὐσία with ὑπόστασις hid a potential Sabellian interpretation of the *symbolum*, that is, an inadequate differentiation of the divine "persons." Such a clear differentiation of the latter did not come about until the Council of Constantinople (381) in the formula μία φύσις τρεῖς ὑποστάσεις.

2) The question that logically follows concerns the relationship between divinity and humanity in the incarnate Son of God, which despite the augmented ἐνανθρωπήσαντα used here, is biblically described as σαρκωθέντα (John 1:14) (*logos-sarx* schema). This led to the explicit denial of Jesus' soul by Apollinaris of Laodicea and of the θεοτόκος title by Nestorius. A final solution in terms of a *logos-anthropos* schema did not come about until the Council of Chalcedon (451) in the formula ἐν πρόσωπον–δύο φύσεις.

*Editions:* ACO 2/1 [323]; 2/3 [394]. – G. L. Dossetti, *Il simbolo di Nicea e di Costantinopoli: Edizione critica* (TRSR 2; Rome: Herder, 1967) [Com].

*Encyclopedia Articles:* W.-D. Hauschild, *TRE* 24 (1994): 444–56.

*Translations:* H. R. Percival, trans., "The Nicene Creed," in *NPNF²* (Peabody, Mass.: Hendrickson, 1995; repr. of 1890 ed.), 14:3.

*Studies:* H. Lietzmann, "Symbolstudien XIII," *ZNW* 24 (1925): 193–202; repr. in idem, *Kleine Schriften* (3 vols.; TU 74; Berlin: Akademie, 1958–1962), 3:248–60. – H. J. Carpenter, "*Symbolum* as a Title of the Creed," *JTS* 43 (1942): 1–11. – W. Rordorf, "La confession de foi et son 'Sitz im Leben' dans l'Église ancienne," *NovT* 9 (1967): 225–38. – D. L. Holland, "The Creeds of Nicea and Constantinople Reexamined," *ChH* 38 (1969): 248–61. – J. N. D. Kelly, *Early Christian Creeds* (3d ed.; London: Longman, 1972), 205–62. – J. N. D. Kelly, "The Nicene Creed: A Turning Point," *SJT* 36 (1983): 29–39. – A. M. Ritter, *TRE* 13 (1984): 399–412. – A. de Halleux, "La réception du symbole œcuménique, de Nicée à Chalcédoine," *EThL* 61 (1985): 1–47. – J. Ulrich, *Die Anfänge der abendländischen Rezeption des Nizänums* (PTS 39; Berlin and New York: de Gruyter, 1994). – R. Staats, *Das Glaubensbekenntnis von Nizäa-Konstantinopel: Historische und theologische Grundlagen* (Darmstadt: Wissenschaftliche Buchgesellschaft, 1996).

# B. Easter Decree

From Polycarp of Smyrna to the Easter controversy under Victor bishop of Rome and Irenaeus of Lyon, the issue of a uniform date for Easter had not been officially resolved. According to Roman and Alexandrian tradition Easter had been observed on the first Sunday after the first full moon of spring; following the Jewish practice, on 14th Nisan; or on the following Sunday, as the Christians of Asia Minor observed it on the basis of the Johannine tradition. The Council of Nicea settled this open question once and for all with a decree that obligated all churches to adhere to the Roman practice.

In form and function, there is hardly any difference between decrees and canons. Both are used to regulate matters of faith and discipline. Hence it may have been because of its significance that the Council of Nicea extrapolated the Easter decree from the twenty canons. The form of the Easter decree nevertheless differs from that of the canons handed down to us, in that it explains the circumstances of the council, the problem, and the discussion instead of merely announcing decisions, as the canons do.

*Editions:* J.-B. Pitra, *Juris ecclesiastici Graecorum historia et monumenta I* (Rome, 1864), 427–40. – V. N. Benesevic, *Ioannis Scholastici Synagoga L titulorum ceteraque eiusdem opera iuridica* (ABAW.PH 14; Munich: Verlag der Bayerischen Akademie der Wissenschaften, 1937–), 1:156.

*Translations:* H. R. Percival, trans., "On the Keeping of Easter," in *NPNF²* (Peabody, Mass.: Hendrickson, 1995; repr. of 1890 ed.), 14:54–55.

*Studies:* J. Schmid, *Die Osterfestfrage auf dem ersten allgemeinen Konzil von Nicäa* (ThSLG 13; Vienna: Mayer, 1905). – F. Daunoy, "La question pascale au concile de Nicée," *EOr* 24 (1925): 424–44. – G. Larentzakis, "Das Osterfestdatum nach dem I. Ökumenischen Konzil von Nikaia (325): Die Rolle von Alexandrien und Rom," *ZKT* 101 (1979): 67–78.

# C. Canons

In a nonsystematic sequence, the council's twenty canons address questions of ecclesiastical structures (4–7, 15, 16), the dignity of the clergy (1–3, 9, 10, 17), public penance (11–14), the readmission of schismatics and heretics (8, 19), and liturgical regulations (18, 20). Canon 3, for instance, stipulates that clerics should have in their house only their mother, sister, or aunt or a woman who is altogether beyond suspicion. Canon 4 regulates the consecration of bishops by at least three bishops. Canon 18 prohibits deacons from administering the Eucharist to a priest. These regulations have not lost their basic validity even today. Canons 8 and 19 regulate the conditions by which the Meletians and Paulinians (followers of Paul of Samosata) may and ought to be readmitted into the church.

Practically all synods and councils before and after Nicea issued such disciplinary canons, along with their creedal decisions, in order to regulate interdiocesan issues.

*Editions:* P.-P. Joannou, ed., *Les canons des conciles œcuméniques (IIe–IXe s.)* (vol. 1/1 of *Discipline générale antique: [IVe–IXe s.];* FCCO 9; Grottaferrata [Rome]: Tipografia Italo-Orientale "S. Nilo," 1962), 23–41.

*Translations:* H. R. Percival, trans., "The Canons of the 318 Holy Fathers Assembled in the City of Nice, in Bithynia," in *NPNF²* (Peabody, Mass.: Hendrickson, 1995; repr. of 1890 ed.), 14:8–45. – J. Stevenson, *A New Eusebius* (rev. ed.; London: SPCK, 1987), 338–44.

*Studies:* W. Bright, *The Canons of the First Four General Council of Nicaea, Constantinople, Ephesus, and Chalcedon, with Notes* (2d ed.; Oxford: Clarendon, 1892). – P. L'Huillier, *The Church of the Ancient Councils: The Disciplinary Work of the First Four Ecumenical Councils* (Crestwood, N.Y.: St. Vladimir's Seminary Press, 1996), 17–100.

# D. Synodal Letter

In order to inform the fellow churches, and as a token of fellowship between the churches, it is reasonable to assume that the Council of Nicea sent a considerable number of synodal letters; only those addressed to the churches of Alexandria and Egypt have been preserved, however. Following custom, it begins with references to the sender and the recipient and a greeting: "To the church of Alexandria . . . and to our well-beloved brethren, . . . throughout Egypt, and Pentapolis, and Libya . . . the holy and great synod, the bishops assembled at Nicea, wish health in the Lord." This was followed by a description of the event, the course of the council, and its resolutions concerning Arius, the Meletian schism, and the decree on the date of Easter. The canons are not listed, although they are referred to in the following way: "If in the presence of . . . our colleague and brother Alexander, anything else has been enacted, . . . he will himself convey it to you in great detail, he having been both a guide and fellow-worker in what has been done." The ending of the letter follows convention, including a request for prayer and with praise to the Trinity as a closing salutation.

*Editions:* "Urkunde 23 zur Geschichte des arianischen Streites," in *Athanasius Werke* (ed. H. G. Opitz; Berlin: de Gruyter, 1934), 3/1:47–51.

*Translations:* H. R. Percival, trans., "The Synodal Letter," in *NPNF²* (Peabody, Mass.: Hendrickson, 1995; repr. of 1890 ed.), 14:53–54. – J. Stevenson, *A New Eusebius* (rev. ed.; London: SPCK, 1987), 347–50.

# IV. ATHANASIUS

Alexander, the patriarch of Alexandria, died on April 17, 328, but not before designating on his deathbed Athanasius, his deacon, as his successor. Athanasius had accompanied him to the Council of Nicea and there demonstrated a firm anti-Arian position. Yet the Meletian schism was still unresolved. Alexander had not implemented the regulations established by the Council of Nicea on the readmission of the Meletians. As a result, a (slim) majority of Egyptian bishops did not acknowledge his supremacy as metropolitan. Hence there was a risk that this party might choose its own bishop in a perfectly legal election; consequently, a few of the bishops devoted to Alexander hurriedly elected Athanasius as the new patriarch and consecrated him on June 8, 328. They did not adhere to all of the stipulations of canon 4 of the Council of Nicea, since they failed to solicit the prescribed written approval of those who could not be present; later on, his opponents reproached him for this. When, however, Emperor Constantine, whom Athanasius informed immediately of his appointment, expressed his approval in a congratulatory letter to the church of Alexandria, the majority of the Egyptian bishops were willing to recognize Athanasius.

Until now it has been traditionally accepted that Athanasius was thirty-three years old when he was consecrated bishop and hence was born ca. 295. Recently, however, Martin[10] and Kannengiesser[11] have appealed to an index according to which Athanasius had not yet attained the required canonical age of thirty at his consecration.[12] In this case, he would have been born only ca. 300. We have virtually no reliable information on his origin, childhood, and adolescence. It seems certain that he was Alexandrian and raised in a non-Christian family. In his version of Eusebius's *Ecclesiastical History* (10.15), Rufinus reports that Bishop Alexander had come to know Athanasius in his childhood at the shore. His attention was drawn to him when he played "baptism" with his playmates, assuming the role of the bishop. When Alexander investigated this in detail, he realized that

---

[10] ThH 27:42³⁴.

[11] C. Kannengiesser, "The Athanasian Decade, 1974–84: A Bibliographic Report," *TS* 46 (1985): 524f.; *EEC* 1:110.

[12] M. Simonetti, *La crisi ariana nel IV secolo* (SEAug 11; Rome: Institutum Patristicum Augustinianum, 1975), 11: "poco più (o meno) che trentenne."

Athanasius had accurately performed the rites, so Alexander acknowledged the baptism to have been carried out legitimately. After consulting with his parents, Alexander placed Athanasius in the care of the priests for his training, and so he grew up "in the temple like Samuel." Whether this story needs to be referred to the realm of pious legends depends on the date of birth one accepts for Athanasius. Since Alexander became bishop in 313, Athanasius the "child" would have been either thirteen or at least eighteen years old.

By contrast, the "Story of the Patriarch of Alexandria" by Severus Ibn al-Muqaffa, preserved in Arabic, can claim greater plausibility.[13] According to this work, Athanasius was the son of a noble and rich Alexandrian widow, who pushed her adult son to get married in order to take over his father's estate. But since Athanasius showed no inclination toward this, she repeatedly sent beautiful girls into his bedroom at night to make marriage and middle-class life palatable to him. When Athanasius woke up, he always chased the girls away. In her desperation, the mother went to a well-known magician in the city, who conversed with Athanasius and then informed the mother that her endeavors were in vain and would remain so because her son had turned to Christianity, where he would become a great man. In order not to lose her son, she went to Bishop Alexander with him, and he baptized both of them. After the mother's death, Alexander received Athanasius as a son, educated him, and later ordained him as a deacon and made him his secretary. Athanasius himself confirms this information insofar as being Alexander's *anagnost* (lector) and secretary, as well as a deacon (from ca. 318/319). His later ascetic and monastic tendencies, which were shaped by his close association with Egyptian monasticism, seem to go back to his adolescent years as well.

Soon after his consecration as bishop, Athanasius (330–334) made visitations throughout his diocese to strengthen his support among the clergy and especially to integrate monasticism ecclesiastically. He was so successful with the latter that in later years, perhaps for the first time ever, he consecrated monks as bishops and found support and shelter in the monasteries. He steadfastly opposed all the endeavors of Constantine to reconcile Arius. As a result, the Meletians, who had installed an anti-bishop, allied themselves with the Arian party associated with Eusebius of Nicomedia and attempted to have Athanasius deposed by means of a criminal court case. Attempts to have him convicted of lèse-majesté (331/332) and murder (332/333) failed because, among other things, Athanasius succeeded in tracking down Bishop Arsenius, who was alleged to have been murdered, in his hideout with the Meletians. As a result, his opponents instituted proceedings in an episcopal court at Caesarea in Palestine (334), which Athanasius simply ignored. The synod of Tyre (335), which Constantine thereupon summoned and which Athanasius attended but left prematurely to travel to Constantinople, deposed him. Constantine rejected his appeal and on November 7, 335, exiled him to Treveri (Trier), possibly because the Eusebians accused him

---

[13] PO I/4, 407f.

of threatening to use the Egyptian grain shipments, which were vital for the capital, so as to exert pressure, but certainly because he was an obstacle to the imperial plans for Arius's reconciliation. In Trier Athanasius formed good relations with Bishop Maximinus and later on also with Paulinus, his successor, who became with him the outstanding defenders of the Nicene faith in the West.

After the death of Emperor Constantine on May 22, 337, Constantine II, his eldest son, issued an amnesty, as the Caesar residing in Trier, for political reasons and allowed Athanasius to return to the East. Constantius II, his brother, recognized his decision, and Athanasius therefore was able to move back to Alexandria again on November 23, 337.

A synod held in 338 also rehabilitated him ecclesiastically and canceled the conviction by the synod of Tyre. The opposing party did not recognize this rehabilitation, however, and therefore incited unrest in the city, complained to the emperor, attempted to isolate Athanasius from Rome, and finally elevated Gregory, a Cappadocian, as antibishop in early 339. On March 18, 339, they expelled Athanasius, who went to Rome, where Marcellus of Ancyra was staying as well. Julius, bishop of Rome, invited the Eusebian party as well to a synod, which the latter declined as the presumptuous act of a jurisdictional overlordship. As a result, the synod, convening in Rome in 341, declared itself in favor of both Athanasius and Marcellus. Only five years later, Emperor Constans forced the repatriation of the exiled bishops, and so Athanasius was not able to move back to Alexandria triumphantly until October 21, 346, after seven years of absence.

The following years seem to have been a more peaceful time of pastoral and literary work without a resolution of the fundamental problems, so that they broke out again from 353 on. In an edict of Arles (353), Emperor Constantius demanded the signing of a letter of the Eastern bishops from the year 347/348, in which Photinus, Marcellus of Ancyra, and Athanasius were summarily characterized as heretics. As a result, the synods of Arles (353) and Milan (355) condemned Athanasius once again. The few who refused to sign were exiled, Paulinus of Trier and Liberius of Rome among them. On February 8, 356, Athanasius barely escaped when imperial troops occupied the church of Theonas, and he found shelter in monasteries that had been closely associated with him since his efforts at the outset of his pontificate.

Constantius's death on November 3, 361, and the failure of George, the anti-bishop, who had already been chased away on October 2, 358, and was murdered on December 24, 361, made it possible for Athanasius to return to his bishopric on February 21, 362, especially since the new emperor, Julian the Apostate, was not interested in Christianity at all. Immediately after his return, he summoned a synod, which addressed the Meletian schism in Antioch and in his *Tomus ad Antiochenos* set the course decisively in terms of the theology of the Trinity and in Christology. This document for the first time conceded the language of three hypostases in God, condemned the teaching of the Holy Spirit's creatureliness and separation from the οὐσία of Christ, and for the first time dealt with the christological explication of the Nicene concepts of the incarnation (σά ρκωσις) and the becoming human (ἐνανθρώπησις) of the Son of God. Emperor

Julian reacted to Athanasius's successful work by banishing him; the prophetic words he spoke while leaving the city on October 24, 362, "My sons, be of good heart, it is only a cloud, and it will soon pass away," were to be fulfilled only too soon. On June 26, 363, Julian fell in battle against the Persians. Athanasius's escape is associated with the famous anecdotal account according to which he fled in a boat heading up the river Nile while those pursuing him moved dangerously close. He had the boat turn around and boldly rode toward them. When the boats met, the soldiers asked innocently whether they had seen Athanasius; the response they were given was truthful but ambiguous, namely, that he was not far and, if they hurried, they would quickly apprehend him.

The subsequent reign of Emperor Jovian and the final expulsion of Athanasius proved to be brief episodes only. Jovian confirmed Athanasius as legitimate bishop of Alexandria; Jovian died on February 17, 364, however, at the same time that the latter returned to Alexandria. Valens, his successor, an Arian of Homoean orientation, thereupon ordered the renewed exiling of all the (Nicene) bishops whom Jovian had reinstated. Consequently, Athanasius left Alexandria on October 5, 365, before the imperial soldiers arrived; by an edict issued on February 1, 366, the emperor reinstated him. During the remaining seven years of his life, Athanasius was left alone. They were filled with contacts with Rome and (from 371 on) with Basil of Caesarea, who was to be handed the baton as leader of the Nicene party. The efforts of the latter to mediate the ecclesiastical reconciliation between Athanasius and Meletius of Antioch were unsuccessful. Athanasius was seventy-eight years old when he died on May 2, 373.

Few church fathers have enjoyed as lengthy an "afterlife" as Athanasius. Since 1568 the Western church has revered him, together with Basil the Great, Gregory of Nazianzus, and John Chrysostom, as one of the "four great ecclesiastical teachers of the East." Johann Adam Möhler's *Kirchenbild*, exerting its influence into the present, was shaped significantly by his research on Athanasius (1827). Ernst Bloch deemed the doctrine of ὁμοουσία to be the "most revolutionary topos" of any religious founder: "The Arians had asserted mere similarity with God.... Instead it was precisely orthodoxy, by condemning the Arian teaching at the Council of Nicea and canonizing the teaching of Athanasius on the homoousia with the Father, that approved for Christ ... the most revolutionary topos that a founder, a parousia ever held."[14]

*Bibliographies:* C. Kannengiesser, "The Athanasian Decade, 1974–84: A Bibliographical Report," *TS* 46 (1985): 524–41. – C. Butterweck, *Athanasius von Alexandrien: Bibliographie* (Opladen: Westdeutscher Verlag, 1995).

*Encyclopedia Articles:* G. Gentz, *RAC* 1:860–6. – M. Tetz, *TRE* 4:333–49. – C. Kannengiesser, "Athanasius von Alexandrien," *GK* 1:266–83. – G. C. Stead, *EECh* 1:93–95. – C. Kannengiesser, *EEC* 1:138–40.

*Collections of Essays:* C. Kannengiesser, ed., *Politique et théologie chez Athanase d'Alexandrie* (ThH 27; Paris: Beauchesne, 1974). – *Kyrios* 14 (1974).

---

[14] E. Block, *Atheismus im Christentum* (Frankfurt: Suhrkamp, 1968), 230f.

*Studies:* E. Schwartz, *Zur Geschichte des Athanasius I–IX* (NGWG.PH 1904), 333–401,
518–47; 1905, 164–87, 257–99; 1908, 305–74; 1911, 367–426, 469–522. – E. Schwartz,
"Zur Kirchengeschichte des vierten Jahrhunderts," *ZNW* 34 (1935): 129–213; repr. in
idem, *Gesammelte Schriften,* vol. 4, *Zur Geschichte der alten Kirche und ihres Rechts*
(Berlin: de Gruyter, 1960), 1–110. – E. Schwartz, *Gesammelte Schriften,* vol. 3, *Zur
Geschichte des Athanasius* (Berlin: de Gruyter, 1959). – D. Ritschl, *Athanasius: Versuch
einer Interpretation* (Theologische Studien 76; Zurich: EVZ, 1964). – L. W. Barnard,
"Athanasius and the Meletian Schism in Egypt," *JEA* 59 (1973): 181–89. – K. M.
Girardet, *Kaisergericht und Bischofsgericht: Studien zu den Anfängen des Donatisten-
streites (313–315) und zum Prozess des Athanasius von Alexandrien (328–346)* (Ant.
1.21; Bonn: R. Habelt, 1975). – W. H. C. Frend, "Athanasius as an Egyptian Christian
Leader in the Fourth Century," in idem, *Religion Popular and Unpopular in the Early
Christian Centuries* (London: Variorum, 1976), 20–37. – M. Tetz, "Zur Biographie des
Athanasius von Alexandrien," *ZKG* 90 (1979): 304–38. – R. Klein, "Zur Glaubwürdig-
keit historischer Aussagen des Bischofs Athanasius von Alexandria über die Religi-
onspolitik des Kaisers Constantius II," in *Proceedings of the Eighth International
Conference on Patristic Studies, Oxford, 3–8 September, 1979* (ed. E. Livingstone;
3 vols.; StPatr 17; Oxford and New York: Pergamon, 1982), 3:996–1017. – D. W. H.
Arnold, *The Early Episcopal Career of Athanasius of Alexandria* (CJAn 6; Notre Dame,
Ind.: University of Notre Dame Press, 1991). – T. D. Barnes, *Athanasius and Con-
stantius: Theology and Politics in the Constantinian Empire* (Cambridge, Mass., and
London: Harvard University Press, 1993). – D. Brakke, *Athanasius and the Politics of
Asceticism* (OECS; Oxford: Clarendon; New York: Oxford University Press, 1995);
repr. as *Athanasius and Asceticism* (Baltimore: Johns Hopkins University Press, 1998).
– C. Kannengiesser, "Athanasius of Alexandria and the Ascetic Movement of His
Time," in *Asceticism* (ed. V. Wimbush; New York: Oxford University Press, 1995),
479–92. – A. Martin, *Athanase d'Alexandrie et l'église d'Égypte au IVe siècle (328–373)*
(CEFR 216; Rome: École Française de Rome, 1996).

## Works

Athanasius's writings, which are also preserved in Coptic, Syriac, and other
languages, thoroughly reflects his episcopal work and his controversies; whether he
mastered the Coptic language, however, has not been clarified for sure up to now.
Of his *Epistulae festales (Festal Letters),* the thirty-ninth, from the year 367, has become famous because it contains the first ever listing of the definitive NT canon.

The character of his apologetic work of two parts, *Contra gentes* and *De
incarnatione,* is determined by the chronological arrangement, which continues
to be a point of discussion today. On the grounds that they lack any mention of
Arianism, Montfaucon and more recently Meijering, van Winden, and Barnes[15]
take it to be an early work, patterned after the traditional apologia prior to the
onset of the Arian controversy. Conversely Tillemont, Schwartz, Schneemelcher,
Kannengiesser, and Tetz place it at the time of the exile in Trier (335–337), with
*Contra gentes* working up older notes. In this case, the work would be a careful defense under the guise of the form of an apologia because at that time Athanasius

---

[15] T. D. Barnes, *Constantine and Eusebius* (Cambridge, Mass.: Harvard University
Press, 1981), 206.

was not yet able to risk an open attack on his opponents. More recently the voices favoring a date at the beginning of his tenure as bishop are on the rise, namely, 328 (Stead), 328–335 (Petterson), and 333 (Kehrhahn). Nordberg's suggestion of a date during the reign of Emperor Julian (361–363) is probably to be dismissed.

The *Orationes contra Arianos* are from the time of his Roman exile (340/341) and, strongly influenced by the theology of Marcellus, deal with the controversial biblical text of Prov 8:22: "The Lord brought me forth as the first of his works, before his deeds of old." The *Historia Arianorum* addresses itself to the monks against the drastic measures of Emperor Constantius (357/358) as the "one who prepares the way of the antichrist." The letters addressed to bishops and emperors all revolve around justifying himself and presenting his opponents as reprehensible. *De decretis nicaenae synodi* (350/351) represents one of the most important sources of the history of the council, the records of which are not preserved. His major work on Egyptian monasticism, *Vita Antonii*, will be addressed later in the context of monastic literature (ch. 8.III).

*Editions:*
*Opera omnia:* PG 25–28.
*Opera varia: Athanasius Werke* (ed. H. G. Opitz; Berlin: de Gruyter, 1934–), 2/1–3/1 [*De decretis Nicaenae synodi, De sententia Dionysii, Apologia de fuga sua, Apologia secunda, Epistula encyclica, De morte Arii, Epistula ad monachos, Historia Arianorum, De synodis, Acta*]. – *Athanasiana syriaca* (ed. R. W. Thomson; 3 vols.; CSCO; Louvain: SCO, 1965–1977), 257–58, 272–73, 324–25 [ET]. – *Athanasius Werke: Die dogmatischen Schriften* (ed. K. Metzler, D. U. Hansen, and K. Savvidis; Berlin: de Gruyter, 1996–1980), 1/1.1–2 [*Epistula ad episcopos Aegypti et Libyae, Orationes I et II contra Arianos*].
*Apologiae: Deux apologies* (ed. J. M. Szymusiak; SC 56 bis; Paris: Cerf, 1987). – *Contre les païens* (ed. P. T. Camelot; SC 18 bis; Paris: Cerf, 1977).
*Contra gentes, De incarnatione: Contra gentes and De incarnatione by Athanasius* (ed. and trans. R. W. Thomson; OECT; Oxford: Clarendon, 1971) [ET].
*De incarnatione: Sur l'incarnation du Verbe* (ed. C. Kannengiesser; rev. ed.; SC 199; Paris: Cerf, 2000).
*Epistulae festales: Lettres festales et pastorales en copte* (ed. L.-T. Lefort; CSCO 150–51; Louvain: Durbecq, 1955). – R.-G. Coquin and E. Lucchesi, "Un complément au corps copte des Lettres festales d'Athanase (Paris, B.N., Copte 176*) (Pl. III)" *OLP* 13 (1982): 137–42. – R.-G. Coquin, *Les Lettres festales d'Athanase* (*CPG* 2102): "Un nouveau complément—le manuscrit IFAO, Copte 25 (Planche X)" *OLP* 15 (1984): 133–58. – *Der zehnte Osterfestbrief des Athanasius von Alexandrien* (ed. R. Lorenz; BZNW 49; Berlin and New York: de Gruyter, 1986) [ *Ep. fest.* 10 Com].
*Expositiones in Psalmos:* G. M. Vian, *Testi inediti dal Commento ai Salmi di Atanasio* (SEAug 14; Rome: Institutum Patristicum Augustinianum, 1978).
*Historia acephala, Syriac index of the festal letters: Histoire "Acéphale" et Index syriaque des Lettres festales d'Athanase d'Alexandrie* (ed. A. Martin and M. Albert; SC 317; Paris: Cerf, 1985).

*Translations:* A. Robertson et al., trans., *Select Works of Athanasius and Letters of Athanasius* (vol. 4 of *NPNF²;* Peabody, Mass.: Hendrickson, 1995; repr. of 1893 ed.) [*Contra gentes, De incarnatione Verbi, Depositio Arii, Epistola Eusebii, Ecthesis, In illud: Omnia etc., Epistola encyclica, Apologia contra Arianos, De decretis, De sententia Dionysii, Vita Antonii, Ad episcopos Aegypti, Apologia ad Constantium, Apologia de fuga, Historia Arianorum ad monachos, Orationes contra Arianos IV, De synodis, Tomus ad Antiochenos, Narratio ad Ammonium, Ad Afros, Letters*]. – C. R. B. Shapland, *The Letters of*

*Saint Athanasius concerning the Holy Spirit* (London: Epworth, 1951) [*Epistolae ad Serapionem*]. – W. G. Rusch, *The Trinitarian Controversy* (SoECT; Philadelphia: Fortress, 1980), 63–129 [*Orationes contra Arianos I*]. – D. Brakke, *Athanasius and the Politics of Asceticism* (OECS; Oxford: Clarendon; New York: Oxford University Press, 1995), 275–334 [Syriac and Coptic Athanasiana: *First* and *Second Letter to Virgins*, *On Virginity*, *Festal Letters*, *Fragments on the Moral Life*].

*Athanasius as a Writer:* L. T. Lefort, "St. Athanase écrivain copte," *Mus* 46 (1933): 1–33. – H.-G. Opitz, *Untersuchungen zur Überlieferung der Schriften des Athanasios* (AKG 23; Berlin: de Gruyter, 1935). – C. Kannengiesser, "L'énigme de la lettre *Au philosophe Maxime* d'Athanase d'Alexandrie," in *ΛΛΕΞΑΝΔΡΙΝΑ—hellénisme, judaïsme, et christianisme à Alexandrie: Mélanges offerts au P. Claude Mondésert* (Paris: Cerf, 1987), 261–76. – C. Stead, "Athanasius' Earliest Written Work," *JTS* NS 39 (1988): 76–91. – K. Metzler and F. Simon, *Ariana et Athanasiana: Studien zur Überlieferung und zu philologischen Problemen der Werke des Athanasius von Alexandrien* (ARWAW 83; Opladen: Westdeutscher Verlag, 1991). – J. D. Ernest, "Athanasius of Alexandria: The Scope of Scripture in Polemical and Pastoral Context," *VC* 47 (1993): 341–62.

*Apologetic Works:* J. C. M. van Winden, "On the Date of Athanasius' Apologetical Treatises," *VC* 29 (1975): 291–95; repr. in idem, *Arche: A Collection of Patristic Studies* (ed. J. den Boeft and D. T. Runia; SVigChr 41; Leiden and New York: Brill, 1997), 176–80. – A. Pettersen, "A Reconsideration of the Date of the *Contra gentes–De incarnatione* of Athanasius of Alexandria," in *Proceedings of the Eighth International Conference on Patristic Studies, Oxford, 3–8 September, 1979* (ed. E. Livingstone; 3 vols.; StPatr 17; Oxford and New York: Pergamon, 1982), 3:1030–40. – E. P. Meijering, "Struktur und Zusammenhang des apologetischen Werkes von Athanasius," *VC* 45 (1991): 313–26.

*Apologia secunda (= Apologia contra Arianos):* L. W. Barnard, *Studies in Athanasius' Apologia secunda* (EHS.T 467; Bern; New York: Lang, 1992).

*Contra Arianos:* C. Kannengiesser, "Athanasius of Alexandria, Three Orations against the Arians: A Reappraisal," in *Proceedings of the Eighth International Conference on Patristic Studies, Oxford, 3–8 September, 1979* (ed. E. Livingstone; 3 vols.; StPatr 17; Oxford and New York: Pergamon, 1982), 3:981–95. – C. Kannengiesser, *Athanase d'Alexandrie évêque et écrivain: Une lecture des traités Contre les Ariens* (ThH 70; Paris: Beauchesne, 1983). – L. Abramowski, "Die dritte Arianerrede des Athanasius: Eusebianer und Arianer und das westliche Serdicense," *ZKG* 102 (1991): 389–413. – E. P. Meijering, "Zur Echtheit der dritten Rede des Athanasius gegen die Arianer (*Contra Arianos* 3,59–67)," *VC* 48 (1994): 135–56. – C. Kannengiesser, "Die Sonderstellung der dritten Arianerrede des Athanasius," *ZKG* 106 (1995): 18–55. – E. P. Meijering, "Zur Echtheit der dritten Rede des Athanasius gegen die Arianer (*Contra Arianos* III 1)," *VC* 50 (1996): 364–86. K. Metzler, *Welchen Bibeltext benutzte Athanasius im Exil? Zur Herkunft der Bibelzitate in den Arianerreden im Vergleich zur ep. ad epp. Aeg.* (Opladen: Westdeutscher Verlag, 1997).

*De incarnatione contra Apollinarium:* G. D. Dragas, *St. Athanasius Contra Apollinarem* (Athens: Church and Theology, 1985). – H. Chadwick, "Les deux traités contre Apollinaire attribués à Athanase," in *ΛΛΕΞΑΝΔΡΙΝΑ—hellénisme, judaïsme, et christianisme à Alexandrie: Mélanges offerts au P. Claude Mondésert* (Paris: Cerf, 1987), 247–60.

*Festal Letters:* A. Camplani, *Le Lettere festali di Atanasio di Alessandria: Studi storico-critici* (Rome: C. I. M., 1989). – C. Kannengiesser, "The Homiletic Festal Letters of Athanasius," in *Preaching in the Patristic Age: Studies in Honor of Walter J. Burghardt, S.J.* (ed. D. G. Hunter; New York: Paulist, 1989), 73–100. – D. Brakke, "Canon Formation and Social Conflict in Fourth-Century Egypt: Athanasius of Alexandria's Thirty-Ninth *Festal Letter*," *HTR* 87 (1994): 395–419.

*Philosophy and Theology:* A. Laminski, *Der Heilige Geist als Geist Christi und Geist der Gläubigen: Der Beitrag des Athanasios von Alexandrien zur Formulierung des trinitarischen Dogmas im vierten Jahrhundert* (EThSt 23; Leipzig: St. Benno, 1969). – T. F. Torrance, "The Hermeneutics of St. Athanasius," *EkklPh* 52.1 (1970): 446–68; 52.2–3 (1970): 89–106; 52.4 (1970): 237–49. – C. Kannengiesser, "Athanasius of Alexandria and the Foundation of Traditional Christology," *TS* 34 (1973): 103–13; repr. in E. Ferguson, ed., *Doctrines of God and Christ in the Early Church* (SEC 9; New York: Garland, 1993), 43–53. – E. P. Meijering, *Orthodoxy and Platonism in Athanasius: Synthesis or Antithesis?* (rev. ed.; Leiden: Brill, 1974). – E. P. Meijering, "Athanasius on the Father as the Origin of the Son," *NAKG* 55 (1974): 1–14. – J. Roldanus, *Le Christ et l'homme dans la théologie d'Athanase d'Alexandrie: Étude de la conjonction de sa conception de l'homme avec sa christologie* (rev. ed.; SHCT 4; Leiden: Brill, 1977). – G. Larentzakis, *Einheit der Menschheit, Einheit der Kirche bei Athanasius: Vor- und nachchristliche Soteriologie und Ekklesiologie bei Athanasius v. Alexandrien* (GrTS 1; Graz: Institut für Ökumenische Theologie und Patrologie, Universität Graz, 1978). – G. D. Dragas, *Athanasiana: Essays in the Theology of St. Athanasius* (London: n.p., 1980). – C. Kannengiesser, "Athanasius of Alexandria and the Holy Spirit between Nicea I and Constantinople I," *ITQ* 48 (1981): 166–80. – A. Louth, "Athanasius' Understanding of the Humanity of Christ," in *Papers Presented to the Seventh International Conference on Patristic Studies Held in Oxford, 1971, 5,* vol. 2, *Monastica et ascetica, orientalia, e saeculo secundo, Origen, Athanasius, Cappadocian Fathers, Chrysostom, Augustine* (ed. E. Livingstone; StPatr 16; TU 129; Berlin: Akademie, 1985), 309–23. – C. Kannengiesser, *Le Verbe de Dieu selon Athanase d'Alexandrie* (CJJC 45; Paris: Desclée, 1990). – A. Pettersen, *Athanasius and the Human Body* (Bristol: Bristol, 1990). – R. K. Tacelli, "Of One Substance: St. Athanasius and the Meaning of Christian Doctrine," *DR* 108 (1990): 91–110. – C. Stead, "Athanasius als Exeget," in *Christliche Exegese zwischen Nicaea und Chalcedon* (ed. J. van Oort and U. Wickert; Kampen, Neth.: Kok Pharos, 1992), 174–84. – P. Widdicombe, *The Fatherhood of God from Origen to Athanasius* (Oxford: Clarendon; New York: Oxford University Press, 2000), 145–249. – A. Pettersen, *Athanasius* (London: Geoffrey Chapman; Harrisburg, Pa.: Morehouse, 1995). – K. Anatolios, "The Soteriological Significance of Christ's Humanity in St. Athanasius," *SVTQ* 40 (1996): 265–86. – K. Anatolios, *Athanasius: The Coherence of His Thought* (London and New York: Routledge, 1998).

*Tomus ad Antiochenos:* M. Tetz, "Über nikäische Orthodoxie: Der sog. *Tomus ad Antiochenos* des Athanasius von Alexandrien." *ZNW* 66 (1975): 194–222. – A. Pettersen, "The Arian Context of Athanasius' *Tomus ad Antiochenos VII," JEH* 41 (1990): 183–98.

# V. HILARY OF POITIERS

Since Athanasius's exile in Trier (335) and the death of Constantine (337), the Arian crisis had increasingly encompassed the western half of the empire as well. On the one hand, Athanasius gained influential support for his theological and ecclesiastical-political line in Trier and Rome; on the other, the originally theological dispute turned increasingly into a power play in the political struggle of the three sons of Constantine. Into this situation came Hilary, bishop of Pictavis (Poitiers) in the province of Aquitania Secunda, from 356 on. Inasmuch as he too was exiled in the other half of the empire and thus assimilated the empire-wide dimension of the problem of Arianism, his fate resembles that of Athanasius; apart from this, however, his is a portrait of contrasts in every way.

Whereas Athanasius gave a stark black-and-white portrayal of stubbornly maintaining the Nicene faith and in summary fashion condemned as Arians all those
who did not agree with him (although his own full theological acceptance of
Nicea did not appear noteworthy in the years immediately following the council),
Hilary in his exile learned to understand the various theological positions and endeavored to bring them into agreement with the Nicene position.

Athanasius's condemnation by the synod of Milan (355), which encountered
major resistance in the West, and the radical Arian reaction this precipitated seem
to have given Hilary the impetus to speak publicly against it.[16] Up to that point, he
had not yet come into the limelight, and so we know hardly anything about his earlier life. Hilary was probably born in Poitiers itself at the beginning of the fourth
century and may have come from the city's upper class. The report in the *Vita* of
Hilary by Venantius Fortunatus (1.3; PL 9:187 A) that he had been married and
was the father of a daughter cannot be verified, and the value of the *Vita* has to be
reckoned as fairly marginal. Hilary's works indicate a good rhetorical, philosophical, and literary education, but it is unclear whether he also enjoyed a Christian upbringing. In the prologue of his work *De Trinitate* (1.1–14), he himself describes his
spiritual development from paganism to Christianity as a path from the philosophical question of the purpose of life and of God to Scripture and faith in Christ. To
what extent this account is to be understood as autobiographical[17] or is part of the
literary topoi,[18] however, has not been clarified to date.

In any case, Hilary was baptized as an adult, assumed the bishopric of
Poitiers in 350, and in 355 incurred the opposition of Arian circles; prominent
among them was Saturninus, bishop of Arles. As a result, a synod at Biterra
(Béziers) under the leadership of Saturninus condemned him in the spring of
356, and Caesar Julian (later "the Apostate") exiled him to Phrygia. The following
four years of his exile were pivotal for his theology and knowledge of the problem
of Arianism. Apparently he enjoyed extensive freedom of movement and maintained correspondence with Gallic bishops. He adopted Origen's theology, which
shaped his spirituality and understanding of Scripture; cultivated contact with
the Homoiousians and thus arrived at a subtly differentiated view of the problem;
and endeavored to find a practicable theological *via media* between radical pro-
Nicene views, with their risk of Sabellianism, and the radical rejection of the
Son's being of the same substance as the Father (anomoeans).

During the time of his exile, three synods were held on this issue: Sirmium
(357), Ariminum (Rimini) (359), and Seleucia (September 359); he himself participated in the third one. The synod of Sirmium met on an issue that was decisive politically and for church policy. Like his father Constantine, Constantius

---

[16] To date this is the unanimous view; H. C. Brennecke, *Hilarius von Poitiers und die
Bischofsopposition gegen Konstantius II* (PTS 26; Berlin and New York: de Gruyter,
1984), 230, and *TRE* 15:316, however, sees it as an improper retroprojection from the time
of exile.

[17] J. Doignon, *HLL* 5:448 and *RAC* 15:140.

[18] M. Simonetti, *EECh* 1:381; H. C. Brennecke, *TRE* 15:315.

united the empire under one rule and had Athanasius, the most obstinate ecclesiastical troublemaker, condemned. By means of a unified, binding theology of the empire, the emperor now sought to restore the ideal unity between the empire and the church, just as his father had done at Nicea. His most influential advisors were the following bishops: Ursacius of Singidunum, Valens of Mursa, and Germinius of Sirmium. The synod passed a theological manifesto (the "second Sirmian formula," after the first one of 351) that clearly subordinated the Son to the Father and prohibited especially the use of the concept of ὁμοούσιος, as well as ὁμοιούσιος. Even Liberius of Rome and Ossius of Córdoba seem to have subscribed to this formula; only a synod in Gaul condemned it, and Hilary, who by correspondence was always in contact with the Gallic bishops, wrote his *Liber primus adversus Valentem et Ursacium*.

The reaction against the second Sirmian formula came from a quarter that could hardly have been anticipated, namely, from Basil, bishop of Ancyra, who replaced Marcellus in 336. Just before Easter 358, he assembled a synod in Ancyra with only twelve bishops who reintroduced the concept of ὅμοιος as a *via media* against the radical Arians, who argued for the absolute dissimilarity of Father and Son (anomoeans), and in place of the Nicene ὁμοούσιος; hence they were called Homoeans. Basil succeeded in gaining the emperor's support for his cause, with the result that in 358 a small synod at Sirmium condemned Aëtius and Eunomius, the leading anomoeans, by appealing to the resolutions of Antioch (341) and Sirmium (351). This synod brought Hilary closer to Homoiousian theology; he became acquainted with Basil of Ancyra, and in his work *De synodis* he recommended this theology to the Gallic bishops (in reply to the request by a Gallic synod of Easter 358 for information concerning the theology and church policy of the East) as an orthodox interpretation of the Nicene position and as a unifying formula between East and West. In this work Hilary not only provided a documentary overview of the post-Nicene oriental confessions of faith but also used the occasion to create a united front in preparation for the empirewide synod planned for 359 and to overcome the division between East and West.

Subsequent events, however, brought to naught his efforts to bring about concord. Constantius forced both the synod of Ariminum and the parallel synod of Seleucia, meeting at the same time, in which Hilary participated in support of the Homoiousians, to accept his Homoean formula. This prompted Hilary to a sharp polemic against the emperor in his *Liber contra Constantium*, in which he charged him with tyranny worse than that of Nero and Decius. This writing was published only after the emperor's death, of course, addressed to the Western bishops.

In 360 Julian, the Western Caesar, was installed as Augustus by his troops, and Hilary returned to Gaul. The connection has been interpreted in different ways: Doignon,[19] "Constantius demanded his return"; Simonetti,[20] "He was allowed to return"; Brennecke,[21] "Possibly as a result of the news about Julian's

---

[19] Doignon, *RAC* 15:141.
[20] Simonetti, *EECh* 1:381.
[21] Brennecke, *TRE* 15:317.

usurpation, Hilary returned to Gaul without explicit approval"; Doignon,[22] "It may be that Constantius pardoned him or simply asked him to leave the East." In any case, the new political constellation now allowed him to pursue his theological course in the West even in church policy, especially when Constantius died on November 3, 361, and Julian the Apostate succeeded him as ruler of the entire empire. In the following years, Hilary actively worked in Gaul and northern Italy at rescinding the resolutions of Ariminum/Seleucia, in accordance with his Homoiousian policy of reconciliation—for instance, at a synod in Paris in 360/361. He had a falling out with Lucifer of Caralis, but after his return from exile and his participation in the synod of Alexandria (362), Eusebius of Vercellae became Hilary's most ardent supporter. Although their attempt to have Bishop Auxentius of Milan deposed by Emperor Valentinan in 364 was unsuccessful, their influence on the anti-Arian reorganization of Gaul and northern Italy certainly remained substantial. Besides his theological writings, some important areas of activity in the latter part of his life were the introduction of the singing of liturgical hymns and the promotion of Gallic monasticism under Martin, his disciple, the later bishop of Tours, whose popularity extends to this day. Hilary died in 367 or 368.[23] On May 13, 1851, Pope Pius IX bestowed on him the honorary title of "teacher of the church." To this day one of the terms of the English courts and the spring semester at the universities of Oxford and Durham are called "Hilary term" because they traditionally commence on or about January 13, the day of Saint Hilary.

Besides Hilary's popular writings already mentioned, his commentaries *In Matthaeum* and *In Psalmos* deserve attention; they reflect his theological development quite well. *In Matthaeum* was written before the exile and is predicated entirely upon Western models (Tertullian, Cyprian, and Novatian). By contrast the *Tractatus super Psalmos* originated in the latter years of his life and is shaped considerably by Origen's exegesis and theology, which he conveyed to the West in this way.

*Bibliography:* F. W. Bautz, *BBKL* 2:835–40.

*Editions: Opera omnia:* PL 9–10. – PLS 1:241–86. – *Contra Constantium: Contre Constance* (ed. A. Rocher; SC 334; Paris: Cerf, 1987). – P. Smulders, *Hilary of Poitiers' Preface to His Opus historicum* (SVigChr 29; Leiden and New York: Brill, 1995) [ET/Com]. – *Tractatus mysteriorum, Fragmenta historica, Libri ad Constantium I–II, Hymni, Fragmenta minora, Spuria: S. Hilarii episcopi Pictaviensis Opera* (ed. A. Feder; CSEL 65; Vienna: F. Tempsky, 1916). – *Tractatus mysteriorum* (ed. J. P. Brisson; new ed.; SC 19 bis; Paris: Cerf, 1967).

*Translations:* E. W. Watson, et al., trans., "On the Councils, or The Faith of the Easterns," "On the Trinity," and "Homilies on the Psalms," in *NPNF²* (Peabody, Mass.: Hendrickson, 1995; repr. of 1899 ed.), 9:1–248 [*De synodis, De Trinitate, Homiliae in Psalmos 1, 53, 130*]. – L. R. Wickham, *Hilary of Poitiers: Conflicts of Conscience and Law in the Fourth-Century Church* (TTH 25; Liverpool: Liverpool University Press, 1997) [*Against Valens and Ursacius*, extant fragments, *Letter to the Emperor Constantius*].

---

[22] Doignon, *HLL* 5:449.

[23] A. J. Goemans, "La date de la mort de saint Hilaire, " *Hilaire et son temps* (Paris: Études Augustiniennes, 1969), 107–11, suggested more specifically November 1, 367, which subsequent research, though otherwise based on his results, did not accept.

*Encyclopedia Articles:* P. Smulders, "Hilarius von Poitiers," *GK* 1:250–65. – H. C. Brennecke, *TRE* 15:315–22. – J. Doignon, *HLL* 5:447–80. – J. Doignon, *RAC* 15:139–67. – M. Simonetti, *EECh* 1:381–82. – M. Clark, *EEC* 1:527–28.

*General Studies:* P. Galtier, *Saint Hilaire de Poitiers, le premier docteur de l'église latine* (BTH; Paris: Beauchesne, 1960). – J. Doignon, *Hilaire de Poitiers avant l'exil: Recherches sur la naissance, l'enseignement, et l'épreuve d'une foi épiscopale en Gaule au milieu du IVe siècle* (Paris: Études Augustiniennes, 1971).

*Collections of Essays: Hilaire de Poitiers, évêque et docteur* (Paris: Études Augustiniennes, 1968). – *Hilaire et son temps* (Paris: Études Augustiniennes, 1969).

*Arianism and Trinitarian Theology:* A. Fierro, *Sobre la gloria en San Hilario: Una síntesis doctrinal sobre la noción bíblica de "doxa"* (AnGr 144; Libreria Editrice dell'Università Gregoriana, 1964). – A. Martínez Sierra, "La prueba escriturística de los arrianos según S. Hilario de Poitiers," *MCom* 41 (1964): 293–376. – C. F. A. Borchardt, *Hilary of Poitiers' Role in the Arian Struggle* (KHSt 12; The Hague: Nijhoff, 1966). – E. P. Meijering, with J. C. M. van Winden, *Hilary of Poitiers on the Trinity: De Tritnitate 1,1–19, 2,3* (PP 6; Leiden: Brill, 1982). – H. C. Brennecke, *Hilarius von Poitiers und die Bischofsopposition gegen Konstantius II* (PTS 26; Berlin and New York: de Gruyter, 1984). – D. H. Williams, "A Reassessment of the Early Career and Exile of Hilary of Poitiers," *JEH* 42 (1991): 202–17. – D. H. Williams, "The Anti-Arian Campaigns of Hilary of Poitiers and the *Liber contra Auxentium*," *ChH* 61 (1992): 7–22.

*Biography:* T. D. Barnes, "Hilary of Poitiers on His Exile," *VC* 46 (1992): 129–40. – P. C. Burns, "Hilary of Poitiers' Road to Béziers: Politics or Religion?" *JECS* 2 (1994): 273–89.

*Theology:* J. M. McDermott, "Hilary of Poitiers: The Infinite Nature of God," *VC* 27 (1973): 172–202. – G. M. Newlands, *Hilary of Poitiers: A Study in Theological Method* (EHS.T 108; Bern and Las Vegas: Lang, 1978). – P. Figura, *Das Kirchenverständnis des Hilarius von Poitiers* (FThSt 127; Fribourg, Switz.: Herder, 1984). – M. Durst, *Die Eschatologie des Hilarius von Poitiers: Ein Beitrag zur Dogmengeschichte des vierten Jahrhunderts* (Hereditas 1; Bonn: Borengässer, 1987). – L. F. Ladaria, *La cristología de Hilario de Poitiers* (AnGr 255; Rome: Editrice Pontificia Università Gregoriana, 1989). – J. Doignon, "Innerer Glaube, Bekenntnis, und schriftliche Festlegung des Glaubens im westlichen Römerreich des vierten Jahrhundert," *TP* 65 (1990): 246–54.

# A. De Trinitate

Hilary's primary work, without a doubt, continues to be his major dogmatic tractate in twelve books, *De Trinitate*. It is the first work of its kind in the Latin church and brings together Eastern and Western theology in the context of the dispute with Arianism. The fourth book begins with the following comment: ". . . in the preceding books which we have written at an earlier time." This led to the conclusion that the first three books had already been published as an independent work before the exile (356) and had not been integrated until later.[24] At

---

[24] Constant; Galtier; J. Borchardt; Doignon, *Hilaire de Poitiers avant l'exil: Recherches sur la naissance, l'enseignement, et l'épreuve d'une foi épiscopale en Gaule au milieu du IVe siècle* (Paris: Études Augustiniennes, 1971), 18.

the same time, however, the view that all twelve books had been written during the exile (356–360) is gaining increasing acceptance.[25] Because the tenor of the work undoubtedly changes between books three and four, Simonetti assumes a change of plans: Hilary first conceived only a brief work, *De fide*, and then planned a second work against the two basic propositions of Arius, found in his letter to Alexander, and finally merged the two. Against this Meijering argues for an integral concept from the start, following the model of the twelve books of Quintilian's *Institutio oratoria*, whose rhetorical rules Hilary followed to a large extent, in any case.

The varied titles under which the work is handed down describe its twofold character: *Contra Arianos* and *De fide* or *De Trinitate*. On the one hand, Hilary intends to defend the orthodox doctrine of the Trinity against Arianism, but beyond this he also wants to develop its theological premises. Both characteristics occur on the bases of baptismal faith and the interpretation of Scripture. Book 1 begins with a proem (1–14) on the search for God's truth from human philosophy to biblical faith. (The earlier assumption that this proem contains autobiographical features has largely been dismissed, as discussed above.) This is followed by identification of the heretics who jeopardize orthodox doctrine, Sabellius and Arius (15–16), as well as of the foundations of an orthodox understanding: faith and the correct application of necessarily earthly trains of thought and examples (17–19). Thereby Hilary isolated the two equally one-sided, extreme positions of the disputed Trinitarian issue, namely, the identification of the Father and the Son in Sabellianism, which is also where an all-too-narrow understanding of the one οὐσία in the ὁμοούσιος might end up, and the absolute differentiation of the Father and the Son as Creator and creature in Arianism. At the same time, he recognized the basic problem of methodology, namely, that concepts used by humans, such as begetting, time, nature, and being, always are inadequate when they are applied to God; indeed the argument from analogy may introduce completely wrong, earthly conceptions into the concept of God. "Therefore every comparison ought to be considered as more helpful to humans than appropriate for God" (19). Chapters 20–36 provide an overview of the contents of the remaining eleven books, and chs. 37–38 conclude bk. 1 with a prayer.

Books 2 and 3 present the orthodox belief in the Trinity in a positive way, whereas bks. 4–12 defend it against the Arian attacks. After a programmatic introduction on the sufficiency and significance of the scriptural evidence (1–5), bk. 2 comments on the baptismal formula of Matt 28:19: the infinity and indescribability of the Father (6–7), the eternal generation and incarnation of the Son (8–28), and the full divinity of the Holy Spirit (29–35). Book 3 broadens the arguments by means of John 14:11, "I am in the Father and the Father is in me" (1–4); the miracles of Jesus (5–8); John 17:1–6, the mutual glorification of the Father and the Son

---

[25] Meslin, Kannengiesser, Simonetti, Meijering, Brennecke, as well as Doignon, *HLL* 5:463. Only P. Smulders has reversed his view: *La Doctrine trinitaire de S. Hilaire de Poitiers* (AnGr 32; Rome: Apud Aedes Universitatis Gregorianae, 1944), 41; *De Trinitate* (2 vols.; CCSL 62–62A; Turnhout, Belg.: Brepols, 1979–1980), vol. 2.

(9–17); the virgin birth of Jesus and his postresurrection appearances as analogies of his eternal generation (18–21); John 17:6, the revelation of the Father by the Son (22–23); and the distinction between human and divine wisdom (24–26).

Books 4–6 deal with the refutation of Arius's letter to Alexander, the main arguments of which are cited in 4.12–13, namely, the denial of the divinity and equal eternality of the Son and the assertion of his creatureliness. Hilary draws his counterarguments from an overwhelming abundance of mostly OT references. The OT theophanies are particularly important in this regard because the Arians used them to bring their authority to bear as arguments for the changeability and hence the creatureliness of the Son.[26] Just as the human birth did not change the Son of God, so also did this not happen in its portent, the theophanies. Rather, the converse is true; according to Prov 8:22, the Son was created "at the beginning of his [the LORD's] work," hence not in his incarnation only, and appeared as such in the OT. Book 7 furnishes the proof of the oneness of the Son's being with the Father's by adducing evidential Scripture references: John 5:18, "he makes himself equal with God"; John 10:30, "I and the Father are one"; John 5:19: "whatever the Father does the Son also does."

Books 8–12 deal with refutation of the basic Arian principles whereby they support the subordination of the Son's nature. Book 8 maintains that the unity of Father and Son takes place on the level of nature, not only through the will; bk. 9, that the Son is accorded *operatio, virtus, honor, potestas, gloria,* and *vita* in the same measure as the Father. Book 10 discusses the place of Christ's sufferings with reference to his divinity. Book 11 maintains that the eschatological submission of the Son to the Father (1 Cor 15:28) does not signify loss or weakness at all but is instead a sign of unity and equality. Book 12 supports the equal eternality of the Son on the basis of the witness of Prov 8:22. The work ends (12.52–57) with a lengthy prayer to God, who transcends all our imaginations and conceptions.

*De Trinitate* very ably makes clear the levels on which the dispute took place in terms of focus and cause: baptismal faith and the witness of Scripture, which in many parts expresses the unity and equality of the Father and the Son but in many others may also be interpreted as subordinationist. In his theology, Hilary appeals primarily to the works of Tertullian and Novatian, whose theology is Trinitarian, but also to Homoiousian theology. Out of this he shapes his own original message, however. In particular, he customarily uses a very demanding exegesis on a highly abstract level, transcending even the material analogies generally also brought to bear by his opponents.

*Editions: De Trinitate* (ed. P. Smulders; 2 vols.; CCSL 62–62A; Turnhout, Belg.: Brepols, 1979–1980). – *La Trinité* (ed. P. Smulders, J. Doignon, G. M. de Durand, C. Morel, and G. Pelland; 3 vols.; SC 443, 448, 462; Paris: Cerf, 1999–2001) [*I–XII*].

---

[26] On this cf. B. Studer, "*Ea specie videri quam voluntas elegerit, non natura formaverit:* Zu einem Ambrosius-Zitat in Augustins Schrift *De vivendo Deo* (ep. 147)," *VetChr* 6 (1969): 91–143, esp. 117–27; repr. in idem, *Zur Theophanie-Exegese Augustins: Untersuchungen zu einem Ambrosius-Zitat in der Schrift De vivendo Deo (ep. 147)* (StAnsPT 59; Rome: Herder, 1971), 1–53, esp. 27–37.

*Translations: The Trinity* (trans. S. McKenna; FC 25; Washington, D.C.: Catholic University of America Press, 1954; repr., 1968).

*Studies:* P. Smulders, *La doctrine trinitaire de s. Hilaire de Poitiers: Étude précédée d'une esquisse du mouvement dogmatique depuis le concile de Nicée jusqu'au règne de Julien (325–362)* (AnGr 32; Rome: Apud Aedes Universitatis Gregorianae, 1944). – M. Simonetti, "Note sulla struttura e la cronologia del De Trinitate di Ilario di Poitiers," *SUSF* 39 (1965): 274–300. – L. F. Ladaria, *El Espíritu Santo en san Hilario de Poitiers* (Madrid: Eapsa, 1977). – E. Cavalcanti, "Filip. 2, 6–11 nel De Trin. di Ilario (De Trin. VIII, 45–47; X, 23–26)," *Comp* 35 (1990): 123–43.

# B. Exegetical Works

Hilary's two biblical commentaries, on the Gospel of Matthew and on the Psalms, reflect the two phases of his life and his theological development. The *Commentarius in Matthaeum* originated before his exile in the eastern part of the empire (356), but the *Tractatus super Psalmos* followed the exile, and the latter exhibits major influence from Greek exegesis, especially Origen's—an observation already made in antiquity. Jerome (*Vir. ill.* 100) writes, "Hilary also wrote a commentary on the Psalms . . . , in which he copied Origen but also added much of his own."

The commentary on Matthew provides a running explanation of the gospel, though in such a manner that the words and deeds of Jesus form the thematic center of the interpretation while the remaining sections represent their context, although they certainly are also needed to understand the main texts. Hilary's primary exegetical interest in the text of the gospel, by means of a timelessly appropriate and therefore also very modern two-step method, focuses on inquiring into the spiritual consequences of Jesus' words and deeds for the church as a whole as well as for the life of the individual. Alongside the immediate directives of Jesus, Hilary makes use of repetitive patterns, such as the boat as a symbol of the church, the wilderness as a symbol of a lack of divine grace, the healing of a person who is ill as an example for the calling of the Gentiles—interpretations that arise freely from the understanding of the *Christus totus,* the church as the body of Christ, and of the individual believer as a member of it.

Hilary also interprets the Psalms christologically-typologically in a traditional way, as prophecies pointing to the Messiah. Jerome (*Vir. ill.* 100) states that Hilary commented on Pss 1–2, 51–62, and 118–150; the commentary preserved for us, however, includes the following additional psalms: 9, 13, 14, 63–69, and 91. Comments in the text itself indicate that the work originally had been even more extensive. Jerome's assessment that Hilary had "copied Origen but also added many things of his own" can easily be verified in a comparison with Origen, even if his commentary on the Psalms is only preserved in fragmentary form.

*Editions: Commentarius in Matthaeum: Sur Matthieu* (ed. J. Doignon; 2 vols.; SC 254, 258; Paris: Cerf, 1978–1979). – *Commentarius in Ps 118: Commentaire sur le psaume 118* (ed. M. Milhau; 2 vols.; SC 344, 347; Paris: Cerf, 1988). – *Tractatus super Psalmos:*

*S. Hilarii episcopi Pictaviensis Tractatus super Psalmos* (ed. A. Zingerle; CSEL 22; Vienna: F. Tempsky, 1981). – *Sancti Hilarii Pictaviensis episcopi Tractatus super Psalmos* (ed. J. Doignon; CCSL 61, 61A; Turnhout, Belg.: Brepols, 1997) [*Tractatus super Psalmos, Instructio Psalmorum, In Psalmos I–XCI*].

*Translations:* W. Sunday, trans., "Homilies on the Psalms," in *NPNF*[2] (Peabody, Mass.: Hendrickson, 1995; repr. of 1898 ed.), 9:236–48 [selections].

*Studies:* C. Kannengiesser, "L'exégèse d'Hilaire," in *Hilaire et son temps* (Paris: Études Augustiniennes, 1969), 127–42.

*Commentarius in Matthaeum:* M. Simonetti, "Note sul Commento a Matteo di Ilario di Poitiers," *VetChr* 1 (1964): 35–64. – W. Wille, *Studien zum Matthäuskommentar des Hilarius von Poitiers* (Hamburg: n.p., 1969). – P. C. Burns, *The Christology of Hilary of Poitiers' Commentary on Matthew* (SEAug 16; Rome: Institutum Patristicum Augustinianum, 1981). – P. Smulders, "Hilarius van Poitiers als exeget van Mattheüs," *Bijdr* 44 (1983): 59–82. – J. Driscoll, "The Transfiguration in Hilary of Poitiers' Commentary on Matthew," *Aug* 29 (1984): 395–420.

*Tractatus super Psalmos:* E. Goffinet, "Kritisch-filologisch element in de Psalmencommentaar van de H. Hilarius van Poitiers," *Revue belge de philologie et d'histoire* 38 (1960): 30–44. – E. Goffinet, *L'utilisation d'Origène dans le Commentaire des Psaumes de saint Hilaire de Poitiers* (Studia hellenistica 14; Louvain: Publications Universitaires, 1965). – N. J. Gastaldi, *Hilario di Poitiers, exegeta del Salterio: Un estudio de su exégesis en los Comentarios sobre los Salmos* (Paris: Beauchesne, 1969). – G. Lutz, *Das Psalmenverständnis des Hialrius von Poitiers* (Trier; n.p., 1969). – A. Orazzo, *La salvezza in Ilario di Poitiers: Cristo salvatore dell'uomo nei Tractatus super Psalmos* (Naples: D'Auria, 1986). – L. F. Ladaria, "Adán y Cristo en los *Tractatus super Psalmos* de San Hilario de Poitiers," *Greg* 73 (1992): 97–122.

# CHAPTER SIX

# Apollinarianism and the Second Phase of Arianism

## I. APOLLINARIS OF LAODICEA

The Trinitarian dogma regarding the Son's and the Father's identical divinity progressed especially after the synod of Alexandria in 362. It immediately drew forth the christological question, logically following from it, of how divinity and humanity are bound up with one another in Christ, so that the result is a true oneness and Christ is not separated into a Son of God in parallel with a Son of Man. The first attempt at an answer to this question came from Apollinaris, bishop of Laodicea, whose solution the church did not accept, however, and whose teaching therefore went down in history as the heresy called Apollinarianism.

The result of his theological efforts should not lead to the wrong conclusion that Apollinaris had been a heterodox theologian from the start. The opposite is true. Apollinaris' father—also named Apollinaris—was a teacher of grammar and had moved from Alexandria to Laodicea where his son was born in 315. He had maintained close ties with Athanasius since the move from Alexandria and kept up an elaborate correspondence with him. On his return from the second exile in 346, Athanasius even stayed with the family in Laodicea as a guest. As a result, George, the bishop of Laodicea, himself an Arian and a former priest in Alexandria, whom Bishop Alexander had deposed because of his support of Arius, excommunicated both of the Apollinarises because of their fidelity to the Nicene position and their associations with Athanasius, its principal defendant (after 346). It is precisely these firm Nicene roots that are of major significance, both for Apollinaris's life and for evaluating his theology. He considered himself a theological follower of Athanasius in matters of Christology and represents the prime example of a strictly orthodox bishop and theologian who, in the urgent problems of his time, sought to penetrate Trinitarian theology, and subsequently Christology, further and to present them clearly. Apollinarianism did not originate as a heterodox current but as a theological attempt at moving orthodoxy forward that the church did not accept; it veered into heresy because Apollinaris himself could not accept the church's decision.

Like his father, Apollinaris also took up teaching as his profession, but during the episcopate of Theodotus of Laodicea the father was a priest and the son a lector of the community. Since both of them attended the lectures of the sophist Epiphanius, the bishop reprimanded them (before 335). It is not clear whether the synod of Constantinople in 360 deposed Bishop George for his support of the Homoiousian confession of Seleucia (359) or whether he died in the course of this year. In any case, Acacius of Caesarea, the leading Homoean bishop at the time, consecrated Pelagius in 360 as the new (Homoean) bishop of Laodicea, whereupon the Nicene party installed Apollinaris as their bishop. The nearby metropolis of Antioch, however, was to become his primary area of ministry during the Meletian schism, which arose at the same time (cf. part 3.II.A.2.b).

The roots of his Christology, which subsequently was condemned, go back to the synod of Alexandria (362), to which he sent some Antiochene monastics as delegates, and to a confession of faith that he sent to Emperor Jovian in 363. Like Basil in the case of Alexandria and Rome, Apollinaris carried on Nicene ecclesiastical policy for many years, consecrated Vitalis, one of his supporters, as bishop of Antioch, and initially was able to obtain the approval of Pope Damasus. Only in 377, when Jerome was still among his audience in Antioch, did the tide turn against him, when, in his *Epist.* 263, addressed to Pope Damasus, Basil the Great called for the sole recognition of Meletius as bishop of Antioch and for Apollinaris's excommunication, as well as that of Paulinus of Antioch and Eustathius of Sebaste. Consequently he was condemned by the synods of Rome (377), Antioch (379), Constantinople (381; canon 1, though without addressing the christological issue), and Rome again (382). Laws were not issued against the Apollinarians until 388, however, after Gregory of Nazianzus had turned to Nectarius, the patriarch of Constantinople, in 387 to entreat the emperor to intervene against the Apollinarians.

Apollinaris died before 392, but Apollinarian churches were widespread until the mid-fifth century. The community in Antioch itself united with the orthodox community in 425.

*Studies:* G. Gentz, *RAC* 1:520–22. – G. L. Prestige, *St. Basil the Great and Apollinaris of Laodicea* (ed. H. Chadwick; London: SPCK, 1956). – E. Mühlenberg, *Apollinaris von Laodicea* (FKDG 23; Göttingen: Vandenhoeck & Ruprecht, 1969). – E. Mühlenberg, *TRE* 3 (1978): 362–71. – C. Kannengiesser, *EECh* 1:58–59. – C. Kannengiesser, *EEC* 1:79–81.

# A. Works

Only a little of Apollinaris's extensive exegetical and theological writings has been preserved, and much of that only in fragments. Most significant are the two letters addressed to Basil the Great, preserved in the latter's corpus of letters (*Ep.* 362 and 364), and excerpts from his Ἀπόδειξις περὶ τῆς θείας σαρκώσεως τῆς καθ᾽ ὁμοίωσιν ἀνθρώπου contained in Gregory of Nyssa's *Antirrheticus adversus Apollinarium*. The latter encountered the Apollinarian teaching for the first time on a trip to Jerusalem in 382, but its refutation probably did not appear until 387. Apart from the fragments of his commentaries on biblical books in the catenas,

his remaining theological writings initially were preserved only pseudepigraphically under the names of orthodox Fathers, such as Gregory Thaumaturgus,
Athanasius, Julius, and Felix of Rome. In this way, unrecognized and unsuspected,
these writings had enduring influence upon the Christology of Cyril of Alexandria and Monophysitism. In the sixth century many of his works were already unmasked, although their complete identification is still not finalized today. Only
recently Enrico Cattaneo attributed three Easter sermons of pseudo-Chrysostom
to him, and Reinhard Hübner did the same with the pseudo-Athanasian work
*Contra Sabellianos.*

*Editions:* H. Lietzmann, *Apollinaris von Laodicea und seine Schule* (TU 1; Tübingen: Mohr,
   1904; repr., Hildesheim and New York: Olms, 1970). – K. Staab, *Pauluskommentare
   aus der griechischen Kirche* (2d ed.; NTAbh 15; Münster: Aschendorff, 1984), 57–82. –
   H. de Riedmatten, "La correspondance entre Basile de Césarée et Apollinaire de
   Laodicée I–II," *JTS* NS 7 (1956): 199–210; 8 (1957): 53–70. – J. Reuss, *Matthäus-
   Kommentare aus der griechischen Kirche* (TU 61; Berlin: Akademie, 1957), 1–54. –
   J. Reuss, *Johannes-Kommentare aus der griechischen Kirche* (TU 89; Berlin: Akademie,
   1966), 3–64. – E. Mühlenberg, "Apollinaris von Laodicea zu Ps 1–150," in idem,
   *Psalmenkommentare aus der Katenenüberlieferung* (3 vols.; PTS 15, 16, 19; Berlin and
   New York: de Gruyter, 1975), 1:1–118. – E. Bellini, *Su Cristo: Il grande dibattito nel
   quarto secolo* (Milan: Jaca, 1978), 15–121.

*Translations:* R. A. Norris Jr., *The Christological Controversy* (SoECT; Philadelphia: Fortress,
   1980), 103–11 [*On the Union in Christ of the Body with the Godhead, Fragments*].

*Studies:* G. Voisin, *L'Apollinarisme: Étude historique, littéraire et dogmatique sur le début des
   controverses christologiques au IVe siècle* (Louvain: J. Van Linthout, 1901). – G. Furlani,
   "Studi apollinaristici," *RSFR* 2 (1921): 257–85; 4 (1923): 129–46. – E. Cattaneo, *Trois
   homélies pseudo-chrysostomiennes sur la Pâque comme œuvre d'Apollinaire de Laodicée: Attribution et étude théologique* (ThH 58; Paris: Beauchesne, 1981). – E. Mühlenberg, "Apollinaris von Laodicea und die origenistische Tradition," *ZNW* 76 (1985):
   270–83. – R. M. Hübner, *Die Schrift des Apolinarius von Laodicea gegen Photin
   (Pseudo-Athanasius, Contra Sabellianos) und Basilius von Caesarea* (PTS 30; Berlin
   and New York: de Gruyter, 1989). – E. Mühlenberg, "Zur exegetischen Methode des
   Apollinaris von Laodicea," in *Christliche Exegese zwischen Nicaea und Chalcedon* (ed.
   J. van Oort and U. Wickert; Kampen, Neth.: Kok Pharos, 1992), 132–47.

# B. Christology

The basic concern of Apollinaris's Christology, as we have already indicated, was to continue the Nicene Trinitarian theology by clarifying the issue of
how the Son of God, the Second Person of the Trinity, was bound up with the
man Jesus, so that the two became genuinely one and did not remain split up as
the Son of God and the Son of Man. For him, such a Christology of separation,
which he attributed to Paul of Samosata according to the witness of Gregory of
Nyssa, and adoptionist Christology, which viewed Jesus, the mere human, as ex-
alted as the Son of God by grace, represented the main heresies. These had to be
avoided at all costs: "If . . . anyone . . . teaches that the Son of God is someone
other than the man born of Mary, is elevated to sonship by grace, so that there are

two sons, one of them the Son of God by nature, namely, from God, and the other one of grace, namely, the man born of Mary, . . . he is condemned by the Catholic Church" (*Ad Jovianum* 3). That the christological issue certainly needed clarification had been demonstrated not least in para. 7 of the *Tomus ad Antiochenos*.[1]

Apollinaris assumed the basic principle that the Second Person of the Trinity and Christ who lived on earth are identical, to the extent that he was accused of construing the flesh of Jesus as having descended from heaven. For him, the basis for this identity and oneness of God and man in Christ was the ὑπόστασις, which he did not distinguish from οὐσία. On this unity he based the personal subsistence of a being. Since self-determination (αὐτοκίνητον) is part of the nature of every being, however, there could be only one such principle (ἡγεμονικόν) in Christ: "Whoever teaches that there are two types of reason in Christ, I mean the divine and the human one, acts as if he were able to engrave letters in a rock with a finger. For if each type of reason is in control of itself because it is motivated by the aspiration unique to its being, it is impossible for two reasons whose strivings are set against each other to exist with one another in one and the same subject (ὑποκείμενον), since each performs according to the nature of its will— for each is self-moving" (fragment 150). From this Apollinaris concluded with strict logic that in Christ the divine ἡγεμονικόν replaced the human one, that, in other words, the Logos took the place of the human soul, at least on the part of its reason, the νοῦς. For him, therefore, Christ was θεὸς ἔνσαρκος or even νοῦς ἔνσαρκος, and so he explained the oneness of God and man in Christ on the level of nature with admirable, and most attractive, logical stringency. Christ was μία φύσις τοῦ Λόγου σεσαρκωμένη, the one incarnate nature of the Logos; hence, for him, the oneness of nature, substance, and person were all on the same level.

How much Apollinaris, through his notion of a dynamic unity of activity in Christ in which the human will was eliminated for the sake of unity, at least posed the necessary question of how two free will powers can be yoked together in one person without tearing apart their unity is demonstrated in the Monothelitic dispute in the wake of the Council of Chalcedon, which dogmatized the two natures of Christ. Apollinaris solved the problem with sharp logic but thereby did away with the unresolved tension of the mystery of the incarnation, and this plunged his theology into heresy.

*Studies:* C. de Raven, *Apollinarianism: An Essay on the Christology of the Early Church* (Cambridge: Cambridge University Press, 1923; repr., New York: AMS, 1978). – G. L. Prestige, *Fathers and Heretics: Six Studies in Dogmatic Faith* (London: SPCK, 1940; repr., 1968), 94–119. – H. de Riedmatten, "La christologie d'Apollinaire de Laodicée," in *Papers Presented to the Second International Conference on Patristic Studies Held at Christ Church, Oxford, 1955* (ed. K. Aland and F. L. Cross; StPatr 2; TU 64; Berlin: Akademie, 1957), 208–34. – R. A. Norris Jr., *Manhood and Christ: A Study in the Christology of Theodore of Mopsuestia* (Oxford: Clarendon, 1963), 79–122. – A. Tuilier, "Le sens de l'Apollinarisme dans les controverses théologiques du IVe siècle," in *Papers Presented to the Sixth International Conference on Patristic Studies Held in Oxford, 1971* (ed. E. Livingstone; StPatr 13; TU 116; Berlin: Akademie, 1975), 295–305.

---

[1] Mansi 3:349–52.

# II. THE "THREE GREAT CAPPADOCIANS"

## Introduction: Their Families and Joint Significance

Because of their extraordinary importance for theology and the church, Basil the Great, his younger brother Gregory of Nyssa, and his fellow student Gregory of Nazianzus were given the honorary title "the three great Cappadocians." They were part of a newly emerging stratum of ecclesiastical leadership, or one that came to the fore more prominently in the course of the fourth century, after the so-called Constantinian shift. They were drawn from families that not only had already been part of the Christian faith for generations but also had actively contributed to the shaping of ecclesiastical life. They belonged to the prosperous and influential upper strata of society and, commensurate with this, had enjoyed an excellent education, which predestined them to engage in the standard public careers of rhetor, lawyer, or statesman.

The grandfather, on the mother's side, of the two brothers, Basil and Gregory, had suffered martyrdom during the Diocletian persecution. Their grandmother on the father's side, St. Macrina the Elder, was a student of Gregory Thaumaturgus, the famous bishop of Neocaesarea, to whom her nephew, Gregory of Nyssa (presumably named after him) left a memorial in a sermon. During the persecution, she and her husband had to flee into the mountains for seven years. As a wealthy landowner, her husband, St. Basil the Elder, was part of the senatorial nobility. Her mother, St. Emmelia, also came from a wealthy Cappadocian family; her brother was a bishop. Besides Basil and Gregory, another three of the ten siblings devoted themselves to the ecclesiastical or ascetic life: their oldest sister, St. Macrina the Younger, who had an enduring influence upon her brothers' lives; Naucratius, who died in his younger years; and St. Peter, their youngest brother, who was bishop of Sebaste.

The family of Gregory of Nazianzus likewise had been Christian for three generations on his mother's side. She owned estates in nearby Arianzus, and Gregory's father, St. Gregory the elder, had preceded him as bishop of Nazianzus. The church also venerates his mother, Nonna, as well as two of his three siblings, Gorgonia and Caesarius, as saints. His cousin, St. Amphilochius, became bishop of Iconium and is considered by many to be the "fourth great Cappadocian."

All three of the "great Cappadocians" turned their backs on their secular careers, not intending to exchange them for ecclesiastical ones but, rather, to devote themselves to an ascetic life of solitariness in the radical following of Christ. All three, however, were called to the episcopal office because, on the basis of their background and education, they possessed the qualifications not only for political but also for ecclesiastical leadership, especially considering that, beginning with the second half of the fourth century, bishops increasingly also assumed public, administrative roles. All three of them gained their individually shaped importance: Basil as an outstanding ecclesiastical politician, Gregory of Nazianzus as a rhetor and theologian, and Gregory of Nyssa more as a philosophical thinker. The first two, together with Athanasius and John Chrysostom, have been reckoned among the "four great teachers of the Eastern church" since the Breviary of Pius V in 1568 and, together with Athanasius, are revered as the "three hierarchs" for their pioneering work on the Trinitarian dogma. By contrast, Gregory of Nyssa is somewhat of an outsider.

That the Cappadocians do not represent a regional phenomenon in the recruitment of leadership personalities in the church of the time can be seen in the Western church from the family of Ambrose, bishop of Milan, as well as Augustine and his mother, St. Monica, who attracted a circle of friends in the spirit of monasticism, which ultimately became a major source for the North African episcopate.

*Reference Works: Biblia patristica: Index des citations et allusions bibliques dans la littérature patristique* (7 vols.; Paris: Centre National de la Recherche Scientifique, 1975–2000), vol. 5.

*Translations:* G. A. Barrois, *The Fathers Speak* (Crestwood, N.Y.: St. Vladimir's Seminary Press, 1986) [*Selections*].

*Studies:* K. Holl, *Amphilochius von Ikonium in seinem Verhältnis zu den grossen Kappadoziern* (Tübingen: Mohr, 1904). – J. F. Callahan, "Greek Philosophy and the Cappadocian Cosmology," *DOP* 12 (1958): 29–57. – B. Otis, "Cappadocian Thought as a Coherent System," *DOP* 12 (1958): 95–124. – J. Bernardi, *La prédication des Pères cappadociens: Le prédicateur et son auditoire* (Paris: Presses Universitaires de France, 1968). – T. A. Kopecek, "The Social Class of the Cappadocian Fathers," *ChH* 42 (1973): 453–66. – T. A. Kopecek, "The Cappadocian Fathers and Civic Patriotism," *ChH* 43 (1974): 293–303; repr. in *Christentum und antike Gesellschaft* (ed. J. Martin and B. Quint; WdF 649; Darmstadt: Wissenschaftliche Buchgesellschaft, 1990), 300–318. – R. C. Gregg, *Consolation Philosophy: Greek and Christian Paideia in Basil and the Two Gregories* (PatMS 3; Cambridge, Mass.: Philadelphia Patristic Foundation, 1975). – G. May, "Die Grossen Kappadokier und die staatliche Kirchenpolitik von Valens bis Theodosius," in *Die Kirche angesichts der Konstantinischen Wende* (ed. G. Ruhbach; WdF 306; Darmstadt: Wissenschaftliche Buchgesellschaft, 1976), 322–36. – A. Rousselle, "Aspects sociaux du recrutement ecclésiastique au IVe siècle," *MEFRA* 89 (1977): 333–70. – W. Eck, "Der Einfluss der konstantinischen Wende auf die Auswahl der Bischöfe im 4. und 5. Jahrhundert," *Chiron* 8 (1978): 561–85. – P. Maraval, "Encore les frères et sœurs de Grégoire de Nysse," *RHPR* 60 (1980): 161–67. – R. P. C. Hanson, *The Search for the Christian Doctrine of God* (Edinburgh: T&T Clark, 1989), 676–737. – C. White, *Christian Friendship in the Fourth Century* (Cambridge and New York: Cambridge University Press, 1992), 61–84. – G. Kontoulis, *Zum Problem der Sklaverei (DOULEIA) bei den kappadokischen Kirchenvätern und Johannes Chrysostomus* (Bonn: R. Habelt, 1993). – J. Pelikan, *Christianity and Classical Culture: The Metamorphosis of Natural Theology in the Christian Encounter with Hellenism* (New Haven, Conn.: Yale Universtity Press, 1993). – A. Meredith, *The Cappadocians* (Crestwood, N.Y.: St. Vladimir's Seminary Press, 1996).

# A. Basil the Great

The details of the chronology of Basil's life, to whom was already attributed the title "the Great" during his lifetime, cannot be precisely determined in all its parts, and it is currently being discussed once again. He was born ca. 329/330 as the eldest son (?)[2] of ten siblings and initially was taught in the classical disciplines by his father, whereas he received his instruction in the Christian faith from his grandmother Macrina. As a student of Gregory Thaumaturgus, she embedded (Origen's) Alexandrian theology in him. In keeping with the current custom of delaying baptism until adulthood, he did not receive baptism. After attending the school of rhetors at Caesarea (beginning in 343?), where he first met Gregory of Nazianzus, he sought out the most famous teachers and places of training, in keeping with his family's status and financial ability. In Constantinople he was with Libanius (346–350?), with whom he later corresponded (*Ep.* 335–359); at the academy in Athens he heard the famous rhetors Prohairesius and Himerius, became acquainted with Julian, the later emperor, and met Gregory of Nazianzus again, with whom he enjoyed a lifelong friendship from this point on and whose life he was to influence significantly, both spiritually and in matters of ecclesiastical politics. After his return from Athens (356?), he briefly taught rhetoric in Caesarea, but he relinquished this occupation and devoted himself fully to a radical Christian, ascetic lifestyle. He was baptized, became a lector, sold all of his possessions, and used the proceeds to fund the support of the poor. The welfare of the "lowly person," especially in the context of contacts with the authorities, was to remain one of his primary concerns and areas of engagement throughout his life.

After his educational travels to study in the monastic centers in Syria, Mesopotamia, Palestine, and Egypt, he settled on one of the family estates called Annesi, on the river Iris in the province of Pontus, together with Emmelia, his mother; Macrina, his sister; and Naucratius, his brother. There a monastic community gathered around him, serving as a model for the founding of future communities. He also developed there his ascetic program and wrote the first two rules laying the foundation for his work as the "father of Eastern monasticism" (cf. ch. 8.I.B). Together with Gregory of Nazianzus, he compiled the *Philocalia,* an anthology of Origen's writings, at this time. For the reasons outlined in the introduction, it was not to be Basil's lot to conclude his life in monastic seclusion, all the more so since, from 364 on, both the Nicene and the Homoiousian churches were increasingly pressured by Emperor Valens's Homoean religious policy (cf. part 3.I.D). These churches urgently needed highly qualified and influential church leaders, and so in 364 Basil yielded to his friends' urging and was ordained a priest in Cappadocian Caesarea. In 359/360 he had already participated in a synod in Constantinople, but later on he had a falling out with Eusebius, bishop of Caesarea, and returned to solitude.

According to his theological conviction, Basil at that time belonged to the Homoiousians, who were inclined toward the Nicene position but strictly rejected the emperor's Homoean confession. Already when he was a presbyter, he assumed in practice the leadership of the bishopric because Bishop Eusebius was

---

[2] According to W.-D. Hauschild (*TRE* 5:302), contra J. Gribomont (*EECh* 1:114 and *EECh* 2:584), who estimates that Naucratius, his brother, was about ten years older.

hardly up to the extremely difficult ecclesiastical-political situation. At the same time, he also began to pursue the two goals that were to determine the rest of his life: combating the Homoean policy of the state, and the reunification of the Eastern (Homoiousian) churches with Nicea and Rome. This was the purpose of the synods in Lampsacus (364) and Tyana (366), as well as of the resistance against Valens (365) by the city of Caesarea.

In the fall of 370 he succeeded Eusebius as bishop of Caesarea, which at the same time also made him metropolitan of the ecclesiastical province of Cappadocia and exarch of the political diocese of Pontus. The authorities, who had already opposed his election because of his public anti-Homoean position, continued their pursuit to force him to align himself with them, in 372 even with the personal efforts of Emperor Valens, albeit without success. On the basis of a panegyric by Gregory of Nazianzus (*Or. Bas.* 43.46–53), this hagiographically noted resistance by Basil was brought to the emperor's attention and cannot be denied as historical fact. It may have to be evaluated, however, in a completely different way, for Valens not only did not depose Basil but also in 372/373 assigned him to a visitation to Armenia. This cannot be explained on the grounds of Basil's social and politically powerful position alone but suggests a correspondingly high regard and goodwill on the part of the emperor. In 372 Basil did indeed have to accept a painful shrinking of his ecclesiastical province because of the division of the province of Cappadocia, but he responded by increasing the bishoprics and appointing brothers, relatives, and friends to be bishops (Gregory of Nazianzus in Sasima, his brother Gregory in Nyssa, and Amphilochius in Iconium).

Especially after the death of Athanasius (373), his main concern continued to be the strengthening of ecclesiastical communion with Rome, particularly by ending the Antiochene schism. Even if he was not entirely successful in these endeavors by the time he died on January 1, 379,[3] he nevertheless contributed substantially, in the few years of his episcopate, as an outstanding and renowned leader of the Cappadocian church and far beyond, to the theological and ecclesiastical-political solution that emerged immediately after his death, because of the death of Valens (August 9, 378) and the assumption of power by Emperor Theodosius (January 19, 379).

Basil has left behind an extensive wealth of writings, which is worth knowing as a whole. These works are consistently focused on practical ecclesiastical life and reflect his own life and work: the famous *Ad adolescentes*, to the young on how they may benefit from Hellenistic literature; several (exegetical) homilies and letters; his rules on ascetic life; and his two major dogmatic treatises, against Eunomius and on the Holy Spirit. The so-called liturgy of Basil, the current form of which originated in the sixth century, at its core goes back to his reforms of Caesarea's liturgy.

---

[3] P. Maraval, "La date de la mort de Basile de Césarée," *REAug* 34 (1988): 25–38, proposes August 377, agreed to by Röder 65[262] (cf. bibliography on II.B.1); Pouchet: September 378.

*Bibliographies:* T. J. Stokes, *A Bibliography of St. Basil the Great: Works Presently Held by the Leddy Library* (Windsor, Ont.: Assumption University Press, 1977). – P. J. Fedwick, "The Most Recent (1977–) Bibliography of Basil of Caesarea," in idem, ed., *Basilio di Cesarea— la sua età, la sua opera, e il basilianesimo in Sicilia: Atti del Congresso internazionale (Messina 3–6 XII 1979)* (Messina: Centro di Studi Umanistici, 1983), 3–19.

*Editions:*
*Opera omnia:* PG 29–32.
*Ad adolescentes: Discorsi ai giovani* (ed. M. Naldini; BPat 3; Florence: Nardini, Centro Internazionale del Libro, 1984).
*De baptismo: Sur le baptême* (ed. J. Ducatillon; SC 357; Paris: Cerf, 1989).
*De jejunio I–II: De jejunio I, II: zwei Predigten über das Fasten* (ed. H. Marti; SVigChr 6; Leiden and New York: Brill, 1989) [Com].
*De origine hominis: Sur l'origine de l'homme: Hom. X et XI de l' "Hexaéméron"* (ed. A. Smets and M. van Esbroeck; SC 160; Paris: Cerf, 1970).
*Fragments on Ps 118: La Chaîne palestinienne sur le Psaume 118: Origene, Eusebe, Didyme, Apollinaire, Athanase, Theodoret* (ed. M. Harl; 2 vols.; SC 189–90; Paris: Cerf, 1972).
*Homiliae: Versione delle omelie di Basilio (I–III)* (ed. C. Lo Cicero; Rome: Universita degli Studi di Roma "La Sapienza": Dipartimento di Filologia Greca e Latina, 1996).
*Homiliae in Hexaemeron: Homélies sur l'Hexaéméron* (ed. S. Giet; 2d ed.; SC 26; Paris: Cerf, 1968). – E. Amand de Mendieta and S. Y. Rudberg, *Eustathius: Ancienne version latine des neuf homélies sur l'Hexaéméron de Basile de Césarée* (TU 66; Berlin: Akademie, 1958). – *Sulla Genesi: Omelie sull'Esamerone* (ed. M. Naldini; Milan: Fondazione Lorenzo Valla: A. Mondadori, 1990) [Com]. – R. W. Thomson, *The Syriac Version of the Hexaemeron by Basil of Caesarea* (2 vols.; CSCO 550–51; Louvain: Peeters, 1995) [ET]. – *Homilien zum Hexaemeron* (ed. E. Amand de Mendieta and S. Y. Rudberg; GCS NF 2; Berlin: Akademie, 1997).
*Homiliae in Isaiam: Commento al profeta Isaia* (ed. P. Trevisan; 2 vols.; CPS 4–5; Turin: Società Editrice Internazionale, 1939).

*Translations:* B. Jackson, trans., *The Treatise De Spiritu Sancto, the Nine Homilies of the Hexaemeron, and the Letters of Saint Basil the Great, Archbishop of Caesarea* (vol. 8 of NPNF²; Peabody, Mass.: Hendrickson, 1995; repr. of 1895 ed.). – *Ascetical Works* (trans. M. M. Wagner; FC 9; New York: Fathers of the Church, 1950) [including *The Long Rules*]. – *Exegetic Homilies* (trans. A. C. Way; FC 46; Washington, D.C.: Catholic University of America Press, 1963) [*On the Hexaemeron, On the Psalms*].

*Encyclopedia Articles:* G. Bardy, RAC 1:1261–65. – W.-D. Hauschild, TRE 5:301–13. – W.-D. Hauschild, 2:7–20. – J. Gribomont, EECh 1:114–15. – F. Norris, EEC 1:169–72. – P. Rousseau, in *Late Antiquity: A Guide to the Postclassical World* (ed. G.W. Bowersock, P. Brown, and O. Grabar; Cambridge, Mass.: Belknap Press of Harvard University Press, 1999), 336–37.

*Collections of Essays:* P. J. Fedwick, ed., *Basil of Caesarea: Christian, Humanist, Ascetic* (2 vols.; Toronto: Pontifical Institute of Mediaeval Studies, 1981). – A. Rauch and P. Imhof, eds., *Basilius: Heiliger der einen Kirche* (Munich: G. Kaffke, 1981). – *Basilio di Cesarea, la sua età, la sua opera, e il basilianesimo in Sicilia* (2 vols.; Messina: Centro di Studi Umanistici, 1983). – J. Gribomont, *Saint Basile, évangile, et Église: Mélanges* (2 vols.; Bégrolles-en-Mauges: Abbaye de Bellefontaine, 1984). – *Mémorial Dom Jean Gribomont (1920–1986)* (SEAug 27; Rome: Institutum Patristicum Augustinianum, 1988).

*General Studies:* M. M. Fox, *The Life and Times of St. Basil the Great as Revealed in His Works* (PatSt 57; Washington, D.C.: Catholic University of America, 1939). – P. Rousseau, *Basil of Caesarea* (Berkeley: University of California Press, 1994). – B. Sesboüé, *Saint Basile et la Trinité—un acte théologique au IVᵉ siècle: Le rôle de Basile de Césarée dans l'élaboration de la doctrine et du langage trinitaires* (Paris: Desclée, 1998). – M. Girardi, *Basilio di Cesarea interprete della Scrittura: Lessico, principi ermeneutici, prassi* (Bari: Edipuglia, 1998).

*Works: Ad adolescentes:* E. Lamberz, "Zum Verständnis von Basileios' Schrift 'Ad adolescents,'" *ZKG* 90 (1979): 221–41. – W. F. Helleman, "Basil's *Ad Adolescentes:* Guidelines for Reading the Classics," in idem, ed., *Christianity and the Classics: The Acceptance of a Heritage* (Lanham, Md. and London: University Press of America, 1990), 31–51.

*Hexaemeron:* Y. Courtonne, *Saint Basile et l'hellénisme: Étude sur la rencontre de la pensée chrétienne avec la sagesse antique dans l'Hexaéméron de Basile le Grand* (Paris: Firmin-Didot, 1934). – R. Lim, "The politics of interpretation in Basil of Caesarea's *Hexaéméron*," *VC* 44 (1990): 351–70. – S. Y. Rudberg, "Notes lexicografiques sur l'Hexaéméron de Basile," in *Greek and Latin Studies in Memory of Caius Fabricius* (ed. S.-T. Teodorsson; SGLG 54; Göteborg, Swed.: AUG, 1990), 24–32.

*Other Works:* V. Limberis, "The Eyes Infected by Evil: Basil of Caesarea's Homily *On Envy*," *HTR* 84 (1991): 163–84. – E. Cavalcanti, "Dall'etica classica all'etica cristiana: Il commento al prologo del Libro dei Proverbi di Basilio di Cesarea," *SMSR* 14 (1990): 353–78. – M. Girardi, "Basilio di Cesarea esegeta dei Proverbi," *VetChr* 28 (1991): 25–60. – E. Junod, "Basile de Césarée et Grégoire de Nazianze sont-ils les compilateurs de la Philocalie d'Origène? Réexamen de la lettre 115 de Grégoire," in *Mémorial Dom Jean Gribomont (1920–1986)* (SEAug 27; Rome: Institutum Patristicum Augustinianum, 1988), 349–60. – R. Hübner, *Die Schrift des Apolinarius von Laodicea gegen Photin (Pseudo-Athanasius, Contra Sabellianos) und Basilius von Caesarea* (PTS 30; Berlin and New York: de Gruyter, 1989).

*Biographical Studies:* S. Giet, *Les idées et l'action sociales de saint Basile* (Paris: Gabalda, 1941). – G. L. Prestige, *St. Basil the Great and Apollinaris of Laodicea* (ed. H. Chadwick; London: SPCK, 1956). – P. Maraval, "La date de la mort de Basile de Césarée," *REAug* 34 (1988): 25–38. – J.-R. Pouchet, "La date de l'élection épiscopale de saint Basile et celle de sa mort," *RHE* 87 (1992): 5–33. – A. Meredith, "Gregory of Nazianzus and Gregory of Nyssa on Basil," in *Papers Presented at the Twelfth International Conference on Patristic Studies Held in Oxford, 1995* (ed. E. Livingstone; StPatr 32; Louvain: Peeters, 1997), 163–69.

*Theology:* M. A. Orphanos, *Creation and Salvation according to St. Basil of Caesarea* (Athens: Gregorios Parisianos, 1975). – P. Scazzoso, *Introduzione alla ecclesiologia di San Basilio* (SPMed 4; Milan: Vita e Pensiero, 1975). – P. J. Fedwick, *The Church and the Charisma of Leadership in Basil of Caesarea* (Toronto: Pontifical Institute of Mediaeval Studies, 1978). – K. Koschorke, *Spuren der alten Liebe: Studien zum Kirchenbegriff des Basilius von Caesarea* (Par. 32; Fribourg, Switz.: Universitätsverlag, 1991). – G. Mazzanti, "Il fondamento biblico della cristologia di S. Basilio Magno," *Vivens homo* 3 (1992): 225–41. – V. H. Drecoll, *Die Entwicklung der Trinitätslehre des Basilius von Cäsarea: Sein Weg vom Homöusianer zum Neonizäner* (FKDG 66; Göttingen: Vandenhoeck & Ruprecht, 1996). – J. T. Lienhard, "*Ousia* and *hypostasis*: The Cappadocian Settlement and the Theology of 'One *hypostasis*,'" in *The Trinity: An Interdisciplinary Symposium on the Trinity* (ed. S. T. Davis, D. Kendall, and G. O'Collins: Oxford and New York: Oxford University Press, 1999), 99–121.

# 1. *Contra Eunomium*

In his *Apologia*, written in 360/361, Eunomius of Cyzicus had justified and defended his anomoean theology of the Trinity. Basil probably came upon this very persuasive and hence dangerous work quite early and realized the necessity of a careful response, which he provided in 363/364 in *Contra Eunomium*, composed of three books (the so-called fourth and fifth books are not Basil's). Each of the three books deals with one person of the Trinity; Basil's method was to go through Eunomius's text meticulously, cite the essential paragraphs verbatim, and then refute them one by one.

After two introductory paragraphs, in which Basil unmasks the dishonest intentions of Eunomius, bk. 1 first dismisses the main thesis, that the Father's attribute of being ἀγέννητος refers to his substance and that the Son's substance as the begotten one therefore has to be different from the Father's. That the Father and the Son, rather, have to be equally eternal can be seen from the contradictions in Eunomius's doctrine of time itself, when he asserts that the Son is creature but begotten "before all time." Book 2 continues this argument by taking the Son's creatureliness and the arguments asserted for it by Eunomius ad absurdum. "Begotten" does not mean that the Son once did not exist, nor does it have anything to do with passions (πάθη), since the latter would imply that God is mutable. Consequently, the Holy Spirit should not be viewed as a creation of the Son. Book 3 therefore distinguishes the differences between the three divine persons on the level of sequence and honor but not of substance. As for the Holy Spirit, it is precisely the names "Holy Spirit" and "Paraclete" that demonstrate the Spirit's divine nature.

*Editions: Contre Eunome* (ed. B. Sesboüé, G.-M. de Durand, and L. Doutreleau; 2 vols.; SC 299, 305; Paris: Cerf, 1982–1983).

*Studies:* E. Cavalcanti, "Il problema del linguaggio teologico nell'Adv. Eunomium di Basilio Magno," *Aug* 14 (1974): 527–39. – P. Rousseau, "Basil of Caesarea, *Contra Eunomium:* The Main Preoccupations," in *Proceedings of the Eighth International Conference on Patristic Studies, Oxford, 3–8 September, 1979* (ed. E. Livingstone; StPatr 17; Oxford and New York: Pergamon, 1982), 77–94. – D. Schmitz, "Formen der Polemik bei Basilius in der Streitschrift '*Adversus Eunomium,*'" *Glotta* 67 (1989): 233–42.

## 2. De Spiritu Sancto

Ten years later, from late 374 to late 375, Basil wrote a treatise specifically on the Holy Spirit, addressed to Amphilochius of Iconium, who apparently had made such a request. The thirty chapters together do not show any systematic structure but rather revolve around the main theme, namely, that the Holy Spirit is worthy of the same honor as the Father and the Son, which points to his consubstantiality with them. The first and last chapters frame the tractate in the form of a letter. The treatise is structured in three parts, each building upon the other. Chapters 2–5 begin with the theological issue; Basil had been criticized by the Pneumatomachians (a term he himself uses to designate them, although it is not possible to determine with certainty whether he already has a specific party in mind) that the doxology he used in the liturgy, "with the Holy Spirit" (σὺν τῷ πνεύματι τῷ ἁγίῳ), instead of the traditional formulation "in the Holy Spirit" (ἐν τῷ ἁγίῳ πνεύματι), inappropriately accords the Holy Spirit the same honor as the Father and the Son. As a first step in response, chs. 6–8 explain the ὁμοτιμία of the

Father and the Son, which among orthodox Christians is uncontested and consistent with their ὁμοουσία. Finally, chs. 9–30, whose structure is subject to a variety of interpretations in its details, substantiate the doctrine of the three hypostases on the same level by safeguarding the μοναρχία of the one God. The evidence provided appeals to the witness of Scripture, the baptismal formula, and the Holy Spirit's part in the creation and in the plan of redemption. The oneness of nature with the Father and the Son therefore entitles the Holy Spirit to the same titles and honors as are accorded them.

In the history of theology, ch. 29 has gained particular importance because here Basil for the first time specifically applies the method of "the evidence of the Fathers" (*argumentum patristicum*). Although the church from the beginning, and increasingly so during the dogmatic disputes of the fourth century, appealed to the well-established witness of tradition, Basil here adduces for the first time the opinions of a whole range of church fathers in support of his argumentation or, more specifically, of the use of σύν in the doxology. Augustine and Cyril of Alexandria (at the Council of Ephesus in 431) continued this method; it has been perpetuated since then until the present and continues to have validity by safeguarding a historically and dogmatically critical appreciation of the material. This method is not a mere stringing together of arbitrarily selected patristic citations without evidential value.

*Editions: Sur le Saint-Esprit* (ed. B. Pruche; rev. ed.; SC 17; Paris: Cerf, 1968). – D. G. K. Taylor, *The Syriac Versions of the De Spiritu Sancto by Basil of Caesarea* (2 vols.; CSCO 576–77; Louvain: Peeters, 1999) [ET].

*Translations:* B. Jackson, trans., "The De Spiritu Sancto," in *NPNF²* (Peabody, Mass.: Hendrickson, 1995; repr. of 1895 ed.), 8:2–50. – *On the Holy Spirit* (trans. D. Anderson, Crestwood, N.Y.: St. Vladimir's Seminary Press, 1980; repr., 1997).

*Studies: De Spiritu Sancto: Der Beitrag des Basilius zum Abschluss des trinitarischen Dogmas* (AAWG.PH 3.39; Göttingen: Vandenhoeck & Ruprecht, 1956). – T. Špidlík, *La sophiologie de s. Basile* (OrChrAn 162; Rome: Pontificium Institutum Orientalium Studiorum, 1961). – H. Dehnhard, *Das Problem der Abhängigkeit des Basilius von Plotin: Quellenuntersuchungen zu seinen Schriften De Spiritu Sancto* (PTS 3; Berlin: de Gruyter, 1964). – R. P. C. Hanson, "Basil's Doctrine of Tradition in Relation to the Holy Spirit," *VC* 22 (1968): 241–55; repr. in E. Ferguson, ed., *Orthodoxy, Heresy, and Schism in Early Christianity* (SEC 4; New York: Garland, 1993), 123–27. – P. Luislampe, *Spiritus vivificans: Grundzüge einer Theologie des Heiligen Geistes nach Basilius von Caesarea* (MBTh 48; Münster: Aschendorff, 1979). – J. M. Yanguas Sanz, *Pneumatología de san Basilio: La divinidad del Espíritu Santo y su consustancialidad con el Padre y el Hijo* (CTUN 37; Pamplona: Ediciones Universidad de Navarra, 1983). – M. A. G. Haykin, *The Spirit of God: The Exegesis of 1 and 2 Corinthians in the Pneumatomachian Controversy of the Fourth Century* (SVigChr 27; Leiden: New York: Brill, 1994).

## 3. Letters

The corpus of letters by Basil numbers 368; thirty-six or thirty-eight of them were not written by him, however. In keeping with general ancient practice, Basil's collection of letters also contains fifteen or seventeen letters addressed to him, namely, by Libanius (336, 338, 340, 341, 345, 346, 349, 352, 354, 355, 357, 358), Apollinaris of Laodicea (362 and 364), Gregory of Nazianzus (367), and Emperor Julian (39 and 40). The authenticity of the latter two is under discussion, however; in the case of *Ep.* 39, the question is whether it is addressed to Basil, and in the case of *Ep.* 40, whether Julian can be its author.

Inauthentic letters that are part of his correspondence, that is, those not written by Basil and also not addressed to him, include the following: 8, 16, 38(?), 41–45, 47, 166, 167, 169–171, 189, 331, 342, 343, 347, 348, 360, 365, and 366.

*Epistulae* 10, 342, 347, and 348 are also found in the corpus of letters of his youngest brother, Gregory of Nyssa, numbered 21, 28, 26, and 27, but they do belong to Basil (cf. II.B.1).

The Maurists (Benedictines of St. Maur) divided the corpus into three major chronological parts: *Ep.* 1–46, before Basil's consecration as bishop (357–370); 47–291, during his episcopacy (370–379); and 292–365, representing letters that cannot be dated with precision. Johannes Quasten (*Patrology* 3:220–26) organizes the letters into eight groups:

a. Letters of friendship: 1, 3, 4, 7, 12–14, 17, 19–21, 27, 56–58, 63, 64, 95, 118, 123, 124, 132–135, 145–149, 152–158, 162–165, 168, 172–176, 181, 184–186, 192–196, 198, 200, 201, 208–210, 232, 241, 252, 254, 255, 259, 267, 268, 271, 278, 282, 285, 320, 332–334.

b. Letters of recommendation: 3, 15, 31–37, 72–78, 83–88, 96, 104, 108–112, 137, 142–144, 177–180, 271, 273–276, 279–281, 303–319.

c. Letters of consolation: 5, 6, 28, 29, 101, 107, 139, 140, 206, 227, 238, 247, 256, 257, 269, 300–302.

d. Canonical letters: 53, 54, 188, 199, 217. The last three, addressed to Amphilochius of Iconium, offer meticulous instructions for the discipline of repentance and were adopted into the universal legislation of the Eastern church.

e. Moral and ascetical letters: 2, 10–11, 14, 18, 22–26, 49, 65, 83, 85, 97, 106, 112, 115, 116, 161, 173, 174, 182, 183, 197, 219–222, 240, 246, 249, 251, 259, 277, 283, 291–299, 366.

f. Dogmatic letters: 9, 38(?), 52, 105, 113, 114, 125, 129, 131, 159, 175, 210, 214, 226, 233–236, 251, 258, 261, 262. The lengthy *Ep.* 38 is also handed down as a tractate among the works of Gregory of Nyssa, titled *Ad Petrum fratrem de differentia essentiae et hypostaseos*. The question of ownership is still a matter of controversy today.

g. Liturgical letters: 93, 207.

h. Historical letters: 204.

A list of Basil's most important partners in correspondence, encompassing the entire Roman Empire, illustrate most impressively the scope and extent of his letter writing:

- Bishop Ambrose of Milan (cf. ch. 7.III): 197;

- Bishop Amphilochius of Iconium, Basil's friend and cousin of Gregory of Nazianzus: 150, 161, 176, 188, 190, 199–202, 217, 218, 231–236, 248;

- Bishop Apollinaris of Laodicea (cf. 6.I): 361, 363;

- Patriarch Athanasius of Alexandria (cf. ch. 5.IV): 61, 66, 67, 69, 80, 82;

- Bishop Barses of Edessa: 264, 267;

- Pope Damasus: 371;

- Bishop Diodore of Tarsus (cf. ch. 7.IV): 135, 160;

- Bishop Epiphanius of Constantia (Salamis) (cf. ch. 7.II): 258;

- Bishop Eusebius of Samosata: 30, 34, 48, 95, 98, 100, 127, 128, 136, 138, 141, 145, 162, 198, 209(?), 213(?), 237, 239, 241, 268;

- Bishop Eustathius of Sebaste: 79, 119, 223;

- Bishop Gregory of Nazianzus, Basil's university friend (cf. II.C): 2, 7, 14, 19, 71, 368;

- Bishop Gregory of Nyssa, Basil's younger brother (cf. II.B): 38, 58;

- Himerius, the famous rhetor under whom Basil studied in Athens: 274, 275(?);

- Patriarch Meletius of Antioch (cf. part 3.II.A.2.b): 57, 68, 89, 120, 129, 216;

- Libanius, the famous rhetor under whom Basil studied in Constantinople: 335, 337, 339, 344, 350, 351, 353, 356, 359 (their correspondence involved a total of twenty-five letters [335–359], of which 342, 343, 347, and 348 are not authentic and 336, 338, 340, 341, 345, 346, 349, 352, 354, 355, 357, and 358 represent letters of Libanius addressed to Basil);

- Patriarch Peter of Alexandria: 133, 266.

In addition, there are a number of letters addressed to unnamed bishops, priests, monks, magistrates, groups of them, and entire congregations; they demonstrate the extent to which Basil brought influence to bear not only upon particular situations but also structurally upon public life, ecclesiastical policy, and religious life:

- rural bishops (54), bishops in the West (90), bishops in Italy (92), bishops in coastal areas (203), Italic and Gallic bishops (243), bishops in Pontus (252), a bishop (282);

- presbyters of Tarsus (113), clerics in Neocaesarea (207), cleric of Samosata (219), cleric of Colonia (227), cleric of Nicopolis (229), presbyter of Nicopolis (238), presbyter of Antioch (253), cleric of Sozopolis (261);

- community of Tarsus (114), Neocaesareans (204), men of Neocaesarea (210), Chalcidians (222), Occidentals (242, 263), Nicopolitans (246, 247), people of Evaesae (251);

- concerning monastic life (22), a female ascetic (46), female ascetics (52), monks (257, 295);

- governor of Neocaesarea (63), a governor (84, 86), governor of Sebaste (306); a *censitor* (83, 284, 299, 312, 313), an officer (106), a *numerarius* (142, 143), a *tractator* (144), councilors of Samosata (183), decurions of Colonia (228), decurions of Nicopolis (230), a *commentariensis* (286), a *comes privatarum* (303), a *principalis* (311), a *notarius* (333).

There is no addressee for the following letters: 35–37, 77, 78, 85, 87, 88, 101, 117, 165, 191, 209, 213, 249, 270, 273, 275, 285, 287–289, 298, 301, 305, 307–310, 314–320, 322, 326, 327, 330–332.

This overview alone shows clearly what a treasure trove Basil's letters offer regarding his person and personal relationships, his politics and ecclesiastical policies, his pastoral and social activities, and his theology and spirituality. Furthermore they also present excellent examples of fine epistolary form and exemplary style. His friend Gregory of Nazianzus praises him in *Ep.* 51 as an expert in the field, and his teacher Libanius considered him to be of even greater quality in epistolary skills than himself and wrote to him so (*Ep.* 338):

> When the carriers handed me your letter and I silently scanned it in its entirety, I smiled and said joyfully, "We are vanquished." "What victory did they win over you," they asked, "and why, being overcome, are you not sad?" "In the beauty of the letters," I responded, "I have been conquered, and Basil has won. But the man is my friend and for this reason I rejoice." When I had said this, they wanted to understand the victory by means of the letter themselves. Alypius read it aloud and those present listened; they concluded that I had not told them a lie. The reader, however, kept the letter and went away in order to show it to others as well, I believe, and scarcely returned it to me again. Therefore write similar letters and be victorious, for that means victory for me!

*Editions: Lettres* (ed. Y. Courtonne; 3 vols.; Paris: Belles Lettres, 1957–1966). – *The Letters* (ed. R. J. Deferrari; 4 vols.; LCL 190, 215, 243, 270; Cambridge, Mass.: Harvard University Press; London: Heinemann, 1961–1964 [ET]). – *Le lettere* (ed. M. Forlin Patrucco; CorPat 11; Turin: Società Editrice Internazionale, 1983) [*1–46* Com]. – B. Gain, *Traductions latines de Pères grecs: La collection du manuscrit Laurentiànus San Marco 584—édition des lettres de Basile de Césarée* (Europäische Hochschulschriften: Reihe 15, Klassische Sprachen und Literaturen 64; Bern and New York: Lang, 1994).

*Translations:* B. Jackson, trans., "The Letters," in *NPNF²* (Peabody, Mass.: Hendrickson, 1995; repr. of 1895 ed.), 8:109–327. – *Letters* (trans. A. C. Way; 2 vols.; FC 13, 28; Washington, D.C.: Catholic University of America Press, 1951–1955; repr., 1965– 1969).

*Studies:* A. C. Way, *The Language and Style of the Letters of St. Basil* (Patst 13; Washington, D.C.: Catholic University of America, 1927). – A. Cavallin, *Studien zu den Briefen des hl. Basilius* (Lund, Swed.: H. Ohlsson, 1944). – B. Treucker, *Politische und sozial-geschichtliche Studien zu den Basiliusbriefen* (Munich: Kommission für Alte Geschichte und Epigraphik, 1961). – P. Mair, "Die Trostbriefe Basileios des Grossen im Rahmen der antiken Konsolationsliteratur" (diss., Universitäts Innsbruck, 1967). – Y. Courtonne, *Un témoin du IVe siècle oriental: Saint Basile et son temps d'après sa correspondance* (Paris: Belles Lettres, 1973). – B. Gain, *L'église de Cappadoce au IVe siècle d'après la correspondance de Basile de Césarée (330–379)* (OrChrAn 225; Rome: Pontificium Institutum Orientale, 1985). – M. S. Troiano, "Sulla cronologia di Ep. 52, Ad alcune religiose di Basilio di Cesarea," *VetChr* 27 (1990): 339–67. – J. Bernardi, "La lettre 104 de S. Basile: Le préfet du prétoire Domitius Modestus et le statut des clercs," in *Recherches et tradition: Mélanges patristiques offerts a Henri Crouzel* (ed. A. Dupleix; ThH 88; Paris: Beauchesne, 1992), 7–19. – P. Devos, "Aspects de la correspondance de s. Basile de Césarée avec s. Eusèbe de Samosate et avec s. Amphiloque d'Iconium," *AnBoll* 110 (1992): 241–59. – J.-R. Pouchet, *Basile le Grand et son univers d'amis d'après sa correspondance: Une stratégie de communion* (SEAug 36; Rome: Institutum Patristicum Augustinianum, 1992).

*Letter 38:* R. Hübner, "Gregor von Nyssa als Verfasser der sog. *Ep. 38* des Basilius: Zum unterschiedlichen Verständnis der οὐσία bei den kappadozischen Brüdern," in *Epektasis: Mélanges patristiques offerts au cardinal Jean Daniélou* (ed J. Fontaine and C. Kannengiesser; Paris: Beauchesne, 1972), 463–90. – P. Fedwick, "A Commentary on Gregory of Nyssa or the 38th Letter of Basil of Caesarea," *OCP* 44 (1978): 31–51. – J. Hammerstaedt, "Zur Echtheit von Basiliusbrief 38," in *Tesserae: Festschrift für Josef Engemann* (JAC.E 18; Münster: Aschendorff, 1991), 416–19.

# B. Gregory of Nyssa

Two individuals had a decisive impact on the life of Gregory of Nyssa: Macrina, his eldest sister, who inspired him and his brothers concerning the ascetic life, and Basil, his older brother, whom he calls his "father and teacher" several times in his works. The extent to which these honorary titles can be adduced to determine the concrete data of Gregory's life remains uncertain, it is true, for his writings contain very few datable references; external attestations are scarce, and to date there is no in-depth modern, scholarly biography of Gregory. What may be considered as certain is that his father died in Gregory's childhood and Basil, his older brother, assumed a certain leadership role. How much younger Gregory was and whether he had been his student in the technical sense when Basil was teaching in Caesarea ca. 356 have to remain open issues.

It is generally assumed that Gregory was born between 335 and 340. Although he did not attend any of the famous schools in Caesarea, Constantinople, or Athens, as did his brother Basil and their friend Gregory of Nazianzus, he acquired a thorough familiarity with rhetoric, philosophy, and the general knowledge of his time, as his works indicate, to the extent that, after he had first become a lector, he preferred to work as a public rhetor. Many passages in his writings give evidence of meticulous observation of his environment and human behavior patterns, as well as in-depth scientific, especially medical, knowledge. On the basis of a remark in *De virginitate* 3 stating that he could no longer be blessed with the fruits of virginity, it is generally assumed that Gregory was married (to Theosebeia?), although there is no further information to corroborate this.

When the province of Cappadocia was divided in 372 and the ecclesiastical province over which Basil presided as metropolitan in Caesarea was thereby severely weakened, Basil, in order to strengthen the Nicene party, responded by increasing the number of bishoprics and appointing brothers and friends as bishops in the remaining province, Cappadocia Prima. Among these was Gregory, whom he appointed to Nyssa, an insignificant little place between Caesarea and Ancyra. The period of his episcopate divides conspicuously into two very different segments. The break came in 379, that is, the year in which Basil, his brother, and Macrina, his sister, died and in which the ecclesiastical-political situation radically changed in favor of the Nicenes when Emperor Theodosius took office. It remains unclear, however, what specific reasons account for the reversal. In any case, Gregory's initial seven years as bishop were marked by many difficulties. Basil complained about Gregory's naivete in ecclesiastical-political and interpersonal matters (*Ep.* 58 and 100) and in 375 refused to send him to Rome with a delegation to negotiate, because he was "completely inexperienced in ecclesiastical matters" (*Ep.* 215). Indeed, in these years Gregory appears to have been so inept that the Homoean opposition in Nyssa succeeded in deposing and exiling him in 376 under the pretence of misappropriation of church property and irregularities associated with his appointment as bishop. He was able to return only on August 9, 378, after the death of Emperor Valens.

In 379, however, the scene changed radically. Gregory suddenly emerged as a sought-after and influential ecclesiastical politician, as a significant theologian on the current dogmatic issues, as a respected speaker, preacher, and exegete; until his life's end, he maintained close relations with Constantinople, the capital, and with the imperial household. At synods in Antioch (379) and Constantinople (381, 382, 383, and 394), he was among the most prominent participants. The synod of Antioch (379) appointed him to make a visitation to the diocese of Pontus; in Ibora and Sebaste he guided the selection of new bishops and, to his surprise, was himself elected as the metropolitan in Sebaste. He succeeded in regaining his mobility, however, by appointing Peter, his younger brother, as bishop. At the second (a later enumeration) ecumenical Council of Constantinople in 381, he delivered an address entitled *De deitate adversus Evagrium*, important for dogmatics. After the death of Meletius, the chairman of the council, he was given the honorable task of delivering the funeral oration. After the council, according to the imperial law confirming the resolutions of the councils (*Codex theodosianus* 16.1, 3), he was reckoned among the "regular bishops," that is, among those who represented the standard of orthodoxy. In 381 he traveled to the Roman province of Arabia and to Jerusalem on behalf of the council in order to settle disputes there. To the synod in Constantinople of 383 he delivered the address *De deitate Filii et Spiritus Sancti*. The imperial court's special appreciation of him can be seen in the invitation he received to deliver the funeral oration for Princess Pulcheria, who died in 385, and for Empress Flacilla. The information about Gregory's life ends with his entry in the list of the participants at the synod in Constantinople in 394; from this it may well be assumed that he died shortly thereafter.

*Encyclopedia Articles:* H. Dörrie, *RAC* 12:863–95. – E. Mühlenberg, 2: 49–62. – D. L. Balás, *TRE* 14:173–81. – J. Gribomont, *EECh* 1:363–65. – D. L. Balás, *EEC* 1:495–98. – P. Rousseau, "Gregory of Nyssa," *LA*, 477.

*General Studies:* A. Meredith, *Gregory of Nyssa* (Early Church Fathers; London and New York: Routledge, 1999).

# 1. Works, Philosophy, and Theology

Gregory's numerous and diverse works, only the most important of which are mentioned here, divide into the following seven categories:

a. treatises on the current christological and Trinitarian issues of his time, against the neo-Arians, Apollinarians, and Macedonians: *Contra Eunomium, Adversus Apollinarium;*

b. exegetical tractates and homilies: *In Hexaemeron, De hominis opificio, In Ecclesiasten, In Canticum Canticorum, De vita Moysis, De oratione dominica, De beatitudinibus;*

c. ascetical and spiritual writings: *De virginitate;*

d. hagiographic works: *Vita Macrinae, Vita Gregorii Thaumaturgi, In Basilium fratrem, In sanctum Ephraim;*

e. sermons and orations delivered at the church's festivals celebrating the Lord and its saints, at funerals, on topics dealing with morality and practical life and on dogmatic questions;

f. the *Oratio catechetica,* a summation of the essential teachings of the Christian faith;

g. thirty letters, of which *Ep.* 21 and 26–28 do not belong to Gregory but to Basil and *Ep.* 30 is addressed to Gregory by his brother Peter; together with the letter corpora of Basil and Gregory of Nazianzus, they contain most of what, on the whole, is the scarce biographical information on Gregory.

With a few exceptions, the chronology of his works cannot be determined with certainty. *De virginitate* can definitely be attributed to the initial segment of the period of his episcopate, up to 379; only after Basil's death did Gregory seem to have developed into a prolific writer, and in many instances he continued his brother's work (*Contra Eunomium, In Hexaemeron, De hominis opificio*). To Basil's *Contra Eunomium* Eunomius had responded with an *Apologia apologiae,* to which Gregory now replied in lieu of his deceased brother. Since he also follows Basil's methodology and each time cites the passages of the writing he is combating, he preserves a good part of the otherwise lost work of Eunomius. A further work was his own *refutatio* of the creed Eunomius had presented at the Council of Constantinople in 381.

Gregory's philosophy was shaped by middle Platonism and early Neoplatonism, which becomes most prominent in the form and content of the dialogue *De anima et resurrectione,* which he fashioned after Plato's *Phaidon* as a dialogue with Macrina, his dying sister. The particularity of Gregory's Platonism consists in using it for the purpose of effectively recasting the Christian body of thought—a characteristic that fundamentally distinguishes him from the other two Cappadocians and, over against them, has rightly earned him the reputation of a profound philosophical thinker.

As in the case of the other two Cappadocians, his theology is based on the Alexandrian tradition of Philo and Origen. From Origen, whom he mentions by name several times in his writings, he borrowed, for instance, the doctrine of the ἀποκατάστασις, the restoration of all things at the end of time into the blissful primordial state, including Satan and the demons (following 1 Cor 15:25, on which he wrote the tractate *Tunc et ipse filius*). The Second Council of Constantinople (553) later condemned this teaching in its anathemas against Origen, though not Gregory of Nyssa. Rather, the Second Council of Nicea (787) still honored him with the honorary title "Father of Fathers." In his ascetical and mystical theology, the ἐπέκτασις (following Phil 3:13) played a significant part, as he explains in exemplary fashion in the *Vita Moysis:* after one puts off earthly passions, salvation consists in ascending to God and in the subsequent infinite progression in knowing the infinite God.

In the modern era, Gregory's sermons have frequently been dismissed with the summary judgment that they "show the pompous pathos of contemporary rhetoric and are not as powerful and vivid as those of the two other Cappadocians"[4]—unfairly so, as more recent investigations demonstrate.

*Bibliographies:* H. Brown Wicher, *Gregorius Nyssenus* (vol. 5 of *Catalogus translationum et commentariorum: Mediaeval and Renaissance Latin Translations and Commentaries, Annotated Lists and Guides;* Washington, D.C.: Catholic University of America Press, 1984). – M. Altenburger and F. Mann, *Bibliographie zu Gregor von Nyssa: Editionen – Übersetzungen – Literatur* (Leiden and New York: Brill, 1988).

*Editions:*
*Opera omnia:* PG 44–46. – *Gregorii Nysseni Opera* (ed. W. Jaeger et al., eds., Berlin: Weidmann; Leiden: Brill, 1921–).
*Ad Theophilum adversus Apolinaristas, Antirrheticus adversus Apolinarium:* E. Bellini, *Apollinare, Epifanio, Gregorio di Nazianzo, Gregorio di Nissa e altri su Cristo: Il grande dibattito nel quarto secolo* (Milan: Jaca, 1978), 321–483.
*De mortuis: Discorso sui defunti* (ed. G. Lozza; CorPat 13; Turin: Società Editrice Internazionale, 1991) [Com].
*De virginitate: Traité de la virginité* (ed. M. Aubineau; SC 119; Paris: Cerf, 1966).
*Epistulae: Lettres* (ed. P. Maraval; SC 363; Paris: Cerf, 1990).
*Homiliae in Ecclesiasten: Homélies sur l'Ecclésiaste* (ed. F. Vinel; SC 416; Paris: Cerf, 1996).

---

[4]B. Altaner and A. Stuiber, *Patrologie: Leben, Schriften, und Lehre der Kirchenväter* (8th ed.; Fribourg, Switz.: Herder, 1978), 306.

*Oratio catechetica: The Catechetical Oration of Gregory of Nyssa* (ed. J. H. Srawley; Cambridge: Cambridge University Press, 1903; London: SPCK, 1917) [Com]. *Vita Macrinae: Vie de sainte Macrine* (ed. P. Maraval; SC 178; Paris: Cerf, 1971). *Vita Moysis: La vie de Moïse, ou Traité de la perfection en matière de vertu* (ed. J. Daniélou; 3d rev. ed.; SC 1 bis; Paris: Cerf, 1955). – *La vita di Mosè* (ed. M. Simonetti; Rome: Fondazione Lorenzo Valla, 1984) [Com].

*Translations:* W. Moore and H. A. Wilson, trans., *Select Writings and Letters of Gregory, Bishop of Nyssa* (vol. 5 of NPNF[2]; Peabody, Mass.: Hendrickson, 1995; repr. of 1893 ed.) [*Against Eunomius, Answer to Eunomius' Second Book, On the Holy Spirit against Macedonius, On the Holy Trinity, On "Not Three Gods", On the Faith, On Virginity, On Infants' Early Deaths, On Pilgrimages, On the Making of Man, On the Soul and the Resurrection, The Great Catechism, On Meletius, Sermon on the Baptism of Christ, Letters*]. – *The Lord's Prayer, The Beatitudes* (trans. H. C. Graef; ACW 18; Westminster, Md.: Newman, 1954). – E. R. Hardy and C. C. Richardson, eds., *Christology of the Later Fathers* (LCC 3; Philadelphia: Westminster, 1954), 233–325 [*An Answer to Ablabius, Address on Religious Instruction*]. – H. Musurillo, *From Glory to Glory: Texts from Gregory of Nyssa's Mystical Writings* (New York: Scribner, 1961; repr., Crestwood, N.Y.: St. Vladimir's Seminary Press, 1979). – *Ascetical Works* (trans. V. Woods Callahan; FC 58; Washington, D.C.: Catholic University of America Press, 1967), 91–122 [*On Virginity, On Perfection, On What It Means to Call Oneself a Christian, On the Christian Mode of Life, The Life of Saint Macrina, On the Soul and the Resurrection*]. – *The Life of Moses* (trans. E. Ferguson; CWS; New York: Paulist, 1978). – *The Soul and the Resurrection* (trans. C. P. Roth; Crestwood, N.Y.: St. Vladimir's Seminary Press, 1993). – *Gregory of Nyssa's Treatise on the Inscriptions of the Psalms* (trans. R. E. Heine; Oxford: Clarendon; New York: Oxford University Press, 1995). – A. Meredith, *Gregory of Nyssa* (Early Church Fathers; London and New York: Routledge, 1999) [Selections].

*Reference Works:* H. R. Drobner, *Bibelindex zu den Werken Gregors von Nyssa* (Paderborn: H. R. Drobner, 1988). – C. Fabricius and D. Ridings, *A Concordance to Gregory of Nyssa* (SGLG 50; Göteborg, Swed.: Distributors, AUG, 1989) [microfiches]. – F. Mann, *Lexicon gregorianum: Wörterbuch zu den Schriften Gregors von Nyssa* (Leiden and Boston: Brill, 1999–).

*Collections of Essays:* J. Daniélou, *L'être et le temps chez Grégoire de Nysse* (Leiden: Brill, 1970). – H. R. Drobner and C. Klock, eds., *Studien zu Gregor von Nyssa und der christlichen Spätantike* (SVigChr 12; Leiden and New York: Brill, 1990).

*Works:* W. Jaeger, *Two Rediscovered Works of Ancient Christian Literature: Gregory of Nyssa and Macarius* (Leiden: Brill, 1954; repr., 1965). – R. Winling, "La résurrection du Christ dans l'*Antirrheticus adversus Apolinarium* de Grégoire de Nysse," *REAug* 35 (1989): 12–43. – R. Winling, "Mort et résurrection du Christ dans les traités *Contre Eunome* de Grégoire de Nysse," *RevScRel* 64 (1990): 127–40, 251–69. – F. Gasti, "La *Vita Macrinae*: Note di lettura," *At.* 69 (1991): 161–83. – P. Maraval, "Grégoire de Nysse pasteur: La *Lettre canonique à Létoios*," *RHPR* 71 (1991): 101–14. – H. M. Meissner, *Rhetorik und Theologie: Der Dialog Gregors von Nyssa De anima et resurrectione* (Patrologia 1; Frankfurt and New York: Lang, 1991). – R. Stupperich, "Eine Architekturbeschreibung Gregors von Nyssa: Zur Diskussion um die Rekonstruktion des Martyrions von Nyssa im 25. Brief," in *Studien zum antiken Kleinasien: Friedrich Karl Dörner zum 80. Geburtstag gewidmet* (ed. A. Schütte et al.; Bonn: Habelt, 1991), 111–24. – F. Dünzl, *Braut und Bräutigam: Die Auslegung des Canticum durch Gregor von Nyssa* (BGBE 32; Tübingen: Mohr, 1993). – B. Pottier, *Dieu et le Christ selon Grégoire de Nysse: Étude systématique du "Contre Eunome" avec traduction inédite des extraits d'Eunome* (Namur, Belg.: Culture et Vérité, 1994). – M. Girardi, "Annotazioni alla esegesi di Gregorio Nisseno nel *De beatitudinibus*," *Aug* 35 (1995): 161–82. – H. J. Sieben, "Die Vita Moisis (II) des Gregor von Nyssa—ein geistlicher Wegweiser," *TP* 70 (1995): 494–525. – R. J. Kees, *Die Lehre von der Oikonomia Gottes in der Oratio catechetica Gregors von Nyssa* (SVigChr 30; Leiden and New York: Brill, 1995). – T. Böhm, *Theoria–Unendlichkeit–Aufstieg: Philosophische Implikationen zu De vita Moysis von Gregor von Nyssa* (SVigChr 35; Leiden and New York: Brill, 1996). – H. R. Drobner, *Archaeologia patristica: Die Schriften der Kirchenväter als Quellen der Archäologie und Kulturgeschichte: Gregor von Nyssa, Homiliae in Ecclesiasten* (Sussidi allo studio delle antichità cristiane 10; Vatican City: Pontificio Istituto di Archeologia Cristiana, 1996). – U. Gantz, *Gregor von Nyssa: Oratio consolatoria in Pulcheriam* (Basel: Schwabe, 1999). – J. Behr, "The Rational Animal: A Rereading of Gregory of Nyssa's *De hominis opificio*," *JECS* 7 (1999): 219–48.

*Philosophy, Mysticism, and Spirituality:* H. U. von Balthasar, *Presence and Thought: An Essay on the Religious Philosophy of Gregory of Nyssa* (trans. M. Sebanc; San Francisco: Ignatius, 1995); trans. of *Présence et pensée: Essai sur la philosophie religieuse de Grégoire de Nysse* (Paris: Beauchesne, 1942; repr., 1988). – H. Merki, ʹΟΜΟΙΩΣΙΣ ΘΕΩ: *Von der platonischen Angleichung an Gott zur Gottähnlichkeit bei Gregor von Nyssa* (Par. 7; Fribourg, Switz.: Paulusverlag, 1952). – J. Daniélou, *Platonisme et théologie mystique: Doctrine spirituelle de saint Grégoire de Nysse* (2d ed.; Theol[P] 2; Paris: Montaigne, 1953). – W. Völker, *Gregor von Nyssa als Mystiker* (Wiesbaden: Steiner, 1955). – D. L. Balás, ΜΕΤΟΥΣΙΑ ΘΕΟΥ: *Man's Participation in God's Perfections according to Gregory of Nyssa* (SA 55; Rome: Herder, 1966). – E. Mühlenberg, *Die Unendlichkeit Gottes bei Gregor von Nyssa: Gregors Kritik am Gottesbegriff der klassischen Metaphysik* (FKDG 16; Göttingen: Vandenhoeck & Ruprecht, 1966). – A. Louth, *The Origins of the Christian Mystical Tradition* (Oxford: Clarendon; New York: Oxford University Press, 1981), 80–97. – A. A. Mosshammer, "Non-being and Evil in Gregory of Nyssa," *VC* 44 (1990): 136–67. – G. Castelluccio, *L'antropologia di Gregorio Nisseno* (Bari: Levante, 1992). – E. Peroli, *Il Platonismo e l'antropologia filosofica di Gregorio di Nissa: Con particolare riferimento agli influssi di Platone, Plotino, e Porfirio* (Milan: Vita e Pensiero, 1993). – C. Desalvo, *L' "oltre" nel presente: La filosofia dell'uomo in Gregorio di Nissa* (Milan: Vita e Pensiero, 1996). – G. Dal Toso, *La nozione di proairesis in Gregorio di Nissa: Analisi semiotico-linguistica e prospettive antropologiche* (Patrologia 5; Frankfurt and New York: Lang, 1998). – J. Zachhuber, *Human Nature in Gregory of Nyssa: Philosophical Background and Theological Significance* (SVigChr 46; Leiden and Boston: Brill, 2000).

*Rhetoric and Literary Style:* H. R. Drobner, "Die Beredsamkeit Gregors von Nyssa im Urteil der Neuzeit," in *Papers of the Ninth International Conference on Patristic Studies, Oxford, 1983* (ed. E. Livingstone; 4 vols.; StPatr 18; Kalamazoo: Cistercian, 1982), 3:1084–94. – C. Klock, *Untersuchungen zu Stil und Rhythmus bei Gregor von Nyssa: Ein Beitrag zum Rhetorikverständnis der griechischen Väter* (BKP 173; Frankfurt: Athenäum, 1987).

*Theology:* W. Jaeger, *Gregor von Nyssa's Lehre vom Heiligen Geist* (ed. H. Dörries; Leiden: Brill, 1966). – R. M. Hübner, *Die Einheit des Leibes Christi bei Gregor von Nyssa: Untersuchungen zum Ursprung der "physischen" Erlösungslehre* (PP 2; Leiden: Brill, 1974). – F. Mateo-Seco, *Estudios sobre la cristología de san Gregorio de Nisa* (Pamplona: Ediciones Universidad de Navarra, 1978). – M. Canévet, *Grégoire de Nysse et l'herméneutique biblique: Étude des rapports entre le langage et la connaissance de Dieu* (Paris: Études Augustiniennes, 1983). – R. E. Heine, "Gregory of Nyssa's Apology for Allegory," *VC* 38 (1984): 360–70; repr. in E. Ferguson, ed., *The Bible in the Early Church* (SEC 3; New York: Garland, 1993), 302–12. – G. L. Kustas, "Philosophy and Rhetoric in Gregory of Nyssa," *Kl.* 18 (1986): 101–46. – A. Siclari, *L'antropologia teologica di Gregorio di Nissa* (StSR 8; Parma: Zara, 1989). – J. A. Brooks, *The New Testament Text of Gregory of Nyssa* (Atlanta: Scholars Press, 1991). – R. D. Young, "On Gregory of Nyssa's Use of Theology and Science in Constructing Theological Anthropology," *Pro ecclesia* 2 (1993): 345–63. – M. Azkoul, *St. Gregory of Nyssa and the Tradition of the Fathers* (Texts and Studies in Religion 63; Lewiston, N.Y.: Mellen, 1995). – B. E. Daley, "Divine Transcendence and Human Transformation: Gregory of Nyssa's Anti-Apollinarian Christology," *StPat* 32 (1997): 87–95.

## 2. Continuing Influence and History of Research

For reasons still to be examined more closely, Gregory, especially in the Western church, has not attained the same importance as the two other "great Cappadocians." Yet the large number of extant manuscripts of his works, as well as translations into Latin and especially Syriac, help us to recognize the admiration and dissemination of his body of thought. In the twentieth century, Gregory became one of the best-researched church fathers because Ulrich von Wilamowitz-Moellendorff, the famous classical philologist, entrusted the critical edition of his works to Werner Jaeger, his student, precisely because of Gregory's remarkable style. He began in Berlin together with Giorgio Pasquali and, after his work at Harvard University (1939), consulted a multitude of international fellow experts. Since his death in 1961, the task is continued partly in Frankfurt (Hermann Langerbeck, Hadwig Hörner) and partly by the Gregor-von-Nyssa Institut in Münster; since 1969 some international colloquia have met at three- or four-year intervals.

*Studies:* M. Harl, ed., *Écriture et culture philosophique dans la pensée de Grégoire de Nysse* (Leiden: Brill, 1971). – H. Dörrie, M. Altenburger, and U. Schramm, eds., *Gregor von Nyssa und die Philosophie* (Leiden: Brill, 1976). – U. Bianchi and H. Crouzel, eds., *Arché e Telos—l'antropologia di Origene e di Gregorio di Nissa: Analisi storico-religiosa* (SPMed 12; Milan: Vita e Pensiero, 1981). – A. Spira and C. Klock, eds., *The Easter Sermons of Gregory of Nyssa* (PatMS 9; Cambridge, Mass.; Philadelphia Patristics Foundation, 1981). – L. F. Mateo-Seco and J. L. Bastero, eds., *El "Contra Eunomium I" en la producción literaria de Gregorio de Nisa* (CTUN 59; Pamplona: Ediciones Universidad de Navarra, 1988) [ET]. – S. G. Hall, ed., *Gregory of Nyssa: Homilies on Ecclesiastes: An English Version with Supporting Studies* (Berlin and New York: de Gruyter, 1993). – H. R. Drobner and A. Viciano, eds., *Gregory of Nyssa: Homilies on the Beatitudes: An English Version with Supporting Studies* (SVigChr 52; Leiden and Boston: Brill, 2000).

## C. Gregory of Nazianzus

We are quite well informed about the chronology of his life and works because Gregory of Nazianzus wrote an extensive *Carmen de vita sua*, and his writings contain numerous references to his biography. He was born either in the small town of Nazianzus, where his father, Gregory the elder (d. 374 as a centenarian), was the bishop for forty-five years, or at the nearby family estate at Arianzus. Beyond this, however, Gregory remains deliberately silent about his childhood, so his date of birth has to be inferred. Traditionally he was thought to have been about the same age as Basil (b. 329/330). Christoph Jungck,[5] along with Bernhard Wyss[6] and Christoph Klock,[7] however, argued for 326, following Clémencet and Sinko, which fits quite well with some of Gregory's remarks in which he appears to be older than Basil. Justin Mossay,[8] on the other hand, is of the opinion that Gregory had already been born ca. 300. But although this early date makes it very difficult to conceive that Gregory and Basil, despite the age difference of thirty years, jointly studied in Caesarea and Athens, Mossay's arguments seem to me entirely compatible with a date of birth in 326: Gregory's claim to be older; that in Constantinople (381) he was considered an "old man"; and that his mother, Nonna, who was of the same age as her husband according to *Or. Bas.* 18.41, must have been fifty years old when Gregory was born.[9] More likely the information of Suda (ca. 1000), that Gregory was ninety years old when he died in 390 ought to be viewed with suspicion.

Gregory enjoyed an outstanding education equal to that of Basil the Great, first in Cappadocian Caesarea, where he probably met the latter for the first time,[10] then in Caesarea in Palestine, in Alexandria, and at the academy in Athens, where he became acquainted with Julian, the later emperor, and again saw Basil, with whom he maintained a lifelong friendship from then on. According to Basil, Gregory returned to his home ca. 356 to teach rhetoric, as did Basil, but under the influence of his friend, he soon turned to the ascetic life and spent some time with him in his monastic community in Annesi on the river Iris (in the province of Pontus), where they jointly compiled the *Philocalia,* a collection of texts from the writings of Origen. He was baptized, and in 361 his father ordained him to the priesthood in order to assist him in the ministry in the diocese of Nazianzus.[11] Because he viewed the ordination as "forced," however, he refused to assume his office and did not return until Easter 362, when, while preaching, he apologized for his hesitation (*Or. Bas.* 1). This was followed by a second apology in the form of an address with a lengthy treatise on the priesthood (*Or. Bas.* 2), which subsequently inspired John Chrysostom to write his famous *De sacerdotio.* At this point, there comes to the fore for the first time one of Gregory's character traits, which was to be part of his whole life and would guide it decisively several times: his love was aimed at erudition and rhetoric, in which he had no equal among the Greek fathers of the fourth century. Because of requests and out of

---

[5] C. Jungck, 1974, 231–33.

[6] B. Wyss, *RAC* 12:794.

[7] C. Klock, 1987, 84. Bibliographic information is given under Gregory of Nyssa.

[8] J. Mossay, *TRE* 14:164f.

[9] Could it be that Gregory's description of his mother as a "spiritual Sarah" points in the same direction?

[10] The statement of earlier patrologists that Gregory had met Basil first in Athens needs to be corrected accordingly, especially by J. Mossay (*TRE* 14:165), who erroneously appeals to *Or. Bas.* 43.13.

[11] Only Justin Mossay ("La date de l'oratio II de Grégoire de Nazianze et celle de son ordination," *Mus* 77 [1964]: 175–86, and again in *TRE* 14:166) moves it to 365 or into the reign of Emperor Julian (361–363) or Valens (364–378).

practical necessity, he neglected these at times. If he was able to withdraw to scholarly leisure, however, he was glad, especially since, given his sensitive character, he was not able to cope with the difficulties of ecclesiastical politics as effectively as Basil.

In the context of increasing the bishoprics and of strengthening the Nicene party in his diocese after the division of the province of Cappadocia, Basil appointed him in 372 as bishop of Sasima, a small but not unimportant town because it was situated at a crossroads. Gregory declined to assume the diocese, however, and instead continued to assist his father in his hometown, Nazianzus, until his death (374). After this he withdrew to Seleucia in Isauria, where he received a call after the death of Emperor Valens (August 9, 378) to lead the small Nicene community in the capital. Since the great majority of Christians in the capital belonged to the Arian confession under Bishop Demophilus, Gregory resided in a private residence (the later Anastasia Church), where he held the famous "five theological orations," in which he explained the Nicene doctrine of the Trinity and which earned him the honorary title "the theologian" (attested for the first time in the council documents of Chalcedon in 451); Jerome was also among his audience. Immediately after his move to Constantinople on November 24, 380, Theodosius forced Bishop Demophilus to leave the city and introduced Gregory as bishop of the capital. The Council of Constantinople (381) acknowledged him as such and, after the death of Meletius of Antioch, elected him as chairman of the council. He was not, however, successful in mediating an acceptable agreement between the various parties of the council regarding both the Meletian schism in Antioch and the *symbolum*. Instead he came under fire to the extent that he was even accused of having been transferred illegitimately to the episcopal see of Constantinople because he already was bishop of Sasima. As a result, Gregory submitted his resignation, which was accepted with approval. He took leave in his famous farewell address (*Or. Bas.* 42) and returned to Nazianzus even before the council ended and there administered the bishopric until Eulalius, his cousin, was installed as bishop in 383. Subsequently he retreated to the family estate near Arianzus, where he presumably died in 390.

The final part of his life, beginning with his call to Constantinople (379), represents Gregory's most prolific period of literary activity. During this time he wrote half of the forty-four extant sermons, most of the 249 letters, and the bulk of his poetry. His remains rested in the left front crossing pillar of St. Peter's in Rome from June 11, 1580, until Pope John Paul II returned them, along with the remains of John Chrysostom, to Patriarch Bartholomew I of Constantinople on November 27, 2004.

*Bibliographies:* F. Lefherz, *Studien zu Gregor von Nazianz: Mythologie, Überlieferung, Scholien* (Bonn; n.p., 1958), 61–108. – E. Bellini, "Bibliografia su San Gregorio Nazianzeno," *ScC* 98 (1970): 165*–81*. – F. Trisoglio, *San Gregorio di Nazianzo in un quarantennio di studi (1925–1965)* (RivLas 40; Turin: Collegio San Giuseppe, 1973). – P. O. Kristeller, F. E. Cranz, and V. Brown, eds., *Catalogus translationum et commentariorum—Mediaeval and Renaissance Latin Translations and Commentaries: Annotated Lists and Guides* (Washington, D.C.: Catholic University of America Press, 1960–), 2:43–192.

*Editions: Opera omnia:* PG 35–38. – *Corpus nazianzenum* (CCSG; Turnhout, Belg.: Brepols, 1988–). – *Contro Giuliano l'Apostata: Oratio IV* (ed. L. Lugaresi; Bpat 23; Florence: Nardini, 1993) [*Contra Julianum IV* Com]. – *La morte di Giuliano l'Apostata: Oratio V* (ed. L. Lugaresi; BPat 29; Florence: Nardini, 1997) [*Contra Julianum V* Com]. – *Le dit de sa vie* (ed. A. Lukinovich and C. Martingay; Geneva: Solem, 1997) [*De vita sua* Com]. – *Corpus nazianzenum 4: Versio arabica antiqua I: Oratio XXI (arab. 20)* (ed. J. Grand'Henry; CCSG 34; Turnhout, Belg.: Brepols, 1996). – *Corpus nazianzenum 5: Versio iberica I: Orationes I, XLV, XLIV, XLI* (ed. H. Metreveli et al.; CCSG 36; Turnhout, Belg.: Brepols, 1998). – *Corpus nazianzenum 6: Versio armenica II: Orationes IV et V* (ed. A. Sirnian; CCSG 37; Turnhout, Belg.: Brepols, 1999).

*Reference Works:* J. Mossay, B. Coulie, C. Detienne, and Cetedoc, *Thesaurus Sancti Gregorii Nazianzeni* (CCSG; Turnhout, Belg.: Brepols, 1990–1991) [microfiches].

*Monograph Series:* Studien zur Geschichte und Kultur des Altertums: 2. Reihe, Forschungen zu Gregor von Nazianz, Paderborn.

*Encyclopedia Articles:* B. Wyss, *RAC* 12:793–863. – B. Wyss, 2:21–36. – J. Mossay, *TRE* 14:164–73. – J. Gribomont, *EECh* 1:361–62. – F. Norris, *EEC* 491–95. – N. McLynn, "Gregory of Nazianzus," *LA*, 476–77.

*Collections of Essays:* C. Moreschini and G. Menestrina, eds., *Gregorio Nazianzeno teologo e scrittore* (Bologna: EDB, 1992).

*General Studies:* A. Benoit, *Saint Grégoire de Nazianze, sa vie, ses œuvres, et son époque* (Marseille: M. Olive, 1876; repr., Hildesheim and New York: Olms, 1973). – E. Fleury, *Saint Grégoire de Nazianze et son temps* (ETH; Paris: Beauchesne, 1930). – P. Gallay, *La vie de saint Grégoire de Nazianze* (Lyon and Paris: E. Vitte, 1943). – R. Radford Ruether, *Gregory of Nazianzus: Rhetor and Philosopher* (Oxford: Clarendon, 1969). – F. Trisoglio, *Gregorio di Nazianzo il teologo* (SPMed 20; Milan: Vita e Pensiero, 1996). – J. Bernardi, *Saint Grégoire de Nazianze: Le théologien et son temps (330–390)* (Paris: Cerf, 1995). – F. Trisoglio, *Gregorio di Nazianzo* (Rome: Tiellemedia, 1999).

*Particular Studies—Life and Works:* M.-M. Hauser-Meury, *Prosopographie zu den Schriften Gregors von Nazianz* (Theoph. 13; Bonn: P. Hanstein, 1960). – M. Kertsch, *Bildersprache bei Gregor von Nazianz: Ein Beitrag zur spätantiken Rhetorik und Popularphilosophie* (2d ed.; GrTS 2; Graz, Austria: Eigenverl. des Inst. f. Ökumenische Theologie u. Patrologie an d. Univ. Graz, 1980). – B. Coulie, *Les richesses dans l'œuvre de saint Grégoire de Nazianze: Étude littéraire et historique* (PIOL 32; Louvain: Université Catholique de Louvain, Institut Orientaliste: Editions Peeters, 1985). – U. Criscuolo, "Gregorio di Nazianzo e Giuliano," in *Talarískos: Studia graeca Antonio Garzya sexagenario a discipulis oblata* (ed. U. Criscuolo; Naples: D'Auria, 1987), 165–208. – E. Junod, "Basile de Césarée et Grégoire de Nazianze sont-ils les compilateurs de la Philocalie d'Origène? Réexamen de la lettre 115 de Grégoire," in *Memorial Dom Jean Gribomont (1920–1986)* (SEAug 27; Rome: Institutum Patristicum Augustinianum, 1988), 349–60. – K. Demoen, *Pagan and Biblical Exempla in Gregory Nazianzen: A Study in Rhetoric and Hermeneutics* (Corpus Christianorum: Lingua patrum 2; Turnhout, Belg.: Brepols, 1996). – C. Moreschini, *Filosofia e letteratura in Gregorio di Nazianzo* (Milan: Vita e Pensiero, 1997). – F. Norris, "Gregory Nazianzen: Constructing and Constructed by Scripture," in *The Bible in Greek Christian Antiquity* (ed. P. Blowers; Notre Dame, Ind.: University of Notre Dame Press, 1997), 149–62.

*Theology:* J. Plagnieux, *Saint Grégoire de Nazianze théologien* (ESR 7; Paris: Éditions Franciscaines, 1951). – J. M. Szymusiak, *Eléments de théologie de l'homme selon s. Grégoire de Nazianze* (Rome: Pontificia Universitas Gregoriana, 1963). – J. Mossay, *La mort et l'au-delà dans saint Grégoire de Nazianze* (Recueil de travaux d'histoire et de philologie 4. ser., 34; Louvain: Bureaux du Recueil, Bibliothèque de l'Université, Publications Universitaires de Louvain, 1966). – T. Spidlík, *Grégoire de Nazianze: Introduction à l'étude de sa doctrine spirituelle* (OrChrAn 189; Rome: Pontificium Institutum Studiorum Orientalium, 1971). – H. Althaus, *Die Heilslehre des heiligen Gregor von Nazianz* (MBTh 34; Münster: Aschendorff, 1972). – D. F. Winslow, *The Dynamics of Salvation: A Study in Gregory of Nazianzus* (PatMS 7; Cambridge, Mass.: Philadelphia Patristic Foundation, 1979). – C. Moreschini, "La persona del Padre nella teologia di Gregorio Nazianzeno," *VetChr* 28 (1991): 77–102.

# 1. Poetry

Although Gregory of Nazianzus was not the first to give poetic form to theological material and Christian themes, he was the first to write a fully developed, extensive poetic oeuvre of 17,000 verses that is unmatched in Greek patristics. His *Carmina,* most of which he wrote after his return from Constantinople, in the secluded leisure that he enjoyed at Arianzus until his death, are composed of didactic poems, hymns, elegies, and epigrams in their traditional meters, from which Gregory does not deviate on the whole, namely, the hexameter, distich, and iambic. He deals with dogmatic, moral, autobiographical, and lyrical themes, with the explicit intent (*Carmina* 2.1.39) of using the poetic form to proclaim the Christian message more pleasantly and more attractively and to provide a comparable Christian expression alongside Hellenistic poetry. With the quality of his poems, Gregory decisively refutes the former polemic charge that Christians lacked education and comparable literature.

Recently *Christus patiens,* the drama handed down under Gregory's name, has again been defended as authentic by André Tuilier and Francesco Trisoglio,[12] without sufficient reasons, to be sure, as Bernhard Wyss[13] counters so aptly. It may be dated to the twelfth century.

*Editions:* H. Beckby, *Anthologia graeca* (2 vols.; 2d ed.; Munich: Heimeran, 1965) [*Epigrammata* Com]. – *Gegen die Putzsucht der Frauen* (ed. A. Knecht; Heidelberg: Winter, 1972) [*Carmina* 1.2.29 Com]. – *De vita sua* (ed. C. Jungck; Heidelberg: Winter, 1974) [*Carmina* 2.1.11 Com]. – *Carmina de virtute 1a/1b* (ed. R. Palla and M. Kertsch; GrTS 10; Graz: Eigenverlag des Instituts für Ökumenische Theologie und Patrologie an der Universität Graz, 1985) [*Carmina* 1.2.9 Com]. – *Über die Bischöfe (Carmen 2,1,12)* (ed. B. Meier; SGKA NF 2. Reihe 7; Paderborn: F. Schöningh, 1989) [*Carmina* 2.1.12 Com]. – *Gegen den Zorn (Carmen 1,2,25)* (ed. M. Oberhaus; SGKA NF 2. Reihe 8; Paderborn: F. Schöningh, 1991) [*Carmina* 1.2.25 Com]. – *Der Rangstreit zwischen Ehe und Jungfräulichkeit (Carmen 1,2,1,215–732)* (ed. K. Sundermann; SGKA NF 2. Reihe 9; Paderborn: F. Schöningh, 1991) [*Carmina* 1.2.1.215–732 Com]. – *Sulla virtù: Carme giambico: [1,2,10]* (ed. C. Crimi, M. Kertsch, and J. Guirau; Pisa: ETS, 1995) [*Carmina* 1.2.10 Com]. – *Ad Olimpiade: Carm. II,2,6* (ed. L. Bacci; Pisa: ETS, 1996

---

[12] A. Tuilier, ed. and trans., *La passion du Christ* (SC 149; Paris: Cerf, 1969), 11–18. F. Trisoglio, *La passione di Cristo* (CTePa 16; Rome: Città Nuova, 1979), 13–16; the 1990 second edition did not take into account the critique by Wyss.

[13] B. Wyss, *RAC* 12:812.

[*Carmina* 2.2.6 Com]). – *Poemata arcana* (ed. D. Sykes and C. Moreschini; Oxford: Clarendon; New York: Oxford University Press, 1997) [ET/Com].

*Translations: Saint Gregory Nazianzen: Selected Poems* (trans. J. McGuckin; Oxford: SLG, 1986). – *Three Poems* (trans. D. M. Meehan and T. P. Halton, FC 75; Washington, D.C.: Catholic University of America Press, 1987) [*Concerning His Own Affairs* II/I/I; *Concerning Himself and the Bishops* II/I/XII; *Concerning His Own Life* II/I/XI]. – *Autobiographical Poems* (trans. C. White; Cambridge Medieval Classics 6; Cambridge and New York: Cambridge University Press, 1996).

*Studies:* M. Pellegrino, *La poesia di S. Gregorio Nazianzeno* (PUCSC 4.13; Milan: Vita e Pensiero, 1932). – F. E. Zehles, *Kommentar zu den Mahnungen an die Jungfrauen (carmen I,2,2) Gregors von Naziarz, V.1–354* (Münster: n.p., 1987). – U. Beuckmann, *Gegen die Habsucht (carmen 1,2,28)* (SGKA NF 2. Reihe 6; Paderborn: F. Schöningh, 1988) [*Carmina* 1.2.28 Com]. – M. Regali, "La datazione del carme II,2,3 di Gregorio Nazianzeno," *SCO* 38 (1988): 373–81. – G. Lozza, "Lettura di Gregorio Nazianzeno, carme II 1,87," in *Metodologie della ricerca sulla tarda antichità* (ed. A. Garzya; Naples: D'Auria, 1989), 451–59. – R. Palla, "Ordinamento e polimetria delle poesie bibliche di Gregorio Nazianzeno," *WSt* 102 (1989): 169–85. – C. Nardi, "Note al primo carme teologico di Gregorio Nazianzeno," *Prometheus* 16 (1990): 155–74. – M. Corsano, "Problemi testuali ed esegetici nel carme 2,1,83 di Gregorio Nazianzeno," *Sileno* 17 (1991): 139–47. – C. Crimi, "*Nazianzenica I*," *Orph.* 12 (1991): 204–9 [*Carmina* 1.2.10.206, 942]. – T. Spidlík, "La théologie et la poésie selon Grégoire de Nazianze," in *Homo imago et amicus Dei = The Man, Image, and Friend of God: Miscellanea in honorem Ioannis Golub* (ed. R. Peric; Rome: Pontificium Collegium Croaticum Sancti Hieronymi, 1991), 97–111. – F. E. Zehles and M. J. Zamora, *Gregor von Nazianz: Mahnungen an die Jungfrauen (Carmen 1,2,2): Kommentar* (SGKA NF 2. Reihe 13; Paderborn: Schöningh, 1996).

# 2. Orations

The Maurist edition encompasses forty-five orations and sermons of Gregory; the thirty-fifth is not attributed to him, however. The time frame for their composition ranges from his consecration as bishop in 362 to his retirement in Arianzus in 383. Half of them are concentrated in the period beginning with his call to Constantinople in 379. Some are orally presented speeches that he himself prepared for publication, and some are literary works in oral form. The latter certainly applies to Or. Bas. 4 and 5, representing invectives against Julian the Apostate, the deceased emperor. All of Gregory's orations stand out not only because of their masterly rhetoric but also, at the same time, because of their skill in presenting solutions to the difficult theological issues of his time clearly and persuasively. This is the case particularly in the five "theological orations" (27–31), which he himself identified as such (28.1) and which, in the main, brought him his honorary title of "theologian." He delivered them during his time in Constantinople (379–381), probably in 380 in the private residence that later became the Anastasia Church, for the cathedral, the Church of the Apostles, still belonged to the Arian bishop. The terms "theological" and "theology" are to be construed in the strictly early-Christian sense of the "doctrine of God"; at issue is the presentation of the orthodox doctrine of the Trinity in dispute with the Young Arians (Eunomians) and Macedonians (Pneumatomachians). Alongside the brilliant defense of the traditional Nicene doctrine of God, he finds the forward-looking formulation of the "procession" (ἐκπόρευσις) of the Spirit from the Father, in distinction to the "generation" (γέννησις) of the Son, and for the first time insists on transferring the concept of consubstantiality (ὁμοούσιος) to the Holy Spirit. Thus he goes beyond Basil and, by means of a more precise terminology, not only sharpens the understanding of the Holy Spirit within the Trinity but also prepares for the pneumatological amendments to the Nicene creed at the Council of Constantinople (381), which followed shortly.

*Editions:* Tyrannii Rvfini Orationvm Gregorii Nazianzeni novem interpretatio (ed. A. Engelbrecht; CSEL 46; Vienna: F. Tempsky, 1910). – *Die fünf theologischen Reden* (ed. J. Barbel; Test. 3; Düsseldorf: Patmos, 1963) [*Orationes theologicae* Com]. – *Discours 1–12, 20–43* (ed. J. Bernardi, P. Gallay, M. Jourjon, G. Lafontaine, C. Moreschini, J. Mossay, and M.-A. Calvet-Sebasti; 9 vols.; SC 247, 250, 270, 284, 309, 318, 358, 384, 405; Paris: Cerf, 1978–1995) [*Orationes*]. – *Orationes theologicae* (ed. H. J. Sieben; FChr 22; Fribourg, Switz., and New York: Herder, 1996) [Com]. – *Sancti Gregorii Nazianzeni Opera: Versio armeniaca* (ed. B. Coulie; CCSG 28; Turnhout, Belg.: Brepols, 1994) [*Orationes* 2, 12, 9 (Armenian)]. – *Sancti Gregorii Nazianzeni Opera: Versio arabica antiqua* (ed. J. Grand'Henry; CCSG 34; Turnhout, Belg.: Brepols, 1996) [*Orationes* 21 (Arabic)].

*Translations:* C. G. Browne and J. E. Swallow, trans., "Select Orations," in *NPNF²* (Peabody, Mass.: Hendrickson, 1995; repr. of the 1894 ed.), 7:203–434. – *Funeral Orations* (trans. L. P. McCauley; FC 22; New York: Fathers of the Church, 1953; repr., Washington, D.C.: Catholic University of America Press, 1968), 1–156. – E. R. Hardy and C. C. Richardson, eds., *Christology of the Later Fathers* (LCC 3; London: SCM; Philadelphia: Westminster, 1954), 113–214 [*Theological Orations*]. – F. W. Norris, L. Wickham, and F. Williams, *Faith Gives Fullness to Reasoning: The Five Theological Orations of Gregory Nazianzen* (SVigChr 13; Leiden and New York: Brill, 1991) [ET/Com].

*Studies:* H.-G. Beck, *Rede als Kunstwerk und Bekenntnis: Gregor von Nazianz* (SBAW.PPH 1977.4; Munich: Verlag der Bayerischen Akademie der Wissenschaften, 1977). – R. Weijenborg, "Some Evidence of Unauthenticity for the Discourse XI in Honour of Gregory of Nyssa Attributed to Gregory of Nazianzus," in *Proceedings of the Eighth International Conference on Patristic Studies, Oxford, 3–8 September, 1979* (ed. E. Livingstone; 3 vols.; StPatr 17; Oxford and New York: Pergamon, 1982), 3:1145–48. – G. Lafontaine and B. Coulie, *La version arménienne des discours de Grégoire de Nazianze: Tradition manuscrite et histoire du texte* (CSCO 446; Louvain: Peeters, 1983). – A. Kurmann, *Gregor von Nazianz, Oratio 4 gegen Julian: Ein Kommentar* (SBA 19; Basel: F. Reinhardt, 1988). – G. H. Ettlinger, "The Orations of Gregory of Nazianzus: A Study in Rhetoric and Personality," in *Preaching in the Patristic Age: Studies in Honor of Walter J. Burghardt, S.J.* (ed. D. G. Hunter; New York: Paulist, 1989), 101–18. – A. Hanriot-Coustet, "Quel est l'auteur du Discours 35 transmis parmi les œuvres de Grégoire de Nazianze?" *RHPR* 71 (1991): 89–99.

# 3. Letters

Following the classical example, Gregory himself published an initial collection of his letters, and he was the only Christian author to bequeath a brief outline of the theory of epistelography, in *Ep.* 51 (cf. ch. 4.IV.excursus). Of the 249 extant letters, *Ep.* 246–248 are also handed down as *Ep.* 169–171 in the corpus of Basil the Great, *Ep.* 243 is inauthentic, and *Ep.* 241 is suspect. In form, all of them are literary letters, but in content, they are largely the day-to-day correspondence of an educated man and bishop. Three of them have gained great theological importance as the "three theological letters" supporting the "five theological orations," namely *Ep.* 101 and 102, dated summer 382 and addressed to the presbyter Cledonius, who led the diocese during the vacancy in the see of Nazianzus following the death of Gregory the elder (374), and *Ep.* 202, addressed to Nectarius (ca. 387), the successor of Gregory and the predecessor of John Chrysostom as patriarch of Constantinople (381–397). Nectarius was not a theologian but at his consecration had been a senator and a catechumen. He accordingly dealt little with the urgent theological questions of his time, although, in contrast to his predecessor and his successor, he successfully avoided disputes with the people of the church and with the imperial household. Gregory sent *Ep.* 202 to him as an admonition to be cautious with the ongoing machinations of the Arians, Macedonians, and Apollinarians, but also as a bit of theological assistance.

If the five theological orations had clarified the one major theological issue of the time of Gregory, namely, the doctrine of the Trinity in dispute with the Arians and Pneumatomachians, the three theological letters address mainly the other issue, namely, Christology in the discussion against Apollinaris. In a decisive and forward-looking way, *Ep.* 101.32 defines the completeness of the two natures in Christ: "For that which he has not assumed he has not healed, but that which is united to his Godhead is also saved" (Τὸ γὰρ ἀπρόσληπτον, ἀθεράπευτον· ὃ δὲ ἥνωται τῷ θεῷ, τοῦτο καὶ σῴζεται). The differentiation of the natures as ἄλλο καὶ ἄλλο in distinction to the three persons in the Trinity as ἄλλος καὶ ἄλλος (101.20–21) supplements the formula. Subsequently the Council of Ephesus (431) appealed to a lengthy paragraph from *Ep.* 101, and in its documents the Council of Chalcedon (451) appropriated it in its entirety.

Generally, Gregory's works and theology have been very widely disseminated and have exerted great influence, as shown by the more than twelve hundred extant Greek manuscripts of his orations, the translations into Latin and some Eastern languages, and the numerous scholia. Alongside individual editions and *editiones minores* of Gregory's writings, the poems and orations have been emerging since 1977 as *editiones maiores* under the patronage of the Görres-Gesellschaft, led by Justin Mossay (Louvain) and Martin Sicherl (Münster) and including numerous international collaborators.

*Editions: Briefe [von] Gregor von Nazianz* (ed. P. Gallay; GCS 53; Berlin: Akademie, 1969) [except *Ep.* 101, 102, 202, 243]. – *Lettres théologiques* (ed. P. Gallay and M. Jourjon; SC 208; Paris: Cerf, 1974) [*101, 102, 202*]. – E. Bellini, *Su Cristo: Il grande dibattito nel quarto secolo* (Milan: Jaca, 1978), 267–319 [*101, 102, 202*].

*Translations:* C. G. Browne and J. E. Swallow, trans., "Letters," in *NPNF²* (Peabody, Mass.: Hendrickson, 1995; repr. of 1894 ed.), 7:437–82 [*Selected Letters*].

*Studies:* P. Gallay, *Langue et style de saint Grégoire de Nazianze dans sa correspondance* (Paris: J. Monnier, 1933). – A. Camplani, "Epifanio (*Ancoratus*) e Gregorio di Nazianzo (*Epistulae*) in copto: Identificazioni e *status quaestionis*," *Aug* 35 (1995): 327–47.

# III. COUNCIL OF CONSTANTINOPLE (381)

On January 19, 379, Emperor Theodosius assumed power, and on August 3 of the same year, he issued the order that only the Nicene creed was accepted empire-wide. When he further called on the entire empire on February 27, 380, to adhere to the Nicene expression of Christianity and replaced Demophilus, the Arian patriarch of Constantinople, with Gregory of Nazianzus immediately after his move to the capital. On November 24, 380, the victory of the faith of Nicea, after more than fifty years of battle for its reception, was sealed. Granted, what was still lacking was its ecclesiastical sanctioning, for according to early Christian opinion, neither an emperor nor a bishop nor even a patriarch was able to lay down valid norms of faith for the entire church by his own absolute power; only a council that is as inclusive as possible—in other words, "ecumenical"—could do this. (This principle also applies to the Council of Constantinople [381]. It did not describe itself as ecumenical, and it was composed exclusively of bishops from the Eastern church. Only the Council of Chalcedon [451] ushered in its recognition as ecumenical.) This was also the reason that after the Council of Nicea (325), confusingly, many synods were held on all sides.

Now, fifty-five years after the Council of Nicea, a simple confirmation of the Nicene creed was no longer sufficient; there had been too much development, both ecclesiastically-politically and theologically. Now Arianism had to be opposed in the form of Eunomianism, and the Meletian schism of Antioch had to be resolved. The resultant theological problems with the doctrine of the Trinity and, for the first time, with Christology, called for a binding clarification: the question of the divinity of the Spirit (Macedonians/Pneumatomachians) and of the kind of unity between the two natures in Christ (Apollinaris). For this reason, Theodosius summoned a synod soon after he moved to Constantinople at the end of 380 or early 381, which met in Constantinople from May to July. One hundred fifty bishops participated, among them Meletius of Antioch as presiding officer; Gregory of Nazianzus; Gregory of Nyssa and Peter, his brother, of Sebaste; Cyril of Jerusalem; and Diodore of Tarsus.

*Editions:* Mansi 3:521–600.

*Encyclopedia Articles:* A. Ritter, *TRE* 19:518–24. – C. Kannengiesser, *EECh* 1:195–96.

*Collections of Essays: ITQ* 48 (1981): 157–267. – *La signification et l'actualité du IIe concile œcumenique pour le monde chrétien d'aujourd'hui* (Chambésy, Switz.: Centre Orthodoxe du Patriarcat Oecuménique, 1982). – T. Piffl-Percevic and A. Stirnemann, eds., *Das gemeinsame Credo* (Innsbruck: Tyrolia, 1983). – J. Saraiva Martins, ed., *Credo in Spiritum Sanctum* (2 vols.; Teologia e filosofia 6; Vatican City: Libreria Editrice Vaticana, 1983).

*Studies:* C. J. Hefele and H. Leclercq, *Histoire des conciles: D'après les documents origineaux* (Paris: Letouzey, 1907–), 2/1:1–48. – E. Schwartz, "Das *Nicaenum* und *Constantinopolitanum* auf der Synode von Chalkedon," *ZNW* 25 (1926): 38–88. – I. Ortiz de Urbina, *Nicée et Constantinople* (HCO 1; Paris: Orante, 1963), 137–242 [ted Mz 1964]. – A. M. Ritter, *Das Konzil von Konstantinopel und sein Symbol: Studien zur Geschichte und Theologie des II. ökumenischen Konzils* (FKDG 15; Göttingen: Vandenhoeck & Ruprecht,

1965). – R. P. C. Hanson, *The Search for the Christian Doctrine of God: The Arian Controversy, 318–381* (Edinburgh: T&T Clark, 1989), 791– 823. – L. Perrone, in *Storia dei concili ecumenici* (ed. G. Alberigo; Brescia: Queriniana, 1990), 57–70.

# A. Symbolum

Along with the Apostles' Creed, the Nicene-Constantinopolitan Creed has united all of the Christian churches to the present day, as if the Council of Constantinople in 381 had adopted and supplemented the *symbolum* of the Council of Nicea of 325. In all likelihood, this was not the case, even if the issue of the sources continues to be difficult. The council documents are not preserved. In its official form, the *symbolum* was transmitted for the first time in the documents of the Council of Chalcedon (451). Epiphanius of Constantia (Salamis) seems to have already been conversant with it before this in his *Ancoratus* (374). A few years ago, however, the research of Bernd Manuel Weischer demonstrated that this represents a later interpolation of the text, and so the commonly accepted view today is that although the Council of Constantinople did not decide on an official *symbolum,* it did discuss and formulate the text available to us through the Council of Chalcedon.[14]

A comparison between the formulations of the Nicene and the Constantinopolitan *symbola* indicates few differences in the first two articles of faith concerning the Father and the Son; the differences consist mostly of transpositions, the tightening up of explanations that are no longer necessary, and supplemental definitions for the purpose of precision. At three points, the confession of Christ is clearly expanded: concerning the role of the Holy Spirit and Mary in the incarnation, the reality and historicity of the suffering and death of Christ, and his eschatological function as ruler and judge. The entire pneumatological section was completely reformulated. It treats the Holy Spirit as equal with the κύριος title of the Father and the Son; the ἐκπόρευσις assimilates the theology of Gregory of Nazianzus, and the ὁμοτιμία assimilates that of Basil the Great. The ecclesiological and eschatological articles are also new additions, whereas the anathemas against misinterpreting the relationship between Son and Father are omitted.

| *Nicene Creed* | *Niceno-Constantinopolitan Creed* |
|---|---|
| Πιστεύομεν εἰς ἕνα θεὸν | Πιστεύομεν εἰς ἕνα θεὸν |
| πατέρα παντοκράτορα | πατέρα παντοκράτορα |
| | ποιητὴν οὐρανοῦ καὶ γῆς |
| πάντων ὁρατῶν τε καὶ ἀοράτων ποιητήν. | ὁρατῶν τε πάντων καὶ ἀοράτων. |
| Καὶ εἰς ἕνα κύριον Ἰησοῦν Χριστόν | Καὶ εἰς ἕνα κύριον Ἰησοῦν Χριστόν |
| τὸν υἱὸν τοῦ θεοῦ | τὸν υἱὸν τοῦ θεοῦ μονογενῆ |

---

14 For a different assessment, see Kannengiesser, *EECh* 1:195f., and DH 150, which apparently are not familiar with Weischer's conclusions. Cf. also the most recent discussion, likewise with a different assessment, between L. Abramowski and A. M. Ritter.

γεννηθέντα ἐκ τοῦ πατρὸς μονογενῆ
τουτέστιν ἐκ τῆς οὐσίας τοῦ πατρός,

θεὸν ἐκ θεοῦ
φῶς ἐκ φωτός
θεὸν ἀληθινὸν ἐκ θεοῦ ἀληθινοῦ,
γεννηθέντα οὐ ποιηθέντα,
ὁμοούσιον τῷ πατρί,
δι' οὗ τὰ πάντα ἐγένετο
τά τε ἐν τῷ οὐρανῷ καὶ τὰ ἐν τῇ γῇ
τὸν δι ἡμᾶς τοὺς ἀνθρώπους
καὶ διὰ τὴν ἡμετέραν σωτηρίαν
κατελθόντα καὶ σαρκωθέντα,


ἐνανθρωπήσαντα


παθόντα

καὶ ἀναστάντα τῇ τρίτῃ ἡμέρᾳ

ἀνελθόντα εἰς τοὺς οὐρανούς,

ἐρχόμενον
κρῖναι ζῶντας καὶ νεκρούς.

Καὶ εἰς τὸ ἅγιον πνεῦμα.

τὸν ἐκ τοῦ πατρὸς γεννηθέντα

πρὸ πάντων τῶν αἰώνων

φῶς ἐκ φωτός
θεὸν ἀληθινὸν ἐκ θεοῦ ἀληθινοῦ,
γεννηθέντα οὐ ποιηθέντα,
ὁμοούσιον τῷ πατρί,
δι' οὗ τὰ πάντα ἐγένετο·

τὸν δι ἡμᾶς τοὺς ἀνθρώπους
καὶ διὰ τὴν ἡμετέραν σωτερίαν
κατελθόντα ἐκ τῶν οὐρανῶν
καὶ σαρκωθέντα ἐκ πνεύματος ἁγίου
καὶ Μαρίας τῆς παρθένου
καὶ ἐνανθρωπήσαντα
σταυρωθέντα τε ὑπὲρ ἡμῶν ἐπι
Ποντίου Πιλάτου
καὶ παθόντα
καὶ ταφέντα
καὶ ἀναστάντα τῇ τρίτῃ ἡμέρᾳ
κατὰ τὰς γραφὰς
καὶ ἀνελθόντα εἰς τοὺς οὐρανούς,
καὶ καθεζόμενον ἐν δεξιᾷ τοῦ πατρός,
και πάλιν ἐρχόμενον μετὰ δόξης
κρῖναι ζῶντας καὶ νεκρούς·
οὐ τῆς βασιλείας οὐκ ἔσται τέλος.
Καὶ εἰς τὸ πνεῦμα τὸ ἅγιον,
τὸ κύριον καὶ ζωοποιόν,
τὸ ἐκ τοῦ πατρὸς ἐκπορευόμενον,
τὸ σὺν πατρὶ καὶ υἱῷ
συμπροσκυνούμενον
καὶ συνδοξαζόμενον,
τὸ λαλῆσαν διὰ τῶν προφητῶν.
Εἰς μίαν ἁγίαν καθολικὴν καὶ
ἀποστολικὴν ἐκκλησίαν.
Ὁμολογοῦμεν ἓν βάπτισμα εἰς ἄφεσιν
ἁμαρτιῶν.
Προσδοκῶμεν ἀνάστασιν νεκρῶν
καὶ ζωὴν τοῦ μέλλοντος αἰῶνος.

Τοὺς δὲ λέγοντας· ἦν ποτε ὅτε οὐκ ἦν
καὶ πρὶν γεννηθῆναι οὐκ ἦν
καὶ ὅτι ἐξ οὐκ ὄντων ἐγένετο
ἢ ἐξ ἑτέρας ὑποστάσεως
ἢ οὐσίας φάσκοντας εἶναι

[ἢ κτιστὸν]
ἢ τρεπτὸν
ἢ ἀλλοιωτὸν τὸν υἱὸν τοῦ θεοῦ,
τοὺς ἀναθεματίζει ἡ καθολικὴ
καὶ ἀποστολικὴ ἐκκλησία.

*Editions:* ACO 2/1 [324]; 2/3 [395]. – G. L. Dossetti, *Il simbolo di Nicea e di Costantinopoli: Edizione critica* (TRSR 2; Rome: Herder, 1967) [Com]. – N. F. Tanner and G. Alberigo, *Decrees of the Ecumenical Councils* (2 vols.; London: Sheed & Ward; Washington, D.C.: Georgetown University Press, 1990), 1:24 [ET].

*Translations:* H. R. Percival, trans., "The Holy Creed Which the 150 Holy Fathers Set Forth, Which Is Consonant with the Holy and Great Synod of Nice," in *NPNF²* (Peabody, Mass.: Hendrickson, 1995; repr. of 1899 ed.), 14:163–65. – J. Stevenson, *Creeds, Councils, and Controversies* (rev. W. H. C. Frend; London: SPCK, 1989), 114–15.

*Encyclopedia Articles:* W.-D. Hauschild, *TRE* 24:444–56.

*Studies:* J. N. D. Kelly, *Early Christian Creeds* (3d ed.; London: Longman, 1972), 296–367. – B. M. Weischer, "Die ursprüngliche nikänische Form des ersten Glaubenssymbols im Ankyrotos des Epiphanios von Salamis: Ein Beitrag zur Diskussion um die Entstehung des konstantinopolitanischen Glaubenssymbols im Lichte neuester äthiopistischer Forschungen," *TP* 53 (1978): 407–14. – A. de Halleux, "La profession de l'Esprit-Saint dans le symbole de Constantinople," *RTL* 10 (1979): 5–39. – B. Schultze, "Die Pneumatologie des Symbols von Konstantinopel als abschliessende Formulierung der griechischen Theologie (381–1981)," *OCP* 47 (1981): 5–54. – T. F. Torrance, *The Incarnation: Ecumenical Studies in the Nicene-Constantinopolitan Creed, A.D. 381* (Edinburgh: Handsel, 1981). – *GOTR* 27 (1982): 359–453. – W.-D. Hauschild, "Das trinitarische Dogma von 381 als Ergebnis verbindlicher Konsensusbildung," in *Glaubensbekenntnis und Kirchengemeinschaft: Das Modell von Konstantinopel (381)* (ed. K. Lehmann and W. Pannenberg; Fribourg, Switz.: Herder; Göttingen: Vandenhoeck & Ruprecht, 1982), 13–48. – A. Kolb, "Das *Symbolum nicaeno-constantinopolitanum*: Zwei neue Zeugnisse," *ZPE* 79 (1989): 253–60. – R. Staats, "Die römische Tradition im Symbol von 381 (NC) und seine Entstehung auf der Synode von Antiochen 379," *VC* 44 (1990): 209–21. – W. Schneemelcher, "Die Entstehung des Glaubensbekenntnisses von Konstantinopel (381)," in idem, *Reden und Aufsätze: Beiträge zur Kirchengeschichte und zum ökumenischen Gespräch* (Tübingen: Mohr, 1991), 150–67. – L. Abramowski, "Was hat das Nicaeno-Constantinopolitanum (C) mit dem Konzil von Konstantinopel zu tun?" *TP* 67 (1992): 481–513. – A. M. Ritter, "Noch einmal: 'Was hat das Nicaeno-Constantinopolitanum (C) mit dem Konzil von Konstantinopel zu tun?'" *TP* 68 (1993): 553–60. – R. Staats, *Das Glaubensbekenntnis von Nizäa-Konstantinopel: Historische und theologische Grundlagen* (Darmstadt: Wissenschaftliche Buchgesellschaft, 1996). – V. Drecoll, "Wie nizänisch ist das Nicaeno-Constantinopolitanum? Zur Diskussion der Herkunft von NC durch Staats, Abramowski, Hauschild, und Ritter," *ZKG* 107 (1996): 1–18.

## B. Tomus *and* Canones

Although the council did not adopt the *symbolum* bearing its name, it nevertheless declared its faith in the official documents, condemned the current

heresies, and settled the disciplinary issues facing it in the forms of an explanation (*tomus*) and four canons (*canones*). The *tomus* has been lost, but its content
can be reconstructed on the basis of canon 1 and the synodal letter of the synod
of Constantinople (382). In the latter, the council fathers affirmed the undiminished validity of the faith of Nicea and the unity of the οὐσία of the Father, the
Son, and the Holy Spirit by rejecting the Sabellian identification of only one
hypostasis, and condemned by name "the Eunomians or anomoeans, the Arians
or Eudoxians, the Semi-Arians or Pneumatomachians, the Sabellians, the followers of Marcellus and Photinus, and the Apollinarians."

Even if unintentionally, the remaining three canons have brought about
far-reaching consequences in the history of the church. Canon 3 bestowed the
second place of honorary primacy, after the bishop of Rome, on the bishopric of
Constantinople as the "new Rome" and thereby relegated the two older patriarchates of Alexandria and Antioch to third and fourth place respectively. Canons 2
and 4 opposed administrative interference by bishops in other ecclesiastical provinces; these were precipitated by the unauthorized consecration of the Cynic
Maximus as bishop of Constantinople by Egyptian bishops (380), which canon 4
declared invalid. Canon 2, as a consequence, determined in general that the
bishop of Alexandria has jurisdiction exclusively over Egypt and that the Eastern
bishops are responsible for the dioceses of the East exclusively (in terms of the
governmental arrangement after the Diocletian reform of the empire). In the
long term, the consequence of these decisions was that, on the one hand, Alexandria sought to assert itself over against Constantinople while Constantinople
watched over the conduct of ecclesiastical affairs in Alexandria like a hawk
in order to, if possible, intervene correctively (John Chrysostom, Nestorius, Eutyches). On the other hand, the restriction of the bishops' jurisdiction according
to areas defined by the government and the more pronounced integration of ecclesiastical structures into those of the state brought about a growing (mid-fifth
century on) rejection of the jurisdictional primacy of the bishop of Rome over
the Eastern dioceses. This became a distant root of the split in the church centuries later.

*Editions:* Theodoret, *Kirchengeschichte* (GCS 44 [19]; Berlin: Akademie, 1954), 5.9.289–94
    [*Tomus*]. – *ACO* 2/1 [324]; 2/3 [395]. – DH 151 [*canon 1*]. – P.-P. Joannou, ed., *Les
    canons des conciles œcuméniques (IIe–IXe s.)* (vol. 1/1 of *Discipline générale antique:
    [IVe–IXe s.]*; FCCO 9; Grottaferrata [Rome]: Tipografia Italo-Orientale "S. Nilo,"
    1962), 42–54. – N. F. Tanner and G. Alberigo, *Decrees of the Ecumenical Councils*
    (2 vols.; London: Sheed & Ward; Washington, D.C.: Georgetown University Press,
    1990), 1:25–30 [*Tomus*], 31–35 [*Canons*] [ET].

*Translations:* H. R. Percival, trans., "Canons of the 150 Fathers Who Assembled at Con-
    stantinople," and "Council of Constantinople, A.D. 382: The Synodical Letter," in
    *NPNF*[2] (Peabody, Mass.: Hendrickson, 1995; repr. of 1899 ed.), 14:171–90 [*Canons,
    Synodical Letter*]. – J. Stevenson, *Creeds, Councils, and Controversies* (rev. W. H. C.
    Frend; rev. ed.; London: SPCK, 1989), 115–18 [*Canons*].

*Studies:* P. L'Huillier, *The Church of the Ancient Councils: The Disciplinary Work of the First
    Four Ecumenical Councils* (Crestwood, N.Y.: St. Vladimir's Seminary Press, 1996),
    101–42.

# CHAPTER SEVEN

# Pastors, Exegetes, and Ascetics

## I. CYRIL OF JERUSALEM

In 381 Cyril, bishop of Jerusalem, participated in the Council of Constantinople, not among those, granted, who substantially determined the theological development but rather among those who, as local bishops affected by the struggles, were forced to decide for one of the theological and ecclesiastical-political directions. Cyril belonged initially to the Homoiousian orientation and later to the Homoousian. Acacius, a Eusebian, who was the responsible metropolitan of Caesarea, consecrated him bishop of Jerusalem in 348, and at the Council of Seleucia (359), Cyril supported the Homoiousian majority. At the Council of Constantinople, however, he retracted his earlier position, which by then had become more closely Macedonian (cf. part 3.III.C); as a result, the council clearly confirmed the legitimacy of his consecration as bishop. This "change of orientation" does not necessarily have to be based on a change in his theology, however, for Hilary of Poitiers, the synod of Paris (360/361), and others also considered both the Homoiousian and the Homoousian views completely compatible theologically.

A few years after his consecration as bishop (on his life before that, we only know that he had been a priest in Jerusalem), Cyril fell out with Acacius, not over doctrinal but instead over disciplinary issues, because he attempted to remove his bishopric of Jerusalem from its dependence upon Caesarea. Acacius thereupon accused him of illegally disposing of church property (similarly to what Gregory of Nyssa experienced at a later time) and called him to account in Caesarea. Since Cyril ignored the summons for more than two years, Acacius relieved him of his duties in 358. The Council of Seleucia (359), for its part, deposed Acacius because he proposed a new Homoean formula, that the Son "according to the Scripture is similar" to the Father (cf. part 3.III.D). Because Cyril supported the Homoiousian majority, he was able to return to Jerusalem. Unfortunately, however, Emperor Constantius associated himself with Acacius's theology, forced the double synod of Ariminum and Seleucia to accept the Homoean formula at Nicea, and then had it ratified by a synod in Constantinople (360). As a result, Cyril had to be exiled again, albeit for a brief period only, because in 361 Emperor Julian, out of disinterest in ecclesiastical disputes, allowed all of the bishops to return to their dioceses. Julian's reign, too, lasted only a few years; his successor, Valens

(364–378), continued the Homoean politics of Constantius, and so the latter's verdicts of banishment came into effect once again. Thus Cyril had to leave Jerusalem for the third time, in this case for fifteen years. After the death of Valens and the final victory of the Nicene party, to which Cyril now gave his allegiance, he was able to reside in Jerusalem without interference until his death on March 18, 387; apart from his participation at the Council of Constantinople in 381, there are no other details available about his later years.

*Editions: Opera omnia:* PG 33:331–1178. – *Cyrilli Hierosolymarum archiepiscopi opera quae supersunt omnia* (ed. W. C. Reischl and J. Rupp; 2 vols.; Munich: Sumptibus Librariae Lentnerianae [G. Keck], 1848–1860; repr., Hildesheim: Olms, 1967).

*Translations: The Works of Saint Cyril of Jerusalem* (trans. A. A. Stephenson; FC 64; Washington, D.C.: Catholic University of America Press, 1970), 141–240 [*Mystagogical Catecheses, Sermon on the Paralytic, Letter to Constantius, Fragments*].

*Encyclopedia Articles:* E. J. Yarnold, *TRE* 8:261–66. – M. Simonetti, *EECh* 1:215. – F. W. Norris, *EEC* 1:312–13.

*Introduction and Surveys:* E. Yarnold, *Cyril of Jerusalem* (Early Church Fathers; London and New York: Routledge, 2000).

*Studies:* J. Mader, *Der heilige Cyrillus, Bischof von Jerusalem, in seinem Leben und seinen Schriften* (Einstedeln, Switz.: Benziger, 1891). – J. Lebon, "La position de saint Cyrille de Jérusalem dans les luttes provoquées par l'arianisme," *RHE* 20 (1924): 181–210, 357–86. – I. Berten, "Cyrille de Jérusalem, Eusèbe d'Emèse, et la théologie semi-arienne," *RSPT* 52 (1968): 38–75. – A. Bonato, *La dottrina trinitaria di Cirillo di Gerusalemme* (SEAug 18; Rome: Institutum Patristicum Augustinianum, 1983). – R. C. Gregg, "Cyril of Jerusalem and the Arians," in idem, *Arianism: Historical and Theological Reassessments* (PatMS 11; Cambridge, Mass.; Philadelphia Patristics Foundation, 1985), 85–109. – J. F. Baldovin, *Liturgy in Ancient Jerusalem* (Alcuin/GROW Liturgical Study 9; Bramcote, Nottingham: Grove, 1989). – P. W. L. Walker, *Holy City, Holy Places? Christian Attitudes to Jerusalem and the Holy Land in the Fourth Century* (Oxford: Clarendon; New York: Oxford University Press, 1990).

# Catecheses

As already indicated, Cyril's significance for patrology does not rest on dogmatic writings but on the *Catecheses* that he gave during the period of Lent and Easter for baptismal candidates or the newly baptized and that were taken down. They became famous not only because they show great theological, spiritual, and stylistic quality but also because they offer extraordinary insight into the liturgical praxis and doctrinal instruction of the time. Twenty-four catecheses have been handed down altogether: a procatechesis at the beginning of the period of immediate preparation for baptism as a baptismal candidate (φωτιζόμενος), eighteen catecheses to the baptismal candidates in the course of Lent, and five "mystagogical" catecheses to the newly baptized (νεόφυτοι) during the week of Easter. In some manuscripts the latter are handed down separate from the other catecheses, and in others they are not attributed to Cyril but to John (until 417), his successor to the see of Jerusalem. It is not altogether clear whether the five mystagogical catecheses belong to John, whether he used Cyril's material, or whether they are Cyril's own work but, in contrast to the first nineteen catecheses, do not come from the beginning but from the end of his tenure as bishop. Since Cyril was considered their undoubted author until the sixteenth century, his authorship may be assumed until compelling evidence to the contrary is adduced.

The procatechesis reflects the typical situation of the growing church at large as the fourth century advanced, when many flocked to the church, no longer directly because of the religious zeal of the earliest centuries but for ulterior, political, societal, or professional reasons. Therefore the procatechesis admonishes the catechumen entering into the actual preparation for baptism to have proper motivation and internal and external disposition. The one who comes to baptism like Simon Magus or like the guest without wedding garments (Matt 22:11–14) will not receive it effectively (2–4). Likewise all the external reasons for receiving baptism, such as to please a woman or a man, a master or a friend, can at best serve as initial incentives (5); the only important thing is the inner preparation to receive the great grace of baptism (6–8). As preparation, this entails, among other things, zealous participation in the exorcisms and catecheses that are intended only for baptismal candidates and those baptized (*disciplina arcani*) (9–15). The procatechesis concludes with the theological explanation of baptism as waters of purification and with the exhortation to build up the temple of Christ (16–17).

The following eighteen catecheses, given during Lent though their precise timing cannot be determined, address the articles of the (Jerusalem) confession of faith, each following the reading of a text. They provide important insight not only into instruction in the faith but also into the *Credo* that was taught and became famous in Jerusalem at this time. Catecheses 1–3 are introductory, addressing the essential questions concerning sin, repentance, forgiveness of sins, and baptism as a participation in the death and resurrection of Christ. Catecheses 4 and 5 initially establish the principles of the Christian view of God and of man, as well as the meaning of faith, in order to follow this with each of the articles of the *symbolum:* the one God (6), the Father, the omnipotent Creator (7–9), the Son, from the incarnation to his return (10–15), the Holy Spirit (16–17), and the church (18). The final three catecheses show that the Jerusalem *Credo* already has moved beyond the Nicene creed, en route to what the Council of Constantinople (381) ultimately established.

The five mystagogical catecheses followed baptism on Easter eve, addressing the newly baptized during the week of Easter. They deal with topics still subject to the *disciplina arcani* as far as the baptismal candidate was concerned, namely, an explanation of the rites of baptism and confirmation (1–3) and of the Eucharist in the celebration of the Mass (4–5).

*Editions:* F. L. Cross, *St. Cyril of Jerusalem's Lectures on the Christian Sacraments* (London: SPCK, 1951; repr., Crestwood, N.Y.: St. Vladimir's Seminary Press, 1986). [*Procatechesis, Mystagogical Catecheses*] [ET]. – *Catéchèses mystagogiques* (ed. A. Piédagnel and P. Paris; 2d ed.; SC 126; Paris: Cerf, 1988) [*Mystagogical Catecheses*]. – *Mystago-*

*gicae catecheses* (ed. G. Röwekamp; FChr 7; Fribourg, Switz., and New York: Herder, 1992) [*Mystagogical Catecheses*].

*Translations:* E. H. Gifford, trans., "The Catechetical Lectures of S. Cyril, Archbishop of Jerusalem," in *NPNF²* (Peabody, Mass.: Hendrickson, 1995; repr. of 1894 ed.), 7:1–157 [*Procatechesis, Catechetical Lectures*]. – *The Works of Saint Cyril of Jerusalem* (trans. L. P. McCauley and A. Stephenson; 2 vols.; FC 61, 64; Washington, D.C.: Catholic University of America Press, 1969–1970) [*Procatechesis, Catecheses, Mystagogical Catecheses*]. – E. Yarnold, *The Awe-Inspiring Rites of Initiation: The Origins of the RCIA* (2d ed.; Edinburgh: T&T Clark, 1994), 70–97 [*Mystagogical Catecheses*].

*Reference Works: Biblia patristica: Index des citations et allusions bibliques dans la littérature patristique*, vol. 4, *Eusèbe de Césarée, Cyrille de Jérusalem, Epiphane de Salamine* (Paris: Éditions du Centre National de la Recherche Scientifique, 1987). – R. L. Mullen, *The New Testament Text of Cyril of Jerusalem* (Atlanta: Scholars Press, 1997).

*Studies:* A. Paulin, *Saint Cyrille de Jérusalem catéchète* (LO 29; Paris: Cerf, 1959). – A. A. Stephenson, "The Lenten Catechetical Syllabus in Fourth-Century Jerusalem," *TS* 15 (1964): 103–16. – H. M. Riley, *Christian Initiation: A Comparative Study of the Interpretation of the Baptismal Liturgy in the Mystagogical Writings of Cyril of Jerusalem, John Chrysostom, Theodore of Mopsuestia, and Ambrose of Milan* (SCA 17; Washington, D.C.: Catholic University of America Press, 1974). – E. J. Cutrone, "Cyril's Mystagogical Catecheses and the Evolution of the Jerusalem Anaphora," *OCP* 44 (1978): 52–64. – G. Hellemo, *Adventus Domini: Eschatological Thought in 4th-Century Apses and Catecheses* (SVigChr 5; Leiden and New York: Brill, 1989). – L. Zappella, "'Elaion-Myron': L'olio simbolo dello Spirito Santo nelle catechesi battesimali di Cirillo di Gerusalemme," *CrSt* 11 (1990): 5–27. – P. Jackson, "Cyril of Jerusalem's Use of Scripture in Catechesis," *TS* 52 (1991): 431–50. – A. Doval, "The Location and Structure of the Baptistery in the *Mystagogic Catecheses* of Cyril of Jerusalem," in *Papers Presented at the Eleventh International Conference on Patristic Studies Held in Oxford, 1991* (ed. E. Livingstone; StPatr 25; Louvain: Peeters, 1993), 1–13. – C. Renoux, "The Reading of the Bible in the Ancient Liturgy of Jerusalem," in *The Bible in Greek Christian Antiquity* (ed. P. Blowers; Notre Dame, Ind.: University of Notre Dame Press, 1997), 389–414.

# *Excursus: Christian Initiation*

Besides the numerous particulars given in the writings of the church fathers and the catecheses of Cyril of Jerusalem, the following works offer detailed information on the ancient church's baptismal practice and theology:

- the New Testament;

- the *Traditio Apostolica* (ch. 3.IV.B.2.B);

- Tertullian, *De baptismo;*

- Ambrose, *Explanatio symboli ad initiandos, De sacramentis, De mysteriis* (ch. 8.IV);

- Augustine, *De catechizandis rudibus;*

- Gregory of Nyssa, *De iis qui baptismum differunt;*

- the *Itinerarium Egeriae* (ch. 8.IV);

- Theodore of Mopsuestia, *Catechetical Homilies* (ch. 7.V.C);

- John Chrysostom, baptismal catecheses (ch. 7.VI.C);

- the Easter sermons, especially those of Asterius the Sophist (d. after 341) and Augustine (ch. 9).

From this ensues the following picture of initiation in three phases, given regional and historical differences in matters of detail:

a. During NT times, baptism could be given immediately, after brief instructions and the confession of faith in Christ (Acts 2:14–42, following Peter's Pentecost sermon; 8:26–39, the baptism of the Ethiopian). Subsequently this practice was not taken up again until the beginning of the medieval period in the missionary work in central and northern Europe and was continued in the modern era.

b. This missionary practice was soon replaced by a more extended time of preparation (catechumenate), not primarily for the purpose of theoretical instruction but especially for the purpose of a change in life, so as to be able to live as a Christian after baptism. Baptism was deemed the only forgiveness of sins, after which the Christian was to live a "perfect" life. In many cases, this meant that the catechumen also had to give up his or profession because he or she was not allowed to continue practicing it if it was associated with the cult of pagan deities, for instance. Everyday sins were forgiven through prayer and good works; initially there was no second repentance for the three cardinal sins (apostasy, fornication, and murder) but only renewed exclusion from the community (excommunication).

In the pre-Constantinian era, the period of the catechumenate generally lasted two to three years but could be shortened in the case of persecution or mortal danger or on the basis of a special testing of the candidate. Overall the catechumens tended to want to receive baptism as soon as possible. They received instruction partly in private, at times from independent Christian teachers, such as Clement of Alexandria, and partly in episcopal catechetical schools, such as the one directed by Origen in Alexandria (cf. ch. 3.V). There was no fixed time for receiving baptism; it always took place at the conclusion of the time of preparation, even if Easter eve already stood out as a particularly suitable time. Shortly before the date of the baptism, the catechumens were accepted into the circle of baptismal candidates (φωτιζόμενοι, *electi, competentes*) and their names entered in an official list. After they presumably had already undergone a certain initiation rite at the beginning of the catechumenate and the catechumens had regularly attended the community's worship service, they now came to the following rites in the immediate preparation for baptism: exorcisms (renunciation of Satan and evil) by breathing and laying hands on them, scrutinies (examination of their Christian lifestyle), and the passing on (*traditio*) and memorization (*redditio*) of the creed and the Lord's Prayer.

Everything else, however, was subject to the *disciplina arcani*, especially the celebration of the Eucharist, in which only those baptized were allowed to share.

The *disciplina arcani* is certainly not to be construed as secrecy in the sense of the mystery religions or the gnostic sects, for Christian teaching and praxis were by all means well-known publicly. Rather, it represented stages of initiation, which reserved the most sacred aspect to the full member for the sake of reverence. This necessarily called for the continuation of instruction after baptism, immediately after which the newly baptized partook of the Eucharist, albeit without having been instructed about it. The catecheses followed the pagan mysteries' initiation insofar as they adopted their terminology and provided it with a Christian reinterpretation in terms of the "mystery of faith."

The era following the "Constantinian shift" basically differed in that a multitude of people, for a variety of reasons, now thronged the church—which had been tolerated initially, then was promoted by the state, and finally became the state church—without the zeal that had characterized the faith in the centuries when a new persecution could break out at any time. This initially led to the practice of delaying baptism. Parents enrolled their children for the catechumenate, but then they waited for them to make their own decision as adults (the three great Cappadocians and Augustine serve as well-known examples). Or adults entered the catechumenate in order to belong to the church at the first level but had themselves baptized only in later years, when in mortal danger or when they had to take up ecclesiastical office (e.g., Ambrose and Nectarius of Constantinople).

The catechumenate thus increasingly lost significance, and the period of immediate preparation for baptism, which was now organized more strictly, as well as its catecheses, became the most important part. The date for baptism was commonly established to be on Easter eve; the preparation of the baptismal candidates, during Lent; and the further catechesis, during the time of Easter. Apart from the special consideration for the changed motivation of the candidates, the rites and content remained basically unchanged.

*Bibliographies:* G. Venturi, "Problemi dell'iniziazione cristiana: Nota bibliografica," *EL* 88 (1974): 241–70. – G. Kretschmar, "Nouvelles recherches sur l'initiation chrétienne," *MD* 132 (1977): 7–32.

*Editions: Monumenta eucharistica et liturgica vetustissima* (ed. J. Quasten; 7 vols.; FlorPatr 7; Bonn: P. Hanstein, 1935–1937). – J. C. Didier, *Le baptême des enfants: Dans la tradition de l'Église* (MCS 7; Tournai and New York: Desclée, 1959). – H. Kraft and H. Hammerich, *Text zur Geschichte der Taufe, besonders der Kindertaufe in der alten Kirche* (2d ed.; KlT 174; Berlin: de Gruyter, 1969).

*Translations:* E. C. Whitaker, *Documents of the Baptismal Liturgy* (ed. M. E. Johnson; 3d rev. ed.; Lodon: SPCK, 2003) [Anthology]. – T. M. Finn, *Early Christian Baptism and the Catechumenate* (2 vols.; MFC 5, 6; Collegeville, Minn.: Liturgical, 1992) [Anthology]. – E. Yarnold, *The Awe-Inspiring Rites of Initiation: The Origins of the RCIA* (2d ed.; Edinburgh: T&T Clark, 1994). [Catecheses of Cyril of Jersualem, Ambrose, John Chrysostom, Theodore of Mopsuestia].

*Encyclopedia Articles:* A. Oepke, βάπτω. βαπτίζω: *TDNT* 1:529–46. – K. Thraede, "Exorzismus," *RAC* 7:44–117. – W. Nagel, "Exorzismus II: Literaturgeschichtlich," *TRE* 10:750–52. – C. Vogel, "Handauflegung I (liturgisch)," *RAC* 13:482–93. – G. Kretschmar, "Katechumenat/Katechumenen I. Alte Kirche," *TRE* 18:1–5. – A. Hamman, "Baptism: Baptism in the Fathers," *EECh* 1:107–8. – F. Cocchini, "Catechesis," *EECh*

1:150–51. – A. Hamman, "Catechumen, Catechumenate," *EECh* 1:151–52. – E. Ferguson, "Baptism," *EEC* 1:160–64. – E. Ferguson, "Catechesis, Catechumenate," *EEC* 1:223–25.

*Manuals:* G. Kretschmar, "Die Geschichte des Taufgottesdienstes in der alten Kirche," *Leit.* 5: 1–348. – B. Neunheuser, *Taufe und Firmung* (2d ed.; *HDG* 4.2; Fribourg, Switz.: Herder, 1983), 9–96. – B. Kleinheyer, *Sakramentliche Feiern I: Die Feiern der Eingliederung in die Kirche* (GDK 7.1; Regensburg: F. Pustet, 1989), 12–95.

*Collections of Essays:* H. Auf der Maur and B. Kleinheyer, eds., *Zeichen des Glaubens—Studien zu Taufe und Firmung: Balthasar Fischer zum 60. Geburtstag* (Zurich, Einsiedeln, and Cologne: Herder, 1972). – S. Felici, ed., *Catechesi battesimale e riconciliazione nei Padri del IV secolo* (Rome: LAS, 1984). – P. F. Bradshaw, ed., *Essays in Early Eastern Initiation* (Alcuin/GROW Liturgical Study 8; Bramcote, Nottinghamshire: Grove, 1988). – A. M. Triacca and A. Pistoia, eds., *Mystagogie: Pensée liturgique d'aujourd'hui et liturgie ancienne* (BEL.S 70; Rome: C.L.V.–Edizioni Liturgiche, 1993). – E. Ferguson, ed., *Conversion, Catechumenate, and Baptism in the Early Church* (SEC 11; New York: Garland, 1993). – M. E. Johnson, ed., *Living Water, Sealing Spirit: Readings on Christian Initiation* (Collegeville, Minn.: Liturgical, 1995).

*Adult Baptism and Infant Baptism:* J. Jeremias, *Infant Baptism in the First Four Centuries* (trans. D. Cairns; London: SCM, 1960; Philadelphia: Westminster, 1962); trans. of *Die Kindertaufe in den ersten vier Jahrhunderten* (Göttingen: Vandenhoeck & Ruprecht, 1958). – K. Aland, *Did the Early Church Baptize Infants?* (trans. G. R. Beasley-Murray; London: SCM, 1963); trans. of *Die Säuglingstaufe im Neuen Testament und in der alten Kirche* (TEH 86; Munich: C. Kaiser, 1961). – A. Strobel, "Säuglings- und Kindertaufe in der ältesten Kirche: Eine kritische Untersuchung der Standpunkte von J. Jeremias und K. Aland," in *Begründung und Gebrauch der heiligen Taufe: Aus der Arbeit einer Studientagung* (ed. O. Perels; Berlin: Lutherisches Verlagshaus, 1963), 7–69. – J. Jeremias, *The Origins of Infant Baptism: A Further Study in Reply to Kurt Aland* (trans. D. M. Barton; Naperville, Ill.: Alec R. Allenson, 1963); trans. of *Nochmals—die Anfänge der Kindertaufe* (Munich: C. Kaiser, 1962). – K. Aland, *Die Stellung der Kinder in den frühen christlichen Gemeinden und ihre Taufe* (TEH 138; Munich: C. Kaiser, 1967). – P. A. Gramaglia, *Il battesimo dei bambini nei primi quattro secoli* (Brescia: Morcelliana, 1973). – E. Nagel, *Kindertaufe und Taufaufschub: Die Praxis vom 3.–5. Jahrhundert in Nordafrika und ihre theologische Einordnung bei Tertullian, Cyprian, und Augustinus* (EHS.T 144; Frankfurt and Cirencester, Eng.: Lang, 1980). – H. Hammerich, *Taufe und Askese: Der Taufaufschub in vorkonstantinischer Zeit* (Hamburg: n.p., 1994).

*Liturgy and the Catechumenate:* A. Stenzel, *Die Taufe: Eine genetische Erklärung der Taufliturgie* (FGTh 7.8; Innsbruck: F. Rauch, 1958). – M. Dujarier, *Le parrainage des adultes aux trois premiers siècles de l'Église: Recherche historique sur l'évolution des garanties et des étapes catéchuménales avant 313* (Paris: Cerf, 1962). – H. Auf der Maur, *Die Osterhomilien des Asterios Sophistes als Quelle für die Geschichte der Osterfeier* (TThSt 19; Trier: Paulinus, 1967). – J. Daniélou, *La catéchèse aux premiers siècles* (ed. R. du Charlat; Paris: Fayard-Mame, 1968).– A. Kavanagh, *The Shape of Baptism: The Rite of Christian Initiation* (New York: Pueblo, 1978; repr., Collegeville, Minn.: Liturgical, 1991). – J. Ries et al., eds., *Les rites d'initiation* (Louvain: Centre d'Histoire des Religions, 1986). – V. Saxer, *Les rites de l'initiation chrétienne du IIe au VIe siècle: Esquisse historique et signification d'après leurs principaux témoins* (Spoleto: Centro Italiano di Studi sull'Alto Medioevo, 1988; repr., 1992). – A. Kavanagh, *Confirmation: Origins and Reform* (New York: Pueblo, 1988). – C. Granado, "La confirmación en el siglo IV: Ambrosio de Milán, Catequesis Jerosolimitanas, Juan Crisóstomo," *EstTrin* 27 (1993): 21–79. – W. Harmless, *Augustine and the Catechumenate* (Collegeville,

Minn.: Liturgical, 1995). – G. Cavalotto, *Catecumenato antico: Diventare cristiani secondo i Padri* (Bologna: n.p., 1996). – M. E. Johnson, *The Rites of Christian Initiation: Their Evolution and Interpretation* (Collegeville, Minn.: Liturgical, 1999).

*Symbolism:* P. Lundberg, *La typologie baptismale dans l'ancienne église* (ASNU 10; Leipzig: A. Lorentz, 1942). – J. Daniélou, *Sacramentum futuri: Études sur les origines de la typologie biblique* (ETH; Paris: Beauchesne, 1950). – J. Ysebaert, *Greek Baptismal Terminology: Its Origins and Early Development* (GCP 1; Nijmegen: Dekker & van de Vegt, 1962). – J. Daniélou, *The Bible and the Liturgy* (Notre Dame, Ind.: University of Notre Dame Press, 1956); trans. of *Bible et liturgie: La théologie biblique des sacraments et des fêtes d'après les Pères de l'Église* (LO 11; Paris: Cerf, 1951).

*Theology and Spirituality:* A. Benoit, *Le baptême chrétien au second siècle: La théologie des Pères* (EHPhR 43; Presses Universitaires de France, 1953). – P. T. Camelot, *Spiritualité du baptême* (2d ed.; LO 30; Paris: Cerf, 1960). – G. W. H. Lampe, *The Seal of the Spirit: A Study in the Doctrine of Baptism and Confirmation in the New Testament and the Fathers* (2d ed.; London: SPCK, 1967). – T. M. Finn, "Baptismal Death and Resurrection: A Study in Fourth-Century Eastern Baptismal Theology," *Worship* 43: (1969) 175–89. – E. Mazza, *Mystagogy: A Theology of Liturgy in the Patristic Age* (trans. M. J. O'Connell; New York: Pueblo, 1989); trans. of *Mistagogia: Una teologia della liturgia in epoca patristica* (BEL.S 46; Rome: C.L.V.–Edizioni Liturgiche, 1988). – K. McDonnell and G. T. Montague, *Christian Initiation and Baptism in the Holy Spirit: Evidence from the First Eight Centuries* (2d rev. ed.; Collegeville, Minn.: Liturgical, 1994). – J. Chalassery, *The Holy Spirit and Christian Initiation in the East Syrian Tradition* (Rome: Mar Thoma Yogam, 1995). – K. McDonnell, *The Baptism of Jesus in the Jordan: The Trinitarian and Cosmic Order of Salvation* (Collegeville, Minn.: Liturgical, 1996). – T. M. Finn, *From Death to Rebirth: Ritual and Conversion in Antiquity* (New York and Mahwah, N.J.: Paulist, 1997).

# II. EPIPHANIUS OF CONSTANTIA (SALAMIS)

In the case of the important church fathers of the fourth century, it may appear as if it was usual that they enjoyed an excellent secular education in their youth, often began with a secular career, and delayed baptism until they entered the ministry of the church. Even if they occasionally warned (theoretically) against the spiritual dangers of a secular education, their philosophical, rhetorical, and literary skills nevertheless inevitably shaped their thought and their writings and enabled them to address the problems of their time in a concrete way. But alongside these there was a second group of bishops in the fourth century who had received an exclusively Christian, biblical education and who not only were hardly conversant with the secular sciences but also did not attach any importance to them. Often they were baptized as children or when they were still young, and were raised in a monastic environment. They are less prominent in patrology because literarily they were not as productive and did not exert as much influence upon theological development as the others. Their number and ecclesiastical importance are not to be underestimated, however, since these bishops numbered in the hundreds, even at the councils.

Part of this latter group was Epiphanius, bishop of Constantia (ancient Salamis, modern Famagusta), on the eastern coast of Cyprus. He was born in or near Eleutheropolis in southern Palestine between 310 and 320[1] and in his early years obtained his education in the Egyptian monasteries, which were to shape the essential features of his entire life. Three elements determined monastic life there: 1) asceticism; 2) the adherence of one group of monasteries to Origen's theology whereas the other rejected it; 3) the rejection of secular sciences as pagan or heretical, replaced by a strictly Bible-based upbringing, and the accompanying conviction that doctrinal truth could not be thought through and substantiated in critical and polemic dispute, but was established in the Bible and in the resolutions of the councils and merely had to be preserved faithfully. Since Egyptian monasticism had aligned itself with Athanasius, the Nicene ὁμοούσιος was considered to be final and unquestioned dogma. One can understand why, in the modern view—but not that of antiquity—this "traditionalistic" orientation and hence Epiphanius's were deemed "retrogressive," "not thought through," and "superficial,"[2] but it is important to guard against projecting such modern, "enlightened" views uncritically on the circumstances of the ancient church. The philosophizing and the purely biblicist orientations have never bedeviled but instead respected and accepted one another. On the one hand, the biblical message on both sides always remained the undeniable premise of all theology; on the other hand, the major problems of the fourth century did indeed result from attempts to penetrate further the question of God logically and philosophically. As a result, the Fathers who decisively determined the theology of the fourth century responded on this level and found a solution that the biblicist orientation at once accepted unquestionably as the church's resolution and defended unreservedly.

After his return to Palestine, roughly at the age of twenty, Epiphanius founded a monastery, in the village of Besanduk, near Eleutheropolis, likely on a parental estate, that he directed for many years. He was also ordained a priest of Besanduk. As a strict adherent of Nicea, he apparently fell out with Eutychius, the Homoean bishop of Eleutheropolis, who at the Council of Seleucia (359) was one of the main supporters of Acacius of Caesarea, and went to Cyprus. In any case, it may be assumed that Epiphanius already lived there for some time before his appointment as bishop of Constantia in 366. For ecclesiastical-political reasons, the island of Cyprus was altogether Nicene. There were attempts to obtain for the Cypriot church an autocephalous status detached from the Antiochene metropolitan, with Constantia as the metropolitan see; Epiphanius successfully accomplished this. Since the patriarchs of Antioch were Eusebians, Cyprus always sided with the Nicenes.

Epiphanius led his diocese for thirty-five years, and during this time, along with his pastoral duties, he took a clear stand on the conflicts of his time. On the

---

[1] The dates of Epiphanius's life cannot be established with absolute certainty. For his date of birth, one also finds the reference to "around 315"; for his consecration, 365 and 367 (376 in B. Altaner and A. Stuiber, *Patrologie: Leben, Schriften, und Lehre der Kirchenväter* (8th ed.; Fribourg, Switz.: Herder, 1978), 315, may be a printing error); for his journey to Jerusalem, 392; and for his death, 403.

[2] Ibid., 315f.

issue of the date of Easter, he supported the Alexandrian date of the Sunday following the first full moon of spring, which the Council of Nicea (325) accepted as the only valid date, although he also tolerated the "Judaizing" practice of the Sunday following the Jewish Passover. On the Antiochene schism, he sided with Paulinus, the Nicene, and his followers, and on the issue of the veneration of images, he wrote against it in tracts that were discussed frequently during the dispute over images (iconoclasm) in the eighth and ninth centuries and therefore were partially preserved.

Epiphanius became most prominent, however, in the first phase of the quarrel over Origen. Presumably because he was raised in an anti-Origenist monastery in Egypt, he had included Origen in his "medicine chest" (*Panarion*) against heresies. While visiting Jerusalem in 393 on the occasion of a church dedication, he entered into a dispute with John, the local pro-Origenist bishop, because he vehemently attacked Origen in his feast day sermon. This was also the cause of the frictions between Rufinus (pro) and Jerome (contra), although initially they were able to settle them. In 400 the disputes flared up again when, as a countermove, Theophilus, the Alexandrian bishop, accused Isidore, his priest, of what to him was heretical Origenism, together with four monks from the Nitrian desert whom Isidore befriended, who on account of their extraordinary height were called "tall brothers" and who criticized Theophilus's leadership and lifestyle. They thereupon turned to John Chrysostom, the bishop of Constantinople, for support, who acted neutral at least, if not seemingly pro-Origenist. In order to forestall his decision, Theophilus summoned a synod to meet in Alexandria and called on the bishops of Palestine and Cyprus to conduct provincial synods. Epiphanius was glad to oblige and in the spring of 402 personally took to Constantinople their decision, which was made in accordance with his understanding of the issue. Upon arrival, he publicly snubbed John by refusing to accept his hospitality and celebrate the Eucharist with him, and instead ordained a deacon without the approval of the latter, conferred with his opponents, and publicly preached against him. When John called on him to leave his area of jurisdiction, Epiphanius boarded a ship because the mood of the people was beginning to turn against him, and he died on his return voyage in early May 402, perhaps on May 12, the day the Eastern and Western churches commemorate him.

# A. Ancoratus

Epiphanius's literary-historical importance is based mainly on his heresiological works, which reflect the conviction of his entire life. Some priests and a layman from Syedra in Pamphylia had requested Epiphanius to instruct them on the orthodox Trinitarian doctrine, especially pneumatology (the correspondence is extant as prelude to his work). In 374 he responded by sending them the tractate *Ancoratus* ("the firmly anchored one") in 120 sections. Here he not only explains the Trinity against the Arians and Pneumatomachians on the basis of baptismal faith and the witness of Scripture (2–75); he also takes the opportunity to provide further instruction, namely, a list of eighty heresies (12–13) forming the basis of the subsequent, detailed treatment in the *Panarion*. He also addresses Christology, disassociating himself from Apollinaris (whose name is not mentioned) (76–82); the resurrection of the dead with body and soul, against pagans and heretics in general, especially against the Manichaeans (83–100); and the Christian God and God's salvation history with humanity, against pagan polytheism (101–118). The work concludes with two *symbola*, the first of which (119) is textually identical to the *Nicaeno-Constantinopolitanum*. It was therefore assumed for a long time that this was the draft of the *symbolum* of Constantinople of 381. In the meantime, however, the majority of scholarship has come to be persuaded that the Nicene creed originally was at this location and later it was exchanged by a copyist. The second *symbolum* (120), as Epiphanius himself states, originates from the baptismal liturgy, probably of the church at Constantia.

# *B.* Panarion

*Panarion*, the "medicine chest" (also cited as *Adversus haereses*) for the healing of those who have been wounded by the snakebite of heresies, written following the *Ancoratus* in 374–377, uses as its model the *Refutatio omnium haeresium* of Hippolytus, supplementing the thirty-two heresies found there with another forty-eight. In addition, Epiphanius made use of Irenaeus's *Adversus haereses*, as well as books of the various sects to the extent that these were available to him. Since he includes citations from the latter, the *Panarion* preserves titles and valuable fragments of otherwise lost heretical writings and other documents. The work is arranged in three *tomoi*: *tomos* 1 in three books with forty-six heresies of "Barbarism, Scythism, Hellenism, Judaism, and Samaritanism"; *tomos* 2 in two books with twenty heresies, among them the gnostic sects, Sabellians, Origenists, and Arians; and *tomos* 3 in two books with eleven heresies, among them the Pneumatomachians and Apollinarians. Each book is prefaced with an *anakephalaiōsis*—a summary with excerpts—not from Epiphanius, which must have originated before 428 because Augustine makes use of it in his *De haeresibus*.

*Editions: Opera omnia:* PG 41–43. – *Opera* (ed. W. Dindorf; 5 vols.; Leipzig: Weigel, 1859–1862). – *Epiphanius* (ed. K. Holl and P. Wendland; 4 vols.; GCS 25, 31, 37, NF 13; vol. 1–3, Leipzig: Hinrichs; vol. 4, Berlin and New York: de Gruyter, 1915–2006). [*Ancoratus, Panarion*]

*Translations: The Panarion of Epiphanius of Salamis* (trans. F. Williams; NHS 35–36; 2 vols.; Leiden and New York: Brill, 1987–1994) [*Panarion, De fide*]. – *The Panarion of St. Epiphanius, Bishop of Salamis* (trans. P. R. Amidon; New York: Oxford University Press, 1990) [*Selected Passages*].

*Reference Works: Biblia patristica: Index des citations et allusions bibliques dans la littérature patristique* (Paris: Centre National de la Recherche Scientifique, 1987), vol. 4.

*Encyclopedia Articles:* W. Schneemelcher, *RAC* 5:909–27. – P. Nautin, *DHGE* 15:617–31. – C. Riggi, *EECh* 1:281–82. – F.W. Norris, *EEC* 1:380–81.

*Studies:* K. Holl, *Der Osten* (vol. 2 of *Gesammelte Aufsätze zur Kirchengeschichte;* Tübingen: Mohr, 1928), 204–24, 310–87. – L. A. Eldridge, *The Gospel Text of Epiphanius of Salamis* (SD 41; Salt Lake City: University of Utah Press, 1969). – B. M. Weischer, "Die Glaubenssymbole des Epiphanios von Salamis und des Gregorios Thaumaturgos im Qērellos," *OrChr* 61 (1977): 20–40. – G. Vallée, *A Study in Anti-gnostic Polemics: Irenaeus, Hippolytus, and Epiphanius* (Waterloo, Ont.: Published for the Canadian Corporation for Studies in Religion by Wilfrid Laurier University Press, 1981). – J. F. Dechow, *Dogma and Mysticism in Early Christianity: Epiphanius of Cyprus and the Legacy of Origen* (PatMS 13; [Belgium]: Peeters; Macon, Ga.: Mercer University Press, 1988). – E. A. Clark, *The Origenist Controversy: The Cultural Construction of an Early Christian Debate* (Princeton, N.J.: Princeton University Press, 1992). – A. Pourkier, *L'hérésiologie chez Épiphane de Salamine* (CAnt 4; Paris: Beauchesne, 1992). – A. Camplani, "Epifanio (*Ancoratus*) e Gregorio di Nazianzo (*Epistulae*) in copto: Identificazioni e *status quaestionis,*" *Aug* 35 (1995): 327–47.

# III. AMBROSE

On the whole, Aurelius Ambrosius may well be remembered best today as the bishop who converted and baptized Augustine. Even if his significant achievements for theology and church were always outshone by those of Augustine in the history of the West's reception, they nevertheless have had an appropriate impact and obtained an appropriate recognition. Together with Augustine, Jerome, and Pope Gregory the Great, Ambrose is regarded as one of the "four great doctors of the Western church." The humanists appreciated his work to such an extent that, along with that of Cicero, Lactantius (the "Christian Cicero"), Augustine, and Jerome, it was among the first to be published after the discovery of the printing press; indeed it appeared in several editions in quick succession. The medieval councils cited him consistently as one of the reliable witnesses of ecclesiastical orthodoxy, as did Thomas Aquinas and Luther. Furthermore, in the East, Ambrose's impact was unlike that of many Latin fathers because he himself emphatically took up Eastern theology; it was not long until his writings were translated into Greek and included in the *florilegia*.

On the basis of his origin, education, and professional development, the life of Ambrose may be considered typical of many bishops of the fourth century, similar to the "three great Cappadocians." He came from a family of the nobility of the city of Rome (of the Aurelians, as his name might suggest?) that had been Christian for generations and took pride in the fact that among its members were numerous distinguished state officials, as well as Soteris the martyr. His father exercised the office of *praefectus praetorio Galliarum* in the provincial capital of Trier and hence was the highest imperial officer—equipped with full legal authority—in Gaul, where Ambrose likely was born in 339,[3] but in keeping with

---

[3] In agreement with E. Dassmann (*TRE* 2:362f), including the date of his consecration, though there are various alternatives available.

contemporary custom, Ambrose had his baptism delayed and remained a cate-chumen until he was an adult. After the early death of his father, his mother and her three children returned to Rome, where, after his initial instruction in Trier, Ambrose received the high-quality philosophical, rhetorical, and literary educa-tion that was customary for the noble and educated circles of his time. This train-ing prepared him for the (juridical) service of the state and is broadly reflected in his writings; it included acquirement of the Greek language, which Ambrose mastered fluently, whereas a few years later Augustine was to learn it reluctantly and with difficulty (*Conf.* 1.14.23). Indeed it can be seen from the church fathers Ambrose, Augustine, and Leo the Great how the knowledge of Greek, which until then had been the κοινὴ διάλεκτος, was lost within a century in the Western part of the Roman Empire: Ambrose was bilingual, Augustine probably knew the ba-sics of Greek, and Leo had not mastered the language at all, so that he needed a translator in the proceedings at the Council of Chalcedon (451).

In keeping with his education and the tradition of the family, Ambrose en-tered the service of the state, where he made a quick career for himself, given his evident abilities, first as *advocatus* at the court of the prefecture of Sirmium, then as adviser to Probus, the local prefect, and already in 370, as a barely thirty-year-old, as consular governor of the province of Aemilia-Liguria, with Milan as the jurisdictional seat. In this capacity, he was also responsible for maintaining public order, which seemed to be seriously threatened during the election of Auxentius, the successor of the (Arian) bishop of the city, because the Arian and Nicene fac-tions of the community could not agree peaceably on a common candidate. As Paulinus, his secretary and biographer, reports (*Vit. Amb.* 6), Ambrose personally hurried into the cathedral to settle the quarrel. Suddenly a child shouted, "Ambrose bishop!" and as a result, "in miraculous and unbelievable unity," all spontaneously agreed that he should be the new bishop of the city. Ambrose was reluctant to accept the vote, however, and attempted to escape; only when the confirmation of Emperor Valentinian I arrived did he accept his fate.

The account of Ambrose's miraculous election and reluctance bears the marks of a topos and in a similar way also occurs in the *vitae* of Augustine, Mar-tin of Tours, and other bishops of the ancient church. All the same, in its basic features, the account probably reflects historical reality. When the governor, who was respected by all and was known as capable and probably also as conciliatory, appeared, the feuding parties may have seen in him the right compromise candi-date. From his family's and his own conviction, he was Nicene, but as a catechu-men, he was not committed to either side—rightly so, as it turned out—and anticipated an integrative episcopate. Conversely, Ambrose had good reasons for being hesitant in accepting the election, for he had not aspired to this office; he was versed in statesmanship but had no pastoral or theological experience what-soever. He was not even baptized, which caused not only the feeling of his own unworthiness but also canonical concerns to surface; it had to be demonstrated first whether the spontaneous acclamation of the people did in fact express their enduring will for the future. Furthermore, the emperor's ecclesiastical-political position would have to be ascertained. Only when all of these concerns were removed did Ambrose receive baptism from a Nicene bishop, by his express desire, and on December 7, 373 (traditionally 374), consecration as bishop. The information by Paulinus (*Vit. Amb.* 9) that after his baptism he received all of the ecclesiastical consecrations in quick succession, within a few days, contradicts the consecrational theology and practice of the ancient church and therefore may not be accurate, all the more so since Paulinus himself rates this as only hearsay (*fertur omnia ecclesiastica officia implesse*).

Ambrose, who in his own words "began to teach you what I myself had not yet learnt" (*Off.* 1.1.4), received his theological training from Simplicianus, a priest in Milan, who after Ambrose's death (397) was to become his successor. He had already become prominent in 355 because he converted Marius Victorinus, the renowned rhetor and philosopher, to Christianity, according to Augustine's own account, as reported to him by Ambrose (*Conf.* 8), and thereby contributed to Augustine's conversion as well. Ambrose fulfilled the pastoral expectations of his community and soon brought about reconciliation among clergy and people, although he himself faithfully adhered to the Nicene position as far as ecclesiastical politics was concerned. When we hear of disputes later on, they do not concern quarrels within the community but between the bishop and the imperial court, in which clergy and people gave their solid support to Ambrose.

The tension erupted in two famous episodes: the dispute concerning the altar of Victoria and Ambrose's firm refusal to relinquish a church in Milan to the Arians. After the death of Emperor Valentinian I (375), who had pursued a neutral religious policy in the West, Ambrose succeeded in influencing Emperor Gratian in the Nicene direction. He even wrote a personal treatise for him against Arianism, *De fide ad Gratianum,* and the first Western tractate on the Holy Spirit, in which he closely followed Didymus of Alexandria, Basil, and Athanasius. Constantine had already ordered the altar of the goddess Victoria, a cultic sign of the basis of Roman world domination, removed from the senatorial curia in Rome, but Julian the Apostate had it erected again. In 382 Gratian had it removed once again, but since he died in 383 in the war against Maximus, the usurper, the Roman senate sent a delegation to the imperial court in Milan, led by its *pontifex maior,* Quintus Aurelius Symmachus, with a letter of petition to have the altar reinstalled. By very logical arguments following the lines of the traditional conviction of Rome's welfare based upon of divine protection, they demanded an ideologically unfettered tolerance of all cults by the state. Ambrose could not acquiesce to this, however, and presented his arguments in a hurriedly written retort: precisely for the sake of its own salvation, the state cannot allow truth and error to exist alongside one another, and the emperor cannot be Christian as a private individual but indifferent in his official capacity. Although Ambrose rejected the use of force as a means of successfully attaining truth and in 385 protested sharply against the execution of Priscillianus the heretic in Trier, a modern "separation of church and state" remained inconceivable for him. The state, and thus the emperor as a person, could recognize only the one true religion and had to promote it, namely, the Nicene creed.

The second dispute occurred a few years later but more publicly and spec-tacularly. Although the synods of Aquileia and Constantinople (381) in principle resolved the Arian issue in the East and the West, its practical effects continued well into the fifth century. Justina, the influential mother of Valentinian II, the young Western emperor, and a number of (Gothic) courtiers remained Arians and before Easter 385 demanded that the small Basilica Portiana be handed over to them for their services. Ambrose refused categorically, and since the negotia-tions ended up in popular unrest in front of the imperial palace, they were broken off without result. A law was thereupon enacted on January 23, 386, probably specifically to break Ambrose's resistance against the authority of the state, to grant the Arians tolerance and the right to hold services, from which the imperial court inferred its further demand for the handing over of one of the churches in Milan. Now, indeed, it was no longer the small Basilica Portiana outside the walls but the larger Basilica Nova within the city. Ambrose again uncompromisingly refused, and so compulsory measures were introduced—the account of this comes from Ambrose himself in *Ep.* 20 to Marcellina, his sister. On Palm Sunday the Basilica Portiana was confiscated, but the community meeting there did not clear the church. Consequently, soldiers surrounded the basilica, in which Ambrose was conducting a worship service, but neither he nor his community re-treated from the church, day or night. Since the imperial court was not interested in an armed conflict with the people and the community's unshakeable enthusi-asm instead spread quickly to the soldiers, the siege was called off on Maundy Thursday or Good Friday.

Both of these scenes demonstrate, first, how successful Ambrose had been at the time of his election in bringing about unity in the strife-torn community that followed him enthusiastically and, second, how even under pressure he did not yield an inch from his conviction in matters of faith and ecclesiastical rights. Beyond this, however, they initiated a development, opposite to the Eastern em-pire, concerning the relationship between church and state. Whereas there the ec-clesiastical structures adapted rather more closely to those of the state and no one disputed the emperor's right to intervene in ecclesiastical affairs, here a division of competences occurred. Although the welfare of the state and the emperor's own profession to protect and promote the one true religion put him under obli-gation, matters of faith and intra-church affairs were exclusively matters of the decision-making powers of the ecclesiastical authorities.

At first glance, a third famous incident, which occurred a few years later, seems to reflect this new situation, namely, the penance of Theodosius. In 390 the military commander of Illyricum was killed by an agitated crowd in the circus of Thessalonica. In his initial anger, Theodosius then ordered the punishment of the guilty, which led to a bloodbath among the people in that circus, whereby the sol-diers took vengeance on behalf of their commander. Theodosius's revocation of the order of punishment came too late. In the view of Ambrose, the emperor thereby became guilty of the mortal sin of murder, and so he appealed to him, in a handwritten letter, to submit to the prescribed penance. Theodosius accepted, attended church for a while as a penitent, and after his public confession of his culpability before the church, he was reconciled (likely at Christmas 390). Neither Ambrose nor the emperor viewed this as a political issue but rather as an intra-church act of discipline that did not cloud their relationship and therefore is to be seen not as a first sign of the church assuming a superordinate position over the state but as a pastoral act.

In spite of all the prominent ecclesiastical-political activity, which was made evident especially in the events described, everyday life for Ambrose during the twenty-four years of his episcopate was filled with pastoral activity, as his writings attest. He not only celebrated holy Mass (he is the first to use this designation in *Ep.* 20.4) on a daily basis but beyond this, at regular intervals throughout the day, led services of the Word, with singing and readings, similar to today's prayers of the hours, as well as nightly times of prayer. On all Sundays and holy days, as well as during the preparation for baptismal candidates, he preached daily with such simple persuasiveness that even the extremely critical Augustine was attracted (*Conf.* 6.3.4). In addition, there was the care of the increasing number of baptismal candidates, who did not always flock to the church because of a pure conviction of faith; the concern about penance, reconciliation, and Christian marriage ceremonies; and the ever-growing charitable organization of the community: care for the poor, the sick, and the imprisoned, as well as the exercise of the public administration of justice, concern for the legal protection of the helpless, and action for a possible pardon in the case of those condemned to death. Given this extreme workload, one may wonder when Ambrose found time to write his works, even if all of them are the fruit of his pastoral work. Augustine reports with disappointment, "Yet I was unable to ask of him what I wanted and in the way I wanted, for crowds of busy men, to whose troubles he was a slave, shut me away from both his ear and his mouth. When he was not with them, and this was but a little while, he either refreshed his body with needed food or his mind with reading . . . for no one was forbidden entry, and it was not his custom to have whoever came announced to him" (*Conf.* 6.3.3). According to Augustine's testimony, Ambrose is the first person of antiquity known to us who departed from the practice of reading aloud, a method otherwise exclusively used, and instead allowed his eyes to move across the pages.

A fifth-century mosaic in the Capella San Vittore in Ciel d'Oro of the Ambrosian basilica in Milan shows his portrait, which may be close to reality: a gaunt, serious ascetic with short hair and full beard, clothed in a long tunic and a simple coat. Like Basil the Great, he gave his estate to the poor and, except for Sundays and holy days, ate only one meal per day "so that he might be able to follow the Lord Christ like a poor soldier with a light pack" (*Vit. Amb.* 38). He died on Easter Saturday (April 4), 397, and was buried the following day in the tomb of the martyrs Gervasius and Protasius, whose forgotten bones he had rediscovered on June 17, 386, amid miraculous attendant circumstances, and transferred to the episcopal basilica on June 19. Today he rests between the two saints, decked in his bishop's garments, enshrined in glass in the basilica's crypt.

*Bibliographies:* P. F. Beatrice et al., eds., *Cento anni di bibliografia ambrosiana (1874–1974)* (SPMed 11; Milan: Vita e Pensiero, 1981).

*Editions:*
*Opera omnia:* PL 14–17. – PLS 1:569–620. – *Opera omnia: Tutte le opere di Sant'Ambrogio* (Milan: Biblioteca Ambrosiana; Rome: Città Nuova, 1977–) [Com]. *De fide: De fide (ad Gratianum Augustum)* (ed. O. Faller; CSEL 78; Vienna: Hölder-Pichler-Tempsky, 1962). *De officiis: Les devoirs* (ed. M. Testard; 2 vols.; Paris: Belles Lettres, 1984–1992) [Com]. *De paenitenta: La pénitence* (ed. R. Gryson; SC 179; Paris: Cerf, 1971). *De Spiritu Sancto, De incarnatione: De Spiritu Sancto libri tres; De incarnationis dominicae sacramento* (ed. O. Faller; CSEL 79; Vienna: Hölder-Pichler-Tempsky, 1964). *Epistulae: Epistulae et acta* (ed. O. Faller and M. Zelzer; 4 vols.; CSEL 82.1–4; Vienna: Hölder-Pichler-Tempsky, 1968–1996). – R. Klein, *Der Streit um den Victoriaaltar: Die dritte Relatio des Symmachus und die Briefe 17, 18, und 57 des Mailänder Bischofs Ambrosius* (TzF 7; Darmstadt: Wissenschaftlische Buchgesellschaft, 1972) [Com]. *Explanatio psalmorum XII: Explanatio psalmorum XII* (ed. M. Petschenig and M. Zelzer; rev. ed.; CSEL 64; Vienna: Verlag der Österreichischen Akademie der Wissenschaften, 1999). *Explanatio symboli, De sacramentis, De mysteriis, De paenitentia, De excessu fratris, De obitu Valentiniani, De obitu Theodosii: Explanatio symboli, De sacramentis, De mysteriis, De paenitentia, De excessu fratris, De obitu Valentiniani, De obitu Theodosii* (ed. O. Faller; CSEL 73; Vienna: Hölder-Pichler-Tempsky, 1955). – R. H. Connolly, *The Explanatio symboli ad initiandos: A Work of St. Ambrose* (Cambridge: Cambridge University Press, 1952) [ET]. *Expositio psalmi CXVIII: Expositio psalmi CXVIII* (ed. M. Petschenig and M. Zelzer; rev. ed.; CSEL 62; Vienna: Verlag der Österreichischen Akademie der Wissenschaften, 1999). *Vita Ambrosii: Vita di Cipriano; Vita di Ambrogio; Vita di Agostino* (ed. C. Mohrmann, A. A. R. Bastiaensen, and L. Canali; 2d ed.; Fondazione Lorenzo Valla, 1981), XXVII–XLII, 51–125, 281–338 [Com]. – *Vita di Sant'Ambrogio: La prima biografia del patrono di Milano* (ed. M. Navoni; Cinisello Balsamo: San Paolo, 1996) [Com].

*Translations:* H. de Romestein, E. de Romestein, and H. T. F. Duckworth, trans., *Ambrose: Select Works and Letters* (vol. 10 of *NPNF²*; Peabody, Mass.: Hendrickson, 1995; repr. of 1896 ed.) [*On the Duties of the Clergy, On the Holy Spirit, On the Death of Satyrus, On the Belief in the Resurrection, On the Christian Faith, On the Mysteries, On Repentance, Concerning Virgins, Concerning Widows, Letters 20, 21, 27, 28, 40, 41, 51, 57, 61–63*]. – *Funeral Orations by Saint Gregory Nazianzen and Saint Ambrose* (trans. L. P. McCauley et al.; introd. M. R. P. McGuire; FC 22; Washington, D.C.: Catholic University of America Press, 1953), 157–332. – *Letters* (ed. M. M. Beyenka; FC 26; Washington, D.C.: Catholic University of America Press, 1954; repr., 1967). – *Theological and Dogmatic Works* (R. J. Deferrari; FC 44; Washington, D.C.: Catholic University of America Press, 1963) [*The Mysteries, The Holy Spirit, The Sacrament of the Incarnation of Our Lord, The Sacraments*]. – B. Ramsey, *Ambrose* (Early Church Fathers; London and New York: Routledge, 1997) [*On Virgins, On Naboth, On the Mysteries, Hymns, Letters Pertaining to the Altar of Victory, Life of Ambrose*].

*Reference Works:* O. Faller and L. Krestan, *Vorarbeiten zu einem Lexikon ambrosianum: Wortindex zu den Schriften des hl. Ambrosius* (Vienna: Verlag der Österreichischen Akademie der Wissenschaften, 1979). – *Thesaurus Sancti Ambrosii* (Corpus Christianorum: Thesaurus patrum latinorum; Turnhout, Belg.: Brepols, 1994).

*Encyclopedia Articles:* W. Wilbrand, *RAC* 1:365–73. – E. Dassmann, *TRE* 2:362–86. – C. Moreschini, "Ambrosius vom Mailand," *GK* 2:101–24. – M. G. Mara, *EECh* 1:28–29. – L. J. Swift, *EEC* 1:41–44.

*Introductions and Surveys:* F. H. Dudden, *The Life and Times of St. Ambrose* (2 vols.; Oxford: Clarendon, 1935). – A. Paredi, *Saint Ambrose: His Life and Times* (trans. J. Costelloe; Notre Dame, Ind.: University of Notre Dame Press, 1964); trans. of *S. Ambrogio e la sua età* (Milan: U. Hoepli, 1960). – N. B. McLynn, *Ambrose of Milan: Church and Court in a Christian Capital* (London and Berkeley: University of California Press, 1994). – C. Pasini, *Ambrogio di Milano: Azione e pensiero di un vescovo* (2d ed.; Milan: San Paolo, 1996). – H. Savon, *Ambroise de Milan* (Paris: Desclée, 1997). – B. Ramsey, *Ambrose* (Early Church Fathers; London and New York: Routledge, 1997). – J. Moorhead, *Ambrose: Church and Society in the Late Roman World* (London: New York: Longman, 1999).

*Collections of Essays:* V. Monachino, *S. Ambrogio e la cura pastorale a Milano nel secolo IV: Centenario di S. Ambrogio, 374–1974* (Milan: Centro Ambrosiano di Documentazione e Studi Religiosi, 1973). – Y.-M. Duval, ed., *Ambroise de Milan—XVIe centenaire de son élection épiscopale: Dix études* (Paris: Études Augustiniennes, 1974). – A. Paredi, *Politica di S. Ambrogio* (Milan: Strenna dell'Istituto Ortopedico, 1974). – *Ricerche storiche sulla chiesa ambrosiana nel XVI centenario dell'episcopato di Sant'Ambrogio IV (1973–1974)* (ArAmb 27; Milan: n.p., 1974). – G. Lazzati, ed., *Ambrosius episcopus* (SPMed 6, 7; Milan: Vita e Pensiero, 1976). – *Ambrogio vescovo di Milano (397–1997)* (Cassago Brianza: Associazione Storico-culturale S. Agostino, 1998). – L. F. Pizzolato and M. Rizzi, eds.; *Nec timeo mori: Atti del Congresso internazionale di studi ambrosiani nel XVI centenario della morte di Sant'Ambrogio. Milano, 4–11 Aprile 1997* (SPMed 21; Milan: Vita e Pensiero, 1998).

*Studies: Ambrosius: Bollettino liturgico ambrosiano* (Milan, 1925–) *[Ambrosius].* – Archivio ambrosiano (Milan: NED, 1950–) [ArAmb]. – E. Dassmann, *Die Frömmigkeit des Kirchenvaters Ambrosius von Mailand: Quellen und Entfaltung* (MBTh 29; Münster: Aschendorffsche Verlagsbuchhandlung, 1965). – R. Johanny, *L'eucharistie, centre de l'histoire du salut chez saint Ambroise de Milan* (ThH 9; Paris: Beauchesne, 1968). – P. Courcelle, *Recherches sur saint Ambroise: "Vies" anciennes, culture, iconographie* (Paris, Études Augustiniennes, 1973). – G. Toscani, *Teologia della Chiesa in Sant'Ambrogio* (SPMed 3; Milan: Vita e Pensiero, 1974). – T. G. Ring, *Auctoritas bei Tertullian, Cyprian, und Ambrosius* (Cass. 29; Würzburg: Augustinus, 1975). – É. Lamirande, *Paulin de Milan et la "Vita Ambrosii": Aspects de la religion sous le Bas-Empire* (Paris: Desclée; Montreal: Bellarmin, 1983). – U. Faust, *Christo servire libertas est: Zum Freiheitsbegriff des Ambrosius von Mailand* (SPS 3; Salzburg: A. Pustet, 1983). – A. Nawrocka, "L'état des études concernant l'influence de l'éthique de Cicéron sur l'éthique de saint Ambroise," *Helikon* 28 (1988): 315–24. – E. Cattaneo, *La religione a Milano nell'età di sant'Ambrogio* (ArAmb 25; Milan: Associazione Storico-culturale S. Agostino, 1974). – S. Mazzarino, *Storia sociale del vescovo Ambrogio* (PRSA 4; Rome: "L'Erma" di Bretschneider, 1989). – W. Berschin, "La *Vita S. Ambrosii* e la letteratura biografica tardoantica," *Aev* 67 (1993): 181–87. – M. Becker, *Die Kardinaltugenden bei Cicero und Ambrosius: De officiis* (Chresis 4; Basel: Schwabe, 1994). – M. Adriaans, *Omnibus rebus ordo: Vorstellungen über die Gesellschaftsstruktur im Werk des Bischofs Ambrosius von Mailand* (Egelsbach and Washington, D.C.: Hänsel-Hohenhausen, 1995). – M. Biermann, *Die Leichenreden des Ambrosius von Mailand: Rhetorik, Predigt, Politik* (Hermes.E 70; Stuttgart: Steiner, 1995). – I. J. Davidson, "Ambrose's *De officiis* and the Intellectual Climate of the Late Fourth Century," *VC* 49 (1995): 313–33. – C. Markschies, *Ambrosius von Mailand und die Trinitätstheologie: Kirchen- und theologiegeschichtliche Studien zu Antiarianismus und Neunizänismus bei Ambrosius und im lateinischen Westen (364–381 n. Chr.)* (BHTh 90; Tübingen: Mohr, 1995). – D. H. Williams, *Ambrose of Milan and the End of the Nicene-Arian Conflicts* (OECS; Oxford: Clarendon; New York: Oxford University Press, 1995). – M. Roques, "L'authenticité

de l'*Apologia David altera:* Historique et progrès d'une controverse," *Aug* 36 (1996):
53–92, 423–58.

*Ecclesiastical Politics:* H. von Campenhausen, *Ambrosius von Mailand als Kirchenpolitiker*
(AKG 12; Berlin: de Gruyter, 1929). – J.-R. Palanque, *Saint Ambroise et l'Empire
romain: Contribution à l'histoire des rapports de l'Église et de l'état à la fin du quatrième
siècle* (Pairs: de Boccard, 1933). – C. Morino, *Church and State in the Teaching of St.
Ambrose* (trans. J. Costelloe; Washington, D.C.: Catholic University of America Press,
1969); trans. of *Chiesa e stato nella dottrina di S. Ambrogio* (Rome: Idea, 1963). – F. Can-
fora, *Simmaco e Ambrogio o di un'antica controversia sulla tolleranza e sull'intolleranza*
(Bari: Adriatica, 1970). – G. Gottlieb, *Ambrosius von Mailand und Kaiser Gratian*
(Hyp. 40; Göttingen: Vandenhoeck & Ruprecht, 1973). – J. Wytzes, *Der letzte Kampf
des Heidentums in Rom* (EPRO 56; Leiden: Brill, 1977). – G. Gottlieb, "Der Mailänder
Kirchenstreit von 385/86: Datierung, Verlauf, Deutung," *MH* 42 (1985): 37–55. –
G. Nauroy, "L'année 386 à Milan: L'affaire des basiliques et l'échec de l'arianisme en
Occident," *MAM* 14 (1988). – G. Nauroy, "Le fouet et le miel: Le combat d'Ambroise
en 386 contre l'arianisme milanaise," *RechAug* 33 (1988): 3–86.

*Philosophy:* P. Courcelle, "Aspects variés du platonisme ambrosien," in *Recherches sur les
"Confessions" de saint Augustin* (ed. P. Courcelle; 2d ed.; Paris: de Boccard, 1968),
311–82. – G. Madec, *Saint Ambroise et la philosophie* (Paris: Études Augustiniennes,
1974). – P. Courcelle, "Die Entdeckung des christlichen Neuplatonismus," in *Zum
Augustin-Gespräch der Gegenwart* (ed. C. Andresen; 2 vols.; 2d ed.; WdF; Darmstadt:
Wissenschaftliche Buchgesellschaft, 1975–1981), 1:125–81.

# A. Exegetical Work

Ambrose's extensive exegetical work developed largely from sermons he
himself reworked, completed, and published. Of the twenty extant commentaries, only one, the largest of all, deals with a NT writing, namely, the *Expositio
Evangelii secundum Lucam;* all the others deal with the OT, which epitomizes his
interest and biblical understanding, which continued to develop over the years, to
be sure. Ambrose was so indebted, first of all, to Philo of Alexandria that he was
called Philo Christianus, and his works *De paradiso, De Cain et Abel, De Noe et
arca,* and *De Abraham* could be construed as Philonic excerpts to the extent that
reconstructions of lost or corrupt Philonic texts from the writings of Ambrose
have been attempted. His second major source was Origen and, in later years,
Basil the Great, especially in the exegesis of the six days of creation. Following his
Alexandrian examples, Ambrose made significant use of allegory and typology,
but as Viktor Hahn has demonstrated, he did not adopt these mechanically but as
the appropriate method for his understanding of the unity of the salvation history of the two Testaments. In his later works, Neoplatonic thought, moral-
paraenetic exegesis, and spiritual-pastoral explanation became more prominent.
Because of his extensive knowledge and adaptation of the Greek fathers, Ambrose
became the major mediator of Greek theology in the West after Hilary of Poitiers,
but this also limited his interpretation of Scripture. With regard to the NT, he
lacked major models, which may also be seen as the reason for his far and away

more modest consideration of the NT. In the exegesis of the NT, he also attended more to the literal meaning of the text.

*Editions: Sancti Ambrosii Opera* (ed. E. C. Schenkl; CSEL; Vienna: F. Tempsky, 1896–) [vol. 1: *Exameron, De paradiso, De Cain et Abel, De Noe, De Abraham, De Isaac vel anima, De bono mortis;* vol. 2: *De Jacob et vita beata, De Joseph, De patriarchis, De fuga saeculi, De interpellatione Job et David, De apologia prophetae David, Apologia David altera, De Helia et ieiunio, De Nabuthae, De Tobia*]. – *Apologia prophetae David: Apologie de David* (ed. P. Hadot and M. Cordier; SC 239; Paris: Cerf, 1977). – *De Nabuthae historia: La storia di Naboth* (ed. M. G. Mara; L'Aquila: Japadre, 1975) [Com]. – *Expositio psalmi CXVIII* (ed. M. Petschenig; rev. M. Zelzer; CSEL 62; Vienna: Verlag der Österreichischen Akademie der Wissenschaften, 1999). – *Explanatio psalmorum XII* (ed. M. Petschenig; rev. M. Zelzer; CSEL 64; Vienna: Verlag der Österreichischen Akademie der Wissenschaften, 1999). – *Expositio Evangelii secundum Lucam: Expositio evangelii secundum Lucan* (ed. C. Schenkl; CSEL 32.4; Vienna: Verlag der Österreichischen Akademie der Wissenschaften, 1902). – *Sancti Ambrosii Mediolanensis Opera* (ed. M. Adriaen; CCSL 14–; Turnhout, Belg.: Brepols, 1957–), vol. 4 [with the Fragments on Isaiah]. – *Traité sur l'Évangile de s. Luc* (ed. G. Tissot; 2 vols.; 2d ed.; SC 45 bis, 52 bis; Paris: Cerf, 1971–1976).

*Translations: Hexameron, Paradise, and Cain and Abel* (trans. J. J. Savage; FC 42; Washington, D.C.: Catholic University of America Press in association with Consortium Books, 1961; repr., 1977). – *Seven Exegetical Works* (trans. M. P. McHugh; FC 65; Washington, D.C.: Catholic University of America Press in association with Consortium Books, 1972), 5–65 [*Isaac, or the Soul; Death as a Good; Jacob and the Happy Life, Joseph, The Patriarchs, Flight from the World, The Prayer of Job and David*].

*Studies:* R. W. Muncey, *The New Testament Text of Saint Ambrose* (TS NS 4; Cambridge: Cambridge University Press, 1959). – J. Pépin, *Théologie cosmique et théologie chrétienne (Ambroise, Exam. I 1,1–4)* (Paris: Presses Universitaires de France, 1964). – V. Hahn, *Das wahre Gesetz: Eine Untersuchung der Auffassung des Ambrosius von Mailand vom Verhältnis der beiden Testamente* (MBTh 33; Münster; Aschendorff, 1969). – H. Auf der Maur, *Das Psalmenverständnis des Ambrosius von Mailand: Ein Beitrag zum Deutungshintergrund der Psalmenverwendung im Gottesdienst der Alten Kirche* (Leiden: Brill, 1977). – E. Lucchesi, *L'usage de Philon dans l'œuvre exégétique de saint Ambroise: Une "Quellenforschung" relative aux commentaires d'Ambroise sur la Genèse* (ALGHJ 9; Leiden: Brill, 1977). – H. Savon, *Saint Ambroise devant l'exégèse de Philon le Juif* (2 vols.; Paris: Études Augustiniennes, 1977). – L. F. Pizzolato, *La dottrina esegetica di Sant'Ambrogio* (SPMed 9; Milan: Vita e Pensiero, 1978). – C. Corsato, *La Expositio euangelii secundum Lucam di Sant'Ambrogio: Ermeneutica, simbologia, fonti* (SEAug 43; Rome: Institutum Patristicum Augustinianum, 1993). – T. Graumann, *Christus interpres: Die Einheit von Auslegung und Verkündigung in der Lukaserklärung des Ambrosius von Mailand* (PTS 41; Berlin and New York: de Gruyter, 1994).

# B. Catechetical Writings

Ambrose's instruction of the many baptismal candidates and neophytes, which, according to Paulinus, "later, after his death, five bishops carried out with difficulty" (*Vit. Amb.* 38), gave rise to three important writings, providing detailed insight into Ambrosian theology, namely, *Explanatio symboli ad initiandos, De sacramentis,* and *De mysteriis.* Whereas the authenticity of *De mysteriis* has never been questioned, that of the two other writings was debated for a long time but generally is accepted now. Doubts emerged from the character of the two works as shorthand notes of some teaching sessions, manifested in the less systematic order and in the repetitiveness. The *Explanatio symboli* was given before baptism, in a session dealing with the *traditio symboli*, and the other catecheses followed, without the possibility of precisely establishing the year; it is likely that they come from Ambrose's later years.

At the very beginning, the *Explanatio symboli* refers to its liturgical place after the scrutinies and after the exorcisms at the time of the *traditio symboli*, which took place in Milan on Palm Sunday in the baptistry of the basilica after dismissal of the catechumens from the community's celebration of Mass (1). It then explains primarily the concept of the *symbolum* and its Latin translation, *conlatio*, as a compilation of short faith formulas by the assembly of the apostles (2). After this they were led in praying the *symbolum*, but without writing it down because of the *disciplina arcani*. Nevertheless the following explanations make it possible to reconstruct the text, which was not the Nicene version but, as Ambrose confirms elsewhere (4; 7), the Roman. After a general introductory paragraph on the orthodox creed over against the heresies of the Sabellians and Arians (3–4), the text of the *symbolum* follows verse by verse (only the first and last words of each verse are noted in the written form), with brief explanations (5–8). It concludes with the reason it is not to be written down: so that the believers learn it by heart and, to that end, meditate on it daily, and so that catechumens or even heretics do not abuse it.

Both *De sacramentis* and *De mysteriis* address in detail the rites of the celebration of baptism and the Eucharist, explaining them item by item in practical terms, according to their meaning in salvation history and their spiritual (mystical) significance. In addition, the fifth and sixth catecheses of *De sacramentis* deal with the Lord's Prayer and the daily prayer. Whereas *De sacramentis* clearly represents instructional notes that have not been reworked, *De mysteriis* has either been revised or, as Bernard Botte and Josef Schmitz argue, was mainly prepared only in writing.

*Editions: Explanatio symboli; De sacramentis; De mysteriis; De paenitentia; De excessu fratris; De obitu Valentiniani; De obitu Theodosii* (ed. O. Faller; CSEL 73; Vienna: Hölder-Pichler-Tempsky, 1955), 1–116. – *Des sacrements; Des mystères; Explication du symbole* (ed. B. Botte; 2d ed.; SC 25 bis; Paris: Cerf, 1961; repr., 1994). – *Spiegazione del Credo; I sacramenti; I misteri; La penitenza* (ed. G. Banterle; Opera omnia 17; Milan: Biblioteca Ambrosiana, 1982), 25–169 [Com]. – *De sacramentis = Über die Sakramente; De mysteriis = Über die Mysterien* (ed. J. Schmitz; FChr 3; Fribourg, Switz., and New York: Herder, 1990) [Com].

*Translations: Saint Ambrose: Theological and Dogmatic Works* (trans. R. J. Deferrari; FC 44; Washington, D.C.: Catholic University of America Press, 1963; repr., 1977) [*The Mysteries, The Sacraments*]. – E. Yarnold, *The Awe-Inspiring Rites of Initiation: The Origins of the RCIA* (2d ed.; Collegeville, Minn.: Liturgical, 1994), 98–149 [*Sermons on the Sacraments*] – B. Ramsey, *Ambrose* (Early Church Fathers; London and New York: Routledge, 1997), 145–60 [*The Mysteries*].

*Studies:* C. Mohrmann, "Le style oral du *De sacramentis* de saint Ambroise," *VC* 6 (1952): 168–77. – L. L. Mitchell, "Ambrosian Baptismal Rites," *StLi* (1962): 241–53; repr. in idem, *Worship: Initiation and the Churches* (Washington, D.C.: Pastoral, 1991), 75–89. – E. J. Yarnold, "The Ceremonies of Initiation in the *De sacramentis* and *De mysteriis* of St. Ambrose," in *Papers Presented to the Fifth International Conference on Patristic Studies Held in Oxford, 1967* (ed. F. Cross; StPatr 10; TU 107; Berlin: Akademie, 1970), 453–63. – E. J. Yarnold, "Did St. Ambrose Know the Mystagogic Catecheses of St. Cyril of Jerusalem?" in *Papers Presented to the Sixth International Conference on Patristic Studies Held in Oxford, 1971* (ed. E. Livingstone; StPatr 12; TU 115; Berlin: Akademie, 1975), 184–89. – C. Calcaterra, *La catechesi pasquale di Ambrogio di Milano: Motivazioni di pastorale liturgica* (ArAmb 24; Milan: n.p., 1973). – H. M. Riley, *Christian Initiation: A Comparative Study of the Interpretation of the Baptismal Liturgy in the Mystagogical Writings of Cyril of Jerusalem, John Chrysostom, Theodore of Mopsuestia, and Ambrose of Milan* (SCA 17; Washington, D.C.: Catholic University of America Press, 1974). – J. Schmitz, *Gottesdienst im altchristlichen Mailand: Eine liturgiewissenschaftliche Untersuchung über Initiation und Messfeier während des Jahres zur Zeit des Bischofs Ambrosius († 397)* (Theoph. 25; Cologne: P. Hanstein, 1975). – C. Jacob, *"Arkandisziplin," Allegorese, Mystagogie: Ein neuer Zugang zur Theologie des Ambrosius von Mailand* (Theoph. 32; Frankfurt: Hain, 1990). – A. Bonato, "Origini della liturgia ambrosiana e riti battesimali nella catechesi mistagogica di Ambrogio," *Aug* 37 (1997): 77–112. – C. Alzati, *Ambrosianum mysterium: The Church of Milan and Its Liturgical Tradition* (trans. G. Guiver; 2 vols.; Joint Liturgical Studies 44; Cambridge: Grove, 1999).

# C. Hymns

Hilary of Poitiers had composed the first Latin hymns for the church but was not successful in introducing them as congregational songs. Only Ambrose popularized them, making them an established part of the liturgy. Since precisely these two built a bridge between the Eastern and Western churches in the fourth century, both of them may also have followed Eastern examples, besides the tradition of Latin poetry. In his *Confessiones* (9.7.15) Augustine recounts that during the siege of the churches during Lent 386, for the first time, "after the custom of the Eastern lands, hymns and canticles should be sung so that the people would not become weak through the tedium and sorrow. From then up to the present day that custom has been maintained, with many, or almost all, . . . the congregations taking it up throughout other parts of the world." This statement of Augustine continues to be relevant in the present. Ambrose became the father of Latin hymn singing, and his songs still are an established part of the church's liturgy of the hours. He probably owes his rapid and decisive success not only to the extraordinary enthusiasm when they were first introduced but also to their popular content and images, which speak to the heart and relate to the times of the day, festivals, liturgical and spiritual rituals, mystical encounters with God, and so forth; their easy meter (the iambic tetrameter, which is the meter used most often in Latin hymns); and the melodies that he personally composed. The hymns were so popular and easy to understand that the believers soon wrote them as well by following his example, as he himself reports (*Aux.* 34).

It is precisely this ease that accounts for the difficulty in determining the authentic ones from the many "Ambrosian" songs that have been handed down. Only four of them are definitely his, as Augustine attests explicitly in his writings:

|  | Today's Liturgical Locus |
| --- | --- |
| *Aeterne rerum conditor* | 1st and 3d week, Sunday, lauds<br>Feast of the Guardian Angel, October 2,<br>office of the readings |
| *Deus creator omnium* | 1st and 3d week, Sunday, 1st vespers |
| *Iam surgit hora tertia*<br>*Intende qui regis Israel* | Easter, terce |

In addition, up to fourteen other hymns are attributed to him:

|  | Today's Liturgical Locus |
| --- | --- |
| *Aeterna Christi munera* | Commemoration of Martyrs, lauds |
| *Agnes beatae virginis*<br>*Amore Christi nobilis* | St. Agnes, January 21, lauds |
| *Apostolorum passio*<br>*Apostolorum supparem*<br>*Grates tibi Iesu novas* | Peter and Paul, June 29, lauds |
| *Hic est dies verus Dei* | Easter, office of the readings |
| *Iesu corona virginum*<br>*Illuminans Altissimus* | Feast of the virgins, 2d vespers |
| *Nunc Sancte nobis Spiritus* | Ordinary time and Christmas, terce |
| *Rector potens verax Deus* | Ordinary time and Christmas, sext |
| *Rerum Deus tenax vigor* | Ordinary time and Christmas, nones |
| *Splendor paternae gloriae*<br>*Victor Nabor Felix pii* | 1st and 3d week, Monday, lauds |

The "Ambrosian hymn of praise," the *Te Deum*, and the *Exultet* definitely did not originate with Ambrose.

*Editions: Inni liturgici ambrosiani: Testo latino, traduzione ritmata, melodia ambrosiana* (ed. G. Molon; Milan: NED, 1992). – *Inni* (ed. M. Simonetti; BPat 13; Florence: Nardini, 1988). – *Hymnes* (ed. J. Fontaine; Paris: Cerf, 1992) [Com]. – B. Ramsey, *Ambrose* (Early Church Fathers; London and New York: Routledge, 1997), 166–73 [ET].

*Studies:* M.-H. Jullien, "Les sources de la tradition ancienne des quatorze *Hymnes* attribués à saint Ambroise de Milan," *RHT* 19 (1989): 57–189. – C. P. E. Springer, "Ambrose's *Veni redemptor gentium:* The Aesthetics of Antiphony," *JAC* 34 (1991): 76–87. – A. Franz, *Tageslauf und Heilsgeschichte: Untersuchungen zu den Ferialhymnen des Ambrosius* (St. Ottilien: EOS Verlag, 1994).

# IV. DIODORE OF TARSUS

At the same time that Alexandrian exegesis blossomed in the West because of Ambrose, the so-called Antiochene school also began its heyday with Diodore of Tarsus. He belonged to the pioneers of Nicene orthodoxy. At the Council of Constantinople (381), he was regarded as one of the "regular bishops," that is, those whose ecclesiastical communion was understood to be the standard of orthodoxy (*Codex theodosianus* 16.1.3). He died greatly respected and in peace with the church; his memory and the transmission of his works, however, obscure the fact that in the fifth century his theology, together with that of his student, Theodore of Mopsuestia, found itself in the maelstrom of the disputes about Nestorius. In his polemical writing *Contra Diodorum et Theodorum* of 438, Cyril of Alexandria identified them as the theological originators of Nestorian Christology, and a synod held in Constantinople (499) posthumously condemned his writings, whereas the Second Council of Constantinople (553)—contrary to the account of Photius (*Bibliotheca* 18)—refused a condemnation in conjunction with the controversy of the Three Chapters, arguing that "it is not our task to judge those who died honorably."[4]

More specific details on Diodore's life are available only for his time in Antioch. He came from a noble family, either from Antioch or from Tarsus, his later episcopal city. His initial education was provided by Silvanus of Tarsus and Eusebius of Emesa; he continued it in Athens, the bastion of ancient education, as did Basil the Great, Gregory of Nazianzus and Emperor Julian the Apostate, with whom he tangled in a controversy in 362/363. Under Bishop Leontius (344–358), he functioned as a lay ascetic in Antioch and then joined Meletius (360–381), who ordained him a priest and with whom he went into exile to Armenia in 372, where he met with Basil the Great. He led an ἀσκητήριον in which he trained young people, among them John Chrysostom and Theodore of Mopsuestia, and thus established the Antiochene school as an institution, not only as a school of thought (cf. ch. 3.V). After the death of Emperor Valens (378), Meletius consecrated him bishop of Tarsus. We have no further details on his life, but since there was a new bishop in Tarsus in 394, he must have died before that.

## Theology and Exegesis

Only fragments have been preserved of Diodore's extensive and diverse work because of the posthumous condemnation mentioned above; only since 1980 has Jean-Marie Olivier made a complete commentary on the Psalms available again. In the *Bibliotheca* (223) of Photius (ca. 820–891) and in the article (δ 1149 A)

---

[4] John of Antioch, *Epistula ad Proclum* (PG 65:878 C).

"Suda" of a Byzantine lexicon (tenth century), however, there are detailed accounts about his writings.

Tractates in which he discussed the philosophies of Plato, Aristotle, and Porphyri regarding their views of God and the world prove him to have been highly educated in the secular disciplines as well; nothing else could have been expected, given his educational career. In *Ep.* 135 Basil the Great (probably before 372) expresses his gratitude to Diodore for the two books of his he sent to him; he lauds Diodore for his terse argumentation and clear disposition in the second book, whereas he critiques the first book for its "confused figures of speech and dialogical niceties," which rather impede the straightness of the argumentation. In any case, Basil thereby also attests to Diodore's rhetorical grasp.

His dogmatic writings against the Arians, Macedonians, and Apollinarians show that Diodore was categorically Nicene and emphasized the distinction between the natures of Christ. If we, like the synod of Constantinople in 499, apply a standard of orthodoxy that—given the absoluteness of truth itself—leaves no room for historical progress in understanding, Diodore can be seen as the theological "father of Nestorianism." With an (ahistorical) criterion such as this, many church fathers could be accused of heresy indeed. If we apply, on the contrary, the correct conception—represented by the Second Council of Constantinople (553) in the case of Diodore and up to today—of a humanly indispensable historical progress in understanding, any theologian may only be judged in accordance with the level of understanding of his own time. Diodore was and is, then, a "pillar of orthodoxy" regardless of what conclusions Nestorius later reached on the basis of his theology in connection with questions that newly arose. Reflection on Christology had only just begun with Apollinaris during Diodore's lifetime and had not yet progressed at all to the explicit issue of the unity of the two natures.

Diodore wrote commentaries on most of the biblical books, all of which follow the typical "Antiochene" method—that is, preferring the literal interpretation without rejecting allegory and typology on principle. (The often mechanically used contrast of "Alexandrian = allegory, Antiochene = literal exegesis" in such a simplistic formulation is by no means accurate at today's level of understanding.) He takes his instruments from secular philology and exegesis, as he learned it in his educational pursuits. He begins his commentary with the ὑπό θεσις, that is, the analysis of the historical setting of the biblical book. This is followed by the διάνοια, an explanatory paraphrase with explication of details, including philological matters brought out by the textual statement. Diodore calls his method θεωρία, in contrast to ἀλληγορία, about which he also wrote a theoretical tract that is no longer extant. Nevertheless, even in his extant writings, he explains the difference clearly: The OT and the NT constitute two parts of the one overall reality (ἀλήθεια) of the entire salvation history and the unity of the divine plan of salvation (πρόνοια) and therefore are of primary historical significance. In addition, the historical realities may contain references to future salvific events (typology) without thereby destroying the historical meaning. For Diodore, this is the fundamental difference between θεωρία and ἀλληγορία: Whereas allegory rejects the literal meaning for the sake of a higher one, θεωρία holds to the literal meaning but also recognizes its prophetic expression based on its correspondence with salvation history. A tropological meaning is also possible, according to Diodore, albeit only where a historical explanation no longer applies.

In Diodore's commentary on the Psalms, which belongs to the category of "questions and answers" (προβλήματα καὶ λύσεις, ἐρωτοαποκρίσεις), his understanding of the biblical text as educating and instructing the reader and his consequently moral interpretation are most evident. Here he also uses the ancient "exegesis of the person"—Theodore of Mopsuestia, his student, does the same at a later point in time—which derives from secular exegesis of the poet and was part of the standard curriculum of ancient education. David does speak the Psalms in a concrete historical situation but, because of the divine inspiration, does so from a different πρόσωπον; hence his words are to be referred to the person so speaking and are to be understood as from that person (God, Christ, the person, the church, etc.). This method will direct Theodore of Mopsuestia and Augustine simultaneously, though independent of one another, to the "Chalcedonian formula" of the two natures in the one person of Christ.

*Editions:* PG 33:1545–1628. – R. Abramowski, "Der theologische Nachlass des Diodor von Tarsus," *ZNW* 42 (1949): 19–69. – J. Deconinck, *Essai sur la chaîne de l'Octateucque, avec une édition des commentaires de Diodore de Tarse* (BEFAR 195; Paris: H. Champion, 1912), 85–173. – *Diodori Tarsensis Commentarii in Psalmos 1–50* (ed. J.-M. Olivier; CCSG 6; Turnhout, Belg.: Brepols, 1980). – K. Staab, *Pauluskommentare aus der griechischen Kirche* (2d ed.; NTAbh 15; Münster: Aschendorff, 1984), 83–112.

*Translations:* K. Froelich, *Biblical Interpretation in the Early Church* (SoECT; Philadelphia: Fortress, 1984), 82–94 [*Commentary on the Psalms—Prologue; Preface to the Commentary on Psalm 118*].

*Encyclopedia Articles:* C. Schäublin, *TRE* 8:763–67. – M. Simonetti, *EECh* 1:236–37. – R. A. Greer, *EEC* 1:331–32.

*Studies:* R. Abramowski, "Untersuchungen zu Diodor von Tarsus," *ZNW* 30 (1931): 234–62 [with Syriac text and German translation of a *Vita Diodori* from the *Ecclesiastical History* by Barhadbesabba]. – E. Schweizer, "Diodor von Tarsus als Exeget," *ZNW* 40 (1941): 33–75. – R. A. Greer, "The Antiochene Christology of Diodore of Tarsus," *JTS* NS 16 (1966): 327–41. – M.-J. Rondeau, "Le 'Commentaire des Psaumes' de Diodore de Tarse et l'exégèse antique du Psaume 109/110," *RHR* 176 (1969): 5–33, 153–88; 177 (1970): 5–33. – R. Devreesse, *Les anciens commentateurs grecs des Psaumes* (StT 264; Vatican City: Biblioteca Apostolica Vaticana, 1970), 302–11. – C. Schäublin, *Untersuchungen zu Methode und Herkunft der antiochenischen Exegese* (Theoph. 23; Cologne: P. Hanstein, 1974). – M. Simonetti, *Lettera e/o allegoria: Un contributo alla storia dell'esegesi patristica* (SEAug 23; Rome: Institutum Patristicum Augustinianum, 1985), 156–67. – J. R. Pouchet, "Les rapports de Basile de Césarée avec Diodore de Tarse," *BLE* 87 (1986): 243–72.

# V. THEODORE OF MOPSUESTIA

The outstanding student of Diodore of Tarsus and the greatest exegete of the Antiochene school was Theodore, the bishop of Cilician Mopsuestia for thirty-six years. In the debate about Nestorius and the subsequent controversy of the Three

Chapters, he was overtaken by a fate similar to that of his teacher. Together with the latter, he was considered a forerunner of Nestorian Christology and ultimately was condemned by the Second Council of Constantinople (553), together with Ibas of Edessa and Theoderet of Cyrrhus. In principle, the same applies to his posthumous condemnation, as in the case of Diodore; what aggravated the situation for Theodore further was that the excerpts of his works that the council seemingly had available as a basis for its condemnation by no means represented a complete and correct picture of his theology. As a result of his condemnation, however, as in the case of Diodore, the majority of Theodore's numerous works were lost, except for some fragments. Only in the nineteenth and twentieth centuries were some of them fully discovered, on the basis of which it is possible to reconstruct his thought more accurately, for the fragments were collected either by his friends or by his foes. A significant number of his works have been preserved in Syriac, since the Syrian church always held Theodore in high esteem and also preserved two catalogues from the thirteenth and fourteenth centuries.

Theodore was born into a prosperous Antiochene family in 350. Much like Basil the Great, he (together with John Chrysostom) attended the lectures of Libanius, the famous rhetor who had returned to his native city in 354. Together with John, he entered the ἀσκητήριον of Diodore of Tarsus in order to lead a monastic life of spiritual studies, especially of the Bible, but three months later he wanted to leave the community in order to get married and become a lawyer. He stayed, however, as a result of John's admonitions, which are preserved (*Ad Theodorum lapsum*). In 383 Patriarch Flavian, the successor of Meletius, ordained him a priest, and beginning in 386 he stayed with Diodore of Tarsus,[5] who had served as bishop there since 378. In 392 he was appointed bishop to the nearby city of Mopsuestia, where he remained until his death in 428.

Prominent in his pastoral work, as his writings also reflect, are his discussions with the heterodox, his biblical exegesis, and his instruction of the catechumens and believers. In 418 Julian of Eclanum and some of his episcopal friends sought shelter with him after being deposed for Pelagianism; initially he did indeed take them in—Julian even translated his commentary on the Psalms into Latin—but then had them condemned by a Cilician synod.

*Bibliographies:* K.-G. Wesseling, in *Biographisch-bibliographisches Kirchenlexikon* (ed. F. W. Bautz; Herzberg: T. Bautz, 1970–), 11:885–909.

*Editions:* PG 66:9–1020. – *Replica a Giuliano imperatore: Adversus criminationes in Christianos Iuliani imperatoris* (ed. A. Guida; BPat 24; Florence: Nardini, 1994) [Com].

*Studies:* R. Devreesse, *Essai sur Théodore de Mopsueste* (StT 141; Vatican City: Biblioteca Apostolica Vaticana, 1948). – F. X. Murphy and P. Sherwood, *Constantinople II et III* (trans. H. J. Sieben; Mainz: Matthias-Grünewald, 1990), 7–130; trans. into German from F. X. Murphy and P. Sherwood, *Constantinople II et III* (HCO 3; Paris: Orante, 1974). – A. Raddatz, *GK* 2:167–78. – J. M. Lera, *DSp* 15:385–400. – M. Simonetti, *EECh* 2:824–25. – R. A. Greer, *EEC* 2:1116–17.

---

[5] Thus suggested for the first time in J. M. Lera, *DSp* 15:385.

# A. Exegesis

According to the extant lists of his works, Theodore commented on the most important OT books and the majority of the NT writings: the entire Pentateuch, Psalms, the major and minor prophets, Job, Ecclesiastes, Song of Songs, Matthew, Luke, John, Acts, and all of the Pauline letters (including Hebrews). Of these the following are preserved in full: the commentary on the twelve minor prophets, as Theodore's only work in the original Greek; the commentary on John in a Syriac translation (besides Greek fragments from the catenas); the commentary on the Psalms, partly in the Latin translation by Julian of Eclanum, partly pieced together from the sections (Pss 1–80) handed down in the catenas; and the commentary on the ten smaller Pauline letters, also in a Latin translation (plus fragments from the catenas on Romans, 1 and 2 Corinthians, and Hebrews).

Theodore's exegetical method essentially perpetuates that of Diodore, his teacher, but he sharpens and deepens it. The one history of humanity developed in two eras (καταστάσεις), with the incarnation of Christ constituting the break between the two. For this reason, the OT is basically to be interpreted with reference to the historical situation of the time; insofar as it prepared the coming of Christ, however, it also has typological meaning. To this end, three criteria must be fulfilled: (a) the OT and NT events must be comparable, (b) they must show concrete salvific power already in the OT, and (c) they must be subordinated to the NT reality. Hence, although Theodore acknowledges the prophecies contained in the Psalms (he is aware that not all of them originated during the time of David, to whom the ancient church traditionally attributes them), the deliverance of Israel from Egypt, Jonah, and others as *typoi* of Christ and of the NT, in reality he hardly ever uses them. As much as the OT and the NT belong together, on the one hand, for him there is such a vast difference between them, on the other, that he is able to juxtapose both Gentiles and the OT over against the NT. From the perspective that the second era of humanity began with the incarnation of Christ and lasts until the eschatological fulfillment, the NT also takes on a more prophetic, futuristic meaning than a reflection of the past. This is true despite his otherwise exclusively literary interpretation, which may appear rather superficial in the case of strongly symbolic texts, such as the Gospel of John.

*Editions:*
*Genesis:* R. M. Tonneau, "Théodore de Mopsueste, interprétation (du livre) de la Genèse (Vat. Syr. 120, ss. I–IV)," *Mus* 66 (1953): 45–64. – T. Jansma, "Théodore de Mopsueste, interprétation du livre de la Genèse: Fragments de la version syriaque (B. D. Add. 17, 189, fol. 17–21)," *Mus* 75 (1962): 63–92 [Com].
*Psalms: Le commentaire de Théodore de Mopsueste sur les Psaumes (I–LXXX)* (ed. R. Devreesse; StT 93; Vatican City: Biblioteca Apostolica Vaticana, 1939). – *Theodori Mopsuesteni Expositionis in Psalmos Iuliano Aeclanensi interprete in latinum versae quae supersunt* (ed. L. De Coninck and M. J. D'Hont; CCSL 88 A; Turnhout, Belg.: Brepols, 1977) [1]. – *Fragments syriaques du Commentaire des Psaumes: (Psaume 118 et Psaumes 138–148)* (ed. L. van Rompay; 2 vols.; CSCO 435, 436; Louvain: Peeters, 1982).
*Ecclesiastes: Das syrische Fragment des Ecclesiastes-Kommentars von Theodor von Mopsuestia: Syrischer Text mit vollständigem Wörterverzeichnis* (ed. W. Strothmann;

GOF 1.28; Wiesbaden: Harrassowitz, 1988). – *Syrische Katenen aus dem Ecclesiastes-Kommentar des Theodor von Mopsuestia: Syrischer Text mit vollständigem Wörterverzeichnis* (ed. W. Strothmann; GOF 1.29; Wiesbaden: Harrassowitz, 1988).
*Minor Prophets: Theodori Mopsuesteni Commentarius in XII prophetas* (ed. H. N. Sprenger; GOF 5.1; Wiesbaden: Harrassowitz, 1977).
*Matthew:* J. Reuss, *Matthäus-Kommentare aus der griechischen Kirche* (TU 61; Berlin: Akademie, 1957), 96–135.
*John: Commentarius in Evangelium Johannis apostoli* (ed. J.-M. Vosté; 2 vols.; CSCO 115, 116; Paris: E Typographeo Reipublicae, 1940).
*Paul: In epistolas B. Pauli Commentarii: The Latin Version with the Greek Fragments* (ed. H. B. Swete; 2 vols.; Cambridge: Cambridge University Press, 1880–1882; repr., Farnborough, Eng.: Gregg, 1969). – K. Staab, *Pauluskommentare aus der griechischen Kirche: Aus Katenenhandschriften gesammelt und herausgegeben* (NTAbh 15; Münster: Aschendorff, 1933; 2d ed., 1984), 113–212.
*Fragments: Theodori Mopsuesteni fragmenta syriaca: E codicibus Musei Britannici Nitriacis* (ed. E. Sachau; Leipzig: Engelmann, 1869).

*Translations:* J. W. Trigg, *Biblical Interpretation* (MFC 9; Wilmington, Del.: Glazier, 1988), 163–77 [*Commentary on Zechariah, Commentary on Galatians*].

*Studies:* H. Kihn, *Theodor von Mopsuestia und Junilius Africanus als Exegeten* (Fribourg, Switz.: Herder, 1880). – L. Pirot, *L'œuvre exégétique de Théodore de Mopsueste, 350–428 après J.-C.* (Rome: Pontifical Biblical Institute, 1913). – M. Simonetti, *Lettera e/o allegoria: Un contributo alla storia dell'esegesi patristica* (SEAug 23; Rome: Institutum Patristicum Augustinianum, 1985), 167–80.

*Old Testament:* M. Simonetti, "Note sull'esegesi veterotestamentaria di Teodoro di Mopsuestia," *VetChr* 14 (1977): 69–102. – D. Z. Zaharopoulos, *Theodore of Mopsuestia on the Bible: A Study of His Old Testament Exegesis* (New York: Paulist, 1989).

*Octateuch:* R. Devreesse, *Les anciens commentateurs grecs de l'Octateuque et des Rois (fragments tirés des chaînes)* (StT 201; Vatican City: Biblioteca Apostolica Vaticana, 1959). – C. Schäublin, *Untersuchungen zu Methode und Herkunft der antiochenischen Exegese* (Theoph. 23; Cologne: Hanstein, 1974). – L. Brade, *Untersuchungen zum Scholienbuch des Teodoros Bar Konai: Die Übernahme des Erbes von Theodoros von Mopsuestia in der nestorianischen Kirche* (GOF 1.8; Weisbaden: Harrassowitz, 1975).

*Gospel of John:* G. Ferraro, " 'L'ora' di Cristo e della Chiesa nel commentario di Teodoro di Mopsuestia al Quarto Vangelo," *Aug* 15 (1975): 275–307. – G. Ferraro, "L'esposizione dei testi pneumatologici nel commento di Teodoro di Mopsuestia al Quarto Vangelo," *Greg* 67 (1986): 265–96. – L. Fatica, *I Commentari a Giovanni di Teodoro di Mopsuestia e di Cirillo di Alessandria: Confronto fra metodi esegetici e teologici* (SEAug 29; Institutum Patristicum Augustinianum, 1988).

*Pauline Letters:* U. Wickert, *Studien zu den Pauluskommentaren Theodors von Mopsuestia als Beitrag zum Verständnis der antiochenischen Theologie* (BZNW 27; Berlin: A. Töpelmann, 1962). – R. A. Greer, *The Captain of Our Salvation: A Study in the Patristic Exegesis of Hebrews* (BGBE 15; Tübingen: Mohr, 1973), 178–263.

# B. Theology

Of Theodore's dogmatic works, dealing primarily with the heresies of his time, only one is still available in full, namely, the *Disputatio cum Macedonianis*, the written form of a dispute with the Macedonians held in Anazarbus, in a Syriac translation. At the beginning of the last century, the Chaldean metropolitan, Addai Scher, briefly owned a Syriac manuscript of Theodore's major christological treatise, *De incarnatione*. He had found it in Seert (Kurdistan) in 1905 but lost it again in 1922 when his library was pillaged. Likewise the treatise *Contra Eunomium*, as well as all of Theodore's other theological writings indicated in the listings, are lost, except for some fragments. For this reason, his exegetical and catechetical works have to serve as primary witnesses of his theology.

Both in his doctrine of the Trinity and in his Christology, Theodore was firmly in the orthodox tradition. But whereas the definitive theological solution regarding the doctrine of the Trinity had already been found through the Cappadocians and the Council of Constantinople (381), the solution for Christology was still lacking, that is, the answer to the question of how divinity and humanity were combined in Christ without merging into one, on the one hand, or remaining separate as two entities, on the other. Theodore assumed the traditional theology of the *homo assumptus* and against Apollinaris clearly emphasized the completeness of the human nature in Christ. This heavy emphasis on the independent, fully human nature runs the danger of teaching a doctrine of two sons, of which he later was accused in connection with Nestorianism; yet a more thorough examination of his writings demonstrates that he did not succumb to this danger. By way of the equally traditional formula *unus atque idem et Deus Verbum . . . et homo*, by means of the exegesis of the person, he finally attained—at the same time as Augustine—the concept of the one πρόσωπον of Christ. For Theodore, το πρόσωπον is not yet to be ascribed the later Chalcedonian content of "person"; here it describes the form in which a nature or hypostasis appears. For this reason, Theodore is able to attribute a *prosōpon* to both natures of Christ, as well as a joint *prosōpon* to the union of the natures. If Theodore's clear opposition to the doctrine of two sons and his emphasis on the unmixed unity of the two complete natures in Christ κατὰ συνάφειαν are taken into consideration, however, he has to be evaluated, as during his lifetime, as an orthodox theologian of his time, when the level of christological development had not yet come to maturity, and not as a forerunner of Nestorianism.

*Edition: La seconde partie de l'histoire de Barhadbesabba 'Arbaia et controverse de Theodore de Mopsueste avec les macedoniens* (ed. F. Nau; PO 9; Paris: Firmin-Didot, 1913; repr., 2003), 635–67 [*Disputatio cum Macedonianis*].

*Translation:* R. A. Norris Jr., *The Christological Controversy* (SoECT; Philadelphia: Fortress, 1980), 113–22 [*On the Incarnation—fragments*].

*Studies:* F. A. Sullivan, *The Christology of Theodore of Mopsuestia* (AnGr 82; Rome: Apud Aedes Universitatis Gregorianae, 1956). – R. A. Greer, *Theodore of Mopsuestia: Exegete and Theologian* (London: Faith, 1961). – R. A. Norris, *Manhood and Christ: A Study in the Christology of Theodore of Mopsuestia* (Oxford: Clarendon, 1963). – G. Koch, *Die Heilsverwirklichung bei Theodor von Mopsuestia* (MThS.S 31; Munich: Huebner, 1965). – J. McWilliam Dewart, *The Theology of Grace of Theodore of Mopsuestia* (SCA 16; Washington, D.C.: Catholic University of America Press, 1971). – A. Grillmeier, *Jesus der Christus im Glauben der Kirche* (2d ed.; Fribourg, Switz.: Herder, 1982),

1:790–814. – R. P. Vaggione, "Some Neglected Fragments of Theodore of Mopsuestia's *Contra Eunomium*," *JTS* NS 31 (1980): 403–70. – A. Grillmeier, *Christ in Christian Tradition* (trans. J. Bowden; 2d rev. ed.; Atlanta: John Knox, 1975–), 2/2: 419–62; trans. of *Jesus der Christus im Glauben der Kirche* (Fribourg, Switz.: Herder, 1965–), 2/2:431–84. – N. El-Khoury, "Der Mensch als Gleichnis Gottes: Eine Untersuchung zur Anthropologie des Theodor von Mopsuestia," *OrChr* 74 (1990): 62–71. – F. McLeod, "Theodore of Mopsuestia Revisited," *TS* 61 (2000): 447–80.

# C. Catechesis

Since their discovery in 1932, the sixteen catechetical homilies by Theodore, extant in a Syriac translation, together with the three writings mentioned in excursus 3, ch. 7.I, are among the most significant sources on Christian initiation, as well as on Theodore's authentic theology. In customary form, the initial ten on the Nicene creed, with special consideration given to the doctrine of the Trinity and Christology, are addressed to the candidates for baptism; the remaining six, dealing with the Lord's Prayer (11), the baptismal liturgy (12–14), and the Eucharist (15–16), are addressed to the newly baptized. It is not absolutely clear whether Theodore delivered these homilies during the period of his priesthood, as the majority of scholars argue, or only during his episcopate (392–428, Lietzmann, Riley); he might also have delivered them on several occasions.[6] In any case, the baptismal catecheses of his contemporary, John Chrysostom, show that in Antioch it was not the bishop, as was usual, but priests who gave the baptismal instruction. If one agrees with Lera's conclusions, it is true, the date for Theodore's catecheses would point to Tarsus, in 388–392, not Antioch, as the locus of the preaching.

*Editions: Commentary of Theodore of Mopsuestia on the Nicene Creed* (ed. A. Mingana; WoodSt 5; Cambridge: Heffer, 1932) [ET/Com]. – *Commentary of Theodore of Mopsuestia on the Lord's Prayer and on the Sacraments of Baptism and the Eucharist* (ed. A. Mingana; WoodST 6; Cambridge: Heffer, 1933) [ET/Com]. – H. Lietzmann, *Die Liturgie des Theodor von Mopsuestia* (APAW.PH; Berlin: Akademie der Wissenschaften, 1933), 915–36 [Com]. – *Les Homélies catéchétiques: Reproduction phototypique du ms. Mingana Syrr. 561* (ed. R. Tonneau and R. Devreesse; StT 145; Vatican City: Biblioteca Apostolica Vaticana, 1949; repr., 1966).

*Translation:* E. Yarnold, *The Awe-Inspiring Rites of Initiation: The Origins of the RCIA* (2d ed.; Collegeville, Minn.: Liturgical, 1994), 165–250 [*Baptismal Homilies 2–4*].

*Studies:* F. J. Reine, *The Eucharistic Doctrine and Liturgy of the Mystagogical Catecheses of Theodore of Mopsuestia* (SCA 2; Washington, D. C.: Catholic University of America Press, 1942). – A. de Lourmel, "Théodore de Mopsueste catéchète," *EtFr* 18 (1968): 65–80. – V.-S. Janeras, "En quels jours furent prononcées les Homélies catéchétiques de Théodore de Mopsueste?" in *Mémorial Mgr G. Khouri-Sarkis* (Louvain: Imprimerie Orientaliste, 1969), 121–33. – H. M. Riley, *Christian Initiation: A Comparative Study of the Interpretation of the Baptismal Liturgy in the Mystagogical Writings of Cyril of Jerusalem, John Chrysostom, Theodore of Mopsuestia, and Ambrose of Milan*

---

[6] Lera, *DSp* 15:388.

(SCA 17; Washington, D.C.: Catholic University of America Press, 1974). – A. Cañizares Llovera, "El catecumenado según Teodoro de Mopsuestia," *Estudios* 52 (1976): 147–93. – J. M. Lera, "*... Y se hizo hombre": La economía trinitaria en las Catequesis de Teodoro de Mopsuestia* (Bilbao: Universidad de Deusto; Mensajero, 1977). – P. Bruns, *Den Menschen mit dem Himmel verbinden: Eine Studie zu den Katechetischen Homilien des Theodor von Mopsuestia* (CSCO 549; Louvain: Peeters, 1995).

# VI. JOHN CHRYSOSTOM

The life of John, the other important student of Diodore and friend of Theodore, who since the fifth century bears the nickname "Chrysostom" ("golden mouth") on account of his extraordinary rhetorical skills, in many ways resembles that of the other great leaders of the fourth-century church, such as Basil the Great and Ambrose. His nickname represents a title of fame that in the Latin church has been accorded only to the bishop of Ravenna, Petrus Chrysologus ("golden word") (ca. 380–450). He was born into a well-to-do Antiochene family, as the son of Secundus, a governmental official, and Anthusa, a devout Christian who was already widowed at the age of twenty. He was offered the best education of his time, together with Theodore of Mopsuestia among others, from Libanius, the famous rhetor. After his baptism in 372, he entered the ἀσκητήριον of Diodore of Tarsus, where he studied the typically Antiochene exegesis of Scripture, deepened his spiritual-ascetical life, and in 375 took on the office of lector.

In his radical pursuit of perfection, this path leading to an ecclesiastical career was no longer adequate. First he moved to another community in the vicinity of Antioch for the next four years and then to a hermitage for two years, where he committed large parts of Scripture to memory. Because he thereby overtaxed his health, however, he returned to Antioch to continue an ecclesiastical career and in 381 was consecrated deacon by Bishop Meletius. As deacon of the diocese of Antioch, comparable to today's vicar-general as far as his duties were concerned, his primary charge was the charitable and social services for the poor, widows, orphans, and virgins; the education of children; and the associated administrative tasks. In all of his writings, John was always stimulated by the current, practical needs of the pastorate. Thus the threefold course for his life was set: his brilliant rhetorical education, which would be reflected in his preaching and make him into the "golden mouth"; his striving for the most thorough, radical following of Christ possible, according to the instructions of Scripture, "be it convenient or not," which caused him to become a martyr; and the realization of the life of faith not in monastic seclusion but in managing the day-to-day problems of pastoral care "in the world."

After John had been in the diaconate for five years, Bishop Flavian, the successor of Meletius, ordained him to the priesthood on February 28, 386, apparently with the express intent of commissioning the rhetor, who had already become famous, to the preaching ministry. Otherwise it would be hard to understand the fact that he preached his first sermon on the very day of his ordination to the priesthood and that it was recorded and is extant today. Preaching and pastoral care became the major work of John's life. More than seven hundred authentic sermons of his twelve years as priest in Antioch and six years as bishop in Constantinople (until his exile) have been handed down. The great majority deal with biblical themes, indeed gradually commenting on entire books of the Bible in sermon series: Genesis and the entire NT, except for the gospels of Mark and Luke, James, and 1 Peter. The three that are proper commentaries on Job, the Psalms, and Galatians may have been the result of edited homilies as well. In addition to the biblical homilies, there are numerous sermons associated with festivals, saints, and practical community concerns; a few dogmatic homilies against the Arians; and, finally, *Adversus Judaeos*, eight homilies against the Jews. In this context, it is to be noted that the anti-Jewish literature of the ancient church has nothing in common with anti-Semitism in the modern sense of racial animosity and, for this reason, has to be classified as anti-Judaism. For John Chrysostom, it is a matter of theological discussion and coexistence between Christianity and its mother religion; in these homilies he maintains the incompatibility of the Christian faith with the Jewish practice of the law, also against the current backdrop of reconversions to Judaism.

After the death of Nectarius, the patriarch of Constantinople, and upon the advice of Eutropius, his powerful first minister, Emperor Arcadius appointed the famed preacher from Antioch as Nectarius's successor on September 27, 397. (Subsequently Eutropius was to play a part in the disagreements between John and the imperial court.) Since the emperor was afraid that Antioch was not prepared to let their great pastor leave, however, he ordered Asterius, the governor of Antioch, to take John to Constantinople without causing a stir. Asterius agreed to meet him outside the city gates without indicating the reasons for it, seated him in a state carriage that was already waiting, informed him of his appointment as bishop of the capital, and had him driven directly to Constantinople. On February 28, 398, Theophilus of Alexandria consecrated him bishop. The emperor's choice quickly proved to be most advantageous for the city's pastoral care. Politically, however, it proved to be fatal, for John was not a politician like Nectarius, his predecessor. As a former senator and after Gregory of Nazianzus stepped down during the Council of Constantinople (381), Nectarius managed his sixteen years in office without problems with the imperial court. On the other hand, the consequence of this seems to have been that, in many respects, he came to terms with the powerful, the clergy and the people succumbed to laxity, and the many monks living in the city went their own ways.

Into this situation came John, who had been a zealot for the cause of Christ since his early years, without regard for politics, power, and wealth. In his position as priest in Antioch, this had not been dangerous politically, but this was not the case in his ecclesiastical position of leadership as bishop of the highly sensitive capital. In spite of this, John began to reform his diocese according to the guidelines of the gospel. Like Ambrose in Milan, he reduced the episcopal court to a level commensurate with a simple lifestyle. When necessary, he sold his own possessions and ecclesiastical property for the poor, suffering, and travelers; with the support of noble women, such as Olympias, he reorganized the administration of deaconesses and widows, exhorted the world's clergy to exemplary conduct, and endeavored to integrate the monks into his episcopal jurisdiction. Most of all, however, he publicly proclaimed the Christian principles of life in his sermons, even if this meant critiquing members of the imperial court or, as already in Antioch, the neglect of church attendance in order to participate in the very popular entertainment of the circus. On the one hand, he understandably succeeded in gaining the vigorous support of the concerned population of the church and of some of the clergy and the monks; on the other, he made bitter enemies of the rest.

His fall was ultimately sparked by some spectacular incidents. When Eutropius, the emperor's first minister, who two years earlier had recommended the appointment of John as bishop, fell into disgrace in 399, John granted him asylum in the church, as it was everyone's prerogative. In a first sermon, he warned the powerful to recognize the transitoriness of their power in the case of Eutropius, and in a second sermon, he justified the church's inalienable right to grant asylum. In 402 he took in the presbyter Isidore from Alexandria, the "tall brothers," and other Egyptian monks, whom Bishop Theophilus had accused of heretical Origenism and who thus turned to John. Although he did not strive for anything other than an unbiased investigation and review of the case, he thereby turned Theophilus of Alexandria and Epiphanius of Constantia (Salamis) into bitter enemies against him because, in their view, he favored heretics. The decisive power in this situation was ultimately that of Eudoxia, the empress, who felt offended by his sermons against luxury and dissipation.

Initially his enemies pushed for John's deposition on the ecclesiastical, rather than on the political, level. The so-called synod of the Oak (according to the venue, the estate of Δρῦς, near Chalcedon) of only thirty-six bishops biased against John, under the leadership of Theophilus, summoned John to give an account. When John did not appear, however, despite three summonses and likely with an awareness that his condemnation had already been decided, the synod relieved him of his office in the fall of 403, and the emperor signed his verdict to be exiled, which was not carried out, however. John's biographer, Palladius, reports that on the day of his deportation "an accident happened in the imperial bedroom" (*Vita* 9), possibly a miscarriage by the empress, which was interpreted as a warning sign from heaven and precipitated the bishop's recall.

Since John continued to preach fearlessly, however, the situation did not improve, and so Arcadius, the emperor, ordered him to leave the city before Easter 404. Because John refused and yet was no longer able to set foot in his cathedral, he held the baptismal service on Easter eve in the baths of Constantius, which the soldiers stormed and ended by force. On June 9, 404, the emperor signed the final decree of exile to Cucusus in Armenia, where John spent three years. Since he continued to maintain lively contacts with Constantinople, Phoenicia, and Persia from there—his entire corpus of letters, encompassing 240 items, comes from this time—his opponents were wary of his potential long-term influence and persuaded the emperor to exile him to remote and inhospitable

Pityus on the east coast of the Black Sea. During this extremely brutal deportation, John died of exhaustion in Pontic Comana on September 14, 407.[7]

Pope Innocent, to whom John personally appealed in two letters, achieved
his rehabilitation in 412; on January 27, 438, his remains were solemnly interred in
the Church of the Apostles in Constantinople. The remains rested in the choir chapel of St. Peter's in Rome from May 1, 1626, until November 27, 2004, when Pope
John Paul II returned them, together with the remains of Gregory of Nazianzus, to
Patriarch Bartholomew I of Constantinople. The Western church has venerated
him since 1568, together with Athanasius, Basil the Great, and Gregory of Nazianzus,
as one of the "four great doctors of the Eastern church," and the Eastern church has
venerated him since Constantine Monomachus (1042–1055), together with Basil
the Great and Gregory of Nazianzus, as one of the three hierarchs.

John has bequeathed the most voluminous work of all the Greek church
fathers, comparable only with Augustine in the West. Over the course of centuries, a considerable number of questionable and inauthentic works have been attributed to his great name, the sifting and separation of which have been
undertaken primarily by José Antonio de Aldama, although this cannot yet
be considered complete. Likewise the so-called Divine Liturgy of Saint John
Chrysostom—in the contemporary Byzantine rite, the almost exclusive liturgical
form of the ecclesiastical year—did not originate with him, even if far more elements of it reach back into his time than assumed hitherto.

*Bibliographies:* K. H. Uthemann, *BBKL* 3:305–26.

*Editions:*
*Opera omnia: Tou en hagiois patros hēmōn Iōannou archiepiskopou Kōnstantinoupoleōs tou
    Chrysostomou tōn heuriskomenōn* (ed. H. Savile; 8 vols.; Eton: In Collegio regali
    excudebat Ioannes Norton . . . regius typographus, 1612–1613). – PG 47–64.
*Ad Theodorum lapsum: A Théodore* (ed. J. Dumortier; SC 117; Paris: Cerf, 1966).
*Ad viduam juniorem: A une jeune veuve: Sur le mariage unique* (ed. B. Grillet and G. H.
    Ettlinger; SC 138; Paris: Cerf, 1968).
*Commentarius in Job: Commentaire sur Job* (ed. H. Sorlin and L. Neyrand; 2 vols.; SC 346,
    348; Paris: Cerf, 1988). – *Kommentar zu Hiob* (ed. and trans. U. Hagedorn and
    D. Hagedorn; PTS 35; Berlin and New York: de Gruyter, 1990).
*Contra Anomoeos: Sur l'égalité du Père et du Fils: Contre les anoméens homélies VII–XII* (ed.
    A.-M. Malingrey; SC 396; Paris: Cerf, 1994).
*De Babyla: Discours sur Babylas* (ed. M. A. Schatkin, C. Blanc, B. Grillet, and J.-N. Guinot;
    SC 362; Paris: Cerf, 1990).
*De inani gloria: Sur la vaine gloire et l'éducation des enfants* (ed. A.-M. Malingrey; SC 188;
    Paris: Cerf, 1972).
*De incomprehensibili Dei natura: Sur l'incompréhensibilité de Dieu: Homélies I–V* (ed.
    J. Daniélou, A.-M. Malingrey, and R. Flacelière; 2d ed.; SC 28 bis; Paris: Cerf, 2000).
*De laudibus Pauli: Panégyriques de s. Paul* (ed. A. Piédagnel; SC 300; Paris: Cerf, 1982).
*De providentia: Sur la providence de Dieu* (ed. A.-M. Malingrey; rev. ed.; SC 79; Paris: Cerf,
    2000).
*De virginitate: La virginité* (ed. H. Musurillo; introd., trans., and notes B. Grillet; SC 125;
    Paris: Cerf, 1966).

---

[7] Leroux's reference (*TRE* 17:125) to "September 21, 407 . . . (Baur II 326–333)" is to
be corrected to "September 14, 407 . . . (Baur II 350–359)."

*Epistulae ad Olympiadem/Vita Olympiadis: Lettres à Olympias* (ed. A.-M. Malingrey; 2d ed.; SC 13 bis; Paris: Cerf, 1968).
*Homiliae in epistulam ad Colossenses: Omelie sulla lettera di S. Paolo ai Colossesi* (ed. C. Piazzino; CPS 6; Turin: Società Editrice Internazionale, 1939).
*Homiliae in Genesim: Sermons sur la Genèse* (ed. L. Brottier; SC 433; Paris: Cerf, 1998).
*Homiliae in Johannem: Le omelie su S. Giovanni Evangelista* (ed. C. Tirone; 4 vols.; CPS 10–13; Turin: Società Editrice Internazionale, 1944–1948).
*Homiliae in quadragesimam: Discorso esortatorio per l'inizio della Santa Quaresima* (ed. M. L. Cervini; CPS 16; Turin: Società Editrice Internazionale, 1953).
*In illud: Vidi Dominum: Homélies sur Ozias* (ed. J. Dumortier; SC 277; Paris: Cerf, 1981).
*In Isaiam: Commentaire sur Isaïe* (ed. J. Dumortier and A. Leifooghe; SC 304; Paris: Cerf, 1983).
*Opus imperfectum in Matthaeum: Opus imperfectum in Matthaeum* (ed. J. van Banning; CCSL 87 B; Turnhout, Belg.: Brepols, 1988).
*Palladius, Dialogus de vita Chrysostomi: Dialogue sur la vie de Jean Chrysostome* (ed. A.-M. Malingrey and P. Leclerq; 2 vols.; SC 341, 342; Paris: Cerf, 1988).
*Quod nemo laeditur: Lettre d'exil à Olympias et à tous les fidèles (Quod nemo laeditur)* (ed. A.-M. Malingrey; SC 103; Paris: Cerf, 1964).

*Translations:* W. R. W. Stephens, T. P. Brandram, and R. Blackburn, trans., *Chrysostom: On the Priesthood, Ascetic Treatises, Select Homilies and Letters, Homilies on the Statues* (vol. 9 of NPNF[1]; Peabody, Mass.: Hendrickson, 1995; repr. of 1889 ed.) [*On the Priesthood; Two Letters to Theodore after His Fall; Letter to a Young Widow; Two Homilies: (I.) On St. Babylas (II.), On St. Ignatius; Two Instructions for Candidates for Baptism; Three Homilies: (I.) That Demons Do Not Govern the World (II. and III.) Concerning the Power of the Tempter; Three Homilies: (I.) Against Marcionists and Manichaeans, on the Passage "Father, If It Be Possible," etc., (II.) On the Paralytic Let Down through the Roof, (III.) To Those Who Had Not Attended the Assembly on the Passage "If Thine Enemy Hunger Feed Him"; Homily against Publishing the Errors of the Brethren; Two Homilies on Eutropius; Treatise to Prove That No One Can Harm the Man Who Does Not Injure Himself; Four Letters to Olympias and One to Presbyters at Antioch; Correspondence of Innocent, Bishop of Rome, with St. Chrysostom and the Church of Constantinople; Twenty-One Homilies on the Statues*]. – T. W. Chambers, trans., *Chrysostom: Homilies on the Epistles of Paul to the Corinthians* (vol. 12 of NPNF[1]; Peabody, Mass.: Hendrickson, 1995; repr. of 1889 ed.). – G. Prevost and M. B. Riddle, trans., *Chrysostom: Homilies on the Gospel of Saint Matthew* (vol. 10 of NPNF[1]; Peabody, Mass.: Hendrickson, 1995; repr. of 1889 ed.). – J. Walker, J. Sheppard, H. Browne, G. B. Stevens, J. B. Morris, and W. H. Simcox, trans., *Chrysostom: Homilies on the Acts of the Apostles and the Epistle to the Romans* (vol. 11 of NPNF[1]; Peabody, Mass.: Hendrickson, 1995; repr. of 1889 ed.). – G. Alexander, J. A. Broadus, and P. Schaff, trans., *Chrysostom: Homilies on Galatians, Ephesians, Philippians, Colossians, Thessalonians, Timothy, Titus, and Philemon* (vol. 13 of NPNF[1]; Peabody, Mass.: Hendrickson, 1995; repr. of 1889 ed.). – P. Schaff and F. Gardiner, trans., *Chrysostom: Homilies on the Gospel of Saint John and the Epistle to the Hebrews* (vol. 14 of NPNF[1]; Peabody, Mass.: Hendrickson, 1995; repr. of 1889 ed.). – *Commentary on Saint John the Apostle and Evangelist: Homilies* (trans. T. A. Goggin; 2 vols.; FC 33, 41; Washington, D.C.: Catholic University of America, 1957–1969) [*Homilies on Saint John*]. – *Discources against Judaizing Christians* (trans. P. W. Harkins; FC 68; Washington, D.C.: Catholic University of America, 1979). – *On the Incomprehensible Nature of God* (trans. P. W. Harkins; FC 72; Washington, D.C.: Catholic University of America Press, 1984). – *Apologist: John Chrysostom* (trans. M. A. Schatkin and P. W. Harkins; FC 73; Washington, D.C.: Catholic University of America Press, 1985) [*Discourse on Blessed Babylas and against the Greeks, Demonstration against the Pagans That Christ Is God*]. – *Homilies on Genesis* (trans. R. C. Hill; 3 vols.; FC 74, 82, 87; Washington,

D.C.: Catholic University of America Press, 1986–1992). – *St. John Chrysostom Commentary on the Psalms* (trans. R. C. Hill; 2 vols.; Brookline, Mass.: Holy Cross Orthodox Press, 1998). – Palladius, *Dialogue on the Life of St. John Chrysostom* (trans. R. T. Meyer; ACW 45; New York: Newman, 1985). – W. Mayer and P. Allen, *John Chrysostom* (Early Church Fathers; London and New York: Routledge, 2000), 55–204 [*On Ephesians, Hom. 11; On Colossians, Hom. 7; Homily on Martyrs; On His Return; On the Statues, Hom. 17; Against the Games and Theatres; Baptismal Instruction 8; On Eutropius; On "I Opposed Him to His Face"; On "My Father's Working Still"; Against the Jews, Oration 1; On 1 Corinthians, Hom. 21; On the Acts of the Apostles, Hom. 3; Concerning Blessed Philogonius; Letters from Exile*].

*Reference Works:* J. A. de Aldama, *Repertorium pseudochrysostomicum* (PIRHT 10; Paris: Centre National de la Recherche Scientifique, 1965). – A.-M. Malingrey and M. L. Guillaumin, *Indices chrysostomici, I: Ad Olympiadem, Ab exilio epistula, De providentia Dei* (AlOm.A 31; Hildesheim and New York: Olms, 1978). – R. A. Krupp, *Saint John Chrysostom: A Scripture Index* (Lanham, Md. and London: University Press of America, 1984).

*Encyclopedia Articles:* P. Stockmeier, "Johannes Chrysostomos," *GK* 2:125–44. – J.-M. Leroux, *TRE* 17:118–27. – A.-M. Malingrey, *EECh* 1:440–42. – R. Aubert, *DHGE* 26:1408–15. – R. Wilken, *EEC* 1:622–24.

*Introductions and Surveys:* C. Baur, *John Chrysostom and His Time* (trans. M. Gonzaga; 2 vols.; 2d ed.; London: Sands, 1960); trans. of *Der heilige Johannes Chrysostomus und seine Zeit* (2 vols.; Munich: Heuber, 1929–1930). – A. Moulard, *Saint Jean Chrysostome: Sa vie, son œuvre* (Paris: Procure Générale du Clergé, 1941; repr., 1949). – D. Attwater, *St. John Chrysostom: Pastor and Preacher* (London: Harvill, 1959). – J. N. D. Kelly, *Golden Mouth: The Story of John Chrysostom—Ascetic, Preacher, Bishop* (London: Duckworth; Ithaca, N.Y.: Cornell University Press, 1995). – W. Mayer and P. Allen, *John Chrysostom* (Early Church Fathers; London and New York: Routledge, 2000).

*Collections of Essays: Chysostomika: Studi e ricerche intorno a S. Giovanni Crisostomo per il XV° centenario della sua morte, 407–1907* (Rome: Pustet, 1908). – P. C. Christou, ed., *Symposion: Studies on St. John Chrysostom* (ABla 18; Thessaloníki: Patriarchikon Hidryma Paterikōn Meletōn, 1973). – C. Kannengiesser, ed., *Jean Chrysostome et Augustin* (ThH 35; Paris: Beauchesne, 1975). – E. A. Clark, *Jerome, Chrysostom, and Friends: Essays and Translations* (New York: Mellen, 1979).

*Studies:* I. Auf der Maur, *Mönchtum und Glaubensverkündigung in den Schriften des hl. Johannes Chrysostomus* (Par. 14; Fribourg, Switz.: Universitäts Verlag, 1959). – P. Rentinck, *La cura pastorale in Antiochia nel IV secolo* (AnGr 178; Rome: Università Gregoriana Editrice, 1970). – R. Kaczynski, *Das Wort Gottes in Liturgie und Alltag der Gemeinden des Johannes Chrysostomus* (FThSt 94; Fribourg, Switz.: Herder, 1974). – J. H. W. G. Liebeschuetz, "The Fall of John Chrysostom," *NMS* 29 (1985): 1–31. – M. A. Schatkin, *John Chrysostom as Apologist: With Special Reference to De incomprehensibili, Quod nemo laeditur, Ad eos qui scandalizati sunt, and Adversus oppugnatores vitae monasticae* (ABla 50; Thessaloníki: Patriarchikon Hidryma Paterikōn Meletōn, 1987). – R. Delmaire, "Les 'lettres d'exil' de Jean Chrysostome: Études de chronologie et de prosopographie," *RechAug* 25 (1991): 71–180. – N. Adkin, "The Date of St John Chrysostom's Treatises on '*Subintroductae*,'" *RBén* 102 (1992): 255–66. – P. Allen, "John Chrysostom's Homilies on I and II Thessalonians: The Preacher and His Audience," in *Papers Presented at the Twelfth International Conference on Patristic Studies Held in Oxford, 1995* (ed. E. Livingstone; StPatr 31; Louvain: Peeters, 1997), 3–21. – W. Mayer, "John Chrysostom and His Audiences: Distinguishing Different Congregations at Antioch and Constantinople," in *Papers Presented at the Twelfth International Conference on Patristic Studies Held in Oxford, 1995* (ed. E. Livingstone; StPatr 31;

Louvain: Peeters, 1997), 70–75. – R. C. Hill, "The Spirituality of Chrysostom's Commentary on the Psalms," *JECS* 5 (1997): 568–79.

*Homilies:* M. von Bonsdorff, *Zur Predigttätigkeit des Johannes Chrysostomus: Biographisch-chronologische Studien über seine Homilienserien zu neutestamentlichen Büchern* (Helsingfors, Finland: Mercators Trickeri Aktiebolag, 1922). – W. Wenk, *Zur Sammlung der 38 Homilien des Chrysostomus Latinus: Mit Edition der Nr. 6, 8, 27, 32 und 33* (Wiener Studien: Beiheft 10; Vienna: Verlag der Österreichischen Akademie der Wissenschaften, 1988). – R. A. Krupp, *Shepherding the Flock: The Pastoral Theology of John Chrysostom* (New York: Lang, 1991). – M. Kertsch, *Exempla chrysostomica: Zu Exegese, Stil, und Bildersprache bei Johannes Chrysostomus* (GrTS 18; Graz: Eigenverlag des Instituts für Ökumenische Theologie und Patrologie an der Universität Graz, 1995).

*Status, Society, and Social Context:* A. J. Festugière, *Antioche païenne et chrétienne: Libanius, Chrysostome, et les moines de Syrie: Avec un commentaire archéologique sur l'Antiochikos (196 ss.) par R. Martin* (BEFAR 194; Paris: de Boccard, 1959). – S. Verosta, *Johannes Chrysostomus: Staatsphilosoph und Geschichtstheologe* (Graz: Styria, 1960). – O. Pasquato, *Gli spettacoli in S. Giovanni Crisostomo: Paganesimo e cristianesimo ad Antiochia e Costantinopoli nel IV secolo* (OrChrAn 201; Rome: Pontificium Institutum Orientalium Studiorum, 1976). – A. González Blanco, *Economía y sociedad en el bajo imperio según san Juan Crisóstomo* (Madrid: Fundación Universitaria Española, 1980). – R. L. Wilken, *John Chrysostom and the Jews: Rhetoric and Reality in the Late 4th Century* (Berkeley and London: University of California Press, 1983; repr., Eugene, Oreg.: Wipf & Stock, 2004). – G. Albert, *Goten in Konstantinopel: Untersuchungen zur oströmischen Geschichte um das Jahr 400 n. Chr.* (SGKA NF 1.2; Paderborn: F. Schöningh, 1984). – A. Stötzel, *Kirche als "neue Gesellschaft": Die humanisierende Wirkung des Christentums nach Johannes Chrysostomus* (MBTh 51; Münster: Aschendorff, 1984). – J. H. W. G. Liebeschuetz, *Barbarians and Bishops: Army, Church, and State in the Age of Arcadius and Chrysostom* (Oxford: Clarendon; New York: Oxford University Press, 1990). – B. Leyerle, "John Chrysostom on Almsgiving and the Use of Money," *HTR* 87 (1994): 29–47.

*Theology:* P. Stockmeier, *Theologie und Kult des Kreuzes bei Johannes Chrysostomus: Ein Beitrag zum Verständnis des Kreuzes im 4. Jahrhundert* (TThSt 18; Trier: Paulinus, 1966). – A. M. Ritter, *Charisma im Verständnis des Johannes Chrysostomos und seiner Zeit: Ein Beitrag zur Erforschung der griechisch-orientalischen Ekklesiologie in der Frühzeit der Reichskirche* (FKDG 25; Göttingen: Vandenhoeck & Ruprecht, 1972). – F.-X. Druet, *Langage, images, et visages de la mort chez Jean Chrysostome* (Namur: Société des Études Classiques; Presses Universitaires, 1990). – M. E. Lawrenz, *The Christology of John Chrysostom* (Lewiston, N.Y.: Mellen, 1997).

# A. De sacerdotio

The most widely known work of John, already available to Jerome in 392 (*Vir. ill.* 129), is his treatise on the priesthood, inspired by Gregory of Nazianzus's *Or. Bas.* 2. Sozomen, the church historian (*Hist. eccl.* 6.3), dates it to the time of John's diaconate (381–386), whereas others argue for the earlier period of his monastic seclusion; on the other hand, most recent editors (Nairn, Malingrey) move it into the time frame of 388–390.

The treatise is arranged in six books, in the form of a literary dialogue with a certain Basil whose identity and historicity cannot be determined. According to bk. 1, the immediate occasion for this work was the decision of the two friends John and Basil to do everything together in life. However, Basil accepted the episcopate with the assumption that John was going to do the same, but then John refused because of the great dignity and responsibility of the office. The dialogue escalates when Basil complains to John about his deceit, and John therefore has to substantiate and defend his behavior. Book 2 first addresses the extraordinary demonstration of Christ's love in the appointment, followed immediately by the difficulties and dangers of the priesthood and the office of the bishop. Though always with the aim of demonstrating that the responsibility of the office demands more than John's abilities are able to provide and of justifying his refusal, bks. 3–6 outline a superb picture of the priest's tasks and their correct administration: the protection of virgins and widows, practicing righteousness, proclamation of the word of God, defending the faith, and responsibility for others, including their errors. Whereas the monk needs only to take care of his own salvation, the priest, in his accountability for his community, requires a much greater measure of learning, zeal, strength, and virtue; for this reason, the punishment for his failure also surpasses the general measure.

*Editions: Sur le sacerdoce: Dialogue et homélie* (ed. A.-M. Malingrey; SC 272; Paris: Cerf, 1980).

*Translations: Six Books on the Priesthood* (trans. G. Neville; London: SPCK, 1964; rev. ed., Crestwood, N.Y.: St. Vladimir's Seminary Press, 1996).

*Reference Works:* A.-M. Malingrey, *Indices chrysostomici II* (AlOm.A 31.2; Hildesheim and New York: Olms, 1989).

*Studies:* W. A. Maat, *A Rhetorical Study of St. John Chrysostom's De sacerdotio* (PatSt 71; Washington, D.C.: Catholic University of America Press, 1944). – H. Dörries, "Erneuerung des kirchlichen Amts im vierten Jahrhundert: Die Schrift *De sacerdotio* des Johannes Chrysostomus und ihre Vorlage, die *Oratio de fuga sua* des Gregor von Nazianz," in *Bleibendes im Wandel der Kirchengeschichte: Kirchenhistorische Studien* (ed. B. Moeller and G. Ruhbach; Tübingen: Mohr, 1973), 1–46. – P. G. Alves de Sousa, *El sacerdocio ministerial en los libros De sacerdotio de san Juan Crisóstomo* (Pamplona: Ediciones Universidad de Navarra, 1975). – A. Houssiau and J.-P. Mondet, *Le sacerdote du Christ et de ses serviteurs selon les Pères de l'Église* (Louvain: Centre d'Histoire des Religions, 1990). – A. Monaci Castagno, "Paideia classica ed esercizio pastorale nel IV secolo," *RSLR* 26 (1990): 429–59. – R. Staats, "Chrysostomus über die Rhetorik des Apostels Paulus: Makarianische Kontexte zu '*De sacerdotio* IV,5–6,'" *VC* 46 (1992): 225–40. – M. Lochbrunner, *Über das Priestertum: Historische und systematische Untersuchung zum Priesterbild des Johannes Chrysostomus* (Hereditas 5; Bonn: Borengässer, 1993).

# B. Homilies on the Statues

At the end of February, that is, shortly before Lent 387, Emperor Theodosius levied a new tax that so aroused the people of Antioch that they got carried away demonstrating on the city streets and the statues of the emperor and his family in the forum were toppled. This constituted insurrection and lèse-majesté, which called for capital punishment. Tisamenus, the city prefect, therefore immediately ordered a number of arrests to be made, legal proceedings to be instituted, and executions to be carried out, and the whole city had to be prepared for the possibility of the most severe punishment, including its total destruction. In this situation of fear and wait-and-see uncertainty, Patriarch Flavian personally traveled to Constantinople to petition the emperor for a pardon, and John delivered twenty-two sermons during Lent, called *Ad populum antiochenum de statuis (On the Statues)*, which represent the apex of his rhetoric. Here he makes his hearers aware in vivid color that they are to be blamed for the current events in Antioch, but he also inimitably succeeds in offering consolation and hope arising from the faith and the expectation of Easter. Regardless of the kind of punishment the emperor metes out, eternal life depends only on a change of heart and on irreproachable conduct, for which John provides concrete instructions in his sermons. The final message on Easter Sunday (April 25) concluded the sermon series with indescribable jubilation, for Flavian returned from Constantinople with the message that the city had been pardoned.

In his edition of 1718–1738, Bernard de Montfaucon extrapolated the twenty-first homily as a separate baptismal catechesis and published it. Migne printed them in the same way, so that there have been only twenty-one homilies since then. In 1909, however, Athanasios Papadopoulos-Kerameus for the first time proposed the reintegration of this homily in its original place; in recent years the publishers of the baptismal catecheses have justified and supported this move with further arguments.

*Editions:* PG 49: 15–222, 231–40.

*Translations:* W. R. W. Stephens, T. P. Brandram, and R. Blackburn, trans., "Twenty-One Homilies on the Statues," in *NPNF[1]* (Peabody, Mass.: Hendrickson, 1995; repr. of 1889 ed.), 9:315–489.

*Studies:* M. A. Burns, *Saint John Chrysostom's Homilies on the Statues: A Study of Their Rhetorical Qualities and Form* (PatSt 22; Washington, D.C.: Catholic University of America Press, 1930). – M. Soffray, *Recherches sur la syntaxe de saint Jean Chrysostome d'après les "Homélies sur les statues"* (Paris: Belles Lettres, 1939). – D. G. Hunter, "Preaching and Propaganda in Fourth Century Antioch: John Chrysostom's *Homilies on the Statues*," in idem, ed., *Preaching in the Patristic Age: Studies in Honor of Walter J. Burghardt, S.J.* (New York: Paulist, 1989), 119–38. – F. van de Paverd, *St. John Chrysostom, the Homilies on the Statues: An Introduction* (OrChrAn 239; Rome: Pontificium Institutum Studiorum Orientalium, 1991).

# C. Baptismal Catecheses

As already mentioned in conjunction with the catechetical homilies of Theodore of Mopsuestia, in Antioch it was customary that the priests—and not the bishop—prepared the baptismal candidates. The eleven famous *Catechesis ultima ad baptizandos* of John, most of which were discovered in the twentieth century (1909/1957), also originated during his time in Antioch. They form two series of three (Piédagnel/Doutreleau) or four (Papadopoulos-Kerameus, Kaczynski) catecheses from 388 and eight (Wenger) or seven (Kaczynski) from one of the years between 389 and 397. The reason for the different arrangement is that one homily is found in the manuscripts of both series, while only the unity of the first three homilies in the first series is undeniably clear. John delivered the four catecheses of the first series thirty and twenty days before Easter, on Wednesday of Holy Week exclusively for the baptismal candidates, and on Easter eve for the entire community together with the newly baptized. The seven catecheses of the second series were delivered at the beginning and toward the end of Lent, on Easter eve, and four of them during the week of Easter. In his edition (1992), Reiner Kaczynski additionally includes the twenty-first homily on the statues— which John delivered on Wednesday of Holy Week (April 21), 387, and which consequently was also addressed to the baptismal candidates—as "Catechesis 1." Whether this arrangement will be successful remains to be seen, of course, for precisely its reintegration into *On the Statues* militates against a special role such as this; otherwise it would be necessary to extrapolate a range of other sermons by John from Lent and Easter and treat them as baptismal catecheses as well.

During preparation of the baptismal candidates, John first expresses his joy over their decision to receive baptism not only on their deathbed (in view of the widespread fourth-century custom to delay baptism). He interprets baptism as rebirth, enlightenment, death, and resurrection with Christ, as being a spiritual bride and essential forgiveness of all sins. Although a second repentance is possible, it is difficult and hopefully not necessary. Before and after baptism, it is important to be victorious in the struggle with evil by means of discipline and moderation, especially in the consumption of alcohol. Several times John warns against swearing, which indicates that this apparently had been a common problem in his community or in the city. He explains the meaning of baptism on Easter eve, of the baptismal rites (exorcisms, chrisms, washings, white garment), and the baptismal *symbolum,* with special emphasis on the correct belief in the Trinity and in Christ over against erroneous Arian and Sabellian interpretations. After baptism John teaches the meaning of the Eucharist and admonishes them to maintain the baptismal grace; in *Catechesis* 2.5, however, he laments already during the week of Easter that the newly baptized, together with many of the other members of the community, preferred the horse races and theater presentations to attending the worship service. Finally, *Catechesis* 2.6 and 2.7 present the martyrs and Abraham as shining examples of, and aids to, faith and the Christian life.

*Editions: Huit catéchèses baptismales inédites* (ed. A. Wenger; 2d ed.; SC 50; Paris: Cerf, 1970) [Com]. – *Trois catéchèses baptismales* (ed. A. Piédagnel and L. Doutreleau; SC 366; Paris: Cerf, 1990).

*Translations: Baptismal Instructions* (trans. P. W. Harkins; ACW 31; Westminster, Md.: Newman, 1963).

*Studies:* J. A. Weaver, *Catechetical Themes in the Post-baptismal Teaching of St. John Chrysostom* (SST 159; Ann Arbor: University Microfilms, 1964). – T. M. Finn, *The Liturgy of Baptism in the Baptismal Instructions of St. John Chrysostom* (SCA 15; Washington, D.C.: Catholic University of America Press, 1967). – H. M. Riley, *Christian Initiation: A Comparative Study of the Interpretation of the Baptismal Liturgy in the Mystagogical Writings of Cyril of Jerusalem, John Chrysostom, Theodore of Mopsuestia, and Ambrose of Milan* (SCA 17; Washington, D.C.: Catholic University of America Press, 1974). – D. Sartore, "Il mistero del battesimo nelle catechesi di S. Giovanni Crisostomo," *Lat.* 50 (1985): 358–95. – P. Devos, "Saint Jean Chrysostome à Antioche dans quatre homélies baptismales (dont *BHG* 1930 w)," *AnBoll* 109 (1991): 137–56. – J.-P. Cattenoz, *Le baptême mystère nuptial: Théologie de saint Jean Chrysostome* (Venasque: Carmel, 1993). – J. Knupp, *Das Mystagogieverständnis des Johannes Chrysostomus* (Munich: Don Bosco, 1995).

# VII. RUFINUS OF CONCORDIA (AQUILEIA)

Epiphanius of Constantia (Salamis), John Chrysostom, and Jerome had been associated with the dispute about Origen and his theology in various ways at the end of the fourth and in the early fifth centuries. Origen supplies Tyrannius Rufinus, however, with his primary significance for the history of literature, since most of Origen's extensive work is available only in the form of Rufinus's translation.

He was born ca. 345 in Concordia, west of Aquileia, the metropolis of northern Italy. Between ca. 358 and 368, together with Jerome, he received the customary grammatical and rhetorical education of his time in Rome. This leads to the conclusion that his family was quite prosperous and must have belonged to the upper class. Upon his return to Aquileia, he joined a local monastic community and received baptism in 371/372, when he was not quite thirty years old. A little later he went to Egypt, to the cradle of monasticism, where he remained for eight years (373–380); visited the desert monasteries; met Melania, the ascetic elder in Alexandria; heard especially Didymus the Blind, among others; and became acquainted with Origen's theology. In 381 he founded a monastery for monks at the Mount of Olives near Jerusalem, in close proximity to the convent established by Melania a few years earlier (374 to 378?),[8] and lived there for sixteen years in close contact with the bishops of Jerusalem. Bishop John ordained him to the priesthood between 390 and 394. When the dispute about Origen erupted in 393, he defended Origen in support of John and thereby evoked the opposition of Epiphanius and Jerome, his old friend, who had lived in Bethlehem since 386. Although the two were publicly reconciled at Easter 397, it would not be long before the Origenist controversy burst open between them once again.

In 397 Rufinus returned to Rome and, in keeping with Basil's rule, translated the apologia for Origen by Pamphilus and Eusebius into Latin, together with his own, fully orthodox *professio fidei* as a prologue and the treatise *De*

---

[8] Cf. N. Moine, "Mélanie l'Ancienne," *DSp* 10:958.

*adulteratione librorum Origenis* as epilogue. In this he took the point of view that Origen had been an orthodox teacher of the church and that the references in his writings contradicting this were falsifications of later interpolations. In the following year (398), he translated Origen's *De principiis* into Latin by smoothing out offensive references in an orthodox way and thereby joined ranks with Jerome's translations of Origen. Jerome did not take kindly to this implied pro-Origenist position and in 399 sent his own very literal and correct Latin version to Rome, accompanied by a very polemical letter (*Epist.* 84). Rufinus, who meanwhile was residing in Aquileia, defended himself (late 400) by means of his *Apologia ad Anastasium papam,* an apologia to Bishop Anastasius of Rome, which in the spring of 401 was followed by the *Apologia adversus Hieronymum* in two books. After Jerome's biting response in his *Adversus Rufinum* (401/402), Rufinus chose not to react further.

The following years, until his death,[9] he used for further translations, most important among them being further works of Origen (homilies on Joshua [in 400]; Judges and Psalms 36–38 [400 or 401]; Genesis, Exodus, and Leviticus [403–404]; the commentaries on Romans [405–406] and the Song of Songs; as well as homilies on Numbers [410]) and Eusebius's *Ecclesiastical History,* which he extended up to the end of Theodosius's reign. Rufinus's literary-critical acumen seems to lack sharpness, for he also translated the dialogue of Adamantius as the work of Origen (398/399 or ca. 400); the sayings of Sextus, the Pythagorean, by assuming the authorship of Pope Sixtus II (before 401); and the *Pseudo-Clementines* as the work of Pope Clement (406 or 407). Before the Goths' invasion of Italy, Rufinus initially fled to Rome (there are indications that he was there in 406; Hammond Bammel suggests he was there from 403 on) and then to a monastery near Terracina, where he wrote his own most important work, *De benedictionibus patriarcharum,* during Lent of 408. After the conquest of Rome in 410, he continued on to Sicily, where he died in Messina between October 411 and spring 412.

In his translation work, Rufinus did not pursue the philosophical goal of producing a literal transmission but aspired to provide his contemporaries with what was needed to manage the problems of their present, by means of the Greek cultural and theological heritage, which was being passed on less and less because of dwindling conversance with the language. This has to be taken into consideration especially in the case of the translations of Origen's works, where he himself admits and justifies his changes. The parallel translations by Jerome are lost and thus cannot be adduced as corrective. But since many of the works Rufinus translated are lost in their original form because of the dispute about Origenism and the perils of the history of transmission, he became their outstanding witness; in the case of Origen—despite all of the reservations—he even represents the main witness of his theology.

---

[9] The study by C. P. Hammond Bammel ("The Last Ten Years of Rufinus' Life and the Date of His Move South from Aquileia," *JThS* NS 28 [1977]: 372–429) demonstrates ably that the dates of the last ten years of Rufinus's life cannot claim absolute certainty.

*Bibliographies:* H. R. Drobner, *BBKL* 8:959–72.

*Editions: Opera omnia: Tyrannii Rufuni Opera* (ed. M. Simonetti; CCSL 20; Turnhout, Belg.: Brepols, 1961). – *De benedictionibus patriarcharum: Les Bénédictions des patriarches [par] Rufin d'Aquilée* (ed. M. Simonetti, H. Rochais, and P. Antin; SC 140; Paris: Cerf, 1968) [Com]. – *De ieiunio I, II: Zwei Predigten über das Fasten (ed. H. Marti; SVigChr 6; Leiden and New York: Brill, 1989) [Com]. – Historia ecclesiastica,* vol. 2/2 of *Eusebius Werke;* ed. T. Mommsen; GCS; Leipzig: Hinrichs, 1908), 951–1040. – *In Psalmos: Il salterio di Rufino* (ed. F. Merlo and J. Gribomont; CBLa 14; Vatican City: Libreria Vaticana, 1972) [Com]. – C. Lo Cicero, *Versione delle omelie di Basilio (I–III)* (Rome: Universita degli Studi di Roma "La Sapienza," 1996). – *Omelie di Basilio di Cesarea tradotte in Latino* (ed. A. Salvini; Naples: D'Auria, 1998).

*Translations:* W. H. Fremantle, trans., "Works of Rufinus," in *NPNF*[2] (Peabody, Mass.: Hendrickson, 1995; repr. of 1892 ed.), 3:403–82, 541–68 [*Opera omnia*]. – *A Commentary on the Apostles' Creed* (trans. J. N. D. Kelly; ACW 20; Westminster, Md.: Newman, 1955). – *The Church History of Rufinus of Aquileia, Books 10 and 11* (trans. P. R. Amidon; New York: Oxford University Press, 1997).

*Encyclopedia Articles:* F. Thelamon, *DSp* 13:1107–17. – J. Gribomont, *EECh* 2:746. – N. Henry, *TRE* 29:460–64. – M. McHugh, *EEC* 2:1002–3.

*Introductions and Surveys:* F. X. Murphy, *Rufinus of Aquileia (345–411): His Life and Works* (SMH NS 6; Washington, D.C.: Catholic University of America Press, 1945). – G. Fedalto, *Rufino di Concordia (345 c.–410/11) tra Oriente ed Occidente* (Rome: Città Nuova, 1990).

*Collections of Essays: Rufino di Concordia e il suo tempo* (2 vols.; AnAl 31; Udine: Arti Grafiche Friulane, 1987). – *Storia ed esegesi in Rufino di Concordia* (AnAL 39; Udine: Arti Grafiche Friulane, 1992).

*Studies:* M. M. Wagner, *Rufinus the Translator: A Study of His Theory and His Practice as Illustrated in His Version of the Apologetica of St. Gregory Nazianzen* (PatSt 73; Washington, D.C.: Catholic University of America Press, 1945). – C. P. Hammond Bammel, "The Last Ten Years of Rufinus' Life and the Date of His Move South from Aquileia," *JTS* NS 28 (1977): 372–429; repr. in idem, *Origeniana et Rufiniana* (VL 29; Fribourg, Switz.: Herder, 1996), IV. – F. Thelamon, *Païens et chrétiens au IVe siècle: L'apport de l'"Histoire ecclésiastique" de Rufin d'Aquilée* (Paris: Études Augustiniennes, 1981). – C. P. Hammond Bammel, *Der Römerbrieftext des Rufin und seine Origenes-Übersetzung* (AGLB 10; Fribourg, Switz.: Herder, 1985). – T. Christensen, *Rufinus of Aquileia and the Historia ecclesiastica, Lib. VIII–IX, of Eusebius* (Copenhagen: Kongelige Danske Videnskabernes Selskab 1989). – N. Pace, *Ricerche sulla traduzione di Rufino del "De principiis" di Origene* (Florence: Nuova Italia, 1990). – É. Junod, "L'auteur de l'*Apologie pour Origène* traduite par Rufin: Les témoignages contradictoires de Rufin et de Jérôme à propos de Pamphile et d'Eusèbe," in *Recherches et tradition: Mélanges patristiques offerts a Henri Crouzel* (ed. A. Dupleix; ThH 88; Paris: Beauchesne, 1992), 165–79. – C. Molè Ventura, *Principi fanciulli: Legittimismo costituzionale e storiografia cristiana nella tarda antichità* (Catania: Prisma, 1992).

# VIII. JEROME

The other great translator of the Latin church, indeed the most important one, was Rufinus's fellow student and later opponent in the dispute about Origen, namely, Sophronius Eusebius Hieronymus (Jerome). For many years both men led a very similar life and at times a shared one. Although Jerome speaks about himself more often than many others in his works, many dates concerning his life and works remain uncertain. On the issue of dating Jerome, therefore, it is always prudent to compare at least the three most recent studies: Jean Gribomont,[10] Pierre Nautin,[11] and Harald Hagendahl and Jan Hendrik Waszink.[12]

Like Rufinus, Jerome was born into a prosperous Christian family of estate owners in Stridon, near Emona (Ljubljana, Slovenia; the exact location of Stridon is unknown). In 360 Jerome went to Rome to study grammar and rhetoric, where he became friends with Rufinus and the famous grammarian Aelius Donatus was his teacher. During his studies he acquired a respectable collection of Latin classics, as well as an extraordinary knowledge of the Latin language and literature, which was to shape him and his writings for life, even if he later felt that "Ciceronianism" and Christianity were incompatible. He personally provides a detail that sheds significant light on his lifestyle at this time, although he was not baptized yet: "While I lived in Rome as a youngster and was being trained in the liberal arts, together with others of my age and who shared a common purpose, I used to visit the tombs of the apostles and martyrs on Sundays, and to enter the crypts[13] frequently, where on either side of the visitors bodies were buried in the walls, dug deep into the earth" (*Commentariorum in Ezechielem libri XVI* 12.50.5, 13.243–254).

Together with Rufinus, he became acquainted with the monastic circles of Rome and felt enthusiastic about the ideals of monastic life. Whereas Rufinus put them into practice immediately upon his return to Aquileia, Jerome, after being baptized while still in Rome, initially seems to have aspired to a career in public service (367/368) in Trier, the imperial residence of Gaul. In his *Confessiones* (8.6.15), Augustine tells of two imperial commissioners at Trier who, while wandering about, came upon a house in which some monks lived. Here they found the *Vita* of Anthony, the Egyptian father of monasticism (which Athanasius wrote [ca. 357/358] shortly after the death of the latter in 355/356 and Evagrius of Antioch translated into Latin before 375), were spontaneously gripped by it and relinquished their court appointments. Even if one does not agree with Pierre Courcelle, who identifies the two as Jerome and Bonosus,[14] the scene does describe the atmosphere in which Jerome soon (ca. 370) decided to end his secular career and lead a life of asceticism and scholarly leisure in his hometown and in the community of his friend Rufinus at Aquileia. This is perhaps comparable to the somewhat later circles around Augustine at Cassiciacum and Tagaste.

---

[10] J. Quasten, *Patrology* (4 vols.; Westminster, Md.: Christian Classics, 1984–1988), 4:212–18, and J. Gribomont, *EECh* 1:430f.

[11] P. Nautin, *TRE* 15:304–15.

[12] H. Hagendahl and J. H. Waszink, *RAC* 15:117–39.

[13] In antiquity, *crypta* denoted the galleries of the catacombs, as this text clearly shows.

[14] P. Courcelle, *Recherches sur les Confessions de saint Augustin* (Paris: E. de Boccard, 1950), 181–87.

The community at Aquileia disbanded, and both Jerome and Rufinus moved to the Eastern sources of monasticism. Whereas Rufinus (373) went to Egypt, Jerome (371?) went to Antioch via Constantinople. There he was received by Evagrius, the later bishop of the original Nicene community of Antioch. He spent some time as a hermit in the desert near Chalcis[15] in eastern Syria but then returned to Antioch. This period in Antioch, until ca. 379/380, decisively determined the course of his life. He acquired good language skills in Greek and Hebrew, which were foundational for his later translation work. He began to read the Bible intensively, which at an earlier time had turned him off, similarly to Augustine, because of its unpolished style, and he listened to the exegetical presentations (377?) of Apollinaris of Laodicea, which became the foundation of his later work in the biblical text and its interpretation. His about-face from his enthusiasm for, if not obsession with, classical literature to Scripture took place in a major life crisis, as he recounts through his famous dream. He dreamed he was standing in judgment before God and heard God's verdict: "You are a Ciceronian, not a Christian; where your treasure is, there your heart is as well (Matt 6:21)" (*Epist.* 22.30). Nevertheless, as an analysis of his works demonstrates, the classics never lost their influence upon Jerome, even if they receded into the background over against Christianity.

Probably in the library Eustathius left behind, Jerome studied the writings of Origen, whose works he was to translate into Latin. Like his host, Evagrius, he joined the old Nicene community and was ordained to the priesthood by Paulinus under the condition that he would not have to relinquish his monastic life, and he began with his literary activity. It is certain that he wrote the first monastic legend of Christian literature during this time, the *Vita* of Paul, the Egyptian hermit, and (according to Nautin) may also have made the earliest translations of Origen's works (homilies on Isaiah, Jeremiah, and Ezekiel). Other scholars, however, date these earliest translations only to the following period in Constantinople, prompted by Gregory of Nazianzus. Together with Bishop Paulinus, he traveled to Constantinople in 379 or 380; there Paulinus wanted to secure his recognition as the legitimate bishop of Antioch from Theodosius, the new Nicene emperor. Although this attempt came to naught because the emperor and the council (381) recognized Meletius, Jerome at this time established contact with the Cappadocians Gregory of Nazianzus, the patriarch of Constantinople, and Gregory of Nyssa, as well as with Amphilochius of Iconium, and began or resumed his translation work. In any case, it was in Constantinople that he undertook the translation and extension of Eusebius's *Chronicle* up to 378, whose influence continued well into the medieval period.

When Gregory of Nazianzus declined the see of Constantinople, Paulinus and Jerome returned to Antioch, though without giving up on their efforts for recognition of the old Nicene community. In the spring of 382, they, together

---

[15] Nautin questions the historicity of the pertinent letters of Jerome and merely recognizes a stay at the periphery of the desert in Maronia, thirty-one miles east of Antioch, in 378/379.

with Epiphanius of Constantia (Salamis), traveled to Rome, with Jerome functioning as the translator. Although a synod meeting in Rome in 382, in which Ambrose of Milan also took part, recognized Paulinus as the only legitimate bishop of Antioch, its decision had no effect in the East. Epiphanius and Jerome stayed with Paula and Marcella, both widows, and Paula's daughter Eustochium, who turned their houses into monasteries, like the mother and the sister of Basil and Gregory of Nyssa, the great Cappadocians. For Jerome, this meant a return to the ascetical circles with which he had already established contact during his studies, as well as the continuation of his own pursuits. These widows were distinguished, wealthy, and educated individuals; Marcella even learned Hebrew in order to be able to study the Bible in the original. When Paulinus and Epiphanius returned eastward in the summer of 383, Jerome, as he himself recounts, remained in Rome as the secretary of Bishop Damasus (*Epist.* 123.9). Nautin questions the accuracy of this information; but on this basis a twelfth-century *Vita* describes Jerome as a cardinal, and later iconography enjoyed presenting him as such.

After the death of Damasus, his benefactor and protector, on December 11, 384, Jerome had hopes of becoming his successor (*Epist.* 45.3). Instead Siricius was chosen, for Jerome had created many enemies in the city because of his ascetical zeal by ruthlessly and fiercely denouncing spiritual and moral abuses. "Jerome was a born satirist by nature; as far as wit, confident observation, and literary elegance, but also viciousness and nastiness, are concerned, he had no equal in his quarrelsome century."[16] Here Jerome's character traits became prominent for the first time, and in the context of the later controversies with Rufinus, Augustine, and others, they became even more pronounced: his attacks were fierce, but he himself was sensitive and easily hurt. In Rome he was treated with such hostility that he had to leave the city; he was even suspected of improper relations with women of his ascetical circles. In August 385 he went by boat from Ostia to Jerusalem; Paula and her daughter Eustochium followed him together with other companions and met him in Reggio di Calabria. From there they traveled via Cyprus and Antioch to Jerusalem, where they arrived in late 385, but they soon left the city again en route to Egypt in order to visit the local monastic settlements and Didymus, the great expert on Origen in Alexandria. In the spring of 386, they returned to Palestine, settled in Bethlehem, and founded a monastery and three convents.

In the following years, Jerome made ample use of the libraries of Origen and Eusebius in Palestinian Caesarea and devoted himself to intensive literary work. Among other things, Jerome produced translations of the Bible, commentaries on Philemon, Galatians, Ephesians, and Titus, and on Ecclesiastes, Micah, Zephaniah, Nahum, Habakkuk, Haggai, Jonah, and Obadaiah, and translations of Didymus's *De Spiritu Sancto*, Origen's homilies on Luke, and the catalogue of Christian writers *De viris illustribus*. In September 393, after the feast of the dedication of a church in Jerusalem, Jerome saw himself embroiled in the dispute

---

[16] H. Hagendahl: *Gn* 40 (1968), 582.

between Epiphanius of Constantia (Salamis) and John of Jerusalem over the theology of Origen. He threw in his lot with Epiphanius, with whom he had already been close for years, whereas his friend Rufinus sided with John. This was not only the beginning of a polemic that would last for years, but Jerome also became involved in a difficult situation ecclesiastically. Without the permission of John, in whose jurisdiction was the monastery at Bethlehem, Jerome's brother had been ordained a deacon by Epiphanius; as a result, John excommunicated the monastery. Jerome defended himself in his work *Adversus Joannem Hierosolymitanum* and sought the support of Theophilus of Alexandria. After multilateral efforts, John finally reconciled Jerome on Maundy Thursday 397, and at the same time Jerome was reconciled with Rufinus once again. It cannot be determined whether the polarization in the dispute about Origen fundamentally changed Jerome's view of Origen. He valued and translated his works before and afterward. The fact that he took sides with Epiphanius in the dispute may initially have been a personal matter, and the polemic against Rufinus was not primarily concerned with Origen's theology, but with the correctness of the translation of *De principiis*, which ignited the further controversy beginning with 397 (cf. VII).

Jerome's relations with other great bishops of his time were subject to tension as well. Since Ambrose in his work *De Spiritu Sancto* drew from Didymus's writing of the same title and in his commentary on Luke drew from Origen's homilies, Jerome translated both works into Latin in order to expose these plagiarisms. Whether indeed his motive was one of vindictiveness, because Ambrose had not supported him and Paulinus at the synod of Rome in 382, can hardly be determined with certainty. The correspondence with Augustine between 400 and 404 became difficult, and during the dispute about Origen between Theophilus and John Chrysostom, he translated letters into Latin for Theophilus (cf. VIII.C).

The years of 403–405 represent a break in Jerome's life; during this time he was not engaged in the literary enterprise because Paula died on January 26, 404, after a lengthy illness. Subsequently he resumed writing commentaries on Zachariah, Malachi, Hosea, Joel, and Amos (406), Daniel (407), Isaiah (408/409), Ezekiel (411–414 or 412–415), and Jeremiah (beginning in 415). The conquest of Rome by Alaric on August 24, 410, and the resultant stream of refugees to Palestine forced another break in his work. In the winter of 415/416 he wrote *Adversus Pelagianos*, against the Pelagians who had been granted shelter with John of Jerusalem.

Jerome died on September 30, 419 or 420. The Western church has venerated him since 1295, together with Ambrose, Augustine, and Gregory the Great, as one of the four "great doctors of the West." Iconography likes to present him as "Jerome in the box" and with a lion at his feet (most popular is the copperplate engraving by Albrecht Dürer). The former refers to his studies in his monastic life; the latter, to the legend of the lion from the paw of which he extracted a thorn and that afterward remained with Jerome out of gratitude, found first in a *Vita* of the ninth century. This represents a travel legend that at a later date is also attributed, for instance, to Henry the Lion (1142–1180), the duke of Saxony and Bavaria.

The famous *Martyrologium hieronymianum*, an important universal index of martyrs and saints for each day of the year, is not Jerome's work; it was compiled from three earlier martyrologies or calendars in northern Italy (around Aquileia?) between 431 and 450.

*Bibliographies: Opera exegetica* (ed. P. Antin; CCSL 72; Turnhout, Belg.: Brepols, 1959), IX–LII. – M. Tilly, *BBKL* 2:818–21.

*Editions:*
*Opera omnia:* PL 22–30. – PLS 2:18–328.
*Adversus Pelagianos: Dialogus adversus Pelagianos* (ed. C. Moreschini; CCSL 80; Turnhout, Belg.: Brepols, 1990).
*Chronicle: Die Chronik des Hieronymus* (vol. 7 of *Eusebius Werke;* ed. R. Helm; 2d ed.; GCS; Berlin: Akademie, 1956).
*Contra Johannem* (ed. J.-L. Feiertag; CCSL 79 A; Turnhout, Belg.: Brepols, 1999).
*Contra Rufinum: Contra Rufinum* (ed. P. Lardet; CCSL 79; Turnhout, Belg.: Brepols, 1982). – *Apologie contre Rufin* (ed. P. Lardet; SC 303; Paris: Cerf, 1983).
*Homiliae: Opera homiletica* (ed. G. Morin; CCSL 78; Turnhout, Belg.: Brepols, 1958).
*In Danielem: Commentariorum in Danielem libri III (IV)* (ed. F. Glorie; CCSL 75A; Turnhout, Belg.: Brepols, 1964).
*In Ezechielem: Commentariorum in Hiezechielem libri XIV* (ed. F. Glorie; CCSL 75; Turnhout, Belg.: Brepols, 1964).
*In Hieremiam: Sancti Evsebii Hieronymi In Hieremiam prophetam libri sex* (ed. S. Reiter; CSEL 59; Vienna: F. Tempsky, 1913). – *In Hieremiam libri VI* (ed. S. Reiter; CCSL 74; Turnhout, Belg.: Brepols, 1960).
*In Isaiam: Commentariorum in Esaiam* (ed. M. Adriaen; 2 vols.; CCSL 73, 73A; Turnhout, Belg.: Brepols, 1963). – *Commentaires de Jerome sur le prophete Isaie* (ed. R. Gryson et al.; 5 vols.; VL 23, 27, 30, 35, 36; Fribourg, Switz.: Herder, 1993–1999).
*In Jonam: Commentaire sur Jonas* (ed. Y.-M. Duval; SC 323; Paris: Cerf, 1985).
*In Matthaeum: Commentariorum in Matheum libri IV* (ed. D. Hurst and M. Adriaen; CCSL 77; Turnhout, Belg.: Brepols, 1969). – *Commentaire sur s. Matthieu* (ed. É. Bonnard; 2 vols.; SC 242, 259; Paris: Cerf, 1977–1979).
*In prophetas minores: Commentarii in prophetas minores* (ed. M. Adriaen; 2 vols.; CCSL 76, 76A; Turnhout, Belg.: Brepols, 1969–1970).
*In Psalmos: Sancti Hieronymi Psalterium iuxta Hebraeos* (ed. H. de Sainte-Marie; CBLa 11; Rome: Abbaye Saint-Jérome, 1954).
*Quaestiones in Genesim, Hebraica nomina, In Psalmos, In Ecclesiasten: Hebraicae quaestiones in libro Geneseos, Liber interpretationis hebraicorum nominum, Commentarioli in Psalmos, Commentarius in Ecclesiasten* (ed. P. de Lagarde, G. Morin, and M. Adriaen; CCSL 72; Turnhout, Belg.: Brepols, 1959).
*Vita S. Hilarionis eremitae, Epitaphium Sanctae Paulae: Vita di Martino [Sulpicio Severo], Vita di Ilarione [Girolamo], In memoria di Paola [Girolamo]* (ed. C. Mohrmann, A. A. R. Bastiaensen, J. W. Smit, L. Canali, and C. Moreschini; ViSa 4; Milan: Fondazione Lorenzo Valla, 1975), 69–237, 291–369 [Com].
*Vita Pauli eremitae: Edizione critica della "Vita Sancti Pauli primi eremitae"* (ed. R. Degòrski; Rome: Typis Pontificiae Universitatis Gregorianae, 1987). – G. Brugnoli, *Curiosissimus excerptor: Gli "Additamenta" di Girolamo ai "Chronica" di Eusebio* (Pisa: ETS, 1995) [Com].

*Translations:* W. H. Fremantle, trans., "Jerome's Apology in Answer to Rufinus," *NPNF²* (Peabody, Mass.: Hendrickson, 1995; repr. of 1892 ed.), 3:482–540. – W. H. Fremantle, G. Lewis, and W. G. Martley, trans., *Jerome: Letters and Select Works* (vol. 6 of *NPNF²;* Peabody, Mass.: Hendrickson, 1995; repr. of 1892 ed.) [*Letters, Life of Paul the First Hermit, Life of St. Hilarion, Life of Malchus the Captive Monk, Against the Luciferians,*

*Against Helvidius, Against Jovinianus, Against Vigilantius, Letter to Pammachius against John of Jerusalem, Against the Pelagians*]. – *The Homilies of Saint Jerome* (trans. M. L. Ewald; 2 vols.; FC 48, 57; Washington, D.C.: Catholic University of America Press, 1964–1966) [*On the Psalms, On St. Mark, Various*]. – *Early Christian Biographies* (trans. R. J. Defarrari et al.; FC 15; New York: Fathers of the Church, 1952), 217–97 [*Life of St. Paul, the First Hermit; Life of Hilarion; Life of Malchus, the Captive Monk*]. – *Dogmatic and Polemical Works* (trans. J. N. Hritzu; FC 53; Washington, D.C.: Catholic University of America Press, 1965) [*On the Perpetual Virginity of the Blessed Mary against Helvidius, The Apology against the Books of Rufinus, The Dialogue against the Pelagians*]. – *Saint Jerome's Hebrew Questions on Genesis* (trans. C. T. R. Hayward; OECS; Oxford: Clarendon; New York: Oxford University Press, 1995). – M. D. Donalson, *A Translation of Jerome's Chronicon with Historical Commentary* (New York: Mellen, 1996). – C. White, *Early Christian Lives* (London and New York: Penguin, 1998), 73–128 [*Life of Paul of Thebes, Life of Hilarion, Life of Malchus*].

*Reference Works:* S. *Hieronymi Presbyteri Opera* (ed. E. Gouder and P. Tombeur; CETEDOC; CChr.ILL 79 A–B; Turnhout, Belg.: Brepols, 1982–1986) [microfiches]. – *Thesaurus Sancti Hieronymi: Series A–Index formarum singulorum operum, Index formarum secundum orthographiae normam collatarum, Tabula frequentiarum, Concordantia formarum* (Turnhout, Belg.: Brepols, 1990) [microfiches].

*Encyclopedia Articles:* P. Nautin, *TRE* 15:304–15. – H. Hagendahl and J. H. Waszink, *RAC* 15:117–39. – J. Gribomont, *EECh* 1:430–31. – R. Aubert, "Jérôme," *DHGE* 27 fasc. 159–60: 1021–27. – M. P. McHugh, *EEC* 1:606–9.

*General Studies:* G. Grützmacher, *Hieronymus: Eine biographische Studie zur alten Kirchengeschichte* (3 vols.; SGTK 6.3.10.1–2; Leipzig: Dieterich, 1901–1908; repr., Aalen: Scienta, 1969). – F. Cavallera, *Saint Jérôme, sa vie et son œuvre* (2 vols.; SSL 1–2; Louvain: "Spicilegium Sacrum Lovaniense," 1922). – P. Antin, *Essai sur saint Jérôme* (Paris: Letouzey & Ané, 1951). – F. X. Murphy, *A Monument to Saint Jerome: Essays on Some Aspects of His Life, Works, and Influence* (New York: Sheed & Ward, 1952). – J. Steinmann, *Saint Jérôme* (Paris: Cerf, 1958; repr., 1985). – P. Antin, *Recueil sur saint Jérôme* (CollLat 95; Brussels: Latomus, 1968). – M. Testard, *Saint Jérôme: L'apôtre savant et pauvre du patriciat romain* (Paris: Belles Lettres, 1969). – J. N. D. Kelly, *Jerome: His Life, Writings, and Controversies* (London: Duckworth; New York: Harper & Row, 1975; repr., Peabody, Mass.: Hendrickson, 1998).

*Collections of Essays:* E. A. Clark, *Jerome, Chrysostom, and Friends: Essays and Translations* (New York: Mellen, 1979). – Y.-M. Duval, ed., *Jérôme entre l'Occident et l'Orient: XVIe centenaire du départ de saint Jérôme de Rome et son installation à Bethléem* (Paris: Études Augustiniennes, 1988). – C. Moreschini and G. Menestrina, eds., *Motivi letterari ed esegetici in Gerolamo: Atti del convento tenuto a Trento il 5–7 dicembre 1995* (Brescia: Morcelliana, 1997).

*Bible and Exegesis:* A. Souter, *The Earliest Latin Commentaries on the Epistles of St. Paul* (Oxford: Clarendon, 1927), 96–138. – W. Hagemann, *Wort als Begegnung mit Christus: Die christozentrische Schriftauslegung des Kirchenvaters Hieronymus* (TThSt 23; Trier: Paulinus, 1970). – Y.-M. Duval, *Le livre de Jonas dans la littérature chrétienne grecque et latine: Sources et influence du Commentaire sur Jonas de saint Jérôme* (2 vols.; Paris: Études Augustiniennes, 1973). – J. Braverman, *Jerome's Commentary on Daniel: A Study of Comparative Jewish and Christian Interpretations of the Hebrew Bible* (CBQMS 7; Washington, D.C.: Catholic Biblical Association of America Press, 1978). – V. Peri, *Omelie origeniane sui Salmi: Contributo all'identificazione del testo latino* (StT 289; Vatican City: Biblioteca Apostolica Vaticana, 1980). – C. Estin, *Les psautiers de Jérôme à la lumière des traductions juives antérieures* (CBLa 15; Rome: San Girolamo, 1984). – P. Jay, *L'exégèse de saint Jérôme d'après son "Commentaire sur Isaïe"* (Paris: Études

Augustiniennes, 1985). – E. A. Clark, "The Place of Jerome's Commentary on Ephesians in the Origenist Controversy: The Apokatastasis and Ascetic Ideals," *VC* 41 (1987): 154–71. – P. Siniscalco, "La teoria e la tecnica del commentario biblico secondo Girolamo," *ASEs* 5 (1988): 225–38. – F. Mali, *Das "Opus imperfectum in Matthaeum" und sein Verhältnis zu den Matthäuskommentaren von Origenes und Hieronymus* (IThS 34; Innsbruck: Tyrolia, 1991). – D. Brown, *Vir trilinguis: A Study in the Biblical Exegesis of Saint Jerome* (Kampen, Neth.: Kok Pharos, 1992). – J. I. Pock, *Sapientia Salomonis: Hieronymus' Exegese des Weisheitsbuches im Licht der Tradition* (Graz, Austria: dbv-Verlag für die Technische Universität Graz, 1992). – A. Kamesar, *Jerome, Greek Scholarship, and the Hebrew Bible: A Study of the Quaestiones hebraicae in Genesim* (Oxford: Clarendon; New York: Oxford University Press, 1993).

*Polemic, Rufinus, and the Origenist Controversy:* J. Brochet, *Saint Jérôme et ses ennemis: Étude sur la querelle de saint Jérôme avec Rufin d'Aquilée et sur l'ensemble de son oeuvre polémique* (Paris: Fontemorng, 1905). – I. Opelt, *Hieronymus' Streitschriften* (BKAW NS 2.44; Heidelberg: Winter, 1973). – E. A. Clark, *The Origenist Controversy: The Cultural Construction of an Early Christian Debate* (Princeton, N.J.: Princeton University Press, 1992). – P. Lardet, *L'Apologie de Jérôme contre Rufin: Un commentaire* (SVigChr 15; Leiden and New York: Brill, 1993).

*Language and Literature:* H. Goelzer, *Étude lexicographique et grammaticale de la latinité de saint Jérôme* (Paris: Hachette, 1884). – P. Courcelle, *Les lettres grecques en Occident de Macrobe à Cassiodore* (2d ed.; Paris: de Boccard, 1948), 37–115. – E. Arns, *La technique du livre d'après saint Jérôme* (Paris: de Boccard, 1953). – H. Hagendahl, *Latin Fathers and the Classics: A Study on the Apologists, Jerome and Other Christian Writers* (AUG 64; Göteborg, Swed.: Elanders boktr. aktiebolag; distr., 1958). – D. S. Wiesen, *St. Jerome as a Satirist: A Study in Christian Latin Thought and Letters* (Ithaca, N.Y.: Cornell University Press, 1964).

*Asceticism and Monasticism:* P. Rousseau, *Ascetics, Authority, and Church in the Age of Jerome and Cassian* (Oxford and New York: Oxford University Press, 1978). – A. de Vogüé, *Histoire littéraire du mouvement monastique dans l'antiquité, Première partie: Le monachisme latin* (Paris: Cerf, 1991–). – C. Krumeich, *Hieronymus und die christlichen feminae clarissimae* (Bonn: R. Habelt, 1993). – B. Feichtinger, *Apostolae apostolorum: Frauenaskese als Befreiung und Zwang bei Hieronymus* (Frankfurt and New York: Lang, 1995). – L. Mirri, *La dolcezza della lotta: Donne e ascesi secondo Girolamo* (Magnano: Qiqajon, 1996). – P. Laurence, *Jérôme et le nouveau modèle féminine: La conversion à la "vie parfaite,"* (Paris: Études Augustiniennes, 1997).

*Other Studies:* Y. Bodin, *Saint Jérôme et l'Église* (ThH 6; Paris: Beauchesne, 1966). – C. Pietri, *Roma christiana: Recherches sur l'église de Rome, son organisation, sa politique, son idéologie de Miltiade à Sixte III (311–440)* (2 vols.; BEFAR 224; Rome: École Française de Rome, 1976). – H. Kech, *Hagiographie als christliche Unterhaltungsliteratur: Studien zum Phänomen des Erbaulichen anhand der Mönchsviten des hl. Hieronymus* (Göppingen: A. Kümmerle, 1977). – A. Ceresa-Gastaldo, ed., *Gerolamo e la biografia letteraria* (Genoa: D.AR.FI.CL.ET., 1989). – S. Rebenich, *Hieronymus und sein Kreis: Prosopographische und sozialgeschichtliche Untersuchungen* (Hist.E 72; Stuttgart: Steiner, 1992).

## A. Bible Translations

The substance of the definitive Latin translation of the Bible, the Vulgate ("generally circulated"), which has been revised as the "Neo-Vulgata" only in

1979 upon commission by the Second Vatican Council, is traced back to Jerome. Whether Pope Damasus appointed him to the task of translation cannot be demonstrated with certainty. In any case, Jerome began it during his years in Rome (382–385) and addressed the foreword to Pope Damasus. Until then there had been different Latin Bibles in the various parts of the church; currently they are being collected and edited by the Vetus Latina Institute in Beuron, Germany (cf. ch. 4.I).

Jerome began the revision of the Latin text of the Gospels by comparing it with the Septuagint. He produced two translations of the OT, one based on Origen's *Hexapla* (cf. ch. 3.V.C.1), encompassing only the Psalms, Job, Proverbs, Song of Songs, Ecclesiastes, and Chronicles (published after 385 at Bethlehem), the second a complete translation based on the Hebrew original, as he himself attests (published 393–404/405). Jerome does not appear to have been sufficiently conversant with Hebrew, however, and so it has to be assumed that he used the *Hexapla* in this case also, since it contained the Hebrew text both in Hebrew and in Greek transliterations.

*Editions: Biblia Sacra iuxta Latinam Vulgatam versionem* (18 vols.; Rome: Typis Polyglottis Vaticanis, 1926–1995). – *Biblia Sacra: Iuxta Vulgatam versionem* (ed. R. Weber; 2 vols.; Stuttgart: Württembergische Bibelanstalt, 1969). – *Nova Vulgata Bibliorum Sacrorum editio* (rev. ed.; Vatican City: Libreria Editrice Vaticana, 1986).

*Reference Works:* F. Kaulen, *Sprachliches Handbuch zur biblischen Vulgata: Eine systematische Darstellung ihres lateinischen Sprachcharakters* (2d ed.; Fribourg, Switz., and St. Louis, Mo.: Herder, 1904). – W. E. Plater and H. J. White, *A Grammar of the Vulgate: Being an Introduction to the Study of the Latinity of the Vulgate Bible* (Oxford: Clarendon, 1926). – B. Fischer, *Novae concordantiae Bibliorum Sacrorum iuxta Vulgatam versionem* (5 vols.; Stuttgart: Frommann-Holzboog, 1977).

*Studies:* F. Stummer, *Einführung in die lateinische Bibel: Ein Handbuch für Vorlesungen und Selbstunterricht* (Paderborn: F. Schöningh, 1928). – H. J. Vogels, *Vulgatastudien: Die Evangelien der Vulgata untersucht auf ihre lateinische und griechische Vorlage* (NTAbh 14.2–3; Münster: Aschendorff, 1928). – G. Q. A. Meershoek, *Le latin biblique d'àprès saint Jérôme* (LCP 20; Nijmegen-Utrecht: Dekker & van de Vegt, 1966). – H. F. D. Sparks, "Jerome as Biblical Scholar," *CHB* 1:510–41. – Institut für neutestamentliche Textforschung and V. Reichmann, *TRE* 6:178–81. – T. Stramare, ed., *La Bibbia "Vulgata" dalle origini ai nostri giorni* (CBLa 16; Vatican City: Libreria Vaticana, 1987). – R. Gryson, "S. Jérôme traducteur d'Isaïe: Réflexions sur le texte d'Isaïe XIV,18–21 dans la Vulgate et dans l'*In Esaiam*," *Mus* 104 (1991): 57–72. – M. Wissemann, *Schimpfworte in der Bibelübersetzung des Hieronymus* (BKAW NS 2.86; Heidelberg: Winter, 1992). – S. Rebenich, "Jerome: The '*vir trilinguis*' and the '*hebraica veritas*,'" *VC* 47 (1993): 50–77.

# B. De viris illustribus

Besides his famous biographies of the emperors, Suetonius, the Roman biographer (d. after ca. 70), published a compendium of biographies of famous authors titled *De viris illustribus* in order to pay tribute to the outstanding literary achievements of the Roman spirit. In deliberate continuity with this, Jerome in

393 collected a catalogue of 135 Christian authors under the same title, beginning with Paul and concluding with himself, so as to demonstrate the outstanding literary achievements of Christianity as well and to refute the charge that only the uncultured turned to Christianity. Jerome did not study all of the authors and works for this purpose, but mainly collected notes and catalogues of works from the Bible and the *Ecclesiastical History* of Eusebius. The book is regarded as an "original patrology," and several have sought to extend it: Gennadius of Marseille (ca. 480/490)[17]; Isidore of Seville (615–618), who augmented it especially with African and Spanish fathers; and Ildefonsus of Toledo (d. 667), with a more local historical interest. Seven of the fourteen exclusively Spanish bishops Ildefonsus added were his predecessors in the see of Toledo, and only eight of them had also engaged in literary work.

*Editions: Hieronymus liber De viris inlustribus, Gennadius liber De viris inlustribus* (ed. E. C. Richardson; TU 14.1a; Leipzig: Hinrichs, 1896). – *Hieronymi De viris inlustribus liber* (ed. G. Herding; Teubner; Leipzig: Teubner, 1924). – *Gli uomini illustri* (ed. A. Ceresa-Gastaldo; BPat 12; Florence: Nardini, Centro Internazionale del Libro, 1988) [Com].

*Translations:* E. C. Richardson, trans., "Jerome: Lives of Illustrious Men," in *NPNF*[2] (Peabody, Mass.: Hendrickson, 1995; repr. of 1892 ed.), 3:359–84. – *On Illustrious Men* (trans. T. P. Halton: FC 100; Washington, D.C.: Catholic University of America Press, 1999).

*Studies:* S. von Sychowski, *Hieronymus als Litterarhistoriker: Eine Quellenkritische Untersuchung der Schrift des h. Hieronymus "De viris illustribus"* (KGS 2.2; Münster: Schöningh, 1894). – C. A. Bernoulli, *Der Schriftstellerkatalog des Hieronymus: Ein Beitrag zur Geschichte der altchristlichen Literatur* (Fribourg, Switz.: Mohr, 1895). – A. Feder, *Studien zum Schriftstellerkatalog des heiligen Hieronymus* (Fribourg, Switz.: Herder, 1927). – P. Nautin, "La date du '*De uiris inlustribus*' de Jérôme, de la mort de Cyrille de Jérusalem, et de celle de Grégoire de Nazianze," *RHE* 56 (1961): 33–35. – A. Ceresa-Gastaldo, "La tecnica biografica del '*De viris illustribus*' di Gerolamo," *Ren.* 14 (1979): 221–36. – S. Pricoco, *Storia letteraria e storia ecclesiastica dal De viris inlustribus di Girolamo a Gennadio* (Quaderni del siculorum gymnasium 6; Catania: Università di Catania, Facoltà di Lettere e Filosofia, 1979). – I. Opelt, "Hieronymus' Leistung als Literarhistoriker in der Schrift *De viris illustribus*,'" *Orph.* NS 1 (1980): 52–75. – P. Nautin, "La liste des œuvres de Jérôme dans le '*De viris inlustribus*,'" *Orph.* NS 5 (1984): 319–34.

## *C. Corpus of Letters*

Jerome's corpus of letters encompasses a total of 154 items and represents an invaluable treasure trove for the knowledge of him as a person and his relations and activities, as well as of contemporary history. Thirty-four of them are not his own, however, but are addressed to him, translated by him, or have been

---

[17] S. Pricoco, "Gennadius of Marseilles," *EECh* 1:342: "is rejected today as inauthentic . . . , but may have been written in the circle and at the time of Gennadius." C. Pietri (*TRE* 12:376) once again confirms the traditional view: "is identified securely in the manuscript tradition."

included in the corpus for other, unknown, reasons: 19, 35, 46, 51, 56, 67, 80, 83, 87, 89–96, 98, 100, 101, 104, 110, 111, 113, 116, 131, 132, 135–137, 144, 148–150. The following are their respective authors:

- Pope Anastasius (95);

- Augustine (56 = Augustine, *Ep*. 28; 67 = Augustine, *Ep*. 40; 101 = Augustine, *Ep*. 67; 104 = Augustine, *Ep*. 71; 110 = Augustine, *Ep*. 73; 111 = Augustine, *Ep*. 74, to Praesidius; 116 = Augustine, *Ep*. 82; 131 = Augustine, *Ep*. 166; 132 = Augustine, *Ep*. 167; 144 = Augustine, *Ep*. 202 A, to Optatus);

- Pope Damasus (19, 35);

- Dionysius of Lydda (94, to Theophilus of Alexandria, translated by Jerome);

- Epiphanius of Constantia (Salamis) (51, to John of Jerusalem, translated by Jerome; 91);

- Pope Innocent (135, to Aurelius of Carthage; 136, 137, to John of Jerusalem);

- Pammachius and Oceanus (83);

- Paula and Eustochium (46, to Marcella);

- Rufinus (80);

- synod of Jerusalem (93, to Theophilus of Alexandria, likely translated by Jerome);

- Theophilus of Alexandria (87, 89, 90, to Epiphanius of Constantia; 92, translated by Jerome; 96, *Ep. pasc.* 16, translated by Jerome; 98, *Ep. pasc.* 17, translated by Jerome; 100, *Ep. pasc.* 21, translated by Jerome; 113, fragment of *Liber enormis,* translated by Jerome).

*Epistulae* 148 belongs to Pelagius, and 149 to an unknown author (Pseudo-Columban); although *Ep*. 150 by Procopios of Gaza is addressed to a certain Jerome, it is not Jerome of Stridon. Thus there remain 120 authentic items from Jerome's pen, to which were added a further item (*Ep*. 27*) in 1981, namely, one of the twenty-nine letters of Augustine recently discovered by Johannes Divjak, and a letter addressed to Jerome (*Ep*. 19*). Also to be included in the broader corpus of letters are the prefaces to the translations, which are handed down and published together with the latter.

Hermann Josef Frede[18] dates the letters from the desert near Chalcis (*Epist.* 5–14) to 374; this type of precision can only be understood as an assumption because of the uncertainty of the chronology of this period, as explained above.

---

[18] H. J. Frede, *Kirchenschriftsteller,* 357.

Their authenticity is rejected by Pierre Nautin because of "some disturbing facts" that "suggest the supposition that he wrote them only after 387 to demonstrate to those slandering him that he had indeed lived together with other monks."[19] As far as I am aware, Nautin is the only one arguing this viewpoint.

The correspondence with Augustine, which is also handed down in the corpus of Augustine's letters, was not blessed with good fortune at the beginning. Augustine corresponded with Jerome (*Epist.* 56 = Augustine, *Ep.* 28) for the first time in 394/395, before his consecration as bishop, with comments and suggestions regarding his translation of the Bible. He suggested that Jerome may wish to indicate the instances when the Latin translation deviates from the Septuagint. One of Augustine's comrades was to carry the letter on his pilgrimage to the Holy Land, which never materialized, however. Augustine nevertheless made the letter accessible to Rufinus, thus annoying Jerome. Hence, when Augustine wrote another letter to Jerome in 400 (*Epist.* 67 = Augustine, *Ep.* 40), he did not deem him worthy of a response. Augustine apologized, and so a correspondence between the two ensued, even if with difficulty at times and interspersed with extended periods of silence, and then mainly on biblical and theological issues:

- *Epist.* 102 = Augustine, *Ep.* 68 (402),

- *Epist.* 103 = Augustine, *Ep.* 39 (397? 403?),

- *Epist.* 105 = Augustine, *Ep.* 73 (403/404),

- *Epist.* 112 = Augustine, *Ep.* 75 (403/404),

- *Epist.* 115 = Augustine, *Ep.* 81 (405?),

- *Epist.* 134 = Augustine, *Ep.* 172 (416),

- *Epist.* 141 = Augustine, *Ep.* 195 (418),

- *Epist.* 142 = Augustine, *Ep.* 123 (410),

- *Epist.* 143 = Augustine, *Ep.* 202 (419).

Although *Ep.* 57, *De optimo genere interpretandi,* from 395 or 396, arose from a particular occasion, it represents, beyond this, a fundamental treatise on Jerome's principles of translation. Here he defends himself against the charge that he had produced a flawed and tendentious translation of a letter by Epiphanius of Constantia (Salamis)—addressed to John of Jerusalem, in which the writer attacked the latter for his Origenism—and thereby placed John at a disadvantage. After clarifying that the translation in question was merely a private favor, not intended for publication, and that it could only have become public as a result of theft and betrayal, Jerome stresses his fundamental principle that a translation needs to provide an apt rendering of the meaning of a text and has to detach itself from slavish, literal rendition.

---

[19] Nautin, *TRE* 15:304.

His correspondence with Theophilus, patriarch of Antioch, beginning in 401, that is, during the second phase of the Origenist controversy about the "tall brothers" and John Chrysostom, preserved valuable, otherwise lost documents pertaining to the controversy.

Further noteworthy letters are *Ep.* 14, 58, and 122 concerning life as a monk, 22 and 130 concerning virginity, 46 and 79 concerning widowhood, 52 concerning the priesthood, and the correspondence with Pope Damasus (15, 16, 18–21, 35, 36).

*Editions: Sancti Eusebii Hieronymi Epistulae* (ed. I. Hilberg and M. Kamptner; 2d ed.; CSEL 54–56; Vienna: Verlag der Österreichischen Akademie der Wissenschaften, 1996). – *SS. Eusebii Hieronymi et Aurelii Augustini epistulae mutuae* (ed. J. Schmid; FlorPatr 22; Bonn: P. Hanstein, 1930). – *Epistolae ex duobus codicibus nuper in lucem prolatae* (ed. J. Divjak; CSEL 88; Vienna: Hölder-Pichler-Tempsky, 1981), 130–33 [*Epist.* 27*]. – *Lettres 1*–29** (ed. J. Divjak et al., BAug 46B; Paris: Études Augustiniennes, 1987), 394–401, 560–68 [*Epist.* 27* Com]. – *Lettere* (ed. C. Moreschini and R. Palla; Milan: Biblioteca Universale Rizzoli, 1989) [*Epist.* 22–24, 39–41, 45, 49, 53, 57, 105, 107, 134].

*Translations:* W. H. Fremantle, trans., "Letters," in *NPNF²* (Peabody, Mass.: Hendrickson, 1995; repr. of 1893 ed.), 6:1–295. – *The Letters of St. Jerome* (trans. C. Mierow and T. C. Lawler; ACW 33; New York: Newman, 1963) [*1–22*]. – C. White, *The Correspondence (394–419) between Jerome and Augustine of Hippo* (Lewiston, N.Y.: Mellen, 1990).

*Reference Works:* J. Schwind, *Index in S. Hieronymi epistulas* (AlOm.A 140; Hildesheim: Olms-Weidmann, 1994).

*Studies:* N. Pronberger, *Beiträge zur Chronologie der Briefe des hl. Hieronymus* (Amberg: H. Böes, 1913). – J. N. Hritzu, *The Style of the Letters of St. Jerome* (PatSt 60; Washington, D.C.: Catholic University of America Press, 1939). – P. Steur, *Het Karakter van Hieronymus van Stridon bestudeerd in zijn brieven* (Nijmegen: Dekker & van de Vegt, 1945). – M. Marcocchi, *Motivi umani e cristiani nell'epistolario di S. Girolamo* (Milan: Ceschina, 1967). – G. Stoico, *L'epistolario di S. Girolamo: Studio critico-letterario di stilistica latina* (Naples: Giannini, 1972). – R. J. O'Connell, "When Saintly Fathers Feuded: The Correspondence between Augustine and Jerome," *Thought* 54 (1979): 344–64. – J. M. Blázquez, "Aspectos de la sociedad romana del Bajo Imperio en las cartas de San Jerónimo," *Gerión* 9 (1991): 263–88. – S. Rebenich, "Der heilige Hieronymus und die Geschichte—zur Funktion der *exempla* in seinen Briefen," *RQ* 87 (1922): 29–46. – R. Hennings, *Der Briefwechsel zwischen Augustinus und Hieronymus und ihr Streit um den Kanon des Alten Testaments und die Auslegung von Gal. 2,11–14* (SVigChr 21; Leiden and New York: Brill, 1994). – G. Menestrina, " '*Domino dilectissimo Hieronymo Augustinus*': Riflessioni sul carteggio Agostino-Gerolamo," in idem, *Bibbia, liturgia, e letteratura cristiana antica* (Brescia: Morcelliana, 1997), 89–177.

*Individual Letters:* N. Adkin, " '*Oras: loqueris ad sponsum; legis: ille tibi loquitur*' (Jerome, Epist. 22,25,1)," *VC* 46 (1992): 141–50. – B. Feichtinger, "Der Traum des Hieronymus—ein Psychogramm," *VC* 45 (1991): 54–77 [*Epist.* 22.30]. – N. Adkin, "Jerome as Centoist: *Epist.* XXII,38,7)," *RSLR* 28 (1992): 461–71. – N. Adkin, " '*Taceo de meis similibus*' (Jerome, *Epist.* LIII,7)," *VetChr* 29 (1992): 261–68. – G. J. M. Bartelink, *Liber de optimo genere interpretandi (Epistula 57): Ein Kommentar* (Mn.S 61; Leiden: Brill, 1980). – J. H. D. Scourfield, *Consoling Heliodorus: A Commentary on Jerome, Letter 60* (OECS; Oxford: Clarendon; New York: Oxford University Press, 1993) [ET/Com]. – R. Hennings, "Rabbinisches und Antijüdisches bei Hieronymus Ep 121,10," in *Christliche Exegese zwischen Nicaea und Chalcedon* (ed. J. van Oort and U. Wickert; Kampen, Neth.; Kok Pharos, 1992), 49–71. – P. C. Miller, "The Blazing Body: Ascetic Desire in Jerome's Letter to Eustochium," *JECS* 1 (1993): 21–45.

# CHAPTER EIGHT

# Monastic and Hagiographic Literature

MANY OF THE FOURTH-CENTURY CHURCH FATHERS presented thus far already reflect the important theological role of monasticism in the history of the church: Athanasius, the Cappadocians, Epiphanius of Constantia (Salamis), Diodore of Tarsus and his disciples, Rufinus of Concordia (Aquileia), and Jerome. Christian monasticism arose in the second half of the third century in Egypt as an anchorite movement (ἀναχωρεῖν = "to withdraw," that is, from the populated Nile Delta into the surrounding desert). In radical following of the gospel, individuals relinquished all of their possessions, indeed social communion, so as to live for Christ alone (μόναχος = "living alone [for Christ]"). This initially occurred in places where the topographical, climatic, and social conditions encouraged it, in the desert areas of Egypt and somewhat later in Syria, that is, in regions with autochthonous wisdom cultures antedating hellenization, which was not pervasive by any means. It did not take long for communities to gather in the desert and thus for cenobitic (κοινὸς βίος = "common life") monasticism to arise—again in the Egyptian desert initially. Finally, in the second half of the fourth century, a cloistered life also began to develop within the civilized areas and cities when seclusion was obtained by isolating a house from its surroundings (*clausura/claustrum* = "enclosed area," hence "cloister"). For the long term, monastic communities needed rules to regulate life together; these would become the initial genre of monastic literature and later on were supplemented with spiritual writings for monks.

The hagiographic literature arising in the fourth century, including pilgrims' accounts in the broader sense of the term, is also closely linked with monasticism. Until then the church had venerated only martyrs as saints and handed down their testimonials in the records, lives, and festal homilies commemorating martyrs. Along with the places in Palestine associated with the life of Christ and the tombs of saints (primarily those of the apostles and martyrs in Rome), the monks became a second group of exemplary Christians to whom pilgrimages were made as "living saints," whose lives were recorded and disseminated. This literature rapidly developed into full-fledged hagiography, recording the life stories of the other great fathers and saints, and where there was no historically reliable data to record, or beyond the historical facts, they supplied pious legends and accounts of miracles. The itineraries (*iter* = "way") served as a guidebook for those who intended to undertake a pilgrimage and, for those not able to undertake a journey such as this, as a travelogue and devotional account of the holy places.

Since their emergence in the middle of the fourth century, both types of literature, the monastic as well as the hagiographic, experienced a flourishing that endured through the remainder of the patristic era and, with especially high points in the medieval period, has continued into the present.

*Reference Works:* W. Johnston, ed., *Encyclopedia of Monasticism* (2 vols.; Chicago and London: Fitzroy Dearborn, 2000).

*Encyclopedia Articles:* J. Gribomont, P. Miquel, and J. Dubois, *DSp* 10:1536–71. – J. Gribomont, *EECh* 1:566–67. – F. von Lilienfeld, *TRE* 23:150–93. – J. Goehring, "Asceticism," *EEC* 1:127–30. – J. Goehring, "Monasticism," *EEC* 2:769–75.

*Introductions and Surveys:* D. J. Chitty, *The Desert a City: An Introduction to the History of Egyptian and Palestinian Monasticism under the Christian Empire* (Oxford: Blackwell, 1966; London: Mowbray, 1977). – B. Lohse, *Askese und Mönchtum in der Antike und in der alten Kirche* (RKAM 1; Munich: Oldenbourg, 1969). – G. M. Colombás, *El monacato primitivo* (2 vols.; BAC; Madrid: Biblioteca de Autores Cristianos, 1974–1975). – K. S. Frank, ed., *Askese und Mönchtum in der Alten Kirche* (WdF 409; Darmstadt: Wissenschaftliche Buchgesellschaft, 1975). – K. S. Frank, *With Greater Liberty: A Short History of Christian Monasticism and Religious Orders* (trans. J. T. Lienhard; CistSS 144; Kalamazoo: Cistercian, 1993); trans. of *Grundzüge des christlichen Mönchtums* (4th ed.; Darmstadt: Wissenschaftliche Buchgesellschaft, 1983). – F. Prinz, *Askese und Kultur: Vor- und frühbenediktinisches Mönchtum an der Wiege Europas* (Munich: Beck, 1980). – M. Augé, *Lineamenti di storia dell'antico monachesimo* (Rome: Pontificia Università Lateranense, 1981). – J.-M. Garrigues and J. Legrez, *Moines dans l'assemblée des fidèles à l'époque des Pères, IVe–VIIIe siècle* (ThH 87; Paris: Beauchesne, 1990). – V. Desprez, *Le monachisme primitif: Des origines jusqu'au concile d'Éphèse* (SpOr 72; Bégrolles-en-Mauges: Abbaye de Bellefontaine, 1998).

*Collections of Essays:* L. Regnault, *Les Pères du désert à travers leurs Apophtegmes* (Sablé-sur-Sarthe: Abbaye Saint-Pierre de Solesmes, 1987). – J. Driscoll and M. Sheridan, eds., *Spiritual Progress: Studies in the Spirituality of Late Antiquity and Early Monasticism* (Rome: Pontificio Ateneo S. Anselmo, 1994). – M. Starowicysi, ed., *The Spirituality of Ancient Monasticism: Acts of the International Colloquium held in Cracow-Tyniec, 16–19th November 1994* (Cracow: Wydawn, Benedyktynów, 1995). – V. L. Wimbush and R. Valantasis, eds., *Asceticism* (Oxford and New York: Oxford University Press, 1995). – A. Guillaumont, *Études sur la spiritualité de l'Orient chrétien* (SpOr 66; Bégrolles-en-Mauges: Abbaye de Bellefontaine, 1996). – H. A. Luckman and L. Kulzer, eds., *Purity of Heart in Early Ascetic and Monastic Literature* (Collegeville, Minn.: Liturgical, 1999).

*Origins:* K. Heussi, *Der Ursprung des Mönchtums* (Tübingen: Mohr, 1936; repr., Aalen: Scientia, 1981). – R. Lorenz, "Die Anfänge des abendländischen Mönchtums im 4. Jahrhundert," *ZKG* 77 (1966): 1–61. – P. Nagel, *Die Motivierung der Askese in der alten Kirche und der Ursprung des Mönchtums* (TU 95; Berlin: Akademie, 1966). – A. Guillaumont, *Aux origines du monachisme chrétien: Pour une phénoménologie du monachisme* (SpOr 30; Bégrolles-en-Mauges: Abbaye de Bellefontaine, 1979). – J. E. Goehring, "The Origins of Monasticism," in *Eusebius, Judaism, and Christianity* (ed. H. W. Attridge and G. Hata; Leiden and New York: Brill, 1992), 235–55; repr. in *Forms of Devotion: Conversion, Worship, Spirituality, and Asceticism* (ed. E. Ferguson; Recent Studies in Early Christianity 5; New York: Garland, 1999), 211–31. – G. E. Gould, "Recent Work on Monastic Origins: A Consideration of the Questions Raised by Samuel Rubenson's *The Letters of St. Antony*," in *Papers Presented at the Eleventh International Conference on Patristic Studies Held in Oxford, 1991* (ed. E. Livingstone; StPatr 25; Louvain: Peeters, 1993), 405–16.

*Greek East:* A.-J. Festugière, *Culture ou sainteté: Introduction au monachisme oriental* (Les moines d'Orient 1; Paris: Cerf, 1961). – *Il monachesimo orientale* (OrChrAn 153; Rome: Pontificium Institutum Orientalium Studiorum, 1958). – Y. Hirschfeld, *The Judean Monasteries in the Byzantine Period* (London and New Haven, Conn.: Yale University Press,1992). – J. Binns, *Ascetics and Ambassadors of Christ: The Monasteries of Palestine, 314–631* (OECS; Oxford: Clarendon; New York: Oxford University Press, 1994). – J. Patrich, *Sabas, Leader of Palestinian Monasticism: A Comparative Study in Eastern Monasticism, Fourth to Seventh Centuries* (Washington, D.C.: Dumbarton Oaks, 1995). – T. Špidlík, M. Tenace, and R. Cemus, *Questions monastiques en Orient* (OCS 259; Rome: Pontificio Istituto Orientale, 1999).

*Latin West:* I. Gobry, *Les moines en Occident* (3 vols.; Paris: Fayard, 1985–1987). – A. de Vogüé, *Histoire littéraire du mouvement monastique dans l'antiquité, Première partie: Le monachisme latin* (5 vols.; Paris: Cerf, 1991–2003). – I. Stahlmann, *Der gefesselte Sexus: Weibliche Keuschheit und Askese im Westen des römischen Reiches* (Berlin: Akademie, 1997). – *Il monachesimo occidentale dalle origini alla Regula magistri* (SEAug 62; Rome: Institutum Patristicum Augustinianum, 1998).

*Egypt:* H. Evelyn-White, *The Monasteries of Wadi 'n Natrûn, Part Two: The History of the Monasteries of Nitria and of Scetis* (New York: Metropolitan Museum of Art Egyptian Expedition, 1932; repr., New York: Arno, 1973). – M. Orban, ed., *Déserts chrétiens d'Égypte* (Nice: Culture Sud, 1993). – L. Regnault, *The Day-to-Day Life of the Desert Fathers in Fourth-Century Egypt* (trans. É. Poirier Jr.; Petersham, Mass.: St. Bede's, 1999); trans. of *Vie quotidienne des Pères du désert en Egypte au IVe siècle* (Paris: Hachette, 1990). J. E. Goehring, *Ascetics, Society, and the Desert: Studies in Early Egyptian Monasticism* (Studies in Antiquity and Christianity; Harrisburg, Pa.: Trinity, 1999).

*Syria:* A. Vööbus, *History of Asceticism in the Syrian Orient: A Contribution to the History of Culture in the Near East* (3 vols.; CSCO 184, 197, 500; Louvain: SCO; 1958–1988). – P. Brown, "Rise and Function of the Holy Man in Late Antiquity," *Journal of Roman Studies* 61 (1971): 80–101; repr. in idem, *Society and the Holy in Late Antiquity* (Berkeley: University of California Press, 1982), 103–52; repr. in E. Ferguson, ed., *Acts of Piety in the Early Church* (SEC 17; New York: Garland, 1993), 254–75. – I. Peña, P. Castellana, and R. Fernandez, *Les reclus syriens: Recherches sur les anciennes formes de vie solitaire en Syrie* (SBF.CMi 23; Milan: Franciscan, 1980). – I. Peña, P. Castellana, and R. Fernandez, *Les cénobites syriens* (SBF.CMi 28; Milan: Franciscan, 1983). – I. Peña, *La straordinaria vita dei monaci siri, secoli IV–VI* (Milan: Cinisello Balsamo, Edizioni Paoline, 1990); trans. of *La desconcertante vida de los monjes Sirios: Siglos IV–VI* (Salamanca: Sígueme, 1985). – S. H. Griffith, "Asceticism in the Church of Syria: The Hermeneutics of Early Syrian Monasticism," in *Asceticism* (ed. V. Wimbush and R. Valantasis; Oxford and New York: Oxford University Press, 1995), 220–45. – P. Brown, "The Rise and Function of the Holy Man in Late Antiquity, 1971–1997," *JECS* 6 (1998): 353–76. – P. Escolan, *Monachisme et Église: Le monachisme syrien du IVe au VIIe siècle, un monachisme charismatique* (ThH 109; Paris: Beauchesne, 1999).

*Gaul, Lérins:* F. Prinz, *Frühes Mönchtum im Frankenreich: Kultur und Gesellschaft in Gallien, den Rheinlanden, und Bayern am Beispiel der monastischen Entwicklung (4. bis 8. Jahrhhundert)* (2d ed.; Munich: Oldenbourg, 1988). – S. Pricoco, *L'isola dei santi: Il cenobio di Lerino e le origini del monachesimo gallico* (Rome: Edizioni dell'Ateneo & Bizzarri, 1978). – R. Nouailhat, *Saints et patrons: Les premiers moines de Lérins* (Paris: Belles Lettres, 1988). – C. M. Kasper, *Theologie und Askese: Die Spiritualität des Inselmönchtums von Lérins im 5. Jahrhundert* (BGAM 40; Münster: Aschendorff, 1991).

*Women's Asceticism:* E. A. Clark, "Ascetic Renunciation and Feminine Advancement: A Paradox of Late Ancient Christianity," *AThR* 63 (1981): 240–57. – B. Ward, "Apophthegmata Matrum," *StPat* 16 (1985): 63–66; repr. in idem, *Signs and Wonders* (VRCS 361; Aldershot, Hampshire, and Brookfield, Vt.: Variorum, 1992), n.p. – B. Ward, *Harlots of the Desert: A Study of Repentance in Early Monastic Sources* (CistSS 106; Kalamazoo, Mich.: Cistercian; London: Mowbray, 1987). – S. Elm, *"Virgins of God": The Making of Asceticism in Late Antiquity* (Oxford and New York: Oxford University Press, 1994). – G. Clark, "Women and Asceticism in Late Antiquity," in *Asceticism* (ed. V. L. Wimbush and R. Valantasis; Oxford and New York: Oxford University Press, 1995), 33–48. – G. Cloke, *This Female Man of God: Women and Spiritual Power in the Patristic Age, AD 350–450* (London and New York: Routledge, 1995). – S. Brock and S. Ashbrook Harvey, eds., *Holy Women of the Syrian Orient* (2d ed.; TCH 13; Berkeley: University of California Press, 1998).

*Terminology:* K. S. Frank, *Angelikos bios: Begriffsanalytische und begriffsgeschichtliche Untersuchung zum "engelgleichen Leben" im frühen Mönchtum* (BGAM 26; Münster: Aschendorff, 1964). – F.-E. Morard, "Monachos, moine: Histoire du terme grec jusqu'au 4e siècle—influences bibliques et gnostiques," *FZPhTh* 20 (1973): 332–411. – E. A. Judge, "The Earliest Use of Monachos for 'Monk' (P. Coll. Youtie 77) and the Origins of Monasticism," *JAC* 20 (1977): 72–89. – P. Miquel, *Lexique du desert: Étude de quelques mots-clés du vocabulaire monastique grec ancien* (SpOr 44; Bégrolles-en-Mauges: Éditions Monastiques, 1986). – J. Goehring, "Through a Glass Darkly: Diverse Images of the Apotaktikoi(ai) of Early Egyptian Monasticism," *Semeia* 58 (1992): 25–45.

*Theology and Spirituality:* E. E. Malone, *The Monk and the Martyr: The Monk as the Successor of the Martyr* (SCA 12; Washington, D.C.: Catholic University of America Press, 1950). – *Théologie de la vie monastique: Études sur la tradition patristique* (Theol[P] 49; Paris: Aubier, 1961). I. Hausherr, *The Name of Jesus* (trans. C. Cummings; CistSS 44; Kalamazoo: Cistercian, 1978); trans. of *Noms du Christ et voies d'oraison* (OrChrAn 170; Rome: Pontificium Institutum Orientalium Studiorum, 1960). – I. Hausherr, *Penthos: The Doctrine of Compunction in the Christian East* (trans. A. Hufstader; CistSS 53; Kalamazoo: Cistercian, 1982). – K. Ware, "The Origins of the Jesus Prayer: Diadochus, Gaza, Sinai," in *The Study of Spirituality* (ed. C. Jones, G. Wainwright, and E. Yarnold; London: SPCK, 1986), 175–84. – T. Špidlík, *The Spirituality of the Christian East: A Systematic Handbook* (CistSS 79; Kalamazoo: Cistercian Studies, 1986); trans. of *La spiritualité de l'Orient chrétien* (OrChrAn 206, Rome: Pontificium Institutum Orientalium Studiorum, 1978). – H. Holze, *Erfahrung und Theologie im frühen Mönchtum: Untersuchungen zu einer Theologie des monastischen Lebens bei den ägyptischen Mönchsvätern, Johannes Cassian und Benedikt von Nursia* (FKDG 48; Göttingen: Vandenhoeck & Ruprecht, 1992). – C. E. Kunz, *Schweigen und Geist: Biblische und patristische Studien zu einer Spiritualität des Schweigens* (Fribourg, Switz.: Herder, 1996). – E. A. Clark, *Reading Renunciation: Asceticism and Scripture in Early Christianity* (Princeton, N.J.: Princeton University Press, 1999).

# I. MONASTIC RULES

*Editions:* H. U. von Balthasar, ed., *Die grossen Ordensregeln* (2d ed.; Zurich: Benziger, 1961). – H. Styblo, "Die *Regula Macharii*," *WSt* 76 (1963): 124–58. – J. Neufville, "Règle des IV Pères et seconde Règle des Pères: Texte critique," *RBén* 77 (1967): 47–106. – A. de Vogüé, *Les Règles des saints Pères* (2 vols.; SC 297–298; Paris: Cerf, 1982) [Com].

*Reference Works:* E. Kasch, *Das liturgische Vokabular der frühen lateinischen Mönchsregeln* (RBS.S 1; Hildesheim: Gerstenberg, 1974). – J.-M. Clément, *Lexique des anciennes règles monastiques occidentales* (2 vols.; IP 7.A–B; Steenbrugge, Belg.: Abbatia Sancti Petri, 1978). – P. Bonnerue, "Concordance sur les activités manuelles dans les règles monastiques anciennes," *StudMon* 35 (1993): 69–96.

*Studies (Literature):* A. Mundó, *Études sur les anciennes règles monastiques latines* (Oslo: n.p., 1964). – M. M. Van Molle, "Essai de classement chronologique des premières règles de vie commune connue en chrétienté," *VS.S* 21 (1968): 108–27. – A. de Vogüé, *Les règles monastiques anciennes (400–700)* (TSMÂO 46; Turnhout, Belg.: Brepols, 1985). – J. Gribomont, "Rules, monastic," *EECh* 2:746–47. – P. Bonnerue, "*Opus* et *labor* dans les règles monastiques anciennes," *StudMon* 35 (1993): 265–91.

# A. Rule of Pachomius

Cenobitic monasticism was established in Egypt at the beginning of the fourth century. Pachomius, its founder, first lived as an anchorite for seven years, according to his *vitae,* and then in 320, as a result of divine inspiration, established the first common-life monastery at Tabennisi, on the right-hand bank of the Middle Nile, in Thebais near Tentyra. His new form of monastic life became so successful so quickly that he established a further eight monasteries for men and two convents for women with a membership of several hundred, all of which he directed as head abbot. The basis for the success of his work was the insight that such communities had to be established on rules applicable to all and obligating everyone equally, members as well as leaders. In this way, the first monastic rule in the history of the church came about, not as a homogeneous plan at a specific point in time and certainly not before the founding of monasteries, but arising from the experiences of common life under a charismatic leader who observed closely, was able to ascertain correctly and evaluate the requirements of communal life, and captured what was appropriate in a rule, with keen knowledge of human nature and empathy. For this reason, it cannot be determined whether the form of the Rule of Pachomius known today had been written during his lifetime (d. May 9, 347)[1] and how many additions made by his successors it contains.

The complete Rule has been preserved only in Jerome's Latin translation. Since more and more Latin Christians entered the Pachomian monasteries, he translated it from the Greek in 404 upon the request of some Alexandrians. The plethora of known manuscripts and the transmission in a *recensio longior* (considered to be the first authentic one) and a *recensio brevior* indicate the popularity the Rule of Pachomius gained in the Latin language domain as well. Its influence upon all the rules in the East and in the West up to Benedict of Nursia is unquestionable. It is arranged in four parts with a total of 193 terse rules: 144 *praecepta,* 18 *praecepta atque instituta,* 16 *praecepta atque iudicia,* and 15 *praecepta ac leges.*

---

[1] According to R. Lorenz, "Zur Chronologie des Pachomius," *ZNW* 80 (1989): 280–83. Traditionally, May 9, 346.

Of the Coptic original, 43 paragraphs of the *praecepta* (88–130) and 18 of the *instituta*, including the proem, have gradually been found in the course of the twentieth century. The Greek translation available to Jerome is lost; only excerpts of it have been handed down and in turn have been translated into Ethiopic.

Because of the history of its origin, the Rule of Pachomius does not offer a systematic ordering of monastic life but rather a collection of individual rules, repeated in many ways but clearly revolving around enduring principles. We have a better understanding of these from the most influential of all rules, that of Benedict of Nursia; nevertheless they originated here. In this context, it is important to remember the goal Pachomius pursued in founding cenobitic monasticism and in his rule: on the one hand, to avoid the dangers of the anchoritic movement, which he knew from his own experience, and, on the other, to enable a much larger number of Christians, who were not suited for the life of a hermit and yet desired to live an ascetic life, to do so in a monastic community.

Scripture is the spiritual basis of the Rule of Pachomius and the standard for everything; the Rule's two supreme characteristics are the intent of all rules to promote the κοινὸς βίος and the moderation they exhibit in every respect. There is no excess, whether in fasting or in working, whether in prayer or in isolation from the outside world. The Rule contains no vows. Obedience is the highest virtue, though not as a personal, heroic effort but as a function promoting and preserving community, from which even the superior is not exempted because he is subject to the rules as much as everyone else. Everything was held in common: the two meal and prayer times in the morning and evening, holy Mass on Sunday, the rhythm of work and rest, clothing and property. Leaving the monastery, too, was permitted only if accompanied by another monk. Each one lived in an individual cell; approximately twenty of them lived in one house and under one superior, thus providing a sphere of privacy and a chance to retreat for reflection, prayer, and meditation. Added to these were centrally located community and work structures (kitchen, dining hall, infirmary) and, at a later point, a church. In the early phase, they jointly attended the church in the village. Only when the membership of the monasteries became too large were the village community and its priest invited to celebrate the Eucharist in the monastery's own church. Everything was enclosed by *one* wall with only *one* gate, monitored by a gatekeeper, who, as "novice master," also introduced the new entrants, who initially lived with him, into the life of the monastery. Numerous rules were work-related, not merely because of the economic necessities of large monastic communities but also because it was appreciated as a constitutive element of personal and spiritual development. At the same time, intellectual interests were not neglected: all the monks had to learn to read. The "secret" of its enduring success may be found in the wisdom and balance pervading the entire Rule.

*Bibliography:* A. Schmidt, *BBKL* 6:1413–19.

*Editions—Works: Pachomiana latina: Règle et épitres de S. Pachome, épitre de S. Théodore, et "Liber" de S. Orsiesius* (ed. A. Boon and L. T. Lefort; Louvain: Bureaux de la Revue, 1932; microfilm repr., London and Ann Arbor: University Microfilms International, 1978) [*Rule, Letters*]. – *S. Pachomii, abbatis tabennensis, Regulae monasticae* (ed. P. B.

Albers; FlorPatr 16; Bonn: Hanstein, 1923). – L. T. Lefort, *Oeuvres de s. Pachôme et de ses disciples* (CSCO 159–60; Louvain: Durbecq, 1956). – H. Quecke, *Die Briefe Pachoms: Griechischer Text der Handschrift W. 145 der Chester Beatty Library: Anhang, Die koptischen Fragmente und Zitate der Pachombriefe* (TPL 11; Regensburg: Pustet, 1975). – *Pachomius: Der Mann und sein Werk* (vol. 2 of *Das Vermächtnis des Ursprungs: Studien zum frühen Mönchtum;* ed. H. Bacht; STGL 8; Würzburg: Echter, 1983) [*Rule* Com]. – J. E. Goehring, *The Letter of Ammon and Pachomian Monasticism* (PTS 27; Berlin and New York: de Gruyter, 1986) [ET/Com].

*Editions—Lives: Sancti Pachomii vitae graecae* (ed. F. Halkin; SHG 19; Brussels: Société des Bollandistes, 1932). – *S. Pachomii vita Bohairice scripta* (ed. L. T. Lefort; 2 vols.; CSCO 89, 107; Louvain: Imprimerie Orientaliste, 1952–1953) [T.bo/Tr.l]. – R. Draguet, "Un morceau grec inédit des Vies de Pachôme, apparié à un texte d'Évagre en partie inconnu," *Mus* 70 (1957): 267–306. – *S. Pachomii vita Sahidice scripta* (ed. L. T. Lefort; CSCO 99–100; Louvain: Imprimerie Orientaliste, 1965). – *Histoire de saint Pacôme* (ed. F. Nau; PO 4.19; Paris: Firmin-Didot, 1907; repr., 1971), 407–511 [T.g/Tr.f]. – F. Halkin and A.-J. Festugière, *Le corpus athénien de saint Pachôme* (Cahiers d'orientalisme 2; Geneva: P. Cramer, 1982).

*Translations:* A. A. Athanassakis, trans., *The Life of Pachomius: Vita prima graeca* (Missoula, Mont.: Published by Scholars Press for the Society of Biblical Literature, 1975) [*First Greek Life*]. – *Pachomian koinonia* (trans. A. Veilleux; 3 vols.; CistSS 45–47; Kalamazoo: Cistercian, 1980–1982) [*Lives, Opera omnia, Works by Disciples*].

*Encyclopedia Articles:* H. Bacht, *DSp* 12:7–16. – A. Veilleux, *Coptic Encyclopedia* 6:1859–64. – J. Gribomont, *EECh* 2:628. – J. E. Goehring, *EEC* 2:845–46.

*Collections of Essays:* A. de Vogüé, *De saint Pachôme à Jean Cassien* (SA 120; Rome: Pontificio Ateneo S. Anselmo, 1996), 17–267. – J. E. Goehring, *Ascetics, Society, and the Desert: Studies in Early Egyptian Monasticism* (Harrisburg, Pa.: Trinity, 1999).

*Studies:* P. Resch, *La doctrine ascétique des premiers maîtres égyptiens du quatrième siècle* (Paris: Beauchesne, 1931). – J. Leipoldt, "Pachôm," *BSAC* 16 (1962): 191–229. – M. M. Van Molle, "Confrontation entre les Règles et la littérature pachômienne postérieure," *VS.S* 21 (1968): 394–424. – A. Veilleux, *La liturgie dans le cénobitisme pachômien au quatrième siècle* (SA 57; Rome: "I. B. C." Libreria Herder, 1968). – F. Ruppert, *Das pachomianische Mönchtum und die Anfänge klösterlichen Gehorsams* (MüSt 20; Münster: Vier-Türme, 1971). – H. Bacht, *Das Vermächtnis des Ursprungs: Studien zum frühen Mönchtum* (2 vols.; STGL 5, 8; Würzburg: Echter, 1972–1983). – H. Chadwick, "Pachomios and the Idea of Sanctity," in idem, *History and Thought of the Early Church* (VRCS 164; London: Variorum, 1982), n.p. – J. E. Goehring, "New Frontiers in Pachomian Studies," in *The Roots of Egyptian Christianity* (ed. B. A. Pearson and J. E. Goehring; Philadelphia: Fortress, 1986), 236–57. – I. Opelt, "*Lingua ab angelo tradita:* Dekodierungsversuch der Pachomiusbriefe," in *Mémorial Dom Jean Gribomont (1920–1986)* (SEAug 27; Rome: Institutum Patristicum Augustinianum, 1988), 453–61. – R. Lorenz, "Zur Chronologie des Pachomius," *ZNW* 80 (1989): 280–83. – T. G. Kardong, "The Monastic Practices of Pachomius and the Pachomians," *StudMon* 32 (1990): 59–78. – J. Weismayer, "Pachomius und die Gemeinschaft der 'Tabennisioten,'" in idem, ed., *Mönchsväter und Ordensgründer: Männer und Frauen in der Nachfolge Jesu* (Würzburg: Echter, 1991), 11–32. – V. Desprez, "Pachomian Cenobitism," *ABenR* 43 (1992): 233–249, 358–394. – J. E. Goehring, "Withdrawing from the Desert: Pachomius and the Development of Village Monasticism in Upper Egypt," *HTR* 89 (1996): 267–85; repr. in *Forms of Devotion: Conversion, Worship, Spirituality, and Asceticism* (ed. E. Ferguson; Recent Studies in Early Christianity 5; New York: Garland, 1999), 233–51. – P. Rousseau, *Pachomius: The Making of a Community in Fourth-Century Egypt* (rev. ed.; TCH 6; Berkeley: University of California Press, 1999).

# B. Rules of Basil the Great

Given his extensive educational visit to the monastic centers of Syria, Mesopotamia, Palestine, and Egypt after his return from Athens (356?), the monastic rules of Basil the Great draw upon the Rule of Pachomius and his own life history. The ecclesiastical circumstances changed substantially in the meantime and influenced his rules as well; thus they took on an entirely different, new shape. At a time when the church had just left behind the era of oppression and had attained its toleration, the Rule of Pachomius was particularly concerned with facing the dangers of anchoritism, and through Athanasius Pachomian monasticism was integrated very early into the church's overall framework. When Basil decided for the ascetic life, the Christianization of the empire had progressed significantly, but the church was also divided over the dispute of the acceptance of the Council of Nicea (325). Eastern monasticism was not integrated; on the contrary, it showed tendencies of an ecclesiological heresy by viewing its own radical ascetic demands as incumbent upon all believers for salvation. This radicalism was based on the situation that is also reflected in the decision of Basil (and Gregory, Augustine, and others) to choose asceticism together with baptism at the same time because, as those who were highly educated in the secular sciences, they were attracted to the earliest Christians' pristine "royal path" of perfection, over against the "worldly" Christianity of their time. Basil's greatness and the enduring achievement that rightly earned him the honorary title "father of Eastern monasticism" consisted in the ecclesiastical integration of an exaggerated and schismatic ascetical enthusiasm, in establishing theologically and spiritually its function within the church, and in bringing order to the monastic rules.

Because of his great authority, Basil's *corpus asceticum* is handed down in eighteen works, only seven of which are accepted as authentic, however: (a) *Sermo de judicio Dei*, (b) *Sermo de fide*, (c) *Regulae morales (Ethica)*, (d) proem of the *Great Asceticon*, (e) *Regulae brevius tractatae*, (f) *Regulae fusius tractatae*, and (g) proem of the *Hypotyposis*. Also included are his *Ep.* 2 and 22 because they are important for Basil's ascetical theology.

(a–b) The two *sermones* represent prefaces to the *Regulae morales* in a later, revised form by Basil himself.

(c) The *Regulae morales* originated in 359/360; in other words, they were written during his stay in Annesi with Gregory of Nazianzus and are the only ones Basil himself named *regulae* (ὅροι). They represent a collection of eighty Scripture references in the form of an index, as it were, intended to guide the reader in his or her reading of the Bible. A later revision made this easier by adding the text to each reference.

Together with their proems, the two rules (d–f) are each called the *Asceticon*. The initial version, from the decade of 360–370, the original of which is lost and preserved only in the Latin translation of Rufinus (after 397) as well as in Syriac versions, was labeled the *Little Asceticon* by Jean Gribomont. It responded to 203 questions. The final revision (the *Great Asceticon*) is dated entirely to the time of Basil's episcopate and is divided into the Longer Rule, with 55 questions and answers, and the Shorter Rule, with 313; in this case, the terms "longer" and "shorter" do not refer to the number of questions answered but to the detailed treatment of the answers (*Regulae fusius/brevius tractatae*).

Basil compiled the *Moralia* and the Rules (g) in revised literary form and gave them the modest title Ὑποτύπωσις ["outline," "draft"] ἀσκήσεως in order to send them, together with a foreword, to his students in Pontus, whom he was not able to visit personally.

As in the case of Pachomius and as is true of all other monastic rules of antiquity, the Rules of Basil do not represent a system but a collection of individual rules based on experience following common, essential principles, as the form of asking (concrete) questions and providing answers—known from the Egyptian *Apophthegmata patrum*—shows. Their first principle is the Pachomian one: Scripture is the exclusive standard for everything. The second principle, however, arises from Basil's own concern to integrate monasticism into the church at large: Scripture points the way to holiness equally for *everyone* in the church. For this reason, Basil prefers to call the monks "those who zealously desire to please God," which applies to them in particular but also to all Christians in general. Hence Basil establishes his rules on the commandment of mutual love. Since God created the human as a creature for community, the monk, too, can only be fulfilled in community. It is on this basis that Basil explains the spiritual-ascetical life in detail: poverty, abstinence, and simplicity as freedom for the Lord; obedience to God's word insofar as it is spoken by divinely appointed authority, not only that of the superiors of the monastery, but also of the husband to the wife, of the master to the slave, of the parents to the children, and of the secular authorities to the citizens of the state; and all other specifics concerning prayer, meals, clothing, work, contacts with the outside world, leadership, repentance, and many others.

Already during his lifetime, Basil's monasticism spread rapidly in the East as well as in the West, as the Latin translation of the Rules and the numerous manuscripts demonstrate. In 1579 Pope Gregory XIII merged the still existing monasteries in Italy into the Basilian Order of Grottaferrata (south of Rome), where it continues to exist today.

*Editions:* PG 31: 619–1428. – *Basili regula* (ed. K. Zelzer; CSEL 86; Vienna: Hölder-Pichler-Tempsky, 1986). – *Il libro delle domande (le Regole)* (ed. G. Uluhogian; CSCO 536–37; Louvain: Peeters, 1993).

*Translations: The Ascetic Works of St. Basil* (trans. W. K. L. Clarke; London: SPCK; New York: Macmillan, 1925). – *Ascetical Works* (trans. M. M. Wagner; FC 9; New York: Fathers of the Church, 1950).

*Studies—Literature:* E. F. Morison, *St. Basil and His Rule: A Study in Early Monasticism* (London and New York: Oxford University Press, 1912). – W. K. L. Clarke, *St. Basil the Great: A Study in Monasticism* (Cambridge: Cambridge University Press, 1913). – F. Laun, "Die beiden Regeln des Basilius, ihre Echtheit und Entstehung," *ZKG* 44 (1925): 1–61. – M. G. Murphy, *St. Basil and Monasticism* (PatSt 25; Washington, D.C.: Catholic University of America Press, 1930). – P. Humbertclaude, *La doctrine ascétique de saint Basile de Césarée* (ETH; Paris: Beauchesne, 1932). – D. Amand, *L'ascèse monastique de saint Basile: Essai historique* (Maredsous, Belg.: Éditions de Maredsous, 1948). – J. Gribomont, *Histoire du texte des ascétiques de s. Basile* (BMus 32; Louvain: Publications Universitaires, 1953). – J. Gribomont, "Le monachisme au IVᵉ s. en Asie Mineure: De Gangres au messalianisme," in *Papers Presented to the Second International Conference on Patristic Studies Held at Christ Church, Oxford, 1955* (ed. K. Aland and F. Cross; StPatr 2; TU 64; Berlin: Akademie, 1957), 400–416. – J. Gribomont, "Les Règles morales de saint Basile et le Nouveau Testament," in *Papers Presented to the Second International Conference on Patristic Studies Held at Christ Church, Oxford, 1955* (ed. K. Aland and F. Cross; StPatr 2; TU 64; Berlin: Akademie, 1957), 416–26. – J. Gribomont, "Le renoncement au monde dans l'idéal ascétique de saint Basile," *Irén* 31 (1958): 282–307, 460–75. – J. Gribomont, "Un aristocrate révolutionnaire, évêque et moine: S. Basile," *Aug* 17 (1977): 179–91. – A. Holmes, *A Life Pleasing to God: The Spirituality of the Rules of St. Basil* (CistSS 189; Kalamazoo: Cistercian, 2000) [ET].

# C. Augustine's Monastic Writings

Augustine belonged to the fourth-century personalities for whom, as in the case of Basil the Great, the decision to become a Christian coincided with the decision for a life in a monastic community. Immediately after his conversion in Milan, he withdrew, from fall 386 to Easter 387, the date of his baptism, to the estate of Cassiciacum, belonging to Verecundus, his friend, situated at the foot of the Alps northeast of Milan. He was joined by his mother, Monica; Navigius, his brother; Adeodatus, his son; Lastidianus and Rusticus, his cousins; Alypius, his friend; and the two youths Licentius and Trygetius. Again, as with Basil in Annisi, this setup functioned more like a learned *otium* than like monastic life in the Pachomian sense, as shown by his works from this period: philosophical dialogues in a Platonic/Ciceronian style concerning the discernibility of truth, happiness, the good, and God and the human person. Although it was characterized by stronger monastic features, the monastic community following his return to Tagaste in 388–391 never lost its scholarly character. Here the intellectual elite of North Africa gathered around Augustine, with the result that its members were continually being appointed bishops. As is well known, this prompted Augustine not only to complain about this disruption of monastic life but, as far as possible, to avoid any city where the episcopal see was vacant (*Serm.* 355.2). When finally he was appointed to be a priest in Hippo, however, where he had fancied himself safe, he petitioned for permission to complete the original intention that led him there, namely, to establish a monastery, which ultimately became the place of the *vita communis* of the clerics of Hippo. Indeed, Augustine went so far as to make the renunciation of possessions a condition for ordination (*Serm.* 355.6; 356.14). He himself always regretted having to give up his monastic life for the restless worries of the episcopal office, and whenever possible withdrew to his monastic community for reflection, even as a bishop. Thus the monastic structure pervaded all of Augustine's postconversion life and yielded his two monastic works: the *Regula ad servos Dei* and *De opere monachorum*.

# 1. Rules

Surprisingly, it is the Rule of Eugippius, written about one hundred years after Augustine's death, that first reports that Augustine had written a monastic rule, and only another fifty years later did a writer identify him as the writer of the rule that is considered the Augustinian. This and the fact that the Rule(s) of Augustine are handed down in a total of nine versions account for the many text-critical problems and those associated with their tradition, authenticity, and dating. In his edition of 1967 and in his two-volume commentary (1980–1988), Luc Verheijen has addressed these issues in an exemplary and pioneering way. They represent the current state of research, which George Lawless (1987) has summarized clearly and accurately. Of the nine versions, four are addressed to communities of men and five to women.

a. Rules for men:

  1) *Praeceptum:* Rule (begins with, *"Haec sunt quae ut observetis praecipimus . . ."*; ends with, *" . . . in temptationem non inducatur"*);
  2) *Ordo monasterii:* Short Rule (begins with, *"Ante omnia, fratres carissimi . . ."*; ends with, *" . . . de vestra salute"*);
  3) *Praeceptum longius:* Longer Rule = *Ordo monasterii* + *Praeceptum;*
  4) *Regula recepta:* the *Praeceptum,* preceded by the first sentence of the *Ordo.*

b. Rules for women:

  5) *Obiurgatio:* A letter chiding the nuns for quarreling among themselves and for disobedience toward their superior (begins with, *"Sicut parate est severitas . . ."*; ends with, *" . . . lacrimas Petri pastoris"*) (*Ep.* 211.1–4);
  6) *Regularis informatio:* the female version of the *Praeceptum* (*Ep.* 211.5–16);
  7) *Epistula longior:* a combination of the *Obiurgatio* and the *Regularis informatio;*
  8) *Ordo monasterii feminis datus:* the female version of the *Ordo monasterii;*
  9) *Epistula longissima:* a combination of a paragraph of the *Obiurgatio* with the *Ordo monasterii feminis datus* and a number of paragraphs of the *Regularis informatio.*

What remains are three primary texts of the Rules of Augustine: *Praeceptum* (1) and *Regularis informatio* (6); *Ordo monasterii* (2) and *Ordo monasterii feminis datus* (8), which are identical in text, except for the different gender; and *Obiurgatio* (5). The four remaining texts are only compilations of these versions; the question of their origin remains unresolved. Likewise, although the suggestions concerning authorship, place of origin, and date of the three primary texts tend in a direction accepted by the majority, they nevertheless are far from being accepted as certain by everyone. The majority tend to accept that all three primary texts originated with Augustine ca. 397; they were initially written for the community of monks at Hippo and later were rewritten as rules for women. But even Verheijen does not concur with every aspect and instead maintains that §§2–10 of the *Ordo monasterii* (2) are the work of Alypius, a friend of Augustine and bishop of Tagaste. On these issues, therefore, the research and argumentation in Verheijen and Lawless should be consulted thoroughly and in detail.

The *Praeceptum* (= *Regularis informatio*) is composed of eight chapters: concerning holding possessions in common according to the need of the individual and without jealousy or pride (1); concerning worthy prayer to be offered at set times in the oratory set aside specifically for this purpose (2); concerning asceticism in food and clothing, again according to an individual's abilities at a given time (3); concerning behavior outside the monastery, especially toward the other sex, as well as the *correctio fraterna* (4); concerning conduct within the monastery: labor, clothing, personal hygiene, sickness, administration (5); concerning disputes and discipline in the monastery (6); concerning obedience and those in authority (7); and final requirements: petitioning for God's grace and an order to listen to the rules weekly (8). The basic idea permeating the Rules of Augustine, as well as those of Pachomius and Basil, is to follow the earliest biblical community (Acts 4:31–35). For this reason, being in community represents the decisive, fundamental value of everything, and all of life is to be functionally ordered to it, without extremes, without personal boasting, and without expecting too much from an individual, under the direction of the words of Scripture itself.

By means of its initial words, the much briefer *Ordo monasterii* (= *Ordo monasterii feminis datus*) emphasizes even more clearly the basis for everything: "Above all else, dearly loved brothers, love God and then the neighbor," which is reminiscent of the Rule of Basil. This is followed, in a total of eleven sections, by precise regulations for monastic life: (1) prayer times (2); work periods (3); personal poverty (4); obedience without inward opposition (5–6); food and reading at table (7); leaving the monastery (8); order of the day (9); *correctio* (10); and affirmation of salvation in Christ to all who faithfully observe this rule (11). Life in a monastic community most of all serves the purpose of overcoming selfishness and orienting one's life to God and fellow human beings. Personal ascetical extravagances, such as those of the anchorites, are neither demanded nor desired. Life in the community is primarily based on three pillars: renunciation of one's possessions by all members of the monastery without exception, joyful obedience, and labor whereby everyone contributes to the welfare of the community.

*Bibliographies:* L. M. J. Verheijen, "La Règle de saint Augustin: Complément bibliographique," *Aug(L)* 36 (1986): 297–303.

*Editions: La Règle de saint Augustin* (ed. L. Verheijen; 2 vols.; Paris: Études Augustiniennes, 1967).

*Translations: Augustine of Hippo: Selected Writings* (trans. M. T. Clark; CWS; London: SPCK; New York: Paulist, 1984), 479–493. – G. Lawless, *Augustine of Hippo and His Monastic Rule* (Oxford: Clarendon; New York: Oxford University Press, 1986).

*Encyclopedia Articles:* A. Zumkeller, *TRE* 4:745–48. – G. Lawless, "Regula," in *Augustine through the Ages* (ed. A. Fitzgerald; Grand Rapids: Eerdmans, 1999), 707–9.

*Studies:* A. Sage, *La Règle de saint Augustin commentée par ses écrits* (2d ed.; Paris: la Vie Augustinienne, 1971). – A. Sage, *The Religious Life according to Saint Augustine* (trans. P. C. Thabault; Brooklyn, N.Y.: New City, 1990); trans. of *La vie religieuse selon saint Augustin* (Paris: la Vie Augustinienne, 1972). – L. de Seilhac, *L'utilisation par s. Césaire d'Arles de la Règle de s. Augustin: Étude de terminologie et de doctrine monastiques* (SA 62; Rome: Editrice Anselmiana, 1974). – L. Verheijen, *Le Règle de saint Augustin* (2 vols.; Paris: Études Augustiniennes, 1967). – A. Zumkeller, *Augustine's Ideal of the Religious Life* (trans. E. Colledge; New York: Fordham University Press, 1986); trans. of *Mönchtum des heiligen Augustinus* (2d ed.; Cass. 11; Würzburg: Augustinus, 1968). T. J. van Bavel, *The Rule of Saint Augustine* (trans. R. Canning; CisstSS 138; Kalamazoo: Cistercian, 1996) [ET/Com]. – G. Lawless, *Augustine of Hippo and His Monastic Rule* (Oxford: Clarendon; New York: Oxford University Press, 1987) [ET/Com]. – A. Mary, *The Rule of Saint Augustine: An Essay in Understanding* (Villanova, Pa.: Augustinian, 1992). – S. Marie-Ancilla, *La Règle de saint Augustin* (Paris: Cerf, 1996). – A. de Vogüé, *Histoire littéraire du mouvement monastique dans l'antiquité, Première partie: Le monachisme latin* (5 vols.; Paris: Cerf, 1991–2003), vols. 2–3.

## 2. De opere monachorum

Upon the request of Aurelius, bishop of Carthage, Augustine wrote the little booklet *De opere monachorum* to bring theological and practical clarity to a dispute that erupted in Carthage ca. 400 over the question of the work of monks. Augustine himself recounts the event in his *Retract.* 2.47:

> Necessity forced me to write a book, *On the Work of Monks:* the fact that when monasteries began to be founded at Carthage, some monks who were obedient to the Apostle [cf. 2 Thess 3:6–12] were making a living by manual work but others wanted to so live on the alms of the faithful that although they were doing nothing to possess or obtain necessities, they thought and boasted that they, in a better way, were fulfilling the precept given to the apostles, in which the Lord says, "Look at the birds of the air and the lilies of the field" [cf. Matt 6:26, 28].

According to Augustine, however, Paul's admonition was to be understood spiritually only.

Against such argumentation, Augustine substantiates the ideal of his own monasteries with the correct interpretation of the two disputed biblical texts by appealing to their contexts and the overall biblical teaching. He first notes that when Paul referred to work, he clearly meant manual labor. The apostles had indeed received the instruction and right from Christ himself to require believers to support them appropriately, but Paul placed greater value on not using this right and instead worked for his subsistence with his own hands out of consideration for the weaker members. This does not release the communities from their obligation for the welfare of the monasteries, but conversely it could not offer a pretext for shying away from work. The reference to freedom to engage in continuous spiritual activity is not relevant here, since it is labor that carries out the mission of the gospel in the first place. Instead the bad example of the monks who shy away from work is contagious, so that a dispensation from work is to be granted only to the one who is not able to do so. The word of the gospel, which the monks misinterpret, does not refer to total inactivity but rather calls for trusting in the provision of God, who will also sustain the believer when he is not able to do so himself. Testing such provision by being lazy, however, is entirely inconsistent with its purpose. In this way Augustine presented in detail the purpose and reason for the maxim *Ora et labora*, which has become famous through the Rule of St. Benedict.

*Editions:* PL 40:547–582. – *Sancti Avreli Avgvstini De fide et symbolo, De fide et operibvs, De agone christiano, De continentia, De bono conivgali, De sancta virginitate, De bono vidvitatis, De advlterinis conivgiis lib. II, De mendacio, Contra mendacivm, De opere monachorvm, De divinatione daemonvm, De cvra pro mortvis gerenda, De patientia* (ed. J. Zycha; CSEL 41; Vienna: F. Tempsky, 1900), 529–96.

*Translations:* H. Brown, trans., "Of the Work of Monks," in *NPNF¹* (Peabody, Mass.: Hendrickson, 1995; repr. of 1887 ed.), 3:503–24. – *Treatises on Various Subjects* (trans. M. S. Muldowney; FC 16; New York: Fathers of the Church, 1952), 321-94.

*Encyclopedia Article:* G. Lawless, "Opere monachorum, De," *Augustine through the Ages* (Grand Rapids: Eerdmans, 1999), 596.

*Study:* K. B. Steinhauser, "The Cynic Monks of Carthage: Some Observations on the '*De opere monachorum*,'" in *Augustine: Presbyter factus sum* (Collectanea augustiniana; New York: Lang, 1993), 455–62.

# II. MONASTIC LITERATURE

## A. *Evagrius Ponticus*

Although the monastic rules reflect cenobitic monasticism, the broader monastic literature also offers insight into the anchorite movement, with the first contribution coming from Evagrius Ponticus. He was born ca. 345 at Ibora, in the province of Pontus, the son of the local *chorepiscopus;* several notable church fathers of his time influenced his life significantly. Basil the Great chose him to be a lector, and after 379 Gregory of Nazianzus ordained him to the diaconate. He may also have obtained his far-reaching literary and theological education from Gregory, for he repeatedly describes himself as his student. In 381 he followed Gregory to Constantinople, where he remained until 383, even under Nectarius, the patriarch. Subsequently he withdrew, initially to the monastery of Rufinus and Melania on the Mount of Olives near Jerusalem, but after a few months he continued his journey to Egypt. First he stayed in Nitria, in lower Egypt, for two years, and then he joined the semi-anchorite community of Kellia in the Nitrian desert, where he remained until his death in 399. During this time he earned his livelihood as a copyist and maintained close contact with the other great monastic fathers in his surroundings, especially with Macarius, the Egyptian who was a student of the great Anthony and led a community of monks in the desert of Scetis (in modern Wādī al-Natrūn) about twenty-five miles away. His contact also extended to Ammonius, one of the four "tall brothers" who, together with John Chrysostom, became entangled in the first phase of the Origenist controversy.

Although Evagrius died earlier, this controversy nevertheless had catastrophic consequences for the preservation of his numerous and important works, because the Second Council of Constantinople (553) condemned him posthumously as an Origenist (on the problematic nature of posthumously condemning a writer who was regarded as orthodox during his lifetime, cf. the comments on Diodore in ch. 7.IV). As a result, the Greek originals of his writings, apart from a few fragments, are lost, unless they were handed down pseudepigraphically under the names of other fathers, especially Nilus of Ancyra (d. ca. 430). All the same, the decisive and enduring influence of Evagrius can hardly be overestimated, since he was the first one to preserve anchoritic spirituality in literary form and made Egyptian monasticism the model for the entire Christian world of the fourth century. For this reason, many of his writings are preserved in Eastern and Latin translations. The *Historia monarchorum in Aegypto,* translated by Rufinus; the *Historia lausiaca* by Palladius, who lived with him for ten years; the *Apophthegmata patrum;* John Cassian; and Maximus the Confessor—all of them wrote about his life in detail, but more than that, they handed down the essentials of his theology.

Evagrius's oeuvre consists primarily of two genres, namely, the commentaries on the Bible, indebted to Origen's allegorical method of interpretation, and monastic, ascetical writings, which are likewise based on Origen's mysticism (as were those of the Cappadocians), without repeating it, of course. The spiritual theology of Evagrius has the anchorite in mind, that is, the question of the purpose of this life and, contingent on this, the question of how the anchorite is able to undertake his or her journey to God by coping with the difficulties and temptations associated with it. In this connection, Evagrius makes the soteriological assumption that in the beginning all creatures had been pure spirit-beings (νόες), created exclusively for the purpose of knowing (γνῶσις) God so as to be made one with him. Since they fell away from beholding God, however, they became souls that God in his mercy relocated into differing bodies and worlds as angels, humans, and demons, so that instead of sharing in knowledge (γνῶσις), they would only share in contemplation (θεωρία). Hence the redemption of the fallen spirit-beings had to take place in the ascent from θεωρία to γνῶσις; in this context, Christ, the only rational being that had not fallen from the γνῶσις of God, is effective as the mediator.

The only goal of monastic life is to attain γνῶσις, which presupposes ἀπά θεια, that is, freedom from all earthly passion; for Evagrius, this certainly assumes a Stoic background. To this end, a monk was to seek ἡσυχία first of all, namely, outward and inward tranquility, in order to begin the battle against πάθη and to be successful in winning it. He attains outward ἡσυχία by renouncing marriage and his earthly goods and withdrawing from worldly communion with people. In doing so, he attains ἀμεριμνία, the freedom from all earthly care. In the seclusion of his small cell, the monk next has to gain inward tranquility as well, which be-

gins by being able to endure solitude and the silence of his cubicle and by not allowing boredom (ἀκηδία) to drive himself outside. As a remedy against boredom,
Evagrius recommends manual work, thus allowing an anchorite to earn his mea-
ger livelihood, as well as tears of repentance and meditation. In this ἡσυχία a
monk is now able to ascend to ἀπάθεια by engaging in the following pursuit: After
leaving behind everything mundane (πράγματα), he combats the thoughts leading
him into temptation by means of πρακτική, the purification of the passionate part
of the soul. According to Evagrius, eight major vices are associated with these
thoughts: gluttony, immorality, greed, sadness, anger, carelessness, vanity, and
pride; through John Cassian and Gregory the Great, these became the seven
deadly sins in the West. Consequently, the battle against sin means practicing the
virtues, which become stronger and stronger: faith, fear of God, abstinence,
steadfastness, hope, passionlessness, love, knowledge, theology, and bliss. This
then opens up the true, spiritual meaning of Scripture for the one who has attained knowledge; in this context, the inner connection between Evagrius's allegorical interpretation of the Bible and his spiritual writings becomes apparent.

As far as the mysticism of Evagrius is concerned, the titles of his main
works speak for themselves: *Praktikos, Gnostikos, Kephalaia gnostica, Sententiae
ad monachos, Rerum monachalium rationes, De malignis cogitationibus, De octo
spiritalibus malitiis, De oratione, Scholia in Psalmos*. Their complex history of
transmission and their status of preservation cannot be addressed here in detail.[2]

*Editions:*
*Opera: Srboy Horn Ewagri Pontacwoy Vark ew Matenagrutiwnk* (ed. B. Sarghissian; Venice:
    S. Ghazar, 1907) [Armenian]. – *Capitula practica, Rerum monachalium rationes,
    Capitula, Spiritales sententiae, De malignis cogitationibus, Sententiae*: PG 40:1219–86.
    – *Tractatus ad Eulogium, De octo spiritibus malis, De oratione, De malignis cogitationi-
    bus*: PG 79: 1093–1234. – *Evagrius Ponticus* (ed. W. Frankenberg; AGWG.PH NF 13.2;
    1912) [Cod. Vatic. syr. N. 178] [*Kephalaia gnostica* with commentary by Babai the
    Great, *Skemmata, Gnosticus, Epistulae, Protrepicus, Paraeneticus*].
*Ad monachos: Studien und Beiträge zur Erklärung und Zeitbestimmung Commodians:
    Nonnenspiegel und Mönchsspiegel des Euagrios Pontikos* (ed. H. Gressmann; TU 39.4;
    Leipzig: Hinrichs, 1913), 152–65.
*De octo spiritibus malitiae: Gli otto spiriti malvagi* (ed. F. Comello; Parma: Pratiche, 1990). –
    *Gli otto spiriti della malvagita: Sui diversi pensieri della malvagita* (ed. F. Moscatelli;
    Cinisello Balsamo: San Paolo, 1996).
*De oratione:* I. Hausherr, *OCP* 5 (1939): 7–71 [Syriac and Arabic].
*Epistula (magna) ad Melaniam:* G. Vitestam, *Seconde partie du traité, qui passe sous le nom
    de "La Grande lettre d'Évagre le Pontique à Mélanie l'Ancienne": Publiée et traduite
    d'après le manuscrit du British Museum Add. 17192* (SMHVL 3; Lund, Swed.: Gleerup,
    1964) [T.sir/Tr.f].
*Fragments:* C. Guillaumont, "Fragments grecs inédits d'Evagre le Pontique," *Texte und
    Untersuchungen* 133 (1987): 209–21.
*Gnostikos: Le gnostique; ou, À celui qui est devenu digne de la science* (ed. A. and C. Guil-
    laumont; SC 356; Paris: Cerf, 1989) [Com].
*Kephalaia gnostica: Les six centuries des "Kephalaia gnostica"* (ed. A. Guillaumont; PO 28.1;
    Paris: Fimin-Didot, 1958).

---

[2] These are accessible fully and clearly in *CPG* 2:2430–82.

*Praktikos: Traité pratique; ou, Le moine* (ed. A. and C. Guillaumont; 2 vols.; SC 170–71; Paris: Cerf, 1971) [Com].

*De malignis cogitationibus: Gli otto spiriti della malvagita: Sui diversi pensieri della malvagita* (ed. F. Moscatelli; Cinisello Balsamo: San Paolo, 1996). – *Sur les pensées* (ed. P. Géhin, C. Guillaumont, and A. Guillaumont; SC 438; Paris: Cerf, 1998) [Com].

*Sententiae ad virginem: Studien und Beiträge zur Erklärung und Zeitbestimmung Commodians: Nonnenspiegel und Mönchsspiegel des Euagrios Pontikos* (ed. H. Gressmann; TU 39.4; Leipzig: Hinrichs, 1913), 143–52.

*Scholia in Ecclesiasten: Scholies à l'Ecclésiaste* (ed. P. Géhin; SC 397; Paris: Cerf, 1993) [Com].

*Scholia in Proverbia: Scholies aux Proverbes* (ed. P. Géhin; SC 340; Paris: Cerf, 1987) [Com].

*Skemmata:* J. Muyldermans, "Evagriana," *Mus* 44 (1931): 37–68, 369–383.

*Translations: The Praktikos: Chapters on Prayer* (trans. J. E. Bamberger; CistSS 4; Spencer, Mass.: Cistercian, 1972). – G. E. H. Palmer, P. Sherrard, and K. Ware, *The Philokalia: The Complete Text, Compiled by St. Nikodimos of the Holy Mountain and St. Makarios of Corinth* (London and Boston: Faber & Faber, 1979–), 1:29–71 [*On Asceticism and Stillness in the Solitary Life, On Discrimination, On Prayer*]. M. Parmentier, "Evagrius of Pontus' 'Letter to Melania,'" *Bijdr* 46 (1985): 2–38; repr. in *Forms of Devotion: Conversion, Worship, Spirituality, and Asceticism* (ed. E. Ferguson; Recent Studies in Early Christianity 5; New York: Garland, 1999), 272–309 [*Ad Melaniam*]. – S. Brock, *The Syriac Fathers on Prayer and the Spiritual Life* (CistSS 101; Kalamazoo: Cistercian, 1987), 66–73 [*Paraeneticus*]. – D. Bundy, "The Kephalaia gnostika," in *Ascetic Behavior in Greco-Roman Antiquity* (ed. V. L. Wimbush; Minneapolis: Fortress, 1990), 175–86 [*Kephalaia gnostica* 1] – M. O'Laughlin, "Antirrheticus (Selections)," in *Ascetic Behavior in Greco-Roman Antiquity* (ed. V. L. Wimbush; Minneapolis: Fortress, 1990), 243–62 [*Antirrheticus* 3–5]. – J. Driscoll, *The Mind's Long Journey to the Holy Trinity: The Ad monachos of Evagrius Ponticus* (Collegeville, Minn.: Liturgical, 1993). – C. Stewart, "Evagrius Ponticus on Prayer and Anger," in *Religions in Late Antiquity in Practice* (ed. R. Valantasis; Princeton, N.J.: Princeton University Press, 2000), 71–80 [*Antirrheticus* 5].

*Encyclopedia Articles:* A. and C. Guillaumont, *DSp* 4:1731–34. – A. and C. Guillaumont, *RAC* 6: 1088–1107. – A. Guillaumont, *TRE* 10:565–70. – J. Gribomont, *EECh* 1:306. – F. W. Norris, *EEC* 1:405–6.

*Studies: Individual Works:* R. Melcher, *Der 8. Brief des hl. Basilius, ein Werk des Evagrios Pontikus* (MBTh 1; Münster: Aschendorff, 1923). – I. Hausherr, *Les versions syriaque et arménienne d'Évagre le Pontique: Leur valeur–leur relation–leur utilisation* (OrChr[R] 22.2; Rome: Pontificium Institutum Orientalium Studiorum, 1931). – A. and C. Guillaumont, "Le texte véritable des '*Gnostica*' d'Évagre le Pontique," *RHR* 142 (1952): 156–205. – I. Hausherr, *Les leçons d'un contemplatif: Le Traité de l'oraison d'Évagre le Pontique* (Paris: Beauchesne, 1960). – M.-J. Rondeau, "Le commentaire sur les Psaumes d'Évagre le Pontique," *OCP* 26 (1960): 307–48. – P. Géhin, "Un nouvel inédit d'Évagre le Pontique: Son commentaire de l'Ecclésiaste," *Byzantion* 49 (1979): 188–98. – G. Bunge, *Das Geistgebet: Studien zum Traktat De oratione des Evagrios Pontikos* (Cologne: Luthe, 1987). – J. Driscoll, "A Key for Reading the *Ad monachos* of Evagrius Ponticus," *Aug* 30 (1990): 361–92. – S. Elm, "Evagrius Ponticus' *Sententiae ad virginem*," *DOP* 45 (1991): 97–120. – J. Driscoll, *The "Ad monachos" of Evagrius Ponticus: Its Structure and a Select Commentary* (SA 104; Rome: Abbazia S. Paolo, 1991) [ET]. – M. O'Laughlin, "The Bible, the Demons, and the Desert: Evaluating the *Antirrheticus* of Evagrius Ponticus," *StudMon* 34 (1992): 201–15. – G. Bunge, "Der mystische Sinn der Schrift: Anlasslich der Veröffentlichung der Scholien zum Ecclesiasten des Evagrios Pontikos," *StudMon* 36 (1994): 135–46. – G. Bunge, "Evagrios Pontikos: Der Prolog des *Antirrhetikos*," *StudMon* 39 (1997): 77–106. – G. E. Gould, "An Ancient Monastic Writing Giving Advice to Spiritual Directors (Evagrius of Pontus, *On Teachers and Disciples*)," *Hallel* 22 (1997): 96–103 [ET]. – V. Desprez and M. André Ducos, "Évagre le Pontique: Réflections (*Skemmata*): Une traducion annotée," *Lettre de Ligugé* 284.2 (1998): 14–29.

*Studies: Sources and Influence:* M. Viller, "Aux sources de la spiritualité de st. Maxime: Les oeuvres d'Evagre le Pontique," *RAM* 11 (1930): 156–84, 239–68. – S. Marsili, *Giovanni Cassiano ed Evagrio Pontico: Dottrina sulla carità e la contemplazione* (SA 5; Rome: Herder, 1936). – G. Bunge, "Evagre le Pontique et les deux Macaires," *Irén* 56 (1983): 215–27, 323–60. – N. Gendle, "Cappadocian Elements in the Mystical Theology of Evagrius Ponticus," *StPat* 16 (1985): 373–384.

*Studies: Spirituality:* A. Levasti, "Il più grande mistico del deserto: Evagrio il Pontico († 399)," *RAMi* 13 (1968): 242–64. – A. Guillaumont, "Un philosophe au désert: Évagre le Pontique," *RHR* 181 (1972): 29–56. – G. Bunge, *Akedia: Die geistliche Lehre des Evagrios Pontikos vom Überdruss* (4th ed.; Würzburg: Der Christliche Osten, 1995). – G. Bunge, *Geistliche Vaterschaft: Christliche Gnosis bei Evagrios Pontikos* (BSPLi 23; Regensburg: Pustet, 1988). – G. Bunge, "*Mysterium unitatis:* Der Gedanke der Einheit von Schöpfer und Geschöpf in der evagrianischen Mystik," *FZPhTh* 36 (1989): 449–69. – R. Augst, *Lebensverwirklichung und christlicher Glaube: Acedia–Religiöse Gleichgültigkeit als Problem der Spiritualität bei Evagrius Ponticus* (Frankfurt and New York: Lang, 1991). – C. Joest, "Die Bedeutung von *akedia* und *apatheia* bei Evagrios Pontikos," *StudMon* 35 (1993): 7–53. – J. Driscoll, "Spiritual Progress in the Works of Evagrius Ponticus," in *Spiritual Progress in the Spirituality of Late Antiquity and Early Monasticism* (ed. J. Driscoll and M. Sheridan; Rome: Pontificio Ateneo S. Anselmo, 1994), 48–84. – A. Guillaumont, "La vision de l'intellect par lui-même dans la mystique évagrienne," in idem, *Études sur la spiritualité de l'Orient chrétien* (SpOr 66; Bégrolles-en-Mauges: Abbaye de Bellefontaine, 1996), 143–50. – L. Dysinger, "The Significance of Psalmody in the Mystical Theology of Evagrius of Pontus," in *Papers Presented at the Twelfth International Conference on Patristic Studies Held in Oxford, 1995* (ed. E. Livingstone; StPatr 30; Louvain: Peeters, 1997), 176–82. – J. Driscoll, "Evagrius, Paphnutius, and the Reasons for Abandonment by God," *StudMon* 40 (1998): 259–86. – J. Driscoll, "Apatheia and Purity of Heart in Evagrius Ponticus," in *Purity of Heart in Early Ascetic and Monastic Literature: Essays in Honor of Juana Raasch, O.S.B.* (ed. H. A. Luckman and Linda Kulzer; Collegeville, Minn.: Liturgical, 1999), 141–59. – W. Harmless, "'Salt for the Impure, Light for the Pure': Reflections on the Pedagogy of Evagrius Ponticus," in *Papers Presented at the Thirteenth International Conference on Patristic Studies Held in Oxford, 1999* (ed. M. Wiles and E. Yarnold; StPatr 37; Louvain: Peeters, 2001), 514–26.

*Studies: Origenism:* A. Guillaumont, "Évagre et les anathématismes antiorigénistes de 553," in *Papers Presented to the Third International Conference on Patristic Studies Held at Christ Church, Oxford, 1959* (ed. F. Cross; StPatr 3; TU 78; Berlin: Akademie, 1961), 219–26. – F. Refoulé, "La christologie d'Évagre et l'origénisme," *OCP* 27 (1961): 221–66. – A. Guillaumont, *Les "Képhalaia gnostica" d'Evagre le Pontique et l'histoire de l'origénisme chez les grecs et les syriens* (PatSor 5; Paris: Seuil, 1962). – A. Dempf, "Evagrios Pontikos als Metaphysiker und Mystiker," *PhJ* 77 (1970): 297–319. – F. Kline, "The Christology of Evagrius and the Parent System of Origen," *Cistercian Studies Quarterly* 20 (1985): 155–83. – M. O'Laughlin, "Elements of Fourth-Century Origenism: The Anthropology of Evagrius Ponticus and Its Sources," in *Origen of Alexandria: His World and His Legacy* (ed. C. Kannengiesser and W. Petersen; Notre Dame, Ind.: University of Notre Dame Press, 1988), 355–73. – G. Bunge, "Hénade ou monade? Au sujet de deux notions centrales de la terminologie évagrienne," *Mus* 102 (1989): 69–91. – M. O'Laughlin, "New Questions concerning the Origenism of Evagrius," in *Origeniana quinta* (ed. R. J. Daly; Louvain: Louvain University Press; Peeters, 1992), 529–34. – S. Rubenson, "Evagrios Pontikos und die Theologie der

Wüste," in *Logos: Festschrift für Luise Abramowski zum 8. Juli 1993* (ed. H. C. Brennecke, E. L. Grasmück, and C. Markschies; BZNW 67; Berlin and New York: de Gruyter, 1993), 384–401.

# B. Symeon of Mesopotamia (Macarius)

Roughly contemporaneous with Evagrius, a second important monastic writer was at work at another Near Eastern center of early monasticism, in Mesopotamia. His writings are handed down under the name of Macarius and for this reason have traditionally been attributed to the Egyptian monastic father of the same name, the student of the great Anthony and founder of the monastic communities in the desert of Scetis. It was already observed in the thirteenth and eighteenth centuries that some of the passages of the works pointed to an Eastern monastic movement that ultimately became heretical, namely, the Messalians or Euchites (from εὐχή = "prayer," hence "those who pray"). They perceived prayer to be the monks' exclusive task and rejected any discipline of, or integration into, the church. For this reason, they were initially condemned by a synod in Constantinople (426), followed by the Council of Ephesus (431), which did so on the basis of excerpts from their manual, *Asceticon*. In 1920 Louis Villecourt demonstrated that precisely these excerpts are cited in the works of Macarius; since then the recognition of the Messalian origin of the writings of "Macarius" has been accepted, and Hermann Dörries identified the writer as Symeon, one of the leaders of Messalianism.

Biographically, the works of Symeon/Macarius divulge only that he was an educated Greek and, together with his monastic community, lived in the vicinity of the upper Euphrates. He presumed the doctrinal decision of the Council of Constantinople (381); in content there are also connections with the work of Basil the Great, and the tractate *De instituto christiano* by Gregory of Nyssa is probably dependent upon Symeon/Macarius. He thus was a contemporary of the great Cappadocians after 380 and before 426, since the *Asceticon* had already been condemned by then.

The writings of Symeon/Macarius are transmitted in four major collections:

- I (= B), containing sixty-four *logoi*, the first one being the so-called Great Letter;

- II (= H), consisting of fifty spiritual homilies;

- III (= C), forty-three homilies, twenty-eight of which are clearly distinct from collection II and eight of which are also found in collection I;

- IV (= W), twenty-six *logoi*, all of which are also found in collection I.

In terms of literary genres, the "Great Letter" represents a treatise; there are also two letters, twenty *erōtoapokriseis,* fifty homilies, and thirty *logia.*

Despite many similarities in matters of detail, the theology and spirituality of Symeon/Macarius differs fundamentally from that of Evagrius Ponticus because of the former's Messalian position. In agreement with the theology of the church at large, he assumes that all human sin is predicated upon original sin. Unlike the common theology of the church, however, he does not acknowledge that this inherited debt is cleansed in baptism, but merely recognizes the latter as the beginning of the spiritual battle against evil, in which the grace of the Spirit has to be gained more and more, for the latter renews the image of God in the human person. Hence, for him, the virtue surpassing all others and on which all others depend is prayer; in the ideal case, this becomes constant prayer. This means, however, that redemption does not primarily result from Christ's sacrifice and from participating in it in the sacrament of baptism, but from success in the battle of prayer and from gaining through it the grace of the Spirit on the basis of an individual's effort. Ἡσυχία is the prerequisite of effective prayer, from which Satan seeks to distract by means of evil thoughts, against which it is necessary to fight. The concrete form of this battle is cenobitic monasticism in poverty and celibacy, on the one hand, for the sake of freedom from earthly bondages so as to enable the soul to unite with God and, on the other, as a sign of disdain for what is transitory. The life of prayer does not isolate the individual from the community but entails the task of διακονία for each other, and this makes the experienced ascetics into the community's competent spiritual and practical leaders.

*Editions:* M. Kmosko, ed., *Liber graduum* (PS 3). – G. L. Marriot, *Macarii Anecdota: Seven Unpublished Homilies of Macarius* (HTS 5; Cambridge, Mass.: Harvard University Press, 1918; repr., New York: Kraus Reprint, 1969). – W. Jaeger, *Two Rediscovered Works of Ancient Christian Literature: Gregory of Nyssa and Macarius* (Leiden: Brill, 1954; repr., 1965) *[I 1]*. – *Neue Homilien des Makarius/Symeon* (ed. E. Klostermann and H. Berthold; TU 72; Berlin: Akademie, 1961) *[III]*. – *Die 50 geistlichen Homilien des Makarios* (ed. H. Dörries, E. Klostermann, and M. Kroeger; PTS 4; Berlin: de Gruyter, 1964) *[II]*. – *Les cinq recensions de l'Ascéticon syriaque d'abba Isaïe* (ed. R. Draguet; 4 vols.; CSCO 289–90, 293–94; Louvain: SCO, 1968), 289:2–8, 14–19 [II 3, 19 T.sir]; 293:1–5, 9–12 [Tr.f]. – *Makarios/Symeon Reden und Briefe* (ed. H. Berthold; 2 vols.; GSC; Berlin: Akademie, 1973) *[I 2–64]*. – *Oeuvres spirituelles* (ed. V. Desprez; SC 275; Paris: Cerf, 1980) *[III Com]*. – *Die syrische Überlieferung der Schriften des Makarios* (ed. W. Strothmann; 2 vols.; GOF.S 21; Wiesbaden: Harrassowitz, 1981) [T.sir/Tr.ted]. – *Schriften des Makarios/Symeon unter dem Namen des Ephraem* (ed. W. Strothmann; GOF.S 22; Weisbaden: Harrassowitz, 1981) [g]. – R. Staats, *Makarios-Symeon Epistula magna: Eine messalianische Mönchsregel und ihre Umschrift in Gregors von Nyssa "De instituto christiano"* (AAWG.PH 3.134; Göttingen: Vandenhoeck & Ruprecht, 1984).

*Translations:* *The Fifty Spiritual Homilies and the Great Letter* (trans. G. Maloney; CWS; New York: Paulist, 1992).

*Encyclopedia Articles:* V. Desprez and M. Canévet, *DSp* 10:20–43. – J. Gribomont, *EECh* 1:514. – O. Hesse, *TRE* 21:730–35.

*Collection of Essays:* W. Strothmann, ed., *Makarios-Symposion über das Böse: Vorträge der Finnisch-Deutschen Theologentagung in Goslar, 1980* (GOF.S 24; Göttingen: Harrassowitz, 1983).

*Transmission of the Text:* H. Dörries, *Symeon von Mesopotamien: Die Überlieferung der messalianischen "Makarios"-Schriften* (TU 55.1; Leipzig: Hinrichs, 1941). – E. Klostermann, *Symeon und Macarius: Bemerkungen zur Textgestalt zweier divergierender Überlieferungen* (ABAW.PH 1943.11; Berlin: In Kommission bei de Gruyter, 1944). – R. A. Klostermann, *Die slavische Überlieferung der Makariusschriften* (GVSH.H 4.3; Göteborg, Swed.: Elanders boktr., 1950). – W. Strothmann, *Textkritische Anmerkungen zu den Geistlichen Homilien des Makarios/Symeon* (GOF.S 23; Göttingen: Harrassowitz, 1981).

*Studies:* G. Quispel, *Makarius, das Thomasevangelium, und das Lied von der Perle* (NovTSup 15; Leiden: Brill, 1967). – E. A. Davids, *Das Bild vom neuen Menschen: Ein Beitrag zum Verständnis des Corpus macarianum* (SPS 2; Salzburg and Munich: Pustet, 1968). – R. Staats, *Gregor von Nyssa und die Messalianer: Die Frage der Priorität zweier altkirchlicher Schriften* (PTS 8; Berlin: de Gruyter, 1968). – A. J. M. Davids, "Der Grosse Brief des Makarios: Analyse einer griechischen Kontroversschrift," in *Heuresis: Festschrift f. Andreas Rohracher, 25 Jahre Erzbischof v. Salzburg* (ed. T. Michels; Salzburg: O. Müller, 1969), 78–90. – H. Dörries, *Die Theologie des Makarios/Symeon* (AAWG.PH 3.103; Göttingen: Vandenhoeck & Ruprecht, 1978). – T. Ihnken, "Zum 13. Kapitel des Grossen Briefes des Makarios/Symeon: Eine Anmerkung," *ZKG* 97 (1986): 79–84. – V. Desprez, "Le baptême chez le Pseudo-Macaire," *EO* 5 (1988): 121–55. – C. Stewart, *"Working the Earth of the Heart": The Messalian Controversy in History, Texts, and Language to AD 431* (OTM; Oxford: Clarendon; New York: Oxford University Press, 1991). – A. Golitzin, "Temple and Throne of the Divine Glory: Pseudo-Macarius and Purity of Heart," in *Purity of Heart in Early Ascetic and Monastic Literature* (ed. H. Luckman and L. Kulzer; Collegeville, Minn.: Liturgical, 1999), 107–29.

# C. John Cassian

The third great monastic writer of the fourth century is John Cassian, whose origins and life, as we know them from his own works, resemble partly those of Rufinus and Jerome and partly those of Epiphanius of Constantia (Salamis). He demonstrates well how much the spirit of Eastern monasticism has stimulated and shaped Western monasticism. Born into an affluent Christian family in Dobrogea (Gennadius, *De viris illustribus* 61: *natione Scythica*) ca. 360, he received a high-quality classical education and was fluent both in Greek and in Latin. While still a *puer* (*Institutiones*, pref. 4), thus presumably ca. 378–380, he entered a monastery near the Church of the Nativity in Bethlehem together with his friend Germanus. Some time later—Cassian describes himself as *adhuc adulescentior* (*Collationes* 14.9)—both traveled to Egypt to acquaint themselves with the monasticism of this region and, after visiting the Thebaid, settled in the desert of Scetis at the time when Evagrius Ponticus provided Egyptian monasticism with decisive spiritual leadership. At the outset of the Origenist controversy, ca. 399,[3] they moved to Constantinople, where John Chrysostom ordained Cassian to the diaconate despite his remonstrations and entrusted him with the

---

[3] Differently in F. Bordolani (*EECh* 1:149): "The violent religious clashes following the letter of Theophilus of Alexandria against the anthropomorphists (ca. 390), led him to leave Egypt for good."

supervision of the treasure of the cathedral. After the fall of John (404), together with Germanus he was sent to Rome with a letter addressed to Pope Innocent. He remained there for several years and formed a friendship with Leo, the archdeacon and later pope. In Rome he was also ordained to the priesthood and lost his friend through death. The final part of his life he spent in southern Gaul, in Massilia (Marseilles), where he founded two monasteries, St. Victor for men and St. Salvator for women. He died after 432.

During the time at the monastery in Massilia, Cassian wrote three works: *Institutiones, Collationes,* and *De incarnatione Domini contra Nestorium* in seven books, which must have been written before the condemnation of Patriarch Nestorius of Constantinople, that is, before summer 431, since it still addresses Nestorius as bishop. This remained the only Western attempt at refuting Nestorian Christology. The first book still opposes Leporius, the monk from Gaul (Massilia?), who tends to be labeled a "pre-Nestorian," despite the fact that he had already been accepted again as orthodox before 430 on the grounds of his *Libellus emendationis sive satisfactionis,* written under the direction of Augustine. Although Cassian's orthodoxy is not in question, his name was added to the list of condemned authors by the Roman church in the *Decretum gelasianum* (early sixth century). The reason for this is that he opposed Augustine in the controversy concerning grace and free will, precipitated in Massilia by Augustine's writings to the monks at Hadrumetum in North Africa, *De gratia et libero arbitrio* and *De correptione et gratia* (427).

*Editions:* Johannis Cassiani De institvtis coenobiorvm et de octo principalivm vitiorvm remediis libri XII; De incarnatione Domini contra Nestorivm libri VII (ed. M. Petschenig: CSEL 17; Vienna: F. Tempsky, 1888) [Institutiones, De incarnatione].

*Translations:* E. C. S. Gibson, trans., "The Twelve Books on the Institutes of the Coenobia," "The Conferences," and "The Seven Books on the Incarnation of the Lord, against Nestorius," in NPNF[2] (Peabody, Mass.: Hendrickson, 1995 repr. of 1894 ed.), 11:161–21 [Institutiones, Collationes, De incarnatione].

*Encyclopedia Articles:* M. Olphe-Galliard, DSp 2:214–76. – A. Hamman, Patrologia 3:486–96. – O. Chadwick, TRE 7:650–57. – F. Bordonali, EECh 1:149. – M. Cappuyns, DHGE 11:1319–48; DHGE 26:1382–84. – P.C. Burns, EEC 1:219.

*Collections of Essays:* A. de Vogüé, De saint Pachôme à Jean Cassien (SA 120; Rome: Pontificio Ateneo S. Anselmo, 1996), 271–522.

*General Studies:* L. Cristiani, Jean Cassien: La spiritualité du désert (2 vols.; Paris: Fontenelle, 1946). – J.-C. Guy, Jean Cassien: Vie et doctrine spirituelle (Paris: Lethielleux, 1961). – O. Chadwick, John Cassian (2d ed.; London: Cambridge University Press, 1968).

*Doctrine of Grace:* A. Hoch, Lehre des Johannes Cassianus von Natur und Gnade: Ein Beitrag zur Geschichte des Gnadenstreits im 5. Jahrhundert (Fribourg, Switz., and St. Louis: Herder, 1895). – D. J. MacQueen, "John Cassian on Grace and Free Will: With Particular Reference to Institutio XIII and Collatio XII," RechTh 44 (1977): 5–28. – R. Harden Weaver, Divine Grace and Human Agency: A Study of the Semi-Pelagian Controversy (PatMS 15; Macon, Ga.: Mercer University Press, 1996).

*Monastic Tradition:* S. Marsili, *Giovanni Cassiano ed Evagrio Pontico: Dottrina sulla carità e la contemplazione* (SA 5; Rome: Herder, 1936). – A. Kemmer, *Charisma maximum: Untersuchung zu Cassians Vollkommenheitslehre und seiner Stellung zum Messalianismus* (Louvain: F. Ceuterick, 1938). – H. O. Weber, *Die Stellung des Johannes Cassianus zur ausserpachomianischen Mönchstradition: Eine Quellenuntersuchung* (BGAM 24; Münster: Aschendorff, 1961). – P. Christophe, *Cassien et Césaire: Prédicateurs de la morale monastique* (Paris: Lethielleux, 1969). – C. Leonardi, "Alle origini della cristianità medievale: Giovanni Cassiano e Salviano di Marsiglia," *StMed* 18.2 (1977): 491–608. – P. Rousseau, *Ascetics, Authority, and the Church in the Age of Jerome and Cassian* (Oxford and New York: Oxford University Press, 1978).

*Spirituality and Theology:* V. Codina, *El aspecto cristológico en la espiritualidad de Juan Casiano* (OrChrAn 175; Rome: Pontificium Institutum Orientalium Studiorum, 1966). – J. Beaudry, *L'humilité selon Jean Cassien* (Montréal: n.p., 1967). – C. Tibiletti, "Giovanni Cassiano: Formazione e dottrina," *Aug* 17 (1977): 355–80. – C. Folsom, "Anger, Dejection, and Acedia in the Writings of John Cassian," *ABenR* 35 (1984): 219–48. – V. Messana, *Povertà e lavoro nella paideia ascetica di Giovanni Cassiano* (Caltanissetta: Seminario, 1985). – M. Zananiri, "La controverse sur la prédestination au Ve siècle: Augustin, Cassien, et la tradition," in *Saint Augustin* (ed. P. Ranson; Paris: Age d'Homme, 1988), 248–61. – L. Giordano, "*Morbus acediae:* Da Giovanni Cassiano e Gregorio Magno alla elaborazione medievale," *VetChr* 26 (1989): 221–45. – G. Summa, *Geistliche Unterscheidung bei Johannes Cassian* (Würzburg: Echter, 1992). – M.-A. Vannier, "Jean Cassien a-t-il fait œuvre de théologien dans le *De incarnatione Domini?*" *RevScRel* 66 (1992): 119–31. – M. Sheridan, "Models and Images of Spiritual Progress in the Works of John Cassian," in *Spiritual Progress: Studies in the Spirituality of Late Antiquity and Early Monasticism* (ed. M. Sheridan and J. Driscoll; SA 115; Rome: Pontificio Ateneo S. Anselmo, 1994), 101–26. – M. Sheridan, "The Controversy over *apatheia:* Cassian's Sources and His Use of Them," *StudMon* 40 (1998): 287–310. – C. Stewart, *Cassian the Monk* (Oxford and New York: Oxford University Press, 1998).

## 1. *De institutis coenobiorum*

On the suggestion of Castor, bishop of Apt in Provence (419–426), Cassian wrote the work titled *Institutiones* (or *De institutis coenobiorum*) in modern editions. It bears no title in the manuscripts and consists of two parts that were also handed down separately and each of which is introduced by a dedicatory address to Castor.[4] Books 1–4 address monastic dress (1), nightly prayer, following Egyptian custom (2), and the singing of psalms during the day, following Palestinian and Mesopotamian examples (3), as well as the ordering of monastic life (4). Following Evagrius Ponticus, bks. 5–12 address the eight cardinal sins: gluttony (5), immorality (6), greed (7), anger (8), sadness (9), carelessness (10), vanity (11), and pride (12).

---

[4] Chadwick (*TRE* 7:650), however, suggests a threefold division: "a. three books on monastic habit, prayers, and the singing of Psalms; b. one book of monastic rules or *Instituta;* c. eight books on the cardinal sins and the means of overcoming them."

*Edition: Institutions cénobitiques* (ed. J.-C. Guy; rev. ed.; SC 109; Paris: Cerf, 2001).

*Translations:* E. C. S. Gibson, trans., "The Twelve Books on the Institutes of the Coenobia," in *NPNF²* (Peabody, Mass.: Hendrickson, 1995; repr. of 1894 ed.), 11:201–90. – *John Cassian: The Institutes* (trans. B. Ramsey; ACW 58; New York: Newman, 2000).

*Studies:* A. de Vogüé, "Les sources des quatre premiers livres des Institutiones de Jean Cassien: Introduction aux recherches sur les anciens règles monastiques anciennes," *StudMon* 27 (1980): 241–311.

## 2. *Collationes*

The twenty-four *collationes,* the number referring to the twenty-four elders of the Apocalypse, followed Cassian's stay in Egypt as a supplement and apex of the *Institutiones.* They take on the form that is familiar from the rules of Basil and the subsequent *Apophthegmata patrum:* Cassian or Germanus, his student, addresses questions to the desert fathers, which the latter answer in keeping with what may be imagined as the actual instruction given to the monks, who came to the spiritual masters with their spiritual and practical problems. The work is divided into three parts, having originated in several successive years: 1–10 (425/426), 11–17 (427), and 18–24 (428/429); they circulated either separately or as a composite. In any case, contentwise they represent a coherent and complete, though not a systematically structured, guide to the monastic life of perfection. The following are their main themes: the goal of monastic life (1), flesh and spirit (4), the eight cardinal sins (5), spiritual battle (7–8), prayer (9–10), perfection (11), chastity (12), charismata and miracles (15), inner freedom (21), and temptations of the flesh (22). *Collatio* 13, "De protectione Dei," has gained particular significance in the history of theology because here Cassian argued against Augustine for what came to be called, beginning in the sixteenth century, a "semi-Pelagian" doctrine of grace; according to this position, the grace of God absolutely had to collaborate with the free will of the human person for his or her salvation, since the starting point of faith was initiated by the individual.

*Editions: Johannis Cassiani Conlationes XXIIII* (ed. M. Petschenig; CSEL 13; Vienna: Apud C. Geroldi filium, 1886). – *Conférences* (ed. E. Pichery; 3 vols.; SC 42, 54, 64; Paris: Cerf, 1955–1959).

*Translations:* E. C. S. Gibson, trans., "The Conferences," in *NPNF²* (Peabody, Mass.: Hendrickson, 1995; repr. of 1894 ed.), 11:295–545. – *John Cassian: The Conferences* (trans. B. Ramsey; ACW 57; New York: Newman, 1997).

*Studies:* A. de Vogüé, "Understanding Cassian: A Survey of the *Conferences,*" *Cistercian Studies Quarterly* 19 (1984): 101–21; trans. of "Pour comprendre Cassien: Un survol des Conférences," *Collectanea cisterciensia* 39 (1977): 250–72. – D. Burton-Christie, "Scripture, Self-knowledge, and Contemplation in Cassian's *Conferences,*" *StPat* 25 (1993): 339–45. – S. Alexe, "Le discernement selon saint Jean Cassien," *StPat* 30 (1997): 129–35. – C. Stewart, "The Monastic Journey according to John Cassian," *Word and Spirit* 19 (1993): 29–40; repr. in *Forms of Devotion: Conversion, Worship, Spirituality, and Asceticism* (ed. E. Ferguson; Recent Studies in Early Christianity 5; New York: Garland, 1999), 311–22.

## 3. Spiritual Theology

In keeping with his own journey through life and his explicit intention, Cassian passed on to the Western church the spirituality of Eastern, especially Egyptian, monasticism as he came to know it there, not as a unified system of thought but as the fruit of his life's experience. For Cassian, the true monastic goal is the life of an anchorite, the *scientia spiritualis*, persisting in prayer alone, in complete denial of everything that is earthly. The cenobitic life as *scientia activa* represents only the first level on this journey to perfection in the battle against the *passiones* and the eight cardinal sins until the monk attains the virtues as well as tranquility (*tranquillitas*—ἡσυχία, ἀπάθεια). The continual reflection on Scripture and increasingly deeper penetration into its meaning, together with the help of the Holy Spirit, leads the way to prayer and ultimately to perpetual prayer, which Cassian terms the "prayer of fire," that is, the contemplation of the presence of God himself, of the fire of love.

# III. LIVES AND HISTORIES OF SAINTS

During its first three centuries, the church venerated only martyrs as saints. For this reason, the hagiographic literature of this period consists of accounts and *passiones* of martyrs, as well as of homilies delivered in their liturgical memory. The second and third centuries, however, had already prepared the ground theologically for the hagiographic developments of the fourth century by broadening the concept of martyrdom to two further forms, namely, those of suffering and of exemplary Christian living. This meant the *confessores* who suffered during the persecution for the sake of Christ's name, though without facing death (cf. Eusebius, *Hist. eccl.* 5.2f.), and the ascetics who, in the complete following of Christ, mortified themselves daily (cf. Clement of Alexandria, *Strom.* 4.3f.). Consequently, the earliest lives of saints recount the story of male and female ascetics:

- *Vita Antonii* by Athanasius (soon after 355/356),

- Lives of Paul of Thebes (378/379) and of Malchus and Hilarion by Jerome (soon after 386),

- *Vita Macrinae* by Gregory of Nyssa (soon after 381),

- *Historia monachorum* (394/395),

- *Historia Lausiaca* by Palladius (419/420),

- *Vita Melaniae iunioris* by Gerontius (ca. 440),

- *Historia religiosa* by Theodoret of Cyrus (ca. 444),

- *Apophthegmata patrum/Verba seniorum* (fifth/sixth century).

Slightly later Martin of Tours also began the veneration of bishops as saints and the recording of their lives, partly because they were ascetics as well and partly to emulate the deep respect for episcopal martyrs that was now being transferred to their witnessing without bloodshed:

- *Vita Gregorii Thaumaturgi* by Gregory of Nyssa (before 394),

- *Vita Martini* by Sulpicius Severus (397 or slightly earlier),

- *Dialogus de vita sancti Joannis Chrysostomi* by Palladius (408),

- *Vita Ambrosii* by Paulinus (422),

- *Vita Augustini* by Possidius (between 432 and 439).

Even if the genre of the Christian *vita* certainly owes much to its pagan models of the ancient cult of heroes, it by no means adopted it unchanged, nor was preoccupied by it; instead, stimulated by the pagan cult, it developed its own Christian form with specifically Christian content. A favorite part of all lives are the integrated accounts of miracles, which, in later legends of saints, are capable of turning into a veritable obsession with miracles, without any historical foundation.

The Latin church of the Middle Ages compiled the *Vita Antonii,* the *Historia monachorum in Aegypto,* the *Verba seniorum* (a collection of sayings similar to the *Apophthegmata patrum*), and the *Historia Lausiaca* by Palladius, together with other works, as the most important witnesses of early Christian monasticism, into a collection titled *Vitae patrum*. Along with the monastic rules, it served as a model and guideline for monastic life.

*Editions: Acta sanctorum quotquot toto orbe coluntur Database on CD-ROM* (Cambridge and Alexandria, Va.: Chadwick-Healey, 2000; print ed., Antwerp: Apud Joannem Mevrsium, 1643–). – *Vite dei santi* (ed. C. Mohrmann; 4 vols.; Milan: Fondazione Lorenzo Valla: A. Mondadori, 1974–1975) [Com]. – F. Halkin, *Hagiographica inedita decem* (CCSG 21; Turnhout, Belg.: Brepols, 1989).

*Translations: Early Christian Biographies* (trans. R. J. Deferrari et al.; FC 15; New York: Fathers of the Church, 1952; repr., Washington, D.C.: Catholic University of America Press, 1981) [Paulinus, *Life of Ambrose;* Possidius, *Life of St. Augustine;* Athanasius, *Life of St. Antony;* Jerome, *Life of St. Paul the Hermit, St. Hilarion, St. Malchus*]. – Theodoret of Cyrrhus, *A History of the Monks of Syria* (trans. R. M. Price; CistSS 88; Kalamazoo: Cistercian, 1985). – Cyril of Scythopolis, *Lives of the Monks of Palestine* (trans. J. Binns; CistSS 114; Kalamazoo: Cistercian, 1991). – R. Doran, *The Lives of Simeon Stylites* (CistSS 112; Kalamazoo: Cistercian, 1992). – T. Vivian, *Journeying into God: Seven Early Monastic Lives* (Minneapolis: Fortress, 1996) [*Coptic Life of Antony, Story of Abba Pambo, Narrative about Syncletia, Life of St. George of Chroiziba, Life of Abba Aaron, Encomium on the Life of Saint Theognius, Life of Onnophrius*]. – J. Petersen, *Handmaids of the Lord: Contemporary Descriptions of Feminine Asceticism in the First Six Centuries* (CistSS 143; Kalamazoo: Cistercian, 1996). – M. S. Mikhail and T. Vivian, "Life of Saint John the Little: An Encomium by Zacharias of Sakhâ," *Coptic Church Review* 18.1–2 (1997): 3–64. – C. White, *Early Christian Lives* (Penguin Classics; London and New York: Penguin, 1998) [*Life of Antony;* Jerome, *Life of Paul of Thebes, Life of Hilarion, Life of Malchus;* Sulpicius Severus, *Life of Martin of Tours;*

Gregory the Great, *Life of Benedict*]. – T. Vivian, K. Vivian, and J. Burton Russell, *The Life of the Jura Fathers* (CistSS 178; Kalamazoo: Cistercian, 1999) [*Life and Rule of Romanus, Lupicinus, and Eugendus*].

*Reference Works: Bibliotheca hagiographica graeca* (ed. Socii Bollandiani; 3 vols.; 3d ed.; Brussels: Société des Bollandistes, 1957; repr., 3 vols. in 1, 1986) *[BHG]*. – *Bibliotheca hagiographica latina antiquae et mediae aetatis* (ed. Socii Bollandiani; 2 vols.; Brussels: Société des Bollandistes, 1898–1901; repr., 1949) *[BHL]*. – *Bibliotheca hagiographica orientalis* (ed. Socii Bollandiani; Brussels: Société des Bollandistes, 1910; repr., 1970) *[BHO]*. – A. Ehrhard, *Überlieferung und Bestand der hagiographischen und homiletischen Literatur der griechischen Kirche von den Anfängen bis zum Ende des 16. Jahrhunderts* (3 vols.; TU 50–52; Leipzig: Hinrichs, 1937–1952). – L. Perria, *I manoscritti citati da Albert Ehrhard: Indice di A. Ehrhard, Überlieferung und Bestand der hagiographischen und homiletischen Literatur der griechischen Kirche, I–III* (Rome: Istituto di Studi Bizantini e Neoellenici, Università di Roma, 1979).

*Encyclopedia Articles:* D. H. Farmer, "Hagiographie I: Alte Kirche," *TRE* 14:360–64. – T. Baumeister and M. Van Uytfanghe, "Heiligenverehrung I–II (Hagiographie)," *RAC* 14:96–183. – V. Saxer, "Hagiography," *EECh* 1:370. – A. Solignac, "*Vitae patrum*," *DSp* 16:1029–35. – D. J. Sahas, "Hagiography," *EEC* 1:507–8.

*Dictionaries: Bibliotheca sanctorum* (ed. Pontificia Università Lateranense; 13 vols.; Rome: Istituto Giovanni XXIII nella Pontificia Università Lateranense, 1961[?]–1970) *[BSS]*. – *Lexikon der Christlichen Ikonographie* (ed. E. Kirschbaum et al.; Rome: Herder, 1968–1976) *[LCI]*. – A. Butler, *Butler's Lives of Saints* (ed. D. H. Farmer; 12 vols.; new ed.; Tunbridge Wells, Kent: Burns & Oates; Collegeville, Minn.: Liturgical, 1995–2000). – D. H. Farmer, ed., *The Oxford Dictionary of Saints* (5th ed.; Oxford and New York: Oxford University Press, 2003).

*Manuals:* R. Aigrain, *L'hagiographie: Ses sources, ses méthodes, son histoire* ([Mayenne]: Bloud & Gay, 1953). – H. Delehaye, *Les légendes hagiographiques* (4th ed.; SHG 18; Brussels: Société des Bollandistes, 1955). – R. Grégoire, *Manuale di agiologia: Introduzione alla letteratura agiografica* (2d ed.; Fabriano: Monastero San Silvestro Abate, 1996).

*Journals: Analecta bollandiana* (Brussels: Société des Bollandistes, 1882–) *[AnBoll]*.

*Collections of Essays:* Subsidia hagiographica (Brussels: Société des Bollandistes, 1886–) [SHG]. – P. Franchi de' Cavalieri, *La Passio SS. Mariani et Jacobi* (StT 3; Rome: Tip. Vaticana, 1900). – P. Franchi de' Cavalieri, *I martirii di S. Teodoto e di S. Ariadne* (StT 6: Rome: Tip. Vaticana, 1901; repr., 1966). – P. Franchi de' Cavalieri, *Note agiografiche* (9 vols.; StT 8–9, 22, 24, 27, 33, 49, 65, 175); Rome: Tip. Vaticana, 1902–1953). – P. Franchi de' Cavalieri, *Hagiographica* (StT 19; Rome: Tip. Vaticana, 1908). – *Hagiographie, cultures, et sociétés, IVe–XIIe siècles: Actes du colloque organisé à Nanterre et à Paris (2–5 mai 1979)* (ed. Centre de recherches sur l'antiquité tardive et le haut Moyen Âge, Université de Paris; Paris: Études Augustiniennes, 1981). – n.a., "L'agiografia latina nei secoli IV–VII," *Aug* 24 (1984): 7–345. – A. Hilhorst, *De heiligenverering in de eerste eeuwen van het christendom* (Nijmegen: Dekker & van de Vegt, 1988). – A. Ceresa-Gastaldo, ed., *Biografia e agiografia nella letteratura cristiana antica e medievale* (Trent: Istituto Trentino di Cultura, 1990).

*Studies:* F. Lanzoni, *Genesi, svolgimento, e tramonto delle legende storiche: Studio critico* (StT 43; Rome: Tipografia Poliglotta Vaticana, 1925). – H. Delehaye, *Sanctus: Essai sur le culte des saints dans l'antiquité* (SHG 17; Brussels: Société des Bollandistes, 1927). – H. Delehaye, *Cinq leçons sur la méthode hagiographique* (SHG 21; Brussels: Société des Bollandistes, 1934). – L. Bieler, ΘΕΙΟΣ ANHP: *Das Bild des "göttlichen Menschen" in Spätantike und Frühchristentum* (2 vols.; Vienna: Höfels, 1935–1936; repr., Darmstadt: Wissenschaftliche Buchgesellschaft, 1976). – B. de Gaiffier, *Études critiques d'hagiographie et d'iconologie* (SHG 43; Brussels: Société des Bollandistes, 1967). – P. Brown, *The Cult of the Saints: Its Rise and Function in Latin Christianity* (Chicago: University of Chicago Press; London: SCM, 1981). – P. Cox, *Biography in Late Antiquity: A Quest for the Holy Man* (London and Berkeley: University of California Press, 1983). – E. Mühlenberg, "Les débuts de la biographie chrétienne," *RTP* 122 (1990): 517–29. – L. Mirri, *La vita ascetica femminile in San Girolamo* (Rome: Pontificia Studiorum Universitas a Sancto Thoma Aquinate in Urbe, 1992). – M. Van Uytfanghe, "L'hagiographie: Un 'genre' chrétien ou antique tardif?" *AnBoll* 111 (1993): 135–88. – L. L. Coon, *Sacred Fictions: Holy Women and Hagiography in Late Antiquity* (Middle Ages Series; Philadelphia: University of Pennsylvania Press, 1997).

# Vita Antonii

For this reason, the earliest *vita* of the history of Christian literature deals with the life of an anchorite, namely, the great Egyptian monastic father Anthony, who died in 355/356 when he was more than a hundred years old. No less a person than Athanasius of Alexandria wrote it soon after Antony's death, in ca. 357/358, during his third exile (356–362) with the Egyptian monks, by whom he was given refuge and support. Athanasius's intention was not the retelling of the biography of this great man as much as the description of an ideal of life and an inspiring example. This may be considered accomplished, for the *Vita Antonii* quickly spread throughout the entire Christian world—Augustine was not the last one to attest to this in his *Confessiones* (6.6.15)—and became an influential model for all later lives. It is known in 165 manuscripts in Greek alone, in a Latin translation by Evagrius of Antioch (before 375), as well as in Coptic, Syriac, Assyrian, and Georgian translations. Because of the differences in the various versions, René Draguet, in his edition of the Syriac text (1980), suggested that the *Vita Antonii* had originally been written in Coptic by a student close to Anthony and was later translated into Greek by an unknown hellenized Copt, not by Athanasius; the Syriac version, however, represents the translation of the original version. Timothy Barnes supported this thesis (1986), but Charles Kannengiesser (1985) dismissed it without giving reasons for it, whereas Martin Tetz (1982) and Andrew Louth (1988) rejected it because of its literary and theological agreement with other, authentic works of Athanasius, which had been observed previously. Luise Abramowski (1988) and Rudolf Lorenz (1989) rejected it for reasons associated with the history of transmission. Adalbert de Vogüé[5] and G. J. M. Bartelink[6] agree with their assessment.

The *Vita* begins with a prologue of a letter in response to an inquiry by monks from outside Egypt who wanted to learn further details about monastic

---

[5] A. de Vogüé, *Histoire littéraire du mouvement monastique dans l'antiquité, Première partie: Le monachisme latin* 1.17.1 (Paris: Cerf, 1991–).

[6] G. J. M. Bartelink, ed. and trans., Athanasius, *Vie d'Antoine* (SC 400; Paris: Cerf, 1994), 32–35.

origins as a guide for their own life. Although this prologue has been understood as literary fiction until now, Martin Tetz considers the possibility that it was historically accurate. This is followed by the history of Anthony's life in ninety-four sections, beginning with his noble origin, youth, call, and initial monastic life, first in his parental home, then at a location near his hometown, guided by the example of an older monk. From there he withdrew farther into solitude, by the age of thirty-five into a cemetery, then into the ruins of a fortress near Pispir for twenty years, and, finally, to the foot of a mountain from where he was able to see Mt. Sinai and where he remained for the rest of his life. Each change of place was accompanied by particularly intense demonic attacks (8, 12f., 51f.) because he drove them from their habitats. First, as Satan himself laments to Anthony (41), the demons had to retreat from the towns because of the growth of Christianity, and now they are even driven from their final place of refuge, the desert, because of the anchorites. In any case, the battle against demons, attacking with the weapons of evil thoughts (23) or of hellish noise (39), against which the ascetic defends with prayer, crossing himself and calling upon the name of Christ, fulfills a fundamental role for an anchoritic life, since a monk thereby follows the practice of the martyrs. At the level of perfection, it ultimately grants the gift of discerning spirits, regardless of the guises in which they might appear and however pious they might be.

Many disciples followed Anthony into the desert to learn from him. In order to make his teaching vivid, Athanasius follows the secular models by using a literary trick. He inserts three dialogues: chs. 16–43, the "great dogmatic address," in which Anthony discusses his entire ascetic program with his students; 69–71, a speech against the Arians, who are alleged to have insisted that Anthony's teaching was in agreement with theirs; and, immediately following, 72–80, a dispute with philosophers. Since the two latter dialogues deal with entirely traditional themes and manners of argumentation, it is not possible to clarify with absolute certainty whether Athanasius placed his own theology in the mouth of Anthony or whether he merely provided literary shape to his statements.

*Bibliography:* C. Butterweck, *Athanasius von Alexandrien: Bibliographie* (Opladen: Westdeutscher Verlag, 1995).

*Editions: La plus ancienne version latine de la vie de s. Antoine par s. Athanase* (ed. H. W. F. M. Hoppenbrouwers; LCP 14; Nijmegen: Dekker & van de Vegt, 1960). – *Vita di Antonio* (ed. C. Mohrmann, G. J. M. Bartelink, P. Citati, and S. Lilla; 4th ed.; ViSa 1; Milan: Fondazione Lorenzo Valla–Mondadori, 1987) [Com]. – *S. Antonii vitae versio sahidica* (ed. G. Garitte; 2 vols.; CSCO 117–118; Paris: E Typographeo Reipublicae, 1949; repr., Louvain: SCO, 1967). – *La vie primitive de s. Antoine: Conservée en syriaque* (ed. R. Draguet; 2 vols.; CSCO 417–418; Louvain: SCO, 1980). – *Vie d'Antoine* (ed. G. J. M. Bartelink; SC 400; Paris: Cerf, 1994) [Com].

*Translations:* A. Robertson et al., trans., "Life of Antony," in *NPNF*[2] (Peabody, Mass.: Hendrickson, 1995; repr. of 1893 ed.), 4:188–221. – *The Life of Saint Anthony* (trans. R. T. Meyer; ACW 10; Westminster, Md.: Newman, 1950). – M. E. Keenan, trans., "Life of St. Anthony," in *Early Christian Biographies* (trans. R. Deferrari et al.; FC 15; New York: Fathers of the Church, 1952), 125–216. – *The Life of Antony and the Letter to Marcellinus* (trans. R. C. Gregg; CWS; New York: Paulist, 1980). – T. Vivian, "Life of

Antony," *Coptic Church Review* 15.1–2 (1994): 1–58 [*Sahidic Coptic version*]. – C. White, *Early Christian Lives* (London and New York: Penguin, 1998), 8–70 [*Latin version*].

*Studies: Antony:* E. Amélineau, "Saint Antoine et les commencements du monachisme chrétien en Égypte," *RHR* 65 (1912): 16–78. – L. von Hertling, *Antonius der Einsiedler* (FGIL 1; Innsbruck: Rauch, 1929). – B. Steidle, ed., *Antonius Magnus Eremita, 356–1956: Studia ad antiquum monachismum spectantia* (SA 38; Rome: Orbis Catholicus, 1956). – R. Staats, "Antonius," *GK* 1:236–49. – T. Orlandi, "Anthony," *EECh* 1:44. – S. Rubenson, *The Letters of St. Antony: Monasticism and the Making of a Saint* (Studies in Antiquity and Christianity; Minneapolis: Fortress, 1995).

*Vita Antonii:* R. Reitzenstein, *Des Athanasius Werk über das Leben des Antonius: Ein philologischer Beitrag zur Geschichte des Mönchtums* (SHAW.PH 1914.8; Heidelberg: Winter, 1914). – J. List, *Das Antoniusleben des hl. Athanasius d. Gr.: Eine literarhistorische Studie zu den Anfängen der byzantinischen Hagiographie* (TBNGP 11; Athens: Sakellarios, 1930). – H. Dörries, *Die Vita Antonii als Geschichtsquelle* (NAWG.PH 1949.14; Göttingen: Vandenhoeck & Ruprecht, 1949), 357–410; repr. in idem, *Gesammelte Studien zur Kirchengeschichte des vierten Jahrhunderts* (vol. 1 of *Wort und Stunde;* Göttingen: Vandenhoeck & Ruprecht, 1966), 145–224. – L. Bouyer, *La vie de s. Antoine: Essai sur la spiritualité du monachisme primitif* (2d ed.; Bégrolles-en-Mauges: Abbaye de Bellefontaine, 1978). – L. W. Barnard, "The Date of S. Athanasius' *Vita Antonii,*" *VC* 28 (1974): 169–75. – R. C. Gregg and D. E. Groh, "Claims on the *Life of St. Antony,*" in idem, *Early Arianism: A View of Salvation* (Philadelphia: Fortress, 1981), 131–59. – G. J. M. Bartelink, "Die literarische Gattung der *Vita Antonii:* Struktur und Motive," *VC* 36 (1982): 38–62. – M. Tetz, "Athanasius und die *Vita Antonii:* Literarische und theologische Relationen," *ZNW* 73 (1982): 1–30. – B. Brennen, "Athanasius' *Vita Antonii:* A Sociological Interpretation," *VC* 39 (1985): 209–27. – G. E. Gould, "The *Life of Anthony* and the Origins of Christian Monasticism in Fourth-Century Egypt," *Medieval History* 1 (1991): 3–11. – V. Desprez, "Saint Anthony and the Beginnings of Anchoritism," *ABenR* 43 (1992): 61–81, 141–72. – D. Brakke, *Athanasius and the Politics of Asceticism* (Oxford: Clarendon; New York: Oxford University Press, 1995; repr., Baltimore: Johns Hopkins University Press, 1998), 201–65. – A. Nugent, "Black Demons in the Desert," *ABenR* 49 (1998): 209–21.

*Versions:* L. T. A. Lorié, *Spiritual Terminology in the Latin Translations of the Vita Antonii, with Reference to the Fourth and Fifth Century Monastic Literature* (LCP 11; Nijmegen: Dekker & van de Vegt, 1955). – T. D. Barnes, "Angels of Light or Mystic Initiate? The Problem of the *Life of Antony,*" *JTS* NS 37 (1986): 353–68. – L. Abramowski, "Vertritt die syrische Fassung die ursprüngliche Gestalt der *Vita Antonii?* Eine Auseinandersetzung mit den These Draguets," in *Mélanges Antoine Guillaumont* (Geneva: Cramer, 1988), 47–56. – A. Louth, "St Athanasius and the Greek *Life of Antony,*" *JTS* NS 39 (1988): 504–9. – R. Lorenz, "Die griechische *Vita Antonii* des Athanasius und ihre syrische Fassung: Bemerkungen zu einer These von R. Draguet," *ZKG* 100 (1989): 77–84. – D. Brakke, "The Greek and Syriac Versions of the *Life of Antony,*" *Mus* 107 (1994): 29–53.

# IV. ITINERARIES

On their travels, Christians throughout time have also visited sites of their faith that they deem worthy of veneration, but Christian pilgrimages per se and their literary witnesses did not emerge until the fourth century. The reasons for this are diverse: the changed political conditions favoring Christianity since Emperor Constantine, the progressive Christianization of the Roman Empire and the increasing acculturation of Christianity in the ancient world, and developments in the history of theology and piety, including the "pilgrimage of life" as an ascetic lifestyle. Yet since all of these elements are part of the history of the church and not of the history of literature and are not required for a closer explanation of the literary witnesses, they may be left aside as far as the details are concerned. The extant works in no way reflect the totality of the pilgrimages of the time. There were pilgrim destinations in all the countries surrounding the Mediterranean: the sites of the life of Christ in Palestine; the monastic areas in Syria and Mesopotamia; the burial places of martyrs and saints in Asia Minor, Constantinople, and Greece; the saints of the deserts and the monks of Egypt; the burial places of the apostles and martyrs in Rome; holy places in Africa, Spain, and Gaul. The largest portion of the numerous pilgrims came from the more immediate surroundings of the places of pilgrimage, however, so that written guides were unnecessary and there was no need to write such. All of the authors of the extant itineraries were travelers from distant places who reported to those who lived far from the place of pilgrimage and stayed at home, and should they undertake the trip themselves, they provided them with a description of the route (*itinerarium*). The stream of pilgrims moved from the West to the East and vice versa. Itineraries have been handed down, however, exclusively by pilgrims from the West, in Latin, and only for the two most significant places in two separate periods of time: for Jerusalem and Palestine from the fourth to the sixth centuries, *Itinerarium burdigalense, Itinerarium Egeriae, Breviarius de Hierosolyma*, and *Itinerarium Antonini Placentini;* and for Rome from the seventh and eighth centuries, *Notitiae ecclesiarum, De locis sanctis, Itinerarium malmesburiense*, and *Itinerarium einsidlense.* The outstanding significance of these works is to be seen in their description of the history of piety and liturgy, on the one hand, and of archaeology, on the other; on the basis of these, it is possible today to understand what is fragmentary and to reconstruct what is lost.

*Editions: Itinera hierosolymitana saeculi IIII–VIII* (ed. P. Geyer; CSEL 39; Vienna: F. Tempsky, 1898). – *Itineraria et alia geographica* (2 vols.; CCSL 175–176; Turnhout, Belg.: Brepols, 1965). – C. Milani, *Itinerarium Antonini Placentini: Un viaggio in terra santa del 560–570 d. C.* (Milan: Vita e Pensiero, 1977) [Com].

*Encyclopedia Articles:* L. Dattrino, *"Breviarius de Hierosolyma,"* EECh 1:128. – V. Saxer, "Itineraries," EECh 1:426–27. – A. Hamman, *"Itinerarium burdigalense,"* EECh 1:427. – P.M. Bassett, "Pilgrimage," EEC 2:921–22.

*Studies:* A. Elter, *Itinerarstudien* (Bonn: Universitäts-Buchdruckerei, 1908). – G. Bardy, "Pèlerinages à Rome vers la fin du IVe siècle," *AnBoll* 67 (1949): 224–35. – B. Kötting, *Peregrinatio religiosa: Wallfahrten in der Antike und das Pilgerwesen in der alten Kirche* (FVK 33–35; Münster: Regensberg, 1950). – R. Gelsomino, *"L'Itinerarium burdigalense* e la Puglia," *VetChr* 3 (1966): 161–208. – E. D. Hunt, *Holy Land Pilgrimage in the Later Roman Empire, AD 312–460* (Oxford: Clarendon; New York: Oxford University Press, 1982). – B. Kötting, *Ecclesia peregrinans—das Gottesvolk unterwegs: Gesammelte Aufsätze* (2 vols.; MBTh 54; Münster: Aschendorff, 1988), 2:225–312. – R. Klein, "Die Entwicklung der christlichen Palästinawallfahrt in konstantinischer Zeit," *RQ* 85

(1990): 145–81. – M. Calzolari, *Introduzione allo studio della rete stradale dell'Italia romana* (AANL.M 9.7.4; Rome: Accademia Nazionale dei Lincei, 1996). – H. R. Drobner, "Die Palästina-Itinerarien der alten Kirche als literarische, historische, und archäologische Quellen," *Aug* 38 (1998): 293–354. – D. Frankfurter, ed., *Pilgrimage and Holy Space in Late Antique Egypt* (Religions in the Graeco-Roman World 134; Leiden and Boston: Brill, 1998).

# Itinerarium Egeriae

Despite the fact that it is only preserved in part, the most famous and most significant account by a pilgrim comes from the pen of one of the few female authors in the history of patristic literature. It has been handed down anonymously in only one manuscript, discovered by G. F. Gamurrini in Arezzo in 1884; the beginning (and two further folios within the extant text) of the *Itinerarium* are missing. Additional fragments of the lost part of the *Itinerarium* can be found in the medieval guide to Palestine *De locis sanctis* by the monk Petrus Diaconus (1137), who composed his work by using the *Itinerarium*, among others.While it had initially been published under the names of Silvia, Eucheria, or Aetheria, the name Egeria has generally established itself today, with the earliest attestation coming most reliably from a letter by Valerius, a monk of Bierzo in the Spanish diocese of Asturica Augusta (Astorga), from ca. 680. Marius Férotin commented (1903) that this letter deals precisely with Egeria's pilgrimage and her *Itinerarium* and that detailed references to the author, as well as to the content of the parts that have been lost, can be extracted from it. Egeria originally came from either Galicia in northern Spain or from southern Gaul (Aquitania/Narbonne) and led a monastic life, although it is not possible to decide whether she was attached to a monastery or whether she had chosen the equally popular form of private asceticism. From Easter 381 to Easter 384, she undertook an extended pilgrimage to Constantinople, Palestine, Syria, Mesopotamia, Arabia, and Egypt. Until the generally accepted results of Paul Devos (1967), the date of the journey had long been contested; the extant part of the account extends from Saturday, December 16, 383, to June 384.

Concerning the lost beginning of the *Itinerarium*, the following can be gathered from the letter of Valerius regarding the course of the journey: It cannot be determined whether Egeria chose to travel from her home to Constantinople by sea or land; from Constantinople to Jerusalem she took the land route, in any case, from Chalcedon through Bithynia, Galatia, Cappadocia, via Tarsus and Antioch, along the coast to Mount Carmel and Jerusalem. She arrived in Jerusalem at Easter 381 and left there for good after Easter 384. During this time, however, she undertook several journeys from Jerusalem, first to the origins of monasticism in Egypt, from where she returned in 382 but definitely before May 18, 383. In the course of 383, she traveled to Samaria, Galilee, and Judea; finally, in December 383 she traveled to Sinai, where the extant part of her *Itinerarium* begins.

The forty-nine chapters of the work are divided into two major parts: chs. 1–23, the chronological travelogue; and 24–49, a very detailed description of the liturgy of Jerusalem and its type of celebration, so that, together with the Armenian lectionary,[7] it represents the most important source in the history of liturgy about this aspect. Egeria's journey led from

- Sinai (Saturday, December 16, to Tuesday, December 19, 383) (1.1–5.10) to

- Pharan (Wednesday, December 20, 383) (5.11),

- Clysma (December 21, 383, to January 1, 384) (6.1),

- Arabia (January 2–7, 384) (7.1–9.3), back to

- Jerusalem (January 384) (9.4–7), then to

- Mount Nebo (February 384) (10.1–12.11),

- Carneas (late February to early March 384) (13.1–16.7),

- Mesopotamia (Antioch – Edessa – Carrhae [Haran], March 25 to April 384) (17.1–21.5) and back to Constantinople, via Antioch and Seleucia (May–June 384) (22.1–23.10).

The presentation of the Jerusalem liturgy contains the following:

- the liturgy of the hours (vigil and matins, sext, nones) with the liturgy of the light at the tenth hour (24.1–7),

- the liturgy for Sunday (vigil, matins, holy Mass until the fifth or sixth hour; the next folio of the manuscript is missing) (24.8–25.6),

- Epiphany with the Octave and the feast forty days after Epiphany (25.7–26),

- the Easter cycle from the eight weeks (!) of fasting to Pentecost, including a feast on the fortieth day after Easter (Ascension?)[8] (27.1–44.1).

Finally, 45.1–47.5 describes in a most instructive way the preparations for baptism in Jerusalem; the account concludes with the dedication of the church on Golgotha, built in memory of Christ's passion and death (48.1–49.3); at this point the manuscript breaks off.

Besides the historians, liturgical experts, and archaeologists, it is especially the linguistic experts who have directed their attention to the *Itinerarium Egeriae* because it does not use polished literary Latin in keeping with classical rules but

---

[7] A. Renoux, ed., *Édition comparée du texte et de deux autres manuscrits* (vol. 2 of *Le codex arménien Jérusalem 121;* PO 36.2; Turnhout, Belg., Brepols, 1971).

[8] Egeria does not refer to Christ's ascension, but the virtually contemporaneous first witnesses for it in the sermons of John Chrysostom (386) and Gregory of Nyssa (before 394) suggest a link. The Armenian lectionary (57) affirms it for Jerusalem.

represents a document in popular language, though its Latin is not directly of the vulgar sort.

*Bibliographies:* C. Baraut, "Bibliografía Egeriana," *HispSac* 7 (1954): 203–15. – M. Staro-wieyski, "Bibliographia egeriana," *Aug* 19 (1979): 297–318. – S. Janeras, "Contributo alla bibliografia Egeriana," in *Atti del Convegno internazionale sulla Peregrinatio Egeriae* (Arezzo: Accademia Petrarca di Lettere, Arti e Scienze, 1990), 355–66.

*Editions: Itinerario de la virgen Egeria (381–384): Constantinopla, Asia Menor, Palestina, Sinaí, Egipto, Arabia, Siria* (ed. A. Arce; BAC 416; Madrid: Editorial Católica, 1980). – *Journal de voyage: Itinéraire* (ed. P. Maraval; rev. ed.; SC 296; Paris: Cerf, 1996) [Com]. – *Pellegrinaggio in terra santa: Itinerarium Egeriae* (ed. N. Natalucci; BPat 17; Florence: Nardini, 1991) [Com]. – *Itinerarium* (ed. G. Röwekamp and D. Thönnes; FChr 20; Fribourg, Switz.: Herder, 1995) [Com].

*Translations: Egeria: Diary of a Pilgrimage* (trans. G. E. Gingras; ACW 38; New York: Newman, 1970). – *Egeria's Travels to the Holy Land* (trans. J. Wilkinson; 3d ed.; Warminster, Eng.: Aris & Phillips, 1999) [ET/Com].

*Reference Works:* W. van Oorde, *Lexicon aetherianum* (Amsterdam: H. J. Paris, 1929; repr., Hildesheim: Olms, 1963). – J. J. Iso Echegoyen, *La Peregrinatio Egeriae: Una concordancia* (Zaragoza: Departamento de Ciencias de la Atiguedad, Universidad de Zaragoza, 1987). – D. R. Blackman and G. G. Betts, *Concordantiae in Itinerarium Egeriae* (AlOm.A 96; Hildesheim and New York: Olms-Weidmann, 1989).

*Encyclopedia Articles:* A. Hamman, *Patrologia* 3:529–32. – A. Hamman, *EECh* 1:263–64. – F. W. Norris, *EEC* 1:362–63.

*Collections of Essays: Atti del Convegno internazionale sulla Peregrinatio Egeriae: Nel centenario della pubblicazione del Codex Aretinus 405 (già Aretinus VI, 3): Arezzo 23–25 ottobre 1987* (Arezzo: Accademia Petrarca di Lettere, Arti e Scienze, 1990).

*Studies:* A. Bludau, *Die Pilgerreise der Aetheria* (SGKA 15.1–2; Paderborn: F. Schöningh, 1927). – P. Devos, "La date du voyage d'Egérie," *AnBoll* 85 (1967): 165–94. – P. Devos, "Égérie à Bethléem: Le 40e jour après Pâques à Jérusalem," *AnBoll* 86 (1968): 87–108. – H. Sivan, "Who Was Egeria? Piety and Pilgrimage in the Age of Gratian," *HTR* 81 (1988): 59–72. – C. Weber, "Egeria's Norman Homeland," *HSCP* 92 (1989): 437–56. – P. Smiraglia, "Un indizio per la cronologia relativa delle due parti dell'Itinerarium di Egeria," in *Studi di filologia classica in onore di G. Monaco* (4 vols.; Palermo: Università di Palermo, Facolta di Lettere e Filosofia, Istituto di Filologia Greca, Istituto di Filologia Latina, 1991), 4:1491–96.

*Philology:* E. Löfstedt, *Philologischer Kommentar zur Peregrinatio Aetheriae: Untersuchungen zur Geschichte der lateinischen Sprache* (Uppsala: Almqvist & Wiksell, 1911; repr., Darmstadt: Wissenschaftliche Buchgesellschaft, 1970). – A. A. R. Bastiaensen, *Observations sur le vocabulaire liturgique dans l'Itinéraire d'Égérie* (LCP 17; Nijmegen: Dekker & van de Vegt, 1962). – G. F. M. Vermeer, *Observations sur le vocabulaire du pèlerinage chez Égérie et chez Antonin de Plaisance* (LCP 19; Nijmegen: Dekker & van de Vegt, 1965). – D. C. Swanson, "A Formal Analysis of Egeria's (Silvia's) Vocabulary," *Glotta* 44 (1967): 177–254. – C. Milani, "Studi sull'*Itinerarium Egeriae*': L'aspetto classico della lingua di Egeria," *Aev* 43 (1969): 381–452. – V. Väänänen, *Le Journal-Épître d'Égérie (Itinerarium Egeriae): Étude linguistique* (Suomalaisen Tiedeakatemian toimituksia B 230; Helsinki: Suomalainen Tiedeakatemia, 1987). – J. Oroz Reta, "Del latín cristiano al latín litúrgico: Algunas observaciones en torno al *Itinerarium Egeriae*," *Latomus* 48 (1989): 401–15.

# CHAPTER NINE

# Augustine of Hippo

ALTHOUGH AUGUSTINE DOES NOT BEAR the honorary title "the Great," as do Popes Leo and Gregory, it is nevertheless uncontested that he remains the most important church father and, for the Western church, the most influential of all. Not only did his *Confessiones* exert an ongoing fascination through the centuries, his overall theological scheme knew neither doubt nor competition until Thomas Aquinas. Even since then his popularity has remained intact, as demonstrated by the hundreds of annual publications on his person, work, and thought, even though command of this special field of patrology becomes increasingly more difficult. Whereas all the other church fathers can be classified according to general themes, in the Western church Augustine subsumed all of the ecclesiastical and theological concerns of his time and decisively defined them, thus justifying and demanding that his treatment be accorded a chapter of its own.

It is common knowledge that although the first three decades of Augustine's life point to great talent, there is no indication that he would determine the history of the world. When he was baptized in Milan at the age of thirty-three, on Easter eve 398, there were varied and turbulent years in his past, which he later assimilated literarily into his world-famous *Confessions (Confessiones)*. All of his other works, among them especially the dialogues written at Cassiciacum, plus the letters and sermons, supplement this information mainly for his post-conversion life. Just a few years after his death (432–439), a *Vita* was produced by Possidius, his student and friend, who lived with him in Hippo and then resided in Calama as bishop from 397 on. While fleeing from the Vandals, however, he happened to be present at Augustine's death in Hippo in 430.

For the writings of Augustine, there are two catalogues unique in the history of literature. Toward the end of his life (426/427), he himself discussed his works in a list that he called *Retractationes (Retractations)* because he not merely briefly put on record the history of their origins and content but also added critical corrections and additions. In the prologue he states his intention: "With a kind of judicial severity, I am reviewing my works—books, letters, and sermons—and, as it were, with the pen of a censor, I am indicating what dissatisfies me." Even if Augustine actually addressed only his ninety-three books and did not get around to the letters and tractates (speeches, sermons), the unique value of the *Retractationes* nevertheless is that it documents his intellectual development in an unprecedented way. Possidius, Augustine's biographer, added a listing (*indiculus*) of his works to his *Vita*, based on the incomplete yet extensive collection of Augustine's personal library. This has likewise proved to be of incalculable value into the present, especially for a knowledge of the lost works of Augustine and for determining the authenticity of recently discovered writings, such as the sermons found in Mainz in 1990.

*Bibliographies: Corpus augustinianum gissense su CD-ROM* (ed. C. Mayer; Basel: Schwabe, 1995) *[CAG]* [the complete works of Augustine and a massive bibliography]. – A. Wilmart, in *Miscellanea Agostiniana: Testi e studi, pubblicati a cura del-l'Ordine eremitano di S. Agostino nel XV centenario dalla morte del santo dottore* (ed. G. Morin and A. Casamassa; 2 vols.; Rome: Tipografia Poliglotta Vaticana, 1930–1931), 2:149–233 *[Indiculus]*. – *Revue des études augustiniennes* (Paris, 1955–) *[REAug]*. – R. Lorenz, "Augustinusliteratur seit dem Jubiläum von 1954," *TRu* NS 25 (1959): 1–75. – R. Lorenz, "Zwölf Jahre Augustinusforschung (1959–1970)," *TRu* NS 38 (1974): 292–333; 39 (1975): 95–138, 253–86, 331–64; 40 (1975): 1–41, 97–149, 227–61. – T. van Bavel, *Répertoire bibliographique de saint Augustin 1950–1960* (IP 3; Steenbrugge, Belg.: Abbatia Sancti Petri,1963). – *Fichier augustinien* (4 vols.; Boston: Hall, 1972). – C. Andresen, *Bibliographia augustiniana* (2d ed.; Darmstadt: Wissenschaftliche Buchgesellschaft, 1973). – T. L. Miethe, *Augustinian Bibliography, 1970–1980: With Essays on the Fundamentals of Augustinian Scholarship* (London and Westport, Conn.: Greenwood, 1982). – H. R. Drobner, *Augustinus von Hippo, Sermones ad populum: Überlieferung und Bestand, Bibliographie, Indices* (SVigChr 49; Leiden and Boston: Brill, 2000).

NOTE: For a listing of editions, translations, and studies of individual works by Augustine, see the chart at the end of the chapter.

*Editions:* PL 32–47 *[Opera omnia]*. – PLS 2:347–1648. – Volumes in the series CSEL, CCL, and BAug [Com]. – *Vita di Cipriano, Vita di Ambrogio, Vita di Agostino* (ed. A. A. R. Bastieaensen; trans. L. Canali and C. Carena; intro. C. Mohrmann; 4th ed.; ViSa 3; Milan: Fondazione Lorenzo Valla: A. Mondadori, 1997), 127–241, 337–449 *[Vita Augustini]*.

*Translations: Anthologies and Series: The Confessions and Letters of Augustin, with a Sketch of His Life and Work* (vol. 1 of *NPNF¹*; ed. P. Schaff; trans. J. G. Pilkington and J. G. Cunningham; Peabody, Mass.: Hendrickson, 1995; repr. of 1886 ed.). – *Augustin: City of God, Christian Doctrine* (vol. 2 of *NPNF¹*; ed. P. Schaff; trans. M. Dods and J. F. Shaw; Peabody, Mass.: Hendrickson, 1995; repr. of 1886 ed.). – *Augustin: On the Holy Trinity, Doctrinal Treatises, Moral Treatises* (vol. 3 of *NPNF¹*; ed. P. Schaff; trans. A. W. Haddan, J. F. Shaw, S. D. F. Salmond, C. L. Cornish, and H. Browne; Peabody, Mass.: Hendrickson, 1995; repr. of 1886 ed.). – *Augustin: The Writings against the Manichaens, and against the Donatists* (vol. 4 of *NPNF¹*; ed. P. Schaff; trans. R. Stothert, A. H. Newman, and J. R. King; Peabody, Mass.: Hendrickson, 1995; repr. of 1886 ed.). – *Augustin: Anti-Pelagian Writings* (vol. 5 of *NPNF¹*; ed. P. Schaff; trans. P. Holmes and R. E. Wallis; Peabody, Mass.: Hendrickson, 1995; repr. of 1886 ed.). – *Augustin: Sermon on the Mount, Harmony of the Gospels, Homilies on the Gospels* (vol. 6 of *NPNF¹*; ed. P. Schaff; trans. W. Findlay, S. D. F. Salmond, and R. G. MacMullen; Peabody, Mass.: Hendrickson, 1995; repr. of 1886 ed.). – *Augustin: Homilies on the Gospel of John, Homilies on the First Epistle of John, Soliloquies* (vol. 7 of *NPNF¹*; ed. P. Schaff; trans. J. Gibb, H. Browne, and C. C. Starbuck; Peabody, Mass.: Hendrickson, 1995; repr. of 1886 ed.). – *Augustin: Expositions on the Book of Psalms* (vol. 8 of *NPNF¹*; ed. P. Schaff; trans. A. C. Coxe; Peabody, Mass.: Hendrickson, 1995; repr. of 1886 ed.). – *Earlier Writings* (trans. J. H. S. Burleigh; LCC 6; Philadelphia: Westminster, 1953). – *Later Works* (trans. J. Burnaby; LCC 8; London: SCM; Philadelphia: Westminster,

1955). – *Augustine of Hippo: Selected Writings* (trans. M. T. Clark; CWS; London: SPCK; New York: Paulist, 1984).– The Works of Saint Augustine: A Translation for the 21st Century (Brooklyn, N.Y.: New City, 1990–) [WSA] [*Opera omnia*, 31 vols. to date].

*Reference Works: Augustinus-Lexikon* (ed. C. Mayer with E. Feldman et al.; rev. K. H. Chelius; Basel: Schwabe, 1986–) *[AugL]*. – D. Lenfant, *Concordantiae augustinianae* (2 vols.; Brussels: Culture & Civilisation, 1965; repr. of 1656–1665 ed.). – A. Cupetioli, *Theologia moralis et contemplativa S. Aurelii Augustini* (3 vols.; Venice: J. Corona, 1738– 1741). – R. W. Battenhouse, *A Companion to the Study of St. Augustine* (New York: Oxford University Press, 1955; repr., Grand Rapids: Baker, 1979). – F. Moriones, *Enchiridion theologicum Sancti Augustini* (Madrid: Editorial Católica, 1961). – W. Hensellek, P. Schilling, N. Winterleitner, and J. Divjak, *Vorarbeiten zu einem Augustinus-Lexikon* (CSEL Beihefte; Vienna: Verlag der Österreichischen Akademie der Wissenschaften, 1973–). – P.-P. Verbraken, *Études critiques sur les sermons authentiques de saint Augustin* (IP 12; Steenbrugge, Belg.: Abbatia Sancti Petri, 1976). – *Catalogus verborum quae in operibus Sancti Augustini inveniuntur* (Eindhoven, Neth.: Thesaurus Linguae Augustinianae, 1976–) [refer to CCL]. – W. Hensellek, P. Schilling, and J. Divjak, *Specimina eines Lexikon Augustinianum: Erstellt auf Grund sämtlicher Editionen des Corpus scriptorum ecclesiasticorum latinorum* (Vienna: Österreichische Akademie der Wissenschaften, 1987–) *[SLA]*. – *Thesaurus augustinianus* (Corpus Christianorum: Thesaurus patrum latinorum; Turnhout, Belg.: Brepols, 1989). – M. Bettetini, "Stato della questione e bibliografia ragionata sul dialogo *De musica* di S. Agostino, 1940–1990," *RFNS* 83 (1991): 430–69. – P.-P. Verbraken, "Mise à jour du fichier signalétique des Sermons de saint Augustin," in *Aevum inter utrumque* (ed. M. Van Uytfanghe and R. Dumeulenaer; IP 23; Steenburgis: Abbatia Sancti Petri; The Hague: Nijhoff, 1991), 484–90. – A. Fitzgerald et al., eds., *Augustine through the Ages: An Encyclopedia* (Grand Rapids: Eerdmans, 1999).

*Encyclopedia Articles:* A. Schindler, *TRE* 4:645–98. – A. Trapé, *EECh* 1:97–101. – C. Mayer, 2:179–214. – G. Bonner, *AugL* 1:519–50. – M. Miles, *EEC* 1:148–54. – R. A. Markus, "Life, Culture, and Controversies of Augustine," in *Augustine through the Ages: An Encyclopedia* (Grand Rapids: Eerdmans, 1999), 498–504.

*Journals: Année théologique augustinienne* (Paris, 1952–) *[AThA]*. – *Augustinianum: Periodicum quadrimestre Instituti Patristici "Augustinianum"* (Rome, 1961–) *[Aug]*. – *Augustiniana: Tijdschrift voor de studie van Sint Augustinus en de Augustijnerorde* (Louvain, 1951–) *[Aug(L)]*. – *Augustinian Studies* (Villanova, Pa., 1970–) *[AugStud]*. – *Augustinus: Revista trimestral publ. por los Padres Agustinos Recoletos* (Madrid, 1956–). – *Revue des études augustiniennes* (Paris, 1955–) *[REAug]*. – *Recherches augustiniennes* (Paris, 1958–) *[RechAug]*.

*Monograph Series:* Cassiciacum: Eine Sammlung wissenschaftlicher Forschungen über den heiligen Augustinus und den Augustinerorden sowie wissenschaftlicher Arbeiten von Augustinern aus anderen Wissensgebieten (Würzburg: Rita, 1936–) [Cass.].

*Collections of Essays: Miscellanea agostiniana: Testi e studi* (2 vols.; Rome: Tipografia Poliglotta Vaticana, 1930–1931). – *Augustinus magister* (3 vols.; Paris: Études Augustiniennes, 1954–1955). – *Sanctus Augustinus: Vitae spiritualis magister* (2 vols.; Rome: Analecta Augustiniana, 1959). – C. Kannengiesser, ed., *Jean Chrysostome et Augustin* (ThH 35; Paris: Beauchesne, 1975). – *Augustiniana: Testi e studi* (Palermo: Augustinus, 1987–). – *Congresso internazionale su S. Agostino* (3 vols.; SEAug 24–26; Rome: Institutum Patristicum Augustinianum, 1987). – J. den Boeft and J. van Oort, eds., *Augustiniana traiectina* (Paris: Études Augustiniennes, 1987). – G. Bonner, *God's Decree and Man's Destiny: Studies in the Thought of Augustine of Hippo* (VRCS 255; London: Variorum, 1987). – P. Ranson, ed., *Saint Augustin* (Paris: Age d'Homme,

1988). – *Agostino d'Hippona: Quaestiones disputatae* (Palermo: Augustinus, 1989). – C. Mayer and K. H. Chelius, eds., *Internationales Symposium über den Stand der Augustinus-Forschung* (Cass. 39.1; Würzburg: Augustinus, 1989). – B. Bruning, ed., *Collectanea augustiniana: Mélanges T. J. van Bavel* (ed. B. Bruning; 2 vols.; Louvain: Louvain University Press, 1990). – J. Schnaulbelt and F. Van Fleteren, eds., *Augustine: Second Founder of the Faith* (Collectanea augustiana 1; New York: Lang, 1990). – J. McWilliam, ed., *Augustine: From Rhetor to Theologian* (Waterloo, Ont.: Wilfrid Laurier University Press, 1992). – L. Alici, R. Piccolomini, and A. Pieretti, eds., *Ripensare Agostino: Interiorità e intenzionalità* (SEAug 41; Rome: Institutum Patristicum Augustinianum, 1993). – J. T. Lienhard, E. C. Muller, and R. J. Teske, eds., *Augustine: Presbyter factus sum* (Collectanea augustiniana 2; New York: Lang, 1993). – F. Van Fleteren, J. C. Schnaubelt, and J. Reino, eds., *Augustine: Mystic and Mystagogue* (Collectanea augustiana 3; New York: Lang, 1994). – F. LeMoine and C. Kleinherz, eds., *Saint Augustine the Bishop: A Book of Essays* (New York; London: Garland, 1994). – L. Alici, R. Piccolomini, and A. Pieretti, eds., *Il mistero del male e la libertà possibile,* vol. 1, *Lettura dei Dialoghi di Agostino;* vol. 2, *Linee di antropologia agostiniana;* vol. 3, *Lettura del De civitate Dei di Agostino;* vol. 4, *Ripensare Agostino* (SEAug 45, 48, 54, 59; Rome: Institutum Patristicum Augustinianum, 1994–1997). – G. Bonner, *Church and Faith in the Patristic Tradition: Augustine, Pelagianism, and Early Christian Northumbria* (VRCS; Brookfield, Vt.: Variorum, 1996). – J. C. Schnaubelt and F. Van Fleteren, eds. *Augustine in Iconography: History and Legend* (New York: Lang, 1999). – G. B. Matthews, ed., *The Augustinian Tradition* (Berkeley: University of California Press, 1999). – L. Perissinotto, ed., *Agostino e il destino dell'Occidente* (Rome: Carocci, 2000). – R. Dodaro and G. Lawless, eds., *Augustine and His Critics: Essays in Honour of Gerald Bonner* (London and New York: Routledge, 2000).

*Works:* G. Madec, *Introduction aux "Révisions" et à la lecture des œuvres de saint Augustin* (Paris: Études Augustiniennes, 1996).

*Biographies:* H. Marrou, *St. Augustine and His Influence through the Ages* (New York: Harper Torchbooks, 1957); repr. in E. Ferguson, ed., *Personalities of the Early Church* (SEC 1; New York: Garland, 1993), 271–352; German trans., *Augustinus: Mit Selbstzeugnissen und Bilddokumenten* (trans. C. Muthesius; Reinbek/Hamburg: Rowohlt Taschenbuch, 1988). – F. van der Meer, *Augustine the Bishop: The Life and Work of a Father of the Church* (trans. B. Battershaw and G. R. Lamb; London and New York: Sheed & Ward, 1961; repr., 1978); trans. of *Augustinus de zielzorger* (Utrecht: Spectrum, 1947). – O. Perler and J.-L. Maier, *Les voyages de saint Augustin* (Paris: Études Augustiniennes, 1969). – A. Trapé, *S. Agostino: L'uomo, il pastore, il mistico* (Fossano: Esperienze, 1976). – V. Paronetto, *Agostino: La vita, il pensiero, la missione* (Milan: Accademia, 1977). – V. Paronetto, *Agostino: Messaggio di una vita* (Rome: Studium, 1981). – J. J. O'Donnell, *Augustine* (Boston: Twayne, 1985). – M. Marshall, *The Restless Heart: The Life and Influence of St. Augustine* (Grand Rapids: Eerdmans, 1987). – C. Lorin, *Pour lire saint Augustin* (Paris: Grasset, 1988). – E. Dassmann, *Augustinus, Heiliger und Kirchenlehrer* (Stuttgart: Kohlhammer, 1993). – S. Lancel, *Saint Augustin* (Paris: Fayard, 1999). – G. Wills, *Saint Augustine* (Penguin Lives; New York: Viking, 1999). – P. Brown, *Augustine of Hippo: A Biography* (2d ed.; Berkeley: University of California Press, 2000) [new ed., with an epilogue]. – G. Bonner, *St. Augustine of Hippo: Life and Controversies* (3d ed.; Norwich: Canterbury, 2002)

*Thought and Theology:* P. Alfaric, *L'évolution intellectuelle de saint Augustin, I: Du manichéisme au néoplatonisme* (Paris: Nourry, 1918). – A. Mandouze, *Saint Augustin: L'aventure de la raison et de la grâce* (Paris: Études Augustiniennes, 1968). – C. P. Mayer, *Die Zeichen in der geistigen Entwicklung und in der Theologie Augustins* (2 vols.; Cass. 24.1–2; Würzburg: Augustinus, 1969–1974). – E. TeSelle, *Augustine the Theologian* (New York: Herder; London: Burns & Oates, 1970; repr., Eugene, Ore.: Wipf &

Stock, 2002). – G. R. Evans, *Augustine on Evil* (Cambridge and New York: Cambridge University Press, 1982). – H. Chadwick, *Augustine* (Past Masters; Oxford and New York: Oxford University Press, 1986). – R. J. O'Connell, *The Origin of the Soul in St. Augustine's Later Works* (New York: Fordham University Press, 1987). – G. B. Mondin, *Il pensiero di Agostino: Filosofia, teologia, cultura* (Rome: Città Nuova, 1988). – A. Vassallo, *Inquietum cor: Con Agostino alla ricerca di Dio* (Palermo: Augustinus, 1988). – M. Vannini, *Invito al pensiero di Sant'Agostino* (Milan: Mursia, 1989). – C. Kirwan, *Augustine* (Arguments of the Philosophers; London and New York: Routledge, 1989). – C. Harrison, *Beauty and Revelation in the Thought of Saint Augustine* (OTM; Oxford: Clarendon; New York: Oxford University Press, 1992). – R. Canning, *The Unity of Love for God and Neighbour in St. Augustine* (Louvain: Augustinian Historical Institute, 1993). – J. M. Rist, *Augustine: Ancient Thought Baptized* (Cambridge and New York: Cambridge University Press, 1994). – T. K. Scott, *Augustine: His Thought in Context* (New York: Paulist, 1995). – D. X. Burt, *Augustine's World: An Introduction to His Speculative Philosophy* (Lanham, Md.: University Press of America, 1996). – G. Madec, *Saint Augustin et la philosophie: Notes critiques* (Paris: Études Augustiniennes, 1996). – B. Stock, *Augustine the Reader: Meditation, Self-Knowledge, and the Ethics of Interpretation* (Cambridge, Mass., and London: Belknap Press of Harvard University Press, 1996). – P. Cary, *Augustine's Invention of the Inner Self: The Legacy of a Christian Platonist* (Oxford and New York: Oxford University Press, 2000).

*Context:* P. Borgomeo, *L'Église de ce temps dans la prédication de saint Augustin* (Paris: Études Augustiniennes, 1972). – P. Brown, *Religion and Society in the Age of Saint Augustine* (London: Faber & Faber; New York: Harper & Row, 1972). – B. Blumenkranz, *Die Judenpredigt Augustins: Ein Beitrag zur Geschichte der jüdisch-christlichen Beziehungen in den ersten Jahrhunderten* (Basel: Helbing & Lichtenhahn, 1973). – A.-G. Hamman, *La vie quotidienne en Afrique du Nord au temps de saint Augustin* (new ed.; Paris: Hachette, 1985). – F. Morgenstern, *Die Briefpartner des Augustinus von Hippo: Prosopographische, sozial- und ideologiegeschichtliche Untersuchungen* (Bochum: Universitätsverlag Dr. N. Brockmeyer, 1993). – J. E. Merdinger, *Rome and the African Church in the Time of Augustine* (New Haven, Conn.; London: Yale University Press; 1997). – C. Harrison, *Augustine: Christian Truth and Fractured Humanity* (Christian Theology in Context; Oxford and New York: Oxford University Press, 2000).

# I. BIOGRAPHY, LITERARY ACTIVITY, AND ESSENTIAL FEATURES OF HIS THOUGHT

## A. Preconversion

### 1. Youth and Education

Augustine was born on November 13, 354, in the town of Tagaste (modern Souk-Ahras in Algeria), situated in the northern African province of Numidia, as the son of Patricius, a non-Christian officer of the Roman curia who was not baptized until shortly before he died (371), and of Monica (Monnica), who was a zealous Christian. Even if little is normally heard about his siblings, he was not an only child but had at least a brother, named Navigius, who later accompanied him to Milan and Cassiciacum and into the monastic community of Tagaste, as well as a sister whose name is unknown. A remark in the *Confessiones* that Monica had "raised sons" (9.9.22: *nutrierat filios*) and the subsequent mention of some nephews and nieces suggest that the family may have been even larger. In keeping with the contemporary practice of delaying baptism until adulthood, Augustine did not receive baptism but, according to custom, was registered as a catechumen at birth and was raised in the Christian faith by his mother. Despite all the aberrations of his life until his conversion, he always perceived himself to be a Christian and in search of Christ, though not as a Catholic, and Monica, his mother, did not become discouraged in firmly leading and accompanying him to the Catholic church. Even when the almost thirty-year-old (383)—with all due caution regarding modern psychological categories that are often applied without adequate care, especially in the case of Augustine—had withdrawn from her maternal love and care, presumably because he perceived it as obtrusive, and secretly traveled to Rome, there was nothing to deter her from setting her house in order and following him to Milan. In the *Confessiones* (3.11.19), Augustine himself recalls his mother's dream, which has become famous and clarifies her motivation: "She saw herself standing upon a certain wooden rule, and coming towards her a young man, splendid, joyful, and smiling upon her although she grieved and was crushed with grief. When he asked her the reasons for her sorrow and her daily tears, . . . she replied that she lamented for my perdition. Then he bade her rest secure and instructed her that she should attend and see that where she was, there was I also. And when she looked, there she saw me standing on the same rule." A little later an unidentified bishop consoled her with prophetic words that have become equally famous: "It is impossible that the son of such tears should perish" (*Conf.* 3.12.21).

Despite their limited financial means, it was his parents' ambition to provide their gifted son with the best possible education as an indispensable prerequisite for any professional career, whether as a teacher, a lawyer, or a politician. After instruction in reading, writing, and arithmetic on the elementary level, his education took place on two levels: language and literary studies with a *grammaticus,* which Augustine completed in his native Tagaste; and the study of dialectics and rhetoric, as well as the other *artes liberales* (arithmetic, music, geometry, astronomy, philosophy), with a *rhetor*. For this purpose he went to nearby Madaurus and in 370 to Carthage, the provincial capital, as the political and cultural center of North Africa. In his *Confessiones* Augustine paints a vivid picture of his schooldays. After he had learned his mother tongue unconsciously and freely, as small children do, the customarily enforced learning in the elementary school, which the parents took for granted and was interspersed with corporal punishment, went against his grain. It also so soured his Greek instruction that he was never fluent in the Greek language, although the precise scope of his knowledge is frequently discussed. He felt enthusiastic for the studies in Latin literature, however, and excelled in this field.

Toward the end of his sixteenth year, Augustine had to return home from Madaurus and spend a year there with enforced leisure because his parents first had to secure the financial means for the planned longer study visit to Carthage. During this time, as he states in the *Confessiones* (2.3.6), Augustine's sexuality awakened, which his father observed with delight in the hope of grandchildren in due course. (He was not to experience the birth of his grandson Adeodatus, however.) It seems almost like an inevitable consequence that during this time of idleness and turbulent personal development, Augustine would join a group of like-minded young men perpetrating all kinds of pranks. When he wrote the *Confessiones* as a bishop, of course, he looked back on this period with nothing but disdain, especially regarding the famous theft of pears that he and his comrades had committed, not for the sake of the fruit itself but because of their common cockiness.

*Studies:* F. G. Maier, *Augustin und das antike Rom* (TBAW 39; Stuttgart: Kohlhammer, 1955). – M. Testard, *Saint Augustin et Cicéron* (2 vols.; Paris: Études Augustiniennes, 1958). – H. Hagendahl, *Augustine and the Latin Classics* (2 vols.; SGLG 20.1–2; Göteborg, Swed.: Universitetet; Stockholm: Almqvist & Wiksell, 1967). – H.-I. Marrou, *Saint Augustin et la fin de la culture antique* (4th ed.; Paris: de Boccard, 1958). – J. Oroz Reta, *San Agustín: Cultura clásica y cristianismo* (BSal.E 110; Salamanca: Universidad Pontificia de Salamanca; Biblioteca de la Caja de Ahorros y M. de P. de Salamanca, 1988). – S. MacCormack, *The Shadows of Poetry: Vergil in the Mind of Augustine* (TCH 26; Berkeley: University of California Press, 1998).

## 2. In Search of the "True Philosophy": Father of a Family and Manichaean

During his studies in Carthage, Augustine not only completed his rhetorical education but also had three decisive encounters that were to set his life's pattern for years. After a series of sexual adventures—apparently of a less serious kind—already in Tagaste and then in Carthage, he maintained an ongoing and committed quasi-marital union with a woman (whose name he never mentions), beginning no later than 372, the year his son Adeodatus was born. An official marriage with this woman was not desirable because of the class difference or for the sake of his career, for he left her only in Milan (after 384) precisely in order to enter into a *matrimonium* befitting his station and beneficial to his career. At the age of nineteen, he read *Hortensius*, Cicero's dialogue, of which only the fragments cited in his *Confessiones* are extant. This kindled the "love for wisdom" (*philosophia*) in him and until his conversion became the basis of his persistent search for it, albeit taking him on many wrong tracks. By "philosophy" a person in antiquity never meant a theoretical construct of ideas alone but always also the correct knowledge of life and lifestyle (ethics), which had already enabled the apologists to proclaim Christianity attractively as the "true philosophy." On the basis of his upbringing, Augustine naturally linked his newly discovered "love for wisdom" with the question of Christ and therefore turned to reading the Bible, which indeed deeply disappointed him because of the barbaric stories of the OT and, compared with Cicero, especially because of its uncultured style.

In this situation he encountered Manichaeism, which apparently offered him everything he searched for: the name of Christ, rationality, and culture instead of mere faith in the authority of the church, rejection of the OT, and a plausible answer to the question *Unde malum?* which had tormented him for a long time. It was based on a materialistic concept of God and a dualistic concept of the world, according to which good and evil exist as two equally eternal antagonistic principles (realms) of light and darkness, whose battleground is the inner being of the human person, since he or she is composed of spirit and matter. For nine years[1] Augustine adhered to this teaching at the lower level of the *auditores,* which did not demand of him the extremely high standards of ethics and asceticism of the *electi,* although these probably substantially contributed to the great attraction of Manichaeism. As a zealous Catholic, Monica was appalled by her son's acceptance of Manichaeism. She wanted nothing to do with a heretic, and so when Augustine returned to Tagaste in 374/375 to work there as a teacher, she barred him from entering the house at times. Only after the dream described above did she resume contact with him for the sake of his salvation. Meanwhile Augustine found shelter and encouragement with Romanianus, one of the wealthy Manichaeans of Tagaste, who provided him with a recommendation when he returned to Carthage a year later, precipitated by the death of a close friend.

The following years of teaching in Carthage increasingly disappointed Augustine; his pupils were ill mannered, and he inwardly distanced himself more and more from Manichaeism, which seemed to be so convincing initially, because its followers were unable to answer his critical questions on the inconsistencies of their system. They put him off until the arrival of their spiritual leader, Bishop Faustus. When he finally arrived, however—Augustine was twenty-nine years old—he proved to be nothing more than a smooth talker without substance who had no answers for Augustine's questions. Nevertheless Augustine did not yet break with Manichaeism officially but had his friends recommend him to Rome, where he hoped for a better living and especially for more compliant pupils.

## 3. Rhetor in Rome and Milan: Skeptic and Platonist

Augustine's stay in Rome, where he arrived in 383, was brief. On the one hand, his pupils disappointed him here as well; although they were more disciplined, they enjoyed cheating their teachers out of their honorarium. On the other hand, there was an unusual opportunity already in the first year to make a major jump in his career. The imperial court in Milan had commissioned Symmachus, the prefect of the city of Rome, to find a *magister rhetoricae* for Milan, whose primary task it was to give public speeches in honor of the emperor and other important personalities and to provide instruction in rhetoric besides.

---

[1] So Augustine himself (*Conf.* 4.1.1); P. Courcelle (*Recherches sur les "Confessions" de Saint Augustin* [new ed.; Paris: E. de Boccard, 1968]; 78) and G. Bonner ("Augustinus [vita]," *AugL* 1:4, 525) calculate ten years.

With the assistance of his Manichaean friends, Augustine was successful in securing the recommendation; and so in the fall of 384 he had already arrived in Milan
to take up his new commission.

Milan was to be Augustine's final station on his way to conversion, even if
he was not able to foresee this personally and a number of factors still had to ac-
crue in the following two years to lead him ultimately to the culminating point in
his development. Most important was Ambrose, the city's bishop. Having inwardly turned away completely from Manichaeism in the meantime but still in
search of wisdom, that is, of Christ, and as a catechumen of the Catholic Church,
Augustine attended the bishop's worship services. As he often confessed later on
(*Conf.* 5.13.23), he did this not so much because he hoped finally to learn the co-
gent truth as because Ambrose warmly welcomed him at his arrival and Augustine wanted to test whether he deserved his great reputation as an orator. Ambrose
justified his reputation even more than Augustine expected, for with his sermons
he not only gained the approval of the trained rhetor, but with his platonizing,
spiritual interpretation of the OT he also won Augustine's heart by opening up for
him for the first time an acceptable meaning for the Bible, against his earlier impression of barbarism in the OT and against the Manichaean critique of the OT.
This led to the final break with Manichaeism, which Monica was delighted to
learn about when she arrived in Milan in the spring of 385. Although Augustine,
"after the manner of the academics," now found himself in a state of fundamental
methodological doubt toward all convictions, for Monica the turning away from
error was already the first hopeful step toward the truth of the church, and she
immediately began actively to promote her son's further progress. To begin with,
this called for a marriage befitting his station, not only for the sake of his professional career but especially in the hope that once he was securely in the haven of
marriage, Augustine would also be able to decide to be baptized (*Conf.* 6.13.23).
Therefore Monica arranged for Augustine's engagement to a young noble girl
from Milan who was still two years younger than the legal age for marriage
(twelve years). He had to break up with his longtime companion immediately, of
course, which caused him considerable pain. She returned to Africa without their
son, Adeodatus, who remained with his father.

In early 386 Augustine's decision making and his inner conflict between
longing for a life of wisdom, namely in asceticism, and his seemingly still undeniable need for sexual fulfillment intensified when he became acquainted with the
writings of the Neoplatonists through a group of friends, probably in the translation of Marius Victorinus, the famous rhetor. After the latter was accorded the
extraordinary honor of a statue in the Forum Romanum, he converted to Christianity in spectacular fashion ca. 355. It was his example that was presented to Augustine (*Conf.* 8.2.3–4) by the priest Symmachus, the same one who in 383 in
Milan had endeavored to achieve the reerection of the altar of Victoria, against the
opposition of Ambrose (cf. ch. 7.III). Platonism for the first time convinced him
of a purely spiritual concept of God as the one who is and who is good and solved
the question of the origin of evil by viewing it as the absence of good and as de-
void of substance. What was still missing was Christ as the redeemer and not only

as the wisest of all humans and the doctrinal authority. For this reason, Augustine again turned to the letters of Paul and discovered him as the teacher of grace in a Platonic synthesis: "Whatever truths I had read in those other words I here found to be uttered along with the praise of your grace" (*Conf.* 7.21.27). For the first time he now realized that he did not have to choose either reason *or* faith as alternatives but that faith *and* reason belonged together as a complementary unity. At a later point he captures their reciprocal function in the famous double formula *Intellege ut credas, crede ut intellegas* (*Serm.* 43.9).

The decisive crisis was finally brought about by the example of Anthony, the Egyptian monastic father, about whom he was told by his African friend Ponticianus. "What do you hear?" Augustine shouted to his friend Alypius, "The unlearned rise up and take heaven by storm, and we, with all our erudition but empty of heart, see how we wallow in flesh and blood!" (*Conf.* 8.8.19), and hurried out into the garden. This is where the now world-famous conversion scene took place. While Augustine paced back and forth distraught, he heard the voice of a child from a neighboring house saying, *Tolle, lege, tolle, lege* ("Take up and read"), and since he was not able to remember a children's game using these words, he understood it as a sign from God, as Anthony had formerly, to open up the Bible. He opened to the letters of Paul at Rom 13:13–14., "not in orgies and drunkenness, not in sexual immorality and debauchery, not in dissension and jealousy. Rather, clothe yourselves with the Lord Jesus Christ and do not think about how to gratify the desires of the sinful nature." "Instantly, in truth, at the end of this sentence, as if before a peaceful light streaming into my heart, all the dark shadows of doubt fled away" (*Conf.* 8.12.29). The historicity of this conversion scene has been the subject of much debate; all the same, this event likely occurred ca. August 1, 386.[2]

## 4. Philosophy and Christianity

The questions of which Platonic books in particular Augustine was conversant with, what influence they had on his thinking, and whether he first converted to Platonism or to the Catholic Church have frequently occupied the experts. Current scholarship assumes that Augustine was primarily influenced by the work of Plotinus and not by Porphyry, as suggested principally by Willy Theiler (1933), and that the alternative question of Platonism or Christianity presupposes a falsely construed ecclesiastical and theological situation in the fourth century. Fourth-century Christianity was shaped platonically from the start, and for Augustine, in the search for wisdom, which, as indicated above, always included the search for Christ, philosophy and Christianity did not represent alternatives but always a unit. To be sure, for him they were not identical, for he could not find Christ in the Platonic writings. Nevertheless, for Augustine, as well as for the church as a whole, Platonism remained the philosophical premise to understanding and

---

[2] Otherwise Bonner, "Augustinus (vita)," 532: at the end of August 386.

explaining faith. This had to be completed and corrected by the biblical message because the former contains incompatible "great errors" (*Retract.* 1.1.4), indeed "nonsense" (*Serm.* 241.6), such as the eternality of the world, the preexistence of the soul, the unnatural and hence forced uniting of the soul with the material body, the cyclical worldview, and others.

*Studies:* C. Boyer, *Christianisme et néo-platonisme dans la formation de s. Augustin* (rev. ed.; Rome: Officium Libri Catholici, 1953). – J. J. O'Meara, *Porphyry's Philosophy from Oracles in Augustine* (Paris: Études Augustiniennes, 1959). – R. Holte, *Béatitude et sagesse: Saint Augustin et le problème de la fin de l'homme dans la philosophie ancienne* (Paris: Études Augustiniennnes; Worcester, Mass.: Augustinian Studies, Assumption College, 1962). – A. H. Armstrong, *St. Augustine and Christian Platonism* (Villanova, Pa.: Villanova University Press, 1967). – E. König, *Augustinus philosophus: Christlicher Glaube und philosophisches Denken in den Frühschriften Augustins* (STA 11; Munich: Fink, 1970). – J. Pépin, *"Ex Platonicorum persona": Études sur les lectures philosophiques de saint Augustin* (Amsterdam: Hakkert, 1977). – L. Wittmann, *Ascensus: Der Aufstieg zur Transzendenz in der Metaphysik Augustins* (Munich: J. Berchman, 1980). – B. Bubacz, *St. Augustine's Theory of Knowledge: A Contemporary Analysis* (New York: Mellen, 1981). – P. F. Beatrice, *"Quosdam Platonicorum libros:* The Platonic Readings of Augustine in Milan," *VC* 43 (1989): 248–81. – R. J. O'Connell, *St. Augustine's Platonism* (Villanova, Pa.: Villanova University Press, 1984). – N. Fischer, *Augustins Philosophie der Endlichkeit: Zur systematischen Entfaltung seines Denkens aus der Geschichte der Chorismos-Problematik* (Bonn: Bouvier, 1987). – G. O'Daly, *Augustine's Philosophy of Mind* (Berkeley: University of California Press, 1987). – U. Wienbruch, *Erleuchtete Einsicht: Zur Erkenntnislehre Augustins* (Bonn: Bouvier, 1989). – E. Roll, *Der platonisierende Augustins* (Stuttgart: Mellinger, 1990). – J. Mader, *Aurelius Augustinus: Philosophie und Christentum* (St. Pölten, Austria: Niederösterreichisches Pressehaus, 1991). – R. J. Teske, "St. Augustine as Philosopher: The Birth of Christian Metaphysics," *AugStud* 23 (1992): 7–32; repr. in *Christianity in Relation to Jews, Greeks, and Romans* (ed. E. Ferguson; Recent Studies in Early Christianity 2; New York: Garland, 1999), 205–30. – D. X. Burt, *Friendship and Society: An Introduction to Augustine's Practical Philosophy* (Grand Rapids and Cambridge: Eerdmans, 1999). – R. Williams, "Insubstantial Evil," in *Augustine and His Critics: Essays in Honour of Gerald Bonner* (ed. R. Dodaro and G. Lawless; London and New York: Routledge, 2000), 105–23.

# B. From Baptism to Ordination

## 1. Christianae vitae otium in Cassiciacum and the Catechumenate

As for Basil, Jerome, and many other contemporaries, Augustine's decision for Christianity meant accepting an ascetic life. At the beginning of the harvest holiday (August 23 to October 15), he withdrew, together with his mother, his son, and several other relatives and friends, to the nearby country estate of Cassiciacum, belonging to his friend Verecundus (possibly modern Cassago di Brianza, nineteen miles north of Milan, at the foot of the Alps). Already before his conversion Augustine had planned for such a tranquil life of cultivated *otium* (cf. *Conf.* 6.14.24), but now it became *christianae vitae otium* (cf. *Retract.* 1.1.1), shaped by prayer, conversations, Bible reading, and literary activity. The conversations gave rise to literary dialogues of a Platonic kind about the issues of concern to Augustine and his companions: *Contra Academicos*, against scepticism; *De vita beata*, based on the knowledge of God; *De ordine*, on the question of evil in the divine providence; and the *Soliloquia*, on the search for God and the immortality of the soul.

At the end of the holiday, he resigned from his office as rhetor and in early 387 returned to Milan in order to be registered as a candidate for baptism at Easter 387, together with Adeodatus, his son, and Alypius, his friend. During the period of his catechumenate, he produced further writings, among them a comprehensively laid out cycle of textbooks on all seven *artes liberales*, though he only completed *De grammatica* (now lost) and *De musica*. On Easter eve, April 24, 387, Augustine, together with his son and his friend, was baptized by Bishop Ambrose in the cathedral of Milan, in the presence of his overjoyed mother.

*Studies:* D. E. Trout, "Augustine at Cassiciacum: *Otium honestum* and the Social Dimensions of Conversion," *VC* 42 (1988): 132–46. – G. Reale et al., *L'opera letteraria di Agostino tra Cassiciacum e Milano* (Palermo: Augustinus, 1987). – M. Sordi et al., *Agostino a Milano: Il battesimo* (Palermo: Augustinus, 1988). – J. P. Burns, "Ambrose Preaching to Augustine: The Shaping of Faith," in *Augustine—Second Founder of the Faith* (ed. J. Schnaubelt and F. Van Fleteran; Collectanea augustinana 1; New York: Lang, 1990), 373–86.

## 2. Monastic Community in Tagaste

Not long after his baptism, Augustine, together with his mother, made preparations to return to Africa from the Roman harbor of Ostia in order to establish a monastic community of Christian *otium* on the parental estates in Tagaste, as did Basil the Great in Annesi. Monica took ill at Ostia, however, and died before November 13, 387, having spent her final days in spiritual conversation with her son—like Macrina with her brother Gregory of Nyssa—and experienced the famous "vision at Ostia" as a mystical pinnacle. Since the voyage to Africa was delayed because of the winter season and the invasion of Italy by the usurper Magnus Maximus, Augustine remained in Rome during the winter and worked on the literary refutation of the Manichaeans. Together with his companions, he finally arrived in Africa in the summer or fall of 388, carried out his plan to establish a monastic community on the parental estates in Tagaste, for which he made all of his possession available, and for three years lived with his companions in a spiritually and literarily most fruitful *otium christianum*.

## 3. Ordination to the Priesthood in Hippo

As Augustine told his church as a seasoned bishop in *Serm.* 355 (425/426), it did not take long for the community to be disturbed by the appointment of members of their resident Christian intellectual elite as bishops, especially when they traveled to cities whose episcopal see was vacant. For this reason, Augustine avoided as much as possible entering a town where there was no bishop. In January

391, however, he went to Hippo Regius to establish another monastic community; here he felt comfortable because Bishop Valerius was in office. During the worship service, the bishop presented his desire to secure a priest for the gathered community, which decided on Augustine by acclamation. Possidius, his biographer (*Vit. Aug.* 4.2–3), reports that Augustine burst into tears over the great dangers of the episcopate but that the people misunderstood this and sought to console him, saying that as a priest he would also become a bishop. Nevertheless Augustine petitioned Valerius for the opportunity to undertake his initial plan, to which the latter responded by donating a garden to him near the cathedral, where he established his monastery, lived in it himself, and there originally may also have written his monastic rule for it (cf. ch. 8.I.C.1).

The primary reason for Augustine's ordination to the priesthood, according to Possidius (*Vit. Aug.* 5.3–5), was Bishop Valerius's insecurity about preaching in Latin, given his upbringing in the context of a Greek family. Although preaching traditionally was exclusively a bishop's prerogative and Augustine's appointment to this function initially triggered criticism, other North African bishops soon emulated Valerius's example. But since Augustine felt that he was not yet sufficiently prepared for this, he asked for a brief interlude in order to study Scripture, a request Valerius granted. He delivered his first sermon to the catechumens of Hippo on March 15, 391; hence the ordination to the priesthood, the date of which we do not know, must have taken place in late 390 or early 391.

# C. Priest and Bishop of Hippo

## 1. Pastor, Ecclesiastical Politician, Theologian, and Ascetic

In order to do full justice to the person and the almost forty years of effectiveness of Augustine as priest and bishop of Hippo (his consecration as bishop occurred between May 395 and August 397, initially as coadjutor of Valerius), we must constantly have him in view as a zealous pastor, an influential ecclesiastical politician, an outstanding theologian, and a spiritual individual at the same time. In the monastic community at Tagaste he had already renounced all personal possessions, and as a priest in Hippo, he lived in the "monastery in the garden." As bishop, he moved into the bishop's residence for practical purposes, but his lifestyle remained altogether ascetic, and even of his diocesan clergy he expected a monastic life in the monastery of the cathedral. *Sermones* 355 and 356, written toward the latter part of his life (425/426), as well as the *Vita* by Possidius (22–26), provide eloquent witness to this.

All of Augustine's actions, including his writings, controversies, and theology, were in the service of pastoral care. None of his works originated as a theoretical construct of an armchair scholar; rather, all of them were written in view of the relevant practical and pastoral needs of his diocese and of his time, frequently in response to concrete questions from far away. This is particularly true of his extensive collections of sermons and letters. Almost six hundred sermons are extant; these were usually taken down in shorthand and then collected in Augustine's own library. Even so this represents only a fraction of the roughly three or four thousand sermons actually delivered during his almost forty years of service, relative to every part of the church calendar, the commemoration of saints, Scripture, Christian doctrine, and correct Christian behavior. As recently as 1990, François Dolbeau identified twenty-six sermons in the city library in Mainz, which until then had been forgotten in part or in whole but which the *indiculus* of Possidius proved to be authentic. In his corpus of sermons, Augustine shows that he was a brilliant speaker, skilled in stirring and gripping formulation, as well as a very empathetic and lucid teacher. Whereas in his polemical works there is much that he sharply intensifies to the point of a misleading one-sidedness so as to heighten their persuasiveness, in his sermons and catechetical writings the presentation is very balanced. Therefore, in order to obtain an accurate picture of Augustine's theology, it is never appropriate to ascertain it from his polemical works alone; they should always be augmented by the pastoral writings.

Agostino Trapé, one of the outstanding twentieth-century experts on Augustine, summarizes the variety of Augustine's industriousness as follows[3]:

(1) for the church in Hippo: sermons, at least Saturday and Sunday, frequently also several days in succession and twice a day; audiences with clergy and people, as well as to decide in legal cases and complaints, which often lasted an entire day; caring for the poor and orphans, training clergy, organizing monasteries for men and women, managing church property, visiting the sick, intervening with governmental authorities on behalf of members of the church; (2) for the church in Africa: frequent journeys to participate in annual synods, to visit fellow brothers and attend ecclesiastical functions; (3) for the worldwide church: dogmatic controversies, responses to many inquiries, books upon books on the most diverse questions addressed to him.

More than anything else, the corpus of letters, containing 299 entries, reflects the variety of Augustine's pastoral, social, political, and personal effectiveness extending over more than forty years (from 386 to his death in 430). As recently as 1981, Johannes Divjak published 29 newly discovered letters, which have been submitted to extensive scrutiny since then.

Even when Augustine disputed with opponents, he first of all sought to win them and only then to vanquish them, because of his concern that no one go astray. The four major controversies he fought not only provide the best organization of his almost forty years of pastoral care, they also contributed substantially to the development of his theology.

*Anthropology:* E. Dinkler, *Die Anthropologie Augustins* (FKGG 4; Stuttgart: Kohlhammer, 1934). – E. L. Fortin, *Christianisme et culture philosophique au cinquième siècle: La querelle de l'âme humaine en Occident* (Paris: Études Augustiniennes, 1959). – A. Maxsein, *Philosophia cordis: Das Wesen der Personalität bei Augustinus* (Salzburg:

---

[3] J. Quasten, *Patrology* (4 vols.; Westminster, Md.; Christian Classics, 1984–1988), 3:331f.; *EECh* 1:98.

Müller, 1966). – R. J. O' Connell, *St. Augustine's Early Theory of Man*, A. D. 386–391 (Cambridge, Mass.: Belknap Press of Harvard University Press, 1968). – L. Hölscher, *The Reality of Mind: Augustine's Philosophical Arguments for the Human Soul as a Spiritual Substance* (London and New York: Routledge & Kegan Paul, 1986). – P. Brown, *Body and Society: Men, Women, and Sexual Renunciation in Early Christianity* (New York: Columbia University Press, 1988), 387–427. – P. Fredriksen, "Beyond the Body / Soul Dichotomy: Augustine on Paul against the Manichees and the Pelagians," *RechAug* 23 (1988): 87–114. – K. E. Børresen, "In Defense of Augustine: How *femina* is *homo*," in *Collectanea augustiniana: Melanges T. J. van Bavel* (ed. B. Bruning; 2 vols.; Louvain: Louvain University Press; Peeters, 1990), 411–28. – J.-M. Girard, *La mort chez saint Augustin: Grandes lignes de l'évolution de sa pensée, telle qu'elle apparaît dans ses traités* (Par. 34; Fribourg, Switz.: Editions Universitaires, 1992).

*History of Theology:* C. Eichenseer, *Das Symbolum apostolicum beim heiligen Augustinus mit Berücksichtigung des dogmengeschichtlichen Zusammenhangs* (KGQS 4; St. Ottilien: EOS, 1960). – W. Wieland, *Offenbarung bei Augustinus* (TTS 12; Mainz: Matthias Grünewald, 1978).

*Ethics and Moral Theology:* J. Mausbach, *Die Ethik des heiligen Augustinus* (2 vols.; Fribourg, Switz.: Herder, 1929). – O. Schaffner, *Christliche Demut: Des hl. Augustinus Lehre von der Humilitas* (Cass. 17; Würzburg: Augustinus, 1959). – J. Brechtken, *Augustinus doctor caritatis: Sein Liebesbegriff im Widerspruch von Eigennutz und selbstloser Güte im Rahmen der antiken Glückseligkeits-Ethik* (MPF 136; Meisenheim/ Glan: Hain, 1975). – S. Budzik, *Doctor pacis: Theologie des Friedens bei Augustinus* (IThS 24; Innsbruck: Tyrolia, 1988). – W. S. Babcock, ed., *The Ethics of St. Augustine* (Journal of Religious Ethics Studies in Religion 3; Atlanta: Scholars Press, 1991). – J. Wetzel, *Augustine and the Limits of Virtue* (Cambridge and New York: Cambridge University Press, 1992).

*Prayer:* M. Vincent, *Saint Augustin: Maître de prière d'après les Enarrationes in Psalmos* (ThH 84; Paris: Beauchesne, 1990). – H. Stirnimann, *Grund und Gründer des Alls: Augustins Gebet in den Selbstgesprächen (Sol. I,1,2–6)* (Fribourg, Switz.: Universitätsverlag, 1992) [with German translation].

*Liturgy:* W. Roetzer, *Des heiligen Augustinus Schriften als liturgie-geschichtliche Quelle: Eine liturgie-geschichtliche Studie* (Munich: Huebner, 1930). – A. E. Zwinggi, "Die Osternacht bei Augustinus," *LJ* 20 (1970): 4–10, 92–113, 120–40, 250–53. – A. E. Zwinggi, "Die Perikopenordnung der Osterwoche in Hippo und die Chronologie der Predigten des hl. Augustinus," *Aug(L)* 20 (1970): 5–34. – A. E. Zwinggi, "Die fortlaufende Schriftlesung im Gottesdienst bei Augustinus," *ALW* 12 (1970): 85–129.

*Preaching and Catechesis:* R. Deferrari, "St. Augustine's Method of Composing and Delivering Sermons," *American Journal of Philology* 43 (1922): 97–123, 193–219. – C. Mohrmann, "Saint Augustin prédicateur," *MD* 39 (1954): 83–96; repr. in idem, *Études sur le latin des chrétiens* (4 vols.; Rome: Storia letteratura, 1958–1977), 1:391–402. – C. Mohrmann, "*Praedicare–tractare–sermo*" in *Études sur le latin des chrétiens* (4 vols.; Rome: Storia e letteratura, 1958–1977), 2:63–72. – C. Mohrmann, *Die altchristliche Sondersprache in den Sermones des hl. Augustinus* (2d ed.; LCP 3; Amsterdam: Hakkert, 1965). – F. Schnitzler, *Zur Theologie der Verkündigung in den Predigten des heiligen Augustinus* (Fribourg, Switz.: Herder, 1968). – S. Poque, *Le langage symbolique dans la prédication d'Augustin d'Hippone* (Paris: Études Augustiniennes, 1984). – E. Reil, *Aurelius Augustinus, De catechizandis rudibus: Ein religionsdidaktisches Konzept* (St. Ottilien: EOS, 1989). – W. Harmless, *Augustine and the Catechumenate* (Collegeville, Minn.: Liturgical, 1995). – G. Madec, ed., *Augustin Prédicateur (395–411): Actes du Colloque International de Chantilly (5–7 Sept, 1996)* (Collection des études Augustiniennes, Série Antiquité 159; Paris: Études Augustiniennes, 1998).

*Theology of Creation:* M.-A. Vannier, *"Creatio," "conversion," "formatio" chez s. Augustin* (Par. 31; Fribourg, Switz.: Éditions Universitaires, 1991). – R. Williams, "'Good for Nothing?' Augustine on Creation," *AugStud* 25 (1994): 9–24.

# 2. Controversies and Their Theology

### a. Manichaeism: Unde malum?

Early on in his priesthood, Augustine continued his battle against the Manichaeans both on the literary front and practically, for instance, by means of a public disputation against Fortunatus, the presbyter of Carthage, who resided in Hippo and there "led the inhabitants astray and blinded them" (*Vit. Aug.* 6.1). In this rhetorical exhibition bout on August 28 and 29, 392, the course of which is preserved in *Contra Fortunatum*, Augustine drove the latter into a corner with his arguments to the extent that he was no longer able to respond and consequently left Hippo in defeat. The conclusion to the debate with Manichaeism was epitomized by a similar public discussion with a Manichaean named Felix in the cathedral of Hippo on December 7 and 12, 404, the records of which Augustine also published. In between there are a number of other anti-Manichaean writings, the most important being *Contra epistulam Manichaei quam vocant Fundamenti* (at the beginning of his episcopacy) and *De natura boni contra Manichaeos* (399), which primarily addressed the following three topics:

- the origin of evil as the lack of good in a creation that is fundamentally good and is created by a good God, against the Manichaean doctrine of two equally eternal realms of good and evil, which since then are in conflict with one another;

- the identification of the God of the OT with the God of the NT, as well as the unity of the two Testaments, against the Manichaean thesis that the OT was the product of an evil God and the NT had been interpolated;

- finally, the greater credibility of the Catholic teaching.

*Works of Augustine (Editions, Translations, Studies): See* nos. 2, 31, 38, 45–47, 53, 67, 74, 76, 98, 110, 116 at the end of the chapter.

*Encyclopedia Articles:* A. di Berardino, "Mani, Manichees, Manichaeism," *EECh* 1:519–20. – P. Perkins, "Mani, Manicheism," *EEC* 2:707–9. – J. K. Coyle, "Anti-Manichean Works," in *Augustine through the Ages: An Encyclopedia* (Grand Rapids: Eerdmans, 1999), 39–41. – J. K. Coyle, "Mani, Manicheism," in *Augustine through the Ages: An Encyclopedia* (Grand Rapids: Eerdmans, 1999), 520–25.

*Studies:* F. Decret, *Aspects du manichéisme dans l'Afrique romaine: Les controverses de Fortunatus, Faustus, et Felix avec saint Augustin* (Paris: Études Augustiniennes, 1970). – E. Feldmann, "Der Einfluss des Hortensius und des Manichäismus auf das Denken des jungen Augustinus von 373" (diss.; Münster, 1975). – F. Decret, *L'Afrique manichéenne (IVe–Ve siècle): Étude historique et doctrinale* (2 vols.; Paris: Études Augustiniennes, 1978). – G. R. Evans, *Augustine on Evil* (Cambridge and New York: Cambridge University Press, 1982). – E. Feldmann, *Die "Epistula fundamenti" der nordafrikanischen Manichäer: Versuch einer Rekonstruktion* (Altenberge: CIS, 1987). – F. Decret, *Essais sur l'église manichéenne en Afrique du Nord et à Rome au temps de saint*

*Augustin: Recueil d'études* (SEAug 47; Rome: Institutum Patristicum Augustinianum, 1995). – N. J. Torchia, *"Creatio ex nihilo" and the Theology of St. Augustine: The Anti-Manichaean Polemic and Beyond* (New York: Lang, 1999).

### b. Donatism: Ecclesiology and Doctrine of Sacraments

After the Diocletian persecution, during which many clerics bowed to the pressure of the state and handed over the church's holy books (*traditores*), and as a direct result of the consecration of Caecilian as the bishop of Carthage by an alleged *traditor* (311/312), an enthusiastic church "of the saints" was established in North Africa under the leadership of Donatus. This church denied the validity of a sinful clergy's exercise of office and the giving of the sacraments and therefore rebaptized; it also rejected a holy church composed of sinful members and therefore considered itself to be the only true church. Although the spread of Donatism was limited to the region of North Africa, the Catholic Church there was pushed into a minority position during the time of Augustine. Although Donatism was certainly a more dangerous problem for the North African church than Manichaeism, it was only in 393 that Augustine began to deal with it, and he did not proceed against it until 400. The reason for this is not only to be sought in the history of his own life but in his initial endeavor to reintegrate the very popular schismatic church of the Donatists into the Catholic Church. This is demonstrated in his first work on this matter, *Psalmus contra partem Donati* (393), telling the story of Donatism and its errors and encouraging reunification in the A-B-C form of a folk song with refrain. Only when Augustine had to be persuaded ca. 400 that the Donatist church, especially its violent arm, the Circumcellions, rejected any rapprochement did he begin to combat them by literary means. At the same time, he proceeded on the front of ecclesiastical policy, not only by attending numerous North African synods concerning this issue but now also by approving the assistance of imperial laws and sanctions against heretics and then applying them. Between 400 and 418 a number of anti-Donatist works originated, many of which are lost and known only on the basis of Augustine's *Retractationes*. The most important ones to mention are the following:

*De baptismo contra Donatistas* (ca. 400), mainly refuting the fundamental thesis of the Donatists that originally caused the schism, namely, that only sinless office bearers could validly fulfill their office and administer the sacraments. Against this Augustine distinguishes between validity and effectiveness. A sacrament administered or received unworthily (initially) may not further the recipient's salvation, but baptism imprints an indelible mark (*character*) in any case, for Christ alone administers the sacraments through his servants. Later Augustine summarizes this theology in his commentary on John (6.7) as a direct result of his explanation of John 1:33 ("this is he who will baptize with the Holy Spirit"), in the following famous words: "When Peter baptizes, Christ baptizes; when Paul baptizes, Christ baptizes; indeed even if Judas baptizes, Christ baptizes."

*De unitate ecclesiae* (also ca. 400), directed against the ecclesiological foundation of the Donatist schism, namely, that only equally saintly members are part of the one holy church. Augustine retorts with the fundamental and, for the church's future, decisive distinction between the sacrosanct holiness of the church as the body of Christ, who constitutes the foundation of its unity (*Christus totus caput et corpus*), and the sinfulness of its members, on account of which the church remains a *corpus permixtum* until its completion. Most important, there is only one church, and it has to be the church universal. Later Augustine developed his ecclesiology around the concept of the threefold *communio:* the earthly church is composed of good and bad individuals as a *communio sanctorum*, without detracting from the holiness of the body of Christ; the dead in Christ constitute the other part of the body of Christ, the *communio iustorum;* and the eschatological church will encompass all who have been called to salvation as the *communio praedestinatorum* (*De civitate Dei* 20.9).

*Gesta collationis Carthaginiensis* and *Breviculus collationis cum Donatistis.* The numerous synods and the imperial legislation against the Donatists culminated in a conference summoned by Marcellinus, the imperial *notarius*, on June 1, 3, and 8, 411, in Carthage. The 286 Catholic bishops who were present, under the leadership of Augustine, proved to be superior in their argumentation, especially because Augustine was able to circumvent the tactics of the 285 Donatist bishops and to move from the isolated, contentious disciplinary cases to the basic theological issues. As a result, an edict by Emperor Honorius (January 30, 412) ordered the suppression of the Donatists by means of governmental sanctions.

*Works of Augustine (Editions, Translations, Studies): See* nos. 9, 13, 15, 21, 23, 30, 33, 39, 51, 68, 89, 102 at the end of the chapter.

*Bibliographies:* É. Lamirande, "Un siècle et demi d'études sur l'ecclésiologie de saint Augustin: Essai bibliographique," *REAug* 8 (1962): 1–125 [also published as a separate booklet]. – É. Lamirande, "Supplément bibliographique sur l'ecclésiologie de saint Augustin," *REAug* 17 (1971): 177–82.

*Translations:* M. A. Tilley, *Donatist Martyr Stories: The Church in Conflict in Roman North Africa* (TTH 24; Liverpool: Liverpool University Press, 1997).

*Encyclopedia Articles:* W. H. C. Frend, "Donatism," *EEC* 1:343–47. – M. Tilley, "Anti-Donatist Works," in *Augustine through the Ages: An Encyclopedia* (Grand Rapids: Eerdmans, 1999), 34–39. – R. A. Markus, "Donatus, Donatism," in *Augustine through the Ages: An Encyclopedia* (Grand Rapids: Eerdmans, 1999) 284–87.

*Donatism:* P. Monceaux, *Saint Augustin et le donatisme* (vol. 7 of *Histoire littéraire de l'Afrique chrétienne depuis les origines jusqu'à l'invasion arabe;* Paris: Leroux, 1923; Brussels: Culture et civilisation, 1966). – A. H. M. Jones, "Were Ancient Heresies National or Social Movements in Disguise?" *JTS* NS 10 (1959): 280–98. – R. Crespin, *Ministère et sainteté: Pastorale du clergé et solution de la crise donatiste dans la vie et la doctrine de saint Augustin* (Paris: Études Augustiniennes, 1965). – E. Lamirande, *La situation ecclésiologique des donatistes d'après saint Augustin: Contribution à l'histoire doctrinale de l'œcuménisme* (Ottawa: Éditions de l'Université d'Ottawa, 1972). – W. H. C. Frend, *The Donatist Church: A Movement of Protest in Roman North Africa* (3d ed.; Oxford: Clarendon; New York: Oxford University Press, 1985). – M. A. Tilley, *The Bible in Christian North Africa: The Donatist World* (Minneapolis: Fortress, 1997).

*Ecclesiology:* F. Hofmann, *Der Kirchenbegriff des hl. Augustinus in seinen Grundlagen und seiner Entwicklung* (Munich: Hueber, 1933; repr., Münster: Stenderhoff, 1978). – J. Ratzinger, *Volk und Haus Gottes in Augustins Lehre von der Kirche* (MThS.S 7;

Munich: Zink, 1954). – S. J. Grabowski, *The Church: An Introduction to the Theology of St. Augustine* (St. Louis: Herder, 1957). – É. Lamirande, *L'Église céleste selon saint Augustin* (Paris: Études Augustiniennes, 1963). – É. Lamirande, *Études sur l'ecclésiologie de saint Augustin* (Ottawa: Éditions de l'Université Saint-Paul; Éditions de l'Université d'Ottawa, 1969). – W. Simonis, *Ecclesia visibilis et invisibilis: Untersuchungen zur Ekklesiologie und Sakramentenlehre in der afrikanischen Tradition von Cyprian bis Augustinus* (FTS 5; Frankfurt: Knecht, 1970). – B. Mondin, "Il pensiero ecclesiologico di sant'Agostino," *Sapienza* 40 (1987): 369–91. – G. Bonner, "Augustine's Understanding of the Church as a Eucharistic Community," in *Saint Augustine the Bishop* (ed. F. LeMoine and C. Kleinhenz; New York: Garland, 1994), 39–63. – T. J. van Bavel, "Church," in *Augustine through the Ages: An Encyclopedia* (Grand Rapids: Eerdmans, 1999), 169–76.

*Sacramental Theology:* C. Courturier, "*Sacramentum et mysterium* dans l'oeuvre de saint Augustin," in *Études augustiniennes* (ed. H. Rondet et al.; Paris: Aubier, 1953), 161–274. – W. Gessel, *Eucharistische Gemeinschaft bei Augustinus* (Cass. 21; Würzburg: Augustinus, 1966). – E. Schmitt, *Le mariage chrétien dans l'œuvre de saint Augustin: Une théologie baptismale de la vie conjugale* (Paris: Études Augustiniennes, 1983). – V. Grossi, *La catechesi battesimale agli inizi del V secolo: Le fonti agostiniane* (SEAug 39; Rome: Institutum Patristicum Augustinianum, 1993). – E. J. Cutrone, "Sacraments," in *Augustine through the Ages: An Encyclopedia* (Grand Rapids: Eerdmans, 1999), 741–47.

### c. Pelagianism: Doctrine of Grace and Predestination

*Studies:* J. P. Burns, *The Development of Augustine's Doctrine of Operative Grace* (Paris: Études Augustiennes, 1980). – G. Bonner, "Pelagianism and Augustine," *AugStud* 23 (1992): 33–51; repr. in *Forms of Devotion: Conversion, Worship, Spirituality, and Asceticism* (ed. E. Ferguson; Recent Studies in Early Christianity 5; New York: Garland, 1999), 191–210. – G. Bonner, "Augustine and Pelagianism," *AugStud* 24 (1993) 27–47; repr. in *Doctrinal Diversity: Varieties of Early Christianity* (ed. E. Ferguson; Recent Studies in Early Christianity 4; New York: Garland, 1999), 211–32. – J. P. Burns, "The Atmosphere of Election: Augustinianism as Common Sense," *JECS* 2 (1994): 325–339. – P.-M. Hombert, *Gloria gratiae: Se glorifier en Dieu, principe et fin de la théologie augustinienne de la grâce* (Paris: Études Augustiniennes, 1996). – D. R. Creswell, *St. Augustine's Dilemma: Grace and Eternal Law in the Major Works of Augustine of Hippo* (New York: Lang, 1997). – W. Harmless, "Christ the Pediatrician: Infant Baptism and Christological Imagery in the Pelagian Controversy," *AugStud* 28 (1997): 7–34. – V. H. Drecoll, *Die Entstehung der Gnadenlehre Augustins* (BHTh 109; Tübingen: Mohr, 1999). – J. Wetzel, "Snares of Truth: Augustine on Free Will and Predestination," in *Augustine and His Critics: Essays in Honour of Gerald Bonner* (ed. R. Dodaro and G. Lawless; London and New York: Routledge, 2000), 124–41.

### (1) Pelagius

The problem of the Donatists had hardly been resolved in principle—even if the actual extinction of this church was a process that took a long time—when the next major controversy began, which was to accompany Augustine throughout the remainder of his life, namely, the doctrine of grace, raised for the first time by Pelagius. Pelagius originally came from Britain and had lived in Rome since ca. 380, where he developed his extremely popular theology in the ascetical circles with which we have already become familiar through Jerome. His theology basically was an optimistic reaction to tendencies of resignation over matters of

shallowness and laxity in the Christian lifestyle, precipitated by the rapidly growing number of believers who flocked to the current state church and also introduced much mediocrity and carelessness. Against this, Pelagius, in a very positive
way, intended to encourage the zealousness of all Christians to a truly Christian
lifestyle by emphasizing the importance of a person's decision of the will for what
is good and for his or her actions. He assumed that by nature, that is, as a creature
in God's image (Gen 1:26f.), the human being possesses the grace and hence the
capability to decide freely for God, to obey God's commandments by following
Christ as the example par excellence (*exemplum*) of the Christian life, and thus to
attain salvation. He therefore understood Adam's sin not as original sin, passed
on from one generation to another, but merely as Adam's personal sin and as a
stimulus to emulate him, which can be resisted by one's determined will. Consequently, the grace of God is received by one's own merits (*merita*) and not on the
basis of the sacraments. This necessarily called for infant baptism, which had increased rapidly in the meantime because of the perception that baptism was essential for salvation, to be rejected as needless.

Initially the Pelagian teaching was not considered heretical because it did
not seem to be concerned with theology proper, that is, with the doctrine of God,
but rather with the issue of ethics. The controversy about it was also not brought
about by Pelagius himself but by Caelestius, his student, who settled in Carthage
after the fall of Rome on August 24, 410. Here Augustine was the first one to recognize the soteriological and christological danger of Pelagianism as a hidden
doctrine of self-redemption, for if a person is able to attain salvation on account
of his creaturely nature and his or her free decision of the will alone, and if Christ
only provided the example to this end, what was the purpose of Christ's death on
the cross? Does this not result precisely in what Paul already warned against in
1 Corinthians (1:17), namely, that the cross of Christ is emptied of its meaning
(*ne evacuetur crux Christi*)? In 412, therefore, Augustine wrote his first anti-
Pelagian work, *De peccatorum meritis et remissione et de baptismo parvulorum*, in
which he stressed the necessity of the prevenient grace of God to the human will
in order to make decisions for what is good, as well as the indispensability of baptism for participation in Christ's death on the cross in order to overcome inherited sin. As the dispute developed further, Augustine wrote further important
works to elaborate more precisely on the relationship of law and grace (*De spiritu
et littera*), as well as on nature and grace (*De natura et gratia*). Keeping the divine
commandments alone, apart from the grace that inspires, does not justify, and
nature and grace are by no means in conflict with one another; instead grace is
what provides nature with freedom and procures its healing (*Retract.* 2.42).

Augustine's doctrine of grace fundamentally assumes that Adam's sin was
not merely his own personal sin but that it turned humanity as a whole into a
*massa damnata* and is passed on from one generation to another, not through
personal imitation (*imitatio*) but with propagation (*propagatio*) through a person's cravings (*concupiscentia*). Whereas human nature in the paradisiacal, original condition, created by God in his own image, was very likely able to decide for
God immediately, human nature corrupted by original sin is no longer able to do

so but needs the prevenient grace of God enabling and encouraging the person to this decision. Compliance with the divine commandments, too, can succeed only with the accompanying grace of God, which ultimately also brings it to completion. A person's free will, however, determines the effectiveness (*efficacitas*) of grace. Through Christ's death on the cross, a person is already redeemed and hence through baptism, which is necessary for salvation, is equipped with the necessary grace; whether the latter will become effective, however, is contingent upon the person's decision and lifestyle. Yet the latter do not represent a compelling claim on the grace of God, which is always given without obligation and freely (*gratuitas*), even though it is true that God saves without merit (*bona merita*) but does not condemn without guilt (*mala merita*) (*C. Jul.* 3.18.35). Augustine's theology of grace becomes problematic and unacceptable for the church when he attributes to the grace of God irresistibility and renders the salvation of the individual completely dependent upon God's predestination, whereby God apparently grants or refuses grace arbitrarily, even if no one is entitled to it. This doctrine of predestination and the transmission of original sin through the *concupiscentia* of the procreative act triggered the two subsequent phases of the Pelagian dispute or formed their central themes.

Initially the pope commented frequently in favor of Augustine's position. His corpus of letters contains three letters by Pope Innocent, dated January 417 (*Ep.* 181–183), deciding in favor of the letters by two synods in Carthage and Milevis, as well as of five bishops (*Ep.* 175–177), one of them Augustine, requesting ratification of their condemnation of Pelagius. The pope excommunicated both Pelagius and Caelestius on January 17, 417. The famous *Serm.* 131, which Augustine probably delivered in September 417, later gave rise to the familiar quotation *Roma locuta—causa finita*, in the sense of a generally recognized, final authority of the see of Rome on doctrine. But this agrees neither with the wording nor with the intent of Augustine's sermon; in fact, the converse was true. Meanwhile, after the synod of Diospolis in Palestine (December 415), Zosimus, too, the successor to Pope Innocent (since March 417), rehabilitated Pelagius because of his extremely obliging manner and skilled defense; nevertheless the Africans considered the matter, against the current position of the pope, as settled with the verdict of Innocent (*causa finita*). Pope Zosimus had to yield to the African pressure, obtaining an imperial edict against Pelagius and Caelestius on April 30, 418, whereupon the Pope condemned Pelagius again in his *Epistula tractatoria.*

*Works of Augustine (Editions, Translations): See* nos. 7, 52, 58, 59, 77, 81, 83, 84, 107 at the end of the chapter.

*Encyclopedia Articles:* J. McWilliam, "Pelagius, Pelagianism," *EEC* 2:887–90. – G. Bonner, "Anti-Pelagian Writings," in *Augustine through the Ages: An Encyclopedia* (Grand Rapids: Eerdmans, 1999), 41–47. – E. TeSelle, "Pelagius, Pelagianism," in *Augustine through the Ages: An Encyclopedia* (Grand Rapids: Eerdmans, 1999), 633–40.

*Studies:* R. F. Evans, *Pelagius: Inquiries and Reappraisals* (New York: Seabury, 1968). – P. Brown, "The Patrons of Pelagius: The Roman Aristocracy between East and West," *JTS* NS 21 (1970): 56–72. – J. P. Burns, "Augustine's Role in the Imperial Action against Pelagius," *JTS* NS 30 (1979): 67–83. – B. R. Rees, *Pelagius: A Reluctant Heretic* (Woodbridge, Suffolk, Eng., and Wolfeboro, N.H.: Boydell, 1988); repr. in idem, *Pelagius: Life and Letters* (Rochester, N.Y.: Boydell, 1998). – B. R. Rees, *The Letters of Pelagius and His Followers* (Woodbridge, Suffolk, Eng., and Wolfeboro, N.H.: Boydell, 1991) repr. in idem, *Pelagius: Life and Letters* (Rochester, N.Y.: Boydell, 1998). – T. DeBruyn, *Pelagius' Commentary on St. Paul's Epistle to the Romans* (OECS; Oxford: Clarendon, 1993). – G. Bonner, *TRE* 26 (1996): 176–85. – C. Mayer, *AugL* 1:828.

## (2) Julian of Eclanum

The *Epistula tractatoria* ushered in the second phase of the Pelagian controversy because Julian, the bishop of Eclanum in southern Italy (modern Mirabella Eclano near Avellino in Campania) and eighteen other bishops refused to sign the condemnation. Julian wrote two letters to Pope Boniface (December 29, 418; September 4, 422), resulting in his excommunication. He therefore sent a complaint to Valerius, the *comes* at Ravenna, who turned to Augustine for a statement of his theological position, as did Pope Boniface. (This and many other instances demonstrate the extraordinary professional authority that Augustine enjoyed already during his lifetime. It was customary to approach Augustine with one's issues by letter or in person, and in all the instances known to us, he resolved them convincingly and enduringly. Many of his works are occasional writings of this sort, and his corpus of letters is replete with the relevant correspondence.)

Augustine responded with two works and made them available to Valerius: *Contra duas epistolas Pelagianorum ad Bonifatium* and *De nuptiis et concupiscentia ad Valerium comitem* (418/419); they also make it possible to reconstruct Julian's theological positions. In these writings Augustine rejects the accusations that he negates free will and that by maintaining original sin and judging disorderly lust as evil, he condemns marriage and devalues baptism. This began a literary exchange of blows, during the course of which Augustine died: Julian's response to the first *De nuptiis et concupiscentia*, followed in four books, whereupon Augustine (421/422) wrote a detailed tractate, *Contra Julianum*, in six books; against the second *De nuptiis et concupiscentia*, Julian wrote a further eight books, which Augustine began to refute in 428 with *Contra secundam Juliani responsionem imperfectum opus*, and which he did not complete. In this phase of the Pelagian dispute, Augustine clarified especially the concept of *concupiscentia*. As far as their institution is concerned, the marital union and the sexual desire of the act of procreation are good and to be affirmed. As a result of Adam's sin, however, *concupiscentia* no longer fits in with its original, God-oriented order but focuses on the physical aspect in a disorderly manner. Although, in the one who is baptized, this guilt is removed through the redemptive act of Christ, it remains as a tendency to disorderly evil and thereby propagates original sin.

*Works of Augustine (Editions, Translations): See* nos. 40, 65, 66, 78 at the end of the chapter.

*Encyclopedia Articles:* V. Grossi, "Julian of Eclanum," *EECh* 1:458. – P. D. Burns, "Julian of Eclanum (ca. 380–455)," *EEC* 1:642–43. – M. Lamberights, "Julian of Eclanum," in *Augustine through the Ages: An Encyclopedia* (Grand Rapids: Eerdmans,1999), 478–79.

*Studies:* P. Brown, "Sexuality and Society in the Fifth Century: Augustine and Julian of Eclanum," in *Tria corda: Scritti in onore di Arnaldo Momigliano* (ed. E. Gabba; Como:

Edizioni New Press, 1983), 49–70. – E. A. Clark, "Vitiated Seeds and Holy Vessels: Augustine's Manichean Past," in idem, *Ascetic Piety and Women's Faith: Essays in Late Ancient Christianity* (SWR 20; Lewiston, N.Y.: Mellen, 1986), 291–349. – E. A. Clark, "From Origenism to Pelagianism," in idem, *The Origenist Controversy: The Cultural Construction of an Early Christian Debate* (Princeton, N.J.: Princeton University Press, 1992), 194–244.

*(3) Monks of Hadrumetum and Massilia*

The third phase of Pelagianism during Augustine's lifetime does not represent a linear continuation of the first two phases, for now it was no longer Pelagius together with his followers opposing the Catholic Church; instead the theological formulation of the issues—brought about by the Pelagian dispute—of grace and especially of predestination continued within the church. The triggering mechanism was Augustine's *Ep.* 194, addressed in 418 to the Roman priest Sixtus, in which he presented his doctrine of grace, for the sake of his arguments' clarity and power of persuasion, with such sharpness that it might have appeared as though the free and unearned grace of God predetermined a person's destiny even without any contribution of his or her own. Among the monks at Hadrumetum (modern Sousse on the eastern coast of Tunisia), the letter became a matter of great concern because they feared that all of their own ascetical efforts to live a life pleasing to God would be rendered invalid thereby. In 426 Augustine addressed these doubts in the tractate *De gratia et libero arbitrio,* in which he made clear once again that although the grace of God precedes a person's decision of the will, makes it possible, and accompanies his or her behavior to completion, the person's free decision is not thereby impeded or rendered superfluous. Some monks at Hadrumetum, however, concluded that this response by Augustine rejected brotherly reprimand, since it is the grace of God that moves the human will. Augustine responded with the writing of *De correptione et gratia,* in which he clarified his doctrine of grace yet again by distinguishing especially the effectiveness of grace before and after the fall. He argued that whereas in a state of harmony with God grace was able to be directly effective, after the fall it encounters the resistance of the human and therefore also avails itself of human assistance. Augustine thus distinguishes between grace as the *adiutorium sine quo non* and reprimand as the *adiutorium quo.*

This apparently settled the concerns of the monks at Hadrumetum; however, in Massilia (Marseilles) in southern Gaul, a real opposition of monks ensued against Augustine's doctrine of grace—precipitated by his two writings addressed to the monks at Hadrumetum. The monks in Gaul continued to insist that the role of grace and predestination, as taught by Augustine, was far overrated over against human decision and merits. In two letters (225 and 226) dated in 429, Augustine's friends, Prosper of Aquitaine and an African by the name of Hilarius, informed him of this; as a result, Augustine (429/430) wrote two further works to the monks in Gaul: *De praedestinatione sanctorum* and *De dono perseverantiae.* Here he emphasizes that predestination does not mean pre*determination* as much as pre*science* and the preparation of grace *(gratiae praeparatio)*; a compulsory premature decision by God about the fate of a person, which eliminates human freedom, does not exist. One is not to succumb to the other extreme, as did Pelagius, of course, by expecting everything from human merit. Without the prevenient and accompanying free grace of God, a person cannot come to faith, let alone persevere in it. In contrast to Hadrumetum and many other controversies in Augustine's life, the monks in Gaul did not accept his theology. In bk. 13 of his *Collationes,* John Cassian opposed it, and Vincent, a monastic priest of Lérins, criticized Augustine sharply in his *Obiectiones;* hence it may be assumed that these two monasteries functioned as the centers of the opposition. Since Augustine died (430) in the meantime, Prosper of Aquitaine and others continued the dispute, also in literary form, until the Second Council of Orange (529), which ultimately condemned what came to be known as Semi-Pelagianism at the beginning of the sixteenth century.

*Works of Augustine (Editions, Translations): See* nos. 22, 58, 85, 86 at the end of the chapter.

*Studies:* G. Nygren, *Das Prädestinationsproblem in der Theologie Augustins* (STL 12; Lund, Swed.: Gleerup, 1956). – G. Bonner, *Augustine and the Modern Research on Pelagianism* (Villanova, Pa.: Villanova University Press, 1972). – G. Philips, *L'Union personnelle avec le Dieu vivant: Essai sur l'origine et le sens de la grace créée* (rev. ed.; BETL 36; Louvain: Louvain University Press, 1989). – A. Trapé, *Natura e grazia* (vol. 1 of *S. Agostino: Introduzione alla dottrina della grazia;* Rome: Nuova Biblioteca Agostiniana: Città Nuova, 1987). – A. Trapé, *Grazia e libertà* (vol. 2 of *S. Agostino: Introduzione alla dottrina della grazia;* Rome: Nuova Biblioteca Agostiniana: Città Nuova, 1990). – R. Harden Weaver, *Divine Grace and Human Agency: A Study of the Semi-Pelagian Controversy* (PatMS 15; Macon, Ga.: Macon University Press, 1996). – J. Lössl, *Intellectus gratiae: Die erkenntnistheoretische und hermeneutische Dimension der Gnadenlehre Augustins von Hippo* (SVigChr 38; Leiden and New York: Brill, 1997).

### d. Arianism

Because of the advance of the Goths and other Germanic tribes that adhered to Arian Christianity, but also because of Germanic soldiers in the Roman forces in North Africa, Augustine also had to deal with Arianism in the later years of his life, beginning in 416. This did not call for the development of a new theology, for the Council of Constantinople (381) had clarified fundamentally the doctrine of the Trinity and Augustine had already completed his major tractate, *De Trinitate,* enabling him to draw from it. He wrote only a few but important works: *Contra sermonem Arianorum* (418), against the *sermo* of an unknown Arian, which he forestalls; and *Contra Maximinum Arianum* (428), against the assertion made by Maximinus, upon his return to Carthage, that he had won the public disputation in Hippo. Beyond the doctrine of the Trinity in these tractates, which, as already indicated, moves entirely within the framework of Augustine's fully developed theology of the Trinity, there are important passages that unfold and apply his Christology, which was not fully developed until ca. 411.

*Works of Augustine (Editions, Translations): See* nos. 18, 71, 98 at the end of the chapter.

*Encyclopedia Articles:* M. R. Barnes, "Anti-Arian Works," in *Augustine through the Ages: An Encyclopedia* (Grand Rapids: Eerdmans, 1999), 31–34.

*Studies:* S. González, *La preocupación arriana en la predicación de san Agustín* (Valladolid: Estudio Agustiniano, 1989). – W. A. Sumruld, *Augustine and the Arians: The Bishop of Hippo's Encounters with Ulfilan Arianism* (Selinsgrove, Pa.; Susquehanna University Press; London and Cranbury, N.J.: Associated University Presses, 1994).

### e. Leporius: A Case of "Pre-Nestorianism"

Shortly before his death, Augustine had to deal with another theological issue that did not yet represent a controversy but the content of which anticipates the Nestorian problem and hence tends to be described as a case of "pre-Nestorianism." From 418 to 428 Leporius, a Gallic priest (of Massilia?), had been excommunicated by the bishop of Massilia because of christological heresy and went to Augustine to obtain theological help. The latter accurately recognized his "pious fear but foolish error: he did not want to confess that God had been born of a woman, that God could have been crucified and suffered in the manner of humans, for fear of believing that deity had been changed into a human or had been corrupted by admixture" (*Ep.* 219.3). Hence the issue was precisely that of the later Nestorian problem of the *communicatio idiomatum;* when this was emphasized excessively, it was in danger of separating the two natures of Christ into two sons. Since Augustine had already resolved this question in his theology of *una persona Christi* as the only and common subject of the doctrine both of Christ's actions and of Christ's divinity and humanity, he was able to instruct Leporius accordingly and, together with him (or for him), wrote a *Libellus emendationis seu satisfactionis.* With this writing and a covering letter (*Ep.* 219), he sent him home and thus contributed to his rehabilitation.

*Editions:* PL 31:1221–30; repr. in P. Glorieux, *Prénestorianisme en Occident* (MCS 6; Tournai and New York: Desclée, 1959), 14–25.

*Studies:* A. Trapé, "Un caso de nestorianismo prenestoriano en Occidente, resuelto por san Agustín," *CDios* 155 (1943): 45–67. – F. de Beer, "Une tessère d'orthodoxie: Le 'Libellus emendationis' de Leporius (vers 418–421)," *REAug* 10 (1964): 145–85. – J.-L. Maier, "La date de la rétractation de Leporius et celle du 'sermon 396' de saint Augustin," *REAug* 11 (1965): 39–42. – F. Gori, "La pericope cristologica del *De Trinitate* X pseudoatanasiano nel *Libellus emendationis* di Leporio," *Aug* 31 (1991): 361–86.

## 3. Choice of Successor and Death

At the age of seventy-two, Augustine decided on September 26, 426, to have a coadjutor elected at a public meeting composed of two further bishops, the clergy, and the people of Hippo, in order to prevent quarrels after his death. A report was made of this meeting as official notification (*Ep.* 213) and sent to Theodosius, the consul, as well as to Emperor Valentinian III. When Augustine himself had become the coadjutor of Valerius, his predecessor in Hippo, he was consecrated bishop during his predecessor's lifetime without the participants' awareness that canon 8 of the Council of Nicea (325) prohibited this. Augustine's designated successor, Eraclius, therefore remained a priest until his predecessor's death, but he unburdened him in his episcopal duties. Augustine died on August 28, 430, in the third month of Hippo's siege by the Vandals, who had been conquering North Africa from the Strait of Gibraltar since 429. The invitation to the Council of Ephesus arrived at Easter 431, attesting to the special empirewide appreciation of Augustine as a theologian. Synods in the eastern part of the empire, although ecumenical, generally took place without the wider inclusion of the Western episcopate; however in this instance, in addition to Augustine, an invitation was sent only to Celestine, bishop of Rome, who had been involved in the controversy previously and dispatched a legate.

Most likely Augustine was buried in the cathedral of Hippo. About 500 of the Catholic bishops who had been exiled from Africa (the Vandals were Arians) took his skeleton with them to Sardinia; in the eighth century Liutprand, the king of the Lombards, acquired it and moved it to Pavia, where they remain to this day in the church of San Pietro in Ciel d'Oro. Together with Ambrose, Jerome, and Pope Gregory the Great, Augustine is one of the "four great doctors of the Western church," and his continued influence in Western theology and in the Western church can hardly be overestimated. The subject of Augustinianism fills entire libraries.

# II. OUTSTANDING WORKS AND THEIR THEOLOGY

## A. Confessiones

Without a doubt, the most famous work of Augustine—one unique in the history of world literature—is his *Confessiones,* in thirteen books; it is the primary source for our knowledge of his life and inner development until his baptism and of the death of Monica, his mother (387). In Latin, *confessio* does not only connote "confession" (i.e., of Augustine's wandering ways up to his conversion); it also means "recognition," namely, of God's greatness and goodness, as Augustine himself explains at various points in his works, for instance, in the new *Sermo moguntinus* 1.1 on Ps 117:1, *Confitemini Domino quoniam bonus:* "In Scripture a confession is customarily expressed and understood in two ways: one regarding your punishment, the other the praise of God." Augustine also understands the title of his book *Confessiones* in this manner, as he affirms in the *Retractationes* (2.6): "The thirteen books of my *Confessions* praise the just and good God for my evil and good acts." The *Confessiones* are organized accordingly into two major parts: bks. 1–9 contain the confession of Augustine's wanderings up to his conversion, ending with the death of his mother, Monica, in Ostia; and bks. 10–13 are in praise of God and God's creation, bk. 11 dealing with one of the great and famous philosophies of the time.

Augustine began the *Confessiones* after the death of Ambrose (April 4, 397); whether he did so because of a concrete external event or merely an inner impulse has been the subject of much discussion, with no consensus reached. It is possible that some friends encouraged him to this end. Part 1 (1–9) was available by the end of 398, and the overall work by 400, which has prompted a discussion concerning the integrity of the work, which is, however, affirmed by the majority. If the presentation of the *Confessiones* is compared with the other contemporaneous sources of Augustine's life, namely, the dialogues of Cassiciacum, a number of discrepancies in the presentations of Augustine's inner development are apparent; this provides another incentive for intensive research. In any case, Augustine may not be blamed for forgetfulness or deliberate falsification; instead it is to be assumed that the bishop's perspective twelve to fourteen years after the events assessed many things differently and made selections and evaluations differently from when he was a new convert. The explicit goal of the *Confessiones* is not an "objective" autobiographical account but the bishop's reflection on life, and so the truth becomes clearer if both sources are viewed together, taking into consideration the different dates of writing and the different intent for writing. The extremely extensive scholarly literature on the *Confessiones* deals mainly with Augustine's biography; his education, inner development, psychology, and philosophy; his concept of God; his worldview; and many other individual issues.

*Works of Augustine (Editions, Translations): See* no. 17 at the end of the chapter.

*Reference Works:* R. H. Cooper, L. C. Ferrari, P. M. Ruddock, and J. R. Smith, *Concordantia in libros XIII Confessionum S. Aurelii Augustini: A Concordance to the Skutella (1969) Edition* (2 vols.; AlOm.A 124.1–2; Hildesheim and New York: Olms, 1991).

*Commentaries:* E. P. Meijering, *Augustin über Schöpfung, Ewigkeit, und Zeit: Das elfte Buch der Bekenntnisse* (PP 4; Leiden: Brill, 1979) [Tr.ted/Com]. – L. F. Pizzolato, et al., *"Le Confessioni" di Agostino d'Ippona* (4 vols. in 3; Lectio Augustini 1–4; Palermo: Augustinus, 1984–1987). – J. J. O'Donnell, *Augustine Confessions* (3 vols.; Oxford: Clarendon, 1992) [Com]. – G. Clark, *Augustine: Confessions, Books I–IV* (Cambridge Greek and Latin Classics; Cambridge: Cambridge University Press, 1995) [Com].

*Encyclopedia Articles:* F. van Fleteren, "Confessions," in *Augustine through the Ages: An Encyclopedia* (Grand Rapids: Eerdmans, 1999), 227–32.

*Surveys:* P. Courcelle, *Recherches sur les Confessions de saint Augustin* (2d ed.; Paris: de Boccard, 1968). – R. J. O'Connell, *St. Augustine's Confessions: The Odyssey of Soul* (2d ed.; New York: Fordham University Press, 1989). – M. Pellegrino, *Le 'Confessioni' di Sant'Agostino: Studio introduttivo* (2d ed.; Rome: Studium, 1972). – L. C. Ferrari, *The Conversions of Saint Augustine* (Villanova, Pa.: Augustinian Institute, Villanova University Press, 1984). – E. Feldmann, *AugL* 1:1134–93. – D. Capps and J. E. Dittes, eds., *The Hunger of the Heart: Reflections on the Confessions of Augustine* (SSSR 8; West Lafayette, Ind.: Society for the Scientific Study of Religion, 1990). – G. Clark, *Augustine: The Confessions* (Landmarks of World Literature; Cambridge: Cambridge University Press, 1993). – N. Fischer and C. Mayer, eds., *Die Confessiones des Augustinus von Hippo: Einführung und Interpretationen zu den dreizehn Büchern* (Fribourg, Switz.: Herder, 1998). – J. J. O'Meara, *The Young Augustine: The Growth of St. Augustine's Mind up to His Conversion* (rev. ed.; New York: Alba, 2001).

*Studies:* P. Fredriksen, "Paul and Augustine: Conversion Narratives, Orthodox Traditions, and the Retrospective Self," *JTS* NS 37 (1986): 3–34. – P. A. Gramaglia, *Agostino, Confessioni 1–2: Interpretazione e autobiografia* (Geneva: Marietti, 1990), 13–94. –

H. Chadwick, "History and Symbolism in the Garden at Milan," in *From Augustine to Eriugena: Essays on Neoplatonism and Christianity in Honor of John O'Meara* (ed. F. X. Martin and J. A. Richmond; Washington, D.C.: Catholic University of America Press, 1991), 42–55. – L. C. Ferrari, "Augustine's 'Discovery' of Paul (Confessions 7, 21, 27)," *AugStud* 22 (1991): 37–61. – C. Starnes, *Augustine's Conversion: A Guide to the Argument of Confessions I–IX* (Waterloo, Ont.: Wilfred Laurier University Press, 1991). – V. J. Bourke, *Augustine's Love of Wisdom: An Introspective Philosophy* (West Lafayette, Ind.: Perdue University Press, 1992). – J. Kreuzer, *Pulchritudo: Vom Erkennen Gottes bei Augustin: Bemerkungen zu den Büchern IX, X, und XI der Confessiones* (Munich: Fink, 1995). – R. J. O'Connell, *Images of Conversion in St. Augustine's Confessions* (New York: Fordham University Press, 1996).

*Form and Literary Structure:* P. Courcelle, *Les Confessions de saint Augustin dans la tradition littéraire: Antécédents et postérité* (Paris: Études Augustiniennes, 1963). – U. Duchrow, "Der Aufbau von Augustins Schriften *Confessiones* und *De Trinitate*," *ZThK* 62 (1965): 338–67. – W. Desch, *Augustins Confessiones: Beobachtungen zu Motivbestand und Gedankenbewegung* (Frankfurt and New York: Lang, 1988). – R. McMahon, *Augustine's Prayerful Ascent: An Essay on the Literary Form of the Confessions* (Athens: University of Georgia Press, 1989). – C. Joubert, "Le livre XIII et la structure des *Confessions* de saint Augustin," *RevScRel* 66 (1992): 77–117. – F. Young, "The *Confessions* of St. Augustine: What Is the Genre of This Work? (1998 St. Augustine Lecture)," *AugStud* 30.1 (1999): 1–16.

*Status Quaestionis:* L. Ferrari, "Reconsiderando las *Confesiones* de Agustín: Treinta años de descubrimientos," *Augustinus* 42 (1997): 279–96.

# B. Biblical Exegesis and Understanding of Scripture

According to the witness of the *Confessiones*, there are two constants throughout all of Augustine's wanderings on his way to baptism: the search for Christ and the deep respect for the Bible as the fundamental source of revelation. Every time Augustine approached the Catholic Church, he turned to Scripture as a matter of course. Even when he turned away from the OT in disappointment over its uncultured style and barbaric content, he still adopted the Manichaeans' biblical text and interpretation in his dealings with them. Ambrose won him over because he knew how to open up an acceptable meaning of the OT for him, with the result that he turned to studying the Bible afresh, especially the Pauline letters, which provided the final impetus leading to his salvation. "Therefore, since we were too weak to find the truth by pure reason and we needed the authority of Holy Writ, I now began to believe that in no way would you have given such surpassing authority throughout the whole world to that Scripture unless you wished that both through it you be believed in and through it you be sought" (*Conf.* 6.5.8). Even if these formulations are those of Augustine as bishop, in terms of content, their witness to the decisive role of Scripture for Augustine at the time of his conversion certainly remained and continued in his life as a Catholic Christian. The communal life at Cassiciacum and Tagaste included the reading and interpretation of Scripture, and after his ordination to the priesthood, he requested time once again to prepare himself for the interpretation of Scripture, which had to be the basis for all preaching as priest and bishop.

After his conversion it was a matter of course that Augustine's initial exegetical works were directed against the Manichaeans. In this context we find his famous saying "I would not believe the gospel if the authority of the Catholic church had not led me to do so" (*Contra epistulam Manichaei quam vocant Fundamenti* 5.6). Hence the final criterion of truth is not one's personal understanding of the Scriptures but the church's doctrinal authority, even though, as Augustine emphasized at about the same time (397) in bk. 2 of *De doctrina christiana*, the sciences (language, literature, history, philosophy, logic, natural sciences, rhetoric, and dialectic) are indispensable for the serious study of Scripture. Here he also develops the theory of signs that was fundamental to his exegesis (cf. below II.F).

The two most important exegetical works of Augustine are the collections of sermons delivered at various places and at very different times and those of lectures taken down by dictation for the sake of completeness; together they constitute a complete commentary on the Psalms and the Gospel of John. In both instances, it is true, dates and places cannot be determined with precision. The *Enarrationes in Psalmos* encompasses a time frame from 392 to 416 or 422; it is Augustine's most extensive work and the only complete commentary on the Psalms of the patristic era. Augustine explains the Psalms mainly from a christological vantage point, for, although they were written by King David according to the general conviction of the ancient church, the praying Christian appropriates them by understanding them—as is true of the entire OT—as Christ-oriented, prophetic words. "All of those verses were spoken by the Lord; while it was the prophet who spoke, he did so as the Lord's representative [*ex persona*]. Even if the prophet speaks on his own [*ex sua persona*], it is the Lord who speaks through him by telling him the truth beforehand" (*Enarrat. Ps.* 56:13). For this reason, following this basic principle, the one who speaks in the Psalms is *Christus totus* for Augustine, either as the Son of God (*ex persona capitis*), as man (*ex persona hominis, carnis*), representing the human race (*ex persona generis humani*), or as the church (*ex persona corporis*), depending upon the context. The criterion applied is always the question of what meaning suggests itself as appropriate (*aptum*) to the context. This kind of textual interpretation had already been developed in classical antiquity for the songs of Homer and other poets in order to explain obscure or unsuitable references and, in general, to pick up the deeper meaning of songs that were considered to be inspired. Augustine had learned this method at school and frequently applied it to biblical exegesis.

The commentary on the Gospel of John (*In Evangelium Johannis tractatus*) consists of 124 lectures; their dating is still subject to debate today, but they fall in the period between 406 and 420, in any case. For Augustine, this commentary, too, has eminently christological meaning, since John, in contrast to the Synoptic Gospels, highlights Christ as the Son of God.

*Works of Augustine (Editions, Translations): See* nos. 3, 19, 34, 37, 41, 53–55, 59, 63, 69, 90–92, 94, 106 at the end of the chapter.

*Reference Works:* D. Lenfant, *Biblia augustiniana* (2 vols., Paris: n.p., 1661–1670).

*Encyclopedia Articles:* J. J. O'Donnell, "Bible," in *Augustine through the Ages: An Encyclopedia* (Grand Rapids: Eerdmans, 1999), 99–103. – K. Pollmann, "Hermeneutical Presuppositions," in *Augustine through the Ages: An Encyclopedia* (Grand Rapids: Eerdmans, 1999), 426–29.

*Works:* T. Raveaux, *Augustinus, Contra adversarium legis et prophetarum: Analyse des Inhaltes und Untersuchung des geistesgeschichtlichen Hintergrunds* (Cass. 37; Würzburg: Augustinus, 1987). – B. Studer, *Zur Theophanie-Exegese Augustins: Untersuchung zu einem Ambrosius-Zitat in der Schrift De videndo Deo (ep. 147)* (SA 59; Rome: Herder, 1971). – M. Vincent, *Saint Augustin, maître de prière, d'après les Enarrationes in Psalmos* (ThH 84; Paris: Beauchesne, 1990). – D. Dideberg, *Saint Augustin et la première épître de saint Jean* (ThH 34; Paris: Beauchesne, 1975). – R. P. Hardy, *Actualité de la révélation divine: Une étude des "Tractatus in Johannis Euangelium" de saint Augustin* (ThH 28; Paris: Beauchesne, 1974). – M.-F. Berrouard, "L'exégèse de saint Augustin prédicateur du quatrième Évangile: Le sens de l'unité des Écritures," *FZPhTh* 34 (1987): 311–38. – D. Wyrwa, "Augustins geistliche Auslegung des Johannesevangeliums," in *Christliche Exegese zwischen Nicaea und Chalcedon* (ed. J. van Oort and U. Wickert; Kampen, Neth.: Kok Pharos, 1992), 185–216.

*Studies:* G. Strauss, *Schriftgebrauch, Schriftauslegung, und Schriftbeweis bei Augustin* (BGBH 1; Tübingen: Mohr, 1959). – A.-M. La Bonnardière, *Biblia augustiniana: A. T.* (7 vols.; Paris: Études Augustiniennes, 1960–1975). – U. Duchrow, *Sprachverständnis und biblisches Hören bei Augustin* (HUT 5; Tübingen: Mohr, 1965). – A. M. La Bonnardière, ed., *Augustine and the Bible* (trans. P. Bright; Bible through the Ages 2; Notre Dame, Ind.: University of Notre Dame Press, 1999); trans. of *Saint Augustin et la Bible* (Bible de tous les temps 3; Paris: Beauchesne, 1986). – A. Pollastri and F. Cocchini, *Bibbia e storia nel cristianesimo latino* (Rome: Borla, 1988), 13–93. – R. J. O'Connell, *Soundings in St. Augustine's Imagination* (New York: Fordham University Press, 1994). – B. de Margerie, *Saint Augustine* (vol. 3 of *Introduction to the History of Exegesis;* trans. Pierre de Fontnouvelle; Petersham, Mass.: St. Bede's, 1995); trans. of *Introduction à l'histoire de l'exégèse* (Paris: Cerf, 1983). – J. T. Lienhard, "Reading the Bible and Learning to Read: The Influence of Education on St. Augustine's Exegesis (the 1995 St. Augustine Lecture)," *AugStud* 27 (1996): 7–25. – P. Bright, ed., *Augustine and the Bible* (Bible through the Ages 2; Notre Dame, Ind.: University of Notre Dame Press, 1999). – T. F. Martin, "*Vox Pauli:* Augustine and the Claims to Speak for Paul, an Exploration of Rhetoric at the Service of Exegesis," *JECS* 8 (2000): 237–72.

# C. Christology and Soteriology

There is no doubt at all that from his earliest childhood Augustine grew up as a catechumen in the home of his pious mother, Monica, and there became familiar with the name of Christ and that his entire long journey to the "true philosophy" was a search for Christ, as he attests himself in the *Confessiones.* This does not mean, of course, that he had gained a correct understanding of Christ before his baptism.

> I sought for a way of gaining strength sufficient for me to have joy in you, but I did not find it until I embraced "the mediator between God and man, the man Christ Jesus." . . . But I had other thoughts: I conceived my Lord Christ only as a man of

surpassing wisdom, whom no other man could equal. . . . But what mystery was contained within those words, "The Word was made flesh," I could not conceive. . . . I acknowledged that in Christ there was a complete man: not merely a man's body, nor an animating principle in the body but without a mind, but a true man. I accounted him a person to be preferred above all other men, not as the person of truth, but because of some great excellence of his human nature and a more perfect participation in wisdom. . . . It was somewhat after this, I admit, that I learned how, with regard to those words, "The Word was made flesh," (John 1:14) Catholic truth is distinguished from the false teaching of Photinus. (*Conf.* 7.18.24–7.19.25)

Thus, at the time of his conversion, Augustine had a purely philosophical, Neoplatonic understanding of Christ. For this reason, the three important studies of the twentieth century, by Scheel, van Bavel, and Newton, investigated especially the influence of philosophy upon Augustine's Christology.

The vocabulary of the *Confessiones* indicates that the Christology of Augustine the bishop had made considerable progress by this time. He viewed the man Jesus Christ within the soteriological category of the mediator and recognized that the incarnation meant the real and complete acceptance of the human by the preexistent true Son of God. In the context of the contemporary formulations of the question and the proposed solutions of how the reality and completeness of the two natures of Christ and their relationship to one another could be defined, this realization ultimately led him, through various preliminary stages, to the famous rediscovery—so decisive for the Council of Chalcedon (451)—of the formulation *Christus una persona in utraque natura*, first expressed in *Ep.* 137 in 411 and prompted by the so-called exegesis of the person, that is, an ancient secular form of interpretation inquiring into the subject of a sentence, a statement, or an action. That Christ is the one subject of all words and actions, both of the human Jesus and of the Son of God, also solves the problem of the *communicatio idiomatum*, the dual appropriation of human and divine attributes, which posed major problems for Leporius and later for Nestorius. Augustine distinguishes between the meaning of the name "Jesus" as the name and that of "Christ" as the redemptive function of the God-man: "Even though Jesus Christ, our Savior, is one, Jesus is nevertheless his proper name. . . . Christ, however, is the name of the sacrament. As he is called a prophet, as he is called a priest, Christ is commended as the anointed one in whom was the redemption of all of Israel" (*In epistulam Johannis ad Parthos tractatus* 3.6).

Augustine's soteriology explains Christ's redemptive work on two levels, namely, those of dogmatics and of devotion to Christ. Christ is the mediator between God and humans in terms of his humanity, on the basis of 1 Tim 2:5: "For there is one . . . mediator between God and men, the man Christ Jesus." This is inextricably bound up, however, with Christ being man *and* God, since mediation logically does not only presuppose two parties; the mediator necessarily also needs to be able to take both sides: "Had he been human only, . . . you would never have gotten there; had he been God only, . . . you would never have gotten there either" (*Enarrat. Ps.* 134:5). Hence the Son of God became human so as to bridge the chasm between God and humanity, not, as in the OT theophanies, by using human apparition as an external tool, of course, but by becoming the God-man. This humility of the Son of God was necessary as an example for humans because the grace of God is made manifest in a unique way in the humility of Christ (*Christus humilis*) and provides the decisive example (*Christus exemplum et magister vitae*) against pride, the original sin of the human being.

Inasmuch as Christ is, finally, the head of his body, the church (*Christus totus*), he not only vouches (against Donatism) the fundamental and unchanging holiness of his church but also is (against Pelagianism) the mediator of all grace. A person receives salvific grace only through sharing in Christ's redemptive act—which has procured all graces—by belonging to the body of Christ through baptism.

*Encyclopedia Articles:* B. E. Daley, "Christology," in *Augustine through the Ages: An Encyclopedia* (Grand Rapids: Eerdmans, 1999), 164–69.

*Christology:* O. Scheel, *Die Anschauung Augustins über Christi Person und Werk: Unter Berücksichtigung ihrer verschiedenen Entwicklungsstufen und ihrer dogmengeschichtlichen Stellung* (Tübingen: Mohr, 1901). – T. J. van Bavel, *Recherches sur la christologie de saint Augustin: L'humain et le divin dans le Christ d'après saint Augustin* (Par. 10; Fribourg, Switz.: Éditions Universitaires, 1954). – J.-L. Maier, *Les missions divines selon saint Augustin* (Par. 16; Fribourg, Switz.: Éditions Universitaires, 1960). – J. T. Newton, "Neoplatonism and Augustine's Doctrine of the Person and Work of Christ: A Study of the Philosophical Structure Underlying Augustine's Christology" (PhD diss., Emory University, 1969). – O. Brabant, *Le Christ, centre et source de la vie morale chez saint Augustin: Étude sur la pastorale des Enarrationes in Psalmos* (RSSR.M 7; Gembloux, Belg.: Duculot, 1971). – W. Geerlings, *Christus Exemplum: Studien zur Christologie und Christusverkündigung Augustins* (TTS 13; Mainz: Matthias Grünewald, 1978). – G. Remy, *Le Christ médiateur dans l'œuvre de saint Augustin* (2 vols.; Paris: Diffusion Librairie H. Champion, 1979). – A. Verwilghen, *Christologie et spiritualité selon saint Augustin: L'hymne aux Philippiens* (ThH 72; Paris: Beauchesne, 1985). – H. R. Drobner, *Person-Exegese und Christologie bei Augustinus: Zur Herkunft der Formel una persona* (PP 8; Leiden: Brill, 1986). – B. E. Daley, "A Humble Mediator: The Distinctive Elements in St. Augustine's Christology," *Word and Spirit* 9 (1987): 100–117. – G. Madec, *La patria e la via: Cristo nella vita e nel pensiero di Sant'Agostino* (trans. G. Lettieri and S. Leoni; Rome: Borla, 1993); trans. of *La patrie et la voie* (Paris: Desclée, 1989). – G. Madec, "Christus," *AugL* 1:845–908. – B. Studer, *The Grace of Christ and the Grace of God in Augustine of Hippo: Christocentrism or Theocentrism?* (trans. M. J. O'Connell; Collegeville, Minn.: Liturgical, 1997); trans. of *Gratia Christi, gratia Dei bei Augustinus von Hippo* (SEAug 40; Rome: Institutum Patristicum Augustinianum, 1993). – O. González de Cardedal, "Cristo en el itinerario espiritual de san Agustín," *Salm* 40 (1993): 21–56.

*Soteriology:* J. Rivière, *Le dogme de la rédemption chez saint Augustin* (3d ed.; Paris: Gabalda, 1933).

# *D.* De Trinitate

"When Augustine contemplated the idea of writing a book on the Trinity, he walked along the shore and saw a boy who made a small pit in the sand, then scooped water from the ocean in a snail's shell and poured it into the pit.

When Augustine asked the boy what he was doing, the boy answered that he was determined to scoop up all of the water in the ocean with the snail's shell and pour it into that pit. When Augustine explained that this was impossible and smiled at the boy's naïveté, the boy told him that his project was much more viable than Augustine's attempt at explaining even the minutest part of the mysteries of the Trinity in his book."[4] This medieval legend, which was handed down first in the collection of 1493 by Petrus de Natalibus, has also gained popularity in artistic presentations because of its touching and apt way of capturing the difficulties that Augustine encountered in writing his monumental work *De Trinitate.* He describes this in the prologue to the work, namely, the dedicatory letter to Aurelius, bishop of Carthage (*Ep.* 174). Over a span of fourteen years (399–412), Augustine wrote twelve books without being satisfied with the result and therefore delayed their publication. As a result, his impatient students and friends, who interpreted his hesitation as an unnecessary urge for perfection, had the manuscript copied and distributed without Augustine's authorization. When he found out, he was so upset that he did not want to complete the writing; nevertheless the urgent requests by his comrades finally persuaded him to do so. Thus by 420 he had added three more books and revised the entire project once more. For this reason, the chronological ordering of the individual ideas of the initial twelve books remains uncertain in the currently available text.

*De Trinitate* is among those of Augustine's works for which the stimulus did not come from the outside but from within, and so he was able to take his time writing it and to prepare himself thoroughly: "As far as possible I have read all who have written before me concerning the Trinity" (*Trin.* 1.4.7). Unfortunately, it is not possible to determine exactly what specific works he had in mind (Tertullian's *Adversus Praxean,* Novatian, Marius Victorinus, Hilary of Poitiers, or also Greek authors). The fifteen books are organized into five major parts: 1–4, the witnesses of Scripture regarding the unity and consubstantiality of the Trinity; 5–7, the teaching on the relations as the distinguishing characteristics of the persons of the Trinity; 8, the knowledge of God through truth, goodness, righteousness, and love; 9–14, the image of the Trinity in the human person; 15, the summary and rounding off of the work and the witnesses of Scripture on the generation of the Son and the Spirit. The crucial and characteristic statements of Augustine's theology of the Trinity are the following:

a. The Trinity constitutes an indivisible unity and always functions as such. In the OT theophanies, it manifests itself in various forms and persons by taking on the form of objects, animals, people, and angels. Further, the Son not only *assumes* the form of a person in the NT but in a unique way *becomes* one; nevertheless it is always all three persons of the Trinity working together.

b. All three divine persons are Being itself, eternal, immutable, and consubstantial. Hence the distinction between them is not in their essence

---

[4] *AASS* 6 (1743): 357f.

but in their relationships (*relationes*), as expressed in their names: Father, beginning and unbegotten; Son, word and image of the Father; Holy Spirit, gift
and love.

c. The Trinitarian formula μία οὐσία τρεῖς ὑποστάσεις, developed by the
Greek church under the leadership of the Cappadocians, is incorrectly rendered
in the literal Latin translation, used by Marius Victorinus, *una essentia–tres
substantiae*. Nor is Augustine satisfied with the translation *tres personae* because,
in the logic of language, the term "person" does not denote relationship but unity.
"All the same the expression 'three persons' is given, not because it is possible
thereby to express the meaning of the tri-une nature of God but in order not to
keep silent" (*Trin.* 5.9.10).

d. As the image of God, a person is the image of the Trinity (cf. Gen 1:26f.).
For this reason, we are able to find in ourselves the Trinitarian God as *memoria,
intelligentia, et voluntas*, or *amor*.

*Works of Augustine (Editions, Translations): See* no. 109 at the end of the chapter.

*Encyclopedia Articles:* R. Williams, "*Trinitate, De*," in *Augustine through the Ages: An Encyclopedia* (Grand Rapids: Eerdmans, 1999), 845–51.

*Studies:* M. Schmaus, *Die psychologische Trinitätslehre des hl. Augustinus* (MBTh 11;
Münster: Aschendorff, 1927; repr., 1967). – M. Schmaus, *Die Denkform Augustins in
seinem Werk "De Trinitate"* (SBAW 6; Munich: Verlag der Bayerischen Akademie der
Wissenschaften, 1962). – U. Duchrow, "Der Aufbau von Augustins Schriften *Confessiones* und *De Trinitate*," ZThK 62 (1965): 338–67. – A. Schindler, *Wort und Analogie
in Augustins Trinitätslehre* (HUT 4; Tübingen; Mohr, 1965). – A.-M. La Bonnardière,
*Recherches de chronologie augustinienne* (Paris: Études Augustiniennes, 1965). – O. Du
Roy, *L'intelligence de la foi en la Trinité selon saint Augustin: Genèse de sa théologie
trinitaire jusqu'en 391* (Paris: Études Augustiniennes, 1966). – E. Hill, *The Mystery of
the Trinity* (London: Chapman, 1985). – G. Ferraro, *Lo Spirito Santo nel De Trinitate
di Sant'Agostino* (Rome: Piemme, 1987). – M. A. Smalbrugge, *La nature trinitaire de
l'intelligence augustinienne de la foi* (ASTh 7; Amsterdam: Rodopi, 1988). – U. R. Pérez
Paoli, *Der plotinische Begriff von* ὑπόστασις *und die augustinische Bestimmung Gottes
als "subiectum"* (Cass. 41; Würzburg: Augustinus, 1990). – J. Arnold, "Begriff und
heilsökonomische Bedeutung der göttlichen Sendung in Augustin's *De Trinitate*,"
*RechAug* 25 (1991): 3–69. – M. Spicer, "El *De Trinitate*, bautismo de la inteligencia,"
*Augustinus* 36 (1991): 259–93. – J. Cavadini, "The Structure and Intention of Augus-
tine's *De Trinitate*," *AugStud* 23 (1992): 103–23; repr. in *Christianity in Relation to
Jews, Greeks, and Romans* (ed. E. Ferguson; Recent Studies in Early Christianity 2;
New York: Garland, 1999), 231–52. – M. R. Barnes, "The Arians of Book V, and the
Genre of *De Trinitate*," *JTS* NS 44 (1993): 185–95. – B. Studer, "History and Faith in
Augustine's *De Trinitate* (the 1996 St. Augustine Lecture)," *AugStud* 28.1 (1997):
7–50. – L. Ayres, "The Christological Context of Augustine's *De Trinitate* XIII:
Toward Relocating Books VIII–XV," *AugStud* 29.1 (1998): 111–39. – M. R. Barnes,
"Re-reading Augustine's Theology of the Trinity," in *The Trinity: An Interdisciplinary
Symposium on the Trinity* (ed. S. T. Davis, D. Kendall, and G. O'Collins; Oxford and
New York: Oxford University Press, 1999), 145–76. – L. Ayres, "The Fundamental
Grammar of Augustine's Trinitarian Theology," in *Augustine and His Critics: Essays in
Honour of Gerald Bonner* (ed. R. Dodaro and G. Lawless; London and New York:
Routledge, 2000), 51–76.

# *E.* De civitate Dei

In the more than one thousand years of the empire's history, the first-time capture of Rome by the Visigoths under Alaric on August 24, 410, literally caused the world to collapse for the Romans—a world in which Rome was the "eternal city," the center of the world, and the embodiment of all culture. In the fourth century Christianity adopted this ideology under a Christian sign whereby the Christian God took the place of the ancient deities in the welfare and protection of the empire. That, after this "end of the world," Christianity was accused of having failed and precipitated the demise of the empire by ousting the ancient gods (for, as long as these had been revered, there had never been a catastrophe like this) was only consistent with this Roman ideology. Many of the affluent and educated Romans fled to North Africa, where they maintained estates, and there challenged Augustine, the leader of African Christianity, to respond to their criticism. Augustine did so by means of his elaborate apologia *De civitate Dei* in twenty-two books, as a *magnum opus et arduum* (bk. 1, prologue). It took fourteen years to complete (413–426): 413, bks. 1–3; 415, bks. 4–5; by 417, bks. 6–10; by 418, bks. 11–14; by 426, bks. 15–22.

Augustine himself best describes the structure and content in his *Retractationes* (2.43):

> The first five of these books refute those persons who would so view the prosperity of human affairs that they think that the worship of the many gods whom the pagans worship is necessary for this; they contend that these evils arise and abound because they are prohibited from doing so. The next five books, however, speak against those who admit that these evils have never been wanting and never will be wanting to mortals, and that these, at one time great, at another time slight, vary according to places, times, and persons; and yet they argue that the worship of many gods, whereby sacrifice is offered to them, is useful because of the life to come after death. In these ten books, then, these two false beliefs, contrary to the Christian religion, are refuted.

> But lest anyone charge that we have only argued against the beliefs of others, and have not stated our own, it is just this that the second part of this work, which consists of twelve books, accomplishes. . . . The first four of the following twelve books, then, deal with the origin of the two cities, one of which is of God, the other of this world; the next four books treat their growth or progress; but the third four books, which are also the last, deal with their destined ends.

Hence this represents a comprehensive apologia and a presentation of a theology of the history of Christianity in two parts.

To those who consider the cult of the gods to be necessary for the well-being of Rome (1–5), Augustine responds with two primary arguments: (a) It is precisely under these deities that Rome disintegrated morally and was assailed from outside. (b) Not they but the Christian God alone is responsible for Rome's greatness. Regarding eternal life, Augustine rejects the usefulness of the cult of the gods (6–10) through a discussion of the philosophies proclaiming such. The second part develops a salvation history of Christianity, structured according to an earthly and an eternal realm. This division is traced back to the fall—indeed to the fall of the angels because of their love of self, from which the fall of man resulted through temptation. For this reason, the earthly *civitas*, stained by evil, continues throughout the history of humanity up to the incarnation of the Son of God, who points the way from the earthly to the divine *civitas* through God's love. Since then, both realms coexist in the world until the consummation, when they will be separated forever into an eternity of hell and salvation.

*Bibliography:* F. D. Donnelly and M. A. Sherman, *Augustine's De civitate Dei: An Annotated Bibliography of Modern Criticism, 1960–1990* (New York; Frankfurt: Lang, 1990).

*Works of Augustine (Editions, Translations): See* no. 16 at the end of the chapter.

*Encyclopedia Articles:* E. L. Fortin, *"Civitate Dei, De,"* in *Augustine through the Ages: An Encyclopedia* (Grand Rapids: Eerdmans, 1999), 196–202.

*Studies:* CDios 167.1–2 (1955–1956). – A. Wachtel, *Beiträge zur Geschichtstheologie des Aurelius Augustinus* (Bonn: L. Röhrscheid, 1960). – J.-C. Guy, *Unité et structure logique de la "Cité de Dieu" de saint Augustin* (Paris: Études Augustiniennes, 1961). – U. Duchrow, *Christenheit und Weltverantwortung: Traditionsgeschichte und systematische Struktur der Zweireichelehre* (FBESG 25; Stuttgart: Klett, 1969), 181–319. – J. Laufs, *Der Friedensgedanke bei Augustinus: Untersuchungen zum XIX. Buch des Werkes De civitate dei* (Hermes.E 27; Wiesbaden: Steiner, 1973). – E. A. Schmidt, *Zeit und Geschichte bei Augustin* (SHAW 1985.3; Heidelberg: Winter, 1985). – G. J. P. O'Daly, AugL 1:969–1010. – G. Lettieri, *Il senso della storia in Agostino d'Ippona: Il "saeculum" e la gloria nel "De Civitate Dei"* (Rome: Borla, 1988). – R. A. Markus, *Saeculum: History and Society in the Theology of St. Augustine* (Cambridge: Cambridge University Press, 1970; repr., 1988). – J. van Oort, *Jerusalem and Babylon: A Study into Augustine's City of God and the Sources of His Doctrine of Two Cities* (SVigChr 14; Leiden and New York: Brill, 1991). – R. Piccolomini, ed., *Interiorità e intenzionalità nel "De civitate Dei" di Sant'Agostino* (SEAug 35; Rome: Institutum Patristicum Augustinianum, 1991). – P. Piret, *La destinée de l'homme—la Cité de Dieu: Un commentaire du "De civitate Dei" d'Augustin* (Brussels: Editions de l'Institut d'Etudes Theologiques, 1991). – B. Studer, "Zum Aufbau von Augustins *De civitate Dei*," Aug(L) 41 (1991): 937–51. – C. Müller, *Geschichtsbewusstsein bei Augustinus* (Cass. 39.2; Würzburg: Augustinus, 1993). – M. Ruokanen, *Theology of Social Life in Augustine's De civitate Dei* (FKDG 53; Göttingen: Vandenhoeck & Ruprecht, 1993). – D. F. Donnelly, ed., *The City of God: A Collection of Critical Essays* (New York: Lang, 1995). – B. Studer, "La *cognitio historialis* di Porfirio nel *De civitate Dei* di Agostino (*civ.* 10,32)," in *La narrativa cristiana antica: Codici narrativi, strutture formali, schemi retorici* (SEAug 50; Rome: Institutum Patristicum Augustinianum, 1995), 529–53. – E. Cavalcanti, ed., *Il De civitate Dei: L'opera, le interpretazioni, l'influsso* (Rome: Herder, 1996). – L. Alici, R. Piccolomini, and A. Pieretti, eds., *Il mistero del male e la libertà possibile, III: Lettura del De civitate Dei di Agostino* (SEAug 54; Rome: Institutum Patristicum Augustinianum, 1996). – M. Vessey, K. Pollmann, and A. D. Fitzgerald, eds., *History, Apocalypse, and the Secular Imagination: New Essays on Augustine's City of God* (Bowling Green, Ohio: Philosophy Documentation Center, 1999; also as AugStud 3.2 [1999]). – G. O'Daly, *Augustine's City of God: A Reader's Guide* (Oxford: Clarendon; New York: Oxford University Press, 1999).

# F. Enchiridion *and* De doctrina christiana

Both of these brief writings of Augustine, from the latter part of his life, have become very popular, enjoy continued influence, and are still very useful today because they succinctly summarize Augustine's entire, mature theology. Like many other works by Augustine, the *Enchiridion,* a "handbook on faith, hope, and love," originated from an inquiry from the outside, as Augustine recounts in the prologue of the book and in the *Retractationes* (2.63). A friend by the name of Laurentius, about whom we have no further information except that he was the brother of Dulcitius (to whom Augustine somewhat later also sent a response [*De octo Dulcitii quaestionibus ex Veteri Testamento*]), asked Augustine ca. 421 for a brief handbook on how God is to be worshiped appropriately. Since Laurentius thereby asked "for one that can be carried in the hand, not one to load your shelves" (1.6), Augustine responded with the foundations of Christianity according to Paul: faith, hope, love. The handbook, however, by no means sets these three themes out evenhandedly; rather, patterned upon the creed, though loosely structured, it addresses faith almost exclusively (3.9 to 30.113). Hope (30.114–116) and love (31.117–32.121) appear at the very end as principles of a Christian lifestyle. Here are to be found Augustine's theology of creation (3.9); the doctrine of evil (3.10–7.22); and soteriology (8.23–32.133), including the doctrine of grace (9.30–32), Christology (10.33–13.41), baptismal theology (13.42–14.49), the doctrine of justification (14.50–53), eschatology (14.54–55, 23.84–93, 29.109–113), pneumatology (15.56), ecclesiology (15.57–16.63), the theology of repentance (17.64–23.83), and the doctrine of predestination (24.94–27.102).

*De doctrina christiana* originated in two parts, thirty years apart: the first part, up to 3.25.35, in 397, the remainder not until 426/427. Augustine interrupted the writing of the *Retractations* for it:

> When I discovered that the books, *On Christian Instruction,* were not completed, I chose to finish them rather than leave them as they were and go on to the reexamination of other works. Accordingly, I completed the third book, which had been written up to the place where mention is made of a passage from the Gospel about the woman who "buried leaven in three measures of flour until all of it was leavened." I then added a last book and thus completed this work in four books. The first three of these are a help to the understanding of the Scriptures, while the fourth explains how we are to present what we understand. (*Retract.* 2.4.1)

The first three books therefore are concerned with a fundamental hermeneutic of Scripture: (a) the dogmatic truths to be recognized in the Bible are God, the Trinity, incarnation and redemption, the church, and eschatology; (b) the three ethical/moral truths, namely faith, love, and hope; (c) the fundamental principles of exegesis. In order to present in a suitable manner what has been understood in the study of the Bible in line with these principles, the following need to be considered (d): rhetoric and secular literature in the service of the true divine wisdom contained in the Bible, as well as the meticulous preparation of the preacher, not only regarding the words of the sermon but also by prayer and his own exemplary life for the purpose of the hearers' sanctification. Three individual themes of this work deserve to be highlighted because they represent central theologoumena of Augustine with particular clarity.

a. The teaching of *frui* and *uti* (1.4.4; 1.22.20; 1.31.34f.), which also plays a major part in his extensive works, such as *De Trinitate* and *De civitate Dei*. As the one who is intrinsically and eternally good, the triune God alone is the *res*, which is to be enjoyed. All the other, created things are intended for human use, with the goal of attaining the enjoyment of God (cf. also *De diversis quaestionibus LXXXIII* 30).

b. The theory of signs (*signa*) (2.1.1–2.4.5). It is of crucial importance to distinguish between things (*res*) and signs (*signa*) and to recognize that signs are things pointing beyond their own existence to other realities. Such signs can come about naturally, such as fire and smoke, or on account of what is established, such as words or Scripture. The latter presuppose intelligence and an intent of expression, just as understanding a sign always calls for intelligence. As part of the created world, natural signs are pointers to the Creator. Beyond this, however, God desires to make himself known by means of intentionally established signs, namely, his words and sacraments. The individual is to understand correctly the intent of what they express.

c. The discussion of the rules of Tyconius (3.30.42–3.37.56). A Donatist layman by the name of Tyconius (ca. 330–390) wrote a *Liber regularum* with seven essential rules of biblical exegesis, among them those of an ecclesiological kind, which Augustine critiques in detail. Here he adopts them in principle, and in other instances he lauds and recommends them.

*Works of Augustine (Editions, Translations): See* nos. 29 and 35 at the end of the chapter.

*Encyclopedia Articles:* J. J. O'Donnell, "*Doctrina christiana, De,*" in *Augustine through the Ages* (Grand Rapids: Eerdmans, 1999), 278–80. – P. Fredericksen, "Tyconius," in *Augustine through the Ages* (Grand Rapids: Eerdmans, 1999), 833–35.

*Studies:* W. R. O'Connor, "The *uti/frui* Distinction in Augustine's Ethics," *AugStud* 14 (1983): 45–62. – G. Martano, "Retorica della *ratio* e retorica della *fides:* Il 4° libro del *De doctrina christiana* di S. Agostino," in *L'umanesimo di Sant'Agostino* (ed. F. Matteo; Bari: Levante, 1988), 537–51. – M. Dulaey, "La sixième règle de Tyconius et son résumé dans le *De doctrina Christiana,*" *REAug* 35 (1989): 83–103. – P. Prestel, *Die Rezeption der ciceronischen Rhetorik durch Augustinus in "De doctrina christiana"* (Frankfurt and New York: Lang, 1992). – *"De doctrina christiana" di Agostino d'Ippona* (Lectio Augustini 11; Palermo: Città Nuova, 1995) [Com]. – D. W. H. Arnold and P. Bright, eds., *De doctrina christiana: A Classic of Western Culture* (Notre Dame, Ind.: University of Notre Dame Press, 1995). – R. A. Markus, *Signs and Meanings: World and Text in Ancient Christianity* (Liverpool: Liverpool University Press, 1996). – K. Pollmann, *Doctrina christiana: Untersuchungen zu den Anfängen der christlichen Hermeneutik unter besonderer Berücksichtigung von Augustinus, De doctrina christiana* (Par. 41; Fribourg, Switz.: Universitätsverlag, 1996). – D. Foster, "*Eloquentia nostra* (DDC IV,VI,10): A Study of the Place of Classical Rhetoric in Augustine's *De doctrina christiana* Book Four," *Aug 36* (1996): 459–94.

*Tyconius:*
*Editions: The Book of Rules of Tyconius* (ed. F. C. Burkitt; TS 3.1; Cambridge: Cambridge University Press, 1894; repr., Nendeln, Liechtenstein: Kraus Reprint, 1967).

*Translations:* K. Froelich, *Biblical Interpretation in the Early Church* (SoECT; Philadelphia: Fortress, 1984), 104–32. – *Tyconius: The Book of Rules* (trans. W. S. Babcock; Texts and Translations 31; Atlanta: Scholars Press, 1989).

*Studies:* P. Bright, *The Book of Rules of Tyconius: Its Purpose and Inner Logic* (Notre Dame, Ind.: University of Notre Dame Press, 1988). – P. Camastra, *Il Liber regularum di Ticonio: Contributo alla lettura* (Rome: Vivera In, 1998). – C. Kannengiesser, "Augustine and Tyconius: A Conflict of Christian Hermeneutics in Roman Africa," in *Augustine and the Bible* (ed. P. Bright; Notre Dame, Ind.: University of Notre Dame Press, 1999), 149–77. – P. Bright, "'The Preponderating Influence of Augustine': A Study of the Epitomes of the *Book of Rules* of the Donatist Tyconius," in *Augustine and the Bible* (ed. P. Bright; Notre Dame, Ind.: University of Notre Dame Press, 1999), 109–28.

# III. LIST OF WORKS (CHRONOLOGY, EDITIONS, ENGLISH TRANSLATIONS, COMMENTARIES)

*Abbreviations: AugL* 2:XI–XXIV. – BAug = Bibliothèque augustinienne. – SC = Sources chrétiennes, which has the Latin text, a French translation, and commentary. – NBA = Nuova biblioteca Agostiniana (Rome: Città Nuova, 1965–), which has an introduction, bibliography, Italian translation, notes, and indices. – WSA = The Works of Saint Augustine: A Translation for the 21st Century (ed. J. Rotelle; Brooklyn, N.Y.; Hyde Park, N.Y.: New City, 1990–)] [ET with notes].

1.  *Acad.*    *De Academicis* (Nov. 386–Mar. 387): *Sancti Aureli Augustini Contra Academicos libri tres; De beata vita liber unus; De ordine libri duo* (ed. P. Knöll; CSEL 63; Vienna: Hölder-Pichler-Tempsky, 1922; repr., New York: Johnson Reprint, 1962), 3–81. – *Dialogues philosophiques,* vol. 1, *Problèmes fondamentaux: Contra Academicos, De beata vita, De ordine* (ed. R. Jolivet; BAug 4; Paris: Desclée de Brouwer, 1939), 14–203. – *Contra Academicos; De beata vita; De ordine; De magistro; De libero arbitrio* (ed. W. M. Green and K. D. Daur; CCSL 29; Turnhout, Belg.: Brepols, 1970), 3–61. – *Dialoghi* (ed. D. Gentili and A. Trapé; 2 vols.; NBA 3.1–2; Rome: Città Nuova, 1970–1976), 1:21–165. – *The Happy Life; Answer to Skeptics; Divine Providence and the Problem of Evil; Soliloquies* (trans. L. Schopp, D. J. Kavanagh, R. P. Russell, and T. F. Gilligan; FC 5; New York: Cima, 1948), 85–225. – *Against the Academics* (trans. J. J. O'Meara; ACW 12; Westminster, Md.: Newman, 1950). – Studies: B. R. Voss, *AugL* 1:45–51. – A. J. Curley, *Augustine's Critique of Skepticism: A Study of Contra Academicos* (New York: Lang, 1996). – T. Fuhrer, *Augustin, Contra Academicos (vel De Academicis) Bücher 2 und 3: Einleitung und Kommentar* (PTS 46; Berlin and New York: de Gruyter, 1997).

2.  *c. Adim.*    *Contra Adimantum Manichaei discipulum* (392): *Sancti Aureli Augustini De utilitate credendi; De duabus animabus; Contra Fortunatum; Contra Adimantum; Contra epistulam fundamenti; Contra Faustum* (ed. J. Zycha; CSEL 25; Vienna: F. Tempsky, 1892), 115–90. – *Six traités anti-manichéens: De duabus animabus, Contra Fortunatum, Contra Adimantum, Contra epistulam Fundamenti, Contra Secundinum, Contra Felicem Manichaeum*

(ed. R. Jolivet and M. Jourjon; BAug 17; Paris: Desclée de Brouwer, 1961), 218–375. – Studies: F. Decret, *AugL* 1:90–94.

3.  *adn. Job*   *Adnotationes in Job: Sancti Aureli Augustini Quaestionum in Heptateuchum libri VII; Adnotationvm in Job liber vnvs* (ed. J. Zycha; CSEL 28.2; Vienna: F. Tempsky, 1895), 509–628. – *Treatises on Marriage and Other Subjects* (trans. C. T. Wilcox, M. Liguori, C. T. Huegelmeyer, J. A. Lacy, R. W. Brown, R. P. Russell, and J. McQuade; FC 27; New York: Fathers of the Church, 1955; repr., Washington, D.C.: Catholic University of America Press, 1969), 385–414. – Studies: W. Geerlings, *AugL* 1:100–104.

4.  *c. adu. leg.*   *Contra adversarium legis et prophetarum* (c. 420): *Il Contra adversaria legis et prophetarum di Agostino* (ed. M. P. Ciccarese; AANL.M 8.25.3; Rome: Accademia Nazionale dei Lincei, 1981). – *Sancti Aurelii Augustini Contra adversarium legis et prophetarum; Commonitorium Orosii; et Sancti Aurelii Augustini Contra Priscillianistas et Origenistas* (ed. K.-D. Daur; CCSL 49; Turnhout, Belg.: Brepols, 1985), 35–131. – *Arianism and Other Heresies: Heresies, Memorandum to Augustine, To Orosius in Refutation of the Priscillianists and Origenists, Arian Sermon, Answer to an Arian Sermon, Debate with Maximinus, Answer to Maximinus, Answer to an Enemy of the Law and the Prophets* (trans. R. J. Teske; WSA 1.18; Hyde Park, N.Y.: New City, 1995), 337–449. – Studies: T. Raveaux, *AugL* 1:107–12. – T. Raveaux, *Augustinus, Contra adversarium legis et prophetarum* (Cass. 37; Würzburg: Augustinus, 1987).

5.  *adult. coniug.*   *De adulterinis coniugiis* (c. 420): *Sancti Avreli Avgvstini De fide et symbolo; De fide et operibvs; De agone christiano; De continentia; De bono conivgali; De sancta virginitate; De bono vidvitatis; De advlterinis conivgiis lib. II; De mendacio; Contra mendacivm; De opere monachorvm; De divinatione daemonvm; De cvra pro mortvis gerenda; De patientia* (ed. J. Zycha; CSEL 41; Vienna: F. Tempsky, 1900), 347–410. – *Problèmes moraux: De bono conjugali, De conjugiis adulterinis, De mendacio, Contra mendacium, De cura gerenda pro mortuis, De patientia, De utilitate jejunii* (ed. G. Combès; BAug 2; Paris: Desclée de Brouwer, 1948), 108–233. – *Treatises on Marriage and Other Subjects* (trans. C. T. Wilcox, M. Liguori, C. T. Huegelmeyer, J. A. Lacy, R. W. Brown, R. P. Russell, and J. McQuade; FC 27; New York: Fathers of the Church, 1955; repr., Washington, D.C.: Catholic University of America Press, 1969), 53–132. – *Marriage and Virginity: The Excellence of Marriage, Holy Virginity, The Excellence of Widowhood, Adulterous Marriages, Continence* (trans. R. Kearney and D. G. Hunter; WSA 1.9; Hyde Park, N.Y.: New City, 1999), 137–85. – Studies: A.-M. La Bonnardière, *AugL* 1:116–25.

6.  *agon.*   *De agone christiano* (beginning of episcopate): *Sancti Avreli Avgvstini De fide et symbolo; De fide et operibvs; De agone christiano; De continentia; De bono conivgali; De sancta virginitate; De bono vidvitatis; De advlterinis conivgiis lib. II; De mendacio; Contra mendacivm; De opere monachorvm; De divinatione daemonvm; De cvra pro mortvis gerenda; De patientia* (ed. J. Zycha; CSEL 41; Vienna: F. Tempsky, 1900), 101–38. – *Le morale chrétienne* (ed. B. Roland-Gosselin; 2d ed.; BAug 1; Paris: Desclée de Brouwer, 1949), 372–435. – *Christian Instruction;*

Admonition and Grace; The Christian Combat: Faith, Hope, and Charity (trans. J. J. Gavigan, J. C. Murray, R. P. Russell, and B. M. Peebles; FC 2; Washington, D.C.: Catholic University of America Press, 1947), 307–53. – Studies: A. Zumkeller, AugL 1:221–27.

7.   an. et or.     De anima et eius origine (c. 420): Sancti Aureli Augustini De peccatorum meritis et remissione et de baptismo parvulorum ad Marcellinum libri tres; De spiritv et littera liber vnvs; De natvra et gratia liber vnvs; De natvra et origine animae libri qvattvor; Contra dvas epistvlas Pelagianorvm libri qvattvor (ed. K. F. Urba and J. Zycha; CSEL 60; Vienna: F. Tempsky, 1913), 303–419. – La crise pélagienne (ed. G. de Plinval, J. de La Tullaye, C. F. Urba, J. Zycha, J. Plagnieux, and F.-J. Thonnard; 2 vols.; BAug 21–22; Brugge, Belg.: Desclée de Brouwer, 1966–1975), 376–667. – Natura e grazia (ed. A. Trapè, I. Volpi, and F. Monteverde; 2 vols.; NBA 17; Rome: Città Nuova, 1981), 2:269–479. – P. Holmes, R. E. Wallis, and B. B. Warfield, trans., "On the Soul and Its Origin," in NPNF¹ (Peabody, Mass.: Hendrickson, 1995; repr. of 1887 ed.), 5:309–71. – Answer to the Pelagians I (ed. J. E. Rotelle; introd., trans., and notes R. J. Teske; WSA 1.23; Hyde Park, N.Y.: New City, 1997), 465–561 [The Nature and Origin of the Soul]. – Studies: A. Zumkeller, AugL 1:340–50.

8.   an. quant.     De animae quantitate (fall 387–July/August 388): Dialogues philosophiques, vol. 2, Dieu et l'ame: Soliloques, De immortalitate animae, De quantitate animae (ed. P. de Labriolle; BAug 5; Paris: Desclée de Brouwer, 1939), 226–397. – Dialoghi (ed. D. Gentili and A. Trapé; 2 vols.; NBA 3.1–2; Rome: Città Nuova, 1970–1976), 2:1–133. – Soliloquiorum libri duo: De inmortalitate animae; De quantitate animae (ed. W. Hörmann; CSEL 89; Vienna: Hölder-Pichler-Tempsky, 1986), 131–231. – The Immortality of the Soul; The Magnitude of the Soul; On Music; The Advantage of Believing; On Faith in Things Unseen (trans. L. Schopp, J. J. McMahon, R. C. Taliaferro, L. Meagher, R. J. Defarrari, and M. F. McDonald; FC 4; Washington, D.C.: Catholic University of America Press, 1947), 49–149. – The Greatness of the Soul: The Teacher (trans. J. M. Colleran; ACW 9; Westminster, Md.: Newman, 1964), 1–112, 189–220. – Studies: J. K. Coyle, "De moribus ecclesiae catholicae et De moribus Manichaeorum"; "De quantitate animae" di Agostino d'Ippona (Lectio Augustini 7; Palermo: Augustinus, 1991), 133–207. – Studies: K.-H. Lütcke, AugL 1:350–56.

9.   bapt.     De baptismo (c. 400): Sancti Aureli Augustini Scripta contra Donatistas (ed. M. Petschenig; CSEL 51; Vienna: F. Tempsky, 1908), 145–375. – Traités anti-donatistes II: De baptismo libri VII (ed. M. Petschenig, G. Finaert, and G. Bavaud; BAug 29; Paris: Desclée de Brouwer, 1964). – J. R. King, trans., "On Baptism, against the Donatists," in NPNF¹ (Peabody, Mass.: Hendrickson, 1995; repr. of 1887 ed.), 4:407–514. – Studies: A. Schindler, AugL 1:573–82.

10.   beata u.     De beata vita (Nov. 13–15, 386): Sancti Aureli Augustini Contra Academicos libri tres; De beata vita liber unus; De ordine libri duo (ed. P. Knöll; CSEL 63; Vienna: Hölder-Pichler-Tempsky, 1922; repr., New York: Johnson Reprint, 1962), 89–116. – Contra Academicos; De beata vita; De ordine; De magistro; De libero arbitrio (ed. W. M. Green and

K. D. Daur; CCSL 29; Turnhout, Belg.: Brepols, 1970), 65–85. – *Dialoghi* (ed. D. Gentili and A. Trapé; 2 vols.; NBA 3.1–2; Rome: Città Nuova, 1970–1976), 167–225. – *Dialogues philosophiques*, vol. 1, *De beata vita* (ed. J. Doignon; BAug 4.1; Paris: Desclée, 1986). – *La felicità; La liberta* (ed. R. Fedriga and S. Puggioni; Milan: Biblioteca Universale Rizzoli, 1995), 29–89. – *S. Aureli Augustini De beata vita* (trans. R. A. Brown; PatSt 72; Washington, D.C.: Catholic University of America Press, 1944). – *The Happy Life; Answer to Skeptics; Divine Providence and the Problem of Evil; Soliloquies* (trans. L. Schopp, D. J. Kavanagh, R. P. Russell, and T. F. Gilligan; FC 5; New York: Cima, 1948), 27–84. – *Augustine of Hippo: Selected Writings* (trans. M. T. Clark; CWS; London: SPCK, 1984), 163–93. – Studies: J. Doignon, *AugL* 1:618–24.

11.  *b. coniug.*  *De bono coniugali* (c. 401): *Sancti Avreli Avgvstini De fide et symbolo; De fide et operibvs; De agone christiano; De continentia; De bono conivgali; De sancta virginitate; De bono vidvitatis; De advlterinis conivgiis lib. II; De mendacio; Contra mendacivm; De opere monachorvm; De divinatione daemonvm; De cvra pro mortvis gerenda; De patientia* (ed. J. Zycha; CSEL 41; Vienna: F. Tempsky, 1900), 187–231. – *Problèmes moraux: De bono conjugali, De conjugiis adulterinis, De mendacio, Contra mendacium, De cura gerenda pro mortuis, De patientia, De utilitate jejunii* (ed. G. Combès; BAug 2; Paris: Desclée de Brouwer, 1948), 22–99. – *Matrimonio e verginità* (ed. A. Trapè, M. Palmieri, V. Tarulli, N. Cipriani, and F. Monteverde; NBA 7.1; Rome: Città Nuova, 1978), 1–63. – C. L. Cornish, trans., "On the Good of Marriage," in *NPNF¹* (Peabody, Mass.: Hendrickson, 1995; repr. of 1887 ed.), 3:395–413. – *Treatises on Marriage and Other Subjects* (trans. C. T. Wilcox, M. Liguori, C. T. Huegelmeyer, J. A. Lacy, R. W. Brown, R. P. Russell, and J. McQuade; FC 27; New York: Fathers of the Church, 1955; repr., Washington, D.C.: Catholic University of America Press, 1969), 1–51. – *Marriage and Virginity: The Excellence of Marriage, Holy Virginity, The Excellence of Widowhood, Adulterous Marriages, Continence* (trans. R. Kearney and D. G. Hunter; WSA 1.9; Hyde Park, N.Y.: New City, 1999), 27–61. – Studies: M.-F. Berrouard, *AugL* 1:658–66.

12.  *b. uid.*  *De bono uiditatis* (c. 414): *Sancti Avreli Avgvstini De fide et symbolo; De fide et operibvs; De agone christiano; De continentia; De bono conivgali; De sancta virginitate; De bono vidvitatis; De advlterinis conivgiis lib. II; De mendacio; Contra mendacivm; De opere monachorvm; De divinatione daemonvm; De cvra pro mortvis gerenda; De patientia* (ed. J. Zycha; CSEL 41; Vienna: F. Tempsky, 1900), 305–43. – *L' ascetisme chretien: De continentia, De sancta virginitate, De bono viduitatis, De opere monachorum* (ed. J. Saint-Martin; 2d ed.; BAug 3; Paris: Desclée de Brouwer, 1949), 234–305. – *Matrimonio e verginità* (ed. A. Trapè, M. Palmieri, V. Tarulli, N. Cipriani, and F. Monteverde; NBA 7.1; Rome: Città Nuova, 1978), 161–219. – C. L. Cornish, trans., "On the Good of Widowhood," in *NPNF¹* (Peabody, Mass.: Hendrickson, 1995; repr. of 1887 ed.), 3:439–54. – *Treatises on Various Subjects* (trans. M. S. Muldowney, M. E. Defarrari, H. B. Jaffee, L. Meagher, and M. F. McDonald; FC 16; New York: Fathers of the Church, 1952), 265–319. – *Marriage and Virginity: The Excellence of Marriage, Holy Virginity, The*

*Excellence of Widowhood, Adulterous Marriages, Continence* (trans.
R. Kearney and D. G. Hunter; WSA 1.9; Hyde Park, N.Y.: New City,
1999), 109–36. – Studies: A. Zumkeller, *AugL* 1:666–71.

13. *breuic.*    *Breviculus conlationis cum Donatistis* (June 1, 3, and 8, 411): *Sancti
Aureli Augustini Scripta contra Donatistas* (ed. M. Petschenig; CSEL 53;
Vienna: F. Tempsky, 1910), 39–92. – *Traités anti-donatistes V: Breviculus collationis cum Donatistis, Ad Donatistas post collationen, Sermo
ad Caesariensis ecclesiae plebem, Gesta cum Emerito Donatistarum
episcopo, Contra Gaudentium Donatistarum episcopum libri duo* (ed.
M. Petschenig, G. Finaert, and E. Lamirande; BAug 32; Paris: Desclée
de Brouwer, 1965), 94–243. – *Concilia Africae a. 345–a. 525* (ed. S. Lancel; CCSL 149; Turnhout, Belg.: Brepols, 1974), 261–306. – Studies:
S. Lancel, *AugL* 1:681–84.

14. *cat. rud.*    *De catechizandis rudibus* (c. 400): *Sancti Aurelii Augustini De fide
rerum invisibilium; Enchiridion ad Laurentium, de fide et spe et caritate;
De catechizandis rudibus; Sermo ad catechumenos de symbolo; Sermo de
disciplina christiana; Sermo de utilitate ieiunii; Sermo de excidio urbis
Romae; De haeresibus* (ed. I. B. Bauer; CCSL 46; Turnhout, Belg.:
Brepols, 1969), 121–78. – *La première catéchèse* (ed. I. B. Bauer and
G. Madec; BAug 11.1; Cahors: Études Augustiniennes, 1991). – S. D. F.
Salmon, trans., "On the Catechising of the Uninstructed," in *NPNF[1]*
(Peabody, Mass.: Hendrickson, 1995; repr. of 1887 ed.), 3:277–314. –
*The First Catechetical Instruction* (trans. J. P. Christopher; ACW 2;
Westminster, Md.: Newman, 1946; repr., 1962). – Studies: J.-P. Belche,
"Die Bekehrung zum Christentum nach Augustins Büchlein *De catechizandis rudibus*," *Aug(L)* 27 (1977): 26–69, 333–63; 28 (1978): 255–87. –
Studies: C. Mayer, *AugL* 1:794–805.

15. *cath. fr.*    *Ad catholicos fratres* (c. 400): *Sancti Aureli Augustini Scripta contra
Donatistas* (ed. M. Petschenig; CSEL 52; Vienna: F. Tempsky, 1909),
231–322. – *Traités anti-donatistes I: Psalmus contra partem Donati,
Contra epistulam Parmeniani libri tres, Epistula ad Catholicos de secta
Donatistarum* (ed. M. Petschenig, G. Finaert, R. Anastasi, and Y. M.-J.
Congar; BAug 28; Paris: Desclée de Brouwer, 1963), 502–707. – Studies: M. Moreau, *AugL*, 808–15.

16. *ciu.*    *De civitate Dei* (414–419): *Sancti Avrelii Avgvstini episcopi De civitate
Dei libri XXII* (ed. E. Hoffmann; 2 vols.; CSEL 40.1–2; Vienna:
F. Tempsky, 1899–1900). – *Sancti Aurelii Augustini episcopi De civitate
Dei libri XXII* (ed. B. Dombart and A. Kalb; 2 vols.; 5th ed.; Stuttgart:
Teubner, 1981); 1929 ed. repr. as *Sancti Aurelii Augustini De civitate
Dei libri I–XXII* (2 vols.; CCSL 47–48; Turnhout, Belg.: Brepols, 1955).
– *La cité de Dieu* (ed. B. Dombart, A. Kalb, G. Bardy, and G. Combès;
5 vols.; BAug 33–37; Paris: Desclée de Brower, 1959–1960). – *La città
di Dio* (ed. A. Trapè, R. Russell, S. Cotta, D. Gentili, and F. Monteverde;
3 vols.; NBA 5.1–3; Rome: Città Nuova, 1978–1991). – M. Dods,
trans., "St. Augustin's City of God," in *NPNF[1]* (Peabody, Mass.: Hendrickson, 1995; repr. of 1886 ed.), 2:ix–511. – *The City of God* (trans.
D. B. Zema, G. G. Walsh, G. Monahan, and D. J. Honan; 3 vols.; FC 8,
14, 24; New York: Fathers of the Church, 1950–1954). – *The City of
God against the Pagans* (trans. G. E. McCracken, W. M. Green, D. S.

Wiesen, P. Levine, E. Matthews Sanford, and W. C. Greene; 7 vols.; LCL
411–17; Cambridge, Mass.: Harvard University Press, 1957–1972). –
*Concerning the City of God against the Pagans* (trans. H. Bettenson;
with new introduction by J. O'Meara; Harmondsworth, Middlesex,
and New York: Penguin, 1984). – *The City of God against the Pagans*
(ed. R. W. Dyson; Cambridge: Cambridge University Press, 1998). –
Studies: G. J. P. O'Daly, *AugL* 1:969–1010.

17. *conf.*   *Confessiones* (Apr. 4, 397–c. 400): *St. Augustine's Confessions* (ed.
W. Watts; 2 vols.; LCL 26–27; London: Heinemann; New York: Macmillan, 1912; repr., London: Heinemann; Cambridge, Mass.: Harvard
University Press, 1988–1989). – *Confessionum, libri XIII* (ed. M. Skutella, H. Jürgens, and W. Schaub; corrected ed.; Teubner; Stuttgart:
Teubner, 1996). – *Les Confessions* (ed. M. Skutella, A. Solignac, E. Tré-
horel, and G. Bouissou; 2 vols.; BAug 13–14; Paris: Études Augustiniennes, 1962–1996). – *Le Confessioni* (ed. M. Pellegrino, C. Carena,
A. Trapè, and F. Monteverde; 3d ed.; NBA 1; Rome: Città Nuova,
1975). – *Sancti Augustini Confessionum libri XIII* (L. Verheijen; CCSL
27; Turnhout, Belg.: Brepols, 1981). – *Confessioni* (ed. R. De Monti-
celli; Milan: Garzanti, 1990) [Com]. – J. G. Pilkington, trans., "The
Confessions of St. Augustin," in *NPNF¹* (Peabody, Mass.: Hendrickson,
1995; repr. of 1886 ed.), 1:27–207. – *Confessions* (trans. V. J. Bourke;
FC 21; Washington, D.C.: Catholic University of America Press, 1953).
– *Augustine: Confessions and Enchiridion* (trans. A. C. Outler; LCC 7;
London: SCM, 1955). – *The Confessions of St. Augustine* (trans. J. K.
Ryan; Garden City, N.Y.: Doubleday, 1960). – *Confessions* (trans. R. S.
Pine-Coffin; London: Penguin, 1961). – *Confessions* (trans. H. Chad-
wick; Oxford World's Classics; Oxford and New York: Oxford Univer-
sity Press, 1991). – *The Confessions* (trans. M. Boulding; WSA 1.1;
Hyde Park, N.Y.: New City, 1997). – Studies: E. Feldmann, *AugL*
1:1134–93.

18. *conl. Max.*   *Conlatio cum Maximino Arrianorum episcopo* (427): PL 42:709–42. –
*Arianism and Other Heresies: Heresies, Memorandum to Augustine, To
Orosius in Refutation of the Priscillianists and Origenists, Arian Sermon,
Answer to an Arian Sermon, Debate with Maximinus, Answer to Maxi-
minus, Answer to an Enemy of the Law and the Prophets* (trans. R. J.
Teske; WSA 1.18; Hyde Park, N.Y.: New City, 1995), 173–227. – Stud-
ies: R. Vander Plaetse and A. Schindler, *AugL* 1:1209–18.

19. *cons. eu.*   *De consensu evangelistarum* (c. 400): *Sancti Aureli Augustini De con-
sensv evangelistarvm libri qvattvor* (ed. F. Weihrich; CSEL 43; Vienna:
F. Tempsky, 1904). – *Il consenso degli evangelisti* (ed. V. Tarulli, P. de
Luis, and F. Monteverde; NBA 10.1; Rome: Città Nuova, 1996). –
S. D. F. Salmond and M. B. Riddle, trans., "The Harmony of the
Gospels," in *NPNF¹* (Peabody, Mass.: Hendrickson, 1995; repr. of 1888
ed.), 6:65–236. – Studies: H. Merkel, *AugL* 1:1228–36.

20. *cont.*   *De continentia* (c. 395 or later; 412): *Sancti Avreli Avgvstini De fide et
symbolo; De fide et operibvs; De agone christiano; De continentia; De
bono conivgali; De sancta virginitate; De bono vidvitatis; De advlterinis
conivgiis lib. II; De mendacio; Contra mendacivm; De opere monachorvm; De divinatione daemonvm; De cvra pro mortvis gerenda; De*

*patientia* (ed. J. Zycha; CSEL 41; Vienna: F. Tempsky, 1900), 141–83. – *L'ascetisme chretien: De continentia, De sancta virginitate, De bono viduitatis, De opere monachorum* (ed. J. Saint-Martin; 2d ed.; Baug 3; Paris: Desclée de Brouwer, 1949), 22–101. – *Matrimonio e verginità* (ed. A. Trapè, M. Palmieri, V. Tarulli, N. Cipriani, and F. Monteverde; NBA 7.1; Rome: Città Nuova, 1978), 319–81. – C. L. Cornish, trans., "Of Continence," in *NPNF¹* (Peabody, Mass.: Hendrickson, 1995; repr. of 1887 ed.), 3:377–93. – *Treatises on Various Subjects* (trans. M. S. Muldowney, M. E. Defarrari, H. B. Jaffee, L. Meagher, and M. F. Mc-Donald; FC 16; New York: Fathers of the Church, 1952), 180–231. – *Marriage and Virginity: The Excellence of Marriage, Holy Virginity, The Excellence of Widowhood, Adulterous Marriages, Continence* (trans. R. Kearney and D. G. Hunter; WSA 1.9; Hyde Park, N.Y.: New City, 1999), 187–216. – Studies: A. Zumkeller, *AugL* 1:1271–76.

21. **correct.**  *De correctione Donatistarum* (= *ep* 185) (417): *S. Avreli Avgvstini Hipponiensis episcopi Epistvlae* (ed. A. Goldbacher; CSEL 57; Vienna: F. Tempsky, 1911), 1–44. – *Le lettere* (ed. L. Carrozzi; NBA 23; Rome: Città Nuova, 1974), 10–75. – J. R. King, trans., "The Correction of the Donatists," in *NPNF¹* (Peabody, Mass.: Hendrickson, 1995; repr. of 1887 ed.), 4:629–51. – *Letters* (trans. W. Parsons; FC 30; Washington, D.C.: Catholic University of America Press, 1955), 141–90. – Studies: J. S. Alexander, *AugL* 2.1–2:27–35.

22. **corrept.**  *De correptione et gratia* (c. 426): Editions: PL 44:915–46. – *Aux moines d'Adrumete et de Provence* (ed. J. Chéné and J. Pintard; Baug 24; Paris: Desclée de Brouwer, 1962), 268–381. – *Grazia e libertà* (ed. A. Trapè, M. Palmieri, and F. Monteverde; NBA 20; Rome: Città Nuova, 1987), 97–189. – P. Holmes, R. E. Wallis, and B. B. Warfield, trans., "On Rebuke and Grace," *NPNF¹* (Peabody, Mass.: Hendrickson, 1995; repr. of 1887 ed.), 5:467–91. – *Christian Instruction: Admonition and Grace; The Christian Combat; Faith, Hope and Charity* (trans. J. J. Gavigan, J. C. Murray, R. P. Russell, and B. M. Peebles; FC 2; Washington, D.C.: Catholic University of America Press, 1947), 237–305. – *Answer to the Pelagians IV* (ed. J. E. Rotelle; introd., trans., and notes R. J. Teske; WSA 1.26; Hyde Park, N.Y.: New City, 1999), 107–45 [*Rebuke and Grace*]. – Studies: A. Zumkeller, *AugL* 2.1–2:39–47.

23. **Cresc.**  *Ad Cresconium grammaticum partis Donati* (c. 405): *Sancti Aureli Augustini Scripta contra Donatistas* (ed. M. Petschenig; CSEL 52; Vienna: F. Tempsky, 1909), 325–582. – *Traités anti-donatistes IV: Contra Cresconium libri 4, De unico baptismo* (ed. M. Petschenig, G. Finaert, and A. C. de Veer; Baug 31; Paris: Desclée de Brouwer, 1968), 70–643. – Studies: M. Moreau, *AugL* 2.1–2:131–37.

24. **cura mort.**  *De cura pro mortuis gerenda ad Paulum episcopum* (424/5): *Sancti Avreli Avgvstini De fide et symbolo; De fide et operibvs; De agone christiano; De continentia; De bono conivgali; De sancta virginitate; De bono vidvitatis; De advlterinis conivgiis lib. II; De mendacio; Contra mendacivm; De opere monachorvm; De divinatione daemonvm; De cvra pro mortvis gerenda; De patientia* (ed. J. Zycha; CSEL 41; Vienna: F. Tempsky, 1900), 621–60. – *Problèmes moraux: De bono conjugali, De conjugiis adulterinis, De mendacio, Contra mendacium, De cura*

*gerenda pro mortuis, De patientia, De utilitate jejunii* (ed. G. Combès; BAug 2; Paris: Desclée de Brouwer, 1948), 462–523. – H. Browne, trans., "On Care to Be Had for the Dead," in *NPNF¹* (Peabody, Mass.: Hendrickson, 1995; repr. of 1887 ed.), 3:537–51. – *Treatises on Marriage and Other Subjects* (trans. C. T. Wilcox, M. Liguori, C. T. Huegelmeyer, J. A. Lacy, R. W. Brown, R. P. Russell, and J. McQuade; FC 27; New York: Fathers of the Church, 1955; repr., Washington, D.C.: Catholic University of America Press, 1969), 347–84. – Studies: M. Klöckener, *AugL* 2.1–2:182–88.

25.  *dial.*    *De dialectica: De dialecta* (ed. J. Pinborg and B. Darrell Jackson; Dordrecht, Neth., and Boston: Reidel, 1975) [ET/Com]. – *Il maestro e la parola* (trans. M. Bettetini; Milan: Rusconi, 1993), 83–123 [Com]. – Studies: J. Pépin, *Saint Augustin et la dialectique* (Villanova, Pa.: Augustinian Institute, Villanova University, 1976). – H. Ruef, *Augustin über Semiotik und Sprache: Sprachtheoretische Analysen zu Augustins Schrift "De dialectica" mit einer deutschen Übersetzung* (Bern: Wyss, 1981).

26.  *disc. chr.*    *De disciplina christiana: Sancti Aurelii Augustini De fide rerum invisibilium; Enchiridion ad Laurentium, de fide et spe et caritate; De catechizandis rudibus; Sermo ad catechumenos de symbolo; Sermo de disciplina christiana; Sermo de utilitate ieiunii; Sermo de excidio urbis Romae; De haeresibus* (ed. R. Vander Plaetse; CCSL 46; Turnhout, Belg.: Brepols, 1969), 207–24. – *Sermons* (trans. E. Hill; WSA 3.10; Hyde Park, N.Y.: New City, 1994), 458–70.

27.  *diu. qu.*    *De diversis quaestionibus octoginta tribus* (388–96): *Melanges doctrinaux: Quaestiones 83, Quaestiones 7 ad Simplicianum, Quaestiones 8 Dulcitii, De divinatione daemonum* (ed. G. Bardy, J.-A. Beckaert, and J. Boutet; BAug 10; Desclée de Brouwer, 1952), 52–379. – *Sancti Aurelii Augustini De diversis quaestionibus ad Simplicianum* (A. Mutzenbecher; CCSL 44 A; Turnhout, Belg.: Brepols, 1975), 1–249. – *La vera religione* (ed. G. Ceriotti, L. Alici, A. Pieretti, and F. Monteverde; NBA 6.2; Rome: Città Nuova, 1995), 7–261. – *Eighty-Three Different Questions* (trans. D. L. Mosher; FC 70; Washington, D.C.: Catholic University of America Press, 1982). – Studies: L. Perrone, *"De diversis quaestionibus octoginta tribus," "De diversis quaestionibus ad Simplicianum," di Agostino d'Ippona* (Lectio Augustini 12; Palermo: Città Nuova, 1996).

28.  *diuin. daem.*    *De divinatione daemonum* (406–408): *Sancti Avreli Avgvstini De fide et symbolo; De fide et operibvs; De agone christiano; De continentia; De bono conivgali; De sancta virginitate; De bono vidvitatis; De advlterinis conivgiis lib. II; De mendacio; Contra mendacivm; De opere monachorvm; De divinatione daemonvm; De cvra pro mortvis gerenda; De patientia* (ed. J. Zycha; CSEL 41; Vienna: F. Tempsky, 1900), 599–618. – *Melanges doctrinaux: Quaestiones 83, Quaestiones 7 ad Simplicianum, Quaestiones 8 Dulcitii, De divinatione daemonum* (ed. G. Bardy, J.-A. Beckaert, and J. Boutet; BAug 10; Desclée de Brouwer, 1952), 654–93. – *La vera religione* (ed. G. Ceriotti, L. Alici, A. Pieretti, and F. Monteverde; NBA 6.2; Rome: Città Nuova, 1995), 625–73. – *Treatises on Marriage and Other Subjects* (trans. C. T. Wilcox, M. Liguori, C. T. Huegelmeyer, J. A. Lacy, R. W. Brown, R. P. Russell, and J. McQuade;

FC 27; New York: Fathers of the Church, 1955; repr., Washington, D.C.: Catholic University of America Press, 1969), 415–40.

29. *doctr. chr.*  *De doctrina christiana* (397 [up to 3.25.35], 426/7): *Sancti Aurelii Augustini De doctrina christiana* (ed. K. D. Daur and J. Martin; CCSL 32; Turnhout, Belg.: Brepols, 1962), 1–167. – *De doctrina christiana libri 4* (ed. W. M. Green; CSEL 80; Vienna: Hölder, 1963). – *La doctrine chretienne* (ed. M. Moreau, I. Bochet, and G. Madec; BAug 11.2; Paris: Études Augustiniennes, 1997). – *L'istruzione cristiana* (ed. M. Simonetti, Rome: Fondazione Lorenzo Valla, 1994) [Com]. – *De doctrina christiana* (ed. and trans. R. P. H. Green; OECT; Oxford: Clarendon, 1995) [ET]. – J. F. Shaw, trans., "St. Augustin's Christian Doctrine," in *NPNF¹* (Peabody, Mass.: Hendrickson, 1995; repr. of 1886 ed.), 2:513–97. – *Christian Instruction; Admonition and Grace; The Christian Combat; Faith, Hope and Charity* (trans. J. J. Gavigan, J. C. Murray, R. P. Russell, and B. M. Peebles; FC 2; Washington, D.C.: Catholic University of America Press, 1947), 1–235. – *On Christian Doctrine* (trans. D. W. Robertson; Indianapolis and New York: Bobbs-Merrill, 1958). – *Teaching Christianity* (trans. E. Hill; WSA 1.11; Hyde Park, N.Y.: New City, 1996). – Studies: L. Alici et al., *"De doctrina christiana" di Agostino d'Ippona* (Lectio Augustini 11; Rome: Città Nuova; Augustinus, 1995).

30. *c. Don.*  *Contra Donatistas* (411): *Sancti Aureli Augustini Scripta contra Donatistas* (ed. M. Petschenig; CSEL 53; Vienna, F. Tempsky, 1910), 97–162. – *Traités anti-donatistes V: Breviculus collationis cum Donatistis; Ad Donatistas post collationen; Sermo ad caesariensis ecclesiae plebem; Gesta cum Emerito Donatistarum episcopo; Contra Gaudentium Donatistarum episcopum libri duo* (ed. M. Petschenig, G. Finaert, and E. Lamirande; BAug 32; Paris: Desclée de Brouwer, 1965), 248–393.

31. *duab. an.*  *De duabus animabus* (392): *Sancti Aureli Augustini De utilitate credendi; De duabus animabus; Contra fortunatum; Contra Adimantum; Contra epistulam fundamenti; Contra faustum* (ed. J. Zycha; CSEL 25; Vienna: F. Tempsky, 1892), 51–80. – *Six traités anti-manichéens: De duabus animabus, Contra Fortunatum, Contra Adimantum, Contra epistulam Fundamenti, Contra Secundinum, Contra Felicem Manichaeum* (ed. R. Jolivet and M. Jourjon; BAug 17; Paris: Desclée de Brouwer, 1961), 52–115. – *Polemica con i Manichei* (ed. F. Decret, L. Alici, and A. Pieretti; NBA 13.1; Rome: Città Nuova, 1997), 201–59. – A. H. Newman, trans., "On Two Souls, against the Manichaens," in *NPNF¹* (Peabody, Mass.: Hendrickson, 1995; repr. of 1887 ed.), 4:91–107.

32. *Dulc. qu.*  *De octo Dulcitii quaestionibus* (425): *Melanges doctrinaux: Quaestiones 83, Quaestiones 7 ad Simplicianum, Quaestiones 8 Dulcitii, De divinatione daemonum* (ed. G. Bardy, J.-A. Beckaert, and J. Boutet; BAug 10; Desclée de Brouwer, 1952), 588–643. – *Sancti Aurelii Augustini De diversis quaestionibus ad Simplicianum* (A. Mutzenbecher; CCSL 44 A; Turnhout, Belg.: Brepols, 1975), 253–97. – *La vera religione* (ed. G. Ceriotti, L. Alici, A. Pieretti, and F. Monteverde; NBA 6.2; Rome: Città Nuova, 1995), 391–447. – *Treatises on Various Subjects* (trans. M. S. Muldowney, M. E. Defarrari, H. B. Jaffee, L. Meagher, and M. F. McDonald; FC 16; New York: Fathers of the Church, 1952), 423–66.

33. *Emer.*   *Gesta cum Emerito Donatistarum episcopo* (Sept. 20, 418): *Sancti Aureli Augustini Scripta contra donatistas* (ed. M. Petschenig; CSEL 53; Vienna: F. Tempsky, 1910), 181–96. – *Traités anti-donatistes V: Breviculus collationis cum Donatistis; Ad Donatistas post collationen; Sermo ad Caesariensis ecclesiae plebem; Gesta cum Emerito Donatistarum episcopo; Contra Gaudentium Donatistarum episcopum libri duo* (ed. M. Petschenig, G. Finaert, and E. Lamirande; BAug 32; Paris: Desclée de Brouwer, 1965), 450–87.

34. *en. Ps.*   *Enarrationes in Psalmos* (392–416): *Sancti Aurelii Augustini Enarrationes in Psalmos* (ed. E. Dekkers and J. Fraipont; 3 vols.; CCSL 38–40; Turnhout, Belg.: Brepols, 1954–1956). – *Esposizioni sui Salmi* (ed. A. Corticelli, R. Minuti, B. di S. Maria di Rosano, V. Tarulli, T. Mariucci, and F. Monteverde; 4 vols.; 2d ed.; NBA 25–28; Roma: Città Nuova, 1982–1993). – *Commento ai Salmi* (ed. M. Simonetti; Milan: Fondazione Lorenzo Valla, 1988) [Com]. – *Augustin: Expositions on the Book of Psalms* (vol. 8 of *NPNF¹*; trans. A. C. Coxe; Peabody, Mass.: Hendrickson, 1995; repr. of 1888 ed.). – *On the Psalms* (S. Hebgin and F. Corrigan; 2 vols.; ACW 29–30; Westminster, Md.: Newman, 1960–1961) [*1–37*]. – *Expositions of the Psalms (1–32)* (trans. M. Boulding; WSA 3.15; Hyde Park, N.Y.: New City, 2000). – *Expositions of the Psalms (33–50)* (trans. M. Boulding; WSA 3.16; Hyde Park, N.Y.: New City, 2000). – Studies: M. Fiedrowicz, *Psalmus vox totius Christi: Studien zu Augustins "Enarrationes in Psalmos"* (Fribourg, Switz.: Herder, 1997). – M. Cameron, in *Augustine through the Ages: An Encyclopedia* (Grand Rapids: Eerdmans, 1999), 290–96.

35. *ench.*   *Enchiridion de fide spe et caritate* (c. 421): *Sancti Aurelii Augustini De fide rerum invisibilium; Enchiridion ad Laurentium, de fide et spe et caritate; De catechizandis rudibus; Sermo ad catechumenos de symbolo; Sermo de disciplina christiana; Sermo de utilitate ieiunii; Sermo de excidio urbis Romae; De haeresibus* (ed. E. Evans; CCSL 46; Turnhout, Belg.: Brepols, 1969), 49–114. – *De la foi* (ed. J. Rivière, G. Madec, and J.-P. Bouhot; 2d ed.; BAug 9; Paris: Desclée de Brouwer, 1988), 102–327. – *La vera religione* (ed. G. Ceriotti, L. Alici, A. Pieretti, and F. Monteverde; NBA 6.2; Rome: Città Nuova, 1995), 449–623. – J. F. Shaw, trans., "The Enchiridion," in *NPNF¹* (Peabody, Mass.: Hendrickson, 1995; repr. of 1887 ed.), 3:229–76. – *Faith, Hope, and Charity* (trans. L. A. Arand; ACW 3; Westminster, Md.: Newman, 1947). – *Christian Instruction; Admonition and Grace; The Christian Combat; Faith, Hope, and Charity* (trans. J. J. Gavigan, J. C. Murray, R. P. Russell, and B. M. Peebles; FC 2; Washington, D.C.: Catholic University of America Press, 1947), 355–472. – *Confessions and Enchiridion* (trans. A. C. Outler; LCC 7; London: SCM, 1955).

36. *ep.*   *Epistulae* (386–430): *S. Avreli Avgvstini Hipponiensis episcopi Epistvlae* (ed. A. Goldbacher; 5 vols.; CSEL 34.1–2, 44, 57–58; Vienna: F. Tempsky, 1895–1923). – *Select Letters* (trans. J. H. Baxter; LCL; London: Heinemann; New York: Putnam's, 1930; repr., London: Heinemann; Cambridge, Mass.: Harvard University Press, 1990) [*2, 4, 10, 15–17, 21, 22, 28, 29, 34, 37, 38, 42, 48, 50, 60, 65–67, 83, 84, 86, 91, 97, 99, 100, 101, 110, 115, 122, 124, 126, 133, 144, 146, 150, 159, 173, 174, 179, 189, 191,*

*192, 200, 203, 209–211, 214, 220, 227, 229, 231, 232, 245, 246, 254, 258, 262, 268, 269*]. – *Le lettere* (ed. M. Pellegrino, T. Alimonti, and L. Carrozzi; 3 vols.; NBA 21–23A; Rome: Città Nuova, 1969–1992). – *Epistolae ex duobus codicibus nuper in lucem prolatae* (ed. J. Divjak; CSEL 88; Vienna: Hölder-Pichler-Tempsky, 1981). – *Lettres 1\*–29\** (ed. J. Divjak et al.; BAug 46B; Paris: Études Augustiniennes, 1987). – J. G. Cunningham, trans., "The Letters of St. Augustin," in *NPNF[1]* (Peabody, Mass.: Hendrickson, 1995; repr. of 1886 ed.), 1:209–593. – *Letters* (trans. W. Parsons; 5 vols.; FC 12, 18, 20, 30, 32; Washington, D.C.: Catholic University of America Press, 1951–1956). – *Letters 1\*–29\** (trans. R. B. Eno; FC 81; Washington, D.C.: Catholic University of America Press, 1989) [Divjak letters]. – Studies: *Les lettres de saint Augustin découverts par Johannes Divjak* (Paris: Études Augustiniennes, 1983). – H. Chadwick, "The New Letters of St. Augustine," *JTS* NS 34 (1983): 425–52. – C. White, *The Correspondence (394–419) between Jerome and Augustine* (Lewiston, N.Y.: Mellen, 1990). – L. F. Bacchi, *The Theology of Ordained Ministry in the Letters of Augustine of Hippo* (San Francisco and London: International Scholars Publications, 1998). – A. Fürst, *Augustins Briefwechsel mit Hieronymus* (JAC.E 29; Münster: Aschendorffsche Verlagsbuchhandlung, 1999). – R. B. Eno, in *Augustine through the Ages: An Encyclopedia* (Grand Rapids: Eerdmans, 1999), 298–310.

37.  *ep. Jo. tr.*    *In epistulam Johannis ad Parthos tractatus decem: Commentaire de la première épître de S. Jean* (ed. P. Agaësse; 4th ed.; SC 75; Paris: Cerf, 1994). – *Commento al Vangelo di San Giovanni* (ed. G. Madurini, L. Muscolino, and F. Monteverde; NBA 24.2; Rome: Città Nuova, 1968), 1627–1855. – *Amore assoluto e "Terza navigazione"; Commento alla prima lettera di Giovanni; Commento al Vangelo di Giovanni* (ed. G. Reale; Milan: Rusconi, 1994), 73–487 [Com]. – H. Browne and J. H. Myers, trans., "Homilies on the First Epistle of John," in *NPNF[1]* (Peabody, Mass.: Hendrickson, 1995; repr. of 1888 ed.), 7:453–529. – *Augustine: Later Works* (trans. J. Burnaby; LCC 8; London: SCM; Philadelphia: Westminster, 1955), 251–348. – *Tractates on the Gospel of John* (trans. J. W. Rettig; FC 92; Washington, D.C.: Catholic University of America Press, 1995), 94–277. – Studies: D. Dideberg, *Saint Augustin et la première épître de saint Jean: Une théologie de l'agapè* (ThH 34; Paris: Beauchesne, 1975). – L. Ayres, "Augustine on God as Love and Love as God," *Pro ecclesia* 5 (1996): 470–87.

38.  *c. ep. Man.*    *Contra epistulam Manichaei quam vocant Fundamenti* (beginning of episcopate): *Sancti Aureli Augustini De utilitate credendi; De duabus animabus; Contra Fortunatum; Contra Adimantum; Contra epistulam Fundamenti; Contra Faustum* (ed. J. Zycha; CSEL 25; Vienna: F. Tempsky, 1892), 193–248. – *Six traités anti-manichéens: De duabus animabus, Contra Fortunatum, Contra Adimantum, Contra epistulam Fundamenti, Contra Secundinum, Contra Felicem Manichaeum* (ed. R. Jolivet and M. Jourjon; BAug 17; Paris: Desclée de Brouwer, 1961), 390–507. – R. Stothert, trans., "Against the Epistle of Manichaeus Called Fundamental," in *NPNF[1]* (Peabody, Mass.: Hendrickson, 1995; repr. of 1887 ed.), 4:125–50.

39. *c. ep. Parm.*   *Contra epistulam Parmeniani* (c. 400): *Sancti Aureli Augustini Scripta contra donatistas* (ed. M. Petschenig; CSEL 51; Vienna: F. Tempsky, 1908), 19–141. – *Traités anti-donatistes I: Psalmus contra partem Donati, Contra epistulam Parmeniani libri tres, Epistula ad Catholicos de secta Donatistarum* (ed. M. Petschenig, G. Finaert, R. Anastasi, and Y. M.-J. Congar; BAug 28; Paris: Desclée de Brouwer, 1963), 208–481.

40. *c. ep. Pel.*   *Contra duas epistolas Pelagianorum* (c. 420): *Sancti Aureli Augustini De peccatorum meritis et remissione et de baptismo parvulorum ad Marcellinum libri tres; De spiritv et littera liber vnvs; De natvra et gratia liber vnvs; De natvra et origine animae libri qvattvor; Contra dvas epistvlas Pelagianorvm libri qvattvor* (ed. K. F. Urba and J. Zycha; CSEL 60; Vienna: F. Tempsky, 1913), 423–570. – *Premières polémiques contre Julien: De nuptiis et concupiscentia contra duas epistulas Pelagianorum* (ed. C. F. Urba, J. Zycha, F.-J. Thonnard, E. Bleuzen, and A. C de Veer; BAug 23; Paris: Desclée de Brouwer, 1974), 312–657. – *Polemica con Giuliano 1: Le nozze e la concupiscenza, Contro le due lettere dei pelagiani, Contro Giuliano* (ed. N. Cipriani, E. Cristini, and I. Volpi; NBA 18; Rome: Città Nuova, 1985), 173–397. – P. Holmes, R. E. Wallis, and B. B. Warfield, trans., "Against Two Letters of the Pelagians," in *NPNF¹* (Peabody, Mass.: Hendrickson, 1995; repr. of 1887 ed.), 5:373–434. – *Answer to the Pelagians II* (ed. J. E. Rotelle; introd., trans., and notes R. J. Teske; WSA 1.23; Hyde Park, N.Y.: New City, 1998), 97–219 [*Answer to the Two Letters of the Pelagians*].

41. *ep. Rm. inch.*   *Epistulae ad Romanos inchoata expositio: Expositio quarundam propositionum ex epistola ad Romanos; Epistolae ad Galatas expositionis liber unus; Epistolae ad Romanos inchoata expositio* (ed. J. Divjak; CSEL 84; Vienna: Hölder-Pichler-Tempsky, 1971), 145–81. – *Opere esegetiche* (ed. S. Caruana, B. Fenati, M. Mendoza, D. Gentili, V. Tarulli, and F. Monteverde; NBA 10.2; Rome: Città Nuova, 1997), 677–721. – *Augustine on Romans* (trans. P. Frederiksen Landes; Chico, Calif.: Scholars Press, 1982), 51–89 [Com].

42. *exc. urb.*   *De excidio urbis Romae: Sancti Aurelii Augustini De fide rerum invisibilium; Enchiridion ad Laurentium, de fide et spe et caritate; De catechizandis rudibus; Sermo ad catechumenos de symbolo; Sermo de disciplina christiana; Sermo de utilitate ieiunii; Sermo de excidio urbis Romae; De haeresibus* (ed. M.-V. O'Reilly; CCSL 46; Turnhout, Belg.: Brepols, 1969), 249–62. – *De excidio urbis Romae sermo* (trans. M. V. O'Reilly; PatSt 89; Washington, D.C.: Catholic University of America Press, 1955) [ET/Com]. – *Sermons* (trans. E. Hill; WSA 3.10; Hyde Park, N.Y.: New City, 1994), 435–44.

43. *exp. Gal.*   *Expositio epistulae ad Galatas* (394–395): *Epistulae ad Romanos inchoata expositio; Expositio quarundam propositionum ex epistola ad Romanos; Epistolae ad Galatas expositionis liber unus; Epistolae ad Romanos inchoata expositio* (ed. J. Divjak; CSEL 84; Vienna: Hölder-Pichler-Tempsky, 1971), 55–141. – *Opere esegetiche* (ed. S. Caruana, B. Fenati, M. Mendoza, D. Gentili, V. Tarulli, and F. Monteverde; NBA 10.2; Rome: Città Nuova, 1997), 567–675. – S. Iodice, *Legge e grazia in S. Agostino* (Naples: Associazione di Studi Tardoantichi, 1977), 213–84 [Com].

44. *exp. prop. Rm.*    *Expositio quarundarum propositionum ex epistula apostoli ad Romanos:*
*Epistulae ad Romanos inchoata expositio; Expositio quarundam propo-*
*sitionum ex epistola ad Romanos; Epistolae ad Galatas expositionis liber*
*unus; Epistolae ad Romanos inchoata expositio* (ed. J. Divjak; CSEL 84;
Vienna: Hölder-Pichler-Tempsky, 1971), 3–52. – *Opere esegetiche* (ed.
S. Caruana, B. Fenati, M. Mendoza, D. Gentili, V. Tarulli, and F. Monteverde; NBA 10.2; Rome: Città Nuova, 1997), 505–65. – *Augustine on*
*Romans* (trans. P. Frederiksen Landes; Chico, Calif.: Scholars Press,
1982), 1–49.

45. *c. Faust.*    *Contra Faustum Manichaeum* (397/8): *Sancti Aureli Augustini De utili-*
*tate credendi; De duabus animabus; Contra Fortunatum; Contra Adi-*
*mantum; Contra epistulam Fundamenti; Contra Faustum* (ed. J. Zycha;
CSEL 25; Vienna: F. Tempsky, 1892), 251–797. – R. Stothert, trans.,
"Reply to Faustus the Manichaean," in *NPNF¹* (Peabody, Mass.: Hendrickson, 1995; repr. of 1887 ed.), 4:151–345.

46. *c. Fel.*    *Contra Felicem Manichaeum* (Dec. 7–12, 404): *Sancti Aureli Augustini*
*De utilitate credendi; De duabus animabus; Contra Fortunatum; Con-*
*tra Adimantum; Contra epistulam Fundamenti; Contra Faustum* (ed.
J. Zycha; CSEL 25; Vienna: F. Tempsky, 1892), 801–52. – *Six traités*
*anti-manichéens: De duabus animabus, Contra Fortunatum, Contra*
*Adimantum, Contra epistulam Fundamenti, Contra Secundinum, Con-*
*tra Felicem Manichaeum* (ed. R. Jolivet and M. Jourjon; BAug 17; Paris:
Desclée de Brouwer, 1961), 644–757.

47. *f. et op.*    *De fide et operibus* (413): *Sancti Avreli Avgvstini De fide et symbolo; De*
*fide et operibvs; De agone christiano; De continentia; De bono conivgali;*
*De sancta virginitate; De bono vidvitatis; De advlterinis conivgiis lib. II;*
*De mendacio; Contra mendacivm; De opere monachorvm; De divina-*
*tione daemonvm; De cvra pro mortvis gerenda; De patientia* (ed. J. Zycha;
CSEL 41; Vienna: F. Tempsky, 1900), 35–97. – *La foi chretienne* (ed.
J. Pegon and G. Madec; BAug 8; Paris: Desclée de Brouwer, 1982),
354–461. – *La vera religione* (ed. G. Ceriotti, L. Alici, A. Pieretti, and
F. Monteverde; NBA 6.2; Rome: Città Nuova, 1995), 675–777. – *Trea-*
*tises on Marriage and Other Subjects* (trans. C. T. Wilcox, M. Liguori,
C. T. Huegelmeyer, J. A. Lacy, R. W. Brown, R. P. Russell, and J. McQuade;
FC 27; New York: Fathers of the Church, 1955; repr., Washington,
D.C.: Catholic University of America Press, 1969), 213–82. – *On Faith*
*and Works* (trans. G. J. Lombardo; ACW 48; New York: Newman, 1988).

48. *f. et symb.*    *De fide et symbolo* (Oct. 393): *Sancti Avreli Avgvstini De fide et symbolo;*
*De fide et operibvs; De agone christiano; De continentia; De bono coniv-*
*gali; De sancta virginitate; De bono vidvitatis; De advlterinis conivgiis*
*lib. II; De mendacio; Contra mendacivm; De opere monachorvm; De*
*divinatione daemonvm; De cvra pro mortvis gerenda; De patientia* (ed.
J. Zycha; CSEL 41; Vienna: F. Tempsky, 1900), 3–32. – *De fide et*
*symbolo* (trans. E. P. Meijering; Amsterdam: Gieben, 1987) [ET/Com].
– *De la foi* (ed. J. Rivière, G. Madec, and J.-P. Bouhot; 2d ed.; BAug 9;
Paris: Desclée de Brouwer, 1988), 18–75. – *La vera religione* (ed.
A. Pieretti; NBA 6.1; Rome: Città Nuova, 1995), 243–93. – S. D. F.
Salmond, trans., "On Faith and the Creed," in *NPNF¹* (Peabody, Mass.:
Hendrickson, 1995; repr. of 1887 ed.), 3:315–33. – *Earlier Writings*

(trans. J. H. S. Burleigh; LCC 6; Philadelphia: Westminster, 1953), 351–69. – *Treatises on Marriage and Other Subjects* (trans. C. T. Wilcox, M. Liguori, C. T. Huegelmeyer, J. A. Lacy, R. W. Brown, R. P. Russell, and J. McQuade; FC 27; New York: Fathers of the Church, 1955; repr., Washington, D.C.: Catholic University of America Press, 1969), 309–45.

49. *f. inuis.*    *De fide rerum invisibilium: Saint Augustine's De fide rerum quae non videntur* (ed. M. F. McDonald; PatSt 84; Washington, D.C.: Catholic University of America Press, 1950) [ET/Com]. – *Sancti Aurelii Augustini De fide rerum invisibilium; Enchiridion ad Laurentium, de fide et spe et caritate; De catechizandis rudibus; Sermo ad catechumenos de symbolo; Sermo de disciplina christiana; Sermo de utilitate ieiunii; Sermo de excidio urbis Romae; De haeresibus* (ed. M. P. J. Van den Hout; CCSL 46; Turnhout, Belg.: Brepols, 1969), 1–19. – *La foi chretienne* (ed. J. Pegon and G. Madec; BAug 8; Paris: Desclée de Brouwer, 1982), 310–41. – *La vera religione* (ed. A. Pieretti; NBA 6.1; Rome: Città Nuova, 1995), 297–335. – C. L. Cornish, trans., "Concerning Faith of Things Not Seen," in *NPNF¹* (Peabody, Mass.: Hendrickson, 1995; repr. of 1887 ed.), 3:335–43. – *The Immortality of the Soul; The Magnitude of the Soul; On Music; The Advantage of Believing; On Faith in Things Unseen* (trans. L. Schopp, J. J. McMahon, R. C. Taliaferro, L. Meagher, R. J. Defarrari, and M. F. McDonald; FC 4; Washington, D.C.: Catholic University of America Press, 1947), 443–69. – Studies: *"De utilitate credendi"; "De vera religione"; "De fide rerum quae non videntur" di Agostino d'Ippona* (ed. O. Grassi et al.; Lectio Augustini 10; Rome: Città Nuova, 1994), 93–109.

50. *c. Fort.*    *Acta contra Fortunatum Manichaeum* (Aug. 28–29, 392): *Sancti Aureli Augustini De utilitate credendi; De duabus animabus; Contra Fortunatum; Contra Adimantum; Contra epistulam Fundamenti; Contra Faustum* (ed. J. Zycha; CSEL 25; Vienna: F. Tempsky, 1892), 83–112. – *Six traités anti-manichéens: De duabus animabus, Contra Fortunatum, Contra Adimantum, Contra epistulam Fundamenti, Contra Secundinum, Contra Felicem Manichaeum* (ed. R. Jolivet and M. Jourjon; BAug 17; Paris: Desclée de Brouwer, 1961), 132–93. – *Polemica con i Manichei* (ed. F. Decret, L. Alici, and A. Pieretti; NBA 13.1; Rome: Città Nuova, 1997), 261–319. – A. H. Newman, trans., "Acts or Disputation against Fortunatus the Manichaean," in *NPNF¹* (Peabody, Mass.: Hendrickson, 1995; repr. of 1887 ed.), 4:109–24. – Studies: F. Decret, *AugL* 1:53–8.

51. *c. Gaud.*    *Contra Gaudentium Donatistarum episcopum: Sancti Aureli Augustini Scripta contra donatistas* (ed. M. Petschenig; CSEL 53; Vienna: F. Tempsky, 1910), 201–74. – *Traités anti-donatistes V: Breviculus collationis cum Donatistis; Ad Donatistas post collationen; Sermo ad Caesariensis ecclesiae plebem; Gesta cum Emerito Donatistarum episcopo; Contra Gaudentium Donatistarum episcopum libri duo* (ed. M. Petschenig, G. Finaert, and E. Lamirande; BAug 32; Paris: Desclée de Brouwer, 1965), 510–685.

52. *gest. Pel.*    *De gestiis Pelagii* (end of 417): *Sancti Aureli Augustini De perfectione iustitiae hominis; De gestis Pelagii; De gratia Christi et de peccato originali libri dvo; De nvptiis et concvpiscentia ad Valerivm comitem*

*libri dvo* (ed. K. F. Urba and J. Zycha; CSEL 42; Vienna: F. Tempsky, 1902), 51–122. – *Natura e grazia* (ed. A. Trapè, I. Volpi, and F. Monteverde; 2 vols.; NBA 17; Rome: Città Nuova, 1981), 2:21–121. – P. Holmes, R. E. Wallis, and B. B. Warfield, trans., "On the Proceedings of Pelagius," in *NPNF¹* (Peabody, Mass.: Hendrickson, 1995; repr. of 1887 ed.), 5:177–212. – *Four Anti-Pelagian Writings* (trans. J. A. Mourant and W. J. Collinge; FC 86; Washington, D.C.: Catholic University of America Press, 1992), 91–177. – *Answer to the Pelagians I* (ed. J. E. Rotelle; introd., trans., and notes R. J. Teske; WSA 1.23; Hyde Park, N.Y.: New City, 1997), 317–81 [*The Deeds of Pelagius*].

53. *Gn. litt.*     *De Genesi ad litteram* (401–415): *Sancti Aureli Augustini De Genesi ad litteram libri duodecim; Eivsdem libri capitvla; De Genesi ad litteram inperfectvs liber; Locvtionvm in Heptatevchvm libri septem* (ed. J. Zycha; CSEL 28.1; Vienna: F. Tempsky, 1894), 3–435. – *La Genese au sens litteral en douze livres* (ed. J. Zycha, P. Agaësse, and A. Solignac; BAug 48–49; Paris: Études Augustiniennes, 1972; repr., 2000). – *La Genesi alla lettera* (ed. L. Carrozzi; NBA 9.2; Rome: Città Nuova, 1989). – *The Literal Meaning of Genesis* (trans. J. H. Taylor; 2 vols.; ACW 41–42; New York: Newman, 1982). – Studies: G. Pelland, *Cinq études d'Augustin sur le début de la Genèse* (Tournai: Desclée, 1972). – R. Arteaga Natividad, *La creación en los comentarios de san Agustín al Génesis* (Zaragoza: n.p., 1994).

54. *Gn. litt. imp.*     *De Genesi ad litteram liber imperfectus* (393): *Sancti Aureli Augustini De Genesi ad litteram libri duodecim; Eivsdem libri capitvla; De Genesi ad litteram inperfectvs liber; Locvtionvm in Heptatevchvm libri septem* (ed. J. Zycha; CSEL 28.1; Vienna: F. Tempsky, 1894), 459–503. – *La Genesi difesa contro i manichei: Libro incompiuto su la Genesi* (ed. A. Di Giovanni, A. Penna, L. Carrozzi; NBA 9.1; Rome: Città Nuova, 1988), 183–265. – *The Literal Meaning of Genesis* (trans. J. H. Taylor; 2 vols.; ACW 41–42; New York: Newman, 1982). – *Saint Augustine on Genesis* (trans. R. J. Teske; FC 84; Washington, D.C.: Catholic University of America Press, 1991), 143–88. – Studies: G. Pelland, *Cinq études d'Augustin sur le début de la Genèse* (Tournai: Desclée, 1972). – G. Pelland et al., *"De Genesi contra Manichaeos"; "De Genesi ad litteram liber imperfectus" di Agostino d'Ippona* (Lectio Augustini 8; Palermo: "Augustinus," 1992), 115–51.

55. *Gn. adu. Man.*     *De Genesi adversus Manichaeos* (c. 389): PL 34:173–220. – *La Genesi difesa contro i manichei: Libro incompiuto su la Genesi* (ed. A. Di Giovanni, A. Penna, and L. Carrozzi; NBA 9.1; Rome: Città Nuova, 1988), 58–181. – *Saint Augustine on Genesis* (trans. R. J. Teske: FC 84; Washington, D.C.: Catholic University of America Press, 1991), 45–141. – Studies: G. Pelland, *Cinq études d'Augustin sur le début de la Genèse* (Tournai: Desclée, 1972). – G. Pelland et al., *"De Genesi contra Manichaeos"; "De Genesi ad litteram liber imperfectus" di Agostino d'Ippona* (Lectio Augustini 8; Palermo: "Augustinus," 1992), 65–113.

56. *gramm.*     *De grammatica: Artium scriptores minores: Cledonius, Pompeius, Julianus, excerpta ex commentariis in Donatum, Consentius, Phocas, Eutyches, Augustinus, Palaemon, Asper, De nomine et pronomine, De dubiis nominibus, Macrobii excerpta* (ed. H. Keil; Grammatici latini 5;

Leipzig: Teubner, 1868; repr., Hildesheim: Olms, 1981), 496–524. – *Il maestro e la parola: Il maestro, La dialettica, La retorica, La grammatica* (trans. M. Bettetini; Milan: Rusconi, 1993), 161–71 [Com].

57. *gr. et lib. arb.* *De gratia et libero arbitrio* (c. 426): PL 44:881–912. – *Aux moines d'Adrumete et de Provence* (ed. J. Chéné and J. Pintard; BAug 24; Paris: Desclée de Brouwer, 1962), 90–207. – *Grazia e libertà* (ed. A. Trapè, M. Palmieri, and F. Monteverde; NBA 20; Rome: Città Nuova, 1987), 19–95. – P. Holmes, R. E. Wallis, and B. B. Warfield, trans., "On Grace and Free Will," in *NPNF¹* (Peabody, Mass.: Hendrickson, 1995; repr. of 1887 ed.), 5:435–65. – *The Teacher; The Free Choice of the Will; Grace and Free Will* (trans. R. P. Russell; FC 59; Washington, D.C.: Catholic University of America Press, 1968), 243–308. – *Answer to the Pelagians IV* (ed. J. E. Rotelle; introd., trans., and notes R. J. Teske; WSA 1.26; Hyde Park, N.Y.: New City, 1999), 69–106 [*Grace and Free Choice*].

58. *gr. et pecc. or.* *De gratia Christi et de peccato originali* (middle of 418): *Sancti Aureli Augustini De perfectione iustitiae hominis; De gestis Pelagii; De gratia Christi et de peccato originali libri dvo; De nvptiis et concvpiscentia ad Valerivm comitem libri dvo* (ed. K. F. Urba and J. Zycha; CSEL 42; Vienna: F. Tempsky, 1902), 125–206. – *La crise pélagienne* (ed. G. de Plinval, J. de La Tullaye, C. F. Urba, J. Zycha, J. Plagnieux, and F.-J. Thonnard; 2 vols.; BAug 21–22; Brugge, Belg.: Desclée de Brouwer, 1966–1975), 52–269. – *Natura e grazia* (ed. A. Trapè, I. Volpi, and F. Monteverde; 2 vols.; NBA 17; Rome: Città Nuova, 1981), 2:123–267. – P. Holmes, R. E. Wallis, and B. B. Warfield, trans., "On the Grace of Christ, and on Original Sin," in *NPNF¹* (Peabody, Mass.: Hendrickson, 1995; repr. of 1887 ed.), 5:213–55. – *Answer to the Pelagians I* (ed. J. E. Rotelle; introd., trans., and notes R. J. Teske; WSA 1.23; Hyde Park, N.Y.: New City, 1997), 383–463 [*The Grace of Christ and Original Sin*].

59. *gr. t. nou.* *De gratia testamenti novi ad Honoratum* (= *ep* 140) (412): *S. Avreli Avgvstini Hipponiensis episcopi Epistvlae* (ed. A. Goldbacher; CSEL 44; Vienna: F. Tempsky, 1904), 155–234. – *Le lettere* (ed. L. Carrozzi; NBA 22; Rome: Città Nuova, 1971), 206–307. – *Letters* (trans. W. Parsons; FC 20; New York: Fathers of the Church, 1953), 58–136.

60. *haer.* *De haeresibus ad Quodvultdeum* (428/9): *Sancti Aurelii Augustini De fide rerum invisibilium; Enchiridion ad Laurentium, de fide et spe et caritate; De catechizandis rudibus; Sermo ad catechumenos de symbolo; Sermo de disciplina christiana; Sermo de utilitate ieiunii; Sermo de excidio urbis Romae; De haeresibus* (ed. R. Vander Plaetse and C. Beukers; CCSL 46; Turnhout, Belg.: Brepols, 1969), 286–345. – *De haeresibus: A Translation with an Introduction and Commentary* (trans. L. G. Müller; PatSt 90; Washington, D.C.: Catholic University of America Press, 1956) [Com]. – *Arianism and Other Heresies: Heresies, Memorandum to Augustine, To Orosius in Refutation of the Priscillianists and Origenists, Arian Sermon, Answer to an Arian Sermon, Debate with Maximinus, Answer to Maximinus, Answer to an Enemy of the Law and the Prophets* (trans. R. J. Teske; WSA 1.18; Hyde Park, N.Y.: New City, 1995), 13–77. – Studies: S. Jannaccone, *La dottrina eresiologica di S. Agostino: Studio di storia letteraria e religiosa a proposito del trattato De haeresibus* (Catania: G. Reina, 1952).

61. *imm. an.*     *De immortalitate animae* (Apr. 1–24, 387): *Soliloquiorum libri duo; De inmortalitate animae; De quantitate animae* (ed. W. Hörmann; CSEL 89; Vienna: Hölder-Pichler-Tempsky, 1986), 101–28. – *Dialogues philosophiques,* vol. 2, *Dieu et l'ame: Soliloques, De immortalitate animae, De quantitate animae* (ed. P. de Labriolle; BAug 5; Paris: Desclée de Brouwer, 1939), 170–219. – *Dialoghi* (ed. D. Gentili and A. Trapé; 2 vols.; NBA 3; Rome: Città Nuova, 1970–1976), 489–547. – *The Immortality of the Soul; The Magnitude of the Soul; On Music; The Advantage of Believing; On Faith in Things Unseen* (trans. L. Schopp, J. J. McMahon, R. C. Taliaferro, L. Meagher, R. J. Defarrari, and M. F. McDonald; FC 4; Washington, D.C.: Catholic University of America Press, 1947), 1–47.

62. *inq. Jan.*     *Ad inquisitiones Januarii* (= *ep* 54–55) (c. 400): *S. Avreli Avgvstini Hipponiensis episcopi Epistvlae* (ed. A. Goldbacher; CSEL 34.2; Vienna: F. Tempsky, 1898), 158–213. – *Le lettere* (ed. L. Carrozzi; NBA 21; Rome: Città Nuova, 1969), 436–97. – *Letters* (trans. W. Parsons; FC 12; New York: Fathers of the Church, 1951), 252–93.

63. *Jo. eu. tr.*     *In Johannis Evangelium tractatus: Sancti Aurelii Augustini In Johannis Evangelium tractatus CXXIV* (ed. R. Willems; CCSL 36; Turnhout, Belg.: Brepols, 1954). – *Commento al Vangelo di San Giovanni: Commento all'epistola ai parti di San Giovanni* (ed. A. Vita, E. Gandolfo, V. Tarulli, and F. Monteverde; NBA 24.1–2; Rome: Città Nuova, 1968). – *Homélies sur l'Évangile de saint Jean* (ed. M. F. Berrouard; 7 vols.; BAug 71–75; Paris: Desclée de Brouwer, 1969–2003). – J. Gibb and J. Innes, trans., "Homilies on the Gospel of John," in *NPNF[1]* (Peabody, Mass.: Hendrickson, 1995; repr. of 1888 ed.), 7:1–452. – *Tractates on the Gospel of John* (trans. J. W. Rettig; 5 vols.; FC 78–79, 88, 90, 92; Washington, D.C.: Catholic University of America Press, 1988–1995). – Studies: M. Comeau, *Saint Augustin exégète du quatrième Évangile* (3d ed.; Paris: Beauchesne, 1930). – M. LeLandais, "Deux années de prédication de saint Augustin: Introduction a la lecture de l'*In Joannem,*" in *Études augustiniennes* (ed. H. Rondet; Paris: Aubier, 1953), 1–95.

64. *adu. Jud.*     *Adversus Judaeos:* PL 42:51–64.

65. *c. Jul.*     *Contra Julianum* (c. 421): PL 44:641–874. – *Polemica con Giuliano 1: Le nozze e la concupiscenza, Contro le due lettere dei pelagiani, Contro Giuliano* (ed. N. Cipriani, E. Cristini, and I. Volpi; NBA 18; Rome: Città Nuova, 1985), 399–981. – *Against Julian* (trans. M. A. Schumacher; FC 35; Washington, D.C.: Catholic University of America Press, 1957). – *Answer to the Pelagians II* (ed. J. E. Rotelle; introd., trans., and notes R. J. Teske; WSA 1.24; Hyde Park, N.Y.: New City, 1998), 221–536 [*Answer to Julian*].

66. *c. Jul. imp.*     *Contra Julianum opus imperfectum: Contra Julianum (opus imperfectum)* (ed. M. Zelzer; 2 vols.; CSEL 85.1–2; 1974–2004). – PL 45:1337–1608 [*IV–VI*]. – *Opera incompiuta* (ed. N. Cipriani, I. Volpi, and F. Monteverde; 2 vols.; NBA 19.1–2; Rome: Città Nuova, 1993–1994). – *Answer to the Pelagians III* (ed. J. E. Rotelle; introd., trans., and notes R. J. Teske; WSA 1.25; Hyde Park, N.Y.: New City, 1999) [*Unfinished Work in Answer to Julian*].

67. *lib. arb.*     *De libero arbitrio* (383–395): *Dialogues philosophiques: De l'âme à Dieu, De magistro, De libero arbitrio* (ed. F. J. Thonnard; 2d ed.; BAug 6; Paris: Desclée de Brouwer, 1952), 136–471. – *De libero arbitrio libri tres* (ed. W. M. Green; CSEL 74; Vienna: Hölder-Pichler-Tempsky, 1956). – *Contra Academicos; De beata vita; De ordine; De magistro; De libero arbitrio* (ed. W. M. Green and K. D. Daur; CCSL 29; Turnhout, Belg.: Brepols, 1970), 211–321. – *Dialoghi* (ed. D. Gentili and A. Trapé; 2 vols.; NBA 3; Rome: Città Nuova, 1970–1976), 2:135–377. – F. De Capitani, *Il "De libero arbitrio" di S. Agostino: Studio introduttivo, testo, traduzione, e commento* (Milan: Vita e Pensiero, 1987) [Com]. – *La felicità; La libertà* (ed. R. Fedriga and S. Puggioni; Milan: Biblioteca Universale Rizzoli, 1995), 91–387. – *Earlier Writings* (trans. J. H. S. Burleigh; LCC 6; Philadelphia: Westminster, 1953), 102–217. – *The Problem of Free Choice* (trans. M. Pontifex; ACW 22; Westminster, Md.: Newman, 1955). – *The Teacher; The Free Choice of the Will; Grace and Free Will* (trans. R. P. Russell; FC 59; Washington, D.C.: Catholic University of America Press, 1968), 63–241. – *On Free Choice of the Will* (trans. T. Williams; Indianapolis: Hackett, 1993). – Studies: *"De libero arbitrio" di Agostino d'Ippona* (ed. G. Madec et al.; Lectio Augustini 6; Palermo: Augustinus, 1990).

68. *c. litt. Pet.*     *Contra litteras Petiliani* (398–401): *Sancti Aureli Augustini Scripta contra donatistas* (ed. M. Petschenig; CSEL 52; Vienna: F. Tempsky, 1909), 3–227. – *Traités anti-donatistes III: Contra litteras Petiliani libri tres* (ed. M. Petschenig, G. Finaert, and B. Quinot; BAug 30; Paris: Desclée de Brouwer, 1967). J. R. King, trans., "Answer to Letters of Petilian, Bishop of Cirta," in *NPNF¹* (Peabody, Mass.: Hendrickson, 1995; repr. of 1887 ed.), 4:515–628.

69. *loc.*     *Locutiones in Heptateuchum: Sancti Aureli Augustini Quaestionum in Heptateuchum libri VII; Adnotationvm in Job liber vnvs* (ed. J. Zycha; CSEL 28.1; Vienna: F. Tempsky, 1895), 507–629. – *Sancti Aurelii Augustini Quaestionum in heptateuchum libri VII; Locutionum in Heptateuchum libri VII; De octo quaestionibus ex veteri testamento* (ed. I. Fraipont and D. de Bruyne; CCSL 33; Turnhout, Belg.: Brepols, 1958), 381–465.

70. *mag.*     *De magistro* (388–391): *Dialogues philosophiques*, vol. 3, *De l'âme à Dieu: De magistro, De libero arbitrio* (ed. F. J. Thonnard; 2d ed.; BAug 6; Paris: Desclée de Brouwer, 1952), 14–121. – *De magistro liber unus* (ed. G. Weigel; CSEL 77.1; Vienna: Hölder-Pichler-Tempsky, 1961). – *Contra Academicos; De beata vita; De ordine; De magistro; De libero arbitrio* (ed. W. M. Green and K. D. Daur; CCSL 29; Turnhout, Belg.: Brepols, 1970), 157–203. – *Dialoghi* (ed. D. Gentili and A. Trapé; 2 vols.; NBA 3; Rome: Città Nuova, 1970–1976), 2:709–95. – *De magistro* (ed. A. Canilli; Milan: Mursia, 1993). – *Il maestro* (ed. M. Parodi and C. Trovò; Milan: Biblioteca Universale Rizzoli, 1996). – *De magistro* (ed. B. Mojsisch; Stuttgart: Philipp Reclam, 1998). – *Earlier Writings* (trans. J. H. S. Burleigh; LCC 6; Philadelphia: Westminster, 1953), 64–101. – *The Greatness of the Soul; The Teacher* (trans. J. M. Colleran; ACW 9; Westminster, Md.: Newman, 1964), 113–86, 221–40. – *The Teacher; The Free Choice of the Will; Grace and Free Will* (trans. R. P. Russell; FC 59;

Washington, D.C.: Catholic University of America Press, 1968), 1–61.
– Studies: F. J. Crossan et al., *"De magistro" di Agostino d'Ippona* (Lectio
Augustini 9; Palermo: "Augustinus," 1993).

71.  *c. Max.*    *Contra Maximinum Arrianum:* PL 42:743–814. – *Arianism and Other
Heresies: Heresies, Memorandum to Augustine, To Orosius in Refutation
of the Priscillianists and Origenists, Arian Sermon, Answer to an Arian
Sermon, Debate with Maximinus, Answer to Maximinus, Answer to an
Enemy of the Law and the Prophets* (trans. R. J. Teske; WSA 1.18; Hyde
Park, N.Y.: New City, 1995), 229–336.

72.  *mend.*    *De mendacio* (395): *Sancti Avreli Avgvstini De fide et symbolo; De fide et
operibvs; De agone christiano; De continentia; De bono conivgali; De
sancta virginitate; De bono vidvitatis; De advlterinis conivgiis lib. II; De
mendacio; Contra mendacivm; De opere monachorvm; De divinatione
daemonvm; De cvra pro mortvis gerenda; De patientia* (ed. J. Zycha;
CSEL 41; Vienna: F. Tempsky, 1900), 413–66. – *Problèmes moraux: De
bono conjugali, De conjugiis adulterinis, De mendacio, Contra mendacium, De cura gerenda pro mortuis, De patientia, De utilitate jejunii* (ed.
G. Combès; BAug 2; Paris: Desclée De Brouwer, 1948), 240–343. –
*Sulla bugia* (ed. M. Bettetini; Milan: Rusconi, 1994) [Com]. – H. Browne,
trans., "On Lying," in *NPNF[1]* (Peabody, Mass.: Hendrickson, 1995;
repr. of 1887 ed.), 3:455–77. – *Treatises on Various Subjects* (trans.
M. S. Muldowney, M. E. Defarrari, H. B. Jaffee, L. Meagher, and M. F.
McDonald; FC 16; New York: Fathers of the Church, 1952), 45–110.

73.  *c. mend.*    *Contra mendacium* (420/1): *Sancti Avreli Avgvstini De fide et symbolo;
De fide et operibvs; De agone christiano; De continentia; De bono
conivgali; De sancta virginitate; De bono vidvitatis; De advlterinis conivgiis lib. II; De mendacio; Contra mendacivm; De opere monachorvm; De
divinatione daemonvm; De cvra pro mortvis gerenda; De patientia* (ed.
J. Zycha; CSEL 41; Vienna: F. Tempsky, 1900), 469–528. – *Problèmes
moraux: De bono conjugali, De conjugiis adulterinis, De mendacio, Contra mendacium, De cura gerenda pro mortuis, De patientia, De utilitate
jejunii* (ed. G. Combès; BAug 2; Paris: Desclée de Brouwer, 1948),
350–453. – H. Browne, trans., "To Consentius: Against Lying," in
*NPNF[1]* (Peabody, Mass.: Hendrickson, 1995; repr. of 1887 ed.), 3:479–
500. – *Treatises on Various Subjects* (trans. M. S. Muldowney, M. E.
Defarrari, H. B. Jaffee, L. Meagher, and M. F. McDonald; FC 16; New
York: Fathers of the Church, 1952), 111–79.

74.  *mor.*    *De moribus ecclesiae catholicae et de moribus Manichaeorum* (388): *La
morale chrétienne* (ed. B. Roland-Gosselin; 2d ed.; BAug 1; Paris:
Desclée de Brouwer, 1949), 136–367. – *De moribus ecclesiae catholicae
et de moribus Manichaeorum libri duo* (ed. J. B. Bauer; CSEL 90; Vi-
enna: Hölder-Pichler-Tempsky, 1992). – *Polemica con i manichei* (ed.
F. Decret, L. Alici, and A. Pieretti; NBA 13.1; Rome: Città Nuova,
1997), 1–199. – R. Stothert, trans., "On the Morals of the Catholic
Church" and "On the Morals of the Manichaeans," in *NPNF[1]* (Pea-
body, Mass.: Hendrickson, 1995; repr. of 1887 ed.), 4:37–89. – *The
Catholic and Manichaean Ways of Life* (trans. D. A. and I. J. Gallagher;
FC 56; Washington, D.C.: Catholic University of America Press, 1965).
– Studies: J. K. Coyle, *Augustine's "De moribus ecclesiae catholicae": A*

Study of the Work, Its Composition, and Its Source (Par. 25; Fribourg, Switz.: University Press, 1978). – J. K. Coyle et al., "De moribus ecclesiae catholicae et de moribus Manichaeorum"; "De quantitate animae" di Agostino d'Ippona (Lectio Augustini 6; Palermo: Augustinus, 1991), 13–130.

75. mus.     De musica (388–391): PL 32:1081–1194. – Dialogues philosophiques, vol. 4, La musique: De musica libri sex (ed. G. Finaert and F.-J. Thonnard; BAug 7; Paris: Desclée de Brouwer, 1947) . – Dialoghi (ed. D. Gentili and A. Trapé; 2 vols.; NBA 3; Rome: Città Nuova, 1970–1976), 2:379–707. – Musica (ed. M. Bettetini; Milan: Rusconi, 1997) [Com]. – Tr.: M. Bettetini, Mi 1992, 83–269 [Com]. – The Immortality of the Soul; The Magnitude of the Soul; On Music; The Advantage of Believing; On Faith in Things Unseen (trans. L. Schopp, J. J. McMahon, R. C. Taliaferro, L. Meagher, R. J. Defarrari, and M. F. McDonald; FC 4; Washington, D.C.: Catholic University of America Press, 1947), 151–379. – Studies: U. Pizzani and G. Milanese, "De musica" di Agostino d'Ippona (Lectio Augustini 5, Palermo: Augustinus, 1990). – A. Keller, Aurelius Augustinus und die Musik (Cass. 44; Würzburg: Augustinus, 1993).

76. nat. b.     De natura boni (399): Sancti Aureli Augustini De utilitate credendi; De duabus animabus; Contra Fortunatum; Contra Adimantum; Contra epistulam Fundamenti; Contra Faustum (ed. J. Zycha; CSEL 25; Vienna: F. Tempsky, 1892), 855–89. – La morale chrétienne (ed. B. Roland-Gosselin; 2d ed.; BAug 1; Paris: Desclée de Brouwer, 1949), 440–509. – Polemica con i manichei (ed. F. Decret, L. Alici, and A. Pieretti; NBA 13.1; Rome: Città Nuova, 1997), 321–407. – G. Reale, Saggezza antica: Terapia per i mali dell'uomo d'oggi (Milan: R. Cortina, 1995). – A. H. Newman, trans., "Concerning the Nature of Good, against the Manichaeans," in NPNF¹ (Peabody, Mass.: Hendrickson, 1995; repr. of 1887 ed.), 4:347–65. – Earlier Writings (trans. J. H. S. Burleigh; LCC 6; Philadelphia: Westminster, 1953), 324–48.

77. nat. et gr.     De natura et gratia (c. 415): Sancti Aureli Augustini De peccatorum meritis et remissione et de baptismo parvulorum ad Marcellinum libri tres; De spiritv et littera liber vnvs; De natvra et gratia liber vnvs; De natvra et origine animae libri qvattvor; Contra dvas epistvlas Pelagianorvm libri qvattvor (ed. K. F. Urba and J. Zycha; CSEL 60; Vienna: F. Tempsky, 1913), 233–99. – Natura e grazia (ed. A. Trapè, I. Volpi, and F. Monteverde; 2 vols.; NBA 17; Rome: Città Nuova, 1981), 1:365–487. – P. Holmes, R. E. Wallis, and B. B. Warfield, trans., "On Nature and Grace," in NPNF¹ (Peabody, Mass.: Hendrickson, 1995; repr. of 1887 ed.), 5:115–51. – Four Anti-Pelagian Writings (trans. J. A. Mourant and W. J. Collinge; FC 86; Washington, D.C.: Catholic University of America Press, 1992), 1–90. – Answer to the Pelagians I (ed. J. E. Rotelle; introd., trans., and notes R. J. Teske; WSA 1.23; Hyde Park, N.Y.: New City, 1997), 203–75.

78. nupt. et conc.     De nuptiis et concupiscentia ad Valerium (419/20): Sancti Aureli Augustini De perfectione iustitiae hominis; De gestis Pelagii; De gratia Christi et de peccato originali libri dvo; De nvptiis et concvpiscentia ad Valerivm comitem libri dvo (ed. K. F. Urba and J. Zycha; CSEL 42; Vienna:

F. Tempsky, 1902), 211–319. – *Premières polémiques contre Julien: De nuptiis et concupiscentia contra duas epistulas pelagianorum* (ed. C. F. Urba, J. Zycha, F.-J. Thonnard, E. Bleuzen, and A. C. de Veer; BAug 23; Paris: Desclée de Brouwer, 1974), 52–289. – *Matrimonio e verginità* (ed. A. Trapè, M. Palmieri, V. Tarulli, N. Cipriani, and F. Monteverde; NBA 7.1; Rome: Città Nuova, 1978), 383–453. – *Polemica con Giuliano 1: Le nozze e la concupiscenza, Contro le due lettere dei pelagiani, Contro Giuliano* (ed. N. Cipriani, E. Cristini, and I. Volpi; NBA 18; Rome: Città Nuova, 1985), 7–171. – R. Holmes, E. Wallis, and B. B. Warfield, trans., "On Marriage and Concupiscence," in *NPNF¹* (Peabody, Mass.: Hendrickson, 1995; repr. of 1887 ed.), 5:257–308. – *Answer to the Pelagians II* (ed. J. E. Rotelle; introd., trans., and notes R. J. Teske; WSA 1.24; Hyde Park, N.Y.: New City, 1998), 11–96 [*Marriage and Desire*].

79. *op. mon.*   *De opere monachorum* – Cf. ch. 8.I.C.2. – H. Browne, trans., "Of the Work of Monks," in *NPNF¹* (Peabody, Mass.: Hendrickson, 1995; repr. of 1887 ed.), 3:501–24. – *Treatises on Various Subjects* (trans. M. S. Muldowney, M. E. Defarrari, H. B. Jaffee, L. Meagher, and M. F. McDonald; FC 16; New York: Fathers of the Church, 1952), 320–94.

80. *ord.*   *De ordine* (Nov. 386–Mar. 387): *Sancti Aureli Augustini Contra Academicos libri tres; De beata vita liber unus; De ordine libri duo* (ed. P. Knöll; CSEL 63; Vienna: Hölder-Pichler-Tempsky, 1922; repr., New York: Johnson Reprint, 1962), 121–85. – *Contra Academicos; De beata vita; De ordine; De magistro; De libero arbitrio* (ed. W. M. Green and K. D. Daur; CCSL 29; Turnhout, Belg.: Brepols, 1970), 89–137. – *Dialoghi* (ed. D. Gentili and A. Trapé; 2 vols.; NBA 3; Rome: Città Nuova, 1970–1976), 227–359. – *Dialogues philosophiques 2: De ordine, L'ordre* (ed. J. Doignon; BAug 4.2; Paris: Études Augustiniennes, 1997). – *The Happy Life; Answer to Skeptics; Divine Providence and the Problem of Evil; Soliloquies* (trans. L. Schopp, D. J. Kavanagh, R. P. Russell, and T. F. Gilligan; FC 5; New York: Cima, 1948), 227–332. – Studies: V. Pacioni, *L'unità teoretica del De ordine di S. Agostino* (Rome: Millennium Romae, 1996).

81. *orig. an.*   *De origine animae* (= *ep* 166) (415): *S. Avreli Avgvstini Hipponiensis episcopi Epistvlae* (ed. A. Goldbacher; CSEL 44; Vienna: F. Tempsky, 1904), 545–85. – *Le lettere* (ed. L. Carrozzi; NBA 22; Rome: Città Nuova, 1971), 718–55. – *Letters* (trans. W. Parsons; FC 30; Washington, D.C.: Catholic University of America Press, 1955), 6–31.

82. *pat.*   *De patientia* (415): *Sancti Avreli Avgvstini De fide et symbolo; De fide et operibvs; De agone christiano; De continentia; De bono conivgali; De sancta virginitate; De bono vidvitatis; De advlterinis conivgiis lib. II; De mendacio; Contra mendacivm; De opere monachorvm; De divinatione daemonvm; De cvra pro mortvis gerenda; De patientia* (ed. J. Zycha; CSEL 41; Vienna: F. Tempsky, 1900), 663–91. – *Problèmes moraux: De bono conjugali, De conjugiis adulterinis, De mendacio, Contra mendacium, De cura gerenda pro mortuis, De patientia, De utilitate jejunii* (ed. G. Combès; BAug 2; Paris: Desclée de Brouwer, 1948), 530–77. – H. Browne, trans., "On Patience," in *NPNF¹* (Peabody, Mass.: Hendrickson, 1995; repr. of 1887 ed.), 3:525–36. – *Treatises on Various Subjects* (trans. M. S. Muldowney, M. E. Defarrari, H. B. Jaffee, L. Meagher, and

M. F. McDonald; FC 16; New York: Fathers of the Church, 1952), 233–64.

83. *pecc. mer.* *De peccatorum meritis et remissione et de baptismo parvulorum ad Marcellinum* (412): *Sancti Aureli Augustini De peccatorum meritis et remissione et de baptismo parvulorum ad Marcellinum libri tres; De spiritu et littera liber unus; De natura et gratia liber unus; De natura et origine animae libri quattuor* (ed. K. F. Urba and J. Zycha; CSEL 60; Vienna: F. Tempsky, 1913), 3–151. – *Natura e grazia* (ed. A. Trapè, I. Volpi, and F. Monteverde; 2 vols.; NBA 17; Rome: Città Nuova, 1981), 1:1–239. – P. Holmes, R. E. Wallis, and B. B. Warfield, trans., "On the Merits and Remission of Sins, and on the Baptism of Infants," in *NPNF¹* (Peabody, Mass.: Hendrickson, 1995; repr. of 1887 ed.), 5:11–78. – *Answer to the Pelagians I* (ed. J. E. Rotelle; introd., trans., and notes R. J. Teske; WSA 1.23; Hyde Park, N.Y.: New City, 1998), 17–137 [*The Punishment and Forgiveness of Sins and the Baptism of Little Ones*]. – Studies: B. Delaroche, *Saint Augustin lecteur et interprète de saint Paul dans le De peccatorum meritis et remissione (hiver 411–412)* (Paris: Études Augustiniennes, 1996).

84. *perf. iust.* *De perfectione iustitiae hominis* (c. 415): *Sancti Aureli Augustini De perfectione iustitiae hominis; De gestis Pelagii; De gratia Christi et de peccato originali libri dvo; De nvptiis et concvpiscentia ad Valerivm comitem libri dvo* (ed. K. F. Urba and J. Zycha; CSEL 42; Vienna: F. Tempsky, 1902), 3–48. – *Natura e grazia* (ed. A. Trapè, I. Volpi, and F. Monteverde; 2 vols.; NBA 17; Rome: Città Nuova, 1981), 1:489–563. – P. Holmes, R. E. Wallis, and B. B. Warfield, trans., "On Man's Perfection in Righteousness," in *NPNF¹* (Peabody, Mass.: Hendrickson, 1995; repr. of 1887 ed.), 5:153–76. – *Answer to the Pelagians I* (ed. J. E. Rotelle; introd., trans., and notes R. J. Teske; WSA 1.23; Hyde Park, N.Y.: New City, 1997), 277–316 [*The Perfection of Human Righteousness*].

85. *perseu.* *De dono perseverantiae:* PL 45:993–1034. – *Aux moines d'Adrumète et de Provence* (ed. J. Chéné and J. Pintard; BAug 24; Paris: Desclée de Brouwer, 1962), 600–765. – *Grazia e libertà* (ed. A. Trapè, M. Palmieri, F. Monteverde; NBA 20; Rome: Città Nuova, 1987), 299–401. – *De dono perseverantiae* (trans. M. A. Lesousky; PatSt 91; Washington, D.C.: Catholic University of America Press, 1956). – P. Holmes, R. E. Wallis, and B. B. Warfield, trans., "On the Gift of Perseverance," in *NPNF¹* (Peabody, Mass.: Hendrickson, 1995; repr. of 1887 ed.), 5:521–52. – *Four Anti-Pelagian Writings* (trans. J. A. Mourant and W. J. Collinge; FC 86; Washington, D.C.: Catholic University of America Press, 1992), 271–337. – *Answer to the Pelagians IV* (ed. J. E. Rotelle; introd., trans., and notes R. J. Teske; WSA 1.26; New York: New City, 1999), 189–240 [*The Gift of Perseverence*].

86. *praed. sanct.* *De praedestinatione sanctorum ad Prosperum et Hilarium* (after 427): PL 44:959–92. – *Aux moines d'Adrumète et de Provence* (ed. J. Chéné and J. Pintard; BAug 24; Paris: Desclée de Brouwer, 1962), 464–597. – *Grazia e libertà* (ed. A. Trapè, M. Palmieri, F. Monteverde; NBA 20; Rome: Città Nuova, 1987), 191–297. – P. Holmes, R. E. Wallis, and B. B. Warfield, trans., "On the Predestination of the Saints," in *NPNF¹* (Peabody, Mass.: Hendrickson, 1995; repr. of 1887 ed.), 5:493–519. – *Four*

*Anti-Pelagian Writings* (trans. J. A. Mourant and W. J. Collinge; FC 86; Washington, D.C.: Catholic University of America Press, 1992), 179–270. – *Answer to the Pelagians IV* (ed. J. E. Rotelle; introd., trans., and notes R. J. Teske; WSA 1.26; New York: New City, 1999), 147–87 [*The Predestination of the Saints*].

87. *praes. dei*  *De praesentia Dei ad Dardanum* (= *ep* 187) (417): *S. Avreli Avgvstini Hipponiensis episcopi Epistvlae* (ed. A. Goldbacher; CSEL 57; Vienna: F. Tempsky, 1911), 81–119. – *Le lettere* (ed. L. Carrozzi; NBA 23; Rome: Città Nuova, 1974), 130–75. *Letters* (trans. W. Parsons; FC 30; Washington, D.C.: Catholic University of America Press, 1955), 221–55. – *Augustine of Hippo: Selected Writings* (trans. M. T. Clark; CWS; London: SPCK; New York: Paulist, 1984), 403–25.

88. *c. Prisc.*  *Contra Priscillianistas* (415): *Sancti Aurelii Augustini Contra adversarium legis et prophetarum; Commonitorium Orosii et Sancti Aurelii Augustini Contra Priscillianistas et Origenistas* (ed. K.-D. Daur; CCSL 49; Turnhout, Belg.: Brepols, 1985), 165–78. – *Arianism and Other Heresies: Heresies, Memorandum to Augustine, To Orosius in Refutation of the Priscillianists and Origenists, Arian Sermon, Answer to an Arian Sermon, Debate with Maximinus, Answer to Maximinus, Answer to an Enemy of the Law and the Prophets* (trans. R. J. Teske; WSA 1.18; Hyde Park, N.Y.: New City, 1995), 79–115.

89. *ps. c. Don.*  *Psalmus contra partem Donati* (c. 394): *Sancti Aureli Augustini Scripta contra Donatistas* (ed. M. Petschenig; CSEL 51; Vienna: F. Tempsky, 1908), 3–15. – *Psalmus contra partem Donati* (ed. R. Anastasi; Padua: CEDAM, 1957) [Com]. – *Traités anti-donatistes I: Psalmus contra partem Donati, Contra epistulam Parmeniani libri tres, Epistula ad Catholicos de secta Donatistarum* (ed. M. Petschenig, G. Finaert, R. Anastasi, and Y. M.-J. Congar; BAug 28; Paris: Desclée de Brouwer, 1963), 150–91.

90. *qu.*  *Quaestiones in Heptateuchum: Sancti Aureli Augustini Quaestionum in Heptateuchum libri VII; Adnotationvm in Job liber vnvs* (ed. J. Zycha; CSEL 28.2; Vienna: F. Tempsky, 1895), 3–506. – *Sancti Aurelii Augustini Quaestionum in Heptateuchum libri VII; Locutionum in Heptateuchum libri VII; De octo quaestionibus ex veteri testamento* (ed. I. Fraipont and D. de Bruyne; CCSL 33; Turnhout, Belg.: Brepols, 1958), 1–377.

91. *qu. eu.*  *Quaestiones evangeliorum* (c. 400): *Sancti Aurelii Augustini De diversis quaestionibus ad Simplicianum* (A. Mutzenbecher; CCSL 44 B; Turnhout, Belg.: Brepols, 1980), 1–118. – *Opere esegetiche* (ed. S. Caruana, B. Fenati, M. Mendoza, D. Gentili, V. Tarulli, and F. Monteverde; NBA 10.2; Rome: Città Nuova, 1997), 287–417.

92. *qu. Mt.*  *Quaestiones XVI in Matthaeum: Sancti Aurelii Augustini De diversis quaestionibus ad Simplicianum* (A. Mutzenbecher; CCSL 44 B; Turnhout, Belg.: Brepols, 1980), 119–40. – *Opere esegetiche* (ed. S. Caruana, B. Fenati, M. Mendoza, D. Gentili, V. Tarulli, and F. Monteverde; NBA 10.2; Rome: Città Nuova, 1997), 419–57.

93. *qu. c. pag.*  *Quaestiones expositae contra paganos* (= *ep* 102) (406–412): *S. Avreli Avgvstini Hipponiensis episcopi Epistvlae* (ed. A. Goldbacher; CSEL 34.2; Vienna: F. Tempsky, 1898), 544–78. – *Le lettere* (ed. L. Carrozzi;

NBA 21; Rome: Città Nuova, 1969), 950–93. – *Letters* (trans. W. Parsons; FC 18; Washington, D.C.: Catholic University of America Press, 1953), 148–77.

94. *qu. uet. t.*   *De octo quaestionibus ex veteri testamento: Sancti Aurelii Augustini Quaestionum in Heptateuchum libri VII; Locutionum in Heptateuchum libri VII; De octo quaestionibus ex veteri testamento* (ed. I. Fraipont and D. de Bruyne; CCSL 33; Turnhout, Belg.: Brepols, 1958), 469–72.

95. *reg.*   *Regula* – Cf. ch. 8.I.C.1. – *Augustine of Hippo: Selected Writings* (trans. M. T. Clark; CWS; London: SPCK; New York: Paulist, 1984), 479–93. – G. Lawless, *Augustine of Hippo and His Monastic Rule* (Oxford: Clarendon; New York: Oxford University Press, 1987).

96. *retr.*   *Retractationes* (426/7): *Sancti Aureli Augustini Retractationum libri dvo* (ed. P. Knöll; CSEL 36; Vienna: F. Tempsky, 1902). – *Les Révisions* (ed. G. Bardy; BAug 12; Paris: Desclée de Brouwer, 1950). – *Sancti Aurelii Augustini Retractationum libri II* (ed. A. Mutzenbecher; CCSL 57; Turnhout, Belg.: Brepols, 1984). – *Le Ritrattazioni* (ed. G. Madec and U. Pizzani; NBA 2; Rome: Città Nuova, 1994). – *The Retractions* (trans. M. I. Bogan; FC 60; Washington, D.C.: Catholic University of America Press, 1968).

97. *rhet.*   *De rhetorica:* C. Halm, *Rhetores latini minores* (Leipzig: Teubner, 1863; repr., Frankfurt: Minerva, 1964), 137–51.

98. *c. Sec.*   *Contra Secundinum Manichaeum* (399): *Sancti Aureli Augustini De utilitate credendi; De duabus animabus; Contra Fortunatum; Contra Adimantum; Contra epistulam Fundamenti; Contra Faustum* (ed. J. Zycha; CSEL 25; Vienna: F. Tempsky, 1892), 905–47. – *Six traités anti-manichéens: De duabus animabus, Contra Fortunatum, Contra Adimantum, Contra epistulam Fundamenti, Contra Secundinum, Contra Felicem Manichaeum* (ed. R. Jolivet and M. Jourjon; BAug 17; Paris: Desclée de Brouwer, 1961), 538–633.

99. *sent. Jac.*   *De sententia Jacobi* (= *ep* 167) (415) *S. Avreli Avgvstini Hipponiensis episcopi Epistvlae* (ed. A. Goldbacher; CSEL 44; Vienna: F. Tempsky, 1904), 586–609. – *Le lettere* (ed. L. Carrozzi; NBA 22; Rome: Città Nuova, 1971), 756–81. – *Letters* (trans. W. Parsons; FC 30; Washington, D.C.: Catholic University of America Press, 1955), 32–49.

100. *s.*   *Sermones:* Bibliographies: H. R. Drobner, *Augustinus von Hippo, Sermones ad populum—Überlieferung und Bestand–Bibliographie–Indices* (SVigChr 49; Leiden and Boston: Brill, 2000). – *Discorsi* (ed. M. Pellegrino, P. Bellini, F. Cruciani, V. Tarulli, F. Monteverde, L. Carrozzi, M. Recchia, A. Quacquarelli, V. Paronetto, and A. M. Quartiroli; 6 vols. in 9; NBA 29–34; Rome: Città Nuova, 1979–1990). – PL 38:332–1484. – PL 39:1493–1638, 1650–52, 1655–59, 1663–69, 1671–84, 1695–97, 1701–6, 1710–36. – PLS 2:417–840. – *Sancti Aurelii Augustini Sermones selecti duodeviginti* (ed. C. Lambot; StPM 4; Utrecht: Spectrum, 1950) *[14, 15, 34, 60, 101, 104, 166, 177, 184, 221, 254, 261, 298, 302, 339, 355, 356, 358].* – *Sancti Aurelii Augustini Sermones de Vetere Testamento, id est Sermones I–L secundum ordinem Vulgatum insertis etiam novem sermonibus post Maurinos repertis* (ed. C. Lambot; CCSL 41; Turnhout, Belg.: Brepols, 1961) *[1–50].* – *Sermons pour la Pâque* (ed. S. Poque; SC 116; Paris: Cerf, 1966) *[59, 121, 211, 212, 227, 231,*

*232, 237, 246, 250, 253, 257, 258]. – Fructus centesimus: Mélanges offerts à Gerard J.M. Bartelink à l'occasion de son soixante-cinquième anniversaire* (ed. A. A. R. Bastiaensen, A. Hilhorst, C. H. Kneepkens, and R. Demeulenaere; IP 19; Steenbrugge, Belg.: Abbatia Sancti Petri, 1989), 105–13 *[283]. – Aevum inter utrumque: Mélanges offerts à Gabriel Sanders* (ed. G. Sanders, M. Van Uytfanghe, and R. Demeulenaere; IP 23; Steenbrugge, Belg.: Abbatia Sancti Petri, 1991), 67–73 *[84]. – Eulogia: Mélanges offerts à Antoon A. R. Bastiaensen à l'occasion de son soixante-cinquième anniversaire* (ed. G. J. M. Bartelink, A. Hilhorst, C. H. Kneepkens, and R. Demeulenaere; IP 24; Steenbrugge, Belg.: Abbatia Sancti Petri, 1991): 51–63 *[76].* – L. De Coninck, B. Coppieters, and R. Demeulenaere, "Saint Augustin peut-il-être l'auteur des sermons *De puero centurionis* et *De filia archisynagogi?" SacEr* 38 (1998–1999): 221–44 [with a critical edition]. – *Sermons on Selected Lessons of the New Testament* (trans. R. G. MacMullen; 2 vols.; A Library of Fathers of the Holy Catholic Church 16, 20; Oxford: J. H. Parker, 1844–1845) [*s* 51–183]. – R. G. MacMullen and P. Schaff, trans., "Sermons on Selected Lessons of the New Testament," in *NPNF¹* (Peabody, Mass.: Hendrickson, 1995; repr. of 1888 ed.), 6:237–545 [*s* 51–147]. – *Commentary on the Lord's Sermon on the Mount with Seventeen Related Sermons* (trans. D. J. Kavanagh; FC 11; New York: Fathers of the Church, 1951), 209–371 [*s* 53, 53A (= Morin 11), 54, 55, 56, 60 (= Lambot 19), 61, 72, 94, 109, 229 (= Denis 6), 260A (= Denis 8), 305A (= Denis 13), 346, 375A (= Denis 4), 375B (= Denis 5)]. – *Sermons for Christmas and Epiphany* (trans. T. C. Lawler; ACW 15; Westminster, Md.: Newman, 1952), [*s* 51, 140, 184–204 (189 = Frangipane 4)]. – *Patristic Homilies on the Gospels: The Sunday Sermons of the Great Fathers* (trans. M. F. Toal; 4 vols.; London: Longmans, Green & Co., 1957–1963; new ed., San Francisco: Ignatius Press, 2000) [*s* 52, 53A (= Morin 1), 63, 63B (= Morin 7), 73, 78, 82, 63A (= Mai 25), 90, 91, 95, 98, 112, 115, 116, 121, 113B (= Mai 13), 132, 137, 144, 219, 222, 224, 223A (= Denis 2), 227, 259, 262, 264, 267, 268, 270, 295, 349, 361, 362, 341A (= Mai 22)]. – *Sermons on the Liturgical Seasons* (trans. M. S. Muldowney; FC 38; Washington, D.C.: Catholic University of America Press in association with Consortium Books, 1959; repr., 1977) [*s* 184–265]. – *Selected Easter Sermons of Saint Augustine* (trans. P. T. Weller; St. Louis: Herder, 1959) [*s* 56, 116, 138, 146, 212, 215, 219, 221 (= *Guelferbytanus* 5), 223, 223A (= Denis 2), 223B (= *Guelferbytanus* 4), 227, 228B (= Denis 3), 229, 229A (= *Guelferbytanus* 7), 229C (= Wilmart 8), 229E (= *Guelferbytanus* 9), 229K (= *Guelferbytanus* 13), 229M (= *Guelferbytanus* 15), 229N (= *Guelferbytanus* 16), 231, 255, 260A (= Denis 8), 260B (= Mai 89), 353, 375A (= Denis 4)]. – *Selected Sermons of St. Augustine* (trans. Q. Howe; New York: Holt, Rinehart & Winston, 1966; London: Golancz, 1967) [*s* 1, 10, 22, 34, 43, 68 (= Mai 126), 73, 81, 150, 161, 183, 184, 194, 201, 213 (= *Guelferbytanus* 1), 224, 241, 273, 274, 300, 340, 348, 349, 355, 360, 364, 374, 375C (= Mai 95), 385, 392]. – *Sermons* (trans. E. Hill; 11 vols.; WSA 3.1–11; Hyde Park, N.Y.: New City, 1990–1997).

| | |
|---|---|
| *s. Caillau* | *Sermones A. B. Caillau et B. Saint-Yves: Sancti Augustini sermones post Maurinos reperti: Probatae dumtaxat auctoritatis nunc primum disquisiti in unum collecti et codicum fide instaurati* (ed. G. Morin; MAg 1; Tipografia Poliglotta Vaticana, 1930), 243–74. – PLS 2:417–43. |
| *s. Casin.* | *Sermones Casinenses: Sancti Augustini sermones post Maurinos reperti: Probatae dumtaxat auctoritatis nunc primum disquisiti in unum collecti et codicum fide instaurati* (ed. G. Morin; MAg 1; Tipografia Poliglotta Vaticana, 1930), 401–19. – PLS 2:531–5. |
| *s. Denis* | *Sermones M. Denis: Sancti Augustini sermones post Maurinos reperti: Probatae dumtaxat auctoritatis nunc primum disquisiti in unum collecti et codicum fide instaurati* (ed. G. Morin; MAg 1; Tipografia Poliglotta Vaticana, 1930), 11–164. |
| *s. Dolbeau* | *Sermones Dolbeau (Moguntini): REAug* 35 (1989): 432. – *REAug* 40 (1994): 290–98. – *REAug* 41 (1995): 281–88. – *RechAug* 28 (1995): 53–65. – F. Dolbeau, *Vingt-six sermons au peuple d'Afrique* (Paris: Études Augustiniennes, 1996) [*s Moguntini*]. – *Newly Discovered Sermons* (trans. E. Hill; WSA 3.11; Hyde Park, N.Y.: New City, 1997). – Studies: B. Löfstedt, "Textkritisches und Sprachliches zu den neugefundenen Augustinpredigten," *SacEr* 38 (1998–1999): 281–87. – H. Chadwick, "The New Sermons of St. Augustine," *JTS* NS 47 (1996): 69–91. |
| *s. Étaix* | *Sermones Étaix: RBén* 86 (1976): 38–48. – *REAug* 26 (1980): 62–87. – *RBén* 98 (1988): 7–17. – *REAug* 39 (1993): 359–70. |
| *s. Frangip.* | *Sermones O. F. Frangipane: Sancti Augustini sermones post Maurinos reperti* (ed. G. Morin; MAg 1; Rome: Tipografia Poliglotta Vaticana, 1930), 169–237. |
| *s. Fransen* | *Sermo I. Fransen: RBén* 84 (1974): 252. |
| *s. frg.* | *Sermonum fragmenta:* Editions: PL 39:1719–23. – PL 110, 107. – C. Lambot, *RBén* 51 (1939): 3–30. |
| *s. frg. Lambot* | *Sermonum Lambot fragmenta: RBén* 79 (1969): 206–14. |
| *s. frg. Verbr* | *Sermonum Verbraken fragmenta: RBén* 84 (1974): 245–70. |
| *s. Guelf.* | *Sermones G. Morin Guelferbytani: Sancti Augustini sermones post Maurinos reperti* (ed. G. Morin; MAg 1; Rome: Tipografia Poliglotta Vaticana, 1930), 441–585. – PLS 536–657. |
| *s. Haffner* | *Sermones Haffner: RBén* 77 (1967): 326–28. |
| *s. Lambot* | *Sermones Lambot:* PLS 2:744–834, 839s. – *RBén* 59 (1949): 55–81. |
| *s. Liver.* | *Sermones F. Liveriani: Sancti Augustini sermones post Maurinos reperti* (ed. G. Morin; MAg 1; Rome: Tipografia Poliglotta Vaticana, 1930), 391–95. – PLS 2:528–31. |
| *s. Mai* | *Sermones A. Mai: Sancti Augustini sermones post Maurinos reperti* (ed. G. Morin; MAg 1; Rome: Tipografia Poliglotta Vaticana, 1930), 285–386. – PLS 2:443–528. |
| *s. Mogunt.* | *Sermones Moguntini:* cf. *s. Dolbeau.* |
| *s. Morin* | *Sermones G. Morin: Sancti Augustini sermones post Maurinos reperti* (ed. G. Morin; MAg 1; Rome: Tipografia Poliglotta Vaticana, 1930), 589–613, 624–664. – PLS 2:657–708. |
| *s. Wilm.* | *Sermones A. Wilmart: Sancti Augustini sermones post Maurinos reperti* (ed. G. Morin; MAg 1; Rome: Tipografia Poliglotta Vaticana, 1930), 673–719. – PLS 2:708–43, 834–39. – A. Wilmart, *RBén* 44 (1932): 201–6 *[317]*. |

101. *c. s. Arrian.*    *Contra sermonem Arrianorum* (418): PL 42:683–708. *Arianism and Other Heresies: Heresies, Memorandum to Augustine, To Orosius in Refutation of the Priscillianists and Origenists, Arian Sermon, Answer to an Arian Sermon, Debate with Maximinus, Answer to Maximinus, Answer to an Enemy of the Law and the Prophets* (trans. R. J. Teske; WSA 1.18; Hyde Park, New York: New City, 1995), 117–71.

102. *s. Caes. eccl.*    *Sermo ad Caesariensis ecclesiae plebem* (Sept. 20, 418): *Sancti Aureli Augustini Scripta contra Donatistas* (ed. Petschenig; CSEL 53; Vienna: F. Tempsky, 1910), 167–78. – *Traités anti-donatistes V: Breviculus collationis cum Donatistis, Ad Donatistas post collationen, Sermo ad Caesariensis ecclesiae plebem, Gesta cum Emerito Donatistarum episcopo, Contra Gaudentium Donatistarum episcopum libri duo* (ed. M. Petschenig, G. Finaert, and E. Lamirande; BAug 32; Paris: Desclée de Brouwer, 1965), 416–45.

103. *s. dom. m.*    *De sermone Domini in monte: Sancti Aurelii Augustini De sermone Domini in monte libros suos* (ed. A. Mutzenbecher; CCSL 35; Turnhout, Belg.: Brepols, 1967). – *Opere esegetiche* (ed. S. Caruana, B. Fenati, M. Mendoza, D. Gentili, V. Tarulli, and F. Monteverde; NBA 10.2; Rome: Città Nuova, 1997), 79–285. – W. Findlay and D. S. Schaff, trans., "Our Lord's Sermon on the Mount," in *NPNF¹* (Peabody, Mass.: Hendrickson, 1995; repr. of 1888 ed.), 6:1–63. – *The Lord's Sermon on the Mount* (trans. J. J. Jepson; ACW 5; Westminster, Md.: Newman, 1948; repr., 1956). – *Commentary on the Lord's Sermon on the Mount: With Seventeen Related Sermons* (trans. D. J. Kavanagh; FC 11; New York: Fathers of the Church, 1951; repr., Washington, D.C.: Catholic University of America Press in association with Consortium Books, 1977), 17–208. – Studies: A. Holl, *Augustins Bergpredigtexegese nach seinem Frühwerk De sermone Domini in monte* (Vienna: Herder, 1960).

104. *Simpl.*    *Ad Simplicianum* (Apr. 4, 397): *Mélanges doctrinaux: Quaestiones 83, Quaestiones 7 ad Simplicianum, Quaestiones 8 Dulcitii, De divinatione daemonum* (ed. G. Bardy, J.-A. Beckaert, and J. Boutet; BAug 10; Desclée de Brouwer, 1952), 410–579. – *Sancti Aurelii Augustini De diversis quaestionibus ad Simplicianum* (A. Mutzenbecher; CCSL 44; Turnhout, Belg.: Brepols, 1970). – *La vera religione* (ed. G. Ceriotti, L. Alici, A. Pieretti, and F. Monteverde; NBA 6.2; Rome: Città Nuova, 1995), 263–389. – *Earlier Writings* (trans. J. H. S. Burleigh; LCC 6; Philadelphia: Westminster, 1953), 370–406. – Studies: *"De diversis quaestionibus octoginta tribus"; "De diversis quaestionibus ad Simplicianum" di Agostino d'Ippona* (ed. L. Perrone; Lectio Augustini 12; Palermo: Città Nuova, 1996).

105. *sol.*    *Soliloquia* (Nov. 386–Mar. 387): *Soliloquiorum libri duo; De inmortalitate animae; De quantitate animae* (ed. W. Hörmann; CSEL 89; Vienna: Hölder-Pichler-Tempsky, 1986), 3–98. – *Dialogues philosophiques*, vol. 2, *Dieu et l'ame, Soliloques, De immortalitate animae, De quantitate animae* (ed. P. de Labriolle; BAug 5; Paris: Desclée de Brouwer, 1939), 24–163. – *Dialoghi* (ed. D. Gentili and A. Trapé; 2 vols.; NBA 3; Rome: Città Nuova, 1970–1976), 361–487. – *Soliloqui* (ed. A. Marzullo; Milan: Ceschina, 1972). – C. C. Starbuck, trans., "So-

liloquies," in *NPNF<sup>1</sup>* (Peabody, Mass.: Hendrickson, 1995; repr. of 1888 ed.), 7:531–60. – *The Happy Life; Answer to Skeptics; Divine Providence and the Problem of Evil; Soliloquies* (trans. L. Schopp, D. J. Kavanagh, R. P. Russell, and T. F. Gilligan; FC 5; New York: Cima, 1948), 333–426. – *Earlier Writings* (trans. J. H. S. Burleigh; LCC 6; Philadelphia: Westminster, 1953), 19–63.

106. *spec.*    *Speculum* (c. 427): *S. Avreli Avgvstini Hipponensis episcopi Liber qvi appellatvr Specvlvm et Liber de divinis scriptvris sive Specvlvm qvod fertvr S. Avgvstini* (ed. F. Weihrich; CSEL 12; Vienna: Geroldi, 1887), 3–285.

107. *spir. et litt.*    *De spiritu et littera ad Marcellinum* (412): *Sancti Aureli Augustini De peccatorum meritis et remissione et de baptismo parvulorum ad Marcellinum libri tres; De spiritv et littera liber vnvs; De natvra et gratia liber vnvs; De natvra et origine animae libri qvattvor; Contra dvas epistvlas Pelagianorvm libri qvattvor* (ed. K. F. Urba and J. Zycha; CSEL 60; Vienna: F. Tempsky, 1913), 155–229. – *Natura e grazia* (ed. A. Trapè, I. Volpi, and F. Monteverde; 2 vols.; NBA 17; Rome: Città Nuova, 1981), 1:241–363. – P. Holmes, R. E. Wallis, and B. B. Warfield, trans., "On the Spirit and the Letter," in *NPNF<sup>1</sup>* (Peabody, Mass.: Hendrickson, 1995; repr. of 1887 ed.), 5:79–114. – *Augustine: Later Works* (trans. J. Burnaby; LCC 8; London: SCM; Philadelphia: Westminster, 1955), 182–250. – *Answer to the Pelagians I* (ed. J. E. Rotelle; introd., trans., and notes R. J. Teske; WSA 1.23; Hyde Park, N.Y.: New City, 1997), 139–202 [*The Spirit and the Letter*]. – Studies: D. Marafioti, *L'uomo tra legge e grazia: Analisi teologica del De spiritu et littera di S. Agostino* (Brescia: Morcelliana, 1983).

108. *symb. cat.*    *De symbolo ad catechumenos: Sancti Aurelii Augustini De fide rerum invisibilium; Enchiridion ad Laurentium, de fide et spe et caritate; De catechizandis rudibus; Sermo ad catechumenos de symbolo; Sermo de disciplina christiana; Sermo de utilitate ieiunii; Sermo de excidio urbis Romae; De haeresibus* (ed. R. Vander Plaetse; CCSL 46; Turnhout, Belg.: Brepols, 1969), 185–99. – C. L. Cornish, trans., "On the Creed: A Sermon to Catechumens," in *NPNF<sup>1</sup>* (Peabody, Mass.: Hendrickson, 1995; repr. of 1887 ed.), 3:367–75. – *Treatises on Marriage and Other Subjects* (trans. C. T. Wilcox, M. Liguori, C. T. Huegelmeyer, J. A. Lacy, R. W. Brown, R. P. Russell, and J. McQuade; FC 27; New York: Fathers of the Church, 1955; repr., Washington, D.C.: Catholic University of America Press, 1969), 283–307. – *Sermons* (trans. E. Hill; WSA 3.10; Hyde Park, N.Y.: New City, 1994), 445–57.

109. *trin.*    *De Trinitate* (399–420): *Sancti Aurelii Augustini De Trinitate libri XV* (ed. W. J. Mountain and F. Glorie; 2 vols.; CCSL 50–50 A; Turnhout, Belg.: Brepols, 1968). – *La Trinità* (ed. A. Trapè, M. F. Sciacca, and G. Beschin; NBA 4; Rome: Città Nuova, 1973). – A. West Haddan and W. G. T. Shedd, trans., "On the Holy Trinity," in *NPNF<sup>1</sup>* (Peabody, Mass.: Hendrickson, 1995; repr. 1887 ed.), 3:1–228. – *The Trinity* (trans. S. McKenna; FC 45; Washington, D.C.: Catholic University of America Press, 1963). – *The Trinity* (trans. E. Hill; WSA 1.5; Brooklyn, N.Y.: New City, 1991).

110. *uera rel.*    *De vera religione* (390): *De vera religione liber unus* (ed. W. M. Green; CSEL 77.2; Vienna: Hölder-Pichler-Tempsky, 1961). – *Sancti Aurelii Augustini De doctrina christiana* (ed. K. D. Daur and J. Martin; CCSL 32; Turnhout, Belg.: Brepols, 1962), 187–260. – *La foi chrétienne* (ed. J. Pegon and G. Madec; BAug 8; Paris: Desclée de Brouwer, 1982), 22–191. – *La vera religione* (ed. A. Pieretti; NBA 6.1; Rome: Città Nuova, 1995), 15–157. – *Earlier Writings* (trans. J. H. S. Burleigh; LCC 6; Philadelphia: Westminster, 1953), 218–83. – Studies: *"De utilitate credendi"; "De vera religione"; "De fide rerum quae non videntur" di Agostino d'Ippona* (ed. O. Grassi et al.; Lectio Augustini 10; Rome: Città Nuova, 1994), 31–92.

111. *uers. mens.*    *Versus in mensa: Carmina in codicibus scripta 2: Reliquiorum librorum carmina* (ed. A. Riese, 2d ed.; Anthologia latina 1.2; Leipzig: Teubner, 1906; repr., Amsterdam: Hakkert, 1964), 40.

112. *uers. Nab.*    *Versus de s. Nabore: Carmina in codicibus scripta 2: Reliquiorum librorum carmina* (ed. A. Riese, 2d ed.; Anthologia latina 1.2; Leipzig: Teubner, 1906; repr., Amsterdam: Hakkert, 1964), 8 = PLS 2:356–.

113. *uid. deo*    *De videndo Deo* (= *ep* 147) (413): *S. Avreli Avgvstini Hipponiensis episcopi Epistvlae* (ed. A. Goldbacher; CSEL 44; Vienna: F. Tempsky, 1904), 274–331. – *Le lettere* (ed. L. Carrozzi; NBA 22; Rome: Città Nuova, 1971), 366–433. – *Letters* (trans. W. Parsons; FC 20; New York: Fathers of the Church, 1953), 170–224. – *Augustine of Hippo: Selected Writings* (trans. M. T. Clark; CWS; London: SPCK, 1984), 361–402.

114. *uirg.*    *De sancta virginitate (c. 401): Sancti Avreli Avgvstini De fide et symbolo; De fide et operibvs; De agone christiano; De continentia; De bono conivgali; De sancta virginitate; De bono vidvitatis; De advlterinis conivgiis lib. II; De mendacio; Contra mendacivm; De opere monachorvm; De divinatione daemonvm; De cvra pro mortvis gerenda; De patientia* (ed. J. Zycha; CSEL 41; Vienna: Tempsky, 1900), 235–302. – *L'ascétisme chrétien: De continentia, De sancta virginitate, De bono viduitatis, De opere monachorum* (ed. J. Saint-Martin; 2d ed.; BAug 3; Paris: Desclée de Brouwer, 1949), 110–227. – *Matrimonio e verginità* (ed. A. Trapè, M. Palmieri, V. Tarulli, N. Cipriani, and F. Monteverde; NBA 7.1; Rome: Città Nuova, 1978), 65–159. – C. L. Cornish, trans., "Of Holy Virginity," in *NPNF¹* (Peabody, Mass.: Hendrickson, 1995; repr. of 1887 ed.), 3:415–38. – *Treatises on Marriage and Other Subjects* (trans. C. T. Wilcox, M. Liguori, C. T. Huegelmeyer, J. A. Lacy, R. W. Brown, R. P. Russell, and J. McQuade; FC 27; New York: Fathers of the Church, 1955; repr., Washington, D.C.: Catholic University of America Press, 1969), 133–212. – *Marriage and Virginity: The Excellence of Marriage, Holy Virginity, The Excellence of Widowhood, Adulterous Marriages, Continence* (trans. R. Kearney and D. G. Hunter; WSA 1.9; Hyde Park, N.Y.: New City, 1999), 63–107.

115. *un. bapt.*    *De unico baptismo contra Petilianum ad Constantinum* (c. 411): *Sancti Aureli Augustini Scripta contra Donatistas* (ed. E. M. Petschenig; CSEL 53; Vienna: F. Tempsky, 1910), 3–34. – *Traités anti-donatistes IV: Contra Cresconium libri 4, De unico baptismo* (ed. M. Petschenig, G. Finaert, and A. C. de Veer; BAug 31; Paris: Desclée de Brouwer, 1968), 664–737.

116. *util. cred.*   *De utilitate credendi* (391): *Sancti Aureli Augustini De utilitate cre-dendi; De duabus animabus; Contra Fortunatum; Contra Adimantum; Contra epistulam Fundamenti; Contra Faustum* (ed. J. Zycha; CSEL 25; Vienna: F. Tempsky, 1891), 3–48. – *La foi chrétienne* (ed. J. Pegon and G. Madec; BAug 8; Paris: Desclée de Brouwer, 1982), 208–301. – *De utilitate credendi ad Honoratum* (ed. A. Hoffmann; FChr 9; Fribourg, Switz.: Herder, 1992) [Com]. – *La vera religione* (ed. A. Pieretti; NBA 6.1; Rome: Città Nuova, 1995), 159–241. – C. L. Cornish, trans., "On the Profit of Believing," in *NPNF¹* (Peabody, Mass.: Hendrickson, 1995; repr. of 1887 ed.), 3:345–66. – *The Immortality of the Soul; The Magnitude of the Soul; On Music; The Advantage of Believing; On Faith in Things Unseen* (trans. L. Schopp, J. J. McMahon, R. C. Taliaferro, L. Meagher, R. J. Defarrari, and M. F. McDonald; FC 4; Washington, D.C.: Catholic University of America Press, 1947), 381–442. – *Earlier Writings* (trans. J. H. S. Burleigh; LCC 6; Philadelphia: Westminster, 1953), 284–323. – Studies: *"De utilitate credendi"; "De vera religione"; "De fide rerum quae non videntur" di Agostino d'Ippona* (ed. O. Grassi et al.; Lectio Augustini 10; Rome: Città Nuova, 1994), 9–30. – A. Hoffmann, *Augustins Schrift "De utilitate credendi": Eine Analyse* (MBTh 58; Münster: Aschendorff, 1997).

117. *util. ieiun.*   *De utilitate ieiunii: Problèmes moraux: De bono conjugali, De conjugiis adulterinis, De mendacio, Contra mendacium, De cura gerenda pro mortuis, De patientia, De utilitate jejunii* (ed. G. Combès; BAug 2; Paris: Desclée de Brouwer, 1948), 584–617. – *Sancti Aurelii Augustini De fide rerum invisibilium; Enchiridion ad Laurentium, de fide et spe et caritate; De catechizandis rudibus; Sermo ad catechumenos de symbolo; Sermo de disciplina christiana; Sermo de utilitate ieiunii; Sermo de excidio urbis Romae; De haeresibus* (ed. S. D. Ruegg; CCSL 46; Turn-hout, Belg.: Brepols, 1969), 231–41. – *De utilitate ieiunii* (trans. S. D. Ruegg; PatSt 85; Washington, D.C.: Catholic University of America Press, 1951) [ET/Com]. – *Treatises on Various Subjects* (trans. M. S. Muldowney, M. E. Defarrari, H. B. Jaffee, L. Meagher, and M. F. Mc-Donald; FC 16; New York: Fathers of the Church, 1952), 395–422. – *Sermons* (trans. E. Hill; WSA 3.10; Hyde Park, N.Y.: New City, 1994), 471–83.

Part Four

# Literature of the Transition from Late Antiquity to the Early Middle Ages (ca. 430 to the Mid-Eighth Century)

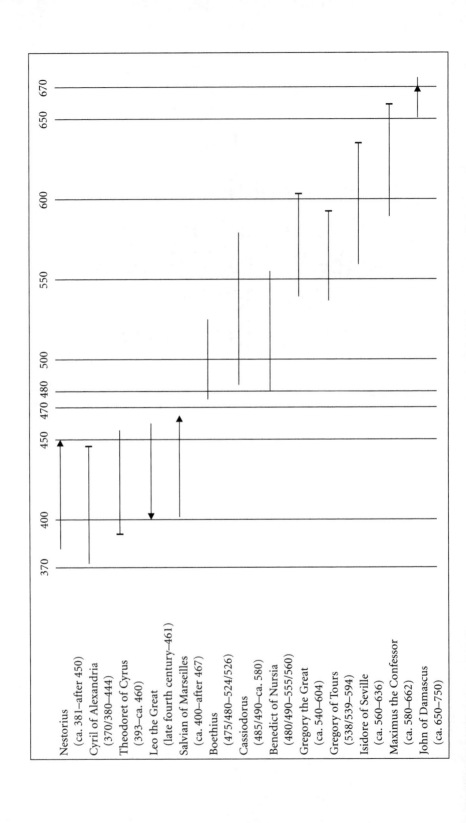

# Retrospective Collections and Progressive Works

THE INTRODUCTION TO PART THREE HAS given reasons for suggesting that the final period of patristic literature began ca. 430. Such a boundary favors Augustine and the Council of Chalcedon (451) as the close of the previous patristic period. The end of the final patristic period is traditionally signaled by the church fathers Isidore of Seville (d. 636) in the West and John of Damascus (d. ca. 750) in the East. Extending it to the seventh or eighth century makes good sense when the history of literature is examined closely. Resolving the complex problem of the division of (late) antiquity and the (early) Middle Ages into periods and separating the history of literature from contemporary political and cultural history becomes unnecessary.

After the collapse of linguistic unity in the transition from the fourth to the fifth centuries and of the unity of the empire as a result of the official end of the western Roman Empire in 476, the former parts of the empire and their respective literature increasingly went their own ways because of the increasing pressure brought on by the migration of peoples. In the West the political and cultural structures of Rome continued to have an effect well into the seventh and eighth centuries, before they were replaced by new, "medieval" ones—apart from the fact that the Roman Empire of the "German nation" continued the notion of Rome until 1806 and that the cultural influence of the Roman Empire continues to be present today. Britain had already been lost once for all in 407 and was only Christianized afresh as a result of the mission undertaken by Gregory the Great (beginning in 596). Since the beginning of the fifth century, the Visigoths had ruled Spain, and since 429 the Vandals had ruled North Africa. Gaul was the region into which the most diverse Germanic, Gothic, and Hun tribes migrated, and so the rule of Rome was practically maintained only in the cities, and by the end of the fifth century the rule of the Franks had spread. Following Odoacer, who in 476 deposed Romulus Augustinus, the final Roman emperor, Theoderic the Great, the Ostrogoth king, established his kingdom in Italy until 526.

The kingdoms of the Goths and the Vandals came to an end in the wars of reunification under Emperor Justinian (518/527–565), who attempted to restore the old Roman unity of the empire in the East and the West. His armies conquered North Africa in 533 and, beginning in 535, Dalmatia and Italy; the wars against the

Goths went on for decades, however, and of Spain he conquered only a small part. But in the long term, Justinian's policy was unsuccessful; beginning in 568, the Lombards penetrated Italy, where only the exarchates of Rome and Ravenna, as well as parts of southern Italy and Sicily, were preserved until the eighth century. From ca. 625 on, Spain belonged to the Visigoths again, and by the end of the seventh century, North Africa had been taken by the Arab conquerers.

In the eastern part of the Roman Empire, the situation changed fundamentally with the advance of Islam beginning in 622; by 750 they had reduced it to Asia Minor, Greece, and the Balkans. For this reason, the political development justifies setting the boundaries of the final period of the patristic era in the mid-seventh century in the West and in the mid-eighth century in the East.

The theological context needs to be taken into consideration as well, extending from Nestorius (428) and the Council of Ephesus (431), via the Council of Chalcedon (451) and the struggles over its acceptance, to the further christological clarifications that were logically built upon such antecedents by the councils of Constantinople (553 and 680–683) in the controversies of the Three Chapters, Monothelitism, and Monergism and by the Council of Nicea (787) in the controversy about images (iconoclasm).

Of decisive importance, however, is that the Christian literature of this period is construed as continuous with, and a component part of, ancient patristic literature even if there are clear signs of the end of an epoch and of a transition to a new era in both the East and the West, reflecting the basic situation of the time. Because of the considerably clearer changes in the West, Latin literature offers vastly more forward-looking works than the literature of the East. In the tension between a great past and the awareness of a new era that is either dawning or already present, it continued, on the one hand, to cultivate the great achievements of the Roman Empire and preserved them for the future; to this extent it bears a traditional and compilatory character. On the other hand, however, it had to cope practically, philosophically, and theologically with this new era, giving rise to important, decisive Christian works that continued to be influential well into the Middle Ages, indeed into the modern period. The monastic Rule of St. Benedict and the works of Gregory the Great serve as good examples.

In this regard the Latin literature of this period differs substantially from the contemporaneous Greek literature of the Christian East, since there was no clear political and cultural break there. The Roman Empire developed imperceptibly into the Byzantine Empire, so that the orientation of Greek patristic literature of late antiquity was much more backward-looking and ended with its most important compiler, John of Damascus, as the progressive spread of Islam finally caused the dawning of the Byzantine "Middle Ages." To be sure, there continue to be important, original, and unique theological, spiritual, and liturgical works, but a large part of the literature is made up of retrospective collections and passes on the great fathers of the past.

Studies: J. Meyendorff, *Imperial Unity and Christian Divisions: The Church, 450–680 A.D.* (Crestwood, N.Y.: St. Vladimir's Seminary Press, 1989). – A. Cameron, *The Mediterranean World in Late Antiquity, AD 395–600* (London and New York: Routledge,

1993). – L. Perrone, *La chiesa di Palestina e le controversie cristologiche: Dal concilio di Efeso (431) al secondo concilio di Costantinopoli (553)* (Brescia: Paideia, 1980). – A. Grillmeier, *Christ in Christian Tradition* (trans. J. Bowden; 2d ed.; London: Mowbray, 1975–), 1:414–568. – J. N. D. Kelly, *Early Christian Doctrines* (5th ed.; London: A. C. Black; San Francisco: Harper & Row, 1977), 310–43. – F. Young, *From Nicaea to Chalcedon* (London: SCM; Philadelphia: Fortress, 1983), 178–289. – J. Meyendorff, *Christ in Eastern Christian Thought* (Crestwood, N.Y.: St. Vladimir's Seminary Press, 1987). – B. Studer, *Trinity and Incarnation: The Faith of the Early Church* (ed. A. Louth; trans. M. Westerhoff; Edinburgh: T&T Clark; Collegeville, Minn.: Liturgical, 1993), 199–238.

# CHAPTER TEN

# Theological Controversies of the Fifth Century

## I. NESTORIUS, CYRIL OF ALEXANDRIA, AND THE COUNCIL OF EPHESUS (431)

The affair concerning Nestorius, leading to the (third ecumenical) Council of Ephesus in 431, developed and reached its climax within a very brief period. Nestorius was likely born in 381 in Germanicia of Syria and possibly was a student of Theodore of Mopsuestia. As a monk and priest, he lived in Antioch and had gained a great reputation for his piety and eloquence, for which he was elected to the politically and ecclesiastically very important episcopal see of the capital, Constantinople, on April 10, 428. In his great zeal for maintaining the purity of the faith, however, he disapproved of the popular form of address for Mary as "the one giving birth to God" (θεοτόκος), which for decades had been used by many of the important church fathers, not for mariological but for christological reasons. Antiochene Christology distinguished sharply between the divine and human natures of Christ and their respective attributes. Thus it is not God who is given birth but the man Jesus, so that Mary should actually be called only "mother of Jesus." But since Nestorius, on the other hand, in no way undervalued the intimate union of the two complete natures in the God-man and therefore also rejected the opposite form of addressing Mary as merely "the one giving birth to man" (ἀνθρωποτόκος), he proposed the title θεοδόκος ("the one receiving God") or Χριστοτόκος ("the one giving birth to Christ") as a *via media*. By this proposal he intended to distinguish clearly, on the one hand, between the attributes of the natures and to indicate, on the other hand, that the man Jesus, who was born of Mary, was united with God.

Nestorius's efforts for such a differentiation, though theologically entirely correct, foundered mainly because of the popularity of the θεοτόκος title. This led to an uprising in the capital, arousing attention far beyond the city, especially in Alexandria, where Cyril had officiated as patriarch since 412. We know very little about Cyril's life before his consecration as bishop. Born in Alexandria between 370 and 380 as the nephew of Theophilus (385–412), the later patriarch, he became a cleric himself and for some time perhaps a monk as well, accompanied his uncle to the so-called synod of the Oak (403), which deposed John Chrysostom, and followed him in the episcopal see of Alexandria on October 17, 412. "From him he not only inherited his power and ambitions but also the energy, political ability, toughness over against his opponents, and lack of scruples."[1] His zealous stance toward Gentiles, Jews, and heretics favored an atmosphere of fanaticism in Alexandria, venting itself in persecutions of the Novatians and Jews and in 415 leading to the murder of the philosopher Hypatia.

Attempts have been made to reduce the motivation for Cyril's intervention against Nestorius to the level of ecclesiastical politics. It is argued that after having already been involved with his uncle and predecessor Theophilus in exiling John Chrysostom, he seized the opportunity to strengthen Alexandria's position after its demotion from second to third place among the patriarchates, behind Rome and Constantinople, at the council held in the latter city in 381. That this was *one* of the reasons for his actions cannot be doubted, but he would not have been able to move against the patriarch of Constantinople without dogmatic leverage. This has led to the conclusion that Cyril used this theological occasion for merely his own ecclesiastical-political goals. Even if it is not possible to decide on which of the two reasons provided the original impetus and proved to be decisive—they worked in combination—it is not appropriate to insinuate that Cyril used pure power politics without serious theological and religious conviction. He had grown up in a different christological tradition in Alexandria, stressing more strongly the unity of the two natures in Christ than did the Antiochene tradition, to the extent that after the Council of Chalcedon (451), it split from the universal church as Monophysite.

Cyril opened the campaign with a letter to the Egyptian monks (*Ep.* 1), who had represented a substantial force in the Egyptian church since Athanasius, together with his paschal letter for 429. During the same year, he turned to Nestorius (*Ep.* 2) for information, and Nestorius responded with a precise and careful presentation of his Christology. In the following year (*Ep.* 4), Cyril, having carefully delineated his own Christology, called on Nestorius to accept the θεοτό κος title. For support both parties turned to the see of Rome, accorded primacy in the empire. After conducting a synod in Rome in 430, Pope Celestine decided in favor of Cyril's position and authorized him, on his behalf, to appeal to Nestorius to recant and, should he not comply within ten days from receipt of the papal decision, to depose him. It was not until November 430, however, after conducting a synod in Alexandria, that Cyril forwarded to Nestorius the papal decree, accompanied by a letter (*Ep.* 17) and twelve anathemas presenting Alexandrian Christology in such radical form that they were unacceptable for an Antiochene. They demanded not only (a) the recognition of the θεοτόκος title for Mary, but also (b) the definition of the unity of the two natures of Christ καθ' ὑπόστασιν, (c) and as ἕνωσις φυσική, not only as συνάφεια κατ' ἀξίαν, and finally (d) the equivalence of πρόσωπον and ὑπόστασις, as well as the *communcatio idiomatum*. The conflict was

---

[1] M. Simonetti, *EECh* 1:214.

not resolved at this level, for Nestorius had requested Emperor Theodosius II to summon a council to decide on this dispute. On November 19, 430, the emperor invited the bishops of the dioceses of the Eastern Empire, as well as Pope Celestine and Augustine of Hippo, to Ephesus at Pentecost (June 7) 431.

The opening of the council was delayed beyond the designated date, however, because neither John, the patriarch of Antioch, nor the papal legates, nor a large number of Syrian and Palestinian bishops had arrived. (Although the imperial court was not yet aware of it, Augustine had already died before the invitations were sent, and the invitations did not arrive in Africa until Easter [April 19] 431). Because of the wars of the Vandals, it was not possible to hold a synod in Africa, and so Bishop Capreolus of Carthage merely sent his deacon, Bassula, as his representative. On June 22, against the objection of Candidian, the imperial commissary, Cyril did not want to wait any longer, although (or because?) he knew that the arrival of the Antiochene bishops was imminent, and opened the council with 154 bishops of his party. Cyril's second letter to Nestorius and his response were read; the former was found to be in accordance with the faith of Nicea, which was accepted as the fundamental and sufficient creedal statement, to which nothing was to be added. Further witnesses were heard, further documents, among them Cyril's letter with the twelve anathemas, were read, and finally Nestorius was condemned and deposed. This session therefore, the decisions of which were later recognized as ecumenically valid council decrees, did not make a decision on the θεοτόκος title or define the heresy it condemned but merely accepted Cyril's Alexandrian Christology as developed in his letters—a procedure that did not solve the christological question but merely delayed it. Cyril's Christology, especially the formulation ἕνωσις καθ' ὑπόστασιν, represented only one of the two juxtaposed theological poles, quite apart from the fact that the scope of the meaning of the terms πρόσωπον and ὑπόστασις continued to lack clarity.

On June 26 John of Antioch arrived and did not recognize Cyril's session; instead he opened the council himself with about 50 bishops and Candidian. They condemned Cyril and his followers and threatened the termination of ecclesiastical communion with them if they did not distance themselves from the twelve anathemas. At the end of June, the emperor thereupon ordered the reopening of the council with both parties, but Cyril and his supporters refused to comply and received decisive support when the papal legates arrived on July 9. In consistent continuation of the Roman decision that had already been made, the latter were authorized to support Cyril, and they confirmed the decrees of the session of June 22, since Nestorius did not recant, as ordered in the wake of Celestine's decision. The joint meeting of both parties never became a reality. Emperor Theodosius thereupon first recognized the decisions of both partial synods, ordered all of the participants to stay in Ephesus until the situation had been clarified, and in early August sent a new commissary by the name of John. Carrying through decisions consistent with both partial synods, he placed Nestorius and Cyril, together with Memnon, the bishop of Ephesus, under arrest and dismissed the fathers of the council to return to their homes. Further negotiations, during which Cyril exercised considerable influence upon the imperial court by means of presents, ended on September 11 with the deposition of Nestorius, who withdrew to a monastery near Antioch. Emperor Theodosius finally declared the council dissolved and allowed the participants, except Cyril, to return home; the latter, however, had already left Ephesus without permission.

For four years Nestorius lived in Antioch until Emperor Theodosius exiled him, initially to Petra in Idumea and then to the Great Oasis in Upper Egypt. There Nestorius outlived both the emperor (d. July 28, 450) and Cyril, his main opponent (d. June 27, 444), and continued to produce theological writings. In April 433, Cyril and John of Antioch settled the dispute by agreeing on the following formulation: "A uniting of both natures occurred, . . . and on account of this union without mingling, we confess that the holy virgin was the one who gave birth to God, because the divine Word became flesh and human" (*DH* 271–273). Cyril's letter (*Ep.* 39), which the Council of Florence deliberately adopted again in the July 6, 1439, bull of union of the Eastern and Western churches, begins with the words of Ps 96:11, "Let the heavens rejoice, let the earth be glad." This understanding did not lead to the rehabilitation of Nestorius, however; indeed, in 438 the emperor ordered all of his works to be burned, so that their availability leaves much to be desired. Yet not all of the Syrian churches accepted the settlement formula of 433, and so some Nestorian churches have been preserved up to now in which important parts of the Nestorian writings have been handed down. In the sixteenth century, some of them were reintegrated into the Catholic Church, namely, the Chaldeans in Iraq, Iran, and Syria. The Malabar St. Thomas Christians in the province of Kerala in southwestern India are Catholic Christians among whom Nestorian elements crept in through the course of history because of their Syrian origin and their peripheral location.

## A. Works and Theology of Nestorius

Gennadius (*De viris illustribus* 53) and Ebedjesus (*Catalogus* 20) attested to the extensive writings of Nestorius; in addition to seven sermons that have been handed down under the name of John Chrysostom, there are eleven letters and numerous fragments. Only one work has been preserved in full, however, the Syriac translation of the *Liber Heraclidis*. This extensive work, written in the latter part of Nestorius's life, was not discovered until 1895 in the patriarchal library at Kotchanes and was issued for the first time in 1910. In it Nestorius offers his autobiography and defends the orthodoxy of his theology. This work made it possible for the first time to gain insight into his original thinking on the disputes beyond the Council of Ephesus and consequently led to a reevaluation of Nestorius that is yet to be completed.

With careful consideration given to the gap of twenty years between his early Christology, which precipitated the dispute and led to the Council of Ephesus, and its later form in the *Liber Heraclidis*, the situation can be presented as follows, especially since the investigations by Luigi Scipioni. By the end of the fourth century and for a considerable part of the fifth century, Eastern and Western theology sought to avoid Monophysite deviations, such as Sabellianism, Arianism, and Apollinarianism and to move beyond such double formulations as εἰς καὶ αὐτός = *unus atque idem,* which had become traditional since Irenaeus, to an apt formulation of the unity of the two complete natures of Christ. After clarifying φύσις and οὐσία as terms associated with the level of nature, the Greek language offered two concepts to this end, namely, πρόσωπον and ὑπόστασις, although the scope of their precise meanings still had to be determined. In Trinitarian theology ὑπόστασις had become the distinctive term of a threefold nature, so that Antiochene theology, especially that of Theodore of Mopsuestia, tended to relate the concept of ὑπόστασις to nature in terms of a concrete reality and to construe πρόσωπον as the sum and subject of all expressions of nature. Hence, for Theodore and Nestorius, both natures of Christ have their own πρόσωπον; in other words, Christ has δύο πρόσωπα. By the union of them into one subject, however, they become one πρόσωπον—a formulation that is capable of signifying "one person" but is not identical to it. The Antiochenes described this kind of unity by means of the term συνάφεια ("contact"), but this is still capable of being misconstrued as a purely external kind of being side-by-side, while Nestorius also used the designation κατ᾽ εὐδοκίαν ("according to favor," "on account of the will"). He certainly accommodated the fundamental Antiochene concern not to blur the completeness and independence of the two natures of Christ. Thus Nestorius did not teach "two sons" before the Council of Ephesus, as the Alexandrian side accused him of doing; he explicitly protested against it, but the other side misconstrued his use of vocabulary as insufficient, indeed wrong, because it did not agree with its conception of solving this issue.

Alexandrian theology did not operate with a different vocabulary; for them, too, the concept of ὑπόστασις was associated with the level of nature and πρόσωπον described the expressions of nature. Since they were primarily concerned with expressing the true, inner unity of the natures of Christ, they deemed the definition ἕν πρόσωπον κατὰ συνάφειαν to be far too weak and so externally oriented that what remained were two sons instead of one. For them, the unity had to be understood on the level of nature, hence as μία φύσις = μία ὑπόστασις. The unity came about καθ᾽ ὑπόστασιν, but this does not yet denote by any means the same as what the Council of Chalcedon defined as the "hypostatic union" twenty years later, for here ὑπόστασις does not signify "person" nor did the Alexandrian church accept this change in meaning at Chalcedon.

The third party, called in as an arbitrator, looked at the problem from an entirely different vantage point, however, because the Latin language and theology did not have a terminological alternative and no later than with Augustine had decided on translating ὑπόστασις as *persona,* since translating it as "substance" rendered the Trinitarian formula impossible. For the meaning of the term *persona* could denote both the external appearance and the acting subject; parallel to the Trinitarian formula, this meaning came through in Augustine's Christology of *una persona in utraque natura.* For this reason, the West, given its exclusively Latin way of thinking by now, actually preferred Cyril's formulation of μία ὑπόστασις = *una persona* = "one subject" to the Nestorian ἓν πρόσωπον = *una persona* = "one external." The more specific distinction of πρόσωπον as signifying "subject" as well, in contrast to Cyril's understanding, and also used in this way by the Antiochene theology, escaped the Roman theologians. Has Nestorius therefore been unjustly condemned as a heretic? If one begins with the assumption of what he intended by his statements, he was orthodox. Yet the crucial point of a dogmatic-historical development is that at a crossroads it has to choose a direction—in this case, a formulation—and reject the other as wrong and hence as heretical. In this sense, Nestorius was rightly expelled as a heretic because his solution was not accepted by the church—despite the fact that, according to current understanding, it was also able to express what the church intended to express—and because Nestorius did not adhere to the church's decision.

*Editions:* F. Loofs, *Nestoriana: Die Fragmente des Nestorius* (with contributions from S. A. Cook and G. Kampffmeyer; Halle: Niemeyer, 1905). – *Le Livre d'Heraclide de Damas* (ed. P. Bedjan; Paris: Letouzey & Ané, 1910; repr., Farnborough: Gregg, 1969) *[Liber Heraclidis]*. – L. Abramowski and A. E. Goodman, *A Nestorian Collection of Christological Texts* (2 vols.; Cambridge: Cambridge University Press, 1972) [T.sir/ET].

*Translations:* *The Bazaar of Heracleides* (trans. G. R. Driver and L. Hodgson; Oxford: Clarendon, 1925; repr., New York: AMS, 1978; Eugene, Oreg.: Wipf & Stock, 2002). – E. R. Hardy and C. C. Richardson, eds., *The Christology of the Later Fathers* (LCC 3; Philadelphia: Westminster, 1954), 346–48 [*First Letter to Celestine*]. – R. Norris, *The Christological Controversy* (SoECT; Philadelphia: Fortress, 1980), 123–31, 135–40 [*First Sermon on the Theotokos, Second Letter to Cyril*].

*Encyclopedia Articles:* M. Simonetti, *EECh* 2:594. – G. Podskalsky, "Nestorius," *GK* 2:215–26. – L. R. Wickham, *TRE* 24:276–86. – S. Ashbrook Harvey, *EEC* 2:809–10.

*Studies:* P. Batiffol, "Sermons de Nestorius," *RBI* 9 (1900): 329–53. – J. F. Bethune-Baker, *Nestorius and His Teaching* (Cambridge: Cambridge University Press, 1908; repr., Eugene, Oreg.: Wipf & Stock, 1999). – F. Loofs, *Nestorius and His Place in the History of Christian Doctrine* (Cambridge: Cambridge University Press; New York: Putnam, 1914; repr., New York: B. Franklin, 1975; Whitefish, Mont.: Kessinger, 2004). – G. L. Prestige, *Fathers and Heretics: Six Studies in Dogmatic Faith* (London: SPCK, 1940; repr., 1968), 120–49. – E. Amann, "L'affaire de Nestorius vue de Rome," *RevScRel* 23 (1949): 5–37, 207–44; 24 (1950): 28–52, 235–65. – L. I. Scipioni, *Nestorio e il concilio di Efeso: Storia, dogma, critica* (SPMed 1; Milan: Vita e Pensiero, 1974). – H. E. W. Turner, "Nestorius Reconsidered," in *Papers Presented to the Sixth International Conference on Patristic Studies Held in Oxford, 1971* (ed. E. Livingstone; StPatr 13; TU 116; Berlin: Akademie, 1975), 306–21. – A. de Halleux, "Nestorius: Histoire et doctrine," *Irén* 66 (1993): 38–51, 163–78. – J. A. McGuckin, *St. Cyril of Alexandria: The Christological Controversy—Its History, Theology, and Texts* (SVigChr 23; Leiden and New York: Brill, 1994; repr., Crestwood, N.Y.: St. Vladimir's Seminary Press, 2004), 126–74. – J. A. McGuckin, "Nestorius and the Political Factions of Fifth-Century Byzantium: Factors in His Personal Downfall," *BJRL* 78 (1996): 7–21.

*Book of Heraclides (Liber Heraclidis):* L. I. Scipioni, *Ricerche sulla cristologia del "Libro di Eraclide" di Nestorio: La formulazione teologica e il suo contesto filosofico* (Par. 11; Fribourg, Switz.: Edizioni Universitarie, 1956). – L. Abramowski, *Untersuchungen zum Liber Heraclidis des Nestorius* (CSCO 242; Louvain: SCO, 1963). – R. C. Chesnut, "The Two Prosopa in Nestorius' *Bazaar of Heracleides*," *JTS* NS 29 (1978): 392–409.

# B. Council Records

In the true sense of the term, council records are preserved for the first time in conjunction with Ephesus (431), whereas the information and records of all previous synods have been handed down in scattered writings. Even in this particular case, however, the records are not the official minutes of the council but a later collection of texts by various compilers and with varying intentions. They have been published in the monumental edition of *Acta conciliorum oecumenicorum* by Eduard Schwartz. The three most important Greek collections are the following: the Collectio Vaticana, the Collectio Seguieriana, and the Collectio Atheniensis. The second represents a partial collection of 146 of the 172 documents contained in the first collection, whereas 58 documents of the 177 in the third collection exceed those in the first one. All three collections can be traced back to an Alexandrian original form favoring Cyril. There are also, however, compilations of the Nestorian counterpart.

All of the Latin translations came about in conjunction with the Three Chapters dispute and the Second Council of Constantinople (553) for the purpose of demonstrating the illegality of the condemnation: (a) the Collectio Turonensis, compiled ca. 560 in Constantinople; (b) the Collectio Casinensis of the Roman deacon Rusticus, likewise translated in Constantinople in 564/565 and copying the Collectio Turonensis in the first part; (c) the Roman Collectio Veronensis, highlighting the role of Pope Celestine; (d) the Collectio Palatina of a Scythian monk in Constantinople or Thrace with a "neo-Chalcedonian" tendency, after 553; and (e–f) the smaller Collectio Sichardiana and (g) Collectio Winteriana.

The records contain the correspondence between the emperor and the participating bishops, the *gesta* of the council, with the list of the participants, decrees, sermons and orations, excerpts from the works of Cyril and Nestorius, as well as collections of *testimonia*. From a theological-historical vantage point, the latter are particularly important for applying "patristic evidence" because at the council Cyril was the first one ever to read out a collection of the Fathers' *testimonia* as a public argument in support of his orthodoxy (cf. I, introduction).

*Editions:* J. Flemming and G. Hoffmann, *Akten der Ephesinischen Synode vom Jahre 449* (AGWG 15; Berlin: Weidmannsche Buchhandlung, 1917; repr., Göttingen: Vandenhoeck & Ruprecht, 1970). – ACO 1/1–5. – B. M. Weischer, *Qērellos 4.1: Homilien und Briefe zum Konzil von Ephesos* (ed. B. M. Weischer; ÄThF 4; Wiesbaden: Steiner, 1979). – N. P. Tanner and G. Alberigo, *Decrees of the Ecumenical Councils* (London: Sheed & Ward; Washington, D.C.: Georgetown University Press, 1990), 37–74 [ET].

*Translations:* H. R. Percival, trans., "The Third Ecumenical Council—the Council of Ephesus, A.D. 431," in NPNF² (Peabody, Mass.: Hendrickson, 1995; repr. of 1890 ed.), 14:191–242 [*Acta* (extracts), *Letters of Cyril to Nestorius, The 12 Anathematisms, Canons, Letter of the Synod to Pope Celestine, Definition against the Messalians*]. – J. Stevenson, *Creeds, Councils, and Controversies* (rev. W. H. C. Frend; rev. ed.; London: SPCK, 1989), 310–12 [*Canons*].

*Encyclopedia Articles:* J. Liébart, *TRE* 9:753–55. – M. Simonetti, *EECh* 2:275–76. – F. W. Norris, *EEC* 1:233–34.

*Studies:* C. J. Hefele and H. Leclercq, *Histoire des conciles: D'après les documents originaux* (Paris: Letouzey, 1907–), 2:1:555–621. – P.-T. Camelot, *Éphèse et Chalcédoine* (HCO 2; Paris: Orante, 1962), 11–75 [ted Mz 1963]. – L. Perrone, in *Storia dei concili ecumenici* (ed. G. Alberigo; Brescia: Queriniana, 1990), 71–107. – A. d'Alès, *Le dogme d'Éphèse* (Paris: Beauchesne, 1931). – B. Studer, "Il concilio di Efeso (431) nella luce della dottrina mariana di Cirillo d'Alessandria," in *La mariologia nella catechesi dei Padri (età postnicena)* (ed. S. Felici; BSRel 88; Rome: LAS, 1989), 49–67. – H.-J. Vogt, "Unterschiedliches Konzilsverständnis der Cyrillianer und der Orientalen beim Konzil von Ephesus 431," in *Logos: Festschrift für Luise Abramowski zum 8. Juli 1993* (ed. H. C. Brennecke, E. L. Grasmück, and C. Markschies; BZNW 67; Berlin and New York: de Gruyter, 1993), 429–51. – R. Teja, *La "tragedia" de Efeso (431): Herejía y poder en la antigüedad tardía* (Santander: Universidad de Cantabria, 1995). – P. L'Huillier, *The Church of the Ancient Councils: The Disciplinary Work of the First Four Ecumenical Councils* (Crestwood, N.Y.: St. Vladimir's Seminary Press, 1996), 143–79.

# C. Works and Theology of Cyril of Alexandria

Cyril's extensive literary work quite clearly divides into two periods of time, before and after the beginning of the Nestorian controversy. Before this he devoted himself to exegesis and refuting Arianism. Of his biblical commentaries, two have been preserved on the Pentateuch (*De adoratione et culta in spiritu et veritate* and *Glaphyra in Pentateuchum*), one on the twelve Minor Prophets, one on the Gospel of John, and numerous fragments of other works on the OT and NT in the catenas. Cyril, too, understands the OT typologically in view of Christ, though not to the same extent as, for instance, Origen and Didymus; instead he allots more room to a literal understanding of the texts. Against Arianism he wrote *Thesaurus de sancta et consubstantiali trinitate* and *Dialogi de sancta trinitate*, explaining the Catholic doctrine of the Trinity entirely along the lines of the Cappadocians and the Council of Constantinople (381).

After the dogmatic letters 1, 2, 4, and 17, mentioned above in conjunction with Nestorius, Cyril followed in 430 with his *Libri V contra Nestorium,* in which he provided a detailed refutation of Nestorian Christology. He also responded to the critique of his *Anathemata* by the bishops Andrew of Samosata and Theodoret of Cyrus by means of the two apologias, *Apologia XII capitulorum contra Orientales* and *Apologia XII anathematismorum contra Theodoretum,* and during his house arrest in Ephesus, he added the *Explanatio XII capitulorum.* Since the outcome of the dispute depended substantially on persuading the emperor and the imperial court, Cyril proved to be a more skillful ecclesiastical politician than Nestorius and thus already in 430 dedicated the *Oratio ad Theodosium imperatorem de recta fide, Oratio ad Arcadiam et Marinam augustas de fide,* and *Oratio ad Pulcheriam et Eudociam augustas de fide* to them. He supplemented the latter after the council in Egypt with the *Apologeticus ad Theodosium imperatorem.* When Diodore of Tarsus and Theodore of Mopsuestia, as forerunners of Nestorian theology, in 438 came into the cross fire of the criticism that was to lead to the Three Chapters dispute and their condemnation by the Constantinopolitan synods of 499 and 553, he identified them as the "fathers" of Nestorianism in his *Contra Diodorum et Theodorum*, preserved only in fragments today. The dialogue *Quod unus sit Christus* represents the final summary of Cyril's Christology. In addition, among the more than one hundred extant letters and numerous homilies, the previously mentioned *Ep*. 39 (*Laetentur coeli*) and *Ep*. 45 and 46 are noteworthy for dogmatics. Cyril's major work from the latter part of his life, *Contra Julianum imperatorem* (after 433), directed against the latter's book *Adversus Galilaeos*, demonstrates his antipagan zeal and perhaps the still existing necessity of explaining and defending Christianity against pagan attacks as well.

Beyond its essential features, presented in connection with the Nestorian controversy above, Cyril's Christology contains two key formulations that would later provide the occasion for the controversy on the Christology of the Council of Chalcedon (451) and for the separation of the Coptic church:

a. Cyril referred to μία φύσις τοῦ θεοῦ λόγου σεσαρκωμένη, convinced that this formulation originated with Athanasius; in reality, however, it came from Apollinaris, whose work was circulated under the name of Athanasius after the condemnation of the former. In spite of all the theological progress and although Cyril clearly rejected the heresy of Apollinaris, he nevertheless did not conclusively move beyond his christological *logos-sarx* schema and did not overcome the danger of subordinating the human nature to the divine instead of coordinating the two.

b. Cyril was fond of the conception that in the unity of Christ the two natures became one. At the Council of Chalcedon (451), therefore, the Alexandrian theologians wanted to impose the formulation ἐκ δύο φύσεων and ultimately were not satisfied with the formulation agreed upon, ἐν δύο φύσεσιν. (In its way of thinking, this formulation, albeit in the opposite way, shows remarkable parallels to the Antiochene conception of Theodore of Mopsuestia and Nestorius, namely, the two πρόσωπα becoming one by being united.)

*Editions:*
*Opera omnia:* PG 68–77. – *Opera* (ed. P. E. Pusey; 7 vols.; Oxford: Clarendon, 1868–1877; repr., Brusells: Culture & civilisation, 1965). – *ACO* 1/1–5; *ACO* 4.1.
*Commentarii in Lucam: S. Cyrilli Alexandrini Commentarii in Lucam* (ed. J.-B. Chabot and R. M. Tonneau; 2 vols.; CSCO 70, 140; Paris: E Typographeo Reipublicae, 1912–1953) [Com].
*Contra Julianum imperatorem: Contre Julien* (ed. P. Burguière and P. Évieux; SC 322; Paris: Cerf, 1985) [*I–II* Com].
*De incarnatione, De recta fide: Deux dialogues christologiques* (ed. G. M. de Durand; SC 97; Paris: Cerf, 1964) [Com].
*De Trinitate: Dialogues sur la Trinité* (ed. G. M. de Durand; 3 vols.; SC 231, 237, 246; Paris: Cerf, 1976–1978).
*Epistulae:* R. Y. Ebied and L. R. Wickham, "The Letter of Cyril of Alexandria to Tiberius the Deacon," *Mus* 83 (1970): 433–82. – R. Y. Ebied and L. R. Wickham, "An Unknown Letter of Cyril of Alexandria in Syriac," *JTS* NS 22 (1971): 420–34 [T.sir/ET]. – *A Collection of Unpublished Syriac Letters of Cyril of Alexandria* (ed. R. Y. Ebied and L. R.

Wickham; 2 vols.; CSCO 359–360; Louvain: SCO, 1975). – *Select Letters* (ed. and trans. L. R. Wickham; OECT; Oxford: Clarendon, 1983) [*4, 17, 41, 44–46, 55* ET].
*Epistulae festales: Lettres festales* (ed. P. Évieux, W. Burns, L. Arragon, M.-O. Boulnois, M. Forrat, B. Meunier, and R. Monier; SC 372, 392, 434; Paris: Cerf, 1991–) [*I–XVII* Com]. – R. Hespel, *Le Florilège cyrillien réfuté par Sévère d'Antioche: Étude et édition critique* (BMus 37; Louvain: Publications Universitaires, 1955).
*Fragmenta apud Severum Antiochenum contra impium grammaticum: Liber contra impium grammaticum* (ed. J. Lebon; 3 vols. in 6; CSCO 93–94, 101–102, 111–112; Paris: E Typographeo Reipublicae, 1929–1938). – J. Reuss, *Johannes-Kommentare aus der griechischen Kirche* (TU 89; Berlin: Akademie, 1966), 188–95. – J. Reuss, *Matthäus-Kommentare aus der griechischen Kirche* (TU 61; Berlin: Akademie, 1957), 103–269. – B. M. Weischer, *Qērellos I: Der Prosphonetikos "Über den rechten Glauben" des Kyrillos von Alexandrien an Theodosios II* (Stuttgart: Steiner, 1993). – B. M. Weischer, *Qērellos III: Der Dialog "Dass Christus einer ist" des Kyrillos von Alexandrien* (ÄThF 2; Weisbaden: Steiner, 1977). – B. M. Weischer, *Qērellos IV.3: Traktate des Severianos von Gabala, Gregorios Thaumaturgos, und Kyrillos von Alexandrien* (ÄThF 7; Weisbaden: Steiner, 1980), 79–117 [two homilies on Melchizedek].

*Translations: Commentary on the Gospel according to S. John* (trans. P. E. Pusey; Library of Fathers of the Holy Catholic Church 48; Oxford: Parker, 1874; London: Smith [late Mozley], 1885) [*Commentary on John*, vol. 1]. – R. P. Smith, *Commentary on the Gospel of St. Luke* (2 vols.; Oxford: Oxford University Press, 1859; repr., with new introduction [United States]: Studion, 1983). – *Five Tomes against Nestorius: Scholia on the Incarnation, Christ Is One, Fragments against Diodore of Tarsus, Theodore of Mopsuestia, the Synousiasts* (trans. P. E. Pusey; Library of Fathers of the Holy Catholic Church 46; Oxford: J. Parker & Rivingtons, 1881). – *Commentary on the Gospel according to S. John* (trans. T. Randell; Library of Fathers of the Holy Catholic Church 48; Oxford: J. Parker, 1885) [*Commentary on John*, vol. 2]. – R. Norris, *The Christological Controversy* (SoECT; Philadelphia: Fortress, 1980), 131–35, 140–45 [*Second Letter to Nestorius, Letter to John of Antioch*]. – *Letters* (trans. J. I. McEnerney; 2 vols.; FC 76–77; Washington, D.C.: Catholic University of America Press, 1987) [*Letters*]. – J. Stevenson, *Creeds, Councils, and Controversies* (rev. W. H. C. Frend; rev. ed.; London: SPCK, 1989), 295–309, 313–17 [*Second and Third Letters to Nestorius, Letter to John of Antioch*]. – J. A. McGuckin, *St. Cyril of Alexandria: The Christological Controversy—Its History, Theology, and Texts* (SVigChr 23; Leiden and New York: Brill, 1994; repr., Crestwood, N.Y.: St. Vladimir's Seminary Press, 2004), 245–363 [*Letter to the Monks of Egypt, Second and Third Letters to Nestorius, Letter to Pope Celestine, Letter to Acacius of Borea, Letter to John of Antioch, Scholia on the Incarnation, Letter to Eulogius, First and Second Letters to Successus*]. – *On the Unity of Christ* (trans. J. A. McGuckin; Crestwood, N.Y.: St. Vladimir's Seminary Press, 1995). – N. Russell, *Cyril of Alexandria* (Early Church Fathers; London and New York: Routledge, 2000) [selections from *Commentary on Isaiah, Commentary on John, Against Nestorius, An Explanation of the Twelve Chapters, Against Julian*].

*Encyclopedia Articles:* G. Jouassard, *RAC* 3:499–516. – E. R. Hardy, *TRE* 8:254–60. – M. Simonetti, *EECh* 1:214–15. – H.-J. Vogt, "Cyril von Alexandrien," *GK* 2:227–38. – L. R. Wickham, *EEC* 1:310–12.

*Introductions:* N. Russell, *Cyril of Alexandria* (Early Church Fathers; London and New York: Routledge, 2000).

*Studies—Individual Works:* G. Jouassard, "L'activité littéraire de S. Cyrille d'Alexandrie jusqu'à 428," in *Mélanges E. Podechard: Études de sciences religieuses offertes pour son émériat au doyen honoraire de la Faculté de théologie de Lyon* (Lyon: Facultés Catholiques, 1945), 148–76. – N. Charlier, "Le '*Thesaurus de Trinitate*' de saint Cyrille d'Alexandrie," *RHE* 45 (1950): 25–81. – A. Vööbus, *Discoveries of Great Import on the Commentary on Luke by Cyril of Alexandria* (Stockholm: ETSE, 1973). – M. Simonetti, "Note sul commento di Cirillo d'Alessandria ai *Profeti minori,*" *VetChr* 14 (1977): 301–30. – W. J. Malley, *Hellenism and Christianity: The Conflict between Hellenic and Christian Wisdom in the Contra Galilaeos of Julian the Apostate and the Contra Julianum of St. Cyril of Alexandria* (AnGr 210; Rome: Università Gregoriana, 1978). – S. Wessel, "Nestorius, Mary, and Controversy, in Cyril of Alexandria's *Homily IV* (*De Maria deipara in Nestorium*, CPG 5248)," *AHC* 31 (1999): 1–49. – R. L. Wilken, "Cyril of Alexandria's *Contra Julianum,*" in *Limits of Ancient Christianity: Essays on Late Antique Thought and Culture in Honor of R. A. Markus)* (ed. W. E. Klingshirn and M. Vessey; Ann Arbor: University of Michigan Press, 1999), 42–55.

*Commentary on the Gospel of John:* L. Fatica, *I commentari a Giovanni di Teodoro di Mopsuestia e di Cirillo di Alessandria: Confronto fra i metodi esegetici e teologici* (SeAug 29; Rome: Institutum Patristicum Augustinianum, 1988). – L. Koen, *The Saving Passion: Incarnational and Soteriological Thought in Cyril of Alexandria's Commentary on the Gospel according to St. John* (AUU 31; Uppsala: [Uppsala University]; Stockholm: Distributed by Almqvist & Wiksell, 1991). – G. Münch-Labacher, *Naturhaftes und geschichtliches Denken bei Cyrill von Alexandrien: Die verschiedenen Betrachtungsweisen der Heilsverwirklichung in seinem Johannes-Kommentar* (Hereditas 10; Bonn: Borengässer, 1996). – D. Pazzini, *Il prologo di Giovanni in Cirillo di Alessandria* (Studi biblici 116; Brescia: Paideia, 1997).

*Studies:* P. Galtier, "Saint Cyrille et Apollinaire," *Greg* 37 (1956): 584–609. – L. R. Wickham, "Cyril of Alexandria and the Apple of Discord," in *Papers Presented to the Seventh International Conference on Patristic Studies Held in Oxford, 1975* (ed. E. Livingstone; StPatr 15; TU 128; Berlin: Akademie, 1984), 379–92. – A. Davids, "Cyril of Alexandria's Early Years," in *The Impact of Scripture in Early Christianity* (ed. J. den Boeft and M. L. van Poll-van de Lisdonk; SVigChr 44; Leiden and Boston: Brill, 1999), 187–201.

*Christology:* A. d'Alès, "Le symbole d'union de 433," *RSR* 21 (1931): 257–68. – J. van den Dries, *The Formula of St. Cyril of Alexandria* MIA ΦΥΣΙΣ ΤΟΥ ΘΕΟΥ ΛΟΓΟΥ ΣΕΣΑΡΚΟΜΕΝΗ (Rome: Pontificia Universitas Gregoriana, 1939). – G. L. Prestige, *Fathers and Heretics: Six Studies in Dogmatic Faith* (London: SPCK; New York: Macmillan, 1940; repr., London: SPCK, 1968), 150–79. – H. Chadwick, "Eucharist and Christology in the Nestorian Controversy," *JTS* NS 2 (1951): 145–64. – J. Liébart, *La doctrine christologique de saint Cyrille d'Alexandrie avant la querelle nestorienne* (Lille: Facultés Catholiques, 1951). – P. Galtier, "L'*Unio secundum hypostasim*' chez saint Cyrille," *Greg* (1952): 351–98. – G. Jouassard, "'Impassibilité' du Logos et 'impassibilité' de l'âme humaine chez saint Cyrille d'Alexandrie," *RSR* 45 (1957): 209–24. – H. M. Diepen, *Douze dialogues de christologie ancienne* (Rome: Herder, 1960). – L. M. Armendáriz, *El nuevo Moisés: Dinámica cristocéntrica en la tipología de Cirilo de Alejandría* (EstOn 3.5; Madrid: Fax, 1962). – R. Norris, "Christological Models in Cyril of Alexandria," *StPat* 13 (1975): 255–68. – P. Imhof and B. Lorenz, *Maria Theotokos bei Cyrill von Alexandrien—zur Theotokos-Tradition und ihrer Relevanz: Eine dogmengeschichtliche Untersuchung der Verwendung des Wortes Theotokos bei Cyrill von Alexandria vor dem Konzil von Ephesus unter Berücksichtigung von Handschriften der direkten Überlieferung* (Munich: G. Kaffke, 1981). – M. Simonetti, "Alcune osservazioni sul monofisismo di Cirillo di Alessandria," *Aug* 22 (1982): 493–511. – L. R. Wickham, "Symbols of the Incarnation in Cyril of Alexandria," in *Typus, Symbol, Allegorie bei den östlichen Vätern und ihre Parallelen im Mittelalter* (ed. M. Schmidt and C. F. Geyer; EichB 4; Regensburg: Pustet, 1982), 41–53. – R. M. Siddals, "Logic and Christology in Cyril of Alexandria," *JTS* NS 38 (1987): 341–67. – G. Gould, "Cyril of Alexandria and the Formula of Reunion," *DR* 106 (1988): 235–52. – A. de Halleux, "Le dyophysisme christologique de Cyrille d'Alexandrie," in *Logos:*

*Festschrift für Luise Abramowski zum 8. Juli 1993* (ed. H. C. Brennecke, E. L. Grasmück, and C. Markschies; BZNW 67; Berlin: de Gruyter, 1993), 411–28. – L. J. Welch, *Christology and Eucharist in the Early Thought of Cyril of Alexandria* (San Francisco: Catholic Scholars; London: International Scholars, 1994). – J. A. McGuckin, *St. Cyril of Alexandria: The Christological Controversy—Its History, Theology, and Texts* (SVigChr 23; Leiden and New York: Brill, 1994; repr., Crestwood, N.Y.: St. Vladimir's Seminary Press, 2004). – B. Meunier, *Le Christ de Cyrille d'Alexandrie: L'humanité, le salut, et la question monophysite* (ThH 104; Paris: Beauchesne, 1997). – J. J. O'Keefe, "Impassible Suffering? Divine Passion and Fifth-Century Christology," *TS* 58 (1997): 39–60. – J. A. Hallman, "The Seed of Fire: Divine Suffering in the Christology of Cyril of Alexandria and Nestorius of Constantinople," *JECS* 5 (1997): 369–91; repr. in *Doctrinal Diversity: Varieties of Early Christianity* (ed. E. Ferguson; Recent Studies in Early Christianity 4; New York: Garland, 1999), 71–94.

*Theology and Philosophy:* E. Weigl, *Die Heilslehre des hl. Cyrill von Alexandrien* (FChLDG 5.2–3; Mainz: F. Kirchheim, 1905). – A. Struckmann, *Die Eucharistielehre des heiligen Cyrill von Alexandrien* (Paderborn: F. Schöningh, 1910). – A. Eberle, *Die Mariologie des heiligen Cyrillus von Alexandrien* (FThSt 27; Fribourg, Switz., and St. Louis: Herder, 1921). – J. Hebensperger, *Die Denkwelt des hl. Cyrill von Alexandrien: Eine Analyse ihres philosophischen Ertrags* (Augsburg: Literar. Institut von Haas & Grabherr, 1927). – H. du Manoir de Juaye, *Dogme et spiritualité chez saint Cyrill d'Alexandrie* (ETHS 2; Paris: J. Vrin, 1944). – A. Kerrigan, *St. Cyril of Alexandria: Interpreter of the Old Testament* (AnBib 2; Rome: Pontificio Istituto Biblico, 1952). – W. J. Burghardt, *The Image of God in Man according to Cyril of Alexandria* (SCA 14; Washington, D.C.: Catholic University of America Press, 1957). – H. M. Diepen, *Aux origines de l'anthropologie de saint Cyrille d'Alexandrie* (Brugge: Desclée de Brouwer, 1957). – A. Dupré la Tour, "La *doxa* du Christ dans les œuvres exégétiques de saint Cyrille d'Alexandrie," *RSR* 48 (1960): 521–43; 49 (1961): 68–94. – R. L. Wilken, *Judaism and the Early Christian Mind: A Study of Cyril of Alexandria's Exegesis and Theology* (New Haven: Yale University Press, 1971). – E. Gebremedhin, *Life-Giving Blessing: An Inquiry into the Eucharistic Doctrine of Cyril of Alexandria* (AUU 17; Uppsala: University of Uppsala Press; Stockholm: Almqvist & Wiksell, 1977). – J.-M. Labelle, "Saint Cyrille d'Alexandrie: Témoin de la langue et de la pensée philosophiques du Ve siècle," *RevScRel* 52 (1978): 135–58; 53 (1979): 23–42. – M.-O. Boulnois, *Le paradoxe trinitaire chez Cyrille d'Alexandrie: Hérmeneutique, analyses philosophiques, et argumentation théologique* (Paris: Études Augustiniennes, 1994). – A. H. A. Fernandez Lois, *La cristología en los Comentarios a Isaias de Cirilo de Alejandria y Teodoreto de Ciro* (Rome: Pontificia Universitas Lateranensis, Institutum Patristicum Augustinianum, 1998).

# II. THEODORET OF CYRUS

At the time the controversy erupted between the Alexandrian and Antiochene Christologies, that is, between Cyril and Nestorius, Theodoret had been the bishop of Cyrus, a town situated ca. 60 miles northeast of Antioch, since 423. He became Cyril's real opponent and the theologian who continued to develop Antiochene Christology up to the Council of Chalcedon in 451. Yet posthumously he met the same fate as did Diodore of Tarsus and Theodore of Mopsuestia, when the Second Council of Constantinople (553) condemned him in the Three Chapters dispute, with the result that many of his works were lost, as was the case with the other two. Theodoret's origins and development resemble those of many of the great church leaders of his time. In 393 he was born into a well-to-do Christian family in Antioch and, as his writings demonstrate, enjoyed an outstanding education and grew up in the church from childhood. Initially he filled the post of lector and after the death of his parents (416) sold his entire estate and withdrew to a monastery near Nicerte, in the vicinity of Apamea (ca. 27 miles west of Gabala) in Syria. In 423 he was appointed bishop of Cyrus, where he worked tirelessly in pastoral care, theology, writing, and ecclesiastical and social politics for four decades, until his death ca. 460.[2] He is among the most prolific and most significant theologians of the Greek church, especially on account of his historical, exegetical, and dogmatic works.

During his early years in the episcopate, Theodoret devoted himself mainly to combating the apparently numerous pagans and heretics in Cyrus itself. Most of his works of this period are lost, however. At the Council of Ephesus (431), he was part of the delegation of John of Antioch and with him rejected the condemnation of Nestorius; for this reason, he was condemned by Cyril's partial council. Already in early 431 John of Antioch had encouraged him to write an *Impugnatio XII anathematismorum Cyrilli,* but because of its subsequent condemnation by the Second Council of Constantinople (553), it is preserved only in Cyril's response to it, *Apologia XII anathematismorum contra Theodoretum.* The extensive work *De theologia sanctae Trinitatis et de oeconomia,* written in the same time frame, survived because it was handed down as two of the writings of Cyril of Alexandria with the titles *De sancta trinitate* and *De incarnatione.* Immediately after the Council of Ephesus, Theodoret published a further work against Cyril's Christology, *Pentalogus contra Cyrillum et concilium ephesinum,* which has been lost except for some fragments. It appears that Theodoret himself drafted the formula of reunion in 433, although he did not join it because doing so would have required acknowledgment of Nestorius's condemnation. Only when John of Antioch and the emperor no longer insisted on this did he come out for reunion in 436. When Cyril attacked Diodore of Tarsus and Theodore of Mopsuestia in 438, however, Theodoret opposed Cyril in a written response, *Pro Diodoro et Theodoro;* only fragments of this writing are preserved today.

Theodoret spent the following decade leading his diocese without interference, until the beginning of the controversy about Eutyches, presbyter of Constantinople, which led to renewed disputes between Alexandria and Constantinople and between Alexandrian and Antiochene Christology and to the Council of Chalcedon (451). In 447 he wrote his most significant dogmatic work, *Eranistes,* against the Monophysitism of Eutyches and thereby understandably gained Alexandria's approval. The pro-Eutyches "robber synod" of Ephesus in 449 deposed him, however, and consequently he had to withdraw to his former monastery near Nicerte. On the other hand, the Council of Chalcedon (451)

---

[2] This is the date now argued by Y. Azéma, "Sur la date de la more de Théodoret de Cyr," *Pallas* 31 (1984): 137–55, 192–93 and *DSp* 15:418f., whereas formerly it was 466.

restored him when he officially acceded to Nestorius's condemnation, for the essentially unchanged theology of Nestorius was now far removed from the Christology of Leo the Great and of the Council of Chalcedon, which had developed further in the meantime, and the latter fulfilled the conditions of Antiochene Christology. Theodoret spent the remaining, relatively uneventful years of his life, until ca. 460, attending to the administration of his diocese and to further literary work. He died at peace with the church. Therefore, what has been said above concerning Diodore of Tarsus (ch. 7.IV) also applies to the evaluation of the posthumous condemnation, by the Second Council of Constantinople (553), of Theodoret's works directed against Cyril, as it led to the painful loss of a significant part of his writings.

*Bibliographies:* K.-G. Wesseling, *BBKL* 11:936–57.

*Editions: Opera omnia:* PG 6:1208–40. – PG 75:1147–90, 1419–78. – PG 80–84. – *CorpAp* 4:2–67; 5:2–247. – *Epistulae: Correspondance* (ed. Y. Azéma; 4 vols.; SC 40, 98, 111, 429; Paris: Cerf, 1955; rev. ed. Paris: Cerf, 1982–) [Com]. – *Graecarum affectionum curatio: Terapia dei morbi pagani* (ed. N. Festa; Florence: Testi Cristiani, 1931) [*I–VI*]. – *Thérapeutique des maladies helléniques* (ed. P. Canivet; 2 vols.; rev. ed.; SC 57; Paris: Cerf, 2000–2001) [Com].

*Translations:* B. Jackson, trans., "The Ecclesiastical History, Dialogues, and Letters of Theodoret," in *NPNF²* (Peabody, Mass.: Hendrickson, 1995; repr. of 1892 ed.), 3:1–348 [*Ecclesiastical History, Dialogues, Letters*]. – *On Divine Providence* (trans. T. Halton; ACW 49; Wilmington, Del.: Glazier, 1988).

*Encyclopedia Articles:* K. Smolak, "Theodoret von Cyrus," *GK* 2:239–50. – E. Cavalcanti, *EECh* 2:827–28. – Y. Azéma, *DSp* 15:418–35. – G. H. Ettlinger, *EEC* 2:1117–18.

*Studies:* A. Grillmeier, *Christ in Christian Tradition* (trans. J. Bowden; 2d rev. ed.; Atlanta: John Knox, 1975–), 2/2:431–84; trans. of *Jesus der Christus im Glauben der Kirche* (Fribourg, Switz.: Herder, 1965–). – S. M. Wagner, "A Chapter of Byzantine Epistolography: The Letters of Theodoret of Cyrus," *DOP* 4 (1948): 119–81. – L. Abramowski, "Der Streit um Diodor und Theodor zwischen den beiden ephesinischen Konzilien," *ZKG* 67 (1955–1956): 252–87. – P. Canivet, *Histoire d'une entreprise apologétique au Ve siècle* (Paris: Bloud & Gay, 1957). – G. Koch, *Strukturen und Geschichte des Heils in der Theologie des Theodoret von Kyros: Eine dogmen- und theologiegeschichtliche Untersuchung* (FTS 17; Frankfurt: J. Knecht, 1974). – F. Young, *From Nicaea to Chalcedon* (London: SCM; Philadelphia: Fortress, 1983), 265–89. – Y. Azéma, "Sur la date de la mort de Théodoret de Cyr," *Pallas* 31 (1984): 137–55, 192–93. – S.-P. Bergjan, *Theodoret von Cyrus und der Neunizänismus: Aspekte der altkirchlichen Trinitätslehre* (AKG 60; Berlin and New York: de Gruyter, 1994). – D. Ridings, *The Attic Moses: The Dependency Theme in Some Early Christian Writers* (SGLG 59; Göteborg, Swed.: AUG, 1995), 197–229.

# A. Exegetical Works

The accolade of being the greatest biblical scholar of the Antiochene school may well be bestowed upon Theodoret, rather than on Theodore of Mopsuestia, not merely because of the extent of his exegetical works but because of their originality and quality. The high regard for him is attested in the catenas, where he is cited most frequently and often first. He used two literary forms: (a) commentaries, in the true sense of the term, on Song of Songs, Daniel, Ezekiel, the twelve Minor Prophets, Psalms, Isaiah, Jeremiah, and the fourteen letters of Paul; and (b) *erōtoapokriseis* on the Octateuch, 1 and 2 Kings, and 1 and 2 Chronicles. All of these exegetical works were produced after 433 and are well preserved because of their noncontroversial nature.

Theodoret always begins his interpretation with a precise examination of the condition of the text by comparing the various Greek translations of the Septuagint and of the Syriac Peshitta and clarifying the basic literary issues, such as authenticity, authorship, date, provenance, circumstances at the time, authorial intent, style, literary genre, and so forth. In the interpretation he pursues clear principles, though not a uniform pattern, and certainly not in keeping with the favorite but oversimplifying contrast of Antiochene = literal, Alexandrian = allegorical; instead he adapts his method to what the text says and to the textual complexities. Much more than for Diodore of Tarsus and Theodore of Mopsuestia, for Theodoret the two Testaments constitute an inseparable, complementary unity, so that he fundamentally construes the OT as pointing to Christ typologically. "Theodoret always strives to maintain a centrist position between allegorical arbitrariness and raw literalism."[3] He interprets the Pauline letters mainly christologically and soteriologically.

*Editions: Interpretatio in Isaïam: Commentaire sur Isaïe* (ed. J. N. Guinot; 3 vols.; SC 276, 295, 315; Paris: Cerf, 1980–1984) [Com]. – *Quaestiones in Octateuchum: Theodoreti Cyrensis Quaestiones in Octateuchum* (ed. N. Fernández Marcos and A. Sáenz-Badillos; Madrid: Consejo Superior de Investigaciones Científicas, 1979). – *Quaestiones in Reges et Paralipomena: Theodoreti Cyrensis Quaestiones in Reges et Paralipomena* (ed. N. Fernández Marcos and J. R. Busto Sáiz; Madrid: Instituto Arias Montano, 1984).

*Translations: Psalms 1–72* (trans. R. C. Hill; FC 101; Washington, D.C.: Catholic University of America Press, 2000) [*Commentary on the Psalms 1–72*]. *Commentary on the Letters of St. Paul* (trans. R. C. Hill; Brookline, Mass.: Holy Cross Orthodox Press, 2001).

*Studies—Individual Works:* F. A. Specht, *Der exegetische Standpunkt des Theodor von Mopsuestia und Theodoret von Kyros in der Auslegung messianischer Weissagungen aus ihren Commentaren zu den kleinen Propheten dargestellt* (Munich: J. J. Lentner, 1871). – K. Jüssen, "Die Christologie des Theodoret von Cyrus nach seinem neuveröffentlichten Isaiaskommentar," *TGl* 27 (1935): 438–52. – J. Lépissier, *Les Commentaires des Psaumes de Théodoret (version slave): Étude linguistique et philologique* (Paris: Imprimerie Nationale, 1968). – P. M. Parvis, "Theodoret's Commentary on the Epistles of St. Paul: Historical Setting and Exegetical Practice" (PhD diss., Oxford, 1975). – B. Croke, "Dating Theodoret's *Church History* and *Commentary on the Psalms*," *Byzantion* 54 (1984): 59–74. – J.-N. Guinot, "La christologie de Théodoret de Cyr dans son Commentaire sur le Cantique," *VC* 39 (1985): 256–72. – M. Simonetti, "La tecnica esegetica di Teodoreto nel *Commento ai Salmi*," *VetChr* 23 (1986): 81–116. – M. Simonetti, "Le *Quaestiones* di Teodoreto su Genesi e Esodo," *ASEs* 5 (1988): 39–56.

---

[3] A. Viciano, "Theodoret von Kyros als Interpret des Apostels Paulus," *TGl* 80 [1990]: 279.

– A. Viciano, *Cristo el autor de nuestra salvación: Estudio sobre el Comentario de Teodoreto de Ciro a las Epístolas Paulinas* (CTUN 72; Pamplona: Ediciones Universidad de Navarra, 1990). – A. Viciano, "Theodoret von Kyros als Interpret des Apostels Paulus," *TGl* 80 (1990): 279–315. – S.-P. Bergjan, "Die dogmatische Funktionalisierung der Exegese nach Theodoret von Cyrus," in *Christliche Exegese zwischen Nicaea und Chalcedon* (ed. J. van Oort and U. Wickert; Kampen, Neth.: Kok Pharos, 1992), 32–48. – A. H. A. Fernandez Lois, *La cristología en los Comentarios a Isaias de Cirilo de Alejandria y Teodoreto de Ciro* (Rome: Pontificia Universitas Lateranensis, Institutum Patristicum Augustinianum, 1998). – J. J. O'Keefe, "'A Letter That Killeth'": Towards a Reassessment of Antiochene Exegesis, or Diodore, Theodore, and Theodoret on the Psalms," *JECS* 8 (2000) 83–104.

*Studies:* G. W. Ashby, *Theodoret of Cyrrhus as Exegete of the Old Testament* (Grahamstown, South Africa: Rhodes University Press, 1972). – J.-N. Guinot, "L'importance de la dette de Théodoret de Cyr à l'égard de l'exégèse de Théodore de Mopsueste," *Orph.* NS 5 (1984) 68–109. – J.-N. Guinot, "Theodoret of Cyrus: Bishop and Exegete," in *The Bible in Greek Christian Antiquity* (ed. and trans. P. Blowers; Notre Dame, Ind.: University of Notre Dame Press, 1997), 163–93; trans. of "Un évêque exégète: Théodoret de Cyr," in *Le monde grec ancien et la Bible* (ed. C. Mondésert; Paris: Beauchesne, 1984), 335–60. – J.-N. Guinot, *L'exégèse de Théodoret de Cyr* (ThH 100; Paris: Beauchesne, 1995).

# B. Eranistes *and the Christology of Theodoret*

Theodoret was the only important theologian to experience the entire theological development from Nestorius and the Council of Ephesus (431) to Eutyches and the Council of Chalcedon (451), and he made a substantial contribution to it. For this reason, his christological writings concentrate on the following focal points: (a) the works mentioned above, directed against Cyril, written between 431 and 438/440, which are preserved inadequately because they were condemned by the Second Council of Constantinople (553), and (b) his most important—because it is his most mature—tractate against the Monophysitism of Eutyches, *Eranistes seu Polymorphus* ("Beggar or the Polymorph"), written in 447. The latter work is a further development of a concept that had already been circulating during the Nestorian controversy, namely, that the current errors are to be explained from the history of heresies and hence the Monophysitism of Eutyches, too, was only an amalgam of the multifaceted heresies that preceded (Gnosticism, Arianism, Apollinarianism). Theodoret demonstrates this in the first three books of *Eranistes*, in the literary form of a dialogue between a Monophysite, appearing in the form of a beggar, and an orthodox believer concerning three essential qualities of Christ: bk. 1, the immutability of his divine nature (ἄτρεπτος); bk. 2, the independence of the two natures (ἀσύγχυτος); and bk. 3, the impassibility of his divine nature (ἀπαθής). Book 4 summarizes the results in forty syllogisms. Besides the mature form of Theodoret's Christology, the particular value of *Eranistes* can be seen in the 298 excerpts of 88 patristic works contained in his argumentation; it thus represents a florilegium of Antiochene Christology opposing Cyril's collection. This florilegium apparently already existed at the time of the Council of

Ephesus and was to be used against Cyril there. That Theodoret's Christology developed not only at the time of the two controversies but on an ongoing basis throughout his life can be shown from his biblical commentaries, sermons, 232 extant letters, and the fifth book of his *Haereticarum fabularum compendium*, written in 453. A comprehensive investigation of his christological thinking requires that all of these works be considered.

In keeping with the essential concern of Antiochene Christology, Theodoret stresses the completeness but also the independence of the two natures of Christ. Against Cyril's ἕνωσις κατὰ φύσιν = καθ' ὑπόστασιν, which he charges with Apollinarianism, he posits the concept of union through the assumption (ἐν τῇ συλλήψει) of the human nature (ἡ ληφθεῖσα) by the divine nature (ἡ λαβοῦσα). As a result of this union, there is only one acting subject (πρόσωπον), namely, Christ, although the two natures retain their respective characteristics. The Word of God does not *become* human (John 1:14) but *covers* itself with humanity; he takes on the *forma servi* (Phil 2:7). In this early form of his Christology, Theodoret is not yet able to transcend the doctrine of the "two sons," of which Nestorius had been accused, because his conception can still be misconstrued as a purely external existence of the two natures alongside one another. The reason for this is the yet unresolved terminological problem of equating πρόσωπον and ὑπόστασις, which he ultimately accepted at the Council of Chalcedon (451). In this way and in the affirmation of Mary's θεοτόκος title, he differs fundamentally from Nestorius.

*Edition: Eranistes* (ed. G. H. Ettlinger; Oxford: Clarendon, 1975).

*Translations:* B. Jackson, trans., "Dialogues: The 'Eranistes' or 'Polymorphus' of the Blessed Theodoretus, Bishop of Cyrus," in *NPNF²* (Peabody, Mass.: Hendrickson, 1995; repr. of 1892 ed.), 3:160–244.

*Studies:* M. Mandac, "L'union christologique dans les œuvres de Théodoret antérieures au concile d'Ephèse," *EThL* 47 (1971): 64–96. – J. L. Stewardson, *The Christology of Theodoret of Cyrus according to His "Eranistes"* (Ann Arbor, Mich.: University Microfilms International, 1977). – P. B. Clayton, "Theodoret, Bishop of Cyros, and the Mystery of the Incarnation in Late Antiochene Christianity" (PhD diss., Union Theological Seminary, 1985).

# *C.* Ecclesiastical History

Eusebius's *Ecclesiastical History*, ending with Constantine's victory over Licinius in 324, had already been supplemented three times before Theodoret: up to 395 in the translation and addition by Rufinus, from 305 to 439 in the ecclesiastical history of Socrates, and from 324 to 425 in the ecclesiastical history of Sozomen. In 449/450 Theodoret wrote his sequel to the Eusebian history of the church in five books, covering the period 325 to 428, that is, to the beginning of the Nestorian controversy, and not extending to include the period of his own life. "Because of prudence or concern about objectivity?"[4] Likely both. The

---

[4] Azéma, *DSp* 15:426.

numerous agreements with the works of Socrates and Sozomen are probably not to be explained as mutual dependence but as the common use of the same sources. As in the case of Eusebius, his goal is historical-theological, though for Theodoret this has to be seen in connection with his conception of the historical propagation of heresies, as described above. Thus his *Ecclesiastical History (Historia ecclesiastica)* takes on a strongly apologetic and antiheretical—mainly anti-Arian—orientation within the overall concept of a purposeful salvation history directed by God's providence. In his pursuit of this idea, Theodoret unfortunately did not attach much importance to accuracy in his historical data and the weighing of his assessments. All the same, the work retains its value as a witness to contemporary historical theology and because of the numerous otherwise unknown documents he assimilates.

*Editions: Historia ecclesiastica: Theodoret Kirchengeschichte* (ed. L. Parmentier and F. Scheidweiler; 2d ed., GCS 44; Berlin: Akademie, 1954). – *Historia religiosa: Histoire des moines de Syrie: Histoire Philothée* (ed. P. Canivet and A. Leroy-Molinghen; 2 vols.; SC 234, 257; Paris: Cerf, 1977–1979) [Com].

*Translations:* B. Jackson, trans., "The Ecclesiastical History," in *NPNF*[2] (Peabody, Mass.: Hendrickson, 1995; repr. of 1892 ed.), 3:33–159. – *A History of the Monks of Syria* (trans. R. M. Price; CistSS 88; Kalamazoo: Cistercian, 1985) [*Historia religiosa*].

*Studies:* A. Güldenpenning, *Die Kirchengeschichte des Theodoret von Kyrrhos: Eine Untersuchung ihrer Quellen* (Halle: Max Niemeyer, 1889). – P. Canivet, "Le Περὶ ἀγάπης de Théodoret de Cyr postface de l'*Histoire Philothée*," in *Papers Presented to the Fourth International Conference on Patristic Studies Held at Christ Church, Oxford, 1963* (ed. F. L. Cross; StPatr 7; TU 92; Berlin: Akademie, 1966), 143–58. – P. Canivet, *Le monachisme syrien selon Théodoret de Cyr* (ThH 42; Paris: Beauchesne, 1977). – G. F. Chesnut, "The Date of the Composition of Theodoret's Church History," *VC* 35 (1981): 245–52. – G. F. Chesnut, *The First Christian Histories: Eusebius, Socrates, Sozomen, Theodoret, and Evagrius* (2d ed.; Macon, Ga.: Mercer University Press, 1986), 199–230. – H. Leppin, *Von Constantin dem Grossen zu Theodosius II: Das christliche Kaisertum bei den Kirchenhistorikern Socrates, Sozomenus, und Theodoret* (Hyp. 110; Göttingen: Vandenhoeck & Ruprecht, 1996).

# III. LEO THE GREAT

In the history of the church, only two popes, Leo (440–461) and Gregory (590–604), have been accorded the honorary title "the Great" by posterity; as far as we are conversant with their life and work, both had much in common. On the basis of their origins and education, they were distinguished, prosperous Romans. In times of collapse or radical change in the political and social order in the western part of the (former) Roman Empire, they preserved and actively promoted not only the affairs of the church but personally assumed the necessary political and societal tasks and maintained Rome's great cultural heritage. Nonetheless we know only as much of Leo's personal biography as can be derived from his corpus of letters as bishop—and there he holds back on all personal matters—

as well as a few additional items of information from the *Liber pontificalis* and from scattered remarks by various authors.

Probably at the end of the fourth century, Leo was born into a Tuscan family that moved to Rome early in the fifth century, or he was born in Rome itself. He chose an ecclesiastical career and may be identified with the Roman acolyte mentioned in Augustine's *Ep.* 191.1 of the year 418. When Nestorius and Cyril turned to Rome in 430, he already held an influential position in the episcopal curia, possibly as an archdeacon, advised Pope Celestine in the disputes, and arranged for John Cassian to write his *De incarnatione Domini contra Nestorium.* During this time he actively supported the fight against the Manichaeans and Arians in Rome, intervened with Celestine in 431 on behalf of Cyril of Alexandria against the ambitions of Juvenal of Jerusalem to elevate his episcopal see to the level of a patriarchate, and may have exerted decisive influence upon Rome's anti-Pelagian position among his predecessors, Innocent (402–417), Celestine (422–432), and Sixtus III (432–440). After the death of Sixtus III, on August 19, 440, he received news from Rome that he had been elected bishop of Rome while on a diplomatic mission of reconciliation in Gaul; he was consecrated bishop in Rome on September 29.

Three areas stand out in the more than twenty years Leo held office:

a. His theology and practice of papal jurisdictional primacy, which rendered him the first pope in the modern sense of the term and, more than anything else, brought him the title "the Great." The backdrop for this is the ancient imperial notion of Rome as an "eternal" city and of the (honorary) priority of the episcopal see of the ancient imperial capital as the first patriarchate—a priority that has never been doubted. When the Western empire of Rome began to disintegrate as a result of migratory pressure during Leo's administration, however, the church remained the only constant institution capable of assuming the previous societal, social, and cultural tasks of the state—under Rome's leadership, of course, now under the leadership of the bishop of the capital. Thus the concept of the "eternal city" began to be transferred to Christianity, like the development toward the medieval papacy as successor and representative of the Roman imperial notion.

Hand in hand with the political development came the perfecting of his predecessors' theology of primacy, which he explains authoritatively in his sermons and letters, written in the context of its practical application to Arles, Thessalonica, and Mauretania. According to Leo, Christ is the founder and real shepherd of the church and as such exercises primacy in the church for all time. Upon Peter, who had been particularly close to him, Christ built his church; through him he gave the missionary mandate to the remaining apostles; and he passed on to him the office of pastor and the task of strengthening his brothers in the faith (cf. Matt 16:13–19; Luke 22:32; John 21:15–19). Peter's successors to his see share in this special commission and authority. Although all of the bishops are accorded the same honor (*honor*), as in the case of the apostles, the same is not true of the authority (*potestas*); rather, the church's hierarchy has the shape of a pyramid, with the bishop of Rome at the top.

At the same time, Leo does not underestimate the church as *communio sanctorum* and *communio sacramentorum,* as well as the communion of priests and bishops as *concordia sacerdotum,* expressed in its synodal structure. Because of their special relationship to Rome, the patriarchates of Alexandria and Antioch are given the next highest ranks; for this reason, Leo never recognized canon 28 of the Council of Chalcedon, which intended to superordinate Constantinople's jurisdiction to that of Alexandria and Antioch. In the one person, the emperor exercises a twofold authority, which, while functioning harmoniously, also needs to be clearly differentiated in terms of function. His imperial *auctoritas sacerdotalis* commissions him to protect the faith and the church and to summon councils and ratify their decisions. At the same time, however, the *potestas imperialis* must respect the church's freedom and is not to attempt to interfere with its internal affairs but, as an indispensable foundation of its existence and welfare, to bring about the external conditions for its continued existence and development.

b. His decisive theological and ecclesiastical-political role in the christological controversy concerning Eutyches, leading to the Council of Chalcedon (451). After the reunion of 433, the balance of power between Alexandria and Constantinople had maintained peace regarding the christological question, which ultimately was yet to be resolved. After the death of bishops Sixtus III of Rome (440), John of Antioch (442), Cyril of Alexandria (444), and Proclus of Constantinople (446), the balance of power changed in such ways that the outbreak of a new controversy was almost a necessity. Proclus, the outstanding theologian and mediatory ecclesiastical politician, was followed by Flavian, a personality weak in leadership; the extremely skilled Cyril was followed by Dioscurus, who was equally zealous but had considerably less political finesse; John was followed by his weak nephew, Domnus; Sixtus III, however, was followed by the strongest leadership of the time, Leo. In addition, there was a change of power at the imperial court, whereby Chrysaphius, the chamberlain and godson of Eutyches, the pro-Alexandrian priest and archimandrite of the great monastery of Job in Constantinople, who was to trigger the controversy, assumed the leading role. At the same time, Pulcheria Augusta, the emperor's sister, who was a virgin and had already been very influential in connection with the Council of Constantinople (431) and the reunion (433), was deprived of power and had to withdraw to a monastery.

On the occasion of the endemic synod in Constantinople,[5] Bishop Eusebius of Dorylaeum brought charges against Eutyches on November 8, 448. The consultations extended throughout the month of November; although various attempts at resolving the issue were made, the consensus was that the formula of reunion of 433, together with the *fides nicaena* and Cyril's second letter to Nestorius, remained binding. Thus the synod ultimately condemned Eutyches because he confessed that before the union Christ consisted of two natures but only of one after it (ἐκ δύο φύσεων . . . πρὸ τῆς ἑνώσεως, μετὰ δὲ τὴν ἕνωσιν μίαν φύσιν).

---

[5] Σύνοδος ἐνδημοῦσα = a gathering of the bishops who happened to be in town.

Eutyches, Emperor Theodosius II, and Flavian by letter turned to Leo in Rome, who on June 13, 449, sent his famous *Tomus ad Flavianum* (*Ep.* 28), which was to be decisive for the future. Already by August 1, however, the emperor had summoned a synod to meet in Ephesus to clarify the issue, to which Leo sent legates as well. Under the leadership of Dioscurus, the council, commencing on August 8, ignored Leo's *Tomus*, rehabilitated Eutyches against the protest of the Roman legates, which was suppressed with the force of arms, and deposed Flavian, who died while still on the way into exile (449 or 450). For this reason, Leo later described the synod as a *latrocinium* ("robber synod") (*Ep.* 95.2: *ACO* 2.4.51) and did not recognize its decisions. The synod also went down in history with this designation.

At the imperial court, Leo unsuccessfully lent his support for convening a new council. Only with the sudden death of Emperor Theodosius, who died childless on July 28, 450, did the situation change fundamentally. Pulcheria, his sister, returned from the monastery, was married on August 24, 450, to a senator named Marcian on the condition that this marriage not be consummated, had him proclaimed emperor, and from then on determined imperial politics. The new emperor now planned to summon the council for which Leo had been striving, but since he accepted Leo's *Tomus* in any case, Leo was no longer keenly interested in it, since the issue per se and the matter of his understanding of the primacy had been settled. Since the emperor, however, had already summoned the council before he became aware of Leo's concerns, the latter did not object to it but insisted that he himself lead the council through his legates. Thus the Council of Chalcedon became the first ecumenical council in the history of the church in which the leadership of the Roman bishop was understood in terms of his primacy. It ratified the Christology of the *Tomus* and out of it formulated its *symbolum*, although quarrels about its acceptance began immediately after the council and were to occupy Leo until the end of his life (461).

c. Leo's two missions to save the city of Rome. When Attila, the king of the Huns, invaded Italy with his hordes in 452, Leo, together with an imperial delegation, traveled to meet him in Mantua and was able to move him to spare the city of Rome. When Genseric, the king of the Vandals, and his people arrived outside Rome in 455, Leo succeeded a second time in having Rome spared from fire and murder, even if it had to endure being looted for two weeks.

These three peaks in Leo's work only describe the tip of his extensive pastoral activity, which could not limit itself to the ecclesiastical realm but increasingly had to fill the political, social, and cultural vacuum in the declining Western Roman Empire. As scholars unanimously point out, he was imbued with the virtues of *moderatio* and *humilitas*. Because of his upbringing and education and his awareness that Christ alone is the Lord of the church whereas he is only his servant, he pursued a constant path of moderation and agreement in matters of theology as well as discipline and politics. Leo died on November 10, 461; Benedict XIV elevated him to the status of doctor of the church on October 15, 1754.

*Bibliographies:* A. Lauras, "Études sur saint Léon le Grand," *RSR* 49 (1961): 481–99.

*Editions: Opera omnia:* PL 54–56. – PLS 3:329–50. – *Epistolae: Epistolae* (ed. W. Gundlach; MGH.AA 3; Berlin: Weidmann, 1892), 15–22. – *Epistulae imperatorum, pontificum, aliorum inde ab a. CCCLXVII usque ad a. DLIII datae: Avellana quae dicitur collectio* (ed. O. Guenther; 2 vols.; CSEL 35; Vienna: F. Temsky, 1895), 117–24. – *ACO* 2/4. – *Tractatus: Sermons* (ed. J. Leclercq and R. Dolle; 4 vols.; 2d ed.; SC 22 bis, 49 bis, 74 bis, 200; Paris: Cerf, 1964–1976) [Com]. – *Tractatus septem et nonaginta* (ed. A. Chavasse; CCSL 138A; Turnhout, Belg.: Brepols, 1973).

*Translations: The Letters and Sermons of Leo the Great, Bishop of Rome* (vol. 12 of *NPNF²*; trans. C. L. Feltoe; Peabody, Mass.: Hendrickson, 1995; repr. of 1895 ed.), 1–205. – *Letters* (trans. E. Hunt; FC 34; New York: Fathers of the Church, 1957; repr., Washington, D.C.: Catholic University of America Press, 1963). – *Sermons* (trans. J. P. Freeland and A. J. Conway; FC 93; Washington, D.C.: Catholic University of America Press, 1996).

*Encyclopedia Articles:* G. Hudon, *DSp* 9:597–611. – B. Studer, *TRE* 20:737–41. – B. Studer, *EECh* 1:479. – G. A. Zinn, *EEC* 2:674–76.

*General Studies:* E. Caspar, *Geschichte des Papsttums von den Anfängen bis zur Höhe der Weltherrschaft, I: Römische Kirche und imperium romanum* (Tübingen: Mohr, 1930), 423–564. – R. Galli, "S. Leone Magno e i suoi scritti," *Did.* 9 (1930): 51–235. – T. Jalland, *The Life and Times of St. Leo the Great* (London: SPCK, 1941). – R. Dolle, *Léon le Grand* (Paris: Cerf, 1961). – N. W. James, "Leo the Great and Prosper of Aquitaine: A Fifth Century Pope and His Adviser," *JTS* NS 44 (1993): 554–84.

*Ecclesiology and Soteriology:* J. Rivière, "Le dogme de la rédemption après saint Augustin," *RevScRel* 9 (1929): 11–42, 153–87. – E. M. Burke, *The Church in the Works of Leo the Great* (Washington, D.C.: n.p., 1945). – L. J. McGovern, *The Ecclesiology of Saint Leo the Great* (Rome: Tip. Dapco, Daily American Publishing, 1957). – J.-P. Jossua, *Le salut, incarnation ou mystère pascal: Chez les Pères de l'Église de saint Irénée à saint Léon le Grand* (Paris: Cerf, 1968), 251–382. – G. Hudon, "L'Église dans la pensée de saint Léon," *EgT* 14 (1983): 305–36.

*Primacy and Conciliarism:* J. Ludwig, *Die Primatworte Mt 16, 18.19 in der altkirchlichen Exegese* (NTAbh 19.4; Münster: Aschendorff, 1952). – W. Ullmann, "Leo I and the Theme of Papal Primacy," *JTS* NS 11 (1960): 25–51. – A. Krömer, "Die Sedes Apostolica der Stadt Rom in ihrer theologischen Relevanz innerhalb der abendländischen Kirchengeschichte bis Leo I" (PhD diss., Fribourg University, 1972). – H. J. Sieben, *Die Konzilsidee der alten Kirche* (Paderborn: Schöningh, 1979), 103–47. – M. Wojtowytsch, *Papsttum und Konzilie von den Anfängen bis zu Leo I. (440–461): Studien zur Entstehung der Überordnung des Papstes über die Konzile* (PuP 17; Stuttgart: Hiersemann, 1981). – S. O. Horn, *Petrou kathedra: Der Bischof von Rom und die Synoden von Ephesus (449) und Chalcedon* (KKTS 45; Paderborn: Bonifatius, 1982). – P. Stockmeier, "*Universalis Ecclesia:* Papst Leo der Grosse und der Osten," in *Kirchengemeinschaft—Anspruch und Wirklichkeit: Festschrift für Georg Kretschmar zum 60. Geburtstag* (ed. W.-D. Hauschild, C. Nicolaisen, and D. Wendebourg; Stuttgart: Calwer, 1986), 83–91.

*Philology and Preaching:* J. Pschmadt, *Leo der Grosse als Prediger* (Elberfeld: Wuppertaler Aktien-Druckerei, 1912). – W. J. Halliwell, *The Style of Pope St. Leo the Great* (PatSt 59; Washington, D.C.: Catholic University of America Press, 1939). – M. M. Mueller, *The Vocabulary of Pope St. Leo the Great* (PatSt 67; Washington, D.C.: Catholic University of America Press, 1943). – F. X. Murphy, "The Sermons of Pope Leo the Great: Content and Style," in *Preaching in the Patristic Age: Studies in Honor of Walter J.*

*Burghardt, S.J.* (ed. D. G. Hunter; New York: Paulist, 1989), 183–97. – W. Blümer, *Rerum eloquentia: Christliche Nutzung antiker Stilkunst bei St. Leo Magnus* (EHS 15.51; Frankfurt and New York: Lang, 1991). – M. Naldini, *I Sermoni di Leone Magno: Fra storia e teologia* (BPat 30; Florence: Nardini, 1997).

*Rome and the Roman Empire:* H. M. Klinkenberg, "Papsttum und Reichskirche bei Leo d. Gr." *Zeitschrift der Savigny-Stiftung für Rechtsgeschichte: Kanonistische Abteilung* 38 (1952): 37–112. – P. Stockmeier, *Leos I. des Grossen Beurteilung der kaiserlichen Religionspolitik* (MThS.H 14; Munich: Hueber, 1959). – J. Oroz Reta, "San León, papa de la Romanidad," *Helm.* 13 (1962): 163–91. – C. Bartnik, "L'interprétation théologique de la crise de l'empire romain par Léon le Grand," *RHE* 63 (1968): 745–84. – J. Fellermayr, *Tradition und Sukzession im Lichte des römisch-antiken Erbdenkens: Untersuchungen zu den lateinischen Vätern bis zu Leo dem Grossen* (Munich: Minerva, 1979). – P. A. McShane, *La Romanitas et le pape Léon le Grand: L'apport culturel des institutions impériales à la formation des structures ecclésiastiques* (Tournai: Desclée; Montreal: Bellarmin, 1979).

*Theology:* A. Guillaume, *Jeûne et charité dans l'église latine des origines au douzième siècle, en particulier chez s. Léon le Grand* (Paris: Laboureur, 1954). – P. Hervé de l'Incarnation, "La grâce dans l'œuvre de S. Léon le Grand," *RTAM* 22 (1955): 17–55, 193–212. – M. B. de Soos, *Le mystère liturgique d'après saint Léon le Grand* (LQF 34; Münster: Aschendorff, 1958). – G. Hudon, *La perfection chrétienne d'après les sermons de s. Léon* (Paris: Cerf, 1959). – B. Studer, "Die Einflüsse der Exegese Augustins auf die Predigten Leos des Grossen," in *Forma futuri: Studi in onore del cardinale Michele Pellegrino* (Turin: Bottega d'Erasmo, 1975), 915–30; repr. in B. Studer, *Dominus Salvator: Studien zur Christologie und Exegese der Kirchenväter* (SA 107; Rome: Pontificio Ateneo S. Anselmo, 1992), 121–39. – R. Fernández, *Antropología de san León Magno* (Pamplona: n.p., 1985). – P. L. Barclift, "Predestination and Divine Foreknowledge in the Sermons of Pope Leo the Great," *ChH* 62 (1993): 5–21.

# Tomus ad Flavianum *and Leo's Christology*

The *Tomus ad Flavianum* of 449, which gained world recognition as the foundation of the christological decision of the Council of Chalcedon (451), is composed of 205 verses (in contrast to previous divisions, according to Arens) and can be organized into five main sections.

a. Introduction with a brief description and evaluation of the situation concerning Eutyches (1–11)

b. (Anti-Docetic) development of the theology of incarnation, adducing texts with Eutyches in mind (12–53)

    1) interpretation of the Apostles' creed: eternal origin of the Son from God the Father and his temporal birth from a virgin (12–29)

    2) scriptural support (30–42)

    3) reinforcement of the above with reference to a difficulty suspected in Eutyches (43–53)

c. Outline of the doctrine of the two natures by means of a series of (self-citations compiled for the *Tomus* (54–157)

1–5) texts from Leo's *Tractatus*, Gaudentius of Brescia, and Augustine (54–151)

6) verdict on the teaching of Eutyches (152–157)

d. Continuation of part II (158–187)

1) Jesus' passion and death as a witness for his human nature (158–162)
2) the significance of the death of Jesus for redemption and the (sacramental) church (163–176)
3) treatment of a specific statement of Eutyches (177–187)

e. Conclusion; determination of a further plan of action and announcement of the commissioned legation (188–205)

Starting with the creed, the fundamental aspect of Leo's Christology is the theologoumenon of the twofold birth of Christ and thus of his twofold consubstantiality with God and humans: "and the same only-begotten and everlasting Son of an eternal Parent was 'born of the Holy Ghost and the Virgin Mary'" (21: *idem vero sempiterni genitoris unigenitus sempiternus natus est de Spiritu Sancto et Maria virgine*). For the God-man to be one, therefore, there had to be a twofold movement of coming together in the incarnation of the Son of God; God divested himself and the human was elevated to a union of personhood: "While the distinctness of both natures and substances was preserved and both met in one person, lowliness was assumed by majesty, weakness by power, mortality by eternity" (54–56: *salva igitur proprietate utriusque naturae et in unam coeunte personam, suscepta est a maiestate humilitas, a virtute infirmitas, ab aeternitate mortalitas*). It can be demonstrated that Leo was conversant with the central christological statements of Augustine, who refers to *una persona Christi in utraque natura* and to the conception used here of the mutual coming together of the natures to become a union; thus it may well be assumed that Leo's Christology is substantially indebted to Augustine. Both natures remain unchanged and unmixed: "The same who is true God is true man, . . . for as God is not changed by condescension, so man is not consumed by sublimity" (91–93: *qui enim verus est Deus, idem verus est homo . . . sicut enim Deus non mutatur miseratione, ita homo non consumitur dignitate*). In Christ, however, only one subject (one person) acts in connection with the two natures (*agit enim utraque forma cum alterius communione*), consequently resulting in the *communicatio idiomatum:* "On account of this unity of person, which is to be understood as existing in both the natures, we read, on the one hand, that 'the Son of Man came down from heaven,' . . . and on the other hand, the Son of God is said to have been crucified and buried" (126–132: *propter hanc ergo unitatem personae in utraque natura intellegendum, et filius hominis legitur descendisse de caelo* [John 3:13], . . . *et rursum filius Dei crucifixus dicitur ac sepultus*).

It is commonly known and readily discernible from his letters that Leo made use of his chancery in writing them, which leads to the question whether others also contributed to the writing of *Tomus ad Flavianum*, especially Prosper of Aquitaine, as Gennadius of Marseilles reports (*Vir. illus.* 4f.). More recent scholarship is inclined to answer the question affirmatively, without denying Leo the original outline of the content.

*Editions:* ACO 2/2.1:24–33. – *S. Leonis Magni Tomus ad Flavianum episc. Constantinopolitanum (Epistula XXVIII): Additis testimoniis patrum et eiusdem S. Leonis M. epistula ad Leonum I Imp. (Epistula CLXV)* (ed. C. Silva-Tarouca; TD.T 9; Rome: Pontificia Universitas Gregoriana, 1932); *S. Leonis Magni epistulae contra Eutychis haeresim* (ed. C. Silva-Tarouca; TD.T 15, 20; Rome: Pontificia Universitas Gregoriana, 1934–1935); *Epistularum romanorum pontificium ad vicarios per Illyricum aliosque episcopos collectio Thessalonicensis* (ed. C. Silva-Tarouca; TD.T 23; Rome: Pontificia Universitas Gregoriana, 1937). – DH 290–95. – N. P. Tanner and G. Alberigo, *Decrees of the Ecumenical Councils* (London: Sheed & Ward; Washington, D.C.: Georgetown University Press, 1990), 77–82 [ET].

*Translations:* E. R. Hardy and C. C. Richardson, eds., *The Christology of the Later Fathers* (LCC 3; Philadelphia: Westminster, 1954), 359–70. – R. Norris, *The Christological Controversy* (SoECT; Philadelphia: Fortress, 1980), 145–55. – J. Stevenson, *Creeds, Councils, and Controversies* (rev. W. H. C. Frend; rev. ed.; London: SPCK, 1989), 336–44.

*Studies:* J. Gaidioz, "Saint Prosper d'Aquitaine et le Tome à Flavien," *RevScRel* 23 (1949): 270–301. – M. J. Nicolas, "La doctrine christologique de saint Léon le Grand," *RThom* (1951): 609–60. – U. Domínguez-Del Val, "S. León Magno y el *Tomus ad Flavianum*," *Helm.* (1962): 193–233. – B. Studer, "*Consubstantialis Patri, consubstantialis matri:* Une antithèse christologique chez Léon le Grand," *REAug* (1972): 87–115. – H. Arens, *Die christologische Sprache Leos des Grossen: Analyse des Tomus an den Patriarchen Flavian* (FThSt 122; Fribourg, Switz.: Herder, 1982). – B. Studer, "*Una persona in Christo:* Ein augustinisches Thema bei Leo dem Grossen," *Aug* 25 (1985): 453–87. – P. L. Barclift, "The Shifting Tones of Pope Leo the Great's Christological Vocabulary," *ChH* 66 (1997): 221–39; repr. in *History, Hope, Human Language, and Christian Reality* (ed. E. Ferguson; Recent Studies in Early Christianity 6; New York: Garland, 1999), 229–48.

# IV. COUNCIL OF CHALCEDON (451)

The Council of Chalcedon and its *symbolum* are widely considered the conclusion of an entire epoch in the history of the church. Strictly from the perspective of the history of dogma, this is rightly so, for the christological formula of *una persona in duabus naturis* of Christ, agreed upon here, continues to be confessed unchanged and without substantial additions by the Catholic Church today. In connection with the larger context of the history of theology, however, the Council of Chalcedon does not represent the conclusion but rather the decisive apex of a trajectory. It extends from the beginning of the formulation of the question concerning the union of the two natures of Christ in the dispute with Nestorius, beginning in 428, via the council itself, the controversial history of the acceptance of its theology, the Three Chapters dispute, and the Second Council of Constantinople (553) to the dispute concerning Monothelitism and the Third Council of Constantinople (*Trullanum,* 680–681).

Brought about by the christological question of the unity of Christ, the God-man, which had not yet been clarified conclusively since Nestorius, as well as the immediate history, from the endemic synod of Constantinople (448) via the "robber synod" of Ephesus and Leo's *Tomus ad Flavianum,* Emperor Marcian summoned a council to meet in Nicea on September 1, 451. Because of concern that new quarrels would break out, Leo would have preferred not to convene a council at all or at least to delay it until the uncertain political situation brought about by the threat of the Huns would allow it to convene in Italy. Since he could not question the emperor's summoning authority, however, he requested that the discussion at least be limited to the dogmatic issue. When the emperor did not agree to this, Leo was forced to consent and delegated four legates, namely, the Roman presbyter Bonifatius; Paschasinus, bishop of Lilybaeum (Marsala, Sicily); Julian, bishop of Kos; and Lucensius, bishop of Asculum (Ascoli). The emperor was not able to be present at Nicea on September 1, 451, however, because of the invasions of the Huns. Since the council was not allowed to begin without him and 450 bishops had assembled, the emperor moved the council to Chalcedon on September 22, right at the gates of Constantinople (in Kadiköy, a section of the present city that is in Asia Minor), where he was able to participate in the council sessions despite urgent governmental business in the capital.

The council met from October 8 to 31, rehabilitated Flavian, deposed Dioscurus, and in its fifth session, on October 22, defined the *symbolum*. It also reinstated bishops Theodoret of Cyrus and Ibas of Edessa, who had been deposed by the "robber synod" of Ephesus (449), and in the seventh (or fifteenth) session passed twenty-eight canons on discipline, of which only twenty-seven were inserted into the collections of conciliar records because Rome did not recognize the twenty-eighth.

*Encyclopedia Articles:* L. R. Wickham, *TRE* 7:668–75. – M. Simonetti, *EECh* 1:159. – F.W. Norris, *EEC* 1:233–34.

*Translations:* H. R. Percival, trans., "The Fourth Ecumenical Council—the Council of Chalcedon, A.D. 451," in *NPNF²* (Peabody, Mass.: Hendrickson, 1995; repr. of 1890 ed.), 14:243–95 [*Acta* (extracts), *Sentence of Condemnation of Dioscorus, Definition of Faith of the Council, Decree on the Jurisdiction of Jerusalem and Antioch, Canons*].

*Studies:* C. H. Hefele and H. Leclercq, *Histoire des conciles: D'après les documents originaux* (Paris: Letouzey, 1907–), 2.1–2:662–880. – A. Grillmeier and H. Bacht, eds., *Das Konzil von Chalkedon: Geschichte und Gegenwart* (3 vols.; 5th ed.; Würzburg: Echter, 1979). – R. V. Sellers, *The Council of Chalcedon: A Historical and Doctrinal Survey* (London: SPCK, 1953; repr., 1961). – P.-T. Camelot, *Éphèse et Chalcédoine* (HCO 2; Paris: Orante, 1962), 77–182 [ted Mz 1963]. – P. Stockmeier, "Das Konzil von Chalkedon: Probleme der Forschung," *FZPhTh* 29 (1982): 140–56. – G. May, "Das Lehrverfahren gegen Eutyches im November des Jahres 448: Zur Vorgeschichte des Konzils von Chalkedon," *AHC* 21 (1989): 1–61. – L. Perrone, in *Storia dei concili ecumenici* (ed. G. Alberigo; Brescia: Queriniana, 1990), 71–107. – R. Norris Jr., "Chalcedon Revisited: A Historical and Theological Reflection," in *New Perspectives on Historical Theology: Essays in Memory of John Meyendorff* (ed. B. Nassif; Grand Rapids: Eerdmans, 1996), 140–58; repr. in *Norms of Faith and Life* (ed. E. Ferguson; Recent Studies in Early Christianity 3; New York: Garland, 1999), 158–77. – J. van Oort and J. Roldanus, eds., *Chalkedon—Geschichte und Aktualität: Studien zur Rezeption der christologischen Formel von Chalkedon* (Louvain: Peeters, 1997).

# A. Symbolum

The dogmatic definition of the council is organized into three parts: (a) In a lengthy introduction, it presents the reason for the council and then appeals to the valid creedal statement of the councils of Nicea (325) and Constantinople (381) as well as to the synodal letters of Cyril. (b) It further identifies the errors to be repelled, namely, the rejection of the θεοτόκος title on the grounds of the doctrine of the "two sons" (Nestorius), on the one hand, and the mixing of the two natures of Christ (Eutyches), on the other. (c) This is followed by the christological definition as such, with an explicit appeal to the tradition of the Fathers. An analysis shows that the sources from which it is composed are the letter of John of Antioch to Cyril on the reunion of 433 (1–6), the *Tomus Leonis* (7–18, 20), Cyril's letters to Nestorius and those of Flavian to Leo (19, 21), and a letter of Theodoret of Cyrus (22f.).

1. Ἑπόμενοι τοίνυν τοῖς ἁγίοις πατράσιν [1] So, following the saintly fathers,
2. ἕνα καὶ τὸν αὐτὸν ὁμολογεῖν υἱὸν [4] we all with one voice teach
3. τὸν κύριον ἡμῶν Ἰησοῦν Χριστὸν [2] the confession of one and the same Son,
4. συμφώνως ἅπαντες ἐκδιδάσκομεν, [3] our Lord Jesus Christ;
5. τέλειον τὸν αὐτὸν ἐν θεότητι [5] the same perfect in divinity
6. καὶ τέλειον τὸν αὐτὸν ἐν ἀνθρωπότητι [6] and perfect in humanity,
7. θεὸν ἀληθῶς καὶ ἄνθρωπον ἀληθῶς [7] the same truly God and truly man,
8. τὸν αὐτὸν ἐκ ψυχῆς λογικῆς καὶ σώματος, [8] of a rational soul and a body;
9. ὁμοούσιον τῷ πατρὶ κατὰ τὴν θεότητα [9] consubstantial with the Father as regards his divinity,
10. καὶ ὁμοούσιον ἡμῖν τὸν αὐτὸν κατὰ τὴν ἀνθρωπότητα, [10] and the same consubstantial with us as regards his humanity;
11. κατὰ πάντα ὅμοιον ἡμῖν χωρὶς ἁμαρτίας [11] like us in all respects except for sin;
12. πρὸ αἰώνων μὲν ἐκ τοῦ πατρὸς γεννηθέντα κατὰ τὴν θεότητα, [12] begotten before the ages from the Father as regards his divinity
13. ἐπ' ἐσχάτων δὲ τῶν ἡμέρων [13] and in the last days
14. τὸν αὐτὸν δι' ἡμᾶς καὶ διὰ τὴν ἡμετέραν σωτηρίαν [14] the same for us and for our salvation
15. ἐκ Μαρίας τῆς παρθένου τῆς θεοτόκου κατὰ τὴν ἀνθρωπότητα [15] from Mary, the Virgin God-bearer, as regards his humanity;
16. ἕνα καὶ τὸν αὐτὸν Χριστὸν υἱὸν κύριον μονογενῆ, [16] one and the same Christ, Son, Lord, Only-begotten, acknowledged
17. ἐν δύο φύσεσιν [17] in two natures
18. ἀσυγχύτως ἀτρέπτως ἀδιαιφέτως ἀχωρίστως γνωριζόμενον [18] which undergo no confusion, no change, no division, no separation;
19. οὐδαμοῦ τῆς τῶν φύσεων διαφορᾶς ἀνηρημένης διὰ τὴν ἕνωσιν [19] at no point was the difference between the natures taken away through the union,

20. σωζομένης δὲ μᾶλλον τῆς          [20] but rather the property of both natures
    ἰδιότητος ἑκατέρας φύσεως               is preserved
21. καὶ εἰς ἓν πρόσωπον καὶ μίαν      [21] and comes together into a single person
    ὑπόστασιν συντρεχούσης                 and a single subsistent being;
22. οὐκ εἰς δύο πρόσωπα μεριζόμενον   [22] he is not parted or divided into two
    ἢ διαιρούμενον,                        persons,
23. ἀλλ' ἕνα καὶ τὸν αὐτὸν υἱὸν       [23] but is one and the same only-begotten
    μονογενῆ                               Son,
24. θεὸν λόγον κύριον Ἰησοῦν Χριστόν, [24] God, Word, Lord Jesus Christ,
25. καθάπερ ἄνωθεν οἱ προφῆται περὶ   [25] just as the prophets taught from the
    αὐτου                                  beginning about him,
26. καὶ αὐτὸς ἡμᾶς Ἰησοῦς Χριστὸς    [26] and as the Lord Jesus Christ himself
    ἐξεπαίδευσεν                           instructed us,
27. καὶ τὸ τῶν πατέρων ἡμῶν          [27] and as the creed of the fathers handed it
    παραδέδωκε σύμβολον.                   down to us.[6]

The definition concludes with the customary anathema against all those who will not accept it.

"The definition of Chalcedon, however, is not so much a compromise or a clever mixture extrapolated from the contrasting views as it is the point where various theological traditions merge."[7] The *symbolum* of Chalcedon may indeed be regarded as the successful climax of, and conclusion to, the unification of Alexandrian and Antiochene Christologies, especially regarding the clarification of the terminology. All the same, with its expression "in two natures" instead of "out of two natures," it laid the groundwork for the centuries-long painful consequences of its acceptance and the splitting off of the Coptic church because, for Alexandrian theology, this had the ring of Dyophysitism whereas, after the agreement on the person as the concept of unity, the Alexandrians' μία φύσις developed into heretical Monophysitism.

Editions: ACO 2. – DH 300–303. – N. P. Tanner and G. Alberigo, *Decrees of the Ecumenical Councils* (London: Sheed & Ward; Washington, D.C.: Georgetown University Press, 1990), 83–87 [ET].

Translations: E. R. Hardy and C. C. Richardson, eds., *The Christology of the Later Fathers* (LCC 3; London: SCM; Philadelphia: Westminster, 1954), 371–74. – R. Norris, *The Christological Controversy* (SoECT; Philadelphia: Fortress, 1980), 155–59. – J. Stevenson, *Creeds, Councils, and Controversies* (rev. W. H. C. Frend; rev. ed.; London: SPCK, 1989), 350–54.

Studies: A. de Halleux, "La définition christologique à Chalcédoine," *RTL* 7 (1976): 3–23, 155–70. – A. Grillmeier, *Mit ihm und in ihm: Christologische Forschungen und Perspektiven* (Fribourg, Switz.: Herder, 1975). – W. H. C. Frend, *The Rise of the Monophysite Movement: Chapters in the History of the Church in the Fifth and Sixth*

---

[6] This translation is from Jaroslav Pelikan and Valerie Hotchkiss, eds., *Creeds & Confessions of Faith in the Christian Tradition* (4 vols.; New Haven: Yale University Press, 2003), 1:181.

[7] P.-T. Camelot, *Éphèse et Chalcédoine* (HCO 2; Paris: Orante, 1962), 159.

Centuries (rev. ed.; Cambridge: Cambridge University Press, 1979). – A. de Halleux, "La réception du symbole œcuménique, de Nicée à Chalcédoine," EThL 61 (1985): 5–47. – A. Baxter, "Chalcedon, and the Subject of Christ," DR 107 (1989): 1–21. – J. Galot, " 'Une seule personne, une seule hypostase': Origine et sens de la formule de Chalcédoine," Greg 70 (1989): 251–76.

# B. Canons and the Synodal Letter

The twenty-eight canons the council passed in its final sessions deal with the most diverse matters of discipline for dioceses, clergy, and monks. Of most interest, however, is only the last, the twenty-eighth canon, passed on October 29, which is missing in the transmission of the council records because Rome never recognized it; indeed it was immediately rejected by Leo. In its third canon the Council of Constantinople (381) had allowed the episcopal see of Constantinople, as the new Rome, the honorary rank of second after Rome, though without encroaching upon the traditional jurisdictional rights of the two other patriarchates of Alexandria and Antioch. Instead it had confirmed the latter explicitly in canon 2. Now, however, by appeal to the council of 381, the patriarchate of Constantinople was being accorded the same rights as ancient Rome. On the one hand, this would curtail the rights of Alexandria and Antioch; on the other, given the present status of the theology of primacy, it would have meant the establishment of a second see of primacy in Constantinople. The papal legates, who were not present when the vote was taken, immediately protested, albeit unsuccessfully, in the following meeting on October 30. In keeping with custom, the council wrote a synodal letter to inform the bishops who were not present, which they handed to the Roman legates for Leo (Ep. 98). Leo hesitated with a response for a considerable time, however, and acknowledged the council's decisions by letter only on March 21, 453, after some correspondence with the emperor and the bishops. Canon 28 indeed was not accepted.

Editions: DH 304–6. – N. P. Tanner and G. Alberigo, Decrees of the Ecumenical Councils (London: Sheed & Ward; Washington, D.C.: Georgetown University Press, 1990), 87–103 [ET].

Translations: J. Stevenson, Creeds, Councils, and Controversies (rev. W. H. C. Frend; rev. ed.; London: SPCK, 1989), 354–64.

Studies: W. Bright, The Canons of the First Four General Councils of Nicaea, Constantinople, Ephesus, and Chalcedon, with Notes (2d ed.; Oxford: Clarendon, 1892). – A. Wuyts, "Le 28ème canon de Chalcédoine et le fondement du primat romain," OCP 17 (1951): 265–82. – V. Monachino, "Genesi storica del canone 28° di Calcedonia," Greg 33 (1952): 261–91; V. Monachino, "Il canone 28° di Calcedonia e S. Leone Magno," Greg 33 (1952): 531–65; repr. in idem, Il canone 28 di Calcedonia: Genesi storica (L'Aquila: Japadre, 1979). – P. L'Huillier, The Church of the Ancient Councils: The Disciplinary Work of the First Four Ecumenical Councils (Crestwood, N.Y.: St. Vladimir's Seminary Press, 1996), 181–328.

# CHAPTER ELEVEN

# Literature of the Latin West

*Studies:* J. Herrin, *The Formation of Christendom* (rev. ed.; Princeton, N.J.: Princeton University Press, 1989). – A. di Berardino, ed., *Dal concilio di Calcedonia (451) a Beda: I Padri latini* (Patrologia 4; Genoa: Marietti, 1996). – P. Brown, *The Rise of Western Christendom: Triumph and Diversity, AD 200–1000* (2d ed.; Malden, Mass.: Blackwell, 2003).

## I. SALVIAN OF MARSEILLES

Salvian's life span coincided fairly closely with the fifth century, and so he experienced the horrors of mass migration and the disintegration of the Roman Empire throughout this period of time and perhaps at its most turbulent focal point, Gaul. His biography, as much (or, rather, as little) as we know of it, and his work were entirely shaped by these events.

He was born in Cologne or Trier ca. 400, and his description of the (third) conquest of Trier by the Franks, through which he lived (ca. 418–420) as a young man, belongs to the most stirring historical testimonials in world literature (*De gubernatione Dei* 6.15.82–89), despite the fact that its reliability has been questioned again lately. There is no doubt that he enjoyed a good education and legal training, as his writings demonstrate, and married a non-Christian by the name of Palladia. Whether he himself was raised in a Christian family or at what point in time he converted to Christianity remains unknown. In any case, after the birth of Auspiciola, their daughter, the couple agreed, for Christian ascetical motives, to continue the marriage in continence, and so it has to be assumed that they had become confessing Christians by then. The specific time of this *conversio* can only be approximated. It led to years of disagreements with his parents-in-law, which still continued when the latter also converted to Christianity. In *Ep.* 4, written seven years after the *conversio*, Salvian endeavored to be reconciled and apparently still lived with his wife and child. Since he belonged to the monastic community of Lérins beginning in 426 at the latest, however, the *conversio* has to be fixed to at least before 420. Beginning in 429 he functioned as a priest in Lérins or Marseilles, but we do not know when or where he was ordained to the priesthood. Furthermore, we have no knowledge of his pastoral ministry. About 467, in *De viris illustribus* (67), his continuation of Jerome's work of the same name, Gennadius of Marseilles makes mention of him as *in senectute bona*, that is, a healthy man of over sixty years of age. Gennadius and Hilarius of Arles also list his works, of which all but three are lost, however: *De gubernatione Dei* (in Gennadius: *De praesenti iudicio*), *Ad ecclesiam* (in Gennadius: *Adversus avaritiam*), and nine letters.

*Bibliographies:* H. R. Drobner, *BBKL* 8:1258–66.

*Editions: Opera omnia: Salviani presbyteri Massiliensis libri qui svpersvnt* (ed. C. Halm; MGH.AA 1.1; Berlin: Weidmann, 1877). – *Salviani presbyteri Massiliensis Opera omnia* (ed. F. Pauly; CSEL 8; Vienna: Apud C. Geroldi Filium, 1883). – *Oeuvres* (ed. G. Lagarrigue; 2 vols.; SC 176, 220; Paris: Cerf, 1971–1975) [Com].

*Translations: The Writings of Salvian the Presbyter* (trans. J. F. O'Sullivan; FC 3; New York: Cima, 1947; repr., Washington, D.C.: Catholic University of America Press in association with Consortium Books, 1977), 25–263 [*The Governance of God, Letters, The Four Books of Timothy to the Church*].

*Reference Works:* Demetrius Barbulius, *Salviani concordantiae* (Pisa: n.p., 1729).

*Encyclopedia Articles:* G. Lagarrigue, *DSp* 14:290–97. – M. Pellegrino, *EECh* 2:754. – M. McHugh, *EEC* 2:1025–26.

*General Studies:* M. Pellegrino, *Salviano di Marsiglia* (Lat. 6.1–2; Rome: Facultas Theologica Pontificii Athenaei Lateranensis, 1940). – E. Griffe, *La Gaule chrétienne à l'époque romaine* (2 vols.; rev. ed.; Paris: Letouzey, 1966).

*Philology:* C. Brakman, "Observationes grammaticae et criticae in Salvianum," *Mn.* 52 (1924): 113–85. – L. Rochus, *La latinité de Salvien* (MAB.L 30.2; Brusells: Palais des Academies, 1934). – O. Janssen, *L'expressivité chez Salvien de Marseille: Étude sur l'usage de quelques particules dans le latin chrétien* (LCP 7; Nijmegen: Dekker & van de Vegt, 1937).

*Political and Historical Context:* G. Sternberg, "Das Christentum des 5. Jahrhunderts im Spiegel der Schriften Salvians von Massilia," *ThStKr* 82 (1909): 29–78, 163–205. – A. Schäfer, *Römer und Germanen bei Salvian* (Breslau: Borgmeyer, 1930). – J. Fischer, *Die Völkerwanderung im Urteil der zeitgenössischen kirchlichen Schriftsteller Galliens unter Einbeziehung des heiligen Augustinus* (Heidelberg: Kemper, 1948). – M. Janelli, *La caduta di un impero nel capolavoro di Salviano* (Naples: Barca, 1948). – E. A. Isichei, *Political Thinking and Social Experience: Some Christian Interpretations of the Roman Empire from Tertullian to Salvian* (Christchurch, N.Z.: University of Canterbury Press, 1964). – A. G. Hamman, "L'actualité de Salvien de Marseille: Idées sociales et politiques," *Aug* 17 (1977): 381–93. – J. Badewien, *Geschichtstheologie und Sozialkritik im Werk Salvians von Marseille* (FKDG 32; Göttingen: Vandenhoeck & Ruprecht, 1980). – G. W. Olsen, "Reform after the Pattern of the Primitive Church in the Thought of Salvian of Marseille," *CHR* 68 (1982): 1–12. – J. Badewien, "Zum Verhältnis von Geschichtstheologie und Theologie bei Salvian von Marseille," in *Papers Presented to the Seventh International Conference on Patristic Studies Held in Oxford, 1975* (ed. E. Livingstone; StPatr 15; TU 128; Berlin: Akademie, 1984), 263–67. – J. M. Blázquez Martínez, "La crisis del Bajo Imperio en Occidente en la obra de Salviano de Marsella: Problemas económicos y sociales," *Gerión* 2 (1985): 157–82.

*Other Studies:* G. Vecchi, *Studi Salvianei I* (Bologna: C. Zuffi, 1951). – L. F. Barmann, "Salvian of Marseille Re-evaluated," *RUO* 33 (1963): 79–97. – R. Kamienik, "Quelques problèmes biographiques concernant Salvien de Marseille restés sans solution," *Annales Université Marie Curie-Sklodowska (Lublin), Section F* 23–24 (1968–1969),

74–110. – W. Blum, "Das Wesen Gottes und das Wesen des Menschen nach Salvian von Marseille," *MTZ* 21 (1970): 327–41. – P. Badot, "La notice de Gennade relative à Salvien," *RBén* 84 (1974): 352–66. – H. Fischer, *Die Schrift des Salvian von Marseille "An die Kirche"* (EHS.T 57; Bern: Herbert Lang; Frankfurt: Lang, 1976). – S. Pricoco, "Una nota biografica su Salviano di Marsiglia," *SicGym* 29 (1976): 351–68. – C. Leonardi, "Alle origini della cristianità medievale: Giovanni Cassiano e Salviano di Marsiglia," *StMed* 18.2 (1977): 491–608. – I. Opelt, "Briefe des Salvian von Marseille," *Romanobarbarica* 4 (1979): 161–82. – R. J. O'Donnell, "Salvian and Augustine," *AugStud* 14 (1983): 25–34. – N. Brox, "*Quis ille auctor?* Pseudonymität und Anonymität bei Salvian," *VC* 40 (1986): 55–65. – P. Badot and D. De Decker, "Salvien de Marseille: Note critique," *Aug* 38 (1998): 223–77.

# De gubernatione Dei

Salvian's work *De gubernatione Dei* ("On the Governance of God") has frequently been compared with Augustine's *De civitate Dei* because they were written for the same situation and question: why does the Christian God not protect the Roman Empire from the barbarians, as would be God's obligation according to the traditional Roman view of the state and religion? The serious differences between the two works indeed already begin with those asking the question. In the case of Augustine, it was the adherents of the old cult of the gods, who accused the Christians of having encouraged the Romans to turn to a powerless God when a catastrophe like the conquest of Rome had never occurred under the rule of the old deities. In the case of Salvian, however, it is the Christians themselves who are despairing of God not taking care of them and to whom God therefore has to explain the reasons and purpose of this misfortune so as to strengthen them in their affliction and at the same time prevent future catastrophes. The strongly oratorical elements of the eight books of *De gubernatione Dei* even suggest that they are based on sermons preached in public. The main reason for the troubles, according to Salvian, is to be found in the Christians' own inappropriate behavior. They were far too gullibly confident that, as Christians (by name) and Romans, they were infinitely superior to the barbarians culturally. Now they have to realize how corrupt their life and culture really are, whereas the barbarians, who did not know Christ (Saxons, Franks, and Huns) or only in the distorted form of Arianism (Goths and Vandals), nevertheless acted more nobly than the Romans in many respects. Therefore, if the barbarians sin, they are more likely to be excused because of their ignorance than are orthodox Christians. In his work Salvian intends to mediate this (painful) self-knowledge in order to interpret the afflictions as God's righteous punishment, on the one hand, and to call Christians to improve their behavior, on the other, so as to avert further misfortune.

Thus Salvian has to provide twofold evidence: (1) that God is truly present in the world, that he cares for and directs it; and (2) that precisely the present hardships are signs of God's welfare because he has imposed them as punishment for the Christians' misdeeds so that they will mend their ways. *De gubernatione Dei* is therefore organized accordingly. From the history of the OT and NT, bks.

1–2 demonstrate God's presence and providence in history. In the next six books, this is followed by a presentation of all the vices of Christians that have rightly brought down God's judgment upon their heads: (3) lack of brotherly love; (4) greed, murder, fornication, oppression of the poor, perjury, and contempt for those who are good; (5) unjust oppression of the rural population, the only reason for the actions of the Bagaudae (organized peasants)[1]; (6) plays and superstition; (7) immorality and arrogance; and (8) idolatry and mistreatment of God's servants. Salvian illustrates these charges with numerous concrete examples and with the divine punishments for these, which can be seen in the conquest of such flourishing Christian cities as Trier and Carthage, for instance. This renders *De gubernatione Dei* an outstanding source for history and the history of culture. His constant comparisons of the Romans' customs with the barbarians' lead to the conclusion that the barbarians are morally superior; for this reason, God grants them victory and admonishes the Christians to return. Book 8 ends abruptly after a few chapters; it is not possible to clarify whether Salvian himself ended it in this fashion or whether the history of its transmission mutilated it.

The historical value of the work, written between 440 and 450, was and continues to be the subject of much discussion, and it may be appropriate not to accept every detail indiscriminately as reliable. Salvian had no intention of an "objective, scholarly" work of history; instead, on the basis of his knowledge, limited as it was in matters of detail, concerning the *Imperium Romanum* and the barbarian peoples, he wrote a historical apologia, to whom his portrayal of customs and his evaluations are especially directed. In many instances there is a lack of precise dates, names, and local knowledge, mainly because they were unimportant to him. Drawing parallels between those situations and valuations and modern times, as has often been done, should be considered inappropriate, in any case.

*Editions: Du gouvernement de Dieu* (ed. G. Lagarrigue; SC 220; Paris: Cerf, 1975) [Com].

*Translations: The Writings of Salvian the Presbyter* (trans. J. F. O'Sullivan; FC 3; New York: Cima, 1947; Washington, D.C.: Catholic University of America Press in association with Consortium Books, 1977), 25–232.

*Studies:* J.-C. Ignace, *Salvien et les invasions du Vème siècle en Gaule d'après le "De gubernatione Dei"* (Toulouse: n.p., 1966). – J. Blänsdorf, "Salvian über Gallien und Karthago: Zu Realismus und Rhetorik in der spätantiken Literatur," in *Studien zu Gregor von Nyssa und der christlichen Spätantike* (ed. H. R. Drobner and C. Klock; SVigChr 12; Leiden and New York: Brill, 1990), 311–32.

# II. BOETHIUS

Even though Salvian of Marseilles lived through the entire period of decline in the western part of the Roman Empire and in his (extant) writings contributed

---

[1] Bands of rebels that presumably were driven from their landholdings because of the state's tax demands.

to the effort to interpret and cope intellectually with the crisis, his personal life history as a young father, a monk, and a priest was sheltered from the politics of his time. By contrast, Anicius Manlius Torquatus Severinus Boethius was born into the old established, tradition-rich Roman lineage of the Anicii between 475 and 480, when the western part of the Roman Empire was dissolving. Since the second century before Christ, they had produced consuls and senators, and from their relatives Pope Gregory the Great was later to emerge. The father of Boethius, too, occupied the office of consul in 487 under Odoacer; after his father's early death, he was taken in by the family of Quintus Aurelius Memmius Symmachus, his subsequent father-in-law, a descendant of the famous senator Symmachus, who at the time of Ambrose had ordered the reerection of the statue of Victoria in the Roman curia. His origin, education, and youth naturally directed Boethius into political paths, which determined his life as well as his tragic death under Theoderic the Great, the king of the Ostrogoths. The latter snatched power from Odoacer in 493 and in 497 was recognized as the legitimate ruler of the West by Anastasius, the emperor of Eastern Rome.

Boethius had enjoyed an outstanding and comprehensive Latin and Greek education,[2] and like many of his status, he endeavored to preserve the cultural heritage of Rome for the future. In ca. 504 he began a complete Latin translation of all the works of Plato and Aristotle for the purpose of demonstrating their essential agreement, as well as commentaries and textbooks of the *artes liberales*. He was the first to refer to the so-called *quadrivium* (arithmetic, music, geometry, and astronomy), to which he devoted himself actively,[3] so that Theoderic initially became aware of him as a (technical) scientist and charged him with the revision of the system of coins and measures and with the construction of clocks. Clearly Boethius demonstrated enormous skills, so much so that it was not long before Theoderic entrusted him with important political tasks. By 510 he was a consul and, extraordinarily, *sine collega;* in 522 he held the highest court and public office as *magister officiorum;* and in the same year, both of his still youthful sons held the office of consul.

Precisely at the apex of his power, however, the political conditions changed, leading to his fall and death. From the start, Theoderic's relations with Eastern Rome fluctuated, both politically and regarding ecclesiastical politics. But the Acacian schism, which arose under Acacius, the patriarch of Constantinople (484), as a result of the disputes concerning acceptance of the Council of Chalcedon, favored Theoderic's position. In 519, however, Emperor Justin (518–527) of the Eastern Roman Empire, a strict orthodox Catholic with a Western orientation, settled the schism and established close ties with the Roman church. This gave impetus to the opposition forces in the senate that were directed against the rule of the Goths, and caused Theoderic to fear a conspiracy against him between Rome and Byzan-

---

[2] The report that Boethius had studied in Athens for a few years is no longer deemed accurate.

[3] *Trivium:* Grammar, rhetoric, dialectics; together they constitute the "seven liberal arts," the foundation of ancient and medieval education.

tium, especially since the Goths had been Arians ever since their conversion by Ulfilas under Constantius II (337–361).

Boethius became caught in this political vortex. When, sometime between 524 and 526, the senator Albinus was accused of treasonable relations with Byzantium, Boethius supported his colleague. Theoderic suspected him of treason as well because he could not tolerate further opposition, given his weakened political situation. He therefore had him imprisoned in Pavia and executed without defense. Today he is buried in the church of San Pietro in Ciel d'Oro in Pavia. He was already considered a martyr during the Carolingian era; Dante placed him as a martyr in paradise among the great doctors of the church (*Paradiso* 10.124–129), and in 1883 the Sacred Congregation of Rites officially permitted his cultus in Pavia. Even if the primary reasons for Boethius's execution were political, his veneration as a martyr is at least able to appeal to the fact that political and ecclesiastical matters could hardly be kept separate and that the opposition between the Arianism of the Goths and the Catholicism of Rome and Constantinople played at least an indirect part.

The four theological writings of Boethius on Trinitarian and christological concerns continued to exert influence for a long time. Initially their authenticity was subject to doubt, however, especially because his main work, *De consolatione philosophiae*, written during his imprisonment, contains no Christian aspects at all. If he did not once seek refuge in his faith in the face of death, can he even be said to have been a Christian? A fragment of Cassiodorus (*Anecdoton Holderi*), however, discovered by Alfred Holder in 1860 and published by Hermann Usener in 1877, undoubtedly demonstrates Anecdoton's authenticity and Boethius's Christianity. The significance of Boethius for the Middle Ages cannot be overestimated. His textbooks passed on the education of antiquity, and for the Middle Ages, limited to a command of Latin only, his translations and commentaries preserved the knowledge of Greek, especially Aristotelian, philosophy. His philosophical works remained foundational for centuries. The theological writings contain definitions, now considered classic, for the philosophical investigation of Christology and the doctrine of the Trinity, and *De consolatio philosophiae* was so popular that translations into the vernacular (Anglo-Saxon and German) were undertaken already in the medieval period (tenth/eleventh century).

*Bibliography:* L. Obertello, *Severino Boezio* (2 vols.; Genoa: Accademia Ligure di Scienze e Lettere, 1974), vol. 2.

*Editions: Opera omnia:* PL 63:537–1364; 64. – *Commentaries on Aristotle's De interpretatione* (ed. C. Meiser; 2 vols.; New York: Garland, 1987); repr. of *Commentarii in librum Aristotelis* ΠΕΡΙ ʽΕΡΜΗΝΕΙΑΣ (ed. C. Meiser, 2 vols., Leipzig: Teubner, 1877–1880). – *De divisione: Trattato sulla divisione* (ed. L. Pozzi; Padua: Liviana, 1969). – *De hypotheticis syllogismis: De hypotheticis syllogismis* (ed. L. Obertello; Brescia: Paideia, 1969). – *De institutione arithmetica, De institutione musica, Geometria: De institutione arithmetica libri duo; De institutione musica libri quinque; accedit Geometria quae fertur Boetii* (ed. G. Friedlein; Leipzig: Teubner, 1867; repr., Frankfurt: Minerva, 1966). – *De institutione arithmetica: Institution arithmétique* (ed. J.-Y. Guillaumin; Paris: Belles Lettres, 1995). – *De institutione musica: De institutione musica* (ed. G. Marzi; Rome: Istituto Italiano per la Storia della Musica, 1990). – *In Isagogen*

Porphyrii commenta: Anicii Manlii Severini Boethii in Isagogen Porphyrii commenta (ed. S. Brandt; CSEL 48; Vienna: F. Tempsky, 1906). – Anicii Manlii Severini Boethii De divisione liber (ed. J. Magee; PhAnt 77; Leiden and Boston, Mass.: Brill, 1998). – Anicii Manlii Severini Boethii De arithmetica (ed. H. Oosthout and I. Schilling; CCSL 94A; Turnhout, Belg.: Brepols, 1999).

Translations: The Theological Tractates: The Consolation of Philosophy (trans. H. F. Stewart, E. K. Rand, and S. J. Tester; new ed.; LCL 74; Cambridge, Mass.: Harvard University Press; London: Heinemann, 1973). – B. Stump, Boethius' In Ciceronis topica (Ithaca, N.Y. and London: Cornell University Press, 1988).

Reference Works: L. Cooper, A Concordance of Boethius: The Five Theological Tractates and the Consolation of Philosophy (Cambridge: The Mediaeval Academy of America, 1928).

Encyclopedia Articles: F. Wotke, RAC 2:482–88. – L. Pozzi, TRE 7:18–28. – C. J. de Vogel, "Boethius," GK 2:251–62. – U. Pizzani, EECh 1:124–25. – W. H. Principe, EEC 1:188–89.

Collections of Essays: M. Gibson, ed., Boethius: His Life, Thought, and Influence (Oxford: Blackwell, 1981). – L. Obertello, ed., Congresso internazionale di studi Boeziani, Pavia, 5–8 ottobre 1980: Atti (Rome: Herder, 1981). – M. Fuhrmann and J. Gruber, eds., Boethius (WdF 483; Darmstadt: Wissenschaftliche Buchgesellschaft, 1984).

Surveys, Introductions, and Influence: E. K. Rand, Founders of the Middle Ages (Cambridge, Mass.: Harvard University Press, 1928; repr., New York: Dover, 1957), 135–80. – H. R. Patch, The Tradition of Boethius: A Study of His Importance in Mediaeval Culture (New York: Oxford University Press, 1935; repr., New York: Russell & Russell, 1970). – P. Courcelle, Les lettres grecques en Occident: De Macrobe à Cassiodore (rev. ed.; Paris: de Boccard, 1948), 257–312. – M. M. Tevis Kinard, A Study of Boethius and His Influence on Medieval Education (Austin, Tex.: n.p., 1967). – F. Gastadelli, Boezio (Rome: Edizioni Liturgiche, 1974). – L. Obertello, Severino Boezio I (Genoa: Accademia Ligure di Scienze e Lettere, 1974). – A. Crocco, Introduzione a Boezio (2d ed.; Naples: Liguori, 1975). – H. Chadwick, Boethius: The Consolations of Music, Logic, Theology, and Philosophy (Oxford: Clarendon; New York: Oxford University Press, 1981; repr., 1990). – L. Obertello, Boezio e dintorni: Ricerche sulla cultura altomedievale (Florence: Nardini, 1989).

Studies—Individual Works: J. Shiel, "Boethius' Commentaires on Aristotle," MRSt(L) 4 (1958): 217–44. – L. M. De Rijk, "On the Chronology of Boethius' Works on Logic," Vivarium 2 (1964): 1–49, 125–61. – G. Schrimpf, Die Axiomenschrift des Boethius (De hebdomadibus) als philosophisches Lehrbuch des Mittelalters (SPAMP 2; Leiden: Brill, 1966). – G. Righi, A. M. S. Boezio: "De syllogismo cathegorico": Studio sul I libro (Milan: Marzorati, 1984). – J.-P. Levet, "Philologie et logique: Boèce traducteur des premiers chapitres du livre I des Analytica priora d'Aristote," RHT 18 (1988): 1–62. – C. Micaeli, Studi sui trattati teologici di Boezio (Naples: D'Auria, 1988). – E. Stump, Boethius's In Ciceronis topica (Ithaca, N.Y.; London: Cornell University Press, 1988). – R. Beinhauer, Untersuchungen zu philosophisch-theologischen Termini in De Trinitate des Boethius (Vienna: VWGÖ, 1990). – S. Ebbesen, "Boethius as an Aristotelian Commentator," in Aristotle Transformed: The Ancient Commentators and Their Influence (ed. R. Sorabij; Ithaca, N.Y.: Cornell University Press; London: Duckworth, 1990), 373–91. – J. Shiel, "Boethius' Commentaries on Aristotle," in Aristotle Transformed: The Ancient Commentators and Their Influence (ed. R. Sorabij; Ithaca, N.Y.: Cornell University Press; London: Duckworth, 1990), 349–72. – A. Galonnier, Anecdoton Holderi ou Ordo generis Cassiodorum: Éléments pour une étude de l'authenticité *boécienne des Opuscula sacra* (Louvain: Éditions de l'Institut Supérieur de Philosophie, 1997).

*Philosophy:* M. Grabmann, *Die Geschichte der scholastischen Methode* (2 vols.; Berlin: Akademie, 1909; repr., 1956), 1:148–77. – K. Bruder, *Die Philosophischen Elemente in den Opuscula sacra des Boethius: Ein beitrag zur Quellengeschichte der Philosophie der Scholastik* (FGPP 3.2; Leipzig; Naumburg: Lippert, 1928). – H. J. Brosch, *Der Seinsbegriff bei Boethius: Mit besonderer Berucksichtigung der Beziehung von Sosein und Dasein* (Philosophie und Grenzwissenschaften 4.1; Innsbruch: Rauch, 1931). – M. Nédoncelle, "Les variations de Boèce sur la personne," *RevScRel* 29 (1955): 201–38. – J. Magee, *Boethius on Signification and Mind* (PhAnt 52; Leiden and New York: Brill, 1989).

*Theology:* V. Schurr, *Die Trinitätslehre des Boethius im Lichte der "skytischen Kontroversen"* (FChLDG 18.1; Paderborn: F. Schöningh, 1935). – E. Dussel, "La doctrina de la persona en Boecio, solución cristológica," *Sapientia: Revista tomista de filosofía* 22 (1967): 101–26. – M. Lluch-Baixauli, *Boezio: La ragione teologica* (Milan: Jaca Book, 1997); trans. of *La teologia de Boecio: En la transicion del mundo clasico al mundo medieval* (Pamplona: Ediciones Universidad de Navarra, 1990). – C. Micaelli, *Dio nel pensiero di Boezio* (Naples: D'Auria, 1995).

# De consolatione philosophiae

Boethius wrote his most important and most famous work, the five-volume *De consolatione philosophiae* (*On the Consolation of Philosophy*), during his incarceration preceding his death, from 524 to 526. It reflects the situation and questions of one who plunged from the zenith of power and fortune to the depths of misfortune: Why does God allow the wicked to be rewarded and the good to be punished? In his despair Boethius initially seeks consolation from the Muses, that is, the arts, which prove to be inadequate. After this *the* philosophy (not a school of thought) appears to him in the form of a venerable woman, comforting him by explaining his questions with logical stringency.

It begins with the undeniable premise that God exists and directs the world as its Creator (bk. 1). Building upon this, progressing in logical conclusions in the following four books, it seeks to clarify the concepts necessary to answer Boethius's basic question, namely, fate, fortune, misfortune, good and evil, and liberty. Books 2 and 3 distinguish between fortune as a superficial manifestation and true fortune. It is not possible for true fortune to depend upon blind fate, that is, upon externally measurable success, power, wealth, or offices; it necessarily has to consist of imperishable things. Human striving for fortune means nothing more than yearning for that which leaves nothing to be desired, hence for perfection. Because of their finiteness, all worldly goods *per definitionem* are imperfect; that which is perfect can only be God himself, and all imperfect things have a share in that. Therefore striving for fortune is striving for God, and true fortune is determined by God alone. In this case, where does evil and the apparent fortune of evil people come from (bk. 4)? Logically, the only possible answer to this is that evil has no existence at all and the human valuation of fortune and misfortune is inadequate from the divine perspective. Contrary to all appearance, the evil person in truth is always unfortunate because he or she has no share in God, who is truly good. This brings up the old problem of the accountability of human behavior, that is, of human freedom and God's providence (bk. 5). Is a person able to escape the prescience of God, or are that person's actions predestined and hence he is not responsible for them? Philosophy answers this question by differentiating between the terms. God's eternal providence is not to be equated with human prescience limited by time. God's omniscience is not based on foresight that predestines the future; but since his being is timeless, he does not foresee but instead the entire history of the world is present for him. Thus human striving—as the philosophy concludes its consolation—necessarily has to consist of combating vices, practicing virtues, and yearning after God, for whom, as judge, our actions are always present.

From the perspective of its form, too, the *Consolatio philosophiae* may be considered a masterpiece bringing together the entire classical literary and philosophical education. Thirty-nine segments of prose alternate with as many poetic segments (meters), following the forms of the Platonic and Aristotelian dialogue and Menippic satire with a lavish use of rhetoric. The fact that what is personified is not a philosophical school but philosophy as such already indicates Boethius's basic understanding of a uniform philosophical construct of ideas, including not only Plato and Aristotle but also the Stoa. This is a purely philosophical work in the ancient sense of philosophy as guidance and coping with life. For this reason, the question was often discussed why a Christian, in the face of death, did not rather posit a Christian legacy or at least one that had been permeated by Christianity more clearly, up to the point that Boethius's Christianity was doubted altogether. A definitive answer may never be found, but it is important to take into account the entire life of Boethius, who devoted himself completely to ancient education and for whom the Christian faith itself was significantly shaped by the terminology and world of thought of (Platonic) philosophy. The *Consolatio*'s concept of God is definitely Christian, and many individual concepts, such as the distinction between God and the world, as well as evil, can be traced back only to Christianity and not exclusively to philosophy.

*Bibliographies:* P. Courcelle, "Bibliographie de la 'Consolatio philosophiae' de 1967 à 1977," in *Convegno internazionale Passaggio dal mondo antico al medio evo da Teodosio a San Gregorio Magno* (Rome: Accademia Nazionale dei Lincei, 1980), 222–24.

*Editions: Anicii Manlii Severini Boethii Philosophiae consolationis libri quinque* (ed. W. Weinberger; CSEL 67; Vienna: Hölder-Pichler-Tempsky, 1934; repr., New York: John Reprint, 1964). – *Anicii Manlii Severini Boethii Philosophiae consolatio* (ed. L. Bieler; CCSL 94; Turnhout, Belg.: Brepols, 1957). – *Philosophiae consolatio* (ed. E. Rapisarda; Catania: Centro di Studi sull'Antico Cristianesimo, Università di Catania, 1961). – *La consolazione della filosofia* (ed. R. Del Re; Rome: Ateneo, 1968). – *La consolazione della filosofia* (ed. V. Banfi; Reggio: Emilia, 1981). – *Trost der philosophie* (ed. E. Gegenschatz and O. Gigon; Munich and Zurich: Artemis, 1990). – *La consolazione della filosofia* (ed. C. Moreschini; Turin: Unione Tipografico-Editrice Torinese, 1994).

*Translations: The Consolation of Philosophy* (trans. R. Green; Library of the Liberal Arts 86; Indianapolis, Ind.: Bobbs-Merrill, 1962). – *The Consolation of Philosophy* (trans. V. E.

Watts; Penguin Classics; Harmondsworth, Eng. and New York: Penguin, 1969). – *The Consolation of Philosophy* (trans. P. G. Walsh; Oxford World's Classics; Oxford and New York: Clarendon, 1999).

*Commentary:* J. Gruber, *Kommentar zu Boethius' De consolatione philosophiae* (TK 9; Berlin and New York: de Gruyter, 1978).

*Poetry:* E. Rapisarda, *Consolatio poesis in Boezio* (2d ed.; Catania: Centro di Studi sull'Antico Cristianesimo, Università di Catania, 1960). – H. Scheible, *Die Gedichte der "Consolatio philosophiae" des Boethius* (BKAW NS 46; Heidelberg: Winter, 1972). – C. Müller-Goldingen, "Die Stellung der Dichtung in Boethius' *Consolatio philosophiae*," *RMP* 132 (1989): 369–95. – G. O'Daly, *The Poetry of Boethius* (London: Duckworth; Chapel Hill: University of North Carolina Press, 1991).

*History of Literature, Philology:* K. Reichenberger, *Untersuchung zur literarischen Stellung der "Consolatio philosophiae"* (Cologne: Romanisches Seminar der Universität Köln, 1954). – E. Rhein, "Die Dialogstruktur der 'Consolatio philosophiae' des Boethius" (PhD diss., Frankfurt, 1963). – P. Courcelle, *La Consolation de philosophie dans la tradition littéraire: Antécédent et postérité de Boèce* (Paris: Études Augustiniennes, 1967). – S. Lerer, *Boethius and Dialogue: Literary Method in the Consolation of Philosophy* (Princeton, N.J.: Princeton University Press, 1985). – F. Troncarelli, "La più antica interpretazione della *Consolatio philosophiae*," *NRS* 72 (1988): 501–50.

*Philosophy:* I. Schwarz, "Untersuchungen zur 'Consolatio Philosophiae' des Boethius" (PhD diss., Vienna, 1955). – V. Schmidt-Kohl, *Die neuplatonische Seelenlehre in der Consolatio philosophiae des Boethius* (BKP 16; Meisenheim am Glan, A. Hain, 1965). – P. Courcelle, "Neuplatonisches in der '*Consolatio philosophiae*' des Boethius," in *Platonismus in der Philosophie des Mittelalters* (ed. W. Beierwaltes; WdF 197; Darmstadt: Wissenschaftliche Buchgesellschaft, 1969), 73–108. – J. Grüber, "Die Erscheinung der Philosophie in der '*Consolatio philosophiae*' des Boethius," *RMP* 112 (1969): 166–86. – P. Courcelle, "Le personnage de philosophie dans la littérature latine," *JS* 43 (1970): 209–52. – P. Courcelle, "Le tyran et le philosophe d'après la 'Consolation' de Boèce," in *Convegno internazionale Passaggio dal mondo antico al medio evo da Teodosio a San Gregorio Magno* (Rome: Accademia Nazionale dei Lincei, 1980), 195–222.

# III. CASSIODORUS

In his endeavor to preserve the heritage of Roman culture, Boethius was supported by a contemporary who was no less important, whose family—even if not equally ancient—was related to the Anicii, as well as to the Symmachi, and whose path in the service of Theoderic the Great led him to Boethius: Flavius Magnus Aurelius Cassiodorus. In other respects, however, their lives and influence were quite different. Whereas Boethius fell out of favor in the prime of his life, Cassiodorus, roughly of the same age, enjoyed a long life of at least ninety-two years and therefore far outlived the rule of the Goths. After their demise and in the context of the renewed unification of the empire under Emperor Justinian, he withdrew to a monastic environment on his estates in southern Italy. There he devoted himself fully to the preservation of Roman education, albeit not so much to philosophy, as in the case of Boethius, as primarily to language, rhetoric, and literature. Fortunately, we are well informed about his life from his own works, especially the *Ordo generis Cassiodororum, Variae*, and *Anecdoton Holderi*.

According to these works, the family of the Cassiodori originated in Syria; the great-grandfather had distinguished himself in the wars against the Vandals and subsequently, in the mid-fifth century, acquired estates at Scyllaceum (modern Squillace in Calabria) in southern Italy, as the family's ancestral seat. Since then his family had increased in power and fortune; his grandfather and his father had held high public offices. Under Odoacer his father was *comes sacrorum largitionum* (administrator of finances), and under Theoderic he held the position of *praefectus praetorio* (governor). As such, he was elevated to the rank of *patricius* between 501 and 507, as was Cassiodorus himself later on. Cassiodorus's year of birth can only be approximated from his *cursus honorum*, which placed him in the service of the Gothic-Roman state for almost thirty years. In his early years of adulthood, he served under his father as *praefectus praetorio* between 503 and 506, with the specific function of a *consiliarius* (councilman), and as such delivered a public speech in honor of Theoderic. On the basis of these data, he must have been born roughly between 485 and 490, possibly even somewhat earlier. From 506 or 507 to 511, he held the office of *quaestor sacri palatii* (minister of justice); as such, he had to edit the formulation of laws, edicts, and all the other official writings on behalf of the king. Here Cassiodorus's linguistic and stylistic skills proved themselves; they presuppose a corresponding education, about which we otherwise have no information but which constitutes a characteristic feature of his life's work as a whole. In 514 he was given the honorary title *consul ordinarius*, and in 523 he followed Boethius as *magister officiorum* (administrative director). After the death of Theoderic (526), he assumed a governorship (possibly as *corrector Lucaniae et Bruttiorum*) and on September 1, 533, was appointed *praefectus praetorio*, which he remained until the conquest of Rome by the Eastern Roman troops under the commander Belisarius (537). Evidently Cassiodorus was a government official who distanced himself from political factions (or manipulated them with sufficient skill) and faithfully served the respective rulers, be it Theoderic, his son Athalaric, who was a minor, and Amalasuntha, his mother, or Theodahad, their rival, murderer, and successor. He was imbued with the ideal of a peaceful association between Roman culture and the rule of the Goths.

Cassiodorus calls the fall of the dynasty of the Eastern Goths his *conversio*, as in the case of Salvian's turn to the monastic life previously. In this case, of course, we are not referring to a religious "conversion" but rather to the important turning point in his life when he returned to private life in order to bring to reality his educational plans, which he had already developed during his governmental career; these plans also had distinctive ecclesiastical or religious features. His intention, together with Pope Agapetus, of establishing a theological academy in Rome comparable to the Eastern schools in Alexandria or Nisibis foundered on the pope's death (536) and the continuing war. The following decade he dedicated to literary efforts, in Ravenna until after 540 and in the company of Pope Vigilius in Constantinople in 550. After 554, as a substitute, as it were, for the failed founding of an academy in Rome, he established a communal monastery on his father's estates on the Gulf of Scyllaceum (ca. three miles to the southeast of modern Squillace), dedicated, in the medieval sense, to the pursuit of studies. Not far to the southwest, on the mountain of Castellum, he also established a community for anchorites. He named the monastery, after his fish ponds, the Monasterium Vivariense, which went down in history by its short name, Vivarium. Cassiodorus himself did not enter his monastery, however, but lived nearby in Christian *otium*, as we know it since the fourth century. Both his private residence and the monastery had a substantial library for their time, supplemented continuously with copies of further works. The monastery's primary task consisted in copying, translating, binding, collecting, and preserving books for the purpose of saving and passing on the ancient treasure of education. Besides the similar, independent efforts of others, Cassiodorus also assigned this task in a pioneering way to monasteries in southern France, Ireland, and England; he saw the monastery as the only institution that was able to achieve this goal in a disintegrating world. Theoretically he thereby also established the foundation for the entire medieval education system. He himself was granted a ripe old age and undiminished creativity. According to its preface, his final work was written when he was ninety-three years old.

*Bibliographies:* A. Momigliano, *Secondo contributo alla storia degli studi classici* (SeL 77; Rome: Storia e Letteratura, 1960; repr., 1984), 219–29.

*Encyclopedia Articles:* D. M. Cappuyns, *DHGE* 11:1349–1408. – R. Helm, *RAC* 2:915–26. – Å. Fridh, *TRE* 7:657–63. – M. L. Angrisani Sanfilippo, *DPAC* 1:617–19. – T. G. Kardong, *EEC* 1:219–20.

*Surveys and Introductions:* J. J. van den Besselaar, *Cassiodorus Senator: Leven en werken van een staatsman en monnik uit de zesde eeuw* (Haarlem: Gottmer, 1950). – J. J. O'Donnell, *Cassiodorus* (Berkeley and London: University of California Press, 1979). – V. A. Sirago, *I Cassiodoro: Una famiglia calabrese alla direzione d'Italia nel V e VI secolo* (Soveria Mannelli: Rubbettino, 1983).

*Collections of Essays:* S. Leanza, ed., *Atti della settimana di studi su Flavio Magno Aurelio Cassiodoro* (Soveria Mannelli: Rubbettino, 1986). – S. Leanza, ed., *Cassiodoro—dalla corte di Ravenna al Vivarium di Squillace: Atti del Convegno internazionale di studi—Squillace, 25–27 ottobre 1990* (Soveria Mannelli: Rubbettino, 1993).

*Culture and Context of Late Antiquity:* G. Bardy, "Cassiodore et la fin du monde ancien," *ATh* 6 (1945): 383–425. – A. Momigliano, "Cassiodorus and Italian Culture of His Time," *PBA* 41 (1955): 207–45; repr. in *Secondo contributo alla storia degli studi classici* (ed. A. Momigliano; SeL 77; Rome: Storia e letteratura, 1960; repr., 1984), 191–218. – P. Riché, *Éducation et culture dans l'Occident barbare, 6e–8e siècle* (4th rev. ed.; PatSor 4; Paris: Seuil, 1995); ET, *Education and Culture in the Barbarian West from the Sixth through the Eighth Century* (trans. of 3d ed.; trans. J. J. Contreni; foreword by R. E. Sullivan; Columbia: University of South Carolina Press, 1976; 1978). – F. Weissengruber, "Cassiodors Stellung innerhalb der monastischen Profanbildung des Abendlandes," *WSt* 80 (1967): 202–50. – S. Krautschick, *Cassiodor und die Politik seiner Zeit* (Bonn: Habelt, 1983). – B. Luiselli, "Cassiodoro e la Storia dei Goti," in *Convegno internazionale Passaggio dal mondo antico al medio evo da Teodosio a San Gregorio Magno* (Rome: Accademia Nazionale dei Lincei, 1980), 225–53.

*Vivarium:* H. Thiele, "Cassiodor, seine Klostergründung Vivarium, und sein Nachwirken im Mittelalter," *SMGB* 50 (1932): 378–419. – P. Courcelle, "Le site du monastère de Cassiodore," *MAH* 55 (1938): 259–307. – P. Courcelle, "Nouvelles recherches sur le monastère de Cassiodore," in *Actes du Ve Congrès international d'archéologie chrétienne: Aix-en-Provence, 13–19 septembre 1954* (SAC 22; Vatican City: Pontificio Istituto di Archeologia Cristiana, 1957), 511–28. – E. Zinzi, *Studi sui luoghi Cassiodorei in Calabria* (Soveria Mannelli: Rubbettino, 1994).

## Works and Significance

Two of the literary works of Cassiodorus stand out: the *Variae* (i.e., *epistolae*) and *Institutiones*. The *Variae* represents a collection of 468 letters, documents, forms, and other literary items from his office, compiled in the years immediately following the end of his public office (538). It is composed of twelve books; somewhat later he added a small tractate, *De anima,* as the thirteenth book. As in the case of the corpora of letters by Leo and Gregory the Great with reference to ecclesiastical administration, so these writings provide an invaluable glimpse into the governmental processes of the Gothic kingdom. Yet they also demonstrate the rhetorical mastery and encyclopedic education of their author, who is able to pull out the most diverse stops of his skill, depending on the addressee and the situation. As a model for a masterly official style, this work has enjoyed extremely wide distribution and continued influence.

To an even greater extent, this is true of the *Institutiones,* a two-part literary introduction to studies, written for the monks of the Vivarium, which was to become the textbook for the entire Middle Ages: *Institutiones divinarum litterarum* and *Institutiones saecularium litterarum.* Part 1 provides instruction on Bible study by furnishing commentaries, practical aids, and methods of study. Part 2 represents a treatment of the seven *artes liberales* and is thus an essential textbook of education as a whole, including a catalogue of the most important literature.

In addition to these, the following writings were noteworthy and influential for the future:

a. the *Historia gothica,* begun before Theoderic's death (526) and completed in 538 in twelve books, which has been preserved only in the excerpts of *Getica,* written in 551 by Jordanes, the Gothic historian, and was supposed to offer a historical legitimation and glorification of Gothic rule;

b. a complete commentary on the Psalms, written over a span of ten years immediately after his *conversio,* in which he analyzes but goes significantly beyond Augustine's *Enarrationes in Psalmos;*

c. the *Historia ecclesiastica tripartita* of 324 to 439, in twelve books, which was a compilation and translation of the ecclesiastical histories of Socrates, Sozomen, and Theodoret and to which Cassiodorus himself wrote the foreword;

d. *De orthographia,* Cassiodorus's final work, which was appended to the *Institutiones* and contains numerous otherwise lost excerpts from eight ancient grammars.

The outstanding significance of Cassiodorus is undoubtedly to be found in his preparation for the medieval system of education. The production of copies by his monastery also preserved numerous ancient works, first for the Middle Ages and then for modern times.

*Editions: Opera omnia:* PL 69:501–1296; 70. – *Anecdoton Holderi:* H. Usener, *Anecdoton Holderi: Ein Beitrag zur Geschichte Roms in ostgothischer Zeit* (Bonn: Carl Georgi, 1877; Hildesheim and New York: Olms, 1969). – L. Viscido, *Ordo generis Cassiodororum, Excerpta: Introduzione, testo critico, traduzione, e commento* (Quaderni del Dipartimento di Scienze dell'Antichità, Università di Salerno 9; Naples: Arte Tipografica, 1992). – *Chronica: Chronica minora saec. IV., V., VI., VII* (ed. T. Mommsen; 3 vols.; MGH.AA 11; Berlin: Weidmann, 1894; repr., 1961): 2:109–61. – *De orthographia:* H. Keil, *Grammatici latini* (8 vols.; Leipzig: Teubner, 1855–1880), 7:143–210. – *Expositio Psalmorum: Expositio Psalmorum* (ed. M. Adriaen; 2 vols.; CCSL 97–98; Turnhout, Belg.: Brepols, 1958). – *Historia Gothorum: Iordanis romana et getica* (ed. T. Mommsen; MGH.AA 5.1; Berlin: Weidmann, 1882; repr., 1961). – *Historia tripartita: Historia ecclesiastica tripartita: Historiae ecclesiasticae ex Socrate, Sozomeno, et Theodorito in unum collectae et nuper de Graeco in Latinum translatae, libri numero duodecim* (ed. W. Jacob and R. Hanslik; CSEL 71; Vienna: Hölder-Pichler-Tempsky, 1952). – *Institutiones: Cassiodori Senatoris Institutiones* (2d ed.; ed. R. A. B. Mynors; Oxford: Clarendon, 1961). – *Variae, De anima: Magni Aurelii Cassiodori Variarum libri XII* (ed. Å. J. Fridh and J. W. Halporn; CCSL 96; Turnhout, Belg.: Brepols, 1973). – *Variae, Orationum reliquiae: Cassiodori Senatoris Variae* (ed. T. Mommsen and L. Traube; MGH.AA 12; Berlin: Weidmann, 1894; repr., 1961), 1–385, 457–84.

*Translations: Cassiodorus: Explanation of the Psalms* (trans. P. G. Walsh; 3 vols.; ACW 51–53; New York: Paulist, 1990–1991). – *The Variae of Magnus Aurelius Cassiodorus Senator* (trans. S. J. B. Barnish; TrTH 12; Liverpool: Liverpool University Press, 1992) [selections].

*Reference Works:* M. Di Marco, *Concordanza del De anima di Cassiodoro* (Soveria Mannelli: Rubbettino, 1992).

*Surveys and Introductions:* P. Lehmann, "Cassiodorstudien," *Phil* 71 (1912): 278–99; 72 (1913): 503–17; 73 (1914–1916): 253–73; 74 (1917): 265–69. – A. van de Vyver, "Cassiodore et son œuvre," *Spec* 6 (1931): 244–92. – P. Courcelle, *Les lettres grecques en Occident de Macrobe à Cassiodore* (2d ed.; Paris: de Boccard, 1948), 313–41. – S. J. B. Barnish, "The Work of Cassiodorus after His Conversion," *Latomus* 48 (1989): 157–87.

*De anima:* F. Zimmermann, "Cassiodors Schrift 'Über die Seele,'" *JPhST* 25 (1911): 414–49. – A. Crocco, "Il '*Liber de anima*' di Cassiodoro," *Sapienza* 25 (1972): 133–68. – F. d'Elia, *L'antropologia di Cassiodoro tra ispirazione agostiniana e suggestioni del mondo classico: Note teoretiche e filologiche sul "De anima"* (Rome: Gesualdi, 1987).

*Historia:* C. Cipolla, "Considerazioni sulle '*Getica*' di Jordanes e sulle loro relazioni colla '*Historia Getarum*' di Cassiodoro Senatore," *MAST.M* 43 (1893): 99–134. – T. Mommsen, "Ostgothische Studien," in idem, *Gesammelte Werke* (8 vols.; Berlin: Weidmann, 1905–1913), 6:362–484. – S. Lundström, *Zur Historia tripartita des Cassiodor* (AUL.T 49.1; Lund, Swed.: C. W. K. Gleerup, 1952). – B. Tönnies, *Die Amalertradition in den Quellen zur Geschichte der Ostgoten: Untersuchungen zu Cassiodor, Jordanes, Ennodius, und den Excerpta valesiana* (Hildesheim and New York: Olms-Weidmann, 1989).

*Institutiones:* M. G. Ennis, *The Vocabulary of the Institutiones of Cassiodorus: With Special Advertence to the Technical Terminology and Its Sources* (SMRL 9; Washington, D.C.: Catholic University of America Press, 1939). – A. van de Vyver, "Les *Institutiones* de Cassiodore et sa fondation à Vivarium," *RBén* 53 (1941): 59–88. – F. Troncarelli, "L'*Ordo generis Cassiodororum* e il programma pedagogico delle *Institutiones,*" *REAug* 35 (1989): 129–34. – P. B. Santiago Amar, "La iniciación a la Biblia en las 'Institutiones divinarum litterarum' de Casiodoro" (PhD diss., Athenaeum Romanum Sanctae Crucis, Rome, 1995).

*Commentary on the Psalms:* U. Hahner, *Cassiodors Psalmenkommentar: Sprachliche Untersuchungen* (MBM 13; Munich: Arbeo-Gesellschaft, 1973). – R. Schlieben, *Christliche Theologie und Philologie in der Spätantike: Die schulwissenschaftlichen Methoden der Psalmenexegese Cassiodors* (AKG 46; Berlin and New York: de Gruyter, 1974). – R. Schlieben, *Cassiodors Psalmenexegese: Eine Analyse ihrer Methoden als Beitrag zur Untersuchung der Geschichte der Bibelauslegung der Kirchenväter und der Verbindung christlicher Theologie mit antiker Schulwissenschaft* (GAB 110; Göppingen: Kümmerle, 1979). – G. P. De Simone, *Cassiodoro e l'Expositio Psalmorum: Una lettura cristologica dei Salmi* (Cosenza: Progetto, 1993; repr., 2000). – P. G. Walsh, "Cassiodorus Teaches Logic through the Psalms," in *Nova et vetera: Patristic Sudies in Honor of Thomas Patrick Halton* (ed. J. F. Petruccione; Washington, D.C.: Catholic University of America Press, 1998), 226–34.

*Variae:* A. Th. Heerklotz, *Die Variae des Cassiodorus Senator als kulturgeschichtliche Quelle* (Heidelberg: P. Braus, 1926). – O. J. Zimmermann, *The Late Latin Vocabulary of the Variae of Cassiodorus: With Special Advertence to the Technical Terminology of Administration* (SMRL 15; Washington, D.C.: Catholic University of America Press, 1944; repr., Hildesheim: Olms, 1967). – Å. J. Fridh, *Études critiques et syntaxiques sur les Variae de Cassiodore* (GVSH.H 6, Ser. A, 4.2; Göteborg, Swed.: Elanders, 1950). – Å. Fridh, *Terminologie et formules dans les Variae de Cassiodore* (SGLG 2; Stockholm: Almqvist & Wiksell, 1956). – Å. Fridh, *Contributions à la critique et à l'interprétation des Variae de Cassiodore* (Göteborg, Swed.: Almqvist & Wiksell, 1968). – M. Reydellet, *La royauté dans la littérature latine de Sidoine Apollinaire à Isidore de Séville* (BEFAR 253; Rome: École française de Rome; Paris: de Boccard, 1981), 183–253. – G. Vidén, *The Roman Chancery Tradition: Studies in the Language of Codex Theodosianus and Cassiodorus' Variae* (SGLG 46; Göteborg, Swed.: AUG, 1984). – V. A. Sirago, *Puglia e Sud Italia nelle "Variae" di Cassiodoro* (Bari: Levante, 1987). – L. Viscido, *Studi sulle Variae di Cassiodoro* (Longobardi: Calabria Letteraria Editrice, 1987). – R. MacPherson, *Rome in Involution: Cassiodorus' Variae in Their Literary and Historical Setting* (Poznan: Wydawn. Nauk. Uniwersytetu im. Adama Mickiewicza w Poznaniu, 1989).

# IV. BENEDICT OF NURSIA

The third individual to make an invaluable contribution to the foundations of the Middle Ages was Benedict of Nursia, a contemporary of Boethius and Cassiodorus, also born between 480 and 490 in Italy. His name and work outshone even those of the two politicians and scholars, earning him the unique honorary title "Father of the West." Indeed, in terms of its historical development, the Christian West is inconceivable without the shaping force of Benedictine monasticism. Yet it is appropriate to see Boethius, Cassiodorus, and Benedict as a threesome, preserving the three most important parts of ancient education and culture in a complementary way. Boethius preserved philosophy. Cassiodorus preserved language and literature, already embedded in a monastic context and in ecclesiastical culture. Benedict ultimately completed these with his Rule by elevating study and intellectual engagement into integral components of monasticism, in contrast to earlier anti-educational monastic ways of life. Benedict's origin and life differentiate him substantially from his two contemporaries, however. He did not come from noble lineage even though he was born into a respected and affluent merchant family in Nursia (modern Norcia in Umbria), as demonstrated by his studies in Rome. At no point did he indicate an interest in a political career or in further philosophical and literary studies.

In the second book of his *Dialogue* (593/594), Pope Gregory the Great composed a hagiographic memorial to him, representing virtually our only source of his biography. Based on the work's objective—to give an account of the miracles of Italian saints in parallel with the Eastern monastic stories—it begins with the *puer senex* topos and is permeated with many miracles. Nevertheless, after the legendary is carefully separated from the historical, this work may well be considered an essentially reliable source because it contains many precise and detailed facts and dates that, in part, can also be supported from other sources. It is also based on the witness of four of Benedict's students, one of whom was the abbot of the Lateran monastery in Rome. In general, the criticism of a work such as this has to guard against exaggerated rationalism, for not every account of miracles belongs *eo ipso* to legend and the evaluations of temptations, battles with demons, visions, and so forth, should not a priori ignore aspects of faith.

According to Gregory's account, Benedict, after a brief period of study, was so disgusted with the unrestrained hustle and bustle of the city of Rome that he withdrew, together with his nurse, to Enfide in the Anio valley (modern Affile on the river Aniene) in the Sabine Hills. There he soon performed his first miracle: his nurse had borrowed a clay sieve from a neighbor and broken it, but because of Benedict's prayer it was joined together again. He remained in Enfide for a brief time only, however, because he yearned for complete solitude and for this reason withdrew to an inaccessible cave in nearby Sublaqueum (modern Subiaco). En route a monk by the name of Romanus gave him a habit, in keeping with the ancient tradition of the anchorites. In the cave, which may still be seen today (*sacro specco*) below the monastery of Sublaqueum, he remained for three years and subsisted on the food that Romanus, the monk, lowered to him in a basket from the ledge. In his immediate surroundings, as we know likewise of the anchorites in the East, he earned the reputation of holiness, but it also brought temptations of the flesh, against which he is said to have fought, for instance, by casting himself naked into underbrush of nettles and thorns, which are still pointed out adjacent to the cave today. Because of his reputation, a monastic community (Vicovaro?) close by asked him to assume its leadership. He failed in this endeavor, however, because its members refused to accept his strict demands. They attempted to kill him by giving him a poisoned drink; he escaped this plot only because he had blessed the glass with the sign of the cross, as was his custom, and the glass shattered as a result. He then withdrew to his cave again.

All the same, the period of Benedict's seclusion came to an end because his fame began to spread and disciples began to gather around him. He established twelve monasteries in the surroundings, each for twelve monks and each led by an abbot. Some noble Romans also began to entrust their young sons to his care, among them the later saints Maurus and Placidus. Gregory characterizes Placidus as still "very childlike," and it was not long before Maurus (unconsciously) began to perform miracles of his own. The handle of a sickle held by a humble Gothic monk of the monastery broke off and fell into the lake; at the behest of Maurus, it resurfaced and reattached itself to the handle. When Placidus went to the lake to fetch water and fell into the water, Benedict sent Maurus to rescue him; the latter did this with such zeal that he did not realize he was walking on the water. Because of his success, however, Benedict again was at the mercy of a less perfect cleric, namely, Florentius, a presbyter of a nearby church. Initially the latter, too, attempted to poison Benedict with laced bread, but a raven carried it away on the divinely inspired command of Benedict. "Since he was not able to put to death the master's body, he sought to corrupt the soul of the brothers" and sent nude female dancers into the monastery's court. Benedict reacted to these new hostilities as he had done previously, by withdrawing from his opponent, leaving Sublaqueum and, together with some of the brothers, moving to Mons Casinus (modern Monte Cassino), above ancient Casinum and ca. eighty-five miles south of Rome, on the Via Latina.

At Mons Casinus Benedict encountered an ancient mountain cult of Apollo (or Jupiter?), and so his founding of a monastery there became a missionary endeavor at the same time. Against the opposition of demons, he replaced the temple with a church dedicated to St. Martin and the altar on the mountaintop with a chapel dedicated to St. John. Benedict never again left the monastery on Mons Casinus, not even on the occasion of the founding of the monastery at Terracina, to which he merely sent some of the brothers. Concerning his sister Scholastica, who was the abbess of a nearby convent, Gregory reports two well-known miracles. On the occasion of her brother's annual visit, she had requested him and his companions to stay with her overnight, which Benedict declined in rigorous compliance with his monastic rule. Scholastica thereupon prayed for a storm that would force him to stay, and her prayer was answered forthwith. And three days later Benedict saw his sister's soul ascend to heaven like a dove. (All of these occurrences were later depicted in the frescoes on the walls and ceiling of the monastery church at Sublaqueum, and they can still be seen. A raven is kept in the garden of the monastery even today.)

A series of events during his time at the monastery on Mons Casinus can be dated and so offers reliable points of reference for this period. The famine in bk. 2 of the *Dialogues,* chs. 21, 28–29 took place during 537/538; Germanus of Capua (ch. 35) died in early 541; Totila, king of the Goths—Gregory reports that Totila's substitute appeared in his place and was exposed miraculously by Benedict even as he entered—visited Benedict in the second half of 546 (chs. 14–15). Sabinus of Canosa came in early 547 (ch. 15), and Zalla, the Goth mentioned in ch. 31, was up to his mischief between 542 and 552. These dates agree with the tradition that

Benedict arrived at Casinum ca. 529/530 and died there ca. 547. Today, however, the date of his death is moved instead to 555 and 560.

*Bibliographies: Bulletin d'histoire bénédictine* (Maredsous, Belg.) *[BHB]*.

*Editions: Dialogues* (ed. A. de Vogüé and P. Antin; SC 260; Paris: Cerf, 1979), 120–249 [*Dialogi II* Com].

*Translation of Dialogues II: Dialogues* (trans. O. J. Zimmerman; FC 39; New York: Fathers of the Church, 1959; repr., Washington, D.C.: Catholic University of America Press in association with Consortium Books, 1977). – *The Life of Saint Benedict* (commentary by A. de Vogüé; trans. H. Costello and E. de Bhaldraithe; Petersham, Mass.: St. Bede's, 1993). – *Early Christian Lives: Life of Antony by Athanasius, Life of Paul of Thebes by Jerome, Life of Hilarion by Jerome, Life of Malchus by Jerome, Life of Martin of Tours by Sulpicius Severus, Life of Benedict by Gregory the Great* (trans. C. White; London and New York: Penguin, 1998), 163–204.

*Encyclopedia Articles:* H. Edmonds, *RAC* 2:130–36. – A. de Vogüé, *TRE* 5:538–49. – S. Zincone, *EECh* 1:119. – T. G. Kardong, *EEC* 1:179–81. – B. Green, in *Encyclopedia of Monasticism* (ed. W. Johnston and C. Renkin; 2 vols.; Chicago and London: Fitzroy Dearborn, 2000), 1:128–32.

*Collections of Essays:* E. von Severus, *Gemeinde für die Kirche: Gesammelte Aufsätze zur Gestalt und zum Werk Benedikts von Nursia* (BGAM.S 4; Münster: Aschendorff, 1981). – P. Tamburrino, ed., *S. Benedetto e l'Oriente cristiano: Atti del Simposio tenuto all'abbazia della Novalesa (19–23 maggio 1980)* (Novalesa: Monastero dei SS. Pietro e Andrea, 1981). – *Atti del 7° Congresso internazionale di studi sull'alto medioevo* (2 vols.; Spoleto: Sede del Centro Studi, 1982). – *Monastica: Discorsi e conferenze tenuti nelle celebrazioni cassinesi per il XV centenario della nascita di San Benedetto (480–1980)* (MCass 46; Monte Cassino: n.p. 1984).

*Studies:* I. Herwegen, *Der heilige Benedikt: Ein Charakterbild* (4th ed.; Düsseldorf: Patmos, 1951). – G. Turbessi, *Ascetismo e monachesimo in S. Benedetto* (Rome: Studium, 1965). – B. Jaspert, "Benedikt von Nursia—der Vater des Abendlandes? Kritische Bemerkungen zur Typologie eines Heiligen," *EuA* 49 (1973): 90–104, 190–207. – A. de Vogüé, *Autour de st. Benoît: La Règle en son temps et dans le nôtre* (VieMon 4; Begrolles en Mauges: Abbaye de Bellefontaine, 1975). – M. Puzicha, "Benedikt von Nursia—ein Mensch 'per ducatum evangelii': Die Gestalt Benedikts bei Gregor d. Gr. im zweiten Buch der Dialoge," *RBS* 17 (1992): 67–84.

# *Rule*

The maxim *Ora et labora* has become the embodiment of Benedictine monasticism and of its spirit, although it is not found in the Rule in this form. Adalbert de Vogüé, the important promoter and researcher of the Rule, agrees with the critical consensus that the famous slogan abbreviates the intent of the entire work of the Rule and needs to be supplemented as follows: *Ora, labora, lege, meditare.*[4] All the same, the easily remembered *Ora et labora* saying may retain its validity because, for Benedict, as well as for Augustine before him, "work"

---

[4] A. de Vogüé, SC 86a:339.

referred not only to manual labor but also to reading and study, and "prayer" not only to the Divine Office but also to penetrating deeper into God and his word through meditation. Why precisely did Benedict's monastic rule become the most successful one in history, rather than that of Augustine or of any others of a substantially earlier date? This essential question can only be answered on the basis of the Rule's profound knowledge of human nature, its clearly critical reflection upon experience, the moderate balance that resulted, and, at the same time, its adaptability: *In qua institutione nihil asperum, nihil grave, nos constituturos speramus*—"By means of these instructions we trust that nothing oppressive and unbearable will be laid down" (Rule of Benedict, prologue 46). In his *Dialogues* (2.36) Gregory the Great assesses the Rule as *discretione praecipuam, sermone luculentam*—"outstanding in its discernment and insightful in its formulation."

The authorship by Benedict cannot be seriously doubted despite the fact that the history of the text and of the transmission had a few surprises in store. In the course of research on the Rule, which has been under way only since 1880, it came to light that the apparent "autograph" of Benedict, rescued during the Lombard conquest of Mons Casinus in 577, was merely a version closely related to the original. Presumably an original never existed because Benedict dictated his Rule to a scribe. For its part, the *textus receptus* did not prove to be a trustworthy transmission of the *textus purus*, which initially had been disseminated very broadly in the Aachen standard codex of Charles the Great soon after 787. Instead it represents a ninth-century amalgamation of a seventh-century *textus interpolatus*, standardizing Benedict's transitional Latin, abbreviating the prologue and other parts of the text, and interpolating explanatory notes. For instance, the Rule originally did not begin with the now famous words *Ausculta, o fili* but with *Obsculta, o fili*. The Rule is not based on a bold design but represents a collection of Benedict's monastic life experiences, written at Mons Casinus toward the end of his life, hence in ca. 550, and edited and supplemented repeatedly, which can be seen especially in the addition of the concluding chapters, 67–73. Precisely for this reason, however, the Rule represents a "unified whole" and thus radiates great care and prudence.

The lengthy prologue, exhorting that the fundamental orientation of the monastic life is to be Christ, is sermonic in nature and uses a host of NT sayings. The Rule is composed of seventy-three chapters, the content of which may be summarized as follows:

- The four types of monks: cenobites and anchorites lead acceptable lifestyles, whereas sarabaites and gyrovagues (small disorderly groups and traveling monks) are rejected (1).

- The abbot and the council of monks. In the monastery the abbot functions as Christ's representative, who is accountable to God alone and follows Christ as his model. For this reason, he is to cultivate greater perfection and exemplariness in striving for God. He is not to make worldly distinctions between monks, and in his function as father, he is to exercise prudence and moderation in particular. In important matters, he is to obtain the counsel of the brothers, who, for their part, are obliged to obey his decisions (2–3).

- The monks' virtues: keeping the commandments, acts of mercy, moderation, prayer, piety, obedience, silence, humility (4–7).

- The ordering of the Divine Office and holy Mass, as well as the correct posture in prayer (8–20).

- The monastery's order of discipline: deans, regulations on sleep, misdemeanors and punishments, reconciliation (21–30).

- Various tasks and duties: cellarer, kitchen duty, care for the sick, lector, food and beverage, seating at table, daily routine, labor (31–49).

- The monastery's relations with the outside: traveling; guests; correspondence; furnishings; admittance of monks, children, and priests; order of rank; selection of the abbot and installation of the prior; doorkeeper; enclosure of the monastery. This is also the section (58.17) in which the famous Benedictine *stabilitas loci* is found, which the new monk has to pledge along with his lifestyle of moral purity (*conversatio morum*) and obedience (*oboedientia*) (50–66).

- Individual supplements, raising many of the issues again that have already been addressed and stating them with greater precision: travels, inability to fulfill a task, discipline and obedience among the brothers, zeal. The conclusion (73) clearly indicates that the Rule is not intended to offer a comprehensive guide for everything and that Scripture and the Fathers offer the essential model (67–73).

Its structure shows that the Benedictine Rule does not contain a rigid system but rather a practical, interrelated arrangement based on experience.

Benedict's Rule is not his own novel "invention"; instead, beyond its rootedness in the Scripture, it is part of the centuries-old monastic tradition of the East as well as of the West, as the text clearly demonstrates: Pachomius, Basil the Great, the *Vitae patrum,* Augustine, and Cassian. The Rule of Benedict has particular affinities with the so-called *Regula magistri,* with which it shares about a third of the text (prologue, chs. 1, 2, 4–7) as well as its general structure and which until 1937 was deemed a seventh-century copy of the former. Since then, however, the hypothesis of Dom Augustine Genestout, the Benedictine monk of Solesmes, has found virtually universal acceptance, that, on the contrary, Benedict's Rule is dependent upon the *Regula magistri,* probably via the *Regula Eugippii,* one of the two oldest text witnesses, written before 534 by Eugippius (d. ca. 535), the abbot of Lucullanum, near Naples and hence not far from Mons Casinus. Benedict's skill and the basis for the outstanding success of his Rule are that he did not merely collect tradition but, in a brilliant way, worked it into a new whole under a strict christocentrism, around which the community of monks (*ecclesiola*) collected as a spiritual family. In addition to the Rule's own qualities, its dissemination has been helped to no small extent, if not indeed decisively, by the witness of the *Dialogue* of Gregory the Great as well as by his sending of Benedictine monks as missionaries to England (596).

### Benedictine Rule (Regula Benedicti)

*Bibliographies:* Regula Benedicti studia: Annuarium internationale (Hildesheim: Gerstenberg, 1972–) *[RBS]*. – A. M. Albareda, *Bibliografía de la Regla Benedectina* (Montserrat: Monestir de Montserrat, 1933). – B. Jaspert, *"Regula magistri—Regula Benedicti:* Bibliographie ihrer historisch-kritischen Erforschung, 1938–1970," StudMon 13 (1971): 129–71; repr. in idem, *Studien zum Mönchtum* (RBS.S 7; Hildesheim: Gerstenberg, 1982), 147–85. – B. Jaspert, *Bibliographie der Regula Benedicti, 1930–1980: Ausgaben und Übersetzungen* (RBS.S 5; Hildesheim: Gerstenberg, 1983).

*Editions:* PL 66:215–932 [Com]. – *La Regola* (ed. A. Lentini; 2d ed.; Monte Cassino: Biblioteca del Monumento Nazionale di Montecassino, 1980) [Com]. – *La Règle de saint Benoît* (ed. A. de Vogüé and J. Neufville; 7 vols.; SC 181–86; Paris: Cerf, 1971–1977) [Com]. – *Vita di San Benedetto e la Regola* (ed. A. Stendardi; Rome: Città Nuova, 1975), 125–273. – *Eugippii regula* (ed. F. Villégas and A. de Vogüé; CSEL 87; Vienna: Hölder-Pichler-Tempsky, 1976). – *Benedicti regula* (ed. R. Hanslik; 2d ed.; CSEL 75; Vienna: Hölder-Pichler-Tempsky, 1977). – *RB 1980: The Rule of Benedict* (ed. T. Fry; Collegeville, Minn.: Liturgical, 1981) [ET]. – *Règle de saint Benoît* (ed. P. Schmitz and A. Borias; 5th ed.; Turnhout, Belg.: Brepols, 1987) [Concordance]. – *La Regola di San Benedetto e le regole dei Padri* (ed. S. Pricoco; Rome: Fondazione Lorenzo Valla, 1995), 115–385 [Com].

*Translations: The Rule of St. Benedict in English* (trans. T. Fry; Vintage Spiritual Classics; New York: Vintage, 1998). – T. G. Kardong, *Benedict's Rule: A Translation and Commentary* (Collegeville, Minn.; Liturgical, 1996).

*Reference Works:* B. Dalman, *Lèxic d'espiritualitat benedictina* (SubMon 18; Montserrat: Abadia de Montserrat, 1987).

*Encyclopedia Articles:* F. Renner, *TRE* 5:573–77.

*Journals: Bulletin d'ancienne littérature chrétienne latine* (Maredsous, Belg., 1921–) *[BALCL]*. – *Benedictina: Fascicoli trimestrali di studi benedettini* (Rome, 1947–) *[Ben.]*. – *Benediktinische Monatsschrift zur Pflege des religiösen und geistigen Lebens* (Beuron, 1919–1958) *[BenM]*. – *The Benedictine Review* (Atchison, Kans., 1946–1965) *[BenR]*. – Benedictine Studies (Baltimore, 1961–) [BenS]. – Benediktinisches Geistesleben (St. Ottilien, 1949–) [BGL]. – *Bulletin d'histoire bénédictine* (Maredsous, Belg., 1907, 1912–) *[BHB]*. – *Revue bénédictine de critique, d'histoire, et de littérature religieuses* (Maredsous, Belg., 1884–) *[RBén]*. – *Regulae Benedicti studia: Annuarium internationale* (Hildesheim, etc., 1972–) *[RBS]*.

*Collections of Essays:* Regulae Benedicti studia: Annuarium internationale, Supplementa (Hildesheim, etc., 1974–) [RBS.S]. – B. Steidle, ed., *Commentationes in Regulam S. Benedicti* (SA 42; Rome: Herder, 1957). – *Hacia una relectura de la Regla de san Benito* (StSil 6; Burgos: de Silos, 1980). – J. Gribomont, ed., *Commentaria in s. Regulam* (SA 84; Rome: S. Paolo, 1982). – B. Jaspert, *Studien zum Mönchtum* (RBS.S 7; Hildesheim: Gerstenberg, 1982). – A. de Vogüé, *Le Maître, Eugippe, et saint Benoît: Recueil des articles* (RBS.S 17; Hildesheim: Gerstenberg, 1984). – A. de Vogüé, *Études sur la Règle de saint Benoît: Nouveau recueil* (Bégrolle-en-Mauges: Abbaye de Bellefontaine, 1996).

*Studies:* I. Herwegen, *Sinn und Geist der Benediktinerregel* (Einsiedeln, Switz.: Benziger, 1944). – O. Porcel, *La doctrina monastica de san Gregorio Magno y la "Regula monachorum"* (Madrid: Consejo Superior de Investigaciones Científicas, 1950; Washington, D.C.: Catholic University of America Press, 1951). – A. Blazovich, *Soziologie des Mönchtums und der Benediktinerregel* (Vienna: Herder, 1954). – G. Holzherr, *Regula Ferioli: Ein Beitrag zur Entstehungsgeschichte und zur Sinndeutung der Benediktinerregel* (Einsiedeln, Switz.: Benziger, 1961). – A. de Vogüé, *La communauté et l'abbé dans la Règle de saint Benoît* (TET; Bruges, Belg.: Desclée de Brouwer, 1961). – S. Pawlowsky, *Die biblischen Grundlagen der Regula Benedicti* (WBTh 9; Vienna: Herder, 1965). – G.-M. Widhalm, *Die rhetorischen Elemente in der Regula Benedicti* (RBS.S 2; 2d ed.; Hildesheim: Gerstenberg, 1977). – P. Miquel, *La vie monastique selon saint Benoît* (Paris: Beauchesne, 1979). – A. de Vogüé, *The Rule of Saint Benedict: A Doctrinal and Spiritual Commentary* (trans. J. B. Hasbrouck; CistSS 54; Kalamazoo: Cistercian, 1983). – U. K. Jacobs, *Die Regula Benedicti als Rechtsbuch* (Cologne: Böhlau, 1987). – M. Kaczmarkowski, "Zur Textstruktur der Mönchsregel des hl. Benedikt von Nursia," in *Aevum inter utrumque: Mélanges offerts à Gabriel Sanders, professeur émérite à l'Université de Gand* (ed. M. Van Uytfanghe and R. Demeulenaere; IP 23; Steenbrugge, Belg.: Abbatia Sancti Petri; The Hague: Nijhoff, 1991), 277–87. – E. DeWaal, *A Life-Giving Way: A Commentary on the Rule of St. Benedict* (Collegeville, Minn.: Liturgical, 1995). – C. Stewart, *Prayer and Community: The Benedictine Tradition* (Traditions of Christian Spirituality; Maryknoll, N.Y.: Orbis; London: DLT, 1998).

### Rule of the Master *(Regula magistri)*

*Editions: La Régle du maître* (ed. A. de Vogüé, J.-M. Clément, J. Neufville, and D. Demeslay; 3 vols.; SC 105–107; Paris: Cerf, 1964–1965) [Com]. – *Eugippii regula* (ed. F. Villegas and A. de Vogüé; CSEL 87; Vienna: Hölder-Pichler-Tempsky, 1976).

*Reference Works:* M. J. Cappuyns, *Lexique de la Regula magistri* (IP 6; Steenbrugge, Belg.: Abbatia Sancti Petri, 1964) [word index].

*Translations: The Rule of the Master* (trans. L. Eberle; CistSS 6; Kalamazoo: Cistercian, 1977).

*Collections of Essays:* B. Steidle, ed., *Regula magistri, Regula S. Benedicti: Studia monastica* (SA 44; Rome: Orbis Catholicus, Herder, 1959).

*Studies:* A. de Vogüé, "La Règle du maître et les Dialogues de s. Grégoire," *RHE* 61 (1966): 44–76. – B. Jaspert, *Die Regula Benedicti–Regula magistri–Kontroverse* (RBS.S 3; 2d ed.; Hildesheim: Gerstenberg, 1977).

# V. GREGORY THE GREAT

*Consul Dei,* "Consul of God," the epitaph of Gregory the Great in the Basilica of St. Peter's in Rome describes most concisely the dual public and ecclesiastical function this pope had to fulfill in response to the demands of his time. He mastered these with such distinction that he is called "the Great," an honor accorded to only a few in the history of the church, and, together with Ambrose, Jerome, and Augustine, is ranked among the "four great doctors of the church." Beginning in 535, Byzantium had once again united Italy with the Roman

Empire; northern and central Italy, however, were lost to the Lombards in 568, so that only the exarchates of Ravenna and Rome, as well as southern Italy and Sicily, remained Roman (Byzantine) territory. In 585 Leovigild, the king of the Visigoths, subjected all of Spain to his rule; his son Recared converted from Arianism to Catholicism in 587. Since Clovis (d. 511), the kingdom of the Franks had become the major power in western Europe, but through acceptance of the Catholic faith (498/499), it had also become the bearer of the church's hope and an integrative factor. In this power play between Byzantium, the Lombards, the Franks, and the Goths, it was Gregory to whom the difficult task fell, from 590 on, to guard the *patrimonium Petri* and to promote the faith in the Western churches. This involved, on the one hand, politics, administration, and social engagement and, on the other, proclamation of the faith and mission. Like many other bishops from the Christian upper strata since the fourth century, who had assumed both governmental and ecclesiastical leadership positions, Gregory was particularly suited and prepared for this, given his background, education, and career.

He was born ca. 540 into a family of patrician rank, related to the Anicii (cf. Boethius in ch. 11.II)—a family with a tradition of both public office and ecclesiastical piety. Two of his predecessors had already served as popes (Felix III [483–492] and Agapetus [535–536]), his father was *regionarius* (presumably an office in the papal administration), and three of his aunts were nuns. Gregory also received a thoroughly "classical" education, which apparently was still available in sixth-century Rome, according to his writings, and chose the *cursus honorum* in keeping with his family's tradition. As *praefectus urbi* in 572/573, he was the highest ranking official of Rome's civilian administration; this required commensurately excellent knowledge and experience, and later on these were to be of great benefit to him in his papal role. In 574 he relinquished his public career, however, and, following the tradition that had been treasured since the Cappadocians and carried out up to Cassiodorus, withdrew to a monastic community in the family estate on the Caelian, one of the seven hills of Rome. He converted the latter into a monastery dedicated to St. Andrew, albeit without serving as its abbot. In addition, he founded six further monasteries on family estates in Sicily. No doubt Gregory introduced a Benedictine atmosphere in his monasteries, for during this time he read the Rule of Benedict and his *Dialogues* attest to his high esteem of Benedict; nevertheless the Rule was not adopted formally. Gregory devoted the years at the monastery to an intensive study of Scripture and the Fathers (Jerome, Augustine, Benedict, John Cassian) and thereby augmented his secular education with an equally sound theological one, which was to be of benefit to him in managing his later office.

As in the case of Basil the Great and Augustine, he was not to be granted the pleasure of completing his life in monastic seclusion; the ecclesiastical hierarchy was desperately in need of his abilities. Throughout his life he longed, albeit for naught, to be able to return from the necessary *vita activa* to the monastic *vita contemplativa*. The Lombards' advances into central Italy increasingly severed Rome from the residence of the Italian exarch at Ravenna, so that the pope was forced by means of an ambassador (*apocrisiarius*) to maintain direct contact with the emperor and the governmental offices in Constantinople in order to negotiate assistance for a beleaguered Italy. To this end, Pope Benedict I (575–579) or Pelagius II (579–590) appointed Gregory in 579 and ordained him a deacon. His stay in the imperial capital completed Gregory's sophisticated political and ecclesiastical-political experiences and enabled him to establish numerous important and life-long relationships—for instance, with Leander of Seville—that were to be of benefit to him at a later time.

In 585/586 the pope recalled him from Constantinople, probably because his expectations for the possibility of diplomatic results remained unfulfilled, and after Gregory had returned to the monastery of St. Andrew as a monk, he made him one of his important advisors. The winter of 589/590 brought a disastrous flood and famine, followed by an epidemic of the plague, to which Pope Pelagius II succumbed on February 7/8, 590.[5] As a deacon, the task of the social and charitable care of the population fell upon Gregory, so enhancing his popularity that he was elected spontaneously as the successor to the episcopal see of Rome; on September 3, 590, when the imperial confirmation had been received, he was consecrated and enthroned. The account of Gregory's hesitation in assuming the office had indeed been part of the hagiographic topoi since the fourth century (Augustine, Martin of Tours), and later legends significantly embellished it with escape attempts; nevertheless the historical core, in any case, is not subject to doubt. This is particularly true of Gregory, who did not want to give up his monastic lifestyle and who was so feeble and sick throughout his pontificate that he spent most of his time in bed and was not able to preach in public any longer. This did not, however, cause him to shy away from his obligations; his chancery's list of 857 letters provides vivid information about the complex, extensive, and difficult tasks he had to deal with during the fourteen years of his pontificate, until his death on March 13, 604.[6]

Five major areas of responsibility required Gregory's attention: (a) caring for the Roman church, the city, and the entire *patrimonium Petri*, not only ecclesiastically and religiously but also politically, socially, and in terms of charity; (b) connections with Eastern Rome; (c) the Lombards; (d) as patriarch of the West, caring for the preservation of the faith and its expansion in the whole area of the patriarchate, extending from North Africa, via Spain and Gaul, to as far as Britain; and (e) his literary activity. The multitude and complexity of these responsibilities allow us to appreciate Gregory's major achievements:

a. Gregory reorganized the Roman curia and the entire administration of the property of the Roman church (*patrimonium Petri*), extending to Campania, Sicily, Sardinia, North Africa, Gaul, and Dalmatia, which provided funds mainly for the support of the steadily increasing numbers of refugees due to the advances of the Lombards. In keeping with the guidelines he himself had established in the *Regula pastoralis*, he applied utmost care to improving the clergy's way of life, to

---

[5] R. Manselli (*TRE* 12:934); according to Bertolini, however, it was February 5.
[6] By appealing to the *Liber pontificalis*, his death is usually dated March 12; the *III idus martias* mentioned there (R. A. Markus, *TRE* 14:136), however, points to March 6.

proper episcopal elections, to reorganizing bishoprics, and to intensifying pastoral care by holding synods and establishing the respective jurisdictional responsibilities. In addition, judicial responsibilities and service as the appeals authority over civilian institutions had already fallen upon the bishops—and to a particular extent upon the bishop of Rome—since the fourth century, but especially since the legislation of Emperor Justinian (527–565).

b. The political and ecclesiastical relations with Eastern Rome under the emperors Maurice (582–602) and Phocas (602–610) developed relatively trouble-free under Gregory's pontificate, no doubt also on account of his excellent contacts from his tenure as *apocrisiarius*. Only in connection with two matters did serious tension arise, namely, in the context of Gregory's peace efforts with the Lombards and in 595, when John, the patriarch of Constantinople, officially assumed the title of οἰκουμενικός ("of the entire world")—a title still borne currently—which Gregory deemed presumptuous and an intrusion into his primacy. Significantly, in juxtaposition to this, he established the title of humility that the popes continue to bear today, *servus servorum Dei*.

c. The Lombards' penetration of Italy naturally represented the most urgent problem both politically and ecclesiastically. Many Lombards were still pagans or, in some cases (including kings), Arian Christians. Only Queen Theodolinda (589–627/628), with whom Gregory maintained correspondence, adhered to the Catholic faith. Gregory was responsible for the entire defense and provisioning of Rome, the negotiations with the Lombards, and the payment of tributes. He realized that Byzantium was not in a position to provide effective assistance and hence sought for a peaceful agreement with the Lombards for the sake of the distressed population. This initiative brought him into serious conflict with the exarch of Ravenna. Gregory also wanted to promote the conversion of the Lombards to the Catholic faith. He was successful insofar as Theodolinda brokered two agreements (598 and 603) between her husband, King Agilulf, and Pope Gregory, and her son Adaloald received a Catholic baptism, overcoming in practice the prohibition against baptism that the agreements had nullified in theory.

d. The outstanding feature of Gregory's effectiveness as the patriarch of the entire church of the former Western Roman Empire is the commissioning of missionaries to Britain, which by then had no longer been subject to Rome for almost two hundred years (since 407) and where apparently all traces of earlier mission work had disappeared. With merely marginal differences, the *Vita* of Whitby and later the *Historia ecclesiastica gentis Anglorum* (2.1) by the Venerable Bede tell the well-known story of Gregory's initial meeting with the Angles at the slave market of Rome before his pontificate. One day he went to the forum, where new commodities had arrived, among them good-looking young boys with fair skin and blond hair. He asked about their place of origin and was told they had come from Britain, from the tribe of the Angles, at which he exclaimed, "Rightly so, for they also have angelic faces [*angeli*]." He also interpreted the name of the province of the Deiri as "saved from the wrath [*de ira*] of God" and the king's name Aelle as a reference to the Allelujah. He immediately planned on evangelizing the Angles personally but was refused by the bishop. In his capacity as pope, he turned his desire into action and in 596 sent Augustine, the prior of his monastery of St. Andrew to Britain together with forty monks. At the court of King Ethelbert of Kent in Canterbury, they met Bertha, the Catholic queen who originally came from Gaul, and found her court chapel dedicated to St. Martin, the most popular Gallic saint. The chapel can still be viewed in Canterbury today. Even if the historicity of the encounter at the Roman forum is debatable, the story aptly depicts Gregory's missionary zeal. Such zeal also extended to the conversion of the Visigoth kingdom in Spain to Catholicism. This took place in 587 (conversion of King Recared) or 589 (Third Council of Toledo) through close contact with Leander of Seville, with whom Gregory had been acquainted since Constantinople. Gregory's efforts also extended to Gaul and the Franks, as well as to the heretical currents in North Africa.

e. Besides the works to be discussed in more detail below, from his days as *apocrisiarius* in Constantinople until 594, Gregory wrote exegetical homilies and commentaries on Ezekiel, 1 Kings, Song of Songs, and the Gospels. After this date, presumably because of his ill health, the only items available are letters. No doubt he also had a lasting influence upon the shape and reform of the liturgy of his time, so that the sacramentary and the antiphonary named after him stand in his tradition although he was not their author.

*Bibliographies:* R. Godding, *Bibliografia di Gregorio Magno (1890–1989)* (Rome: Città Nuova, 1990).

*Editions: Opera omnia:* PL 75–79. – PLS 4:1525–85. – *Gregorii Magni Opera* (Rome: Città Nuova, 1992–). – *Expositiones in Canticum canticorum, Expositiones in librum primum Regum* (ed. P. Verbraken; CCSL 144; Turnhout, Belg.: Brepols, 1963). – *Expositiones in Canticum canticorum: Commentaire sur le Cantique des cantiques* (ed. R. Bélanger; SC 314 [1984]) [Com]. – *Expositiones in librum primum Regum: Commentaire sur le premier livre des Rois* (ed. A. de Vogüé and C. Vuillaume; SC; Paris: Cerf, 1989–) [Com]. – *Homiliae in Ezechielem: Sancti Gregorii Magni Homiliae in Hiezechihelem prophetam* (ed. M. Adriaen; CCSL 142; Turnhout, Belg.: Brepols, 1971). – *Homélies sur Ezéchiel* (ed. C. Morel; 2 vols.; SC 327, 360; Paris: Cerf, 1986–1990) [Com]. – *Vita:* LP 1:312–14. – H. Grisar, "Die Gregorbiographie des Paulus Diaconus in ihrer ursprünglichen Gestalt, nach italienischen Handschriften," *ZKT* 11 (1887): 158–73. – *The Earliest Life of Gregory the Great by an Anonymous Monk of Whitby* (ed. and trans. B. Colgrave; Lawrence: University of Kansas Press, 1968; Cambridge: Cambridge University Press, 1986). – *Homiliae in Evangelia* (ed. M. Fiedrowicz; 2 vols.; FChr 28.1–2; Fribourg, Switz.: Herder, 1997–1998) [Com]. – *Homiliae in Evangelia* (ed. R. Étaix; CCSL 141; Turnhout, Belg.: Brepols, 1999).

*Translations: Forty Gospel Homilies* (trans. D. Hurst; CistSS 123; Kalamazoo: Cistercian, 1990).

*Encyclopedia Articles:* P. Cannata, in *Bibliotheca sanctorum* (13 vols.; Rome: Istituto Giovanni XXIII nella Pontificia Università Lateranense, [1961?] – ca. 1970), 7:222–87. – R. Gillet, *DSp* 6:872–910. – R. Manselli, *RAC* 12:930–51. – R. A. Markus, *TRE* 14:135–45. – R. Gillet, *DHGE* 21:1387–1420. – V. Recchia, *EECh* 1:365–68. – G.A. Zinn, *EEC* 1:488–91.

*Surveys and Introductions:* F. H. Dudden, *Gregory the Great: His Place in History and Thought* (2 vols.; London and New York: Longmans, Green, 1905; repr., New York:

Russell & Russell, 1967). – E. Caspar, *Geschichte des Papsttums von den Anfängen bis zur Höhe der Weltherrschaft* (2 vols.; Tübingen: Mohr, 1933), 2:306–514. – R. Manselli, *Gregorio Magno* (Turin: G. Giappichelli, 1967). – J. Richards, *The Consul of God: The Life and Times of Gregory the Great* (London and Boston: Routledge & Kegan Paul, 1980). – V. Paronetto, *Gregorio Magno: Un maestro alle origini cristiane d'Europa* (Rome: Studium, 1985). – R. A. Markus, *Gregory the Great and His World* (Cambridge and New York: Cambridge University Press, 1997).

*Collections of Essays:* R. A. Markus, *From Augustine to Gregory the Great: History and Christianity in Late Antiquity* (VRCS 169; London: Variorum, 1983). – P. Catry, *Parole de Dieu, amour et Esprit-Saint chez saint Grégoire le Grand* (VieMon 17; Bégrolles-en-Mauges: Abbaye de Bellefontaine, 1984). – J. Fontaine, R. Gillet, and S. Pellistrandi, eds., *Grégoire le Grand: Chantilly, Centre culturel Les Fontaines, 15–19 septembre 1982—actes* (Paris: Centre National de la Recherche Scientifique, 1986). – *Gregorio Magno e il suo tempo: XIX Incontro di studiosi dell'antichità cristiana in collaborazione con l'École française de Rome, Roma, 9–12 maggio 1990* (2 vols.; SEAug 33–34; Rome: Institutum Patristicum Augustinianum, 1991). – J. C. Cavadini, ed., *Gregory the Great: A Symposium* (Notre Dame, Ind., and London: University of Notre Dame Press, 1995). – V. Recchia, *Gregorio Magno papa ed esegeta biblico* (Bari: Dipartimento di Studi Classici e Cristiani, Università di Bari, 1996).

*Thought and Theology:* C. Dagens, *Saint Grégoire le Grand: Culture et expérience chrétiennes* (Paris: Études Augustiniennes, 1977). – G. R. Evans, *The Thought of Gregory the Great* (Cambridge: New York: Cambridge University Press, 1986). – C. Straw, *Gregory the Great: Perfection in Imperfection* (TCH 14; Berkeley: University of California Press, 1988). – J. Modesto, *Gregor der Grosse: Nachfolger Petri und Universalprimat* (STG 1; St. Ottilien: EOS, 1989). – M. Fiedrowicz, *Das Kirchenverständnis Gregors des Grossen: Eine Untersuchung seiner exegetischen und homiletischen Werke* (RQ.S 50; Fribourg, Switz.: Herder, 1995). – B. McGinn, *The Growth of Mysticism* (New York: Crossroads, 1994; London: SCM, 1996).

*Exegesis:* V. Recchia, *L'esegesi di Gregorio Magno al Cantico dei cantici* (Turin: Società Editrice Internazionale, 1967). – P. Meyvaert, "The Date of Gregory the Great's Commentaries on the Canticle of Canticles and on I Kings," *SacEr* 23 (1979): 191–216. – V. Recchia, *Le omelie di Gregorio Magno su Ezechiele (1–5)* (QVetChr 8; Bari: Adriatica, 1974). – S. Mueller, *"Fervorem discamus amoris": Das Hohelied und seine Auslegung bei Gregor dem Grossen* (St. Ottilien: EOS, 1991). – D. Wyrwa, "Der persönliche Zugang in der Bibelauslegung Gregors des Grossen," in *Sola scriptura: Das reformatorische Schriftprinzip in der säkularen Welt* (ed. H. H. Schmid and J. Mehlhausen; Gütersloh: G. Mohn, 1991), 262–78. – V. Recchia, "I moduli espressivi dell'esperienza contemplativa nelle *Omelie su Ezechiele* di Gregorio Magno: Schemi tropi e ritmi," *VetChr* 29 (1992): 75–112. – S. C. Kessler, *Gregor der Grosse als Exeget: Eine theologische Interpretation der Ezechielhomilien* (IThS 43; Innsbruck: Tyrolia, 1995).

*Missions:* G. Jenal, "Gregor der Grosse und die Anfänge der Angelsachsenmission (596–604): Angli e Sassoni al di qua e al di là del mare," *SSAM* 32 (1986): 793–849. – A. Furioli, "San Furioli, San Gregorio Magno, e l'evangelizzazione degli Anglosassoni," *ED* 42 (1989): 471–93.

*Administration and Politics:* M. Vaes, "La papauté et l'église franque à l'époque de Grégoire le Grand (590–604)," *RHE* 6 (1905): 537–56, 755–84. – E. Spearing, *The Patrimony of the Roman Church in the Time of Gregory the Great* (Cambridge: Cambridge University Press, 1918). – E. H. Fischer, "Gregor der Grosse und Byzanz: Ein Beitrag zur Geschichte der päpstlichen Politik," *ZSRG.K* 36 (1950): 15–144. – O. Giordano, *L'invasione longobarda e Gregorio Magno* (Bari: Adriatica, 1970). – V. Recchia,

*Gregorio Magno e la società agricola* (VSen NS 8; Rome: Studium, 1978). – M. Rey-dellet, *La royauté dans la littérature latine de Sidoine Apollinaire à Isidore de Séville* (BEFAR 253; Rome: École Française de Rome; Paris: de Boccard, 1981), 441–503. – J. Herrin, *The Formation of Christendom* (rev. ed.; Princeton, N.J.: Princeton University Press, 1987), 145–82. – G. Jenal, "Gregor der Grosse und die Stadt Rom (590–604)," in *Herrschaft und Kirche: Beiträge zur Entstehung und Wirkungsweise episkopaler und monastischer Organisationsformen* (ed. F. Prinz; MGMA 33; Stuttgart: A. Hiersemann, 1988), 109–45.

# *A.* Moralia in Job

During his work as *apocrisiarius* in Constantinople, Gregory, encouraged by Leander, his friend from Seville, lectured on the book of Job in the monastic community in which he lived; later on he completed, revised, and stylistically standardized these lectures into a comprehensive commentary in thirty-five books, as he himself writes in the letter accompanying the copy for Leander (*Ep.* 5.53 a). It cannot be determined precisely, however, when he published the work in the complete form available to us today. Markus[7] assumes that "it was available no later than 591." Adriaen,[8] appealing to the relevant source references, only specifies that Gregory wrote to Leander in 591 (*Ep.* 1.41) about the books already being copied but that Leander did not actually receive a copy until 595, which later on must have been supplemented again because *Moralia in Job* 27.11 refers to the mission to the Anglo-Saxons. All that is certain is that *Moralia in Job* was published after 579 and before 600/602.

That the person of Job presents itself for moral exegesis is obvious and has many patristic examples. Although Gregory initially intends an interpretation in keeping with the threefold meaning of Scripture, literal, allegorical, and moral, he adheres to it only in the first three books. Increasingly with bks. 4 and 5, he almost skips the literal interpretation, and the moral exegesis becomes dominant; for this reason, today's common title, *Moralia in Job*, quickly superseded the original name, *Expositio in Job*. In keeping with the threefold meaning of Scripture, Job, in the literal sense, represents the historical person, struck by suffering and testing; in the allegorical/typological sense, he represents Christ and his body, the church; and morally he represents the human person in his misery. With the assistance of the angels and the preaching of the church's shepherds, the person's way to God leads through the temptations of the devil to a knowledge of self, yielding first of all the fruit of humility, purity of heart, fear of God, and remorse and thus rendering effective Christ's redemptive act for the individual person. Although Gregory is indebted in many ways to his reading of Augustine, he distinguishes himself significantly in one respect: he allows much more room to the free will and decision of the individual in relation to the grace of God.

---

[7] R. A. Markus, *TRE* 14:138.

[8] M. Adriaen, ed., *Moralia in Job* (3 vols.; CCSL 143, 143A, 143B; Turnhout, Belg.: Brepols, 1979–1985).

*Editions: Morales sur Job* (ed. R. Gillet, A. de Gaudemaris, and A. Bocognano; SC 32 bis, 212, 221, 476; Paris: Cerf, 1952–1989) [*I–II, XI–XVI, XXVIII–XXIX* Com]. – *Moralia in Job* (ed. M. Adriaen; 3 vols.; CCSL 143, 143A, 143B; Turnhout, Belg.: Brepols, 1979–1985). – *Moralia in Iob* (ed. M. Adriaen et al.; vol. 1 of *Gregorii Magni Opera;* 1 vol. in 4; Rome: Città Nuova, 1992–2001).

*Studies:* R. M. Hauber, *The Late Latin Vocabulary of the Moralia of Saint Gregory the Great: A Morphological and Semasiological Study* (SMRL 7; Washington, D.C.: Catholic University of America Press, 1938). – L. Weber, *Hauptfragen der Moraltheologie Gregors des Grossen: Ein Bild altchristlicher Lebensführung* (Par. 1; Fribourg, Switz.: Paulusdruckerei, 1947). – P. Catry, "Épreuves du juste et du mystère de Dieu: Le commentaire littéral du *Livre de Job* par saint Grégoire le Grand," *REAug* 18 (1972): 124–44. – P. Aubin, "Intériorité et extériorité dans les Moralia in Job de saint Grégoire le Grand," *RSR* 62 (1974): 117–66. – V. Recchia, "Il metodo esegetico di Gregorio Magno nei '*Moralia in Job*' (ll. I, II, IV, 1–47)," *Invigilata lucernis* 7–8 (1985–1986): 13–62. – M. Baasten, *Pride according to Gregory the Great: A Study of the Moralia* (Studies in the Bible and Early Christianity 7; Lewiston, N.Y.; Queenston, Ont.: Mellen, 1986). – J. P. Cavallero, "La técnica didáctica de San Gregorio Magno en los *Moralia in Job,*" *Helm.* 41 (1990): 129–88.

# *B.* Regula pastoralis

"What Benedict's Rule was to the monks of the Middle Ages, the Pastoral Rule of Gregory the Great was to the clergy of the world"—this oft repeated opinion may be passed on with confidence, because for centuries the *Regula pastoralis* became the essential textbook of spirituality and pastoral matters for bishops and priests. Already during Gregory's life it had spread throughout Italy, Spain, France, and England and, in a Greek translation, to Constantinople, Antioch, Jerusalem, and Alexandria. In the dedicatory letter to John, bishop of Ravenna,[9] that preceded the text, Gregory himself explains the occasion for, and structure of, the work: John had rebuked him for hesitating to assume the episcopate, and this small book was intended to delineate his motives, namely, his fear of that high and difficult office. Thus Gregory places himself in the tradition of Gregory of Nazianzus and John Chrysostom, who also wrote such justifications. On the basis of this letter and one addressed to Leander of Seville (*Ep.* 5.53), it can be established that it was written at the beginning of his pontificate, and since a synodal letter from February 591 (*Ep.* 1.24) contains citations from it, the time can be narrowed further to the months between September 590 and February 591. In content, the *Regula* is anticipated in the *Moralia in Job,* although it remains an open question whether it had "progressed significantly" by the time Gregory's pontificate began and was not completed "until the earliest months of his pontificate."[10]

---

[9] Since the letter's prescript mentions only the name itself, another theory argues for the identification of John as the patriarch of Constantinople.

[10] Markus, *TRE* 14:136.

"The book has a four-part structure: . . . [I] how someone attains to the pastorate, . . . [II] how he orders his life, . . . [III] how he manages his teaching ministry, . . . [IV] how he seeks to acknowledge his weakness daily, so that one's assumption of office does not lack humility" (*Epistula ad Joannem*). Thus the eleven chapters of part 1 consider the seriousness and responsibility of the pastoral office, tearing one away—Gregory himself suffered this—from contemplation. They analyze the necessary prerequisites for those who are to assume this office or, on the other hand, who are not to enter into or even aspire to it. The eleven chapters of part 2 present the character traits and lifestyle of a good pastor: personal transparency and exemplary conduct, the gift of discernment, sympathy, wisdom in judgment and in behavior toward those entrusted to one's care, and the cultivation of one's own spirituality. (Here again the tension between the *vita activa* and *vita contemplativa*, which Gregory himself senses so strongly, comes to the fore; a good pastor has to endure this and understand how to combine the two). The number of chapters—forty—shows that part 3 represents the main focus of the work, preaching. In the first chapter, Gregory establishes a lengthy list of pairings of people, based on contrasts adopted from the *Moralia* (30.3.13)—people who must be addressed appropriately in preaching: men and women, young and old men, poor and rich, happy and sad, healthy and sick, and so forth. The following thirty-four chapters meticulously adhere to this ordering and explain the appropriate method of preaching for each of the juxtaposed pairs. Chapters 37–39 conclude the book with general advice intended for all; the final chapter (40) exhorts the pastor on the necessity of his own example in what he proclaims by his words. Book 4 is so brief that it creates the impression that Gregory had to rush to complete the work as a whole, for it contains only a terse admonition for the pastor's humility and in size is no more extensive than a chapter in the preceding books.

*Editions: Regula pastoralis: Wie der Seelsorger, der ein untadeliges Leben führt, die ihm anvertrauten Gläubigen belehren und anleiten soll* (ed. G. Kubis; Graz: Styria, 1986). – *Règle pastorale* (ed. B. Judic, F. Rommel, and C. Morel; 2 vols.; SC 381–382; Paris: Cerf, 1992) [Com].

*Translations:* J. Barmby, trans., "The Book of Pastoral Rule of Saint Gregory the Great, Roman Pontiff, to John, Bishop of the City of Ravenna," in *NPNF²* (Peabody, Mass.: Hendrickson, 1995; repr. of 1895 ed.), 12:1–72. – *Pastoral Care* (trans. H. Davis; ACW 11; Westminster, Md.: Newman, 1950; repr., 1955).

*Studies:* L. La Piana, *Teologia e ministero della parola in S. Gregorio Magno* (Palermo: Edi Oftes, 1987). – J. Speigl, "Die Pastoralregel Gregors des Grossen," *RQ* 88 (1993): 57–76.

# *C.* Dialogi (Dialogues)

Whereas the *Moralia in Job* addressed monks and the *Regula pastoralis*, pastors, Gregory's *Dialogues* is directed to all the (Italian) people of the church. Its intent is to edify them with examples of the model lives of the saints of their native country, to encourage their imitation, and, through the miracles of the saints, to demonstrate to the people that God is also manifesting his power in the world in their present difficult history. Gregory's letter of July 593, addressed to Bishop Maximian of Syracuse (*Ep.* 3.50), clearly indicates that he was urged to this undertaking by the brothers with whom he lived and that he thus addressed an apparent spiritual need. He followed such popular examples as the *Apophthegmata patrum,* which was also widely circulated in the West in a Latin translation, Rufinus's *Vita patrum,* Palladius's *Historia Lausiaca,* Sulpicius's *Vita Martini,* and the sixth-century *Gesta martyrum.* He chose the traditional literary form of a dialogue with a fictitious interlocutor, a deacon by the name of Peter. Gregory of Tours wrote his *Libri miraculorum* about Gallic saints at the same time and for a similar purpose.

As attested by, for instance, the letter to Maximian mentioned above, Gregory collected the material for the *Dialogues* from oral sources; hence modern historians reproach him for having adopted miracle accounts all too uncritically. This critique, voiced from an "enlightened" perspective, in fact misjudges Gregory's intention. Instead of writing a historical work, he intended to provide spiritually edifying literature, which has been vindicated by its centuries-long success. The date of composition for the *Dialogues* can be narrowed down with fair accuracy from the hints contained in it and in correspondence. Gregory began working on the *Dialogues* after his accession to the pontificate, especially in 593 and 594, and must have completed the work before November 594 because it shows no awareness of the death of Bishop Maximian of Syracuse.

From the sixteenth to the eighteenth centuries, the authenticity of the *Dialogues* was discussed at length, but the issue was settled by the Maurists. Since then it has been considered an authentic work of Gregory. In his 1982 contribution to the Gregory Colloquium in Chantilly, however, Francis Clark provided new stimulus to the discussion and since then has argued for their pseudonymity in various publications. Meanwhile a number of experts have responded to the issue, albeit without achieving a unanimous decision.

The *Dialogues* divides into four books, which Adalbert de Vogüé subjected to an astute structural analysis in the introduction to his edition and thus deciphered their exceedingly artistic and well-thought-out structure.[11] Apparently everything revolves around the number fifty, which Gregory several times in his works construes as a symbol of divine (eternal) rest, in parallel with the Jewish Year of Jubilee. Books 1–3 tell of the life and miraculous deeds of Italian saints, whereas bk. 4 consists of a tract on eschatology. Books 1 (twelve chapters) and 3 (thirty-eight chapters) provide the frame for bk. 2 (thirty-eight chapters) as their center, which deals exclusively with Benedict of Nursia, with bk. 1 presenting twelve saints in each chapter and bk. 3 presenting thirty-seven saints. Altogether, therefore, there are fifty saints, and together with the sixty-two chapters of bk. 4, there are one hundred

---

[11] A. de Vogüé and P. Antin, eds., *Dialogues* (3 vols.; SC 251, 260, 265; Paris: Cerf, 1978–1980), 1:51–55.

and fifty chapters. The symbolism of numbers goes beyond this, however, because the two books in the middle symmetrically have thirty-eight chapters each, bks. 1 and 2 amount to fifty, bks. 3 and 4 to one hundred. Contentwise, bk. 1 concludes with a descent into the netherworld, bk. 2 with an ascension, and bk. 3 with a view of the end times, which bk. 4, finally, explains theologically.

*Editions: Dialogues* (ed. A. de Vogüé and P. Antin; 3 vols.; SC 251, 260, 265; Paris: Cerf, 1978–1980) [Com].

*Translations: Dialogues* (trans. O. J. Zimmerman; FC 39; New York: Fathers of the Church; Washington, D.C.: Catholic University of America Press, 1959).

*Studies:* A. J. Kinnirey, *The Late Latin Vocabulary of the Dialogues of St. Gregory the Great* (Studies in Medieval and Renaissance History 4; Washington, D.C.: Catholic University of America Press, 1935). – P. Boglioni, "Miracle et nature chez Grégoire le Grand: Epopées, légendes, et miracles," *CEMéd* 1 (1974): 11–102. – A. Vitale Brovarone, "La forma narrativa dei *Dialoghi* di Gregorio Magno: Problemi storico-letterari," in n.t. (*AAST.M* 108; Turin: Accademia delle Scienze di Torino,1974), 95–173. – A. Vitale Brovarone, "Forma narrativa dei *Dialoghi* di Gregorio Magno: prospettive di struttura," *AAST.M* 109 (1975): 117–85. – G. Cracco, "Uomini di Dio e uomini di Chiesa nell'alto medioevo: Per una reinterpretazione dei 'Dialogi' di Gregorio Magno," *RSSR* 12 (1977): 163–202. – J. M. Petersen, *The Dialogues of Gregory the Great in Their Late Antique Cultural Background* (STPIMS 69; Toronto: Pontifical Institute of Mediaeval Studies, 1984). – F. Clark, *The Pseudo-Gregorian Dialogues* (2 vols.; SHCT 37–38; Leiden: Brill, 1987). – W. D. McCready, *Signs of Sanctity: Miracles in the Thought of Gregory the Great* (STPIMS 91; Toronto: Pontifical Institute of Mediaeval Studies, 1989). – F. Clark, "The Renewed Controversy about the Authorship of the Dialogues," in *Gregorio Magno e il suo tempo: XIX Incontro di studiosi dell'antichità cristiana in collaborazione con l'École française de Rome, Roma, 9–12 maggio 1990* (2 vols.; Rome: Institutum Patristicum Augustinianum, 1991), 2:5–25. – A. de Vogüé, "Les dialogues, œuvre authentique et publiée par Grégoire lui-même," in *Gregorio Magno e il suo tempo: XIX Incontro di studiosi dell'antichità cristiana in collaborazione con l'École française de Rome, Roma, 9–12 maggio 1990* (2 vols.; Rome: Institutum Patristicum Augustinianum, 1991), 2:27–40.

# *D.* Registrum epistularum

All of the church fathers' corpora of letters, be it that of Cyprian, those of the three great Cappadocians, or of Jerome, Augustine, Leo the Great, or Cassiodorus, are relevant and vivid mirrors of their time and are of inestimable value to the historian as sources. The number of letters Gregory the Great wrote (normally by dictation) during his tenure of four years is unknown, for the original register of the papal administration, the *Liber diurnus*, in which his correspondence was entered daily, was lost in the ninth century. During the eighth century, however, copies were made of it, which have been preserved in three collections: P with 54 letters, C with 200, and R with 684, amounting to 847 genuine and 10 questionable items. Like the original collection, they are divided into fourteen books, in keeping with the period of indiction[12] from September 1 to August 31

---

[12] The taxation cycle of five years (beginning in 313: fifteen) introduced by Emperor Diocletian (297), which the papal administration routinely adopted from Pelagius II (584) on.

of each year (not including the letters accompanying his works). Since the number of the letters handed down varies between 16 and 240 per year, it is to be assumed that during his pontificate Gregory wrote several thousand letters on the most diverse tasks of his pontificate: to fellow bishops, to the emperor and officials, regarding personnel decisions, privileges, and many others. As in the case of Leo the Great and Cassiodorus, the style of the letters is shaped by the office, and so they are permeated with frequently recurring formulations, to which Gregory generally adds a few personal words.

*Editions: Gregorii I papae Registrum epistolarum* (ed. P. Ewald and L. M. Hartmann; 2 vols.; MGH.AA 1–2; Berlin: Weidmann, 1887–1893). – *S. Gregorii Magni Registrum epistularum* (ed. D. Norberg; 2 vols.; CCSL 140–140A; Turnhout, Belg.: Brepols, 1982). – *Registre des lettres* (ed. P. Minard; SC; Paris: Cerf, 1991–) [Com]. – *Registrum epistularum* (ed. V. Recchia; vol. 5 of *Gregorii Magni Opera*; 1 vol. in 4; Rome: Città Nuova, 1996–).

*Translations:* J. Barmby, trans., "Register of the Epistles of Saint Gregory the Great," in NPNF[2] (Peabody, Mass.: Hendrickson, 1995; repr. of 1895 ed.), 12:73–243; 13:1–111.

*Studies:* M. B. Dunn, *The Style of the Letters of St Gregory the Great* (PatSt 32; Washington, D.C.: Catholic University of America Press, 1931). – J. F. O'Donnell, *The Vocabulary of the Letters of Saint Gregory the Great* (SMRL 2; Washington, D.C.: Catholic University of America Press, 1934). – D. Norberg, *In Registrum Gregorii Magni studia critica: Commentatio academica* (2 vols.; Uppsala: Almqvist & Wiksell, 1937–1939). – D. Norberg, "Qui a composé les lettres de saint Grégoire le Grand?" *StMed* 3.21 (1980): 1–17. – D. Norberg, *Critical and Exegetical Notes on the Letters of Gregory the Great* (VHAAH.FF 27; Stockholm: Almqvist & Wiksell, 1982). – E. Pitz, *Papstreskripte im frühen Mittelalter: Diplomatische und rechtsgeschichtliche Studien zum Brief-Corpus Gregors des Grossen* (BGQMA 14; Sigmaringen: Thorbecke, 1990).

# VI. GREGORY OF TOURS

"I have not become a bishop of the Romans but of the Lombards," lamented Gregory the Great in a letter of January 591 to the ex-consul John (*Ep.* I 30). For the final two important church fathers of the West, Gregory of Tours and Isidore of Seville, this was actually true. In origin and education, they were Romans, but they served as bishops to the Franks and the Goths. Whereas in Italy and North Africa the structures of the Roman Empire continued to have an effect until the eighth century, in Gaul and Spain the relationship had been reversed already in the sixth and seventh centuries: the Franks and the Goths constituted the people of the state providing the structure, in whom *romanitas* continued to have an effect only at a certain educational stratum. The works of the last Latin church fathers therefore fed on the ancient patristic tradition, but they were already in a new environment and led on finally to the medieval church and culture.

Born on November 30, 538 or 539, in Arverna (modern Clermont-Ferrand) to a family of senatorial nobility, Gregory's life coincides almost precisely with that of his contemporary Gregory the Great, although it shows considerable differences because of the differing situation in Gaul. The scope and quality of their education are poles apart. Whereas Gregory the Great still enjoyed a comprehensive Roman education, Gregory of Tours was tutored by his episcopal uncles, whose education had a primarily ecclesiastical orientation. Already at the age of fourteen he had decided on an ecclesiastical career, and no later than 563 was a deacon under his uncle Nicetius of Lyons,[13] and in August 573 followed his cousin Eufronius as the twenty-second holder of the episcopal see of St. Martin of Tours. Thus he continued an extended family tradition, for, as he himself reports (*Historia Francorum* 5.49), "all but five bishops" came from his family. Until 585 Gregory's episcopacy of more than twenty years was shaped by the battles for the city of Tours by three Franconian regional kingdoms. In this situation he courageously defended the independence and rights of the church, even against the threats of the rulers. He was able to hold his ground, finally mediated peace, and became an important adviser to the kings. He died in 594, probably on November 17, the day on which he is venerated.

*Encyclopedia Articles:* B. K. Vollmann, *RAC* 12:895–930. – L. Pietri, *TRE* 14:184–88. – M. Simonetti, *EECh* 1:365. – P. C. Burns, *EEC* 1:498–99.

*Translations: Life of the Fathers* (trans. E. James; 2d ed.; TTH 1; Liverpool: Liverpool University Press, 1991). – *Glory of the Martyrs* (trans. R. Van Dam; TTH 3; Liverpool: Liverpool University Press, 1988). – *Glory of the Confessors* (trans. R. Van Dam; TTH 4; Liverpool: Liverpool University Press, 1988).

*Collections of Essays: Gregorio di Tours* (CCSSM 12; Todi: Accademia Tudertina, 1977). – N. Gauthier and H. Galinié, eds., *Grégoire de Tours et l'espace gaulois: Actes du Congrès international, Tours, 3–5 novembre 1994* (Tours: Revue Archéologique du Centre de la France, 1997).

*Studies:* L. Pietri, *La ville de Tours du IVe au VIe siècle: Naissance d'une cité chrétienne* (CEFR 69; Rome: École Française de Rome, Palais Farnèse, 1983), 247–334. – G. de Nie, *Views from a Many-Windowed Tower: Studies in Imagination in the Works of Gregory of Tours* (Amsterdam: Rodopi, 1987). – B. Saitta, *Gregorio di Tours e i Visigoti* (Catania: CUECM, 1996).

# Historia Francorum *and* Libri miraculorum

At first glance, the two major extant works seem to have little in common, but on closer examination, they prove to be two parts of the same concept. At a time that Gregory clearly perceives as the end of ancient Roman culture and as the dawn of a new era, he understands history as God's activity among people and thus as part of revelation, in which, on principle, there is no distinction between political/profane and miraculous events. The record of the *gesta Dei per homines* (*Vitae patrum* 9 pref.), as a pedagogical witness, cooperates in God's salvific plan and activity; for this reason, the present or most recent events for

---

[13] The dates differ considerably in L. Pietri (*TRE* 14:184–88) and B. K. Vollmann (*RAC* 12:895–930), who depends on B. Krusch (*Historia Francorum* [ed. B. Krusch, W. Levison, and W. Holzmann; 2d ed.; MGH.SRM 1.1; Hannover: Hahn, 1951]).

Gregory are far more important than those of long ago. In his writings, therefore, he collects, brings up to date, and expands on recent events much more extensively, indeed as fully as possible.

In continuity with the chronicles of the world by Eusebius and Jerome, Gregory actually conceived his historical work, *Decem libri historiarum*—later appropriately labeled merely *Historia Francorum*—as a universal history from creation to the present. The first book, however, goes up to the death of Martin of Tours (397), and the closer Gregory comes to his own time, the more extensively and more detailed his presentation becomes as a history exclusively devoted to the kingdom of the Franks: bks. 2–4 to the death of King Sigebert I in 575; bks. 5–10, formed like a chronicle, to the summer of 591. Thus it represents the outstanding source for our understanding of the early history of the Franconian kingdom, especially since Gregory recorded much on the basis of his own knowledge and eyewitness reports. His overall historical concept supports the notion of a divine history of salvation, in which—entirely different from Salvian's but paralleling Cassiodorus's history of the Goths—providence assigned a major role to the Franks as a people. Since the Jews and the Romans forfeited their mission as bearers of salvation because of their own guilt, the Franks have now been chosen. Because of their disputes, they, too, are in danger of losing out on God's grace, but God's wonderful saving work, which continuously manifests itself, especially in the present, does not let their hope wane.

For this reason, the *Libri miraculorum* is an integral part of Gregory's historiography. Book 1 treats the miracles of the Lord, the apostles, and especially the Gallic martyrs. Book 2 concerns Julian, the martyr who died near Arverna, whom Gregory himself had held in high regard since childhood. Books 3–6 concern St. Martin of Tours, although only bk. 3 summarizes his *vita* and miracles up to Gregory's assumption of office whereas bks. 4–6, similar to the *Historia*, present a precise chronicle of the miracles at the tomb of St. Martin in Tours during Gregory's pontificate. Book 7, *De vita patrum*, offers twenty-three biographies of Gallic saints, again mostly from his own area around Arverna and Tours. Book 8, *In gloria confessorum*, concerns miracles of Gallic saints. Since, for Gregory, both historiography and hagiography fulfill the same purpose, namely, recognizing God's saving work on the basis of the most direct and extensive knowledge of one's own history possible, the *Libri miraculorum* also contain considerable historical material because Gregory was concerned with accurate references about times and places, names, sources, and so forth. One thing is clearly far from his mind, however: the polished stylistic form following the rules of late antiquity. Nevertheless, by means of deliberate *rusticitas*, not only was he able to conceal his own shortcomings in this area, but an analysis of his work instead suggests that he saw the use of elevated colloquial language as the appropriate form of his time for his intended readership.[14]

*Editions: Opera omnia:* PL 71. – *Historia Francorum* (ed. B. Krusch, W. Levison, and W. Holtzmann; 2d ed.; MGH.SRM 1.1; Hannover: Hahn, 1951). – *Gregorii episcopi*

---

[14] In assessments of Gregory's work and style, the opinions of scholars vary widely.

*Turonensis Miracula et opera minora* (ed. B. Krusch and M. Bonnet; 2d ed.; MGH.SRM 1.2; Hannover: Hahn, 1969). – *La storia dei Franchi* (ed. M. Oldoni; 2 vols.; Rome: Fondazione Lorenzo Valla, 1981).

*Translations: The History of the Franks* (trans. L. Thorpe; Penguin Classics; Harmondsworth, Eng. and Baltimore: Penguin Books, 1974).

*Studies:* M. Bonnet, *Le latin de Grégoire de Tours* (Paris: Hachette, 1890; repr., Hildesheim: Olms, 1968). – J. M. Wallace-Hadrill, "The Work of Gregory of Tours in the Light of Modern Research," *THS* 5.1 (1951): 25–45; repr. in idem, *The Long-Haired Kings and Other Studies in Frankish History* (New York: Barnes & Noble; London: Methuen, 1962), 49–70. – M. Vieillard-Troiekouroff, *Les monuments religieux de la Gaule d'après les œuvres de Grégoire de Tours* (Paris: Honoré Champion, 1976). – M. Weidemann, *Kulturgeschichte der Merowingerzeit nach den Werken Gregors von Tours* (2 vols.; Mainz: Verlag des Römisch-Germanischen Zentralmuseums; Bonn: In Kommission bei R. Habelt, 1982). – M. Heinzelmann, "Hagiographischer und historischer Diskurs bei Gregor von Tours?" in *Aevum inter utrumque: Mélanges offerts à Gabriel Sanders, professeur émérite à l'Université de Gand* (ed. M. Van Uytfanghe and R. Demeulenaere; IP 23; Steenbrugge, Belg.: Abbatia Sancti Petri; The Hague: Nijhoff, 1991), 237–58.

*Historia Francorum:* F.-L. Ganshof, *Een historicus uit de VIe eeuw: Gregorius van Tours* (Brussels: Koninklijke Vlaamse Academie voor Wetenschappen, Letteren en Schone Kunsten van Belgie, 1966). – J. Schneider, "Die Darstellung des Paupers in den Historien Gregors von Tours," *JWG* 4 (1966): 57–74. – E. H. Walter, "Hagiographisches in Gregors Frankengeschichte," *AKuG* 48 (1966): 291–310. – M. Oldoni, "Gregorio di Tours e i *'Libri historiarum,'*" *StMed* 3.13 (1972): 563–700. – F. Thürlemann, *Der historische Diskurs bei Gregor von Tours: Topoi und Wirchlichkeit* (GWZ 39; Bern: Lang, 1974). – B. Vetere, *Strutture e modelli culturali nella società merovingia: Gregorio di Tours—una testimonianza* (Galatina: Congedo, 1979). – M. Reydellet, *La royauté dans la littérature latine de Sidoine Apollinaire à Isidore de Séville* (BEFAR 253; Rome: École Française de Rome; Paris: de Boccard, 1981), 345–437. – R. Sonntag, *Studien zur Bewertung von Zahlenangaben in der Geschichtsschreibung des frühen Mittelalters: Die Decem libri historiarum Gregors von Tours und die Chronica Reginos von Prüm* (Kallmünz: M. Lassleben, 1987). – W. Goffart, *The Narrators of Barbarian History (A. D. 550–800): Jordanes, Gregory of Tours, Bede, and Paul the Deacon* (Princeton, N.J.: Princeton University Press, 1988), 112–234. – K. A. Winstead, "The Transformation of the Miracle Story in the *Libri Historiarum* of Gregory of Tours," *MAe* 59 (1990): 1–15. – A. H. B. Breukelaaer, *Historiography and Episcopal Authority in Sixth-Century Gaul: The Histories of Gregory of Tours Interpreted in Their Historical Context* (FKDG 57; Göttingen: Vandenhoeck & Ruprecht, 1994). – M. Heinzelmann, *Gregor von Tours (538–594), "Zehn Bücher Geschichte": Historiographie und Gesellschaftskonzept im 6. Jahrhundert* (Darmstadt: Wissenschaftliche Buchgesellschaft, 1994).

*Libri miraculorum:* J. Schlick, "Composition et chronologie des *De virtutibus Sancti Martini* de Grégoire de Tours," in *Papers Presented to the Fourth International Conference on Patristic Studies Held at Christ Church, Oxford, 1963* (ed. F. Cross; StPatr 7; TU 92; Berlin: Akademie, 1966), 278–86. – M. Carrias, "Études sur la formation de deux légendes hagiographiques à l'époque mérovingienne: Deux translations de saint Martin d'après Grégoire de Tours," *RHEF* 57 (1972): 5–18. – O. Giordano, "Sociologia e patologia del miracolo in Gregorio di Tours," *Helikon* 18–19 (1978–1979): 161–209. – R. Van Dam, *Saints and Their Miracles in Late Antique Gaul* (Princeton, N.J.: Princeton University Press, 1993).

# VII. ISIDORE OF SEVILLE

Despite his outstanding importance for the Spanish/Visigoth church of his time and, through his writings, for the Middle Ages, only a few particulars on Isidore's life have been handed down. He came from a Roman family, possibly of Greek origin, from Carthago Nova (modern Cartagena), a town in southeastern Spain, where he was likely born ca. 560. Perhaps because of the Byzantine occupation of the town in the context of the reunification of the empire under Emperor Justinian in 552 or 555, his family moved to Hispalis (modern Seville), where Isidore likely attended the local episcopal school. There he obtained a thorough education, which was to find expression in his encyclopedic work. Like several members of his family, he chose an ecclesiastical career and ultimately succeeded his elder brother, Leander (who befriended Gregory the Great in Constantinople), to the metropolitan see of Seville between 599 and 601. He experienced the conversion of the Visigoths from Arianism to Catholic Christianity (587/ 589), and his episcopate of thirty-five years witnessed the battles for the national unification of Spain and the final expulsion of the Romans (621). Further, after two centuries of battles and invasion, and as the senior metropolitan and president of the Fourth Council of Toledo (633), he decisively influenced the reorganization and integration of the Catholic Church in the kingdom of the Visigoths. He died in 636, probably on April 4; in 1722 Pope Innocent XIII bestowed upon him the honorary title "doctor of the church."

The writings Isidore left are encyclopedic, encompassing the entire knowledge of his time and preserving it for the Middle Ages. They include a history of the Goths, Vandals, and Suevians; a chronicle that carries forward the works of Eusebius and Jerome; exegetical textbooks; a series of writings in the field of natural history (*De natura rerum, Differentiae, Synonyma*); *De haeresibus,* a compilation of the writings of Augustine and Jerome; a book titled *De ecclesiasticis officiis;* and a monastic rule. Of particular importance for patrology is *De viris illustribus,* his continuation of the literary-historical work of Jerome and Gennadius of Marseilles by the same title. He supplemented it mainly with Spanish authors; Ildefonsus of Toledo (d. 667) later supplemented it with another fourteen Spanish personalities, seven of whom were bishops of Toledo.

*Bibliography:* B. Altaner, "Der Stand der Isidorforschung: Ein kritischer Bericht über die seit 1910 erschienene Literatur," in *Miscellanea isidoriana: Homenaje a s. Isidoro de Sevilla en el XIII centenario de su muerte, 636—4 de abril—1936* (Rome: Typis Pontificiae Universitatis Gregorianae, 1936), 1–32. – J. N. Hillgarth, "The Position of Isidorian Studies: A Critical Review of the Literature since 1935," in *Isidoriana: Colección de estudios sobre Isidoro de Sevilla, publicados con ocasión del XIV centenario de su nacimiento* (Leon: Centro de Estudios San Isidoro, 1961), 11–74. – A. Segovia, "Informe sobre bibliografía Isidoriana (1936–1960)," *EstEcl* 36 (1961): 73–126. – W. Haubrichs, "Zum Stand der Isidorforschung," *ZDP* 94 (1974): 1–15. – J. N. Hillgarth, "The Position of Isidorian Studies: A Critical Review of the Literature since 1975," *StMed* 24 (1983): 817–905.

*Editions: Opera omnia:* PL 81–84. – PLS 4:1801–66. – *Commonitiuncula ad sororem:*
*S. Isidori Hispalensis episcopi Commonitiuncula ad sororem auctori* (ed. A. E. Anspach;
SEHL 4; El Escorial: Typis Augustinianis Monasterii Escurialensis, 1935). – *De*
*differentiis verborum: Diferencias* (ed. C. Codoñer Merino; Paris: Belles Lettres, 1992).
– *De ecclesiasticis officiis: Sancti Isidori episcopi Hispalensis De ecclesiasticis officiis* (ed.
C. M. Lawson; CCSL 113; Turnhout, Belg.: Brepols, 1989). – *De haeresibus: S. Isidori*
*Hispalensis episcopi De haeresibus liber* (ed. A. C. Vega; SEHL 5; Madrid: Typis
Augustinianis Monasterii Escurialensis, 1940). – *De natura rerum: Traité de la nature*
(ed. J. Fontaine; Bordeaux: Féret, 1960). – *De ortu et obitu patrum: De ortu et obitu*
*patrum = Vida y muerte de los santos* (ed. C. Chaparro Gómez; Paris: Belles Lettres,
1985). – *De variis questionibus: Liber de variis quaestionibus adversus Judaeos seu*
*ceteros infideles vel plerosque haereticos iudaizantes ex utroque Testamento collectus* (ed.
P. A. C. Vega and A. E. Anspach; SEHL 6–9; Madrid: Typis Augustinianis Monasterii
Escurialensis, 1940). – *De viris illustribus: El "De viris illustribus" de Isidoro de Sevilla*
(ed. C. Condoñer Merino; Salamanca: Consejo Superior de Investigaciones Científicas, Instituto "Antonio de Nebrija," Colegio Trilingüe de la Universidad, 1964)
[Com]. – *Epistulae: The Letters of St. Isidore of Seville* (ed. G. B. Ford; 2d ed.; Amster-
dam: Hakkert, 1970). – E. Anspach, *Taionis et Isidori nova fragmenta et opera* (Madrid:
C. Bermijo, 1930), 23–183. – *Historia Gothorum, Chronica: Chronica minora saec. IV.,*
*V., VI., VII.* (ed. T. Mommsen; 3 vols.; MGH.AA 9, 11, 13; Berlin: Weidmann,
1892–1898), 2:241–506. – *Historia Gothorum: Las historias de los Godos, Vandalos, y*
*Suevos de Isidoro de Sevilla* (ed. C. Rodríguez Alonso; León: Centro de Estudios e
Investigacion "San Isidoro," 1975) [Com]. *Sententiae: Isidorus Hispalensis Sententiae*
(ed. P. Cazier; CCSL 111; Turnhout, Belg.: Brepols, 1998). *Versus (Poems): Isidori*
*Hispalensis Versus* (ed. J. M. Sánchez Martín; CCSL 113A; Turnhout, Belg.: Brepols,
2000).

*Translations: Isidore of Selville's History of the Kings of the Goths, Vandals, and Suevi* (trans.
G. Donini and G.B. Ford Jr.; 2d rev. ed.; Leiden: Brill, 1966). – *The Letters of St. Isidore*
*of Selville* (trans. G. B. Ford Jr.; Amsterdam: A. M. Hakkert, 1970).

*Encyclopedia Articles:* J. Fontaine, *DSp* 7/2:2104–16. – R. J. H. Collins, *TRE* 16:310–15. –
R. Tenberg, *BBKL* 2:1374–79. – R. Aubert, *DHGE* 26 fasc. 150:214–18. – J. Fontaine,
*EECh* 26:214–18. – M. McHugh, *EEC* 1:593–94.

*Collections of Essays: Miscellanea isidoriana: Homenaje a s. Isidoro de Sevilla en el XIII*
*centenario de su muerte, 636—4 de abril—1936* (Rome: Typis Pontificiae Universitatis
Gregorianae, 1936). – M. C. Díaz y Díaz, ed., *Isidoriana: Colección de estudios sobre*
*Isidoro de Sevilla* (Léon: Centro de Estudios "San Isidoro," 1961).

*Surveys and Introductions:* L. Araujo Costa, *San Isidoro: Arzobispo de Sevilla* (Madrid:
Editorial Tradicionalista, 1942). – I. Quiles, *San Isidoro: Biografia, escritos, doctrinas*
(Buenos Aires: Espasa-Calpe Argentina, 1945). – J. Madoz, *San Isidoro de Sevilla:*
*Semblanza de su personalidad literaria* (Léon: Consejo Superior de Investigaciones
Científicas, Centro de Estudios e Investigaciones S. Isidoro, 1960). – J. Perez de
Urbel, *San Isidoro de Sevilla: Su vida, su obra, y su tiempo* (3d ed.; Léon: Universidad
de León, Secretariado de Publicaciones: Cátedra de San Isidoro de la Real Colegiata
de León, 1995). – H.-J. Diesner, *Isidor von Sevilla und seine Zeit* (AzTh 52; Stuttgart:
Calwer, 1973). – H.-J. Diesner, *Isidor von Sevilla und das westgotische Spanien*
(ASAW.PH 67.3; Berlin: Akademie, 1977). – R. Collins, *Early Medieval Spain: Unity*
*in Diversity, 400–1000* (2d ed.; Basingstoke, Eng.: Macmillan, 1995). – J. Fontaine,
*Isidore de Séville et la culture classique dans l'Espagne wisigothique* (3 vols.; 2d ed.;
Paris: Études Augustiniennes, 1983).

*Studies:* G. von Dzialowski, *Isidor und Ildefons als Litterarhistoriker: Eine quellenkritische*
*Üntersuchung der Schriften "De viris illustribus" des Isidor von Sevilla und des Ildefons*

*von Toledo* (KGS 4.2; Münster: H. Schöningh, 1898). – P. Séjourné, *Le dernier Père de l'Église—saint Isidore de Séville: Son rôle dans l'histoire du droit canonique* (Paris: Beauchesne, 1929). – J. R. Geiselmann, *Die Abendmahlslehre an der Wende der christlichen Spätantike zum Frühmittelalter: Isidor von Sevilla und das Sakrament der Eucharistie* (Munich: Hueber, 1933; repr., Hildesheim, Zurich, and New York: Olms, 1989). – P. J. Mullins, *The Spiritual Life according to Saint Isidore of Seville* (SMRL 13; Washington, D.C.: Catholic University of America Press, 1940). – G. Mancini, *Osservazioni critiche sull'opera di Isidoro* (Pisa: Goliardica, 1955). – J. de Churruca, *Las Instituciones de Gayo en san Isidoro de Sevilla* (Bilbao: Publicaciones de la Universidad de Deusto, 1975). – F.-J. Lozano Sebastián, *San Isidoro de Sevilla: Teología del pecado y la conversión* (Burgos: Aldecoa, 1976). – M. Reydellet, *La royauté dans la littérature latine de Sidoine Apollinaire à Isidore de Séville* (BEFAR 253; Rome: École Française de Rome; Paris: de Boccard, 1981), 505–97. – F.-J. Lozano Sebastián, *San Isidoro y la filosofía clásica* (León: Editorial Isidoriana, 1982). – G. Gasparotto, *Isidoro e Lucrezio: Le fonti della meteorologia isidoriana* (Verona: Libreria Universitaria, 1983). – A. Carpin, *Il sacramento dell'ordine: Dalla teologia isidoriana alla teologia tomista* (Bologna: ESD, 1988), 7–74. – J. Fontaine, *Tradition et actualité chez Isidore de Seville* (London: Variorum, 1988). – A. Carpin, *L'eucaristia in Isidoro di Siviglia* (Bologna: ESD, 1993). – P. Cazier, *Isidore de Seville et la naissance de l'Espagne catholique* (ThH 96; Paris: Beauchesne, 1994).

# Etymologiae *and* Sententiae

Of all the writings of Isidore, two stand out that became textbooks of theological and secular knowledge for the Middle Ages because of their encyclopedic character. In twenty books the *Etymologiae* collects the entire linguistic, historical, cultural, scientific, but also theological knowledge of his time, beginning with the knowledge acquired at school, namely, the seven "liberal arts" (grammar, rhetoric, dialectics, arithmetic, geometry, music, and astronomy), then through medicine, jurisprudence, chronology, history, the church, theology, state affairs, language, anthropology, natural science, geography, architecture, and agriculture, to military affairs, plays, navigation, domestic matters, and food. Only bk. 10 contains nothing but etymologies; the work as a whole, however, has been given this name because of Isidore's essential conviction, adopted from antiquity, that language and its analysis provide access to understanding reality. At Isidore's death this work was still incomplete; Braulio, his student and bishop of Saragossa (631–651), completed and published it ca. 630.

The *Sententiae* constitutes the complementary theological work to the *Etymologiae* and represents the first major witness to the extensive continuing influence of the *Moralia in Job* by Gregory the Great. From this source Isidore compiles a three-part (dogmatics, spirituality, morality), comprehensive religious ethics for Visigoth Christianity, which had now become fully integrated into the affairs of the state.

*Editions: Etymologiae: Isidori Hispalensis episcopi Etymologiarum sive originum libri XX* (ed. W. M. Lindsay; 2 vols.; Scriptorum classicorum bibliotheca; Oxford: Clarendon; New York: Oxford University Press, 1911; repr., 1985). – *Etymologies* (ed. P. K. Marshall, M. Reydellet, and J. André; Paris: Belles Lettres, 1981–1984) [*II, IX, XVIII*]. –

G. Gasparotto, *Agricoltura dei Romani: Isidoro di Siviglia, Etimologiae l. XVII—de agricultura* (Verona: Libreria Universitaria, 1996) [*XVII* Com].

*Reference Works:* A.-I. Magallón-García, *Concordantia in Isidori Hispalensis Etymologias: A Lemmatized Concordance to the Etymologies of Isidore of Sevilla* (4 vols.; AIOm.A 120.1–4; Hildesheim and New York: Olms-Weidmann, 1995).

*Studies:* J. Sofer, *Lateinisches und Romanisches aus den Etymologiae des Isidor: Untersuchungen zur lateinischen und romanischen Wortkunde* (Göttingen: Vandenhoeck & Ruprecht, 1930). – A. Borst, "Das Bild der Geschichte in der Enzyklopädie des Isidor von Sevilla," *DA* 22 (1966): 1–62. – B. Recaredo García, *Espiritualidad y "lectio divina" en las "Sentencias" de san Isidoro de Sevilla* (Zamora: Monte Casino, 1980). – W. Schweikard, "'*Etymologia est origo vocabulorum*': Zum Verständnis der Etymologiedefinition Isidors," *Historiographia linguistica* 12 (1985): 1–25.

# CHAPTER TWELVE

# Literature of the Greek East

## I. CATENAS

The catenas represent perhaps the most typical example of the mostly retrospective and collating character of Greek literature of the final period of
patristics. Catenas are continuous comments on biblical books in which the
biblical text is not explained by means of actual and original theology but by
verbatim excerpts of one or several older, proven commentaries, collated by a
compiler. At times it seems that Alexandrian and Antiochene commentaries are
deliberately juxtaposed in order to compare differing interpretations. Procopius of Gaza (465 to shortly after 530) appears to have been the originator of
this type of literature, drawing his compilation mainly from Origen's Ἐκλογαι
ἐξηγητικαί on the Octateuch, the books of Kings, Proverbs, Ecclesiastes, and
Song of Songs. The catenas became so popular that in many instances they replaced the transmission of complete original works. Precisely for this reason,
they have become valuable for modern scholarship because they at least preserve
(large) parts of otherwise lost writings (cf. above on Melito of Sardis, ch. 3.II;
Origen, ch. 3.V.C; Apollinaris of Laodicea, ch. 6.I; Diodore of Tarsus, ch. 7.IV;
Theodore of Mopsuestia, ch. 7.V; Cyril of Alexandria, ch. 10.I; and Theodoret
of Cyrus, ch. 10.2). The common Western designation "catena" (Latin *catena* =
"chain") originated in 1321 as the description of a commentary (*Catena aurea*)
by Thomas Aquinas of excerpts such as this from the Gospels. He himself
superscribed *expositio continua,* and the original Greek and Latin names for a
catena were ἐκλογαι, συναγωγή, συλλογή, *excerpta,* and *collectanea.* According to
the form, there are three types:

    a. The most frequent form is the *marginal catena,* in which the biblical
text, often in larger letters, is written toward the center of the page, along the
inner right-hand margin of the page, or in the center of the folio, whereas the
excerpts appear on the three or four available margins of the folio. Numbers or
symbols linking the excerpts to the respective text are usually, though not always, written in bolder letters. Since the attribution is subject to erroneous
sources in the history of transmission, they have to be examined critically, in
any case.

b. In the case of the scarcer *columnar catenas,* text and commentary are placed side by side in two columns per page, each taking up half of a folio.

c. In the *text catenas,* first the biblical text and then the explanations are written across the entire folio in alternating fashion.

The method of continuously copying a certain number of exemplars of commentaries distinguishes the catenas from the genre of biblical scholia, in which explanations of varying provenance are written in the margin of the text. They also differ from the florilegia, which can compile the most diverse kinds of sources, even if such elements do find a place in the later development of the catenas. In the case of his catenas on the Octateuch, Procopius of Gaza had summarized the comments from the original documents because of their abundance and then added his own remarks.

Beginning in the seventh century, Syriac, Armenian, and Coptic catenas translated the Greek biblical commentaries in part or provided excerpts of commentaries in their respective language. Also in the Latin language domain, scholia and *exposita* began to emerge, albeit only occasionally. They did not become popular, however, until the Carolingian era, and they led to the thriving medieval form of the gloss. Since the patristic writings excerpted there have been preserved completely in other ways, in contrast to the Greek catenas, they only bear corroborative witness to their knowledge and history of reception. They gained major significance in the time of the Reformation, however, as collections of authoritative witnesses against the Reformers' interpretation of the Bible; for this reason, Greek catenas were also translated into Latin. Although the primary interest in the catenas revolves around the reclamation of otherwise lost works, modern scholarship not only compiles lost original works on this basis but also publishes individual catenas in their original form as generally verifiable text witnesses.

*Editions:* J. A. Fabricius, *Bibliotheca graeca: Notitia scriptorum veterum graecorum, quorumcunque monumenta integra aut fragmenta edita exstant, tum plerorumque e MSS ac deperditis* (14 vols.; Hamburg: Christian Liebzeit & Theodor Christoph Felginer, 1715–1728), 7:727–88. – J. A. Fabricius and G. C. Harles, *Bibliotheca graeca* (14 vols; 4th ed.; Hamburg: Apud Carolvm Ernestvm Bohn, 1790–1809; repr., Hildesheim: Olms, 1966–1970), 8:637–700. – J. A. Cramer, *Catenae graecorum patrum in Novum Testamentum* (8 vols.; Oxford: E Typographeo Academico, 1838–1844; repr., Hildesheim: Olms, 1967).

*Octateuch:* J. Deconinck, *Essai sur la chaîne de l'Octateuque: Avec une édition des commentaires de Diodore de Tarse qui s'y trouvent contenus* (BEHE.H 195; Paris: H. Champion, 1912). – R. Devreesse, *Les anciens commentateurs grecs de l'Octateuque et des Rois* (StT 201; Vatican City: Biblioteca Apostolica Vaticana, 1959). – F. Petit, *Catenae graecae in Genesim et in Exodum* (CCSG; Turnhout, Belg.: Brepols, 1977–). – F. Petit, *La chaîne sur la Genèse* (4 vols.; Louvain: Peeters, 1991–1996).

*Job:* U. and D. Hagedorn, *Die älteren griechischen Katenen zum Buch Hiob* (4 vols.; PTS 40, 48, 53, 59; Berlin and New York: de Gruyter, 1994–2004).

*Psalms:* R. Cadiou, *Commentaires inédits des Psaumes: Études sur les textes d'Origène contenus dans le manuscrit Vindobonensis 8* (CEA; Paris: Belles Lettres, 1936). – R. Devreesse, *Les anciens commentateurs grecs des Psaumes* (StT 264; Vatican City:

Biblioteca Apostolica Vaticana, 1970). – M. Harl, *La chaîne palestinienne sur le psaume 118 (Origène, Eusèbe, Didyme, Apollinaire, Athanase, Théodoret)* (2 vols.; SC 189–190; Paris: Cerf, 1972). – E. Mühlenberg, *Psalmenkommentare aus der Katenenüberlieferung* (3 vols.; PTS 15, 16, 19; Berlin and New York: de Gruyter, 1975–1977) [*Didymus, Apollinaris*]. – J.-M. Oliver, "Les fragments 'Métrophane' des chaînes exégétiques grecques du psautier," *RHT* 6 (1976): 31–78. – G. Dorival, *Les chaînes exégétiques grecques sur les Psaumes* (4 vols.; SSL 43–46; Louvain: Peeters, 1986–1995). – C. Curti, "La catena palestinese sui Salmi graduali," *Paideia* 45 (1990): 93–101.

*Proverbs, Ecclesiastes, Canticle of Canticles:* M. Faulhaber, *Hohelied-, Proverbien- und Prediger-Catenen* (ThSLG 4; Vienna: Mayer, 1902). – O. Hoppmann, *Die Catene des Vaticanus gr. 1802 zu den Proverbien analysiert* (Leipzig: Hinrichs, 1912). – S. Leanza, "Le catene esegetiche sull'Ecclesiaste," *Aug* 17 (1977): 545–52. – S. Leanza, *Procopii Gazaei Catena in Ecclesiasten necnon Pseudochrysostomi Commentarius in eundem Ecclesiasten* (CCSG 4; Turnhout, Belg.: Brepols; Louvain: Louvain University Press, 1978). – S. Lucà, "La catena dei 3 Padri sull'Ecclesiaste," in *Studi in onore di Anthos Ardizzoni* (ed. E. Livrea and G. A. Privitera; 2 vols.; Rome: Ateneo & Bizzarri, 1978), 1:557–82. – S. Leanza, *Un nuovo testimone della Catena sull'Ecclesiaste di Procopio di Gaza, il Cod. Vindob. Theol. Gr. 147* (CCSG, 4 Supplementum; Turnhout, Belg.: Brepols; Louvain: Louvain University Press, 1983). – S. Lucà, *Anonymus in Ecclesiasten commentarius qui dicitur Catena trium patrum* (CCSG 11; Turnhout, Belg.: Brepols, 1983). – A. Labate, "Nuove catene esegetiche sull'Ecclesiaste," in *Antidōron: Hulde aan Dr. Maurits Geerard bij de voltooiing van de "Clavis patrum graecorum"* (Wetteren: Cultura, 1984), 241–63. – A. Labate, *Catena Hauniensis in Ecclesiasten in qua saepe exegesis servatur Dionysii Alexandrini* (CCSG 24; Turnhout, Belg.: Brepols, 1992).

*Prophets:* M. Faulhaber, *Die Propheten-Catenen nach römischen Handschriften* (BibS[F] 4.2–3; Fribourg, Switz., and St. Louis: Herder, 1899).

*Gospels:* J. Reuss, *Matthäus-, Markus- und Johannes-Katenen* (NTAbh 18.4–5; Münster: Aschendorff, 1941). – J. Reuss, *Matthäus-Kommentare aus der griechischen Kirche* (TU 61; Berlin: Akademie, 1957). – J. Reuss, *Johannes-Kommentare aus der griechischen Kirche* (TU 89; Berlin: Akademie, 1966). – B. Ehlers, "Eine Katene zum Johannes-Evangelium in Moskau, auf dem Athos (Dionysiu), in Athen und Oxford (050)," in *Materialien zur neutestamentlichen Handschriftenkunde* (ed. K. Aland et al.; ANTF 3; Berlin: de Gruyter, 1969–), 96–133. – J. Reuss, *Lukaskommentare aus der griechischen Kirche* (TU 130; Berlin: Akademie, 1984).

*Paul:* O. Lang, *Die Catene des Vaticanus gr. 762 zum Ersten Korintherbrief* (Leipzig: Hinrichs, 1909). – K. Staab, "Die griechischen Katenenkommentare zu den katholischen Briefen," *Bib* 5 (1924): 296–353. – K. Staab, *Die Pauluskatenen* (Rome: Verlag des Päpstlichen Bibelinstituts, 1926). – K. Staab, *Pauluskommentare aus der griechischen Kirche: Aus Katenenhandschriften gesammelt und herausgegeben* (NTAbh 15; Münster: Aschendorff, 1933; 2d ed.; Münster: Aschendorff, 1984).

*Reference Works:* G. Karo and J. Lietzmann, *Catenarum graecarum catalogus* (NGWG.PH 1902; Göttingen: K. Gesellschaft der Wissenschaften zu Göttingen, 1902). – M. Geerard and F. Glorie, *Clavis patrum graecorum* (7 vols.; Corpus Christianorum; Turnhout, Belg.: Brepols, 1974–2003), 4:185–259.

*Studies:* H. Lietzmann, *Catenen: Mitteilungen über ihre Geschichte und handschriftliche Überlieferung* (Fribourg, Switz.: Mohr, 1897). – R. Devreesse, *DBSup* 1:1084–1233. – M. Richard, *Opera minora* (3 vols.; Turnhout, Belg.: Brepols; Louvain: Louvain University Press, 1976–1977). – C. Curti, *EECh* 1:152–53. – E. Mühlenberg, *TRE* 17:14–21.

# II. PSEUDO-DIONYSIUS THE AREOPAGITE

"A few men became followers of Paul and believed. Among them was Dionysius, a member of the Areopagus" (Acts 17:34). Under the pseudonym of this Dionysius the Areopagite, an author, who remains unknown to this day, wrote four famous and important works. Except for the doubts of Hypatius of Ephesus (532) and a few others, these works were generally considered to be authentically those of the disciple of Paul mentioned in the Acts of the Apostles. For this reason, their Latin translation by Abbot Hilduin of St. Denis in Paris (827–835; revised again by John Scotus Erigena in 852) was held in high regard throughout the Middle Ages and exerted considerable influence. A legendary *Vita Dionysii* by the same abbot even identified him with the patron saint of Paris. The humanists Lorenzo Valla (1457) and Erasmus of Rotterdam (1504) exposed the *Corpus dionysiacum* as pseudepigraphic because it can be demonstrated incontrovertibly that it is dependent upon the Neoplatonism of Syrianus (first half of fifth century) and Proclus, his student (412–485). On the other hand, Severus of Antioch cites it already in 510 or 518/528; hence it has to be dated to the late fifth or early sixth century. In addition, there are clear indications of substantial influence from Plato's *Parmenides* and from the Christian Platonism of Gregory of Nyssa. Since then many scholars have postulated numerous hypotheses on the identity of Pseudo-Dionysius, none of which has been persuasive until now, however. Nevertheless, even today this question is still able to elicit sufficient attention for an international daily paper (1992) to publish a major journalistic article on the occasion of a critical edition and translation of his works.[1] This much may be concluded from these writings: their author probably was a Syrian Christian who had been living in Athens for a long time, where, as is well known, a circle of Syrian scholars gathered near the end of the fifth century.

*Bibliography:* J.-M. Hornus, "Les recherches récentes sur le pseudo-Denys l'Aréopagite," *RHPR* 35 (1955): 404–48. – K. F. Doherty, "Toward a Bibliography of Pseudo-Dionysius the Areopagite: 1900–1955," *MSM* 33 (1956): 257–68. – J.-M. Hornus, "Les recherches dionysiennes de 1955 à 1960," *RHPR* 41 (1961): 22–81. – K. F. Doherty, "Pseudo-Dionysius the Areopagite: 1955–1960," *MSM* 40 (1962): 55–59. – S. Lilla, "Introduzione allo studio dello Ps. Dionigi l'Areopagita," *Aug* 22 (1982): 568–77.

*Encyclopedia Articles:* R. Roques, P. Sherwood, A. Wenger, A. Rayez, P. Chevallier, H. Weisweiler, G. Dumeige, A.-A. Fracheboud, S. de St.-Anthonis, J. Turbessi, M. de Gandillac, A. Ampe, A. Combès, R. Marcel, J. Krynen, E. de Vièrge du Carmel, P.-H. Michel, S.-P. Michel, and O. de Veghel, *DSp* 3:244–429. – R. Roques, *RAC* 3:1075–1121. – R. Aubert, *DHGE* 14:265–310. – G. O'Daly, *TRE* 8:772–80. – S. Lilla, *EECh* 1:238–40. – J.A. Brooks, *EEC* 1:335–36.

*Surveys and Introductions:* V. Poletti, *Dionigi Areopagita: Sintesi dottrinali e brani scelti dalle opere* (Faenza: F.lli Lega, 1967). – S. Lilla, "Introduzione allo studio dello Ps. Dionigi

---

[1] K. Flasch, "Strahl des göttlichen Dunkels: Die Entlarvung des Pseudo-Dionysius Areopagita ist ein wissenschaftliches Unikum," *Frankfurter Allgemeine Zeitung*, February 8, 1992, supplement "Bilder und Zeiten."

l'Areopagita," *Aug* 22 (1982): 533–77. – A. Louth, *Denys the Areopagite* (Outstanding Christian Thinkers Series; London: G. Chapman; Wilton, Conn.: Morehouse-Barlow, 1989). – Y. de Andia, ed., *Denys l'Aréopagite et sa postérité en Orient et en Occident* (Paris: Études Augustiniennes, 1997).

## Works and Theology

The *Corpus dionysiacum* consists of four treatises by one and the same unknown author—*De divinis nominibus, De mystica theologia, De caelesti hierarchia, De ecclesiastica hierarchia*—and ten theological letters. Its writer refers to a further seven works that he allegedly wrote but about which we have no knowledge at all, and scholarship therefore considers them to be fictitious. As pseudepigraphic writings, they were probably intended to appear as part of an even more extensive theological construct in order to lend them even greater authority. All of the subsequent writings appearing under the name of Dionysius the Areopagite later on do not belong to the author of the *Corpus*. From the very noteworthy theology and philosophy of Pseudo-Dionysius overall, two trains of thought stand out, each of them associated with two of the treatises:

a. The absolute transcendence and unknowability of God, which compel theology and spirituality onto the path of a *theologia negativa* and a mysticism of darkness (1–2). All of the divine names that Pseudo-Dionysius addresses, in keeping with the OT, Plato, and Neoplatonism, as well as with the Alexandrian and Cappadocian church fathers, namely, goodness, light, beauty, love, being, life, wisdom, truth, power, righteousness, salvation, peace, and so forth, are unable to express anything about the altogether unknowable being of God. For this reason, all the names of God describe only his activity and not his being, which is nameless. In this context, following Proclus, Pseudo-Dionysius deals in great detail with the problem of evil, which cannot be accorded existence because God alone *is;* consequently, evil can only be understood as the absence of good. This theology of God's absolute transcendence, again in keeping with the Alexandrian and Cappadocian church fathers, rigorously leads to a mysticism of darkness rather than to enlightenment. In order to be in union with God, the human person has to penetrate more and more into the unknowability of God by understanding that in doing so, he or she has to relinquish all sensory impressions, every experience and thought. For this reason, the mystical union with God consists in the human's perfect ignorance.

b. The step-by-step (hierarchical) but unified structure of creation as a whole, in which God is the head of the heavenly hierarchy as well as of the earthly (ecclesiastical) one (3–4). The heavenly hierarchy (this currently very popular word was coined by Pseudo-Dionysius) is composed of three triads:

- seraphim, cherubim, thrones (*Cael. hier.* 7);

- rulers, powers, dominions (*Cael. hier.* 8);

- principalities, archangels, angels (*Cael. hier.* 9).

They continue in the two triads of the ecclesiastical hierarchy:

- bishops, priests, deacons (*Cael. hier.* 5);

- monks, community, levels of purification (*Cael. hier.* 6).

The purpose and goal of this hierarchical ordering of the whole cosmos is the ascent to, and union with, God, which are passed down from above through purification, enlightenment, and initiation and in the same manner enable the ascent from below.

The continued effects of the *Corpus dionysiacum* can hardly be overestimated. The list of theologians and mystics upon whom its influence can be demonstrated reads like a who's who of church history: Maximus the Confessor, Gregory the Great, John Scotus Erigena, Hugh and Richard of St. Victor, Peter Abelard, William of St. Thierry, Isaac d'Étoile, Robert Grosseteste, John Wyclif, Albertus Magnus, Thomas Aquinas, Master Eckehart, Johannes Tauler, Nicholas of Cusa, and John of the Cross.

*Editions: Opera omnia: The Armenian Version of the Works Attributed to Dionysius the Areopagite* (ed. and trans. R. W. Thomson; 2 vols.; CSCO 488–489; Louvain: Peeters, 1987) [ET]. – *Corpus dionysiacum* (ed. B. R. Suchla, G. Heil, and A. M. Ritter; 2 vols.; PTS 33; 36; Berlin and New York: de Gruyter, 1990–1991). – *De caelesti hierarchia: La hiérarchie céleste* (ed. R. Roques, G. Heil, and M. de Gandillac; 2d ed.; SC 58; Paris: Cerf, 1970) [Com].

*Translations: Dionysius the Areopagite: On the Divine Names and the Mystical Theology* (trans. C. E. Rolt; London: SPCK; New York: Macmillan, 1920; repr., Berwick, Me.: Ibis, 2004). – *The Divine Names and Mystical Theology* (trans. J. D. Jones; Mediaeval Philosophical Texts in Translation 21; Milwaukee: Marquette University Press, 1980). – *Pseudo-Dionysius: The Complete Works* (trans. C. Luibheid; CWS; New York: Paulist, 1987).

*Reference Works:* A. van der Daele, *Indices pseudo-dionysiani* (Receuil de travaux d'histoire et de philologie 3.3; Louvain: Bibliothèque de l'Université, 1941). – P. Chevallier, "Index complet de la langue grecque du Pseudo-Aréopagite," in idem, *Dionysiaca* (2 vols.; Paris: Desclée de Brouwer, 1937–1950), 2:1585–1660.

*Studies:* I. Stiglmayr, *Das Aufkommen der Pseudo-Dionysischen Schriften und ihr Eindringen in die christliche Literatur bis zum Laterankonzil, 649* (IV. Jahresbericht des öffentlichen Privatgymnasiums an der Stella Matutina zu Feldkirch; Feldkirch: Im Selbstverlage der Anstalt—Druck von L. Sausgruber, 1895), 3–96. – E. Corsini, *Il trattato De divinis nominibus dello Pseudo-Dionigi e i commenti neoplatonici al Parmenide* (PFLUT 13.4; Turin: G. Giappichelli, 1962). – D. Rutledge, *Cosmic Theology: The Ecclesiastical Hierarchy of Pseudo-Denys* (London: Routledge & Keegan Paul, 1964). – P. Scazzoso, *Ricerche sulla struttura del linguaggio dello Pseudo-Dionigi Areopagita* (PUCSC 3.14; Milan: Vita e Pensiero, 1967). – R. F. Hathaway, *Hierarchy and the Definition of Order in the Letters of Pseudo-Dionysius* (The Hague: Nijhoff, 1969). – S. Gersh, *From Iamblichus to Eriugena: An Investigation of the Prehistory and Evolution of the Pseudo-Dionysian Tradition* (SPAMP 8; Leiden: Brill, 1978). – S. Lilla, "Zur neuen kritischen Ausgabe der Schrift *Über die göttlichen Namen* von Ps. Dionysius Areopagita," *Aug* 31 (1991): 421–58. – B. R. Suchla, "Textprobleme in der Schrift Περὶ θείων ὀνομάτων des Ps. Dionysius Areopagita," *Aug* 32 (1992): 387–422. – P. Rorem, *Pseudo-Dionysius: A Commentary on the Texts and an Introduction to Their Influence* (New York; Oxford: Oxford University Press, 1993). – P. Rorem and J. C. Lamoreaux, *John of Scythopolis and the Dionysian Corpus: Annotating the Areopagite* (OECS; Oxford and New York: Clarendon, 1998).

*Mysticism:* R. Roques, *DSp* 2:1885–1911. – W. Völker, *Kontemplation und Ekstase bei Pseudo-Dionysius Areopagita* (Wiesbaden: Steiner, 1958). – J. Vanneste, *Le mystère de Dieu: Essai sur la structure rationelle de la doctrine mystique du pseudo-Denys l'Aréopagite* (Paris: Desclée de Brouwer, 1959). – A. Louth, *The Origins of the Christian Mystical Tradition: Plato to Denys* (Oxford: Clarendon; New York: Oxford University Press, 1981), 159–78. – P. Rorem, *Biblical and Liturgical Symbols within the Pseudo-Dionysian Synthesis* (STPIMS 71; Toronto: Pontifical Institute of Mediaeval Studies, 1984). – P. Rorem, "The Uplifting Spirituality of Pseudo-Dionysius," in *Christian Spirituality: Origins to the Twelfth Century* I (ed. B. McGinn and J. Meyendorff; London: Routledge & Keegan Paul; New York: Crossroad, 1986; repr., 1992), 132–51. – C. A. Bernard, "La doctrine mystique de Denys l'Aréopagite," *Greg* 68 (1987): 523–66. – I. E. M. Andreggen, "La *Teología mística* de Dionisio Areopagita," *Teol* 29 (1992): 169–79. – B. McGinn, *The Foundations of Mysticism: Origins to the Fifth Century* (London: SCM, 1994), 157–82. – D. Turner, *The Darkness of God: Negativity in Christian Mysticism* (Cambridge and New York: Cambridge University Press, 1995), 19–49.

*Philosophy:* H. Koch, *Pseudo-Dionysius Areopagita in seinen Beziehungen zum Neuplatonismus und Mysterienwesen* (FChLDG 1.2–3; Mainz: Kirchheim, 1900). – G. della Volpe, *La dottrina del Areopagita e i suoi presupposti neoplatonici* (Rome: Ferri, 1941). – M. Schiavone, *Neoplatonismo e cristianesimo nello Pseudo Dionigi* (Milan: Marzorati, 1963). – E. von Ivánka, *Plato Christianus: Übernahme und Umgestaltung des Platonismus durch die Väter* (Einsiedeln, Switz.: Johannes, 1964), 223–89. – P. Spearritt, *A Philosophical Enquiry into Dionysian Mysticism* (Bösingen, Switz.: Rotex, 1968; with bibliographic additions, 1975). – B. Brons, *Gott und die Seienden: Untersuchungen zum Verhältnis von neuplatonischer Metaphysik und christlicher Tradition bei Dionysius Areopagita* (FKDG 28; Göttingen: Vandenhoeck & Ruprecht, 1976). – G. Shaw, "Neoplatonic Theurgy and Dionysius the Areopagite," *JECS* 7 (1999): 573–99.

*Theology:* P. Chevallier, *Jésus-Christ dans les œuvres du Pseudo-Aréopagite* (Paris: Plon, 1951). – A. Brontesi, *L'incontro misterioso con Dio: Saggio sulla teologia affermativa e negativa nello Pseudo-Dionigi* (Brescia; Morcelliana, 1970). – H. Goltz, ΊΕΡΑ ΜΕΣΙΤΕΙΑ: *Zur Theorie der hierarchischen Sozietät im Corpus areopagiticum* (Erlangen: Lehrstuhl für Geschichte und Theologie des christlichen Ostens an der Universität Erlangen, 1974). – V. Muñiz Rodríguez, *Significado de los nombres de Dios en el Corpus dionysiacum* (Salamanca: Universidad Pontificia, 1975). – C.-A. Bernard, "Les formes de la théologie chez Denys l'Aréopagite," *Greg* 59 (1978) 39–69. – E. Stein, *Wege der Gotteserkenntnis: Dionysius der Areopagite und seine symbolische Theologie* (Munich: Kaffke, 1979). – E. Bellini, "Teologia e teurgia in Dionigi Areopagita," *VetChr* 17 (1980): 199–216. – M. Ninci, *L'universo e il non-essere*, vol. 1, *Transcendenza di Dio e molteplicità del reale nel monismo dionisiano* (Temi e testi 30; Rome: Storia e Letteratura, 1980). – R. Roques, *L'univers dionysien: Structure hiérarchique du monde selon le Pseudo-Denys* (Paris: Aubier, 1954; repr., Paris: Cerf, 1983). – Y. de Andia, *Henosis: L'union à Dieu chez Denys l'Aréopagite* (PhAnt 71; Leiden and New York: Brill, 1996). – J. N. Jones, "Sculpting God: The Logic of Dionysian Negative Theology," *HTR* 89 (1996): 355–371.

# III. MAXIMUS THE CONFESSOR

Reliable information about the biography of Maximus is only available beginning in 626, in connection with the controversy about Monothelitism and Monergism, in which he took part with a substantial theological intervention and also faced death as a "confessor." All further data on his earlier life come from a well-known tenth-century Greek *vita*, on which a Georgian *vita* also depends, and from a seventh- or eighth-century Syriac *vita*, edited by Sebastian Brock in 1973. Both sources, however, appear to have been written from conflicting viewpoints and with tendentious intent: the Greek, in order to praise Maximus as the orthodox confessor of Dyophysitism; and the Syriac, to disparage him as the opponent of Monophysitism. Nevertheless, neither *vita* is without historical value, even if it is difficult to decide, especially for the years before 626, which of the two accounts is to be considered accurate and therefore both have to be allowed to stand side by side.[2] Where they lack historical documentation, the Greek sources seem to supplement it along the lines of familiar hagiography. There are two further Greek accounts of his martyrdom, one of them from the pen of Anastasius the *apocrisiarius*, his student and companion in suffering.

According to the Greek sources, Maximus was born into a noble family in Constantinople ca. 580; according to the Syriac sources, he was born in Palestine as Moschion, son of a Samaritan trader and a Persian female slave. He is said to have chosen a civil-service career at the imperial court and attained the influential position of imperial secretary but relinquished it in 614 in order to become the abbot of the monastery of Chrysopolis outside Constantinople. His later work *Ambigua* resulted from his dialogues with John, bishop of Cyzicus on the southern coast of the Sea of Marmara (according to the Greek version; *Ambigua* actually originated in Africa after 626). By contrast, the Syriac version has him enter the monastery of St. Chariton in Jerusalem at the age of ten, where the name Maximus was given to him and where he studied the writings of Origen. Because of the Arab invasion, in 614 he left Jerusalem, went to Cyzicus, and from there established close relations with the imperial household. There is agreement, therefore, on the following credible points, based on the subsequent life of Maximus: his monastic lifestyle, his relations with the imperial court, and his stay in Cyzicus.

In 626 Maximus evaded the encroaching Persians and Arabs, possibly via Cyprus and Crete, and went to North Africa, where, in connection with Monophysitism, he continued to deal with the problem of Monothelitism or Monergism, having written minor dogmatic treatises on this previously. This controversy has to be understood in the broader context of the search for a correct understanding and an appropriate conceptuality of the unity of the two natures of Christ, extending from Nestorius and the Council of Ephesus (431), via the Council of Chalcedon (451) and the Second Council of Constantinople (553), to the Third Council of Constantinople (*Trullanum*, 680/81). Antiochene Christology, stressing primarily the completeness and independence of the two natures of Christ, and Alexandrian Christology, by contrast stressing primarily the unity of the two natures, constituted the two opposing parties. Between these

---

[2] A. Ceresa-Gastaldo (*EECh* 1:547) decides in favor of the Syriac *vita*. The German translation of Murphy/Sherwood (*GÖK* 3:188f.) does not incorporate it, though Breukelaar cites it in the bibliography without analyzing it.

a middle course had to be found for an agreeable solution by a consideration of the appropriate elements of the two viewpoints. As is characteristic and necessary for the process of knowledge concerning controversial developments such as this, the parties move forward by approaching the opposing positions in turn, thereby assimilating both, and finally arriving at an acceptable middle course. Together with the θεοτόκος title, Alexandrian theology became dominant in Ephesus. In the formula of one person in two natures, Chalcedon had so embraced the Antiochene concern that the Egyptian and other Monophysite churches were unable to accept it and separated from the Catholic Church. By condemning the Three Chapters, the Second Council of Constantinople moved closer to the Alexandrian position again. Under the external pressure of the Persian and Arab invasion, against which the Roman Empire also desperately needed religious unity for its internal strength, the efforts for a theological agreement and reunification with the Monophysites at the time of Maximus were continued by the endeavor to do justice to the Alexandrian theology by speaking of two natures (in keeping with the Chalcedonian view, which was not to be rescinded) but of only one action (ἐνέργεια) and one will (θέλησις) in Christ.

In 626, the year Maximus went to Africa, Sergius, patriarch of Constantinople (610–638), for the first time presented his theology of the action of Christ in a letter to Cyrus, bishop of Phasis, leading in 633 to a pact of reunion with the Coptic church. The formula of reunion encountered the vigorous objection of the Palestinian monk Sophronius, who was on a return journey from Africa, where he met Maximus, to Constantinople. In order to preempt further arguments, Patriarch Sergius in 634 informed Cyrus, now patriarch of Alexandria, of a decision (ψῆφος), according to which the actions of Christ were not to be articulated numerically at all. But history teaches us that the prescribed disregarding of an unresolved problem such as this cannot silence it forever. In the same year, Sophronius ascended to the episcopal see of Jerusalem. Traditionally a new bishop sent so-called synodal letters to the other patriarchs for the purpose of assuming or continuing ecclesiastical communion and presenting his own confession of faith. In his letter to Sergius, patriarch of Constantinople, Sophronius used this opportunity expressly to reject the theology of only one ἐνέργεια in Christ. In 638 Sergius took up his ψῆφος in a detailed presentation (ἔκθεσις), which Emperor Heraclius signed and the endemic synod approved.

When Sergius died the same year, he was followed by Pyrrhus, who, after his politically motivated removal (641), engaged and occupied Maximus with the controversy. From Africa the latter maintained close contact with the leading ecclesiastical and political offices of the empire and was among the most sought after theologians of his time. In July 645 a spectacular public disputation took place in Carthage between Maximus and Pyrrhus, the records of which are preserved; the latter was defeated and agreed to renounce his errors in the presence of the pope. Maximus accompanied him to Rome and remained there as the most influential theologian of Pope Martin (649–653), under whom the disputes were to reach their critical apex. In 648 Emperor Constans II (641–668), in continuity with Sergius's ψῆφος of 634, prohibited any discussion on the actions and the will of Christ in a doctrinal decree (τύπος περὶ πίστεως). Pope Martin, however, disregarded the imperial edict and summoned a synod to meet in the Lateran on October 5, 649; under the overall theological leadership of Maximus, it condemned the doctrines of Monothelitism and Monergism on October 31. Since all of the emperor's efforts at motivating the pope to support his religious policy in the following years failed, he had Martin and Maximus arrested in Rome on June 17, 653, brought them to Constantinople, and condemned them for high treason. The case against Maximus ended in 655 with his exile to Bizye in Thrace. But since Maximus was not to be persuaded even in exile, despite the emperor's ongoing efforts, he was taken to court again in Constantinople in the spring of 662 in order finally to break his resistance, together with Anastasius, his student, and the former papal secretary of Constantinople of the same name. They were condemned to the "Persian punishment" of mutilating the tongue and cutting off the right hand because they resisted the imperial edict. Maximus was then exiled to the Colchian part of Lazika on the Black Sea, where he succumbed to his suffering in the castle of Schemaris on August 13, 662. Eighteen years later the Third Council of Constantinople (680/681) rehabilitated him and ratified his theology, and so the church venerates him as a holy confessor.

*Bibliographies:* P. Van Deun, "Maxime le Confesseur: État de la question et bibliographie exhaustive," *SacEr* 38 (1998–1999): 485–565.

*Encyclopedia Articles:* I.-H. Dalmais, *DSp* 10:836–47. – P. Hauptmann, "Maximus Confessor," *GK* 2:275–88. – D. de Vocht, *TRE* 22:298–304. – A. Ceresa-Gastaldo, *EECh* 1:547–48. – G. C. Berthold, *EEC* 2:742–43.

*Biographies:* R. Devreesse, "La vie de saint Maxime le Confesseur et ses recensions," *AnBoll* 46 (1928): 5–49. – W. Lackner, "Zu Quellen und Datierung der Maximosvita (*BHG*[3] 1234)," *AnBoll* 85 (1967): 285–316. – C. v. Schönborn, *Sophrone de Jérusalem: Vie monastique et confession dogmatique* (ThH 20; Paris: Beauchesne, 1972). – C. N. Tsirpanlis, "Acta S. Maximi," *Theol(A)* 43 (1972): 106–24. – S. Brock, "An Early Syriac Life of Maximus the Confessor," *AnBoll* 91 (1973): 299–346. – J. M. Garrigues, "Le martyre de saint Maxime le Confesseur," *RThom* 76 (1976): 410–52.

## Works and Theology

More than ninety works by Maximus have been preserved, including exegetical, ascetic, dogmatic, and mystagogical writings and forty-five letters. His Christology is, naturally, stamped with the dispute of Monothelitism and Monergism. His theological rationale for the two actions of Christ is rooted deeply in his overall understanding of anthropology, soteriology, and mysticism. For him, will (θέλησις), power (δύναμις), and action (ἐνέργεια) are parts of nature (φύσις, οὐσία), and so, for the sake of the completeness of his two natures and of redemption, Christ had to possess them twice. In Christ, however, they uniquely combine in such a way that Christ's self-determining (αὐτεξούσιος) human will, in contrast to Adam and his descendants, freely (ἑκούσιος) accepted both the divine will and the human πάθη, whereas since Adam's sin the human being is subject to a changeable nature and to πάθη. The human being, too, can and must ascend again to the knowledge (γνῶσις) of God by combating and laying aside the πάθη by means of virtue—a path that has been opened up precisely through Christ's voluntary suffering. With this tradition Maximus is positioned in the tradition of the Alexandrian theologians, especially Origen, and of the great Cappadocians, but also of Evagrius Ponticus and Pseudo-Dionysius the Areopagite, for whose work he wrote the scholia, thus contributing to its extraordinary continued influence.

*Bibliographies:* M. L. Gatti, *Massimo il Confessore: Saggio di bibliografia generale ragionata e contributi per una ricostruzione scientifica del suo pensiero metafisico e religioso* (Milan: Vita e Pensiero, 1987).

*Editions: Opera omnia:* PG 90–91. – *Ambigua: Maximi Confessoris Ambigua ad Johannem: Iuxta Johannis Scotti Eriugenae latinam interpretationem* (ed. E. Jeauneau; CCSG 18; Turnhout, Belg.: Brepols; Louvain: Louvain University Press, 1988). – *Capita de caritate: Capitoli sulla carita* (ed. A. Ceresa-Gastaldo; VSen NS 3; Rome: Studium, 1963). – *Disputatio cum Pyrrho: Dispute de Maxime le Confesseur avec Pyrrhus* (ed. M. Doucet; 2 vols.; Montreal: n.p., 1972). – *Epistulae:* R. Devreesse, "La fin inédite d'une lettre de saint Maxime: Un baptême forcé de Juifs et de Samaritains à Carthage en 632," *RevScRel* 17 (1937): 25–35. – R. Devreesse, "La lettre d'Anastase l'apocrisiaire sur la mort de s. Maxime le Confesseur et de ses compagnons d'exil: Text grec inédit," *AnBoll* 73 (1955): 5–16. – P. Canart, "La deuxième lettre à Thomas de s. Maxime le Confesseur," *Byzantion* 34 (1964): 415–45. – *Expositio in Psalmum LIX, Expositio orationis dominicae: Maximi Confessoris opuscula exegetica duo* (ed. P. van Deun; CCSG 23; Turnhout, Belg.: Brepols; Louvain: Louvain University Press, 1991). – *Quaestiones ad Thalassium: Maximi Confessoris Quaestiones ad Thalassium: Una cum latina interpretatione Joannis Scotti Eriugenae iuxta posita* (ed. C. Laga and C. Steel; 2 vols.; CCSG 7, 22; Turnhout, Belg.: Brepols; Louvain: Louvain University Press, 1980–1990). – *Quaestiones et dubia: Maximi Confessoris Quaestiones et dubia* (ed. J. H. Declerck; CCSG 10; Turnhout, Belg.: Brepols; Louvain: Louvain University Press, 1982). – *Scholia Dionysii:* PG 4:13–576. – *Vita virginis: Vie de la vierge* (ed. M.-J. van Esbroeck; 2 vols.; CSCO 478–79; Louvain: Peeters, 1986).

*Translations: The Philokalia: The Complete Text Compiled by St. Nikodimos of the Holy Mountain and St. Makarios of Corinth* (ed. and trans. G. E. H. Palmer, P. Sherrard, and K. Ware; London and Boston: Faber & Faber, 1979–), 2:48–305 [*Four Hundred Texts on Love, Two Hundred Texts on Theology and the Incarnate Dispensation of the Son of God Written for Thalassios, Various Texts on Theology, the Divine Economy, and Virtue and Vice, On the Lord's Prayer*]. – *Maximus the Confessor: Selected Writings* (trans. G. C. Berthold; CWS; London: SPCK, 1985) [*Four Hundred Chapters on Love, Commentary on the Our Father, Chapters on Knowledge, The Church's Mystagogy*]. – A. Louth, *Maximus the Confessor* (Early Church Fathers; London and New York: Routledge, 1996) [*Difficulty 1, 5, 10, 41, 71; Opuscule 3, 7; Letter 2*].

*Collections of Essays:* F. Heinzer and C. von Schönborn, eds., *Maximus Confessor: Actes du symposium sur Maxime le Confesseur, Fribourg, 2–5 septembre, 1980* (Par. 27; Fribourg, Switz.: Editions Universitaires, 1982).

*Surveys and Introductions:* I.-H. Dalmais, "Saint Maxime le Confesseur et la crise de l'origénisme monastique," in *Théologie de la vie monastique* (Paris: Aubier, 1961), 411–21. – W. B. Green, "Maximus Confessor: An Introduction," in *Spirit and Light: Essays in Historical Theology* (ed. M. L'Engle and W. B. Green; New York: Seabury, 1976), 75–96. – B. R. Suchla, *Die sogenannten Maximus-Scholien des Corpus dionysiacum areopagiticum* (NAWG 1980.3; Göttingen: Vandenhoeck & Ruprecht, 1980). – F.-X. Murphy and P. Sherwood, *Constantinople II et III* (HCO 3; Paris: Orante, 1973); German: *Konstantinopel II und III* (trans. N. Monzel and E. Labonté; Mainz: Matthias Grünewald, 1990). – A. Nichols, *Byzantine Gospel: Maximus the Confessor in Modern Scholarship* (Edinburgh: T&T Clark, 1993). – A. Louth, *Maximus the Confessor* (Early Church Fathers; London and New York: Routledge, 1996). – J.-C. Larchet, *Maxime le Confesseur: Médiateur entre l'Orient et l'Occident* (Paris: Cerf, 1998).

*Studies:* H. U. von Balthasar, *Die "Gnostischen Centurien" des Maximus Confessor* (FThSt 61; Fribourg, Switz.: Herder, 1941). – P. Sherwood, *An Annotated Date-List of the Works of Maximus the Confessor* (SA 30; Rome: "Orbis Catholicus," Herder, 1952). – I.-H. Dalmais, "Un traité de théologie contemplative: Le Commentaire du Pater de S. Maxime le Confesseur," *RAM* 29 (1953): 123–59. – P. Sherwood, *The Earlier Ambigua of Saint Maximus the Confessor and His Refutation of Origenism* (SA 36; Rome: "Orbis Catholicus," Herder, 1955). – C. De Vocht, "Un nouvel opuscule de Maxime le Confesseur, source des chapitres non encore identifiés des cinq centuries théologiques (CPG 7715)," *Byzantion* 57 (1987): 415–20. – P. M. Blowers, *Exegesis and Spiritual Pedagogy in Maximus Confessor: An Investigation of the Quaestiones ad Thalassium* (CJAn 7; Notre Dame, Ind.: University of Notre Dame Press, 1991).

*Anthropology:* J. Loosen, *Logos und Pneuma im begnadeten Menschen bei Maximus Confessor* (Münster: Aschendorff, 1941). – I. Hausherr, *Philautie: De la tendresse pour soi à la charité selon saint Maxime le Confesseur* (OrChrAn 137; Rome: Pontificium Institutum Orientalium Studiorum, 1952). – J.-M. Garrigues, *Maxime le Confesseur: La charité, avenir divin de l'homme* (ThH 38; Paris: Beauchesne, 1976). – F. Heinzer, "Anmerkungen zum Willensbegriff Maximus' Confessors," *FZThPh* 28 (1981): 372–92. – L. Thunberg, *Man and the Cosmos: The Vision of St Maximus the Confessor* (Crestwood, N.Y.: St. Vladimir's Seminary Press, 1985). – J. P. Farrell, *Free Choice in St. Maximus the Confessor* (South Canan, Pa.: St. Tikhon's Seminary Press, 1989). – L. Thunberg, *Microcosm and Mediator: The Theological Anthropology of Maximus the Confessor* (2d ed.; Chicago: Open Court, 1995). – P. M. Blowers, "Gentiles of the Soul: Maximus the Confessor on the Substructure and Transformation of the Human Passions," *JECS* 4 (1996): 57–85.

*Christology, Soteriology, and Trinitarian Theology:* J.-M. Garrigues, "L'énergie divine et la grâce chez Maxime le Confesseur," *Istina* 19 (1974): 272–98. – J.-M. Garrigues, "La Personne composée du Christ d'après saint Maxime le Confesseur," *RThom* 74 (1974): 181–204. – F.-M. Léthel, *Théologie de l'agonie du Christ: La liberté humaine du Fils de Dieu et son importance sotériologique mises en lumière par saint Maxime le Confesseur* (ThH 52; Paris: Beauchesne, 1979). – F. Heinzer, *Gottes Sohn als Mensch: Die Struktur des Menschseins Christi bei Maximus Confessor* (Par. 26; Fribourg, Switz.: Universitätsverlag, 1980). – P. Piret, *Le Christ et la Trinité selon Maxime le Confesseur* (ThH 69; Paris: Beauchesne, 1983). – G. Bausenhart, *"In allem uns gleich ausser der Sünde": Studien zum Beitrag Maximos' des Bekenners zur altkirchlichen Christologie, mit einer kommentierten Übersetzung der "Disputatio cum Pyrrho"* (TSTP 5; Mainz: Matthias Grünewald, 1992). – V. Karayiannis, *Maxime le Confesseur: Essence et énergies de Dieu* (ThH 93; Paris: Beauchesne, 1993).

*Spirituality and Mysticism:* W. Völker, *Maximus Confessor als Meister des geistlichen Lebens* (Wiesbaden: Steiner, 1965). – R. E. Asher, "The Mystical Theology of St. Maximus the Confessor," *Australian Biblical Review* 29 (1978): 87–95. – P. M. Blowers, "Maximus the Confessor, Gregory of Nyssa, and the Concept of 'Perpetual Progress,'" *VC* 46 (1992): 151–71. – J.-C. Larchet, *La divinisation de l'homme selon saint Maxime le Confesseur* (Paris: Cerf, 1996). – K. Savvidis, *Die Lehre von der Vergöttlichung des Menschen bei Maximos dem Bekenner und ihre Rezeption durch Gregor Palamas* (St. Ottilien: EOS, 1997).

*Theology:* H. U. von Balthasar, *Kosmische Liturgie: Das Weltbild des Maximus des Bekenners* (2d ed.; Einsiedeln, Switz.: Johannes, 1961; repr., 1988); ET, *Cosmic Liturgy* (trans. B. Daley; San Francisco: Ignatius, 2003). – S. L. Epifanovsky, *Saint Maximus the Confessor and Byzantine Theology* (Farnborough: n.p., 1971). – A. Riou, *Le monde et l'Église selon Maxime le Confesseur* (ThH 22; Paris: Beauchesne, 1973). – V. Croce, *Tradizione e ricerca: Il metodo teologico di San Massimo il Confessore* (SPMed 2; Milan: Vita e Pensiero, 1974). – A. Louth, *Wisdom of the Byzantine Church: Evagrios of Pontos and Maximos the Confessor* (Paine Lectures in Religion 1997; Columbia: Department of Religious Studies, University of Missouri, 1997).

# IV. JOHN OF DAMASCUS

Traditionally the patrology of the Greek church fathers concludes with John, who was born into the Arab-Christian Mansur family in Damascus ca. 650 and died ca. 750 in the Mar Saba monastery near Jerusalem. The reasons for the inclusive dates of this period have been explained in the introduction to part 4. In 635 the Arabs had conquered Damascus, but since the caliphs initially pursued a tolerant religious policy toward Christianity, John, who grew up with Yazid, the later caliph (680–683), and had received a thorough classical education with a Greek teacher, held important court appointments, as did his father and grandfather before him. When Caliph 'Abd al-Malik (685–705) began to discriminate against Christians and removed them from their offices, John withdrew to the monastery of Mar Saba in 700, where he spent the rest of his life. Bishop John of Jerusalem (706–717) ordained him to the priesthood. During his time in the monastery, John devoted himself to study and to producing numerous important theological writings, the distribution and influence of which may be appraised from the fact that they were translated into a number of other languages soon after his death. The most important and most extensive writing is the *Source of Knowledge,* composed of three books on philosophy (*Capitula philosophica or Dialectica*), heresies (*De haeresibus*), and a summation of the true faith (*Expositio fidei or De fide orthodoxa*). John attained fame as a hymn writer, and among his sermons the homilies on Mary stand out, as do the three discourses on images, which proved to be of decisive future influence. The authenticity of the *Sacra parallela* (or *Hiera*), a biblical-patristic florilegium of texts on morality and asceticism, is subject to debate, and the widely known romance *Barlaam and Josaphat,* which was extremely popular in the Middle Ages, in all probability did not originate with him.

Emperor Leo III (717–741) began the iconoclastic dispute in 726/727, which, with a few breaks, was to last until 843, by delivering speeches against images and having the icons of Christ removed from the Chalke Gate of the palace in Constantinople. Whereas Patriarch Germanus (730) had to pay dearly for his resistance by being deposed, John was able to defend the veneration of images unhindered outside the empire by means of his three famous discourses, which laid the theological foundation for the future. Although he was condemned by the synod of Hieria (754), which was opposed to images, the seventh ecumenical council in Nicea (787) not only rehabilitated him but based itself entirely on his theology of images. John died in his monastery ca. 750. The approximate dates of his life are derived from the following: the tradition according to which he was more than one hundred years old; the synod of Hieria (754), which condemned him posthumously; and his playmate Caliph Yazid (born ca. 642–647). By the decree of August 19, 1890, Pope Leo XIII included him among the doctors of the church.

In keeping with his time, John was primarily a compiler who adhered to the traditions of the preceding theologians. At the beginning of his largest work, *Source of Knowledge*, he goes so far as to say that he did not wish to add "anything of his own" (*Dialectica* pref. 60). Nevertheless all researchers agree that he in no way merely mechanically compiled and repeated. The wealth alone of assimilated material and its expert selection and systematization demonstrate his creativity, and in many instances, especially in the discourses on images, he develops a new, original theology based on tradition.

*Bibliography:* J. M. Hoeck, "Stand und Aufgaben der Damaskenos-Forschung," *OCP* 17 (1951): 5–60. – A. Kallis, "Handapparat zum Johannes-Damaskenos-Studium," *OS* 16 (1967): 200–213.

*Editions: Opera omnia: Die Schriften des Johannes von Damaskos* (ed. B. Kotter; PTS; Berlin: de Gruyter, 1969). – Writings on Islam: *Ecrits sur l'Islam* (ed. R. Le Coz; SC 383; Paris: Cerf, 1992) [Com]. – *Schriften zum Islam* (ed. R. Glei and A. T. Khoury; Würzburg: Echter; Altenberge: Oros, 1995) [Com]. – Homilies on the Nativity and the Dormition: *Homélies sur la nativité et la dormition* (ed. P. Voulet; SC 80; Paris: Cerf, 1961) [Com].

*Translations:* S. D. F. Salmond, trans., "Exposition of the Orthodox Faith," in *NPNF²* (Peabody, Mass.: Hendrickson, 1995; repr. of 1899 ed.), 9:1–101. – *Barlaam and Ioasaph* (trans. G. R. Woodward and H. Mattingly; LCL 34; New York: Macmillan; London: Heinemann, 1914; repr., Cambridge, Mass.: Harvard University Press; London: Heinemann, 1967; 1983). – *Writings* (trans. F. H. Chase; FC 37; New York: Fathers of the Church, 1958) [*The Fount of Knowledge, On Heresies, The Orthodox Faith*].

*Encyclopedia Articles:* M. Richard, "Florilèges damascéniens," *DSp* 5:476–86. – B. Studer, *DSp* 8:452–66. – A. Kallis, *GK* 2:289–300. – B. Kotter, *TRE* 17:127–32. – K.-H. Uthemann, *BBKL* 3:331–36. – B. Studer, *EECh* 1:442–43. – R. Aubert, "Jean Damascène," *DHGE* 26:1458–59 . – G. C. Berthold, *EEC* 1:625–26.

*Introductions:* J. Nasrallah, *Saint Jean de Damas: Son époque, sa vie, son œuvre* (Harissa, Lebanon: Saint Paul, 1950).

*Studies:* J. Szövérffy, *A Guide to Byzantine Hymnography* (2 vols.; Brookline, Mass.; Leiden: Classical Folia Editions, 1978–1979). – B. Kotter, *Die Überlieferung der Pege Gnoseos des hl. Johannes von Damaskos* (SPB 5; Ettal: Buch-Kunstverlag, 1959). – G. Richter, *Die Dialektik des Johannes von Damaskus: Eine Untersuchung des Textes nach seinen Quellen und seiner Bedeutung* (SPB 10; Ettal: Buch-Kunstverlag Ettal, 1964).

*Theology and Philosophy:* J. Bilz, *Die Trinitätslehre des hl. Johannes von Damaskus* (FChLDG 9.3; Paderborn: F. Schöningh, 1909). – C. Chevalier, *La mariologie de saint Jean Damascène: Prix du concours international de l'Institut catholique de Paris (1934)* (OrChrAn 109; Rome: Pontificium Institutum Orientalium Studiorum, 1936). – B. Studer, *Die theologische Arbeitsweise des Johannes von Damaskus* (SPB 2; Ettal: Buch-Kunstverlag, 1956). – K. Rozemond, *La christologie de saint Jean Damascène*

(SPB 8; Ettal: Buch-Kunstverlag Ettal, 1959). – A. Kallis, *Der menschliche Wille in seinem Grund und Ausdruck nach der Lehre des Johannes Damaskenos* (Naussa, Greece: n.p., 1965). – A. Siclari, *Giovanni di Damasco: La funzione della "Dialectica"* (Perugia: Benucci, 1978). – F. R. Gahbauer, "Die Anthropologie des Johannes von Damaskos," *TP* 69 (1994): 1–21.

*Response to Islam:* D. J. Sahas, *John of Damascus on Islam: The "Heresy of the Ishmaelites"* (Leiden: Brill, 1972). – A.-T. Khoury, "Apologétique byzantine contre l'islam (VIIIe-XIIIe siècle)," *POC* 29 (1979): 242–300; 30 (1980): 132–74; 32 (1982): 14–49. – P. Khoury, *Jean Damascène et l'islam* (Würzburg: Echter, 1994).

## Discourses concerning Images

Like the fourth- and fifth-century controversies over Trinitarian theology and Christology, the iconoclastic dispute was partly based on unclear terminology—in this case, the terms εἰκών and προσκύνησις. The term εἰκών could include the conception that an image included the reality portrayed. Against this, as in the OT and in Islam, there is to be no image of the invisible and incomprehensible God, and making and revering an image of God are idolatry. With reference to God, however, προσκύνησις meant what is expressed by "worship" in English, which befits God alone, and not the human person or even an object. The contribution of John's three famous discourses concerning images is to be seen in his understanding of this terminological problem and in his forward-looking clarification of the concepts by means of a sharp differentiation, which was adopted by the Second Council of Nicea (787).

An image is always the likeness (ἀντιτύπος) of a prototype (πρωτοτύπος), similar to the latter but necessarily different—otherwise they would be identical. Yet the concept and meaning of the image cannot be deduced merely from human representations; they are rooted in the Trinity and the economy of salvation, so that there are three types of images: personal, those preparing for reality, and those reproducing reality. (1a) The Son of God—here John takes up Alexandrian theology—is the original image of the Father; (1b) the human person, "created in the image and likeness of God" (Gen 1:26f.), is the image of the image of God. (2) The second meaning of an image—here John uses the familiar terminology of typological exegesis of the Bible—refers to the types (τύποι) of the OT that modeled the future salvation in Christ. The common understanding of this is not only that these typoi are "shadows of things to come" but that God's salvific grace is already visualized in them. (3) Finally, on the third and lowest level, there are images of representation, hence references and remembrances of the reality that is represented and that is at once similar and different. Thus, by definition, the pictorial presentation of God does not encompass God. Furthermore, in Christianity it obtains its justification from the incarnation of God, against the OT prohibition of images. God as such is able to be grasped and represented in a picture.

John initially differentiates the concept of προσκύνησις as simple "admiration," befitting creatures, and as "worship" (προσκύνησις κατὰ λατρείαν), befitting God alone. In no way does the προσκύνησις of images of God and his saints refer to the object, however, but always to the person represented, who, according to ancient tradition, is present, as it were, in the representation of the image. Only because of the presence of the Spirit of God do images possess grace and effect. The precise date for the discourses concerning images continues to be debated for the following reasons: The removal of Germanus, the patriarch of Constantinople (730), preceded the second discourse, and the second and third discourses quote from the first one; furthermore there are no clear indications concerning their date. Whereas earlier on they were moved closer to the beginning of the iconoclastic dispute (726–730), the editor of John's *Opera omnia*, Bonifatius Kotter (1975), allocates the first one to January 730, the second "shortly after the first, perhaps still in 730 or soon thereafter," and the third to an undetermined later time. More recently, however, a late dating for the third discourse, if not all three, has gained acceptance, namely, the years following 741.[3] In any case, they represent a typical example of John's theological method of achieving new solutions to the relevant questions of his time by adopting and continuing the theology of the Fathers.

*Editions: Die Schriften des Johannes von Damaskos* (ed. B. Kotter; PTS 17; Berlin: de Gruyter, 1975).

*Translations: On the Divine Images: Three Apologies against Those Who Attack the Holy Images* (trans. D. Anderson; Crestwood, N.Y.: St. Vladimir's Seminary Press, 1980).

*Theology of Icons:* H. Menges, *Die Bilderlehre des hl. Johannes von Damaskus* (Kallmünz: M. Lassleben, 1937). – G. Ladner, "The Concept of Image in the Greek Fathers and the Byzantine Iconoclastic Controversy," *DOP* 7 (1953): 1–34. – J. Pelikan, *The Spirit of Eastern Christendom (600–1700)* (vol. 2 of *The Christian Tradition: A History of the Development of Doctrine*; Chicago: University of Chicago Press, 1974), 91–145. – J. Meyendorff, *Christ in Eastern Christian Thought* (Washington, D.C.: Corpus; repr., Crestwood, N.Y.: St. Vladimir's Seminary Press, 1975), 173–92. – T. Nikolaou, "Die Ikonenverehrung als Beispiel ostkirchlicher Theologie und Frömmigkeit nach Johannes von Damaskos," *OS* 25 (1976): 138–65. – V. Fazzo, "Rifiuto delle icone e difesa cristologica nei discorsi di Giovanni Damasceno," *VetChr* 20 (1983): 25–45. T. F. X. Noble, "John Damascene and the History of the Iconoclastic Controversy," in *Religion, Culture, and Society in the Early Middle Ages: Studies in Honor of Richard E. Sullivan* (ed. T. F. X. Noble and J. J. Contreni; Kalamazoo: Medieval Institute Publications, Western Michigan University, 1987), 95–116. – J. Pelikan, *Imago Dei: The Byzantine Apologia for Icons* (Washington, D.C.: National Gallery of Art; Princeton, N.J.: Princeton University Press, 1990). – M. Barasch, *Icon: Studies in the History of an Idea* (New York: New York University Press, 1992), 183–253. – J. R. Payton Jr., "John of Damascus on Human Cognition: An Element of His Apologetic for Icons," *ChH* 65 (1996): 173–83.

*History of the Iconoclastic Controversy:* S. Gero, *Byzantine Iconoclasm during the Reign of Leo III: With Particular Attention to the Oriental Sources* (CSCO 346; Louvain: SCO, 1973). – P. Brown, "A Dark Age Crisis: Aspects of the Iconoclastic Controversy," *English Historical Review* 88 (1973): 1–34; repr. in idem, *Society and the Holy in Late Antiquity* (Berkeley: University of California Press, 1982), 251–301. – S. Gero, *Byzantine Iconoclasm during the Reign of Constantine V: With Particular Attention to the Oriental Sources* (CSCO 384; Louvain: Corpussco, 1977). – G. Dumeige, *Nicée II* (HCO 4;

---

[3] Stein 1980; Speck 1981.

Paris: Orante, 1977); German trans., *Nizäa II* (trans. E. Labonté; Mainz: Matthias Grünewald, 1985). – L. D. Davis, *The First Seven Ecumenical Councils (325–787): Their History and Theology* (Wilmington, Del.: Glazier, 1983; repr., Collegeville, Minn.: Liturgical, 1990), 290–322. – J. M. Hussey, *The Orthodox Church in the Byzantine Empire* (Oxford History of the Christian Church; Oxford: Clarendon; New York: Oxford University Press, 1986), 30–68. – J. Herrin, *The Formation of Christendom* (Princeton, N.J.: Princeton University Press, 1987; repr., 1989), 307–44. – P. Schreiber, "Der byzantinische Bilderstreit: Kritische Analyse der zeitgenössischen Meinungen und das Urteil der Nachwelt bis heute," in *Bisanzio, Roma, e l'Italia nell'alto medioevo: 3–9 aprile 1986* (Spoleto: Centro Italiano di Studi sull'Alto Medioevo, 1988), 319–407. – V. Fazzo, "I Padri e la difesa delle icone," in *Complementi interdisciplinari di patrologia* (ed. A. Quacquarelli; Rome: Città Nuova, 1989), 413–55. – P. A. Yannopoulos, in *Storia dei concili ecumenici* (ed. G. Alberigo; Brescia: Queriniana, 1990), 145–51. – J. A. McGuckin, "The Theology of Images and the Legitimation of Power in Eighth Century Byzantium," *SVTQ* 37 (1993): 39–58. – A. Giakalis, *Images of the Divine: The Theology of Icons at the Seventh Ecumenical Council* (SHCT 54; Leiden and New York: Brill, 1994).

Part Five

# Literature of the Christian East

# CHAPTER THIRTEEN

# Independent Bodies of Literature

THE MAIN AREA OF DISTRIBUTION of ancient Christianity coincided with the territory of the Roman Empire and its imperial church. For this reason, the writings of the church fathers in the two primary languages, Greek and Latin, naturally make up the lion's share of all the patristic literature. In addition to this, however, there also were autochthonous languages within the empire. The expansion of Christianity did not stop at the borders of the empire, and so in the eastern regions of the empire, both within and outside its boundaries, there also developed a number of independent, albeit comparatively limited, bodies of writings in Syriac, Coptic, Ethiopic, Armenian, and Georgian. To a large extent, the works in these languages functioned as translation literature; all of them, however, also produced original and in part very significant writings. To what extent these churches and bodies of literature engaged in a lively exchange with the Latin and Greek churches of the empire depended largely on the time of their origin as well as their political and geographic situation. Whereas the Syriac and Coptic literature contributed greatly to the overall theological development, the others were rather marginal—the Ethiopic literature because of its geographical remoteness, the Armenian because it only emerged in the fifth century, and the Georgian on account of the continued decline of the Roman Empire and its resultant isolation. In any case, they represent an independent type of literature that cannot be integrated into the major streams of Latin and Greek literature. For this reason, their separate treatment is justified and required. Sometime later Arabic and Old Church Slavonic were added as secondary patristic languages; although they were no longer part of the patristic era, or barely so, as translation literature they attained great importance for the transmission of the patristic texts. They preserve important textual witnesses for the purpose of ascertaining the original text of works whose original is lost or that are no longer fully extant.

*Syrians:*
> Bardesanes (Bardaisan) (154–222)
> Tatian (pre-155–post-172)
> Aphraates (ca. 337/345)
> Ephraem Syrus (ca. 306–373)
> Evagrius Ponticus (ca. 345–399)
> Titus of Bostra (pre-362–pre-378)

Cyrillonas (end of 4th c.)
Symeon of Mesopotamia (Macarius) (pre-380–ca. 426)
Balaeus (Balai) (5th c.)
Rabbula of Edessa (d. 435)
Ibas of Edessa (bishop 435–457)
Barsauma (d. 496)
Narsai (399–502)
Philoxenus of Mabbug (ca. 440–523)
James of Sarug (ca. 451–521)
Severus of Antioch (baptized 488, d. 538)
John of Ephesus (ca. 507–588)
Mar Aba (bishop 540–552)
Romanos Melodos (d. 560)
Peter Callinicus (d. 591)
Babai the Great (ca. 550–628)
Gregory ibn al-'Ibrī (Gregory Bar Hebraeus) (1225/1226–1286)
Abhdisho (Ebedjesus) bar Berikha (bishop 1291–1318)

*Egyptians (Copts):*
Anthony (251–356)
Peter of Alexandria (bishop 300–311)
Alexander of Alexandria (bishop 311–328)
Athanasius of Alexandria (295/300–373)
Theophilus of Alexandria (bishop 385–412)
Cyril of Alexandria (370/380–444)
Shenoute of Atripe (348–454/466)

*Armenians:*
Mesrop Mashtots (361/362–439/440)
Eznik of Kolb (first half of 5th c.)
John Mandakuni (484/485–498/499)
Agathangelos (second half of 5th c.)
Elisaeus (ca. 660)
Mambre Vercanol (7th c.?)
Moses of Korene (first half of 9th c.?)
Gregory of Narek (944–ca. 1010)

*Arabs:*
Severus ibn al-Muqaffa (pre-955–post-987)

*Bibliographies:* S. Voicu, "Lingue orientali e patristica greca," *Aug* 16 (1976): 205–15. –
M. Albert, R. Beylot, R. – G. Coquin, B. Outtier, and C. Renoux, *Christianismes orien-taux: Introduction à l'étude des langues et des littératures* (ICA 4; Paris: Cerf, 1993).

*Editions:* Corpus scriptorum christianorum orientalium (Paris, etc., 1900–) [CSCO]. –
Patrologia orientalis (Paris, etc., 1903–) [PO].

*Translation Series:* Eastern Christian Texts in Translation (Louvain: Peeters, 1997–) .

*Journals: Acta orientalia* (Copenhagen, etc., 1922–) *[AcOr].* – *Le Muséon: Révue d'études orientales* (Louvain, 1882–) *[MUS].* – *Oriens christianus* (Rome, 1901–) *[OrChr].* – *Orientalia* (Rome, 1920–) *[Or].* – *Orientalia christiana periodica* (Rome, 1935–) *[OCP].* – *Orientalia lovaniensia periodica* (Louvain, 1970–) *[OLP].* – *Orientalistische Literaturzeitung* (Berlin, 1898–) *[OLZ].* – *Parole de l'Orient* (Kaslik, Lebanon, 1970–) *[ParOr].* – *Proche-Orient chrétien* (Jerusalem, 1951–) *[POC].* – *Revue de l'Orient chrétien* (Paris, 1895–) *[ROC].* – *Rivista degli studi orientali* (Rome, 1907–) *[RSO].* – *Studi e ricerche sull'Oriente Cristiano* (Rome, 1978–) *[SROC].*

*Series:* Göttinger Orientforschungen (Wiesbaden: Harrassowitz, 1971–) [GOF]. – Orientalia christiana analecta (Rome: Pontificium Institutum Orientalium Studiorum, 1923–) [OrChrAn].

*Encyclopedia Articles:* G. Kretschmar, "Kirchensprache," *TRE* 19:74–92. – P. Siniscalco, "Languages of the Fathers," *EECh* 1:472.

*Dictionaries:* J. Assfalg and P. Krüger, *Kleines Wörterbuch des christlichen Orients* (Wiesbaden: Harrassowitz, 1975); French trans., *Petit dictionnaire de l'Orient chrétien* (trans. Centre informatique et Bible; Turnhout, Belg.: Brepols, 1991). – K. Parry et al., *The Blackwell Dictionary of Eastern Christianity* (Oxford and Malden, Mass.: Blackwell, 1999).

*Manuals:* C. Brockelmann, J. Leipoldt, F. N. Finck, and E. Littmann, *Geschichte der christlichen Litteraturen des Orients* (2d ed.; Die Literaturen des Ostens in Einzeldarstellungen 7.2; Leipzig: C. F. Amelang, 1909; new ed. with updated bibliography by N. Nagel, Leipzig: Zentralantiquariat der Deutschen Demokratischen Republik, 1972). – A. Baumstark, *Die christlichen Literaturen des Orients* (2 vols.; Leipzig: Göschen, 1911). – G. Furlani, "Letterature dell'Oriente cristiano," in *Le civiltà dell'Oriente: Storia, letteratura, religioni, filosofia, scienze, e arte* (ed. G. Tucci; 4 vols.; Rome: Casini, 1956–1962), 2:191–228. – A. Guillaumont, J. Doresse, R. Schneider, and H. Berbérian, "Chrétienté orientale," in *Histoire des littératures* I (ed. R. Queneau; 3 vols.; 2d ed.; Paris: Gallimard, 1968–1978), 751–821.

# I. SYRIAC LITERATURE

In scope and content, the most significant national Christian literature of antiquity was produced in Syria, a Roman province since its conquest by Pompey in 65–62 B.C.E., extending from the Taurus Mountains in the north to Arabia in the south, from the Mediterranean coast in the west to the Euphrates in the east. Together with Mesopotamia and parts of Persia, this region coincides with the area in which the Syriac language mainly spread, even if the political province itself was subdivided and reorganized several times later on. As the territory closest to—indeed encompassing—Palestine, its christianization, according to the Acts of the Apostles, occurred directly in the context of the first wave of missions by the apostles and especially by Paul. In the third century Syria was already among the most extensively christianized regions of the Roman Empire.

The Syriac language generally was a late development, centered around Edessa, of Aramaic, and so of the language of Jesus and the earliest community of Jerusalem, though with major Akkadian, Hebrew, Persian, and Greek influences. It is a Semitic language with its own alphabet and script (from right to left), closely related to other Semitic alphabets (e.g., Hebrew), and contains twenty-two consonants. In written form the vowels are indicated by markings, as in the Hebrew language. The modern script called Estrangelo (Greek στρογγύλος, "round") did not emerge, however, until the early fifth century as a standardized form; until then it had similarities with the Hebrew square script. The Syriac language spread throughout the entire Syrian territory mentioned above, including Mesopotamia and into Persia. It has been the language of the Nestorian, Jacobite, Melkite, Maronite, Chaldean, and Malabar churches up to the present time, although it was separated into two alphabets in the eighth century, namely, the Jacobite (in the case of the Jacobite and Maronite western Syrians) and the Nestorian (in the case of the eastern Syrians).

The oldest witnesses to Syriac in general are non-Christian inscriptions of the first and second century from the region of Edessa; its first Christian literary witnesses date from the second century C.E., from the same region. The latter are mainly gnostic and heterodox Jewish texts that are also extant in Coptic and Greek translations—for example, the NT apocrypha, such as the *Gospel of Thomas*, the *Acts of Philip*, the *Acts of Thomas*, and the *Pseudo-Clementines*, as well as the *Odes of Solomon* (cf. ch. 2.IV) and the *Didascalia*. In contrast to the other Eastern literature of the patristic era, consisting mainly of translations, the Syriac literature is largely original, and its reciprocal relations with the Greek church are strong.

The Syriac Christian literary history divides into four phases:

*Phase One:* Its beginnings and initial peak, which extended from the second to the fourth centuries, Edessa and Nisibis serving as the centers, were characterized by bilingualism (Syriac-Greek) within the boundaries of the Roman Empire and by important authors outside the empire, in Mesopotamia and Persia. Three of the most important writers of this first phase, which, as already mentioned, was shaped by bilingualism, were already dealt with in the framework of Greek patrology because their works in Greek or in translated form exerted enduring influence there: Tatian, the apologist (second century; cf. ch. 3.I.C), and the monks Evagrius Ponticus (345–399; cf. ch. 8.II.A) and Symeon of Mesopotamia (Macarius) (ca. 380–426; cf. ch. 8.II.B). Aphraates and Ephraem Syrus, generally acknowledged to be the most important figures of Syriac Christian literature, will be introduced in more detail after this general overview.

Bardesanes (Bardaisan; 154–222), considered to be the first Syriac writer, is credited with having introduced the hymns that were so typical for the entire Syrian theology. Granted, Ephraem later opposed him, together with Marcion and Mani, as their intellectual father (cf. B below). Besides the mainly Persian martyrdom records of the third to the sixth centuries, of particular interest are the four books against the Manichaeans by Bishop Titus of Bostra, written in 363, and the poet Cyrillonas (late fourth century); the Syriac translations of the Bible; and the legend concerning the founding of the church of Edessa.

The oldest Syriac translation of the Gospels is Tatian's second-century *Diatessaron*, addressed previously (cf. ch. 3.I.C.2). Additionally, ca. 300 a very literal translation of the Gospels, distinct from the former in form, was produced

(Old Syriac). In the mid-fifth century both versions were replaced by the Peshitto ("the simple one"), a translation of the entire Bible that continues to be valid today and that later translations of both the OT and the NT have not been able to replace. The OT versions of the *Peshita* indeed seem to go back to the second century C.E.

Eusebius of Caesarea (*Hist. eccl.* 1.3; 2.1.6–8] (cf. ch. 5.I.C) and *Itinerarium Egeriae* 19.6 (cf. ch. 8.IV) report that the archives of Edessa owned and displayed an (apocryphal) Syriac correspondence between Jesus and King Abgar of Edessa in which the latter entreated the Lord to come to Edessa to escape pestering by the Jews and to heal him. In his response letter, Jesus promises to send a disciple after the completion of his earthly mission. No earlier than at the end of the fourth century, for Eusebius and the *Itinerarium* do not mention it, this apocryphal correspondence was incorporated into the *Doctrina Addai*, a comprehensive legend of the founding of the church of Edessa, for the purpose of legitimizing its apostolicity and orthodoxy as well as its hierarchical and liturgical rules. After the ascension of Jesus, the Apostle Thomas is said to have sent Judas Thaddaeus (Addai), who healed King Agbar, as a result of which the king and the people turned to Christianity. Subsequently Addai personally gave the church of Edessa its constitution and its liturgical order. Later insertions include an apocryphal exchange of letters between Abgar and Emperor Tiberius, a legend about the discovery of the cross, and a story about Abgar's emissary who had sketched a portrait of Jesus and brought it personally to Edessa. This later famous icon of Christ of Edessa is first mentioned, however, in 593 by Evagrius Scholasticus (*Hist. eccl.* 4.27).

*Phase Two:* In the second phase, from the fifth to the seventh centuries, Syriac Christian literature initially developed in two blocks, one in eastern Persia, its center being Seleucia-Ctesiphon on the Tigris, and the other encompassing the eastern provinces of the Roman Empire, with Antioch as its point of orientation. The translations of the most important Greek fathers emerged during this time, as well as such important original works as the *Liber graduum* and the *Spelunca thesaurorum* ("Treasure Cave"). Writers such as the *chorepiscopus* Balaeus and the bishops Rabbula (d. 435) and Ibas of Edessa (d. 457) are also part of this period; in the general history of the church, they have become famous especially because, together with Theodore of Mopsuestia, they were condemned as forerunners of Nestorian Christology in the so-called Three Chapters dispute of the Second Council of Constantinople (553), although Ibas had been recognized as orthodox and rehabilitated by the Council of Chalcedon (451).

In the late fifth century, the controversies over the reception of the theology of the Council of Chalcedon (451) were followed by the split of the Syriac church into a Persian-Nestorian and a Western-Monophysite part. Among the important writers of the Persian-Nestorian church of this period are the metropolitan of Nisibis Barsauma (d. no later than 496); Narsai, its outstanding theologian and founder of a school at Nisibis (399–502); the eastern Syrian *catholicus* Mar Aba (d. 552); and Babai the Great (ca. 550–628), a monk and archimandrite of the large monastery on Mount Izla (north of Nisibis). Important among the

Monophysites were Bishop Philoxenus of Mabbug (d. 523), a crusader for their cause; Jacob of Sarug (451–521), a moderate Monophysite and notable preacher; Patriarch Severus of Antioch (d. 538), who pursued a moderate *via media* between Chalcedonianism and Nestorianism; John of Ephesus (ca. 507–588), a church historian and hagiographer; and Peter Callinicus (d. 591), a Jacobite patriarch of Antioch.

*Phase Three:* The third phase of Syriac literature continued into the tenth century; because of the Islamic conquests of the country, however, its decline had already begun in the seventh century.

*Phase Four:* The fourth phase (tenth to sixteenth centuries) consists of the last strands of Syriac ecclesiastical literature, although it enjoyed a certain renaissance once again in the twelfth and thirteenth centuries; its primary representative is Gregory ibn al-'Ibrī (Gregory Bar Hebraeus) (1225/1226–1286), the head of the Syrian Orthodox church of this period. Of particular significance for patrology is the catalog of Nestorian Syrian writings, comparable to Jerome's *De viris illustribus,* written by Abhdisho (Ebedjesus) bar Berikha (d. 1318), the Nestorian metropolitan of Nisibis. Like Jerome, he concludes with his own works and represents an indispensable treasure trove for the lost works of Nestorius and other Nestorian writers.

Syriac since then has been the only liturgical language of the Nestorian, Jacobite, Melkite, Maronite, Chaldean, and Malabar churches.

*Bibliographies:* P. B. Dirksen, *An Annotated Bibliography of the Peshitta of the Old Testament* (Monographs of the Peshitta Institute 5; Leiden; Brill, 1989). – S. P. Brock, *Syriac Studies: A Classified Bibliography (1960–1990)* (Kaslik, Lebanon: Parole de l'Orient, 1996); compiled from *ParOr* 4 (1973): 393–465; 10 (1981–1982): 291–412; 14 (1987): 289–360; 17 (1992): 211–301.

*Editions: Patrologia syriaca* (ed. R. Graffin; 3 vols.; Paris: Firmin-Didot, 1894–1926). [PS]

*Translations:* B. P. Pratten, trans., "The Memoirs of Edessa and Ancient Syriac Documents," in *ANF* (Peabody, Mass.: Hendrickson, 1995; repr. of 1886 ed.), 8:645–743. – S. P. Brock, *Syriac Fathers on Prayer and the Spiritual Life* (CistSS 101; Kalamazoo: Cistercian, 1987). – S. P. Brock and S. Ashbrook Harvey, *Holy Women of the Syrian Orient* (rev. ed.; TCH 13; Berkeley: University of California Press, 1998). – T. M. Finn, *Early Christian Baptism and the Catechumenate: West and East Syria* (MFC 5; Collegeville, Minn.: Liturgical, 1992).

*Vocabulary:* R. Payne Smith et al., *Thesaurus syriacus* (2 vols.; Oxford: Clarendon, 1879–1901; repr., Hildesheim: Olms, 1981). – J. P. Margoliouth, *Supplement to the Thesaurus syriacus of R. P. Smith* (Oxford: Clarendon, 1927; repr., Hildesheim: Olms, 1981).

*Dictionaries:* J. Payne Smith, *A Compendious Syriac Dictionary: Founded upon the Thesaurus syriacus of R. Payne Smith* (Oxford: Clarendon, 1903; repr., 1967, 1979; repr., Oxford: Oxford University Press, 1985). – J. Brun, *Dictionarium syriaco-latinum* (Beirut: Typographia PP. Soc. Jesu, 1895; 2d ed.,1911). – C. Brockelmann, *Lexicon syriacum* (2d ed.; Halle: M. Niemeyer, 1928; repr., Hildesheim: Olms, 1966). – L. Costaz, *Dictionnaire syriaque-français: Syriac-English Dictionary* (Beirut: Imprimerie Catholique, 1963).

*Grammars:* R. Duval, *Traité de grammaire syriaque* (Paris: F. Vieweg, 1881; repr., Amsterdam: Philo, 1969). – T. Nöldeke, *Kurzgefasste syrische Grammatik* (2d ed.; Leipzig:

C. H. Tauchnitz, 1898; repr., Darmstadt: Wissenschaftliche Buchgesselschaft, 1966); ET, *Compendious Syriac Grammar* (London: Williams & Norgate, 1904; repr., Winona Lake, Ind.: Eisenbrauns, 2001). – C. Brockelmann, *Syrische Grammatik mit Litteratur, Chrestomathie, und Glossar* (Berlin: Reuther & Reichard; New York: Lemcke & Buechner, 1899); *Syrische Grammatik mit Paradigmen, Literatur, Chrestomathie, und Glossar* (7th ed.; Leipzig: Harrassowitz, 1955). – M. H. Goshen-Gottstein, *A Syriac-English Glossary with Etymological Notes: Based on Brockelmann's Syriac Chrestomathy* (Wiesbaden: Harrassowitz, 1970). – L. Palacios, *Grammatica syriaca: Ad usum scholarum iuxta hodiernam rationem linguas tradendi concinnata* (rev. V. Camps; Rome and New York: Desclée, 1954). – L. Costaz, *Grammaire syriaque* (Beirut: Librairie Orientale, 1955; 3d ed., Beirut: Dar el Machreq, 1992). – J. F. Healey, *First Studies in Syriac* (Birmingham, Eng.: University of Birmingham, 1980). – J. Joosten, *The Syriac Language of the Peshitta and Old Syriac Versions of Matthew: Syntactic Structure, Inner-Syriac Developments, and Translations Technique* (Studies in Semitic Languages and Linguistics 22; Kinderhook, N.Y.: Brill, 1996). – M. Pazzini, *Grammatica siriaca* (Studium Biblicum Franciscanum Analecta 46; Jerusalem: Franciscan, 1999).

*Journals: L'Orient syrien* (Paris, 1954–1967) *[Orsyr]*. – *Hugoye: Journal of Syriac Studies* (online; Washington, D.C.: Syriac Computing Institute, 1998–).

*Collections of Essays: Symposium syriacum, 1972, célébré dans les jours 26–31 octobre 1972 à l'Institut pontifical oriental de Rome: Rapports et communications* (OrChrAn 197; Rome: Pontificium Institutum Orientalium Studiorum, 1974). – *Symposium syriacum, 1976, célébré du 13 au 17 septembre 1976 au Centre culturel Les Fontaines de Chantilly, France: Communications* (OrChrAn 205; Rome: Pontificium Institutum Orientalium Studiorum, 1978). – *III Symposium syriacum, 1980: Les contacts du monde syriaque avec les autres cultures (Goslar, 7–11 Septembre 1980)* (ed. R. Lavenant; OrChrAn 221; Rome: Pontificium Institutum Studiorum Orientalium, 1983). – *IV. Symposium syriacum, 1984—Literary Genres in Syriac Literature: Groningen-Oosterhesselen, 10–12 September* (OrChrAn 229; Rome: Pontificium Institutum Studiorum Orientalium, 1987). – *V Symposium syriacum: Leuven, Katholieke Universiteit, 29–31 aout 1988* (ed. R. Lavenant; OrChrAn 236; Rome: Pontificium Institutum Studiorum Orientalium, 1990). – *VI Symposium syriacum, 1992: University of Cambridge, Faculty of Divinity, 30 August–2 September 1992* (ed. R. Lavenant; OrChrAn 247; Rome: Pontificio Istituto Orientale, 1994). – *Symposium syriacum VII: Uppsala University, Department of Asian and African Languages, 11–14 August 1996* (ed. R. Lavenant; OrChrAn 256; Rome: Pontificio Istituto Orientale, 1998). – S. P. Brock, *Syriac Perspectives in Late Antiquity* (VRCS 199; London: Variorum, 1984). – H. J. W. Drijvers, *East of Antioch: Studies in Early Syriac Christianity* (VRCS 198; London: Variorum, 1984). – S. P. Brock, *Studies in Syriac Christianity: History, Literature, and Theology* (VRCS 357; Hampshire, U.K.; Brookfield, Vt.: Variorum, 1992). – H. J. W. Drijvers, *History and Religion in Late Antique Syria* (VRCS 464; Aldershot, Eng.; Brookfield, Vt.: Variorum, 1994). – G. J. Reinink and A. C. Klugkist, eds., *After Bardaisan: Studies on Continuity and Change in Syriac Christianity in Honour of Professor H. J. W. Drijvers* (Orientalia lovaniensa analecta 89; Louvain: U. Peeters en Departement Oosterse Studies, 1999).

*Encyclopedia Articles:* A. di Berardino and B. Bagatti, "Syria," *EECh* 2:807–9. – F. Rilliet, "Syriac," *EECh* 2:809–11. – S. H. Griffith, "Syria, Syriac," *EEC* 2:1100–1102.

*Introductions and Surveys:* S. H. Moffett, *Beginnings to 1500* (vol. 1 of *A History of Christianity in Asia;* 2d ed.; Maryknoll, N.Y.: Orbis, 1998).

*History of the Literature:* J. S. Assemani, *Bibliotheca orientalis clementino-vaticana* (4 vols.; 2d ed.; Rome: Typis Sacrae Congregationis de Propaganda Fide, 1719–1728; repr., Hildesheim and New York: Olms, 2000). – W. Wright, *A Short History of Syriac Literature* (London: Adam & Charles Black, 1894; repr., Folcroft, Pa.: Folcroft Library

Editions, 1978). – R. Duval, *La litterature syriaque* (vol. 2 of *Anciennes littératures chrétiennes;* 3d ed.; Paris: Victor Lecoffre, 1907; repr., Amsterdam: Philo, 1970); Spanish trans., *La literatura siriaca* (2 vols.; Pamplona: Imprenta, Lib. y Enc. Diocesana, 1913). – A. Baumstark, *Geschichte der syrischen Literatur mit Ausschluss der christlich-palästinensischen Texte* (Bonn: A. Marcus & E. Weber, 1922; repr., Bonn: de Gruyter, 1968). – O. Bardenhewer, *Geschichte der altkirchlichen Literatur,* vol. 4, *Das fünfte Jahrhundert mit Einschluss der syrischen Literatur des vierten Jahrhunderts* (2d ed.; Fribourg, Switz.: Herder, 1924; repr., Darmstadt: Wissenschaftliche Buchgesellschaft, 1962), 318–421. – J.-B. Chabot, *Littérature syriaque* (Paris: Bloud & Gay, 1934). – I. Ortiz de Urbina, *Patrologia syriaca* (2d ed.; Rome: Pontificium Institutum Orientalium Studiorum, 1965). – S. P. Brock, "An Introduction to Syriac Studies," in *Horizons in Semitic Studies* (ed. J. H. Eaton; Birmingham, Eng.: Department of Theology, University of Birmingham, 1980), 1–33. – P. Bettiolo, "Lineamenti di patrologia siriaca," in *Complementi interdisciplinari di patrologia* (ed. A. Quacquarelli; Rome: Città Nuova, 1989), 503–603.

*Studies:* E. R. Hayes, *L'école d'Édesse* (Paris: Presses modernes, 1930). – A. Vööbus, *History of Ascetism in the Syrian Orient: A Contribution to the History of Culture in the Near East* (3 vols.; CSCO 184, 197, 500; Louvain: SCO, 1958–1988). – A. Vööbus, *History of the School of Nisibis* (CSCO 266; Louvain: SCO, 1965). – R. Murray, *Symbols of Church and Kingdom: A Study in Early Syriac Tradition* (rev. ed.; Piscataway, N.J.: Gorgias, 2004). – J.-M. Sauget, "L'apport des traductions syriaques pour la patristique grecque," *RTP* 110 (1978): 139–48. – W. Cramer, *Der Geist Gottes und des Menschen in frühsyrischer Theologie* (MBTh 46; Münster: Aschendorff, 1979). – S. P. Brock, "The Prayer of the Heart in the Syrian Tradition," *Sobornost* 4 (1982): 131–42; repr. in *Forms of Devotion: Conversion, Worship, Spirituality, and Asceticism* (ed. E. Ferguson; Recent Studies in Early Christianity 5; New York: Garland, 1999), 133–44.

# A. Aphraates

The circumstances of the life and the person of Aphraates remain largely obscure, especially since he himself explains that he wants to be secondary to his work (*Demonstrationes* 22.26). Both the handwritten transmission of his works and the tradition of literary history attribute to him the honorary designation "the Persian sage," confirmed by the content and vocabulary of his works. He lived in the western part of the Persian Sassanian Empire (Mesopotamia). From his twenty-two "Instructions" (*Demonstrationes*), arranged acrostically according to the same number of letters of the Syriac alphabet, it emerges that he wrote them in 337 (1–10) and 344 (11–22) and in 345 added a twenty-third instruction as a supplement. He addressed them to the "sons of the covenant," that is, the ascetics to whom he himself also belonged. Apart from the evident high regard that he already enjoyed during his lifetime, it remains an open question whether he held an ecclesiastical office. The marginal note in a manuscript dated to 1364 according to which, during the persecution under Emperor Julian (361–363), he was the bishop of the monastery of Mar Mattai, founded ca. five miles northeast of Mossul (on the Tigris) and named after its founder, must be ruled out for chronological reasons.

The popularity and importance of the *Demonstrationes* are shown in its numerous translations. Besides the Syriac original, nos. 1–19 are also found in Armenian under the name of Jacob of Nisibis because the text tradition frequently also calls Aphraates Jacob; no. 6 is found in Georgian; and no. 5 and fragments of no. 8 are found in Ethiopic. The Ethiopic version may not have been translated directly from Syriac but via an Arabic version, fragments of which have been preserved under the name of Ephraem.

The outstanding importance of the *Demonstrationes* for modern research is that it provides a unique glimpse into the history and theology of an ancient church that was not hellenized but was entirely part of the Jewish-Christian tradition. In typically Syriac form, continually interspersed with hymns and prayers, the first ten *demonstrationes* address topics of faith as well as of the spiritual and ecclesiastical life: faith (1), love (2), fasting (3), prayer (4), wars (5), the sons of the covenant (6), the penitent (7), the resurrection of the dead (8), humility (9), and the shepherds (10). *Demonstrationes* 5 reflects the preparations for war by Shâpûr II against the Roman Empire, preparations that Aphraates interprets as vain, following the apocalyptic vision of Daniel. In *Demonstrationes* 7 Aphraates solemnly admonishes office bearers to prove themselves as good leaders of souls, as father confessors, and as good disciples of Christ the physician, for their failure would lead the sinner to death.

The second series of *demonstrationes* emerged in a situation that politically was altogether different. In 344 Shâpûr II began a bloody persecution of Christians, while tolerating the Jews. This led to the strong Jewish communities in Mesopotamia polemicizing against the Christians, arguing that God was standing idly by, watching their persecution, whereas God was protecting the Jews from the same, in order to show that the Jews alone were his chosen people. To the external pressure they thus added the inner doubt about the correctness of the Christian faith. Against this, Aphraates stresses frequently that he must and will strengthen the Christians in their faith by persuading them of the falsehood of the Jewish polemic as he hands them powerful counterarguments against it in order also to face the danger that, under the pressure of persecution, Christians might convert to unmolested Judaism. For this reason, Aphraates presents the decisive theological and practical differences between the Christian and the Jewish faiths: circumcision (11), the Passover (12), the Sabbath (13), the difference in foods (15), the nations in place of the one nation (16), that the Messiah is the Son of God (17), against the Jews, concerning virginity and holiness (18), and against the Jews who argue that they are destined to be gathered (19). Thereby he seeks to demonstrate that the Christian church is the messianic fulfillment of Judaism and that Judaism, as the typological preliminary stage, is outdated. Circumcision has its fulfillment in baptism, the Passover in Easter, the law in the gospel, and the people of Israel in the church. *Demonstrationes* 21, about the persecution, completes the series by encouraging Christians and at the same time rejecting the inappropriate ridicule of the Jews, who ignore their own history, in which, as the OT bears witness, their own righteous ones had to endure persecution as well.

*Demonstrationes* 14, about exhortation, offers a loosely arranged summary of the exhortations of a provincial synod, directed to the church's office bearers and addressed to the Christian community of the capital, Seleucia-Ctesiphon. *Demonstrationes* 20 deals with providing for the poor, and 22 with death and the last days. *Demonstrationes* 23, "About the Grapes," which was subsequently added in 345, addresses the continuity of God's salvation history with humans, in which the Jews were chosen first but whose blessing then was transferred to the true vine of Christ.

*Editions: The Homilies of Aphraates, the Persian Sage* (ed. and trans. W. Wright; London: Williams & Norgate, 1869) [ET]. – J. Parisot, ed., *Aphraatis sapientis Persae Demonstrationes* (PS 1.1; Paris: Firmin-Didot, 1894; repr., Turnhout, Belg.: Brepols, 1980). – F. Nau, ed., *Liber legum regionum* (PS 1.2; Paris: Firmin-Didot, 1907). – F. M. Esteves Pereira, ed., in *Orientalische Studien: Theodor Nöldeke zum siebzigsten Geburtstag (2. März 1906)* (ed. C. Bezold; 2 vols.; Giessen: A. Töpelmann, 1906), 877–92 [5 ethiop]. – G. Garitte, *Bedi K'art'lisa* 17–18 (1964): 82–7 [6 georg]. – G. Garitte, "La version géorgienne de l'entretien VI d'Aphraate," *Mus* 77 (1964): 301–66 [6 georg]. – *La version arménienne des œuvres d'Aphraate le Syrien* (ed. G. Lafontaine; 3 vols. in 6; CSCO 382–383, 405–406, 423–424; Louvain: SCO, 1977–1980) [*1–19* T.armen]. – J.-M. Sauget, "Entretiens d'Aphraate en arabe sous le nom d'Ephrem," *Mus* 92 (1979): 61–69 [*frgg* arab]. – T. Baarda, *NTS* 27 (1981): 632–40 [*8 ethiop* ET].

*Translations:* J. Gwynn, trans., "Select Demonstrations," in *NPNF²* (Peabody, Mass.: Hendrickson, 1995; repr. of 1898 ed.), 13:343–412 [*Demonstrations 1, 5, 6, 8, 10, 17, 21, 22*].

*Other Translations: French: Les Exposés* (ed. M.-J. Pierre; 2 vols.; SC 349, 359; Paris: Cerf, 1988–1989) [Com]. – *Italian: Le piu belle pagine* (trans. G. Ricciotti; Milan: ARA–G. Gasparini, 1926). – *German: Aphrahat's des persischen Weisen Homilien* (trans. G. Bert; TU 3.3–4; Leipzig: Hinrichs, 1888) [Com]. – *Unterweisungen* (trans. P. Bruns; 2 vols.; FChr 5.1–2; Fribourg, Switz.: Herder, 1991).

*Encyclopedia Articles:* A. Vööbus, *JAC* 3:152–55; repr. in *RAC.S* 4:497–506. – G. G. Blum, *TRE* 1:625–35. – R. Lavenant, *EECh* 1:54. – P. Bruns, *LTK* 1:802–3. – R. J. Owens, *EEC* 1:71–72.

*General Studies:* P. Schwen, *Afrahat: Seine Person und sein Verständnis des Christentums* (NSGTK 2; Berlin: Trowitsch, 1907; repr., Aalen: Scientia Verlag, 1973).

*Bible and Exegesis:* O. E. Evans, "Syriac New Testament Quotations in the Works of Aphraates and Contemporary Sources" (M.A. thesis, University of Leeds, 1951). – T. Baarda, *The Gospel Quotations of Aphrahat, the Persian Sage: Aphrahat's Text of the Fourth Gospel* (Amsterdam: Vrije Universiteit, 1975). – R. J. Owens, *The Genesis and Exodus Citations of Aphrahat, the Persian Sage* (Monographs of the Peshitta Institute, Leiden 3; Leiden: Brill, 1983). – K. A. Valavanolickal, *The Use of the Gospel Parables in the Writings of Aphrahat and Ephrem* (Frankfurt and New York: Lang, 1996).

*Philology:* E. Hartwig, *Untersuchungen zur Syntax des Afraates* (Leipzig: Drugulin, 1893). – L. Haefeli, *Stilmittel bei Afrahat dem Persischen Weisen* (LSS NS 4; Leipzig: Hinrichs, 1932; repr., Leipzig: Zentralantiquariat der DDR, 1968). – A. Vööbus, "Methodologisches zum Studium der Anweisungen Aphrahats," *OrChr* 46 (1962): 25–32. – G. Nedungatt, "The Authenticity of Aphrahat's Synodal Letter," *OCP* 46 (1980): 62–88. – K. Samir and P. Yousif, "La version arabe de la IIIe Démonstration d'Aphrahat," *Actes du deuxième Congrès international d'études arabes chrétiennes*

(Oosterhesselen, septembre 1984) (ed. K. Samir; OrChrAn 226; Rome: Pontificium Institutum Studiorum Orientalium, 1986), 31–66.

*Response to Judaism:* S. Funk, *Die haggadaischen Elemente in den Homilien des Aphraates* (Vienna: Selbstverlag des Verfassers, 1891). – F. Gavin, "Aphraates and the Jews," *JSOR* 7 (1923): 95–166. – J. Neusner, *Aphrahat and Judaism: The Christian-Jewish Argument in Fourth-Century Iran* (StPB 11; Leiden: Brill, 1971; repr., Atlanta: Scholars Press, 1999). – J. G. Snaith, "Aphrahat and the Jews," in *Interpreting the Hebrew Bible: Essays in Honour of E. I. J. Rosenthal* (ed. J. A. Emerton and S. C. Reif; Cambridge and New York: Cambridge University Press, 1982), 235–50.

*Sacramental Theology:* E. J. Duncan, *Baptism in the Demonstrations of Aphraates the Persian Sage* (SCA 8; Washington, D.C.: Catholic University of America Press, 1945). – T. Jansma, "Aphraates' Demonstration VII §§ 18 and 20: Some Observations on the Discourse on Penance," *ParOr* 5 (1974): 21–48. – F. Pericoli Ridolfini, "I sacramenti negli scritti del Sapiente Persiano," *SROC* 2.3 (1979): 157–71. – F. S. Pericoli Ridolfini, "Battesimo e penitenza negli scritti del 'Sapiente Persiano,'" in *Catechesi battesimale e riconciliazione nei Padri del IV secolo* (ed. S. Felici; BSRel 60; Rome: LAS, 1984), 119–29.

*Theology:* H. L. Pass, "The Creed of Aphraates," *JTS* 9 (1908): 267–84. – D. Ploij, "Der Descensus ad inferos in Aphrahat und den Oden Salomos," *ZNW* 14 (1913): 212–31. – I. Ortiz de Urbina, *Die Gottheit Christi bei Afrahat* (OrChr[R] 87; Rome: Pontificium Institutum Orientalium Studiorum, 1933). – A. Vogel, "Zur Lehre von der Erlösung in den Homilien Aphraats: Die Deutung der Christuserlösung als Vollendung der alttestamentlichen Heilsgeschichte bei Aphraat, dem Persischen Weisen" (diss., Pontificia Universitas Gregoriana, 1966). – F. Pericoli Ridolfini, "Note sull' antropologia e sull'escatologia del 'Sapiente Persiano,'" *SROC* 1.1 (1978): 5–17; 1.2 (1978): 5–16. – F. Pericoli Ridolfini, "Problema trinitario e problema cristologica nelle Dimostrazioni del Sapiente Persiano," *SROC* 2.2 (1979): 99–125. – M.-J. Pierre, "L'âme ensommeilée et les avatars du corps selon le Sage Persan: Essai sur l'anthropologie d'Aphraate," *POC* 32 (1982): 233–62; 33 (1983): 104–42. – P. Bruns, *Das Christusbild Aphrahats des Persischen Weisen* (Hereditas 4; Bonn: Borengässer, 1990). – W. L. Petersen, "The Christology of Aphrahat, the Persian Sage," *VC* 46 (1992): 241–56.

# B. Ephraem Syrus

Ephraem, with the epithet "of Nisibis" or simply Syrus, "the Syrian," is indisputably the most productive, the most significant, and by far the most cited author of Syriac Christian literature overall. Born ca. 306 as the son of Christian parents in or near Nisibis, he joined the ascetic "sons of the covenant"— Aphraates was also among them—after his baptism and traditionally bears the title of deacon. Under Jacob (d. 338), the first bishop of Nisibis, whom he revered as his own teacher, he himself functioned as a teacher in Nisibis. Much of his famous *Carmina nisibena* (1–34), as well as the hymns *De paradiso, Contra haereses,* and *De fide,* originated at this time. During Ephraem's lifetime, the city of Nisibis heroically withstood three sieges by the Persians (338, 346, 350); the results of the Persian campaign by Emperor Julian the Apostate (April–June 363)—Julian was killed in battle and Jovian, his successor, left Nisibis to the Persians—were catastrophic for the city. Ephraem lauds these events, in his *Hymns against Julian* and in the *Hymns on the Church* prefacing the former, as hard but just punishment for Julian's return to the ancient cults of the gods and his proceedings against the Christians. Since, in their peace accord with Jovian, the Persians insisted on the resettlement of most of the Roman population from Nisibis, Ephraem moved to Edessa as well in 364, where he spent the remaining ten years of his life as a teacher at the local exegetical school, until his death on June 9, 373. What role he played in the founding of the famous "school of the Persians" in this context, attributed to him by many sources, remains obscure. In any case, the years in Edessa seem to have been filled with unceasing labor, even if it is not possible to state with certainty which of his numerous works were written during this period of time; what is certain, however, is that the commentary on the *Diatessaron* (cf. ch. 3.I.C.2) and the anti-Arian *Hymns on Faith* originated at that time.

The influence and importance of Ephraem extend far beyond the Syriac language realm. Although he himself wrote exclusively in Syriac, already during his lifetime he was cited by both the Greek and the Latin churches—quite unique in this context. Jerome included him in *De viris illustribus* (115) and reports that Ephraem's works were recited in church after the scripture reading; he himself had read a Greek translation of Ephraem's writing on the Holy Spirit. The historian Sozomen attests that a large part of Ephraem's works was extant in a Greek translation in the early fifth century (*Hist. eccl.* 3.16.4). In the broad tradition of Ephraem Graecus, however, much that is inauthentic has crept in today; the same also applies to the Latin and Armenian text tradition. His continued relevance in the Western church is underscored by the conferral of the honorary title "doctor of the church" by Pope Benedict XV on October 5, 1920, thereby ranking him among the greatest Fathers of the church.

Ephraem's literary fame is derived mainly from his artistic theological, ascetical, and liturgical hymns, *memre* (metrical homilies), and *madrash* (songs), which probably attain their artistic apex in the final six anti-Arian *Hymns on the Faith* (81–87). The latter contain meditations about the traditional legend of the origin of pearls in a shell by fertilization with the heavenly dew as an image of Mary's virginal conception. In this way, Ephraem took the typical and already traditional Syrian form of doing theology to its full flowering. It is said to have had its inception with Bardesanes, the first Syrian writer, and plays an important role with most of the Syrian theologians, one of the outstanding examples being Romanos Melodos of Emesa (d. 560). Syrian theology basically thinks less in terms of concepts and discursive argumentation, as practiced especially by the Latin church though to a lesser extent by the Greek church as well. Instead its ideas are expressed in stories, pictures, and symbols that are best rendered in the form of poems, hymns, and prayers. This way of thinking constitutes the essential feature of Ephraem's theology. For him the root of all theological error is based on the attempt to understand God by means of philosophical, rationalistic thought, whereas God is to be sensed only through pictures and symbols, by means of which both "books of revelation," namely Holy Scripture and creation, point to him. In his Christology therefore Ephraem begins with the biblical titles of Christ (king, shepherd, bridegroom, physician), and in the doctrine of the Trinity he begins with nature (sun, fire, light, warmth, father and son relating like a tree and fruit). In his soteriology he compares paradise with Noah's ark and Mount Sinai and describes redemption as "the way from wood to wood" (from the tree of paradise to the cross of Christ). Certainly, such metaphorical language can also be found among the Greek and Western fathers; its fullness, poetic quality, and theologically central role in Ephraem, however, transcends them by far.

Beyond this, Ephraem is demonstrably a master of Syriac literary prose, as evidenced by his five refutations against Marcion, Mani, and Bardesanes and by his homilies and letters.

*Bibliographies:* M. Roncaglia, "Essai de bibliographie sur saint Éphrem," *ParOr* 4 (1973): 343–70. – K. Samir, "Compléments de bibliographie éphremienne," *ParOr* 4 (1973): 371–91.

*Editions: Diatessaron/Exegesis: Commentaire de l'Évangile concordant: Version arménienne* (ed. L. Leloir; 2 vols.; CSCO 137, 145; Louvain: Durbecq, 1953–1954). – *Saint Ephrem's Commentary on Tatian's Diatessaron: An English translation of Chester Beatty Syriac MS 709* (Oxford: Oxford University Press on behalf of the University of Manchester, 1993). – *In Genesim et Exodum commentarii* (ed. R. M. Tonneau; 2 vols. in 1; CSCO 152–153; Louvain: Durbecq, 1955). – *Commentaire de l'Évangile concordant: Texte syriaque (Ms Chester Beatty 709)* (ed. L. Leloir; Dublin: Hodges Figgis, 1963). – *An Exposition of the Gospel* (ed. G. A. Egan; 2 vols.; CSCO 291–292; Louvain: SCO, 1968) [ET]. – *Commentaire de l'Évangile concordant: Texte syriaque (Manuscrit Chester Beatty 709): Folios additionels* (ed. L. Leloir; CBM 8; Louvain: Peeters, 1990).

*Hymns and Sermons: Sancti Ephraem Syri Hymni et sermones* (ed. T. J. Lamy; 4 vols.; Mecheln, Belg.: H. Dessain, 1882–1902). – *Hymnen De fide* (ed. E. Beck; 2 vols.; CSCO 154–55; Louvain: Durbecq, 1955). – *Hymnen Contra haereses* (ed. E. Beck; 2 vols.; CSCO 169–70; Louvain: Durbecq, 1957). – *Hymnen De paradiso und Contra Julianum* (ed. E. Beck; 2 vols. in 1; CSCO 174–75; Louvain: SCO, 1957). – *Hymnen De nativitate (Epiphania)* (ed. E. Beck; 2 vols. in 1; CSCO 186–87; Louvain: SCO, 1959). – *Hymnen De ecclesia* (ed. E. Beck; 2 vols. in 1; CSCO 198–99; Louvain: SCO, 1960). – *Sermones de fide* (ed. E. Beck; 2 vols.; CSCO 212–13; Louvain: SCO, 1961). – *Carmina nisibena* (ed. E. Beck; 2 vols. in 4; CSCO 218–19, 240–41; Louvain: SCO, 1961–1963). – *Hymnes de saint Ephrem: Conservées en version arménienne* (ed. L. Mariès and C. Mercier; PO 30.1; Paris: Firmin-Didot, 1961). – *Des heiligen Ephraem des Syrers Hymnen De virginitate* (ed. E. Beck; 2 vols. in 1; CSCO 223–24; Louvain: SCO, 1962). – *Des heiligen Ephraem des Syrers Hymnen De ieiunio* (ed. E. Beck; 2 vols. in 1; CSCO 246–47; Louvain: SCO, 1964). – *Des heiligen Ephraem des Syrers Paschahymnen (De azymis, De crucifixione, De resurrectione)* (ed. E. Beck; 2 vols. in 1; CSCO 248–49; Louvain: SCO, 1964). – *Des heiligen Ephraem des Syrers Sermo de Domino nostro* (ed. E. Beck; 2 vols.; CSCO 270–71; Louvain: SCO, 1966). – *Des Heiligen Ephraem des Syrers Sermones* (ed. E. Beck; 4 vols. in 8; CSCO 305–6, 311–12, 320–21, 334–35; Louvain: SCO, 1970–1973) – *Memre sur Nicomédie* (ed. C. Renoux; PO 37; Turnhout, Belg.: Brepols, 1975).

*Other Works:* C. W. Mitchell, A. A. Bevan, and F. C. Burkitt, *S. Ephraim's Prose Refutations of Mani, Marcion, and Bardaisan* (2 vols.; London: Published for the Text and Translation Society by Williams & Norgate, 1912–1921; repr., Farnborough, Eng.: Gregg, 1969) [ET]. – S. P. Brock, "Letter to Publius," *Mus* 89 (1976): 261–305 [ET]. – B. Outtier, *Textes arméniens relatifs à s. Éphrem* (2 vols.; CSCO 473–74; Louvain: Peeters, 1985).

*Dubia et Spuria:* E. Beck, *Hymnen auf Abraham Kidunaya und Julianos Saba* (2 vols.; CSCO 322–23; Louvain: SCO, 1972). – E. Beck, *Nachträge zu Ephraem Syrus* (2 vols.; CSCO 363–64; Louvain: SCO, 1975). – E. Beck, *Sermones in hebdomadam sanctam* (2 vols.; CSCO 412–13; Louvain: SCO, 1979).

*Ancient Biographies: Sancti Ephraem Syri Hymni et sermones* (ed. T. J. Lamy; 4 vols.; Mecheln, Belg.: H. Dessain, 1882–1902), 2:3–89. – Pseudo-Gregory of Nyssa, *In Sanctum Ephraim,* PG 46:819–50. – Symeon Metaphrastes, PG 114:1253–68. – *Vies géorgiennes de s. Symeon Stylite l'ancien et de s. Éphrem* (ed. G. Garitte; 2 vols.; CSCO 171–72; Louvain: Durbecq, 1957). – *A Metrical Homily on Holy Mar Ephrem by Mar Jacob of Sarug* (ed. J. P. Amar; PO 47.1; Turnhout, Belg.: Brepols, 1995) [ET].

*Translations:* J. Gwynn, trans., "Hymns and Homilies of Ephraim the Syrian," in *NPNF²* (Peabody, Mass.: Hendrickson, 1995; repr. of 1898 ed.), 13:113–341 [*Nisibene Hymns, 19 Hymns on the Nativity, 15 Hymns for the Feast of the Epiphany, The Pearl: 7 Hymns on the Faith, 3 Homilies*]. – *The Harp of the Spirit: Eighteen Poems of Saint Ephrem* (trans. S. P. Brock; 2d ed.; London: Fellowship of St. Alban and St. Sergius, 1983; San Bernardino, Calif.: Borgo, 1984). – *The Emperor Julian: Panegyric and Polemic* (ed. and trans. S. N. C. Lieu and J. M. Lieu; 2d ed.; Liverpool: Liverpool University Press, 1989), 87–128 [ET/Com]. – *Ephrem the Syrian: Hymns* (trans. K. E. McVey; CWS; New York: Paulist, 1989) [*Hymns on the Nativity, Hymns against Julian, Hymns on Virginity and on the Symbols of the Lord*]. – *Hymns on Paradise* (trans. S. Brock; Crestwood, N.Y.: St. Vladimir's Seminary Press, 1990). – *St. Ephrem's Commentary on Tatian's Diatessaron: An English Translation of Chester Beatty Syriac MS 709 with Introduction and Notes* (ed. and trans. C. McCarthy; JSemS.S 2; Oxford: Oxford University Press on behalf of the University of Manchester, 1993). – *Selected Prose Works* (ed. K. McVey; trans. E. G. Mathews and J. P. Amar; FC 91; Washington, D.C.: Catholic University of America Press, 1994) [*Commentary on Genesis, Commentary on Exodus, Homily on Our Lord, Letter to Publius*].

*Translations to Other Languages: French: Commentaire de l'Évangile concordant ou Diatessaron* (ed. L. Leloir; SC 121; Paris: Cerf, 1966). – *Hymnes sur le paradis* (ed. R. Lavenant; SC 137; Paris: Cerf, 1968). – *Les Chants de Nisibe* (trans. P. Fhégali and C. Navarre; Paris: Cariscript, 1989). – G. A. M. Rouwhorst, *Les Hymnes pascals d'Éphrem de Nisibe: Analyse théologique et recherche sur l'évolution de la fête pascale chrétienne à Nisibe et à Edesse et dans quelques églises voisines au quatrième siècle* (SVigChr 7.2 Leiden and New York: Brill, 1989). – *Célébrons la Pâque: Hymnes sur les azymes, sur la crucifixion, sur la résurrection* (trans. D. Cerbelaud and A.-G. Hamman; CPF 58; Paris: Migne, 1995). *Italian: Inni alla vergine* (trans. G. Ricciotti; Turin: Società Editrice Internazionale, 1939). – *German: Ausgewählte schriften des hl. Ephräm von Syrien* (trans. P. Zingerle; 3 vols.; BKV¹ 7, 21, 40; Kempten: Kösel, 1870–1876). – *Des heiligen Ephräm des Syrers Ausgewählte Schriften* (trans. O. Bardenhewer and A. Rücker, 2 vols.; BKV² 37, 61; Munich: Kösel, 1919–1928). – *Hymnen über das Paradies* (trans. E. Beck; SA 26; Rome: "Orbis Catholicus," Herder, 1951) [Com]. – *Lobgesang aus der Wüste* (trans. E. Beck; Sophia: Quellen östlicher Theologie 7; Fribourg, Switz.: Lambertus, 1967). – E. Beck, "Brief an Hypatios," *OrChr* 58 (1974): 76–120 [Com]. – E. Beck, "Rede gegen eine philosophische Schrift des Bardaisan," *OrChr* 60 (1976): 24–68 [Com]. – *Reden über den Glauben: Ausgewählte nisibenische Hymnen* (trans. S. Euringer, A. Rücker, and W. Cramer; SKV 10; Munich: Kösel, 1984). – E. Beck, "Der syrische Diatessaronkommentar," *OrChr* 67 (1983): 1–31; 73 (1989): 1–37; 74 (1990): 1–24; 75 (1991): 1–15; 76 (1992): 1–45; 77 (1993): 104–19 [Com].

*Reference Works:* F. C. Burkitt, *S. Ephraim's Quotations from the Gospel* (TS 7.2; Cambridge: Cambridge University Press, 1901; repr., Nendeln, Liechtenstein: Kraus Reprint, 1967). – *L'Évangile d'Éphrem d'après les œuvres édités: Recueil des textes* (ed. L. Leloir; CSCO

180; Louvain: SCO, 1958). – G. A. Egan, *An Analysis of the Biblical Quotations of Ephrem in "An Exposition of the Gospel" (Armenian Version)* (CSCO 443; Louvain: Peeters, 1983).

*Collections of Essays: XVIe centenaire de saint Éphrem (373–1973)* (Special issue of *ParOr* 4.1–2; Kaslik, Lebanon: Université Saint-Esprit, 1973).

*Encyclopedia Articles:* E. Beck, D. Hemmerdinger-Iliadou, and J. Kirchmeyer, *DSp* 4/1:788–822. – E. Beck, *RAC* 5:520–31. – L. Leloir, *DHGE* 15:590–97. – R. Murray, *TRE* 9:755–62. – F. Rilliet, *EECh* 1:276–77. – A. de Halleux, *GK* 1:284–301. – W. Cramer, *LTK* 708–10. – K. McVey, *EEC* 1:376–77.

*Introductions:* B. Outtier, "Saint Éphrem d'après ses biographies et ses œuvres," *ParOr* 4 (1973): 11–33. – A. de Halleux, "Mar Ephrem, théologien," *ParOr* 4 (1973): 35–54. – A. de Halleux, "Saint Éphrem le Syrien," *RTL* 14 (1983): 328–55. – P. S. Russell, "St. Ephraem, the Syrian Theologian," *Pro ecclesia* 7 (1998): 79–90. – S. H. Griffith, "A Spiritual Father for the Whole Church: St. Ephraem the Syrian," *Sobornost* 20.2 (1998): 21–40.

*Anthropology, Cosmology, and Spirituality:* W. Cramer, *Die Engelvorstellungen bei Ephräm dem Syrer* (OrChrAn 173; Rome: Pontificium Institutum Orientalium Studiorum, 1965). – N. El-Khoury, *Die Interpretation der Welt bei Ephraem dem Syrer: Beitrag zur Geistesgeschichte* (Mainz: Matthias Grünewald, 1976). – E. Beck, *Ephräms des Syrers Psychologie und Erkenntnislehre* (CSCO 419; Louvain: SCO, 1980). – T. Bou Mansour, "La liberté chez Éphrem le Syrien," *ParOr* 11 (1983): 89–156; 12 (1984–1985): 3–89. – S. P. Brock, *The Luminous Eye: The Spiritual World Vision of Saint Ephrem* (rev. ed.; CistSS 124; Kalamazoo: Cistercian, 1992). – T. Bou Mansour, *La pensée symbolique de saint Éphrem le Syrien* (Bibliothèque de l'Université Saint-Esprit 16; Kaslik, Lebanon: Université Saint-Esprit, 1988).

*Bible and Diatessaron:* L. Leloir, *Doctrines et méthodes de s. Éphrem d'après son Commentaire de l'Évangile concordant (original syriaque et version arménienne)* (CSCO 220; Louvain: SCO, 1961). – S. Hidal, *Interpretatio syriaca: Die Kommentare des heiligen Ephräm des Syrers zu Genesis und Exodus mit besonderer Berücksichtigung ihrer auslegungsgeschichtlichen Stellung* (Coniectanea biblica: Old Testament Series 6; Lund, Swed.: Gleerup, 1974). – T. Kronholm, *Motifs from Genesis 1–11 in the Genuine Hymns of Ephrem the Syrian, with Particular Reference to the Influence of Jewish Exegetical Tradition* (Coniectanea biblica: Old Testament Series 11; Lund, Swed.: Gleerup, 1978). – W. L. Petersen, *The Diatessaron and Ephrem Syrus as Sources of Romanos the Melodist* (CSCO 475; Louvain: Peeters, 1985). – K. A. Valavanolickal, *The Use of the Gospel Parables in the Writings of Aphrahat and Ephrem* (Frankfurt and New York: Lang, 1996). – S. H. Griffith, *"Faith Adoring the Mystery": Reading the Bible with St. Ephraem the Syrian* (Milwaukee: Marquette University Press, 1997).

*Sacramental Theology:* G. Saber, *La théologie baptismale de saint Éphrem: Essai de théologie historique* (Kaslik, Lebanon: Université Saint-Esprit de Kaslik, 1974). – E. Beck, *Dōrea und Charis, die Taufe: Zwei Beiträge zur Theologie Ephräms des Syrers* (CSCO 457; Louvain: Peeters, 1984). – P. Yousif, *L'eucharistie chez saint Éphrem de Nisibe* (OrChrAn 224; Rome: Pontificium Institutum Orientale, 1984).

*Historical Studies:* A. Vööbus, *Literary, Critical, and Historical Studies in Ephrem the Syrian* (Stockholm: ETSE, 1958). – E. Beck, *Ephräms Polemik gegen Mani und die Manichäer im Rahmen der zeitgenössischen griechischen Polemik und der des Augustinus* (CSCO 391; Louvain: SCO, 1978). – S. H. Griffith, "Images of Ephraem: The Syrian Holy Man and His Church," *Traditio* 45 (1989–1990): 7–33; repr. in *Doctrinal Diversity: Varieties of Early Christianity* (ed. E. Ferguson; Recent Studies in Early Christianity 4; New York: Garland, 1999), 299–325.

*Theology:* E. Beck, *Die Theologie des hl. Ephraem in seinen Hymnen über den Glauben* (SA 21; Vatican City: Libreria Vaticana, 1949). – E. Beck, *Ephraems Reden über den Glauben: Ihr theologischer Lehrgehalt und ihr geschichtlicher Rahmen* (SA 33; Rome: "Orbis Catholicus," Herder, 1953). – J. Martikainen, *Das Böse und der Teufel in der Theologie Ephraems des Syrers* (Åbo, Finland: Stiftelsens für Åbo Akademi Forskningsinstitut, 1978). – E. Beck, *Ephräms Trinitätslehre im Bilde von Sonne: Feuer, Licht, und Wärme* (CSCO 425; Louvain: Peeters, 1981). – J. Martikainen, *Gerechtigkeit und Güte Gottes: Studien zur Theologie von Ephraem dem Syrer und Philoxenos von Mabbug* (GOF.S 20; Wiesbaden: Harrassowitz, 1981). – G. A. M. Rouwhorst, *Les Hymnes pascals d'Éphrem de Nisibe: Analyse théologique et recherche sur l'évolution de la fête pascale chrétienne à Nisibe et à Edesse et dans quelques églises voisines au quatrième siècle* (SVigChr 7.1; Leiden and New York: Brill, 1989). – P. S. Russell, "Ephraem the Syrian on the Utility of Language and the Place of Silence," *JECS* 8 (2000): 21–38.

# II. COPTIC LITERATURE

The term "Coptic" has no other meaning than "Egyptian," derived from the Arabic *qobti,* which in turn gave rise to the Greek term Ἀιγύπτιος. Hence Coptic is the Egyptian language in its most recent stage of development. The oldest form of Egyptian, hieratic, was written either in hieroglyphics or in the hieratic cursive script until the eighth century B.C.E. In the eighth century, through disappearance and the use of ligatures, it evolved into the demotic (δῆμος = "people"), that is, the common script, which continued to be used until the third century B.C.E. Beginning in the fourth century B.C.E., the Greek culture and language attained a dominant influence under the Ptolemies, so much so that the Greek alphabet and a wealth of Greek terms were adopted. In addition to the twenty-four letters of the Greek alphabet, however, seven demotic letters were retained, so that the Coptic alphabet is made up of thirty-one letters: alpha to omega, in the form of the majuscule letters of late antiquity, plus shâi *(sh),* fâi *(f),* châi *(h)* (Bohairic only), hori *(h),* dshandsha (hard *dsh*), kjima (soft *dsh*), and ti.

Coptic has two primary dialects: Sahidic in Upper Egypt and Bohairic in Lower Egypt. In addition, there are eight further local dialects with subdialects, such as Akhmimic in Upper Egypt and the Middle Egyptian dialects of Fayumic and Memphitic. From the third to the eighth centuries C.E., Sahidic was the dominant literary language, and from the ninth to the twelfth centuries, it was Bohairic. Coptic continues to exist only as the liturgical language of the Coptic church, since the tenth century, when it was entirely replaced by Arabic as the common Egyptian language.

Coptic literature remains primarily a translation literature. Its earliest texts come from the fourth century C.E.—translations of the OT and the NT, gnostic and Hermetic writings (among them especially the famous gnostic library of Nag Hammadi; cf. ch. 3.IV.A.1.a)—and later on there are also many works of the monastic, spiritual-moral, and homiletical Greek literature (among them the famous Passover sermon of Melito of Sardis; cf. ch. 3.II). Unfortunately, important parts of the Coptic library of Manichaean writings, found in 1930 by Carl Schmidt at Medinet Madi, perished during World War II.[1] The first original Coptic literature emerged in the context of Egyptian monasticism. Of the Coptic original of the letters of Anthony (251–356; cf. *Vit. Ant.* 8.3), only fragments are preserved; seven of them are extant, however, in their entirety in Georgian and Arabic translations. Another thirteen letters attributed to him and handed down in Arabic originated from his circle of students. The life and works of Pachomius, the father of cenobitic monasticism in Egypt, were introduced above in connection with the monastic rules of ancient Christianity (cf. ch. 8.I.A). The *Apophthegmata patrum*, which probably emerged first in the early fifth century and is an anonymous collection of spiritual instructions and anecdotes of the desert fathers and mothers (there are three women among them as well), reflects the anchoritic life and body of thought of the fourth and fifth centuries. Also worth mentioning are the *Historia monachorum in Aegypto*, the fictitious travelogue of a group of Palestinian monks in Egypt in 394/395, which is often combined with the *Historia Lausiaca* of Palladius, and a *Vita* of St. Onuphrius, written by Paphnutius, his disciple.

Coptic sermons, letters (especially the annual Easter letters), and catecheses of the following Alexandrian patriarchs have been preserved: Peter (300–311), Alexander (311–328), Athanasius (328–373; cf. ch. 5.IV), and Theophilus (385–412); preserved, too, are sermons, exegeses, and encomia by Cyril of Alexandria (412–444; cf. ch. 10.I). Also belonging to the original Coptic literature are the late apocryphal gospels and associated literary pieces, such as the *History of Joseph the Carpenter*, which originated ca. 400, acts of the apostles, and apocalypses, as well as numerous Coptic legends about martyrs.

The dispute with the Council of Chalcedon (451), which led to the separation of the Coptic church from the Catholic imperial church, produced a further flowering of dogmatic and polemical literature; the attacks by Islamic Arabs, however, soon (from 750) brought this to an end. Since then Coptic literature remains limited largely to the liturgical writings of the church.

*Bibliographies: Coptic Bibliography* (ed. Unione accademica nazionale, Corpus dei manoscritti copti letterari; Rome: Centro Italiano Microfiches, 1982–) *[CoptBibl]. – Coptic Bibliography: Supplement* (Rome: Centro Italiano Microfiches, 1992) *[CoptBibl.S]. –*

---

[1] Cf. C. Schmidt and H. Polotsky, *Ein Mani-Fund in Ägypten: Originalschriften des Mani und seiner Schüler, mit einem Beitrag von H. Ibscher* (SPAW.PH 1; Berlin Akademie der Wissenschaften, in Kommission bei W. de Gruyter, 1933); H. H. Schaeder, review of C. Schmidt and H. Polotsky, *Ein Mani-Fund in Ägypten, Gn* 9 (1933): 337–62; A. Böhlig, "Die Bedeutung der Funde von Medinet Madi und Nag Hammadi für die Erforschung des Gnostizismus," in A. Böhlig und C. Markschies, *Gnosis und Manichäismus: Forschungen und Studien zu Texten von Valentin und Mani sowie zu den Bibliotheken von Nag Hammadi und Medinet Madi* (BZNW 72; Berlin and New York: de Gruyter, 1994), 113–242. Bibliography: M. Tardieu, *Études manichéennes: Bibliographie critique, 1977–1986* (Teheran and Paris: Institut Français de Recherche en Iran, 1988); G. B. Mikkelsen, *Bibliographia manichaica: A Comprehensive Bibliography of Manichaeism through 1996* (Turnhout, Belg.: Brepols, 1997).

W. Kammerer with E. Mullet Husselmann and L. A. Shier, *A Coptic Bibliography* (Ann Arbor: University of Michigan Press, 1950; repr., New York: Kraus Reprint, 1969).

*Dictionaries:* W. E. Crum, *A Coptic Dictionary* (Oxford: Clarendon, 1939; repr., Oxford and New York: Clarendon, 1962; repr., Oxford: Clarendon, 1979). – R. Kasser, *Complé- ments au dictionnaire copte de Crum* (Bibliothèque d'études coptes 7; Cairo: Institut Français d'Archéologie Orientale, 1964). – W. Westendorf, *Koptisches Handwörter- buch* (Heidelberg: Winter Universitätsverlag, 1965–1977). – G. Roquet, *Toponymes et lieux-dites égyptiens enregistrés dans le dictionnaire copte de W. E. Crum* (Bibliothèque d'études coptes 10; Cairo; Institut Français d'Archéologie Orientale, 1973). – J. Cerný, *Coptic Etymological Dictionary* (Cambridge and New York: Cambridge University Press, 1976). – R. Smith, *A Concise Coptic-English Lexicon* (2d ed.; Atlanta: Scholars Press, 1999). – W. Vycichl, *Dictionnaire etymologique de la langue copte* (Louvain: Peeters, 1983).

*Grammars:* G. Steindorff, *Koptische Grammatik mit Chrestomathie, Wörterverzeichnis, und Literatur* (3d ed.; Berlin: Reuther & Reichard, 1930; repr., Hildesheim: Gerstenberg, 1979). – W. C. Till, *Koptische Grammatik (saidischer Dialekt): Mit Biographie, Les- estücken, und Wörterverzeichnissen* (2d ed.; Leipzig: Verlag Enzyklopädie, 1961; repr., Leipzig: VEB Verlag Enzyklopædie, 1989). – T. Orlandi, *Elementi di lingua e lettera- tura copta: Corso di lezioni universitarie* (Milan: Goliardica 1970). – H. J. Polotsky, *Collected Papers* (Jerusalem: Magnes, Hebrew University, 1971). – C. C. Walters, *An Elementary Coptic Grammar of the Sahidic Dialect* (Oxford: Blackwell, 1972). – J. Vergote, *Grammaire copte* (2 vols. in 4; Louvain: Peeters, 1973–1983). – T. O. Lambdin, *Introduction to Sahidic Coptic* (Macon, Ga.: Mercer University Press, 1983). – T. Orlandi, *Elementi di grammatica copto-saidica* (Rome: C.I.M., 1983).

*Encyclopedia: The Coptic Encyclopedia* (8 vols.; New York: Macmillan; Toronto: Collier Macmillan Canada, 1991).

*Journals: Enchoria: Zeitschrift für Demotistik und Koptologie* (Wiesbaden, 1971–). – *Journal of Coptic Studies* (Louvain, 1990–). – *Kemi: Revue de philologie et d'archéologie égyptiennes et coptes* (Paris, 1928–). – *Coptic Church Review* (Lebanon, Pa., 1980–).

*Series:* Cahiers de la Bibliothèque copte (Louvain: Peeters, 1982–) [CBCo]. – Coptic Stud- ies (Leiden, etc.: Brill, 1978–1990) [CoptSt].

*Collections of Essays: The Future of Coptic Studies: International Congress of Coptic Studies (1976: Cairo, Egypt)* (ed. R. M. Wilson; CoptSt 1; Leiden: Brill, 1978). – *Nag Hammadi and Gnosis: Papers Read at the First International Congress of Coptology (Cairo, Decem- ber 1976)* (ed. R. McL. Wilson; NHS 14; Leiden: Brill, 1978). – *[Proceedings,] Internatio- naler Kongress für Koptologie, Kairo, 08.-18. Dezember 1976* (Enchoria 8; Wiesbaden: In Kommission bei Harrassowitz, 1978). – *Acts of the Second International Congress of Coptic Study, Roma, 22–26 September 1980* (ed. Tito Orlandi and Frederik Wisse; Rome: C.I.M., 1985). – *Coptic Studies: Acts of the Third International Congress of Coptic Studies, Warsaw, 20–25 August, 1984* (ed. W. Godlewski; Warsaw: PWN- Éditions scientifiques de Pologne, 1990). – *Actes du IVe Congrès copte: Louvain-la- Neuve, 5–10 septembre 1988* (ed. M. Rassart-Debergh and J. Ries; Louvain: Université Catholique de Louvain, Institut Orientaliste, 1992). – *Acts of the Fifth International Congress of Coptic Studies: Washington, 12–15 August 1992* (ed. T. Orlandi; 2 vols.; Rome: C.I.M., 1993). – *Ägypten und Nubien in spätantiker und christlicher Zeit: Akten des 6. Internationalen Koptologenkongresses, Münster, 20.–26.* (ed. S. Emmel; Weisbaden: Reichert, 1999). – *Coptic Studies on the Threshold of the New Millennium: Proceedings of the Seventh International Congress of Coptic Studies, Leiden, August 27–September 2, 2000* (ed. M. Immerzeel, J. van der Vliet, M. Kerston, and C. van Zoest; Louvain and Dudley, Mass.: Uitgeverij Peeters en Dep. Oosterse Studies, 2004). – B. A. Pearson and J. E. Goehring, eds., *The Roots of Egyptian Christianity* (Studies in Antiquity and Christianity; Philadelphia: Fortress, 1986). – L. S. B. MacCoull, *Coptic Perspectives on Late Antiquity* (VRCS 398; Aldershot, Eng. and Brookfield, Vt.: Variorum, 1993). – A. Camplani, ed., *L'Egitto cristiano: Aspetti e problemi in età tardoantica* (SEAug 56; Rome: Institutum Patristicum Augustinianum, 1997).

*Encyclopedia Articles:* E. O'Leary, *DACL* 9/2:1599–1635. – M. Krause, "Koptische Literatur," in *Lexikon der Ägyptologie* (ed. W. Helck and W. Westendorf; 7 vols.; Wiesbaden: O. Harrassowitz, 1972–1992), 3:694–728. – M. Krause and K. Hoheisel, *RAC.S* 1/2:14–88. – T. Orlandi, *EECh* 1:199–201. – M. Krause, *LTK* 6:360–62. – L. S. B. MacCoull, "Copts," *EEC* 1:289–90.

*History of the Literature:* F. Pericoli Ridolfini, "Letteratura copta," in *Storia delle letterature d'Oriente* (ed. O. Botto; 4 vols.; Milan: F. Vallardi, 1969), 1:765–800. – S. Morenz, "Die koptische Literatur," in *Der nahe und der mittlere Osten* (2d ed.; HO 1.2; Leiden and New York: Brill, 1970), 239–50. – T. Orlandi, "Coptic Literature," in *The Roots of Egyptian Christianity* (ed. B. A. Pearson and J. E. Goehring; Philadelphia: Fortress, 1986), 51–81. – T. Orlandi, "La patrologia copta," in *Complementi interdisciplinari di patrologia* (ed. A. Quacquarelli; Rome: Città Nuova, 1989), 457–502.

*Roman Egypt:* R. S. Bagnall, *Egypt in Late Antiquity* (Princeton, N.J.: Princeton University Press, 1993). – A. K. Bowman, *Egypt after the Pharoahs, 332 BC–AD 642: From Alexander to the Arab Conquest* (2d ed.; Berkeley: University of California Press; London: British Museum Press, 1996).

*Studies:* C. D. G. Müller, "Die alte koptische Predigt: Versuch eines Überblicks" (PhD diss., Universität Heidelberg, 1954). – T. Baumeister, *Martyr invictus: Der Martyrer als Sinnbild der Erlösung in der Legende und im Kult der frühen koptischen Kirche* (Münster: Regensberg, 1972). – C. W. Griggs, *Early Egyptian Christianity from Its Origins to 451 C.E.* (CoptSt 2; Leiden: New York: Brill, 1990; repr., Leiden and Boston: Brill, 2000). – M. Johnson, *Liturgy in Early Christian Egypt* (Alcuin/GROW Liturgical Study 33; Cambridge: Grove, 1995). – A. Grillmeier, *The Church of Alexandria, with Nubia and Ethiopia after 451* (vol. 2, part 4 of *Christ in Christian Tradition;* trans. O. C. Dean, London: Mowbray, 1996); trans. of *Die Kirche von Alexandrien mit Nubien und Athiopien nach 451* (vol. 2, part 4 of *Jesus der Christus im Glauben der Kirche;* Fribourg, Switz.: Herder, 1990). – D. Frankfurter, *Religion in Roman Egypt: Assimilation and Resistance* (Princeton, N.J.: Princeton University Press, 1998).

# Shenoute of Atripe

Certainly the most significant and prolific writer of original Coptic literature was Shenoute, the abbot of the monastery of Atripe, near Akhmim (Upper Egypt); later the monastery was named after him the "monastery of Shenoute" (*Deir Anba Shenouda*) and today is known as the White Monastery (*Deir el Abiad*). Still, relatively little is known about the external data of his life, and everything known about him comes exclusively from Coptic sources; the Greek sources do not mention him. In a sermon from the year of the Council of Ephesus (431), in which he participated in the entourage of Cyril of Alexandria, he remarks that he had been reading the Bible continually for sixty years and proclaiming it for forty-three years, which is interpreted to mean that he was a monk since 371 and archimandrite since 388. According to the *Vita* of his student and successor as the abbot of the White Monastery, Besa, whose letters and homilies are also preserved, Shenoute was born in the village of Shenalolet, near Akhmim, the son of small farmers and as a child tended to the sheep. Already as a child (ca. 360) he is said to have entered the monastery of Atripe, founded and led by Pjol, his maternal uncle, succeeded him as abbot following his uncle's death (ca. 385), and died on a seventh of July (his present commemoration day) at the age of 118. Besa's reference to the year of indiction[2] allows for the years 451–452 or 466; but since Shenoute considerably outlived Nestorius, who according to references in his writings did not die until after the Council of Chalcedon (451), he himself must have died on July 7, 466, and hence was born in 348. An inscription from the White Monastery itself confirms the year of his birth but indicates the year of his death as 454.

Shenoute understood the leadership of his monastery, encompassing houses for both men and women and which he led to great success with strict discipline, as the primary mission of his life. Beyond this he also actively supported the cause of the neighboring population. He assisted them in surviving the economic crises of the fifth century, defended them against rapacious nomads and the exploitation by big landowners, and thus became a sought-after adviser even of ecclesiastical and state agencies beyond the immediate region.

Shenoute's literary legacy reflects his wide-ranging activities and importance: homilies and catecheses for the monks, correspondence with various church and state courts, and theological tractates on Nestorianism, Gnosticism, and Origenism against Meletians and pagans. Because of the difficulties in the transmission and editing of his works, a comprehensive literary and theological estimation of them is at its early stages, but Shenoute seems generally a zealous proponent of strict morality, piety, and asceticism as well as of Alexandrian Christology, rigorous orthodoxy, and church discipline against every form of paganism, heresy, and schism. Also, the opinion that he incorporated in his writings nothing of Greek education and thought no longer seems tenable.

*Bibliographies:* P. J. Frandsen and E. Richter Aerøe, "Shenoute: A Bibliography," in *Studies in Egyptology and Linguistics: In Honour of H. J. Polotsky* (ed. H. B. Rosén; Jerusalem: Israel Exploration Society, 1964), 147–76.

*Editions:* H. Guerin, "Sermons inédits de Senouti," *RdE* 10 (1902): 148–64; 11 (1905): 15–34. – *Sinuthii archimandritae Vita et Opera omnia* (ed. J. Leipoldt and E. W. Crum; 6 vols.; CSCO 41, 42, 73, 96, 108, 129; Paris, etc.: E Typographeo Reipublicaè, etc, 1906–1951; repr., 6 vols. in 2; Louvain: Durbecq, 1951–1954) [*Life and Works*]. – *Oeuvres de Schenoudi: Texte copte et traduction française* (ed. E. C. Amélineau; 2 vols.; Paris: Leroux, 1907–1914) [*Works*]. – *Le quatrième livre des entretiens et épîtres de Shenouti* (ed. É. Chassinat; Mémoires publiés par les membres de l'Institut français d'archéologie orientale 23; Cairo: Institut Français d'Archéologie Orientale, 1911). – P. Du Bourguet, "Entretien de Chénouté sur les devoirs des juges," *BIFAO* 55 (1955): 85–109. – *Letters and Sermons of Besa* (ed. K. H. Kühn; 2 vols. in 1; CSCO 157–58;

---

Louvain: Durbecq, 1956) [ET]. – P. Du Bourguet, "Entretien de Chénouté sur des problèmes de discipline ecclésiastique et de cosmologie," *BIFAO* 57 (1958): 99–142. – *Pseudo-Shenoute on Christian Behaviour* (ed. and trans. K. H. Kühn; 2 vols. in 1; CSCO 206–7; Louvain: SCO, 1960) [ET]. – P. Du Bourguet, "Diatribe de Chenouté contre le demon," *BSAC* 16 (1961): 17–72 [Com]. – K. Koschorke, S. Timm, and F. Wisse, "Schenute: *De certamine contra diabolum*," *OrChr* 59 (1975): 60–77. – *La version éthiopienne de la Vie de Schenoud* (ed. G. Colin; 2 vols.; CSCO 444–45; Louvain: Peeters, 1982) [*Vita*]. – *Shenute: Contra Origenistas* (ed. T. Orlandi; Rome: C.I.M., 1985) [*Contra Origenistas*].

*Translations: The Life of Shenoute/Besa* (trans. D. N. Bell; CistSS 73; Kalamazoo: Cistercian, 1983) [*Vita*].

*Translations to Other Languages: Sinuthii archimandritae Vita et Opera omnia* (trans. H. Wiesmann; 6 vols.; CSCO 41, 42, 73, 96, 108, 129; Paris, etc.: E Typographeo Reipublicae, etc., 1906–1951; repr., 6 vols. in 2; Louvain: Durbecq, 1951–1954 [*Life and Works*, Latin trans.]).

*Encyclopedia Articles:* T. Orlandi, *EECh* 2:776. – K. H. Kühn, "Shenute, Saint," in *The Coptic Encyclopedia* (8 vols.; New York: Macmillan, Toronto: Collier Macmillan, Canada, 1991), 7:2131–33. – H. R. Drobner, *BBKL* 9:153–54.

*Studies:* J. Leipoldt, *Schenute von Atripe und die Entstehung des national ägyptischen Christentums* (TU 25.1; Leipzig: Hinrichs, 1903). – J. F. Bethune-Baker, "The Date of the Death of Nestorius: Schenute, Zacharias, Evagrius," *JTS* 9 (1908): 601–5. – L. T. Lefort, "Catéchèse christologique de Chenoute," *Zeitschrift für ägyptische Sprache und Altertumskunde* 80 (1955): 40–55. – H.-F. Weiss, "Zur Christologie des Schenute von Atripe," *BSAC* 20 (1969–1970): 177–209. – J. Timbie, "The State of Research on the Career of Shenoute of Atripe," in *The Roots of Egyptian Christianity* (ed. B. A. Pearson and J. E. Goehring; Philadelphia: Fortress, 1986), 271–306. – Rebecca Krawiec, *Shenoute and the Women of the White Monastery: Egyptian Monasticism in Late Antiquity* (Oxford and New York: Oxford University Press, 2002).

# III. ETHIOPIC LITERATURE

According to the Lukan account of Acts (8:27–39), the first conversion and baptism of an Ethiopian took place under the Apostle Philip. He was a Diaspora Jew, in service to the Ethiopian Queen Candace, returning from his pilgrimage to Jerusalem (Aksum, the capital of the Ethiopian kingdom at the time, was situated on the fourteenth degree latitude, about four hundred miles north of the modern capital Addis Ababa). Because of Ethiopia's trade relations with the Roman Empire, the following centuries saw the establishment of early Christian communities in such trade colonies. Mission work in Ethiopia did not officially begin until about the middle of the fourth century, however, with the conversion of King Ezana and King Shizana by two Syrian laymen, the brothers Frumentius and Edesius (cf. Rufinus, *Hist. eccl.* 1[10].9f.). Since Frumentius later was consecrated bishop by Athanasius in Alexandria, geographically the closest patriarchate, the Ethiopian church came under the jurisdiction of Alexandria until 1959.

The Ethiopian language belongs to the Semitic language group, with its own alphabet deriving from Southern Arabic. In contrast to Southern Arabic with its boustrophedon, the writing of lines from right to left and from left to right alternately, Ethiopic has retained only the direction from left to right. Originally the alphabet consisted of thirty consonants, to which vowels were added in the early fourth century. But instead of indicating the vowel pointing above or under the line, as in other Semitic languages (e.g., Hebrew, Syriac), each consonant was given seven different modifications to indicate the vowel to follow. Hence a consonant and a vowel are expressed by a common sign. Subsequently, further modifications were added for diphthongs. Numbers were no longer written in Southern Arabic but in Greek. The ancient Christian literature is written in the classical form of Ethiopic, the so-called Geez.

The Ethiopic Christian literature, too, remains largely translation literature and as such is relatively limited in scope. Immediately after the christianization of the kingdom, the translation of the Bible from the Greek language was begun but not with continuity, so that it was not completed until the second half of the seventh century and therefore shows major variations. Further translations included the following:

- OT and NT apocryphal writings, such as *Jubilees, Enoch,* the *Greek Apocalypse of Ezra,* the *Martyrdom and Ascension of Isaiah,* the apocryphal correspondence of King Abgar of Edessa with Jesus (cf. ch. 1.III.A and ch. 4.IV.excursus 2.3), the *Apocalypse of Peter,* and the Shepherd of Hermas (cf. ch. 1.IV.B);

- the treatise *De antichristo* by Hippolytus of Rome (cf. ch. 3.IV.B.2);

- monastic literature, such as the monastic rule of Pachomius (cf. ch. 8.I.A) and the *vitae* of Paul of Thebes (Paul the Hermit) and of the Egyptian monastic father Anthony (cf. ch. 8.III);

- the *Physiologus,* a fourth-century work on the symbolism of nature, attributed to Epiphanius of Constantia (Salamis) (cf. ch. 7.II), numerous editions and translations of which considerably influenced Christian art;

- homilies of John Chrysostom;

- a collection of twenty-nine anti-Nestorian writings, introduced by two works of Cyril of Alexandria, *De recta fide,* addressed to Emperor Theodosius and to his two younger sisters Arcadia and Marina, and the dialogue *Quod unus sit Christus.* The entire collection is entitled "Querellos" (Cyrillos). After Cyril, though, the remainder of the collection is composed of homilies by various anti-Nestorian writers or by authors used for this purpose.

The Islamic conquest of the Ethiopian kingdom, beginning with the eighth century, meant the demise of Geez as the national language, which continues to exist only as a liturgical and ecclesiastical-literary language.

*Editions: Qērellos I: Der Prosphonetikos 'Über den rechten Glauben' des Kyrillos von Alexandrien an Theodosios II* (ed. B. M. Weischer; Glückstadt: Augustin, 1973). – *Qērellos II:*

*Der Prosphonetikos "Über den rechten Glauben" des Kyrillos von Alexandrien an Arkadia und Marina* (ed. B. M. Weischer; Stuttgart: Steiner, 1993). – *Qērellos III: Der Dialog "Dass Christus einer ist" des Kyrillos von Alexandrien* (ed. B. M. Weischer; Wiesbaden: Steiner, 1977). – *Qērellos IV.1: Homilien und Briefe zum Konzil von Ephesos* (ed. B. M. Weischer; Wiesbaden: Steiner, 1979). – *Qērellos IV.2: Traktate des Epiphanios von Zypern und des Proklos von Kyzikos* (ed. B. M. Weischer; Wiesbaden: Steiner, 1979). – *Qērellos IV.3: Traktate des Severianos von Gabala, Gregorios Thaumaturgos, und Kyrillos von Alexandrien* (ed. B. M. Weischer; Wiesbaden: Steiner, 1979).

*Dictionaries:* C. F. A. Dillmann, *Lexicon linguae aethiopicae cum indice latino* (Leipzig: T. O. Weigel, 1865; repr., New York: F. Ungar, 1955; Osnabrück: Biblio, 1970). – S. Grébaut, *Supplément au Lexicon linguae aethiopicae d'August Dillmann (1865) et édition du Lexique de Juste d'Urbin (1850–1855)* (Paris: Imprimerie Nationale, 1952). – G. da Maggiora, *Vocabolario etiopico-italiano-latino ad uso dei principianti* (Asmara: Scuola Tipografico Francescana, 1953). – W. Leslau, *Comparative Dictionary of Ge'ez (Classical Ethiopic): Ge'ez-English / English-Ge'ez, with an index of the Semitic Roots* (Wiesbaden: Harrassowitz, 1987).

*Grammars:* A. Dillmann, *Grammatik der äthiopischen Sprache* (2d ed.; rev. and enlarged by C. Bezold; Leipzig: H. Tauchnitz, 1899; repr., Graz: Akademische Druck- und Verlagsanstalt, 1959); [ET] *Ethiopic Grammar* (trans. J. A. Crichton; London: William & Norgate, 1907; repr., Amsterdam: Philo, 1974). – M. Chaîne, *Grammaire éthiopienne* (Beirut: Imprimerie Catholique, 1907; repr., 1938). – C. Conti Rossini, *Grammatica elementare della lingua etiopica* (Rome: Istituto per l'Oriente, 1941). – T. O. Lambdin, *Introduction to Classical Ethiopic (ge'ez)* (Harvard Semitic Studies 24; Missoula, Mont.: Scholars Press, 1978).

*Journals: Annales d'Éthiopie* (Paris, 1955–). – *Cahiers de l'Institut éthiopien d'archéologie* (Addis-Ababa, 1965–) *[Aet].* – *Journal of Ethiopian Studies* (Addis Ababa, 1963–) *[JetS].* – *Rassegna di studi etiopici* (Rome, 1941–) *[RSEt].*

*Encyclopedia Articles:* G. Lanczkowski, *JAC* 1:134–53; repr. in *RAC.S* 1/2:94–134. – F. Heyer, *TRE* 1:572–96. – O. Rainieri, *EECh* 1:289–91. – G. Fiaccadori, *LTK* 1:1149–54. – M. J. Blanchard, "Ethiopia," *EEC* 1:391–92. – D. Bundy, "Ethiopic Christian Literature," *EEC* 1:392–93. – G. Haile, *Encyclopedia of Monasticism* (ed. W. M. Johnston; 2 vols.; Chicago and London: Dearborn, 2000), 1:454–60.

*Manuals:* I. Guidi, *Storia della letteratura etiopica* (Rome: Istituto per l'Oriente, 1932). – E. Cerulli, *La letteratura etiopica: L'Oriente cristiano nell'unità delle sue tradizioni* (3d ed.; Florence: Sansoni; Milan: Accademia, 1968). – L. Ricci, "Letterature dell'Etiopia," in *Storia delle letterature d'Oriente* (ed. O. Botto; 4 vols.; Milan: Vallardi, 1969), 1:801–911.

*Historical Studies:* M. E. Heldman, ed., *African Zion: The Sacred Art of Ethiopia* (New Haven, Conn.: Yale University Press, 1993). – H. Brakmann, ΤΟ ΠΑΡΑ ΤΟΙΣ ΒΑΡΒΑΡΟΙΣ ΕΡΓΟΝ ΘΕΙΟΝ: *Die Einwurzelung der Kirche im spätantiken Reich von Aksum* (Bonn: Borengässer, 1994).

# IV. ARMENIAN LITERATURE

The Armenian language (close to Indo-Germanic and Persian) and culture in the area of modern eastern Anatolia, the southern Caucasus, and northwestern Iran, goes back to the migration of the Armenian (Thraco-Phrygian) peoples from the west in the seventh century B.C.E. Although the historicity of the christianization of Armenia by the apostles Judas Thaddaeus and Bartholomew, a tradition that can only be demonstrated beginning in the fifth century C.E., is debatable, there are some references to Armenian Christians already in the late second century. Further, the existence of Christian communities and ecclesiastical structures are securely attested in the consecration of Gregory the Illuminator as the bishop of Armenia by Leontius of Caesarea (Cappadocia) in 314. Naturally, an original Armenian literature could only emerge after the invention of an alphabet of its own, which Bishop Mesrop Mashtots developed ca. 422. Since Armenian is a language rich in sounds, it encompasses thirty-eight letters, which also explains why previous attempts to write Armenian in Syriac (eastern Armenia) or Greek (western Armenia) letters were unsuccessful. Because of medieval migrations, Armenian today is divided into two dialects, the eastern (Asian) dialect and the western dialect of the Turkish-Armenians, who became known in Europe especially through the Mechitarist *collegia* of Venice and Vienna.[3] The Armenian script runs from left to right; the accents stem from the Greek alphabet.

Armenian patristic literature extends from the early fifth century to the tenth century and thus, in terms of time, goes far beyond Latin and Greek patristics; this can be explained by the isolated situation of the national church. As in the case of all the national bodies of literature, Armenian literature consists mainly of translations from Greek and Syriac, beginning with the Bible and the biblical Apocrypha, via the great Greek and Syrian Fathers Aphraates, Athanasius, Basil the Great, Ephraem Syrus, Ephraim, Epiphanius of Constantia (Salamis), Eusebius, Gregory of Nazianzus, Gregory of Nyssa, Irenaeus, John Chrysostom, Cyril of Alexandria and Cyril of Jerusalem, Severian of Gabala, and Theodoret of Cyrhus, all the way to Plato, Aristotle, and Philo of Alexandria. Voicu structures the translation literature into three phases:

- the "golden era" of the first half of the fifth century, producing translations in which the Armenian language form is carefully observed;

- the "silver era" of the late fifth and early sixth centuries, the language of which moves away from the classical form and seeks to translate the originals as literally as possible, even through the introduction of neologisms;

- the third phase, the "Hellenophile school," from the second half of the sixth century to the first half of the eighth century, which pursues the strict adherence to the original to the extent that even the Armenian language rules are violated in favor of following the forms of the original as closely as possible.

The original Armenian literature from the fifth to the tenth century yields a fairly extensive corpus as well; a first phase produced more theological and his-

---

[3] An Armenian Uniate order under the Benedictine Rule, founded in 1701 by Mechitar of Sebaste, which devotes itself mainly to Armenian studies and to publishing books.

torical works, and a second phase produced more homiletical and exegetical ones. The theological literature deals mainly with Christology, in which the Armenian church went its own way, separate from Nestorianism and Monophysitism but also without accepting the Council of Chalcedon. The historical writings are largely limited to the local history of the church of Armenia and its immediate relations, and philosophy takes on greater prominence only in the seventh and eighth centuries. For the Western church, the names of most Armenian authors have little significance. Their impact on the theology and the church outside Armenia is negligible.

*Bibliographies: Annual Bibliography of Armenian Studies* (Los Angeles, 1979–). – V. Mistrih, "Bibliographie arménienne, 1969–1971," *Studia orientalia christiana: Collectanea* 17 (1982): 61–235. – A. Salmaslian, *Bibliographie de l'Arménie* (rev. and augmented ed.; Yerevan, Armenia: L'Académie des Sciences de la R.S.S. de l'Arménie, 1969). – V. Nersessian, *An Index of Articles on Armenian Studies in Western Journals* (London: Luzac, 1976). – G. Uluhogian, *Bibliography of Armenian Dictionaries* (Bologna: Pàtron, 1985).

*Vocabulary:* G. Awetik'ean, X. Siwrmélean, and M. Awgerean, *Nor bargirk` haykazean lezui* (2 vols.; Venice: I Tparani Srboyn Ghazaru, 1836–1837; repr., Yerevan, Armenia: Erevani Hamalsarani Hratarakch`ut`yun, 1979– 1981).

*Dictionaries:*
*French:* P. Aucher, *Dictionnaire abrégé français-arménien et arménien-français* (2 vols.; Venice: Imprimerie de la Susdite Académie, 1812–1817). – A. de Nar Bey (A. Calfa), *Dictionnaire arménien-français* (4th ed.; Paris: L. Hachette, 1893; repr., Paris: Klincksieck, 1972).
*English:* P. Aucher, *A Dictionary: English and Armenian* (2d ed.; Venice: Press of the Armenian Academy of S. Lazarus, 1868). – M. Bedrossian, *New Dictionary Armenian-English* (Venice: St. Lazarus Armenian Academy, 1875–1879; repr., Beirut: Librairie du Liban, 1974). – M. G. Kouyoumdjian, *A Comprehensive Dictionary Armenian-English* (Cairo: Sahag-Mesrob, 1950).
*Italian:* E. Ciakciak, *Dizionario armeno-italiano* (2 vols. in 1; Venice: Tip. Mechit.-aristica di S. Lazzaro, 1837).
*Latin:* I. Mískgian, *Manuale lexikon latino-armenum ad usum scholarum* (Rome: I Bazmalezuean Tparan S. Zhoghovoy Taratsman Hawatoy, 1893). – B. Reynders, *Lexique comparé du texte grec et des versions latine, arménienne, et syriaque de l'"Adversus haereses" de saint Irénée* (2 vols.; CSCO 141–142; Louvain: Durbecq, 1954). – B. Reynders, *Vocabulaire de la "Démonstration" et des fragments de saint Irénée* (Chevetogne: Chevetogne, 1958).
*German:* D. Froundjian, *Armenisch-Deutsches Wörterbuch* (Munich: R. Oldenbourg, 1952; repr., Hildesheim and New York: Olms, 1987).

*Grammars:* A. Meillet, *Altarmenisches Elementarbuch* (Heidelberg: Winter, 1913; repr., 1980). – H. Jensen, *Altarmenische Grammatik* (Heidelberg: Winter, 1959). – F. C. Roszko, *A Classical Armenian Grammar (Morphology, Syntax, Texts, Vocabulary)* (Indianapolis: Catholic Seminary Foundation of Indianapolis, 1970). – D. Van Damme, *A Short Classical Armenian Grammar* (Orbis biblicus et orientalis: Subsidia didactia 1; Fribourg, Switz.: University Press; Göttingen: Vandenhoeck & Ruprecht, 1974). – R. Godel, *An Introduction to the Study of Classical Armenian* (Wiesbaden: Reichert, 1975). – R. W. Thomson, *An Introduction to Classical Armenian* (2d ed.; Delmar, N.Y.: Caravan Books, 1989). – M. Minassian, *Manuel pratique d'arménien ancien* (Vaduz, Lichtenstein: Fondation des Frères Ghoukassiantz; Paris: Klincksieck, 1976). – F. Feydit,

*Cahiers de grammaire arménienne* (4 fascicules; Bazmavep 125; Venice: Tipolitografia Armena, 1956–1977). – R. Schmitt, *Grammatik des Klassisch-Armenischen mit sprach-vergleichenden Erläuterungen* (Innsbruck: Institut für Sprachwissenschaft der Universität Innsbruck, 1981).

*Journals: Handes Amsorya: Zeitschrift für armenische Philologie* (Vienna, 1887–) *[HandAm].* – *Journal of the Society for Armenian Studies* (Los Angeles, 1984–). – *Revue des études arméniennes [REArm]* (Paris, 1920–1933, 1964–).

*Encyclopedia Articles:* G. Klinge, *RAC* 1:678–89. – W. Hage, *TRE* 4:40–57. – M. Falla Castelfranchi and S. J. Voicu, *EECh* 1:79–81. – M. van Esbroeck, *LTK* 1:999–1004. – C. Cox, "Armenia," *EEC* 1:116–18. – R. Darling Young, "Armenian Christian Literature," *EEC* 1:118–19.

*History of the Literature:* J. Karst, *Geschichte der armenischen Literatur* (Leipzig: n.p., 1930). – O. Bardenhewer, *Die letzte Periode der altkirchlichen Literatur mit Einschluss des ältesten armenischen Schrifttums* (vol. 5 of *Geschichte der altkirchlichen Literatur;* Fribourg, Switz.: Herder, 1932; repr., Darmstadt: Wissenschaftliche Buchgesellschaft, 1962), 177–219. – H. Thorossian, *Histoire de la littérature arménienne des origines jusqu'à nos jours* (Paris: Thorossian, 1951). – G. Deeters, G. Solta, and V. Inglisian, *Armenische und kaukasische Sprachen* (HO 1.7; Leiden: Brill, 1963), 157–250. – K. Sarkissian, *Introduction à la littérature arménienne chrétienne* (Cahiers d'études chrétiennes orientales 2; Paris: Le Monde non Chrétien, 1964). – K. Sarkissian, *A Brief Introduction to Armenian Christian Literature* (London: Faith, 1960; Bergenfield: Barour, 1980). – R. W. Thomson, "The Formation of the Armenian Literary Tradition," in *East of Byzantium: Syria and Armenia in the Formative Period* (ed. N. Garsoïan et al.; Washington, D.C.: Dumbarton Oaks, Center for Byzantine Studies, Trustees for Harvard University, 1982), 135–50. – S. P. Hairapetian, *Hay hin ew mijnadarean grakanut'ean patmut'iwn: History of Ancient and Medieval Armenian Literature* (Los Angeles: Hairapetian, 1986). – S. J. Voicu, "La patristica nella letteratura armena (V–X sec.)," in *Complementi interdisciplinari di patrologia* (ed. A. Quacquarelli; Rome: Città Nuova, 1989), 657–96. – R. W. Thomson, *Studies in Armenian Literature and Christianity* (VRCS 451; Aldershot, Eng.; Brookfield, Vt.: Variorum, 1994).

# V. GEORGIAN LITERATURE

Despite the fact that important trade routes between Europe and Asia led through Georgia (known as Iberia in antiquity), the contact with Christianity came relatively late for this country. A bishop by the name Stratophilus, from the Greek colony of Pitzunda (Pityous/Bichvint) in western Georgia (ancient Colchis), situated on the coast of the Black Sea, attended the Council of Nicea (325). At a later time John Chrysostom was to be exiled there (cf. ch. 7.VI). Christianity probably reached that region by sea, for the actual evangelization of Georgia was likely initiated by St. Nino at the time of Emperor Constantine, according to the account in the *Ecclesiastical History* of Rufinus (1[10].11), broadly accepted today as the most reliable. The first documented bishop was John (335–ca. 363). Until the sixth century, the Georgian church was under the sovereignty of the neighboring Armenian church, which also influenced the development of Georgian literature.

The Georgian language is an independent Caucasian language, belonging neither to the Indo-Germanic nor to the Semitic or Tauric language groups. It has its own alphabet of thirty-eight letters and its own script, the precise age of which is still subject to debate. In any case, the earliest witnesses to Georgian literature only begin in the second half of the fifth century, with inscriptions and translations of the Bible and liturgical texts, followed by patristic writings on exegesis, dogmatics, polemics, asceticism, homiletics, poetry, canon law, and hagiographic literature. To a large extent, in antiquity Georgian remained translation literature from the Armenian, Syriac, and Greek languages, and later also from the Arabic, and the original Christian literature in Georgian produced mainly hagiographic materials. Especially notable among the latter are the *Vita* of St. Nino and the *Martyrdom of Saint Shushanik*, written ca. 480.

*Dictionaries:* R. Meckelein, *Georgisch-Deutsches Wörterbuch* (Berlin and Leipzig: de Gruyter, 1928). – E. Cherkesi, *Georgian-English Dictionary* (Oxford: Printed for the trustees of the Marjory Wardrop Fund, University of Oxford, 1950). – J. Molitor, *Altgeorgisches Glossar zu ausgewählten Bibeltexten* (Monumenta biblica et ecclesiastica 6; Rome: Pontificium Institutum Biblicum, 1952). – K. Tschenkéli and Y. Marchev, *Georgisch-Deutsches Wörterbuch* (4 vols.; Zurich: Amirani, 1960–1974). – J. Molitor, *Glossarium ibericum* (6 vols.; CSCO 228, 237, 243, 265, 280, 373; Louvain: SCO, 1962–1976). – T. Gvarjaladze and I. Gvarjaladze, *Georgian-English Dictionary: 10,000 Words* (Tbilisi, Georgia: Ganat'leba, 1965). – O. Xuc'išvili, *K'art'ul-germanuli lek'sikoni: Georgisch-Deutsches Wörterbuch* (Tbilisi, Georgia: Ganat'leba, 1977). – T. T'oraže, *K'art'uli-inglisuri lek'sikoni—4700 sitqva: Georgian-English Dictionary* (Tbilisi, Georgia: Gamomc'emloba "Mnat'obi," 1994).

*Grammars:* F. Zorell, *Grammatik zur altgeorgischen Bibelübersetzung mit Textproben und Wörterverzeichnis* (Rome: Päpstliches Bibelinstitut, 1930; repr., 1978). – H. Fähnrich and A. Schanidse, *Altgeorgisches Elementarbuch* (trans. H. Fähnrich; Tbilisi, Georgia: Universitätsverlag, 1982); trans. of *Jveli k'art'uli enis gramatika* (Tbilisi, Georgia: T'bilisis Universitetis Gamomc'emloba, 1976). – R. Zwolanek and J. Assfalg, *Altgeorgische Kurzgrammatik* (Orbis biblicus et orientalis 2; Fribourg, Switz.: Universitätsverlag; Göttingen: Vandenhoeck & Ruprecht, 1976).

*Journals: Bedi K'art'lisa: Revue de karthvélologie* (Paris, 1948–1984) *[BeKa]. – Revue des études géorgiennes et caucasiennes* (Paris, 1985–) *[REGC]*.

*Encyclopedia Articles:* R. Janin, *DTC* 6/1:1239–89. – G. Garitte, *DSp* 6:244–56. – M. Falla Castelfranchi, *EECh* 1:344–45. – M. van Esbroeck, *EECh* 1:345. – J. Assfalg and D. M. Marshall, *TRE* 12:389–96. – R. Aubert, *DHGE* 20:681–83. – J. Assfalg, *LTK* 4:490–92. – O. Lordkipanidse and H. Brakmann, *RAC* 17:12–106. – C. Cox, *EEC* 1:460.

*History of the Literature:* G. Peradze, "Die alt-christliche Literatur in der georgischen Überlieferung," *OrChr* 3.3–4 (1928–1929): 109–16, 282–88; 5 (1930): 80–98, 233–36; 6 (1931): 97–107, 241–44; 8 (1933): 86–92, 180–98. – J. Karst, *Littérature géorgienne chrétienne* (Paris: Bloud & Gay, 1934). – M. Tarchnischvili and J. Assfalg, *Geschichte der kirchlichen georgischen Literatur* (StT 185; Vatican City: Biblioteca Apostolica Vaticana, 1955). – K. Kekelidze, *Etiudebi dzveli k'art'uli literaturis istoridan [Studies on the History of Ancient Georgian Literature]* (14 vols.; Tbilisi, Georgia: Stalinis saxelobis T'bilisis Saxelmcip'o Universitetis Gamomc'emloba, 1945–1986). – K. Kekelidze, *K'art'uli literaturis istoria* (2 vols.; Tbilisi, Georgia: Saxelmcip'o Gamomc'emloba "Sabcot'a Sak'art'velo," 1960). – K. Kekelidze, *Histoire de la littérature géorgienne I* (4th ed.; Tbilisi, Georgia: n.p., 1960). – I. Abuladze, *Žveli k'art'uli agiograp'iuli literaturis*

*żeglebi* (6 vols.; Tbilisi, Georgia: Sak'art'velos SSR Mec'nierebat'a Akademiis Gamomc'emloba, 1963–1989). – D. M. Lang, *Landmarks in Georgian Literature: An In-
augural Lecture Delivered on 2 November 1965* (London: School of Oriental and
African Studies, University of London, 1966). – M. van Esbroeck, *Les plus anciens
homéliaires géorgiens: Étude descriptive et historique* (PIOL 10; Louvain: Université
Catholique de Louvain, Institut Orientaliste, 1975). – H. Fähnrich, *Georgische Literatur* (Aachen: Shaker, 1993). – G. Deeters, G. Solta, and V. Inglisian, *Armenische und
kaukasische Sprachen* (HO 1.7; Leiden: Brill, 1963), 129–55.

# VI. ARABIC LITERATURE

The Arabic language intersects with the patristic era insofar as the Muslim
conquest of the Near East, North Africa, and Spain coincided with the final
period of ancient Christian literature. By the time of the death of John of Damascus (ca. 750; cf. ch. 12.IV), regarded as the last of the Greek fathers, Islam had
conquered all of Armenia, Syria, Palestine, Egypt, North Africa, and Spain. John
was born and raised in this environment, and as long as Christianity was tolerated by Islam (until ca. 700), he, like his father and grandfather, held important
offices at the court of the caliph, with whom he had been friends since childhood.
Nevertheless Arabic belongs to the secondary patristic languages, for there are no
original Arabic patristic texts; extant are only translations from Greek, Aramaic,
Syriac, Coptic, and in Spain some from Latin.

Essentially the Christian Arabic language is not distinct from the classical
Arabic of the Qur'an. Even the earliest documents, written in a local dialect, in
the Syrian-Palestinian territory are not unaffected by classical Arabic, but a thorough alignment does not come about until the eleventh century; all the same, a
thoroughly Christian "technical" vocabulary is retained. The Arabic script is derived from Nabataean, an Aramaic dialect of southeastern Palestine, and therefore resembles Syriac. The earliest Christian inscriptions are found in Zebed
(512) and Harran (568); but whether pre-Islamic Christian literature, such as a
translation of the Bible, ever existed, remains subject to debate.

The earliest manuscripts of Arabic Christian literature come from 885. Its
first phase included translations of biblical and hagiographic works, patristic
writings, canon law and liturgical texts, and linguistic and scientific works. This
was followed by original Arabic Christian literature in the various churches
(Melkites, Maronites, western and eastern Syrians [Nestorians, Jacobites, Chal-
deans], Copts, and Arabic-speaking Armenians) in thousands of writings—some
of them historically significant—until the nineteenth century. Later on translations were undertaken from Arabic into Georgian and, beginning in the twelfth
century, into Ethiopic. The wealth of Christian Arabic literature can be explained by the number and expansion of the Arabic-speaking churches, on the
one hand, and by its function of introducing Greek philosophy and science into
Arabic culture, on the other. Particularly significant, for instance, is the *History of
the Patriarchs of Alexandria* by Severus ibn al-Muqaffa; among other things, this
is presumably the most reliable source for the *Vita* of Athanasius of Alexandria

(cf. ch. 5.IV). Further, the importance of Christian Arabic literature for patristics is based also on the fact that it preserves numerous otherwise lost pieces of patristic writings.

*Bibliographies:* R. Caspar et al., "Bibliographie du dialogue islamo-chrétien," *Islamochristiana* 1 (1975): 125–81; 2 (1976): 187–249.

*Dictionaries:* E. W. Lane, *An Arabic-English Lexicon* (8 vols.; London: Williams & Norgate, 1863–1893; repr., 2 vols.; Cambridge: Islamic Texts Society, 1984). – G. Graf, *Verzeichnis arabischer kirchlicher Termini* (2d ed.; CSCO 147; Louvain: Durbecq, 1954). – H. Wehr, *Arabisches Wörterbuch für die Schriftsprache der Gegenwart* (5th rev. ed.; Wiesbaden: Harrassowitz, 1985; repr., 1998); [ET] *A Dictionary of Modern Written Arabic: Arabic-English* (ed. J. M. Cowan; 4th enlarged ed.; Ithaca, N.Y.: Spoken Language Services, 1994). – M. Ullmann et al., *Wörterbuch der klassischen arabischen Sprache* (Wiesbaden: Harrassowitz, 1957–). – *Vocabolario arabo-italiano* (3 vols.; Rome: Istituto per l'Oriente, 1966–1973). – G. Schregle, *Arabisch-Deutsches Wörterbuch* (Wiesbaden: Steiner, 1981–).

*Grammars:* L. Veccia Vaglieri, *Grammatica teorico-pratica della lingua araba* (3d ed.; 2 vols.; Rome: Istituto per l'Oriente, 1941–1961). – J. Blau, *A Grammar of Christian Arabic, Based Mainly on South-Palestinian Texts from the First Millennium* (3 vols.; CSCO 267, 276, 279; Louvain: SCO, 1966–1967). – W. Fischer, *A Grammar of Classical Arabic* (trans. J. Rodgers; 3d ed.; New Haven: Yale University Press, 2002); trans. of *Grammatik des klassischen Arabisch* (3d ed.; Wiesbaden: Harrassowitz, 2002). – M. Gaudefroy-Demombynes and R. Blachère, *Grammaire de l'arabe classique* (3d ed.; Paris: Maisonneuve Larose, 1984). – C. P. Caspari, *A Grammar of the Arabic Language* (trans. W. Wright; 3d rev. ed.; ed. W. R. Smith and M. J. de Goeje; Cambridge: Cambridge University Press, 1991; repr., 1995).

*Journals: Al-Andalus: Revista de la Escuelas de Estudios Árabes de Madrid y Granada* (Madrid, 1933–1978). – *Arabica* (Leiden, 1954–). – *Bulletin d'arabe chrétien* (Heverlee, Belg., 1976–) *[BACh].* – *Mélanges de l'Institut dominicain d'études orientales du Caire* (Cairo, 1954–) *[MIDEO].* – *Mélanges de la Faculté orientale de l'Université Saint-Josèph* (Beirut, 1906–1921) *[MFOB].*

*Encyclopedia Articles:* M. Höfner, *RAC* 1:575–85. – B. Spuler, *TRE* 3:577–87. – M. van Esbroeck, C. Nardi, and B. Bagatti, *EECh* 1:65–67. – M. van Esbroeck, *LTK* 1:906–7. – S. H. Griffith, "Arabia," *EEC* 1:98. – J. P. Amar, "Arabic Christian Literature," *EEC* 1:98–99.

*Manuals:* C. Brockelmann, *Geschichte der arabischen Literatur* (2 vols.; 2d ed. with supplement; Leiden: Brill, 1943–1949). – C. Brockelmann, *Geschichte der islamischen Völker und Staaten* (6 vols.; Hildesheim: Olms, 1977). – G. Graf, *Geschichte der christlichen arabischen Literatur* (5 vols.; StT 118, 133, 146–47, 172; Vatican City: Biblioteca Apostolica Vaticana, 1944–1953). – F. Sezkin, *Geschichte des arabischen Schrifttums bis ca. 430 H.* (Leiden: Brill, 1967–).

*Studies:* I. Shahid, *Byzantium and the Arabs in the Fourth Century* (Washington, D.C.: Dumbarton Oaks Research Library and Collection, 1984). – K. Samir, ed., *Actes du deuxième Congrès international d'études arabes chrétiennes* (OrChrAn 226; Rome: Pontificium Institutum Studiorum Orientalium, 1986). – I. Shahid, *Byzantium and the Arabs in the Fifth Century* (Washington, D.C.: Dumbarton Oaks Research Library and Collection, 1989). – S. H. Griffith, *Arabic Christianity in the Monasteries of Ninth-Century Palestine* (VRCS 380; Aldershot, Eng.: Variorum; Brookfield, Vt.: Ashgate, 1992). – I. Shahid, *Byzantium and the Arabs in the Sixth Century* (Washington, D.C.: Dumbarton Oaks Research Library and Collection, 1995–).

# VII. PALEOSLAVIC LITERATURE

The original tribal areas of the Slavs were probably nestled between the rivers Vistula and Dnieper. Their westward migration had already begun by ca. 500 B.C.E.; it was not until the fourth and fifth centuries C.E., however, that the Goths and Huns forced them into southern Europe. From the late sixth century, they took possession of the Roman regions of Noricum, Pannonia, Dalmatia, and the Balkan Peninsula as far as Greece. Their christianization began in 863 under the Greek brothers Cyril and Methodius, who for this reason were given the honorific title "apostles of the Slavs" and, along with St. Benedict, were declared to be "patrons of Europe" in 1980. Since Slavic did not have a script of its own, Cyril developed from the Greek minuscule and elements of oriental alphabets the so-called Glagolitsa for vernacular liturgy and ecclesiastical literature. It spread from Moravia to Bohemia, Macedonia, Bulgaria, the Croatian coast, Serbia, and Bosnia and all the way to Romania and southern Russia. Although it was increasingly displaced by the new Cyrillic alphabet beginning in the tenth century, it persisted in Croatia, where the original round Glagolitsa gave rise to the present angular form beginning in the thirteenth century.

All this is after the patristic era; but since Cyril and Methodius began to translate not only the Bible and liturgical books of the church but also works of the church fathers into Old Church Slavonic, this provided a not insignificant secondary tradition of patristic works. In Byzantium the ninth century marks the transition from the majuscule to the minuscule script, so that many texts have only been preserved in their Slavonic translation. Among the favorite writers were Basil the Great, John Chrysostom, and Gregory of Nazianzus, especially because of their liturgies, as well as *De fide orthodoxa*, a dogmatic manual by John of Damascus. The following are also worth mentioning:

- extensive *Hexaemeron* of John Exarchus (mid-ninth century), a compilation of works with the same title by Basil, Severian of Gabala, John Chrysostom, and further sources;

- translation of *De libero arbitrio* of Methodius of Olympus (early tenth century), of which only a few fragments have been preserved in Greek;

- *Topographia christiana* of Cosmas Indicopleustes;

- *Paraenesis* of Ephraem Syrus (first half of tenth century);

- commentary on Daniel by Hippolytus of Rome, only the larger part of which is extant in Greek but which is preserved in full in Old Church Slavonic;

- *Scala paradisi* of John Climacus;

- baptismal catecheses of Cyril of Jerusalem;

- works of Pseudo-Dionysius the Areopagite (ninth/tenth century).

*Collections of Texts:* F. W. Mares, *An Anthology of Church Slavonic Texts of Western (Czech) Origin: With an Outline of Czech-Church Slavonic Language and Literature and with a Selected Bibliography* (Munich: Fink, 1979).

*Dictionaries:* F. Miklosich, *Lexicon palaeoslovenico-graeco-latinum* (rev. ed.; Vienna: G. Braumueller, 1862–1865; repr., Aalen: Scientia, 1963, 1977). – L. Sadnik and R. Aitzetmüller, *Handwörterbuch zu den altkirchenslavischen Texten* (s'-Gravenhage: Mouton, 1955; repr., Heidelberg: Winter, 1989). – *Lexicon linguae palaeoslovenicae* (Prague: Československé Akademie Věd, 1966–). – T. A. Lysaght, *Material towards the Compilation of a Concise Old Church Slavonic-English Dictionary* (Wellington: Victoria University Press with Price Milburn, 1978).

*Grammars:* P. Diels, *Altkirchenslavische Grammatik: Mit einer Auswahl von Texten und einem Wörterbuch* (2d ed.; Heidelberg: Winter, 1963). – A. Leskien, *Handbuch der altbulgarischen (altkirchenslavischen) Sprache: Grammatik–Texte–Glossar* (9th ed.; Heidelberg: Winter, 1969). – A. Tovar, *Antiguo eslavo eclesiástico (antiguo búlgaro): Paradigmas gramaticales, textos, léxico* (2d ed.; Madrid: Editorial de la Universidad Complutense, 1987). – N. S. Trubetzkoy, *Altkirchenslavische Grammatik: Schrift-, Laut-, und Formensystem* (SÖAW.PH 228.4; Vienna: In Kommission bei R. M. Rohrer, 1954). – H. H. Bielefeldt, *Altslavische Grammatik: Einführung in die slawischen Sprachen* (Halle: Niemeyer, 1961). – H. G. Lunt, *Old Church Slavonic Grammar* (7th rev. ed.; Berlin and New York: de Gruyter, 2001).

*Journals: Byzantinoslavica* (Prague, 1929–) *[BySl]. – Revue des études slaves* (Paris, 1921–) *[RESl]. – Ricerche slavistiche* (Rome, 1952–; NS 2003–). – *Studia slavica Academiae scientiarum hungaricae* (Budapest, 1955–) *[SSH]. – Zeitschrift für slavische Philologie* (Leipzig, 1924–) *[ZSlP].*

*Encyclopedia Articles:* R. Rogosic, *LTK²* 4:906–8. – I. Dujcev, *DPAC* 2:2575–81. – F. W. Mares, *LMA* 5:1178–80.

*History of the Literature:* A. S. Archangelskij, *Tvorenija otcov Cerkvi v drevne-russkoj pis'mennosti: Izvlecenija iz rukopisej i opyty istoriko-literaturnych izucenj I–IV* (Kazan, Russia: Tip. Imp. Universiter, 1889–1890). – M. Murko, *Geschichte der älteren südslawischen Literaturen* (Die Literaturen des Ostens 5.2; Leipzig: C. F. Amelang, 1908; repr., Munich: Trofenik, 1971).

# Supplementary Bibliography

by William Harmless, SJ

## General Bibliography

*Dictionaries & Encyclopedias of Early Christianity:* J.A. McGuckin, *The Westminster Handbook to Patristic Theology* (Louisville: Westminster John Knox, 2004).
*General Dictionaries for Theology and Church:* P. Levillain, ed., *The Papacy: An Encyclopedia* (3 vols.; New York: Routledge, 2001). – J. Pelikan and V. Hotchkiss, eds., *Creeds and Confessions of Faith in the Christian Tradition* (4 vols.; New Haven: Yale University Press, 2003). – J. Bowden, ed., *Encyclopedia of Christianity* (New York: Oxford University Press, 2005).
*General Encyclopedias for Classical Antiquity and Byzantium:* J. Roberts, ed., *Oxford Dictionary of the Classical World* (New York: Oxford University Press, 2005).
*Patrologies and Histories of Literature:* F. Young, L. Ayres, and A. Louth, eds., *The Cambridge History of Early Christian Literature* (Cambridge and New York: Cambridge University Press, 2004).
*Series of Translations:*
The Ancient Christian Commentary on Scripture (ed. T. C. Oden and C. H. Hall; Downers Grove, Ill.: InterVarsity, 1998–).

> The Ancient Christian Commentary revives the medieval tradition of the *glossa ordinaria*—taking the biblical text verse by verse and citing excerpts from the Fathers' commentary. Projected to be 27 volumes, it draws on ancient commentaries in Greek, Latin, Syriac, and Coptic.

The Early Church Fathers series (ed. C. Harrison; London and New York: Routledge, 1996–).

> This series focuses each volume on an individual church father (e.g., Origen, Tertullian, Athanasius, Jerome, Chrysostom, Maximus the Confessor); each volume has a lengthy introduction followed by new translations of major (and often previously untranslated) works.

Popular Patristics Series (ed. J. Behr; Crestwood, N.Y.: St. Vladimir's Seminary Press, 1977–).

> Volumes focus on individual works (e.g., Irenaeus's *On the Apostolic Preaching*, Cyril of Alexandria's *On the Unity of Christ*).

*Surveys and Manuals (History, Philology, Theology):*

H. Chadwick, *The Church in Ancient Society: From Galilee to Gregory the Great* (Oxford History of the Christian Church; Oxford and New York: Oxford University Press, 2002).

> A well-written comprehensive one-volume survey of the history of the early church.

P. F. Esler, ed. *The Early Christian World* (2 vols.; London and New York: Routledge, 2000).

> This collection of essays surveys early Christianity from a variety of angles: its social and intellectual world, its art and worship, its leaders and their clashes. Volume 2 closes with profiles of church fathers: Origen, Tertullian, Perpetua, Constantine, Antony, Athanasius, Jerome, Ambrose, Augustine, and Ephrem.

G. R. Evans, ed., *First Christian Theologians: An Introduction to Theology in the Early Church* (The Great Theologians; Oxford: Blackwell, 2004).

> This volume offers brief chapters that survey the biography, writings, and theology of individual church fathers. Chapters are authored by leading specialists.

*The Cambridge Ancient History* (Cambridge and New York: Cambridge University Press, 1970–).

> Three volumes are of relevance to early Christian studies:
>
> Vol. 11: A. K. Bowman, P. Garnsey, and D. Rathbone, eds., *The High Empire, A.D. 70–192* (2001).
>
> Vol. 13: A. Cameron and P. Garnsey, eds., *The Late Empire, A.D. 337–425* (1998).
>
> Vol. 14: A. Cameron, B. Ward-Perkins, and M. Whitby, eds. *Late Antiquity: Empire and Successors, A.D. 425–600* (2001).

*Patrology as a Subject:* D. Brakke, "The Early Church in North America: Late Antiquity, Theory, and the History of Christianity," *ChH* 71 (2002): 473–91.

# PART ONE

## *Chapter One: Biblical Apocrypha*

*Formation of the Biblical Canon:* C. Helmer and C. Landmesser, eds., *One Scripture or Many? Canon from Biblical, Theological, and Philosophical Perspectives* (Oxford and New York: Oxford University Press, 2004).

*Biblical Apocrypha—Gospels:* D. R. Cartlidge, *Art and the Christian Apocrypha* (London and New York: Routledge, 2001). – B. Ehrman, ed., *Lost Scriptures: Books That Did Not Make It into the New Testament* (New York: Oxford University Press, 2003). – H.-J. Klauck, *Apocryphal Gospels: An Introduction* (trans. Brian McNeil; London: T&T Clark, 2003).

*Protevangelium of James:* M. F. Foskett, *A Virgin Conceived: Mary and Classical Representations of Virginity* (Bloomington: Indiana University Press, 2002). – T. Horner, "Jewish Aspects of the *Protoevangelium of James*," *JECS* 12 (2004): 313–35.

*Coptic Gospel of Thomas:* A. Siverstev, "The *Gospel of Thomas* and Early Stages in the Development of Christian Wisdom Literature," *JECS* 8 (2000): 319–40. – A.D. Deconinck, "The Original *Gospel of Thomas*," *VigChr* 56 (2002): 167–99. – N. Perrin, *Thomas and Tatian: The Relationship between the Gospel of Thomas and the Diatessaron* (Academia biblica 5; Leiden and Boston: Brill, 2002).

*Apocryphal Acts of Peter:* F. Bovon, "Canonical and Apocryphal Acts of Apostles," *JECS* 11 (2003): 165–94. – C. M. Thomas, *The Acts of Peter, Gospel Literature, and the Ancient Novel: Rewriting the Past* (New York: Oxford University Press, 2003).

*Apocryphal Acts of Paul:* S. J. Davis, *The Cult of Saint Thecla: A Tradition of Women's Piety in Late Antiquity* (OECS; Oxford and New York: Oxford University Press, 2001).

*Letter of Barnabas:* J. N. Rhodes, *The Epistle of Barnabas and the Deuteronomic Tradition: Polemics, Paraenesis, and the Legacy of the Golden-Calf Incident* (WUNT 188; Tübingen: Mohr Siebeck, 2004).

# Chapter Two: Postapostolic Literature

*The Apostolic Fathers—Editions:* B. D. Ehrman, ed., *The Apostolic Fathers* (LCL 24–25; Cambridge, Mass.: Harvard University Press, 2003). [1 and 2 Clement, Ignatius, Polycarp, *Didache*, Barnabas, Papias, Quadratus, *Epistle to Diognetus, Shepherd of Hermas*].

*The Apostolic Fathers—Studies:* F. A. Sullivan, *From Apostles to Bishops: The Development of the Episcopacy in the Early Church* (New York: Paulist, 2001).

*First Clement:* O. M. Bakke, *"Concord and Peace": A Rhetorical Analysis of the First Letter of Clement with an Emphasis on the Language of Unity and Sedition* (WUNT 143; Tübingen: Mohr Siebeck, 2001). – G. D. Dunn, "Clement of Rome and the Question of Roman Primacy in the Early African Tradition," *Aug* 43 (2003): 1–24. – C. Breytenbach and L. L. Welborn, eds., *Encounters with Hellenism: Studies on the First Letter of Clement* (AGJU 53; Leiden and Boston: Brill, 2004)

*Ignatius of Antioch:* P. A. Harland, "Christ-Bearers and Fellow-Initiates: Local Cultural Life and Christian Identity in Ignatius' Letters," *JECS* 11 (2003): 481–99. – H. O. Maier, "The Politics of the Silent Bishop: Silence and Persuasion in Ignatius of Antioch," *JTS* NS 55 (2004): 503–19.

*Polycarp of Smyrna:* K. Berding, *Polycarp and Paul: An Analysis of Their Literary and Theological Relationship in Light of Polycarp's Use of Biblical and Extra-biblical Literature,* SVgrChr 62 (Leiden and Boston: Brill, 2002). – P. A.

Hartog, *Polycarp and the New Testament: The Occasion, Rhetoric, Theme, and Unity of the Epistle to the Philippians and Its Allusions to New Testament Literature* (WUNT 134; Tübingen: Mohr Siebeck, 2002).

*Didache*—Edition: A. Milavec, *The Didache: Text, Translation, Analysis, and Commentary* (Collegeville, Minn.: Liturgical, 2004) [ET, com].

*Didache*—Studies: R. E. Aldridge, "The Lost Ending of the *Didache*," *VC* 53 (1999): 1–15. – J. A. Draper, "Ritual Process and Ritual Symbol in *Didache* 7–10," *VC* 54 (2000): 121–58. – H. van de Sandt and D. Flusser, eds., *The Didache: Its Jewish Sources and Its Place in Early Judaism and Christianity* (Minneapolis: Fortress, 2002). – A. Milavec, *The Didache: Faith, Hope and Life of the Earliest Christian Communities, 50–73 C.E.* (New York: Paulist, 2003). – M. Del Verme, *Didache and Judaism: Jewish Roots of an Ancient Christian-Jewish Work* (New York: T&T Clark, 2004).

# PART TWO

## Introduction: The Impact of Persecution

*Christianity and the Pagan World / Philosophy / Culture:* A. D. Lee, *Pagans and Christians in Late Antiquity: A Sourcebook* (London and New York: Routledge, 2000). – R. L. Wilken, *Christians as the Romans Saw Them* (2d ed.; New Haven: Yale University Press, 2003). – G. Clark, *Christianity and Roman Society* (Key Themes in Ancient History; Cambridge and New York: Cambridge University Press, 2004). – A. Smith, *Philosophy in Late Antiquity* (London and New York: Routledge, 2004).

*Jews and Christians:* D. Boyarin, *Border Lines: The Partition of Judaeo-Christianity* (Philadelphia: University of Pennsylvania Press, 2004). – M. Goodman, *Jews in a Greco-Roman World* (New York: Oxford University Press, 2004).

## Chapter Three: Greek Literature

*Greek Apologists: Editions:* Aristide, *Apologie* (ed. B. Pouderon, M.-J. Pierre, B. Outtier, and M. Guiorgadzé; SC 470; Paris: Cerf, 2003).

*Justin Martyr—Editions:* Dialogue avec Tryphon: Edition critique, traduction, commentaire (ed. P. Bobichon, 2 vols.; Par. 47.1–2; Fribourg, Switz.: Academic Press Fribourg, 2003).

*Justin Martyr—Studies:* T. J. Horner, *Listening to Trypho: Justin Martyr's Dialogue with Trypho Reconsidered* (Contributions to Biblical Exegesis and Theology 28; Leuven: Peeters, 2001). – D. Boyarin, "Justin Martyr Invents Judaism," *ChH* 70 (2001): 427–61. – P. Widdicombe, "Justin Martyr's Apophaticism," *StPatr* 36 (2001): 313–19. – C. D. Allert, *Revelation, Truth, Canon, and In-*

*terpretation: Studies in Justin Martyr's Dialogue with Trypho* (SVigChr 64; Leiden: Brill, 2002). – P. L. Buck, "Justin Martyr's *Apologies:* Their Number, Destination, and Form," *JTS* NS 54 (2003): 45–59. – A. Hofer, "The Old Man as Christ in Justin's *Dialogue with Trypho*," *VC* 57 (2003) 1–21. – A. Y. Reed, "The Trickery of the Fallen Angels and the Demonic Mimesis of the Divine: Aetiology, Demonology, and Polemics in the Writings of Justin Martyr," *JECS* 12 (2004): 141–71.

*Tatian of Syria:* R. F. Shedinger, *Tatian and the Jewish Scriptures: A Textual and Philological Analysis of the Old Testament Citations in Tatian's Diatessaron,* CSCO 591 (Louvain: Peeters, 2001). – J. Joosten, "The Gospel of Barnabas and the Diatessaron," *HTR* 95 (2002): 73–96. – K. L. Gaca, "Driving Aphrodite from the World: Tatian's Encratite Principles of Sexual Renunciation," *JTS* NS (2002) 28–52. – E. J. Hunt, *Christianity in the Second Century: The Case of Tatian* (Routledge Early Church Monographs; New York: Routledge, 2003). – J. Joosten, "The Dura Parchment and the Diatessaron," *VC* 57 (2003): 159–75. – U. B. Schmid, "In Search of Tatian's Diatessaron in the West," *VC* 57 (2003): 176–99.

*Melito of Sardis—Studies:* L. H. Cohick, *The Peri Pascha Attributed to Melito of Sardis: Setting, Purpose, and Sources* (Providence, R.I.: Brown Judaic Studies, 2000). – H. M. Knapp, "Melito's Use of Scripture in *Peri Pascha:* Second-Century Typology," *VC* 54 (2000): 343–74. – *Translation:* A. Stewart-Sykes, trans., *On Pascha: Melito of Sardis* (Popular Patristics Series; Crestwood, N.Y.: St. Vladimir's Seminary Press, 2001).

*Martyrdom:* D. Boyarin, *Dying for God: Martyrdom and the Making of Christianity and Judaism* (Figurae: Reading Medieval Culture; Stanford, Calif.: Stanford University Press, 1999). – J. W. van Henten and F. Avemarie, eds., *Martyrdom and Noble Death: Selected Texts from Greco-Roman, Jewish, and Christian Antiquity* (Context of Early Christianity; London and New York: Routledge, 2002). – A. McGowan, "Discipline and Diet: Feeding the Martyrs in Roman Carthage," *HTR* 96 (2003): 455–76. – J. Leemans, W. Mayer, P. Allen, and B. Dehandschutter, eds., *"Let Us Die That We May Live": Greek Homilies on Christian Martyrs from Asia Minor, Palestine, and Syria (c. AD 350–AD 450)* (London and New York: Routledge, 2003). – J. E. Salisbury, *The Blood of the Martyrs: Unintended Consequences of Ancient Violence* (London and New York: Routledge, 2004).

*Gnosticism:* H. W. Attridge, "Valentinian and Sethian Apocalyptic Traditions," *JECS* 8 (2000) 173–211. – A. H. B. Logan, "Gnosticism," in *The Early Christian World* (ed. P. F. Esler; 2 vols.; London and New York: Routledge, 2000), 2:907–28. – A. L. Molinari, *I Never Knew the Man: The Coptic Acts of Peter (Papyrus berolinensis 8502.4): Its Independence from the Apocryphal Acts of Peter, Genre and Legendary Origins* (Bibliothèque copte de Nag Hammadi: Section "Études 5"; Québec: Presses de l'Université Laval, 2000). – R. Valantasis, "Nag Hammadi and Asceticism: Theory and Practice," *StPatr* 35 (2001): 172–90. – H.-G. Bethge, ed., *For the Children, Perfect Instruction: Studies in Honor of Hans-Martin Schenke on the Occasion of the Berliner*

*Arbeitskresis für koptisch-gnostische Schriften's Thirtieth Year*, NHS 54 (Leiden and Boston: Brill, 2002). – B. A. Pearson, *Gnosticism and Christianity in Roman and Coptic Egypt* (Studies in Antiquity and Christianity; New York: T&T Clark, 2004). – J. A. Kelhoffer, "Basilides's Gospel and *Exegetica* (*Treatises*)," *VC* 59 (2005): 115–34.

*Montanism:* C. Trevett, "Montanism," in *The Early Christian World* (ed. P. F. Esler; 2 vols.; London and New York: Routledge, 2000), 2:929–51. – W. Tabbernee, "To Pardon or Not to Pardon? North African Montanism and the Forgiveness of Sins," *StPatr* 36 (2001): 375–86. – W. Tabbernee, "Portals of the Montantist New Jerusalem: The Discovery of Pepouza and Tymion," *JECS* 11 (2003): 87–93.

*Irenaeus of Lyons:* J. Behr, *Asceticism and Anthropology in Irenaeus and Clement* (OECS; Oxford and New York: Oxford University Press, 2000). – J. Behr, "Irenaeus on the Word of God," *StPatr* 36 (2001): 163–67. – D. J. Bingham, "Knowledge and Love in Irenaeus of Lyons," *StPatr* 36 (2001): 184–99. – E. F. Osborn, *Irenaeus of Lyons* (Cambridge: Cambridge University Press, 2001). – A. Y. Reed, "'Εὐαγγέλιον: Orality, Textuality, and the Christian Truth in Irenaeus' *Adversus haereses*," *VC* 56 (2002): 11–46. – J. Driscoll, "Uncovering the Dynamic of *Lex orandi–lex credendi* in the Baptismal Theology of Irenaeus," *Pro ecclesia* 12 (2003): 213–25. – M. C. Steenberg, "Children in Paradise: Adam and Eve as 'Infants' in Irenaeus of Lyons," *JECS* 12 (2004): 1–22.

*Hippolytus of Rome—Translation:* A. Stewart-Sykes, ed., *Hippolytus: On the Apostolic Tradition* (Popular Patristics Series; Crestwood, N.Y.: St. Vladimir Seminary Press, 2001). – *Studies:* J. A. Cerrato, *Hippolytus between East and West: The Commentaries and the Provenance of the Corpus* (OTM; New York: Oxford University Press, 2002). – P. Bradshaw, M. E. Johnson, and L. E. Phillips, eds., *The Apostolic Tradition: A Commentary* (Hermeneia Series; Minneapolis: Fortress, 2002). – J. F. Baldovin, "Hippolytus and the Apostolic Tradition: Recent Research and Commentary," *TS* 64 (2003): 520–42.

*Patristic Exegesis:* P. M. Blowers et al., eds., *In dominico eloquio = In Lordly Eloquence: Essays on Patristic Exegesis in Honor of Robert Louis Wilken* (Grand Rapids: Eerdmans, 2002). – C. A. Bobertz and D. Brakke, eds., *Reading in Christian Communities: Essays on Interpretation in the Early Church* (Notre Dame, Ind.: University of Notre Dame Press, 2002). – C. Kannengiesser, ed., *Handbook of Patristic Exegesis: The Bible in Ancient Christianity* (2 vols., Bible in Ancient Christianity 1–2; Leiden and Boston: Brill, 2004). – J. J. O'Keefe and R. R. Reno, *Sanctified Vision: An Introduction to Early Christian Interpretation of the Bible* (Baltimore: Johns Hopkins University Press, 2005).

*Clement of Alexandria—Editions: Les Stromates (Stromate IV)* (ed. A. van den Hoek and C. Mondésert; SC 463; Paris: Cerf, 2001).

*Clement of Alexandria—Studies:* J. L. Kovacs, "Divine Pedagogy and the Gnostic Teacher according to Clement of Alexandria," *JECS* 9 (2001): 3–25. –

A. Choufrine, *Gnosis, Theophany, Theosis: Studies in Clement of Alexandria's Appropriation of His Background* (Patristic Studies 5; New York: Peter Lang, 2002). – D. T. Runia, "Clement of Alexandria and the Philonic Doctrine of the Divine Power(s)," *VC* 58 (2004): 256–76.

*Origen—Editions: Homélies sur les Nombres* (ed. L. Doutreleau; SC 461; Paris: Cerf, 2001).

*Origen—Translations: Commentary on the Epistle to the Romans* (trans. Thomas P. Scheck; 2 vols.; FC 103–4; Washington, D.C.: Catholic University of America Press, 2001–2002). – *Homilies on Joshua* (trans. Barbara J. Brucel; FC 105; Washington, D.C.: Catholic University of America Press, 2002). – *The Commentaries of Origen and Jerome on St. Paul's Letter to the Ephesians* (ed. R. Heine, OECS; Oxford and New York: Oxford University Press, 2003). – *Tertullian, Cyprian, Origen: On the Lord's Prayer* (trans. A. Stewart-Sykes; Popular Patristics Series; Crestwood, N.Y.: St. Vladimir's Seminary Press, 2004) [*De oratione*].

*Origen—Reference Works:* J. A. McGuckin, ed., *The Westminister Handbook to Origen* (Louisville: Westminster John Knox, 2004).

*Origen—Studies:* R. A. Layton, "Recovering Origen's Pauline Exegesis: Exegesis and Eschatology in the *Commentary on Ephesians*," *JECS* 8 (2000): 373–411. – F. Norris, "Origen," in *The Early Christian World* (ed. P. F. Esler; 2 vols.; London and New York: Routledge, 2000), 2:1005–26. – L. Perrone, "Prayer in Origen's *Contra Celsum:* The Knowledge of God and the Truth of Christianity," *VC* 55 (2001): 1–19. – F. Ledegang, *Mysterium ecclesiae: Images of the Church and Its Members in Origen* (BETL 156; Leuven: Leuven University Press, 2001). – M. J. Edwards, *Origen against Plato* (Ashgate Studies in Philosophy & Theology in Late Antiquity; Burlington, Vt.: Ashgate, 2002). – R. E. Heine, *The Commentaries of Origen and Jerome on St. Paul's Epistle to the Ephesians* (OECS; Oxford and New York: Oxford University Press, 2002). – L. Perrone, *Origeniana octava—Origen and the Alexandrian Tradition: Papers of the 8th International Origen Congress, Pisa, 27–31 August 2001* (Leuven: Leuven University Press; Peeters, 2003). – B. Dunkle, "A Development in Origen's View of the Natural Law," *Pro ecclesia* 13 (2004): 337–51.

*Pamphilus of Caesarea (and Eusebius of Caesarea)—Editions: Apologie pour Origène* (ed. R. Amacker and E. Junod; SC 464–65; Paris: Cerf, 2002) [*Apologeticum pro Origene*]

# Chapter Four: Beginnings of Latin Literature

*Tertullian—Editions: Contre Marcion (Livre V)* (ed. R. Braun and C. Moreschini; SC 483; Paris: Cerf, 2004) [*Adversus Marcionem* V].

*Tertullian—Translations: Christian and Pagan in the Roman Empire: The Witness of Tertullian* (ed. R. D. Sider; Washington, D.C.: Catholic University of America Press, 2001), 63–161 [*Apology, Testimony of the Soul, Spectacles, To the Martyrs, The Crown, Flight in Time of Persecution*]. – G. D. Dunn,

*Tertullian* (The Early Church Fathers; London and New York: Routledge, 2004) [*Adversus Judaeos, Scorpiace, De virginibus velandis*]. – *Tertullian, Cyprian, Origen: On the Lord's Prayer* (trans. A. Stewart-Sykes; Popular Patristics Series; Crestwood, N.Y.: St. Vladimir's Seminary Press, 2004) [*De oratione*].

*Tertullian—Introductions:* D. Wright, "Tertullian," in *The Early Christian World* (ed. P. F. Esler; 2 vols.; London and New York: Routledge, 2000), 2:1027–47. – G. D. Dunn, *Tertullian* (The Early Church Fathers; London and New York: Routledge, 2004), 3–61.

*Tertullian—Studies:* Jérôme Alexandre, *Une chair pour la gloire: L'anthropologie réaliste et mystique de Tertullien* (ThH 115; Paris: Beauchesne, 2001). – G. D. Dunn, "Rhetoric and Tertullian's *De virginibus velandis*," *VC* 59 (2005): 1–30.

*Cyprian of Carthage—Editions:* A Démétrien (ed. J.-C. Fredouille; SC 467; Paris: Cerf, 2003) [*Ad Demetrianum*].

*Cyprian of Carthage—Translations:* A. Stewart-Sykes, *Tertullian, Cyprian, Origen: On the Lord's Prayer* (Popular Patristics Series; Crestwood, N.Y.: St. Vladimir's Seminary Press, 2004) [*De domenica oratione*].

*Cyprian of Carthage—Studies:* J. P. Burns, "Confessing the Church: Cyprian on Penance," *StPatr* 36 (2001): 338–48. – J. P. Burns, *Cyprian the Bishop* (Routledge Early Christian Monographs; New York: Routledge, 2002). – G. D. Dunn, "Infected Sheep and Diseased Cattle, or the Pure and Holy Flock: Cyprian's Pastoral Care of Virgins," *JECS* 11 (2003) 1–20. – G. D. Dunn, "The White Crown of Works: Cyprian's Early Pastoral Ministry of Almsgiving in Carthage," *ChH* 73 (2004): 715–40. – G. D. Dunn, "Heresy and Schism according to Cyprian of Carthage," *JTS* NS 55.2 (2004): 551–76.

*Lactantius—Translations: Divine Institutes* (trans. A. Bowen and P. Garnsey, TTH 40; Liverpool: Liverpool University Press, 2003).

# PART THREE

# *Introduction: Essential Features of the History of the Fourth Century*

*Political History:* S. N. C. Lieu and Dominic Montserrat, eds., *From Constantine to Julian: Pagan and Byzantine Views* (London and New York: Routledge, 1996). – B. Lançon, *Rome in Late Antiquity, AD 313–604* (New York: Routledge, 2000). – P. R. L. Brown, *Poverty and Leadership in the Later Roman Empire* (Hanover, N.H.: University Press of New England, 2001). – D. Rohrbacher, *The Historians of Late Antiquity* (London and New York: Routledge, 2002). – C. Kelly, *Ruling the Later Roman Empire* (Revealing Antiquity; Cambridge, Mass.: Belknap Press of Harvard University Press, 2004). – S. Swain and M. Edwards, eds., *Approaching Late Antiquity: The Transformation from Early to Late Empire* (New York: Oxford University Press, 2004).

*Constantine:* H. D. Drake, *Constantine and the Bishops: The Politics of Intolerance* (Ancient Society and History; Baltimore: Johns Hopkins University Press, 2000). – B. Leadbetter, "Constantine," in *The Early Christian World* (ed. P. F. Esler; 2 vols.; London and New York: Routledge, 2000), 2:1069–87. – R. R. Holloway, *Constantine and Rome* (New Haven: Yale University Press, 2004). – C. M. Odahl, *Constantine and the Christian Empire* (Roman Imperial Biographies; New York: Routledge, 2004).

*Julian the Apostate:* M. B. Simmons, "Julian the Apostate," in *The Early Christian World* (ed. P. F. Esler; 2 vols.; London and New York: Routledge, 2000), 2:1251–72. – A. Murdoch, *The Last Pagan: Julian the Apostate and the Death of the Ancient World* (Stroud, Eng.: Sutton, 2003).

*Church History:* H. Chadwick, *The Church in Ancient Society: From Galilee to Gregory the Great* (Oxford History of the Christian Church; New York: Oxford University Press, 2002). – P. Rousseau, *The Early Christian Centuries* (London: Longman, 2002). – P. R. L. Brown, *The Rise of Western Christendom: Triumph and Diversity, A.D. 200–1000* (2d ed; Malden, Mass.: Blackwell, 2003). – H. Chadwick, *East and West—The Making of a Rift in the Church: From Apostolic Times until the Council of Florence* (Oxford History of the Christian Church; New York: Oxford University Press, 2003).

*The Expansion of Christianity:* M. R. Salzman, *The Making of a Christian Aristocracy: Social and Religious Change in the Western Roman Empire* (Cambridge, Mass.: Harvard University Press, 2004). – C. Rapp, *Holy Bishops in Late Antiquity: The Nature of Christian Leadership in an Age of Transition* (TCH 37; Berkeley: University of California Press, 2005).

*Synods:* P. R. Amidon, "Paulinus' Subscription to the *Tomus ad Antiochenos*," JTS NS (2002): 53–74. – H. Hess, *The Early Development of Canon Law and the Council of Serdica* (New York: Oxford University Press, 2002).

*History of Theology:* R. L. Wilken, *The Spirit of Early Christian Thought: Seeking the Face of God* (New Haven: Yale University Press, 2003). – J. Behr, *The Formation of Christian Theology* (Crestwood, N.Y.: St. Vladimir's Seminary Press, 2001–).

*Trinitarian Theology:* S. T. Davis, D. Kendall, and G. O'Collins, eds., *The Trinity: An Interdisciplinary Symposium on the Trinity* (Oxford and New York: Oxford University Press, 1999). – L. Ayres, *Nicaea and Its Legacy* (Oxford and New York: Oxford University Press, 2004).

*Christology:* S. T. Davis, D. Kendall, and G. O'Collins, eds., *The Incarnation: An Interdisciplinary Symposium* (New York: Oxford University Press, 2002). – D. Fairbairn, *Grace and Christology in the Early Church* (OECS; New York: Oxford University Press, 2003). – S. T. Davis, D. Kendall, and G. O'Collins, eds., *The Redemption: An Interdisciplinary Symposium* (New York: Oxford University Press, 2004). – P. Gavrilyuk, *The Suffering of the Impassible God: The Dialectics of Patristic Thought* (OECS; New York: Oxford University Press, 2004)

*Anomoeans:* R. P. Vaggione, *Eunomius of Cyzicus and the Nicene Revolution* (OECS; New York: Oxford University Press, 2001).

*Homoousians (Nicenes):* A. H. B. Logan, "Marcellus of Ancyra (Pseudo-Anthimus), 'On the Holy Church': Text, Translation, and Commentary," *JTS* NS 51 (2000): 81–112. – L. Ayres, *Nicaea and Its Legacy: An Approach to Fourth-Century Trinitarian Theology* (New York: Oxford University Press, 2004).

## Chapter Five: First Phase of Arianism

*Arius:* R. Williams, *Arius: Heresy and Tradition* (rev. ed.; Grand Rapids: Eerdmans, 2002).

*Athanasius—Translations:* K. Anatolios, *Athanasius* (The Early Church Fathers; London and New York: Routledge, 2004), 87–242 [*Orations against the Arians* (selections), *On the Council of Nicaea, Letter 1 to Serapion on the Holy Spirit, Letter 40* to Adelphius].

*Athanasius—Introductions:* D. Brakke, "Athanasius," in *The Early Christian World* (ed. P. F. Esler; 2 vols.; London and New York: Routledge, 2000), 2:1103–27. – K. Anatolios, *Athanasius* (The Early Church Fathers; London: New York: Routledge, 2004), 1–86.

*Athanasius—Studies:* D. Brakke, "Athanasius' *Epistula ad Epiphanium* and Liturgical Reform in Alexandria," *StPatr* 36 (2001): 482–88. – L. Ayres, "Athanasius' Initial Defense of the Term Ὁμοούσιος: Rereading the *De decretis*," *JECS* 12 (2004): 337–59. – J. D. Ernest, *The Bible in Athanasius of Alexandria* (The Bible in Ancient Christianity 2; Leiden: Brill, 2004). – J. Behr, *The Nicene Faith: True God of True God* (vol. 2, pt. 1, of *The Formation of Christian Theology;* Crestwood, N.Y.: St. Vladimir's Seminary Press, 2004).

*Eustathius of Antioch—Editions: Eustathii Antiocheni, patris nicaeni, Opera quae supersunt omnia* (ed. J. H. Declerck; CCSG 51; Turnhout, Belg.: Brepols, 2002).

*Hilary of Poitiers—Editions: La Trinité* (ed. G.-M. de Durand, G. Pelland, and C. Morel; 3 vols.; SC 443, 448, 462; Paris: Cerf, 1999–2001). – *Tractatus super Psalmos: In Psalmum CXVIII* (ed. J. Doignon, R. Demeulenaere; CCSL 61A; Turnhout, Belg.: Brepols, 2002).

*Hilary of Poitiers—Studies:* D.H. Williams, "Defining Orthodoxy in Hilary of Poitiers' *Commentarium in Matthaeum*," *JECS* 9 (2001): 151–71. – C. L. Beckwith, "The Condemnation and Exile of Hilary of Poitiers at the Synod of Béziers (356 C.E.)," *JECS* 13 (2005): 21–38.

## Chapter Six: Second Phase of Arianism and Apollinarism

*Apollinaris:* K. McCarthy Spoerl, "Apollinarius on the Holy Spirit," *StPatr* 37 (2001): 571–92. – B. E. Daley, "'Heavenly Man' and 'Eternal Christ':

Apollinarius and Gregory of Nyssa on the Personal Identity of the Savior," *JECS* 10 (2002): 469–88.

*The Three Cappadocians:* J. T. Lienhard, "*Ousia* and *hypostasis:* The Cappadocian Settlement and the Theology of 'One *hypostasis*," in *The Trinity: An Interdisciplinary Symposium on the Trinity* (ed. S. T. Davis, D. Kendall, and G. O'Collins; Oxford and New York: Oxford University Press, 1999) 99–121. – R. Klein, *Die Haltung der kappadokischen Bischöfe Basilius von Cäsarea, Gregor von Nazianz, und Gregor von Nyssa zur Sklaverei* (Stuttgart: Steiner, 2000). – S. R. Holman, *The Hungry Are Dying: Beggars and Bishops in Roman Cappadocia* (Oxford Studies in Historical Theology; New York: Oxford University Press, 2001). – N. Thierry, *La Cappadoce de l'antiquité au Moyen Âge* (Bibliothèque de l'antiquité tardive 4; Turnhout, Belg.: Brepols, 2002). – R. Van Dam, *Families and Friends in Late Roman Cappadocia* (Philadelphia: University of Pennsylvania Press, 2003). – J. Behr, *The Nicene Faith: One of the Holy Trinity* (vol. 2, pt. 2, of *The Formation of Christian Theology;* Crestwood, N.Y.: St. Vladimir's Seminary Press, 2004). – A. Sterk, *Renouncing the World yet Leading the Church: The Monk-Bishop in Late Antiquity* (Cambridge, Mass.: Harvard University Press, 2004).

*Basil of Caesarea—Translations:* N. V. Harrison, *St. Basil the Great: On the Human Condition* (Popular Patristics Series; Crestwood, N.Y.: St. Vladimir's Seminary Press, 2005) [*Two Homilies on the Origin of Humanity, Homily Explaining That God Is Not the Cause of Evil; Homily against Anger; Homily on the Words "Be Attentive to Yourself"; Letter* 233 to Amphilochius, *Long Rules* (selections)].

*Basil of Caesarea—Studies:* D. Woods, "Dating Basil of Caesarea's Correspondence with Arintheus and His Widow," *StPatr* 37 (2001): 301–7. – S. M. Hillerbrand, "A Reconsideration of the Development of Basil's Trinitarian Theology: The Dating of *Ep.* 9 and *Contra Eunomium*," *VC* 58 (2004): 393–406.

*Gregory of Nyssa—Edition: Discours catéchétique* (ed. R. Winling; SC 453; Paris: Cerf, 2000) [*Oratio catechetica*]. – *Sur les titres des Psaumes* (ed. J. Reynard; SC 466; Paris: Cerf, 2002).

*Gregory of Nyssa—Studies:* J. Zachhuber, *Human Nature in Gregory of Nyssa: Philosophical Background and Theological Significance* (SVigChr 46; Boston: Brill, 1999). – H. R. Drobner, "Gregory of Nyssa as Philosopher: *De anima et resurrectione* and *De hominis opificio*," *Dionysius* 18 (2000) 69–101. – D. Krueger, "Writing and the Liturgy of Memory in Gregory of Nyssa's *Life of Macrina*," *JECS* 8 (2000): 438–510. – M. R. Barnes, *The Power of God: Dynamis in Gregory of Nyssa's Trinitarian Theology* (Washington, D.C.: Catholic University of America Press, 2001). – M. R. Barnes, " 'The Burden of Marriage' and Other Notes on Gregory of Nyssa's *On Virginity*," *StPatr* 37 (2001): 12–19. – J. Leemans, "On the Date of Gregory of Nyssa's First Homilies on the Forty Martyrs of Sebaste (I A and I B)," *JTS* NS 52 (2001): 93–97. – A.A. Mosshammer, "Gregory of Nyssa as Homilist," *StPatr* 37 (2001): 212–39. – J. W. Smith, "Macrina, Tamer of Horses and Healer of

Souls: Grief and the Therapy of Hope in Gregory of Nyssa's *De anima et resurrectione,*" *JTS* NS 52.1 (2001): 37–60. – R. Cross, "Gregory of Nyssa on Universals," *VC* 56 (2002): 372–410. – H. R. Drobner, "The Critical Edition of Gregory of Nyssa's *In Hexaemeron:* A Preliminary Report," *Dionysius* 20 (2002): 95–138. – J. Rexer, *Die Festtheologie Gregors von Nyssa: Ein Beispiel der reichskirchenlichen Heortologie* (Patrologia: Beiträge zum Studium der Kirchenväter 8; Frankfurt and New York: Lang, 2002). – J. W. Smith, "A Just and Reasonable Grief: The Death and Function of a Holy Woman in Gregory of Nyssa's *Life of Macrina,*" *JECS* 12 (2004): 57–84. – S. Coakley, ed., *Rethinking Gregory of Nyssa* (Directions in Modern Theology; Oxford: Blackwell, 2003). – M. Laird, *Gregory of Nyssa and the Grasp of Faith* (OECS; New York: Oxford University Press, 2004). – P. Rousseau, "The Pious Household and the Virgin Chorus: Reflections on Gregory of Nyssa's *Life of Macrina,*" *JECS* 13 (2005): 165–86. – L. Turcescu, *Gregory of Nyssa and the Concept of Divine Persons* (American Academy of Religion Academy Series; New York: Oxford University Press, 2005). – J. Zachhuber, "Once Again: Gregory of Nyssa on Universals," *JTS* NS 56 (2005): 75–98.

*Gregory of Nazianzus—Editions: Sancti Gregorii Nazianzeni Opera: Versio armeni-aca* (ed. B. Coulie; Corpus nazianzenum 1, 3; CCSG 28, 38; Turnhout, Belg.: Brepols, 1994–) vols. 1, 3 [*Orationes* 2, 12, 9; 21, 8; 7]. *Studia nazianzenica* (ed. B. Coulie; Corpus nazianzenum 8; CCSG 41; Turnhout, Belg.: Brepols, 2000). *Sancti Gregorii Nazianzeni opera: Versio iberica II, III* (4 vol.; ed. H. Metreveli; Corpus nazianzenum 9, 17; CCSG 42, 52; Turnhout, Belg.: Brepols, 2000–2004) [*Orationes* 15, 24, 19; 43]. – *Opera: Versio arabica antiqua II, III* (ed. L. Tuerlinckx; Corpus nazianzenum 10, 19; CCSG 43, 57; Turnhout, Belg.: Brepols, 2001–) [*Orationes* 1, 45, 44; 40]. – *Gregorii Pres-byterii Vita sancti Gregorii Theologi* (ed. X. Lequeux; Corpus nazianzenum 11; CCSG 44; Turnhout, Belg.: Brepols, 2001). – *Sancti Gregorii Nazianzeni Opera: Versio syriaca* (3 vols.; ed. J.-C. Haelewyck; Corpus nazianzenum 14, 15, 18; CCSG 47, 49, 53; Turnhout, Belg.: Brepols, 2001–2005) [*Orationes* 13, 27, 38, 39, 41]. – *Sancti Gregorii Nazianzeni Opera: Versio iberica III* (ed. H. Metreveli et al.; Corpus nazianzenum 12; CCSG 45; Turnhout, Belg.: Brepols, 2001) [*Oratio* 38]. – *Basili Minimi in Gregorii Nazianzeni oratio-nenm xxxviii commentarii* (ed. T. S. Schmidt; Corpus nazianzenum 13; CCSG 46; Turnhout, Belg.: Brepols; Louvain: Louvain University Press, 2001) [*Oratio* 38]. – *Pseudo-Nonniani In IV orationes Gregorii Nazianzeni commentarii* (ed. T. Otkhmezuri; Corpus nazianzenum 16; CCSG 50; Turnhout, Belg.: Brepols; Louvain: Louvain University Press, 2002) [ET].

*Gregory of Nazianzus—Translations: On God and Man: The Theological Poetry of St. Gregory of Nazianzus* (trans. Peter Gilbert; Popular Patristics Series; Crestwood, N.Y.: St. Vladimir's Seminary Press, 2001). – *On God and Christ: The Five Theological Orations and Two Letters of Cledonius* (trans. L. Wickham; Popular Patristics Series; Crestwood, N.Y.: St. Vladimir's Seminary Press, 2002). – *Select Orations* (trans. Martha Vinson; FC 107; Washington, D.C.: Catholic University of America Press, 2004) [*Orationes* 6, 9, 10, 11, 13, 14, 15, 17, 19, 20, 22, 23, 24, 25, 26, 32, 35, 36, 44].

*Gregory of Nazianzus—Studies:* J. McGuckin, *Saint Gregory of Nazianzus: An Intellectual Biography* (Crestwood, N.Y.: St. Vladimir's Seminary Press, 2001). – J. A. McGuckin, "Autobiography as Apologia in St. Gregory of Nazianzus," *StPatr* 37 (2001): 160–77. – F. Gautier, *La retraite et le sacerdoce chez Grégoire de Nazianze* (Bibliothèque de l'École des hautes études: Section des sciences religieuses 114; Turnhout, Belg.: Brepols, 2002). – F. Trisoglio, *La salvezza in Gregorio di Nazianzo* (Cultura cristiana antica: Studi; Rome: Borla, 2002). – A. Richard, *Cosmologie et théologie chez Grégoire de Nazianze* (Collection des études augustiniennes, Série antiquité 169; Paris: Institut d'Études Augustiniennes, 2003).

## *Chapter Seven: Pastors, Exegetes, and Ascetics*

*Cyril of Jerusalem:* A. J. Doval, *Cyril of Jerusalem, Mystagogue: The Authorship of the Mystagogic Catecheses* (PatMS 17; Washington, D.C.: Catholic University of America Press, 2001). – A. Doval, "Cyril of Jerusalem's Theology of Salvation," *StPatr* 37 (2001): 452–61. – G. Frank, "'Taste and See': The Eucharist and the Eyes of Faith in the Fourth Century," *ChH* 70 (2001): 619–43. – J. W. Drijvers, *Cyril of Jerusalem: Bishop and City* (SVigChr72; Leiden and Boston: Brill, 2004).

*Epiphanius of Constantia (Salamis)—Editions: The Armenian Texts of Epiphanius of Salamis: De mensuris et ponderibus* (ed. M. E. Stone; CSCO 583; Louvain and Sterling, Va.: Peeters, 2000).

*Ambrose—Editions: De officiis* (2 vols.; ed. I. J. Davidson; OECS; New York: Oxford University Press, 2001) [ET].

*Ambrose—Studies:* I. Davidson, "Ambrose," in *The Early Christian World* (ed. P. F. Esler; 2 vols.; London and New York: Routledge, 2000), 2:1175–1204. – C. A. Satterlee, *Ambrose of Milan's Method of Mystagogical Preaching* (Collegeville, Minn.: Liturgical, 2002). – G. Maschio, *La figura di Cristo nel Commento al salmo 118 di Ambrogio di Milano* (SEAug 88; Rome: Institutum Patristicum Augustinianum, 2003). – M. L. Colish, *Ambrose's Patriarchs: Ethics for the Common Man* (Notre Dame, Ind.: University of Notre Dame Press, 2005).

*Diodore of Tarsus—Translation: Commentary on Ps 1–51* (trans. R. C. Hill; Writings from the Greco-Roman World; Atlanta: SBL, 2005).

*Diodore of Tarsus—Studies:* J. J. O'Keefe, "'A Letter That Killeth': Towards a Reassessment of Antiochene Exegesis, or Diodore, Theodore, and Theodoret on the Psalms," *JECS* 8 (2000): 83–104.

*Theodore of Mopsuestia—Translations: Commentary on the Twelve Prophets* (trans. R.C. Hill; FC 108; Washington, D.C.: Catholic University of America Press, 2004).

*Theodore of Mopsuestia—Studies:* S. Gerber, *Theodor von Mopsuestia und das Nicänum: Studien zu den katechetischen Homilien* (SVigChr 51; Boston: Brill, 2000). – R. C. Hill, "Theodore of Mopsuestia: Interpreter of the Prophets," *SacEr* 40 (2001): 107–29. – C. Leonhard, "Şūrat Ktāb: Bemerkungen zum sogenannten *Rituale* des Theodor von Mopsuestia am Beginn der katechetischen Homilien 12–16," *VC* 56 (2002): 411–33. – F. G. McLeod, "The Christological Ramifications of Theodore of Mopsuestia's Understanding of Baptism and the Eucharist," *JECS* 10 (2002): 37–75. – R. C. Hill, "His Master's Voice: Theodore of Mopsuestia on the Psalms," *HeyJ* 45 (2004): 40–53. – F. G. McLeod, *The Roles of Christ's Humanity in Salvation: Insights from Theodore of Mopsuestia* (Washington, D.C.: Catholic University of America Press, 2005)

*John Chrysostom—Translations: Old Testament Homilies* (trans. Robert C. Hill; 3 vols.; Brookline, Mass.: Holy Cross Orthodox Press, 2003) [*Homilies on Hannah, David, and Saul; Homilies on Isaiah and Jeremiah; Homilies on the Obscurity of the Old Testament, Homilies on the Psalms.*] – *Eight Sermons on Genesis* (trans. R. C. Hill; Boston: Holy Cross Orthodox Press, 2004).

*John Chrysostom—Studies:* P. Allen and W. Mayer, "John Chrysostom," in *The Early Christian World* (ed. P. F. Esler; 2 vols.; London and New York: Routledge, 2000), 2:1128–50. – W. Mayer, "Patronage, Pastoral Care, and the Role of the Bishop at Antioch," *VC* 55 (2001). – A. Valevicius, "Les 24 homélies *De statuis* de Jean Chrysostome," *REAug* 46 (2000): 83–91. – W. Pradels, "The Sequence and Dating of the Series of John Chrysostom's Eight Discourses *Adversus Iudaeos*," *ZAC* 6 (2002): 90–116.

*Didymus the Blind:* R. A. Layton, *Didymus the Blind and His Circle in Late-Antique Alexandria: Virtue and Narrative in Biblical Scholarship* (Urbana: University of Illinois Press, 2004).

*Jerome—Editions: Débat entre un luciférien et un orthodoxe* (ed. A. Canellis; SC 473; Paris: Cerf, 2003) [*Altercatio Luciferiani et orthodoxi*]. – *Commentarii in epistulas Pauli apostoli ad Titum et ad Philemonem* (ed. F. Bucci; CCSL 77C; Turnhout, Belg.: Brepols, 2003).

*Jerome—Translations:* S. Rebenich, *Jerome* (The Early Church Fathers; London and New York: Routledge, 2002), 61–136 [*Letters 1, 15, 31, 40, 127, 128, Preface to the Chronicle of Eusebius, Life of Malchus, Preface to the Book of Hebrew Questions, Lives of Famous Men* (selections), *Preface to the Vulgate Version of the Pentateuch, Against Vigilantius* (selections)].

*Jerome—Introductions:* D. Brown, "Jerome," in *The Early Christian World* (ed. P. F. Esler; 2 vols.; London and New York: Routledge, 2000), 2:1151–74. – S. Rebenich, *Jerome* (The Early Church Fathers; London and New York: Routledge, 2002), 3–59.

*Jerome—Studies:* R. A. Layton, "From 'Holy Passion' to Sinful Emotion: Jerome and the Doctrine of Propassio," in *In dominico eloquio = In Lordly Eloquence: Essays on Patristic Exegesis in Honor of Robert Louis Wilken* (ed. P. M. Blowers et al., Grand Rapids: 2002), 280–93.

# Chapter Eight: Monastic and Hagiographic Literature

*Early Monasticism—Historical Surveys:* M. Dunn, *The Emergence of Monasticism: From the Desert Fathers to the Early Middle Ages* (Oxford: Blackwell, 2000). – C. Stewart, "Monasticism," in *The Early Christian World* (ed. P. F. Esler; 2 vols.; London and New York: Routledge, 2000), 1:344–66. – W. Harmless, *Desert Christians: An Introduction to the Literature of Early Monasticism* (New York: Oxford University Press, 2004).

*Early Monasticism—Reference Works:* Juan Laboa, ed., *The Historical Atlas of Eastern and Western Monasticism* (Collegeville, Minn.: Liturgical, 2004).

*Early Monasticism—Studies:* – W. Harmless, "Remembering Poemen Remembering: The Desert Fathers and the Spirituality of Memory," *ChH* 69 (2000): 483–518. – B. McNary-Zak, *Letters and Asceticism in Fourth-Century Egypt* (Landam, Md.: University Press of America, 2000). – D. Brakke, "The Making of Monastic Demonology: Three Ascetic Teachers on Withdrawal and Resistance," *ChH* 70 (2001): 19–48. – G. Gould, "The Preservation of Some Authentic Material in a Latin Collection of *Apophthegmata patrum*," *StPatr* 35 (2001) 81–89. – D. Caner, *Wandering, Begging Monks: Spiritual Authority and the Promotion of Monasticism in Late Antiquity* (TCH 33; Berkeley: University of California Press, 2002). – J. L. Hevelone-Harper, *Disciples of the Desert: Monks, Laity, and Spiritual Authority in Sixth-Century Gaza* (Baltimore: Johns Hopkins University Press, 2005).

*Early Monasticism—Archeology:* E. S. Bolman, ed., *Monastic Visions: Wall Paintings in the Monastery of St. Antony at the Red Sea* (New Haven: Yale University Press; Atlanta: American Research Center in Egypt, 2002). – D. Bar, "Rural Monasticism as a Key Element in the Christianization of Byzantine Palestine," *HTR* 98 (2005): 49–65.

*Early Monasticism—Theology and Spirituality:* J. Chryssavgis, "Abba Isaiah of Scetis: Aspects of Spiritual Direction," *StPatr* 35 (2001): 32–40. – T. Špidlik, *Prayer* (vol. 2 of *The Spirituality of the Christian East;* trans. A. P. Gythiel; CistSS 206; Kalamazoo: Cistercian Publications, 2005).

*Rule of Pachomius:* J. E. Goehring, "The Provenance of the Nag Hammadi Codices Once More," *StPatr* 35 (2001): 234–53. – W. Harmless, *Desert Christians: An Introduction to the Literature of Early Monasticism* (New York: Oxford University Press, 2004), 115–63.

*Rules of Basil the Great:* A. M. Silvas, "Edessa to Cassino: The Passage of Basil's Asketikon to the West," *VC* 56 (2002): 247–59.

*Augustine's Monastic Writings:* G. Lawless, "Thematic Similarities Common to Scripture and the Latin Classics in *The Rule of St. Augustine*," *AugStud* 34 (2003): 233–44. – G. Lawless, "*Ex Africa semper aliquid novi:* The Rules of Saint Augustine," *AugStud* 36 (2005): 239–49.

*Evagrius Ponticus—Translations:* W. Harmless and R. R. Fitzgerald, "The Sapphire Light of the Mind: The *Skemmata* of Evagrius Ponticus," *TS* 62 (2001) 493–529 [*Skemmata*]. – *The Ad Monachos: Translation and Commentary* (trans. J. Driscoll; ACW 59; New York: Paulist, 2003) [*Ad monachos*]. – R. E. Sinkewicz, ed., *Evagrius of Pontus: The Greek Ascetic Corpus* (OECS; New York: Oxford University Press, 2003) [*Foundations of Monastic Life; To Eulogius; On the Eight Thoughts; The Monk (Praktikos); To Monks in Monasteries and Communities and Exhortation to a Virgin; On Thoughts (Peri logismōn); Chapters on Prayer; Reflections; Exhortations 1–2 to Monks; Thirty-Three Ordered Chapters*].

*Evagrius Ponticus—Studies:* R. Darling Young, "Evagrius the Iconographer: Monastic Pedagogy in the *Gnostikos*," *JECS* 9 (2001): 53–72. – C. Stewart, "Imageless Prayer and the Theological Vision of Evagrius Ponticus," *JECS* 9 (2001): 173–204. – D. Bertrand, "Force et faiblesse du νοῦς chez Évagre le Pontique," *StPatr* 35 (2001): 10–23. – L. Dysinger, "The *logoi* of Providence and Judgment in the Exegetical Writings of Evagrius Ponticus," *StPatr* 37 (2001): 462–71. – C. Stewart, "Evagrius Ponticus on Monastic Pedagogy," in *Abba: The Tradition of Orthodoxy in the West* (ed. J. Behr; Crestwood, N.Y.: St. Vladimir's Seminary Press, 2003), 241–71. – A. Casiday, "Review Article: Gabriel Bunge and the Study of Evagrius Ponticus," *SVTQ* 48 (2004): 249–98. – A. Guillaumont, *Une philosophe au désert: Évagre le Pontique* (Paris: Librairie Philosophique J. Vrin, 2004). – W. Harmless, *Desert Christians: An Introduction to the Literature of Early Monasticism* (New York: Oxford University Press, 2004), 311–72. – L. Dysinger, *Psalmody and Prayer in the Writings of Evagrius Ponticus* (OTM; New York: Oxford University Press, 2005).

*Symeon of Mesopotamia (Macarius):* A. Orlov and A. Golitzin, " 'Many Lamps Are Lightened from the One': Paradigms of the Transformational Vision in Macarian Homilies," *VC* 55 (2001): 281–98. – M. Plested, *The Macarian Legacy: The Place of Macarius-Symeon in the Eastern Christian Tradition* (OTM; Oxford and New York: Oxford University Press, 2004).

*John Cassian:* C. M. Chin, "Prayer and *otium* in Cassian's *Institutes*," *StPatr* 35 (2001): 24–29. – C. Leyser, *Authority and Asceticism from Augustine to Gregory the Great* (OHM; New York: Oxford University Press, 2001). – A. M. C. Casiday, "Cassian, Augustine, and *De incarnatione*," *StPatr* 38 (2001): 41–47.

*Other Early Monastic Texts—Editions:* Barsanuphius and John of Gaza, *Correspondance* (ed. F. Neyt, P. de Angelis-Noah, and L. Regnault; 3 vols. in 5; SC 426, 427, 450, 451, 468; Paris: Cerf, 1997–2002) [*Ep. 1–848*].

*Other Early Monastic Texts—Translations:* The Desert Fathers: Sayings of the Early Christian Monks (trans. Benedicta Ward; Penguin Classics; London: Penguin, 2003) [*Verba seniorum*]. – Abba Isaiah of Scetis, *Ascetic Discourses* (ed. J. Chryssavgis and P. Penkett; CistSS 150; Kalamazoo: Cistercian Publications, 2002). – Barsanuphius and John of Gaza, *Letters from the Desert: A Selection of Questions and Responses* (trans. John Chryssavgis; Popular Patristics Series; Crestwood, N.Y.: St. Vladimir's Seminary Press, 2003).

*Lives and Histories of Saints—Translations:* T. F. Head, ed., *Medieval Hagiography: An Anthology* (Garland Reference Library of the Humanities 1942; New York: Garland, 2000). – See also "*Coptic Literature—Translations*" below.

*Lives and Histories of Saints—Studies:* J. Howard-Johnston and P. A. Hayward, eds., *The Cult of the Saints in Late Antiquity and the Middle Ages: Essays on the Contribution of Peter Brown* (New York: Oxford University Press, 2000).

*Vita Antonii—Translations: The Life of Antony: The Coptic Life and the Greek Life* (trans. T. Vivian and A. N. Athanassakis; CistSS 202; Kalamazoo: Cistercian Publications, 2003) [John of Shmūn, *Encomium on Saint Antony;* Serapion of Thmuis, *A Letter to the Disciples of Antony; Coptic Life of Antony; Greek Life of Antony*].

*Vita Antonii—Studies:* C. Stewart, "Anthony of the Desert," in *The Early Christian World* (ed. P. F. Esler; 2 vols.; London and New York: Routledge, 2000), 2:1088–1101. – W. Harmless, *Desert Christians: An Introduction to the Literature of Early Monasticism* (New York: Oxford University Press, 2004), 57–114.

*Itineraries:* G. Frank, *The Memory of the Eyes: Pilgrims to the Living Saints in Christian Late Antiquity* (TCH 30; Berkeley: University of California Press, 2000). – S. J. Davis, *Cult of St. Thecla* (OECS; New York: Oxford University Press, 2001). – L. Ellis and F. Kidner, eds., *Travel, Communication, and Geography in Late Antiquity: Sacred and Profane* (Burlington, Vt.: Ashgate, 2004). – M. Dietz, *Wandering Monks, Virgins, and Pilgrims: Ascetic Travel in the Mediterranean World, A.D. 300–800* (University Park: Pennsylvania State University Press, 2005).

*Itinerarium Egeriae—Edition: Journal de voyage: Itinéraire* (ed. P. Maraval; SC 296; Paris: Cerf, 2002).

*Itinerarium Egeriae—Studies:* E. D. Hunt, "The Date of the *Itinerarium Egeriae,*" *StPatr* 38 (2001): 410–16.

# Chapter Nine: Augustine of Hippo

*Collections of Essays:* G. Madec, *Lectures augustiniennes* (Collections des études augustiniennes: Série antiquité 168; Paris: Institut d'Études Augustiniennes, 2001). – P.-Y. Fux, J.-M. Roessli, O. Wermlinger, eds., *Augustinus Afer, saint Augustin—africanité et universalité: Acts du Colloque internationale Alger-Annaba, 1–7 avril 2001* (2 vols.; Par 45.1–2; Fribourg, Switz.: Éditions Universitaires, 2003). – K. Pollman and M. Vessey, eds., *Augustine and the Disciplines: From Cassiciacum to Confessions* (New York: Oxford University Press, 2005).

*Biographies:* S. Lancel, *Saint Augustine* (trans. Antonia Nevill; London: SCM, 2002).

*Thought and Theology:* H. Chadwick, *Augustine: A Very Short Introduction* (New York: Oxford University Press, 2001).

*Augustine's Context:* L. I. Hamilton, "Possidius' Augustine and Post-Augustinian Africa," *JECS* 12 (2004): 85–105. – P. R. L. Brown, "Augustine and a Crisis of

Wealth in Late Antiquity (St. Augustine Lecture, 2004)," *AugStud* 36 (2005) 5–30.

*Philosophy:* E. Stump and N. Kretzmann, eds., *The Cambridge Companion to Augustine* (Cambridge Companions to Philosophy; Cambridge and New York: Cambridge University Press, 2001). – A. I. Bouton-Touboulic, *L'ordre caché: La notion d'ordre chez saint Augustin* (Collection des études augustiniennes: Série antiquité 174; Paris: Institut d'Etudes Augustiniennes, 2004).

*Augustine the Bishop:* D. E. Doyle, *The Bishop as Disciplinarian in the Letters of St. Augustine* (Patristic Studies 4; New York: Lang, 2002). – É. Rebillard, "*Nec deserere memorias suorum:* Augustine and the Family-Based Commemoration of the Dead," *AugStud* 36 (2005): 99–111.

*Anthropology:* B. Schmisek, "Augustine's Use of 'Spiritual Body,'" *AugStud* 35 (2004): 237–52. – J. C. Cavadini, "Feeling Right: Augustine on the Passions and Sexual Desire," *AugStud* 36 (2005): 195–217.

*Ethics:* D. G. Hunter, "Augustine, Sermon 354A*: Its Place in His Thought on Marriage and Sexuality," *AugStud* 33 (2002): 39–60. – D. G. Hunter, "Augustine and the Making of Marriage in Roman North Africa," *JECS* 11 (2003) 63–85.

*Preaching and Catechesis:* L. Ayres, "'Remember That You Are Catholic' (*serm.* 52.2): Augustine on the Unity of the Triune God," *JECS* 8 (2000): 39–82. – W. Harmless, "The Voice and the Word: Augustine's Catechumenate in the Light of the Dolbeau Sermons," *AugStud* 35 (2004): 17–42. – H. R. Drobner, "The Chronology of Augustine's *Sermones ad populum* III: On Christmas Day," *AugStud* 35 (2004): 43–53. – H.R. Drobner, "Christmas in Hippo: Mystical Celebration and Catechesis," *AugStud* 35 (2004): 55–72. – M. Cameron, "*Totus Christus* and the Psychagogy of Augustine's Sermons," *AugStud* 36 (2005): 59–70.

*Augustine and Manichaeism:* J. Van Oort, O. Wermelinger, and G. Wurst, eds., *Augustine and Manichaeism in the Latin West* (Nag Hammadi and Manichaean Studies 49; Leiden: Brill, 2001).

*Augustine and Donatism:* J. Alexander, "Donatism," in *The Early Christian World* (ed. P. F. Esler; 2 vols.; London and New York: Routledge, 2000), 2:952–74. – M. Tilley, "Theologies of Penance during the Donatist Controversy," *StPatr* 35 (2001): 330–37.

*Ecclesiology:* J. Carola, "Augustine's Vision of Lay Participation in Ecclesial Reconciliation," *AugStud* 35 (2004): 73–93. – M. C. McCarthy, "An Ecclesiology of Groaning: Augustine, the Psalms, and the Making of the Church," *TS* 66 (2005): 23–48.

*Augustine and Pelagianism:* C. C. Burnett, "Dysfunction at Diospolis: A Comparative Study of Augustine's *De gestis Pelagii* and Jerome's *Dialogus adversus Pelagianos*," *AugStud* 34 (2003): 153–73.

*Confessions—Translations: Augustine's Childhood* (trans. G. Wills; New York: Viking, 2000) [*Conf.* 1]. – *Augustine's Memory* (trans. G. Wills; New York: Viking, 2002) [*Conf.* 10] (2002). – *Augustine's Sin* (trans. G. Wills; New

York: Viking, 2003) [*Conf.* 2]. – *Augustine's Conversion* (trans. G. Wills; New York: Viking, 2004) [*Conf.* 8].

*Confessions—Studies:* J. P. Kenney, "Saint Augustine and the Limits of Contemplation," *StPatr* 38 (2001): 199–218. – J. M. Quinn, *A Companion to the "Confessions" of St. Augustine* (New York: Peter Lang, 2002). – K. Paffenroth and R. P. Kennedy, eds., *A Reader's Companion to Augustine's Confessions* (Louisville: Westminster John Knox, 2003). – *Le Confessioni di Agostino (402–2002)—bilancio e prospettive: XXXI Incontro di studiosi dell'antichità cristiana, Roma, 2–4 maggio 2002* (Rome: Institutum Patristicum Augustinianum, 2003). – A. Kotzé, *Augustine's Confessions: Communicative Purpose and Audience* (SVigChr 71; Leiden and Boston: Brill, 2004). – J. P. Kenney, *The Mysticism of Saint Augustine: Re-reading the "Confessions"* (London and New York: Routledge, 2005).

*Biblical Exegesis and Understanding of Scripture—Studies:* T. F. Martin, "*Psalmus gratiae Dei*: Augustine's Pauline Reading of Psalm 31," *VC* 55 (2001): 137–55. – M.-F. Berrouard, *Introduction aux homélies de Saint Augustin sur l'evangile de Saint Jean* (Collection des études augustiniennes; Série Antiquité 170; Paris: Institut d'Etudes Augustiniennes, 2004). – I. Bouchet, *"Le firmament de l'Écriture": L'herméneutique augustinienne* (Collection des études augustiniennes: Série Antiquité 172; Paris: Institut d'Études Augustiniennes, 2004).

*Augustinian Christology:* L. Ayres, "Augustine, Christology, and God as Love: An Introduction to the Homilies on 1 John," in *Nothing Greater, Nothing Better: Theological Essays on the Love of God* (ed. K. Vanhoozer; Grand Rapids: Eerdmans, 2001), 67–93. – C. W. Griffin and D. L. Paulsen, "Augustine and the Corporeality of God," *HTR* 95 (2002): 97–118. – D. J. Jones, *Christus sacerdos in the Preaching of St. Augustine: Christ and Christian Identity* (Patrologia 14; Frankfurt and New York: Lang, 2004). – L. Ayres, "Augustine on the Rule of Faith: Rhetoric, Christology, and the Foundation of Christian Thinking," *AugStud* 36 (2005): 33–49. – M. Lamberigts, "Competing Christologies: Julian and Augustine on Jesus Christ," *AugStud* 36 (2005): 159–94.

*De Trinitate—Studies:* A. Louth, "Love and the Trinity: Saint Augustine and the Greek Fathers (2001 St. Augustine Lecture)," *AugStud* 33 (2002): 1–16.

*De civitate Dei—Studies: Lettura del De civitate Dei libri I-X* (SEAug 86; Rome: Institutum Patristicum Augustinianum, 2003). – P. Curbelié, *La justice dans La cité de Dieu* (Collection des études augustiniennes: Série Antiquité 171; Paris: Institut d'Études Augustiniennes, 2004). – R. Dodaro, *Christ and the Just Society in the Thought of Augustine* (Cambridge: Cambridge University Press, 2004).

*Enchiridion—Studies: Fede e vita: De fide et symbolo, De agone christiano, Enchiridion* (SEAug 91; Rome: Institutum Patristicum Augustinianum, 2004).

*Tyconius—Edition: Le livre des règles* (ed. J.-M. Vercruysse; SC 488; Paris: Cerf, 2004) [*Liber regularum*].

## Augustine: List of Works (editions, English translations)

11. *b. coniug.* (*De bono coniugali*): *De bono coniugali, De sancta virginitate* (ed. P.G. Walsh; OECT; Oxford and New York: Oxford University Press, 2001) [ET, com].

34. *en. Ps.* (*Enarrationes in Psalmos*): *Expositions of the Psalms: 51–72* (trans. M. Boulding; WSA 3.17; Hyde Park, N.Y.: New City, 2001). – *Expositions of the Psalms: 73–98* (trans. M. Boulding; WSA 3.18; Hyde Park, N.Y.: New City, 2002). – *Expositions of the Psalms: 99–120* (trans. M Boulding; WSA 3.19; Hyde Park, N.Y.: New City, 2003). – *Expositions of the Psalms: 121–150* (trans. M. Boulding; WSA 3.20; Hyde Park, N.Y.: New City, 2004).

36. *ep.* (*Epistulae*): *Sancti Aurelii Augustini Epistulae I-LV* (ed. K. D. Daur; CCSL 31; Turnhout, Belg.: Brepols, 2004). – *Sancti Aurelii Augustini epistulae LVI-C* (ed. K. D. Daur; CCSL 31A; Turnhout, Belg.: Brepols, 2005). – *Augustine: Political Writings* (trans. E. M. Atkins and R. Dodaro; Cambridge Texts in the History of Political Thought; Cambridge: Cambridge University Press, 2001) [*Ep.* 51, 66, 86, 87, 88, 90, 91, 95, 100, 103, 104, 105, 133, 134, 136, 138, 139, 152, 153, 154, 155, 173, 185, 189, 204, 220, 229, 250, 1*, 10*; *s* 13, 302, 335C; *Sermon on the Sack of Rome*]. – *Letters 1–99* (trans. R. J. Teske; WSA 2.1; Hyde Park, N.Y.: New City, 2001). – *Letters 100–155* (trans. R. J. Teske; WSA 2.2.: Hyde Park, N.Y.: New City, 2003). – *Letters 156–210* (trans. R. J. Teske; WSA 2.3; Hyde Park, N.Y.: New City, 2004). – *Letters 211–270, 1*–29** (trans. R. J. Teske; WSA 2.4; Hyde Park, N.Y.: New City, 2005).

43. *exp. Gal.* (*Expositio epistulae ad Galatas*): *Augustine's Commentary on Gala-tians: Introduction, Text, Translation, and Notes* (ed. E. Plumer; OECS; New York: Oxford University Press, 2003) [ET, com].

53. *Gn. litt.* (*De Genesi ad litteram*): *On Genesis* (trans. Edmund Hill; WSA 1.13; Hyde Park, N.Y.: New City, 2003), 153–506 [*Literal Meaning of Genesis*].

54. *Gn. litt. imp.* (*De Genesi ad litteram liber imperfectus*): – *Sur la Genèse au sens littéral livre inachevé* (ed. P. Monat; BAug 50; Paris: Institut d'Études Augustiniennes, 2004), 156–383. – *On Genesis* (trans. Edmund Hill; WSA 1.13; Hyde Park, N.Y.: New City, 2003), 103–51 [*Unfinished Literal Com-mentary on Genesis*].

55. *Gn. adu. Man* (*De Genesi adversus Manichaeos*): *Sur la Genèse contre les manichéens* (ed. P. Monat; BAug 50; Paris: Institut d'Études Augustiniennes, 2004), 396–505. – *On Genesis* (trans. Edmund Hill; WSA 1.13; Hyde Park, N.Y.: New City, 2003), 23–102 [*On Genesis: A Refutation of the Manichees*].

63. *Jo. eu. tr.* (*In Johannis evangelium tractatus*): *Homélies sur l'Évangile de saint Jean CIV–CXXIV* (ed. M.-F. Berrouard; BAug 75; Paris: Institut des Études Augustiniennes, 2003).

109. *trin.* (*De Trinitate*): *On the Trinity* (ed. G. B. Matthews; Cambridge Texts in the History of Philosophy; Cambridge and New York: Cambridge Univer-sity Press, 2002) [*De Trinitate* 8–15].

# PART FOUR

## Chapter Ten: Theological Controversies of the Fifth Century

*Nestorius / Council of Ephesus:* S. Wessel, *Cyril of Alexandria and the Nestorian Controversy: The Making of a Saint and of a Heretic* (OECS; New York: Oxford University Press, 2004).

*Cyril of Alexandria—Theology:* S. A. McKinion, *Words, Imagery, and the Mystery of Christ: A Reconstruction of Cyril of Alexandria's Christology* (Leiden: Brill, 2000). – D. Keating, "The Twofold Manner of Divine Indwelling in Cyril of Alexandria: Redressing an Imbalance," *StPatr* 37 (2001): 543–49. – T. G. Weinandy and D. Keating, eds., *The Theology of St. Cyril of Alexandria: A Critical Appreciation* (Edinburgh: T&T Clark, 2003). – D. A. Keating, *The Appropriation of Divine Life in Cyril of Alexandria* (OTM; New York: Oxford University Press, 2004).

*Theodoret of Cyrus—Translations: Commentary on the Song of Songs* (trans. R. C. Hill; Early Christian Studies 2; Brisbane: Australian Catholic University Press, 2001). – *Eranistes* (trans. G. H. Ettlinger; FC 106; Washington, D.C.: Catholic University of America Press, 2003).

*Theodoret of Cyrus—Studies:* R.C. Hill, "Theodoret Wrestling with Romans," *StPatr* 34 (2001): 347–52. – T. Urbainczyk, *Theodoret of Cyrrhus: The Bishop and the Holy Man* (Ann Arbor: University of Michigan Press, 2002).

*Leo the Great:* G. D. Dunn, "Divine Impassibility and Christology in the Christmas Homilies of Leo the Great," *TS* 62 (2001): 71–85.

*Severus of Antioch—Introduction/Translations:* P. Allen and C. T. R. Hayward, *Severus of Antioch* (The Early Church Fathers; London and New York: Routledge, 2004).

## Chapter Eleven: Literature of the Latin West

*Translations: Early Christian Latin Poets* (trans. C. White; The Early Church Fathers; London and New York: Routledge, 2000). – Quodvultdeus of Carthage, *The Creedal Homilies: Conversion in Fifth-Century North Africa* (trans. T. M. Finn; ACW 60; New York: Paulist, 2004).

*Caesarius of Arles—Editions: Sermons sur l'Écriture (Sermons 81–105)* (ed. G. Morin and J. Courreau; SC 447; Paris: Cerf, 2000).

*Boethius:* John Marenbon, *Boethius* (Great Medieval Thinkers; New York: Oxford University Press, 2003).

*Cassiodorus—Editions: Commentaria minora in Apocalypsin Johannis variorum auctorum* (ed. R. Gryson; CCSL 107; Turnhout, Belg.: Brepols, 2003) [*Complexiones in Apocalypsim Johannis*].

*Benedict of Nursia:* F. Clark, *The "Gregorian" Dialogues and the Origins of Benedictine Monasticism* (SHCT 108; Leiden and Boston: Brill: 2003). – A. Böckmann, *Perspectives on the Rule of St. Benedict: Expanding Our Hearts in Christ* (trans. M. Burkhard and M. Handl; Collegeville, Minn.: Liturgical, 2005).

*Gregory the Great—Editions: Commentaire sur le premier livre des Rois* (ed. A. de Vogüé; SC 449, 469, 482; Paris: Cerf, 2000–2004), vols. 4–6 [*In librum primum Regum expositiones*]. – *Morales sur Job 4–6 Livres XXVIII–XXIX)* (ed. C. Straw; SC 476; Paris: Cerf, 2003) [*Moralia in Iob*]

*Gregory the Great—Translations: The Letters* (trans. J. R. C. Martyn; Toronto: Pontifical Institute of Medieval Studies, 2004).

*Gregory the Great: Introduction/Translations:* J. Morehead, *Gregory the Great* (The Early Church Fathers; London and New York: Routledge, 2005).

*Gregory of Tours:* M. Heinzelmann, *Gregory of Tours: History and Society in the Sixth Century* (trans. C. Carroll; Cambridge and New York: Cambridge University Press, 2002).

*Isidore of Seville—Editions: Versus* (ed. J. M. S. Martín; CCSL 113A; Turnhout, Belg.: Brepols, 2000). – *Chronica* (ed. J. C. Martín; CCSL 112; Turnhout, Belg.: Brepols, 2003).

# Chapter Twelve: Literature of the Greek East

*Justinian:* M. Maas, ed., *The Cambridge Companion to the Age of Justinian* (Cambridge and New York: Cambridge University Press, 2005).

*Pseudo-Dionysius the Areopagite:* J. P. Williams, *Denying Divinity: Apophasis in the Patristic Christian and Sōtō Zen Buddhist Traditions* (New York: Oxford University Press, 2001).

*Maximus the Confessor—Editions: Liber asceticus* (ed. P. van Deun; CCSG 40; Turnhout, Belg.: Brepols, 2000). – *Ambigua ad Thomam una cum Epistula secunda ad Eundem* (ed. B. Janssens; CCSG 48; Turnhout, Belg.: Brepols, 2002). – *Maximus Confessor and His Companions: Documents From Exile* (ed. P. Allen and B. Neil, OECT; Oxford and New York: Oxford University Press, 2003) [*Record of the Trial; Dispute at Bizy; Letter of Maximus to Anastasius; Letter to the Monks of Cagliari; Letter of Anastasius Apocrisarius to Theodosius of Gangra, Commemoration, Against the People of Constantinople*].

*Maximus the Confessor—Translations: On the Cosmic Mystery of Jesus Christ* (trans. P. M. Blowers and R. L. Wilken; Popular Patristics Series; Crestwood, N.Y.: St. Vladimir's Seminary Press, 2003) [*Ambiguum 7, 8, 42; Ad Thalassium 1, 2, 6, 17, 21, 22, 42, 60, 61, 64; Opusculum 6*].

*Maximus the Confessor—Studies:* P. M. Blowers, "The Passion of Jesus Christ in Maximus the Confessor: A Reconsideration," *StPatr* 37 (2001): 361–77. – A. G. Cooper, "St. Maximus the Confessor on Priesthood, Hierarchy, and Rome," *Pro ecclesia* 10 (2001): 346–67. – L. Thunberg, "Spirit, Grace, and

Human Receptivity in St. Maximus the Confessor," *StPatr* 37 (2001): 608–17. – J. P. Williams, "The Incarnational Apophasis of Maximus the Confessor," *StPatr* 37 (2001): 631–35. – B. De Angelis, *Natura, persona, libertà: L'antropologia di Massimo il Confessore* (Quaderni dell'Assunzione; Rome: Armando, 2002). – P. G. Renczes, *Agir de Dieu et liberté de l'homme: Recherches sur l'anthropologie théologique de saint Maxime le Confesseur* (Cogitatio fidei; Paris: Cerf, 2003). – A. E. Kattan, *Verleiblichung und Synergie: Grundzüge der Bibelhermeneutik bei Maximus Confessor* (SVigChr 63; Boston: Brill, 2003). – D. Bathrellos, *The Byzantine Christ: Person, Nature, and Will in the Christology of Saint Maximus the Confessor* (OECS; New York: Oxford University Press, 2005). – A. G. Cooper, The *Body in St. Maximus the Confessor: Holy Flesh, Wholly Deified* (OECS; New York: Oxford University Press, 2005).

*John of Damascus: Translations: Three Treatises on the Divine Images* (trans. A. Louth; Popular Patristics Series; Crestwood, N.Y.: St. Vladimir's Seminary Press, 2003).

*John of Damascus: Studies:* A. Louth, *St. John Damascene: Tradition and Originality in Byzantine Theology* (OECS; Oxford and New York: Oxford University Press, 2002).


# PART FIVE


## *Chapter Thirteen: Independent Bodies of Literature*

*Syriac Literature—Editions:* W. Wright and N. McLean, eds., *The Ecclesiastical History of Eusebius in Syriac* (Piscataway, N.J.: Gorgias, 2003).

See also the works listed under "*Gregory of Nazianzus—Editions*" above.

*Syriac Literature—Translation: The Book of Steps: The Syriac Liber graduum* (trans. R. A. Kitchen and M. E. G. Parmentier; CistSS 196; Kalamazoo, Mich.: Cistercian Publications, 2004).

*Ephraem Syrus:* S. Brock, *From Ephrem to Romanos: Interactions between Syriac and Greek in Late Antiquity* (Variorum Collected Studies Series 664; Aldershot, Eng., and Brookfield, Vt.: Ashgate, 1999). – K. E. McVey, "Ephrem the Syrian," in *The Early Christian World* (ed. P. F. Esler; 2 vols.; London and New York: Routledge, 2000), 2:1228–50. – S. H. Griffith, "The Thorn among the Tares: Mani and Manichaeism in the Works of St. Ephraem the Syrian," *StPatr* 35 (2001): 395–427. – F. Graffin, *Ephem de Nisibe: Hymnes sur la nativité* (SC 459; Paris: Cerf, 2001). – T. Buchan, *Blessed Is He Who Has Brought Adam from Sheol: Christ's Descent to the Dead in the Theology of Saint Ephrem the Syrian* (Gorgias Dissertations 13; Piscataway, N.J.: Gorgias, 2004).

*Isaac of Nineveh:* H. Alfeyev, *The Spiritual World of Isaac the Syrian* (CistSS 175; Kalamazoo: Cistercian Publications, 2000).

*Coptic Literature—Translations: St. Macarius the Spiritbearer: Coptic Texts Relating to Saint Macarius the Great* (trans. T. Vivian; Popular Patristics Series; Crestwood, N.Y.: St. Vladimir's Seminary Press, 2005) [*Sayings of Saint Macarius of Egypt, Virtues of Saint Macarius of Egypt, Life of Saint Macarius of Scetis*]. – *Four Desert Fathers: Pambo, Macarius of Egypt and Macarius of Alexandria: Coptic Texts Relating to the Lausiac History of Palladius* (trans. T. Vivian; Popular Patristics Series; Crestwood, N.Y.: St. Vladimir's Seminary Press, 2005) [Coptic Palladiana].

*Shenoute of Atripe:* C. T. Schroeder, "Purity and Pollution in the Asceticism of Shenute of Atripe," *StPatr* 35 (2001): 142–47. – S. Emmel, *Shenoute's Literary Corpus* (2 vols., CSCO 599–600; Peeters, 2003). – C. T. Schroerder, "'A Suitable Abode for Christ': The Church Building as Symbol of Ascetic Renunciation in Early Monasticism," *ChH* 73 (2004): 472–521.

*Armenian Literature:* A. J. Hacikyan, ed., *From the Oral Tradition to the Golden Age* (*The Heritage of Armenian Literature;* Detroit: Wayne State University Press, 2000). – E. G. Mathews, *The Armenian Commentaries on Exodus-Deuteronomy Attributed to Ephrem the Syrian* (2 vols.; CSCO 587–88; Leuven: Peeters, 2001).

*Georgian Literature: See* works listed under *"Gregory of Nazianzus—Editions"* above.

*Arabic Literature—Editions/Translations:* Yahya ibn 'Adi, *The Reformation of Morals* (ed. S. H. Griffith; Eastern Christian Texts 1; Provo, Utah: Brigham Young University Press, 2002). – *The Arabic Life of Severus of Antioch Attributed to Athanasius of Antioch* (ed. Y. N. Youssef and P. Allen; PO 49; Turnhout, Belg.: Brepols, 2004).

See also works listed under *"Gregory of Nazianzus—Editions"* above.

# Index of Subjects

Innocent III, Pope, 5
Innocent XIII, Pope, 526
*Institutiones* (Cassiodorus), 502
*Institutiones* (John Cassian), 373
Irenaeus, 47, 52–53, 54, 105, 111, 112, 115,
 117–22, 465
"I-sayings," 25
Isidore of Seville, 5, 227, 305, 348, 457, 522,
 526–29
Islam, 458, 544, 554, 565, 570, 576
itinerant prophet, 56
itineraries, 381–85
*Itinerarium Egeriae*, 300, 382, 383–85, 553

Jacob of Nisibis, 559
Jacob of Sarug, 554
Jacobite church, 552, 554
Jaeger, W., 283
James of Sarug, 550
Jaschke, H.-J., 119
Jerome, 4, 50, 117, 130, 136, 145, 148, 152,
 166, 178, 207, 223, 227, 260, 263, 285,
 305, 333, 337–38, 339–51, 352–57,
 372, 554
 literary work, 342–43
Jerusalem, 32, 384
Jerusalem liturgy, 384
Jesus Christ
 descent into Hades, 27, 28, 29
 divinity, 147, 243, 262
 as fulfillment of Old Testament, 141,
 234–35
 generation of, 243, 259, 289
 humanity, 50, 262
 redemptive work, 416–17
 return (Parousia), 27
 two natures, 291, 469, 477, 480, 484, 488,
 537–38, 539
 virgin birth, 28
Jesus-sayings, 26
Jews, 71, 83, 130
 Diaspora, 69, 130
 *See also* Judaism
Joachim and Anna (Mary's parents), 22, 24
John Cassian, 141, 366, 367, 372–76, 409,
 479
John Chrysostom, 4, 71, 93, 178, 202, 204,
 205, 249, 267, 285, 290, 295, 300, 305,
 319, 322, 326, 327–37, 366, 372, 462,
 518, 574, 578
John Climacus, 578
John Exarchus, 578
John Mandakuni, 550
John of Antioch, 463–64, 473, 480, 487

John of Damascus, 5, 457, 458, 542–46,
 576, 578
John of Ephesus, 550, 554
John of Jerusalem, 343, 542
John of the Cross, 535
John Paul II, Pope, 285, 330
John Scotus Erigena, 535
Joseph, 24
Joseph of Arimathea, 29
Josephus, 73, 227
Jovian, Emperor, 197, 249, 263, 559
Jubilee, 521
Judaism, 9, 71–72, 306
 apologetics of, 73
 and Christianity, 162, 227
 and Gnosticism, 107
 Hellenistic, 69
 *See also* Jews, Judaism
Judas Thaddaeus, 572
Julian (later emperor) 191, 268, 274, 284
Julian of Eclanum, 322, 323, 407–8
Julian of Kos, 486
Julian the Apostate, 192, 197–98, 215,
 248–49, 251, 254, 255–56, 288, 296,
 309, 319, 559–60
Julian the martyr, 524
Julius Africanus, 226
Julius of Rome, 212, 248, 264
Jungck, C., 284
justice, 311
justification, 422
Justin, 28, 74, 77–82, 83–84, 94–95
Justinia, 310
Justinian, Emperor, 148, 457, 499, 514, 526
Juvenal of Jerusalem, 479

Kacynski, R., 336
Kannengiesser, C., 246, 250, 379
kingdom of God, 39, 188
Klock, C., 284
knowledge, 112, 367
Koine Greek, 69. *See also* Greek language
Kotter, B., 545

Lactantius, 182–84, 223, 229, 307
Lagerlöf, S., 22
Laodiceans, 35
*lapsi*, 168, 170, 180
Latin, 122, 149–50, 154, 188, 356, 384–85,
 458, 549
 translation of the Bible, 151–52, 346–47
Laurentius, 422
Lawless, G., 362
Leander, 515, 517, 518

# Index of Ancient Sources

**Benedict**

*Rule*

**Boethius**

*De consolatione philosophiae*

**Council of Constantinople**

*Canones*

**Council of Nicea**

*Canones*

***1 Clement***

**Clement of Alexandria**

*Stromata*

*Paedagogus*

*Protrepticus*

***Codex theodosianus***

**Cyprian**

*De catholicae ecclesiae unitate*

*De lapsis*